# Stephen A. Douglas

Stephen A. Douglas, about 1859

# Stephen A. Douglas

Robert W. Johannsen

New York
OXFORD UNIVERSITY PRESS
1973

Copyright © 1973 by Oxford University Press, Inc.
Library of Congress Catalogue Card Number: 72-92293
Printed in the United States of America

For Lois
and
Nancy and Bob

# Preface

Stephen A. Douglas was a man of his times. Born during the first vivid expression of American nationalism, the Second War for Independence, he died just as that nationalism encountered its most serious threat. His life spanned the formative period of American development, the cataclysmic middle decades of the nineteenth century, which were marked by social change and transition, rapid economic and technological growth, and fervent national feelings. He reflected the qualities that have been identified with the Jacksonian era and shared its fundamental beliefs—a deep conviction that America was swiftly moving to a position of strength and power commensurate with its potential, guided by an inexorable force that some called Manifest Destiny and that Douglas often described as a natural law of expansion; and an unshakable faith in democracy and democratic institutions, in the enlightenment of the people and in the wisdom of the majority, for Douglas an almost obsessive devotion to "the voice of the many." Springing from a deep-seated New England heritage, growing to maturity in the individualistic frontier society of the west, and marrying into the proud aristocratic tradition of the slaveholding south, Douglas had a feel for the nation that few others could boast. His interests were national, and this fact shaped everything he said and did. Like the prairies of his adopted state, his vision was broad and unfettered, and, like all true exponents of the American mission, his look was westward. To Douglas, the Union was sacred, the symbol of all human progress. He was Young America personified, a representative man in the Emersonian sense.

Periods of change are often hard on those who have to live through them. Douglas was no exception. Old patterns and attitudes were giving way before new ones, and many aspects of the transition were only dimly understood or appreciated. The dynamic character of American society, the upheavals and dislocations, created problems and issues that to Douglas seemed only to distract Americans from their onward and upward course. But even he had to come to terms with them eventually, as he discovered that not all problems could be easily solved by a majority decision. He held tenaciously to his Jacksonian beliefs and devoted his last years to a desperate effort to preserve them in the face of new challenges, at a time when they had lost some of their vitality. Impatient to serve the expansion and growth of his country and its institutions, he became locked instead in a life-and-death struggle for the very existence of the Union itself. He died as his beloved country stood on the threshold of bloody civil war, a casualty of the conflict just as surely as if he had been struck down on the battlefield.

Douglas was a man of action rather than intellect. His energy, nervous and impulsive, was a source of wonder. His emotions were volcanic, as the victims of his sarcasm and denunciation were quick to discover. A consummate politician, he was ambitious, reckless, and sometimes unscrupulous. All the turbulence of Jacksonian politics found expression in his public character. He knew how to appeal to the passions and prejudices of the people; he was the master of an eloquent, vigorous manner of speaking. Whenever he made a speech it was as if he were addressing an excited crowd at some railway station. He was often compared to a prizefighter, and one contemporary thought it was as exciting to hear Douglas in debate as it was to witness the acting of the older Booth. Those who were unable to see beneath the surface dismissed him as an unprincipled demagogue. Douglas was a political pragmatist, basing his actions always on a strong sense of realism, but he was also a man of principle. He was happiest when he was the center of controversy; he loved furor, and he had more than his share. During the last decade of his life, he was probably the most widely known political figure in the nation. There were few Americans who did not know his name. He was praised and condemned, vilified and idolized, inspiring fierce loyalty on the one hand and bitter hatred on the other. Douglas was a person toward whom few people could feel neutral or apathetic.

Like his period, Douglas was a man of paradox and contradiction. He was not introspective, as were many of his contemporaries, and he seldom confided his innermost feelings and motivations. He baffled many in his own time and has puzzled historians and biographers since. "Never was a man really less known, appreciated and estimated at his actual value," commented a New Englander in 1857. Douglas will doubtless continue to be, as he has always been, the subject of speculation, uncertainty and dispute, for it is doubtful that the key to his personality will ever be found to the satisfaction of all. Certainly I make no claims of discovery. This is, first of all, the story of a man's life, but it is also more than that, for in Douglas' story is revealed the America in which he lived.

A word of warning to the reader: In the pages that follow, the original spellings and grammatical constructions (sometimes bizarre and unique) have been retained in all quotations. In order to avoid tedious repetition, I have dispensed with the use of [*sic*].

A great many people—librarians, archivists, colleagues, and students—have contributed to the preparation of this account. Although they may be unsung, their assistance is neither forgotten nor unappreciated. This book owes much to the help and encouragement of Martin F. Douglas, grandson of Stephen A. Douglas, and his family of Greensboro, North Carolina, who not only granted me access to their rich collection of Douglas material, but also extended the gracious hospitality of their home during my several visits. I am also grateful to Robert Rosenthal, Director of Special Collections at the University of Chicago Library and custodian of the vast collection of Douglas manuscripts there, for his continued interest in the project and his efforts to do everything possible to ease the task of research.

To the John Simon Guggenheim Foundation, whose generosity enabled me to devote a full year, undistracted by other responsibilities, to the study of the Little Giant, and to the Graduate College of the University of Illinois, for its support during the early stages of the work and for a semester's appointment to its Center for Advanced Study, I owe a large debt of gratitude. For their help in research I wish to extend special thanks to the four graduate students in history at the University of Illinois who served as my research assistants at various times: George W. Pilcher of the University of Colorado; Eugene H. Berwanger of Colorado State University; Ronald D. Rietveld of California State College, Fullerton; and Roger D. Bridges of the Illinois State Historical Library. My thanks also to Judy Grieve, who typed the entire manuscript with rare competence and efficiency and to the editors of *Civil War History*, the *Journal of American History*, the *Journal of Southern History*, and the

*New England Quarterly* for permission to use material that originally appeared in their journals.

Finally I wish to acknowledge the encouragement and valuable assistance of my good friend and editor, Sheldon Meyer of Oxford University Press. In a category all by herself is my wife Lois, who not only read and criticized the entire manuscript, but who also provided unwavering moral support, bolstered my will whenever energy seemed to flag, protected me from distractions both within and outside the family, and helped me maintain a proper perspective during periods of administrative concern.

R. W. J.

*Champaign, Ill.*

# Contents

# Stephen A. Douglas

# I

## "Here I first learned to love liberty"
## 1813—1833

For days the citizens of Brandon, Vermont, had been preparing for the visit of the town's most celebrated native son. Private residences and public buildings were gaily decorated with flags and streamers, and a platform had been erected in front of the Brandon House. Notices were circulated announcing the event, and on the appointed day, Saturday, July 28, 1860, two thousand persons, virtually the town's entire population, gathered on the streets. At half past four in the afternoon, the train from Rutland arrived. A few moments later Stephen A. Douglas, Senator from Illinois and candidate for the presidency of the United States, stepped on the platform. A twenty-one gun salute thundered its welcome, and a band struck up "Hail Columbia," then "Hail to the Chief." The nation was in the midst of a presidential campaign, and there was some anxiety lest Douglas, a lifelong Democrat, be accorded a less than cordial reception in Republican-dominated Vermont. Such fears soon dissipated as political differences were lost in the enthusiasm. Democrat or not, the native son had "won for himself a proud position among the leading statesmen of his time, and a name and fame world-wide."

A procession of carriages, Douglas in the lead, moved from the station through "most of the principal streets" toward the Brandon House. An honor guard, assembled from the local company of the state militia, marched alongside. On the way, the procession paused before the small, brown, story-and-a-half house at the north end of the village in which Douglas had been born more than forty-seven years before. A crowd of people, gathered at the house, manifested "great enthusiasm" as the Senator viewed "this relic of his boyhood days." [1]

From a platform erected before the Brandon House, Douglas paid tribute to his Vermont heritage and recalled his childhood. "There are the mountains, yonder are the same hills; the streets are here, and the corners are as then. Yet almost all is changed. . . . Around me all, all is changed; boys are grown to be old men, and I am to-day welcomed by those who are sons of those who knew me when a boy." To the delight of the people gathered before the platform, Douglas announced, "I am proud of being a native of Vermont. Here I first learned to love liberty. . . . Liberty loves the mountains. All history attests that the mountains can never be conquered." Surrounded by the memories of earlier years, he reminisced, "One of your number goes to the West; in a little while you almost forget him, and think of him perhaps only as a wanderer, or an adventurer; but he can never forget you. Here is his birthplace, the scenes of his childhood, his native hills, his parents, brothers or sisters, or their graves. Can he forget these?"

In the evening, Douglas and his wife Adele (who won "golden opinions for herself") held a public reception in the hotel parlors while the band played in the park across the street and a display of fireworks lit the sky. The following day, Sunday, the Senator spent an hour in the house where he had been born and visited the small graveyard behind the Congregational Church, where his father and grandfather lay buried. He may not have won many votes in this Republican stronghold, but he left behind him the admiration and goodwill of the town's population. [2]

Brandon's citizens had glimpsed the man who, in the thirty years since he left his native town, had become the most prominent, most controversial figure in American politics. Douglas' visit to Vermont was part of a larger campaign tour of New York and New England. His reputation had long since preceded him, and thousands flocked to the stations along the way to see and hear him. One New England reporter was reminded of a prize fighter. "He has excellent prize fighting qualities," he wrote, "Pluck, quickness and strength; adroitness in shifting his positions, avoiding his adversary's blows, and hitting him in unexpected places in return." The description was apt, albeit partisan. Douglas' physical appearance belied his strength and position. Diminutive in height, he stood only five feet four inches tall. A massive head, broad shoulders, full chest and short, stubby legs completed the picture, inviting ridicule among the unwarry but formidable to those who had encountered the force of his obsessive energy. His eye was quick and penetrating under a large projecting brow and thick masses of dark brown hair, his visage stern and heavy. His was an appearance not easily forgotten.[3]

ii

"I learn from my mother," Douglas wrote in 1838, "that I was born in the town of Brandon in the County of Rutland and State of Vermont on the 23d of April, 1813." [4]

Brandon was still a frontier town in 1813. Settlement of the area had been slow, and not many years before travelers had complained of the primitive state of the roads and noted the town's large number of log houses. Lying east of Lake Champlain, in the shadow of the great mountain ridge that bisects Vermont, the countryside retained its early isolation, nurturing among its farmers a spirit of independence and individualism. Radicalism and religious heresy, it was said, flourished unchecked among the hills and valleys of western Vermont, but this was the judgment of more conservative travelers from the older eastern settlements. The fires of religious revivalism swept the area, and the principles of Jeffersonian democracy took root during the early years of the Republic, setting the region apart from much of the rest of New England. Interest in politics was deep-seated; partisan animosity ran high. Democracy in local government was pure, and the people were jealous of their rights. The statehouse had been built in Montpelier only five years before; up to that time, the legislature had rotated its meetings among the state's communities.[5]

The year 1813 was a critical one for the yeomen of western Vermont. With the nation at war, their settlements lay exposed on the flank. Less than two months after Douglas' birth, British forces made a foray along the shores of Lake Champlain, evoking a fierce nationalistic spirit among the settlers. Vermont alone among the New England states declined to send delegates to the Hartford Convention. In the midst of the emergency, Vermonters pledged their allegiance to the young Republic and revealed their vision of its future in a tribute to the "Union of the States—Oceans the boundary, eternity the duration, and infamy to those who advise their dissolution." It was a conviction and a pledge that would dominate Douglas' life.[6]

Stephen A. Douglas, the sixth generation of his family to be born in New England, was descended from strong and distinguished Puritan stock. Like many other western Vermont settlers, the Douglasses had migrated from Massachusetts and Connecticut.[7] The first member of the family of whom there is record was William Douglass, born in Scotland in 1610, who emigrated to New England in 1640. A cooper by trade, William lived in Boston and Ipswich before moving his family to New London, Connecticut, in 1660, where he became a landowner of means and a holder of town offices. In 1676 he served as a commissary officer during King Philip's War.

The Douglass family remained in Connecticut for two generations. Following the last French war, Asa Douglass, great grandson of William and great grandfather of Stephen A. Douglas, moved north and west in 1766 to the cheaper lands along the Massachusetts–New York boundary. Clearing some thirty acres of land, he built a large farmhouse near what later became Stephentown, New York. It is not known whether religious considerations provided an additional impetus for the move, but with their removal to the north, the Douglasses seem to have lost their previous orthodox religious associations. Eleven years later, sixty-one-year-old Asa Douglass struck his blow for freedom when he led a company of thirty men at the Battle of Bennington.

The twelfth of Asa's thirteen children, and his youngest son, was Benajah Douglass. With his brothers, Benajah helped to work the family farm until after his marriage, when he continued the northward movement begun by his father. After a brief residence in Ballston, New York, he purchased nearly 400 acres of farmland near Brandon in July 1795, and there he remained until his death over thirty-four years later. His eldest son bore the name of his wife's father, Stephen Arnold. Stephen Arnold Douglass foreswore agricultural pursuits for medicine, studying for a time at Middlebury College and with a Brandon physician before beginning his own practice. Early in 1811, he married Sarah Fisk, the youngest daughter of Nathaniel Fisk, a prosperous farmer and a resident of the Brandon area since 1784; two years later his first son, and second child, was born in the simple, frame dwelling on the north edge of the village. The son, like the father, bore the name of Stephen Arnold.[8]

Stephen A. Douglas never knew his father, who died in his thirty-second year, when Douglas was just over two months old. "I have often been told," Douglas later wrote, "that he was holding me in his arms when he departed this world." [9] Upon her husband's sudden death, Mrs. Douglass moved with her two children to a small farm in Arnold Hollow, about three miles northwest of Brandon.

Although Douglas did not know his father, he knew his grandfathers well. Nathaniel Fisk died in 1827, when Douglas was fourteen years

old. It was from Benajah Douglass that he acquired many of his characteristics, both physical and temperamental. Benajah was described as of
less than "middling height," with large head and body, and short neck
and limbs. Self-confident and noted for his practical common sense, he
was given to "much speaking" and in a meeting could always be
counted upon for a "word of exhortation." He early developed an interest in politics, serving in the Vermont General Assembly for five terms
and as town selectman and justice of the peace. At a time when membership in the Methodist Church was locally unpopular, he helped to
found the first Methodist society in Brandon. A penchant for controversy
frequently involved him in bitter feuds, both political and religious, resulting on one occasion in his expulsion from the church for a brief time.
When he died in 1829, at age sixty-nine, Benajah's estate testified to his
affluence as a farmer and public figure; among his legacies was a modest
sum bequeathed to his grandson.[10]

iii

When the widowed Sally Douglass left Brandon with her two small
children, she joined her brother Edward Fisk, on the latter's farm. Edward was a bachelor—"an industrious, economical, clever old bachelor," Douglas later wrote—who needed someone to keep his house.
Since Edward's farm was contiguous to that inherited by Douglas'
mother, and since "each was so situated as to need the aid of the other,"
the farms were merged, and Sally took over the management of her
brother's household. Here, under the eye of his uncle, Douglas grew to
adolescence. In time, however, he came to resent the living arrangement.
"I thought it a hardship that my uncle would have the use of my mother's
farm and also the benefit of my labour without any other equivalent
than my boarding and clothes." Work on the farm was hard; the soil
was rocky and unproductive, the water supply poor and undependable.
While he performed his tasks without complaint, Douglas regarded his
uncle as "rather a hard master." [11]

Douglas' chores kept him on the farm for eight or nine months of the
year, but for three months each year he attended the Arnold District
School, an interlude he always anticipated with delight. His schoolmates
and teacher later remembered him as a studious child, with a quality of
perception and a retentive memory that enabled him to excell in mathematics and Latin grammar. Not all his time was spent in farm work or
in the classroom. He developed the recreational pastimes normal to a

young boy—fishing in Otter Creek with a pin hook, swimming in the
creek's deep holes and playing in the woods with neighboring children.
Another uncle, Jonathan Fisk, encouraged Douglas' interest in woodworking by providing a small workshop for the lad on his near-by
farm.[12]

In this environment Douglas developed the physical and personal
characteristics which would distinguish him in later years. Quick, alert,
and proudly self-reliant, he made friends easily, combining a natural
magnetism with a consuming energy. His horizons were limited, and
only rarely did his thoughts pass beyond the quiet valley where he was
born. Many years later, he recalled that he thought his valley "was the
very centre of civilization, and that beyond the mountains that bounded
his horizon there was nothing, but barbarism and filibustering." [13] But
Douglas also nurtured a strong ambition which would not rest. His position in his uncle's household, he felt, discouraged his development and
held him back. Resentment of his uncle made him restless, especially as
he watched the sons of well-to-do farmers in the neighborhood leave
their homes for jobs or school elsewhere.

In his fifteenth year, Douglas made his first important decision: he
would leave home, family, and friends to see "what I could do for myself
in the wide world among strangers." His mother remonstrated with him,
but Douglas was not dissuaded. He wished to learn a trade, most especially to follow his natural talent for working in wood. Mrs. Douglass
finally consented, "with the thought that the way to cure the boy's lik-
ing for a trade . . . was to put him at it." As Douglas later expressed it,
"[She] warned me of the dangers and temptations to which young men
are exposed, and insisted upon my selecting some trade or engaging in
some business that would give me a steady home and regular employment. I promised to comply with her wishes, that is, keep good company, or in other words keep out of bad company, avoid all immoral and
vicious practices, attend church regularly, and obey the regulations of
my employer; in short I promised everything she wanted, if she would
consent to my leaving home." Douglas' "wide world" lay fourteen miles
north of Brandon village in the town of Middlebury. In the spring of
1828 he set out for Middlebury in search of his fortune.[14]

In later years a different version of the circumstances of Douglas' departure for Middlebury, for which there is little evidence, became popular. An understanding, it was said, existed between Douglas and his
uncle that the latter would provide him with the means for pursuing his

education. Uncle Edward, however, up to that time considered to be a confirmed bachelor, suddenly married. The arrival of a son and heir dashed Douglas' hopes that he would receive his uncle's support for a college education. Edward Fisk tried to persuade Douglas to give up his plans for college and remain on the farm, but there was now no alternative for the young man but to leave home and make his own way in the world.[15]

Middlebury, situated at the falls on Otter Creek and at the time an important industrial and agricultural center, was about twice the size of Douglas' native Brandon. Douglas found employment with Nahum Parker, a local cabinetmaker, and entered upon his duties with spirit and determination, sawing table legs, making washstands and bedsteads and aspiring to no other distinction than that related to his trade, at least for the time being. But the novelty soon wore off, and differences of opinion developed between the headstrong youth and his employer, partly over the nature of the apprentice's duties in the Parker shop and home. "I was willing to do anything connected with the shop but could not consent to perform the duties of a servant in the house," Douglas later wrote. His relationship with Parker was terminated and, after eight months in Middlebury, Douglas returned home.[16]

Douglas' sojourn in Middlebury, although brief, was not without importance to his development. While living with the Parkers, he undertook an ambitious reading program, particularly in works related to politics, and he often spent his evenings and Sundays in political discussion with other young men in the community. In 1828 an acrimonious presidential contest between Andrew Jackson and John Quincy Adams aroused an intense political interest in western Vermont, as in other parts of the country. For the first time, Douglas was dazzled by Old Hickory, and a lifelong attachment to the Tennessean's politics was begun. Parker, his employer, was an Adams man, a fact which did little to harmonize relations between the two. "From this moment," Douglas noted, "my politics became fixed, and all subsequent reading, reflection and observation have but confirmed my early attachment to the cause of Democracy." Not content with limiting his convictions to the level of discussion, Douglas, with his friends, pulled down the famous coffin handbills, issued by Adams' partisans to call attention to Jackson's execution of five militiamen for desertion during the War of 1812, as fast as they were posted on the village walls and fences.[17]

Douglas returned to Brandon still attached, as he wrote, "to the life of

a mechanic." He immediately found a place in the woodworking shop of
Deacon Caleb Knowlton, a position he retained for about a year. It was
a year of change for Douglas. In the spring of 1829, his grandfather Benajah died. His uncle Edward had married, and life on the Fisk farm became even less satisfactory than before. Douglas had reached a point
when a re-assessment of his goals and ambitions seemed necessary, when
new and critical decisions had to be made.

During the winter of 1829–30, Douglas fell ill, and he was advised
that his health was "too feeble" for him to continue working in the
shop. He had retained his interest in reading during his year with
Knowlton; and the desire for a college education, in preparation for a
professional career, gradually supplanted his earlier ambition to follow
the woodworking trade. Deacon Knowlton released him from his apprenticeship, and the youth entered the Brandon Academy, a school that
had been organized in 1806 to prepare the town's young men for teaching or for admission into college. Douglas was exposed to English studies, mathematics and the classical languages; he was also active in the
school debating society.[18]

Like most schoolboys, Douglas became enthralled with the great
deeds of the past. His favorite books were those which detailed the ex-
ploits of Alexander, Caesar, and Napoleon. His interest in the giants of
history, however, was matched by a growing excitement with the politics of the present. Politics was very much a part of Douglas' life during
his early years. Growing up in the atmosphere of the town meeting, he
developed a strong attachment to local democracy and self-government.
His grandfather's political career had brought political discussion into
the family circle, and the lad was impressed with the position Benajah
commanded in the community because of his membership in the state
assembly. These were turbulent times politically, and the interest which
the 1828 campaign had aroused continued to occupy Douglas' attention.
Politics was in flux; old political alignments were blurred and new ones
had not yet crystallized. Vermont had been dominated for over a decade
by the legatees of Thomas Jefferson's party, but Jackson's triumph ended
political unity and injected a new vitality into political discussion. In
1829, the appearance of the Anti-Masonry movement in the state added
to the confusion. At the same time, Vermonters expressed increasing
concern over the existence of an institution far to the south which
seemed to negate their convictions of free opportunity for all. During the
campaign of 1828, when Douglas was tearing down coffin handbills in

Middlebury, an editor in near-by Bennington, William Lloyd Garrison, was not only urging Adams' election, but was also voicing his opposition to slavery.

These were not only years of political change for Vermont; they were characterized by social and economic unrest as well. The state's agricultural economy was in transition, natural resources were beginning to dwindle, and the pattern of small household industry was declining. Symptomatic of these changes was an increased movement of Vermonters from the state, especially of the young men. In the face of declining opportunities for professional advancement, many citizens left for other parts of the country, little knowing where they would settle or what they would do when they got there.[19]

Douglas remained in the Brandon Academy through most of 1830; it was his last year in Vermont. In February, a young man from upstate New York, who had come to Brandon earlier on business, took Douglas' sister for a bride. Julius N. Granger was not quite twenty years old when he married Sarah Douglass. Shortly afterward, the two returned to the Granger family home near Canandaigua, Ontario County, New York. Several months later, Granger's fifty-five-year-old father, Gehazi Granger, a widower, arrived in Brandon to claim Douglas' mother for a wife. They were married in late November of 1830. When they returned to New York a few days later, the elder Grangers were accompanied by seventeen-year-old Stephen.

Years later, Douglas suggested that Vermont was a glorious place for a man to be born in, provided he emigrated when he was very young. Although spoken half in jest and resented by Vermonters for a long time afterward, the remark had an apt application to Douglas' early years. "I love the old green mountains and valleys of Vermont, where I was born, and where I played in my childhood," he said in 1858.[20] The green mountains and valleys provided him with a strong, stable foundation, but Douglas, ambitious, energetic, and with no strong ties to the soil from which he sprang, looked elsewhere for the opportunities to build on this foundation.

iv

Canandaigua, on the northern tip of the lake after which it was named, in the verdant hills of the Finger Lakes country of western New York, was first settled in the late eighteenth century by Yankees from Connecticut, Massachusetts, and Vermont. In the center of a rich agricultural region and at the intersection of important transportation routes, the town had achieved an economic importance. Its elegant, aristocratic homes, neat gardens, and broad tree-shaded streets were evidence of wealth and prosperity. The completion of the Erie Canal in 1825 dampened the town's economic growth, but Canandaigua remained a significant cultural center and the seat of wealthy landlords and their agents. By the late 1820's it boasted a population of about 3000 people.

The opening of the Erie Canal brought economic maturity to western New York, but it also ushered in a period of political, social, and religious ferment. Canandaigua and Ontario county lay in the heart of the "Burned-Over District." In 1826, William Morgan, who had revealed his plans to publish an exposure of the secrets of Freemasonry, was abducted from the Canandaigua jail and disappeared under mysterious circumstances, an incident that was quickly followed by the spread of Anti-Masonic feeling and that formed the basis for an Anti-Masonic political movement. At the same time, the great evangelist Charles Grandison Finney inaugurated a series of religious revivals that would set the area aflame, culminating in a grand revival in near-by Rochester in 1831. Twelve miles north of Canandaigua, near Palmyra, a young Vermont-born farm boy named Joseph Smith unearthed and translated the golden plates and, in 1830, organized the Mormon Church. Throughout, Canandaigua remained a conservative island in this swirling sea of optimism, enthusiasm, and excitement.[21]

Douglas came to the Burned-Over District in December 1830, and for the next two and a half years he was exposed to the movements and countermovements that gave the area its characteristic flavor. The Granger family farmstead lay a few miles northeast of Canandaigua, on the road between Manchester and Clifton Springs, its neat, white, two-story house set back from the roadway in a grove of trees. Soon after his arrival Douglas, anxious to continue his formal education, enrolled as a student in the Canandaigua Academy.

Canandaigua Academy traced its existence back to 1795, but the school had not flourished until the 1820's. With the appointment of Henry Howe, a graduate of Middlebury College, as principal in 1828, the Academy became self-supporting for the first time, and it was soon recognized as one of the leading institutions of learning in the Genesee Country. Among some it was reputed to be the best classical academy west of Albany. The course of study emphasized Latin and Greek classics, but also offered work in English, mathematics, and French. During Howe's regime, a program for the preparation of common school teachers was added to the curriculum.[22]

Douglas boarded at the Academy, spending his Sundays at the Granger home. In his own words, "I devoted myself zealously to my studies, the Greek and Latin languages, mathematics, rhetoric, logic, &c., and made considerable improvement." The Academy records indicate that in his last term at the school (which he did not complete), Douglas commenced reading Sallust and Livy and began instruction in French. A classmate later noted that Douglas was less interested in rhetoric and belle-lettres than he was in logic and mathematics and apparently took little interest in writing, for he never competed for the annual essay award. In his after-school hours he read Gibbon's *Decline and Fall of the Roman Empire* and Hume's *History of England.* A serious, if not a brilliant, student, he was, as Henry Howe later remembered him, diligent and successful in his studies.[23]

Politics continued to fascinate him, and he early secured the reputation of being the politician among his schoolmates. He was active in the school debating club, and on more than one occasion he defended Andrew Jackson before small audiences. When Douglas delivered his maiden speech in the House of Representatives years later, his former roommate at the Academy, Marcius Willson, noted that it was quite similar to Douglas' defense of Jackson at the school. Not all of his early oratorical ventures were as serious. On one occasion, he and a group of fellow students engaged in some experiments with laughing gas, secured from a local dentist. One of his companions later reminded Douglas of his "taking the 'Gass,' and vehemently speaking the poem, then commonly known among us as 'Attella.' "[24]

Many of Douglas' classmates were sons of Canandaigua's legal and political leaders, and his friendship with them gained him entrance into their homes. The atmosphere in which he lived was politically charged. His contacts further whetted his own interest in state and national politics. Few towns could boast such a distinguished group of citizens. Among them was Francis Granger, whose father, Gideon, had been a distant cousin of Douglas' stepfather and whose mansion was (and is) one of Canandaigua's showplaces. Gideon Granger had served as Postmaster General in the cabinets of Presidents Jefferson and Madison; his son had been a member of the New York state legislature, candidate for lieutenant governor and governor on the Anti-Masonic ticket, and in

1834 would be elected to Congress. In 1841 he would be appointed Postmaster General by President William Henry Harrison. John Canfield Spencer, prominent Canandaigua attorney, had been a member of the state legislature and of Congress. In the late 1820's he was selected as one of three persons to revise the statutes of New York, a task on which he was engaged when Douglas became acquainted with him. In July 1831, Alexis de Tocqueville and his companion, Gustave de Beaumont, spent two days in Canandaigua as Spencer's guests, and it is possible that Douglas met them.[25] Spencer later edited the first American edition of *Democracy in America*. In 1841, he was appointed Secretary of War in the cabinet of President Tyler. Other Canandaigua citizens with whom Douglas became acquainted included Mark H. Sibley, legislator, Congressman, and widely reputed to be a brilliant lawyer; and Nathaniel W. Howell, First Judge of Ontario County (a post he held during Douglas' residence in Canandaigua), who also had been a member of the state legislature and of Congress.

Canandaigua's leaders were members of the National Republican or Anti-Masonic parties. The town had been in the center of Anti-Masonic excitement, and for years following, the Anti-Masonic party, of which both Granger and Spencer were members, enjoyed an almost undisputed leadership in local politics. In the election of 1832, William Wirt, the Anti-Masonic candidate for the presidency, carried Ontario County by a margin of almost two to one over Andrew Jackson. The majority was even more decisive in Canandaigua.[26]

Surrounded by such an array of legal and political talent, Douglas was logically drawn to the study of law. He began to read law casually while still a student at the Academy, and on January 1, 1833, he left the school to devote his full time to legal study. He entered the law office of Walter and Levi Hubbell and for the next six months applied himself to his books, a "quiet, studious, and exemplary young man," according to one of the partners. His choice of the Hubbells was probably governed by political considerations, for Levi was one of the few Democratic attorneys in the town. Because admission to the New York bar stressed a classical as well as a legal education, Douglas maintained his interest in classics. "I pursued my law studies diligently five days in a week, and the sixth I spent in reviewing my classical studies."

Douglas' association with the Hubbells did not deprive him of his contacts with the town's leading lawyers, in spite of their political differences. Francis Granger opened his excellent library to Douglas and even provided a room in the porter's lodge on his estate where Douglas could study and sleep. Spencer, Sibley, and Howell frequently entertained the town's young law students, providing an opportunity for the youths to talk with "those old-fashioned, most learned members of the bar, who were not mere lawyers, but superb scholars." Each Saturday, the students in Spencer's law office were critically examined on their week's studies, and, although Douglas was not a member of the group, he was allowed to join the examinations.[27] Douglas' early knowledge of the law was gained from some of New York state's best legal minds.

But Douglas was a young man in a hurry. New York law required four years of classical education and three of legal study before a candidate could qualify for his own practice. Douglas, after a thorough examination of his training in the classics, was allowed a credit of three years, but he still faced a four-year program before he could be admitted to the bar.[28] Although his family had financed his Academy education and his law studies, there was no guarantee that this financial support could continue for several more years.

In June 1833, Stephen A. Douglas made the most important decision of his young life. "Finding myself in straightened pecuniary circumstances," he later wrote, "and knowing my mother's inability to support me through a regular course of law studies, which would continue about four years longer . . . I determined upon removing to the western country and relying upon my own efforts for a support henceforth. My mother and relatives remonstrated, urging that I was too young and inexperienced for such an adventure; but finding my resolution fixed and unchangeable, they reluctantly consented, and kindly furnished me with three hundred dollars, the last of my patrimony, with which to pay expenses. On the 24th of June, 1833 (being 20 years of age) I bid farewell to my friends, and started alone for the 'great west,' without having any particular place of destination in view." [29]

With the $300 in his pocket, and letters of introduction from Francis Granger and Mark Sibley, twenty-year-old Douglas turned his face to the west.

# II

## "I have become a *Western* man"
## 1833—1836

In the early morning darkness of a November day in 1833, the stage for Jacksonville left the small Mississippi River town of Alton, Illinois, climbed the steep bluffs behind the town, and headed out across the prairie. Aboard the four-horse post coach was Stephen A. Douglas, sleeping, on the last lap of his western journey. At sunrise, near where the town of Jerseyville now stands, Douglas awoke. "It was the first time my eyes ever beheld a Prairie," he recalled, "and I shall never forget the impressions & emotions produced by the scene." [1]

Douglas' journey had begun five months before, in late June, when he left family and home and embarked on his excursion to the "great west." He knew only that he wanted to establish himself in his chosen profession, the law; the location depended upon the opportunities he found. At Buffalo he boarded a lake steamer, and, following the monotonous, tree-covered shoreline of Lake Erie, he arrived in Cleveland the next day. [2] Through his letters of introduction, Douglas immediately made the acquaintance of Sherlock J. Andrews, twelve years his senior, like Douglas a native New Englander and, since 1825, a practicing lawyer in the lake city. Although he had not intended to remain in Cleveland, Douglas was impressed with the prospects which that city seemed to offer and decided to stay. Andrews placed his law office and library at Douglas' disposal and offered to take the young man into his firm as a partner at the end of the year of study required by Ohio law for admission to the bar. Douglas resumed his studies with "increased spirit and zeal." [3]

Sickness, however, altered Douglas' plans. He was prostrated with what he described as "an Inflammatory fever accompanied with the rheumatism." For weeks he lay ill, attended by his physician, cared for by his landlady ("even Mother herself could not have taken better care of or exhibited more kindness towards me") and cheered by the few acquaintances he had made in Cleveland. His dwindling resources were bolstered by the receipt of $200 from his parents, and his long convalescence was brightened by the visits of two classmates from Canandaigua Academy who had come to Cleveland to study in the Andrews law office. By mid-September he was well enough to report in a cheerful letter home that he was free from pain, gaining strength, "and in a fair prospect of being about in a very few days." Douglas' slow recovery afforded him much time for thought and reflection. It now seemed inadvisable to remain in Cleveland. Valuable time had been lost, and Andrews had taken other law students into his office. Douglas' doctor advised him to return to Canandaigua, but this was out of the question. The prospect of settling in St. Louis occurred to him. In September Douglas wrote his family, "As for St. Louis, I cannot make any calculation now upon going there or any other place; I shall put off all those things untill I get entirely well and then take a new start." By October he was once again on his feet. Using the money he had received from home, Douglas paid his doctor and boarding house bills and, with $30 left in his pocket, continued his way west, a course of action he later recalled as "reckless and adventurous." [4]

Douglas' illness was later the subject of a rare moment of introspection. Reflecting on his state of mind as he lay on his sickbed in Cleveland, Douglas wrote in 1838, "I felt satisfied with the past and no particular hopes or apprehensions of the future. I thought I was on the dividing line between this world and the next, must continue to exist in the one or the other, was willing to take either and felt no choice which." Far from home and family, cared for by strangers, he "enjoyed more peace and contentment of mind, more perfect freedom from all care and trouble, except occasional bodily pain, and more negative happiness than during any other similar period of my life." [5]

From Cleveland Douglas took passage on a canal boat on the recently completed Ohio Canal, traversing the state to Portsmouth, on the Ohio River. Boarding a steamboat, he continued down the Ohio, lingering for a few days in Cincinnati and Louisville—just long enough, apparently, to convince himself that no opportunities awaited him there. The river was filled with emigrants moving west, undeterred by a cholera epidemic that spread along the Ohio in the summer and autumn of 1833. Disease was not the only hazard to western travel. Near the mouth of the Ohio, Douglas' craft struck a snag and was detained for a week while repairs were made to its machinery; nearing St. Louis, the ship was saved from fire by its crew and passengers.[6]

St. Louis was a busy and prosperous river port when Douglas landed there in the fall of 1833. The river front was lined with steamboats, the levee piled high with merchandise, and the streets crowded with people. His money almost gone, Douglas again sought employment in a local law office, hoping that he might continue his studies while paying expenses through the performance of menial office tasks. The difficulties of finding a suitable situation in a strange city, without letters of introduction, were soon evident. He called on Edward Bates, former Missouri Congressman and state legislator, who received him "kindly and politely," but there was no opening in his office. Bates offered the young man the free use of his law library, but without employment Douglas was forced, reluctantly, to reject the offer. He decided instead to seek some smaller country town where, if his chances for employment were no better, at least his expenses would be less.

Illinois had been much discussed among the emigrants on the river, and undoubtedly Douglas' interest was aroused by the tales he heard. He had recently read of central Illinois in a book of western travels, and the glowing terms in which this area was described further whetted his interest. With barely enough money to make the trip, Douglas decided to make his last effort in this land of opportunity. The short trip from St. Louis to the river town of Alton was made by steamboat; after spending his first night on the soil of what was to become his adopted state, Douglas set out for the town that bore the name of the Hero of New Orleans.[7]

ii

"I dwell with pleasure and perhaps with a pardonable pride upon the incidents connected with my early history in the West," wrote Douglas in 1854.[8] When he arrived in Jacksonville in November 1833, his prospects were not bright. Far from home, without friends, and with only a few dollars in his pocket, he faced the immediate necessity of employment. He was not yet twenty-one years of age. But youth is resilient; Douglas was ambitious and resolute, and these handicaps seemed small indeed.

Jacksonville in 1833 was a gateway to Illinois' fastest growing area; it boasted a population of 1200 people and was the seat of the state's most populous county. Illinois had been settled first in the south, by border state farmers, but by the early 1830's settlement began to penetrate the fertile prairies of the central and northern portions. The end of the Black Hawk Indian War in 1832, the development of transportation on the Illinois River, and the opening of navigation on the Great Lakes brought civilization to this Illinois frontier in rapid strides. A new stream of migration from New England and New York entered the state, and central Illinois became a meeting ground between north and south, with a mixed population that would play a significant role in the area's political development.

The area was rich with opportunity. Nature was bountiful and the rewards were great; no person, commented an early guide, could possibly fail, provided he was endowed with "talent, tact and industry." Young men of enterprise, it was said, whether in law, medicine, or engineering, would succeed better and more quickly there than anywhere else in the country. When Douglas arrived the area was in the midst of an impressive economic growth, and Jacksonville itself was enjoying new building construction and rapidly rising property values. The town was, according to a local booster, "one of the loveliest villages in the whole Valley of the Mississippi." 9

Douglas had $5.00 in his pocket when he stepped from the stage in Jacksonville. He augmented these resources by selling a few of the schoolbooks he had brought with him, took up lodgings in the private home of Joseph Heslep, and then sought out one of the town's leading attorneys. Murray McConnel befriended the young man, and in doing so he established a relationship that would continue throughout Douglas' life, but he had no employment to offer. He advised Douglas to go to the small Illinois River town of Pekin and to open a law office there, in what promised to become an important marketing and shipping center for a growing agricultural hinterland. To give the youth a start, McConnel furnished him with a number of law books. Douglas was assured that in this frontier society a law license was of no consequence, that he could practice before a justice of the peace without one, and that he could easily procure a license whenever he desired to do so. Following McConnel's advice, Douglas travelled to Meredosia, on the Illinois River, where he awaited a steamboat that could take him upriver. After a week of waiting, he learned that the only boat expected on the river at that time of year had blown up; no other boats would make the trip until the following spring. His money almost gone, Douglas once again faced the necessity of immediate employment. As an expedient, he determined to obtain subscribers and open a school. He rode with a farmer to the near-by village of Exeter, where he was informed that a school could probably be obtained in Winchester, ten miles distant. "I thought this was rather poor encouragement," he later wrote, "but what was to be done? I was out of money, and still in too feeble health to perform any very arduous labor; and must do something to live; for I was too proud to beg." Taking leave of his farmer friend, and with "my cloak on my arm," Douglas walked to Winchester.[10]

Schools on the Illinois frontier of the 1830's were highly informal institutions. Anyone with a modicum of education who could secure enough pupils to make it profitable was qualified as a teacher. Since the pupils were expected to learn only the barest essentials of reading, writing, and arithmetic, the intellectual demands on the teacher were not great. The landlord of Winchester's single tavern introduced Douglas to the townsfolk, and within a short time the youth had obtained a subscription list of forty scholars. In the meantime he served as clerk at an auction sale, and for two and a half days' work he earned $2.50. Early in December 1833, Douglas opened his school, and he continued teaching until the following March. He lived with Edward G. Miner, the town's merchant, who, like Douglas, was a native of Vermont. In the small apartment behind Miner's store, Douglas spent his first winter in the west.[11]

Douglas continued to devote himself diligently to his law studies, using the few books he had obtained from McConnel, read avidly all the newspapers he could secure, and talked politics with the men of the town as they gathered in the store on the cold winter evenings. Following McConnel's advice, he applied his meager knowledge of the law in practice before the local justice of the peace. When out of the classroom, he wrote, "I was either mingling with the people and forming acquaintances or pettifoging in the Justices Court." By the end of his school term, he boasted that he had become "pretty generally known as a lawyer," a sad commentary, perhaps, on the state of the legal profession on this central Illinois frontier. During that same winter, Winchester's citizens organized a lyceum. Meeting weekly in the schoolhouse, the lyceum provided Douglas with a wide circle of friends, as well as with his first audiences.[12]

This small collection of buildings clustered about a partially enclosed

town square provided the opportunity for the career Douglas had been seeking. When he closed his school in March 1834, he concluded that the "changes of fortune" he had experienced and the "bold steps" he had taken would prove to be the most fortunate developments in his life. Separation from family and friends demonstrated the value and importance of forming acquaintances, and he hoped, he wrote, to draw a lesson that could become "a living guide during my whole life." Twenty-five years later, as he canvassed the state in his most important political campaign, he paid tribute to the settlers of Winchester who had first befriended him and who had helped give him his first start in life.

His enthusiasm for the frontier state mounted, and he was soon writing letters home that rivaled the claims of the most extravagant boosters. "Illinois possesses more natural advantages, and is destined to possess greater artificial and acquired advantages, than any other State in the Union or on the Globe." It was "the Paradise of the world," and he congratulated himself on having found it. The physical characteristics of the land—the remarkable fertility of the soil, the beauty of the rolling prairie, interspersed with timber—were not alone in forming his decision to stay. The character of the people and "the Political principles that prevail here" were congenial. He lost no time in identifying with them. Opportunities were manifold, inviting Douglas to action. "I have become a *Western* man," he wrote his family in December 1833, "have imbibed Western feelings principles and interests and have selected Illinois as the favorite place of my adoption." [13]

### iii

To secure a license to practice law in Illinois in 1834, a candidate had only to be examined by two judges of the state supreme court and to be certified as to his good moral character. There was no residence requirement, nor was a particular course or period of study specified. At the close of his school term, Douglas had earned enough money to meet his expenses and to purchase a small library of his own. His discussions with Winchester's citizenry and his rudimentary practice before the local justice of the peace had brought him some public notice. He was ready, he judged, to become a full-fledged attorney and to embark on a legal career. That he knew little law seemed not to have given him a moment's concern. In March 1834, Douglas appeared before Judge Samuel D. Lockwood of the Illinois Supreme Court and, after a brief examination, obtained his certificate. It was obvious to both examiner and candidate

that his knowledge of the law was not all it could have been, for Judge Lockwood granted the license with the suggestion that Douglas apply himself more closely to his law studies in the future.

The state's judicial system at the time was marked by a spirit of ease and informality. The people were less interested.in learning and erudition in their judicial officers than they were in congeniality. Courts were frequently held in log cabins and barrooms, as well as in the more formal surroundings of the county courthouse, and judges tried at all times to cater to the people. Law suits were most often small, simple cases, and few demands were made on the intellectual capabilities of the legal fraternity.

Legal business was most lucrative in the county seat, so Douglas, with his new license in hand, moved immediately to Jacksonville. He sought a partnership first of all with an established attorney, a common practice for neophyte lawyers, but without success (one attorney, when approached, complained that Douglas did not know enough law to write out a declaration). Undismayed, Douglas took an office in the courthouse, which shared the same building with the town market, and fastened his sign to the wall. He grandly announced, in a letter home, that he was permanently located in Jacksonville as an "attorney and counsellor at law and Soliciter in chancery." Most of Jacksonville's attorneys were opposed to the party of Andrew Jackson, while a majority of the voters in Morgan County had cast their ballots for Jackson in 1832. The opportunities for a young Democratic lawyer seemed encouraging. A visitor to Jacksonville, himself a lawyer, commented, in June 1834, that "the prospects for my profession here are better than I expected . . . the bar is a very weak one. . . . Their business is done in a very loose irregular manner, & neither the court or bar appear to be versed in rules of equity, law or practice." [14]

Hopeful prospects, however, did not necessarily mean a successful practice. Although Douglas wrote, many years later, that he had obtained a "liberal share of law business" during his first few months as an attorney, the testimony of a Jacksonville resident at the time indicated otherwise. "Clients were rare visitants at his office," wrote Daniel Roberts. He had almost no practice at the bar, nor did he acquire a substantial reputation as a lawyer, a state of affairs that was not entirely the consequence of an insufficient knowledge of the law. Douglas, Roberts wrote, was not a "close keeper of his office," but was always out among "the boys," arguing politics.

Politics remained Douglas' real interest. By the time he moved to Jacksonville, he had already earned a local reputation as a political debater. While teaching school the previous winter, Douglas had attended a meeting of the Winchester lyceum that was devoted to a discussion of President Jackson's bank policy. There was, in Douglas' words, "considerable excitement" in the county over Jackson's veto of the Second United States Bank bill in 1832, the appointment of Roger B. Taney as Secretary of the Treasury, and the subsequent removal of deposits from the national bank. A well-known Jacksonville attorney was imported to discuss the issue before the lyceum. In his address he denounced Jackson's veto as arbitrary and tyrannical, and he characterized the removal of deposits as both dangerous and unconstitutional. This was more than Douglas could take. "I could not remain silent when the old hero's character, public and private, was traduced, and his measures misrepresented and denounced." He plunged into the debate, defending the President with a "zeal and warmth" that won the gratitude of Jackson's partisans. The news of Douglas' defense quickly spread, bringing a notoriety that surprised even him.

Douglas was remarkably well informed on the political questions of his day, and his legal study soon had to compete for attention with his strong political interests. He read carefully the congressional debates, as reported in the local press, and studied the Federalist Papers, the debates of the Constitutional Convention, works of John Adams, Alexander Hamilton, and Thomas Jefferson, and Gales and Seaton's history of the Second United States Bank. By the time he began his law practice in Jacksonville, his political opinions had become "firmly established." Political alignments were fluid and party lines were still flexible; it was not surprising that the lure of politics should prove greater than that of the law. The Jackson party in Morgan County lacked vigorous and dedicated leadership; it was into this void that Douglas moved.[15]

Douglas' youth and physical appearance contrasted with his strength and determination. When the editor of the town's Democratic newspaper first met Douglas, he was momentarily disarmed by the youthful appearance of the boy. With short legs and a disproportionately large head, Douglas reminded people of a scrappy bantam cock. All who came to know him, however, were impressed with his instinct for leadership. His convictions were strong, and he possessed an irresistible desire to impress those convictions on others. "It was as natural and spontaneous with him to reason, to argue, to seek to convince, as it is to all men to eat," wrote one who knew him in Jacksonville. Nor was Douglas lacking in those personal traits that make for good politics—he called people by their first names, and to those who supported him he gave the impression that he was "the frank, personal friend of each one of them." Dressed in Kentucky jeans, he mingled with the people "in street and saloon," ready to debate with utter confidence the political questions of the day.

Jacksonville in the 1830's provided Douglas an ideal stage on which to build his political ambitions. An island of New England influence in a countryside that had been settled primarily by border state southerners, the town had become a cultural center in frontier Illinois. Described as a "faithful transcript of New-England," Jacksonville boasted schools, churches, a lyceum, and a circulating library, as well as a number of benevolent societies, all assets which Douglas proudly enumerated in a letter to his former principal at Canandaigua Academy. He found the moral and religious character of the population more elevated than he expected in a frontier society, and he felt that the area had all the appearances of "an old settled Country." Illinois College had been founded a few years before by a group of Yale graduates and, under the able leadership of Edward Beecher, had already acquired the reputation of a high quality educational institution, lending a cultural tone to the community.

Although Douglas found Jacksonville's New England atmosphere congenial, his real affinity was with the farmers of the countryside. His Jacksonian principles were not always acceptable to the transplanted New Englanders, and their espousal of abolitionism repelled Douglas. The leveling tendencies of this inchoate society, on the other hand, attracted him. "The people of this country," he declared enthusiastically, "are more thoroughly Democratic than any people I have ever known. They are democratic in principle and in Practice as well as in name." Equality and equal rights prevailed, and "no man acknowledges another his superior unless his talents, his principles and his good conduct entitle him to that distinction." His own "ardent and fervent attachment" to democracy and "the principles which are the result of it" found ready acceptance among the settlers.[16]

Jackson's war on the Second United States Bank dominated political discussion in central Illinois during the spring of 1834. The withdrawal of government deposits from the Bank weakened the institution and caused it to contract its credit, a policy that was keenly felt in the specu-

lative atmosphere of the west. Financial uncertainty and hardship stiffened resistance to Jackson's program and caused many Democrats to
waver in their support of the President. The recharter of the Bank
seemed necessary to alleviate the distress, but some Jacksonians argued
that the Bank had deliberately created a panic in order to impress the
people with the need for a new charter. The impact on the Jackson
party of what Douglas called the Bank's "reign of Terror" was both a
source of anxiety and a challenge. "All the *weak bretheren* among the
friends of the Administration," he reported, *"deserted* and many others
were scared, and the party were about to be used up." A memorial asking Congress to restore the deposits and to recharter the Bank stirred the
Jacksonians to action and provided the occasion for Douglas' political
debut. At an overflow meeting in the courthouse, several of Jacksonville's leading lawyers presented the case against Jackson. The task of rebuttal fell to Douglas. In an hour-long speech, he defended Jackson's
policy toward the Second United States Bank. "I was rather severe in my
remarks upon the opposition," he later wrote, and the effect was unmistakable. One of the pro-Bank attorneys stalked angrily from the hall
when Douglas' effort was received with rousing cheers. Following his remarks, Douglas presented a series of resolutions condemning the Bank
and affirming an increased confidence in the "purpose, integrity, firmness
and patriotism of our venerable Chief Magistrate." They passed unanimously. Douglas was then borne from the hall on the shoulders of the
crowd and, it has been said, was dubbed, for the first time, the "Little
Giant " [17]

The Jacksonville meeting was a significant step in the organization of
the Democratic party in Morgan County, a project to which Douglas
now dedicated himself. The party was not well defined, for the county's
political talent was almost exclusively on the side of the opposition. The
Democrats lacked an effective public speaker, and that gave Douglas an
opportunity he quickly seized. "The name of Jackson," commented the
*Sangamo Journal,* was "potent in Illinois," but, while Andrew Jackson
enjoyed great popularity, many of those identified with the Democratic
party held to a "watered-down" type of Jacksonism and were not willing
to support the President in all of his actions. The opposition, known frequently as the "Federal Party," but soon to be referred to as the Whigs,
wooed the lukewarm Jacksonians with some effect. Although to Douglas
Democratic affiliation was a matter of rigid definition, he recognized
that expedience and compromise were necessary for effective party orga-

nization. One of the resolutions he had presented declared that the party
had no objection to the establishment of a national bank "upon such
principles as are consistent with the rights of the States, and the Constitution of the United States, and with such restrictions that it cannot interfere with the politics of the country," an obvious gesture to those
Democrats who felt that Jackson's removal of the deposits was not entirely in the best interest of the nation. Looking beyond the confines of
his county, Douglas proposed that Democrats in other counties hold similar meetings and asked that the proceedings of the Jacksonville meeting
be published in newspapers throughout the state. Douglas' role in the effort to strengthen the Democratic party was conceded by the opposition
press, which singled him out for attack. The *Illinois Patriot,* a Jacksonville paper, devoted so much space to Douglas that the youth wondered
if he were not "morally bound to pay the editor for his abuse according
to the usual prices of advertisements." As a result of this publicity,
Douglas' name became known throughout the area; he was placed in
the situation, he wrote, of being supported by one party and opposed by
the other. One side effect of this new political notoriety was that his law
business suddenly increased in volume.[18]

The need for party organization became more evident during the state
elections in 1834. Douglas, with his new-found prominence in local politics, played an active part in the campaign. No clear distinction was
made between the Jackson party and the opposition; the contest rather
became a struggle between two factions in the Democratic party: the
"whole hog" Jacksonians and the "milk and cider" Jacksonians. The
former were the loyal supporters of the President and all his policies; the
latter, while ardent admirers of Old Hickory, had become disturbed over
the President's Bank war, his veto of certain internal improvement bills
dealing with the Illinois area, and the growing possibility that Martin
Van Buren would be designated as Jackson's heir apparent. The party
confusion was reflected in the choice of candidates. The two most prominent candidates for the governorship were William L. Kinney and Joseph Duncan. Kinney was a "whole hog" Jacksonian who had made an
unsuccessful bid for the governor's office in 1830, a rough, vigorous Baptist farmer-preacher who electioneered "with a Bible in one pocket and a
bottle of whiskey in the other." Duncan was one of Illinois' Congressmen. Elected in 1826, he was originally an ardent supporter of Jackson,
but since 1831 he had gradually moved away from his Jacksonian allegiance, opposing many of the administration's measures and supporting

the efforts to override Jackson's vetoes. The extent of Duncan's defection from the Jacksonian ranks, however, was not well known in Illinois, and many voters supported him under the impression he was still a "reliable" Democrat. In the race for Congress from Illinois' Third District, which embraced the entire northern half of the state, two Jackson men, Benjamin Mills and William L. May, vied with one another for Duncan's vacated seat. The only marked difference between the two seemed to be Mills' preference for Richard M. Johnson of Kentucky as successor to the President, while May argued that the choice should be left to a national convention, a position that was interpreted as favoring Van Buren. Such a state of affairs could only confuse the voter and persuade him to cast his vote on a personal rather than a party basis. "It is difficult to catch the hang of parties here," wrote one Jacksonville resident, "for although there is considerable party feeling there is very little party organization."

The Bank question dominated discussion during the election campaign, and the pressure on the money market heightened the excitement. County meetings were held in which resolutions supporting or condemning Jackson's Bank policy were passed, and many political candidates saw fit to issue public statements in which they discussed their positions. Every Saturday, farmers from the surrounding countryside (Jacksonians for the most part) crowded into Jacksonville to hear the local candidates and to discuss the issues with one another. Each Saturday was "a kind of seventh day political jubilee for the Jackson party." Candidates harangued the people from wagons, logs, or stumps; following the speeches, there was general and unrestrained drinking, as each candidate sought to prove that his generosity was greater than that of any others. Before nightfall, the streets were filled with rowdy, boisterous, noisy men, staggering through town cheering their favorite candidates or galloping on their horses. Politics was a rough-and-tumble game in which physical strength and endurance commanded a premium. Douglas made at least one campaign speech in the Jacksonville courthouse during such an occasion, and in it he spiritedly endorsed the candidacy of William L. May.[19]

The election results further demonstrated to the Jacksonians the necessity for better party organization. Opponents of the Bank were generally successful, but some "milk and cider" Jacksonians won office simply by posing as true, reliable Democrats. Duncan was elected to the governorship; although he was a partisan of the Bank, one Democratic newspaper hailed his election on the vague assurance that he had shown "a friendship and support of the leading acts of the President." To Douglas, Duncan was nothing more than a *"Traitor."* Two of the three representatives to the state legislature from Morgan County, all elected as Democrats and supported by Douglas, soon made clear their opposition to Jackson's policies. Even William L. May, who won election to Congress, wavered in his support of the Old Hero. Kinney, defeated for the governorship, urged Jacksonians to act together henceforth, "for we have two faced men enough in this country." The opposition, Douglas reported, had become "more abusive than ever & bragged that the *'Jackson party was used up.'*" To the young Jacksonville attorney, there was but one course to follow. The Jacksonians cried out for leadership; the party demanded organization. "Up to this time," he wrote, "I had never dreamed of being a candidate for any Office, but had acted the part I did because I conceived it to be right. But seeing the opposition were determined to put me down, and to starve me out as they expressed themselves, I thought it best to carry the war into 'Africa' as of old." [20]

iv

Vandalia, on the banks of the Kaskaskia River, had been Illinois' state capital since 1820. A collection of frame and log structures, the town had known prosperity as a market center for southern Illinois when flatboats had carried produce down the river. In 1834, however, there was little to recommend the community. Its 800 inhabitants included state officers and the usual entourage that gathered about the land office, the federal court, and the county seat. The National Road, scarcely more than a track, connected the town with the east, and a second thoroughfare from Kentucky passed through to the northwest. But settlement had bypassed Vandalia, and the town had languished. The ten-year-old statehouse was already dilapidated, inconvenient for the transaction of business, and a disgrace to the state. Some state legislators, representing the rapidly developing areas to the north, were determined to relocate the state capital in some more central spot.

Like other western capitals, Vandalia was transformed during the weeks of the legislative session, when legislators, lobbyists and office-seekers invaded the town and swamped its meager lodging facilities. In December 1834, the political alignment of the legislature reflected the uncertainty of party lines, but it was clear that the friends of Jackson enjoyed a majority. Douglas, anxious to strengthen the Democratic organization, was irresistibly drawn to the scene of action, where for the first time he witnessed the rough informality of western lawmaking. National issues dominated much of the discussion. Acting Governor W. L. D. Ewing opened the session with a stinging denunciation of the Second United States Bank. Both houses of the legislature subsequently passed resolutions condemning the Bank, opposing its recharter, and endorsing Jackson's position. Not all of the debate was confined to the legislative halls. The question of the United States Bank was hotly debated in the lobby, or "third house," as well. Douglas soon discovered that members of the lobby were frequently more influential than the legislators. Among the opponents of Jackson's Bank policy was the tall, first-term representative from Sangamon County. Abraham Lincoln must have encountered Douglas in the halls of the capitol, but there is no record of their first meeting. Neither apparently took any particular notice of the other.[21]

In his effort to strengthen the Jackson party, Douglas found a valuable ally in John Wyatt, the only state representative from Morgan County whose Democracy was, according to Douglas, above suspicion. Wyatt had his own score to settle, and he was not unwilling to use Douglas to achieve his ends. John J. Hardin, a Jacksonville attorney, had been appointed state's attorney two years before, partly through the influence of a group of Morgan County Democrats, including Wyatt. In the 1834 election, however, Hardin had opposed the Jacksonians, apparently with some effect, for Wyatt was the only survivor of the group. Indignant at Hardin's "ingratitude," Wyatt swore revenge. State's attorneys were appointed by the governor for four-year terms; Hardin's term had two more years to run, and there was no likelihood that he would be dismissed in the meantime. The only alternative was to "repeal" Hardin out of office, to alter the law and make the office elective by the legislature.

Wyatt's desire for revenge coincided with Douglas' political ambitions. The two men had conferred in Douglas' office in Jacksonville, where Douglas drafted a bill "repealing the Old States attornies out of office, and making them Elective by joint ballot of both houses of the Legislature." Douglas also had other plans. If the state's Supreme Court judges could be relieved of the duty of holding circuit courts, a new set of circuit judges could be appointed. Judge Lockwood, a pillar of the opposition in Morgan County, would be confined to the supreme bench, and a more congenial person could be appointed to hold court in Jacksonville. Through these measures, Wyatt and Douglas agreed, "the opposition would be used up in this part of the State."

Wyatt introduced the bill into the lower house early in the session, arguing that the change in the selection of state's attorneys was in conformity with "the republican principle . . . of throwing these things more nearly before the people." Although it aroused considerable discussion, the bill passed the lower house by a party vote. Its fate in the state senate, where the margin between the parties was narrower, was less certain, although Hardin was advised by a friend following the house passage to prepare his resignation as state's attorney and hold it in readiness. The senate judiciary committee, to which the bill was referred, objected strongly to the change, concluding that "the idea . . . that the House of Representatives should participate in making appointments to office, because that brings the appointment nearer to the people, is altogether fallacious, and not founded upon any very exalted opinion of the intelligence and integrity of the Executive and Senate." After repeated attempts to sidetrack the legislation, the bill squeaked through the upper house.

Veto power over state legislation was held by the council of revision, composed of the governor and the four judges of the state supreme court, a majority of which was sufficient to nullify a law. On January 30, 1835, Douglas' bill was returned to the house "as improper to become a law of this State." Governor Duncan and two judges of the supreme court (one of them Samuel Lockwood) had objected to the bill. The legislature passed the bill over the council's objections, and on February 10 the two houses met in joint session to elect state's attorneys for the six judicial districts of the state. The results surprised no one; Douglas was elected state's attorney for the First Judicial District over Hardin by a margin of four votes. Wyatt's vengeance was complete, and Douglas had taken the first step of his political career.

While his state's attorneys bill was pending, Douglas wrote a second bill, one making county recorders and surveyors elective by the people. The council of revision found the bill objectionable, but their veto was overridden easily by the legislature. Douglas also assisted in drafting legislation revising the state's judicial system by creating a new set of circuit court judgeships. This effort likewise met with success. The members of the supreme bench were no longer required to perform circuit duty; as a result, Douglas wrote, "we got an impartial and pretty clear fellow in the place of Lockwood my old enemy." [22]

Several years later, Douglas wrote with unconvincing modesty that he had not expected to be a candidate for the office of state's attorney, nor had he had any desire for the office. The charge of the opposition, however, that the bill had its origin "in Wyatt's malice and my selfishness and ambition" altered the picture. His friends swore that if the bill were successful, "little Douglas" would be the man to defeat Hardin. However it happened, Douglas was elated. "I occupy precisely the position I have long wished for *Politically* and *Professionally*," he wrote to his family, assuring his mother that "I am doing as well in my *'profession'* as could be expected of a Boy of twenty one." He attributed his triumph over Hardin to "the *Lord,* and the *Legislature,* and *Gen Jackson.*"

Douglas' election provoked considerable discussion throughout the district. The Whigs regarded as an outrage Hardin's displacement by an untried youth who had resided in Illinois barely over a year. One of the supreme court judges (probably Lockwood himself) protested that the election was wrong. "What business," he asked, "has such a stripling with such an office? He is no lawyer, and has no law-books." In virtually every succeeding session of the state legislature attempts were made to repeal Douglas' bill, but without success. Several years later, looking back on his first office with a perspective gained from experience and reflection, Douglas doubted the wisdom of his state's attorneys bill; "all Legislative elections," he then wrote, "ought to be abolished, and the officers either appointed by the Governor and Senate, or elected by the people." [23]

v

The First Judicial District encompassed eight counties, sprawling across central Illinois to the Mississippi River on the west. No district could have been more ideally suited to a young man with political aspirations. The counties lay within the fastest growing section of the state, and among them were the state's two most populous counties, Morgan and Sangamon. As state's attorney, Douglas traveled with the circuit court, meeting in each of the eight counties and remaining long enough to form valuable political acquaintances. As the legal representative of the state, he attracted attention wherever he went and became known to some of the leading lawyers of the district. The courtroom provided him with an important sounding board for his political convictions. It was not likely that the juries he addressed would soon forget him.

It was his responsibility, Douglas wrote, "to prossecute all criminals in each county in the Circuit, and also all civil actions in which the People are concerned, the Pres & Directors of the State Bank, any county, or the Auditor of Public &c." This required a more complete knowledge of the law than he had thus far acquired. As soon as he was elected, he secured all the standard works on criminal law that were available and applied himself "assiduously to study and practice." The office paid a salary of $250 per year; with his fees, Douglas estimated that his annual income would reach the handsome figure of $500 or $600. Fortunately, no court sessions were scheduled from late October until early March, which allowed him to devote the winter months to problems of party organization and to attend the legislative sessions as a member of the lobby.

Douglas' official duties began when he appeared in the Sangamon circuit court a month after his election. Within two months he had visited each of the eight counties within his district. A friend recalled Douglas' departure from Jacksonville as he set out on his circuit, mounted on a horse furnished by Wyatt, his short legs barely reaching below the saddle skirts and his law books stuffed into the saddle bags. "He was not," commented this person in marvelous understatement, "a striking figure on horse-back." [24]

In spite of his youth and inexperience, Douglas was moderately successful as a state's attorney. While the statement of an early biographer, that not a single indictment drawn by Douglas was ever quashed, was obviously an exaggeration, there is evidence that the young lawyer achieved some local fame and reputation as a prosecutor. Some of his success was undoubtedly due to the able assistance of such men as Josiah Lamborn, who held the office of attorney general during part of Douglas' term, and some can be attributed to simple luck rather than legal skill. After his first six weeks on the circuit, he proudly informed his family, "Whilst on my present Tour I have sent two men to the State Prison and have not had an Indictment quashed, to the great mortification of my enemies, and the gratification of my friends." For the benefit of those at home, he painted a dramatic picture of his single-handed efforts to secure justice for the people of Illinois. "I find myself on a new theatre of action," he wrote, "and I may say a very important and critical one, when conducting an important trial alone, with three or four of the best Lawyers in the State on the opposite side ready to take advantage of every circumstance, never asking favors nor granting them." Not all were so impressed with Douglas' prowess. A Bloomington attorney, with whom Douglas stayed during the sessions of the McLean court, later wrote that Douglas "never amounted to much as a lawyer." As a state's attorney, he continued, "he was not a success, and I don't believe he convicted one case out of ten that he was interested in."

Most of the cases which Douglas tried involved minor infractions of the law, and only a small proportion were jury trials. Illinois courtrooms in the 1830's were highly informal. The judges, who were often not far removed in experience and ability from the farmers they served, abdicated much of their responsibility to the juries. Jurors were often moved by the passions of the moment and an innate sympathy for the underdog. They seldom convicted for minor offenses, and even in more serious cases they usually found extenuating circumstances justifying the crime. In that atmosphere, Douglas' scanty knowledge of the law probably aided rather than hindered him. His speaking ability proved a considerable asset, for he addressed his juries as he would political audiences. His own law practice, meager to begin with, suffered even more.

One of Douglas' early cases as state's attorney has become almost legendary. At his first court in McLean County, Douglas received a number of indictments from the grand jury and spent most of one night hastily writing them up so that the grand jurors could be discharged. When court opened, John T. Stuart, a member of the legislature, a Whig and a friend of Hardin, moved that all of Douglas' indictments be quashed on the ground that the state's attorney had misspelled the name of the county in each one of them. Stuart's manner was "very pompous," and his statement included "some rather contemptuous remarks imputing ignorance to the writer of the indictments." Members of the bar and the spectators sensed a plan to disgrace the young attorney publicly, and he himself became discouraged at what seemed to be an inauspicious beginning to his career. Asked by the judge (Stephen T. Logan, one of Lincoln's legal mentors) for his reply, Douglas declared that the burden of proof was on Stuart. He demanded that evidence be introduced to sustain the contention that the county name had been misspelled. No copy of the law establishing the county was available in Bloomington, the county seat, so the court adjourned for two days while a messenger was dispatched to near-by Peoria to procure a copy of the statutes. Few gave Douglas' case any chance for success. The opposition lawyers felt that the young man who had helped push the state's attorneys bill through the legislature and who had himself upset one of the leading lawyers of the district would now receive his due. Douglas' demand for evidence was regarded as a delaying tactic, which indeed it was. When the volume of statutes was finally produced, Stuart found to his (and Douglas') astonishment that the county name was spelled as in the indictments. Douglas' indictments were immediately sustained, and the court enjoyed a laugh at Stuart's expense. For Douglas, the incident proved to be one of vital importance to his reputation, for now the spectators and the jurors regarded it as a deliberate plan laid by the state's attorney to trap the able lawyers against whom he was contending, an impression Douglas was careful not to dispel. He later compared the statute with the original enrolled bill in the office of the secretary of state and found, as he had suspected, that there was a misprint in the printed version. Though he was as surprised as Stuart at the outcome of the case, Douglas drew a political lesson from the incident: "Admit nothing, and require my adversary to prove everything material to the success of his cause." [25]

Douglas traveled the circuit twice as state's attorney. His briefs were drawn up with a carelessness that would have been disastrous in a more sophisticated society. He was constantly subjected to the insinuations of the opposition lawyers that he was too young and inexperienced for the job, and courtroom proceedings were frequently distracted by heated personal battles between Douglas and his opponents. In one weird case, argued in Jacksonville early in 1836, Douglas engaged in a lengthy debate with the opposing counsel over the question of his legal qualifications. The case involved the members of an isolated rural family who, in the heat of religious frenzy, had attempted to make a human sacrifice. A neighbor had intervened, but he had almost lost his own life in the process. The discussion between Douglas, who was the prosecutor on behalf of the state, and his opponent revolved about the question of temporary insanity. Douglas contended that the members of the family were responsible for their acts, even though he conceded that they suffered an "insanity produced by religious excitement." The jury sided with Douglas and found the defendants guilty. Thomas Ford, the presiding judge and later to become governor of the state, set aside the verdict as contrary to law and evidence and ordered a new trial, maintaining that the accused suffered insanity and therefore were not responsible for their acts. The verdict of the jury, the judge declared, was influenced more by the controversy between Douglas and the defense counsel than by the evidence.[26]

Douglas' term as state's attorney disillusioned him with the law, while it opened his eyes to the possibilities of a political career. The highly touted prospects for professional advancement in this frontier society proved elusive. "Out of the long list of Lawyers that come to this country and settle," Douglas wrote in 1835, "there is not one out of an hundred who does *one half* the business enough to pay his expenses the first year . . . practicing Law in the Sucker State will not make a man rich the first year or two." [27] For a young man in a hurry, the road to legal prominence and success seemed too long and tortuous. The dream of his youth, that he would seek a career in the law, quickly faded. His experience on the circuit and his involvement in the political discussions at the state capital, on the other hand, persuaded him that the way to power and success was through politics. The times were propitious, and opportunities seemed abundant. Political ambition stirred within him, and he soon began the hard-driving, relentless pursuit of political power that would dominate the rest of his life.

# III
## "The voice of the many and the doctrine of equal rights"
### 1835—1837

i

"If you have an opportunity of selling your farm immediately," Douglas wrote to his family shortly after his arrival in Illinois, "be sure and embrace it, and all come on at once. . . . There are greater bargains to be had now and better locations than there will be at any future time. Land far superior to yours in beauty, in fertility, in location and in every other respect may be had at one dollar & twenty five cents per acre. And these very land [s] five or ten years hence will be worth from five to fifty dollars per acre." [1] His family did not move from New York to Illinois, but Douglas persisted in his attempts at persuasion, reflecting in his enthusiasm the spirit of buoyancy and speculation that gripped the frontier state in the 1830's.

Two years before Douglas wrote, the last Indian resistance in Illinois had been subdued and the way cleared for the advance of population into the northern portions of the state. The development of transportation, on the Great Lakes as well as on the Ohio and Mississippi rivers, brought thousands of people within reach of these new lands. Southern Illinois was passed by, as the settlers sought out the rich bottom lands of the Sangamon and Illinois rivers. The Military Tract, a slim finger of land lying between the Illinois and Mississippi rivers that had been reserved for veterans of the War of 1812, filled rapidly. The population of the state almost tripled between 1830 and 1840.

With the farmers came the land speculators. "The West is *boiling*

36

with speculation," wrote an Illinois-bound emigrant in 1835. Four new land offices were opened, at Quincy, Danville, Galena, and Chicago, to keep pace with the increasing demand for public land, and the volume of land sales fluctuated widely as the speculators shifted their activities from one district to another. Town site promotion and speculation in town lots produced as much excitement as did the traffic in farmland.

Few of the new settlers were as enthusiastic as Douglas. To his step-father he wrote of the delightful climate, the rolling prairie, the rich productive soil, "and the great and unexampled advantages it offers to those who may choose to emigrate to it." The young cattle feeding on the green prairie grass, the brooks "of ever living water" winding their way through the countryside, the fields of corn, wheat, and oats all were evoked in his letters home. The lure of quick, easy profit in this "Garden of the World" completely captured Douglas' imagination. "The most money is made here," he wrote from Jacksonville in 1835, "by speculat-ing in Lands, for which this year presents the finest opportunities that have ever been afforded in this State." Nor was back-breaking toil neces-sary for economic success. "With the capital you can bring with you," he advised his family, "you will be able to make a fortune in Lands without laboring any yourself." Later, he again informed his stepfather, "Without performing a particle of labor you might make four fold the money you now do off your farm by all your labor and industry." [2]

Apparently swayed by Douglas' enthusiasm, Julius Granger visited Illinois in 1835, and when he returned to New York, he left a sum of money with Douglas for investment. Douglas purchased town lots in Jacksonville, which by April 1836 had so increased in value that Doug-las proudly informed his brother-in-law that "I can now sell your Lots at from fifty to an hundred per cent advance—or for between three & four hundred dollars—which by the by is a pretty good interest." Douglas converted some of his own small earnings into real property, purchasing farmland in Pike County and town lots in Meredosia, Bloom-ington, Virginia, and Beardstown. [3]

The speculative fever raised serious economic problems in the state. New settlers found no common or sufficient medium of exchange with which they could transact business. Speculators desired an expansion of credit, and an increased supply of currency which could only be provided by new banking institutions. Neighboring states, gripped by the same speculative mania, had authorized banks of issue, and Illinois residents feared that their notes would soon flood the state unless new banking organizations were provided. Douglas shared this point of view. "I am no friend to the Banking System," he wrote, "but under existing circumstances a Bank may be necessary in this State in self defense." He was (and remained) a hard-money man, but like many Jacksonians he recognized the need for a state banking institution that could meet the demand for currency and credit. When the legislature met in December 1834, a group of Whigs and Democrats combined to create Illinois' second state bank. Response to the sale of the bank stock was immediate; within a few days after subscriptions began, Douglas reported, "Capitalists are rushing in from all quarters to take our Bank stock which it is supposed will be very profitable." [4]

The increasing population, the settlement of the northern counties, the stimulation of public land sales, and the rise of speculation dominated the first half of the 1830's in Illinois. These were also years of political ferment and confusion. As the economy burgeoned and the population became more heterogeneous, the political attitudes of the settlers matured, and the close relation between state and national politics became more apparent. The dominance of the earlier settled southern portions of the state was challenged by the newly settled central and northern counties. Many of the new settlers brought with them notions of political party organization which seemed foreign to the state's older leaders. A more rigid political organization, through such eastern devices as the convention system, became the weapon by which the new settlers made their challenge effective. Stephen A. Douglas, a fledgling Jacksonian just embarking on his career, was a central figure in this movement, and he reflected the new political forces that were at work in the state.

ii

The fortunes of the Jackson party in Illinois had reached a critical juncture by the spring of 1835. The local elections the year before had demonstrated the fluidity of party lines and had revealed sharp cleavages among the followers of Old Hickory. A governor had been elected largely on the strength of his Jacksonian pose, though in fact he was not in sympathy with much of the President's program. The differences between the "whole hog" Jacksonians and the "milk and cider" Jacksonians became more pronounced, as the former found themselves defeated at the polls by men whose Jacksonism was suspect. The appearance of the Whig party, although as yet highly disorganized, emphasized the need to purge from the Democratic ranks all but true, unquestioning followers of Jackson. The approaching presidential election of 1836 made unity in the party all the more essential.

The question of the succession created division in the Democratic ranks, and the rifts that developed among national rivals were keenly felt in Illinois. Partisans of Kentucky's Richard Mentor Johnson, though they had lost the vice presidential nomination for their candidate in 1832, were determined to put him forth once again, this time for the higher office. Convinced that Jackson's successor should be a westerner, they prepared to do battle with the supporters of Martin Van Buren. The "opposition," a label indiscriminately applied to Whigs and to "milk and cider" Jacksonians, looked to erstwhile-Jacksonian Hugh Lawson White of Tennessee.

The loosened party lines, the dissatisfaction of some Democrats with Jackson's policies, and the rivalry for the presidential succession marked this as an important period of transition in Illinois politics. To the young, vigorous Jacksonians who were arriving in the state, but one course seemed open to the party: the struggle in the next election must be made on the basis of principle rather than personality. Loyalty to Andrew Jackson was no longer enough; to be a Democrat also must mean devotion to the principles and policies which Jackson professed. The instrument by which party organization would be strengthened was the nominating convention, a device brought to the state by the emigrants from New England and New York, where it had already developed. Its introduction into Illinois provided a strong link between national and state politics and encouraged party organization on national rather than local principles.

Although Douglas later boasted that he introduced the convention system into his county, he shared that honor with Jacksonville editor S. S. Brooks. The two men were instrumental in calling the first Democratic party convention in Morgan County early in April 1835. With Douglas' friend John Wyatt in the chair, the meeting resolved that "it is desirable . . . that the principles which have characterized the administration of Andrew Jackson . . . shall continue to be maintained in the person of his successor." The national convention, scheduled to meet in Baltimore the following month, was supported as "the best and surest means of harmonizing the conflicting interests of our widely extended country." A state convention, to meet in Vandalia on April 27 to select delegates to the Baltimore meeting, was proposed, and six county men were chosen to go to Vandalia with instructions to support Martin Van

Buren for President and Richard M. Johnson for Vice President. Resolutions expressing "undiminished confidence" in Jackson and gratitude to Thomas Hart Benton "for his unyielding devotion to the interests of the West" concluded the discussion. Douglas delivered the principal address on behalf of the resolutions, following which they were unanimously adopted.[5]

Douglas' role in the Morgan County convention revealed his new position in Democratic party politics. Barely twenty-two years old and just beginning his term as state's attorney, he rapidly received political recognition. Three weeks after the county meeting, he wrote home, "Huzza for Martin Vanburen & the National Convention. The whigs are making a tremendous effort here to divide the Democratic party by bringing out Judge White. But it wont do. We are determined to all go together and act in concert with our brethren in other parts of the Union." The idea of the party convention quickly gained support. Within a few weeks following the initial meeting in Morgan County, conventions were held in several other counties. The state convention at Vandalia was poorly attended (only five counties were represented, with barely a dozen delegates), and Democrats from the northern and central counties dominated the proceedings. Nevertheless, it was clear that a revolution in party organization was in the making in Illinois, and that Stephen A. Douglas would play an important part in that revolution.[6]

The appearance of the convention system aroused the opposition of Whigs and "milk and cider" Jacksonians. The party convention, they said, was an eastern device, undemocratic and alien to the ways of the west. Its use was identified with Martin Van Buren and the machinations of officeholders to put the "Red Fox" in the White House. The Baltimore convention, which nominated Van Buren, was "nothing more nor less than an effort of the *few* to govern the *many,* and to relieve the People of the troublesome task of choosing a President for themselves," commented the Whig *Sangamo Journal.* Supporters of White, regarding themselves Jacksonians still, rejected Van Buren because "he is an eastern man and has no interest in common with the western people." Conventions, the opposition declared, were got up by the officeholders in an attempt to control public sentiment, a charge that struck home, for much of the impetus for the convention system did indeed come from men like Congressman May, George Forquer of the Springfield land office, and Douglas himself. The proscriptive power of the new party organization was demonstrated almost immediately, when Archer G. Hern-

222

don, father of Lincoln's future law partner, was literally read out of the Democratic party for his support of White. "Does it follow," Herndon appealed, "because I support Judge White I must consequently oppose the measures of our beloved President?" To the new managers of the party, however, there was no room for such flexibility.[7]

Another round of county conventions followed the nomination of Van Buren and Johnson at the Baltimore convention in May. Many of the counties appointed committees of "correspondence and vigilance" to promote unity of action throughout the state, and once again Stephen A. Douglas and Morgan County took a lead. A state convention to select presidential electors gathered in Vandalia early in December 1835, during the first week of the legislative session—a convenience to those delegates who were also legislators—and offered an occasion for the first full-scale debate on the merits of the convention system.

Douglas, present as a delegate from Morgan County, was placed on the committee to select five presidential electors and also on the committee to prepare an "address" to the Democrats of the state. Resolutions endorsing the nomination of Van Buren and Johnson, approving Jackson's administration, and opposing those who would create dissension in the party were introduced and passed. "All power of right, rests with the people, and emanates directly from them," the delegates resolved. They recommended "union and concert of action, and a frequent recurrence to primary principles . . . for without a frequent interchange of political sentiment, expressed by the people, and repeated by the delegates, properly authorized, the democracy cannot ensure that success in their elections, which the purity and integrity of their principles, entitle them to claim." One proposal, however, urging the nomination of all state officers by the convention, aroused immediate debate. Democrats from the newer sections of the north clashed with the "old fashioned" Democrats of the south over the desirability of party discipline.

With Ebenezer Peck of Chicago, Douglas spoke at some length in favor of conventions. He recalled the operation of the convention system in New York, where he had had an opportunity to observe it in action, and argued "that it was the only way to manage elections with success." In many other states of the east and south, he added, conventions were being held with great success. It was a mistake to suppose, as some had, "that the people of the West had too long enjoyed their own opinions to quietly submit to the regulations of a convention." The system had been accepted in Morgan County, where it worked with success. In conclusion, Douglas "hoped to hear no more objections about the people not being prepared for the system. It was the duty of politicians and statesmen to prepare the people for every service, where their own best interests, and the success of the party, and democracy were at stake."

Douglas' effort won a glowing tribute from Chicago delegate John D. Caton, who thanked Douglas for the distinguished and valuable service he had rendered the party during his short residence in the state. If all of our young men, Caton observed, "would use the same exertions to introduce sound principles and to give the party the benefit of their experience, we should soon hear no more of the silly objection, that the people are not prepared for the Convention system."

The arguments in favor of the convention system fell hard on the ears of Democrats from the older sections of the state. The convention was branded as "anti-republican," as a "contrivance to cheat the people out of their votes, and to give power and consequence to the party managers." The claims of the Van Buren supporters "to the exclusive democracy of the country" were ridiculous and arrogant. The opposition managed to defeat the proposal to nominate state officers in the convention, but the question continued to be argued with vigor in the legislature and in the lobby. Douglas, not a member of the assembly, participated in the discussion in the lobby, although his arguments were not always well received. At the end of December, an anti-convention member of the legislature reported that "my friend duglas, when he went to address the Lobby the last time on the Convention Sistem the Lobby adjourned on him & would not here him speeke."

The clash from the first assumed sectional characteristics; not only was it a struggle between the northern and southern, the newer and the older, sections of the state, but it also became part of an east-west hostility. The party convention was identified as an eastern device, promoted for the benefit of the New York "magician" at the expense of the west and of western interests. "Van Burenism and 'New Yorkism' are beginning to be understood as synonymous here," commented the *Sangamo Journal.* Two of the five presidential electors chosen at the convention were from New York. Peck had lived in New York for a short time, as had both Douglas and Caton. "It is a remarkable fact," the editor commented, "that no man who has been born and raised west of the mountains, or south of the Potomac, has yet ventured publicly to vindicate 'the wholesome system of Conventions.' " Douglas had earlier boasted of his new western orientation, but in this quarrel he was identified with the east. The party convention, to Douglas, was a symbol of political maturity; regardless of its origin, it was essential if the party wished to develop into a strong instrument for democracy.[8]

When the state convention adjourned, the debate continued in the legislature. There discussion of the convention system became involved with the question of the presidential succession. In December 1835, the state senate, by the close vote of 13 to 12, approved resolutions nominating Hugh Lawson White for the presidency and disapproving of "the convention system attempted to be forced upon the American people by the Van Buren party." Douglas, in Vandalia as a member of the lobby, protested that the resolutions had been passed "by the most fraudulent means" and that the state was by no means favorably inclined to White's candidacy. The action of the upper house on behalf of White was countered by the passage of pro-Van Buren resolutions in the lower house in January 1836. An attempt to amend the resolutions by declaring the "practice of holding conventions for the nomination of all elective officers" to be "opposed to republican institutions, and dangerous to the liberties of the people" was defeated. The Van Buren resolutions passed by an easy margin.[9]

Douglas' importance to the discussion of the convention system is undoubted; the adoption of the convention by the Democratic party may be credited in part to his exertions in Morgan County, in the state convention, and as a lobbyist at the state capital. Perhaps one indication of his role in the movement was the attention given him by the opposition press. His youth, his short stature, and his pretensions to party leadership invited ridicule even at this early date. The *Sangamo Journal* scornfully referred to him as "Squire Douglas," and in a letter published in the *Journal,* purportedly written by Congressman William L. May but probably a fabrication, Douglas was accused of "laboring under a mental derangement." "He must be dismissed from service," the letter stated, "and put upon half pay; and to prevent any clashing in our present arrangements, I am about to have a post office established at the head of the Morn Star for his special benefit."

On the last day of December, as the legislature debated the convention system, the committee appointed by the Democratic convention to prepare a party statement issued its address "To the Democratic Republican citizens of Illinois." Douglas was among the signers of the document. Indeed, some later admirers credited him with its authorship, but, whether or not Douglas wrote the address, he subscribed to its sentiments. The convention system was defended as necessary "to embody and give effect to the popular will." Martin Van Buren, the nominee of the Baltimore convention, was hailed as the man best qualified to carry on the "principles which have marked, distinguished and elevated the political course of Andrew Jackson." The address concluded with an enumeration of the principles which identified Jackson and his party: strict construction, "preserving the rights of states, and the supremacy of the general government"; a vigorous foreign policy that would vindicate the rights and claims of American citizens; the "humane and wise" removal of the Indians "from within the borders of civilization"; a reduction in the price of the public lands; and firm resistance to the United States Bank.[10] The address not only served the Democratic party, it provided Douglas with one of his earliest platforms.

### iii

Douglas was so busy promoting the convention system during the spring of 1836 that he neglected his duties as state's attorney, failing even to appear in court. It was an important year for the reorganized Democracy, as it faced its first trial in the state, and Douglas was eager to make the necessary investment of time and energy in order to ensure its success. With S. S. Brooks, his Jacksonville friend, he urged that a party convention be summoned—the first in the county to be composed of delegates appointed by precincts—to nominate candidates for the state legislature, two senators and six representatives, and the several county offices. The number of aspirants for each seat was large, and the Whigs who observed the proceedings were confident that Douglas would not succeed in his effort to discipline the party. In neighboring Sangamon County, the Whig press was prepared to report the failure of the "slaves of the magician" to impose their will on Morgan County Democrats. The Whigs, however, were disappointed. The meeting was conducted with "dignity and decorum," and the nominations were received with approbation by the delegates. Although the *Sangamo Journal* scoffed at the "fine sport" provided by the "Van Buren Dictators," the Whigs themselves followed suit and quickly came to agreement on a ticket of their own.

Douglas was not willing to confine his organizational efforts to the county level, as he in fact had already demonstrated. Before its adjournment, the Morgan meeting endorsed a proposal for a Third Congressional District convention to be held later in the spring, in Peoria.

Douglas was among those chosen to represent the county at the meeting. Few of the counties in the district were as well organized as Morgan County. Only five of the district's nineteen counties were represented at Peoria, and the Morgan County delegation clearly dominated the proceedings. Undeterred by the imperfect representation, which proved, commented the Whigs, that Douglas' organizing efforts lacked popular support, the delegates nominated incumbent Congressman William L. May for another term.[11]

Soon after the county's legislative ticket had been nominated, the election campaign was under way. John J. Hardin, the able Jacksonville attorney who had lost his office of state's attorney to Douglas, was selected to head the slate of Whig candidates, causing some reshuffling among the Democrats. The obvious person to oppose Hardin seemed to be Douglas himself. He had bested the Whig before the state legislature. Could he not repeat his performance before Morgan County voters? One of the Democratic nominees (Samuel Pettit, not Brooks as some accounts aver) promptly withdrew his candidacy, and Douglas was named to his place. Considerations of political strategy quickly overcame any scruples Douglas might have had for a strict observance of the convention system. "Really," the *Sangamo Journal* suggested, "the Van Buren men of Morgan must not possess a very fastidious taste, if they can swallow such a dose as this."

Douglas lost no time in taking to the stump. His selection as a candidate for the legislature's lower house, he modestly reported to his family, was much against his will, but "in this as in other things I yielded to the solicitations of my friends." His friends, no doubt, had little difficulty in persuading him. He was confident that he would be elected and imparted some of the excitement he felt to his family in New York. "I find no difficulty in adopting the Western mode of Electioneering by addressing the people from the Stump." He had, he wrote, already met his opponent Hardin in "a number of pitched battles" in which he had come out the "conqueror." It would be, he predicted, a warm contest but the "warmer the better for I like excitement." Although national and party issues played a role in the contest, the principal issue of the campaign transcended party lines. The rapid growth of the state in population, the building of new towns, and the opening of new areas to agricultural development raised the cry for internal improvements—the construction of canals and railroads. The cry was not unique to Illinois, nor was the response. One traveler to the state during the 1836 campaign noted that "Internal Improvement seems now to be the order of the day in Northern Illinois. . . . [It is] the hobby of most of the stump-speakers." Party doctrine was shunted aside as candidates of both parties urged a large-scale internal improvement program by the quickest, easiest plan. As the campaign continued, the idea became fixed in the popular mind, and it was clear that the new legislature would be responsible for bringing the dreams of the state's promoters to reality.

If any Democrats had doubted the efficacy of the convention system, the results of the state election in August 1836 should have dispelled their doubts. The popular Hardin was the only Whig candidate for state representative elected from Morgan County. Douglas and four other Democrats won handily, and the Little Giant proved himself the leading vote-getter. Although the fluidity of party lines in some parts of the state and the uncertain party affiliations of some candidates prevent an accurate breakdown of the votes, the results of the state election gave Jacksonians cause for rejoicing.[12]

The presidential campaign was much less exciting than the contest for the state offices. The Whig opposition, disorganized and generally committed to the candidacy of Hugh Lawson White, must have recognized the futility of its appeal. The White electoral ticket was composed of anti-Van Buren Jackson men, which hampered the Whigs in their attack on the party of Old Hickory. Their confusion was compounded shortly after the state election, when the candidacy of William Henry Harrison was seriously proposed. In September, an Edwardsville meeting urged the White electors to cast their votes for Harrison, if the latter received greater support than White in other states. As election day neared, support for Harrison increased, while many original White backers, Jacksonians still, drifted back into the Democratic ranks. By late October, the opposition ticket bore the label "Union Anti-Van Buren Electoral Ticket" and was headed by both White and Harrison. Harrison, portrayed as the friend of the west and of the small farmer, gained ground rapidly, and by the eve of the election he was regarded as the principal Whig candidate. Although his name aroused more enthusiasm than White's did, especially among those who regarded White as the candidate of John C. Calhoun and the nullifiers, the boom came too late. To the Democrats the issue was clear. The question, commented the *Illinois State Register,* the state's leading Democratic paper, was "whether we will forever bend our necks to the yoke of northern federalists and monopolists on the one hand and southern nullifiers on the other, or whether we will perpetuate the principles of Gen. Jackson's administration, which have produced such general prosperity to the whole country and to the west in particular." The triumph of Martin Van Buren at the polls in Illinois surprised no one; to Douglas, the Democratic victory was vindication of his struggle for party organization.[13]

Members of the Tenth General Assembly gathered in Vandalia soon after the election. The old statehouse, decrepit and neglected, had been abandoned and a new frame building was being built to house the legislature, a gesture by Vandalia's citizens to keep the capital in their town. The plaster was still wet, the rooms were damp, and, in spite of the additional stoves which were provided, the legislators complained of discomfort. Vandalia had changed little since Douglas first traveled to the capital two years before. One legislator solemnly announced to his wife, "This is the dullest, dreariest place"; another complained of the poor and crowded accommodations; still a third commented, "I would rather be any place in the world than here."

Although the legislature contained a Democratic majority, the *Sangamo Journal* generously declared that it embraced "more talent than any legislative body ever before assembled in Illinois"—in view of the session's achievements, a rather bold and reckless tribute. Sixty-six of the ninety-one members of the lower house were without any previous legislative experience, the result of a reapportionment and of the stiffening party lines. Serving with Douglas were Abraham Lincoln of New Salem, soon to move to Springfield, who was one of the few members with experience; Augustus C. French, later to become Illinois' first Yankee-born governor; James Semple and James Shields, who would later take seats in the United States Senate; and Edward Dickinson Baker, John J. Hardin, John A. McClernand, William A. Richardson, and Robert Smith, all future Congressmen. Semple was elected speaker (although both Douglas and Lincoln voted consistently for Newton Cloud, Democrat from Morgan County).[14]

Partisan lines were drawn immediately as the assembly devoted its first weeks to a heated discussion of national politics. Governor Joseph Duncan, in his message to the legislature, bitterly assailed the Jackson administration, accusing the President of establishing a "despotism more absolute than that of any civilized government in the world" and calling on the representatives to rebuke Jackson's course. The President's policy of appointments and removals and his withdrawal of the deposits from the Second United States Bank came under blistering attack. For the

Democrats, Duncan's charges (described as a "declaration of war against General Jackson") were an especially bitter pill, since the governor had been elected two years before as a Jacksonian; for Duncan, the attack marked his transition into the ranks of the opposition. A committee composed entirely of "Van Buren men" was immediately appointed by the speaker to consider the governor's accusations and to vindicate Jackson. Douglas was a member of the committee.

The report, written by John A. McClernand, was the occasion for Douglas' debut as a legislator. The committee exonerated Jackson from Duncan's charges and offered resolutions approving his administration. The Whigs countered with resolutions of their own, declaring that it was a waste of time and money to discuss questions "which merely involve national politics." Douglas was not content, however, to allow Duncan's message to go unanswered from the floor. The governor's charges, he shouted, had aroused his "honest indignation" and he felt compelled to expose them. In a speech which exhibited many of the characteristics of his later oratorical style, he accused Duncan of hurling a firebrand into the house in order to stir up strife and dissension among his opponents. He denounced the Whig resolutions as an "artful maneuver" and "a finesse cunningly devised to snare the unwary, and worthy of those only who are engaged in a cause that cannot stand upon its own merits." The people, he confidently asserted, surely had more intelligence and sagacity than to be duped by "such shallow artifices of intriguing politicians." The words were strong, but Douglas was on safe ground. The house supported him by passing the committee's resolutions quickly and easily.[15]

A further preliminary to the legislative session was the election of a United States Senator. The Whigs, without a candidate of their own, smiled "complacently at the angry snarls of the contending Van Buren candidates" as several Democrats of varying orthodoxy vied for the position. Although his record as a Jacksonian was not above suspicion, Richard Montgomery Young was elected. He received Douglas' vote on all the ballots. Douglas hailed Young's election as a Jacksonian triumph and demonstrated his delight at the traditional post-election celebration, where the "corn juice" ran freely. Douglas and James Shields, wrote the brother of William Cullen Bryant, who was spending the winter in Vandalia, "to the consternation of the host and the intense merriment of the guests, climbed up on the table, at one end, encircled each other's waists, and to the tune of a rollicking song, pirouetted down the whole length

of the table, shouting, singing, and kicking dishes, glasses, and everything right and left, helter skelter." Young was later presented with a
bill for $600, covering the food, liquor, and breakage. Douglas' adapta-
tion to frontier customs was complete.[16]

With partisan questions disposed of, the members of the assembly
turned their attention to what they considered their most important
task: the creation of a state-financed system of general internal improvements. Previous legislatures had chartered large numbers of private railroad companies, but the failure of these private interests to attract sufficient capital caused the people to look to the state. County meetings had
been held through the summer of 1836, and an internal improvements
convention was scheduled to meet in Vandalia on the eve of the opening
of the general assembly. Congress, as early as 1822, had authorized the
construction of a canal connecting Lake Michigan with the Illinois
River, but the project had become a political football and languished.
Construction had barely begun on the Illinois and Michigan Canal by
1836. The new interest in railroads presented the canal advocates with a
formidable challenge, especially in the southern part of the state, where
the people saw in railroad construction an opportunity to counter the
fast-growing north. Other states were embarking on ambitious internal
improvements schemes, and Illinois, it was thought, must keep up. The
people of the state were exhorted to build for the future, to prepare for
the glorious destiny that awaited them. In all the discussions there was a
tone of haste and urgency, and it was shared by members of the Tenth
General Assembly. The legislature, urged one newspaper, must respond
to the popular demand and discharge its duty to the state with "zeal and
energy." Governor Duncan, in his opening address to the assembly,
looked forward to the time when "the whole country shall be intersected
by canals and railroads, and our beautiful prairies enlivened by thousands of steam engines, drawing after them lengthened trains freighted
with the abundant productions of our fertile soil."

The internal improvements convention met simultaneously with the
opening of the legislature, and many of the delegates were members of
the assembly who shared Duncan's vision. After two days of deliberation, resolutions were passed demanding the improvement of the principal rivers and the construction of a railroad system by the state. Douglas, according to one source, was selected by the convention to present
an internal improvements plan to the legislature. Early in the session he
introduced several resolutions providing for the completion of the Illi-

nois and Michigan Canal, the construction of a railroad connecting the
terminus of the canal with the Ohio River (the so-called Central Railroad project), the construction of a second railroad from Quincy eastward to the Indiana state line in the direction of the Wabash and Erie
Canal, and the improvement of the Wabash and Illinois rivers. Additional surveys were to be made for other works of general utility, although Douglas later commented that he was unwilling to go further
than the projects he specified. The improvements were to be constructed
and owned by the state and would be financed by a loan effected on the
faith of the state. Douglas' proposal reflected his own interest in the development of the central and northern sections of the state, as well as his
conviction that the internal improvements system must be general and
varied, embodying canal, railroad, and river projects. Such a modest system, however, did not meet the expansive and comprehensive notions of
many of his colleagues.[17]

The internal improvements committee of the lower house, to which
Douglas' resolutions were referred, reported a system that differed considerably from Douglas' plan. The Illinois and Michigan Canal (which
was already under construction) was dropped from the bill and a number of river and railroad projects were added. The whole was estimated
to cost about $7,500,000. The salutary effect of such an internal im-
provements program on the growth of the state was described in detail.
An "overcautious system of legislation" was disapproved on the grounds
that it would stop emigration to the state and that it would actually result in an exodus to other states where more liberal systems had been enacted. The committee's bill was immediately subjected to a flurry of
amendments, particularly from those who were interested in adding further projects and from those Whigs who were opposed to construction
by the state and wanted the work done by private companies. "Let
Douglass and his Vanburen coajutors have the fame of supporting &
passing the *involvement Bill,*" wrote one Jacksonville Whig to Hardin,
"It will be Glory enough for you to vote against it." Douglas, however,
was himself disturbed at the extent and magnitude of the proposed system, but to oppose the bill was to court popular disapproval. "So strong
was the current of popular feeling in its favor," Douglas later wrote,
"that it was hazardous for any politician to oppose it." The question of
internal improvements was not a partisan one (except, perhaps, as it
concerned the manner of constructing and financing the works), but
Douglas was anxious to secure as much partisan advantage out of the

debate as possible. Writing to his constituents in Morgan County, he charged the Whig members of the delegation with opposition to any system of internal improvements, a serious charge in view of the fact that one of the railroads originally proposed by Douglas was to pass through the county. Petitions instructing the county delegation to support the bill were circulated and signed by members of both parties. When the bill was finally approved by the lower house on the last day of January, Douglas' vote was cast with the majority in the affirmative. His opposition to the "mammoth bill" had become well known, he wrote a year later, after the Panic of 1837 had placed the internal improvements system in a somewhat different perspective, but "from my known sentiments in favor of the doctrine of instruction, I did not feel myself at liberty to disobey." His vote, he noted, was that of his constituents, not his own. Douglas, for all his youth, was an adept student of the political game.

The final passage of the internal improvements system was wildly received. Land speculators, wrote one Jacksonville citizen, "are on the alert night and day to catch the first news from Vandalia so that they can profit by the changes which the Legislature shall make in passing the great Mamoth Bill for internal improvements." Vandalia was illuminated, bonfires were built, and fire balls were thrown. "All was joy! joy!" commented the *Register*. "Illinois," predicted the editor, "must shortly take her place far in advance of her Western Sisters." Whigs vied with Democrats in their enthusiasm, forecasting a population for Illinois of over two million within fifteen years. "The names of those who have been conspicuous in bringing forward and sustaining this law, will go down to the future as great benefactors"—a marked contrast to the remarks made a few years later, when the state's leaders would seek to disassociate themselves from the bill that had propelled Illinois to the brink of bankruptcy.[18]

While considerations of economy proved no deterrent to the passage of the internal improvements program (the legislature authorizing a loan that amounted to eight times the total expenses of the state government from its inception to 1836), Douglas and others in the assembly expressed concern over the cost of the Illinois and Michigan Canal. Construction had begun in the summer of 1836 according to a plan that called for a lake-fed "deep cut" canal that would parallel the Illinois River to the vicinity of Peru. Douglas challenged the feasibility of this admittedly expensive method of construction, suggesting instead a "shal-

low cut" that would terminate at Lake Joliet and the construction of
locks and dams on the Des Plaines and Illinois rivers from that point on.
No member of the lower house, it was later reported, manifested a
greater hostility to the "deep cut" plan or a greater partiality for the
"shallow cut" or "slack water" plan than Douglas. A speech in support
of his proposal was reported by the opposition to be unequaled for its
ridicule, exaggeration, and abuse, Douglas apparently insinuating that
those who supported the "deep cut" did so because of their interest in
town site speculations. Douglas' attack, however, was unsuccessful, and
the "deep cut" plan was re-confirmed. Rather than jeopardize the canal
project altogether, he dropped his opposition, but he pointed out that he
could not be held to account if the "deep cut" plan failed. The immediate consequence of his opposition was a crucial delay in the construction
of the canal, a factor which also rendered him unpopular among some of
the strong supporters of the canal in those sections of the state which it
would serve.[19]

The debate over the internal improvements program quite naturally
led to another discussion of the state's banking system. In order to meet
the annual interest bill on the loan (now $8 million), the legislators de-
termined to make the banks a part of their internal improvements program. "One is the handmaid of the other," commented the *Sangamo
Journal,* "and since the internal improvement system is based upon
credit it cannot be carried on without the aid of banks." If the state
could become the owner of bank stock, it was thought, the obligation of
financing the internal improvements loan could be met easily. Bills were
introduced increasing the capital stock of the banks and providing for
large subscriptions by the state, the necessary funds to be provided by
another loan, this one of $3 million. Additional state directors were
added to the board of the state bank, and the banks were officially designated the fiscal agents of the state. Although the state owned over half
of the bank stock, it still held only a minority voice on the directorate.
Douglas, true to his Jacksonian convictions, opposed the entire program.
The close alliance between bank and state smacked too strongly of the
recent experience with the Second United States Bank. Democrats also
charged that the state bank was enriching a small group of financiers,
some of whom lived outside the state and most of whom were Whigs.
The bank program appealed to many vested interests, and in spite of
Douglas' opposition, it passed both houses by substantial majorities.
Douglas also led the opposition to a measure, supported by some south-

ern Illinois Democrats, that would enlarge the powers and privileges of the Bank of Illinois at Shawneetown, but once again his efforts proved futile. The anti-bank element, however, was able to carry a resolution providing for an investigation of the affairs of the recently chartered state bank at Springfield, although the opposition resorted to every delaying tactic to prevent a vote, including a strong pro-bank speech by Abraham Lincoln. Douglas voted consistently for the investigation and against the bank.[20]

Douglas proved an active, diligent, and conscientious legislator. Not one to allow his lack of experience to relegate him to the background, he was active in the deliberations on many of the crucial measures of the session, and he voted on 191 of the 249 roll calls, a respectable record for a beginner. He was appointed to the chairmanship of the committee on petitions, a tedious but highly significant assignment, and much of his time was necessarily devoted to the consideration of countless petitions, ranging from requests from individuals to change their names to demands for the creation of new counties. Ten days after the session began, he made an important contribution to the definition of legislative power, when he reported against a divorce petition. The granting of divorces, he declared, was a judicial function, which the legislative branch was not competent to exercise. His report closed with a resolution declaring that it was unconstitutional and foreign to the duties of legislation for the legislature to grant bills of divorce. After the word "unconstitutional" was softened to "inexpedient," the resolution passed. No divorces were granted by the legislature during the session (although forty-two had been granted up to that time), and Douglas' criticism virtually put an end to this legislative practice thereafter.

Throughout the session, Douglas acted on his basic Jacksonian convictions. His opposition to enlarging the powers of banks, his support of a hard-money policy, and his belief that internal improvement projects were the responsibility of the state rather than of private corporations placed him in the forefront of the Jacksonian ranks. He supported an effort to broaden the elective power by providing for the election of county clerks and county treasurers and fought for the replacement of oral voting by the secret ballot. When he found he could not prevent the chartering of corporations of all descriptions, a system of legislation he described as "unjust, impolitic and unwise," he attempted to add to each charter a clause reserving the right of the legislature to alter, amend, or repeal it "whenever the public good shall require it." [21]

Nor was Douglas oblivious to the wishes and demands of his constituents. He successfully staved off an attempt to create a new county out of
portions of Sangamon and Morgan counties by reporting, as chairman of
the petitions committee, that the number of petitioners from his county
was vastly outnumbered by the number from Sangamon County. Therefore, he maintained, the division should be restricted to the latter, but he
insisted, to the gratification of the Sangamon delegation, that the whole
question be submitted to the voters of that county.

A more serious issue involved the permanent location of the state capital. Vandalia was originally chosen as the temporary capital; as the
population in the northern and central sections of the state increased so
did dissatisfaction with this location. The issue came to climax when it
was linked with the question of internal improvements. The Sangamon
County delegation (known familiarly as the "Long Nine") labored zealously to shift the seat of government to Springfield. Logrolling of the
boldest kind was resorted to, as the delegation supported all the amendments to the internal improvements act (including an appropriation to
those counties which would be bypassed by the proposed projects), presumably in return for support for Springfield's pretensions. Lincoln, who
participated in the trading, later opposed efforts to repeal the internal
improvements act because "Sangamon county had received great and important benefits, at the last session of the Legislature, in return for giving support, thro' her delegation to the system of Internal Improvement." Douglas, eager to prevent the capital from going to a rival
county, registered his "decided and uncompromising opposition" to the
relocation of the capital. He circulated reports of lawlessness in Springfield, hoping to forestall a decision, and when the legislature gathered in
joint session to select the capital, he voted consistently for Jacksonville.
His efforts were to no avail, and Springfield proved an easy winner.
Springfield not only secured the seat of government, but it soon also
gained two new and distinguished citizens, as both Lincoln and Douglas
shortly made plans to move to the new capital.[22]

The legislative session also brought the twenty-three-year-old Douglas
face to face with the slavery question for the first time in his career. Late
in December, Governor Duncan transmitted resolutions passed by the
legislatures of Virginia, Alabama, Mississippi, New York, and Connecticut "in relation to domestic slavery." The resolutions were referred to a
special joint committee, and, in mid-January, the committee reported to
the house. After a preamble which denounced the purposes of the aboli-

tionists and denied that the national government held the power "to strike the fetters" from the slaves, resolutions were proposed which disapproved the formation of abolition societies, held that "the right of property in slaves is sacred to the slave-holding States by the Federal Constitution," and contended that the national government could not abolish slavery in the District of Columbia "against the consent of the citizens." Numerous amendments were offered by members of the house, including both Douglas and Lincoln, and after considerable discussion the amended resolutions were passed by the lopsided vote of 77 to 6. Douglas voted in the affirmative, thus registering his first formal protest against the activities and purposes of the abolitionists, while Lincoln's was one of the few negative votes.

The legislative session closed as it had begun—with an endorsement of Andrew Jackson. On March 3, the eve of Van Buren's inauguration, the assembly approved a resolution endorsing "the firm, consistent, independent and able manner" in which the President had discharged the duties of his office and tendering to Jackson its "respect, esteem and best wishes for his future welfare and happiness." Three days later, the first session of the Tenth General Assembly adjourned, and Douglas returned to Jacksonville, $408 richer for his three months' service.[23]

iv

Shortly after the adjournment of the Tenth General Assembly, Douglas resigned his seat in the lower house. On March 9, 1837, he was appointed Register of the Springfield Land Office by President Van Buren. On the day before his appointment, Douglas penned an angry letter to the editor of the *Illinois Patriot,* a Jacksonville Whig paper, answering the charge that he had entered into a nefarious arrangement to gain the Register's office. The accusation, made on February 22, six days before the final vote in the legislature on the relocation of the capital, specified that Douglas had sold out Jacksonville's interests in return for the support of the Sangamon County delegation for the land office appointment. The charge, Douglas retorted, was a "fabrication, false as the heart that conceived it and the hand that penned it." He denied that he had made any arrangement with the Sangamon delegation and reminded the editor of his strong opposition to the removal of the capital to Springfield. The recommendation for his appointment to the land office, signed by several members of the legislature, he declared, "was got up by my friends without my solicitation or knowledge."

Douglas' appointment had its background in a situation considerably more complex than the capital relocation issue. The incumbent in the land office, George Forquer, was widely recognized as a member of the ruling junto of the Jacksonian party. Like Douglas, he had supported Richard M. Young, a man whose past was tinged with Whiggism and who had at one point actively courted Whig support, for election to the United States Senate. Douglas' support of Young did not square with his exertions to achieve party regularity, but, as a member of the legislature, he did not occupy as vulnerable a position as Forquer. William L. May, Democratic Congressman representing northern and central Illinois who harbored ambitions of his own for the senatorial seat, immediately attacked Forquer and sought his removal. He was aided by the fact that Forquer was in ill health and in a poor condition to defend himself against the charges. His effectiveness as a party leader already impaired, Forquer was persuaded by Young to offer his resignation. Young then turned the tables on May by recommending Douglas as Forquer's successor. He secured supporting recommendations from several Democratic members of the legislature and sent them to the Secretary of the Treasury, Levi Woodbury, in late February. Within a year Forquer was dead of tuberculosis, and Douglas had assumed a firm position in the ruling group of the party. Senator Young became a staunch supporter of the Van Buren administration, and with Douglas he initiated a "war" against May which resulted in the utter repudiation of the Congressman by the Jacksonian party.[24]

The announcement of Douglas' appointment to the Springfield Land Office was not made in the local press until April 1, and the office, closed at the time of Forquer's resignation, was not reopened by Douglas until after the spring term of the courts in the First Circuit. When he assumed his new duties in the land office, the *Sangamo Journal* commented, "We are told the *little man* from Morgan, was perfectly astonished, at finding himself making money at the rate of from one to two hundred dollars per day!" Although Douglas qualified for the highest income allowed the Register by law, $3000 yearly, he found his new appointment profitable from more than a pecuniary point of view. He was in a better position than before to carry on his own land speculations, and, as he wrote his brother-in-law, he could "make a better investment" than he could have done at a previous time. But a post in the land office was also important politically. It offered an opportunity to develop a wide and valuable acquaintance with voters and brought to its holder prestige and high standing among local politicians. In Illinois, as in other frontier states, complaints were frequent that local politics were dominated by a "land office clique." In an area where population was increasing and land sales were booming, the land office appointees assumed roles of prime political significance.

This was the way Douglas regarded his appointment—as an important step in the development of his own political career—and he made the most of it. His small, active, and wiry figure became a familiar sight in the dusty streets of the capital. Slovenly in dress, his pockets crammed with newspapers, pamphlets, and other political documents, he soon made the acquaintance of virtually every resident of the town. His quickness in conversation and his "exuberant flow of animal spirits," it was said, rendered him a delightful companion at social functions as well as in political gatherings. His fondness for wrestling and his clumsy efforts at dancing in the "village frolics" enhanced his popularity. The responsibilities of his office did not weigh heavily on him, for he continued to attend meetings of the court in the First Circuit, associating with attorneys in the various county seats in order to handle his legal business.[25]

Douglas' primary task, however, still remained the organization of the Democratic party. The prospect of the 1838 elections, when Illinois voters would select a governor and a slate of Congressmen, necessitated further promotion of the convention system on the state and congressional district level. "We have no doubt," declared the *Register,* "that unless the Jackson party unite on some *one* man to run for the office, they will have to stand another anti-Jackson Governor and another anti-Jackson Message, like the present incumbent and his message last winter." Douglas, through his influential position in the land office, argued the importance of adhering, without doubt or question, to the policies of the Van Buren administration, and he urged that this adherence be reflected on all levels of local politics. "Mr. Douglas," wrote the editor of Springfield's opposition organ, "has given the Van Buren party to understand that they must go against all banks and for an entire specie currency. He has received a number of new collars, stamped and branded. Step up, boys."

In July, Douglas shifted his activities to the state capital. Governor Duncan had summoned the legislature into special session, and, although no longer a member, Douglas was in Vandalia to push his convention scheme. A meeting of the Democratic members of the assembly, at which he was present, resolved that "there should be concert of action and union of sentiment among the members of the democratic party throughout the state." A state convention was scheduled to meet in Vandalia in December to nominate candidates for the state offices, and a central party committee was appointed to correspond with county groups throughout the state, thus providing the party with its first organizational apparatus. Douglas was named to a special committee charged with the preparation of an address to the party's rank and file. Action by the party was made more urgent when a gubernatorial ticket was selected by a Whig caucus. The lines were now drawn, it was said, between the supporters of caucus nominations and nominations by the people in conventions. Governor Duncan's message to the special session, in which he inveighed against the evils of party spirit, added impetus to the determination of Democratic convention supporters. The struggle, however, was not an easy one. Sentiment against party conventions remained strong among Democrats from southern Illinois; the device was still identified with "northern & eastern politicians." During the latter months of 1837, Douglas continued the fight on his home ground in Sangamon County, strongly defending the convention system before a meeting of county Democrats. With several other party leaders, he purchased an interest in the *Illinois Republican,* a Democratic paper which could, it was hoped, counteract the influence of the well-established Whig organ in Springfield, and for a time he directed its editorial policy.[26]

The campaign of Douglas and other Democratic leaders for party organization and discipline soon faced other obstacles more formidable than the opposition of some of the older politicians. In May the *Illinois State Register* reported that a large number of New York banks had suspended payment, but the paper expressed confidence that the west would be spared from its effects. The Bank of England, "and its Branch, the Bank of the United States," were held responsible for the dislocation. A week later the news was more alarming. The number of banks that had stopped payment had increased; the panic had spread as far west as Cincinnati, and it seemed quite possible that banks generally in all the states would follow the example of those in the large eastern cities. The full force and seriousness of the panic became apparent by early June. On June 3, the press reported that the State Bank of Illinois had suspended specie payment. Overtrading, extravagant living, and speculation were blamed for the distress. "Too many people have been anxious to get rich in a day," commented one paper. "The rich and beautiful lands of the

West have been mostly entered . . . *not* by the Agriculturist but by the
Speculator." The land had not been cultivated; nothing had been added
to the wealth of the state. The enthusiasm with which the state had
greeted the passage of the internal improvements program turned into
an acid bitterness. The program itself was now impossible of fulfillment.
Douglas was in a strategic position to observe and appreciate the impact
of the distress on the state. Land sales at the Springfield Land Office had
reached an all-time high in 1836, totaling over $480,000. During
Douglas' first year in the office the sales plummeted to one-quarter of
the 1836 total, and in 1838 they fell even further, to $68,835. The fol-
lowing year they dropped to $30,000.

The efforts of the Democratic press to blame the panic on Nicholas
Biddle and the moneyed aristocracy of England seemed unconvincing to
most of the state's voters. Of much more effect was the opposition's
pointed reminder that the distress "follows immediately *after* the accession of Martin Van Buren to the Presidential chair." The extermination
of the United States Bank had been responsible for an expansion of
paper currency and for "all the rage for speculations." If the Democrats
"did not bring about the present state of things," asked the *Sangamo
Journal,* "who did?"

The task of perfecting Democratic party organization in the face of
this deepening distress was massive in its proportions and a challenge to
young Douglas. In November, the address of the party to the voters of
Illinois, which Douglas had a hand in preparing, was published. It was a
vibrant declaration of the Jacksonian faith and an urgent call to Jacksonians to join together in the "organization of the Democratic strength
by Convention." Party members were warned not to "yield to the illu-
sive semblance of their adversaries," but were cautioned to recognize the
opposition for what it really was. Stripped of all their disguises, the
Whigs remained the advocates of the "privileges of Property," standing
in antagonistic opposition to the advocates of the "rights of the People."
The recent history of the Federal, or Whig, party had revealed the arts
and intrigues with which its members sought to confuse and mislead the
people. The party of privilege was all the more dangerous "for the multitude of its names and vascillation of its members." If the principles of
the Democracy were worth preserving, the committee declared, the party
must now marshal its strength in their behalf. Democrats must "yield all
minor differences" and "resort to the efficacious instrumentality of a State
Convention." The "midnight caucus" of the opposition should be met by

the "free and consentaneous voice of every member" of the Democratic
party. Only by concert and unity of action could the people prevent the
revival of the United States Bank, "which has fattened on their substance,
and sported at their sufferings." The issue was drawn between consolidation, monopoly, and property privilege on the one hand, and equal distribution of the favors of the federal government and a strict construction of the Constitution on the other. In such a contest, "the voice of the
many and the doctrine of equal rights" must surely prevail.[27]

# IV

## "An utter aversion to Hard Cider"
## 1837—1840

i

On September 15, 1837, Congressman May complained to the Secretary
of the Treasury "that the Register of the Land Office at Springfield, Illinois, has been recently, and is perhaps at present engaged in a political
electioneering tour through my district, getting up meetings of the voters to organize a Convention of Delegates, to nominate a candidate for
Congress, who are to be pledged against me, should my name be presented to the Convention." Levi Woodbury, the Treasury Secretary,
promptly communicated May's charges to Douglas and asked for an explanation. Douglas professed ignorance of any basis for May's accusation.
He had indeed traveled extensively through May's district, he wrote, but
only in order to take care of his extensive legal business at the meetings
of the court in the First Judicial District, an area which only coinciden-
tally corresponded to a greater part of May's constituency. He innocently
declared that "no political meetings were held and of course no delegates were appointed and pledged as stated by Mr May, in any county
that I was in during the time I was there." The charge, he suggested,
clearly had its source in the jealous partisanship of a petty opposition
newspaper "in this Town." Douglas hastened to add, however, that his
denial should not be regarded as agreement that such political activity
was in any way improper. "I feel myself as free to mingle with my fellow citizens and express my opinions of men and measures (not even ex-
cepting Mr May) as I should if I have never received an Office at the
hands of the Government." [1]

That Congressman May had fallen from favor among Jacksonians became obvious by the fall of 1837. The feud between May and Senator Young, which apparently had its origin in May's opposition to Young for the senatorship, became more intense. May held Young responsible for the attacks on him and expressed his determination not to be driven from the Democratic ranks, but Stephen A. Douglas played a key role in the estrangement. When Douglas assumed a share of the editorial responsibility of the *Illinois Republican* (a fact that was supposed to be confidential), it was reported that he hated May and would use the paper's columns to secure the Congressman's ouster. During the summer, he turned over to Young evidence that May had made overtures to Douglas early in the legislative session in order to gain support for election to the Senate. "The fact is," Douglas wrote to Lewis W. Ross, "our Party will never support Col May again for Congress." Doubts as to the orthodoxy of May's political beliefs increased. Word came from Washington that not only May but also the other two Illinois Congressmen had voted to lay the subtreasury bill on the table. In the election for public printer, May had cast his ballot for William Allen, editor of the Washington *Madisonian,* who was known as the "bank candidate," over the old Jacksonian, Francis Preston Blair. In a circular to his constituents, printed in the *Madisonian,* May took strong ground against Van Buren's independent treasury proposal and charged the administration with bringing ruin on the people. By mid-November, the *Register* accused May of advocating "the principles of the Federal party" and of having deserted the ranks of the Democracy. It was clear that May would have to go.[2]

The party convention became the weapon to secure May's defeat. From the *Illinois Republican,* and thus very probably from Douglas himself, came the proposal that Democrats in the Third Congressional District meet in convention to select a candidate for Congress, a suggestion that Douglas had made privately months before. Primary elections to select delegates to the district convention, the paper noted, could be held in the various counties during the fall terms of the court. Something other than his legal business, then, was responsible for Douglas' tour of the First Judicial District during the fall of 1837. The opposition complained that the movement for a district convention was for the sole benefit of a particular candidate, and the *Jacksonville News,* edited by Douglas' friend Brooks, presented a list of possible candidates that included Douglas' name. Even the *Chicago Democrat,* suspecting that something was afoot, speculated that the purpose of the convention was to oust May and to "procure the nomination of some subservient instrument of the junto" in Springfield. The realization slowly grew that the young Register of the Springfield Land Office was the chief "wire-puller." [3]

Douglas had done his work well, and his efforts bore fruit. The Third District convention, which met in Peoria early in November and was one of the first such conventions in the state, was hardly representative of the Democratic party in northern Illinois. Only fourteen of the thirty-five counties in the district were represented, and of the forty delegates present, thirty-one were from east and south of the Illinois River. The fifteen delegates from Morgan and Sangamon counties easily dominated the proceedings and dictated the result. Winning a majority of the delegates (twenty-three), Douglas was declared the Democratic nominee for Congress from the Third District, although he had not yet attained the constitutional age for members of Congress.

Douglas' nomination immediately came under fire. Some Democrats regarded the convention as a farce, and Congressman May protested vehemently. Douglas was attacked for "his most pernicious and jacobinical notions of loco focoism," and conservative Democrats were warned against supporting him.

A series of letters appeared in the *Sangamo Journal* soon afterward, supposedly written by an anonymous conservative Democrat, which purported to reveal the inside story of Douglas' nomination at Peoria. There is evidence that at least one of these letters was written by Abraham Lincoln. The nomination of Douglas, according to the story, had its origin in the desire of one member of the Democratic junto for Douglas' position in the land office. Although not named, he was presumed to be Springfield Democrat John Calhoun. In order to vacate the office, Calhoun, it was related, persuaded Douglas to seek the congressional nomination, convincing him of his political genius and of the glorious career that awaited him. "You may be President of these United States just as well as not," Calhoun was supposed to have said to Douglas. The whole story was a spoof on Douglas' youth and ambition. "History gives no account," he was allegedly told, "of a man of your age occupying such high ground as you now do." The ruling clique of the party then, by devious and nefarious means, secured Douglas' nomination, offering up the young Register for sacrifice in order to remove him from his office in Springfield. Douglas, the writer concluded, "is a clever enough young man; but he cannot be elected." Douglas erupted and replied in kind, denying that he had entered into a "corrupt bargain" for the nomination. "My acts have been misrepresented, my opinions perverted, my motives impugned, and my character traduced in language as unkind and ungentlemanly as it was unjust and untrue." He demanded that the editor of the *Journal* reveal the name of the "infamous, villainous liar" and "cowardly scoundrel" who had penned the letters.

That Douglas' nomination could arouse such a level of accusation is an indication that he was taken seriously, not only by the Democrats, but by the Whigs as well. The Whig *Journal,* minimizing Douglas' strength as a vote-getter, concluded, rather unconvincingly, that "no nomination could have suited *us* better." The official organ of the Democracy was highly pleased. Douglas had demonstrated his ability in the last legislature; he was a distinguished debater and firm in his principles. "Although comparatively a young man, Mr. Douglass is old in political integrity." [4]

ii

The election of 1838 in Illinois was fought on national issues. Hard times were everywhere in evidence, and discontent with the Van Buren administration ran high. Several months before, the President had proposed the independent treasury, or subtreasury, system, a complete "divorce" between government and banks, as one solution to the deepening depression. According to the plan, the government, accepting and disbursing only silver and gold coin, would keep its funds in its own vaults and make no use of bank credit, either in the form of bank notes or bank deposits. This extension of hard-money policy was received with mixed feelings by westerners. If the system were approved, government funds would be removed from their banks, the amount of specie on which paper money could be issued would be reduced, and the banks generally would have less power over the currency. Because the plan ran counter to the dreams of economic expansion nurtured by western communities in the 1830's, the independent treasury created additional difficulties for those who sought to tighten the organization of the Democratic party in Illinois.

Douglas had announced his unqualified support of Van Buren's scheme early. In August 1837 he wrote, "I believe the whole [banking] system is founded in error, and must undergo a thorough & radical reform. . . . There should be a Divorce granted between the Banking system and the Government, and the Public revenue should be collected in the current coin of the U. S. as fixed by the Constitution." Not all Democrats followed Douglas' hard-money convictions. In Congress, a move to table the subtreasury bill was supported by all three of Illinois' Democratic Congressmen, a clear sign that on the question of Van Buren's banking reform the Democratic party in Illinois might be badly divided. Douglas moved swiftly. A party convention, summoned in mid-December to nominate candidates for state offices, endorsed Van Buren's fiscal program without equivocation. Its members were influenced by a pre-convention address to the party which Douglas helped to prepare.[5]

The Whigs of the Third Congressional District selected John Todd Stuart of Springfield to challenge Douglas' bid for election to the House of Representatives. The law partner of Abraham Lincoln, Stuart had made the race two years before but had been beaten by the Democrat May. Douglas was regarded as no match for the older, more experienced, and better-known Stuart, and the Whigs had little doubt that they could capture the seat. "We have adopted it as part of our policy here, to never speak of Douglass at all," Lincoln wrote to a political friend. "Isn't that the best mode of treating so small a matter?" [6]

Douglas and Stuart both conducted strenuous speaking tours throughout the sprawling Third District, visiting the county seats during the spring terms of the circuit court, when lawyers and farmers crowded into the towns. The experience was not entirely new to Douglas, for he had traveled the circuit before as state's attorney, appealing to juries and addressing these same farmers who had sat in judgment on his cases. The campaign for Congress, however, was Douglas' first real challenge. Ridiculed for his youth and his diminutive size (his opponent stood well over six feet in height), and carrying the onus of the depression and the growing unpopularity of Van Buren's administration, Douglas had need of all the talent and skill he could muster. But these obstacles never weighed heavily. Instead, his eagerness, impatience, and unstinted confidence became evident to all who saw and heard him. "Ask Mother," he wrote home to his brother-in-law, "what she should think if the People of Illinois should be so foolish as to send her 'prodigal Son' to Congress, and give him an opportunity to visit her on his way. If she has no serious objection to it, I believe the people have some idea of doing so at the next August Election just for the fun of the thing."

In true frontier style, Douglas and Stuart frequently traveled together, took their meals at the same table, and sometimes slept in the same bed. Moving about the district on horseback, they often partook of the hospitality of isolated farmers and their families. The two candidates debated the issues of the election from the same platform, appearing in such towns as Jacksonville, Carrolton, Rushville, and Macomb. In Bloomington Stuart became ill; according to local tradition, his law partner substituted for him and discussed the issues with Douglas in front of the courthouse. If true, this was the first time Lincoln and Douglas faced one another in debate. Both candidates were usually accompanied by a number of supporters (also attorneys making the circuit), including David Davis, Edward Dickinson Baker, Josiah Lamborn, and Stephen T. Logan, who continued to argue the issues before the local crowds after the featured speakers had departed.

Douglas took leave of Stuart and the circuit court in late May and, amid charges that the "Peoria Bantling" had abandoned the campaign to his opponent out of fear, he spent considerable time among the Irish laborers in the construction camps along the canal line. After speaking in Chicago, Douglas returned to the south, and he devoted much of the remaining campaign to Morgan and Sangamon, the most populous counties in the district. His speeches were well received, and his impact on the crowds was greater than the Whigs had expected. One who heard Douglas in this campaign later wrote that "there was something captivating in his manly straightforwardness and uncompromising statement of his political principles." His power to speak to the people in their own language, his use of frontier metaphors, and his determination to stand by his own convictions made him an effective stump speaker. Throughout the campaign, he remained on the best of terms with his opponent. The bitterness of their political exchanges on the platform was seldom carried over into their relationship off the platform. Only occasionally did the candidates allow their emotions to get the better of them, as when, late in the campaign, Stuart became angry at Douglas' language, grabbed his opponent, tucked him under his arm, and carried him around the Springfield markethouse. Douglas, in return, gave Stuart's thumb such a bite that Stuart carried the scar for many years afterward.[7]

Douglas concentrated his arguments on a denunciation of banking and a defense of the independent treasury system. In answer to those Whigs who used the depression as an issue against the Democrats, Douglas declared, "The question is not how we got into the present difficulties, but how we shall get out of [them]." He traced the history of the Whig party and emphasized the differences between the "old republican and federal parties." His position, he maintained, was that of General Jackson; Stuart, on the other hand, supported Henry Clay, who would without doubt be Van Buren's opponent at the next presidential election. A new national bank, as proposed by Clay, Douglas felt would ruin the nation. He denounced all banks with an "unconquerable hostility" that was widely commented upon by the Whig press. In summary, the Jacksonian candidate announced that he was for pre-emption rights (pointing out that Clay had voted against a pre-emption bill), for a divorce of banks from the government, and for sustaining Van Buren in his proposal to create an independent treasury.

Douglas was assailed by his opponents not only for his stand on the fiscal question, but also for his record in the previous legislature. His opposition to the "deep cut" plan for constructing the Illinois and Michigan Canal and his preference for the "shallow cut" was interpreted by the Whigs to be opposition to the canal itself. A Chicago paper termed him "one of the most violent opponents of the Illinois and Michigan Canal"; a Galena paper predicted that the northern counties would give a strong and decisive vote against Douglas because he was an "enemy" of the canal. Douglas' belief that the legislature should reserve the right to alter or repeal corporation charters if the public interest seemed to demand it was denounced in the Whig press as irresponsible, disorganizing, and "incompatible with every principle of law and true republicanism." The Democratic candidate, it was clear to the opposition, was a loco-foco of the worst sort, a "radical mobocrat." Moreover, Douglas continued to hold his land-office appointment throughout the campaign. "Is not Douglass paying his expenses with the money he gets from the Public Treasury as a salary for an office, the duties of which he neglects to perform. What else is this than electioneering on the Public money?" queried a Jacksonville paper. Some of the early confidence of the Whig campaigners disappeared by the end of the contest. Lincoln, concerned over the congressional campaign, admonished a party worker, "if we relax an *iota,* we shall be beaten." Douglas was tireless. After making his final appeal in Morgan and Sangamon counties, he was off once again to the canal line, where he remained until after the election.[8]

The election returns came in slowly and uncertainly, but from the beginning it was apparent that the result would be a close one. Five days after the election, the *Sangamo Journal* conceded that Douglas had probably been elected. Douglas himself was confident. Following the election, he returned to Springfield from Chicago by stage, "riding always on the outside, at least when he entered the towns, magnificently smoking a cigar—'*He had used up Mr. Stuart to the tune of 2,000'!!*" The Democratic press was more cautious in claiming victory for its candidate. Both sides agreed that the contest was uncomfortably close. Almost three weeks after the polls had closed the Whigs in Springfield were still conceding the election to Douglas. Others began to have doubts. "A few votes either way will make or unmake a Representative," commented the *Quincy Whig*. On September 1, the *Journal,* for the first time, reported that Stuart might have won the election, but that the "issue is still involved in uncertainty." Stuart did indeed win. The official returns were not announced by the secretary of state's office until early September; in the following weeks, the returns underwent fifteen corrections certified from the counties. The final tabulation gave Stuart a majority of 36 votes over Douglas, out of a total vote of 36,495. The Democratic candidate for governor, Thomas Carlin, was more fortunate; he defeated his Whig opponent by less than 1000 votes out of a total in excess of 60,000.

Douglas was gravely disappointed, but he found consolation in the close race he had run and in the emergence of a stronger Democratic party. "The late crisis," he wrote in November, "has had a salutary effect upon the noble cause; has purged the party of all those weather cocks that change from Party to Party as self interest would impel them, and left the Democratic Party in a purer, health[i]er & stronger condition than it has ever been at any former period." [9]

Of the thirty-four counties in the Third Congressional District, Douglas carried only twelve, including six along the canal line and five in the Military Tract and along the lower Illinois River. His extra exertions among the canal workers had paid handsome dividends, for he carried four of the canal line counties by more than 62 per cent of the vote. The Whigs were not long in finding an explanation. Douglas' surprising strength, they charged, came not from any intrinsic merit in his campaign for the independent treasury system, nor from the fact that the Democratic party had achieved such outstanding strength in the northern counties. Douglas' vote stemmed rather from the alien Irish canal laborers who had been persuaded to vote the Democratic ticket. "A terrible display of Irish politics & foreign influence," moaned one Whig. The protests grew stronger and louder even though the official returns indicated Douglas' defeat. The Irish at work on the canal "come in the spring—work during the summer—and leave the state in the fall

—many never return. They are transient persons, and neither *citizens* or *inhabitants.*" Since the state constitution specified only six months' residence in the state as a qualification for the franchise, there was little doubt in the minds of those who protested that the aliens had a right to vote, but such a right, they declared, was dangerous "to our institutions" and a threat to the two party system. The basis for representation "according to the loco foco dictionary," commented the *Quincy Whig* bitterly, "means Douglass mounted on the shoulders of two Irishmen, addressing a Chicago rabble upon the glorious privilege of a free country, and the right of unnaturalized foreigners to control the elections of Illinois."

Douglas had been singularly successful in marshaling the Irish labor vote behind his candidacy. His audiences in the construction towns were appreciative and enthusiastic, probably because he skillfully appealed to their national pride. He extolled the patriotism of Ireland, the virtues of the Irish people, the bravery of her sons and the beauty of her daughters, and, stretching credulity to the limit, he even claimed descent from a line of patriotic Irish sires. At the close of the campaign, Douglas reportedly told a friend, "I expect to get all their votes." The Whig protests against the alien vote in 1838 touched a sensitive nerve in state politics and gave the opposition an issue and a goal for the coming presidential election.[10]

In general, however, the Whigs were encouraged by the election results. Although they lost the governorship, they carried both houses of the state legislature. The close victory in the Third Congressional District, which had previously sent nominal Jacksonians to the House of Representatives, was viewed as part of a larger swing away from the Democratic party. In spite of the cries of Douglas' supporters that the election was marked by numerous irregularities, the governor declared Stuart the victor and granted him the certificate of election (although after the period of time stipulated by law). The Whigs staged a great victory celebration in Springfield shortly afterward; numerous toasts were drunk and speeches were made by William L. May (who now openly identified with the Whigs), Hardin, Baker, and Lincoln. The course of future Whig strategy was reflected by Lincoln, who, in speaking of President Van Buren, cried out, "Crucify him!"

The Democrats in the district found cause for their own celebration. A public testimonial banquet was tendered to Carlin and Douglas in Quincy, and those who gathered were lavish in their praise of the Little

Giant. "His untiring zeal, his firm integrity and high order of talents," read one of the toasts, "have endeared him to the democracy of the state and they will remember him two years hence." Senator Young delivered the principal address of the evening: he denounced the "odious character and dangerous tendency" of the United States Bank, condemned Whig hostility toward foreign voting as having been conceived in the spirit of the alien and sedition laws, and alluded to the dangerous character the question of abolition had assumed. The United States Bank, foreign voting, and abolition—these were the issues which the Illinois Democratic party would continue to argue in the important months that followed.

As the election returns sifted in, rumors of irregularities in the voting multiplied. The extremely narrow margin of votes between Stuart and Douglas encouraged backers of the latter to urge that the election be contested. Douglas, advised the *Chicago Democrat,* was bound "by the sacred consideration of the *rights of the people*—not merely his own rights" to make the challenge. The argument was persuasive, but before proceeding he sought the advice of certain national Democratic leaders. To Francis Preston Blair he wrote for information on the manner of contesting the election, asking what preliminary steps must be taken. He had, he informed Blair, received a majority of the votes cast in the election, but his opponent had been granted the certificate of election. The question in the campaign, he wrote, "was made directly before the people between Democratic & Federal principles and particularly between the *subTreasury* & a *National Bank.*" If the next presidential election should be thrown into the House of Representatives, he pointed out, Illinois' vote would be doubtful if Stuart's election were not challenged. From Thomas Hart Benton, to whom he had also written, Douglas received reassuring word that the Missouri Senator would "cheerfully" aid him in his effort to contest the election.

Reports of election irregularities continued to come in. The canal commissioners, it was reported, had not only passed the word that Douglas was an enemy to the canal; they had also misspelled Douglas' name in the poll-books in order to disqualify the votes given him. Others had allegedly posed as Democrats, urging the voters to cast their ballots for "John A. Douglas" or "James A. Douglas." Election judges were, in some cases, not properly sworn; election clerks were accused of refusing to report votes for Douglas. Stuart's incorrect ballots, Democrats charged, were all being counted for him. Governor Duncan's non-compliance with the law in granting Stuart his certificate of election after the time required had elapsed added strength to Douglas' decision. As the state government prepared to move from Vandalia to Springfield, the election returns were carefully boxed and stored. Douglas' investigators charged that they were prevented access to the records, heightening their suspicion that Stuart had not received a majority of the votes. The Whigs refused to believe that all the mistakes in the poll-books favored Douglas, and they warned that if the Democratic candidate pressed his contest additional votes for Stuart might very well be found.[11]

Douglas formally announced his decision to challenge the election in a letter to Stuart early in March 1839. He proposed several alternatives for Stuart's consideration: that the corrected returns be canvassed by state officers and that all votes for "Stuart" and "Douglass" be counted without regard to the first names or the spelling; that persons designated by the two candidates canvass the returns; that the same persons visit each county and examine the original poll-books; or that both candidates sign a joint resignation and run the race over. Stuart replied simply that he had no doubts of his election; he invited Douglas to contest the election, with the clear understanding that Douglas would be responsible for all the delays and expense that would result. Douglas accepted the invitation. "I feel it my duty to my country," he wrote, "to those kind friends who have sustained me, and to myself, to contest the election in vindication of the right of a majority of the people to rule." He alerted his supporters in the district to examine the poll-books in their counties and sent a close friend, Charles H. Lanphier, whose brother-in-law was the proprietor of the *State Register,* to check the results. Haste was urged, for Douglas intended to carry the challenge to the floor of the House of Representatives when Congress met in December. Meanwhile, Stuart's friends were not idle. A committee of Whigs, including Lincoln, began to search out mistakes that might be counted for Stuart and announced the intention of making an issue of the alien and non-resident vote that was cast for Douglas in the counties along the canal line. The results of the investigation were apparently not as encouraging as Douglas had hoped for in November; it became clear that he was not going to Washington with his challenge. Without making a public announcement, he quietly abandoned his decision to contest Stuart's seat. Instead he indicated he would attend the session of the state legislature as a lobby member and devote his energies to the approaching presidential election.[12]

By casting doubt on the validity of Stuart's election, Douglas had proved his point. He had, moreover, demonstrated his vote-getting power and had become well known throughout the district. He could not, at this stage of his career, risk a rebuff at the hands of Congress. Local problems were uppermost in his thinking. The Whigs seemed determined to pursue the issue of alien voting, a prospect that caused some anxiety in the Democratic ranks. The continuing financial crisis and the close election in 1838 demonstrated that there was much work to be done if Illinois were to remain faithful to the Democratic party in the election of 1840. Democrats had carried Illinois for Van Buren in 1836 in the face of a disorganized Whig party; now they faced an efficiently organized Whig opposition. Douglas' talents were needed at home, not in Congress.

iii

Springfield, in 1839, was a town of about 3000 population. The move of all the state offices from Vandalia early in the summer brought the town a measure of prosperity in the midst of hard times. A statehouse was under construction, its square littered with piles of stone and "eloquent with the music of scores of pick axes." In addition to the legislature, the state supreme court and the United States courts for the District of Illinois met in Springfield. Political leaders, lawyers, and businessmen from all parts of the state converged on the town. New business houses and residences were being erected, contrasting sharply with the streets deep in mud (one editor proposed that rice be cultivated in the town's thoroughfares) and the freely wandering hogs.

The opening of the legislature in December also marked the beginning of Springfield's social season. One of the town's popular meeting places was the home of Ninian Edwards, where Elizabeth Todd Edwards and her sister Mary Todd, a cousin of John J. Hardin recently arrived from Kentucky, gave tone to the town's social life. Although differing from them in politics, Douglas was a frequent and welcome visitor in the Edwards' home.

Douglas found little time for social life in his busy career in politics and the law. Yet he was not aloof, and to those who knew him well he was accomplished "as a society man." His rapid rise to prominence and his determined, hard-driving ambition marked him as a man of influence and opened many doors to him. He had a bright, convivial nature, loved a good time, and possessed a certain amount of social grace, all qualities which made him an acceptable companion to the town's fairer members. In mid-December 1839, Springfield's citizens held a cotillion at the new and impressive American House, to welcome the members of the legislature and their wives. Douglas was listed as one of the managers, as much a gesture to his social standing as to his political importance.

As a visitor to the Edwards' home, it was perhaps expected that he should be among those young men who became enamored of Mary Todd's charms. The two were frequently seen together, walking about the town or visiting at the Edwards' house. Rumors circulated that he was courting Miss Todd, and testimony gathered years after his death actually had Douglas proposing marriage to her. There is no evidence that their relationship went beyond that of friendship. In any case, Douglas soon gave way to a more serious rival. Years later, Mary told one of her relatives, "I liked him well enough, but that was all." Douglas did not solicit Mary Todd's hand; his attention to the vivacious young Kentuckian was matched by equal attention to Julia Jayne (later Mrs. Lyman Trumbull) and to Sarah Dunlap of Jacksonville (later Mrs. John A. McClernand). Politics consumed his full attention, and there was little chance for a rival.[13]

In fact, Douglas was busier than ever during this winter of 1839–40. On December 9, Democrats from all parts of the state gathered in Springfield to nominate candidates for presidential electors and to organize the party for the coming campaign. The call had gone out two months before in response to an unprecedented flurry of activity in the Whig ranks. Whigs began to hold meetings in anticipation of the presidential contest as early as January 1839, and in February Whig members of the state legislature met to discuss ways of organizing for the campaign. A state convention gathered in Springfield in October "to secure a concert of action among the whigs of Illinois." Delegates were selected for the national convention of the party at Harrisburg and candidates for electors were chosen, pledged to support the national nominee whomever he might be. Not to take any chances, the body approved both Henry Clay and William Henry Harrison. By their early entrance into the campaign, the Whigs gained a jump on their rivals. The call for the Democratic convention immediately went out; the *Register* cautioned, "This is no time for the Democracy to rest in security." The initiative, however, had been seized by the Whigs, and the Democrats were forced into an unfamiliar and uncomfortable defensive role.[14]

Douglas rose to the challenge. On March 2 he had resigned his position in the Springfield land office in order to spend the remainder of the year in political maneuvering and planning. Once he had determined not to contest Stuart's election, he was able to devote his full energy to strengthening the Democratic position. A special election in the fall to fill a vacancy in the local delegation to the general assembly spurred Douglas to behind-the-scenes activity. Capitalizing on resentment of the Whig leadership in Springfield, he proposed that the Whigs in newly created Menard County support the Democratic candidate, Thomas J. Nance of Petersburg. Failing in this, he persuaded the Whig Bowling Green, formerly of New Salem and one of Lincoln's early benefactors, to run for the office in defiance of the Whig "junto" decision to support John Bennett. Two other Whigs also announced their candidacies, threatening to split the party vote. "I am afraid of our race for Represen-tative," wrote Lincoln, complaining that someone was "tampering" with members of his party. It was obvious that Douglas was doing the tam-pering. The maneuver was successful, for Nance was elected over Ben-nett.[15]

The issues that would divide the electorate in the presidential election of 1840 began to appear early in the preceding year. Speaking at a cele-bration of Jackson's victory at New Orleans on January 8, John A. McClernand narrowed the issues to two—*"Monopolies* and *Aboli-tion."* On the same occasion, Douglas defined the principles of his party in language reminiscent of the Old Hero himself—"Founded upon the inalienable rights of man—political equality, freedom of thought, of speech, and of conscience, appealing to the intelligence and virtue of the people, like the dews of Heaven, [they] shed their blessings upon all alike." Two months later, Douglas addressed several hundred persons at the courthouse in Springfield, portraying the "principles and their ef-fects, of the two great political parties, as with a pencil of light." He de-fended the Virginia resolutions of 1798, identified the Whigs with the Federalists, and, because of their charges against alien voting, portrayed them as supporters of the alien and sedition laws. After the speech, sev-eral "grey headed veterans who had struggled with the immortal Jeffer-son" took him by the hand and confirmed the truth of his statements. Resolutions recognizing the Virginia resolutions as a "true exposition of Democratic principles" were immediately passed.

County Democratic organizations held their meetings in the fall months of 1839, selecting delegates for the state convention in Decem-ber and further developing the issues for the contest that lay ahead.

Douglas was called to the chair of the Sangamon convention in mid-November. He was also among those chosen to represent the county in the state convention. Resolutions, typical of those approved by the county organizations, strongly endorsed President Van Buren for having "pursued the path which Jefferson and Jackson marked out." The independent treasury plan, effecting a complete separation of bank and government, was upheld and the efforts of abolitionists to interfere with the domestic institutions of the south were condemned. The county activities revealed the extent and success of the party's efforts to improve its organization. A state central committee had been appointed early in the year, and committees of correspondence were established in each county. Through the committees, the county organizations were coordinated and the party operated as a smooth and efficient unit. The Whigs, however, were not far behind. Writing of the two parties at this time, Thomas Ford commented that "no regular army could have excelled them in discipline."

Two hundred and fifty Democratic delegates gathered in Springfield on December 9 for their state convention, the largest ever held in the state. Douglas was appointed to the important committee on address and was given a place on the state central committee. Resolutions were approved endorsing the independent treasury and supporting Van Buren for the presidency, but it was the address of the convention that summarized the position of the party to the state's electorate. Inasmuch as Douglas played an important part in drafting the address, the document also reflected his own political position. States' rights and a strict construction of the Constitution stood at the center of the Democratic creed. The national government was one of strictly limited and delegated powers; the state governments were "the pillars of the Republic." In an allusion to the recent Bank war, the committee charged that chartered monopolies were dangerous to the liberties of the people and subversive of state authority, but it drew an important distinction between the proper and improper uses of banks. Finally, in a burst of partisan zeal, the address warned Democrats that "political infidelity" was an evil. Men might change, but the principles of the Democratic party were immutable. "Democracy protects equally, *the entire mass of society,* and can therefore outlive any individual who may abandon her cause." With this call to action, Douglas and the party spokesmen went to the people.[16]

The campaign of 1840 in Illinois followed the national pattern. Some of the fiercest campaigning revolved about the personalities of the Whig and Democratic standardbearers. Monster rallies, parades, and barbecues were held throughout the state. The Whigs, quietly dropping their earlier opposition to party organization, had achieved a discipline that aroused both surprise and admiration. The hard times proved to be their greatest and most effective weapon. "All the disaffected and disappointed of all differences of opinion and incongruities," moaned one Democratic politician, "have joined forces for Harrison." The unprecedented zeal and unanimity with which Whigs argued their cause, the "money, labor and unremitting exertion" which they employed, alarmed party leaders. The Democratic party was blamed for all the misdeeds of "visionary speculators" and for the "wild and useless" internal improvements system (although Whigs had been equally responsible for the latter). Yet, in Illinois, the discussion of principles attained an importance that was not evident in other parts of the country. To bring the issues directly to the voters, a group of Whigs, led by Abraham Lincoln, challenged the Democrats to meet them in debate "in order that the public may see with whom are the facts, and with whom the arguments." [17]

Lincoln's proposal would merely formalize joint discussions among Whigs and Democrats that were already under way. In November, shortly after they returned to Springfield from their tour of the judicial circuit, Lincoln and Douglas became involved in an angry political discussion in the rear of Joshua Speed's store. Douglas suggested that the discussion be continued in a public debate. So much interest was aroused that additional speakers were recruited and three days set aside for the exchange. Cyrus Walker, a Whig candidate for presidential elector, led off on the first afternoon, November 19, and he was followed by Douglas. The crowd returned in the evening to hear Lincoln, also a candidate for elector, and his address was followed by further remarks by both Douglas and Walker. The meeting lasted until after midnight. "Between the two Whig speakers," commented the *State Register,* "our Democratic 'little giant' . . . had a rough time of it." Douglas complained that this was a case of *"two-pluck-one,"* but, according to the not entirely disinterested *Register,* his arguments remained unanswered. The *Register* further expressed annoyance at Lincoln's "clownish manner" and advised that he "correct this *clownish* fault, before it grows upon him." Unfortunately, none of the speeches were recorded. Years later, Joseph Gillespie recalled that Lincoln did not come up to the requirements of the occasion. "He was conscious of his failure," Gillespie continued, "and I never saw any man so much distressed." On the following evening, Douglas opened the debate with a strong indictment of the Second United States Bank, and again Lincoln replied. On the third evening, Edmund R. Wiley, a prominent local merchant and a Democrat, and Edward Dickinson Baker concluded the discussion. The independent treasury plan was the principal area of disagreement among the debaters.[18]

The Democrats eagerly accepted Lincoln's more formal challenge. On December 18 Lincoln opened the debate with a speech in which he attacked the independent treasury as "a new and corrupt system of tactics." Douglas answered for the Democrats with what the Whigs termed "a school-boy device." Several more Democrats followed on succeeding days before Lincoln returned to answer their arguments. Writing to Stuart, Lincoln noted scornfully, "The Democratic giant is here; but he is not now worth talking about." Nonetheless, he devoted considerable time to answering Douglas' earlier speech in an address that was reprinted and widely distributed as a Whig campaign document. After defending the Bank and denouncing the independent treasury as a scheme that would bring ruin and bankruptcy to the nation, he attacked Douglas' attempt to justify the policies of the Van Buren administration. Douglas, Lincoln reminded his audience, had "indulged himself in a contemptuous expression of pity for me," but, he added, "when I saw that he was stupid enough to hope, that I would permit such groundless and audacious assertions to go unexposed, I readily consented, that on the score both of veracity and sagacity, the audience should judge whether he or I were the more deserving of the world's contempt." [19]

The three-day discussion proved so effective that Lincoln and Douglas decided to repeat their performance in other parts of the state. Each man warmed to the task of refuting the other's arguments, both displaying the form that would characterize their more celebrated encounter at a later time. In March 1840, an estimated 1,000 people gathered in Jacksonville to hear the debaters conclude a week of political oratory. Baker and Josiah Lamborn warmed up the audience with a preliminary discussion. Lincoln then followed, "dealing out the usual quantum of abuse upon the administration of Gen. Jackson," and Douglas responded. The two men continued their debate later in the evening, when Lincoln charged the Van Buren administration with corruption, offering as proof a long list of defaulters taken from the report of the Secretary of the Treasury. Douglas challenged his opponent to show that any of the de-

faulters had been appointed by Van Buren and then, shifting to the attack, "proved Abolitionism upon Harrison so strong, that many of his
[Harrison's] friends declared that they would not support him until he
. . . denounces the Abolitionists." The Whigs, however, reported that
Douglas' speech contained nothing shocking and that the lie was
promptly given to Douglas' charges against Harrison by an "Old Soldier" present. Several days later Douglas was in Winchester, debating
the issues of the election with John J. Hardin. Hardin, looking at the
political struggle that lay ahead, predicted, "It will be a hot summers
work."

On the last day in April, the circuit court sat in Tremont, Tazewell
County, and Lincoln and Douglas, who were both in attendance, took
the occasion to continue their debate. Lincoln, in picturesque language,
depicted the prosperous and happy condition that prevailed in the country before the war against the United States Bank and exposed "the hideous deformity and injurious effects" of the independent treasury. In an
attempt to counter Douglas' charge of abolitionism against Harrison,
Lincoln accused Van Buren of having supported free Negro suffrage in
New York state. "He related," according to the account of a spectator,
"many highly amusing anecdotes which convulsed the house with laughter." Douglas, according to the Whig *Journal,* could only rave "incoher-
ently about high tariff, people's money, . . . U.S. Bank, blasphemy, Tom
Benton, &c." The "Big Giant" had used up the "little giant." The *Register,* of course, disagreed, predicting that "a few more such speeches as
. . . Lincoln's will soon place Van Buren in the majority."

Douglas continued to travel the circuit, attending court and making
political speeches. He wrote to Lewis Ross in late June that the prospects of Democratic victory became brighter each day. "Energy and activity are all that is necessary to gain the victory," he advised, but he
warned, "Let us not relax our exertions because we feel confident of success." With diligence, he was convinced, Van Buren could carry the state
by a greater majority than in 1836. "We keep up the fire wherever we
go."

Congressman John T. Stuart, Douglas' opponent of two years before,
entered the fray in September, and a debate between Douglas and Stuart
in Springfield followed soon afterward. Stuart charged that Van Buren
was sending federal marshals around the country counting chickens, tur-
keys, and other poultry with the intention of imposing a direct tax on
them all. Douglas denied that Van Buren favored direct taxation and,

with characteristic confidence, cited chapter and verse to show that the portion of the census law requiring a count of poultry had been proposed by a Whig and that Stuart himself had made no objection to it when it passed the House of Representatives. A month later, Douglas took on ex-Governor Duncan in debate, again in Springfield, discussing Van Buren's conduct in the New York constitutional convention, his attitude toward the War of 1812 (which the Whigs claimed he opposed), and the "slang of a palace, and extravagant furniture, and a hundred other ridiculous charges." Between debates, Douglas continued to travel throughout the state, making speeches on behalf of the Democrat ticket. In Carlinville, he attended a public hanging, availing himself of the occasion by delivering a campaign speech to the crowd that had gathered to witness the execution. Contrary to rumor, he did not speak from the gallows. By the close of the campaign, he had addressed 207 meetings.[20]

Bearing the brunt of the Democratic campaign during the eight months he spent on the stump, the twenty-seven-year-old Douglas displayed many of the qualities that would mark his public speaking in later years. He proved to be remarkably well-informed on the issues of the day, the result of his wide and avid interest in reading. His ability to retain facts and figures and to recite them in extemporaneous discussion never failed to astound his audiences. That he was sometimes careless in his references did not matter, for there were few, if any, in attendance who could catch him up. Fearless, energetic, and bold, either in attacking the opposition or in defending his position, Douglas developed a speaking style that was stark and realistic, with few rhetorical flourishes and seldom quotable. He had only one objective, the triumph of his party, and he spoke only to that end.

Politics to Douglas, as a contemporary later wrote, was a trade, and he pursued it with a single-minded devotion. When caught misrepresenting facts for political effect, he seldom worried, oftentimes conceding his mistake and admitting that he could not always be right. Lincoln and other Whig campaigners frequently quoted from William M. Holland's campaign life of Van Buren, published in 1835, to prove that Van Buren, in the New York constitutional convention, had supported a property qualification for the suffrage of whites and free Negroes alike. Lincoln repeatedly charged that a white man, even if he should be a Revolutionary War veteran, could be disfranchised by such a provision, while a free Negro who qualified could cast a ballot. Douglas just as repeatedly declared Holland's book to be a forgery. In order to settle the dispute, one Whig sent a copy of the book to the President, inquiring whether or not it was a true biography. Van Buren reportedly replied that "it was correct, so far as it went into his Life." At the next opportunity, following Douglas' declaration that the volume was fraudulent, Lincoln read the letter from Van Buren. Douglas seized the book and threw it far out into the audience, loudly damning both the author and his work. He later publicly admitted his error.[21]

The seriousness with which Douglas engaged in political warfare was demonstrated by another campaign incident. Little love was lost between Douglas and the editor of the Whig organ in Springfield, Simeon Francis. Each delighted in attacking and misrepresenting the other, Francis through the columns of his newspaper, the *Sangamo Journal,* and Douglas in his speeches or through the issues of *Old Hickory,* a Democratic campaign paper with which he was frequently identified as a contributing editor. Early in March, for example, *Old Hickory* described Francis as a "compound of *goose fat* and *sheep's wool,*" and declared that Douglas could not be "injured by the croaking of all the *Old Grannies* about the Journal office." These statements resulted from an altercation that ruffled Springfield society. As Lincoln told it, "Douglas, having chosen to consider himself insulted by something in the 'Journal,' undertook to cane Francis in the street. Francis caught him by the hair and jammed him back against a marketcart, where the matter ended by Francis being pulled away from him. The whole affair was so ludicrous that Francis and everybody else (Douglas excepted) have been laughing about it ever since." Francis, who stood six feet tall, published a mocking account of the affair, attributing his lack of serious injury at Douglas' hands "to the fact that the stick was too heavy for him to wield, our head too high for him to hit, or that he adopted a retreat too soon for his success." Needless to say, the account of the fracas in the rival *State Register* described an entirely different result.[22]

Douglas' activities in the 1840 campaign extended beyond his speechmaking. As a member of the Democratic state central committee, he was responsible for the direction of the party's appeal. Early in the year he signed the prospectus of *Old Hickory,* and he urged party workers in the counties to solicit subscriptions from all the voters in their neighborhoods. The rumor that Douglas was an editor of the paper was denied, but it was obvious that he exercised a great deal of editorial control. Although most concerned with the state-wide campaign, he continued to direct party activities in Sangamon County as well, and he signed the call for a county convention to meet in April. To his surprise, the convention nominated him for the lower house of the legislature, a nomination he felt obliged to decline. While he publicly announced that "considerations of a private nature" prevented his acceptance, it was clear that he had no desire to stand for election in a predominantly Whig constituency.[23]

Democratic campaign strategy emphasized national issues. To the dismay of some, such pressing local issues as the mounting state debt and the ill-advised internal improvements system were pushed into the background. The contest for the presidency, proclaimed *Old Hickory,* was to be one of principle. Democratic campaigners expressed confidence that the people were able to understand "the principles connected with the theory and practice of government," and it was on this assumption that they carried their arguments to the voters. But for the Whigs there was a lighter side to the campaign. Parades, rallies, barbecues, and mass meetings were staged throughout the state. The log cabin and hard cider jug were everywhere in evidence. The Whig campaign reached a climax in early summer when the party sponsored a Young Men's Convention and Old Soldier's Meeting in Springfield. Delegations, with bands, glee clubs, and fireworks, converged on the capital from all over the state. A gala parade through the town streets was followed by a gigantic barbecue where the delegates partook of "plain, substantial, log-cabin fare."

Unable to match the pageantry of the Whigs, the Democratic state central committee canceled its own plans for a Young Men's Convention. The Democratic party, the committee announced, "is emphatically a sober and reflecting party." But the party's annoyance with the Whig techniques could not be easily suppressed. Douglas was one of a committee of nine Democrats charged with issuing an address to the people of the state concerning the presidential campaign, in the hope that it might help to bring the voters to their senses. Never before had an election campaign been marked by such extraordinary spectacles. The people, the committee protested, "are treated as though they are the dupes of passion, of vain and ostentatious outward shows, and fit subjects of artifice and deception." Much was made of the fact that the Whigs had scheduled their celebration (unwittingly, to be sure) on the birthday of George III. Martial music, the roar of cannon, the multitude satiated with stimulants and fed with costly food, belied the Whig charge that the nation was suffering an unprecedented economic depression. The committee called upon the voters of the state to exercise their cool and deliberate judgment, to join in the "holy and patriotic" Democratic cause. The document hardly ruffled the Whig demeanor. Douglas, commented a Chicago paper, "appears to have an utter aversion to Hard Cider." [24]

Still the Whig efforts fell short. In spite of the cider jugs and log cabin floats, Illinois remained faithful to the Democracy. In the preliminary trial of strength, the August elections for the state legislature, the Democrats won handily. Although the Whigs doubled their efforts in the following weeks, their exertions were to no avail. Martin Van Buren won the state by a close margin over William Henry Harrison. Illinois was one of only seven states to endorse the President in what was otherwise a Whig year. Douglas could rest assured that the result was due in no small measure to his own untiring efforts and effective leadership.

iv

Douglas' satisfaction was all the sweeter because of his involvement during the campaign in two controversial local issues, each of which probably had some impact on the election results. The first was the continuing argument over the right of aliens to vote in Illinois elections, and the second involved the efforts of Governor Carlin to remove the Whig incumbent from the office of secretary of state.

Following the close contest for Congress in 1838, and convinced that Douglas' large vote was due to heavy support from the Irish along the canal line, the Whigs determined to bring the question of alien voting to a test in the state courts. Since the Democrats undoubtedly would enlist alien support in the presidential campaign of 1840, it was urgent that a court decision be secured before the August and November elections. There was little doubt that the problem would be decided favorably, for three of the four state supreme court justices were Whigs while the fourth was a Democrat of doubtful orthodoxy.

In May 1839, two Whigs, one a Galena newspaper editor and the other a judge of election in 1838, brought a case against alien voting before the circuit court in Jo Daviess county. A statement of facts, agreed upon by the two parties, was admitted, but no arguments were made and no briefs submitted. The election judge was charged with having knowingly received the vote of an unnaturalized person, a native of Ireland, in the election of 1838. The case was continued to the October term of the circuit court, at which time Judge Daniel Stone, a former Whig member of the state legislature, ruled against the defendant and

denied the authority of the state to confer the right to vote upon an unnaturalized alien. The decision caused an uproar among the Democrats,
who until it was rendered had taken no particular notice of the case. In
calm understatement, the *State Register* commented that "the case is one
of the very highest importance." The case was promptly appealed to the
state supreme court, where it was placed on the docket for the December
1839 term.

Stephen A. Douglas, although busily engaged with party affairs and
involved in the opening debates of the campaign with Lincoln and other
Whigs, was selected to defend the appellant and the right of aliens to
vote. Douglas was assisted by Murray McConnel, his old friend and
benefactor from Jacksonville, while the case for the Whigs was argued
by Schuyler Strong and Justin Butterfield. Upon the decision of the
court, wrote a Douglas biographer, "hung the future success or defeat
of the Democratic party."

Douglas argued that naturalization had no necessary connection with
the elective franchise. While naturalization came under the exclusive authority of Congress, the suffrage did not. Each state, he reminded the
court, had the right to determine its own voting qualifications. The Illinois constitution stipulated simply that all free white male inhabitants
above the age of twenty-one years could, after a six months' residence,
vote in all elections. Naturalization could neither confer nor withhold
the ballot. After hearing the arguments on both sides, the court took the
case under advisement until the next term, in June 1840. The Democrats were not encouraged with their prospects for winning the case, especially since rumors circulated almost immediately that the three Whig
justices had already made up their minds to rule against alien voting.

The court reassembled in Springfield in June, amidst all of the excitement and tumult that attended the mammoth Whig convention. The
parades, banners, log cabins, and cider jugs, Democrats feared, would be
difficult for the judges to resist. Before the court opened, Douglas
learned that a majority of the judges had agreed on a decision upholding
the judgment of the circuit court. In desperation, he examined minutely
the record of the case which had been sent up by the clerk of the circuit
court, and, to his amazement, he discovered a clerical error that had
gone unnoticed before. The case had originally been filed in May
1839—but the date of the election at which the alien's vote had been
cast was recorded as August 6, 1839, several months later. Obviously,
the clerk should have written August 6, 1838. Douglas immediately

filed a motion to dismiss the case, on the ground that, first, "the record in the case shows an improbable state of facts; all the facts having occurred after the case was adjudicated and decided in the Court below," and that, second, "this is a fictitious case, having no foundation in fact; the cause of action being alleged to have occurred at a time when the Court must judicially take notice, by the laws of the State, that no general election could take place." For the second time in his brief legal career, Douglas was saved in the courtroom by a clerical error. The court refused to dismiss the case but had no other choice than to continue it until the facts could be cleared up. The "alien case," as it was now widely and commonly referred to throughout the state, was postponed until the next, or December, term of the supreme court, after the crucial state and national elections. The democratic party was saved by what one contemporary called "a great feat of dexterity and management." That feat was Douglas'. Few believed Van Buren would have won the election in Illinois if the court had decided against alien voting before the election.

The election returns did not lull the Democrats into a false sense of security. Fully expecting the Whig majority on the court to rule against the right of aliens to vote when the case came up for consideration in December, the victorious Democrats began to discuss, more seriously than ever before, the proper role of the court in state government. Following the election, proposals for a sweeping reform of the judiciary were broached. There were indications that the composition of the supreme court would be placed at the top of the agenda of the new state legislature.[25]

The state supreme court fell into further disfavor with the Democrats over the celebrated "secretary of state case," which involved the attempts of the Democratic governor to remove the Whig incumbent from that office. Alexander P. Field, a six-foot-tall attorney, had been appointed secretary of state by Governor Ninian Edwards in 1829. At that time Field was a Jacksonian, but in the intervening years he had strayed from the party, and by 1838 he had moved completely into the Whig ranks. Soon after his inauguration, Democratic Governor Thomas Carlin removed Field from office and appointed John A. McClernand in his stead. The Whig-controlled state senate refused to confirm McClernand's appointment, on the ground that no vacancy existed and that therefore the governor had no power to appoint him. The Whigs pointed out that the constitution of the state did not specify the term for which the secretary of state was to be appointed. The incumbent must remain in office during good behavior or until the legislature should limit his term. Carlin protested this interpretation but did nothing further until after the legislature adjourned. At that time, the governor once again appointed McClernand to the office.

When Field refused to vacate the office, the case was taken to the courts for settlement. McClernand brought a *quo warranto* proceeding against Field in the Fayette County circuit court in the spring of 1839, before the capital had been officially moved to Springfield. Sidney Breese, the circuit judge and a good Democrat, decided in McClernand's favor. Appeal was immediately taken to the state supreme court, but before it could be considered, Field moved the files of the secretary of state's office, including the state seal, to the new capital in Springfield. They were placed for safekeeping with a mercantile establishment that had often served as Whig party headquarters in the town.

Stephen A. Douglas, already busy with the "alien case" and working hard to organize the Democratic party for the coming campaign, was drawn into the case. As McClernand's counsel, he applied to the Sangamon circuit court for a writ to recover the files and seal. Opposing him was Abraham Lincoln, who argued on behalf of Field. Douglas lost his case when the circuit judge decided in favor of Field.

While Douglas argued McClernand's right to the office of secretary of state before the circuit court, he was involved in the greater and more significant task of representing the Democratic appointee before the state supreme court. McClernand's case was ably argued by Jesse B. Thomas, James Shields, McClernand himself, and Attorney General Wickliffe Kitchell in addition to Douglas, but Douglas seems to have borne the greater part of the argument. The arguments were heard from July 19 to 23. Although the struggle between Field and McClernand for possession of the files of the office had aroused some excitement in Springfield, the final determination of the question by the supreme court, at least judging by the small number of spectators in the courtroom, aroused little interest. The arguments, according to the *Sangamo Journal,* revealed the high caliber of legal authority in the state. "The counsel for the respective parties," the paper boasted, "were well prepared, and the authorities presented by them to the Court, and the ingenuity and force of argument exhibited, made us feel proud of the legal talent engaged in the controversy."

Douglas' argument, printed in detail in the Democratic press, revealed his concern for preserving the purity of the institutions of government. His strong belief in a strict construction of the Constitution, his confidence in the "intelligence and virtue of the people, and their capacity for self-government," and his conviction that the responsibility and accountability of public officers to the people "is essential to the very existence of republican institutions," ran throughout his presentation. His speech was delivered with a clarity, boldness, and documentation that excited even the admiration of his opponents. "It must be conceded, that, in this country," he began, "all power is inherent in, and derivable from the people; that our government was instituted by them, for their mutual benefit and protection; and that the government possesses no powers, except those granted, by the people, in the constitution." "Is the office to be held," he asked, "during the pleasure, or in other words, during the life of the incumbent, or is he subject to removal?" Regarding the issue as one involving the principle of "life office," Douglas analyzed the constitutions of the United States and of Illinois, cited the authority of John Marshall and James Madison, and appealed to "the spirit of Republicanism." The conclusion, he declared, is "irresistible, that the governor had the constitutional right to remove A. P. Field, and to appoint John A. McClernand in his place." The court, he maintained, was not being asked to overturn established practices or to lay down new rules of constitutional interpretation, but merely to confirm already existing principles and usages. In a final burst of oratory, Douglas hoped "the wheels of Government will move on in the old beaten track, its functions and duties settled and defined, and the principles of the constitution maintained in their purity." If the court should endorse "life office," he warned, old principles will be discarded and new ones substituted in their stead, "and the ship of State left floating upon the ocean without star or compass to direct her course." The Whig court was little impressed with Douglas' logic. In a decision that filled 106 printed pages, the court upheld Field's right to continue in office.

The Democrats immediately attacked the decision. Judge Theophilus W. Smith, the lone Democrat on the bench, dissented from the majority opinion and upheld McClernand's right to the office, while a second judge, Thomas C. Browne, disqualified himself because of a family relationship to McClernand. The majority opinion, therefore, was the opinion of the remaining two judges, Samuel D. Lockwood and William Wilson. The Democratic press charged the Whigs with a conspiracy to keep Field in office for life and accused the court of opening the door to

"Federal trickery and subterfuge." Field himself was widely referred to as "King Alexander I." The decision, however, proved a boomerang for the Whigs. The Democrats took the "life office" issue into the 1840 campaign and kept it constantly before the electorate. According to one contemporary, the decision raised "a great flame of excitement" and undoubtedly was a factor in the Democratic victory. With the pending decision in the "alien case," the verdict of the court in the "secretary of state case" increased the determination of many Democrats to seek some kind of judicial reform during the next session of the state legislature.

For Douglas, the chapter did not close with the court's decision. Governor Carlin was not reconciled to Field's continued tenure in the office of secretary of state. He made another effort to replace him in February 1840, but once again the state senate refused to concur, citing the supreme court decision as their reason. During the following months Field's arrogance and his propensity for liquor made him more odious to the Democrats and reduced his usefulness to the Whig party. At the opening of the new, Democratic-controlled legislature in November 1840, Carlin made a fourth attempt to oust Field. This time the state senate agreed with him, but it was not McClernand who received the appointment. Instead, Carlin rewarded the man who had so ably argued the case against "life office" before the supreme court—Stephen A. Douglas. On the last day of November, Douglas' name was confirmed by the state senate, and he entered upon the discharge of his new duties. The *State Register* wrapped it all up: "Thus has ended this long mooted question in the triumph of correct principles over error and party zeal." [26]

# V

## "The common law
## is a beautiful system"
## 1840—1843

i

"Douglas at the bar," wrote William H. Herndon, "was a broad liberal-minded gentleman, a good lawyer, courteous, was not very well read in the law but his great good common sense carried him along with the best of the bar." Although he had once expressed doubts about the prospects of a legal career, the law continued to be an important part of Douglas' life. As he turned to politics and became more concerned with problems of party organization, his law practice, never lucrative, receded into the background. Yet he never gave it up completely, for, however small, it supplemented his sometimes meager income as a politician and officeholder. His legal activity revived between March 1839, when he resigned from the Springfield land office, and November 1840, when he was appointed secretary of state, a time when he was forced to rely entirely on his law practice for a livelihood. While he spent much of his time directing Democratic party strategy and campaigning for its candidates, he also enjoyed his greatest success as a lawyer. His near-miss in the race for Congress in 1838 had brought him valuable publicity, aiding his legal as well as his political reputation, and, in a day when a man's politics determined even his choice of legal counsel, Douglas became one of the leading Democratic lawyers in central Illinois. Traveling the circuit brought him into contact with other lawyers from around the state and provided him with audiences for his political electioneering. Douglas' contacts were further augmented and his law practice probably assisted by his membership in the Masonic lodge. He was received into the lodge during the spring of the busy year of 1840. At the first convocation of the Grand Lodge of Illinois the following October he was elected Grand Orator, although he seems to have been too busy ever to qualify for that office.

Others of Douglas' contemporaries agreed with Herndon's impression of his courtroom manner. In December 1839, Douglas examined John M. Palmer for admission to the bar, and Palmer later recalled the "cheerful kindness" which made Douglas so popular. Isaac N. Arnold remembered Douglas as a strong jury lawyer, distinguished for his ability to seize the real points in a case and happiest in the examination of witnesses. Technically, he was not regarded as a "close lawyer." He spent little time in the preparation and study of his cases and often seemed to rely on an intuitive knowledge of the law. As a trial lawyer, however, all agreed that he achieved striking success. Juries were regarded almost as political audiences, and Douglas employed the same tactics in addressing juries that brought him success on the stump. He made use of "all his privileged makeshifts" to win his cases and frequently resorted to bluff. "He might distort evidence, motive, manner, law; everything was regarded fair that tended to win the jury," wrote one biographer, "and in that respect his charming personality and his transcendent ability to cross-examine an unfriendly witness had more than a little to do." The informality of the courtroom enabled Douglas to capitalize on his popularity with the people. A visiting lawyer described the Sangamon circuit court as Douglas argued a case. The spectators were busily chewing and spitting tobacco, and the judge, Stephen T. Logan, was distinguishable from them only by his seat at the bench. Dressed in clothing "like that worn by a woodchopper," his hair "standing nine ways for Sunday," Logan sat with chair tilted back and feet propped high in front, puffing on a corncob pipe. In spite of the court's informality, however, an examination of Douglas' briefs reveals a thorough, if not profound, knowledge of constitutional law.[1]

Contrary to usual practice, Douglas did not enter into any lasting legal partnerships. He seemed to prefer working alone. While he was register of the Springfield land office, with little time to devote to his law practice, he formed a partnership with John D. Urquhart of Springfield, but this arrangement lasted only until October 1839, when the partnership was dissolved by mutual consent. On at least two occasions, Douglas entered into local partnerships in other parts of the judicial circuit—with William R. Archer in Pike County and George F. Markley in McLean County—but these affiliations applied only to business in the two counties. While he avoided the close relationships usually involved in partnerships, Douglas frequently worked with other lawyers on specific cases. On one occasion, a murder trial in Dewitt County in May 1840, Lincoln and Douglas appeared as co-counsel. It was the only time the two rivals argued the same side in a law case. The two men had been hurling verbal brickbats at one another as they debated the issues of the election campaign throughout the judicial circuit, but they took time out for a brief respite to work together in the courtroom. Their client was acquitted. Lincoln received a ninety-day note for $200 for his services and, after a year and a half of non-payment, was forced to sue for his fee. Douglas, on the other hand, demanded and received his $200 payment either before the trial commenced or immediately after its conclusion.

With political feelings and emotions running high, it is not surprising that political disagreements and rivalries were often taken to the courts for adjudication. Douglas, doubling as a political leader and practicing lawyer, was involved in a high proportion of such cases. The "alien" and "secretary of state" cases were the most important examples of his involvement in attempts to settle political questions by court action, but there were other, less significant instances. In most of them, political disagreement had led to violence. A hard-fought contest for probate justice of the peace in Springfield in 1837 erupted into violence following a series of vicious denunciations of one of the contestants, Dr. Anson G. Henry, in the columns of the *Republican*. Partisans of Dr. Henry attempted to invade the *Republican* office, but they were repulsed by George Weber, the editor; Jacob M. Early, Democrat, physician, and Methodist preacher; and Douglas. The next day, the sheriff of Sangamon County called on Weber, insults were exchanged, and in the subsequent melee the sheriff was stabbed. Both the attackers and the attacked were arrested. Douglas, who, it was said, had written the original inflammatory articles, defended Weber in the trial and secured an acquittal for his client.[2]

The Democratic district convention that nominated Douglas for Congress provided the background for a celebrated murder trial during the following year. Henry L. Truett, the son-in-law of Congressman May (whom Douglas had just bested in the convention), accosted Dr. Early in Spottswood's Hotel in Springfield, brandished a pistol, and demanded

to know if Early had been the author of certain resolutions derogatory to
his father-in-law. Early, remaining silent, attempted to protect himself
with a chair, but without success. Truett fired, and Early fell. He died
three days later. Douglas was appointed prosecuting attorney *pro tem.* to
try Truett, although he later turned the case over to the newly elected
states' attorney, Daniel Woodson, and thenceforth acted as Woodson's
assistant. Early's associations with Douglas had been close, for he had
been one of Douglas' most loyal supporters. Truett's defense was handled by Lincoln and Stuart, with the assistance of three additional attorneys. The case excited great interest partly because of its political
character and partly because Douglas and Stuart were stumping the district for Congress at the same time that they were involved in the trial.
Douglas and Woodson presented what seemed to many observers to be
an airtight case against Truett. Lincoln, however, was successful in creating a reasonable doubt of his client's guilt by maintaining that Early
possessed a deadly weapon, the chair, and that Truett shot only in self-
defense. The jury was convinced, and Truett, to Douglas' shock and surprise, was acquitted. The Truett-Early murder case was the most famous
confrontation between Lincoln and Douglas in the courtroom.

While Douglas was arguing both the "secretary of state" and "alien"
cases, he was called upon to defend the party in still a third instance. In
January 1840, charges were brought against John Pearson, judge of the
Seventh Judicial District and a Democrat, by Whig members of the
state legislature. He was accused of violating the right of trial by jury, of
acting in an arbitrary and oppressive manner, of making threats from
the bench, and of unjustly quashing indictments. Demands were made
for his impeachment as the Whigs sought to make an election issue of
Pearson's conduct. The lower house of the legislature agreed to sit in
committee of the whole to hear and investigate the charges. Douglas
was among those selected to defend Pearson. The charges were answered
ably and convincingly, for, after a few days, the house decided that there
was not enough evidence against Pearson to warrant his removal from
the bench. Thirty-two members of the Whig opposition, including Lincoln, protested the decision. Pearson was later held in contempt by the
state supreme court, and again Douglas came to his defense.[3]

Douglas' record before the Illinois state supreme court was an impressive one, adding to his reputation as a successful lawyer. Between 1835
and 1840 he argued fifteen cases before the supreme court, all but two of
them following his campaign for Congress in 1838. Of the fifteen cases,

Douglas won twelve and lost three. His appointment to the office of secretary of state ended his appearances before the highest state court, except for four cases argued over a decade later, in 1851. At the same time, his interest in the practice of law languished, and as his political career began to flourish it all but disappeared. He continued to maintain a law office, moving it from Springfield to Chicago in 1847, but it no longer represented a deep professional commitment and was probably more a hedge against the future than anything else. Douglas and Lincoln were admitted to practice before the United States Circuit Court at the same time, and in 1849 both were admitted to practice before the United States Supreme Court. There is no record that Douglas ever appeared before the latter body.[1]

ii

In December 1840, Gustave Koerner, a young German immigrant who had settled in Illinois seven years before, traveled to Springfield, seeking appointment as messenger to carry the state's electoral vote to the national capital. He was introduced to Stephen A. Douglas, and years later he recalled that first meeting. Douglas, he wrote, "was of very small size, but broad-shouldered and muscular." When sitting, he appeared of medium height, but "his legs were very short." His massive and "intellectual" head was crowned with thick black hair, his light blue or gray eyes sparkled and his mouth and chin were firm. "He was pleasant in conversation, and toward those he liked and wanted to persuade he was full of blandishment. . . . The word was not much used then, but he had a 'magnetism' about him almost irresistible." It was Douglas who saw to it that Koerner received the appointment.

The secretary of state's office was only a temporary stop for Douglas. The duties of the position were perfunctory, and Douglas took little interest in their execution. He maintained a register of the official acts of the governor, as required by law, and, when asked, transmitted information to the state legislature. In February 1841, for example, Douglas and James Shields, the state auditor, acting as a board of auditors, investigated the conduct of the state house commissioners (both Whigs) and audited the accounts for work done on the new statehouse in Springfield. Douglas accepted the appointment as secretary of state purely for political reasons. The job brought him a steady income and enabled him to remain close to the wheels of state government. His appointment also marked a final victory for the Democratic party in the "secretary of state" case and was an act of defiance against the Whig-dominated state supreme court.[5]

While the controversy over the governor's power to remove the secretary of state was thus resolved, in spite of the supreme court's pronouncement, the "alien" case remained undecided. The case had been continued from the June term, 1840, when Douglas had discovered the error in the report of the lower court. It was common knowledge that the Whig majority of the court had already prepared its decision on the constitutional aspects of the case when the error was discovered, and all signs pointed to a decision adverse to the Democrats in December. Anticipating defeat on the alien question, the Democratic members of the legislature, emboldened by their decisive victory in the August election, gathered in Springfield "inflamed with the highest degree of resentment" against the judiciary. The excitement of the 1840 campaign, the Democratic victory in the state, and the Whig triumph in the nation resulted in an intense degree of partisan feeling among the legislators. Democrats, especially, expressed a hard determination to make their supremacy in state politics more secure. With the prospect of defeat on the alien question facing them, with the memory of the court's position on the "secretary of state" case still fresh, members of the dominant party cast a vengeful eye on the state's highest tribunal.

On December 10, Adam W. Snyder, whose senate district contained a large foreign vote, introduced a bill calling for a sweeping reorganization of the state's judicial system. The legislation would discontinue the office of circuit court judge, would create five additional justices of the state supreme court, and would require the justices (nine in number) to hold circuit court in addition to their duties on the supreme bench. The bill was a blatant political move to entrench the Democratic party in the judicial branch. By increasing the number of supreme court judges from four to nine (the additional judges to be elected by the Democratic-controlled legislature), the party would gain a two-to-one majority on the court. The bill was immediately denounced by the Whigs. Many believed that the measure would backfire on its supporters because of its radical and revolutionary character. "We think loco focoism has struck the last blow at the credit and reputation of our State," the *Journal* concluded. John J. Hardin, a member of the lower house, was convinced "the Locos are cutting their throats this winter." Even some Democrats balked at supporting the reorganization of the court.

The bill passed the state senate by an easy majority on January 9 and was immediately sent to the house, where a bitter struggle ensued. While the battle raged, the court reconsidered the "alien" case and issued its final decision. The Whig judges now sidestepped the constitutional aspects of the case, altering the stand they were prepared to take six months before. In an obvious effort to forestall the Democratic effort to reorganize the supreme court and to render the reform legislation unnecessary, the court ruled simply that if a voter took the oath prescribed by law his vote could not be rejected, that the alien whose vote had been challenged in Galena was by law qualified to cast a ballot. Only the Democratic judge, Theophilus Smith, upheld the constitutional right of aliens to vote.

The decision, far from placating the Democrats, created an uproar. The Whig judges were denounced by the disappointed members of the majority party for having evaded the constitutional question. The day after the decision, an angry Douglas addressed a crowded audience "in the lobby" on the necessity for judicial reform. The reorganization of the supreme court was now more necessary than before, he cried. He condemned the judges' evasion of the constitutional aspects of the case, pointing out that they had "prepared an opinion last summer against the right of aliens to vote; which opinion they had *suppressed,* and yesterday gave a different opinion, avoiding the *constitutional* question." Douglas boldly accused the judges of having disposed of the case without deciding it; their decision, he declared, had been motivated solely by a desire to squelch the pending reorganization bill. A decision on the constitutional question, he charged, had been postponed to a time when the political climate of the state would be more agreeable to the opinions of the judges. Douglas urged support of the judiciary bill and argued its constitutionality. The three Whig judges denied Douglas' charge that they had been prepared to rule on the constitutional aspects of the "alien" case six months before, a denial which the Democratic judge, Theophilus Smith, supported. Douglas and several others immediately published letters attesting to the fact that Smith had informed them to the contrary during the previous term of the court.[6]

The controversial bill passed the lower house a few days after the court decided the "alien" case, and it was sent at once to the council of revision. The reaction of the council was not difficult for the Democrats to predict. A week after its passage, the bill was returned to the senate with the council's veto. Only Governor Carlin had approved it. The legislation was easily passed again by the senate, but the bill's backers despaired of getting it through the house with the required majority. If the party should fail, wrote Sidney Breese, then judge of the circuit court, the question would be taken to the people, "the great and final arbiters in all matters of this sort." Snyder complained that some Democrats were being "bought up" by the opposition. The apprehensions, however, proved needless. When the bill was brought up for passage, it mustered exactly the vote required and became law, in part because of Douglas' own efforts to organize and discipline the affirmative vote. Thirty-four members of the lower house, including Lincoln, entered their protest against the passage of the bill.

The final passage of the judiciary bill was cheered by Democrats as a great triumph over the Whigs and the "present corrupt supreme court." "The Judges of the Supreme Court," declared the *State Register,* "are no longer to be idle drones, wandering about our streets doing nothing, and receiving a salary of fifteen hundred dollars per annum." Adam Snyder rejoiced "in now having a court that will decide all questions of a political character upon that broad basis of liberality which suits, and conforms to, the principles we mutually entertain." There was little attempt to conceal the political purposes for which the legislation was passed. The Whigs vowed unceasing war against the spirit of "Destructiveism, which threatens to uproot all our institutions."

Although not a member of the legislature, Douglas worked for the bill in the lobby and behind the scenes, becoming so closely identified with it that the measure was known to some as the "Douglas bill." Its passage had important implications for the future of the Democratic party. Douglas regarded it as necessary to strengthen party bonds in the face of a growing opposition. The bill became a new test for party loyalty, and those few Democrats who had voted against it found themselves in an increasingly uncomfortable position. Judge Smith, who not only had opposed the bill in the council of revision but who also had sided with his Whig colleagues in denying Douglas' charges, was now cast out of the party. With a Democratic majority on the court, the alien vote in Illinois could not be effectively challenged, and a major source of Democratic strength would be protected. Just to make sure, the legislature passed a law later in February 1841, specifically granting to aliens the right to vote.

The reform of the judiciary was actually not as revolutionary as the Whigs maintained. The political excitement aroused by the bill obscured the fact that the legislation merely returned the state's judicial system to the situation that had existed until six years before. Supreme court judges had been withdrawn from holding circuit courts in 1835, when a new set of circuit judges was provided for. As a result, the supreme court judges had lost much of their influence and the court itself had been weakened as a branch of the state government. The reorganization would, it was thought, restore vigor to the judiciary and enable the judges to act with greater independence than before.[7]

Douglas was well rewarded for his efforts on behalf of the judiciary bill. Five days after its final approval, the legislature met in joint session to elect the additional judges. Sidney Breese, Thomas Ford, Samuel H. Treat, Walter B. Scates—and Stephen A. Douglas—were elevated to the supreme bench. Of the five, Douglas' name was the only one to arouse comment throughout the state. For Douglas to be one of the beneficiaries of the legislation he had so strenuously pushed smacked too strongly of a political deal for many to accept graciously. There was some evidence to support these misgivings. The office of secretary of state was apparently part of the shuffle, used by Douglas as a lever to achieve his election to the court. Douglas' old benefactor, Murray McConnel, who had himself hoped for a judgeship, revealed that Douglas' nomination in the Democratic caucus (euphemistically called the "Slaughter Pen") was brought about "by a manouver and by force of bargain and the hope of a Secretaries office." John A. McClernand seemed in line once again for the office vacated by Douglas, and on the day after the election "a most furious effort on the part of the wire movers" to secure McClernand's appointment was reported. Another name was injected into the discussion when a Belleville newspaper suggested, "I think the people understand the game—they understand the creation of a supreme judgeship with 1500 dollars salary for the promotion of Stephen A. Douglass—and leaving the office of Secretary of State vacant for the promotion of our Representative Lyman Trumbull." Trumbull did, in fact, succeed Douglas.

Some Democrats were not convinced that Douglas, at the age of twenty-seven, was ready to act the part of a supreme court justice. "Dug a great *Supreme Squire*," wrote McConnel somewhat incredulously, "I till you we are a great people." Snyder commented that "Douglas is talented, but too young for the office." He added, however, that "we could not do much better than elect him." Douglas' election to the court was as much recognition of his political importance to the Democratic party as it was the result of any political deal. No one had the temerity to suggest that it was recognition of a superior legal talent. The people had simply "repaid him for being wronged out of his seat in Congress."

During the seven years that he had resided in Illinois, Douglas had risen to a position of considerable power in state politics. From the time he first took up the defense of Old Hickory as a schoolteacher in Winchester, Douglas had been in the thick of state politics. As states' attorney, member of the legislature, register of the Springfield land office, candidate for Congress, and secretary of state, he had built a formidable political following as well as a state-wide reputation for vigorous political leadership and adeptness. Each stage in his brief career fit into a deliberate pattern of movement up the ladder of political success. He was, as one correspondent put it, the "Generalissimo" of the Illinois Democratic party: "What a profound set of men the locofocos must be in the law, to select little Stephen as their greatest judicial light. But Douglass is the tallest chap in the lot, and when he says 'stand aside,' none of the party dare say otherwise than 'so mote it be.' The truth is the whole party are afraid of him; and they all obey his nod most implicitly." [8]

### iii

The day after his election to the supreme court, Douglas resigned the office of secretary of state. He waited until the last day of the winter term before assuming his place on the bench. He was then assigned to the Fifth Judicial Circuit, a nine-county area in the west central part of the state between the Illinois and Mississippi rivers, which included most of the Military Tract. Quincy, a busy Mississippi River town and county seat of Adams County, was the most important community in the circuit. It was here that Douglas made his home, although he continued to spend several months each year in Springfield. An area of scattered farms and small towns, the circuit was one of the fastest growing regions in the state, its population increasing from about 8000 in 1830 to almost 68,000 ten years later. Among the newcomers were members of the Church of Jesus Christ of Latter-Day Saints, the Mormons, who began moving into Adams and Hancock counties in large numbers late in the 1830's. Still, the area seemed to Douglas to be isolated and off the beaten track. Most of his time would be spent holding court in the small nondescript county towns—Lewistown, Rushville, Mt. Sterling, Macomb, Oquawka, Monmouth, and Knoxville—and he often complained that because they were "off the road," news from the state capital was slow and uncertain.

If Douglas' report to his parents can be believed, he looked upon his judicial post as a respite from the exciting political struggles in which he had recently been involved. "I assure you," he wrote shortly after his election to the court, "that I have been so completely engrossed with the excitements and strifes of partizan conflicts and official stations, that office and honors have lost their charms, and I desire and seek repose and the society of friends." Admitting to some pecuniary embarrassment, he reviewed his recent activities with an uncharacteristic modesty. "I have thus far led a life of extraordinary activity, and have endured great efforts of Mind and body, and have yet left a Constitution strong healthy and unimpaired. But this, and whatever of character and of fame I may have acquired are all I have left."

The tone of humility in Douglas' remarks was deceiving. That he exaggerated his loss of interest in "office and honors" soon became evident. Those who knew Douglas could not but believe that his election to the supreme court would only be a way-station, another step in the realization of his political ambitions. "I have now commenced upon a new theatre," he informed his parents, "and expect to devote all the energies of my mind to my Judicial duties and my private affairs for at least a few years to come." His tenure on the bench was to be significant, but temporary. Many years later, he jokingly observed that his acceptance of the judgeship in 1841 was "among my youthful indiscretions," but at the time the position had a political importance that did much to advance his reputation. The state's congressional districts were to be redrawn following the 1840 census, and perhaps Douglas recognized the desirability of becoming better known in an area that was not so thoroughly Whig in politics as was Sangamon County.[9]

Among the objections of the Whigs to the reorganization of the state supreme court had been the argument that cases in the circuit courts would pile up and justice would be delayed in the absence of a separate set of circuit judges. The judges of the supreme court, dividing their time between their circuit duties and their responsibilities as the highest state tribunal, would be unable to keep abreast of legal business in the circuit courts. Almost as if he were determined to refute the Whig assertions, Douglas attacked the circuit court dockets with vigor and characteristic energy. Writing from Fulton County in April 1841, he boasted that he had cleared the circuit court docket in that county for the first time in seven years, disposing of between 300 and 400 cases. The dispatch with which he discharged his judicial duties aroused even the admiration of some Whigs. One of them, writing from Schuyler County, had reservations over Douglas' "hop, skip and jump" through the docket, but nevertheless expressed satisfaction with the "qualities of readiness and promptitude in the despatch of business" which he had displayed. The young judge was "fast advancing to a high reputation" as a judicial officer. Similar reports of Douglas' energetic approach to his duties came from other counties. In Knox County, he called case after case on the docket. Finding none of the attorneys ready to take them up, Douglas asked the sheriff to adjourn the court until the next morning, when each case on the docket would be called and either tried or dismissed. Douglas' announcement was followed by a sudden flurry of activity among the local lawyers. True to his word, each case was settled as it was brought up. Not only did Douglas complete the business in his own circuit courts, but he also filled in for fellow judges who were unable to meet their courts. In 1842, Douglas presided over the Cook County circuit court at a special term, in place of Judge Smith, and earlier he had held court in Morgan County for Judge Lockwood. During his two years on the bench, he presided over thirty-eight sessions of the circuit courts. There is little doubt that he earned his salary.

"The members of the Bar and the people generally," Douglas confided to a friend, "have received and treated me with great kindness and courtesy." He was agreeably disappointed that even many of his political opponents seemed satisfied with the manner in which he discharged his duties. Whig party leaders, however, remained unconvinced that the judicial reform had been necessary, or that Douglas had been a wise choice for the bench. In Quincy, Douglas was attacked for his lack of legal experience. Never able to make his bread by the law, the *Quincy Whig* charged, Douglas "has but little standing except as a mere partisan politician." Douglas himself added fuel to the fire by removing all circuit court clerks who were Whigs and replacing them with Democrats.[10]

As a circuit judge, Douglas' knowledge of the law was never severely tested. The cases that were brought before him were of a routine nature, with civil suits outnumbering criminal suits. Few of his decisions attracted wide notice. In the spring of 1843, his decision in the Adams circuit court which dealt with the redemption of lands sold under mortgage foreclosure decree was published in the press outside the circuit. In the same court, he decided that the state's bankruptcy law was unconstitutional. On another occasion, Douglas ruled against the assessment of the property of nonresidents at a higher rate than that of residents. Perhaps the most controversial of his pronouncements was a decision upholding the creation by the state legislature of a new county where even the residents opposed the law and refused to organize. The contest became involved in partisan rivalries. In rendering his decision Douglas sided with the Democrats against the Whigs, leaving himself open once again to the angry charges of the opposition. The entire incident grew out of a bitter county seat fight in Adams County, and it continued to dominate the columns of Quincy newspapers for several weeks after Douglas had handed down his decision.[11]

Twice each year Douglas joined his eight colleagues in Springfield for the terms of the state supreme court. Altogether he attended four terms of the higher court. The summer term in July was frequently brief, the result perhaps of central Illinois' midsummer weather. The December term usually lasted until February, thus affording the judges opportunity to participate in the political discussions of the state legislature. The business of the supreme court was almost literally taken over by the new judges. None of the four older judges was responsible for many of the opinions, most of the decisions being prepared by Samuel H. Treat, Sidney Breese, Walter B. Scates, and Douglas. Douglas himself wrote twenty-two opinions during his period of service on the supreme bench.

Douglas' decisions were brief, explicit, and clear, and he delivered them in a straightforward manner without embellishment. They revealed his pragmatic approach to the law. His interpretation of the law was broad and liberal. On only one occasion did he depart from terse legal language. In the case Penny v. Little, argued during the December 1841 term, Douglas dealt with the character of the common law as it had been extended to the Northwest Territory, and hence to what had become the state of Illinois. "The common law," he declared, "is a beautiful system; containing the wisdom and experience of ages. Like the people it ruled and protected, it was simple and crude in its infancy, and became enlarged, improved, and polished, as the nation advanced in civilization, virtue, and intelligence. Adapting itself to the condition and circumstances of the people, and relying upon them for its administration, it necessarily improved as the condition of the people was elevated." Transplanted from England to the colonies, the common law was improved and modified by American legislation and the reports of American courts, and it was this American product, Douglas maintained, that had been extended over the Northwest Territory in 1787. It

was the common law adapted "to our peculiar institutions, and the habits and customs of the people" that formed a basis for the legislation of
both the territory and the state. The law to Douglas was ever-changing
as circumstances and experience themselves changed; judicial action, he
thought, should reflect this flexibility. Like all other institutions, the law
had to be adapted to the needs, wants, and desires of the society in
which it existed, a fundamental conviction on which Douglas was to
base much of his later political activity.[12]

His position on the law's flexibility was further revealed in his reaction to small technical errors or variances which appeared in the records
of cases brought before him. Twice he ruled that such variances were
immaterial and that the cases based upon them could not stand. As an
attorney, Douglas had won his point in the courtroom on at least two
occasions by seizing upon just such errors in the record, but he was now
on the other side of the bench and exercising new prerogatives.[13] Under
the new judicial system, it was inevitable that the supreme court justices
might hear and pass upon appeals from their own decisions in the lower
courts. Douglas delivered the opinion of the court in four cases that had
been appealed from his own circuit decisions. In three, he affirmed his
earlier judgment, but in one case he reversed his prior opinion.[14]

iv

The Fifth Judicial District was one of the most exciting in the state
during the years when Douglas rode the circuit. Not only did it include
the town of Nauvoo and the growing Mormon community, but it also
included, in Adams and Knox counties, strong centers of abolitionist
feeling. Because of the district's proximity to the slave state of Missouri,
incidents involving fugitive slaves and the underground railroad occurred with increasing frequency.

The slavery issue had always been an important one to Illinois, in
spite of the fact that both the Northwest Ordinance and the 1818 state
constitution had made the area free. Initially settled by people from the
upper south, and sharing a boundary with two slave states, Illinois became the scene of heated discussion over slavery during its early statehood years. Attempts were made to introduce the institution and to convert Illinois by means of constitutional reform into a slave state. Slaves
were actually held in the state as late as the 1840's, as indentured ser-
vants, and free Negroes always encountered a hostile reception. After
1824 the movement for a slave state died out, but discussion of the ques-

tion continued. The next decade brought significant changes in the popular attitude toward slavery. The movement of population into the central and northern counties from New England and the Middle Atlantic states coincided with the rise of militant abolitionism. Many of the new settlers brought strong antislavery attitudes with them. In Illinois the newcomers encountered the older southern heritage, and the question of slavery and the Negro became an important issue between the two groups.

Abolitionism in Illinois was religious and ecclesiastical in character. Some of its chief agents were northern clergymen who found fresh fields of endeavor in the state. Two "islands of abolitionism" were the towns of Galesburg and Quincy, both of which were in Douglas' judicial district. Here the memory of the abolitionist Elijah P. Lovejoy, martyred in Alton four years before Douglas' appointment to the bench, was still fresh. In Quincy, the Reverend David Nelson, a Presbyterian preacher who had been driven from Missouri, ran an institute for training missionaries which had strong abolitionist overtones. Local antislavery societies had appeared, and in 1837 the Illinois Anti-Slavery Society was organized, stimulated by the national debate over the receipt by Congress of abolitionist petitions and the annexation of Texas. The Illinois legislature took cognizance of the growing movement the same year, when it approved several anti-abolition resolutions. Douglas, then a member of the legislature, supported the resolutions; it was his first formal protest against the abolition movement. Although he represented the new stream of migration from the northern states, he did not sympathize with the antislavery cause.[15]

Douglas first encountered the fugitive slave problem in the fall of 1842, when, sitting in circuit court in Knox County, he quashed an indictment against a justice of the peace for assaulting the "conductor" of a group of fugitive slaves. A more important case which came up at about the same time forced Douglas to deal directly with the fugitive slave question. In August 1842, Richard Eells, a prominent Quincy physician and well-known abolitionist, was apprehended and charged with harboring, secreting, and assisting a fugitive slave. The charge was sustained in the justice of the peace's court, and Eells was bound over to the circuit court for trial. Dr. Eells' case was argued before Judge Douglas in Quincy, but because of the illness of a material witness, Douglas postponed the trial until the following spring term. For two days, in April 1843, the arguments were presented. Eells' defense cited the United

States Supreme Court decision in the case of *Prigg v.* Pennsylvania, handed down the previous year, in which the Court had ruled that the power and duty of apprehending fugitive slaves lay exclusively with the federal government. Illinois' fugitive slave law, Eells' counsel argued, was therefore unconstitutional and void. Judge Douglas denied the validity of the defense argument. The object of the Illinois law, he maintained, was not to return fugitive slaves, but to preserve the peace of the state. As a police regulation, the statute was constitutional, notwithstanding the fact that it aided in the execution of the laws of the United States. The jury returned a verdict of guilty. Douglas sentenced Eells to pay a fine of $400, imposing the fine, he said, rather than the imprisonment allowed by the law in order that the case might serve as a warning to future offenders. Should another case follow, Douglas cautioned, he would imprison the guilty party to the fullest extent of the law. Douglas' decision won support from both the Democratic and the Whig press. The *Quincy Whig* commented, "We hope this will prove a warning to the abolitionists for the future."

The Eells case was appealed to the state supreme court, where it was heard in February 1844, after Douglas had left the bench. The higher court sustained Douglas' decision. In the "syllabus" of the case, as it was reported to the supreme court, Douglas' position was further summarized. The police power of a state, he maintained, embraces the power of regulating the internal affairs of the state in all its civil and criminal polity. The state of Illinois, under this police power, could prevent the introduction of Negro slaves into the state and could punish those individuals who made the attempt. He declared that the state therefore had the right to legislate on the subject of fugitive slaves, and that this right was not taken away by the legislation of Congress on the same subject. The constitutionality of the state law against aiding fugitive slaves was upheld. The case was appealed to the United States Supreme Court, where it was not heard until the 1850's, long after Eells himself had died. Although the appeal was ably handled by Ohio's Salmon P. Chase, the national tribunal upheld the state court.[16] Douglas' role in the case provided him with his first opportunity to suggest the use of the local police power as a means for regulating the slavery question.

Litigation concerning fugitive slaves, the security of free Negroes, and the indentured system that practically enslaved Negroes in Illinois continued to occupy the attention of the state courts. The growing disregard of the state's laws against harboring and assisting fugitive slaves may be dated from the Eells case in 1842. In a case involving a Negro who was held as a slave without proof of indenture, the state supreme court decided in the December 1840 term (before Douglas' election to the court) that "the presumption of law in this state is in favor of liberty, and every person is supposed free, without regard to color." The holding of slaves in Illinois, the court insisted, was repugnant to state law and hence illegal. A similar case came before the court again in the summer of 1841, when Abraham Lincoln, representing the defendant, argued that the Negro girl in question was free by virtue of the Northwest Ordinance and the Illinois state constitution. The court (with Douglas concurring) sustained Lincoln's argument on behalf of freedom and reaffirmed its earlier stand.[17]

v

The Mormons began moving into Illinois in large numbers in 1839. Their Church had been organized in 1830 by Joseph Smith, a young up-state New York farm boy whose family had settled near the town of Palmyra. Close by was Canandaigua, the scene of Douglas' youth and education, and it is likely that Douglas' first contacts with the Mormons were made during this early period in his life. By the time Douglas left Canandaigua for Illinois, in 1833, the Church had already become a center of controversy. Two years before, the Mormons had moved to Kirtland, Ohio, and by the middle 1830's they had moved again to the western counties of Missouri. In each location, the members of the Church had to face the hostility of their neighbors. Opposition in Missouri flared into violence and bloodshed, culminating in Governor Lilburn Boggs' "extermination order" in 1838. "The Mormons," the governor ordered, "must be treated as enemies, and *must be exterminated or driven from the state* if necessary for the public peace—their outrages are beyond all description." Forced to flee, the Mormons turned eastward toward Illinois, where they felt they would be received with sympathy and toleration. During 1839, thousands of Church members began moving into Adams and Hancock counties. A town site on the banks of the Mississippi, renamed Nauvoo, was selected as the new center of the Church.

The Mormons' first impact on Illinois was political. Following the close contest between Douglas and Stuart in the Third District congressional race, both the Whig and Democratic parties welcomed the new settlers. Sensing the voting potential of the refugees, party leaders vied with one another for their favor. The Whigs had the first advantage. Expelled from Missouri by a Democratic governor, and their petitions rebuffed by the Democratic administration of Martin Van Buren, the Mormons heeded Smith's directives and cast their vote in the 1840 election for the Whig ticket. One Whig paper cheerfully accepted the Mormon votes as antidote to the alien vote received by the Democrats. Whig enthusiasm was tarnished, however, by a curious development in the Nauvoo precinct, where some 200 Mormons were persuaded to strike the name of Abraham Lincoln from the electoral ticket. The trick was immediately blamed on Douglas, who, it was said, had been in Nauvoo on election day, a report strongly denied by the *State Register*.[18] It is clear that Douglas was not willing to let the Mormon vote go to the Whigs by default.

During the legislative session of 1840–41, the Mormons sought to consolidate their position in the state, while the Democrats, with a majority in the legislature, saw their opportunity to win support from the Church members. Legislation of amazing liberality was passed, granting the Church a security that was soon to arouse controversy. A charter was approved for Nauvoo that made that city virtually independent of the state government. The Church was incorporated, and a military force, the Nauvoo Legion, was created, answerable only to the governor. Later critics charged that the measures were "anti-republican" and "capable of infinite abuse by a people disposed to abuse them" but they excited little interest at the time and passed without opposition. Managing the legislation were Sidney Little, the Whig senator from McDonough and Hancock counties, and Stephen A. Douglas, at that time secretary of state. Apparently the Mormons were more grateful for Douglas' support than for Little's, for shortly afterward they granted Douglas the Freedom of the City of Nauvoo.[19]

Following his election to the court, Douglas strengthened his contacts with the followers of Joseph Smith. Early in May he addressed the townspeople in Nauvoo, praising the Mormons for the improvements they had made in their town and commending them for their enterprise and industry. Joseph Smith concluded that "Judge Douglass has ever proved himself friendly to this people." At the same time, Douglas appointed John C. Bennett, mayor of Nauvoo, to be master in chancery for Hancock County, an appointment that was loudly denounced by non-Mormons. Bennett, described by Thomas Ford as "probably the greatest scamp in the western country," was a recent convert to the Church and reputedly a man of unsavory character. Within two years, in fact, he was to break with the Church. Before his visit to Nauvoo, Douglas rendered an opinion, one of his first judicial acts concerning the Mormons, that the officers and men of the Nauvoo Legion were exempt from all military duty not required by Church authorities, further emphasizing the independence of that body from state control. The Mormons lavished their praise on Douglas, and from this time on he was able to count on their full support. The Whigs, losers in the struggle, became increasingly anti-Mormon in their attitudes.[20]

Following an election day fracas in Davies County, Missouri, in 1838, Joseph Smith and five of his followers were arrested and charged with treason against the state of Missouri. Before their trial could be completed, the six men escaped to Illinois. Attempts were later made to extradite Smith by the Missouri authorities, and an indictment was drawn by Governor Boggs naming the six "fugitives from justice." It was not served on Smith until June 5, 1841, when the sheriff of Adams County arrested the Mormon leader in a small town south of Nauvoo. Smith was returned to Quincy, where he obtained a writ of *habeas corpus.* Judge Douglas arrived in Quincy that same evening, was apprised of Smith's arrest and consented to give him a hearing in Monmouth, where he was scheduled to hold court a few days later.

The trial opened on June 9. The courtroom was filled with spectators and, according to Smith, "great excitement" prevailed in the town. To argue his defense, Smith had secured the services of some of the ablest Whig attorneys in the area, including Orville H. Browning, Cyrus Edwards, Sidney Little, and Archibald Williams. As the arguments began, the crowd of spectators became so intense that Douglas ordered the sheriff of Warren County to hold them back. When the sheriff hesitated, Douglas fined him $10. A few minutes later a second order was issued, the sheriff replying that he had directed a constable to prevent the spectators from crowding the prisoner and witnesses, whereupon Douglas imposed a second $10 fine. Orville Browning carried the burden of the defense argument. In an eloquent and impassioned plea, interrupted once by the sudden nausea of one of the prosecuting attorneys, Browning described the Church as an abused and persecuted institution and detailed the atrocities which had been committed against its members in Missouri. So effective was Browning's eloquence that even Judge Douglas was reported to have wept. In reporting the scene, one anti-Mormon paper asked, "Were there any onions about?"

Douglas delivered his opinion the next day. Without considering the validity of the charges against Smith, Douglas dismissed the case on procedural grounds. The indictment against Smith, he ruled, was invalid since it had been returned to the governor once without being served. On whether evidence in the case was admissible or not, Douglas refused to decide, "as it involved great and important considerations relative to the future conduct of the different states." Since no precedent existed as far as he could determine, he felt he had to examine the subject further before rendering a decision. Douglas then ordered that Smith be liberated. Before the Mormon leader could be brought to court again, new indictments would have to be drawn in Missouri and new writs would have to be served in Illinois. Douglas' decision, while generally conceded to be correct, aroused strong suspicions that he had entered into a political arrangement with the Prophet. Whig newspapers sharply accused him of openly courting the Mormon vote.[21]

The incident resulted in an increased tension between the Mormons and their "Gentile" neighbors in western Illinois. For Governor Carlin's part in directing that the writ be served on Smith, the Mormons were said to be "pronouncing vengeance upon the State." The Whigs, forgetting their earlier efforts to woo the Mormon vote, stepped up their attacks on the Church as the 1842 elections approached. Douglas, now identified with the Mormons, became a target for many of the opposition's blasts, and his relationship with the Church leaders during the months following the Monmouth trial did little to allay the criticism. His appointment of partisans of the Church to court positions in Hancock County, particularly in the anti-Mormon town of Warsaw, only intensified the attacks. Early in 1842, Joseph Smith, at a meeting of the Nauvoo city council, "prophesied" that Judge Douglas would never set aside a law of the council. The full measure of Mormon gratitude appeared in a letter of Smith to the Nauvoo *Times and Seasons,* published on the first day of the new year. "Douglass," Smith wrote, "is a *Master Spirit,* and *his friends are our friends*—we are willing to cast our banners on the air, and fight by his side in the cause of humanity, and equal rights—the cause of liberty and the law." Smith's statement, published on the first day of an important election year, was reprinted and discussed in Whig journals throughout the state, with the sharpest barbs reserved for the Judge of the Fifth Circuit.[22]

The 1842 election campaign, highlighted by the visit of Martin Van Buren to Illinois, began early. Whigs selected Joseph Duncan again as their candidate for the governorship. The Democrats, continuing their practice of convention nominations, chose Adam W. Snyder, a southern Illinois man who had won the favor of the north by supporting the Illinois and Michigan Canal. Before the campaign could get under way, however, Snyder died and his place on the ticket was taken by Thomas Ford, a member, with Douglas, of the state supreme court. The Mormons, whose support of Snyder had been promised by Smith, transferred their loyalty to Ford. The Whigs, who had prepared an elaborate campaign against Snyder, found themselves disarmed by the turn of events. The election was to have been fought on the Mormon issue, since Snyder had been chairman of the judiciary committee which had reported the Mormon charters favorably to the legislature. Ford was not nearly so vulnerable. Undaunted, Duncan raised his "crusade" against the Mormons and against the Democracy for receiving the support of the Church. The Whig campaign became a shrill and desperate outcry against the "miscreants." Party newspapers carried lurid accounts of "enormities" committed in Nauvoo, and the "corrupt bargain" between Joseph Smith and the Democratic party, principally in the person of Judge Douglas, was denounced.

Although not a candidate for office, Douglas became the target of Whig charges during the campaign, probably because he was thought to be more vulnerable than others on the Mormon issue, but also in recognition of his power in the party. Unwilling to remain on the sidelines when his own actions were so loudly assailed, Douglas left the bench momentarily in the summer of 1842 to aid Ford's campaign—"two political Judges are now brawling about the State," commented one Whig paper—and tangled immediately with his old antagonist, ex-Governor Duncan. Duncan accused Douglas of "having corruptly sustained" the Mormons in his capacity as circuit judge. Speaking in Jacksonville to an audience that included ex-President Martin Van Buren, he pointed out that Douglas had been the guest of Joseph Smith in Nauvoo and had "sat in the Synagogue with the Prophet." Duncan went further and charged that Douglas had avowed his belief in Mormon doctrine, citing as proof Douglas' statement, made in a private conversation the year before, that there was as much true religion among the Mormons as in any other church. Douglas' comment was that of a person who had developed no strong religious preferences of his own, but it was apparently sufficient to damn him among anti-Mormons. Duncan recalled that Douglas once expressed his belief that the Mormons had been misrepresented, that they were generally upright and correct in their conduct. Following up Duncan's attack, the *Sangamo Journal* speculated that Douglas would "go into the water with Joe Smith before the election."

Douglas replied in kind, inveighing against Duncan's demagoguery and cautioning against the Whig effort to promote anti-Mormon prejudice. He warned that anti-Mormons in the state's western counties were arming themselves to repeat the Missouri scenes of violence against the Church members, a charge that was scoffingly dismissed in the Whig press. In answering the Whig emphasis on the Mormon issue, Douglas followed his party's line. "As to the Mormons as a religious body," the *State Register* had declared, "our policy has always been to let them alone. . . . Every man has a right to worship God as he pleases." [23]

The Democrats won the August election, and Thomas Ford was an easy victor over Duncan. "We are again beaten in Illinois," moaned the *Sangamo Journal*. "No one can doubt hereafter, the omnipotence of Joe Smith's power." Whigs were urged to increase their strength for the next election rather than submit to the rule of "that prince of knaves and impostors" and his Democratic allies. But Smith was not the only cause for Whig defeat. Duncan placed greater responsibility for his downfall on Martin Van Buren, whose timely visit to the state had given the Democracy an undue advantage. The lack of enthusiasm within the Whig party and the unpopularity of Duncan with many Whig voters were factors that were conveniently overlooked. His job completed, Douglas returned to his judicial duties.

Although Missouri authorities had never been reconciled to their failure to secure Smith's extradition, Douglas was not called upon again to rule from the bench on the Mormon difficulties. In May 1842, ex-Governor Boggs was shot and wounded in what was obviously an assassination attempt. Charging the Mormon Prophet with responsibility for the deed, Boggs secured another writ against Joseph Smith. Smith was arrested in August but was taken before his own Nauvoo municipal court, where he was immediately freed on a writ of *habeas corpus.* The exercise of this power by the local court angered non-Mormon citizens in the area and embarrassed Governor Carlin. Smith felt it expedient to remain in hiding in order to avoid re-arrest. Meanwhile, in October, rumors circulated that he had given himself up and would be brought before Judge Douglas in Carthage, there to test the validity of his arrest. The rumors were false. At the same time, one of the Mormon elders learned, reputedly from Douglas himself, that Smith would be served an illegal writ, intentionally issued by Governor Carlin to draw him out of hiding. When he should appear before Douglas in Carthage and be released on *habeas corpus* he would be served with a legal writ and be borne away to Missouri "without further ceremony." This report, too, was without foundation. Smith did surrender himself in December 1842, after he had received assurances that he could not be held on a Missouri requisition for a crime committed in that state while he was in Illinois. He traveled to Springfield, consulted immediately with Justin Butterfield (whom he engaged as his counsel), Governor Ford, and Douglas before he was tried before the United States District Court and released. Smith's troubles with the state of Missouri were by no means over, but Judge Douglas was no longer involved.

On May 18, 1843, shortly before he left the court, Douglas dined with Joseph Smith and several of the elders of the Church. After dinner, he asked Smith to relate the history of the Church's persecution in Missouri. According to William Clayton, one of those present, Douglas "listened with the greatest attention, and then spoke warmly in deprecation of Governor Boggs and the authorities in Missouri." Smith, in conclusion, prophesied that unless the United States should redress the wrongs committed against "the saints" in Missouri, the government would be overthrown. "Judge," declared Smith, directing his remarks to Douglas, "you will aspire to the presidency of the United States; and if you ever turn your hand against me or the Latter-day Saints, you will feel the weight of the hand of the Almighty upon you; and you will live to see and know that I have testified the truth to you; for the conversation of this day will stick to you through life." Douglas, recorded Clayton, "appeared very friendly and acknowledged the truth and propriety of President Smith's remarks." [24]

Douglas resigned his seat on the bench on June 28, 1843, after serving as a judge for a little over two years. While he never ranked as an outstanding legalist, he nevertheless gave general satisfaction as a member of the supreme bench, and few people had cause to complain of his performance. His knowledge of the law and of basic legal principles was not profound, but he demonstrated an intuitive or pragmatic approach which made him equal to any situation. He made up in energy and quickness for what he lacked in depth and understanding. "He has a good knowledge of the law and furthermore can apply himself to any subject he takes hold of as readily as any man in the State," commented

one observer. "And what he does not understand to-day, if he thinks necessary, he will be thoroughly conversant with tomorrow." His personality and courtroom manner brought him popularity with the people and
with the younger members of the bar. His manners were cordial, frank,
and hearty, recalled Isaac Arnold. "The poorest and humblest found him
friendly. He was . . . hale-fellow well-met with the rudest and poorest
man in the Court-Room." Douglas' energetic approach to his judicial responsibilities provoked wide comment. He seemed to make less work out
of his judicial duties than his colleagues on the bench did, yet he frequently accomplished much more. The dispatch with which he cleared
the dockets in the circuit courts won the praise of even his opponents.
The *Illinoian,* long a critic of Douglas, conceded that he had presided
over the court "with much dignity." Douglas' energy inspired one correspondent to dub him "a perfect 'steam engine in breeches.' "

Some of Douglas' judicial practices did not arouse the admiring praise
of the older legal hands. The atmosphere in his courtroom was one of
shirt-sleeved informality. "He is the most *democratic* judge I ever knew,"
wrote one individual. "While a case is going on he leaves the bench and
goes among the *people* and among the members of the bar, takes his
cigar and has a social smoke with them, or often sitting in their laps."
Cyrus Walker, a Whig attorney in Douglas' circuit, took particular exception to Douglas' habit of leaning back in his chair with his feet elevated on the bench. Irritated, Walker swore he would never practice in
Douglas' court and, so far as is known, kept his promise. A minister
writing many years later told of his disgust with some of Douglas' "bad
decisions." "Hoping to effect more good in another profession," he left
the law for theology and became a Presbyterian preacher.[25]

Holding court ten months out of the year was an arduous task for
young Douglas, especially since he maintained his leadership in the
Democratic party and continued to play an active role in state politics.
His service on the bench, however, contributed mightily to his political
career and, in one important respect, marked him for the rest of his life.
From this time forth, he was known as Judge Douglas.

# VI

## "A President-making session"
## 1843—1844

i

Although Douglas confided to his family, shortly after his election to the bench, that "office and honors" had lost their charms, it had been manifestly impossible for the young judge to remain aloof from political life. During his term as supreme court judge, he continued to follow national politics with close interest. Van Buren's defeat for the presidency in 1840, Harrison's death after only one month in office, and John Tyler's accession to the presidential office brought change and transition to national politics. Old alignments began to break, and new ones were forming. For both parties, but perhaps for the Democratic more than the Whig, the first years of the 1840's were critical. John Tyler's veto of a Whig bank bill in August 1841 was, Douglas wrote, "a perfect windfall to the Democrats." Tyler, he commented, had met the question nobly, but, he added, "we should be cautious how we commit ourself in his favor." The political signs in other states were encouraging. The Whigs would soon be in the minority in the nation again, Douglas predicted, "and [at] that moment their power is gone & their party dissolved." The times called for caution and restraint, but they also offered opportunity.

The United States Senate term of Richard Montgomery Young was drawing to a close in 1842. Six years before, as a new state legislator, Douglas had supported Young's election, and in return Young had secured Douglas' appointment in the Springfield Land Office. Douglas, however, felt no particular loyalty toward Young. The Senator, it was charged, was leaning toward President Tyler, thereby casting suspicion on his Democratic orthodoxy. Harry Wilton, former United States marshal for Illinois and an early friend of Douglas', was the first person to urge Douglas to seek election to Young's Senate seat, but it is unlikely that much persuasion was necessary. As early as March 1842 Douglas wrote that he had not mentioned his candidacy to anyone who did not first introduce the subject, but that many of his friends had promised him support. Within a few months Douglas' name was widely discussed throughout the state as a strong candidate for the Senate.

Douglas was not the only person who aspired to the office. Besides Young himself, who hoped to be re-elected, John A. McClernand and a colleague on the bench, Sidney Breese, were active as candidates. Only Breese caused Douglas concern, for he had begun early to solicit support among members of the state legislature. "This is a pretty strong game & may do mischief if no [t] counteracted," Douglas advised one of his supporters. To some, however, Douglas' reputation as a popular vote-getter and as a party leader would more than offset Breese's efforts. The Whig *Sangamo Journal,* observing the race from the sidelines, was ready to place its wager on the twenty-nine-year-old judge. "Let all those candidates have a clear field and a fair start and we'll bet a ginger cake against an 'apple' on Douglass." [1]

The appearance of three challengers for the Senate, all of them from central or southern Illinois, produced serious tensions within the Democratic party. Once again charges were raised that Democratic politics were controlled by a "Springfield clique," of which Douglas was reputed to be the prominent member. A principal critic, John Wentworth, editor of the *Chicago Democrat,* sought, among other things, to reduce the power of the *Illinois State Register* and its publisher, William Walters. Walters had not only become Douglas' supporter, but he had also controlled the public printing for the preceding six years. Another of Wentworth's targets was Ebenezer Peck, a Chicagoan who had been elected clerk of the supreme court by the new judges. Walters, Peck, and Douglas ("the ablest wire-puller") were the leaders of the "unprincipled, selfish clique" which imposed its arbitrary dictation on "the honest portion of the Democratic party." To complicate matters further, the charge was made that the clique had induced Breese to withdraw from the governor's race against Ford on the promise that he would be selected as Young's successor.

Once again Douglas tasted narrow defeat. After nineteen ballots, the Democratic caucus on December 16 declared Sidney Breese to be the party's nominee, by a vote of 56 to Douglas' 51. Young had dropped out of the balloting, and McClernand had withdrawn his name early. The *State Register* declared that the "utmost harmony and good feeling" had prevailed in the meeting, although to Whig observers this harmony was only on the surface. Douglas failed in his bid, the *Journal* suggested, only because certain unauthorized persons were allowed in the caucus to vote for Breese. Hardin maintained that if the election had been postponed a month Douglas would have been the victor.

Douglas' youth was undoubtedly a factor in his defeat. He would not attain the constitutional age for United States Senator until after the beginning of the new senatorial term, although his friends urged that even should there be a called special session of the Senate, Douglas need not take his seat until after his thirtieth birthday. However, there is strong probability that Douglas himself had determined to acquiesce in Breese's nomination in return for the latter's support for the Senate in 1846. Even though the two men probably agreed to such an arrangement, the bitterness which their rivalry had provoked lingered on, resulting in a coolness between them that persisted for many years.

Young's rejection and Breese's election was interpreted outside the state as having national political implications. The Washington *Globe* saw signs of a schism in the Illinois Democratic party between supporters of Tyler and their opponents. Walters denied that there was "a Tyler or anti-Tyler party in the State of Illinois." Tyler's organ in the national capital attributed Young's defeat to the intervention of Missouri's Thomas Hart Benton, a charge that was quickly denied by Young himself. Young did, however, maintain that his views had been misrepresented in the columns of the *State Register,* an accusation that evoked a lengthy reply from Walters. Perhaps to soothe Young's feelings, the legislature promptly elected him to the state supreme court, although it was rumored that the judgeship had been promised when he withdrew from the Senate race.

On New Year's Eve, the victorious Judge Breese followed an old custom: he celebrated his triumph with a grand ball at the American House in Springfield. Three to four hundred gentlemen were present, far outnumbering the disappointingly small turnout of ladies. A correspondent of the New York *Herald* reported the event for his newspaper. "Judge Douglass, his [Breese's] opponent, was present," he wrote, "and took an active part in the dancing; he is a small, black-eyed, black hair and whiskers, lively, intelligent, active bachelor of about 30 years of age." [2]

The state's financial distress, the result of the Panic of 1837, continued to concern Douglas during his judicial term. Work on the ambitious internal improvements system had ceased, and the Illinois and Michigan Canal was still unfinished. The state had defaulted on its interest payments, indebtedness mounted, and many people despaired of ever salvaging the state's credit. There was increasing talk of repudiation. Banking facilities were inadequate and the state suffered from a lack of circulating medium. The legislature had legalized the suspension of specie payment by the state bank, but instead of reducing its note issue, as expected, the bank increased it. Both the value of the bank's stock and the credit of its notes declined rapidly.

The state's economic condition was hotly debated in the 1842 election. Both parties rejected repudiation, but each sought to fasten the blame for the crisis on the other. The internal improvement system, so enthusiastically supported five years before, became a stigma. The Democrats increased their attacks on the state banks, especially the "unholy alliance" of bank and state, and in their election pronouncements they declared against a national bank and in favor of the independent treasury system. When Thomas Ford was elected to the governorship, it was clear that the new administration would be forced to deal first with the state banking situation. Sentiment in favor of putting the banks into liquidation was overwhelming. A minority of the Democrats, led by secretary of state Lyman Trumbull, supported the outright repeal of the bank charters.

Governor Ford, who favored a compromise by which the banks and the state would dissolve their partnership, proposed a bill which would legalize suspension for another six months and allow the banks to surrender their state bonds in return for the bank stock which the state held. Ford's bill was shown to McClernand, chairman of the house finance committee, who immediately called a meeting of his committee. Governor Ford, James Shields, and Judge Douglas were invited to attend. All the members of the committee agreed to Ford's plan except one, "and he was soon argued out of his objections by Judge Douglass." With the committee's endorsement, the bill passed the legislature by a large margin. Trumbull's opposition to the compromise cost him his job as secretary of state and brought him into conflict with Douglas. Speaking before the "lobby," the young judge denounced Trumbull as a dangerous and radical repudiator. Ford's bill, after its passage by the legislature, went to the council of revision, where Douglas, sitting on the council by virtue of his judicial position, promptly and inexplicably voted against the very legislation he had helped to pass. He was the only member to cast a negative vote, "for no other reason," according to one biographer, "than that when called upon to review it judicially, he fancied it still smattered of repudiation by the state." [3]

Ford, in his *History of Illinois,* provided a classic description of the successful professional politician during this turbulent period in the state's history. Always in the forefront of any contest, men of this type were the principal orators, the writers for newspapers, and the organizers and disciplinarians of their party, working night and day to bring success to the organization. "They are always much despised by the opposite party in politics; and are always selected as especial objects of abuse and detraction." Any such politician, Ford concluded, who possesses sense and tact, who knows how far he can go in advocating his party's position, and who knows how to abuse the opposition without giving personal offense is bound to succeed. If Ford did not have Douglas in mind when he penned these words, the description is nonetheless apt. During his term on the bench, Douglas assumed an ever more controversial and important role in state politics. As a party boss he became the target not only of the Whig opposition, but also of elements in his own party who, resentful of the power he held, denounced him as the leading "wirepuller" of the "Springfield clique." Others eagerly sought his advice, as he continued to urge a tighter organization of the party on the local level. By making full use of the convention system and by establishing a network of committees down to the precinct level, Douglas advised one friend, "you can have the most perfect organization in the whole county & the Whigs need know nothing about it." More to the point, such efforts would be amply rewarded with success. "By producing a perfect organization . . . & becoming well acquainted with the committee men in each Precinct," he suggested, "you can have any man you please nominated for the Legislature & can in all probability elect him." [4]

ii

Illinois gained four new congressional seats as a result of the census of 1840, increasing its delegation in the lower house of Congress from three to seven. The Whigs took heart, since the state's population in-

crease was concentrated in central and northern Illinois, where the
Whig party was strong, and a redistricting would undoubtedly reflect
this fact. For the same reason, the Democratic *State Register* urged that
a general ticket system be adopted. Congressmen would continue to represent their districts, but they would be elected by the state at large, thus
assuring, the *Register* pointed out, "the election of seven democratic
members of Congress." The proposal was not adopted (partly because of
Douglas' strong opposition to it), but the Democratic majority in the
legislature drew the new district lines so as to give the party a better
than even chance in all but one of the new districts. The Seventh, or
Springfield, District, was regarded as "hopelessly Whig."

The new Fifth District corresponded roughly to Douglas' Fifth Judicial District. The northern counties, including the Mormons in Hancock,
were struck off and the district was extended to the south. Seven of the
ten counties lay in the Military Tract between the Illinois and Mississippi rivers; the remaining three were east of the Illinois River. The settlement of New Englanders and New Yorkers in the northern part of
the district was thus offset by the large number of Kentuckians and
other southerners who inhabited the southern portions. The town of
Quincy dominated the congressional district as it had the judicial circuit,
although Peoria was a fast-growing rival. Both towns were receiving sizable numbers of foreign-born, especially Germans, which gave them a
cosmopolitan character that contrasted sharply with that of the rural sections.

Several individuals quickly announced their candidacies for the Democratic congressional nomination in the new district, including ex-Governor Thomas Carlin, A. W. Cavarly of Greene County, W. A.
Richardson, and former Senator Young. Conspicuously absent from the
list was Stephen A. Douglas. Although many of his friends had urged
him to run, Douglas had actually published his intention not to be a
candidate for Congress. One of his close friends and early biographers
later revealed that Douglas planned to resign his judgeship for health
reasons and to spend the summer of 1843 in the Indian country to the
west recouping his strength. If such plans were known at the time, they
were undoubtedly a smokescreen, for there were few who did not believe
that Douglas would seize the opportunity offered by the redistricting to
make a third bid for election to the national Congress. The number of
candidates for the nomination alarmed some members of the party,
Douglas probably among them. The district was thought to be closely

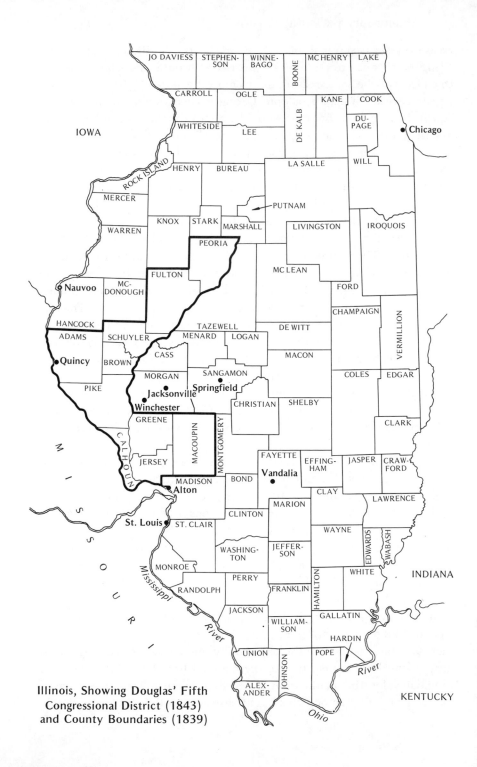

Illinois, Showing Douglas' Fifth
Congressional District (1843)
and County Boundaries (1839)

divided between Whigs and Democrats, and the Democratic party leaders warned that defeat would follow unless all the aspirants would agree to support the convention's choice.

On June 5, 1843, delegates from the district's ten counties gathered in the small Pike County town of Griggsville. The Whigs had already selected Orville Hickman Browning, an able Quincy attorney, necessitating a careful and sound choice on the part of the Democrats. The first ballot was inconclusive, Carlin leading with fifteen votes, Cavarly following with ten, and Douglas, who was not an announced candidate, trailing with seven. Richardson and Young received only token support. A half-hour recess was called, and, when the delegates reconvened, a second ballot was taken. Douglas received twenty-five votes and was promptly declared the party's nominee for Congress. Resolutions opposing a high protective tariff and a United States Bank and favoring the independent treasury were approved, all national rather than local issues. "We have for our prevailing motto," the delegates concluded, "the Jeffersonian doctrine of the 'Greatest good to the greatest number.' "

What took place during the thirty-minute break was not recorded, but it must have been clear to the delegates that only Douglas of all the candidates possessed the stature and ability required to face Browning. In view of Douglas' party leadership and his control over its machinery, it is difficult to believe that the movement was spontaneous. Douglas was holding court in Knoxville when he was informed of his nomination. He accepted without hesitation. As soon as the term of the court closed he resigned from the bench. Considering the alacrity with which Douglas embarked on his election campaign, it is doubtful that his nomination caught him by surprise.[5]

Douglas' selection was lauded by the Democratic press, although the ease and rapidity with which it had been made occasioned some surprise. The nominee, declared the *Quincy Herald,* was an "uncompromising advocate of the rights of the people, and the defender of the creed that they are 'capable of self-government,' " who could do more for the state than any other man could possibly accomplish. Few comments went as far as that of the *People's Advocate* of Carrollton, Cavarly's home town. "Against Judge Douglass, not a single objection can be raised by any one who is a democrat, for his political integrity is as unspotted as the vestal's fame—as untarnished and pure as the driven snow."

The Whigs opened fire on Douglas immediately. His nomination, they asserted, had been engineered by the friends of Governor Ford, who were anxious to get rid of a possible rival for the United States Senate. His nomination for Congress, at least, would put an end to his senatorial ambitions. Douglas was nothing more than a "political adventurer" in the eyes of the opposition party. His Quincy residence had never been considered permanent. A man of "unsettled and migratory habits," Douglas moved wherever he could secure an office and was no more a resident of the district than were other transient persons who put up at the town's public houses. The *Peoria Register,* in a remarkably perceptive observation, conceded that Douglas would be difficult to defeat, for he was a man of no "ordinary ambition." Proper ambition should be honest in its intentions, satisfied with present good, and "not always hankering after things that lie beyond." Douglas obviously did not fit this mould, for he "is possessed of those reaching aspirations that are not quieted by an office which should suit a man of ordinary ambition." [6]

Douglas' record as a legislator and as a judge was assailed. Seven years before, the state's politicians had vied with one another for the credit of passing the ambitious internal improvements program. In 1843, they were equally anxious to disavow any connection with the legislation that had proved so disastrous to the state's economy. Douglas was attacked for his vote in favor of the internal improvements system, although he had announced at the time that he supported the program with considerable misgivings. For his opposition to the removal of the capital from Vandalia to Springfield, he was branded a "northern man with southern principles," a charge that had reference only to sectional differences within Illinois, but one that would soon assume a larger meaning.

The Congressional campaign in the Fifth District, however, was not fought primarily on local issues. Both parties, in their district conventions, had focused their resolutions on national problems. The Whigs especially were sensitive to national developments. Having carried the nation in a wild burst of enthusiasm in 1840, the party three years later was despondent, in the minority, and locked in a bitter struggle with the Chief Executive. Reflecting the party's concern, the questions of a United States Bank, the protective tariff, and the distribution of the proceeds from public land sales were discussed in persuasive detail in a campaign circular written by Lincoln and issued by the state Whig committee. Each of these measures had been met with a presidential veto. Angered and frustrated, the Whigs carried their struggle with John Tyler into the congressional election campaign. Stephen A. Douglas, the *Quincy Whig* complained, had been nominated because he would blindly follow the dictates of his party "in destroying the tariff—opposing the establishment of a National Bank—and defeating that beneficial measure of distribution." A "warm and violent partisan," he would "tear down every measure the whig party would build up."

Following Douglas' nomination, the candidates issued an arduous speaking schedule that called for almost daily speeches in a score of towns up to the eve of election in early August. Years later, Browning recalled, "We travelled together, often in the same conveyance, and spoke together from the same stand on an average of two hours each per day, and that repeated every day with the exception only of the Sabbath." Douglas was in his element, engaged in the kind of political warfare he enjoyed so much and fought so well. Younger than Browning by seven years, his easy informality in both dress and demeanor contrasted sharply with the formality of his opponent. Browning, dignified and deliberate, became known throughout the district for his dress coat, ruffled shirt, and large cuffs. Although a Kentuckian, he had more difficulty relating to the border state farmers than Douglas did. Partisan spirit ran high—the Whigs smarting under their setbacks nationally and the Democrats eager to recover the leadership they lost in 1840—and personal attacks had become common in state campaigns. As they embarked on their campaign, Douglas and Browning agreed to maintain their discussions on a higher level, "not to violate with each other the courtesies and proprieties of life; and not to permit any ardor or excitement of debate to betray us into coarse and unmanly personalities." According to Browning's recollection, not an unkind word passed between the candidates during the canvass, and the contest closed on the same friendly relations that had existed before.[7]

Douglas argued unequivocally against banks of all kinds and asserted that a national bank was a monster more to be feared than "the great Nahant Sea-Serpent." He was, he declared, a believer in a strictly hard-money system. The United States Banks had been and would continue to be destructive of the best interests of the people and dangerous to their liberties. Popular liberty stood in even graver danger when the bank was linked with a high protective tariff. Appealing to his agrarian audiences, Douglas charged that the Whig tariff bills discriminated against agriculture, favored the rich at the expense of the poor, and were injurious to western interests. He insisted on a tariff for revenue only and called for a return to the levels of the 1833 compromise tariff which Clay himself had engineered. The question of the tariff was, in turn, closely tied to that of distribution. By distributing the proceeds from the public land sales, the need for the tariff to meet government expenses would become greater. The government would be deprived of an important source of revenue. At a time when many state governments were wallowing in debt, the prospect of distribution was alluring, but Douglas denounced the scheme and pointed out that the amount the state would receive would be negligible, while the adverse effects of the plan on public land policy as well as on fiscal policy would be detrimental to the interests of its citizens.

The demands of the rigorous speaking schedule, the summer heat, and the excitement of the campaign sapped the energies of the candidates. Election day, August 7, found them both prostrated with exhaustion. Douglas, however, was cheered by the election results. Not only did he win his own seat in Congress; of the state's seven Congressmen, all but one were Democrats. The lone Whig was Douglas' old rival, John J. Hardin, who won an easy victory in the Seventh, or Springfield, District. Douglas' margin over Browning was the narrowest in the state. Out of 17,000 votes, he had a majority of only 461, carrying 6 of the 10 counties in the district. The gloom in the Whig camp was thick. Although they attributed their defeat to the gerrymandered districts, their protests covered the weakened condition into which the party had slipped. "I confess that I am getting tired of this continued warfare without success," confided one discouraged Whig from Douglas' district.

One explanation for the narrowness of Douglas' victory margin concerned the behavior of the Mormon voters. Most of the Mormons lived in Hancock County, outside Douglas' district, but scattered settlements had been established in Adams County, to the south. Early in the campaign, the Church leaders decided to support the Whig candidates in both the Fifth and Sixth Districts. The decision was changed a few days before the election, and word was sent out to support the Democratic candidates at the polls. The change was effected in Hancock County, where Joseph P. Hoge, the Democratic candidate, received almost 74 per cent of the vote, but news of the shift did not reach the Adams County Mormons in time, and Browning consequently received almost the entire Mormon vote there. The reasons for the last-minute change on the part of the Mormons are not clear. Governor Ford asserted that Hyrum Smith, brother of the Prophet, had received a revelation that the state militia would not be sent against the Mormon communities if Mormons voted Democratic. More likely it was because of Governor Ford's refusal to comply with the latest extradition request for Joseph Smith. To complicate matters even further, the rumor circulated that Ford himself had influenced the Mormons to vote against Douglas because the governor recognized in Douglas a potential rival for the United States Senate.[8]

The Democrats had good reason to rejoice over the results of the congressional elections. John A. McClernand achieved a lopsided victory in the Second District, and in the Fourth District the voters selected John Wentworth, editor of the *Chicago Democrat*. Robert Smith of Alton, Orlando B. Ficklin of Charleston, and Joseph P. Hoge of Galena completed the roster of Democratic Congressmen. All were untried and inexperienced in national legislation, but the *State Register* was confident that they would make their influence felt in Congress on behalf "of our hitherto much neglected State." For the state's lone Whig in Congress came words of despair. "How will you act and feel," Hardin was asked, "surrounded as you will be on all sides with red mouthed Locos and colleagues ready to endorse every foul lie and scandal that may be promulgated to injure and destroy us as a party?" [9]

Douglas' election to Congress closed an era in his career and opened new doors to his ambition. For ten years his activity had pointed toward this day. The groundwork had been carefully prepared. At the age of thirty, he had not only become an acknowledged leader, but also a controversial political figure. For the next eighteen years, surely one of the most crucial periods in the nation's history, Douglas' name would be linked with all the great movements of national political life.

iii

Illinois' new Congressmen had less than four months to settle their affairs and make the trip to Washington. The first session of the twenty-eighth Congress was scheduled to convene on December 4. Douglas had additional reasons for haste. Five years before, when he made his first race for Congress, he had planned a triumphal visit to his family home in New York, but defeat had intervened. He now hurried eastward to Canandaigua, stopping in Cleveland for a few days on the way. It was just ten years since he had followed the same route westward. At home he received all the adulation his victory deserved; he also gained some badly needed rest before plunging into the unfamiliar life of national politics.[10]

Douglas looked forward to his new task with enthusiasm. He found his five Democratic colleagues congenial company, and he anticipated great achievements on behalf of Illinois and the west. Early in the year, Illinois' Senator Samuel McRoberts had died, and James Semple, a member with Douglas of the state supreme court, had been appointed to take his place. "I am glad we will spend the winter in Washington together," Douglas wrote Semple, "and propose that we make a mess of the entire delegation. They are all good fellows and would make pleasant companions."

Washington in 1843 still lacked the proper earmarks of a national capital. Crude, raw, dirty, unfinished, the city invited the savage comment of travelers, especially those from Europe, who expected more. Charles Dickens had stopped in Washington the year before and described the city in his customary biting sarcasm. "Spacious avenues that begin in nothing, and lead nowhere," he wrote, "streets, mile long, that only want houses, roads, and inhabitants; public buildings that need but a public to be complete; and ornaments of great thoroughfares, which only lack great thoroughfares to ornament—are its leading features." Few people, he speculated, would live in Washington who were not obliged to live there. Others were less critical. Over a decade before, the discerning and not always sympathetic pen of Mrs. Trollope described the city as "light, cheerful and airy" and compared the capital to a fashionable watering-place. Horace Greeley, in Washington to report the opening of Congress for his newspaper, praised the imposing public buildings, the spacious dwellings, and the "noble plain" on which the city was built; nonetheless, the "City of Magnificent Distances" was, Greeley felt, a "magnificent mistake," owing to the large amounts of money already spent and yet needed to complete and maintain it.

The capitol, although imposing from the outside, was to Greeley "a series of blind, gloomy and crooked labyrinths, through which a stranger threads his devious way with difficulty." The House of Representatives met in what even Dickens described as a beautiful semicircular hall. Each member had his own writing desk and chair, an arrangement that tended to "long sittings and prosaic speeches." In front, and raised above the floor of the hall, was the canopied chair of the presiding officer; in the balcony was a ladies' gallery, where the women "come in, and go out, as at a play or concert." The hall's handsome carpeting, however, was mottled "by the universal disregard of the spittoon," and the acoustics were bad.[11]

Here, early in December, the members of the House assembled. It was an auspicious group, including men whose names would become well known and even commonplace in the political struggles to come. Two Georgians, Howell Cobb and frail Alexander H. Stephens, both, like Douglas, serving their apprenticeship in national politics; Robert Dale Owen, son of the Utopian, and future cabinet member Caleb B. Smith, from Indiana; crafty John Slidell of Louisiana, also a newcomer to Congress; Maine's Hannibal Hamlin, a future Vice President; Robert C. Winthrop and the venerable and respected ex-President, John Quincy Adams, from Massachusetts; Jacob Thompson of Mississippi; New Hampshire's John P. Hale; Thomas L. Clingman and David S. Reid from North Carolina, the latter to become one of Douglas' closest friends; the outspoken abolitionist Joshua R. Giddings of Ohio; Andrew Johnson of Tennessee, on the threshold of a long career in national politics; and Vermont's Jacob Collamer gave the assemblage a distinction that had not been matched for years. As a result of a general reapportionment throughout the country, the House contained a high proportion of new, youthful, and inexperienced legislators for whom it would be a training ground in political leadership.

The Illinois members soon found that much of a Congressman's life was sheer drudgery. Their desire, wrote John Wentworth, was "to distinguish themselves as practical business men, attending to the business, wants and interests of their constituents rather than as speech-makers," but they were unprepared for the pressures that beset them. They were not only accosted on the street by those who sought favors, but they found their desks piled with letters, notes, and circulars which required perusal and answers. "Having a seat in Congress," Hardin commented, "is not the thing it is cracked up to be." Determined to act together as much as possible, the members of the delegation called on President Tyler early in the session to pay their respects. They were received with politeness by the President, who discussed questions of western policy with them. Next they made the rounds of the executive departments, paying particular attention to the contract and appointment offices of the Post Office Department—key offices if the interests of their constituents were to be properly promoted.

By the middle of January, the new Representatives had settled into a routine, although they had some difficulty adjusting to it. "Our mode of life is well calculated to injure our health until we get acclimated," Wentworth wrote. "The Hours of eating here," added Hardin, "destroy all business habits & the Hours of the House destroy a man's health."

Breakfast was usually taken at eight in the morning. The morning hours were spent writing letters, reading the papers, visiting the departments on constituents' business, and attending committee meetings. The executive departments were scattered over the city, and in each one crowds of favor-seekers were encountered. Although Congressmen were given priority, the whole proved extremely time-consuming. Wentworth estimated that a western Representative visited an average of six departments in a week.

The House convened at noon and adjourned any time between four and eight in the evening. After adjournment there were frequent caucuses that lasted into the night—"all this without a dinner to which one has been used from his boyhood." If the evenings were free of meetings, they were spent writing letters and chatting with colleagues over tea. The schedule was an arduous one; little wonder that the rate of illness among Congressmen was high.

Not all of a Congressman's life was devoted to the demands of politics and business. Although Washington society left much to be desired, there were compensations for the drudgery. Congressmen frequently complained of the small number of ladies in the capital, since many members left their families at home. "There is very little gaiety here this winter & not so many ladies from abroad as formerly," Hardin wrote to Mrs. Browning. Nonetheless, the distractions were there for those who wished to enjoy them. Dinner parties were constantly scheduled, bringing members of Congress, the executive branch, and the diplomatic corps into convivial fellowship. Every two weeks, President Tyler gave a "public levee" in the White House, where the guests could dance to the music of the Marine Band. "The President's family," according to Wentworth, "is remarkable fond of dancing and the President himself never seems happier than when the whole house is moving with the accents of music." Formal calls, balls, and parties filled out the social life of the nation's lawmakers. The bachelors (and four of the seven members of the Illinois delegation were unmarried) found themselves in special demand, so much so that they formed a society "for mutual protection" headed by Pennsylvania's Senator James Buchanan. For some, inevitably, the distractions of social life proved too great a temptation. "Washington has made many a man great," reported Wentworth, "but the number it has ruined is immensely greater." [12]

On December 4, the opening day of the session, Douglas was sworn in as a member of the House of Representatives. The day before he had attended a caucus of all the Democratic members of the House and had supported, with the rest of the Illinois delegation, the nomination of John W. Jones of Virginia for Speaker. The Democratic party, which enjoyed just under a two-thirds majority of the membership, easily organized the House. When the committees were finally announced, Douglas learned that he had been placed on the Committee on Privileges and Elections, an important assignment since the legality of the election of four state delegations had been challenged. Later, in February, he was given a seat on the judiciary committee.

The first session of the twenty-eighth Congress was, in the words of one of its members, a "President-making session." The efforts of the Democrats to find a winning combination for the next presidential election pervaded the deliberations. Victory for the Democratic party in 1844 seemed certain, and the rivals for the nomination looked upon Congress as an arena in which to test their strength. Martin Van Buren, defeated in 1840, commanded the strongest position; he was the favorite of the west and of the Illinois delegation, and representative of the Jacksonian tradition. John C. Calhoun was busy building support for his candidacy, and President Tyler, though elected on a Whig ticket in 1840, was angling for Democratic favor. The organization of the House of Representatives was regarded as having "an importance next to the Presidential election itself." When Jones was elected speaker the action was interpreted as a victory for the Van Buren forces. Silas Wright, New York Senator and a Van Buren manager, speculated that, with Van Buren leading the field, "our future troubles for this session will be rather to settle preferences for 1848 than 1844." Not everyone agreed with Wright, but there was wide agreement that it would be a "very stormy session." [13]

Congress' preoccupation with the approaching presidential election was disillusioning to the young members of the Illinois delegation; they had come to Washington fired with zeal to accomplish great things for their state and section. Van Buren supporters, it was reported, were determined to get through the session with as little action as possible. "Appearances are not auspicious," commented one paper two weeks after the session opened, "for the accomplishment of much good by the present Congress." The inability to act, however, was not so much a conscious policy of the Van Buren majority as it was a commentary on the divided opinion within the party. The Calhoun men were unreconciled; the followers of Richard M. Johnson and Tyler were dissatisfied. "There cer-

tainly are strong symptoms of a thorough rupture in the loco party,"
wrote Hardin a little hopefully.

Even the conditions under which the members labored on the House
floor seemed ill-suited to the achievement of sound legislation. Horace
Greeley, who observed the deliberations of the House a week after its organization, described the chamber as a "noisy Bedlam . . . somebody
speaking and nobody listening, but a buzz of conversation, the trotting
of boys, the walking about of Members, the writing and folding of letters, calls to order, cries of question, calls for Yeas and Nays" all adding
up to "large opportunities for headache, meagre ones for edification."
Hardin, already disappointed with the Congressman's life, confided, "I
would prefer speaking in a pig pen with 500 hogs squealing—or
speak in a prairie against a thunder storm, or talk to a mob when a fight
is going on . . . than to try to fix the attention of the House." Some of
the scenes in the House, he added, would disgrace the "meanest western
grocery." The slowness with which the House moved exasperated the
eager westerners. Equally appalling to the newcomers was the high ab-
sentee rate among House members and the nonchalant way many of
them regarded their responsibilities.[14]

iv

Although they sometimes seemed more concerned with the maneuverings of presidential hopefuls for the 1844 election, the nation's lawmakers still found plenty of issues to occupy their attention. As soon as the
session opened, seventy-six-year-old former President John Quincy
Adams gave notice that he would once again seek the repeal of the
"gag" rule imposed years before on abolition petitions. The validity of
the congressional elections in four states which had adopted "general
ticket" systems had to be decided early in the session. Appropriations for
western river and harbor improvements, an issue which the new western
members were determined to press, were urged. The troublesome tariff
issue demanded action and proved a crucial divisive force among Democrats. The Van Buren leaders sought to postpone action on the tariff
until after the party's nominating convention in May, while Calhoun's
southern followers were equally determined to resolve the issue at the
earliest moment. The Illinois Representatives, many of whom, like
Douglas, had campaigned on the promise of tariff reform, were ready to
act with the south. Little wonder that the old Jacksonian Amos Kendall

reported to Van Buren that "a most restless and dissatisfied spirit exists in Congress." [15]

To the consternation of the Whigs, the House first turned to pay tribute to the Old Hero, who from his retirement at the Hermitage still exerted a strong influence over the rank-and-file Democracy. On December 6, Pennsylvania's Charles J. Ingersoll introduced a bill that would refund, with interest, the $1000 fine imposed on Andrew Jackson nearly thirty years before by Judge Dominick A. Hall, United States District Judge for Louisiana, for contempt of court. The case had grown out of Jackson's declaration of martial law during his defense of New Orleans against the British in 1815. Ingersoll's bill was a gesture of gratitude to the old soldier as well as a means of easing the ex-President's financial straits, but its importance to the Democratic party in this election year was unmistakable. The bill had been discussed in the previous session, but passage had been prevented by the Whig majorities. The Illinois legislature a year before had passed resolutions instructing the state's congressional delegation to support the refunding bill, but Governor Ford, who sent Jackson a copy of the resolutions, was discouraged that justice would be done Old Hickory before the election of a Democratic Congress.

Stephen A. Douglas' first major speech as a member of Congress was delivered, appropriately, in defense of Andrew Jackson and the refunding bill. Securing the floor on January 6, 1844, he launched into an address replete with emotion, legal technicalities, and high-flying rhetoric. On occasion he seemed to be addressing the House as he would the jury in a frontier courtroom. With an air of authority that would remind his listeners that he had recently occupied a place on the bench, Douglas examined the circumstances surrounding the case. In his declaration of martial law, Jackson "did not violate the Constitution, nor assume to himself any authority which was not fully authorized and legalized by his position, his duty, and the unavoidable necessity of the case." But even if he had transgressed his authority, Douglas argued, his citation for contempt of court was "unjust, irregular, and illegal." Every unlawful act, he pointed out, "is not necessarily a contempt of court." "The doctrine of contempts only applies to those acts which obstruct the proceedings of the court, and against which the general laws of the land do not afford adequate protection. . . . The mere declaration of martial law is not of that character. . . . It was a matter over which the civil tribunals had no jurisdiction, and with which they had no concern, unless some specific crime had been committed, or injury done; and not even then, until it was brought before them, according to the forms of law." Jackson's action, however, had been justified. Douglas recalled the events surrounding the British attack on New Orleans and demonstrated that the city's salvation had depended upon Jackson. "There are exigencies in the history of nations as well as individuals, when necessity becomes the paramount law to which all other considerations must yield. . . . In cases of war and desolation, in times of peril and disaster, we should look at the substance, not the shadow of things. . . . Talk not to me about rules and forms in court, when the enemy's cannon are pointed at the door, and the flames encircle the cupola!" In a moving statement of personal conviction, Douglas declared, "I admire that elevation of soul which rises above all personal considerations, and, regardless of consequences, stakes life and honor and glory upon the issue, when the salvation of the country depends upon the result." And in final eulogy, he invoked the character of the Hero of New Orleans, Douglas' own guiding star: "His stern, inflexible adherence to Democratic principles, his unwavering devotion to his country, and his intrepid opposition to her enemies, have so long thwarted their unhallowed schemes of ambition and power, that they fear the potency of his name on earth, even after his spirit shall have ascended to heaven."

It was a striking debut for a freshman Congressman. John Quincy Adams, impatient with the entire debate over the refunding bill, noted Douglas' effort with the diary comment, "an eloquent, sophistical speech, prodigiously admired by the slave Democracy of the House." Reporters commented on the zeal and personal conviction with which Douglas had defended Jackson. The speech was reprinted in Illinois, where William H. Herndon described it as a "grand flourish." A copy of the speech, sent to the Hermitage, was said to have been endorsed by Old Hickory himself, "This speech constitutes my defense; I lay it aside as an inheritance for my grandchildren."

Two days after Douglas spoke, on the anniversary of the Battle of New Orleans, the bill passed the House by the lopsided margin of 158 to 28. House Democrats gathered that night in a celebration supper and congratulated themselves on their great moral victory. Jackson himself wrote that "no vote the whiggs can give can blot out the *triumphant vote of the Representative House.*" Fears that the bill would be rejected by the Senate, where the Whigs enjoyed a small majority, proved unfounded.[16]

During the debate over the bill refunding Jackson's fine, Douglas, as a member of the Committee on Privileges and Elections, was wrestling with the dispute over the election of four state delegations by general ticket. The act reapportioning the members of the House of Representatives among the states according to the 1840 census, passed by a Whig-controlled Congress in June 1842, specified that Congressmen must be elected by districts. In New Hampshire, Missouri, Mississippi, and Georgia this section of the law had been defied when the new members were chosen in at-large elections. The Whigs, reduced to a hopeless minority in the lower house, challenged the right of the Representatives from the four states to their seats. The dispute was referred to the Committee on Privileges and Elections, chaired by Tennessee's Aaron V. Brown, where the Whigs had little hope that their position would be upheld.

Douglas was selected to write and deliver the committee's majority report, an unusual and heavy responsibility for a new member of the House. That the report would favor seating the challenged Congressmen was a foregone conclusion, since all but two of the twenty-one Representatives involved were Democrats. Placing his argument on the broad ground of states' rights and the separation of powers between Congress and the state legislatures, Douglas expressed his own convictions as well as those of the Democratic majority. "Congress has no more authority to direct the form of state legislation," he wrote, "than the states have to dictate to congress its rule of action. Each is supreme within the sphere of its own peculiar duties—clothed with the power of legislation, and a discretion as to the manner in which it shall be exercised, with which the other cannot interfere by ordering it to be exercised in a different manner." The section of the apportionment law requiring district elections was "not a *law* made in pursuance of the Constitution of the United States, and valid, operative, and binding upon the States." The members from the four states were elected in conformity with the Constitution and were therefore entitled to their seats. Douglas' report, presented on January 22, touched off a bitter debate. The Whigs, according to Adams, revealed the "absurdities" of the report, while Douglas "vainly attempted to defend" himself against their attacks. The report, the Whigs charged, was tantamount to nullification.

Douglas concluded the debate on February 14, and he sought to answer the criticisms. He resented the charge that political motives or considerations had had anything to do with the committee's decision. It was, he emphasized, a judicial question, and he, as author of the report, had seen his duty as that of "an honest, impartial, and conscientious judge." Warming to his task, Douglas turned the accusation back upon his opponents who "with sanctimonious and puritanical faces" and with "very bad grace" had themselves attempted to make party capital for the presidential election. The fundamental question to be decided, he maintained, was whether four "independent sovereign States of this Union" should be disfranchised and their Representatives sent from the chamber. Although he had opposed the general ticket system in Illinois, he defended those states which had adopted it. The mode of electing members of the House, he argued, was a right reserved to the states; Congress had no power to compel any state to adopt either the district or general ticket system of election. Since the Constitution itself prescribed that Congress shall be the judge of the qualifications of its own members, the House may rightfully sit in judgment on the apportionment act passed by the previous Congress, as "the only tribunal authorized to decide upon the constitutionality of the law."

Douglas' words were harsh and impassioned, delivered in the same frenetic style and with the same frontier informality that had characterized his speaking in Illinois. Adams was outraged and insulted by the spectacle. Douglas, he wrote, "now raved out his hour in abusive invectives upon the members who had pointed out its [the report's] slanders, and upon the Whig party. His face was convulsed, his gesticulation frantic, and he lashed himself into such a heat that if his body had been made of combustible matter it would have burnt out. In the midst of his roaring, to save himself from choking, he stripped off and cast away his cravat, unbuttoned his waistcoat, and had the air and aspect of a half-naked pugilist. And this man comes from a judicial bench, and passes for an eloquent orator!"

Douglas' speech left the House in utter confusion. Dozens of members sought the floor, and it seemed as if "one quarter of the House would be speaking at a time." But Douglas had effectively closed the discussion. The vote was taken, and all the members from the four states were declared duly elected and entitled to their seats.[17]

Douglas' spirited defense of General Jackson and states' rights established his Democratic orthodoxy and brought him to the attention of his congressional colleagues, but it did little to satisfy the hungry demands of his constituents. The neglect (real and imagined) of Illinois and the west by the national legislature remained a sore point. The charge had been made repeatedly during the congressional campaigns, and citizens of the prairie state looked to their new House delegation to end this neglect. The opportunity came early in the session, when the House routinely undertook to refer the various portions of President Tyler's message to the appropriate committees for consideration.

Although a strict constructionist and long opposed to making internal improvements at federal expense, Tyler proposed that "every consideration of public policy" be given to the lakes and rivers of the west, consistent with the Constitution—a brief and vague allusion ("dark, no-meaning words," according to Adams), but one upon which the western members of the House were determined to capitalize. Virginia's Henry A. Wise sought to refer the suggestion to the Committee on Commerce, but objections were immediately voiced by some of the western members. Douglas proposed instead that a select committee be designated to consider the improvement of western rivers and lake harbors. In support of his suggestion, he made a strong plea for national unity, denouncing those who would arouse sectional interests and loyalties. Western men should, to be sure, act in "solid phalanx," but he denied that the interests of the west were hostile to those of the other states. "The Mississippi river and its tributaries," he pointed out, "connect not only the Western but some of the Middle States with those bordering on the Gulf of Mexico; whilst the northern Lakes unite the great Western valley and the Atlantic coast in the strong bonds of commercial interest."

Douglas insisted on a select committee because the question required an accurate and detailed knowledge "of the condition of the country, its resources, its navigable streams, the obstructions to be removed, and the trade, commerce, and varied interests connected with the proposed improvements." Obviously, Douglas felt, if the west were to receive beneficial consideration it must be at the hands of those who best knew the problem. To the objections of southern strict constructionists, Douglas argued that the improvement of "those great natural and national channels of commerce, and trade, and travel" would not violate the most rigid interpretation of the Constitution. Douglas' proposal was not adopted. Instead the question was referred to the commerce committee, but the flurry of debate early in the session forecast the struggle that would develop.[18]

Debate on a bill for the improvement of western rivers and harbors began in April. Almost immediately the legislation encountered problems. Signs of division among the western members appeared as attempts were made to increase the amount of appropriation for particular areas. The inclusion of the Illinois River in the bill was extremely important to Douglas, Hoge, and Wentworth, the three northern Illinois Congressmen, but it evoked bitter opposition from those (notably southerners) who assumed a strict constitutional position, as well as from some westerners, who for various local reasons were unwilling to support it. A river lying wholly within one state, it was argued, could not constitutionally be improved by the national government. The improvement of the Illinois River, which, with the Illinois and Michigan Canal, would connect the lakes with the Mississippi River, would draw commerce away from canals which had been dug across Ohio and Indiana. Efforts were made to strike out the Illinois River, bringing Douglas to his feet once again.

A general system of internal improvements by the federal government, he argued, was not contrary to the principles of the Democratic party, as some had charged. To prove his point, Douglas found support in a careful analysis of Jackson's messages, apparently thinking that an appeal to Old Hickory would effectively end the argument. He drew a sharp distinction between the improvement of natural waterways and the support of "artificial works"—roads, turnpikes, railways, and canals. The former was constitutionally sound, while the latter was contrary to the Constitution and principles of the Democratic party. "By a wonderful confusion of ideas," he maintained, his opponents had associated "the right to protect commerce and navigation upon our navigable waters, with the power to construct artificial means of communication—ordinary roads and canals—within the limits of a State." The power of Congress to make appropriations for internal improvements was clear; "the propriety of its exercise depends upon the *nationality* of the object to be effected by it." The Illinois River passed this test. One of the finest navigable streams in the world, the river provided an uninterrupted connection between the northern lakes, the Atlantic Ocean, and the Gulf of Mexico, a connection essential to the foreign and inland commerce of the nation and indispensable to the defense of the country during wartime. With a gesture toward the growing excitement over the Oregon country, Douglas contrasted the ease with which the British could collect their fleet from all over the world in one continuous line from Montreal to Chicago with the difficulties the United States would encounter if the Illinois River were not maintained.

Douglas' statements sparked a furious counterattack from South Carolina's Robert Barnwell Rhett and Isaac Holmes. Rhett and Holmes, noted the ever-observant Adams, charged "against Douglas and against the whole system of internal improvement, federalism, consolidation, and despotism." Holmes, referring to Douglas as the gentleman from *"all noise,"* rejected the latter's appeal to Jackson as an authority. When Douglas suggested Calhoun instead, Holmes angrily retorted that he was "no man's man . . . when the Constitution of the country was concerned."

Voting on amendments to the bill began soon afterward. The appropriation for the Ohio River was increased, Douglas voting in the affirmative. An attempt to include the Wabash River in the bill was defeated, but Douglas and four other members of the Illinois delegation did not vote on the measure. The *Sangamo Journal* later severely criticized the five for "skulking" out of the chamber in order to avoid committing themselves on the amendment. This desertion of the Wabash amendment, the paper commented, exasperated the Indiana members and prevented Douglas from exercising any influence with them in his effort to keep the Illinois River in the bill. The next day, Douglas once again became involved in an angry exchange of words, this time with the Ohio and Indiana delegations. He charged the members of the two states with having entered into a "combination" to oppose the appropriation for the Illinois River, "for pitiful local jealousies of a superior work." The charge was heatedly denied, and for a time strong words flew back and forth. Douglas' colleague McClernand eventually interceded, deplored the personal nature of the debate, and hoped the controversy would end. Douglas resentfully told McClernand that he felt he could take care of himself and had no fear of the " 'hunters,' individually or collectively."

On April 20, the House voted to remove the Illinois River from the bill and then hastily approved the appropriation measure. The final vote revealed a serious split in the Illinois delegation. The unity of action among the state's Congressmen, which had been widely anticipated at election time, proved to be illusory on the firing line. The bill included the improvement of the Ohio River and of the Missouri, Mississippi, and Arkansas rivers; an additional sum was appropriated for the improvement of Chicago's harbor. Douglas, Hoge, and Wentworth voted in the affirmative in spite of their disappointment at the loss of the Illinois River appropriation, but the three Democratic Congressmen from southern Illinois, McClernand, Smith, and Ficklin, were solid in their opposition, citing constitutional scruples and the meager amount appropriated for the Ohio River as their reasons.[19]

Beyond his part in the discussions of Jackson's fine, the general ticket election, and the improvement of western rivers and harbors, Douglas participated little in the debates of the House. Soon after his speech on the general ticket elections in mid-February, he became seriously ill with a recurrence of the "bilious fever" that had prostrated him following his congressional campaign several months before. He was absent from the House from the middle of February until early April. While some of his colleagues expressed their concern for his recovery, Douglas only chafed at this enforced absence from the halls of Congress. "The great difficulty in being sick here," Wentworth wrote, "is the great and increasing excitement to get out." Douglas continued to conduct routine business from his sickbed, but his recovery was not complete for some time. Even after he returned to his seat in April, when he threw himself into the debate over the rivers and harbors bill, his attendance was sporadic.[20]

During Douglas' absence much had happened—the continuing fight over the "gag" rule, debate over the tariff, the repeal of the distribution bill, and an unsuccessful attempt to revive the independent treasury. In spite of being on the sidelines during much of the session, however, Douglas had every reason to be satisfied with his first experience as a national legislator. He had tackled the responsibilities of his position with characteristic energy, and his constituents had no cause for complaint with the manner in which he looked after their interests. More importantly from the standpoint of his own career, he had made an impact on many of his fellow Congressmen, and he had placed his political convictions before the nation through his defense of Jackson, of states' rights, and of the constitutionality of federal internal improvements appropriations. But Douglas' contribution was not limited simply to these areas. The question of the presidential succession hung over Congress' deliberations and kept the Democratic party in turmoil. Although not fully recognized at the time, the new issue of national expansion—the annexation of Texas and the occupation of the Oregon country—had become involved in the party's future. Douglas made the transition from local to national politics quickly and easily. Nothing demonstrated this better than his part in bringing these questions to resolution.

# VII

## "Polk, Dallas, and Texas"
### 1844—1845

i

By 1844 Douglas' politics had been tested in a decade of activity in Illinois and in one session of Congress. In his state, he had achieved the reputation of a strict party man, a disciplinarian, a leader whose energies were directed toward strengthening the party structure. The Democratic party in Illinois owed him much. Douglas' role as the pragmatic, consummate politician told only half the story, however. His organizational skill was balanced by a growing devotion to politics based on principle. Douglas was preeminently a Jacksonian, and his adherence to the tenets of what became known as Jacksonian Democracy grew as his own career developed. His Jacksonian faith was also influenced by the conditions and circumstances of the rural, frontier environment in which he moved. He never hesitated to adapt his principles to the needs of his own society.

Popular rule, or what he would later call popular sovereignty, lay at the base of his political structure. Like most Jacksonians, Douglas believed that the people spoke through the majority, that the majority will was the expression of the popular will. His contributions to party development in Illinois and his almost obsessive insistence on party regularity were based ultimately on his conviction that through the political party the popular will could be voiced most effectively. He recognized, however, the dangers inherent in an unrestricted and unrestrained majority and insisted that a scrupulous regard for the rights of the minority be observed. The Constitution of the United States, to which Douglas paid an unquestioning homage, was the bulwark for the protection of minority rights and a check against the exercise of power by the majority. Although he could not always be properly classified as a strict constructionist, he insisted that the limits of federal authority be recognized. States' rights had a strong and positive meaning for Douglas, but he never allowed his feeling to force him into rigid and unrealistic positions. Popular self-government, he believed, must be preserved and protected where it was most effective, on the local level, and he wished to see as few restrictions on the exercise of local self-government as possible, consistent always with the Constitution and the laws. Government and the law were evolutionary, shifting and changing as the times themselves changed, but always progressing. Principle and pragmatism both occupied significant places in Douglas' political outlook.

As a good Jacksonian, Douglas matched his belief in popular, local self-government with strong notions of equality, and he followed the party line in denouncing the forces of inequality and privilege. He opposed the Second United States Bank and fought consistently against all efforts to reestablish that institution. He extended his dislike to all banks, a stance that was reinforced by the unfortunate association of state banks with the vast internal improvements program into which Illinois plunged in the 1830's. Most of his early career coincided with the distress that followed the Panic of 1837, and the impact of the hard times on his state influenced his attitude toward economic and fiscal policy. His opposition to banks and banking was confirmed and his dislike of an inflated paper currency underscored. From the early days of his career, Douglas was a hard-money man.

Douglas' attacks on inequality led him also into opposition to the protective tariff. In the principle of protection, Douglas recognized a lack of balance between the interests of industry and those of agriculture. His economic thought, like his political thought, was rooted in the simple agrarian pattern of the past. Faithful to the needs and desires of the agricultural community he represented, Douglas was convinced the tariff discriminated against the farming population of the west. His devotion to western interests was also reflected in his struggle for the improvement of his section's commercial arteries, the great rivers and their tributaries and the inland lakes. The western lakes and rivers, he argued, were as important to the nation's economic well-being as the great eastern seaports were. Once again he denounced inequality, and he found ample justification in the Constitution for improvement at federal expense of the arteries on which his section depended. In answer to his strict constructionist critics, he appealed to Jackson's own statements and drew a distinction between natural and artificial works. Douglas' position on the tariff and internal improvements frequently drew him into sectional conflicts, but he never allowed his arguments to obscure the larger importance of the Union. He denounced efforts to set one section against another and entreated his colleagues in Congress to be moved only by broad national considerations. The much-vaunted western-southern alliance in Congress had little practical meaning for Douglas. On the tariff he sided with the south, but on the question of internal improvements he had to face a fierce southern opposition.

From the time he had ripped down the coffin handbills as a youth in Vermont, Douglas cherished a desire to meet Andrew Jackson. As he espoused Jackson's cause and became identified in Illinois as a leader of the Jackson party, his determination to meet the old General grew. His opportunity came during the summer of 1844, in the midst of the campaign for the presidency. While attending a grand Democratic rally in Nashville, where he had been invited to speak, Douglas visited the near-by Hermitage. Democratic politicians from all parts of the country made the pilgrimage to Jackson's home, and during the 1844 campaign the Hermitage was especially crowded. In the company of William Walters, editor of the *State Register,* and others from Illinois, Douglas was introduced to Jackson by Clement Comer Clay, former Governor and Senator of Alabama. Jackson, old and feeble, recalled Douglas' speech in Congress on the bill to refund the fine imposed at New Orleans during the War of 1812. He thanked Douglas for his effort, adding generous words of praise for the arguments Douglas had mustered on his behalf. Douglas, speechless, "convulsively" shook Jackson's hand and left the room.[1]

Douglas' visit to the Hermitage emphasized his Jacksonian allegiance, but it came at a time when the lines of Jacksonian politics in the Democratic party were being loosened. Douglas, no less than other western Democrats, espoused the new and controversial issues of national expansion. Even as he shook the Old Hero's hand, he had already begun to move beyond the issues he had argued so forcefully in a decade of state political activity into a new area of political decision.

ii

The issue of territorial expansion was not new to the 1840's. Ever since Americans had crossed the Mississippi River and had pressed up against the hither edge of the "Great American Desert," they had looked beyond it, to the far western reaches of the continent. Explorers, fur traders, missionaries had all brought back stories of opportunity in the west. The United States had early expressed its interest in the Pacific coastal regions, gradually strengthening its claim to the Oregon country, the area between the forty-second parallel and the southern boundary of Russian America. In 1818 a joint occupation agreement with Great Britain left the question of ultimate sovereignty to future negotiation. Renewed for an indefinite period in 1828, the agreement provided Americans with a firm foothold in the far northwest. Meanwhile, Americans were moving into the northern borderlands of Mexico. Although encouraged initially by the Mexican government, the movement of Americans into Texas soon reached alarming proportions. Mexican fears and anxieties were realized in 1836, when the transplanted Americans in Texas succeeded in establishing an independent Texas nation. Their desire for annexation to the United States received a sympathetic response in many parts of the country, but action was postponed because of the fierce opposition of the militant antislavery movement.

By the time Douglas took his seat in the House of Representatives in December 1843, the issue of territorial expansion had reached irresistible dimensions. The Panic of 1837 had increased the restlessness of Mississippi valley farmers, and Oregon, with its fertile valleys and apparently limitless markets, beckoned from the western horizon. American trading and commercial interests looked with increased longing at the ports and harbors on the Pacific. British activity in the Oregon country aroused suspicion and hostility, and some fear that the disputed area would soon be overrun by Britain's armed legions, exposing the American flank to the danger of enemy attack. There were rumors of secret negotiations between the British and Texas that would place that new republic within the British sphere. Southerners regarded the annexation of Texas as necessary to the expansion of their plantation-slave economy and were fearful lest Britain, with its antislavery notions, gain influence with the Texans. The times were ripe for expansion. The Jacksonian enthusiasm, the reform spirit in all its various manifestations, provoked an increased interest in national growth, of which expansion was regarded as an important part, and many Americans talked of the nation's manifest destiny.

The accession of John Tyler to the presidency gave the question of national expansion a new impetus. In his message to the first session of the twenty-eighth Congress, he urged the settlement of the Oregon boundary and emphasized the validity of the American claim to all the territory between 42° and 54°40′ north latitude. He told the congress that military protection should be provided for the hundreds of American citizens who were making the long trek to the Pacific coast and proposed that the laws of the United States be extended over them. The hostilities between Texas and Mexico must be ended, he declared, through the intercession of the United States if necessary, and every attempt should be made to prevent the interference of other powers in Texas affairs. While Tyler did not openly recommend annexation, his administration was at that moment engaged in negotiations with the Texas Republic. The Illinois delegation found encouragement in Tyler's remarks. One of them described the message as a "truly western document, sound upon every question of western interest."

Illinoisans had already placed themselves on the side of expansion. Emigrant companies were formed in the state, and many of its citizens were moving west. In November 1842, an Alton meeting vigorously protested the omission of the Oregon boundary question from the Webster-Ashburton negotiations and demanded that Oregon be occupied. Several months later, in February 1843, a series of meetings was held in Springfield to express the interest of the people in "the settlement and occupation of the Territory of Oregon." Formal resolutions were adopted, declaring the unquestioned right of the United States "to the whole Oregon Territory" and viewing with concern the activities of the British in the Pacific Northwest. Douglas took time out from his judicial duties to address the meeting. It was his first public expression on behalf of expansion. Commenting on the meeting, in which both Democrats and Whigs took part, the *Sangamo Journal* announced, "Happily the Oregon question is not a party one." In the Senate, Semple offered a resolution giving notice to Great Britain that the joint occupation agreement would be abrogated (it was rejected by a decisive vote), and John Wentworth kept up a steady fire on behalf of Oregon in the House. When the Illinois legislature instructed the state's delegation to support the claim to all of Oregon, it was Wentworth who presented the resolution to the lower house.[2]

Of no less concern to the people in the state was the issue of Texas annexation. Rumors that an annexation treaty was being negotiated brought the issue surging to the fore, and Texas soon crowded out all other questions. Annexation, Senator Breese was informed, had become a passion. To John Reynolds, it was a "flame that is burning from one end of the State to the other." Reflecting the position of the state's Democratic party, the *State Register* offered three reasons why Texas should be annexed: first, as part of the Louisiana Purchase, Texas had once been paid for but had been subsequently lost through the "blundering diplomacy" of John Quincy Adams; second, the admission of Texas would strengthen the Union and "by giving that country the protection of our laws, the benefits of our institutions and a full share of the blessings which flow from our happy form of Government, [would] increase the sum of human happiness"; and finally, annexation would forestall British designs and throw open the middle and southern portions of the continent to American influence and expansion. Late in May 1844, a large meeting in Springfield endorsed these arguments. The two issues, Oregon and Texas, were frequently linked, and both were related to the fear of growing British power. "The greatest curse with which the earth is afflicted," warned the *Register,* was the extent of British dominion. The United States would soon be surrounded by British power—in Canada, in Oregon, in Texas, and on the sea—and battalions of runaway Negroes and savage Indians were ready to move at the bidding of British commanders.[3]

Douglas had aligned himself early with the expansionists. Although he did little to advance the cause during his first session in Congress, primarily because of his prolonged illness and absence from the House, he devoted much of his time to a study of the west. As a program for western development took shape in his mind, the issue of expansion became increasingly important to him. He sought to familiarize himself with the reports of explorers, the diplomatic background, and the natural history of the areas in question. Late in April 1844, Orson Hyde, a leader in the Mormon Church, sought Douglas' advice on Mormon plans to emigrate to Oregon. Douglas, Hyde reported, "is ripe for Oregon and the Californias." He talked of his interest in a bill that would encourage emigration to Oregon but expressed pessimism that such legislation could pass Congress at the current session. Douglas gave Hyde a map of Oregon and a copy of John C. Frémont's report of his second expedition to the west, promising to send copies also to Joseph Smith. He offered to attend to any business the Church might have in Congress and indicated a willingness to discuss the "subject of Oregon, Texas and California" with Smith on his return to Illinois.[4]

To Douglas, territorial expansion was a party issue. Although many

Whigs participated in the Oregon and Texas movements, their general lack of zeal gave the Democrats a great advantage. As the fever mounted, the Whigs became more defensive. The Oregon question, insisted William H. Herndon, was espoused by the Democrats to obscure the real issues, a subterfuge he urged his fellow party members to expose. It was inevitable that the issue should become entangled with the presidential contest in 1844.

In the fall of 1843, Martin Van Buren's prospects for the Democratic nomination seemed secure. The Illinois delegation to the Baltimore convention, Governor Ford predicted, would be unanimous in support of the New Yorker. The names of Calhoun, Tyler, and Richard M. Johnson had been advanced in the state earlier, but none had aroused any particular interest. Calhoun had withdrawn his name when the House of Representatives was organized by Van Buren's supporters. For a time it seemed likely that a Tyler movement might develop in Illinois; however, the President's chances soon evaporated. Johnson had some following among southern Illinois Democrats, but his name was more frequently suggested for the vice presidency. Both Wentworth and Walters asked Van Buren for statements that might be printed in their respective newspapers. The former felt the election might turn on the pre-emption issue; Walters asked for Van Buren's position on the tariff, "a question which enters deeply into the politics of Illinois." Not a word was said about Texas.[5]

In February 1843, when the Democrats met at Springfield to select their delegates to the party's national nominating convention, Douglas seemed securely behind Van Buren's candidacy. Still on the bench, he clearly dominated the proceedings. Discussion focused on the method of selecting delegates, one group favoring their nomination by a committee of the state convention and Douglas urging that the delegates be chosen and instructed by meetings in each judicial district. Douglas argued persuasively that delegates selected in this way would be fresh from the people and thus more reflective of the wishes of the party members. The convention agreed. Douglas' resolutions were adopted, and the meeting adjourned without endorsing a presidential candidate. Governor Ford assured Van Buren that Douglas "is a friend of yours," and that his strategy sprang from a desire to advance "your pretensions by conciliating adverse interests." But Douglas' strategy may also have stemmed from doubts at this early time of Van Buren's "availability" in 1844, for the district system had been strongly proposed elsewhere as a device for stopping Van Buren. Certainly, the adjournment of the state convention without a strong endorsement of the ex-President was regarded as a setback for the Van Buren forces.[6]

As the Texas issue gathered momentum, Van Buren's western supporters became restive. His continued silence on the issue, it was thought, meant that this interest in expansion was less than wholehearted. By February 1844 there were signs that the ardor of Illinois Democrats for the New Yorker had cooled, a disturbing development to the Whigs, whose campaign strategy had been planned around the assumption that he would be nominated. Douglas, whose support of Van Buren had earlier seemed unshakable, began looking elsewhere, to Lewis Cass, James K. Polk, or some other annexationist Democrat. He was joined in the search by other members of the Illinois House delegation. When Van Buren finally broke his silence, he effectively ended any possibility that he might receive the nomination. In his famous letter to Congressman W. H. Hammet, the ex-President maintained that it was inexpedient to speak of annexation so long as a state of hostilities existed between Texas and Mexico. The statement cleared the air and ended all doubts. The *State Register,* reflecting Douglas' position, called for a candidate who would be pledged to immediate annexation. The chances for nominating a western expansionist suddenly brightened, and Douglas spoke more strongly of Cass. Joining with others from his section, he urged that Cass endorse annexation in a public letter. Cass' views on the Oregon question, his strong anti-British feeling, and his support of annexation presented an ideal combination to the western Democracy.[7]

The Democratic national convention opened in Baltimore on May 27. Since most of the delegates stopped in Washington on their way, members of Congress seized the opportunity to influence their thinking. A Van Buren supporter complained that Illinois' delegates were being met by the state's congressional delegation and spirited away to their private lodgings in order to prevent them from talking with Van Buren's managers. John C. Rives, after listening to one Illinois delegate talk about Texas, feared that the entire delegation would be lost. Douglas was singled out as one who was doing all he could against Van Buren.

Instructed for Van Buren by their district conventions, a majority of Illinois' delegates felt obligated to cast their first ballots for the ex-President, but they made certain that he could not get the nomination by supporting the two-thirds rule. After the first ballot, Van Buren never received more than two of the state's nine votes. On the eighth ballot,

Cass received the support of all but one of the Illinois delegates. On the next ballot, however, the entire delegation switched to James K. Polk, and the Tennessean was nominated. George M. Dallas of Pennsylvania received the vice presidential nomination. The platform was all that the Illinoisans, and Douglas, could wish. Among its planks were a veiled opposition to the protective tariff, a declaration that Congress had no power to charter a United States Bank, a vigorous endorsement of states' rights, and an urgent call for the "re-occupation" of Oregon and the "re-annexation" of Texas.

Polk's nomination and the adoption of a platform that blended Jacksonian issues with the new issue of expansion won the plaudits of Illinoisans. Resolutions approved at a mass Texas meeting in Springfield praised the convention delegates for expressing the "sober second thought" of Illinois Democrats in their selection of Polk. Polk's nomination, however, threw the Whigs off stride. Not expecting Van Buren to be passed over, they had invested considerable time and money in attacks on the former President. Anti-Van Buren speeches and documents had been circulated throughout the country. With Polk's selection, the Whigs were forced to shift their strategy, but they made up for their surprise by the bitterness of their denunciations of the Democratic candidate.[8]

The floor of Congress became the campaign's first battleground. Presidential politics entered the debate on the civil and diplomatic appropriation bill in the House on June 3, soon after the adjournment of the Baltimore convention. Illinois' lone Whig Congressman, resentful that his plans had been upset by Van Buren's rejection, delivered a blistering attack on Polk. Douglas took the floor in defense of the Tennessean. "He is emphatically a Young Hickory," he declared. "No man living possesses General Jackson's confidence in a greater degree, or displayed more zeal and ability in defending his fame from the slanders of his enemies, and in carrying out the great republican principles with which his administration was identified." Douglas touched upon the three elements of the Demcratic platform which were uppermost in his mind—the tariff, Oregon, and Texas—and revealed for the first time his commitment to "spread-eagle" nationalism and the optimistic expectations of manifest destiny and the American mission.

In reviewing Polk's position on the tariff, Douglas reiterated his opposition to a system of high, protective duties. The imposition of prohibitory duties, he insisted, would stop the flow of foreign goods into the

United States, deprive the government of needed revenue, and necessitate a ruinous policy of direct taxation. He advocated instead a moderate tariff that would raise sufficient revenue to support the government while at the same time providing incidental protection "to the products of American labor." But the tariff question was not Douglas' primary concern in the 1844 campaign.

It was to the subject of national expansion that Douglas warmed as he lashed out against the Whigs and British, expressing the faith of an ardent western expansionist. That Polk was sound on the Oregon question Douglas dismissed as a truism. The nation's title to all of Oregon was, without the shadow of a doubt, "perfect and indisputable." The time for "bold, immediate, speedy action" had arrived. "We have slumbered in false security for the last thirty years, in the vain hope that the whole question would be amicably settled by negotiations," he declared. The delay had only strengthened the British hand. He denounced the efforts to settle the boundary along the forty-ninth parallel as an abject surrender of American rights and shrugged off the fear of involvement in a war with Great Britain. Why should America quail before British power, appease her wrath, and purchase her mercy "with the fairest and richest portion of our beloved country?" War was not to be feared. The Oregon country, he believed, was vital to the commercial and military interests of the United States. Its acquisition would protect the nation's expanding commerce in the Pacific and would facilitate a direct trade with China and the East Indies. The area's natural resources were inexhaustible, its fertile soil and genial climate well adapted to agricultural pursuits. Americans ought never to shrink from conflict, he concluded. "Let us rather act upon the maxim of Old Hickory—'Ask nothing but what is right, and submit to nothing that is wrong;' and then, if need be, put our trust in the God of battles."

The "re-annexation" of Texas, Douglas shouted, was also an imperative duty. Aside from the fact that Texas had originally been part of the Louisiana Purchase, only to be surrendered by John Quincy Adams in 1819, its union with the United States was essential for economic and military reasons. Again the villainous British lion crouched in the background, ready to leap on the young Republic. It was obvious that Great Britain had designs on Texas. If these designs were not thwarted, American cotton would be excluded from the British market and Texas cotton would take its place. Cotton planters would be forced to turn to other forms of agricultural activity, thereby increasing agricultural production at the same time that the market would be restricted and the demand diminished. Texas and northern Mexico would be flooded with British goods, to the exclusion of American manufactures. The effects of British influence in Texas, in short, would be ruinous to American agricultural, manufacturing, and commercial interests.

Texas (and, Douglas added, Cuba as well) was vital to America's security. Great Britain was encircling the United States with a network of fortifications, from Oregon through Canada to New Brunswick, Nova Scotia, "and even part of Maine" in the east, and to Bermuda and the Bahamas on the Atlantic coast. "To these let her add Cuba and Texas," Douglas warned, "and the work is done." The young Congressman cheerfully accepted the prospect of war, even welcomed it. "It is time," he added, "England was taught that North America has been set apart as a nursery for the culture of republican principles, and that there is no room here for a monarchy or its dependencies." National interest and patriotism, national glory and security demand the extension of the principles of civil and religious liberty over "a large portion of the continent." The issues of the election campaign were clear: "With POLK and DALLAS as our standard-bearers—Oregon and Texas, democracy and freedom, inscribed upon our banner—we are ready to rush to the battle, with *victory or death* as our watchword."

Soon after Douglas' appeal to national patriotism and destiny, the issues became even clearer. The Texas treaty, upon which Tyler and Calhoun had lavished so much effort, was defeated in the Senate, a "deliverance by the special interposition of Almighty God," according to John Quincy Adams. Tyler, however, was not ready to surrender. A few days later, he placed the issue before the House of Representatives. "The responsibility," he announced, "of deciding this question is now devolved upon you." [9]

### iii

The first session of the twenty-eighth Congress adjourned on June 17, and its members scurried home to participate in the election campaigns and to fight for their own return to the national legislature. Less than two months remained before the August elections.

Douglas' campaign for re-election had already begun. A month before the adjournment of Congress a district convention in Pittsfield unanimously endorsed Douglas for a second term. His bid for the nomination had not been unchallenged. Both ex-Governor Carlin and Alfred Cavarly, two former competitors, had actively sought the nomination. Carlin, resentful of Douglas' control over the party, threatened to run "on his own hook" if he should be "jockeyed in the convention" as he was the year before. By convention time, however, opposition had withered away, and Douglas received the enthusiastic support he had every reason to expect.

The Democratic party in Illinois was torn by personal dissension during the spring of 1844, in part a reflection of the rivalries for the presidential nomination, in part the result of a tightening grip on the party organization by Democratic leaders. Governor Ford, it was said, nurtured political ambitions that placed him at odds with the party's ruling clique (including Douglas). A quarrel involving the completion of the Illinois and Michigan canal ruffled the ranks and alienated Ford from other Democrats. Ford's effort to interest British investors in the canal elicited a sharp response from the Washington *Globe* in an article Ford was convinced had been written by Douglas. Douglas remained silent in the face of Ford's charges, and the paper later denied that any member of Congress had been involved in the attack. The incident, if anything, worked to Douglas' advantage during the campaign.[10]

The Fifth District, according to predictions, would be one of the few hotly contested districts in the state. Douglas' slim victory the year before encouraged the Whigs to believe that, with a little more effort, the congressional seat could be won. Their hopes, however, rested with Orville H. Browning, who was conceded to be the only Whig who could upset the Little Giant. Although Browning wavered in his decision, his reluctance to be a candidate became apparent, and the Whigs were forced to look elsewhere. David M. Woodson, a Greene County lawyer and a former member of the state legislature, received the nomination.[11]

Woodson was no match for Douglas. Both candidates traveled extensively about the district, but the Whig's efforts were at best half-hearted. The Whig press almost completely ignored the congressional contest, concentrating its attention on the presidential election. Douglas hit the Texas and Oregon issues hard, emphasizing the growing British threat, and alluded with less vigor to the tariff issue. The *Quincy Whig,* in one of its few outbursts, complained that there was little difference between the Democrats and the Whigs on the Oregon issue; more to the point was Douglas' willingness to plunge the nation into a war with Mexico over Texas, and his opposition, on all the test votes, to the 1842 tariff bill. Douglas flooded the district with congressional documents, especially his speeches on refunding Jackson's fine and Polk's nomination, and brought in Gustave Koerner, by then a prominent leader in Belleville, to persuade the German population in Quincy to support him. The election proved disastrous to the Whigs. Douglas defeated Woodson by over 1700 votes and carried every county in the district but one.[12]

Following his victory in the congressional race, Douglas concentrated his efforts on the presidential contest. The Whigs had earlier been confident that Henry Clay would carry Illinois. "If we cannot carry Illinois in November 1844 for Gallant Hal, by Singing, Speaking truth, telling facts and publishing documentary evidence," wrote William H. Herndon, "we then intend giving her up to hardness of heart." Polk's nomination on an expansionist platform, however, cast a pall over the Whig camp. The *Quincy Whig,* reflecting a wider concern, bitterly criticized Douglas for laying aside "the old issues between the parties" and for springing new ones on the people. The August elections, a first test for the new issues, resulted in a Democratic sweep. The Democrats gained large majorities in the state legislature, and all the Democratic incumbent Congressmen were re-elected. Hardin, who had not been renominated, gave way to Edward Dickinson Baker, the lone successful Whig. "Great and Glorious Triumph of the Cause of Human Liberty," crowed the *State Register* after the election, "Downfall of British Whiggery, Abolitionism, & Church-burning Federalism."

Although victory in November appeared certain, Douglas did not relax his efforts. There were still some factors which, he feared, might reduce the Democratic advantage. For the first time nativist arguments entered the campaign significantly, filling the columns of the state's newspapers and reflecting the growth of the Native American movement nationally. Illinois Democrats, dependent upon the foreign vote, denounced the movement, while the Whigs remained silent, an attitude that was interpreted as approbation. Douglas made special efforts to counter the nativist appeal.

In June 1844, the Mormon Prophet, Joseph Smith, was murdered by a mob in the Carthage jail where he had sought refuge. An announced candidate for the presidency, he had become the focus of bitter controversy among dissident Mormons as well as among the anti-Mormons of western Illinois. Angry meetings had been held at which his enemies swore to exterminate the Church leadership. In the face of this danger, Smith and his brother Hyrum surrendered to the state authorities, only to be murdered in jail. The question of the Mormon vote in the state and national elections had been a matter of speculation. "Their vote," predicted one Whig early in the year, "will about turn the scale in the State." Smith's murder, however, added an unexpected ingredient to the campaign. Democrats immediately demanded that the Prophet's murderers be brought to justice, while the Whigs slipped into an increasingly anti-Mormon stance. In the Fifth District, the Mormons sided once again with Douglas and contributed to his decisive victory in the congressional race. There was little doubt after mid-summer which party would receive the Mormon vote in November.[13]

Douglas' campaign activities extended beyond the boundaries of his own state, a sign that his name was becoming known elsewhere in the nation. His greatest effort was in Polk's own state, where a great mass meeting of Democrats from all parts of the Union was held in Nashville in August. "Call upon the whole Democracy to attend the *great mass-meeting,*" Polk had suggested, "and thousands would seize the occasion to make a pilgrimage to the Hermitage." Douglas was among those invited to speak. An estimated 50,000 people attended the rally, and with Democratic orators speaking simultaneously in different parts of the camp ground, the meeting assumed the character of a religious revival. Douglas, according to the *Nashville Union,* was prevented "by temporary indisposition" from addressing the crowd at the beginning, as he was scheduled to do, but he did speak on a later day. Following the mass meeting, Douglas traveled through Tennessee, speaking for Polk at a number of localities. He concluded his tour with a two-hour speech on "the subjects of Annexation, and the evils and injustice of a protective tariff" before the courthouse in Nashville. "As a popular debater," commented the local paper, "Judge Douglas is equalled by few men. He is clear, succinct and pointed, and brings directly home all his strong arguments and connecting facts to the bosoms and understanding of his hearers."[14]

Stopping in St. Louis on his return to Illinois, Douglas held a large audience "in a breathless silence" for three hours. He denounced the Whig tariff of 1842 as "not a protective tariff in reality, but an act for the oppression and plunder of the American laborer for the benefit of a few large capitalists." After a brief review of the Oregon dispute, he plunged into the question of Texas annexation. Our national honor and faith, he declared, require the annexation of Texas, the safety of the southwestern frontier and the maintenance of our rights in Oregon demand it, and the interests of every section of the Union render it necessary. Once again Douglas raised the British bogy and dismissed the threat of war with Mexico. If war should result, he added, "then let it come—it would be a just war on our part, and a war in waging which, we had nothing to fear." At the conclusion of the speech, the enthusiasm of the crowd erupted in "three whole-souled cheers, and three additional ones, for Polk, Dallas, and Texas." The "Young Giant of Illinois," one Missouri editor noted, was an "intellectual giant" indeed.

Douglas, in declining an invitation to campaign in Michigan, wrote confidently early in October that the election was "already settled, and the only question now to be determined is the extent of our majority." The last weeks of the campaign he spent in his home state, where he brought his efforts to a conclusion in Springfield on the eve of the election.[15]

Polk carried Illinois by over 13,000 votes, a dramatic increase over the narrow margin by which Van Buren had carried the state four years before. Democrats, rejoicing at Clay's defeat, chortled that "the same old coon cannot be revived." Whigs, plunged into deep gloom, charged that gross frauds had been perpetrated at the polls and once again raised the question of alien voting. Foreigners, they maintained, "are the *Serviles* of the locofocos and always will be." The Democratic party had, they maintained, proved itself destitute of American feelings and patriotism. In their desperation, some Whigs turned to nativism. Suggestions that the Whig party be abandoned in favor of the newly organized nativist American party gained ground. Abraham Lincoln, a defeated Clay elector, was said to be one of the supporters of the nativist movement.[16]

The election of 1844 in Illinois turned on the issues of the tariff and Texas. Douglas had struck hard at the Whig tariff of 1842, declaring that any tariff based on protection was hostile to the best interests of American farmers and laborers. It was the Texas issue, however, that caught the enthusiasm of his audiences. Although the Oregon question was dear to the hearts of westerners, it played almost no role in the campaign. Texas, wrote James Shields, became "more exciting and more absorbing than the Oregon question." [17] To Douglas, however, the issues could not be separated, for they were both essential parts of a single national impulse, interdependent in their relationship. The acquisition of all of Oregon, as he declared in one campaign speech, depended upon the annexation of Texas. The former would inevitably follow the latter. Texas was the issue of the moment and stood high in the order of priorities, but Oregon was not far behind.

iv

Douglas was in his seat on December 2 when the second session of the twenty-eighth Congress was called to order. It was with new stature and prestige that he had returned to Washington. Decisively re-elected, recognized beyond his own state for his campaign efforts, Douglas, it was thought, would likely have considerable influence with the new President. Indeed, there was some talk that Douglas would be invited to sit in Polk's cabinet, possibly as Attorney General. "No man, of his age and experience, in the whole Union," wrote the editor of the *Register,* "would make a more able Cabinet officer." Echoing these sentiments, a Missouri paper announced that Douglas was "the favorite now of the Democracy of the Northwest" and would soon occupy the same place in the party as that once held by Thomas Hart Benton. The speculation was ended by Douglas himself. He would not, he wrote, abandon his seat in Congress "for any office within the gift of the Executive." Eagerly anticipating a chance at the spoils, Illinois Democrats now bombarded him with letters seeking support for favors and patronage.[18]

That Douglas had no desire to trade his congressional seat for an executive appointment was clear. Not quite so clear was whether he would remain content with his post in the lower house. The Democratic sweep of the legislative elections raised anew the question of Douglas' elevation to the Senate. The death of Samuel McRoberts in March 1843 had left one of the state's Senate seats vacant. James Semple was appointed to the position later in the year, but the last two years of McRoberts' unexpired term had yet to be filled by the legislature. As early as January 1844, Douglas was mentioned as a candidate. At first Douglas did nothing to discourage the suggestion. Instead he asked his friends to make discreet inquiries concerning his chances without divulging his own connection with the move. Within a few weeks some Whigs were openly predicting that Douglas would be elected to the Senate if the Democrats carried the August elections.

Douglas, to the disappointment of some of his friends, soon thought better of running for the Senate. He had no desire to test his popularity for an unexpired term when the full prize would be available two years hence, nor did he wish to antagonize Semple. It would be unwise, wrote one friend, for Douglas to alienate Semple and thereby endanger his claims, "which no man has the temerity to question," to election for a full term in two years. "I am doing all I can to prevent it," wrote an-

other friend of his efforts to dissuade the legislators from placing Douglas' name in contention, "as I know you do not wish it now inasmuch as
you will be sure of it after Semple's term expires." As he had done with
Breese, Douglas arranged with Semple to keep his name out of the contest in return for Semple's support in 1846. When Semple was selected
by the legislature to fill the seat, Douglas' own promotion to the United
States Senate was virtually assured.[19]

Douglas was now better known in Washington than he had been a
year before and more inclined to participate in the winter's social affairs.
The White House remained the center of social life in the capital, and
Douglas was present at many of the receptions and levees which the Ty-
lers sponsored. An eligible bachelor, Douglas was observed at these functions "flirting with the ladies." One in particular caught his eye and
fancy. Phoebe Gardiner, an eighteen-year-old cousin of Mrs. Tyler, was a
guest in the White House for the winter season. Her presence had an
immediate impact on the bachelors, and within one week she received
her first proposal of marriage. Douglas, it was said, pursued "Phoebe the
Coquette" at the various balls and receptions with such determination
that all of Washington society became aware of his intentions. Despite
the fact that her family urged her to encourage Douglas' interest, she
soon gave him up for another. Even so, Douglas did not lack for com-
panionship, for he was soon seen in the company of a frequent White
House guest, Mary Corse, who boasted of her conquest and her skill "at
having cut Phoebe out." One reporter commented that Douglas had better get married and thus carry out his doctrine of annexation.[20]

It was annexation of a different kind, however, that consumed Douglas' energies during the brief second session. The defeat of the Texas
treaty proved only a temporary setback to the annexationists. In his message in December, President Tyler urged that the question of annexation
be resolved, not by a treaty as before attempted, but by means of a joint
resolution of Congress. The question, he said, had been referred to the
people during the presidential election and a majority had declared in
favor of immediate annexation. Congress had its instructions in most unmistakable terms. Although the 1844 election was not the referendum
on the Texas issue which Tyler supposed it to be, the Democratic victory
had contributed mightily to annexationist strength. Most members of
the victorious party in Congress recognized, as did Tyler, that their first
duty would be to add Texas to the Union.[21]

On December 12, the chairman of the House Committee on Foreign

Relations, Pennsylvania's C. J. Ingersoll, reported joint resolutions for the annexation of Texas. Ingersoll's proposal, reflecting Tyler's position, was substantially that of the rejected treaty. Because they faced the same difficulties encountered by the treaty, the resolutions were not popular, and other plans were introduced. Shortly afterward, Weller of Ohio submitted resolutions that altered some of the terms of Ingersoll's proposal, and four days later, on December 23, Douglas followed with still another set of resolutions. Others were to follow, but discussion in the House revolved at first about Ingersoll's, Weller's, and Douglas' plans for the annexation of Texas.

Douglas made no attempt to meet the wishes of President Tyler, but rather prepared his resolutions in close consultation with those who could speak for the President-elect, especially Aaron V. Brown of Tennessee, chairman of the House Committee on Territories, in whose room the draft was developed. Douglas' proposal also received the endorsement of Andrew Jackson. With these advantages, his resolutions were regarded as the strongest of those presented and received the widest support.

Douglas, unlike Ingersoll and Weller, based his resolutions on the Louisiana treaty of 1803, by which he claimed Texas had been "ceded and conveyed" to the United States. Under the terms of the treaty, the nation was obligated to incorporate the inhabitants of that territory into the Union as soon as possible. He did not, as did many of his Democratic confreres, base his argument on the invalidity of the 1819 treaty with Spain, by which the United States had surrendered its claim to Texas. While the United States lost its rights to Texas by that instrument, Douglas explained, the nation was not released from its obligation to fulfill the terms of the 1803 treaty whenever Texas demanded it. That time had now arrived. Texans desired admission into the Union, and Congress was obligated to grant it.

Douglas' resolutions met, or bypassed, some of the objections that had been charged against earlier plans for annexation. The question of securing Mexico's assent was ignored completely, and the difficult problem of boundaries was to be left to presidential negotiation. A feasible plan for the payment of the Texas debt was advanced. Further, the slavery issue was answered by the implicit declaration that the Missouri Compromise had long ago settled the matter with respect to Texas. Texas, according to Douglas' reasoning, had been a part of the Louisiana Purchase at the time the line separating free from slave territory was agreed upon, a convenient response to the critics of slavery who challenged the annexation of Texas. Years later he recalled that, while he did not approve of the principle involved in the Missouri Compromise, he was convinced that its extension over Texas was necessary to prevent the outburst of a serious slavery agitation. Douglas' plan was based on some questionable assumptions regarding the 1803 treaty with France, but by skirting a discussion of the validity of the 1819 negotiation with Spain (in which John Quincy Adams had played the principal part), he placed the legal argument for annexation on stronger ground.[22]

The scene in the House now became one of parliamentary maneuvers, stormy debates, and inconclusive caucuses. It was clear that a majority of the members desired the annexation of Texas in some form, but agreement on the details seemed remote. Ingersoll's resolutions were taken up, Weller moved his as an amendment, and Douglas proposed his as an amendment to the amendment. The debate thus proceeded on Douglas' resolutions. Douglas was not prepared to defend his proposition immediately, either because of "indisposition," as he pleaded, or because he did not have his papers with him, as noted by Adams. To gain time he agreed to a proposal, made by South Carolina's Robert Barnwell Rhett, that his preamble be withdrawn so that the first resolution, declaring simply that Texas be annexed, could be acted upon. If that resolution should be approved, Rhett maintained, there would be little difficulty in arranging the terms of the annexation. Rhett's suggestion was rejected, and debate on Douglas' plan began. The Whigs led off on the attack.

After an hour-long speech by Robert Winthrop, in which the Massachusetts Representative vigorously maintained the unconstitutionality of annexation by joint resolution, Douglas succeeded, "above many competitors," in obtaining the floor. What followed was one of the Little Giant's major congressional addresses. He denounced the tactics of the opposition and especially Winthrop's charge that the annexation proposal had been devised by an "accidental President," one not elected by the people. Douglas skillfully turned the charge around and reviewed the efforts made during John Quincy Adams' administration to secure Texas, chiding the Massachusetts Representative for his unkind remarks against his own colleague (a reminder that Adams himself had not been elected to the presidency by the people). The Texas question, Douglas pointed out, was not a new one, but "had for a long time engrossed the attention of the American people and government."

Douglas concentrated his defense on the assertion, boldly stated in his resolutions, that the United States had an obligation under the 1803 treaty to admit Texas into the Union. He cited treaties, documents, and diplomatic correspondence to demonstrate that the Rio del Norte (Rio Grande) had been considered the western boundary of Louisiana by the French, Spanish, and Americans. Under the terms of the Louisiana cession, the inhabitants of Texas were "naturalized and adopted as citizens of the United States," to be incorporated into the Union as soon as possible. To fulfill these terms, "the sacred faith and honor of this nation were solemnly and irrevocably pledged." The "fatal" treaty with Spain in 1819 surrendered the territory west of the Sabine and broke the national faith. "The American republic was severed," Douglas charged, "and a part of its territory joined to a foreign kingdom." But while the nation lost its right to Texas by that negotiation, it did not lose its obligation to the people of Texas. Under the terms of the 1803 treaty Texans retained the right to demand admission into the Union, and the United States was morally obligated to accede to these demands. "The opponents of annexation," Douglas remarked scornfully, "can discourse eloquently and feelingly upon the sanctity of treaty stipulations and the sacred observance of national faith, when there is an outstanding bond in the hands of some banker for the payment of a small pittance of money; but when human rights, the rights of person and property— or religious freedom—the glorious privileges of American citizenship, are all involved in the guaranty, the doctrine of repudiation loses its horrors and its infamy."

Responding to the constitutional argument raised by some Whigs, Douglas argued a broad construction of the Constitution. The power to admit new states, taken in conjunction with Congress' authorization to make all laws which shall be necessary to the execution of its powers, gave annexation a firm and explicit constitutional sanction. As for the advantages annexation would bring to the country—the stimulation of industry, the opening of new markets for manufactures, the extension of commerce and navigation, the augmentation of political power, and the securing of safer and more natural boundaries—Douglas did no more than list them. "It is sufficient argument with me," he said, "that our honor and violated faith require the immediate annexation of Texas to the Union." He placed his argument almost entirely on moral considerations. Significantly, he made no mention of the slavery question.[23]

Douglas' speech, wrote a Richmond newspaper correspondent, "proves that he has not only deep legal research, natural eloquence, and a most argumentative mind, but that he possesses the power of condensation to a degree which is extraordinary in one of his extreme youth, trained as a public speaker in the Far West, where condensation is by no means in vogue." William H. Polk, brother of the President-elect, recalling Douglas' efforts in Tennessee during the campaign, declared that he had never heard him speak so well as he did before the House. The Whigs, however, rushed to the attack. His application of the Missouri Compromise line to Texas was denounced as meaningless, since virtually all of Texas lay south of the line. In basing his argument for annexation on the treaty obligations of 1803, Douglas had, according to one Whig member, revived a dead treaty by strangling three live ones. John Quincy Adams branded Douglas' constitutional argument as fallacious and maintained that the power to annex Texas was not at all incident to the power to admit new states.

Debate on the annexation resolutions continued for three weeks after Douglas delivered his address. Kentucky's Linn Boyd introduced new resolutions paraphrasing closely a set offered earlier by Milton Brown, Whig Representative from Tennessee. They were concise and simple and avoided some of the questions of interpretation raised by Douglas. Douglas accepted Boyd's resolutions as a substitute for his own but, since they followed Brown's so closely and since Brown was a Whig and liable to attract Whig support, Brown's resolutions were eventually agreed upon by the annexationists. On January 25, all the resolutions except Brown's were rejected. On the question of slavery, Brown had provided that the state or states lying south of the Missouri Compromise line should be admitted with or without slavery, as the people of each might prescribe. Douglas asked Brown to modify the clause by adding the prohibition of slavery in any states formed out of that part of Texas lying north of 36°30' latitude, thus making explicit the application of the Missouri Compromise to Texas. Brown accepted Douglas' modification. It was in this form that the joint resolutions for annexation finally passed the House.

After a month's debate, the Senate returned the House resolutions with only slight amendment, the House concurred, and, on March 3, 1845, President Tyler, on his last day in office, announced that he had signed the joint resolutions annexing Texas. "A loud burst of plaudits" rocked the House. The Lone Star had joined the national firmament.[24]

# VIII

## "I would make this
## an *ocean-bound republic*"
## 1845–1846

i

Douglas came home to Quincy late in April 1845. Although he had won praise for his role in the Texas triumph and was thought by many to be a strong man with the new administration, he was greeted with murmurs of discontent. Many of his former rivals for party leadership cast covetous eyes toward his growing national prominence. There were also hints of a split in the congressional delegation itself.

One formidable adversary appeared unexpectedly in the towering figure of Thomas Hart Benton. The Missouri Senator, many thought, had sacrificed his claim to the leadership of the western Democracy by his firm support of Van Buren and by his obstructionist role in the Texas debates. Douglas, although youthful and inexperienced, had been mentioned as a successor to Benton, destined to assume Benton's role as a western leader.

Douglas had taken issue with Benton on both the Baltimore nomination and Texas annexation, thus incurring the Missourian's displeasure. During the summer of 1844 Douglas was denounced in the columns of the *Missourian*, Benton's St. Louis paper, and during the short session of Congress he endured the attacks of "the tools of Col. Benton at Washington." That Douglas did not reciprocate is indicated by his successful support of the editor of the *Missourian* for appointment to public office by President Polk. Walters, Springfield's Democratic editor, raised a

furor when he charged that Illinois' House delegation had split over the
Benton-Douglas differences and that some, notably John A. McClernand, had encouraged Benton's attacks against Douglas out of jealousy
for the rising fame of the " 'giant' of Illinois." Other papers chimed in,
denouncing anyone who was "willing to become the cat's paw of the
Missouri Senator, to destroy the political fame of Illinois' favorite." Vigorous denials of Walters' charges were issued by McClernand and his
southern Illinois supporters, and by the end of May the *State Register*
was ready to end the controversy. James Shields helped to smooth the
waters. In a letter to McClernand, he urged the southern Illinois Congressman to stand with Douglas. "If you two keep together you may
defy any thing." [1]

Some questions raised by the incident, however, persisted. Walters
clung to the notion that the Illinois House delegation had been rocked
by dissension. Why, he asked, had bills for Illinois and the west (particularly for the improvement of western waterways) been lost, if not because of disunity among the state's Congressmen? The Democratic
sweep of six of the seven newly apportioned congressional districts had
aroused great expectations for the state, but the hoped-for results had not
been achieved. Walters called on Douglas for an explanation. An additional irritant appeared when Polk allowed the Congressmen to control
new appointments in the state, thus ruling out any influence over patronage from party leaders at home. A coolness developed between the
two men which Walters attributed to the fact that Douglas had moved
from Springfield to another district. The difficulty went deeper than that.
The *Quincy Herald* aspired to be Douglas' organ at the same time that
the *State Register's* influence in state and party politics showed signs of
decline. There were indications that Douglas and the *Herald* intended to
challenge the Springfield influence, even down to the choice of state
printer, a position Walters had held for many years. Douglas was further
accused of conspiring with McClernand, Lyman Trumbull, and John
Wentworth for control of the party to the exclusion of others. A bargain
had been struck, it was charged, whereby Douglas and McClernand were
to be elected Senators, Trumbull would receive the governorship, and
Wentworth would lead the Illinois delegation in the lower house of
Congress. In the ensuing contest between the two men there was little
doubt that Walters received the worst of it.

Douglas did not answer Walters' charges until late in June. The latter's attacks against the delegation, he finally wrote, "were so palpably

unjust and so inconsistent with the facts" that he had decided to ignore them. The attacks had continued, however, until he could no longer remain quiet. He pointed out that it was Tyler's veto that defeated the appropriations for western improvements, not Congress, and he accused Walters of trying to screen Tyler by casting odium on the state's delegation. Walters had further attacked the Democratic Congressmen for supporting a resolution that he contended would deprive Illinois of its school fund. The resolution in question empowered the Secretary of the Treasury to withhold the proceeds of the sales of public lands to which a state might be entitled if that state were in default to the United States government. Douglas disagreed completely that this resolution could affect the school fund, maintaining that the latter was "a sacred fund, secured by an express compact, irrevocable except by common consent." Walters' interpretation of the resolution was, he wrote, "repugnant to common sense."

Douglas' argument failed to convince the unhappy editor. He published Douglas' letter and then devoted several issues to answering it in detail. His discontent reached the boiling point when he discovered that, while Douglas' letter was reprinted in the press throughout the state, his own answering arguments were not. Walters concluded the struggle with the publication of a savage attack against Douglas (written by a Peoria resident) in which Douglas was characterized as arrogant, pompous, and unmindful of the truth. Douglas was charged with being "so entirely absorbed with the contemplation of his rising greatness" that he ignored the interests of his constituents. "His mind may have been in the other end of the Capitol, or in the White House." It was Walters' own political death warrant; not long afterward he resigned from the editorship of the *State Register*.[2]

The summer and fall of 1845 also witnessed the closing chapter in the story of the Mormons in Illinois. Characteristically, Douglas played an important role in the final events. His relations with the Mormons and their leaders had remained cordial even after his election to Congress, and he was frequently consulted by them on matters of national policy. He sympathized with their efforts to recover their losses in Missouri and once suggested that the Mormons sue the state for a redress of grievances.

The rapidly deteriorating relations between the Mormons and their neighbors, intensified by Smith's death the year before, continued to upset western Illinois. Irritations multiplied, accompanied by violence and destruction of property on both sides. Demands were soon made that the Mormons vacate their Illinois homes. The sheriff of Hancock County, a partisan of the Mormons and a former Douglas-appointed clerk of the circuit court, added to the excitement when he raised a posse in Nauvoo to maintain order. Governor Ford, convinced that "neither party in Hancock could be trusted with the power to keep the peace," conferred with Congressmen Hardin and Douglas, William B. Warren (clerk of the Supreme Court) and state attorney general James A. McDougall. The four, it was agreed, should move hastily into the Mormon settlements with an armed volunteer force in order to halt the disorder and to negotiate the removal of the Mormons from Illinois.

Douglas, holding the rank of Major and Aide-de-Camp to Hardin (who commanded the force), acted as the intermediary with the Mormon leadership. In the company of the sheriff, he persuaded Brigham Young to meet formally with the negotiators to discuss the terms of Mormon removal from Illinois. Plans for removal had been discussed by the Mormons for some time prior to the final crisis, and Vancouver Island, in the Oregon country, had frequently been mentioned as a new area of settlement. In response to their inquiries, Douglas had assured them that Vancouver Island was claimed by the United States and that he saw no objection to its occupation by the Church. Preparations should be made at once, the commissioners urged, for the departure of the Mormons during the following spring. The Church leaders agreed, and their decision was immediately communicated to the governor and to the anti-Mormon citizens of Hancock County. An uneasy peace followed. The volunteer force was disbanded, except for a small detachment which remained in the area throughout the winter.

As preparations were made for the Mormon exodus to some point "west of the Rocky Mountains," Douglas received appeals from the Church leaders for assistance and support. Proposals had been made in Congress for the construction of blockhouses along the Oregon Trail to protect the emigrants, and for the establishment of a monthly mail service with the settlements in the far west. Brigham Young hoped that Douglas might secure contracts for the construction work and the transportation of the mail for the Mormons as they moved west. "Should you procure us the job," he promised, "we will remember you when the territory we settle becomes a State in the Union." No appropriations were made, but Douglas continued to serve as a contact for the Mormons in Congress for many years afterward. One Mormon delegate to Washington later commented that Douglas was "a better friend to us than any other member of Congress." [3]

ii

The brief lame-duck second session of the twenty-eighth Congress had been a significant one for Douglas. The young Illinois politician opened his first term in Congress with a vigorous defense of Jackson and Jacksonian principles; he closed it with an equally vigorous appeal to America's expansive destiny. Nothing more clearly demonstrated the national faith during these exciting years. Jacksonian democracy and national expansion provided a firm foundation for the ambitions of the Little Giant, who now saw his future in large dimension.

During these few months, Douglas formulated a program for western expansion and development that would influence his course in national politics for many years afterward. His attention focused initially on the annexation of Texas, but Texas was only a part of his larger vision. In his speech on annexation, made on January 6, he alluded to the forces which compelled a reappraisal of America's role on the continent and in the world, demonstrating an insight into the wider meaning of the technological changes of the day than many of his contemporaries could appreciate. At the same time he revealed his own dream of America's greatness.

> The application of steam power to transportation and travel [he declared] has brought the remotest limits of this confederacy, now comprising twenty-six states . . . much nearer to the centre than when they were but thirteen. The revolution is progressing, and the facilities and rapidity of communication are increasing in a much greater ratio than our territory or population.
>
> Our federal system is admirably adapted to the whole continent; and while I would not violate the laws of nations, nor treaty stipulations, nor in any manner tarnish the national honor, I would exert all legal and honorable means to drive Great Britain and the last vestiges of royal authority from the continent of North America, and extend the limits of the republic from ocean to ocean. I would make this an *ocean-bound republic,* and have no more disputes about boundaries or red lines upon the maps.

Such notions were not new to Douglas. What was new was the opportunity he now had to implement ideas and policies he had often expressed. Writing to Douglas at this time, James Shields recalled earlier discussions, "in the wild apparent enthusiasms of pearly youth," when they had talked of "extending a territory to the Rocky Mountains, thus securing a military pass, under civil jurisdiction thence opening a way to the occupation of Oregon, thence acting on the fertile territory south." "You," he reminded Douglas, "are actively and powerfully engaged in turning those dreams into solemn realities. . . . It is working out the destiny of a mighty people." [4]

John Tyler devoted only a small portion of his message to the Oregon question when he addressed the second session in December 1844. Emigrants to the Oregon country, he suggested, should be protected along their journey by a line of fortifications, places of rest as well as safety for the travelers. Pending the completion of negotiations with Great Britain over the boundary question, Congress should extend the "aegis of our laws" over Americans on that distant frontier. Douglas eagerly took the cue. Efforts to assert American rights to the "whole Oregon Territory" during the previous session had met with little success. The Baltimore platform of the Democratic party, however, revived the hopes of the western expansionists and provided a mandate for the early consideration of the Oregon question by Congress.

Douglas moved quickly to translate this mandate into legislative action. In a speech before the House on January 31, he briefly outlined his program for expansion. Texas and Oregon, he declared, "were like man and wife: when separated, the welfare and happiness of both were seriously injured; but when once united, they must be kept together forever." Organize a territorial government in Oregon, he urged, and settle the boundary question once and for all. But Oregon was closely and significantly linked to other aspects of national development. If once secured, it must be made easily and safely accessible. A territorial government should be erected in Nebraska, that vast empty space stretching westward from the Missouri River; military posts should be established along the trails for the protection of the emigrants; and, finally, surveys of the western country should be authorized for the construction of a Pacific railroad. The American people, Douglas admonished, must shoulder the obligations of expansion, to "make the area of liberty as broad as the continent itself." The oceans were boundaries which "the God of nature had marked out." But while Douglas placed his argument on the soaring flight of the American eagle, on the responsibility to fulfill America's destiny, he also appealed to hard economic and political realities. The "unscrupulous aims of Great Britain at universal dominion" must be checked, American commerce must be expanded and protected, and Britain's ships driven from China as well as from the Gulf of Mexico.[5]

Three days before Douglas spoke, Asa Whitney's first proposal for a

Pacific railroad was submitted to Congress. Whitney, a New York merchant engaged in the China trade, envisioned immense possibilities for American commercial and political expansion with the construction of a railroad from Lake Michigan to the Pacific coast. "To the interior of our wide-spread country," he wrote, "it would be as the heart is to the human body." Not only would American and European commerce be channeled to the great markets of China by this road, but American cities would be relieved of misery, vice, crime, and taxation, and the west settled by an "industrious and frugal people." Whitney asked Congress for a generous grant of land to construct and maintain his project.

Congress took no action on Whitney's memorial, but the suggestion caught fire. Whitney traveled extensively through the west, issued elaborations of his plan, and corresponded with Douglas. Douglas seized the opportunity to develop his western program further and to publicize his own plans for a Pacific railroad. He wrote an open letter to Whitney that was immediately published and circulated as a pamphlet.

Douglas objected to Whitney's preference for a railroad route from Milwaukee, on Lake Michigan, to the mouth of the Columbia River. Chicago, with its eastern rail connections, he argued, made better sense as a terminus. In the west he preferred San Francisco Bay, "if that country could be annexed in time," an early indication that Douglas looked also to the acquisition of the Mexican borderlands. He rejected Whitney's plan for financing the road, since it would "postpone the peopling of the country." He further stated that "your scheme is too magnificent —the trust too great—the grant of lands too extensive—and the power over the rights and interests of the people, states, territories, and government, too monstrous to be confided to any citizen, no matter how virtuous, enlightened and patriotic." Let Congress instead grant to each of the states and territories through which the road would pass alternate sections of land, extending for a reasonable distance on each side of the line. The states and territories could develop their own plans and means of construction, consistent with Douglas' belief that such tasks were a matter of local responsibility. The other alternate sections could be opened to settlement, thus ensuring a regular and orderly occupation of the country along the road. By following such a plan, not one, but "a continuous line of rail roads to the Pacific ocean" could be built.

The Pacific railroad fit neatly into Douglas' concept of national destiny; it was essential to the greatness that awaited America. The railroad would promote American commercial expansion as the India and China trade, "the vast commerce of the Pacific ocean," passed over its route. In addition, it would play an indispensable role in "subduing the wilderness, and peopling it with a hardy and industrious population." Migration to the west was mounting in volume each year. "To those vast multitudes, who wish to change their condition, and select new homes, the promised land is westward."

Douglas' plan for a Pacific railroad, however, was not an isolated policy. It was a part of a broader national program for growth and development, inextricably linked to other specific proposals which Douglas advanced in the same document. Territorial governments should be established in Oregon, "extending from the Rocky Mountains to the Pacific," and in Nebraska, "extending from the western borders of Iowa and Missouri to Oregon." In order to ensure a "continuous line of settlements from the Mississippi to the Pacific" and to encourage the peopling of the west, Douglas urged that the lands west of the Missouri River "be donated in tracts of 160 acres, to the actual settler." It was this program to which Douglas became dedicated. His first efforts toward its realization came in the short second session of his first congressional term.[6]

On December 11, 1844, John Quincy Adams noted in his diary that Douglas had asked leave to introduce a bill establishing a new territory "with a strange name." Douglas presented his first bill to organize Nebraska Territory shortly afterward. The House Committee on Territories gave it brief consideration, but no further action was taken on it. A similar fate awaited Douglas' proposal to line the routes of travel to the west with military fortifications. A bill to establish military posts in Nebraska and Oregon "to protect the commerce of the United States with New Mexico and California, and the emigration and trade to Oregon, against Indian agression and depredations" was introduced late in January and referred to the Committee on Military Affairs, where it subsequently died. Both of these bills, he thought, were essential to the occupation and settlement of Oregon. "The only certain mode of maintaining our rights to Oregon, is to connect the settlements there with those on this side of the mountains." Douglas' attempt to promote the settlement of the vast empty spaces west of Missouri, however, aroused little comment—only a small amount of speculation on the question, "Where can Nebraska be?"[7]

Two bills relating more directly to Oregon were introduced into the House early in the session. The first, sponsored by Ohio's Alexander Duncan, provided for the organization of a territorial government in Oregon, an alarming move to some since it bypassed the joint occupation treaty and the disturbing boundary question. The second, presented on the same day (December 16) by Douglas, authorized the purchase of copies of Robert Greenhow's *History of Oregon and California, and the Other Territories on the North-West Coast* for distribution to members of Congress.

Greenhow, a librarian in the State Department, first prepared his work in 1840 and published it in expanded form in 1844; in it he attempted to prove the validity of the American claim to all of Oregon through the publication of both Spanish and American documents. A bill to purchase 1500 copies of the book had passed the Senate in the previous session, at which time Senator James Buchanan had declared that the book "extricated that portion of this territory north of forty-nine degrees from the embarrassed position in which it had been placed by the blundering diplomacy of our negotiators and the blundering speeches of our statesmen." Douglas urged that the book be read by every member of Congress before the discussion of any bills relating to Oregon. Greenhow's history, he asserted, would "save territory enough beyond the Rocky mountains to form three or four States." After some debate, which included an impassioned plea on behalf of manifest destiny by Douglas' colleague, John Wentworth, the bill passed both houses of Congress. The book, immediately published in a second edition to meet the new demand, subsequently exercised a considerable influence on the boundary discussions in Congress.[8]

The debate on Duncan's bill was wild and stormy. Opponents of the organization of a territorial government that would include all of Oregon emphasized the nation's treaty obligations and urged that proper notice be given to Great Britain of the abrogation of the joint occupation agreement before any action respecting Oregon be taken. The expansionists would have none of it. Douglas charged into the fray, inspiring Adams to note in his diary that "Douglas, of Illinois, raved an hour about democracy and Anglophobia and universal empire."

Douglas expressed surprise that the bill should have aroused opposition. After the passage of the Texas resolution by so large a majority, he declared, he had supposed that the bill to extend the government of the United States over Oregon would receive the unanimous support of the House. He was disturbed by those who argued that far-distant Oregon could never form a part of the American nation, and suggested that the answer to their argument might be found in the federal system and in technology. Our system of government was "as well adapted to the whole American continent as it was to the thirteen original States of the Union." The secret of America's future was precisely in that system which "provided that different confederacies might be organized into the same republic, divided into States with sovereign powers for local and domestic purposes, but united together for general power and common defence." Improvement in the means of communication and the development of steam power had brought the extremities of the continent closer together, "nearer together, in time at least, than the original States were when this republic was formed." The nation might safely be extended to the edges of the continent, he concluded, "and even further if necessary."

As he had in the Texas debates, Douglas brushed aside the fear that expansion might lead the United States into war. "Why should it produce war?" he asked. "Was it not our own country, and was not our title to it beyond dispute?" War with the British held no terrors for the young Congressman. Military posts must be established and naval forces dispatched to the coast ready to repel British aggression and to "punish any invasion of our rights." The establishment of a boundary between Great Britain and the United States through diplomatic channels was hopeless. "Every man in his senses knows that there is no hope of our getting possession of this country by negotiation." Other means must be employed. A territorial government, backed by military force, must be established in Oregon. "Then the whole question would be settled." He would never, he pledged, yield an inch of Oregon to Great Britain or to any other power.

Douglas ended his speech with a familiar burst of Anglophobia. Britain was quietly surrounding the United States with a network of possessions and fortifications; the Canadas were in her hands, she was intriguing for Texas and California and had her eye on Cuba. Britain's policy, Douglas declared, was apparent even to a blind man. "It was to check the growth of republican institutions on this continent, and the rapidity with which we have progressed, not only in political power, but in trade and national glory." American growth, he pointed out, had produced "a great moral effect in Europe." Crowned heads tottered on their thrones. In desperation, in order to preserve themselves, they found it necessary to check the onward growth of the United States. The Union was sacred; every inch of its territory, including all of Oregon, must be maintained "at all hazards."

Douglas' speech brought the opposition to its feet. The haste which

Douglas urged and his anti-British bluster were denounced. John Quincy Adams characterized Douglas' statements as "extremely belligerent," and in an answering speech he deplored the "precipitation and rashness" which seemed to drive the proponents of Oregon. In the haste to bring the bill to a vote, there was not even time to read Greenhow's book, which Douglas had after all urged every member to read before passing on the Oregon bill. Adams argued that the notice of the termination of the agreement with Great Britain should be served before any legislation establishing a territorial government in Oregon could be considered. The next day, Adams' colleague, Robert Winthrop, told the House that Douglas had "seemed to work himself up to a dangerous state of excitement, and chafed himself into a towering passion." The whole discussion, he concluded, was "unwise, ill-timed, and impolitic," and would very likely jeopardize peaceful negotiations between the two nations.

In the debate the right of the United States to Oregon was not at issue; the manner in which that right should be exercised and the steps that should be taken to secure Oregon provided the focal point of disagreement. In counseling haste, in proposing the establishment of a territorial government in Oregon before any other steps were taken, and in breathing war-like defiance against British power in North America, Douglas reflected the radical western expansionist position.

Unable to halt the bill in its course, the opposition turned to amendments to secure their ends. On February 3 two significant amendments were added, one prohibiting slavery in the new territory and a second extending the long fought-for notice of the abrogation of the joint occupation treaty. Douglas supported both amendments. In its amended form, the bill passed the House, but its supporters failed in all their attempts to secure its passage in the Senate before the adjournment of Congress on March 3.[9]

Polk established the theme of his administration quickly. Inauguration day, moaned a Whig correspondent, "was in keeping with all the melancholy events of the campaign." Summer-like weather gave way, on March 4, to rain and mud, and the new President, shielded by an umbrella, delivered his inaugural address from the steps of the capitol. Although he devoted more time to Texas, he made it clear that Oregon occupied a primary place in his thinking. He pledged himself to assert and maintain "by all constitutional means" the right of the United States to the Oregon country and urged that "the jurisdiction of our laws and the benefits of our republican institutions" be extended over the Americans who lived on that far frontier.

Action, however, gave way to the more pressing problems of the moment. Washington, complained the *New-York Tribune*'s correspondent, was full of the "most desperate characters," attracted by the inauguration. The Empire Club celebrated the new administration by discharging a cannon, which shattered the windows of downtown buildings, and an intoxicated horseman, painted like an Indian and wearing a ring in his nose, wove his way through the inauguration crowd. Two inaugural balls capped the festivities, one for the "aristocracy of Loco-Focodom," at ten dollars a ticket, and a second for the "unwashed," at half the price. With the new Democratic President seated in the presidential chair, members of Congress scattered to their homes and the office-seekers moved into the capital. Douglas lingered in Washington, busying himself with letters of recommendation to the new administration on behalf of personal and political friends.[10]

iii

Douglas returned to an Illinois that was afire with agitation. Democrats in the state were loud in their demand for all of Oregon and were eager to submit to "an appeal to arms" rather than compromise what was a clear and indisputable right to 54°40'. The issue in Illinois was not a partisan one: Whigs joined the Democrats in numerous Oregon meetings during the spring and summer, and fiery orators from both parties denounced British avarice and cupidity and condemned Britain's traditional "aggression on the weaker nations." A rumor, circulated in midsummer, that a treaty had been signed in Washington, with Polk's endorsement, fixing the boundary at the forty-ninth parallel sent the advocates of all of Oregon into a frenzy of passionate oratory. An open breach between western Democratic leaders and the Polk administration was threatened.

On June 3 people from all parts of the state gathered in Springfield for a gigantic demonstration that extended over three days. The resolutions approved there left no room for accommodation or compromise. A galaxy of speakers, including two eminent Whigs, John J. Hardin and Edward Dickinson Baker, reiterated the expansionist arguments. Douglas was "loudly" called for and, although he pleaded "an unusual hoarseness" that would prevent him from speaking at length, he held the attention of the crowd for an hour and a half without cessation. His object, he told his audience, was not to get up a war fever, but he called upon the people to meet war if it should come, "like men conscious of our rights and able to maintain them." A war with Great Britain over Oregon would be "no child's play," for it could not end while the British retained a foothold in North America. "Let us blot out old boundary lines" and make "an ocean bound Republic." Once again he argued the hopelessness of negotiation over the boundary, expressing his fear that negotiation would lead to compromise. Britain was arming in Canada and on the Great Lakes, and the only way to meet this challenge in Oregon was by erecting fortifications, encouraging emigration, and establishing a territorial government. Later in the month Douglas supported the American claim to Oregon before an audience in Chicago, and in early July he was in southern Illinois, where he delivered "one of his usual bursts of eloquence" in the town of Marion.[11]

The prospect of war with Great Britain persuaded Douglas that the Mississippi Valley and the Great Lakes region should be placed on a war footing. He urged that western defenses be strengthened against British attack from the west and north. Among the most important measures was the rapid completion of the Illinois and Michigan Canal, the only channel through which naval ships might be moved from the ocean to the lakes. The completion by the British of the Rideau and Welland canals, connecting the St. Lawrence River with Lakes Ontario and Erie, would enable the British "to spread their fleets over the whole chain of the Northern Lakes, and put all the towns and cities on the American shore, from Sacketts Harbor to Chicago, at the mercy of the enemy." Open the ship canal from Lake Michigan to the Illinois River, establish a naval yard at Chicago, fortify the Straits of Mackinac. Lake Michigan would then "constitute a grand harbor for our vessels, inaccessible to the foe by water or land." Attacks could be launched on land and water against the British while the latter's ships were still locked in the winter's ice, and Upper Canada would easily fall to the United States. Lest his proposals be misinterpreted, Douglas carefully added that it was not his purpose to "indulge in dreams or schemes of foreign conquest," for this was alien to the American mission. Territorial expansion, and hence the extension of the "area of freedom," was unavoidable and "would result as natural consequences from causes over which we have no control, and which we had no disposition to arrest."

Douglas' demand that western defenses be strengthened was not new.

Earlier in the year he had written to Governor Ford of the necessity of such measures, borrowing heavily from ideas expressed by Matthew Fontaine Maury, then a lieutenant in the United States Navy. Maury, writing under the name of "Harry Bluff," had called attention to the exposed condition of the lakes in case of war with Great Britain, and he had communicated his concern to Douglas. Douglas' letter and Maury's statements were transmitted by Ford to the Illinois legislature. In July Douglas was reported to be making his own inspection tour of lake defenses from the Illinois River to Detroit, in the company of Colonel Joseph G. Totten.[12]

The question of internal improvements thus became involved in the Oregon question. For Douglas the relationship was especially close. In the summer of 1845 he found an opportunity to press their relationship in the movement to promote a political alliance between west and south. Discouraged by the defeat of western improvements, western leaders looked to the south for support. Southerners, in turn, had been bidding for western backing in their own struggle against the tariff. A closer cooperation between west and south, based on mutual economic interest, seemed both desirable and possible, and a great convention was scheduled to meet in Memphis to apply the cement to it. Illinois was involved in the plans from the beginning, as interests in both the northern and southern parts of the state hoped for an endorsement of their improvement projects. Douglas, anxious to find a forum for his plans for western defense, recognized his chance to place internal improvements for western inland waters upon the high plane of patriotism and national interest. At the great Springfield meeting in June, he urged that Illinois be fully represented at Memphis, and the audience responded by naming him as one of the delegates.

The Memphis convention met in July, but it adjourned until November in order to develop a broader representation and a fuller agenda. The most distinguished delegate present was clearly John C. Calhoun, who was unanimously elected president of the meeting. Four days of discussion resulted in the approval of a memorial to Congress which embraced a grand and sweeping design for internal improvements. Questions of constitutional interpretation were wisely kept in the background. While the Illinois delegates secured all they asked for in the memorial, Douglas' insistence that the question was linked with that of Oregon went unrecognized.[13]

The passage by the House of Representatives of a bill organizing a territorial government in Oregon brought the boundary question into its final stage and persuaded even the British that an accord should be sought. The first move was made by Polk in July, when he instructed Secretary of State James Buchanan to offer a settlement along the forty-ninth parallel, little expecting that the offer would be accepted. Although it was not made public, the gesture sparked the rumors of a treaty settlement that swept Illinois in the summer. Richard Pakenham, British minister in Washington, rejected the proposal without referring it to his government. The air was thus cleared for the administration to stand on the Democratic platform's demand for all of Oregon, and so the burden of further negotiation was shifted to the British. Although Polk had misgivings about the validity, and even the wisdom, of the extreme American claim, he believed that his success as a national and party leader depended upon acceptance of the Western expansionist position.[14]

Douglas arrived in Washington in late November, determined to continue his battle for a settlement at 54°40'. The Oregon question weighed heavily on his mind. It was, he wrote, "the great measure of the day." The Washington *Union,* the official organ of the new administration, confidently declared that there would be no wavering among Democrats, and it called on all honest and patriotic Whigs to stand fast as well. The President's message was anxiously awaited. Douglas was almost immediately placed in an advantageous position from which to direct the struggle in the House. In recognition of his deep concern for western expansion and development, he was elected chairman of the Committee on Territories.

To the delight of western Democrats, Polk supported the full American claim. He revealed the offer he had made during the summer but pointed out that it had been extended only "in deference to what had been done by my predecessors." The offer had been rejected, the proposition was withdrawn, and the title to the whole of Oregon was now asserted. The responsibility to maintain this title rested with Congress, Polk advised, and he suggested several ways in which this might be done. The laws of the United States must be extended to the disputed territory, an Indian agency should be established there and blockhouses erected along the trails to protect the emigrants, a monthly overland mail ought to be initiated, and, most important, the joint occupation agreement should be terminated with the required year's notice.[15]

The President's statement was variously interpreted. That Polk did not contemplate war over Oregon seemed obvious to the Whig *National Intelligencer,* while John C. Calhoun, just returned to the Senate by South Carolina, was convinced that "if the recommendation of the Message be carried out into acts, the termination will be war with England." Douglas disagreed with the South Carolinian. "There is no prospect of war," he wrote, "England cannot fight us at this time—she does not risk such a contest." The western expansionists, encouraged by the prospect of full administration support, hastened to carry Polk's recommendations into action. Douglas offered resolutions referring the elements of Polk's message to the appropriate committees, declaring that it was essential that the committees begin their work without delay. For his own Committee on Territories, he reserved Polk's suggestions relating to the protection of Americans in Oregon and to the extension of jurisdiction over the Oregon country.[16]

A flurry of activity followed. A petition from American settlers in Oregon, asking for a territorial government, was read and, on Douglas' motion, referred to the Committee on Territories. A memorial from the legislative committee of Oregon's provisional government, asking that the protection of United States law be extended over the territory, was submitted to the House soon thereafter. Douglas tried to persuade John Quincy Adams to present it, but he was unsuccessful. Missouri's James B. Bowlin introduced legislation organizing a territorial government in Oregon which was practically identical to the bill passed by the House at the last session. It was referred to Douglas' committee, where such a government was already being discussed. On December 19, Douglas himself reported a bill from his committee that would protect the rights of Americans in Oregon. On the last day of December a bill for the construction of forts along the trails to Oregon was reported out of the Committee on Military Affairs. At the same time, a joint resolution giving notice of the termination of the joint occupation agreement was under discussion in the Committee of Foreign Relations.

Possibility of compromise on the boundary question seemed remote as the western expansionists in the House, acting boldly and forcefully, took command of the situation. Calhoun was convinced that a majority in Congress favored peaceful negotiation, but, he moaned, "things have been so managed on our part" that it would be difficult to avoid war with Great Britain. One of Calhoun's correspondents was convinced that the western states desired war with England in order to wipe out their debts to English creditors, and that Douglas, as one of the "heavy land

Holders" in Illinois, was acting solely from selfish motives. Robert Winthrop sought to slow down the momentum of the expansionists with several resolutions declaring that the differences between the United States and Great Britain over Oregon were still subject to negotiation and compromise. No sooner had Winthrop completed his presentation when Douglas was on his feet with two brief resolutions reflecting the western position. The title to any part of the Oregon territory south of 54°40', he insisted, was *"not* open to compromise so as to surrender any part of said territory," and the question "should not be left to arbitration." The two sets of resolutions were not debated, but they served as a confrontation between the two opposing points of view.[17]

Douglas' legislation for the protection of Americans in Oregon won high praise from the administration organ: "Perhaps no bill could have been devised by human ingenuity better calculated to facilitate and stimulate emigration to Oregon," commented the *Union,* "It is one of these masterly measures which indicate a master mind." It encountered a cooler reception among his House colleagues. The bill was characteristically comprehensive, reflecting not only Douglas' broad western outlook, but also his liberal interpretation of the jurisdiction of the territorial committee. He proposed that the laws of Iowa Territory be extended to all of Oregon and that a judge be appointed who could hold court in the disputed area. Grants of land were to be made to settlers, troops raised, blockhouses erected, and officials appointed to administer Indian affairs. The last section of the bill advised the President to give immediate notice to Great Britain of the termination of the joint occupation agreement. Members of the House seemed more disturbed by Douglas' assumption of wide responsibility in the territorial committee than by his declaration that the American right to 54°40' was clear and unquestionable. An unsuccessful attempt was made to recommit various sections of the bill to other committees, but not before Douglas angrily retorted that "there seemed to be a game playing to object to the Oregon bill when it came up, and to say to the Committee on Territories, You have reported on subjects which you ought not to have reported on, and which belong to other committees." As Douglas suspected, it was as much a tactic to delay the expansionists as it was an objection to the scope of his committee.

Debate on the Oregon question did not focus on Douglas' bill; it was provoked by the proposal of the Committee on Military Affairs to raise two regiments of riflemen. Since Douglas' bill also provided for an expansion of the army, a relationship with the Oregon question was immediately drawn. Douglas pressed the debate and suggested the postponement of his own bill so that it would not interrupt the discussion. In calm, considered language he commented on the "terror" the Oregon question held for some of his colleagues. Directing his remarks to southern members of his own party, he expressed the hope that the "same spirit and the same enthusiasm" would be shown on behalf of Oregon as had been displayed on behalf of Texas. The contest with Great Britain over Oregon, he was confident, would prove as bloodless as that with Mexico over Texas had been. Congress need only act firmly and decisively. Douglas encountered opposition from two directions. No action extending American jurisdiction over Oregon could be taken, declared John Quincy Adams, until after notice of the termination of the joint occupation agreement were given—a position in which Douglas later acquiesced. Robert Winthrop, Adams' colleague, objected to any move whatsoever, on the ground that the possibility of negotiation with England had not yet been exhausted. On January 5 the Committee on Foreign Relations reported a joint resolution serving notice to Great Britain, and debate shifted to this new development. Douglas did not enter the discussion until the latter part of the month.[18]

The resolution simply stated that the President should "forthwith cause notice" to be extended to Great Britain that the convention between the two countries would be abrogated. Opponents of Polk and all of Oregon argued that the convention could be terminated only by treaty, but they opposed such action until possibilities of negotiation had been fully explored. Southerners like South Carolina's Robert Barnwell Rhett and Jefferson Davis of Mississippi joined with northern Whigs like Winthrop in repelling the arguments of the expansionists. Joshua Giddings, Ohio's famed abolitionist, and John Quincy Adams supported the western Democrats. Few were as extreme as Douglas, who now pushed his Anglophobia to new lengths.

Much of the ground covered by Douglas in his speech on January 27 was by this time familiar to his audience. His arguments for the annexation of all of Oregon were based upon considerations of manifest destiny as well as upon the importance of the northwest Pacific coast to the commercial growth of the United States, two aspects of the question that were inseparable to Douglas. He emphasized historical precedent and justification, quoting at length from documents that supported his position and revealing the extensive historical research that had come to characterize his speeches. He took exception to the argument that the notice was a hostile measure, tantamount to a declaration of war, and charged his opponents with standing against the only possible peaceable remedy to the contest. Douglas pushed his argument further than he had done before. "I choose to be frank and candid in the declaration of my sentiments on this question," he announced. "For one, I never will be satisfied with the valley of the Columbia, nor with 49°, nor with 54°40', nor will I be, while Great Britain shall hold possession of one acre on the northwest coast of America." England, Douglas argued, never had a valid title "to one inch of that country." "The value of the Oregon territory," he shouted, "is not to be measured by the number of miles upon the coast, whether it shall terminate at 49°, or at 54°40', or reach to 61° and the arctic ocean. It does not depend on the character of the country nor the quality of the soil. It is true, that consideration is not unworthy of attention; but the great point at issue, the great struggle between us and Great Britain, is for the freedom of the Pacific ocean, for the trade of China and of Japan, of the East Indies, and for maritime ascendancy on all these waters." In order to maintain these interests, "we must not only go to 54°40', but we have got to exclude Great Britain from the coast *in toto.*"

Douglas supported his demand by seizing upon a statement made by Polk in his message, in which the President had reasserted the Monroe Doctrine. The United States, Polk had warned, could never consent to the establishment of a European colony on any part of the North American continent. "When I saw that declaration in the President's message," Douglas stated, "I was willing to forgive him from the bottom of my heart for the offer of the 49th parallel in August last." Any treaty with Great Britain fixing the northern boundary of Oregon, whether at 49° or at 54°40', would violate this declaration. Douglas was convinced by Polk's words that no such treaty would be drawn. "He who knows the character of the man—he who knows the stern integrity of his political character—he who knows the consistency of his whole public life —he who knows his fidelity to his principles, must know that, during his four years, this 'settled policy' will not be unsettled by him." Douglas concluded with his familiar admonition to stand fast against Britain's imperial ambitions. Oregon was "the key to the Pacific"; its surrender would guarantee British ascendancy on the seas and, he warned, eventually on the land as well. Douglas' speech placed him among the most extreme and uncompromising of the expansionists.

The debate continued almost daily until both the House members and the public began to weary of it, but Douglas himself took no further part in the discussion. A final vote was taken on February 9 amid much confusion ("cries of '54°40' forever'—clapping of hands and stamping of feet"). The resolution, as finally passed, included a paragraph stating that it should not be construed as interfering with the efforts to negotiate an amicable settlement of the controversy, a statement that must have been repugnant to Douglas. Nevertheless, Douglas cast his vote in favor of passage.[19]

The discussion of the Oregon question in the House was not terminated by the passage of the notice resolution. At least two other measures remained to be disposed of, Douglas' bill for the protection of American settlers in Oregon and the proposal to establish a territorial government in Oregon. Both bills were being discussed in the Committee on Territories. President Polk was impatient with the delay in their consideration, and late in March he conferred with Douglas and others in the White House to emphasize the importance of acting promptly. Neither of the bills, however, inspired Douglas to the full exposition of his views on the Oregon question that had characterized his support of the notice resolution. He had established his position, and there was little need for further elaboration.

Douglas' measure for the protection of Americans in Oregon had been altered by a majority of the territorial committee, over Douglas' protest, to omit specific boundaries. (Douglas had originally prescribed 54°40' as the northern limit of American jurisdiction.) He felt strongly enough about this omission to withhold his signature from the committee report, submitting his own minority report, but he supported the omission on the floor of the House. It was either prescribe no boundaries, he reluctantly admitted, or lose the bill altogether. In a remarkable statement of pragmatic philosophy, Douglas declared that he had learned "if he wished to gain an object, it was sometimes better to yield a little that one might desire, in order to get the support of a majority, rather than being impracticable, and insisisting upon his own peculiar views to hazard the whole, and lose the object he had in view." When asked to reconcile this position with the adamant, uncompromising stand he had taken on the Oregon boundary question, Douglas replied that there were some things—national rights and honor—which could not be compromised. He found, he said, the omission of boundaries in the bill "extremely hard to accept," but had decided that "he might yield something, for the sake of obtaining a greater good hereafter." The good of the country, the safety of Americans on the northwest coast, and the peace of the world demanded this legislation. At the same time, by committing the government to no specific boundary, the bill did not surrender the nation's right to all of Oregon. Douglas struck a neat balance between principle and pragmatism. The bill passed the House on April 18 and was sent to the Senate, where it died.[20]

A sizable group of young southern representatives sided with the western expansionists, but others, following Calhoun's lead, were opposed to pressing the contest with Great Britain or agreed with Georgia's Robert Toombs, who commented privately that "the country is too large now, and I don't want a foot of Oregon or an acre of any other country, especially without 'niggers.' " Such attitudes, Douglas charged, not only violated a solemn party pledge, but also compromised the national honor. He frequently attacked his southern Democratic colleagues for their failure to support the demand for all of Oregon with the same ardor they had displayed for Texas annexation. His pointed allusions and barbed comments produced several sharp exchanges with such men as Alabama's William L. Yancey and George S. Houston, South Carolina's Isaac E. Holmes (recognized as Calhoun's mouthpiece in the House), and James A. Seddon of Virginia. Texas and Oregon, Douglas often emphasized, were equal parts of a single grand scheme, and he had no patience with those who based their manifest destiny on sectional considerations. How, he asked, can members of the House think it "consistent with honor and patriotism to protect that portion of the country's rights that lie in one section of the Union, and abandon that portion of the country's rights that lie in another portion of the Union?" No Democrat, he added, could consent to anything less than 54°40'. When reminded that Polk had offered a settlement on the forty-ninth parallel, he excused the President by pointing out that the government had been pledged to do so by previous negotiations. But a renewal of that offer would be nothing less than "a treasonable proposition." "The negotiation, which Mr. Polk found in progress when he came into office, and by which he was embarrassed, was now ended," Douglas told the House, "and if ever it was commended again upon that principle, in violation of the pledges given by the Democratic party to the American people, sooner let his tongue cleave to the roof of his mouth than he would defend that party which should yield one inch of Oregon."

Such outbursts delighted the Whigs and attracted attention in the press. Douglas, in the heat of debate, vest open and hands hooked in his suspenders, became the object of amused comment, as he took on the southern phalanx, at times questioning even the party loyalty of the great South Carolinian himself. When, following one exchange, Douglas and Yancey exchanged profuse mutual apologies for the charges they had just hurled at one another, the *New-York Tribune* correspondent registered mild disappointment.[21]

Douglas was bound to be trapped by his own extremism on the Oregon question. His demand for 54°40' was not simply a political ploy or a party maneuver; it was a matter of deep conviction, reflecting the emotional expansionism and wild Anglophobia of the western section he represented. Douglas' manifest destiny was not narrowly conceived, nor was it founded solely on idealistic premises, for he saw in national expansion the route to economic and commercial leadership in the world. Great Britain, a reactionary monarchical force in an age of democracy, was America's greatest rival and a threat to her national security. The young Illinois Representative exemplified the fierce devotion to democratic institutions, the deep faith in America's future greatness, and the exciting development of economic and commercial power that characterized his time. These were factors that could not be slowed or compromised. The success of the Texas annexation movement encouraged Douglas to find equal success in an uncompromising stand on Oregon. But Oregon differed markedly from Texas. By ignoring the realities of the diplomatic situation involved in the Oregon controversy, Douglas deprived himself of an important element of political flexibility. His concession to pragmatic politics in April was undoubtedly a reflection of his gradual awakening to some of these realities, as well as a recognition that the demand for all of Oregon was losing its public appeal. He soon retreated from the extremes he had assumed in his January speech.

The negotiation and settlement of the Oregon question was a deep disappointment to Douglas. Indeed, he was stunned by the rapid turn of events during the spring of 1846. The resolution extending notice to Great Britain, as it finally passed both houses of Congress, reflected the conciliatory attitude of the Senate. The result was unacceptable to the western expansionists. John A. McClernand voiced their sentiments when he described the wording as a veiled instruction to the President to seek a compromise and to sacrifice American rights. A great national question, he declared, had been degraded to a "miserable party level." Although the resolution in its final form passed the House of Represen-

tatives by the decisive vote of 142 to 46, all six of Illinois' Democratic
Representatives opposed it. Douglas and his western colleagues, stubborn
to the end, suffered what one correspondent described as "the sorrow of
defeat and the loneliness of desertion."

Events moved quickly following the passage of the resolution. Early in
June 1846, the British responded with a new offer, proposing to settle
the boundary along the forty-ninth parallel with the stipulation that the
Hudson's Bay Company should enjoy free navigation of the Columbia
River south of that line. Polk regarded the offer as unsatisfactory, but
after consulting with his cabinet he submitted the British terms to the
Senate for advice. By a decisive vote, the Senate urged the President to
accept the offer, and on June 15 a treaty was signed by the two nations
settling the boundary. The promptness with which the Senate ratified the
treaty, and the support which it received outside of Congress, indicated
how far the nation had moved from the earlier extreme demands. Only
a hard core of 54°40' men, including Douglas, remained unplaced.
Two days after the treaty was signed Douglas had a long conversation on
the Oregon question with Polk in the White House. The President
explained that he stood on the same ground he had taken in his annual
message and that his actions had been entirely consistent. Douglas was
not convinced.[22]

As a last echo of the Oregon debate, there remained the bill organizing a territorial government for Oregon. Douglas reported the measure
from his committee early in August, but it excited little discussion. It
was, he said, "a simple proposition for the establishment of a territorial
government west of the Rocky Mountains." When some members questioned the omission of specific boundaries for the proposed territory,
Douglas, responding in a curiously subdued manner, declared that he
was ashamed of the boundary settlement at the forty-ninth parallel. He
did not wish to increase the humiliation by recording it in an act of
Congress. The House respected Douglas' disappointment; after approving several amendments, including one that would prohibit slavery in
the new territory, the bill was passed. It died in the Senate for lack of
consideration. "This was too bad," wrote the correspondent of the *National Intelligencer,* "for Judge Douglass had drawn the bill with great
care, and it was a very good bill as it passed the House. I am afraid
there was a little—the least taste in life—fifty-four forty malevolence in this!" [23]

## iv

The Oregon question placed a strain on Democratic party unity at a time when the party could ill afford it. Polk had entered office amid rumblings of discontent among Democrats and predictions of serious party splits. Van Buren's rejection by the Baltimore convention alienated many northern Democrats, some of whom expressed uneasiness lest the new administration be dominated by southern influence. Polk's replacement of Francis Preston Blair's *Globe* with the new *Union,* edited by the Richmond newspaper editor Thomas Ritchie, as the administration organ seemed to signal a break with the past that many Jacksonians found disturbing. Thomas Hart Benton, a Van Buren supporter, emerged as a source of potential opposition to the new President, while southerners sought to strengthen the role of their spokesman, John C. Calhoun, in the administration. Hostility between northern and southern Democrats was growing, Polk was informed, and "a war between them is inevitable." The instability of the party in Illinois, dramatized in the summer of 1845, reflected the condition of the party nationally. Polk's dispensation of the patronage evoked criticism. The new concern for territorial expansion that characterized the 1844 campaign overshadowed the older issues of Jacksonian democracy, marking a transition that was symbolized by the Old Hero's death in June 1845. New alignments were taking shape, and many political observers looked to the twenty-ninth Congress as a testing ground for the contending factions. When the session opened in December, Vice President Dallas predicted that it would be "the most important, disturbed, and protracted" in the nation's history. He was not far wrong.

Polk had been dismayed by the heated and prolonged discussion of the Oregon boundary question. He could not believe that it represented deep-seated convictions. Instead, he was convinced that the struggle involved nothing more than political maneuvering for the next presidential election. Too many Democrats, he confided to his diary, "have been more concerned about the Presidential election in '48, than they have been about settling Oregon either at 49° or 54°40'." The party rivalries and divisions, he feared, would defeat his recommendations and render his administration "unsuccessful and useless." [24]

There were other matters to command Congress' attention. One of these was the final disposition of the Texas question. Others were the

two perennials, the tariff and internal improvements. All three issues excited sectional debate and contributed further to the strain on party
unity.

In his opening message to Congress, Polk announced that the people
of Texas had complied with the terms of the annexation resolution. He
urged that Texas be admitted as a state without delay. On December 10,
Douglas, as chairman of the Committee on Territories, reported a joint
resolution admitting Texas on an equal footing with the original states.
The resolution encountered small but spirited opposition. Massachusetts'
Julius Rockwell, a member of Douglas' committee who had voted
against reporting the resolution, spoke strongly against the admission of
Texas as a slave state. He moved instead that it be recommitted to the
territorial committee with instructions to report an amendment prohibiting slavery in the new state. Rockwell's motion was defeated, and Douglas' resolution passed the House by an overwhelming margin. Douglas
had little to say during the discussion, but he later spoke out sharply and
contemptuously against those who would introduce the slavery question
into House debates. Such agitation, he warned, could only bring harm to
all sections of the country as well as to the slave himself. He had, he declared, "no favor to the fanatics upon either extreme" and would denounce all combinations that sought to "keep up heart-burnings and
jealousies between the North and South." [25]

Aside from announcing his intention to vote for a reduction in the
tariff, Douglas had little to say on the issue. The repeal of the Whig tariff of 1842 was, however, considered one of the important measures of
the session. Its replacement with a revenue tariff, urged by both the
Democratic platform and the President in his message, was considered
essential to the interests of south and west. The people of the west, commented the *Illinois State Register,* had been "defrauded" by the "iniqui-
tous" Whig legislation. "Let their members never cease their efforts until
it is repealed." The opposition of southern members to the extreme demands of the western expansionists, however, raised some doubts about
the degree to which westerners would cooperate with the south in supporting new tariff legislation. "The course pursued by the Southern democracy about Oregon," wrote Georgia's Howell Cobb, who had stood
with the 54°40' men, "has had the effect of alienating the good feelings
of many of our northern and western democrats." But while they said
little in its support, Douglas and other western representatives voted in
the affirmative when the new tariff bill (the so-called Walker tariff)

passed the House early in July. The *Union* exulted that the "free trade states" of the west, burying their disappointment over Oregon, had remained true to their principles and interests. Confident that the 54°40′ men in the Senate would follow the example of their counterparts in the House, the editor declared that he would as soon suspect "Judge Douglass of tergiversation on this great question of the age, as any of these western democrats." Douglas' steadfast adherence to the Democratic party line had become well known. He was, in fact, asked by the President himself to exert his influence on Senator Semple when it was feared one vote might decide the fate of the tariff bill in the Senate.[26]

The price exacted by some westerners for their support of the tariff was equal southern backing for river and harbor improvements. Internal improvements, however, proved to be a poor issue on which to test party unity. Disappointed by their failure to secure federal appropriations during the latter days of Tyler's administration, western supporters of river and harbor improvements struck early in the session. The report of the Memphis convention, over which Calhoun himself had presided, persuaded them that the power and prestige of the South Carolinian would bring the south to their side. Calhoun, seeking unity between south and west, encouraged this belief. Douglas, frustrated and defeated in his earlier attempts to secure appropriations for western improvements, hoped that the connection between the Oregon question and the need for western defenses would bring success to his efforts. The river and harbor improvements bill, however, very soon departed from the relatively simple proposals of the Memphis convention and became a lavish attempt to satisfy the demands of Congressmen eager to please their constituents. Scores of amendments were defeated, including one by Douglas that would have authorized the national government to purchase the Illinois and Michigan Canal from Illinois for military and defensive purposes.

Discussion inevitably became involved in constitutional interpretation, and it soon was obvious that southern support would not be forthcoming. Douglas cited the authorization of Presidents Jefferson, Madison, Monroe, Jackson, and Van Buren for improvements identical to those included in the bill. "There were some powers in the Government that, by this time, ought to be conceded," he suggested. When such powers had been exercised for so long, "the policy which embodied them should at least be considered a settled policy." He disclaimed all support for a general system of internal improvements (that, after all, was Whig doctrine), but he strongly maintained the constitutionality of the improvement of rivers, harbors, and navigable waters. Not everyone could see a distinction. His argument only embroiled him in heated discussions with southern representatives over the definition of Democratic principles.

Southerners were not the only ones who took exception to the bill. There were signs of defection in the western ranks as well. The *State Register* complained of the many unsound items included in the legislation, and when the bill came to a vote two members of the Illinois delegation, McClernand and Ficklin, voted against it. Southern Illinois was not prepared to join with the north on this issue. The bill passed the House with only minimal southern support and eventually cleared the Senate. Predictably, President Polk, after having consulted with several western representatives, including McClernand, returned the legislation with his veto.

The veto of the river and harbor improvements bill was the second blow suffered by Douglas at the hands of the President. Soon after the veto message was read to the House, Douglas responded. There was nothing in the message, he said, that would cause him to change his opinion regarding the bill. He found Polk's constitutional position on internal improvements to be "sound and orthodox." Douglas agreed that the government was one of limited powers, "possessing none except those which were expressly granted, or were necessary to carry the enumerated powers into effect." He was, he declared, prepared to adopt this "construction" with respect to rivers and harbors as well as "banks, tariff, distribution, and all the other great measures of the day." But what puzzled Douglas was the application of these constitutional principles to the works provided for in the bill. Polk, he charged, had not made clear the extent to which the provisions of the bill violated his constitutional scruples. Although he conceded that some of its terms were objectionable even to him (the appropriation for the improvement of the St. Louis harbor, for example), Douglas found the bill in the main sound and defensible. He rejected any distinction between foreign and domestic commerce, between salt and fresh water, and argued that Congress had a constitutional right to protect commerce on all navigable waters, seaboard and inland. He feared that the veto implied a discrimination against the west. "The West will never submit to an odious and unjust discrimination," Douglas warned, "which lavishes millions on the seaboard, and excludes the lakes and rivers from all participation. They must all be placed on the same footing, and share alike in the favors and burdens of government." [27]

Douglas found little support for his stand against the veto. Back home, the *State Register* defended the President's action. If he erred, "he erred on the side of safety." Other Democratic papers in the state followed the *Register*'s example. Douglas' own statements on the veto struck one Whig editor as anomalous, for they "evince a purpose not to go with the President, nor yet to break from him." The comment accurately described Douglas' dilemma. On both the Oregon question and the river and harbor improvements issue, he had suffered defeat and disappointment. The disappointment was all the more painful because in each case defeat had been administered by a Democratic President. Yet he could not split with the party leadership; he could only swallow his frustration and look for new causes.

Douglas could and did recover quickly. In spite of these setbacks he enjoyed greater prominence than ever before, both in Illinois and in the national capital. His party, beset with factional rivalries and threatened with disunity, was not so fortunate. Although the Washington *Union* declared the session to be the "most successful first Congressional session of a new administration in the history of the country," the cracks were showing. The *Union* was not unaware of the dangers ahead. The party, it warned, must follow the principles of the Constitution, not the "factiousness of men." [28]

# IX

## "A just war"
## 1846—1847

i

Douglas, recalled Alabama Congressman Henry W. Hilliard, was "already one of the leading members of the House" when Hilliard first took his seat in December 1845. Although small, Douglas was "distinctly a man of large faculties," impressing Hilliard with his strength, activity, and unaffected manner. He appeared younger than his thirty-two years; "his boyish appearance, his ready wit, his fine memory, his native rhetoric, above all, his suavity and heartiness" made him a favorite among his fellow Congressmen. Newspaper correspondents often made much of his short stature and frequently made Douglas the target of amused comment. But all agreed that the second-term Congressman had proved a formidable foe in debate; his sobriquet "Little Giant" was well merited.

For all his youth and inexperience, Douglas' reputation as a party leader was in rapid ascent. When the twenty-ninth Congress opened, his name was advanced as a candidate for Speaker of the House, on the ground, in part, that the post should go to a westerner. John W. Davis of Indiana was elected instead, but Douglas was entrusted with the chairmanship of the territorial committee, a large responsibility for a newcomer to Congress at a time when territorial matters occupied an increasing share of Congress' attention. His deep involvement in the issues facing the national legislators also brought him recognition from the White House. Although Douglas was greatly disturbed with some of the President's positions, Polk was impressed with the young Illinois Representative. Douglas was frequently called to the White House for consultation, and on one such visit the President "told him that he could, if he would, lead the Democratic party in the House. " [1]

Douglas' growing prestige in Washington strengthened his position at home and rendered his renomination and re-election to a third term in Congress a certainty. For Fifth District Democrats, the nominating convention in Rushville in January 1846 was a mere formality. Douglas was unanimously selected and his "unwavering course in sustaining democratic principles" enthusiastically approved. Outside the district, William Walters strongly urged Douglas' re-election in the editorial columns of the *State Register*. Douglas, Walters wrote, had acquired a high reputation in Congress and had raised Illinois "to a proud eminence in the estimation of the Democracy of the Union." His inflexible stand on the Oregon question and his support of a revenue tariff were singled out as strong reasons for his re-election.

The Whigs made only a half-hearted attempt to unseat Douglas. Isaac Vandeventer, defeated earlier for the state legislature, was nominated, but the campaign in his behalf was lackluster and desultory. The most serious charge leveled against Douglas was the old complaint that he had never identified himself with his district, spending most of his time when not in Congress "in the large cities, or at places where he can the more conveniently enjoy life." The interests of his constituents were neglected, the Whigs charged, by Douglas' "desire to soar above the clouds on some national question." Douglas was unable to campaign in his district, since Congress remained in session beyond election day, but he was re-elected with a higher proportion of the vote than he had received two years before.[2]

Douglas' election to a third congressional term was little more than insurance against his political future, for in 1846 his eye was fixed on election to the United States Senate. His name had been prominently mentioned in the last two senatorial contests, but he had preferred to bide his time until his election could be assured. The groundwork was carefully laid, and, if the widely circulated reports can be credited, he had arranged for the support of both the incumbent Senators, Sidney Breese and James Semple. In the fall of 1846, Semple announced that he would not be a candidate for re-election. "I was never so sick in all my life as at present," he wrote shortly after the adjournment of Congress. "We have not yet heard a word of who is likely to take my place here, but suppose it will be Douglas." Breese wrote that there was no doubt of Douglas' election, an opinion with which Douglas modestly agreed.

Douglas began his campaign early, and it quickly became obvious that he would brook no opposition in his effort to be elected. The extent of his power and the organization of his followers was soon felt. "Dug's friends *feel confident,* that no combination of circumstances can arise to prevent his election to the Senate," commented one Whig as early as January 1845. Douglas shared this confidence, but he was determined to leave nothing to chance. He returned to Illinois in the fall and traveled extensively throughout the state, talking and corresponding with his supporters and with members of the state legislature. "This contest will be a good lesson to teach me my real friends," he wrote. All threats of rival candidacies, he decided, should be eliminated.[3]

Governor Ford, who denied that he was a candidate, charged that Douglas had deliberately aroused opposition against his administration, "lest I might be in his way." Douglas was more concerned with rumors of a secret movement to prevent his election by persuading several men from different parts of the state, among them former Senator Richard M. Young, to announce their candidacies after he left for Washington. Young's potential candidacy was dealt with in characteristic fashion by the Little Giant. Early in the following January, Douglas, in the company of Sidney Breese, called on President Polk to urge Young's appointment as Commissioner of the General Land Office. Polk, after some hesitation, finally yielded, but only after Douglas assured him that Young's appointment was the unanimous desire of the Illinois delegation in Congress. The Senate confirmed the appointment within hours after Young's name had been sent in. That evening, Polk received three angry Illinois representatives, including John A. McClernand, protesting that Young's name had been proposed without their knowledge. McClernand charged that Douglas had made a bargain with Young by which the latter promised not to oppose him for the Senate. Polk was disgusted with Douglas' conduct, but was unable to withdraw the nomination. Both Illinois Senators, he wrote, "have acted badly towards the delegation and towards me. There has been a want of fairness and open dealing in the matter that is unworthy of members of Congress." [4]

The opposition which Douglas feared most was that threatened by McClernand, whose voice in southern Illinois was especially strong, but by mid-November even this threat seemed to have dissipated. Douglas' prospects became increasingly more certain. "Douglass will be elected easy," predicted Charles H. Lanphier, Walters' successor as editor of the

*Register.* The public mind, wrote another correspondent, had clearly settled in Douglas' favor. Still Douglas did not relax. "I have learned," he wrote state supreme court justice John D. Caton, "that a candidate is never in so much danger as when he and his friends regard his success as perfectly sure." To be beaten, he confided, "would not only be a defeat, but would be followed by much more serious consequences to myself, and greatly impair my power of usefulness to my party & country." Douglas regarded his election to the Senate as a crossroads in his career, and he was desperate for success.[5]

Douglas need not have worried. His organizational efforts paid off when, in December 1846, he was unanimously nominated by the Democratic caucus of the legislature. No other Democrat dared oppose him. A short time later he was elected United States Senator, defeating his Whig opponent by the lopsided vote of 100 to 45. Reporting the result, the *New-York Tribune* correspondent noted that the "Little Giant has at last reached the goal of his ambition." The night of the election, Douglas' supporters celebrated their triumph with the largest levee ever held in Springfield, the arrangements for which had been made by Douglas before he left for Washington. Eating, drinking, and dancing continued until early morning, and when the party was over, Douglas was poorer by $1500. In a special election later in 1847, William A. Richardson, a former Schuyler county legislator who had been handpicked by Douglas, was elected by Fifth District voters to Douglas' vacant seat in the House.[6]

ii

Relations between the United States and Mexico had been deteriorating for some time before James K. Polk assumed the presidency in March 1845. Several issues, dating back many years, had placed unusual strains on relations between the two countries, but it was the question of Texas annexation that produced the final crisis during Polk's first year in office. Unreconciled to the loss of Texas in 1836, Mexico regarded its annexation by the United States as an act of hostility, and, soon after the passage of the annexation resolution, it broke off diplomatic relations. Mexican bitterness was increased by disagreement over the Texas boundary. Following its achievement of independence, Texas claimed the Rio Grande as its southern and western boundary, a claim which the United States assumed with annexation. For Mexico, all of Texas was still national territory, but, practically, she insisted that Texas' boundaries were those which had prevailed before 1836—the Nueces River, not the Rio Grande.

Texas formally accepted annexation on July 4, 1845. Soon afterward, United States army troops, commanded by Zachary Taylor, were ordered into Texas with instructions to extend federal protection to the area west of the Nueces. Although Texas had never established effective control over the disputed area, it became clear that the United States would assert its claim to the Rio Grande boundary. Mexico responded with demands for an immediate declaration of war against the United States, and measures were taken to increase Mexican military strength. During the summer of 1845, rumors that a Mexican invasion of Texas was imminent circulated throughout the United States.

During that summer, as relations between the United States and Mexico approached the breaking point, Douglas was home with his constituents, making speeches for all of Oregon. He recognized the impact that war with Mexico might have on the success of his own expansionist program and was determined not to miss the opportunity afforded by the rapidly moving events. On August 21 he wrote to President Polk from Quincy that "we are inclined to the opinion that the next mail will bring the news of a declaration of war." He proposed that a regiment be raised from among the mountain men and Santa Fe traders, individuals familiar with the Rocky Mountains and the southwest, to march immediately for Santa Fe and California. Writing again to Polk four days later, Douglas assumed that hostilities between the two nations had already begun. He urged the President to repel any Mexican invasion of Texas and to inflict such punishment on Mexico "as will teach them to respect our rights in the future." A war with Mexico, however, should not be confined to defensive operations. "The Northern Provinces of Mexico including California," he wrote, "ought to belong to this Republic, and the day is not far distant when such a result will be accomplished. The present is an auspicious time." Again he urged that an expedition be raised immediately to occupy New Mexico and California. "Such a movement will meet with the enthusiastic support of the whole west." Momentarily diverted from his campaign for all of Oregon, Douglas asked Polk for authority to raise a regiment of Illinois volunteers.[7]

Reports of the opening of hostilities, however, proved to be premature. Polk had learned that the Mexican government was willing to negotiate the difficulties between the two nations. Anxious to avoid war if

possible, he appointed John Slidell, a member of Congress from Louisiana, as minister to Mexico, with a view to the resumption of diplomatic relations and the settlement of the grievances on both sides. One
of the objects of Slidell's mission, Polk wrote in his diary, would be the
adjustment of the boundary through the purchase "for a pecuniary consideration" of Upper California and New Mexico. In his official instructions, Slidell was empowered to offer a cancellation of unpaid claims
against Mexico in return for Mexican recognition of the Rio Grande
boundary. Polk's plans encountered difficulties almost immediately.
When the nature of Slidell's mission became known in Mexico, opinion
there turned against the government for encouraging what was regarded
as an insult to Mexican independence and integrity. Slidell was not received, but this was not enough to save the government. While the
American envoy waited, convinced of Mexican bad faith, the government was toppled in a swift and successful revolution and was replaced
by a more bellicose leadership. After additional delays, Slidell was rebuffed a second time. America's course of action with respect to the annexation of Texas, he was told, was not and could not be a subject for
negotiation.

News of Slidell's rejection by the Mexican government was received
by Polk with annoyance and impatience. The Oregon question was as
yet unresolved, and Congress was in the midst of debate on the termination of the joint occupation agreement. War with the British still
seemed a possibility. Nevertheless, Polk acted without hesitation. Taylor's army was ordered to take up positions along the Rio Grande, but
beyond that Polk was for the moment unwilling to go. When Congress
passed the joint resolution on Oregon giving notice to Great Britain,
and the British government responded with its proposal that the boundary be negotiated, the peaceful settlement of the Oregon question
seemed imminent. Slidell, back in Washington, advised the President "to
take the redress of the wrongs and injuries which we had so long borne
from Mexico into our own hands." Polk promised that a message on the
subject would soon be sent to Congress.

On May 9, dispatches from Taylor arrived in the national capital, describing the first clash between Mexican and American troops, a patrol
action in the disputed territory east of the Rio Grande in which the
United States suffered its first casualties. A week before, Douglas had
complained that "all yet remains in doubt & uncertainty" and that "the
intentions of the administration in this respect are a profound secret."

"We are," he wrote, "in a state of quasi war with that country, and are left to conjecture as to what is to be the sequel." He expected "a crisis soon." Polk's intentions became clear on May 11, when he sent his war message to Congress. Reviewing the accumulated grievances between the two countries, the President declared that "after reiterated menaces, Mexico has passed the boundary of the United States, has invaded our territory, and shed American blood upon the American soil." "As war exists, and, notwithstanding all our efforts to avoid it, exists by the act of Mexico herself," he continued, "we are called upon, by every consideration of duty and patriotism, to vindicate, with decision, the honor, the rights, and the interests of our country." [8]

Congress responded to the President's statement with alacrity and enthusiasm. On the day before, Sunday, the House Committee on Military Affairs agreed on legislation appropriating $10 million and authorizing the enlistment of 50,000 volunteer troops to meet the emergency. The next afternoon, following the President's message, the bill was amended to recognize that "by the act of the Republic of Mexico, a state of war exists between that Government and the United States." Within an hour, it was passed by an overwhelming margin, with only fourteen negative votes. "The entire national sentiment was exhibited . . . in the House of Representatives," wrote Vice President Dallas. Sent to the Senate, the measure encountered opposition from John C. Calhoun. Denying that the President had the power to declare war, the South Carolina Senator insisted that time be taken to read and examine all the documents supporting Polk's message. His protests were unavailing. The bill passed the Senate with minor amendments, was approved by the House later the same day, and on Wednesday, May 13, received the President's signature. [9]

Having obliged Polk with a declaration of war, the House then debated the issues involved. Ohio's Columbus Delano, one of the fourteen opponents, denounced the conflict as an "illegal, unrighteous, and damnable war" and complained that no debate had been allowed on the bill. "If the people had any common sense," he concluded, "they would hold responsible the authors of this war, which was conceived in fraud, and was to be consummated in iniquity." Delano's remarks stirred Douglas to an angry rebuttal. Apologetic that his statement was "desultory and without preparation," he delivered a long, impassioned, and bold defense of the administration's Mexican policy. "Patriotism emanates from the heart," he declared, "it fills the soul; inspires the whole man with a devotion to his country's cause." Those who condemned the justice of the war, he charged, were "traitors in their hearts." "Patriots may differ as to the expediency of a declaration of war, or the wisdom of a course of policy which may probably lead to such a result," he continued, "but honor and duty forbid divided counsels after our country has been invaded, and American blood has been shed on American soil by a treacherous foe." Partisan strife should be subordinated to "the triumph of our country." Citing documents and reading from books that he had at hand, Douglas reviewed America's relations with Mexico to show that ample cause for war had existed for years, independent of the incident on the Rio Grande frontier. The repeated insults, indignities, and injuries perpetrated by Mexicans against the United States had been met with patience and forbearance, but with little effect.

Douglas focused on the principal argument of the war's opponents —that the Rio Grande was not in fact the boundary between Texas and Mexico. On the contrary, he pointed out, Texas was always understood to be a part of the Louisiana Purchase, its western boundary clearly recognized as the Rio Grande by both the French and Spanish. "A multitudinous collection of old maps and musty records, histories and geographies" would attest to this fact. The clincher, however, was a statement made by John Quincy Adams in a dispatch written in 1819 when he was Secretary of State: "our title as far as the Rio del Norte [Rio Grande] was as clear as to the island of New Orleans." Was the "venerable gentleman from Massachusetts" engaged in "an unholy, unrighteous, and damnable cause" when he thus demonstrated the American title to the Rio Grande boundary? But, Douglas continued, justification of the nation's position rested on "better and higher evidence." The Republic of Texas had held the disputed territory "by virtue of a successful revolution—a declaration of independence, setting forth the inalienable rights of man—triumphantly maintained by the irresistible power of her arms, and consecrated by the precious blood of her glorious heroes." At the conclusion of that revolution, Mexico herself had recognized the validity of the Texas claim.

Douglas' remarks drew him into an exchange with Adams, to the delight of the gallery and not altogether to the credit of the aged statesman. "The contrast was marked," wrote one witness, "between the feeble and bald-headed statesman and the boyish face and figure of the black-eyed and black-haired partisan." Adams had voted against the declaration of war and had expressed his approval of Delano's strictures against the war party. When Douglas quoted his 1819 statement in support of the American claim to the Rio Grande, the ex-president was caught off guard. That dispatch, he replied to Douglas, had been written when he was Secretary of State. He had simply "endeavored to make out the best case I could for my own country, as it was my duty." He had not, in any case, claimed the river in its full extent as the boundary. "I only claimed it a short distance up the river, and then diverged to the northward some distance from the stream." When pressed by Douglas to name the point at which the boundary left the river, Adams conceded that he had never specified the exact spot. Douglas reminded him that he had claimed the river as the boundary in general terms, without qualification; even under Adams' interpretation the area which had been occupied by General Taylor's troops was clearly within the United States. Adams then denied that Mexico's recognition of the Rio Grande boundary after the Texas Revolution had any validity, because Santa Anna was a prisoner and under duress when he signed the treaty. "It is a strange doctrine," Adams contended, "that the acts of a prisoner, while in duress, are to be deemed valid after he has recovered his liberty." But, Douglas countered, how else can treaties of peace be concluded with conquered nations? Are defeated governments incompetent to make peace because they are in duress? Douglas reminded the Massachusetts Congressman that he was confusing the "legal maxims relative to civil contracts" with transactions between nations. The rights of a nation, in time of war, "are not identical with those of a citizen, under the municipal laws of his own country, in a state of peace." Was not Santa Anna's treaty with Texas later repudiated by Mexico? asked Adams. Douglas readily conceded the fact, but he observed that he was not aware of any treaty or compact entered into by Mexico that had not afterward been repudiated. This was, he declared, precisely one of the nation's grievances against its southern neighbor. Douglas had the last word. It was a new experience, commented one observer, to see John Quincy Adams in retreat.

Both Delano and Adams taunted Douglas for his extreme position on the Oregon question, pointing out that even his own party did not support him. Douglas rose to the bait with a familiar expression of fealty to the Union. He was as willing, he said, to fight for 54°40' as he was to fight for the Rio Grande. "My patriotism is not of that kind which would induce me to go to war to enlarge one section of the Union out of mere hatred and vengeance towards the other." "To me," he emphasized, "our country and all its parts are one and indivisible."

"One of the most successful and triumphant of any he has delivered in the House," observed the *State Register* of Douglas' speech, proving that Douglas was equal to a contest with "Old Man Eloquent." Printed, it was circulated in many parts of the country and was thought to be particularly effective in persuading "wavering Whigs" to support the administration.[10]

Illinoisans greeted the outbreak of the war as zealously as did Douglas, even reflecting his admonition that partisanship should be submerged in the spirit of patriotism. "The enthusiasm of the people is unbounded," declared one Whig editor. Whigs throughout the nation, boasted the *Sangamo Journal,* "have united in the support of the war with all their power and influence." Leaders in both parties urged citizens of the state to respond to Governor Ford's May 25 proclamation calling for thirty companies of volunteers. Within ten days the quota was filled. By mid-summer, seventy-five companies had been raised, "each furious to go." When entire companies were refused because facilities to care for them were lacking, the men were bitter and resentful of the authorities. Illinois ultimately sent six regiments to Mexico, two more than had been originally authorized.

Among those supporting the war was Douglas' long-time Whig opponent, John J. Hardin. In spite of their many encounters the two had become good friends, and the war seemed to cement their friendship. Since early February, Hardin had been corresponding with Douglas about the impending conflict with Mexico. He was anxious, he wrote, that the United States acquire California, by force if necessary, and suggested that an expedition of mounted riflemen be sent over the Santa Fe trail to accomplish the task. In the face of repeated Mexican insults, the United States had no alternative but to declare war. Offering his services, he asked Douglas' aid in securing a commission. "I take it for granted," Douglas replied, "that you will have a high command," and added, "I shall claim to be your Representative during this war." Hardin assumed command of one of Illinois' regiments, and less than a year later he was fatally wounded at Buena Vista.[11]

Douglas exerted his influence with the President to press for the appointment of personal and party friends to military offices. On at least one occasion Polk was compelled to restrain Douglas' ardor for limiting the appointments to faithful Democrats. "I told him that we were at war with a Foreign country and that I thought it improper to make politics a test in appointments in the army," Polk wrote. His greatest problems in the matter of military appointments, the President later confided, were with the Illinois delegation. Against Polk's advice, Douglas' close friend, James Shields, resigned his post as Commissioner of the General Land Office to accept a commission as brigadier general of volunteers, and for a time Senator Semple considered leaving Congress for the battlefield. The state's lone Whig in the lower house, Edward Dickinson Baker, resigned his seat to accept the command of one of Illinois' volunteer regiments. The contagion soon affected the Little Giant himself. A brief remark in one of Hardin's letters triggered Douglas' imagination: "Cant you adjourn Congress and go along with us?" [12]

That Douglas gave serious thought to Hardin's suggestion was immediately evident. "I hope to be with you in some capacity," he responded to Hardin on June 16, "a high privates place will suit me about as well as anything." Douglas' modesty, however, was short-lived. A few days later, several members of the Illinois delegation called on the President to recommend Douglas for brigade major. Hardin was delighted. "I am exceedingly pleased with the expression of your determination to join my command," Hardin wrote, later reporting that all of his officers as well "seem pleased with your joining us." The President, however, interceded. Summoning Douglas to the White House, Polk asked him to withdraw his application and urged him to remain at his seat in Congress. He objected to the appointment of members of Congress to offices created by their own votes, he told Douglas, but it is also likely that he recognized Douglas' value in Congress and was reluctant to lose such an ardent supporter of the war. Douglas, Polk noted, "is a sensible man, and he received what I said to him well." Within a few hours, Douglas withdrew his application. [13]

The report that Douglas sought a military appointment raised some eyebrows, since it coincided with his attack on Polk's role in the Oregon settlement. "How dearly these 54°40' froth-spouters love the people," exclaimed the *New-York Tribune* correspondent, "and how much they would sacrifice for securing our territory against alienation, when their mouths are thus hermetically sealed against Executive delinquency by the degrading acceptance of office." Reactions at home were equally strong. "Mr. Polk, it would seem," wrote the editor of the *Sangamo Journal*, "is taking the most effectual means to dispose of the 'phifty-

fore-phorties.' " Douglas' pursuit of spoils, he concluded, proved his willingness to abandon consistency and honor. In order to spike such reactions, Douglas penned a letter for circulation in the Illinois press. He
would not, he assured his followers, abandon his seat in Congress to go
to Mexico. "When I heard of so many of my friends volunteering their
services, I felt a very strong desire to go with them." "One night's reflection," he added, "convinced me that I ought not to vacate my seat in
Congress even for a portion of the remnant of the session to accept that
or any other appointment." [14]

iii

Members of Congress enjoyed only a brief respite between the first
and second sessions of the twenty-ninth Congress. The first session had
been a remarkably full one, and the people demanded information and
explanations. The final resolution of the Texas issue, the settlement of
the Oregon boundary, the declaration of war against Mexico, and the
passage of internal improvement and tariff legislation focused attention
on the nation's lawmakers. The retreat from $54°40'$ and the veto of the
river and harbor bill had aroused the ire of western Democrats, and
many Congressmen returned to Washington smarting from the attacks
of their constituents. "The western members," observed one paper, "are
dead against Polk." No one was more aware of the situation than the
President himself. Harmony and concert of action among Democrats, he
confided, had disappeared. "In truth faction rules the hour, while principle & patriotism is forgotten."

Douglas, returning to Washington strong and confident, was an exception. Re-elected to a third House term before the last session had
ended, he had made a quick trip to Georgia to attend the wedding of
fellow Congressman Orlando B. Ficklin, then returned to Illinois to lay
the groundwork for his election to the Senate. The second session was
barely under way when his efforts bore fruit. "Douglas feels well since
his election to the Senate," commented one Washington correspondent,
"A contented smile plays round his mouth and lights up his
countenance." [15]

Although his earlier disappointment with Polk had been acute, Douglas assumed the role of defender of Polk's war measures in the House.
On numerous occasions he was summoned to the White House to confer
with the President on matters relating to wartime legislation. Douglas
was one of several House members whose advice Polk sought on his pro-

posal to revive the rank of lieutenant general. "I explained to them my embarrassment in conducting the war with the present officers," Polk wrote. He discussed his objections to Zachary Taylor and Winfield Scott and the "impossibility of conducting the War successfully when the General in Chief of the army did not sympathize with the Government." Douglas appreciated Polk's dilemma, but, with his colleagues, he saw little hope for legislation that would authorize the appointment of a lieutenant general over Taylor and Scott. When the issue came before the House he voted in the affirmative, but Polk's proposal went down to defeat.

Douglas later defended the President against charges of hostility toward Taylor. A resolution thanking Taylor for his capture of Monterrey, with a Democratic amendment justifying the war, provoked a vigorous discussion of the administration's attitude toward Taylor, as well as a debate over the purposes of the conflict. Whigs angrily accused the administration of sacrificing Taylor "to the purposes of the President and the party" and spoke out boldly against the war itself. Douglas sprang to Polk's defense. Frequently interrupted by cries of "Go it, Douglass," he rebutted the conspiracy charge and defended the justice of the Mexican War. It was a "greater honor," he pointed out, "to thank General Taylor for his gallantry in a just war than in an expedition for plunder." If the statement that the war was being fought "in defence of the honor and vindication of the just rights of the United States" were withheld, then Congress would be branding Taylor as "a pirate and a bandit." The Whigs, though momentarily silenced, were not persuaded by the circumlocutions of Douglas' logic.[16]

As chairman of the Committee on Territories, Douglas expressed special concern for the organization of civil governments in the occupied portions of New Mexico and California. Polk, in his annual message, had requested appropriations to defray the costs of maintaining American authority in the occupied areas, a request his opponents interpreted as a recommendation for permanent possession before a treaty was made. When General Kearny declared New Mexico to be a part of the United States and established a government there, members of Congress questioned the President's right to authorize military officers to set up civil governments in conquered territory. Was Polk, asked one Congressman, "an emperor, sending forth his Agrippa and his Marcellus as his proconsuls, to establish and govern the provinces they might conquer by force of arms?"

Douglas again defended the President. Mexican government in the occupied areas, he pointed out, had been superseded, and the military commanders had an imperative duty to replace it, in conformity "with the universal usage of civilized nations when engaged in war." One of the rights "growing out of conquest was to govern the subdued provinces in a temporary and provisional manner, until the home Government should establish a government in another form." Whether or not Polk had authorized the organization of the government was immaterial. Although Polk later conceded that General Kearny had exceeded his authority, he did not contradict Douglas' statement. Instead he called Douglas to the White House to inform him confidentially of his position, so that Douglas "might be prepared to meet any attacks which might be made by the opposition." Whig opponents of the war sneeringly dismissed the Illinois Representative as "the pliant apologist of party and power." Douglas, they said, could never achieve the heights of statesmanship as long as he "shows himself in White-house livery, cracking the Executive whip in the face of those who oppose its usurpations." [17]

Douglas believed that measures relating to the prosecution of the war held precedence over all other legislation. He expressed annoyance when other issues distracted members of the House. When the backers of internal improvement legislation tried a second time to pass a river and harbor bill, Douglas had little to say except that he favored the measure. Polk vetoed the bill a second time, but Douglas made no comment. Later he told the President that he disagreed with him on the question of river and harbor improvements, but that "he felt no great interest on the subject." [18] Douglas' accommodation with Polk, however, did not extend to the administration's organ, the Washington *Union*. When the *Union* attacked John Wentworth for opposing Polk's proposal for a tax on coffee and tea, Douglas bristled, and, while he disagreed with Wentworth, he defended his colleague against the attacks. It was a small matter, but Douglas, in the mood for a fight, developed it into a large and time-consuming issue, leading the House into the very distraction he so deplored. Douglas, chortled one Whig, "whose neck is somewhat chafed by wearing the Executive collar, intends to come out against the Executive organ." Douglas, maintaining that the *Union*'s comments had brought the entire House into disgrace and contempt, persuaded the House to appoint an investigating committee, with himself as its chairman. His anger soon cooled, however, and the investigation was never made. One House member politely informed Douglas that this time "prejudice had somewhat got the better of the gentleman's uniformly good judgment." [19]

### iv

In the waning moments of the first session, on August 8, 1846, President Polk sent a special message to the House of Representatives, asking that an appropriation of $2 million be placed at his disposal to compensate Mexico for concessions that might be made in a peace treaty. In the confusion of the usual last-minute attempts to dispose of unfinished business, a bill granting the President's request was introduced.

The circumstances of the hour were not conducive to serious and reasoned discussion. The President's proposal had come without warning, and some members thought the subject too important to crowd into the session's last efforts. Many Congressmen were anxious to leave for their homes after an unusually long and tiring session. It was an election year, and some of them had not yet had an opportunity to campaign among their constituents. The air was hot and oppressive; the humidity had turned the House into a steam bath. The bill was brought up for debate in the evening, as newspaper fans fluttered and shouts for ice water interrupted the business.

The bill came under immediate Whig attack. Although they wished to hasten the conclusion of peace, the Whigs viewed Polk's request as a move to convert the conflict from a defensive war to one for the acquisition of territory. The uses to which the sum would be put had not been defined by the President, declared New York Congressman Hugh White, nor had any evidence been suggested that the additional money was necessary. Suspecting that it might be applied to the acquisition of territory from Mexico, White expressed his opposition to the appropriation unless it could be "so amended as to forever preclude the possibility of extending the limits of slavery." White's objections were echoed by Robert Winthrop, who added that he was "uncompromisingly opposed to extending the slaveholding territory of the Union."

After some additional discussion, David Wilmot took the floor. The young Pennsylvania Democrat answered the Whig charges, defending the necessity of the war and denying that it was a war of conquest. However, he had no objection to the acquisition of territory "provided it were done on proper conditions." Wilmot agreed that under no circumstances should slavery be extended. "If free territory comes in," he

argued, "God forbid that he [I] should be the means of planting this institution upon it." As he concluded his remarks, he offered an amendment to the appropriation bill, the famous Wilmot Proviso, that slavery
should never exist in any territory acquired from Mexico.

The debate continued on into the night. The galleries gradually filled
as spectators sensed that something important was going on, and several
cabinet members appeared in the House. Nearly every Congressman was
on his feet. Several northern members declared their support for Wilmot's amendment, while a South Carolinian regarded it as premature
and irrelevant to the President's request. John Quincy Adams rose.
While the members crowded around to catch his words, he expressed his
approval of Wilmot's amendment, but announced that he would support the appropriation in any case, with or without the Proviso. As the
hour for adjournment approached, a number of amendments was defeated in favor of a modified version of the appropriation bill with Wilmot's amendment attached. The House then passed it by a close vote.
Although the bill was sent immediately to the Senate, it was brought up
too close to adjournment to be given the consideration it demanded, and
it died.[20]

Douglas took no part in the debate on either the appropriation bill or
on Wilmot's amendment. His position on the Proviso, however, was consistent throughout. He voted for laying the amended measure on the
table, against the bill's engrossment, and against its final passage. In all
instances he was on the losing side. On the final vote, he was one of only
four northern Democrats to oppose passage.

The approval of the Wilmot Proviso had its origin in the growing opposition of disgruntled western Democrats and unreconciled Van Buren-
ites to the Polk administration. Those who supported the Proviso, commented the *State Register,* were "not governed in their course by a love
of the slave or a horror of the extension of the 'area of slavery,' but by
an inveterate hatred of the administration." The veto of the river and
harbor improvements bill and the defeat of the western expansionists on
the Oregon boundary question were traced to growing southern power
in the government and provoked many Democrats to revolt. The Wilmot Proviso enabled western Democrats to express their resentment
against Polk, without at the same time surrendering their desire for territorial expansion. Yet Douglas, a leader in the struggle for all of Oregon and one of the most outspoken critics of Polk's stand on the boundary question, refused to join the revolt. In spite of his disappointments,

he could not support a measure he was convinced would splinter the party. He was more aware than most politicians of southern power in the administration, but to counter it with the Proviso was to encourage the very sectional forces he feared. Moreover, it introduced a dangerous element into political discussion. The agitation of the slavery question, Douglas had argued, was unwise, improvident, and a dangerous distraction from the nation's more pressing problems. The New York *Herald* echoed Douglas' anxiety. The slavery question, the paper predicted, would be the ground for a coming sectional contest, "the absorbing element of all the elements in dispute between the North and the South." Polk, like Douglas, was dismayed with Wilmot's "mischievous & foolish amendment." "What connection slavery had with making peace with Mexico," he confided, "it is difficult to conceive." [21]

The full impact of the Wilmot Proviso was not felt in the House until the next session, when Douglas renewed his efforts to provide Oregon with a territorial government. He reintroduced his earlier bill, which prohibited slavery in the proposed territory, and it was taken up for discussion by the House early in January 1847. The slavery prohibition had excited little comment in the last moments of the previous session, but the Wilmot Proviso intervened in the meantime, and it changed the picture. The slavery question as it related to Oregon now became a live issue. Douglas attempted to push it into the background by pointing out that the extension of the Northwest Ordinance to Oregon automatically prohibited slavery, but southern representatives were not to be stilled. Eager to strip the Wilmot Proviso of its force, they insisted that Douglas base the slavery prohibition on the fact that Oregon lay north of 36°30', and they urged that the principle of the Missouri Compromise be applied to the territories on the Pacific. Supporters of the Proviso objected. The Missouri Compromise, declared Maine's Hannibal Hamlin, "had no more application to the Territory of Oregon than it had with the East Indies," an early announcement that for some northerners the Missouri Compromise principle could no longer serve as an answer to the problem of slavery and expansion. Nevertheless, Armistead Burt of South Carolina, acting on Calhoun's instructions, offered an amendment that placed the prohibition of slavery in Oregon on the ground that the territory lay north of the Missouri Compromise line.

Although Burt's amendment was defeated by the House, Douglas supported it as an expedient solution to the slavery issue, at the same time objecting to discussion of the issue in relation to matters of such vital importance. When an Alabama Congressman asked if there was one northern man willing to stand by the principle of the Missouri Compromise, Douglas broke the long silence that followed with the statement that he had recognized the Compromise at the time of the annexation of Texas and that "he was ready to recognize it now, and should be ready at all times." He would, he announced, seek to replace the total prohibition of slavery contemplated by the Wilmot Proviso "in all the new territory we might acquire" with the extension of the Missouri Compromise line. Douglas' Oregon bill finally passed, but only after an angry debate over the power of Congress to legislate for the territories.[22]

While the Oregon bill was under consideration, the battle over the Wilmot Proviso resumed amid dire predictions of its impact on party and nation. The controversy, warned the editor of the Washington *Union,* would not only "shiver" the Democratic party but would also "alienate the feelings and weaken the ties which should bind this holy Union together forever." Polk was more direct. "The slavery question," he wrote, "is assuming a fearful & most important aspect." Its consequences, he feared, could only be the destruction of the party and perhaps of the Union itself. The *State Register* blamed it all on "the disorganizing spirit of abolitionism." [23]

The issue came up on February 1, when the appropriation bill (now providing $3 million, and known as the Three Million Bill) was brought before the House by the Committee on Foreign Relations. David Wilmot, over the loud objections of the House, read his amendment, although it was not formally offered at this time. Instead, the bill was postponed, presumably to give the administration time to apply pressure on the Proviso's supporters. Sitting as the committee of the whole, the House debated the measure and Wilmot's amendment (which had not yet been introduced) for a week following February 8, to the virtual exclusion of all other business. On February 15 the debate was closed and the voting began. Confusion and disorder followed, and on several occasions the chairman was forced to suspend the proceedings until order could be restored. Attempts were made to forestall the introduction of the Proviso as an amendment, but Hamlin finally broke through the parliamentary snarl. Douglas was on his feet immediately with an amendment to the Proviso recognizing the extension of the Missouri Compromise, "that there shall be neither slavery nor involuntary servitude in any territory acquired under this act, or as the result of the existing war with Mexico, which lies north of 36° and 30' north lati-

tude, commonly known as the Missouri compromise line." Douglas'
move was decisively defeated, 82 to 109. A rash of amendments followed, deepening the confusion, before the committee of the whole approved the Proviso and reported the amended bill to the House. The
Three Million Bill, with its crucial amendment, was promptly passed.[24]

The Senate rejected the Proviso and passed the Three Million Bill
without it. On the last day of the session, the question was once more
before the House. Wilmot again moved his amendment to the Senate
version, and again the House, in committee of the whole, approved it.
Before the final vote was taken, Douglas made a last appeal to his colleagues, reaffirming his opposition to the Proviso. If the question of slavery in a territory "to be received hereafter into the Union" had to be resolved at this time, he declared, he favored the adoption of the Missouri
Compromise line. However, he saw no immediate necessity for settling
the question, and he strongly disapproved of tying a blanket solution to
the problem as a condition to a wartime money bill. Such a move ignored the unique needs and circumstances of specific areas and assumed
that conditions would be alike in all territory acquired from Mexico.
The time to deal with this issue, Douglas argued, was when Congress organized governments for the new territory. Only then could the slavery
question be dealt with properly. Slavery, he pointed out, had been abolished in Mexico and thus would be prohibited in any Mexican territory
annexed by the United States. Congress could, if it wished, repeal this
prohibition, but only when territorial governments should be established
there. "Why, then," Douglas asked, "should so exciting a question be
pressed now?" His appeal apparently had some effect. When the Proviso
was brought before the House, it failed by a narrow margin, five votes,
and the Three Million Bill, as passed by the Senate, was approved.[25]

Although disposed of for the time, few people believed that the question raised by the Wilmot Proviso had been settled. It was Douglas' first
serious bout with the slavery issue, and he unhesitatingly placed it in the
perspective of his larger goals. The extension of the Missouri Compromise line, a move he had supported with reference to Texas earlier, was
"the most proper arrangement," if it meant preventing a serious and distracting outburst over the extension of slavery. But it was only an expedient. He preferred to postpone the issue until it could be discussed with
specific reference to the organization of territorial governments. Douglas'
opposition to the Proviso, and particularly his support of the Missouri
Compromise principle, aroused the ire of the antislavery press. The

*New-York Tribune* listed his name among the "Betrayers of Freedom" and predicted ultimate victory for the Proviso's supporters. In Illinois the denunciations were bitter and extreme. For his earlier role in the annexation of Texas and his support of the Mexican War, Douglas was charged by one antislavery editor with being "the most servile tool that has crawled in the slime and scum of slavery at the foot of the slave power." Such "dough-faced renegades," protested the *Chicago Journal* later, "should be branded with the mark of Cain." When he defended the Missouri Compromise, he was denounced as "willing to gratify the south in their cherished desire of forming more Slave States in the south west." [26]

Douglas was not disturbed by the diatribes of the abolitionist press. What did disturb him was that the issue raised by the Wilmot Proviso cut across party lines. It was a question that exploded party distinctions, and to Douglas it was all the more dangerous for that. Congress adjourned in March 1847, full of foreboding. As its members dispersed, they surely recognized the immensity of the problems that lay ahead.

# X

## "The vexed question
## of slavery in new territories"
## 1847—1848

i

The frustration and dissatisfaction felt by many congressmen following the adjournment of the twenty-ninth Congress did not bother Douglas. Re-elected to a third term in the House and almost immediately elevated to the United States Senate, he had consolidated his position in the affairs of party and nation. The future appeared bright and secure. With the confidence of a man whose outlook was assured, Douglas at the age of thirty-four now took an additional momentous step. He ventured into the uncertain area of matrimony.

Women had not played an important part in Douglas' life. His hard-driving and highly disciplined political ambition allowed him little time for social life. He had been drawn occasionally into society and had cultivated friendships among the women he encountered, both the wives of colleagues and their unattached friends and relatives. But these attachments were never deep. Douglas found little time and inclination to make strong and lasting friendships, with men or women, and even those he did make lacked the warmth and intimacy common to such relationships. His was a solitary life, and to many of those who knew him he seemed destined to remain a bachelor.

Part of Douglas' problem was his appearance and personality. Physically, he was anything but commanding; one woman who observed him described his figure as "short, stout, and thick." He compensated for his lack of stature by developing a boisterous and exuberant manner and a nervous energy that frequently put people off. "Every inch of him has its own alertness and motion," wrote another woman. "His figure would be an unfortunate one were it not for the animation which constantly pervades it." Deficient in elegance, his bearing contained "a dash of the rowdy." His manners were described by some as downright coarse. Informal and careless of his dress, Douglas smoked cigars, drank whiskey, and worst of all, chewed tobacco, the one "bond of brotherhood among all western men." [1]

Yet to others Douglas was "a great ladies' man" who was considered among Congress' most eligible bachelors. Washington's gossip columnist, Mrs. Anne Royall, whose judgment of people often depended upon their financial support of her newspaper, regarded Douglas as very much "in the market." He must have been one of her most faithful subscribers, for she accorded him an unusually glowing description. He is, wrote Mrs. Royall, rather under middle height, with a light figure of the finest symmetry. "His face is partly round and much of the Grecian contour. His features are delicate and regular, of the middling shade, comely and pleasing. His eye is a deep blue, large, mild and steady, and has great expression—chiefly penetrative. His forehead is high, and square, and bespeaks intelligence and thought. His hair is a dark brown, and his neat modest brow gives a sweetness and innocence to his countenance that words cannot convey." Douglas could not have asked for a better press. [2]

A fellow Congressman played an important part in bringing an end to his solitary existence. When Douglas first appeared in Congress in December 1843, he was assigned a seat next to a young North Carolinian, David S. Reid, who, like Douglas, was serving his first term in the House of Representatives. The same age and strikingly similar in physical appearance, the two men became fast friends. When Reid's uncle, Robert Martin, a prosperous North Carolina planter, visited Washington later in the session with his daughter, Reid introduced Douglas to his cousin Martha. Douglas' acquaintance with Martha was renewed later when he spent some time at Reid's home in Rockingham County, North Carolina. The friendship between Douglas and Martha Martin blossomed, with Reid's encouragement, into a deep attachment, and Douglas began making regular visits to her plantation home.

In 1847 Martha was twenty-two years old, twelve years younger than Douglas. She was descended from a family that had long been prominent in North Carolina politics. Her father, Colonel Robert Martin, was the nephew of Alexander Martin, who had been an officer in the Revolutionary army, governor of North Carolina, and a member of the United States Senate from 1793 to 1799. Her uncle, Thomas Settle, had served in the lower house of Congress from 1817 to 1821. For generations the family had owned and operated large plantations along the upper Dan River. Colonel Martin owned some 800 acres along the Dan, on which he grew cotton, corn, and tobacco. Reputed to be one of the wealthiest planters in the area, he maintained a home on the river plantation as well as a residence in nearby Wentworth, the county seat of Rockingham County.

Martha, one of two daughters of Colonel Martin, was raised in the fashion befitting her social class. She was educated at finishing schools in Philadelphia and Washington, where she studied French, mathematics, and natural philosophy, took music lessons, and was instructed by a French dancing master. Small, hazel-eyed, with fair and graceful features, Martha was not only intelligent, she also possessed a simple charm and keen wit. She was frail, and her health had always been delicate. When her sister, Lucinda, died in September 1846, Martha's nerves gave way and she became ill, forcing the postponement of one of Douglas' planned visits. By the following February, she had recovered sufficiently to travel to Washington, probably with her father, there to witness Douglas in action on the House floor. While delivering a speech, wrote a newspaper correspondent, Douglas' *"ardent* and *wrapt gaze"* was so frequently directed toward the ladies' gallery as to attract the notice of all in the hall. "Every one could see that he thought ten times more of the subject in the Gallery than the one before the House." [3]

Soon after Congress' adjournment in March 1847, Douglas traveled to North Carolina, a journey delayed by a train derailment south of Petersburg, Virginia. On April 7, he married Martha Martin at her Dan River plantation home. News of Douglas' marriage was a source of particular delight to his friends. From far-off Mexico came a congratulatory message from old associates in command of Illinois troops. "It is all now that you require," Douglas was assured, "to make your ascent up the uncertain clift of political fame, not only certain but rapid." [4]

Several years before, Martha's father, attracted by reports of new and productive lands in the southwest, had established a cotton plantation on the Pearl River in Lawrence County, Mississippi. On the day after Douglas' marriage, Robert Martin offered this plantation, with its slaves, to the newlyweds as a wedding present. Douglas dissuaded him. As a man of northern birth and background, he argued, he was unfamiliar with plantation and slave property and therefore incompetent to care for it properly. Less explicit was his conviction that a southern plantation acquired on the eve of his senatorial career might prove to be a political liability. He preferred that Colonel Martin should retain the property. If it had not been disposed of in the meantime, Douglas suggested, disposition of the property might be made in his will, a tactic that would eliminate any question of Douglas' acceptance.[5]

After spending a few days on the North Carolina plantation, Douglas and his wife set out for Illinois. Because of the delicacy of Martha's health, the entire trip was made in her private carriage, with frequent stops for rest. They arrived in Quincy by mid-May. After a short visit with friends, they made a steamboat excursion up the Mississippi to the falls of St. Anthony, where Douglas narrowly escaped serious injury in a hiking mishap.

Douglas now made another important decision. With his election to the Senate, it was no longer necessary to maintain his residence in Quincy. He had never developed a strong attachment to the Mississippi River town and had spent most of his time in Washington or in Springfield, a source of considerable irritation to his Whig opposition. In the summer of 1847, following their return to Illinois, Douglas and his wife moved to the burgeoning lake city of Chicago, taking up temporary quarters in the fashionable Tremont House while planning a more permanent home on the shores of Lake Michigan. The dramatic growth of the state was in the north, and Chicago, it was said, would soon become the west's most important city, a fitting base for Illinois' new Senator.[6]

Douglas was no stranger to Chicago. Nine years before, during his first congressional campaign, he had publicly debated his Whig opponent, John T. Stuart, in the city. Although Stuart won the election in 1838, Douglas carried Chicago and Cook County by a two-to-one majority. His support of the Illinois and Michigan Canal had not been forgotten, and later, when he supported Great Lakes harbor improvements and insisted on having a ship canal linking the lakes with the Mississippi River built at Federal expense, he won the acclaim of Chicago's citizens. His relations with Chicago's Congressman John Wentworth had been close. Now, with his election to the Senate, he could transfer his residence to Wentworth's district.

Douglas decided to settle in Chicago at a propitious time. In 1847, the city was on the threshold of a new era in its spectacular growth.

When Douglas had campaigned there nine years before, Chicago had been a town of but 4000 inhabitants. Now it boasted a population of more than four times that figure. First incorporated in 1833, the town was born in the boom times of the mid-1830's. Encouraged by the passage of the Illinois and Michigan Canal bill in 1836, speculators had flocked to Chicago. Property values advanced to dizzy heights as Chicagoans anticipated the commercial dominance of their location, linking the Great Lakes with the Mississippi River system and controlling the trade of the west. The Panic of 1837 dimmed these visions, real estate values declined, and population growth was slowed. The hopes, however, still remained, and when prosperity returned, Chicago's growth enjoyed a more stable basis. In 1847, the city, stretching for three and a half miles along Lake Michigan, numbered just under 17,000 inhabitants. The number of vessels arriving and departing, carrying goods destined for eastern and Canadian lake ports, was rapidly increasing, and a network of stage lines connected Chicago with the hinterland. Street improvements were being carried out, a breakwater was under construction, and a new city water system was in operation. The canal was approaching completion (it would be opened to traffic in 1848), and plans for linking Chicago with both east and west by rail were in their final stages. The prospect that Chicago would soon "become the first city in the West" was about to be realized.[7]

The future of Chicago was a lively topic of discussion when Douglas moved there in 1847. The only measures "necessary to establish the commercial advantages of Chicago upon a secure foundation," wrote the compiler of an early business directory, "are judicious works of improvement." To dramatize Chicago's bid for primacy in the economic development of the northwest, and to urge the extension of the internal improvements system to the Great Lakes, a carefully planned convention met in Chicago in the summer of 1847. Two years before, at Memphis, a similar meeting had emphasized the northwest's ties with the south, but southern opposition to river and harbor improvements and Polk's vetoes of internal improvement legislation had intervened. The Chicago River and Harbor Convention that met on July 5 was attended by thousands of persons from the lake states, New York, and New England, marking a new orientation for western aspirations. The constitutional objections of the President and of southern politicians (especially John C. Calhoun, who had been prominent in the Memphis convention) were brushed aside, and the convention issued a strong call for the promotion and protection of internal trade. The need for a nationally owned and operated Pacific Railroad, following a central route, was emphasized. Nothing could more effectively have focused attention on the future of Chicago and the upper west—or served as a warning to the south that this future lay with the states of the north and northeast. Although he may have been in the state at the time, Douglas apparently did not attend the convention. His absence, suggested one delegate, may have resulted from an article in the Washington *Union* "throwing cold water on the Convention" for its apparent Whiggish orientation.[8]

Douglas' faith in Chicago's future was nonetheless firm. He began almost immediately to purchase land in the city from a speculator in Illinois and Michigan Canal lands. Over the next two years he bought additional tracts of canal land west and south of the city limits, as well as the valuable property along the lake on which he planned to build his residence. These purchases marked the beginning of what would soon become a rather substantial investment in Chicago land.[9]

Not long afterward, Douglas' property interests were expanded beyond his home state. In June 1848, his father-in-law died. By the terms of his will, Colonel Martin left his Mississippi plantation, including over 2500 acres and in excess of 100 slaves, to his daughter "for her separate and exclusive use," and to her heirs. "I would remind my dear Daughter," Martin had stated in his will, "that her husband does not desire to own this kind of property and most of our collateral connection already have more of that kind of property than is of advantage to them." He asked that, in the event Martha left no children, the slaves be given the net proceeds of the last crop and sent to Liberia. If, however, Martha had children, the property should pass to them, "as nearly every head of a family among them have expressed to me a desire to belong to you and your children rather than go to Africa." "To set them free where they are," Martin had concluded, "would entail on them a greater curse." The plantation was located along the Pearl River, southeast of the town of Monticello in Lawrence County, and produced cotton, corn, and a small amount of sugar cane. According to the bequest, Douglas was to serve as manager of the property, for which he would receive 20 per cent of its annual income. He soon became involved in the business of the plantation, corresponding with the New Orleans commission house which handled the cotton and receiving regular reports from the overseer on the condition of the land and the behavior of the slaves.[10]

ii

Douglas and his wife left Chicago for the east early in the fall of 1847. He addressed a meeting of Illinois bondholders in New York, assuring them that every dollar of the state's debt would be paid, stopped in Philadelphia, and arrived in Washington early in November, where he called on President Polk in the White House. After a quick trip to his wife's home in North Carolina, Douglas appeared in his Senate seat to answer the roll call on the first day of the thirtieth Congress.[11]

The war with Mexico was in its last stages. The campaigns in northern Mexico had virtually ended with the defeat of the enemy at Buena Vista early in the year. The expedition to the Pacific had accomplished its purpose, and Mexico's northern borderlands, Upper California and New Mexico, were under American occupation. A new offensive against the Mexican capital had been launched from Vera Cruz in March, and by September the United States flag flew over Mexico City.

Peace with Mexico, however, seemed remote when members of Congress received Polk's annual message early in December. Nicholas Trist, chief clerk in the State Department, had been dispatched to Mexico months before with instructions to negotiate a settlement with the Mexicans, but his mission had been complicated by quarrels with General Scott and the refusal of the Mexican government to deal with him. Frustrated by the lack of progress and sensitive to the continuing Whig attacks on his policies, Polk decided in October to recall Trist to Washington. Further negotiation, the President concluded, would have to be initiated by the Mexicans themselves.

Trist's failure persuaded Polk to seek a more vigorous prosecution of the war. Having failed to achieve a settlement on the basis of the cession of California and New Mexico to the United States, which had been Trist's instructions, Polk hinted that additional territorial indemnities might be asked. In answer to those who were demanding all of Mexico, however, he disclaimed any intention "to make a permanent conquest of the Republic of Mexico, or to annihilate her separate existence as an independent nation." He proposed the organization of territorial governments for California and New Mexico, but pointed out that other Mexican provinces were under American occupation as well. Their disposition, he suggested, would depend upon the "future progress of the war, and the course which Mexico may think proper hereafter to pursue." Before he submitted this new hard line to Congress, Polk had been careful to discuss it with some of the congressional leaders. Douglas was among those summoned to the White House for consultation, and Polk later noted that the new Illinois Senator had read and approved those portions of his message dealing with Mexico.[12]

For the next three months, discussion of the Mexican war—its justification, prosecution, and termination—dominated congressional deliberations. The issue was complicated by the fact that 1848 was a presidential election year, so much of the rhetoric was more designed to advance political fortunes than to clarify the problems. Polk's hint that additional Mexican territory might be sought provoked a number of resolutions in the Senate which inevitably brought the question of slavery back into the discussion. Daniel S. Dickinson of New York proposed that such additional contiguous territory be annexed as would strengthen the nation's political and commercial relations on the continent, an open-ended suggestion that could conceivably result in the annexation of all Mexico. Of greater import was Dickinson's proposal that in organizing territorial governments for the area, all matters of domestic policy, including slavery, be left to the legislatures elected by the people of the territories, an early expression of popular sovereignty. Reflecting the views of southern leadership, John C. Calhoun objected to the enlargement of war aims. "To conquer Mexico, and to hold it either as a province or to incorporate it in the Union," he declared, "would be inconsistent with the avowed object for which the war has been prosecuted." Calhoun, it was clear, was concerned with the impact territorial expansion might have on the future of slavery.

Douglas was impatient with the time-consuming discussion of what he regarded as essentially abstract questions. He objected to the postponement of "the business of the country, or the necessary measures of legislation for the prosecution of the war" in favor of issues that would have "no practical bearing on our legislation." The argument over how much territory should be taken from Mexico, or whether slavery should exist or not, Douglas insisted, evaded the real questions with which the Senate had to deal if the war were to be speedily and successfully terminated. He reserved his harshest words for Calhoun, questioning his real motives and likening him to Talleyrand, whose dictum was "that language was given to man by the Deity to enable him to *conceal,* not to express, his ideas." [13]

A bill authorizing additional enlistments for service in Mexico, the so-called Ten Regiment Bill, provided the focal point for an almost in-

terminable discussion of the origins and justification of the war. The subject had been debated before, and few new arguments were presented.
The bill, however, provided the Whigs with an opportunity to launch
their campaign against the Democratic administration and to revive
most of their old accusations against Polk. Douglas was again pushed to
the limit of his patience. He was unprepared, he said, to hear individuals
who had supported war measures earlier now denounce the war as unjust, unnecessary, and unconstitutional. Polk's policy toward Mexico had
not changed. "The causes and the objects of the war remain unchanged."
Douglas could only conclude that hope of success in the presidential
election had pre-empted the sound judgment of many members of the
Senate.

Douglas' maiden speech in the Senate on February 1, 1848, was an
attempt to settle once and for all some of the disputed questions concerning the character of the war. His arguments had been carefully prepared to impress his new Senate colleagues as well as to shed light on
the issues. The galleries filled, and a number of members of the House of
Representatives came over. Douglas, however, was not in his usual form.
Surrounded by an array of books, he promised to "state no fact for the
accuracy of which I have not the most conclusive authority in the books
before me." His tone was scholarly, lacking the warmth and spontaneity
which people had come to expect of him.

Douglas reiterated his conviction that the United States was fighting
"a war of self-defence, forced upon us by our enemy, and prosecuted on
our part in vindication of our honor, and the integrity of our territory."
"Conquest," he added, "was not the motive for the prosecution of the
war; satisfaction, indemnity, security, was the motive—conquest and
territory the means." The major part of his argument dealt with the
question of whether American blood had been shed on American soil in
the spring of 1846, perhaps in part an answer to Abraham Lincoln's examination of the same question in the House of Representatives only
two weeks before. With frequent reference to the books before him,
Douglas reviewed in tiresome detail the history of Texas settlement, the
character of the Texas revolution, and the question of the boundary,
with particular emphasis on the area lying between the Nueces River
and the Rio Grande. "One thing is certain," he concluded, "Mexico
never dreamed of any other boundary than that of the Rio Grande or
the Sabine. She was in possession of the country to the Rio Grande, and
claimed the right to conquer to the Sabine."

Douglas returned to his old form when he answered Whig charges that Polk's order to General Taylor to move his force to the Rio Grande was the real cause of the war. Not so, Douglas insisted. Reading from Taylor's dispatches, he showed that the General himself had advised the move "as a peace measure, calculated to facilitate and hasten the settlement of the boundary question." It was, Douglas urged, a "right and wise" move. Douglas could not resist sarcasm when he pointed out that the men who denounced the order as bringing on the war were the same persons who were urging Taylor's election to the presidency. He concluded with harsh words for those who would make the world believe the war to be unnecessary and unjust. Little wonder that the nations of Europe, already jealous of American greatness, should "denounce us as a nation of robbers and pirates." Their only triumph, he warned, will be to render the nation infamous in the eyes of Christendom. "Whose heart did not swell and pulsate with patriotic pride," Douglas asked, "as he heard the shout of the glorious victories achieved by our countrymen wafted from the plains and mountains of Mexico, striking terror to the hearts of all enemies of republican institutions, and demonstrating that ours is the first military, as well as civil power, upon the globe?" He described the proud and grateful emotions he experienced at the response of the many thousands to the call for volunteers. "Was that response prompted by a love of plunder and robbery; or was it a patriotic response from the hearts of freemen, burning with a fervent desire to avenge their country's wrongs and vindicate her rights?" [14]

By the time the Ten Regiment Bill was approved in mid-March, the peace treaty had been submitted to the Senate for ratification. Trist, defying Polk's order for his recall, had remained in Mexico. The Mexican government, faced with the threat of new and stiffer peace terms, appointed commissioners to treat with Trist and, after a series of meetings, the Treaty of Guadalupe Hidalgo was drawn up. Mexico recognized the Rio Grande boundary of Texas and ceded half a million square miles of its territory—New Mexico and California—to the United States, while the United States assumed the claims of its citizens against Mexico, agreed to pay Mexico for damages caused by Indian tribes, and gave Mexico $15 million.

After consulting with his cabinet, Polk placed the treaty before the Senate late in February, "with a view to its ratification." Discussion of the treaty, conducted in secret in executive session, was complicated by the Senators' knowledge that Trist had exceeded his authority in drafting it and by the expansionists' desire for a greater amount of Mexican territory. Whigs who wished no territory were joined in their opposition to the treaty by Democrats who wished more. Polk was concerned lest the treaty be defeated, or so altered as to ensure its rejection by Mexico. He strongly suspected that the Senators were actuated more by the presidential election than they were by the nation's interests.[15]

Douglas supported the demand for the acquisition of a large part of Mexico, although his statements lacked the bold and aggressive tone they had assumed during the Oregon debates. The *State Register,* reflecting extreme expansionist sentiment in Illinois, called for the conquest, subjugation, and annihilation of Mexican sovereignty. Douglas did not go that far, but he was careful not to rule out the possibility that the acquisition of all of Mexico might prove desirable. His unshakable conviction that the war was necessary and just was matched by an equally strong belief that the peace should be a harsh one. "The results of this war," he wrote in December 1847, "have not been more glorious than its origin was *just* on our part. Forced upon us by an enemy who spurns our repeated proffers of peace, let it be prosecuted until Mexico shall feel that her very existence among the nations of the earth depends on her making ample reparation for the past, and strictly observing the principles of justice and friendship in the future." On the question of the acquisition of all of Mexico, however, he maintained an open mind. To oppose "the whole of Mexico," as some Democrats had done, "may prove to have been unwise as an act of patriotism as well as policy." Douglas was not prepared to assume such a position, nor to commit the party to it. "I wish to be left free to act as circumstances and future developments may render necessary." [16]

Although there is no record of the debates on the treaty, it is clear from the proceedings that Douglas favored the acquisition of more territory than the Treaty of Guadalupe Hidalgo provided. The Senate made only minor adjustments in the document. At Polk's suggestion, Douglas voted with the majority to delete the tenth article, which dealt with Mexican land grants in Texas and the southwest, and the final, secret article, which would have extended the time for the exchange of ratifications. He was not successful in his attempt to delete the sections that provided for the protection and control of the Indian tribes in the area to be annexed. An effort was made to add the Wilmot Proviso to the treaty, but Douglas joined with others to defeat it. A proposal by Jefferson Davis to increase the amount of territory taken from Mexico by adding Coahuila and the larger parts of Tamaulipas, Nuevo Leon, and Chihuahua received Douglas' strong support, but Davis' motion was decisively defeated. Thirty-eight Senators, more than the necessary two-thirds, approved the treaty on March 10, while only fourteen voted against ratification. Douglas was in the minority, favoring rejection. He was joined by his senior colleague, Sidney Breese, who had earlier urged "the *complete subjugation* of Mexico." Illinois was the only state whose Senators both voted against the treaty. "I rejoice that you went against the Trist treaty," wrote one western Democrat to Douglas. "That accursed thing has silenced much of our thunder." [17]

Polk's prediction that a dozen Democratic Senators would vote against the treaty because they wished more territory was not realized. Of the fourteen negative votes, seven were cast by Whigs who desired less territory. The seven opposition Democrats, six of them from the west, were, like Douglas, expressing their conviction that more, perhaps all, of Mexico should have been acquired. Once again, Douglas found himself at odds with the administration on the question of expansion. The Illinois Senators, commented the New York *Herald,* "are not favourites at the White House. They would not turn for 49 when Mr. Polk abandoned 54 40. . . . They now refuse, after making grandiloquent, fire-eating, war speeches; after declaring themselves for 'an ocean-bound republic,' to go for the treaty feloniously made by Mr. Trist." The *Herald*'s comment was off the mark, for Douglas' relations with the President remained close in spite of their differences. Despite his setbacks on both the Oregon and Mexican questions, Douglas continued to pursue his expansionist goals. Two months after the treaty was ratified, he accompanied John L. O'Sullivan, editor of the *Democratic Review,* to the White House to urge the President to "take early measures with a view to the purchase of the Island of Cuba from Spain." [18]

iii

The Treaty of Guadalupe Hidalgo added over 500,000 square miles to the United States. With the new lands came new problems, and with them an urgency that would make their solution difficult and complicated. Problems of continental transportation and communication, of Indian policy, and of frontier defense demanded attention. With the expansion of the boundary to the Pacific coast, the nation's geographic configuration had been drastically altered, and older programs and attitudes no longer sufficed. The most pressing and immediate problem sprang from the necessity to organize some kind of government for the new lands. The results of the Mexican War brought the question of territorial government into sharp focus and seriously challenged the adequacy of the traditional territorial system. The Wilmot Proviso had anticipated the crisis that now faced the American people. With the ratification of the Treaty of Guadalupe Hidalgo, the question of slavery's expansion into the west was no longer abstract. It was deeply involved in the practical need for government in the Mexican cession. Oregon, as yet unorganized, was inevitably drawn into the debate.

Douglas' concern for the problems of territorial government was closely linked with his interest in national expansion. The extension of the national domain also meant the extension of the institutions of American democracy, and the territorial system became the vehicle by which these institutions would be planted on the frontier. His interest in western growth and development was deeply rooted. "From early youth," he once recalled, "I have indulged an enthusiasm, which seemed to others wild and romantic, in regard to the growth, expansion, and destiny of this republic." This enthusiasm led him into a serious study of the needs and desires of the west and its people. "The great west and the Pacific coast presented a theatre for new and wonderful events," he continued. "I studied carefully everything that pertained to them—every mountain and valley, plain and river, was the subject of peculiar interest and inquiry, until I felt that I understood the geography and topography of the country between the Mississippi and the Pacific ocean, quite as accurately as of the old states of the Union." [19]

Although the debates over the application of the traditional system of territorial government to the new western lands revolved principally about the slavery question, there was implicit in them a deeper, more fundamental constitutional problem. What was the proper relationship between the territories and the national government, and what precisely was the extent of Congress' power over the territories? The Constitution did not provide easy answers to these questions. The one provision that seemed to apply, Article IV, Section 3, was vague and ambiguous. Since the Ordinance of 1787 had organized the nation's first territory, Congress' power over the territories had been regarded as absolute. The government that was first established in the Northwest Territory, with its tight, imperial control by the national government, served as a model for future territorial legislation. The system was gradually liberalized, partly through the demands of the westerners themselves for a greater share in their local government, but rigid limits to self-government in the territories still remained.

Douglas had been appointed chairman of the Committee on Territories in the House of Representatives in December 1845, and when he entered the Senate two years later he was selected for the corresponding post. The Senate committee was a relatively new one, with the scope of its responsibilities still undefined. Douglas regarded the committee as vital to the formulation of national policy for the west, and he adopted a sweeping view of its duties that often brought him into conflict with the chairmen of the more established committees. The Committee on Territories, he had told the House earlier, had been constituted "to take charge of the Territorial business . . . and its province included military affairs, judicial affairs, post office affairs, and everything else which related to the Territories." Some of his colleagues objected to this comprehensive view. Douglas replied, "If the Committee on Territories had not the right to take cognizance of all laws necessary to the organization of Territories, and to the protection of our citizens there, they had no rights; because every branch of this subject might come within the purview of other committees." At the same time that he insisted on a broad definition with respect to the territories, he also argued the jurisdiction of his committee over the admission of new states. Douglas carried these views with him into the Senate, convinced that the Committee on Territories, and he as its chairman, must necessarily play a central role in all matters pertaining to western development.[20]

Douglas revealed his support of the traditional pattern of federal-territorial relationships early in his career. He also made it clear, however, that Congress could not impose restrictions on the people of a territory when they sought admission to the Union as a state. Early in 1845, in the debate over the Florida statehood bill, he defended the right of the people of Florida to include in their state constitution sections forbidding the emancipation of slaves and prohibiting the immigration of free Negroes, on the ground that they dealt with institutions and regulations that were local and domestic in character. Congress had no right to interfere. "The people of each State," he declared, "are to form their constitution in their own way and in accordance with their own views." As long as the government created by the proposed state constitution was republican in character, Congress could not block its passage. While insisting that the people of a new state should be left free to form and regulate their own domestic institutions without congressional interference,

Douglas was not yet prepared to concede the same freedom to the people of a territory. In one of his earliest statements on the territorial system, he disclosed his commitment to the prevalent view:

> The father may bind the son during his minority; but the moment he attains his majority, his fetters are severed, and he is free to regulate his own conduct. So with the Territories; they are subject to the jurisdiction and control of Congress during their infancy, their minority; but when they attain their majority, and obtain admission into the Union, they are free from all restraints and restrictions, except such as the constitution of the United States has imposed on each and all of the States.[21]

On other occasions, Douglas had shown similar support of the territorial system as it had evolved over the years, and, like most others, he agreed that authority over the affairs of the territories rested in Congress and the national government. One of the restrictions on territorial action that proved most galling to frontier settlers was the power of Congress to disallow or veto territorial legislation. Douglas himself had introduced bills into Congress providing for the disallowance of territorial laws, declaring that "experience has sanctioned as sound and wise" the policy of the congressional veto, although one such action, disallowing certain banking laws of Iowa and Wisconsin territories, seems to have resulted more from a desire to prevent the operation of a Wisconsin bank in Illinois. In drafting bills providing for the organization of new territories, Douglas reaffirmed the traditional territorial form. His bills for the creation of Nebraska and Oregon territories followed precedent closely. In the latter instance, Iowa's territorial government, based on the Northwest Ordinance but embodying all the changes that had developed since, was used as a model, it being in his view the "most perfect" of all territorial organizations.

Douglas' support of the traditional system was not based on an unquestioned devotion to precedent; it was highly pragmatic in character. His goal was to secure the organization of governments for the western frontier in the quickest and easiest way possible. He frequently expressed great annoyance at the efforts of his colleagues to postpone consideration of territorial matters in favor of other legislation. Douglas sought to make the passage of territorial bills an automatic process. Yet the territorial system, to Douglas, required constant adaptation to differing conditions of time and place. In answer to southerners who insisted that the Congress should observe the terms of the Ordinance of 1787, which restricted the number of states to be created out of the Northwest Territory to five, Douglas declared that the provisions of the Ordinance were not obligatory on Congress and that the Ordinance had been superseded and "virtually annulled," with respect to the admission of new states, by the Constitution, a position that opened the way for future changes.[22]

That Douglas did not hesitate to support the exercise of congressional authority over the internal concerns of the territories was clear from his firm adherence to the extension of the Missouri Compromise line, although, again, his position resulted not so much from any deep convictions regarding territorial government as from his belief that the extension of the line was simply an easy and expedient way of settling a troublesome question. In spite of his declaration that Congress could not rightfully place restrictions on new states, his efforts to extend the Missouri Compromise line did just that. Douglas' position on the rights of territories and new states was a mixture of principle and pragmatism, and by 1848 no clear and consistent pattern in his thinking had emerged.

Territorial matters occupied much of Douglas' attention during his first session in the Senate. He renewed his earlier effort to organize Nebraska Territory and introduced bills for the creation of Minnesota Territory and the admission of Wisconsin as a state. Only the last was successful. More pressing were the questions of territorial government in Oregon and the provision of government for the Mexican cession, both of which became entangled with the slavery issue.

Douglas' prior attempts to organize a territorial government for Oregon had failed, and in 1848, two years after the Oregon treaty was ratified, United States law still had not been formally extended to the area. Although they had created their own provisional government early in the 1840's, Oregonians grew restive and impatient with Congress' delay. As the population increased, the pressures for action became more acute. Petitions and memorials were dispatched to Congress, and some individuals made the long trek eastward to plead their case. In the meantime, Oregon's provisional government, out of necessity, was strengthened. Administrative officers were elected and laws were promulgated, including the prohibition of slavery. This provided the settlers with a degree of self-government they were later reluctant to give up.

On January 10 Douglas introduced a new bill for the organization of Oregon Territory. In substance it resembled the Wisconsin and Iowa territorial bills, except for one significant section, which recognized the un-usual governmental situation existing in Oregon. The provisional gov-ernment had extended the laws of Iowa Territory over Oregon (one settler having had a copy of Iowa's territorial statutes in his possession), an action validated by the twelfth section of Douglas' bill. The section further stated that the laws passed by the provisional government should continue to be valid so long as they were not incompatible with the act creating the territory and until they might be altered, modified, or re-pealed by the legislature of the new territory. This was an important rec-ognition by Douglas and his committee of the government established by the people themselves and of the laws they had provided to meet their own needs, including the one which prohibited slavery. By this provision, Douglas placed control over slavery, as well as over other sub-jects of local importance, in the hands of the people who lived in the territory, a significant step away from the traditional federal-territorial relationship he had supported previously. The circumstances in Oregon, however, were unique; there was no indication that he would be willing to extend the same privilege to other territories.

Douglas left the Senate in May to electioneer in the presidential cam-paign, confident, apparently, that his bill would not be brought up for discussion until late in the session. An urgent memorial from Oregon to the President, however, warning of the dangers of Indian attacks, forced an early consideration of Douglas' measure. When, late in May, Polk transmitted the memorial to Congress, he strongly urged that laws be passed promptly to establish a territorial government in Oregon, and on the last day of the month Senate debate on the bill began. Douglas' ab-sence from the Senate proved critical. Indiana's Senator Jesse Bright, a member of the territorial committee, assumed the leadership in the dis-cussion of the bill, but the committee, hampered by the absence of its chairman, proved unable to cope effectively with the stormy debate that ensued.[23]

Disagreement centered on the twelfth section, which dealt with the slavery question. Since there were few, if any, illusions that slavery could or would exist in Oregon, virtually everyone agreed that the subject was of no practical concern to the area. However, with the organization of the Mexican cession in the offing, the Oregon bill loomed as a test case. Neither northerners nor southerners were willing to see anything in-cluded in the bill that might seriously compromise their position on slavery in the lands acquired from Mexico. Southerners opposed the inclusion of any slavery restriction. The issue, wrote John C. Calhoun, was "the most vital to us of all questions," revealing the dangerous situation in which the south had been placed. Northern freesoilers, on the other hand, supported efforts, such as that of New Hampshire's Senator Hale, to extend the slavery prohibition of the Ordinance of 1787 to Oregon. Polk, worried about the safety of Oregon's settlers as well as about the outcome of the presidential election, prevailed upon Bright to introduce an amendment extending the Missouri Compromise line to the Pacific in an attempt to break the deadlock, but his move had little effect on the discussion. Prospects for an early passage of the bill dimmed as the debate over slavery focused increasingly on the larger question of Congress' power in the territories.[24]

It soon became apparent that new and different tactics would have to be employed. The territorial committee, which was also attempting to shape a proposal for the governments of California and New Mexico, found itself completely frustrated by the disagreement on the slavery question and by the absence of its chairman. That Douglas dominated the committee seemed clear from the inability of the committee members to function efficiently in his absence. In early July, Bright, alluding to the uncertainty of Douglas' return "during the residue of the session," proposed that the committee membership be increased temporarily, but the Senate rejected the suggestion. Several days later, John M. Clayton of Delaware, also a member of Douglas' committee, urged that a special committee be formed to resolve the disagreements. The debate, Clayton pointed out, had not revealed any ground on which the Senate could agree, and the Committee on Territories, with but four active members, was proceeding too slowly to be of any use. After Bright formally proposed that the territorial committee be discharged from further consideration of Oregon, California, and New Mexico, Clayton's suggestion was eagerly accepted by the Senate, and Clayton himself was selected as chairman of the new committee.

The result of Clayton's move was the introduction of a long and cumbersome compromise bill, providing territorial governments for Oregon, California, and New Mexico in one package. The sections dealing with Oregon were substantially the same as those in Douglas' bill. California and New Mexico were given territorial governments patterned after the first stage of government in the Northwest Ordinance, ignoring the evolution of the territorial system since that time. "The inhabitants of New Mexico and Upper California," it was said, "are made up of persons not acquainted with legislation." The slavery question was neatly side-stepped. No law could be passed "respecting the prohibition or establishment of African slavery," and all questions relating to slavery were to be referred to the local courts, with the right of appeal to the Supreme Court of the United States. The bill was hardly satisfactory, but it won the approval of the President and was hailed by the Washington *Union* as "the Rainbow of Peace."

Douglas returned to his seat soon after debate on Clayton's compromise began. He gave the measure his full support, voting against the attempts of northern freesoilers to extend the slavery prohibition of the Northwest Ordinance to the new territories and against all the efforts to postpone the organization of the Mexican cession, but he said little on its behalf. Early on July 27, after a continuous and exhausting session of twenty-one hours, the Senate passed the bill. Many of those who supported it did so without enthusiasm and with many qualms. The effort, however, marked an important step in the adaptation of the territorial system to the controversial slavery issue, providing the germ of a new pattern of organization which the *Union* labeled "the principle of non-intervention." [25]

After having devoted so much of their time and energy to the passage of the Clayton bill, the members of the Senate were little prepared for the cursory treatment accorded it by the House. On the day after its Senate passage, the House tabled the compromise without reading it and proceeded to the consideration of its own Oregon bill, preferring to defer the organization of California and New Mexico to a later time. The House bill prohibited slavery in Oregon by extending the provisions of the Northwest Ordinance over the territory and by recognizing the validity of the laws passed by the provisional government, a combination that proved acceptable to a majority of House members. The bill passed on August 2 and was promptly sent to the Senate, where it was referred to Douglas' committee.

Douglas' anxiety for the organization of Oregon Territory prompted him to move quickly, although he still hoped to lay the groundwork for a settlement of the slavery issue in the Mexican cession as well. Racing against time as the end of the session approached, he reported the bill with several amendments, seeking once again to secure recognition of the Missouri Compromise principle. To the section prohibiting slavery in Oregon, he proposed to add the words, "inasmuch as the said territory is north of the parallel of 36°30′ of north latitude, usually known as the

'Missouri compromise.' " When the amendment was defeated, he altered its wording to give greater strength to the Missouri Compromise and to make more explicit its role in future territorial organizations. The Compromise, Douglas wrote, "is hereby revived, and declared to be in full force and binding, for the future organization of the Territories of the United States, in the same sense, and with the same understanding with which it was originally adopted." Once again Douglas' effort to recognize the continuing force of the Missouri Compromise was vigorously denounced by northern freesoilers, although the amendment passed the Senate by a substantial majority. When the House refused to concur in the extension of the Missouri Compromise, Douglas desperately sought the appointment of a conference committee that might resolve the differences, but the Senate decided instead to abandon the amendment. The House bill passed without change, and on August 14, the last day of the session, Polk affixed his signature to it.[26]

Douglas rejoiced that Oregon had finally been given a territorial government, but he was disappointed in his hope that the explosive slavery question would be settled for the entire west by the Oregon bill. But if the debates over Oregon taught him anything, they taught him that new ways of thinking had to be developed to meet the challenge of the slavery issue. His adherence to the traditional lines of the territorial system was shaken, and his effort to revive a twenty-eight-year-old sectional compromise had been frustrated. In addition, he discovered that, to a growing body of northern opinion, the principle of the Missouri Compromise was no longer acceptable. Yet in the very attempt to extend the Compromise to the far west a new formula was suggested. Douglas had argued that the extension of the line 36°30′ merely reinforced the slavery prohibition that had already been passed by the people who lived in Oregon; in the territory south of that line, he pointed out, the fate of the institution would be left to the states to be carved from it, as the terms of the Missouri Compromise had originally provided. The principle of popular decision, implicit in his argument, gained credence in his thinking.

iv

The question of slavery in the western territories, first raised by David Wilmot in 1846 and argued with increased vehemence during the next two years, took its toll on the Democratic party. Weakened already by divisions over expansion and war, internal improvements and the tariff, the party ranks wavered before the onslaught of sectional issues that seemed to transcend party loyalties. Democrats were concerned for their party long before the election year of 1848 brought these issues to angry focus. "Did you ever see a Party so completely at Sixes & Sevens as the Demo. Party now is?" Martin Van Buren was asked early in 1847. The party had become a collection of warring factions, and no clear leadership for 1848 emerged. "The next Presidency," moaned an Illinois Congressman, "is all in a cloud." Some hoped that the thirtieth Congress might produce a candidate who could unite the ranks, but others despaired that the party could ever close its wounds. "I foresee a session of great distraction and confusion," Calhoun had written prophetically. "The old party organization cannot much longer hold together." [27]

In no state was the condition of the Democracy so chaotic as it was in New York. The divisions in the New York party ran deep, but they had been aggravated by recent political developments. Two factions battled for leadership. The Barnburners, or radical wing, were followers of Martin Van Buren, hostile to the Polk administration, disturbed at the growth of southern influence in both the party and the government, and holding a freesoil, antislavery position on the territorial question. Not only had Van Buren been defeated in the 1844 convention, but his supporters had been overlooked by Polk in the dispensation of the patronage. The Barnburners opposed the Mexican War, supported the Wilmot Proviso, and were in part responsible for the failure of the Clayton compromise. On the other side stood the Hunkers, conservative in their stand on the slavery question and supporters of the administration. The two groups reached the parting of the ways in the fall of 1847. The Hunkers secured control of the state Democratic convention at Syracuse, in spite of a bitter challenge from the Barnburners, and proceeded to name the state ticket. The Barnburners, refusing to act with their rivals, held their own convention several weeks later and nominated a separate slate. The immediate result of the schism in the party was the success of the Whigs in the November state elections.

The condition of the New York party caused serious concern among Democratic leaders, for similar divisions began to appear in less extreme form in other states. The key to success in the 1848 presidential election clearly lay with the situation in New York. John Wentworth reflected wider opinion when he predicted that "any man that can unite the party in New York can be elected" to the presidency. Douglas watched the developments in the Empire State closely. One troubled New Yorker wrote him that the rift in the party "has created a degree of bitterness in our ranks hardly to be conceived," and warned that the split might reach Illinois. The party's only hope, he informed Douglas, was to name a candidate "upon which both wings of our party in this State can unite." [28]

It had long been obvious that the questions raised by David Wilmot in 1846 would provide the principal issue in the election of 1848. Should Congress allow the extension of slavery to the new western territories? Does Congress indeed have the power to legislate with respect to slavery in the territories? Presidential hopefuls began placing themselves on record months before the Democratic convention was scheduled to meet. Late in August 1847, James Buchanan, Polk's Secretary of State, endorsed the extension of the Missouri Compromise line to the Pacific. John C. Calhoun, speaking on the Oregon bill, demanded that the question of slavery in the territories be met in the terms of the Constitution itself. The territories, he insisted, as long as they remained in a territorial condition, should be open to the citizens of all the states.[29] From the leaders of New York's distracted party came additional statements, each reflecting opinion among Democrats on a broader scale. Silas Wright, lieutenant of Van Buren and leader of the Barnburners, declared his unqualified support of the Wilmot Proviso. New York Senator Daniel S. Dickinson, a Hunker, denied that Congress had a right to legislate for the domestic affairs of the people of the territory without their consent and proposed that all questions relating to the domestic policy of the territories, including slavery, be left to the legislatures chosen by the people of the territories.[30]

Dickinson's proposal was developed more fully by Lewis Cass in his Nicholson letter, the most widely publicized of pre-election pronouncements. Writing to A. O. P. Nicholson of Tennessee in December 1847, the Michigan Senator denounced the Wilmot Proviso and narrowly analyzed the constitutional provisions dealing with the powers of Congress in the territories. Slavery did not exist in the Mexican cession, nor was it likely that the institution could thrive there. Certainly, he pointed out, the Constitution could not establish slavery in the new area. Only the action of the legislatures of the territories themselves could give it legal existence. "Leave to the people, who will be affected by this question," Cass wrote, "to adjust it upon their own responsibility, and in their own manner, and we shall render another tribute to the original principles of our government, and furnish another guaranty for its permanence and prosperity." Although Cass grounded his argument in constitutional interpretation, he may also have hit upon his doctrine as an expedient alternative to the Wilmot Proviso. His formula, which appealed especially to moderate Democrats as a means for extricating the party from the dangers of sectionalism, soon caught on. To many westerners, Cass' statement held the promise of an expanded self-government for the territorial settler.[31]

Cass' name had been linked with the presidential nomination before. In 1844, Douglas had considered him an acceptable alternative to Van Buren, and he continued to regard him as a strong presidential possibility. "We must have a Western President," Douglas was informed two years later, and "General Cass is *the* man." In the intervening years, however, Cass' stock among some westerners had dropped. His perfunctory response to the Chicago River and Harbor convention in 1847, and his opposition to the acquisition of all of Mexico, alienated many would-be supporters. By early 1848, Douglas himself was being proposed for the presidential nomination. The choice, urged one New Yorker, should go to "the ardent defender of our claim to the *'whole of Oregon,'* the author of a Resolution for the *'Annexation of Texas,'* the advocate for a bold and vigorous prosecution of the *'War with Mexico'* "—in other words, to Stephen A. Douglas. With Douglas as the candidate, "the vexed question of *Slavery in new Territories,* as between *Northern & Southern* Democrats would be suffered to lie dormant through the campaign." The suggestion was echoed in Illinois. Wentworth, anticipating a deadlock in the national convention, speculated that "Illinois stands just as good a chance to get the nomination finally, in the shape of Judge Douglas, as any other State." [32]

The concern of Illinois politicians was more realistically devoted to heading off a split in the Democratic ranks along the lines of the New York division. Wentworth's own course was the cause of much anxiety. As he had supported the Wilmot Proviso, it was feared he might press for an endorsement of the freesoil position by the Illinois party. The selection of delegates to the national convention by districts, which Wentworth preferred, would give an advantage to the Proviso men and strike deep into party unity. Democratic leaders urged, instead, that delegates be elected by a state convention, thus preserving unity and excluding "fire brands from the Nat. Convn. and the bosom of the democracy of our State." Although it was strongly suggested that the Illinois delegation be uninstructed on the presidential nomination, the belief gained support among westerners that the nomination of New Hampshire's old

Jacksonian, Levi Woodbury, was the only one that would satisfy all the elements of the party.[33]

By mid-May, delegates to the national convention began to arrive in Washington on their way to Baltimore, virtually all, the *Union* nervously assured itself in an exercise of wishful thinking, prepared "to conciliate, to unite, to act together for the common cause." The Senate conveniently adjourned—on the excuse that the summer carpets were to be laid—so that its members could go to Baltimore for the opening of the convention on May 22. Both the personal rivalries for the nomination and the divisions generated by the Wilmot Proviso heightened the tension and rendered the outcome of the meeting uncertain. The New York split threatened to engulf the party, for both the Barnburners and the Hunkers sent delegations to Baltimore. Each demanded recognition, and an explosion over the question of their admission was feared.

Douglas reflected the uncertainty of many Democrats. Party matters, he wrote, were in a "glorious state of confusion," and he was frankly puzzled over which way to turn. Deciding to take no part in the controversy between the party's factions, he was determined to "stand entirely aloof," not from policy, as he confessed, "but because I do not know what course we ought to pursue." His effort to remain detached from the party's squabbles, however, was tempered by suspicion of the Barnburners' motives. The Barnburners, he was convinced, would oppose Cass, Buchanan, Polk, and even Woodbury. They did not, he suggested, wish to be seated in the convention. "Their policy is to be refused admission at Baltimore and to make that refusal the pretext for separating" from the party. The decision on the seating of New York's delegates, Douglas predicted, "will have much to do in controlling the nomination & election." As for his own preference among the candidates, he decided to remain uncommitted as long as possible. "I have great doubt who ought to be our man." Of one thing, however, Douglas was certain. "We have a fearful struggle before us." [34]

The New York dispute was referred to the credentials committee on the first day of the meeting. The committee decided that neither side would be heard until both pledged themselves to support the nominee of the convention. This the Barnburners refused to do. The convention later agreed to admit both delegations and to divide New York's vote between them. Although this outraged the Hunkers, the decision proved even more unacceptable to the Barnburners, who promptly withdrew from the convention. "Much confusion & no little bitterness exists,"

Polk's private secretary informed his chief. With the withdrawal of the Barnburners, and with the decision to invoke the two-thirds rule once again, the knottiest problems of the convention seemed to be solved, however. Balloting for the presidential nominee began soon afterward, and after four ballots Lewis Cass was declared the winner. General William O. Butler of Kentucky was nominated for Vice President. The Illinois delegation supported the winners on all the ballots.

The platform as finally approved avoided the dangerous question of slavery in the territories. The principles of previous Democratic platforms were reaffirmed; in addition, the Mexican War was declared to be just and necessary, and the French people were congratulated on the success of their recent revolution. This was not enough for the southerners. Under the leadership of Alabama's William Lowndes Yancey, a minority of the resolutions committee protested the absence of any guarantee to the south on the slavery question. A platform that avoided "what is really the most exciting and important political topic now before the country" was judged unacceptable. Disagreeing with Cass' position that slavery might be excluded from the territories by the people who inhabit them, Yancey insisted that a resolution be added to the platform that would endorse "the doctrine of non-interference with the rights of property," whether in states or territories, but his proposal was defeated. In the absence of a precise statement on the issue, the party's position was interpreted as southerners feared it would be, as supporting the views developed by Cass in his Nicholson letter.[35]

The withdrawal of the Barnburners from the Democratic convention, and the excitement felt throughout the north on the question of slavery in the territories, gave credence to the New York *Herald*'s prediction that there would be a revolution in political parties before the November election. In a move that had obviously been planned well in advance, the Barnburners met at Utica late in June and nominated Van Buren for the presidency on a platform that included the Wilmot Proviso. Feelings of revenge against Cass (who, it was believed, had engineered Van Buren's defeat in the 1844 convention) and against the Polk administration played no small part in the strategy. The movement caught on in other northern states, resulting in the formation of the Free-Soil party at a convention in Buffalo early in August. Van Buren's nomination was confirmed, with Charles Francis Adams added to the ticket as a vice presidential candidate. The platform of the new party was unequivocal on the slavery question—"the *only* safe means of preventing the extension of Slavery into territory now free, is to prohibit its existence in all such territory by an *act of Congress.*" To southern demands for slavery's protection, the delegates answered, "No more Slave States and no more Slave Territory." [36]

The appearance of the Free-Soil party in the campaign was ominous. Polk regarded the movement of the Barnburners as a dangerous attempt to organize geographical parties on the slavery question, "more threatening to the Union than anything which has occurred since the meeting of the Hartford convention in 1814." Douglas' earlier suspicions were borne out, and he no longer felt any uncertainty regarding the party split. By withdrawing from the convention and nominating their own ticket, the Barnburners had challenged the authority of the regular party organization and could no longer be considered Democrats. Douglas fully concurred in the President's belief that members of the dissident faction ought to be removed from office.

Douglas was more concerned with the impact of the freesoil revolt on politics in his own state, but events swiftly proved his concern to be groundless. John Wentworth, whose influence and prestige the Free-Soilers had hoped to enlist in their cause, realistically endorsed the Cass ticket. Wentworth had just won renomination for Congress in spite of heavy pressure from administration supporters to oust him. His success, some hinted, was due in part to Douglas' timely help. Wentworth's subsequent orthodoxy may have resulted from an arrangement between the two men. With the state's leading Proviso Democrat withholding his support from the Van Buren movement, the Free-Soilers were discouraged in their effort to take Illinois out of the Democratic column. Douglas, whose leadership in the party was daily becoming more evident, became a special target for the bolting group. He was savagely denounced during the campaign for his "disgraceful servility to the slave influence," presumably for his opposition to the Proviso and his attempts to compromise the slavery issue, and was declared "recreant to principle and duty, and unworthy of the confidence of a free people." [37]

As he had done four years before, Douglas took the stump in the 1848 campaign. Once again his efforts were directed toward the south. In mid-April he left his seat in the Senate briefly to address the North Carolina Democratic state convention in Raleigh and to lend his support to the nomination of David S. Reid, his friend and relative, for the governorship. Douglas' speech, commented one North Carolina politician, "was the greatest popular effort I ever heard." He covered old familiar ground—the vindication of Polk's administration, the causes of the Mexican War, and the lack of principle among Whigs—and ended with a soul-stirring reference to "the seven thousand brave men sent by his own beloved state to the fields of Mexico, to meet the diseases of the climate and the balls and bayonets of the common foe." Reid won the nomination, and Douglas received the praises of North Carolina Democrats, although one Raleigh newspaper protested the invitation of a member of Congress from a non-slaveholding state to instruct the people of a slave state in their duty.[38]

The death of his father-in-law, Colonel Robert Martin, on his North Carolina plantation afforded Douglas an additional opportunity to speak in the south during the early summer of 1848. Douglas was named one of the executors of Martin's estate. In administering Martha's inheritance of her father's plantation property in Mississippi, Douglas found it necessary to look after certain legal matters connected with the transfer of the property in that state. He decided to combine family business with electioneering. Forced to leave Washington just before his Oregon bill was to be brought up, and before the Baltimore convention, Douglas first heard of Cass' nomination in North Carolina. On his way to Mississippi he talked with local Democratic leaders, and he sent a detailed report of his soundings to Cass. North Carolina Democrats, he wrote, were pleased with the nomination and confident that they would carry their state in November, "unless Taylor should be nominated by the Whigs." Not so in South Carolina, where the greater number of people he contacted seemed "doubting & hesitating what they would do." In Georgia, Alabama (where, he wrote, Yancey's influence seemed small), and Mississippi, Democratic hopes were high. "The South are satisfied with your views on the slavery question," Douglas informed Cass, but, he added, "Write no more letters." The one element of uncertainty which he encountered among southern Democrats was the impact Zachary Taylor's nomination by the Whigs might have on their states. News of Taylor's selection did not reach Douglas until later, but his choice as the Whig candidate had seemed certain long before.

Douglas' greatest effort on his southern tour was made in New Orleans, where he spoke at a Democratic ratification meeting early in June. He sang the praises of Cass and Butler and emphasized the perfidy of Whig leaders. The election should not be fought, he insisted, on "mere personal issues" but should be waged on principles, so that the "issue between the two parties may be clearly understood, and the verdict of the people distinctly proclaimed." In Taylor's home state he warned his audience that the election of a southern President would not provide security for the south or its institutions. Coming to grips with what he regarded as the central issue of the campaign, Douglas reiterated his opposition to the Wilmot Proviso. In a statement he later came to regret, he declared, "When I am required by my constituents to support that measure, as much as I value their confidence, as highly as I appreciate the distinctions they have conferred on me, I will not hesitate to resign my post and retire to a private station."

On the question of slavery in the territories, Douglas supported the doctrine suggested in Cass' Nicholson letter, although he placed his arguments more on pragmatic than on constitutional grounds. The merits or demerits of slavery, he said, were irrelevant to the question. Slavery was a local institution, and its "burdens or advantages . . . belong to those who chose to retain it, and who alone have the right to determine when they will dispense with it." "We tried slavery once in Illinois," he continued. "It did not suit our circumstances or habits, and we turned philanthropic, and abolished it." In one of his earliest clear statements in support of popular sovereignty, Douglas argued, "I hold that the control of this subject [slavery] belongs entirely with the State or Territory which is called upon to determine upon what system or basis its institutions and society shall be organized. The general government cannot touch the subject without a flagrant usurpation." If the people of California desire slavery, they should not be prevented from having it. If the people of Oregon do not want slavery, it should not be imposed upon them. "Such are my sentiments. Such is the democratic creed."

Douglas received other invitations to speak in the south, but he delivered only one other address before returning to Washington. On July 4 he spoke in Montgomery, reiterating "the inconsistencies, sinister motives, and fraudulent intentions" of the Whigs. By mid-July he was back in his Senate seat.[39]

Following the adjournment of Congress in August, Douglas again traveled to his wife's family home in North Carolina. He intended to return to Illinois before the November election, but an attack of "the fever and ague" forced a change of plans. To the great disappointment of Illinois Democrats, he was unable to campaign in his own state. His presence, as it turned out, was not needed, for Cass carried the state, although for the first time the Democrats were in the minority. Van Buren cut deeply into Democratic strength, especially in the northern part of the state, where his support was stronger than in any other area of the country, but his vote was not sufficient to give the Whigs their hoped-for victory. Nationally, however, the Whigs finally had something to cheer about, for Zachary Taylor carried the nation and won the presidency. The lesson of the election was clear. The slavery question had assumed frightening proportions, and its resolution could not be postponed much longer. Governments would have to be established in the new western territories and the issue raised by the Wilmot Proviso decided. Cass' doctrine of popular sovereignty won increasing acceptance among Democrats. "Whether the peculiar institution . . . shall be introduced into our new territories," commented an Illinois Democratic paper, following the election, "is a question which the Democracy of the nation would leave for decision with the people who reside in the territories, in the full conviction that they are quite as capable of governing themselves, as we are of governing them." To Stephen A. Douglas, it became increasingly apparent that this was the only practical alternative to the dangerous agitation that seemed to threaten both his party and the Union.[40]

# XI

## "Non-interference
is the true doctrine"
1848—1849

i

The defeat of the Clayton compromise and the passage of the Oregon
territorial bill still left unsolved the problem of governmental organization in the Mexican cession. The debates in Congress on the Wilmot
Proviso and the heated discussions in the 1848 election campaign made
it further apparent that the problem could not be solved until some kind
of accord could be reached on the larger question of slavery in the territories. The agitation of the slavery question, President Polk concluded,
was simply "mischievous & wicked," and he imputed a lack of patriotism
to those who carried it on. He was convinced that it was nothing more
than "a mere political question on which demagogues & ambitious politicians hope to promote their own prospects for political promotion." But
Polk, anxious to consolidate the gains secured by the war with Mexico,
failed to appreciate the depth of feeling in the north and south. The agitation held disastrous portents for the future equilibrium of American
politics as well as for the unity of the nation itself. The President might
argue, as he did in his message to the lame-duck Congress in December,
that the issue was more abstract than practical and that slavery could
not flourish in the newly acquired territory in any case, but to many
Americans the question involved more than a simple abstraction. Southern acquiescence in the Wilmot Proviso, the Washington *Union* declared, would result in the advance of abolitionism "until it strikes at the
whole institution in each State, without regard to the property, the lives,

235

the safety of the whites." To Calhoun, the time had arrived when the south had to choose between disunion and submission. He wondered "whether the alienation between the two sections has not already gone too far to save the Union." One northern correspondent despaired that the differences between north and south could ever be successfully compromised. Repugnance to slavery's extension, he pointed out, was not confined to the abolitionist element. "Some of the firmest opponents are men who despise, as cordially as the southern men detest, the canting abolitionist." [1]

The impact of the sectional disagreement on the nation's political structure was equally troubling. The quarrel over the Proviso, the defection of the Free-Soilers, and Cass' defeat in November shook the foundations of the Democratic party and challenged its already tenuous unity. Triumphant Whigs gleefully reported the "dissolution of the Locofoco party" as a national party. Their confident declaration that "the Whigs are the only national party in this Union" rang hollow, however, for the seeds of disunity had already sprouted within their own ranks. Whigs seemed as perplexed in triumph as the Democrats were divided and discouraged in defeat.[2]

For Douglas, as for the President, the course of events proved acutely disturbing. He was persuaded that the polarization on the territorial question represented the work of an imprudent and fanatical minority. He was equally convinced that his own path lay somewhere in the middle, between the two extremes. His concern for the future of his party and for the unity of the nation was overriding; his duty, as he saw it, was to seek solutions to the problem that could be accepted by both sides. Douglas was also worried lest the southern outbursts result in a strengthening of abolitionism in the north, a matter of immediate concern to him.

In April 1848, a proslavery mob attacked the Washington newspaper offices of the abolitionist *National Era,* a graphic example to Douglas of the excesses that could result from the inflammatory statements of southern radicals. Douglas seized the occasion to upbraid the southern extremists for the imprudence of their course. Their speeches, he warned, extreme and breathing a wild and reckless fanaticism, were helping to strengthen abolitionism in the north.

"I have never desired to enlist," Douglas pointed out, "and never shall enlist under the banners of either of the radical factions on this question. I have no sympathy for abolitionism on the one side, or that extreme course on the other which is akin to abolitionism." He protested that in the struggle between those "two ultra parties," those who belonged to neither were "being made instruments—puppets—in this slavery excitement." Yet it was with the latter group that the responsibility for finding an acceptable settlement of the issue rested. Douglas' statements gave little comfort to the southern radicals. John C. Calhoun objected to being branded a fanatic, and he declared that Douglas' course was "at least as offensive" as that of any abolitionist Senator. From Mississippi's fiery Senator Henry S. Foote came the warning that Douglas' determination to remain "clear of all union with the two leading factions" would ultimately prove to be his political downfall. There was no room in the growing struggle, this Senator maintained in 1848, for one who followed a middle course.

Slavery, Douglas argued persistently, was a local institution, domestic in its character. "In the North," he maintained, "it is not expected that we should take the position that slavery is a positive good—a positive blessing. If we did assume such a position, it would be a very pertinent inquiry, Why do you not adopt this institution? We have moulded our institutions at the North as we have thought proper; and now we say to you of the South, if slavery be a blessing, it is your blessing; if it be a curse, it is your curse; enjoy it—on you rest all the responsibility!"

Douglas, in disavowing affiliation with either extreme, did not disguise his belief that some southern indignation was just. He recalled his support of the gag rule, and he pledged his "vote for any other measure necessary to protect your [southern] rights." His repugnance for abolitionism was deep; his distrust of the growing freesoil movement, which he felt was fraught with danger for the Union, was clear, although he failed to appreciate the strength of principle which tied many of its members. "May God prevent that this country is to be ruled by a faction which comes into power by pandering to feelings and prejudices combining men from all parties, with no one principle in common!" Such a calamity, he maintained, could only be averted by bending every effort to quiet the agitation through a practical settlement of the question.[3] Douglas' pragmatic view of the political crisis was laudably assessed by a Whig journal. The Senator approached "the most difficult public questions with a determination to settle them; presenting them to a legislative mind in a practical form; seeking on all occasions to divest the subjects which he handles of all ultraism . . . and constantly manifesting a desire to act for the good of the whole country."[4]

Recognizing the necessity for a practical solution of the territorial question was one thing; finding such a solution was quite another. By the end of the first round of debate on the issue of slavery in the territories, several alternatives had been presented, but none seemed to hold the key to an acceptable settlement. The Wilmot Proviso was one alternative. Another, the controversial Clayton compromise, sought to place the ultimate decision regarding slavery in the Mexican cession in the hands of the Supreme Court, but whatever promise this arrangement may have had was abruptly terminated by the peremptory rejection of the compromise by the House of Representatives. Efforts had also been made to extend the Missouri Compromise line to the Pacific, a move endorsed by President Polk and strongly supported by Douglas as an expedient, practical, and immediate means for bringing the question to solution, but these efforts likewise had failed. The debates both within and outside of Congress revealed the emergence of three basic positions on the constitutional aspects of the question of slavery in the territories. As the discussions continued these positions became crystallized, and, with only slight modification, they remained at the center of sectional controversy for over a decade thereafter.

The first of these positions was that of the northern Free-Soilers, which was based in part on the traditional interpretation of congressional authority over the territories, implicit in the Wilmot Proviso. Congress, the Free-Soilers argued, possessed a clear constitutional power over slavery in the territories and could legitimately bar its introduction or allow its existence there. The power was solely that of the national legislature and could not be delegated to any other body. As antislavery thought became stronger and more influential, many Free-Soilers moved beyond this initial premise, maintaining that Congress indeed had power only to prohibit slavery in a territory, and that slavery could exist in a territory only if it had flourished there at the time of acquisition (which was clearly not the case with the lands acquired from Mexico). With this view, moral principle took on the character of constitutional sanction.

Southern proslavery and states' rights advocates were quick to respond to the freesoil argument. Their position, expressed by John C. Calhoun in a series of resolutions presented to the Senate early in 1847, and further developed during the debates over the Oregon territorial bill, explicitly denied Congress' power to legislate on the question of slavery in the territories. Inasmuch as the territories were the common property of all the states, Calhoun maintained, Congress, or the federal government, was constitutionally obligated to recognize the equality of all the states in the territories and could not legislate against the slaveholding states by forbidding the introduction of slavery. To prevent slaveholders from moving to the territories with their property was to exercise an unwarranted discrimination between citizens of different states and thus to destroy the equality of states. No power on any level could inhibit the existence of slavery in any territory. On the contrary, the federal government must extend to slave property the same degree of protection afforded other kinds of property.

The third view was that of Lewis Cass, as developed in his Nicholson Letter. Others had anticipated the Michigan Senator in his statement, but it was with Cass that the position was at this time most closely identified. Popular sovereignty—contemptuously branded as "squatter sovereignty" by some of its critics—held that only the people who lived in the territories could and should determine the status of slavery within their boundaries. Congress had no authority to legislate on the question. Slavery, it was argued, was a local and internal institution, of concern primarily to those who actually lived in the territories. Like all such local and internal matters, it was to be regulated and controlled by the people themselves, through their own democratic processes. Popular sovereignty represented, additionally, an effort to reconcile Calhoun's denial of congressional authority over the territories with the desire of many northerners to prevent the extension of slavery. Although it had not been formally adopted by the Democratic party as part of its election platform in 1848, it was regarded as party doctrine even though it was not approved by all Democrats.[5]

Both the Calhoun and the Cass doctrines denied the power of Congress to decide the slavery question during the territorial period, and each was referred to by its adherents as "non-intervention." To Cass' followers, however, the term meant non-intervention by Congress only; to Calhoun, it was defined more broadly to mean non-intervention with slavery by either Congress or the territorial legislature. The two concepts were often confused, and the common label frequently was employed by the Democratic party to disguise the deep and radical differences that divided its members on the territorial question.[6]

For Douglas, both the freesoil doctrine and that of Calhoun were unacceptable, for they argued, he felt, from essentially sectional rather than national premises. Neither was acceptable to the other. They represented

the "two ultra parties" which he assiduously sought to avoid. Neither
one, Douglas was convinced, could provide a settlement to the crisis and
quiet the agitation. In the 1848 campaign, Douglas had given passing
endorsement to popular sovereignty in his election statements. Its appeal
for him had grown, and he would soon move to a more complete commitment to the doctrine in the months to come. To Douglas, as to many
Democrats, Cass' position offered an answer that avoided the stigma of
"ultraism." At the same time it conformed closely to long-accepted tenets of local self-government. Never bothered for long by the niceties of
constitutional interpretation, and not a deep thinker himself, Douglas
looked upon popular sovereignty as essentially pragmatic and expedient.
As a western program, with strong support from the frontier itself, popular sovereignty seemed to provide the path for which Douglas searched
—it was a plan that, by avoiding extremes, would restore unity to his
party, end the threat to the Union itself, and enable the American people to get on with the development of the vast continent that lay before
them. Popular sovereignty became an integral part of his plans for the
growth and expansion of the west.

ii

Leaving Martha, who was expecting their first child, in North Carolina, Douglas returned to Washington in November, took up lodgings at
Willard's Hotel, and prepared for the opening of the second session of
the thirtieth Congress. He called immediately at the White House,
where he apologized to the President for his "hasty and imprudent" remarks at their last interview, an action that gave Polk much pleasure.
Douglas, the President noted in his diary, "has been one of my most ardent and active political supporters & friends, and I am much gratified
that our former relations are restored." Later that evening, Polk read to
Douglas those portions of his message to Congress that would urge the
settlement of the slavery question and the establishment of government
in the Mexican cession by accepting non-intervention as the "true doctrine," by extending the line of the Missouri Compromise, or by referring the question to the Supreme Court. Douglas approved the draft and
expressed his delight with the President's position.[7]

Cass' defeat in November cast an air of uncertainty over the capital.
The territorial question would demand the immediate attention of Congress, but there was little hope that the issue could be settled to the satisfaction of all the parties involved. Vice President Dallas was convinced

that the Democratic strategy would be "to try hard to do nothing," leaving the troublesome slavery question to harass the new Whig administration. Developments in the west, however, had added a new urgency to the problem. The discovery of gold in California early in 1848 was followed by the movement of hordes of gold seekers to the Pacific coast. It was clear that the extension of government over the area could not be postponed much longer. The rapid increase in population resulted in new demands for congressional action, accompanied frequently by threats of separation if Congress should continue to be dilatory in its responsibility. President Polk, for whom the acquisition of California had been a primary goal, was particularly apprehensive that the gains of the Mexican War might now be lost by default.[8]

Some hoped that the urgency of California's needs would lay the Wilmot Proviso "flat on its back"; others, encouraged by the recent election returns and the strength of the freesoil movement, were convinced that the Proviso would be reintroduced with greater determination than ever before. John A. McClernand, Douglas' spokesman in the House, argued that the only practical solution to the problem was to refer the slavery question to the people immediately interested, thus affirming their right and capacity to govern themselves, a position that was echoed by the Democratic press in the state. McClernand could not agree with the southern view that Congress had no power to legislate for the territories in this regard, but, with other Illinois Democrats, he was persuaded that the implementation of Cass' doctrine of popular sovereignty would achieve the same result as that desired by the Provisoists. Delaware's Whig Senator Clayton, still bemoaning the defeat of his compromise in the previous session, was also prepared to support a plan that would allow the people to settle the slavery question to suit themselves. "I am sure *they* will exclude slavery," he wrote, "& thus relieve us from the trouble forever." But Congress, he added, would probably do little during the coming session.

Clayton's pessimism was shared by many of the lawmakers in the capital. The Whigs, exulting in their triumph, were nonetheless perplexed and confused; the Democrats were divided. None of the projects that had been advanced to settle the territorial question seemed in a position to succeed. Only one thing was certain. The "slavery topic," Dallas wrote, "will agitate the whole of this session." [9]

Douglas lost no time in renewing his efforts to bring governmental organization to the southwest. On the first day of the session he announced his intention to introduce bills for the admission of California as a state and for the territorial organization of New Mexico. During the ensuing week he altered his proposal, and on December 11 he introduced a bill that would organize the entire Mexican cession as one gigantic state of California, since he was firmly convinced that no territorial bill could be passed at this session. Douglas' strategy was a bold and unprecedented one, designed to meet the pressing need for governmental organization on the Pacific coast without at the same time confronting the controversial problem of whether slavery could or could not exist under territorial administration. By bypassing the territorial stage and providing for immediate statehood for the entire area, the bill would place the slavery decision in the hands of the people who lived there. No one disputed the right of the people of a new state to decide the question. For those who would argue that the proposed state was too large, Douglas' bill reserved to Congress the right to create additional states out of the territory that lay east of the Sierra Nevada mountains, thus leaving a permanent state of California along the coast. Douglas pointed out that he presented this new plan "merely as a suggestion," in the hope that an extension of law and order to California might result from it. He expressed his willingness to support the Clayton compromise once again, if it should be revived during the session, or an extension of the Missouri Compromise line "if it be the wish of the Senate."

Douglas was praised for trying, but few felt that his effort would be successful. The House of Representatives, it was predicted, would refuse any settlement short of the "absolute, unconditional, and uncompromising proviso." Indeed, two days after Douglas introduced his bill, the House reaffirmed the Wilmot Proviso in a resolution that passed by an easy margin, and a week later it received a territorial bill that would extend the slavery prohibition of the Northwest Ordinance over the area. Joshua Giddings, Ohio's outspoken abolitionist, objected strongly to Douglas' proposal as containing "one of the grossest frauds ever perpetrated upon a free people." By providing that all the laws of the United States not locally inapplicable should be extended over the new state (usually regarded as a routine provision in statehood bills), Douglas' measure would in effect allow the domestic slave trade to flourish there.[10]

Southerners greeted Douglas' bill with equal suspicion and hostility. When Douglas moved that his bill be referred to his own Committee on Territories, he was immediately challenged by a group of southern Senators. Bills creating new states, they pointed out, had traditionally been referred to the Senate Committee on the Judiciary; furthermore, questions of statehood involved legal and constitutional matters and were therefore more appropriately the concern of that committee. Douglas reminded his colleagues that referral to the judiciary committee had indeed prevailed in the past, but only because the Senate lacked a Committee on Territories. He cited the practice of the House in support of his position, and he pointed out that the Wisconsin statehood bill, contrary to Senate precedent, had been referred to his committee in the last session. Douglas was overruled, but only by a 25-to-24 vote. He was "much wounded by the decision," for he knew that it had sealed the fate of his bill. Four of the five members of the judiciary committee came from slave states, and South Carolina's Senator Butler, the committee chairman, had expressed strong objections to his proposal. Predictably, the judiciary committee reported his bill back to the Senate in early January with the recommendation that it not pass. One southern member, Solomon Downs of Louisiana, disagreed with the majority of the committee, arguing that "a bill might have been made out of it" that would have obviated the committee's objections.[11]

Douglas regretted that he had not been consulted by the committee before the presentation of its report, and he expressed a willingness to modify the language of his bill in order to satisfy some of the committee's objections. In response to the committee's argument that it was unconstitutional for a state to be admitted before it had organized a government, he sought, rather unpersuasively, to prove the contrary by citing doubtful historical precedents. But more importantly, he threw constitutional arguments and precedents aside to argue that the needs of California were urgent and could not be postponed. California must either be admitted as a state or be left "exposed to all the horrors of anarchy and violence." He hoped that "Colt's pistols will not continue to be the common law of the land." Douglas' plea was impressive, but it had little effect. Several days later he was presented with a book, gilt-edged and bound in morocco, on the back of which was inscribed, "Colt's Common Law of California, From the Author." Inside the book was a brace of elegant revolvers.[12]

The hostility expressed by both the freesoilers and the southern radicals pushed Douglas to the limit of his patience; he lashed out once again at the spirit of sectionalism which pervaded the discussions. Directing his remarks to both sides, he shouted, "Do not insult one section of the Union by bringing forward your prohibition of slavery, nor defy the other by threats of disunion." Only by banishing the question of slavery from the halls of Congress could it be settled. Bring the territories into the Union as states, he urged, and "let the people of such States settle the question of slavery within their limits, as they would . . . any other domestic institution, according to their own will." Douglas leveled his charges at those who sought to array the north against the south, indicating that he too could argue from a moral base. "Neither the North nor the South," he declared, "have any right to enforce their peculiar notions upon the people of those territories. I do not speak of constitutional rights. I do not choose to go into abstractions and metaphysical reasoning, but I speak of those moral rights which are violated when we go to dictating forms of government to a people who are about ready to assume the position of an independent State." [13]

While the judiciary committee deliberated over his bill, Douglas remained in close consultation with President Polk regarding the strategy to be employed in providing government for California. The members of the cabinet agreed with the President that the area encompassed in Douglas' bill was too large and its population too scattered for a single state, but they also agreed that Douglas' proposal to circumvent the territorial stage by admitting California directly as a state was the most feasible plan for settling the slavery question. In fact, it represented the only hope for a settlement during the session. Douglas was summoned to the White House on several occasions for extended discussions. He finally agreed to modify his plan by providing statehood for California alone, but only after it became clear to him that his original bill was doomed. Government for New Mexico could be the subject of a separate bill. Such an effort, he was assured, would have the full backing of the administration.[14]

Shortly after the judiciary committee made its report, Douglas introduced a substitute for his original bill, the details of which had been worked out with Senator Downs, that would admit only California as a state. As for New Mexico, Douglas toyed briefly with the idea of transferring all of that territory south of 36°30′ on both sides of the Rio Grande to the state of Texas (in return for Texas' surrender of its claim to territory north of that line), thereby confirming the Missouri Compromise principle and, incidentally, settling the troublesome Texas boundary question. The suggestion appealed to Polk, but Calhoun firmly rejected it. In spite of the administration's efforts to persuade members of the

Senate to support Douglas' new California bill, it received a cold reception. A fight developed once again over whether the bill should be referred to the judiciary committee or to the more favorable Committee on Territories. It was finally resolved by the decision to submit the bill to a select committee, a decision in which Douglas concurred. A committee of seven was immediately named by the Vice President, including Douglas as chairman, John M. Clayton of Delaware, Jefferson Davis of Mississippi, George E. Badger of North Carolina, Reverdy Johnson of Maryland, John Niles of Connecticut, and George W. Jones of Iowa.[15]

There was little prospect that this new effort would succeed. Polk feared "that the extremes of the South headed by Mr. Calhoun and the extremes of the North headed by Hale & Giddings" would unite to prevent any legislation for California from passing. It was certainly clear by the time the select committee was chosen that any attempt to settle the crisis along the lines suggested by Douglas would be firmly resisted by Calhoun and his followers. The reaffirmation of the Wilmot Proviso in the House of Representatives early in the session, followed by the passage of a resolution calling for the prohibition of the slave trade in the District of Columbia, had spurred the radical southerners to action. In mid-December, a caucus of southern Senators and Representatives was called to unite the south in opposition to the northern attacks against slavery. After several stormy meetings, an address, written by Calhoun, was adopted and issued. Although it failed to receive the approval of even a majority of the southerners in Congress, the purport of the address was ominous. The calamitous consequences for the south of the northern agitation against slavery were reviewed. If the north could not be brought to a policy that would terminate the conflict between the sections peaceably, Calhoun warned, "nothing would remain for you but to stand up immovably in defense of rights, involving your all—your property, prosperity, equality, liberty, and safety." On the day that Douglas' bill was committed to the select committee, Calhoun gleefully wrote, "The South is more roused that I ever saw it on the subject." He was strongly opposed to Douglas' proposal to admit California as a state and was even reported to have told Douglas "that it would never do to settle this question of slavery." More moderate southerners denounced the South Carolinian for his intransigence and for his opposition to Douglas' bill, but even some of Calhoun's critics conceded that the south had a "point of honor" that must be saved.[16]

When the select committee, after a hurried deliberation, made its report at the end of January, Douglas' attempt to secure the admission of California as a state entered a third stage. Two states were to be created in a single bill: California, with oddly meandering boundaries, as soon as the people there should draft a constitution and establish a government; and New Mexico, with an outlet to the Pacific, as soon as its population should be sufficiently large to warrant statehood. Slavery was not mentioned, but those laws of the United States that were "not locally inapplicable" were to be extended over both areas. Because California's admission was regarded as imminent, it would undoubtedly be a free state; presumably, the delay in the admission of New Mexico would enable the southern slaveholders to gain a foothold there. Five of the seven members of the select committee, including three from slave states, had concurred in the new bill (Badger and Niles dissenting), and Douglas was encouraged that it would be favorably received by the Senate. If, at the end of January, he had high hopes that a settlement could be reached, however, they were soon dashed. The bill proved no more acceptable to southerners than his earlier ones, and, with less than five weeks remaining in the session, the Senate seemed in no mood to consider this latest effort. Douglas made repeated efforts to bring the bill up for discussion, but he was frustrated at every turn. The Washington *Union,* reflecting the administration's position, argued that the only alternatives were Douglas' proposal or no action at all. The Senate clearly indicated its choice for the latter.

As the time for adjournment approached, Douglas became desperate. Time after time he reminded the Senate of California's need for government. "All I ask is action," he pleaded, "and I will cheerfully vote for any bill approved by a majority of the Senate." He warned his colleagues that he would move a consideration of his California bill on each remaining day of the session.[17]

Before Douglas could carry out his threat, the discussion entered a final phase. In the course of debate on the civil and diplomatic appropriation bill, Senator Isaac P. Walker, from the new state of Wisconsin, offered an amendment that would extend the Constitution and laws of the United States over the territory acquired from Mexico and would authorize the President to establish a temporary government there. Inasmuch as it would automatically abrogate Mexican law in the area, including the stricture against slavery, the amendment had southern backing. By following the same strategy as that employed by Wilmot three years before—that is, attaching an amendment to an appropriation bill—

southerners hoped to counter the freesoilers and open the Mexican cession to slavery. They were joined by those who, like Walker and Douglas, recognized the urgency of California's need and despaired of securing a statehood bill at this session. Walker's move, however, was immediately complicated when Tennessee's Whig Senator John Bell proposed to substitute a bill for California statehood, prepared by Whigs in the House, for the amendment, thereby achieving the result for which Douglas had labored so long. Southern radicals were shocked. Butler expressed disbelief that Bell could expect to admit a new state in an amendment without the careful consideration usually devoted to such legislation, and Calhoun called the Tennessee Senator to order. Facing a combined northern and southern opposition, Bell's effort was soundly defeated; only four Senators, including Douglas, supported it.

Debate on the Walker amendment monopolized the few remaining days of the session. In defense of his move, Walker expressed his fear that the sectional agitation was leading the nation to disaster. His amendment, he said, was a peace offering. To his northern critics, he declared, "If the Constitution will extend slavery to the land, then let it go. If by that Constitution slavery is extended, I am willing to stand by that Constitution." For his stand, Walker also faced the angry denunciations of his constituents, and he was soon formally censured by the Wisconsin legislature. The Senate debate opened the floodgates of sectional bitterness; angry rhetoric engulfed the chamber. Daniel Webster, fearsome and overbearing, expounded his conviction that the Constitution could not be so extended to the territories. He was answered by Calhoun, feeble and sick but still breathing fire, who declared with equal conviction that the Constitution followed the flag. Douglas, again brushing aside all constitutional questions and disclaiming any intention of entering into a "metaphysical discussion," supported Walker, although he still preferred his own statehood bill. "We had better give to the people of California as much law as we can in the bill that is now before us." As the hour for adjournment drew closer, tempers became shorter and invective more frequent. In the final stages of the debate, the battle was suddenly interrupted when Douglas, securing the floor, declared, "I wish to make one more effort to give a government to California." He moved that the Senate take up consideration of the bill recently passed by the House, providing a territorial government for California and extending the antislavery provisions of the Ordinance of 1787 to it. He was all but howled down when he admitted that he had been unable even to get his own Committee on Territories to consider the legislation. "I have tried to get up State bills, territorial bills, and all kinds of bills, in all shapes, in the hope that some bill, in some shape, would satisfy the Senate," he lamented. "But thus far, I have found their taste in relation to this matter too fastidious for my humble efforts." His last hope for success, he concluded, was in the Walker amendment.[18]

The amendment passed the Senate on the last day of February, Douglas and only three other free state Senators voting for it, but it immediately encountered a firm wall of opposition in the House. There it was replaced by a substitute amendment that would continue the military government and the existing laws in California and New Mexico until July 4, 1850, unless Congress were to provide a government for the area sooner. The House substitute reached the Senate following the hour of adjournment of March 3. A conference committee had been unable to reach agreement and both chambers seemed immovable. Meeting well past midnight into the early hours of March 4, the Senate was the scene of angry and tumultuous confusion, sparked by bitter epithets and threats of violence. As the sun rose on the first day of the new administration, the weary Senators finally agreed to recede from the Walker amendment by a vote of 38 to 7. Douglas, one of the seven, had held out to the bitter end. The Senate adjourned at 7 a.m., with its members in a state of complete exhaustion.[19]

Douglas' aim throughout the stormy session had been to provide the new territories with organized government. All other considerations were secondary to this goal, including the question of slavery. While he moved toward popular sovereignty as the "true doctrine," he was willing to support any proposal that would still the agitation in Congress. He regarded his plan for California statehood as the most feasible, for it circumvented completely the issue of slavery in the territories, but he was willing to support an extension of the Missouri Compromise and even the organization of a territory on the basis of the antislavery clauses of the Northwest Ordinance. While he reacted with great impatience to the protracted debate over the slavery issue and denounced those in both north and south who were responsible for it, he gradually came to realize that the question could not easily be put aside. Whether he liked it or not, Douglas was forced to accept the fact that slavery had assumed new and portentous dimensions in the nation's political life.

Douglas' overriding concern for California during the session obscured his quest for some workable basis on which to extend the laws and institutions of the United States to new territories. He did not deny Congress' power to legislate for the territories in matters pertaining to slavery, but he thought its exercise to be unwise in view of the bitter disagreements which that question aroused. Still, non-intervention operated only for new states, leaving the issue unsettled for the territorial period. In a discussion over the reception of antislavery resolutions passed by the New York legislature, Douglas indicated that he was prepared to move that final step and allow the territories, as territories, to determine the slavery question for themselves. He denied "the propriety of Congress interfering to restrain" the people of the territories from deciding the question for themselves, "upon the great fundamental principle that the people are the source of all power; that from the people must emanate all government; that the people have the same right in these Territories to establish a government for themselves that we have to overthrow our present Government and establish another if we please." He would resist, he stated, encroachments from either the north or the south on this principle, opposing both the extension of slavery to an area where it was not wanted and the attempt to restrain a people from establishing it if they should so desire. Douglas' views were echoed back home by the state's official party organ. "We have ever believed," wrote the editor of the *Register,* "that if the settlement of that vexed and exciting question, was left to the decision of the people of the territories themselves, it would be safely and correctly settled." It was not a clear statement of popular sovereignty, but the germ of Douglas' later doctrine was present.[20]

Douglas' speculations on the relationship between Congress and the territories were focused solely on the lands acquired from Mexico, where the slavery question was unsettled. He was not yet ready to question the traditional view of the power of Congress to legislate for the territories in those areas where slavery was not an issue. While the battle raged over California, Douglas was quietly leading a bill for the organization of Minnesota Territory through the upper chamber. At the opening of the session, he had also announced his intention of bringing up for consideration a bill organizing Nebraska Territory, but this plan was soon dropped. The Minnesota bill aroused little interest, the only disagreement being over an unsuccessful amendment added by the House to postpone the effective date of the bill to March 10, thereby preventing Polk from making the first territorial appointments. A portion of the new territory lay within the area covered by the Northwest Ordinance, but no attempt was made to inject the slavery question into the discussion. Douglas assured the Senate that the bill "provides for the simplest form of territorial government, and does not contain a single peculiar provision." It passed easily.[21]

The short second session of the thirtieth Congress had been an exhausting experience. Not the least of those affected was the President himself. Weakened by illness and despondent over the bitter struggle which characterized the closing days of his administration, Polk left the presidency without seeing the organization of the vast territories which he had secured for the nation. Almost as if to emphasize the closing of an era, he died at his Nashville home on June 15, a short three months after he left the capital. Yet his administration was little short of remarkable for its achievements, a conclusion that would gradually dispel the unpopularity he suffered during his final hours in office. Douglas, who was as close to Polk as anyone could be, sought to place his administration in its true perspective. Although he had differed with the President, sometimes sharply and bitterly, Douglas found in him the highest qualities of heart and conscience. He had presided over and directed one of the great periods of American history; his deeds bore the stamp of his integrity, sincerity, and practical virtue. "The prejudices of communities, like the passions of men," Douglas told a Chicago audience shortly after Polk's death, "sometimes cloud the understanding and obscure the sense of justice." "When we trace the changes which have taken place within the last four years in our domestic policy—in the development of our national resources—in the expansion of our commerce—in the enlargement of our territory—in the augmentation of our power—and in the respect and awe with which the renown of our arms has impressed the world—the mind is startled and dazzled as if beholding at one panoramic view the mighty work of ages." [22]

If the events of early 1849 signaled the end of an era, they also marked the beginning of a new one. The struggle in Congress during the short session was, in many respects, a dress rehearsal for future combat. For Douglas, the session had proved highly significant. No other junior Senator so dominated the discussions in the upper house. With his full, rich voice and easy fluency, he was ranked as one of the Senate's foremost debaters. Always self-possessed and confident, he won respect and affection through his familiar, friendly manner and his utter lack of pretentiousness. "He never put on what vain and self-conscious Senators imagine to be airs of Senatorial dignity," wrote one reporter. "His dignity was of that solid, American sort which can unconsciously take care of itself without airs of any kind." [23]

The excitement of the winter session was enhanced for Douglas when he received word that Martha had given birth to their first child, on January 28 at the Martin plantation in North Carolina. A son, he was named Robert Martin, for his maternal grandfather. Though to Douglas it was an event of no ordinary importance, the increase in his family hardly ruffled his composure. When the session finally closed, Douglas traveled to North Carolina for a brief visit before returning to Illinois to face his constituents for the first time in eighteen months. Martha and the baby remained in North Carolina. Her health, never good, did not permit the long trip to Chicago and she recovered her strength slowly. Danger of cholera in Chicago persuaded Douglas even more that his family should remain in the south. As for himself, he "never enjoyed better health," he wrote late in July. He had found a sure cure for cholera—Dr. Bird's Sulphur Pills—which, he was convinced, could "cure the cholera in an hour." He took one pill each day and enjoyed "perfect protection," enduring only a bout with dysentery later in the summer. Martha's cousin and Douglas' close friend, David Reid, sent reassuring letters from North Carolina on the condition of his wife and son, "the finest looking little fellow I ever saw." When Martha joined Douglas in Washington for the next session of Congress, little Robert remained on the Dan River plantation under the watchful care of his grandmother.[24]

iii

The questions raised by the Wilmot Proviso and the need for government in the Mexican cession were not argued only in Congress. They were fought with equal heat and determination in the state capitals as well. State legislatures, both north and south, leaped into the struggle, debating the Proviso and passing resolutions either endorsing or attacking the freesoil statement. Illinois was no exception. The Democratic party gained heavy majorities in both houses of the Illinois legislature in the 1848 election, but the figures were deceptive. Many Democrats from the northern counties of the state openly identified themselves with New York's Barnburners and with the freesoil movement. Van Buren's Free-Soil ticket received strong support in the north, winning a plurality in Douglas' new home town of Chicago, although the defection had not

prevented Cass from carrying the state. While many freesoil sympathizers, like Chicago's Congressman John Wentworth, had supported the
regular Democratic ticket, they were not willing to submerge their feelings in local discussions of the slavery question. Following the election,
Wentworth's *Chicago Democrat* advised the north to stand firm against
slavery extension, in the hope that the southerners might be converted
to their position.[25]

The disaffected Democrats were hopeful that, with the aid of the
Whig minority in the legislature, they might commit the state to the
freesoil cause. The Whigs hoped that the expiration of Sidney Breese's
senatorial term would give them an opportunity to weaken the state's
Democratic phalanx, but, more dramatically, they expressed the hope
that Douglas himself could be unseated. The statement Douglas had
made in New Orleans, that he would unhesitatingly resign his Senate
seat if he should ever be required by his constituents to support the Wilmot Proviso, was eagerly seized upon by his opposition. "We say by all
means," commented the *Quincy Whig,* "let his sincerity in this matter
be put to the test." Soon after the election, it became clear that an attempt would be made in the state legislature to commit Illinois' congressional delegation to the support of the Proviso, a scheme the *State Register* charged had been concocted by Wentworth himself in the belief that
both Senate seats could then be filled by freesoilers, including perhaps
himself. The combined vote of Taylor and Van Buren, a majority in the
recent election, was, Whigs maintained, an expression in favor of the
Proviso and provided the legislature with its mandate. Douglas' opposition to the Proviso and his strenuous efforts to secure a government for
California in the early weeks of the new session provided further incentive to the freesoilers. He was charged with a "shameful subserviency to
the slave holding interest," even though his efforts had drawn him into
heated disagreements with southern Senators.[26]

The legislators lost no time in implementing their strategy to unseat
Douglas. The first days of the session were taken up with a discussion of
the Wilmot Proviso and several proposed resolutions of instruction, with
the freesoil Democrats from northern Illinois assuming the leadership.
Both houses finally concurred in a brief and direct version that originated in the state senate. Illinois' United States Senators were instructed
"to use all honorable means in their power, to procure the enactment of
such laws by congress, for the government" of the territories acquired
from Mexico "as shall contain the express declaration, that there shall be

neither slavery, nor involuntary servitude in said territories." The votes approving the resolution were close—14 to 11 in the senate and 38 to 34 in the house.[27] Attempts were made to unite the Democrats in support of the resolution, but they were to no avail. Freesoil Democrats as well as those Democrats who supported Cass, commented one of the resolution's backers, "were all honest advocates of free soil and opposed the extension of slavery, differing only as to the proper and more appropriate means to be used to effect the object," a forecast of the view that popular sovereignty itself would limit the extension of slavery to the territories. At least one opposition member took a strong stand in favor of popular sovereignty. The people of the territories, he pointed out, "are capable of self-government." "Their domestic concerns, their peculiar institutions, and their legislative interests, should be entrusted to them, and not vauntingly usurped." [28]

Reaction to the resolution was mixed. To one Whig paper, it was "Simon pure Wilmot proviso." The *State Register,* however, disagreed. The resolution, the editor declared emphatically, *"by no means recognized the principle of the Wilmot proviso,"* since the latter stipulated that slavery should be forever excluded from the new territory. By requiring the exclusion of slavery from the territories only, the statement recognized that slavery could exist in the states to be formed from the territories if the people should desire it. "This is infinitely less objectionable than the Wilmot proposition." [29]

Douglas' reaction to the instructions immediately became a matter for speculation. "It is confidently expected that Douglas will resign," wrote one hopeful member of the opposition. Whigs discussed the possibility of electing his successor, if the split in the Democratic ranks should persist, and the local politicians jockeyed for position. Every freesoil Democrat who supported the resolution, it was reported, was a candidate for Douglas' seat. Rumors began to fly. One was that Douglas had written to a member of the legislature, announcing his intention to resign. Another declared that Douglas would resign and leave Illinois, to establish residence in either North Carolina or Mississippi where he would tend the plantation and slave property owned by his wife, "a martyr in the cause of the South." Still another report, said to have been Whig-inspired, stated that Douglas would not obey the instructions on the ground that they were not supported by a majority of his own party. "To resign, or not to resign, that is the question," began "Douglass' Soliloquy," published by the *Chicago Journal.*[30]

Democrats were confident that Douglas would remain in the Senate. "His plain duty is to retain his position in the Senate, which he will undoubtedly do," one editor predicted. To make certain, another resolution was submitted to the legislature lauding Douglas' "patriotism, integrity and undoubted talents" and requesting him to remain in the United States Senate. The resolution created such a furor, however, that it was immediately withdrawn. The judgment of the state's leading Whig paper ultimately proved correct. Douglas would remain at his post. "Like many ardent politicians in the heat of political excitement, he may have said things which his cooler judgment will condemn." Douglas himself received reassuring word from at least one constituent, "Your course in Congress meets with great applause here, as it does in every other part of the country & Union, and I have predicted that about the year 1860 you will be elected President of the United States." At the end of January, Douglas presented the resolution of instructions to the United States Senate, where, on his motion, it was laid on the table. Later, in a spirit of rationalization, he explained his reaction to the resolution on the ground that it "did not go to the extent of the Wilmot proviso" and that it was little more than a "party trick" perpetrated by a combination of Whigs and freesoil Democrats. Knowing that if he did resign he would be replaced by a freesoiler who would "carry out abolition doctrines," he concluded that it was his duty to remain in the Senate.[31]

While Douglas made it clear by his actions that the instructions would not alter his course in Congress, he did feel compelled to define and clarify his position before his constituents. An article (which he may have written) defending his stand was printed in the *State Register* in mid-June, and in the following October he delivered a speech in Springfield, giving a lengthy and detailed summary of his record on the territorial and Proviso questions. He placed his opposition to the Wilmot Proviso largely on its relationship to the peace treaty with Mexico. It was, he believed, a "mischievous and wicked measure," designed to embarrass the administration, hinder the prosecution of the war, and prevent the conclusion of an honorable peace. Attaching the condition that slavery should never exist in the territory won from Mexico would have defeated the treaty, for no Senator from a slaveholding state could then have voted for it. Its adoption "was well understood to be a decision against the acquisition of any territory from the Republic of Mexico, by way of indemnity or otherwise." In addition, Douglas emphasized, the

Proviso struck at the constitutional right of states to decide the slavery question for themselves at the time of their admission, a right that was recognized even by those who supported the Proviso. States erected from the territory acquired from Mexico could not have exercised this right, since the area would have been secured on the condition that it should remain forever free of slavery. The Proviso, he concluded, was a measure he "had ever opposed and would never support not even under the pressure of instructions."

Whether slavery should be prohibited in the territories while they remain territories "is entirely a different question" from that of the Proviso. The latter "breathed its last gasp" when the treaty with Mexico was ratified and the ratifications were exchanged between the two countries. Those who supported the Proviso, he declared, had now determined "to keep up the agitation for political and partizan purposes, upon an entirely different question under the same name." Douglas reviewed his support of the Missouri Compromise, a measure that had "harmonised and tranquilised the whole country" and that "had become canonised in the hearts of the American people, as a sacred thing, which no ruthless hand would ever be reckless enough to disturb." Upon his own motion, the Compromise had been extended over Texas, and in keeping with its principle he had voted for the prohibition of slavery in Oregon Territory. At the time the Oregon bill was approved, he recalled, "the constitutional right of congress to legislate upon the subject of slavery in the territories was not violently resisted, if indeed it was seriously questioned." The same reasons which had induced him to support the principle of the Missouri Compromise on the earlier occasions persuaded him to support its extension to New Mexico and California. So far as the slavery question was concerned, its extension would have had no practical effect. The physical condition of the country, he believed, was such that the area would in fact remain forever free, "by the decree of the people themselves, whatever might be the action of Congress." With the agitation over the Wilmot Proviso, however, "things assumed entirely a different aspect."

Douglas did not deny the constitutional power of Congress to prohibit slavery in the territories, but he saw no necessity for such a measure. He opposed the Wilmot Proviso not on constitutional grounds, but on practical grounds. Such a measure would clearly be anathema to southerners, many of whom now disclaimed the right of Congress to interfere with the institution in the newly acquired area. Since the territory was already free by the action of Mexico, no congressional prohibition was necessary to prevent the extension of slavery into it. "As a question of policy," Douglas declared, "on the part of those who desired to prevent the extension of slavery, non-interference was the true doctrine." "With the South," he reiterated, "the doctrine of non-interference was a matter of principle—with the north, it should have been one of policy as well as principle—and the result of this doctrine must inevitably have been the establishment of freedom in all our territories." The people of California, he predicted, would decide the question, just as the people of Oregon (in their provisional government) had decided it, "if left to themselves to do as they pleased." He had, Douglas emphasized, "great faith in that great fundamental principle, upon which all free governments rest, that the people were capable of self-government."

Douglas' position on the question of slavery in the territories was clearly in a transitional stage. The traditional view that Congress possessed the power and the right to prohibit slavery in the territories, to which he had subscribed in earlier years, still persisted in his thinking, although he was persuaded that the exercise of that power would be unwise and injudicious in view of the sharp differences of opinion that had arisen on it. He had supported the principle of the Missouri Compromise and seemed reluctant, even at this late stage, to concede its failure. The Wilmot Proviso and the agitation it initiated, however, had shaken his confidence in the efficacy of the Compromise. The only practical solution was non-intervention. The south would support it, and it would, at the same time, achieve the ends for which many northerners argued. By withholding congressional action on slavery in the territories, the sectional agitation would be allayed without loss to either side. But while he urged the doctrine of non-intervention, he also spoke confidently of the ability of the people of the territories to settle the slavery question for themselves, a position to which he would give increasing attention in the months to come. The great danger of the time was in the continued agitation of the slavery question, by which "the north was arrayed against the south, the slave-holding states against the non-slave-holding, sectional prejudices were excited, unfounded fears and groundless alarms aroused, until each section had been worked up to a perfect frenzy." Douglas repeated his alarm at the growth of "northern and southern fanaticism," and he once again announced his determination to check its course.[32]

iv

Douglas' response to the legislature's instructions strengthened his position in the state. His Springfield speech won praise from both Whig and Democratic journals and, it was said, "administered rather cold comfort to those who are looking for his empty shoes." The Whigs had early decided that Douglas' resignation would be of little benefit to either their party or the state. His successor most assuredly would be a Democrat with but "a tithe of his talents." [33] The expiration of Sidney Breese's senatorial term in March 1849 provided Douglas with a further opportunity to influence the course of state politics.

Relations between Douglas and Breese had always been superficially cordial, but the two men had never been close, each one distrusting the other. An able Senator, conscientious and hard-working, Breese was a colorless man whose efforts were seldom fully appreciated by his constituents. His challenger was Douglas' old friend and political companion, James Shields, who possessed all the color that Breese lacked. Irish-born, vain, and impetuous, Shields had served a successful career as a minor officeholder in Illinois before he was appointed, through the efforts of both Douglas and Breese, Commissioner of the General Land Office by President Polk. In 1846, Polk tendered him a commission as Brigadier General of Volunteers. Seriously wounded in Mexico, Shields returned to the country a war hero, and the adulation and praise that were heaped upon him, as well as an official Washington reception and the presentation of a sword by the state of South Carolina, stirred his political ambition once again. Polk offered him the governorship of the new Oregon Territory, but he was after bigger game. In June 1848, he wrote Douglas of his intention to run for the Senate, and he asked his friend to aid in the campaign.

Douglas and Shields in earlier years had developed a close and confidential friendship, and they often speculated together on the true paths to political success. The war had temporarily interrupted their association, but with the war's end Shields was eager to re-establish it along its former lines. "You have no competitor of your age in the nation," he wrote to Douglas, in obvious flattery. "So sure as you and I live you will be president before ten years." Shields proposed a continuation of "the most close alliance of friendship and confidence . . . that each shall make the other's cause his own." Sweep aside all obstacles at home, with energy and application engage in "lofty and manly exertions," and "we can accomplish any thing attainable." [34] Douglas was not so easily swayed. The enthusiasm was all on one side. When Shields was feted in Washington, Douglas was absent from the capital traveling south to take care of his late father-in-law's estate, and there is no record of any letters he may have written urging Shields' election. In spite of the ties of friendship, Douglas remained aloof, and he declined to take an active part in the contest.

Shields' candidacy was not warmly received among the state's political leadership. The politicians and officeholders, it was said, preferred Breese's re-election, while John A. McClernand had built a small but vigorous support for his own candidacy among some of the state's influential Democratic newspapers. Reports that the national administration favored Shields over Breese, which Polk blamed on Buchanan, were vigorously denied by the President. A majority of the Democratic members of the state legislature had, according to one report, given their private pledges to the incumbent Breese. Shields, however, held two advantages over his opposition. His war record (which he dramatically advertised) aroused the sympathy and support of rank-and-file party members, who in turn instructed their legislators to give him their full backing. Shields also benefited from his own equivocation on the question of the Wilmot Proviso and slavery extension. Northern Illinois Democrats were determined to fill Breese's seat with a freesoiler, but they were prevented from selecting one from their own ranks because the north, in Stephen A. Douglas, already held one of the Senate seats. Political custom dictated the choice of a man from southern Illinois. The statement of one freesoil paper, that no person could be elected who was not a supporter of the Wilmot Proviso, was followed by vague reports that Shields (a resident of Belleville), although "a Democrat of the deepest dye," was pledged to "no-slavery-extension principles." Shields did little to clarify his position before the election. Later Douglas wrote that Shields had agreed fully with the position he himself had taken on the slavery question in his Springfield speech in October 1849. "But the people do not know it," Douglas added. "At the North he is understood one way & at the South the other." [35]

Early in the legislative session, Shields was nominated by the Democratic caucus over Breese and McClernand, and soon afterward he was easily elected United States Senator over a weak and ineffectual Whig opponent. One prominent Whig attributed Shields' victory to the war and "that Mexican bullet." "What a wonderful shot that was! The ball went clean through Shields without hurting him, or even leaving a scar, and killed Breese a thousand miles away." Vice President Dallas regretted the defeat of his friend Breese. "Nothing climbs now-a-days," he wrote his wife, "but the epaulette and sword." [36]

Shields' opponents were not prepared to acquiesce so readily in the election results. During the campaign they had cast doubt on his eligibility for a Senate seat, maintaining that he had not been a naturalized citizen of the United States for the required number of years. When Shields' name was called at the opening of the short special session of the Senate following President Taylor's inauguration, Wisconsin's Senator Isaac P. Walker (a friend of Breese's) moved that his eligibility be investigated. At Douglas' instigation, Shields was first sworn in and admitted to his seat, following which his credentials were referred to a select committee. On March 13, the committee reported that Shields had not been a citizen for the required nine years at the time of his election (his naturalization dating from October 1840), and that his election was therefore void. There followed several days of excited discussion, an "excellent *impromptu*" according to one reporter, in which Douglas played a leading part.

Douglas took issue with the committee's conclusions, arguing that Shields was eligible and that his election was valid, a position for which he received lavish praise in the press. "In a constitutional argument," noted the New York *Herald,* "he has completely worsted some of those —among them Webster, Calhoun and Berrien—who have heretofore been considered as pre-eminent authorities on such subjects—a triumph . . . so overwhelming that the gentlemen I have named were necessitated to recede from the positions they had taken." Citing prececents and undoubtedly recalling his own race for the Senate before he had attained the constitutional age, Douglas argued persuasively that a Senator need only have reached the constitutional age and have been a citizen the necessary number of years by the time he assumes the functions of the office. Inasmuch as Shields would fulfill the citizenship requirement by December 1849, when the Senate would meet in regular session, Douglas proposed that the whole question be postponed. The encomiums of the capitol reporters proved premature, for Douglas' Senate colleagues were much less impressed with his performance than they were. His proposal failed, and on March 15 the report of the select committee was approved.[37]

The excitement grew when Breese revealed that he had received a threatening letter from Shields shortly before the opening of the special session. Recalling Breese's charges that he was ineligible for a Senate seat ("and thus, too, after I had poured out my blood like water in the battle fields of my country"), Shields declared that "had I been defeated by you on that ground I had sworn in my heart that you never should have profited by your success." If Breese should persist, he warned further, "let the consequences fall on your own head." Shields lamented that Breese had treated him unfairly by making public the letter, which he conceded had been hastily and imprudently written. "Why didn't you tell Shields to say he was *drunk* when he wrote to Breese that unfortunate letter!" Douglas was asked by a friend. Following the submission of the committee report, Shields threw himself on the mercy of the Senate, convinced that the "whole of this affair was concocted in Illinois," and when it became clear that the report would be endorsed he attempted to resign his seat.[38]

The action of the Senate was watched closely in Illinois. When the election of Shields was declared void, speculation as to how his seat should be filled and by whom ran hot and heavy. The governor, Augustus C. French, was bombarded with suggestions. Some maintained that he held the power to appoint a Senator; others declared that the seat could only be filled by the legislature in a special session. Both groups claimed Douglas' endorsement. In answer to Governor French's appeal for advice, Douglas clarified his position. He had argued against the Senate resolution because he had feared that, by declaring Shields' election to be void, the Senators were in fact denying the power of the governor to fill the vacancy by appointment. Noting, however, that several backers of the Senate resolution disagreed with this interpretation, Douglas was persuaded that the language of the Constitution defining the appointive power of the governor was "sufficiently broad & comprehensive to include every description of vacancy which might occur during the recess of the Legislature." The framers of the Constitution had intended "to insure a full delegation from each State." "If this view of the subject be correct," he concluded, the vacancy was clearly one that could be filled by executive appointment.[39]

Governor French, however, was under heavy pressure from would-be aspirants for the Senate and so preferred not to get involved in the intra-party rivalries. Railroad lobbyists in the state were extremely anxious that a special session be called in order to give them an opportunity to rush their schemes. The governor, in spite of Douglas' advice, yielded, and he called the legislature together in October. In a stormy session of the Democratic caucus, Shields was nominated on the twenty-first ballot and was elected to the Senate once again.[40]

# XII

## "The Union will not be put in peril"
## 1849–1850

i

By the fall of 1849, sectional hostility had moved to a new and dangerous extreme. The utter failure of Congress to reach a settlement on the slavery question during the previous winter left both northerners and southerners bitter and frustrated. The prospect of a settlement seemed remote, and the danger of a rupture between the sections imminent. Talk of secession had become more widespread and earnest, "something more than a bag of wind." "Wherever you see a Southern man, he talks of dissolution, and a Southern confederacy," commented one Washington reporter. "It is, with him, a matter of pride, of duty, of devotion to his country." Moderate southerners were being drawn into the vortex, and the contagion was spreading to the border states.

Southern fears were real and sincere. Many in the south conceded that the question of whether slavery could or would exist in California and New Mexico was an abstraction. At the same time, however, they were convinced that the exclusion of slavery from those areas would bring disaster in its train. The admission of free states from the Mexican cession, with the expected admission of Oregon and Minnesota without slavery, would disturb the balance between free and slave states and submerge the south in the national councils. The abolition of slavery in the District of Columbia and of the domestic slave trade would follow. The efforts of northerners to flout the law requiring the rendition of fugitive slaves was "an ominous sign of the times." With its new strength, the north would not hesitate to attack slavery in the southern states themselves, either through an alteration of the Constitution or by act of Congress. "This," concluded one moderate southern Congressman, "is as good a time to resist as any other." It was, for many alarmed southerners, the only time to resist, and the path of resistance was clearly marked out. "The only safety of the South from abolition universal," according to a Georgian, "is to be found in an early dissolution of the Union." [1]

Actions in some southern states gave substance to the threat. Calhoun's Address had been avidly received in the deep south, and many southern Whigs who had withheld their support from it had now become disenchanted with Taylor's apparent lack of sympathy for their cause. They joined with the Democrats in protest. Prodded by Calhoun, a Mississippi state convention called for a meeting of delegates from all the slave states to be held in Nashville in June 1850, in order to "devise and adopt some mode of resistance to these aggressions." The Mississippi convention members reviewed the southern position and, in a series of resolutions, they indicated that the territorial question was not the section's only concern. The attacks on slavery in the District of Columbia in the House of Representatives had broadened southern fears. The convention held that Congress not only had no power to prohibit the introduction of slavery into the territories (all territories, not simply those gained from Mexico), but that it was also powerless to abolish slavery in the District of Columbia or to interfere with the domestic slave trade. Any such actions would violate the Constitution and "afford evidence of a fixed and deliberate design . . . to interfere with the institution of slavery in the States." The resolutions concluded with a thinly veiled threat of secession if protection should not be afforded to the south. In the months that followed, other states joined in the movement. Southern Whigs closed ranks with southern Democrats, and there were signs that the political parties might be reorganized along sectional lines. By the time the new Congress met, Calhoun was confident that "the North must give away, or there will be a rupture." [2]

Northern freesoilers, however, showed no signs of "giving away." If anything, their determination stiffened in the face of the southern threats. They were joined by northern Whigs, in a spirit which Alexander H. Stephens described as "down right aggressive." Northern moderates, anxious to find a middle ground on which all could stand, conceded that some in the north seemed as anxious for disunion as their counterparts in the south. It was against the south, however, that the moderates' resentment was particularly directed. Southern threats seemed designed to drive off those northerners who sought a settlement. "Every northern

man who fights for them is slaughtered," commented one Douglas supporter, but "even the outrages of the South must not drive us from the
integrity of our position." "We might as well be . . . preparing for the
storm." [3]

The feeling that the thirty-first Congress might well decide the question of whether the Union should continue to exist spread rapidly
throughout the country. In anticipation of the struggle, people flocked to
the national capital to witness what some thought might well be the
death throes of the Republic. "Every body, it would seem, that can make
or feign business at Washington is now here," wrote an Illinois Congressman. The tension was overpowering, and the pressure "felt all around."
The already cramped legislative halls were swamped with visitors, dram-
atizing the overcrowding of the Senate chamber and the wretched acoustics of the House, and giving rise to plans for the enlargement of the
capitol "if the government is to stay here." [4]

Douglas arrived in Washington a week late, "looking badly" and
thinner than usual (the result of his late summer illness). He found himself to be a center of attention almost immediately. His arrival had been
anxiously awaited by those who hoped that he might find a way out of
the difficulties. Douglas, it was said, was "not only a man of nerve and
of sound practical sense," but his position, "equally distant from both extremes," admirably qualified him for the "too often ungrateful task of
mediator." Moreover, his re-election to the chairmanship of the Committee on Territories placed him in a post of considerable power and influence in the Senate, and in any discussion of territorial policy he was
bound to play a leading part.

Douglas scornfully rejected the southern secession threat and denounced those who would countenance disunion. When a petition from
a group of Pennsylvania Quakers arrived asking that steps be taken for a
peaceable dissolution of the Union he became furious. The petition
amounted to "moral treason" and deserved only to be thrown out of the
Senate. When Senator John P. Hale mischievously proposed that it be
referred to the Committee on Territories, Douglas warned that his committee would not consider it. He was convinced that the people of the
country, regardless of section, were anxious that the crisis be settled. "I
do not think it so important to them how it is settled, as that it should
be settled, and peace and quiet restored to the country." He was determined, he said, to keep the Senate in continuous session until March 4,
1851, if that should be necessary. [5]

The session began inauspiciously. Neither party could muster a sufficient majority to organize the House of Representatives, although the Democrats held a slight plurality. Day after day the House members sought to elect a Speaker, but without success. In the meantime, legislative business was at a standstill. Senators, watching the days slip by as the crisis deepened, marked time. Finally, on December 22, after sixty-three ballots, House members agreed on Georgia Democrat Howell Cobb. Two days later, on Christmas Eve, President Taylor presented his annual message. Although he gave disappointingly small space to the territorial question, Taylor suggested that California and New Mexico be admitted as states as soon as their populations requested it. California's application, he noted, was imminent, while that of New Mexico would not be far in the future. By obviating the territorial stage and by awaiting the action of the people, Taylor hoped that "all causes of uneasiness may be avoided." It was the plan Douglas had proposed earlier.[6]

Taylor confined his thoughts to the territorial question; he took no cognizance of the other sectional issues which southerners now related to it. To many his plan was simply a "no-action" policy on the slavery issue, since both California and New Mexico were already free by Mexican law. Douglas' proposal to admit two states had been peremptorily pushed aside, but the administration was hopeful that Taylor's suggestion might have a chance. A strong objection to Douglas' proposal had been the absence of action in the west—the Congress could not admit a state until the people had at least framed a constitution. During the first months of the Taylor administration, however, events on the Pacific moved rapidly toward removing this objection.

Shortly after his inauguration, Taylor received a letter from Edward Dickinson Baker, the new Whig Congressman from Illinois, urging that the administration actively encourage the organization of a state government in California before the meeting of Congress in December, thus giving the Whig party a solid foundation in the new area. The idea had already occurred to the administration. Taylor dispatched Georgia Congressman Thomas Butler King to California as his special agent, with instructions to aid and encourage Californians in the formation of a state government. On the day before King's arrival in San Francisco, a constitutional convention was called. The convention met as scheduled, and by mid-October it had drafted a constitution that organized California as a free state. The constitution received an overwhelming endorsement at the polls, and state officers and a state legislature were selected at the same time. By the time Congress met, a state government was ready to go into operation and two new Senators were on their way to Washington.[7]

The situation in New Mexico was more complicated. Irritated by continued military rule, and discouraged by Congress' inaction, the New Mexicans scheduled a convention to meet in Santa Fe in September 1849, to form a government and to elect a delegate to represent New Mexico in Congress. In an obvious attempt to win southern support, no mention was made of the slavery question or of the disputed boundary with Texas. The Taylor administration, which favored statehood rather than a territorial government, determined, however, to follow the same course in New Mexico as it had adopted in California. A special agent was dispatched to Santa Fe with explicit instructions to advance the cause of statehood. In spite of sharp differences of opinion over the feasibility of statehood, the New Mexicans met in a constitutional convention in May 1850, and drafted a constitution with a sharply worded rejection of slavery. The document was later ratified and a full complement of state officers elected; the new state legislature selected two Senators, who promptly set out for the national capital.[8]

Although the focus of attention remained on California and New Mexico, a third voice was raised. After fleeing from Illinois in 1846, the Mormons had settled in the Salt Lake basin, where they had worked hard to build a new community on the inhospitable desert wastes surrounding the lake. The results were phenomenal. Following the end of the Mexican War, when it became evident that the area had become a part of the United States, Mormon leaders sought to reconcile their theocratic governmental system with the inevitable extension of American authority. In the spring of 1849 they petitioned Congress for the establishment of a territorial government. In their attempts to secure congressional recognition, the Mormons turned to Douglas, whose assistance and sympathy during their Illinois days had not been forgotten. "With a pleasing remembrance of our former acquaintance, and the Philanthropic feelings you have ever manifested towards us as a people," Brigham Young urged Douglas to support the Mormon plea. Their strategy soon shifted, however, and the idea of territorial organization was dropped in favor of statehood. The Mormon settlements, lying athwart the trails to the California gold fields, were particularly susceptible to outside influences. Statehood would preserve Mormon authority and protect the community from rule by unsympathetic officeholders. A constitution was drafted for a proposed state of Deseret, with wide-ranging boundaries that included much of the Territory of New Mexico and an outlet on the Pacific in southern California. A delegate was dispatched in the summer of 1849 to press Congress for the admission of Deseret to the Union. The constitution which he carried contained no prohibition of slavery, for, as he later explained, "there are some two hundred slaves now there, and it was necessary to conciliate that interest, small as it was, in the formation of the constitution." Douglas was asked to give the effort his full support and cooperation. President Taylor for a time considered the possibility of joining the Mormon settlements to California in a single state, and he sent an agent to Salt Lake City to propose such a scheme, but nothing came of it.[9]

With the settlers in California, New Mexico, and the Salt Lake basin all moving toward the establishment of their own state governments, the territorial question assumed a new urgency. The dominance of free state groups in both California and New Mexico impressed even southerners with the necessity for a speedy settlement, if any semblance of a slave interest in those areas was to be salvaged. Moreover, Taylor himself had hinted broadly that he would not feel compelled to exercise his veto power if the Wilmot Proviso principle should receive congressional endorsement. The threat of secession hung ominously in the air as the only alternative to a settlement that would satisfy both north and south, and there was a growing belief that the Nashville convention would unite the south in support of such drastic action. The responsibility of finding a settlement rested with those who, like Douglas, regarded disunion as the greatest of all calamities that could befall the nation.

ii

With the House of Representatives left hopelessly divided by the protracted speakership contest, congressional leadership fell to the United States Senate. The Senate, however, was not immune from divisive forces. Meetings of the Democratic caucus were stormy affairs, highlighted by southern success in removing Thomas Hart Benton from his chairmanship of the Committee on Foreign Relations—presumably because his position on the slavery question was unsound. Douglas was angry. If Benton had been excluded because "he believed that congress possessed the power to legislate upon the subject of slavery in the territories, when opposed to the exercise of the power," then the same rule, Douglas charged, would apply to himself, as it would indeed to many of the other senators present. He registered a strong protest against making the slavery question a test of faith in the Democratic party. To placate Douglas, southern leaders weakly denied that Benton was excluded because of his opinions regarding slavery and then proposed to give Douglas Benton's place on the Committee on Foreign Relations, an offer which he scornfully rejected. It was the first of many angry confrontations between Douglas and the southern leadership.[10]

Douglas became the target of southern ire a short time later, when he opposed a demand for information bearing on the administration's involvement in the California and New Mexico statehood movements. Alabama's youthful Senator Jeremiah Clemens charged Douglas with duplicity, saying that he opposed the Wilmot Proviso while trying to pass the "same principle which that proviso involves." "Are we to be treated like sick children," Clemens asked Douglas, "who are induced to take the medicine offered them by giving the pill a coat of sugar?" Douglas, Clemens asserted, had demonstrated what southerners long suspected, "that the northern Democrats wanted to shield the President from this investigation, because the slavery question was involved in it." The true feeling of the north had been unmasked. Leveling his charge directly at Douglas, the Alabama Senator shouted, "God deliver me from such friends as the northern Democrats!" Douglas could not deceive the south any longer "that he is still a friend of the South." [11]

Undismayed by the southern accusations, Douglas was determined to assume a leadership in the struggle to provide governmental organization to the west and to bring the issue to an acceptable settlement. Much would depend, however, upon the role played by his own Committee on Territories and upon the power it would be able to wield over the pending legislation. Probably in anticipation of its increased influence, the membership of the committee had been selected with care. Three of its five members were from slave states. One of these, Andrew P. Butler of South Carolina, was a prominent spokesman for the southern cause who also held the chairmanship of the powerful judiciary committee. Another, however, Sam Houston of Texas, could hardly be relied upon by the southern leadership, while the third, Kentucky's Whig Senator Joseph R. Underwood, was strongly inclined toward a compromise of the territorial question. The fourth member, James Cooper of Pennsylvania, stood apart from most of his northern Whig colleagues, feeling that slavery need not necessarily be excluded from the west. The makeup of the committee gave little satisfaction to northern antislavery sentiment, but its conservatism made it an ideal vehicle for the development of a compromise on the sectional issue.

The presentation of the Mormon memorial for the creation of either a territory or state of Deseret, and the introduction by Senator Henry S. Foote of a bill establishing territorial governments in California, New Mexico, and Deseret, provided Douglas with the opportunity to define his committee's function and to establish it as the key committee in the crisis. His motions to refer both documents to his committee were vigorously challenged by southerners, who again preferred the more sympathetic judiciary committee. If the southern effort should succeed, Douglas asked, what was the object in having a Committee on Territories at all? "If a bill forming a new State out of the Territories, or a bill creating territorial governments is not to go to that committee, what, then, is there left to be sent to it?" He cited the practice in the House of Representatives and insisted that all business relating to the territories and to the admission of new states properly belonged to his committee. Douglas hoped that a test question could be made on the committee's responsibilities, and he added, "If it is the sense of the Senate, I am entirely willing to be relieved from all my duties on that committee." His arguments were persuasive. Both the Deseret memorial and Foote's bill were referred to his committee, the former by an ample margin, the latter by a bare majority. In both instances, opposition came almost solidly from the slave states. Douglas' committee now had the entire territorial question before it. He was confident that California could soon be admitted as a state, boasting that his prediction that the people there would decide against slavery if left to themselves had been borne out. Even the Whigs and Free-Soilers, he thought, would now support its admission. Although the all-absorbing slavery question was still fraught with danger, "my wishes and judgment concur in the belief that we will be able to save the Union." [12]

While Douglas' committee deliberated, opinion in Congress began to moderate. With the certainty that California would be a free state, those who had insisted on the Wilmot Proviso earlier seemed less likely to insist on it now. Moderate southerners, alarmed at the determination evinced by their more radical colleagues, felt a genuine fear for the future of their section. The conviction gained ground that no settlement of the territorial question could succeed unless it was linked to the other issues that disturbed the sections, especially the move to abolish the slave trade in the District of Columbia and the need for more effective fugitive slave legislation. No one saw this need more clearly than Henry Clay, aged and in ill health but eager to resume his role as the Great Pacificator. "I have been anxiously considering whether any comprehensive plan of adjustment can be devised and proposed to adjust satisfactorily the distracting question," he wrote on January 24. A private conference with Daniel Webster produced the agreement of his long-time colleague, and on January 29 he presented his compromise resolutions to the Senate.[13]

"I hold in my hand a series of resolutions which I desire to submit to the consideration of this body," Clay told the Senate. "Taken together, in combination, they propose an amicable arrangement of all questions in controversy between the free and the slave States, growing out of the subject of slavery." First, California ought, with suitable boundaries, to be admitted to the Union as a state, "without the imposition by Congress of any restriction in respect to the exclusion or introduction of slavery within those boundaries." Second, territorial governments should be established for the remaining portion of the Mexican cession, "without the adoption of any restriction or condition on the subject of slavery." Slavery, Clay added, did not exist by law in the area, nor was it likely to be introduced there. The third and fourth resolutions provided for the reduction of Texas' western boundary and for the payment by the United States of the debt contracted by Texas before its annexation. The fifth resolution declared the inexpediency of abolishing slavery in the District of Columbia, and the sixth provided for the prohibition of the slave trade there. The seventh stated that a more effective fugitive slave law should be passed. Congress, declared the eighth and final resolution, has no power to prohibit or obstruct the domestic slave trade. In conclusion, Clay pointed out that his resolution provided for equal concessions from both sides, and therefore ought to be acceptable to both.[14]

There was little that was new in Clay's compromise. Bills had already been introduced into Congress in almost all the areas covered by the resolutions. The question of California's admission and the organization of New Mexico and Deseret into territories was at that moment being considered by Douglas' committee. By combining the various issues into a single package and by presenting the package as a conciliatory measure, however, Clay had provided a new and more realistic basis for discussion. Union men, northerners and southerners, Whigs and Democrats, took heart. Bipartisan caucuses, in which Clay, Webster, Douglas, and Cass took leading parts, met with increasing frequency to map plans for settling the crisis. Still, Clay's resolutions met with skepticism from some quarters. They were criticized for their vagueness and for the fact that, even if adopted, they would be no more binding than an expression of opinion. It was feared that Clay had a political motivation in presenting them and that they would soon become embroiled in Whig intraparty rivalries. Clay's contention that the Mexican interdict against slavery in the disputed territories remained valid was challenged as a major stumbling block in the acceptance of his compromise. Reluctantly, the Washington *Union* declared Clay's effort to be a failure. "We must now look to clearer, and more generous, and more intrepid minds to save the Union from the horrors which he so eloquently predicted." [15]

In the meantime, Douglas had been busy in his committee, working on the outlines of his own compromise proposal. Early in February the press carried reports of what was labeled as the "Douglas Compromise," but whether Douglas himself released the plan to the newspapers or whether it was the result of a leak from the territorial committee is not known. All its details had not yet been precisely determined, the reports conceded, but it was announced that Douglas awaited only an opportune moment to present his program to the Senate. Douglas' proposal contained five parts. First, California was to be admitted as a free state, in accordance with its own wishes, with the Sierra Nevada mountains as its eastern boundary. Second, the provisional government of Deseret would be legalized as a territorial government, to extend over the entire Great Basin area. Third, the government established by the people of New Mexico would be recognized also as a territorial government. The boundaries of New Mexico would include the land east of the Rio Grande that was claimed by Texas, with the exception of the "Paso del norte," and Texas was to be compensated for its loss. Fourth, a new slave state was to be carved out of Texas and admitted as an offset to the free state of California, thereby maintaining the balance between free and slave states. Finally, territorial officials were to be appointed for Deseret and New Mexico in the same manner as provided for in all other territories. There was speculation that all of the items in his plan would be embodied in a single bill, which, if true, would indicate that Douglas was taken early with the notion of an "omnibus" bill, an idea he later repudiated.

Douglas' proposal was confined to the territorial question, the one aspect of the conflict with which he was most concerned. By recognizing governments already established by the people of Deseret and New

Mexico, he further confirmed his developing idea of popular sovereignty—that the people of the territories should be allowed to determine their own domestic institutions without dictation from Congress. He had done the same in the case of Oregon earlier, when the latter's provisional government, with its prohibition of slavery, was officially recognized in its territorial act. New Mexico had spoken out against slavery, but the Mormons in Deseret had taken no action on the institution.

Douglas' compromise proposal excited little interest. The slavery agitation, commented the New York *Herald,* would "derive no little fermentation" from Douglas' plan, so there was small likelihood that it would succeed. Freesoilers in Douglas' own state took alarm at his move and denounced his suggestion that a new slave state should be admitted as a balance to California. Clay's compromise resolutions were "far preferable." Douglas' compromise was not reported from his committee, nor was it submitted to the Senate, for Clay's resolutions swept the debate in other directions.[16]

Douglas, however, was far from inactive. Although his plan was not as comprehensive as Clay's, he was nonetheless convinced that no settlement would be successful which did not treat the entire territorial question as a single problem. He strongly disagreed with the administration's proposal, supported in the Senate by Thomas Hart Benton, that California be treated as a separate issue, even though he had fought for California's admission on this basis in the previous session. In the California question, if treated alone, lurked the danger of party disruption and even, perhaps, of disunion. Only by linking California with the organization of territorial governments in Deseret and New Mexico, he felt, could northerners and southerners be induced to act together and a true compromise be achieved. A crisis in the House of Representatives enabled him to promote his position there.

On February 18, Wisconsin's James D. Doty proposed that the House Committee on Territories prepare a bill admitting California, separate from and without consideration of the other territorial issues. Southerners leaped to the challenge, and an acrimonious debate ensued, threatening to destroy all hopes of compromise and tie up the House in a fruitless filibuster. Douglas immediately consulted with his two closest supporters in the Illinois delegation, William A. Richardson, a member of the House Committee on Territories, and the influential McClernand, chairman of the House Committee on Foreign Relations. He persuaded them to join two of the south's most respected Whig Congressmen, Alexander H. Stephens and Robert Toombs, in seeking legislation that would combine the California and territorial questions along the lines then being considered by his Senate committee. At Douglas' instigation, a meeting was held at the home of Speaker Howell Cobb, at which Kentucky's Linn Boyd, chairman of the territorial committee, and Ohio's John K. Miller were also present. Douglas was asked to attend, but he preferred to remain behind the scenes. Plans were made to introduce bills that would admit California as a free state, organize the remaining area into two territories on the popular sovereignty basis already proposed by Douglas, reduce Texas' western boundary, and provide a money payment to compensate Texas for her loss. The group also agreed to oppose the abolition of slavery in the District of Columbia. The territorial proposals were virtually identical with Douglas' compromise. The deliberations of the two territorial committees would be coordinated, and identical legislation, to be written by Douglas, would be introduced in the House and Senate. More important, a bipartisan alliance between the northwest and the south on behalf of compromise had been effected.[17]

Meanwhile, Douglas' attention was drawn in another direction as he worked to set the stage for compromise. Some northern Democrats felt a growing concern over the support given to the extreme southern position by the Washington *Union,* the party's official organ. The fear was more imagined than real, and it probably stemmed from a quarrel between the editor, Thomas Ritchie, and his assistant, Edmund Burke. Burke wrote Douglas in February that "old Ritchie is determined to go with the disunionists," and he announced that Ritchie's course might force Burke to quit the paper. Although Ritchie supported Clay's resolutions and had urged compromise, Douglas explored the possibility of establishing a new paper in Washington that would be more friendly to the northern Democracy. He approached Francis Preston Blair, Jackson's old editor, and asked him if he would undertake a new paper that would defeat the southern conspiracy to destroy the Union and restore the party to its former Jacksonian purity. Blair was not opposed to the suggestion, but nothing more came of the talk. Ritchie, perhaps sensing the movement and anxious to retain the government printing contract, became more emphatic in support of compromise and more laudatory of Douglas' efforts.[18]

iii

Debate on Clay's resolutions began early in February, when Clay himself, feeble and suffering a debilitating cough, delivered a stirring defense of his compromise to a packed Senate chamber. The crush soon became unbearable and the air fetid and suffocating, but Clay continued. Never before, he declared, had he spoken "under feelings of such deep solicitude," never before had he been "so oppressed, so appalled, so anxious." Vividly recounting the horrors of disunion, he begged his colleagues to pause "at the edge of the precipice, before the fearful and disastrous leap is taken in the yawning abyss below, which will inevitably lead to certain and irretrievable destruction."

For the next eleven weeks, the words flowed virtually unchecked as the members of the Senate placed their views on record. Only occasionally did the debate reach the oratorical heights achieved by Clay's opening speech. The discussion followed several interrelated threads, and they became so entangled that it was difficult to perceive which one the Senators were addressing. Clay's resolutions provided one thread; a second was introduced when President Taylor transmitted a copy of California's constitution to the Senate. Douglas immediately moved its referral to the Committee on Territories, but the Senators were not willing to dispose of it so quickly. On the last day of February, Tennessee's Whig Senator John Bell presented still another set of compromise resolutions to the Senate. Unlike Clay, Bell was content to limit his proposals to the territorial issue. Two new slave states were to be created out of Texas, California was to come in as a free state, and the area between Texas and California would be organized into two territories, "without any restriction as to slavery." Throughout the discussion, the hotheaded Senator Foote argued monotonously that all the compromise plans should be turned over to a select committee, a move which he made in part to circumvent their consideration by the Committee on Territories, but which also stemmed from his unwillingness to see the different portions of the slavery issue considered separately. Finally, on March 25, Douglas reported his bills for the admission of California and for the creation of Utah and New Mexico territories. An attempt was made to take up these threads in alternate fashion, but they became so hopelessly entwined as to challenge the shrewdest parliamentarian. It mattered little; the arguments related to one were equally applicable to any of the others. "If it be true," commented the *Union*, "that in a multitude of counsellors there is wisdom, or in a variety of schemes any prospect of adjust-ment, it may be hoped that the Union may be saved, even on the brink of the precipice." [19]

One of the most controversial parts of Clay's compromise was his as-sumption that the Mexican prohibition of slavery in the new territories still remained in force—a view that countered Calhoun's constitu-tional argument, and one that met with strong southern objections. It was to this point that Douglas spoke early in the debate. Once again his statements brought him into sharp disagreement with the southern ex-tremists. Douglas agreed with Clay. He had no doubt that slavery was prohibited by existing law in California and New Mexico as certainly as it was in Massachusetts or New York. Because of this fact, he reminded the Senate, he had always opposed the efforts of the free states to pass the Wilmot Proviso; it was unwise and unnecessary for the accomplish-ment of their object. With slavery already prohibited, the Proviso could only result in useless sectional discord, the irritation of one section by another. He did not agree with the south that Congress had no power to prohibit or establish slavery in the territories, but he did object to the exercise of that power. So much Douglas had said before; now he went one step further. To prohibit slavery in the territories was no violation of the rights of southern states, he charged, nor was the establishment of slavery in the territories a violation of the rights of northern states. "Talk to me about the rights of the North, or the rights of the South! Neither has any rights there, so far as the institution of slavery is con-cerned." Under the principle of self-government, each community, whether it be the incipient state of California or the territory of New Mexico, should settle the question for itself. For Congress to exercise its power over slavery in the territories, Douglas added, would be to violate "the great and fundamental principle of free government, which asserts that each community shall settle this and all other questions affecting their domestic institutions by themselves, and in their own way; and for the Congress of the United States to interfere and do it for them when they were unrepresented here, was a violation of their rights, of which they would have reason to complain."

Douglas' statement, his first forceful declaration of popular sover-eignty, was a logical extension of his plan to recognize the governments already set up by the people of California, New Mexico, and Deseret, and to give congressional sanction to their actions on slavery. It was to this point that Douglas' thinking had been moving. Popular sovereignty was the only proper and practical solution to the crisis. Although he presented it as a compromise, it must have been evident that popular sovereignty, as applied to the territories in question, would award the victory to the north, for Douglas' remarks brought angry rebuttals from Butler and Jefferson Davis. The latter reaffirmed the southern position that the south had a right to go into any of the territories of the United States with its slave property. While he conceded that a sovereign state could decide the slavery question for itself, he utterly denied Douglas' contention that a territory could do likewise. Davis continued his denunciation of Douglas' position in a set speech on Clay's resolutions that consumed the better part of two days. Even the Wilmot Proviso, he declared, was preferable to Douglas' popular sovereignty—"the will of the conglomerated mass of goldhunters, foreign and native." The Proviso "attempts to rob me of my rights, whilst acknowledging them, by the admission that it requires legislation to deprive me of them"; Douglas' doctrine "denies their existence." Southern abhorrence for Douglas' solution to the territorial issue was clear and unequivocal.[20]

Douglas did not again address himself to the crisis until a month later, when he delivered his major speech of the session. In the meantime, the nation was treated to a succession of dramatic and awesome statements. On March 4, the dying Calhoun was assisted into the crowded and expectant Senate chamber to make what all knew would be his last speech. Too ill to deliver it himself, he had written it out to be read by Virginia's Senator James M. Mason. Slumped in his chair, his face thin and ghastly, Calhoun listened attentively and immovably as Mason read to the hushed audience. Retracing the steps by which the Union was brought to its present danger, he placed the responsibility for the crisis at the feet of those who had brought the agitation of the slavery question to the point where the south could no longer remain "as things now are, consistently with honor and safety, in the Union." How, then, can the Union be preserved? The task belonged to the north: to concede an equal right to the south in the acquired territory, to enforce faithfully the fugitive slave legislation, to cease the agitation of the slavery question, and to restore to the south, by constitutional amendment, the power "she possessed of protecting herself" before the equilibrium between the sections should be destroyed. Calhoun rejected Clay's resolutions as inadequate. He proposed no specific program, and his vagueness in calling for a constitutional amendment raised many questions. Douglas, for example, thought Calhoun simply sought to guarantee the admission of a slave state with every free state in order to maintain a perfect balance in the Senate.

Three days after Calhoun's speech, the third member of the great triumvirate replied to the southern leader. Daniel Webster had earlier consulted with Clay concerning the latter's course, and then he and Calhoun had conferred regarding the positions they would assume in their addresses. Once again the Senate chamber, as well as all the approaches to it, was crowded with an "eager multitude." "I wish to speak to-day," Webster began, "not as a Massachusetts man, nor as a northern man, but as an American, and a member of the Senate of the United States." He would speak, he declared, for the preservation of the Union. Slavery was excluded from California and New Mexico by the "law of nature," a law that settled the question forever with a "strength beyond all terms of human enactment." The Wilmot Proviso was, therefore, totally useless and unnecessary, and its enactment, achieving no constructive purpose, would only arouse the south. Denouncing the extremists on both sides, Webster concluded with an emotional denial that there could be any such thing as peaceable secession. "I would rather hear of natural blasts and mildews, war, pestilence, and famine, then to hear gentlemen talk of secession."

Webster's speech not only gravely disappointed many of his constituents; it aroused their undisguised anger. They had their say four days later, when, on March 11, William H. Seward, the new Senator from New York and intimate of the Taylor administration, took the floor. There was little doubt that he spoke for the extreme antislavery element, and his remarks carried ominous overtones. California must be admitted as a free state, and the "proviso of freedom" must be extended to the territories; he supported the abolition of slavery in the District of Columbia, and he stood opposed to the fugitive slave law. In short, Seward rejected the whole idea of compromise; he saw no threat of disunion and therefore no necessity for compromise. But the one statement that set southerners (and many northerners) on edge more than any other was Seward's contention that "there is a higher law than the Constitution" which would regulate the slavery question. A moral question had arisen, "transcending the too narrow creeds of parties." Slavery must soon give way, emancipation was inevitable and near.[21]

When Douglas followed Seward, on March 13 and 14, his remarks seemed anticlimatic, although in terms of later events, and his own future career, they were extremely significant. The nation was still specu-

lating on the events of the previous two weeks, still attempting to
fathom the real import of the addresses of Calhoun, Webster, and Seward. Douglas took up their arguments in an attempt to answer some of
them, but his statements made only a slight stir. A *New-York Tribune*
correspondent, curious to witness the Little Giant in action, found Douglas "of small size, hale and healthy," with thick black hair and a shrewd
and resolute countenance. Strong of voice, he was "by no means an unpleasant speaker." Douglas' speech, however, was verbose, highly detailed, and even tedious in places. Much of what he said he had covered
earlier. But the thirty-seven-year-old Illinois Senator had already earned
a reputation as "one of the best and readiest debaters in the Senate," and
those who anticipated a "splendid effort on the slavery question" were
not altogether disappointed.[22]

Douglas preferred to speak to his motion referring California's constitution to his Committee on Territories, rather than to Clay's compromise
resolutions. He praised the Kentuckian for the "matchless moral courage" and "self-sacrificing spirit" with which he stood between the two
hostile factions, but it was the territorial question that drew Douglas' attention. Douglas also granted Webster a share of moral courage for having sacrificed "his pride to his conscience," although he devoted the first
part of his remarks to a tiresome refutation of the Massachusetts Senator's charges against the northern Democratic party for its part in the
annexation of Texas. Seward also received Douglas' partisan jibes for
having represented Taylor as a supporter of the Wilmot Proviso in
1848. It was Calhoun, however, who received the full brunt of Douglas'
attack. Leaving partisanship behind, he turned to "those very interesting
questions called 'southern rights,' and 'northern aggressions' " and declared his disagreement, *"in toto,"* with the South Carolinian. He denied
that the south had any rights in the territories; then, with equal force,
he denied that the north was guilty of aggressions against the south in
this regard. "The territories," he said, "belong to the United States as
one people, one nation, and are to be disposed of for the common benefit
of all, according to the principles of the Constitution. Each State, as a
member of the Confederacy, has a right to a voice in forming the rules
and regulations for the government of the territories; but the different
sections—North, South, East, and West—have no such right." To
Calhoun's assertion that it was up to the north to do justice to the south,
Douglas replied that there were none more scrupulous in the observance
of the principles of justice than the northern states. But, he warned, the

northern states would "consent to no amendment of the Constitution which shall be presented under a threat to dissolve the Union."

What Calhoun and his southern cohorts could not appreciate, Douglas declared, was that "the cause of freedom has steadily and firmly advanced, while slavery has receded in the same ratio," rendering the suggestion that there be a balance between free and slave states unworkable and unrealistic. Directing his remarks as much to northern Provisoists as to the south, he pointed out that freedom's advance had been in spite of, not because of, the enactment of national legislation. A law passed by Congress "to operate locally upon a people not represented, will always remain practically a dead letter upon the statute book, if it be in opposition to the wishes and supposed interests of those who are to be affected by it," an idea to which Douglas would return on later occasions with telling effect. Only popular sovereignty—"that great Democratic principle, that it is wiser and better to leave each community to determine and regulate its own local and domestic affairs in its own way"—provided a satisfactory solution to the slavery question, although Douglas predicted that it would result in the expansion of the area of freedom. No person, regardless of his sectional origin, was barred from the territories, but certain institutions and forms of property were. For example, the banker could not take his bank into some territories, nor could the whiskey dealer take his stock into others, because local laws prohibited it. By this principle, slavery had been excluded from Oregon Territory, from California, and, indeed, from Douglas' own state of Illinois, whose citizens, he reminded the Senate, had once owned slaves in defiance of the Ordinance of 1787. "Unalterable provisions in favor of freedom" or "arbitrary enactments" of Congress would prove unavailing, Douglas told the north. "Slavery can never be exterminated—liberty can never be established and perpetuated—by such means. The desire for free institutions must first find an abiding place in the hearts of the people, and show itself in all their works." It mattered not whether the question related to states or territories; popular sovereignty belonged equally to both. "Have the people of the territories of the United States no rights?" he asked. "I had supposed that the principle was universally conceded in this country, that all men have certain inherent and inalienable rights; and I have yet to learn upon what grounds the people of the territories are to be excluded from the benefit of this principle."

Douglas offered small comfort to the south. The area between the Mississippi and the Pacific, he predicted, would soon be filled with a "hardy, enterprising, and industrious" population, enough to form seventeen new free states. There was no alternative, whether Congress prohibited slavery there or not, for the area was already free by the laws of nature and of God, and where nature would not work for freedom the will of the people would. Where, Douglas queried, is the territory so adapted to slavery that new slave states might be formed from it? He answered his own question, "There is none—none at all." As if to drive his point deeper, he hoped that before long Delaware, Maryland, Virginia, Kentucky, Missouri, North Carolina, and Tennessee would adopt gradual emancipation and join the ranks of the free states.

As he had done many times before, Douglas placed the responsibility for the agitation with the extremes in both north and south. "Pride of opinion" and the unwillingness of each side to understand the problems of the other prevented a practical settlement of the issues. "It is as impossible to get a Carolinian to comprehend and appreciate the character of the people and institutions of the North, as it is for an Abolitionist to understand the true condition of things in the South." Rejecting both extremes, he concluded with a paean to his own great west, the most national of all areas, in words that touched his innermost convictions. "There is a power in this nation greater than either the North or the South—a growing, increasing, swelling power, that will be able to speak the law to the nation. . . . That power is the country known as the great West—the Valley of the Mississippi, one and indivisible from the gulf to the great lakes, and stretching, on the one side and the other, to the extreme sources of the Ohio and Missouri—from the Alleghenies to the Rocky mountains. There, sir, is the hope of this nation —the resting-place of the power that is not only to control, but to save, the Union. . . . This is the mission of the great Mississippi valley, the heart and soul of the nation and the continent." [23]

Douglas' speech reflected the conservatism that had come to be identified with his views on the slavery question. From his home at Wheatland, James Buchanan praised the speech for its "surpassing ability" and "patriotic, liberal & enlightened spirit." While he could not concur in all the positions taken by Douglas, he felt that the speech would do great good throughout the country. Douglas had not committed himself to Clay's compromise (pleading lack of time as his reason for not discussing it), but he had hinted at his general support. He was convinced that the territorial issues were the most important and most urgent. Throughout his speech ran the thread of popular sovereignty; there was no longer any doubt that this principle had assumed a critical importance in his view of the crisis. Douglas took a more pronounced stance against the extension of slavery than he ever had before, which must have heightened the suspicion of his motives that was already held by southerners, but his position was based on a practical and realistic appraisal of the facts of western settlement, including a recognition of the oft-expressed wishes of western settlers. It was an antislavery view that sprang solely from his devotion to local self-government. Where he had only hinted before, he was now explicit—popular sovereignty would advance the cause of freedom. Alluding briefly to the instructions of his own state legislature, Douglas assured the Senate that he had no desire to "break loose" from the expressed wishes of his constituents. Maintaining his opposition to a congressional prohibition of slavery in the territories, he hoped that his state would soon recognize that his proposals were "safe, prudent and discreet," while at the same time they achieved the result that the legislature desired. With a characteristic boastfulness, he declared that, if his earlier efforts to secure the organization of California and New Mexico had not encountered the combined opposition of the northern and southern extremists, "the whole of the territory acquired from Mexico would, at this moment, have been dedicated to freedom forever." Douglas ended his remarks on a note of optimism. The excitement, he felt, was subsiding and reason was in the ascendancy. "The Union will not be put in peril; California will be admitted; governments for the territories must be established; and thus the controversy will end, and I trust forever." [24]

On March 25, Douglas reported his two long-awaited bills for the admission of California and for the organization of territorial governments in New Mexico and Utah (preferring the latter name to Deseret). He had written the bills and laid them before his committee as early as the previous December but had not secured the consent of the committee to submit them until late in March. Even then, there was a difference of opinion among the committee members. Each one, he told the Senate, reserved the right to state his own opinions on the proposed legislation and to act accordingly, even to the point of offering amendments to the bills. Douglas admitted that he was the only member who was responsible for all the provisions. Before reporting, he consulted with Clay and Cass, both of whom agreed with Douglas that he should offer separate bills rather than combining the question in a single piece of legislation. California was, of course, to be admitted as a free state, in accordance with its constitution. The second bill provided for the organization of New Mexico and Utah territories, without provision as to slavery, and the settlement of the Texas boundary. In general, the bills followed Douglas' earlier "compromise" and were identical with a plan proposed a short time later in the House of Representatives by McClernand (who conceded that "the plan is not of my authorship"). Popular sovereignty was further established in the bills' terms. The Utah government was substituted for the proposed state of Deseret, primarily to forestall anti-Mormon opposition, but the provisional laws there were to continue in force. The provisions for New Mexico merely legalized the territorial plan proposed by its settlers. The Mormon delegate in Washington expressed great disappointment with the plan, but Douglas was able to persuade him that no other arrangement could possibly succeed.[25]

Douglas was heartened by the reactions to his bills. "The skies are brightening," commented the Washington *Union*. "We hail this movement as the sure harbinger of an early settlement of the question." Douglas, the paper continued, was entitled to the gratitude of the country for his "arduous and perservering labors in this great work of pacification." His two bills, with Mason's proposal for a more effective fugitive slave law, provided a compromise that would surely satisfy the "moderate and patriotic of all portions of the Union." One Illinois Congressman wrote, "Douglas stands very high with the senate." The real struggle, however, was just beginning. "We are just getting into the agitation," one paper warned, "and God only knows when, or how, or by what process, we are to get out." [26]

# XIII
## "The common ground
## of justice and compromise"
## 1850

i

Douglas' efforts to settle the sectional controversy received the general endorsement of his constituents, as sentiment favoring compromise grew in Illinois among all except the most adamant freesoilers. Southern disunion threats alarmed citizens of the state, and both Whigs and Democrats agreed that their first duty was to the Union. The Wilmot Proviso as a requirement for the settlement of the territorial issue no longer seemed so important when contrasted with the danger of disunion. Reports from the Illinois delegation in Congress of southern intransigence in the crisis, and of Douglas' frequent altercations with southern extremists, tended to solidify support behind the efforts to achieve a settlement. "The Southerners are insolent, overbearing & bullying beyond all endurance," wrote Congressman William H. Bissell. From the Senate, Shields reported that southern Senators "pounded on the North until it became insufferable. . . . The Ultra pro-slavery man is intolerable. The Ultra Free-Soil man is still worse. It should be our effort to keep the middle course between two extremes." Richardson, appalled to hear members of Congress speak earnestly of disunion, urged his constituents to stand by the Union and defend it to the last. In the northern part of the state, however, many freesoilers remained unreconciled. For John Wentworth, the time for compromise had passed. Proviso meetings were held in the spring of 1850, protesting the drift toward compromise, but their appeal was not what it had been earlier. Even the *Chicago Tribune* severed its relationship with the freesoil movement.[1]

Douglas became the special target of the agitators. With a total lack of understanding for his position, they pictured him as a servile tool of the south and as an advocate of slavery extension. The fact that his views were most sharply challenged by the very men whom he was charged with serving seems to have made little impression. The attacks reached a climax at a "nonpartisan" freesoil meeting held in Chicago late in February, which was presided over by the city's mayor. There the freesoilers denounced Douglas for his reported compromise plan, especially the suggestion that an additional slave state be created out of Texas. They firmly endorsed the Wilmot Proviso and called for the abolition of slavery in the District of Columbia. Once again, they demanded Douglas' resignation. This time not only Democratic papers, but the Whig press as well sprang to Douglas' defense. One Whig editor, a caustic critic of Douglas in earlier times, conceded Douglas' view that the Proviso was not necessary to guarantee freedom in the territories. Douglas himself immediately responded to the meeting in an angry letter, protesting the "studied suppression of all I say and do upon the slavery questions and the constant publication of what I have neither said nor done." The misrepresentation of his views was a source of frustration to Douglas. Branded as a "doughface" and a "slavery extensionist" by some of his freesoil constitutents, he hoped that in time they would realize they had been deceived in their interpretation of his position. The state's leading Whig paper dismissed the Chicago meeting as the work of a "knot of politicians" who were bent on driving Douglas from the Senate. As Whigs and Democrats came together in Illinois in support of compromise, so did they in other parts of the north, to the despair of the extreme freesoil element. Charles Sumner moaned that "both the old parties are coming together on substantially the same principle," that is, non-intervention. He looked to Calhoun and his followers to aid the freesoilers in driving them "from this shelter," but the southern effort was hampered by the death of the eminent South Carolinian at the end of March.[2]

Whether the compromise forces could be driven from their "shelter" became increasingly problematical. Throughout the early months of the year, Henry S. Foote maintained that all the compromise measures should be submitted to a select committee. The idea, Foote later revealed, had originated with Ritchie and had been shaped in consultation with Clay and Virginia Representative Thomas H. Bayly. Foote at first suggested that Clay's resolutions could be combined in a single compromise bill by such a committee. Clay, opposed to such an "omnibus" approach, preferred that each of the resolutions be taken up in succession, although he agreed that those dealing with the territorial governments and with the Texas boundary might be so combined. Douglas disagreed with Foote's proposal, at least so far as the territorial question was concerned, but he promised he would raise no objection if the Senate wished to create a select committee. He preferred, however, that the California and territorial issues be considered separately from the other resolutions, thus maintaining the influence of his own committee.

Foote's persistence eventually won out. On April 18, following one of the most exciting scenes ever witnessed in the Senate, when Foote, overcome by anger, advanced on Benton with a drawn pistol, the Senate formally approved the creation of a select committee of thirteen. The membership included six Democrats and six Whigs (equally divided between north and south); the thirteenth member, Henry Clay, would serve as chairman. Douglas, because he opposed the creation of the committee, declined to be a member. He had repeatedly urged the Senate to bring his bills for California and the territories to a vote, but without success. Since copies were already on each Senator's desk, he saw no point in referring them to a select committee only to have them reported again. If the Senate wished to combine his two bills into one, as it seemed likely Clay's committee would do, he suggested that a motion to that effect could easily be made. While he opposed the committee, he acquiesced in its appointment. "If I cannot have my own way, I will not delay the Senate by preventing the majority from having theirs." The movement, he was convinced, was a farce, the committee's verdict cut and dried, but he would rather, he said, "laugh at the farce than wrangle and quarrel, and make it a tragedy instead of a farce." [3]

On May 8, Clay presented the report of the Committee of Thirteen to the Senate. Douglas received a hint as to the nature of the report on the day before, in a private conversation with Clay in the Senate chamber. In response to Douglas' inquiry, Clay, who had earlier favored separate bills, said that his committee would simply recommend that Douglas' two bills be united into a single act, and that, therefore, no legislation on the subject would be formally reported. When Douglas suggested that the select committee itself combine them, Clay protested that such a course would not be fair to Douglas; he had written the legislation and should receive full credit for his labors. Douglas, however, persisted in his suggestion. He had no such pride of authorship in the bills, he said, as to insist that the committee defer to his part in their preparation. At the same time, he was anxious that the most effective strategy for their adoption be effected. He was convinced, he frankly told Clay, that the bills could not pass Congress as a single measure, since uniting them would also unite their opponents. If the select committee should report his bills as one measure, the Senate would then have the matter before it in two forms—as one bill, proposed by Clay, and as two bills, proposed by Douglas. If the former should fail, as Douglas was persuaded it would, the Senate could easily take up the latter. After some further remonstrance in favor of doing Douglas justice for having written the bills, Clay agreed that they would be combined by the committee. And so they were when Clay delivered his report to a waiting but sparsely attended Senate the next day.[4]

Of the three bills submitted by the committee, two were based on legislation already before the Senate. The first combined the question of California's statehood, territorial governments for Utah and New Mexico, and the Texas boundary in a single bill, known from that time on as the omnibus bill. In making his presentation, Clay acknowledged that his committee, "availing themselves of the arduous and valuable labors of the Committee on Territories," had simply united Douglas' two bills. As Douglas later put it, the committee "took my two printed Bills & put a wafer between & Reported them back without changing or writing a single word, except one line." But the one change was crucial. Against the opposition of both Clay and Cass, the committee had inserted a clause prohibiting the territorial legislatures of Utah and New Mexico from acting on the subject of slavery, a clause that could be supported by both northern and southern extremes for different reasons, but one which violated Douglas' principle of popular sovereignty. The second committee bill was Mason's legislation for the more effective rendition of fugitive slaves. Finally, in the only bill written by the committee, the slave trade in the District of Columbia was to be prohibited.[5]

After the short respite afforded by the committee's deliberations, the Senate prepared for a new fight over the omnibus bill. The battle lines were drawn once again, and debate on the bill consumed the next two and a half months. Virtually every Senator insisted on having his say, and the business of the nation became submerged in a welter of words. Southern hostility to the compromise was apparent immediately, a hostility that was stiffened by the meeting of the Nashville Convention early in June. Calhoun's death had moderated the initial thrust of the convention, but the delegates still found sufficient warrant to denounce Clay's compromise and to endorse the extension of the Missouri Compromise line as the best plan for adjusting the crisis. President Taylor stubbornly adhered to his own proposal in spite of Clay's anxious effort to secure the cooperation of the White House. Bitterly disappointed with the President's refusal to support his compromise, Clay angrily criticized the Chief Executive. "Here are five wounds . . . bleeding and threatening the well being, if not the existence of the body politic. What is the plan of the President? Is it to heal all these wounds? No such thing." Northern radicals saw in the bill an effort to convert all the territories into a "slave pasture." Clay himself became discouraged, writing at the end of May that "the Administration, the Abolitionists, the Ultra Southern men, and the timid Whigs of the North" were all combined against the bill. Douglas' prediction that the omnibus bill could never pass seemed close to fulfilment.[6]

Douglas' goal was to secure the passage of his bills, either in their original form or combined. A clear choice was now before the Senate. A week after Clay made his report Douglas sought to commit his colleagues to one or the other. Reminding the Senate that the bills were virtually the same in either case (except for the controversial provision restricting the territorial legislatures from acting on the slavery question), he moved that the omnibus bill be laid on the table. His motion failed, but only by a narrow margin. Douglas then turned to the one change Clay's committee had made in his territorial bill.

The efforts of Jefferson Davis to modify the prohibition on action relating to slavery so as to allow the territories to provide protection to slave property brought Douglas to his feet and enabled him to argue forcibly for popular sovereignty. Slavery, like all other questions relating to the domestic policy of the territories, "ought to be left to the decision of the people themselves." "We ought to be content with whatever way they may decide the question, because they have a much deeper interest in these matters than we have, and know much better what institutions suit them than we, who have never been there, can decide for them." For the first time, Douglas was challenged to indicate the precise point at which the people of a territory might exercise this right. Popular sovereignty, carried to its fullest extent, Davis maintained, would mean that one man in a territory could determine the fundamental law for all time to come. "Without determining the precise number," Douglas retorted, "I will assume that the right ought to accrue to the people at the moment they have enough to constitute a government." The fact that Congress was debating a bill to provide a territorial government for Utah and New Mexico surely indicated that the people in those territories had reached that stage. Davis' real object, Douglas charged, was to extend slavery to an area from which it was already barred by existing law, a move to which Douglas could never assent. Douglas did not rest his case only on principle; he added an element of expedience. No compromise bill in which the word "slavery" was mentioned, he warned, would ever pass. "If you prohibit; if you establish; if you recognize; if you control; if you touch the question of slavery, your bill cannot, in my opinion, pass this body." The only bill that could pass, and thus bring the crisis to a settlement, was one that left the question open, "but leaves the people to do as they please, and to shape their institutions according to what they may conceive to be their interests both for the present and the future." Douglas' arguments were unavailing. His attempt to strike the offending words from the bill failed.

During the discussions Douglas often found himself in the uncomfortable position of arguing one way out of conviction and voting another in deference to the instructions of the Illinois legislature. The contradiction, however, was not as deep as it may have seemed, which, perhaps, accounts for the fact that he chose this occasion to follow the dictates of his constituents. Although he voted for amendments of Chase and Seward that would apply the Wilmot Proviso to the territories, he recognized that neither could succeed. In each case, the amendment merely confirmed his own view that slavery already was excluded from the area and that the people had already expressed their opposition to its introduction. Practically, the difference between these amendments and his own efforts to secure recognition for popular sovereignty was small, at least to Douglas. At the same time, he voted consistently against southern moves to provide protection to slavery in the area. He preferred, he often said, that the bill remain silent on the slavery question, thereby leaving the decision to the people. However, "if we are to take cognizance of the subject of slavery there, then I am compelled to vote according to my view of what is right under my instructions." [7]

Debate on the omnibus bill continued unabated through June and July, the heat of the discussions matching the rising temperatures outside. The energy of some members of Congress began to flag under the constant pressure. Virginia's Senator Hunter, reflecting a growing weariness in the Senate, complained of being worn down "under the worry and excitement around me." A plethora of amendments was offered, most of them unsuccessful, and few of the bill's details escaped extended argument. Four amendments to the territorial provisions of the bill, three of them offered by southerners, were successful, although Douglas and others did not feel that they altered the basic nature of the legislation. Georgia's Senator Berrien proposed that the clause prohibiting action by the territorial legislatures with respect to slavery be altered to read "no law shall be passed . . . establishing or prohibiting African slavery." By this more precise language, southerners felt that the territorial legislatures would have the power to protect slave property. Like the clause it replaced, the phrase violated popular sovereignty, and Douglas voted in the minority against the change. On June 6, David Yulee of Florida, seeking to secure the southern view that slavery existed in the territories by virtue of the Constitution, offered an amendment extending the Constitution and laws of the United States to the area, in phraseology derived from the ill-fated Clayton compromise. His amendment passed, but to those northerners who supported it, like Douglas, the change was unimportant. The Constitution, Douglas maintained, was already there. Several days later, the freesoiler John P. Hale succeeded in amending the bill so as to place the appellate power of the Supreme Court on the same basis in the territories as in the states, a move that would take the final decision in cases involving title to slaves out of the hands of the territorial courts. Although it passed almost without debate and disagreement, Hale's amendment, according to one scholar, was the most important change effected in the bill, as it established a pattern for later territorial legislation. On the same day, Louisiana's Pierre Soulé introduced an amendment providing that states created out of the territories would be admitted with or without slavery, as their constitutions would prescribe. Douglas believed that the amendment, an attempt to commit northerners to the admission of new slave states if they should so apply, was immaterial and unnecessary, since the right already existed. "I have always held," he said, "that the people have a right to settle these questions as they choose, not only when they come into the Union as a State, but that they should be permitted to do so while a Territory." Soulé's amendment passed by a substantial margin.[8]

While Douglas assented to amendments of the territorial provisions of the bill so long as they conformed to his popular sovereignty position, he fought to preserve the admission of California in precisely the manner in which he had written and reported it, and exactly as it had been reported by the Committee of Thirteen. At one point he announced his intention of amending the section in order to allow the admission of two additional states from California, but he quickly changed his mind. He repelled southern efforts to reduce California's representation in the lower house from two representatives to one and strongly opposed Soulé's attempt to prevent the admission of California until the new state should relinquish its title or claims to the public domain. Responding to Soulé's challenge, Douglas occupied the Senate floor for two days with an excessively detailed discussion of the terms under which new states had been admitted since the early days of the Republic, concluding with a statement with which few of his auditors would disagree. "I am aware," he said, "that these dry details must have been tedious and wearisome to the Senate."

Douglas angrily rejected southern hints that he had written a faulty bill, pointing out the care with which he discharged his tasks as chairman of the Committee on Territories. "When it becomes my duty . . . to report a bill for the admission of a new State, I review the precedents under our own Constitution. I examine the practice in other cases, and trace the history of our legislation upon the subject from the formation of the Government. I look into the action of all the departments of the Government, and examine the decisions of the courts; and when I find there is one unbroken chain of authority upon the subject, running through our entire history as a nation, I do not hesitate to bring in a bill in accordance with the examples of those who have gone before." Charging the south with promulgating "antiquated notions of State sovereignty," he denounced the persistent southern efforts to forestall California's admission by raising technicalities that had never been applied to other states. Putting his finger on the difficulty, he concluded that California's only sin in the eyes of the south "was that she chose, in the plenitude of her wisdom and power, to exclude the institution of slavery from her borders."

Douglas' defense of his bill won high praise in spite of its detailed and technical nature. One congressman thought it was the ablest speech Douglas had ever delivered. "There is probably no man in the Senate so familiar with the Statutory law of the U. S. as Mr. Douglas," wrote the *New-York Tribune* correspondent. Webster was to follow Douglas, but after the latter's "completely triumphant refutation" of Soulé's argument, "a speech from Mr. Webster seemed almost superfluous." Douglas, the "Young Giant of the West," another correspondent reminded his readers, "speaks with great energy and precision, enunciating every word distinctly, and commands the attention of the Senate." [9]

By mid-July it was apparent that the supporters of compromise were making little headway against the delaying tactics of the opposition. "Our hopes of the compromise grow feebler every day and the general opinion is that it must fail," wrote Illinois Congressman Thomas L. Harris. After seven and a half months of debate and deliberation, the compromise seemed doomed. The sudden death of President Taylor on July 9 provided a slim ray of hope to the backers of the omnibus bill. Taylor, an implacable foe of the bill, was succeeded by Millard Fillmore, whose close relations with Clay and Webster augured well for a settlement. But even the new support from the White House could not save the omnibus bill. Once the threat of a presidential veto had been removed, there seemed less need for combining the California, territorial, and Texas boundary issues. The weakness of Clay's approach had been dramatically revealed during the debates. Now Douglas' original strategy of treating the problems separately achieved new popularity. On July 17, Daniel Webster, in his role as administration spokesman, asked Douglas what he should do if California were to be admitted in a separate bill. Douglas replied that he would immediately take up the territorial bills, with the Texas boundary question, and push them through the Senate separately. The groundwork was at last laid for a final resolution of the problem. [10]

In the last stages of the debate, the Senate turned to the question of Texas' boundary. Douglas said little during the debates on the boundary issue, other than to defend the terms of his original bill. He denied Texas' claim to the east bank of the upper Rio Grande, unless, as he said sarcastically, Texas' "getting her own force captured amounted to a conquest." Now he seemed willing to modify his stand slightly, if by so doing the possibility of passing the compromise would be enhanced. In caucus, the supporters of the omnibus bill concluded that the act would be strengthened by referring the boundary issue to a joint commission for settlement. An amendment to that effect was offered by James W. Bradbury of Maine. Douglas indicated his support to Bradbury's amendment, but he was absent from the Senate when it failed by a tie vote. Bradbury renewed his effort immediately, in slightly modified form, but it was almost as immediately amended by Georgia's William C. Dawson, to provide that New Mexico's territorial government should not go into effect east of the Rio Grande until the commission's report had been accepted by Texas. Clay accepted Dawson's proviso, but Douglas did not. The proviso, Douglas pointed out, would in effect grant the disputed area to Texas. Dawson deferred to Douglas in the hope that the latter might prepare a more acceptable version, but apparently none was formally offered. As proceedings in the Senate became more confused, Benton, visibly upset, declared that Dawson had turned his proviso over "to the Senator from Illinois, who either alters the prescription or writes it all over." "I do not know what was done," he continued, "but it is said he operated upon it," following which it was handed to Texas' Senator Rusk. A consultation between Dawson and Rusk ensued. At any rate, Dawson's amendment narrowly passed, with Douglas voting in the negative; Bradbury's amended proposal was then approved with Douglas' support.[11]

As the struggle rapidly approached its climax, Douglas made one final effort to restore popular sovereignty to Utah and New Mexico. Although he had failed once to delete the restriction on territorial legislation respecting slavery, Douglas was asked by Clay to renew his motion to strike out the limitation in a last-minute effort to save the bill. Instead of doing it himself, Douglas asked Moses Norris of New Hampshire to make the motion. The move encountered severe southern opposition, but, on the last day of July, it passed. With the deletion of the restrictive clause, the territorial provisions were returned to Douglas' original version, except for the Yulee, Hale, and Soulé amendments, which Douglas did not regard as crucial. Popular sovereignty was at last fully recognized in the proposed territories of Utah and New Mexico.[12]

The fate of the omnibus bill, however, had already been sealed. Douglas' faith in the bill had never been deep. The prolonged debates over its provisions merely confirmed him in his belief that it could not pass. Fillmore shared his belief. Having presided over the Senate debates, a task that had severely challenged his parliamentary skill, he had become aware both of the gravity of the crisis and of the impracticality of the omnibus bill as a compromise. The passage of the Bradbury-Dawson amendment, it was widely assumed, cleared the track for the triumph of the omnibus bill. On the last day of July, the Senate was crowded once again with visitors, confident that they would witness the final termination of the long months of debate. The crowd combined with the hot summer weather to turn the Senate into a sweltering, steaming chamber.

No one could have anticipated the curious turn which events took that day. Instead of bringing the omnibus bill to its final success, the Bradbury-Dawson amendment served as the instrument of its destruction.

Senator James A. Pearce of Maryland, who shared Douglas' concern for the impact Dawson's proviso would have on the ultimate boundary settlement, as well as on the organization of New Mexico Territory, determined to eliminate the admendment from the bill. His plan was known to President Fillmore, although it is not clear that the precise strategy followed by Pearce had the sanction of the Chief Executive. He played a dangerous game. Knowing no other way to accomplish his end, Pearce moved that the entire section dealing with the organization of New Mexico and with the Texas boundary question be stricken from the bill. If he should succeed in this, he told the Senate, he intended to restore the stricken provisions with the exception of Dawson's proposal. The opponents of the compromise immediately sensed their opportunity to defeat the bill, and the worst fears of the compromisers were soon realized. Pearce's motion to strike out the sections passed, 33 to 22. Following an unsuccessful attempt by Douglas to replace Dawson's proposal with one that would be acceptable to all, including Pearce and the Texas Senators, Pearce's motion to restore the New Mexico sections (except for Dawson's proviso) to the omnibus bill narrowly failed. Clay's bill had been shorn of one of its three components; it now remained to dismember what was left. David R. Atchison of Missouri proposed that the sections relating to the admission of California next be removed from the bill; his motion carried. All that remained was the organization of Utah Territory. Crushed by the turn of events, Clay walked out of the chamber. Douglas supported both of Pearce's motions and opposed Atchison's, registering his disapproval of the Dawson proviso and sticking with the omnibus bill to the end.[13]

The opponents of compromise were jubilant. "The omnibus is overturned," declared Benton, "and all the passengers spilled out but one." Only Utah remained as a "monument of the herculean labors of the immortal thirteen." Jefferson Davis, Hale, Seward, Butler, Yulee, Chase —northerners and southerners who had worked hard to frustrate the compromise—exulted at their victory. Massachusetts' Robert Winthrop, who took Webster's seat when Webster was appointed to Fillmore's cabinet, crowed that the compromise was dead. Henry Clay, dejected and fatigued, left Washington for Newport, where he hoped to regain his strength. "The future is dark and portentous," wrote one Congressman;

"this is a most lame and impotent conclusion of four or five months labour," commented another. For Douglas, however, the defeat of the omnibus bill was not a disaster. "I regrett it very much, altho I must say
that I never had very strong hopes of its passage," he wrote. "By combining the measures into one Bill the Committee united the opponents of
each measure instead of securing the friends of each. I have thought
from the beginning that they made a mistake in this respect." The omnibus bill had been lost, but his California and territorial bills, reported
separately from his committee, still remained.[14]

ii

With Clay's departure from the Senate, Douglas assumed the leadership of the compromise forces. Actually his role scarcely changed, since
he had already been recognized as the leading strategist in the compromise camp. Moreover, as chairman of the Committee on Territories his
responsibility for the legislation was a logical one. As soon as the dis-
memberment of the omnibus bill had been accomplished, Douglas took
over its remains. After he secured approval for a slight modification of
Utah's southern boundary, the Utah bill was ordered to be engrossed for
a third reading, and on the following day, August 1, it passed. On the
same day, Douglas called up his bill for California's admission as a free
state. Senator Downs objected, complaining that "we have had the subject discussed in our ears for so long a time that it has become quite disagreeable to hear it." Hunter moaned that "we have been kept here
week after week, and we are worn out." But Douglas persisted, optimistic that a compromise could now be passed in the form of separate bills.
"The Utah Bill has passed the Senate in the precise words in which I
wrote it," he stated. "We are now engaged on my California Bill." In
the meantime, he and Pearce were preparing a bill on the Texas boundary question. "We shall then take up the Bill for New Mexico & pass it
just as I reported it four months ago. . . . When they are all passed you
see they will be collectively Mr. Clays compromise, & separately the
Bills reported by the committee on Territories four months ago." [15]

On August 5, Pearce presented the Texas boundary bill, in which
Texas was to be heavily compensated for surrendering her claims to the
area east of the Rio Grande. Four days later it was approved by the Senate. Shortly afterward, Douglas was able to bring the California bill to a
vote. Southern attempts to extend the Missouri Compromise line to the
Pacific were beaten back. Douglas was chided for opposing the extension

now when he had favored it previously, but he effectively answered his southern critics by pointing out the changes that had occurred in the meantime. On August 13, the California bill passed the Senate in spite of the unswerving opposition of the southern ultras, and Douglas' long struggle to bring organized government to California was finally over. As soon as the California vote was announced, Douglas moved the consideration of his bill for the organization of New Mexico Territory. Two days later, after a desultory debate, it passed. By mid-August, just over two weeks after the omnibus bill had met its fate, Douglas had successfully guided its various parts through the Senate.[16]

The speed with which the bills were passed, in contrast to the long debate on Clay's bill, was little short of astonishing. Senators were obviously weary, compromise sentiment had been strengthened, especially among northern Senators, and Taylor's death had released some Whigs from their opposition. But most of all, the triumph was a tribute to the leadership of the thirty-seven-year-old Illinois Senator. The apparent ease and rapidity with which the bills were passed masked the energy which the "bantling" (as the New York *Herald* called Douglas) had exerted in marshalling his forces, while it glossed over the anxieties he suffered. His perserverance in moving calls of the Senate and adjournments, and his constant motions for the yeas and nays, forestalled his opponents and allowed him to consolidate his support. His attendance on the floor of the Senate was obligatory at all times; he was even forced to take his meals there. The order with which he brought up the bills was carefully calculated to bring them maximum support. The troublesome Texas boundary issue was settled first, followed by California, and, finally, New Mexico. There is a logic to the order that, if it had not been heeded, might have brought a different result.

Reviewing the summer's work, Douglas pointed out that the important point had been to secure the passage of the bills; whether they were passed jointly or separately "was a matter of small moment." "I had no idea of losing the great measures which my judgment approved, and upon which I believed the peace and quiet of the country depended." The identification of the omnibus bill with Henry Clay, Douglas felt, had been one factor in its defeat. The Taylor administration was jealous of Clay's leadership, and some Democrats feared his presidential ambitions if his bill should succeed. "But let it always be said of old Hal," Douglas asserted, "that he fought a glorious & a patriotic battle. No man was ever governed by higher & purer motives." At the same time,

Douglas was loath to assume credit for the success. In a spirit of abnegation, he declared that "no man and no party has acquired a triumph, except the party friendly to the Union triumphing over abolitionism and disunion." Others more readily credited Douglas for his achievement. "If any man has a right to be proud of the success of these measures," stated Jefferson Davis, "it is the Senator from Illinois." Coming from one of Douglas' staunchest adversaries, this was high praise indeed.[17]

Two measures remained to complete the compromise. The bills to abolish the slave trade in the District of Columbia and to provide for a more effective rendition of fugitive slaves had both been reported by the Committee of Thirteen, although the latter had been introduced earlier as separate legislation. The debate on the fugitive slave bill occupied the Senate for barely a week before it was passed on August 26. Although he supported the bill, Douglas was absent from the Senate during the entire debate. Assured that the final vote would probably not be taken for two weeks, he left the capital for a few days on a business trip. A note for $4000, in payment of property he had recently purchased in Chicago, had fallen due in New York, and he felt obliged to arrange the matter personally with the directors of his bank. While dining with a group of Illinois friends at the Astor House, he received word that the bill had been advanced to final passage. He returned to Washington, although not as hurriedly as he later recalled, but not in time to vote. The bill to abolish the slave trade in the District of Columbia was not taken up until early September. Douglas' role in the debate, which spread over a period of five days, was minimal. His only participation was a defense of Illinois' constitutional restriction against the immigration of free Negroes into the state. "We do not wish to make our State an asylum for all the old and decrepit and broken-down negroes that may emigrate or be sent to it," he declared. "We desire every other State to take care of her own negroes, whether free or slave, and we will take care of ours." When the bill came up for final passage on September 16, Douglas was among those voting in favor of it.

The Compromise of 1850, nine months in the making, had at last been accomplished. On the day the District of Columbia bill passed, Douglas summed it all up. "The measures," he told the Senate, "are right in themselves, and collectively constitute one grand scheme of conciliation and adjustment. . . . The success of a portion of them only would not have accomplished the object; but all together constitute a fair and honorable adjustment. Neither section has triumphed over the other. The North has not surrendered to the South, nor has the South made any humiliating concessions to the North. Each section has maintained its honor and its rights, and both have met on the common ground of justice and compromise." He was proud, he modestly asserted, to have had the opportunity to play "an humble part" in the enactment of the measures.[18]

Douglas had good reason to be gratified with the result. Aside from the settlement of the crisis and the stature which his leadership had gained for him, Douglas could point to the success of his own formula for quieting the slavery agitation: popular sovereignty. Without concerning himself with questions of constitutional interpretation, and instead placing his arguments on moral, pragmatic, and expedient grounds, he had achieved a recognition of the right of the people in the territories, as in the states, to decide the slavery question for themselves. He was confident that, in doing so, they would enlarge the area of free institutions and contribute to the growing strength of the "great West."

When the Senate had completed its work, attention shifted to the House of Representatives. The Senators watched developments in the House closely, and during the debates several of them, including Douglas, were frequently seen in the hall. Douglas maintained close contact with Linn Boyd of Kentucky, chairman of the House Committee on Territories, advising him and supplying him with information. Through McClernand he was able to exert his influence in favor of a speedy approval of the Senate bills. After some suspenseful skirmishing, the Texas boundary and New Mexico bills (which the House combined into a "little omnibus") passed on September 6. On the following day, both the California and Utah bills were approved. Although the House had yet to concur in the two final bills of the Compromise, the passage of the first four dealing with the territorial question signaled a festive outburst.

Saturday night, September 7, was given over to joyous celebration in the capital. "The good news spread like the sunshine chasing the shadow of a cloud." A salute of 100 guns was fired, rockets and fireworks were exploded, the National Hotel was brightly illuminated, and the Marine Band played patriotic airs. Joined by several hundred shouting citizens, the bandsmen marched through the city serenading the men who had played a part in the Compromise. Foote, Cass, Cobb, Douglas, Houston, Rusk, and Webster were all called out of their lodgings, and all delighted the crowd with extemporaneous speeches. Douglas responded to the music and cheers by speaking "with a glow of enthusiasm which made the welkin ring with applause, of the spirit of conciliation which had carried the day." The bonds of union were stronger than ever, he declared. "We are united from shore to shore; and while the mighty West remained as the connecting link between the North and the South, there could be no disunion." Bells rang, bonfires blazed, and "all countenances, except those of the real abolition and disunion revolutionists, beamed with joy and gladness." Liquor flowed freely. One eyewitness reported that it was declared the duty of every patriot to get drunk. That the advice was heeded was evident the next morning when Foote complained of diarrhea from "fruit" he had eaten the night before, and Douglas was prostrated with a headache from a "cold." Never before had so much excitement followed the passage of a law.[19]

iii

The exertions of the spring and summer had been harder on Douglas than on most of the Senators, for he had had to bear the brunt of the struggle for the Compromise. Its effects were telling. He was exhausted and yearned to return to Illinois. Before the adjournment, however, he suddenly developed a vicious abscess on his hip, said to have been caused "by unwearied sittings in the Senate." His hip became swollen and extremely painful and, on his doctor's order, he was confined to his bed. He was not able to leave for Chicago until almost a week after the adjournment, and even then he was cared for on the journey by one of the members of the Illinois House delegation, perhaps Thomas L. Harris. There was much to do at home, and little time remained before Congress would convene again in December.[20]

Douglas' role in the crisis brought him recognition throughout the north. He must have been pleased with the attention he received outside his own state. Early in the year the New York *Herald* included his name in a list of possible candidates for the presidency in 1852. A friend in New York City wrote him that he had a large number of admirers there, and he received invitations to meet with the Tammany Society. Even the usually hostile *New-York Tribune* described him as a "useful and active working member of the Senate . . . replete with statistical information" and knowledgeable "in the practical business of legislation." Daniel Webster praised his efforts in a Massachusetts speech, and a Buffalo newspaper regarded him as "one of the ablest men in the country," with a future "full of high hope and promise." He was placed "in the foremost rank among the leading minds of the nation," with a record in

Congress that "has uniformly been characterized by moderation, and never-failing good sense." Sidney Breese, with whom his relations had not always been cordial, wrote from Illinois that "no one from the West stands higher than you do in the public esteem and I look forward to the time when you will reach the highest pinnacle of human ambition." In March 1851, the grateful citizenry of California presented Douglas with a massive, jewel-studded gold watch, suitably engraved, "California knows her friends."[21]

Still, Douglas received disquieting reports from his state. During his long absence from Illinois, his political fences had fallen into neglect and badly needed repairing. Although he had weathered the storm that followed the passage of the legislative instructions, he still received reports of movements and combinations designed to oust him from the Senate. His term had over two more years to run, but there was already talk of his chances for re-election. "There is a considerable force in the Military tract against you," wrote a friend from Quincy. "The People are with you, but the politicians are not." From deep in southern Illinois came similar warnings: "There is a strong party against you in southern Illinois, and the prospect now is that you will be defeated unless you canvass the state." One paper speculated that the real ground of opposition to the Compromise among some politicians was their desire to defeat Douglas for re-election. It became clear that he would have little rest at home during the short interval between sessions. Before he left Washington, Douglas had already promised that he would campaign for Harris' re-election in his congressional district.[22]

Despite his general antislavery stance during the compromise debates and his constant battles with southern extremists, Douglas still failed to impress the freesoil opposition in his own state. Although concentrated in the north and especially in his home town of Chicago, the attacks against his course were occasionally echoed in the Whig press downstate. In July, the *Quincy Whig* criticized Douglas for his slaveholding connections, and it reprinted an article from a Mississippi newspaper which alluded to his property intersts in that state. Although the reprinted article took Douglas to task for voting in favor of slavery's prohibition in the territories, it was the fact that Douglas "owned" slaves that drew the *Whig*'s fire. In rebuttal, Douglas penned a defense, pointing out that the Mississippi plantation (including its slaves) belonged to his wife, and not to him. According to Mississippi law the property of a married woman was her separate estate and could not be controlled by her husband. The defense was published in the *Register.* In a covering note to Lanphier, Douglas avowed their intention to liquidate the Mississippi holdings and concentrate all their property in Illinois. They never did so, and his opponents continued to use the southern plantation and slaves to link Douglas with the slave interest. Douglas attributed the persistent freesoil opposition to a bad press, especially in Chicago. Wentworth's *Chicago Democrat,* which had strongly opposed the Compromise, was clearly hostile, and the *Chicago Tribune* was not much better. The fact that he had voted in accord with the legislative instructions on several occasions, he complained, had gone virtually unnoticed in Illinois. He wanted it made clear, he wrote to Lanphier, that he had done so, but that he also continued to adhere firmly to popular sovereignty.[23]

To meet the need for a friendly newspaper in Chicago, Douglas undertook negotiations in the summer for the establishment of a new Democratic press there to which he promised considerable financial support. Edmund Burke of New Hampshire, who had recently assisted Ritchie on the *Union,* was suggested as a possible editor, but Burke declined the offer. Douglas turned next to his old friend Isaac R. Diller of Springfield. Diller at first resisted Douglas' proposal, and by the time he changed his mind Douglas himself had cooled. When Ebenezer Peck and his son established the *Democratic Argus* shortly afterward, it was widely reported that Douglas was one of its financial supporters. The *Argus,* however, did not satisfy Douglas, for he continued to explore the idea of setting up his own organ in Chicago. He later apparently considered the purchase of the *Chicago Tribune* in the hope that it might be transformed into a *"genuine* democratic paper." The Springfield *Register* continued to act as Douglas' spokesman, and the *Quincy Herald* continued to receive his financial contributions, for which the editor pledged undying support.[24]

Although the freesoilers were disappointed with the omission of the Wilmot Proviso from the territorial bills, for which they held Douglas responsible, their rejection of the Compromise centered on the fugitive slave law. The law became the target of bitter press attacks and the subject of numerous protest meetings throughout northern Illinois. Although he had taken no part in the debate on the bill and was absent from the Senate when it was voted upon, Douglas had declared his approval of the measure and had indicated that, had he been present, his vote would have been affirmative. His name was consequently linked with the law by his opponents. The president of Knox College published an open letter to Douglas, and in it he asked if the people might not rightfully disobey the fugitive slave law. The most dramatic outburst against Douglas and the law, however, occurred in Chicago, when the city council formally denounced it as "cruel and unjust" and relieved the police and the citizens of the city from its enforcement. In a resolution aimed at Douglas, the council branded those free state Senators and Representatives "who aided and assisted in the passage of this infamous law, and those who basely sneaked away from their seats, and thereby evaded the question" as "fit only to be ranked with the traitors." [25]

Douglas arrived in Chicago at just this moment. Shocked by the council's action, he interrupted a mass meeting that had been called to ratify the resolution to announce that he would speak in defense of the law and of the Compromise generally on the following night. On October 23, "a tremendous concourse of people" gathered at the City Hall to hear his remarks. In spite of his physical weakness, he spoke for three and a half hours. Defending the Compromise measures as being fair and just to all parts of the nation, Douglas deplored the renewal of the agitation in the two extremes of the Union. In the deep south, the Compromise was condemned as a disgraceful surrender to northern abolitionism, while among some northerners it was denounced as a total abandonment of the rights of freemen to the slave power. "We have fallen on evil times," he declared, "when passion, and prejudice, and ambition, can so blind the judgments and deaden the consciences of men, that the truth cannot be seen and felt." Douglas reminded his audience that he had written the California, Utah, and New Mexico bills, and, assuming full responsibility for them, he defended the "great fundamental principle" on which they were predicated—"that every people ought to possess the right of forming and regulating their own internal concerns and domestic institutions in their own way." He pointed out that wherever slavery had been excluded and free institutions established it had been done by the voluntary action of the people interested, in spite of (even in defiance of) the attempted interference by Congress. Similar actions had already been taken by the people of California and New Mexico, and he was confident that slavery would not take root there. He supported the law abolishing the slave trade in the District of Columbia, not as a "concession to the North," but because he believed it to be "right in itself." He was disappointed, he said, that not one word had been uttered in commendation of this feature of the Compromise or of those who supported it.

Passing to the fugitive slave law, Douglas pointed out its similarity to the old law of 1793, which it was designed to amend, especially with respect to the writ of habeas corpus and the right of trial by jury. He denied that the writ of habeas corpus, not mentioned in the bill, had been suspended, and argued the contrary, that habeas corpus was necessary to carry the law into effect and to prevent the rights of freemen from being violated under it. "The sole object of the writ of habeas corpus is to ascertain by what authority a person is held in custody; to release him, if no such authority be shown; and to refrain from any molestation of the claimant, if legal authority be produced." Jury trial must take place in the state whose laws were alleged to have been violated, that is, in the state from which the fugitive fled. Southern state courts bore the responsibility of seeing that jury trial was granted in cases where the freedom of a slave was in question. Interrupted frequently by questions from the audience, Douglas responded by reviewing the terms of the act in detail. He concluded that "in some respects, the law guards the rights of the negro, charged with being a fugitive from labor, more rigidly than it does those of a white man who is alleged to be a fugitive from justice." Emphasizing the need for providing "all the safeguards, that the wit of man can devise, for the protection of the innocent and the free," he conceded that the law did not accomplish "all this." Such failings, however, applied equally to white men and Negroes. He felt that the new law would prevent the kidnapping of free Negroes by southerners, since it forced the latter to establish their legal right to the fugitive.

The real objection, Douglas asserted, was not to the fugitive slave law, nor to the 1793 statute, but rather to the Constitution itself. "You would not care a farthing about the new law . . . if there was a hole in it big enough for the fugitive to slip through and escape. Habeas corpuses—trials by jury—records from other States—pains and penalties—the whole catalogue of objections, would be all moonshine, if the negro was not required to go back to his master." Members of the audience readily agreed. To the argument that the Constitution, in providing for the surrender of fugitive slaves, violated the laws of God, Douglas replied that "no government ever existed on earth in which there was a perfect equality, in all things, among those composing it." Many provisions of the Constitution, as well as of the state constitutions, violated the "principle of absolute equality among men, when considered as component parts of a political society or government." These provisions were, in his opinion, "unwise and unjust, and . . . subversive of Republican principles," but he was not prepared to say that they were either sanctioned or condemned by divine law.

Douglas' speech was delivered with force and conviction, and its impact was profound. Patient, calm, and careful in his choice of language, he invited questions from the audience and dealt with them in detail. When he had finished, he presented several resolutions of his own, declaring that it was the obligation of all citizens to respect and execute laws of Congress enacted in pursuance of the Constitution. His resolutions were thunderously approved "with much unanimity" by the gathering. Further action was taken at the suggestion of an old-line Whig, when the audience voted to repudiate the city council's action. But the most striking result of Douglas' presentation came on the following night, when the council repealed its own resolutions with only one dissenting vote. It was a personal triumph of the most impressive kind, gained in the midst of opposition.

Some of the opponents of the fugitive slave law remained unconvinced by his "ingenious and able defence," but they expressed their gratitude for Douglas' clear exposition of its provisions. Reports of Douglas' triumphant confrontation with the critics of the Compromise spread rapidly. His speech, published as a pamphlet, was circulated throughout the north. "That one single man should, by his moral courage and his intellectual resources," declared the Washington *Union,* "so successfully turn the tide of opinion in a meeting of 4,000 citizens . . . is a feather in his cap which any orator might desire to wear." "With such champions, the Union may defy every attack." Douglas' vindication was complete when the state legislature, meeting a few weeks later, repealed its Wilmot Proviso instructions and, by overwhelming margins, endorsed Douglas' course on the Compromise.[26]

From Chicago, Douglas traveled south to Jacksonville and Springfield, where he delivered a similar speech. In early November he left the state to return to the east. His mother had hoped that he might visit her at her home in upstate New York on his way, but he did not plan to do so. After a brief stopover in Washington, he journeyed to North Carolina, where he joined his wife and son, resting until Congress opened in December. He was tired. His effort in Chicago had climaxed a year of unparalleled exertion. He was also sick of the agitation over slavery. When he later expressed his determination "never to make another speech on the slavery question," he meant it. Confident that the Compromise had placed the Union once again on a sound and enduring foundation, he prepared to turn to other matters.[27]

# XIV
## "The spirit of the age"
## 1850–1853

Providing organized government to the far reaches of the American frontier was but one of Douglas' concerns, although it always ranked very high in his order of priorities. As the Senate's watchdog over the territories, a role he largely defined for himself, his responsibilities extended to all matters that pertained to western development. His vision was always directed toward a greater and stronger America, and western expansion and growth were inseparable from the need to strengthen the nation in other ways, internally through the improvement of transportation and communication, and externally through the pursuit of a vigorous foreign policy.

The slavery agitation, Douglas felt, was a dangerous distraction from the achievement of these higher national goals. The Union was indispensable to his program, and he loudly condemned anything that threatened its existence. The passage of the Compromise measures was a tribute to his political skill and to his determination to preserve national unity. At the same time, the Compromise of 1850 cleared the air and opened the way for new and vital measures of national development. Even as he struggled with questions that struck at the very heart of the Union, Douglas continued to labor for measures that would carry the American people closer to the strength and power that was their destiny.

An important element in Douglas' program was his dream of connecting the Mississippi valley with the Pacific by a railroad that could be integrated with the valley's river system, the Great Lakes, and the eastern railroads to form a massive national transportation network. He had earlier rejected Asa Whitney's Pacific Railroad proposal, preferring his own plan which included the organization of territorial government in the intervening country and the grant of lands to the states and territories through which the road would pass, in order to aid in its construction. Although the Illinois legislature had endorsed Whitney's proposal, Douglas continued to argue that the interests of the west (and hence of the nation) would be served better by his own plan. Four years after his reply to Whitney, a railroad convention in St. Louis gave him the opportunity to press his position.

At a meeting in Chicago in October 1849, Douglas was not only selected as a delegate to the St. Louis convention, but several resolutions he had submitted were endorsed as instructions to the delegation. In these he urged a central railroad route over South Pass, connecting Council Bluffs, Iowa, with the Pacific. Steamboat navigation would connect Council Bluffs with points on the Missouri and Mississippi rivers. Douglas suggested, however, that three branch railroads be constructed joining the terminus with Chicago, St. Louis, and Memphis. The first would clearly become the most important, since rail lines from the east, both existent and contemplated, would converge at Lake Michigan's southern tip.

The St. Louis convention, obviously called to promote that city's ambitions for a Pacific railroad, attracted little interest outside the immediate area. Douglas was unexpectedly chosen as president of the convention, an "honor" bestowed upon him, he later charged, in order to muzzle him. In his opening statement, he called upon the delegates to set aside sectional prejudice in deliberating on the nation's need for a Pacific railroad, but his words made little impression. His own plan was coolly received by the St. Louis partisans, and it was even rejected by one member of the Illinois delegation, who charged Douglas with concocting a "cunningly devised strategem" to enhance the position of Chicago and northern Illinois. Thomas Hart Benton challenged Douglas' suggestion, arguing instead for a railroad built west from St. Louis, and Douglas rose immediately to reply. Commenting "with some severity" on Benton's remarks, he was "very pointed in his strictures" on the "grasping policy" of St. Louis. The full fury of the Missourians descended immediately upon his head. Missouri Congressman James B. Bowlin joined the fray, and the St. Louis press viciously attacked Douglas for "advocating sectional claims." Douglas promptly resigned the presidency of the convention.

In spite of the attacks, Douglas was vindicated in the convention's final action, for Benton's resolutions were replaced by a set based on Douglas' earlier proposal, the so-called Chicago Plan, a triumph not only for his railroad ambitions but a satisfying personal victory over the doughty Senator from Missouri. Returning to Illinois, Douglas reviewed his position further in a speech in Springfield, following which the legislature rescinded its earlier endorsement of Whitney's plan and gave full support to Douglas' proposal.[1]

The St. Louis convention did little to advance the cause of a Pacific railroad, fanning as it did the rivalries between Illinois and Missouri. Douglas' efforts also brought him into conflict again with his erstwhile Senate colleague, Sidney Breese, for Breese had endorsed Whitney's plan in a report submitted by the Senate Committee on Public Lands. Nevertheless the furor over the Pacific railroad subsided in the following months, partly because of the sectional disagreement over the organization of the Mexican cession, and partly because Douglas turned to another bit of unfinished railroad business. As he struggled for state and territorial organization and led the fight for the Compromise of 1850, Douglas also found time to bring to fruition his dream of a rail connection between the Great Lakes and the Mississippi River system that would run the length of his state of Illinois.

The Illinois Central Railroad was closely linked in Douglas' mind to his proposals for a Pacific railroad. His dedication to the former in part explains his opposition to the ambitions of St. Louis for the eastern terminus of a transcontinental railroad. Nor was the Illinois Central project unrelated to his struggle against sectionalism and to his support of the Compromise of 1850. The project's significance was by no means local in character. By extending the Central Railroad to the Gulf of Mexico, north and south would be bound by new economic ties in the Mississippi valley. The unity of this heartland would be enhanced, just as the unity of Douglas' own state would be strengthened. To accede to St. Louis' aspirations would be to separate the interests of central and southern Illinois from those of the northern part of the state, as well as to divide the Mississippi valley along an east-west axis. The Illinois Central would accomplish in an economic way what the Compromise of 1850, on a larger scale, achieved in a political way. No small factor in Douglas' thinking was his faith in the future of Chicago as the nation's great commercial hub, linking east and west as well as north and south. With Chicago as a terminus for both the Pacific railroad and the Illinois Central Railroad, with its importance as a lake port and as the terminal of eastern railroads, the interests of the nation would converge on the prairie state. Douglas himself stood to gain personally from his land investments in Chicago (although most of his interests there developed after he fought for the Illinois Central), but the political advantages that would accrue from his plan far outweighed considerations of pecuniary gain.

The Illinois Central Railroad was a vestige of the internal improvement mania that had swept Illinois a decade and a half before. Douglas' name was not even identified with the project until the late 1840's, when he entered the United States Senate. Its early promotion developed from the speculative ventures of Darius B. Holbrook, a Bostonian, and Sidney Breese. Holbrook and Breese, impressed with the commercial possibilities of the point of land at the confluence of the Ohio and Mississippi rivers, determined to found a town there, to be known as Cairo, and conceived the idea of a railroad from Galena, in northern Illinois, to Cairo to aid their townsite speculation. A charter was secured from the legislature early in 1836, but when a subsequent legislature passed the vast internal improvements program the charter was surrendered to the state on condition that the railroad should be financed by the state and that it should terminate at Cairo. When the internal improvements program collapsed, the project was abandoned. At that time only a small amount of work had been done on it.

Holbrook and Breese maintained their interest in Cairo and the railroad. In 1843, another charter, incorporating the officers of their organization, the Cairo City and Canal Company, as the Great Western Railway Company, was secured from the legislature. All property, rights, and work already accomplished on the railroad were to be turned over to the new company. The state's interests in the project were protected by provisions stipulating that the annual income of the road would go to the state (once the company had met its obligations) and that all unsold lands donated to the company from whatever source would revert to the state five years after the road's completion. The latter provision reflected Breese's confidence that Congress would provide part of the public domain to support construction. Breese's election to the Senate the same year placed him in an advantageous position to press for governmant aid. Still no work on the road was accomplished, and in 1845 the legislature repealed the charter.

Breese and Holbrook wished to secure for their company a pre-emption right to lands along the proposed route. A bill to this effect was accordingly drawn up by Breese and early in 1844 was reported to the Senate by the Committee on Public Lands. Before its introduction, however, Breese sought to enlist Douglas' support for the measure. Douglas, who had entered the House of Representatives at the same time Breese took his Senate seat, strongly objected to the scheme. He distrusted Holbrook and suspected the honesty of his motives. Breese's bill, he felt, would retard the settlement of Illinois without providing the state with the railroad. He had no faith that Holbrook and his associates were sincere in their proposal to achieve its construction. It seemed clear to Douglas that the sole function of the project was to increase the value of investments in Cairo. As an alternative, he suggested that land grants be made directly to the state, not to "an irresponsible private corporation."

As Breese continued to push his pre-emption plan, Douglas became more thoroughly committed to his alternative proposal. The competition between the two plans was closely followed by Illinoisans. During the summer before he entered the Senate, Douglas argued his position in many parts of the state, and he urged the citizens to memorialize Congress on behalf of his proposal. That same summer he established his residence in Chicago, and shortly afterward he brought that city into the picture. Impressed by the argument that the railroad project was strictly local in character and that the national government was therefore constitutionally unable to render assistance, Douglas proposed that an additional terminus be provided at Chicago. By this move, the railroad would no longer be considered as "calculated to throw the whole trade upon the Gulf of Mexico at the expense of the cities on the Lakes and the Atlantic seaboard," but would "connect the lower Mississippi with the Lakes, the St. Lawrence with the Gulf of Mexico, and the upper Mississippi valley with both." Breese later charged Douglas with attempting to improve the value of his Chicago speculations, but Douglas also had political objectives in view. A Chicago terminus would bring needed support to the railroad project from northern Illinois, but, more importantly, it would strengthen his position and increase his popularity in an area of predominantly freesoil sentiment. He was confident also that eastern support would be secured if the railroad connected with the Great Lakes. His move proved sound; Chicago and northern Illinois backed his plan with an impressive fervency. Douglas later maintained that the addition of a Chicago terminus secured crucial votes from Pennsylvania, New York, and New England.[2]

When Congress met in December 1847, both Breese and Douglas introduced their respective bills in the Senate, the one seeking a pre-emption grant, the other asking a donation of public land. While the Senate proved receptive, Douglas' bill being passed in May 1848 and Breese's during the short second session early in 1849, it became clear that neither could succeed in the House as long as they remained in competition. Holbrook took no chances. In 1849, the Illinois legislature was persuaded to renew his charter with added provisions, including the right to build the line to Chicago and the granting to the company of all lands which the state might receive for the railroad. Under this charter, Holbrook's company would gain regardless of whether Breese or Douglas should succeed. Holbrook made his move none too soon, for the same legislature also defeated Breese for the Senate in favor of James Shields, who was known to favor Douglas' plan. In the waning weeks of Breese's last session, Holbrook desperately bombarded him with letters urging the passage of the pre-emption bill at all costs before the expiration of his term. When the bill passed the Senate, Breese was importuned to exert all his pressure on the House. In return, Holbrook wildly offered Breese the presidency of the railroad company, an appointment as counselor for the company at an annual retainer of $1200, a house in Cairo, and a private fortune on his investment in the townsite. Negotiations with investors, including Washington banker W. W. Corcoran, Holbrook wrote optimistically, were proceeding, and money would be available to the company as soon as Breese's bill should become law. Everything "depends on the value we can give to our investments at Cairo." It was as Douglas had suspected; Holbrook was primarily concerned with Cairo, and only secondarily interested in building a railroad. As adjournment neared, Holbrook urged Breese to confer with Douglas in the hope that some kind of compromise could be worked out. The Illinois House delegation, he reminded Breese, "will do what Douglass advises." But Breese was not ready to meet with his rival, so his efforts on behalf of the bill fell short. Congress adjourned before final action was taken, and Breese returned to private life.

Although Breese's defeat aided Douglas, the renewal of Holbrook's charter by the legislature was greeted with undisguised wrath by the Little Giant. Speaking in Chicago just before he left for the St. Louis convention, Douglas angrily denounced the action and despaired that a bill for the Central Railroad could ever pass Congress under the circumstances. Shortly afterward, with characteristic firmness, he persuaded

Holbrook's Cairo City and Canal Company, represented by former Connecticut Congressman John A. Rockwell and agent George W. Billings, "to execute to the State of Illinois a full & complete release & surrender of the charter of the Great Western Rail Road Co." together with all the rights granted to the company by the legislature. Douglas' persuasive power was strengthened by his threat to introduce legislation in Congress for the construction of a railroad that would completely bypass Cairo if the release were not forthcoming. When Congress convened in December 1849, the way was clear for Douglas' own railroad proposal.[3]

On January 3, 1850, Douglas introduced his bill granting the right of way and a donation of public lands to Illinois to aid in the construction of the Central Railroad. It was immediately referred to the Senate Committee on Public Lands, of which Shields was a member. The committee reported favorably in mid-February, with some amendments that had been worked out by Douglas and Shields, but it was not until late April that it was brought up for consideration. At that time it stood twenty-second on the Senate calendar. When Douglas pointed out that the measure was identical with one that passed the Senate two years before, the bill was taken up out of order. For three days, while Clay's select committee deliberated on a compromise of the slavery question, the Senate debated Douglas' bill. On May 2 it passed, 26 to 14.

Two important changes were made in the bill during the debate, both of which were supported by Douglas. At the instigation of Iowa's Senator George W. Jones, the northern terminus of the railroad was moved a few miles, from Galena, Illinois, to Dubuque, Iowa. Galena, a short distance from the Mississippi and the center of a declining lead mining industry, was less suitable than Dubuque, which lay on the river. The latter city would more easily connect with other railroads projected westward across Iowa, as well as channel the northern river commerce into the Illinois Central.

More significant was the extension of the railroad southward from the mouth of the Ohio River to Mobile, Alabama. This move had been contemplated by Douglas as early as 1848, when his earlier version failed in the House of Representatives by only a few votes. He recognized that a connection with the Gulf of Mexico would more than likely overcome the constitutional scruples of southern opponents to the measure. It would also elevate the project to one of national scope and serve more effectively as a binding force between north and south. When Douglas left Illinois for Washington in the fall of 1849, he traveled south to visit his wife's plantation in Mississippi. He used the occasion to stop in Mobile, where he conferred with the officers of the virtually defunct Mobile and Ohio Railroad, a line that had been planned to connect the Gulf with the Ohio River but that had failed for lack of capital. Douglas proposed that the line be extended to Mobile in his bill and that a grant of lands be sought not only for Illinois but for Mississippi and Alabama as well. Both state legislatures subsequently instructed their congressional delegations to support the measure, and on the first day of debate in the Senate, Alabama's Senator William R. King introduced an amendment (which Douglas later claimed he had written) providing for the extension.[4]

With these changes, Douglas' bill encountered little difficulty in the Senate. The original proposal for a Central Railroad had been skillfully altered to bring it the greatest amount of support. The branch to Chicago (which Douglas regarded as the main line), the extension to Dubuque, and the connection with the Gulf brought crucial support to the project from the northeast, the west, and the deep south. Even so, one reporter suggested that the bill would not have received Senate approval had all the Senators been in their seats. A number of Senators, he wrote, left the chamber before the final vote was taken out of deference to Douglas and Shields, "whose adroit management of the bill had commanded their admiration." Whether true or not, a large number of Senators did not vote on the bill, although among them were some supporters of the legislation. Attendance in the Senate during the debate was poor. It may be that many members took advantage of the lull in the compromise struggle to tend to other business. As it passed the Senate, Douglas' bill provided for a grant to the three states of six alternate sections of land along the entire route of the road, as well as a 200-foot right-of-way. In cases where lands within the strip had already been sold, the state was allowed to locate indemnity lands elsewhere. The sections retained by the government within the strip were to be sold for double the minimum price, $2.50 an acre. Construction of the railroad was to begin within two years and be completed within ten, or the lands would revert to the government.[5]

Illinois greeted the Senate's passage of the bill with enthusiasm, but the rejoicing was tempered by the realization that the real struggle for the legislation yet remained. Twice before, bills to accomplish the Central Railroad had failed in the House of Representatives. More receptive to local pressures, and in some cases more inclined to adhere to party lines, House members had been reluctant to sanction the dispensation of government largesse for what seemed to be a local internal improvements project. Fear that the pattern might be repeated prompted Douglas and the members of the Illinois House delegation to exert their utmost pressure on the House and to devise every strategem which their ingenuity allowed. Much of the story of the bill's treatment in the House still remains shrouded in mystery, but it is clear that private bargaining and logrolling, carried on through personal contacts and behind closed doors, greatly contributed to the bill's eventual success.

Danger signals were raised almost immediately. Missouri Representative Bowlin, with whom Douglas had clashed at the railroad convention, was chairman of the House Committee on Public Lands. His opposition to any bill that would bypass the interests of St. Louis was well known. Congressman Edward D. Baker, from Illinois' Galena district, was upset with Douglas' removal of Galena as the terminus in favor of Dubuque. Indiana Representatives insisted that appropriations be made for railroads in that state. Supporters of the Central Railroad were indeed "in some tribulation" and feared the bill would be clogged with other projects in an effort to defeat it. More serious was the strong possibility that the bill would not even be brought up for a vote. On the last day of July, the day the omnibus bill was rejected by the Senate, the bill dropped to the bottom of the House calendar. Ninety-seven other bills held higher priority.

In spite of his deep involvement with the Compromise measures in the Senate, Douglas was frequently on hand in the House to direct the campaign for his railroad bill. He enlisted the invaluable aid of Thomas H. Bayly, Representative from Virginia, chairman of the powerful Ways and Means Committee and a leading figure in the compromise forces, who manipulated the bill to the head of the calendar. According to Douglas' own perhaps apocryphal account, related verbally later and not recorded until after his death, this was accomplished by repeated motions to clear the Speaker's table and go into the committee of the whole, thus dropping the pending legislation to the bottom of the calendar and moving each bill up one place. Whatever the strategy was, it succeeded, for on September 17 Douglas' bill passed the House, 101 to 75.[6]

The manipulation of the calendar did not by itself assure passage. Crucial to the bill's success was the support of the northeastern states. While the extension of the line to Chicago brought favorable reactions from that section, the extension of the other end to the Gulf of Mexico caused some misgivings. Much of the credit for securing the support of northeastern Congressmen belonged to John Wentworth, whose freesoil tendencies opened many doors that were closed to Douglas. Wentworth later wrote of an arrangement with Daniel Webster and his close friend Representative George Ashmun, whereby northeastern support of the railroad bill was traded for western support of the tariff. The possibility of such a deal was confirmed by another Illinois Congressman at the time. More discreet forms of persuasion were undoubtedly practiced. In late June, Holbrook, returning to New York from a trip to Washington, wrote that "if the Bill should pass . . . I shall have expended a large sum in effecting the object," and Breese later, in a letter to Douglas, commented, "It was the votes of Massachusetts and New York that passed the bill, and you and I know how they were had." [7]

Northeastern support of Douglas' bill may also be traced to the heavy financial investment of that section in Illinois. A large portion of the state debt, in the form of internal improvement bonds, was held by New York and Massachusetts financial interests. Since the collapse of the state's internal improvements program, these bonds had depreciated in value. The construction of the Illinois Central Railroad offered new hope to these investors, for Douglas believed that the lands granted to the state ought to be applied to the payment of the state debt. "The Lands will make the Road & pay the State debt both," he wrote early in October. The passage of the bill, Douglas maintained, would enable Illinois "to fulfil its obligations and extinguish its debt without being compelled to resort to onerous and oppressive taxation." The connection between the land grant and the state debt was clearly appreciated by the bill's supporters. In August, Congressman Bayly ordered, through Washington banker W. W. Corcoran, $5000 worth of Illinois state bonds for himself and an additional $12,000 for his father-in-law, undoubtedly part of the arrangement between Douglas and Bayly. A short time later, Douglas himself placed an order with Corcoran. "I fix no limit to the amount," he wrote the banker, "for I am satisfied that it is a good investment, and consequently desire as many as you are willing to purchase & hold for me."

Eastern land investments in Illinois provided an additional inducement for support of the bill. Webster, a consistent advocate of the railroad, had been an Illinois landowner since the 1830's, and many eastern-based land companies had invested heavily in the state. John

Rockwell, a Connecticut investor in the Cairo City and Canal Company, and Ashmun were urged by Holbrook to impress every New England member of the House with the importance of the Central Railroad, and apparently they did their job well. The constitutional scruples and sectional anxieties of the hesitant northeastern Congressmen were overcome, and a majority of them supported Douglas' bill.[8]

The passage of the Illinois Central Railroad bill was a political and personal triumph for Douglas, matching his success in the struggle for the Compromise of 1850. Indeed, as Douglas saw it, his railroad, establishing a direct line of communication between the upper Mississippi and the Great Lakes and the Gulf of Mexico, was as much a part of the sectional compromise as were the bills dealing with the slavery question, for it united north and south with one great bond of union. It was, he wrote, "one of the most gigantic enterprises of the age."

While the bill's passage was testimony to his energy, acumen, and growing political stature, Douglas also had much help in securing the final result. Years later, he commented with indefensible braggadoccio that "if any man ever passed a bill, I did that one," but in 1850 he was more willing to grant the credit to his colleagues in the House. When the *Chicago Tribune* lauded him as the man responsible, Douglas replied modestly that the credit was due the Illinois members in the House, where the real battle was fought. "Their talents, energy, and unanimity, and their influence with their fellow members from other states, operated to insure success." When Sidney Breese, who had long been identified with the project, protested that principal recognition should go to him, Douglas reiterated his conviction that chief credit belonged to the Illinois House delegation.

At the same time Douglas was loath to recognize the contributions which Breese and Holbrook had made to the project, maintaining that they had been motivated primarily by a desire to benefit themselves. Holbrook had worked hard for the success of Douglas' bill, but Douglas' distrust of the speculator ran deep. Following the passage of the bill in the House, Holbrook conferred with Douglas in Washington and, according to Douglas, announced that he would ask the Illinois legislature to reject the release that had been executed earlier on behalf of his company. Douglas was suffering from the abscess on his hip at the time, and, he later recalled, he chased Holbrook from his room with his crutches. If such a rejection had been Holbrook's intention, he was unsuccessful, for in February 1851 the legislature accepted the release. The release, Doug-

las insisted, was Holbrook's "essential service" to the bill, for it enabled
its supporters *"to cut loose from the odium which attached to his name
and his operations."* [9]

Douglas' success, greeted with wild enthusiasm in Illinois, strengthened his political position throughout the state. When he returned home
in October he was invited to congratulatory banquets and universally
praised for his efforts, in marked contrast to the simultaneous denunciations he endured from the freesoilers for his part in the Compromise of
1850. "The destiny of Illinois will be onward," commented one paper,
and there were few in the state who did not share in this optimism. Because of Douglas' insistence that the land grant be used to liquidate the
state debt, quotations on Illinois bonds rose sharply following the passage of the bill. The credit of the state had never stood higher. Douglas'
promotion of the Illinois Central, however, did not end with the struggle in Congress. The means by which the state would dispose of the land
grant in return for the railroad's construction had yet to be determined.
In anticipation of a speedy decision, Douglas submitted to the President
an application, supported by Senators from Kentucky, Tennessee, Mississippi, and Alabama, asking that all land sales be suspended within
twenty-five miles of each side of the proposed railroad, a request which
Fillmore speedily granted. [10]

Three groups vied for the privilege of receiving the grant and building the road. The final selection would be made by the state legislature.
Holbrook had been hopeful that the grant would be made to his Cairo
City and Canal Company and that the legislature could be persuaded
not to accept the company's release. Only a few days after the House
acted on the bill, Holbrook approached Robert J. Walker, Secretary of
the Treasury in Polk's cabinet, with the suggestion that Walker assume
the presidency of the railroad company. Walker sought Douglas' advice
and encountered the Senator's deep hostility toward Holbrook. Douglas
was not alone. Shields warned that Holbrook and Breese were trying "to
get all the lands in their own hands." Congressman William H. Bissell
was more outspoken. "The Cairo Company concern," he wrote, "is rot-
ten, all through. It stinks, and has long stank in the nostrils of the people of Illinois; and everything connected with it has not only become
distasteful, but odious, absolutely odious to them." Attempts were made
by the company to win over the legislators, but the cause was hopeless
from the beginning. As for Walker, he was later selected by the railroad
to negotiate a construction loan in Europe.

Before he returned to Illinois after the adjournment of Congress, Douglas conferred with Julius Wadsworth, Illinois' financial agent in New York, in an attempt to find a plan "by which the greatest advantage can be realized to the State." Wadsworth proposed that the Illinois bondholders assume responsibility for the construction of the road. Douglas, for a time, seemed favorably inclined to this plan. He suggested to Wadsworth that each bondholder be circularized to this effect. The bondholders, however, were scattered throughout the east and in Great Britain, and the time was so short before the legislature would meet that Wadsworth soon found it impossible to carry through his proposal. A hastily drawn scheme was placed before the legislature, but Douglas and others rejected it as too speculative in nature.

A third group, made up of New York and Boston capitalists, most of whom had extensive holdings in Illinois bonds, became interested in the Illinois Central soon after the final hurdles were cleared in Congress. Included in the group were David Neal, George Griswold, John Murray Forbes, John Thayer, Jonathan Sturges, Robert Schuyler, Morris Ketchum, Franklin Haven, J. W. Alsop, and G. W. Ludlow. These men represented an impressive network of business, banking, railroad, and steamship interests. Schuyler was president of five railroads; Ketchum headed a locomotive manufacturing works, and Alsop and Ludlow directed the Panama Railroad and the Pacific Mail Steamship Company. Others in the group were involved in the Michigan Central Railroad and the Great Western (later the Wabash) Railroad. Douglas, disenchanted with Wadsworth's scheme, threw his support behind the efforts of this group to secure the Illinois Central charter. He had, in fact, been in touch with some members of the group since January 1850. A powerful lobby was organized, headed by George W. Billings, former agent of Holbrook's company, and assisted by Mason Brayman, a prominent Illinois lawyer, and Congressmen Wentworth and Bissell, to serve the group's interests in Springfield. When the legislature convened, the case for the eastern promoters was formally presented by Robert Rantoul, Jr., soon to be elected by Massachusetts to succeed Webster in the United States Senate. The talent and resources mustered by the capitalists proved irresistible. The legislature accepted the release executed by Holbrook's company and, in February 1851, incorporated the Illinois Central Railroad, turning over the land grant to the new company. According to the terms of the charter, 7 per cent of the gross revenue of the railroad was to be paid annually into the state treasury to aid the state in meeting its obligations.[11]

Douglas did not play an open part with the legislature in securing the charter for the eastern group, but he was active behind the scenes. Stopping in New York on his return to Illinois, he talked with some of the capitalists involved and urged the prompt construction of the road. Some of them were no strangers to Douglas. His friendship with the promoters of the project to build a rail line across the Isthmus of Panama, including William H. Aspinwall, who later became a director of the Illinois Central, dated back at least to 1848. His relations with the steamship interests had also been close; he had backed legislation for government subsidies to various steamship lines, and there is some evidence that he now expected reciprocal aid in the construction of the Illinois Central. His involvement with the nation's leading transportation and financial interests opened a new area of support to his political ambitions which he would soon exploit. When the backers of the Illinois Central celebrated their success with a banquet in New York, Douglas was among those honored. The nation, his state, and the stockholders in the company, he pointed out, would all share in the benefits of the great railroad system. His own private interests were not ignored, for he later sold some of his Chicago lakefront property to the Illinois Central for its right-of-way at a considerable profit.[12]

ii

Douglas' faith in the cohesive power of railroads, his dream of building a strong and progressive nation with the Mississippi valley heartland as its focal point, and his long-standing commitment to the economic and political development of the west gave direction to his thought and action during the early 1850's. In typical western fashion, he looked to the national government as the essential agent and prime mover in this development. Schooled in the states' rights view and sensitive to the inviolability of local self-government, like most westerners he believed that the proper role of the national government was to aid, and not to control. The government stood as a giant benefactor, encouraging national growth through a wise and impartial dispensation of its resources and protecting, but never infringing upon, the right of the people to govern themselves. Of its resources, the public domain, Douglas thought, could be used most effectively as an instrument for strengthening the

ties that bound the nation together and for speeding the realization of
its virtually unlimited potential. When he secured the land grant to Illinois for aid in railroad construction, Douglas broke new ground. His
success opened the way for other states. In the months that followed the
struggle for the Illinois Central land grant he supported similar efforts
to aid and encourage railroad construction.

Not only states but individuals as well, Douglas believed, should benefit from the vast national domain. When Congress convened in December 1849, he introduced a bill that would grant 160 acres of the public
domain to actual settlers, provided they resided on the land and cultivated it for a period of four years. Douglas was not alone in his effort to
secure homestead legislation, nor was he among the first. Two Illinois
Congressmen, Robert Smith and Orlando Ficklin, had introduced homestead legislation into the lower house of Congress as early as 1844 and
1846, respectively, and Tennessee's Andrew Johnson had already
emerged as an early champion of a free land policy. Long argued by
such pioneers in the land reform movement as Horace Greeley, the
movement for free homesteads received an impetus from the growth of
antislavery feeling in the north following the Mexican War. A homestead policy, it was thought, would provide an effective deterrent against
the expansion of slavery into the western territories.

Both Daniel Webster and Sam Houston supported free homesteads
with resolutions of their own in January 1850, but it was Seward's proposal that a portion of the public domain be set aside for Hungarian refugees that inspired Douglas' eloquent defense of a free land policy. Gratified that his bill would have the support of both Massachusetts and
Texas, Douglas believed that it was the "true policy" of the government
to grant the public lands, in limited quantities, to actual settlers who
should reside on them for a prescribed number of years. He appealed to
the Senate to consider the interests of the pioneer farmer—"the man
who goes into the wilderness, and makes the first settlement, who erects
his house, who makes his improvements, who undergoes the privation to
which pioneers are subject"—as superior to those of the mere speculator. Opposing Seward's plan, Douglas would place the foreign-born emigrant on an equal basis with the native-born citizen. In his remarks, he
gave an early indication of his opposition to prejudice against the foreigner. "I wish to see every foreigner," he argued, "who comes to make
his home with us, welcomed in our midst, and put upon an equality
with our own citizens; I wish to see him received with open arms, with

generosity, with hospitality." But Seward, he maintained, would ignore the interests of native-born citizens. By placing immigrants and natives on the same footing, "we should have no foreign and native parties— no demagogism on the question." A free homestead policy, binding all together in the "bonds of fraternal affection," would speed the settlement of the west, strengthen the nation, and be equally advantageous to north and south, to old states and new states.

Douglas' bill, thought Horace Greeley, did not provide adequate safeguards against speculation, but others regarded it as a "statesmanlike measure" and the "true bill," providing for the emigrants who flee from oppression as well as "our own citizens who escape from the social slavery of our large settlements." No action was taken by the Senate on Douglas' bill during the session, so the initiative passed to others.[13]

While Douglas' attempt to secure homestead legislation was unsuccessful, his support of a free land policy found more specific applications. He gave strong backing to a donation land act that would grant 320 acres of land to every male settler in Oregon (double if he should be married) and to a new military bounty land bill that would extend the privilege of securing free land to veterans of the War of 1812 and of Indian wars since 1790. Both acts passed, the latter with an amendment (proposed by Douglas) that would include veterans of the Black Hawk War. In 1852, he revived an earlier proposal for the settlement of volunteer troops along the Oregon and California trails, granting to each volunteer a section of land upon the expiration of his term of service. The measure would not only provide protection to the emigrants, but would also serve as an important preliminary to the construction of a Pacific railroad and the settlement of the Great Plains.[14]

Douglas' interest in western development was closely related to his concern for the advancement of science and technology. Both were important elements in the unfolding national destiny of which he spoke so enthusiastically. Receptive to new ideas, he frequently used his position and influence in Congress to secure their acceptance by others. The prospect of linking the Atlantic and Pacific coasts with a magnetic telegraph fascinated Douglas. He read materials in the Library of Congress dealing with the telegraph, familiarized himself with its scientific aspects, and became a strong supporter of government aid to the construction of a transcontinental telegraph line. Henry O'Reilly's petition for federal assistance received Douglas' endorsement in 1848, and he continued to fight for O'Reilly's project in the following years. With California's Senator John Weller he sought, in early 1853, an extension of the telegraph from Missouri's western boundary to San Francisco, but southern suspicions that his effort was a subtle move to determine the route of a Pacific railroad defeated his proposal.[15]

The advent of steam power had revolutionized transportation, and Douglas was eager to place this technological advance in the service of national growth and unity through a network of intersectional railroads. He was equally convinced that steam power, if properly and speedily utilized, would bring mastery of the seas to the United States. In 1848 Douglas argued for the passage of government steamship subsidies on the ground that it would facilitate the construction of mail steamers that could challenge the British for the supremacy of the sea lanes. Such vessels could easily be converted into fighting ships, thus enhancing the strength and efficiency of the navy. The advantages of steam power over sail, he maintained, were so obvious that all naval officers "should be newly educated, to make them familiar with the march of science." Two years later Douglas supported a memorial from balloonist John Wise, asking an appropriation for the development of "aerial navigation." He found Wise's contention that balloons could be utilized for purposes of war as well as for the transportation of passengers and mail worthy of study and deserving of government support, but he was unable to persuade the Senate. Senator Bright of Indiana, chairman of the Committee on Roads and Canals, firmly declared that "navigating the air . . . does not find a friend in me." North Carolina's Senator Mangum jokingly suggested that Douglas be made chairman of a select committee to look into it, "as the honorable Senator from Illinois has indicated a high degree of scientific attainment in these matters, to the edification and amusement of the Senate." Douglas had read Wise's book on the subject and was, he said, very favorably impressed. He implored the Senate to take the matter seriously, but without success.[16]

"Two great objects of individual and general prosperity," began a document endorsed by Douglas in 1851, are "the development of the natural resources of our country, and the promotion of practical science." To accomplish the former, he sought unsuccessfully to secure grants of the public domain to the states to support geological surveys. To achieve the latter, he endorsed the efforts of educational reformer Josiah Holbrook to introduce "practical science" as a subject of primary instruction in the schools. "The more this knowledge becomes individual, making every farmer acquainted with the character and capabilities of his own fields, and all classes familiar with the natural wealth immediately surrounding them, the more thoroughly will it be promoted, the more widely diffused." "Agriculture and mechanism" were the two leading objects of human pursuit; educational institutions should, therefore, be designed to offer instruction in the sciences relating to these two branches of learning. Echoing Holbrook's concern was an Illinois educator, Jonathan Baldwin Turner, whose proposal for a national system of industrial universities which would provide instruction for farmers and mechanics was first formally presented in a speech at Granville, Illinois, in 1851. Douglas became interested in Turner's plan, and when the latter proposed that grants of land be made to the states to endow industrial universities, he offered Turner his encouragement and support. Douglas was among those urging the creation of an Agricultural Bureau in the executive branch of the national government. His activities in the cause of scientific agriculture were soon to become more widely known.[17]

Douglas' interest in the promotion and dissemination of practical scientific knowledge found expression in his long association with the Smithsonian Institution. In a democracy, he maintained, it was imperative that the people be informed of the marvelous advances in science and technology that were being made. The Smithsonian admirably filled this role. It was essential that the nation keep pace with what Douglas often termed the "spirit of the age" if it were to fulfill its manifest obligations as the seat of progress and enlightment. Practical and popular science was a prerequisite to national greatness. As a member of the House of Representatives in 1846, Douglas was an enthusiastic supporter of the Smithsonian's establishment, and through his efforts the initial legislation was amended to provide for the deposit of one copy of every copyrighted book, map, chart, musical composition, print, cut, or engraving in the library of the institution. In recognition of his interest, Douglas was appointed a Regent of the Smithsonian in February 1854, a position he held until his death. Joseph Henry, the eminent American scientist and the institution's first secretary, became a close friend. Special tribute was later paid to Douglas' warm advocacy of the "extension of the bounds of science" and for his devotion to the objects of the institution.[18]

iii

Douglas' vision of a strong America was not limited to domestic growth and development. It also required a vigorous foreign policy. The spread-eagle nationalism and bitter Anglophobia that characterized his role in the Texas and Oregon questions continued to influence his view of America's role in the world. The American people, he told a gathering of Irish sympathizers early in 1852, were "the most peculiar and superior people upon the face of the earth," in part because the United States was "a cross of all nations" and "the result of improvement—of continued crossing." National superiority, the manifest destiny for which Douglas argued, demanded certain obligations and responsibilities.

Great Britain was Douglas' *bête noire,* the greatest obstacle to American expansion and development, a rival for hegemony in the New World and for commercial leadership in the world at large, and a natural enemy. "I cannot recognize England as our mother," he told the Senate. "If so, she is and ever has been a cruel and unnatural mother." Unmindful of Americans in their "infancy," she evidenced no pride or joy "at our ever-blooming prosperity and swelling power, since we assumed an independent position." Her literature is full of "lurking and insidious slanders and libels" against the American character and institutions. Even abolitionism, the most serious threat to the security of the Union, had its origin and inspiration in England. Douglas' Anglophobia, commented one paper, bordered on insanity. "England and Englishmen are his particular antipathy." Douglas' hatred of England became an obsession, coloring and distorting his approach to American foreign policy.

Delaware's Senator John M. Clayton once taunted Douglas for his boasts "that we are a *giant* Republic." The Illinois Senator himself, Clayton declared, "is said to be a 'little giant,' . . . and everything that he talks about in these latter days is *gigantic."* But Douglas' convictions of national greatness were not shallow, and his oft-stated contrast between the "old, antiquated notions which belong to the stationary and retrograde movements of the Old World" and the "youthful, uprising aspirations of the American heart" was sharply drawn and deeply felt. "Europe," he insisted, "is antiquated, decrepit, tottering on the verge of dissolution." Its monuments "are the relics of past greatness; the broken columns erected to departed power." Europe was one vast graveyard— "here a tomb indicating the burial of the arts; there a monument marking the spot where liberty expired; another to the memory of a great man, whose place has never been filled." In the United States by contrast, everything is "fresh, blooming, expanding, and advancing." Douglas saw a fundamental antagonism between the Old World and the New, between democracy and aristocracy, and he scornfully rejected the arguments of those who would pattern American policy on European models. Some Americans, he believed, were incapable of comprehending America's growth. Those who had first argued that the nation could not extend beyond the Alleghenies, then the Mississippi, and finally the Pacific were unaware that "the same laws which have carried us forward must inevitably carry us further in the process of time." [19]

Douglas found a new forum for his manifest destiny in the question of America's role in Central American, Isthmian, and Caribbean affairs. The expansion of the United States to the Pacific and the discovery of gold in California inevitably focused attention on Central America, especially as efforts to provide a Pacific railroad stalled. Attempts were made almost immediately to secure government aid for the construction of a Panama Railroad as an important transportation link to the Pacific coast. In December 1848, Douglas submitted a memorial to the Senate, signed by William H. Aspinwall (owner of the Pacific Mail Steamship Company who was later to be involved in the Illinois Central Railroad), asking for a twenty-year government contract to carry supplies on the proposed railroad. A Panama Railroad, it was argued, would greatly advance the interests of the United States in its struggle against Great Britain for commercial supremacy in the Pacific. Douglas, in addition, was confident that "in a few years more we shall have a large empire upon the Pacific" for the support of which such a railroad would be essential. A bill implementing Aspinwall's request was defeated in the Senate, however, partly because some Senators preferred a route across Mexico's Isthmus of Tehuantepec.[20]

At the same time, a more ambitious project developed for the construction of an inter-ocean canal across Nicaragua, but its planners became entangled with British interests in the area. Early in 1848, the British seized the Nicaraguan seaport town of San Juan del Norte, logically considered to be the eastern terminus of the proposed canal. Similar moves were later made to control the western terminus of the canal. Frustrated by these developments, and by Britain's determination to exercise a "protectorate" over the Mosquito Indians along Nicaragua's eastern coastline, the canal's backers sought and received diplomatic aid from the United States government. Douglas expressed little interest in the Nicaragua canal, but the opportunity to consolidate American influence in Central America and simultaneously to defy the British appealed to his notions of manifest destiny.

In 1849, Elijah Hise, Polk's envoy to Guatemala, sought to forestall

British activity by concluding a treaty with Nicaragua, giving both the United States and Nicaragua a virtual monopoly over the proposed canal and granting the United States the right to occupy the country in defense of the canal. It was, Hise later wrote to Douglas, "a substantial annexation of the State of Nicaragua to the American Union." President Taylor soon replaced Hise with the noted archeologist and ethnologist, E. George Squier. Squier also drafted a treaty with Nicaragua, less sweeping than that of Hise and more in keeping with the Taylor administration's decision not to seek a monopoly over the canal. Both treaties were unauthorized, and neither was ever acted upon by the Senate. Discussion of them, however, forced an Anglo-American confrontation in Central America and compelled the two nations to seek a peaceful settlement of their rival interests. John Clayton, as Taylor's Secretary of State, took the initiative. The result was the Clayton-Bulwer Treaty, signed in April 1850, and submitted soon afterward to a Senate already deeply preoccupied with the slavery compromise.[21]

Douglas was opposed from the first to the Clayton-Bulwer Treaty. In the ratification debates he emerged as one of its most bitter critics. Earlier in the year, he had taken the initiative in promoting a Senate investigation of the administration's handling of Central American affairs. Suspecting the Whig administration of pro-British leanings, he submitted a resolution asking the President to lay before the Senate all the correspondence and other papers dealing with diplomatic developments in the area. Newspapers had carried reports of Hise's treaty-making activities, by which the United States had been granted extensive concessions in Nicaragua, and Douglas demanded to know why Hise's treaty had not been referred to the Senate. Squier himself had become alarmed at the prospect of an American surrender to British interests, and he encouraged Douglas in his investigation. When it became clear that Clayton was negotiating a formal treaty with Great Britain, Douglas feared that American rights might be surrendered.

To Douglas, the future course of American growth was at stake. In a conversation with Clayton and Senator William R. King, chairman of the Senate Committee on Foreign Relations, he conveyed his objections to the Secretary of State. When the treaty was submitted to the Senate in April, his worst fears were realized. He opposed the treaty, he informed Clayton and King, "because its objects and provisions were at war with all those principles which had governed all my actions in relation to the affairs of this continent." It amounted to an alliance with

Great Britain and a pledge that "we would never annex any portion of Central America." His objections, he later recalled rather cryptically, occasioned his withdrawal from the foreign relations committee (to which he had been elected in December 1850) "under circumstances not agreeable to my feelings and pride." Douglas was joined in his opposition by two former members of Polk's cabinet. "As well might you stop the current of the Mississippi as arrest the onward march of the American people over this continent," wrote Robert J. Walker to Douglas. James Buchanan urged resistance to the treaty "to the utmost extremity," and he added, "It is, I have no doubt, our destiny to over-run & annex the whole of North America before the close of the present century." The treaty, however, was easily ratified and, to Douglas' consternation, with some Democratic support.[22]

Douglas' opposition did not cease with the treaty's ratification. When it was revealed that the British did not regard its terms as affecting their interests in the Belize Settlement or the Bay Islands, an interpretation in which Clayton had apparently acquiesced, attacks on the treaty began anew. Bulwer, in fact, believed the treaty had tacitly set aside the Monroe Doctrine. When, in 1852, the British government announced the creation of a new colony, the "Colony of the Bay Islands," out of what it maintained were dependencies of British Honduras, a full-scale debate on the treaty developed in the Senate, this time without the injunction of secrecy.

Aroused to white heat by these developments, Douglas angrily denounced the treaty, and when Clayton, who had by then returned to the Senate, sought to defend himself, Douglas viciously turned his denunciations against the former Secretary of State. Douglas based his attack on the "memorable declaration" of President Monroe which recently, he observed, had "assumed the dignified appellation of the 'Monroe doctrine.'" Every provision of the Clayton-Bulwer Treaty, he shouted, was "a practical negation and repudiation" of the Monroe Doctrine. The terms of the treaty had not restricted British power in Central America, as many of its supporters had said it would; on the contrary, it had resulted in the expansion of British colonization efforts. "The right of European Powers to intervene in the affairs of American States is recognized." The Hise treaty, which would have firmly established American interests in the area, Douglas charged, had been deliberately suppressed by Clayton. He declared his unwillingness to enter into treaties with any European power "by the terms of which, we should pledge the faith of this Republic not to do in all coming time that which in the progress of events our interests, duty, and even safety may compel us to do." Who can say, he asked, "that the time will not arrive when our interests and safety may require us to possess some portion of Central America?" Douglas gave full vent to his Anglophobia in defense of his expansionist goals. He recalled his opposition to the Oregon Boundary Treaty, which he maintained was an earlier violation of the Monroe Doctrine, and his opposition to the clauses in the Treaty of Guadalupe Hidalgo by which the United States was limited in its annexation of Mexican territory. Turning his attention to Cuba, he declared himself ready to support the annexation of the island if the Cuban people should ever desire it, but he announced his determination to seize the island by force if Spain should seek to transfer Cuba to England or any other European power.

"The whole system of European colonization rests upon seizure, violence, and fraud." By contrast, Douglas pointed out, "We have never acquired one inch of territory, except by honest purchase, and full payment of the consideration." American policy "is generous, honorable, and justifiable," while that of the British "is illiberal, unkind, unjust." Summing up his view of America's role in world affairs and of the goals of American foreign policy, Douglas concluded:

> I do not wish to annex any more territory now. But I avow freely that I foresee the day when you will be compelled to do it, and cannot help it, and when treaties cannot prevent the consummation of the act. Hence my policy would be to hold the control of our own action, give no pledges upon the subject, but bide our time, and be at liberty to do whatever our interest, our honor, and duty require when the time for action may come. An old, decrepit nation, tottering and ready to fall to pieces, may well seek for pledges and guarantees from a youthful, vigorous, growing Power, to protect her in her old age. But a young nation, with all of her freshness, vigor, and youth, desires no limits fixed to her greatness, no boundaries to her future growth. She desires to be left free to exercise her own powers, exert her own energies, according to her own sense of duty, in all coming time.

As for the immediate problem of British encroachment in Central America, he urged that the government protest the creation of the new colony, making it clear that the United States "in no event or contingency" could acquiesce in the action. If done "with becoming discretion and firmness," he had no fear that it would lead to hostilities. Once that is accomplished, "let us free ourselves from entangling alliances by the annulment of the Clayton and Bulwer treaty." [23]

Douglas' statements were of the kind people had come to expect from him, yet, even for Douglas, the vindictiveness seemed excessive. Armed with government documents from which he read copious and lengthy extracts, he dipped deep into history, which he occasionally insisted on interpreting rather loosely. Efforts to correct his documentation were scornfully brushed aside. The British were convinced that he was part of an intrigue to defeat the treaty's implementation and that he was in correspondence throughout with Nicaraguan revolutionaries, all for the sake of promoting his own presidential ambitions.

His speeches on the Central American question evoked wide interest. The spectators who crowded the galleries were not disappointed. Their "laughter and scarcely-suppressed applause" punctuated his comments. Douglas, one reporter wrote, had admirably vindicated "the great principle of an American policy for the American continent as the cardinal doctrine in our foreign relations." Douglas' nationalism—what Edward Everett called his "bellicose and annexing propensities"—fell in large part on receptive ears. Those who listened forgot his small stature; "you see and feel the tall intellect, booming up, and looking forward to the future." "No man has grasped the idea of American destiny with such prescience and ability," declared a spectator. "The onward, intrepid spirit and will of the times, spoke out in his voice." Still, one newspaper correspondent, while admiring his boldness and courage, wrote, with some justification, that only "careless readers (and they are the majority in this hurrying age)" would regard Douglas' arguments as "pointed and effective." [24]

Some of Douglas' constituents expressed great impatience with his preoccupation with Anglo-American rivalries in Central America while the "vital interests of the great West" lay neglected. But to Douglas, Central America was not remote from western interests. In the first place, one of the existing transportation routes to the Pacific coast crossed it. Central America and Cuba also occupied strategic locations with respect to the mouth of the Mississippi River and must, he thought, be prevented from falling into unfriendly hands. The mouth of the Mississippi, he once said, was in the narrow channel between Florida and Cuba, and no foreign power should be given an opportunity to control it.[25]

Douglas was also mindful of the importance of the Great Lakes and the St. Lawrence River to his state and to the west. He pressed equally hard for the advancement of American interests in that direction. Reciprocity, or free trade, between Canada and the United States had long been discussed, and in 1849 legislation dealing with it was introduced into Congress, only to run afoul of the sectional argument over slavery in the territories. With the inauguration of a Whig administration, talks with the British were resumed. It was not a Whig, however, who revived the reciprocity measure in the Senate, but Stephen A. Douglas. Douglas' bill, introduced in the midst of the compromise discussions in 1850, combined reciprocal trade with the free navigation of the St. Lawrence River and its various ship canals. It was carefully fashioned to give it the greatest chance for success. To meet southern objections he included hemp and sugar among the enumerated articles; stone and marble were added to bring support from the New England states.

The bill's essential provision, Douglas believed, was the free navigation of the St. Lawrence River. The commerce of the lake states depended upon it, since the present outlets to the sea were no longer adequate to handle the traffic. Douglas assured Senator Seward that he was not trying to diminish the trade through New York state; he pointed out that the Erie Canal was simply crowded beyond its capacity. Sir Henry Lytton Bulwer, Britain's minister to the United States, conceded his country's willingness to grant free navigation, but he preferred that it be done by a separate convention. Douglas, however, refused to drop the provision from the bill. "I have had Mr. Douglas spoken to upon the subject," Bulwer wrote to Lord Palmerston, "with a view of dissuading him from the addition . . . but he says that without this provision the Bill will be lost in the Senate, and that with it he is sure of success." He suspected, as he wrote later, that Douglas refused in order to gain "the credit for the measure" for himself.[26]

Douglas pushed hard, but without success. Southerners still hesitated, and many Whigs refused to surrender their protective tariff principles. The early prediction that "the agitation of the negro question" would force a postponement of the question proved accurate. Douglas made a last attempt to bring his bill before the Senate in September, after the passage of the Compromise measures, but he was defeated in a test vote. Ironically, the British hopes for the bill's success hinged on Douglas. He was, wrote a Canadian diplomat, "the only person whose constituents had any direct interest in the measure." Douglas' illness in the closing days of the session brought the matter to an end. "All hopes . . . fell with Sen [ato]r Douglas upon his sick bed." Reciprocity between the two nations was forced to wait until 1854, when a formal treaty provided virtually the same terms as Douglas' bill.[27] Although Douglas for once found himself on the same side as the British, their motives differed. To the latter, free trade between Canada and the United States was an alternative to annexation; to Douglas, it was a first step toward political union.

iv

America's mission, Douglas argued, not only consisted of the annexation of new territories and the relentless drive for unchallenged hegemony in the western hemisphere. The United States must also provide an example to the world, supporting democracy and democratic movements wherever they might occur. "The United States of America is the only republic upon earth, or the only one that deserves the name. All republicans throughout the world have their eyes fixed upon us. Here is their model. Our success is the foundation of all their hopes." When, in 1848, Europe was convulsed by revolutions ostensibly aimed at replacing monarchical forms with democratic ones, Douglas recognized new opportunities for the fulfillment of the national mission. Barely a month after the Paris populace forced the abdication of King Louis-Philippe and proclaimed a republic, Douglas insisted that the Senate offer its congratulations and sympathies to the French people without delay. The leaders of the uprising, he declared, were second only to the Continental Congress in skill and wisdom; their work, accomplished almost without bloodshed, was one of great moral force. Uprisings in the German states evoked similar statements of support and sympathy from other Democratic leaders.

The struggle of the Hungarians against Austrian domination, however, captured American sympathies most completely. The movement to establish an independent Magyar state was compared with America's own revolution, and Louis Kossuth, the leader of the revolt, was likened to George Washington. When the movement was crushed, Americans offered their country as a haven for the defeated leaders. Seward's effort to provide free homesteads for Hungarian refugees, to which Douglas had taken strong exception, was one manifestation of the popular concern. Kossuth, who had fled to the Ottoman Empire, became the object of much solicitude. Early in 1851 Congress passed a resolution empowering the government to carry the Hungarian leader to the United States in an American vessel.[28]

Kossuth landed in New York early in December, receiving a wild ovation such as that city had not witnessed since Lafayette's visit twenty-five years before. It soon became clear that Kossuth was not simply seeking asylum in the United States, but that he was actively soliciting support for his cause. The revelation hardly affected his reception, and his appeals were answered by contributions of money and arms. In the meantime, Congress debated the proper mode of receiving the visitor. With a presidential election less than a year away, the question quickly became involved in partisan politics, as both Whigs and Democrats vied with one another in support of the revolutionary. A resolution presented by Seward welcoming Kossuth on behalf of the American people was passed, and plans were made for a gala congressional reception.

Speaking in support of Seward's resolution, Douglas declared that it was America's obligation "to demonstrate to all mankind" that she "sympathizes with the popular movement against despotism, whenever and wherever made." A great movement was in progress "which threatens the existence of every absolute government in Europe" to which the nation should not close its eyes. The armed intervention of Russia against the Hungarian uprising was such a violation of the "laws of nations," Douglas stated, as to authorize the United States to intervene. He did not propose American intervention in European affairs at that moment, but argued emphatically that the United States had the right "to interfere or not, according to our convictions of duty." To maintain otherwise was to give consent to Russia's attempt "in violation of the international code, to destroy the liberties of an independent nation." The suggestion that an alliance with England should be sought "to restrain the march of Russia over the European Continent" aroused Douglas' Anglophobia. England, he charged, was as responsible as any European power for the failure of the recent revolutionary movements. America had no need of such an ally "to maintain the principles of our Government." "I wish no alliance with monarchs." In conclusion, Douglas presented his rule for the conduct of American foreign policy: "The peculiar position of our country requires that we should have an *American policy* in our foreign relations, based upon the principles of our own Government, and adapted to the spirit of the age. We should sympathize with every liberal movement—recognize the independence of all

Republics—form commercial treaties, and open diplomatic relations with them—protest against all infractions of the laws of nations, and hold ourselves ready to do whatever our duty may require when a case shall arise." An independent foreign policy, sympathy with liberal democratic movements throughout the world, readiness to intervene on behalf of these movements—these were essential ingredients in the national mission, and Douglas was prepared to implement them on behalf of Hungarian freedom.[29]

After spending almost three weeks in the New York area, Kossuth began a triumphal tour that took him as far west as St. Louis. He arrived back in Washington on December 30, and on the following day he conferred briefly with President Fillmore. Later in the day he talked with Douglas for an hour and a half. If he had expected assurances of immediate governmental support and intervention, he was sadly disappointed. Fillmore cast cold water on Kossuth's hopes, and, with the election in the offing, Douglas was too shrewd a politician to add to what he had already said publicly. Southerners were hesitant to endorse Kossuth, and the enthusiasm with which the Hungarian was received by abolitionists and freesoilers embarrassed some northerners. If Kossuth's reception in New York was wild and unrestrained, his reception in official Washington was cool and cautious. Unofficially, his hosts in the national capital feted him with all the trappings afforded a visiting dignitary.

On the evening of January 7, some 250 Congressmen, cabinet members, and members of the diplomatic corps gathered at the National Hotel to do honor to the Hungarian patriot. The champagne flowed freely and the rhetoric became more colorful as the evening wore on. Seward applauded loudly and stamped his feet following Kossuth's brief opening remarks, and Secretary of State Daniel Webster rejoiced at the prospect of seeing "our American model upon the Lower Danube and on the mountains of Hungary." Others declared themselves ready to pledge America's armed forces to strike a blow for liberty. Douglas followed with a more prudent and carefully prepared speech, cautiously avoiding any commitment to immediate intervention in European affairs. "Whether I would or would not interfere in the struggles of Europe, must depend upon the peculiar circumstances of the case—the principles involved and the consequences to follow."

Douglas was less restrained in his description of the United States as a model for all the world to emulate. American institutions, he judged, were the "most successful in advancing the great interests of humanity

—in promoting civilization and intelligence—in developing and elevating the intellectual, moral and physical condition of the people." No other nation "upon the face of the globe" had done more "to elevate the condition of the people—to render them intelligent, peaceable, and happy" or had done more "for the cause of civilization, religion, and morality, in the same space of time." Without committing the nation to intervention, Douglas declared that "I would remonstrate to all mankind, by our every act and word, that we do sympathize, ardently, with the liberal movement throughout the globe." Such were the dimensions of Douglas' belief in America's manifest destiny.

The occasion offered a further opportunity to attack England, and Douglas was not unaware of the political effect his remarks would have. For a time he seemed more interested in the struggle of the Irish than with that of the Hungarians. England "must do justice to Ireland, [applause,] and to the Irish exiles, [great applause,]" before she could command his respect. "So long as she imprisons and banishes for life, Irish patriots for no other crime than that which has made the illustrious Hungarian our national guest," he shouted, "she must look elsewhere for allies and assistance." "Let her restore O'Brien, Mitchell, Meagher, and their associates to liberty in their nation and to the English people, and assimilate her institutions to ours." It was a speech well-tailored to an election year.[30]

v

For Douglas, the early years of the 1850's were probably among the most satisfying of his life. In 1843 he had entered Congress, a thirty-year-old freshman Representative; less than ten years later he was a United States Senator with national influence and power and a leader in the Democratic party. His rise had been little short of meteoric. Unwilling to play the passive role usually assigned to new members of Congress, he had literally forced his way into the front ranks of American political life, often to the consternation of older, more seasoned politicians. He was brash, aggressive, and frequently impudent, and if he was not always right, he was at least heard. Assuming for himself the position as spokesman for the west and for western interests, he soon became a force to be reckoned with in the development of national legislation. His intense partisanship as well as his zealous promotion of his section's welfare led him into the highest councils of the nation. President Polk, with whom Douglas strongly disagreed on some questions, had early recognized the young Congressman's potential. Douglas' frequent visits to the White House and his frequent mention in the President's diary attest to the value which Polk placed on his advice. Even under a Whig administration, his influence remained strong. He was frequently asked to intercede with both Taylor and Fillmore on behalf of men who wished appointments in states other than his own, and some Illinois Whigs sought his assistance in determining the character of the local patronage. Unabashed in his support of the appointment of Democrats by a Whig administration, he once urged that a new Illinois postmastership be awarded to a Democrat on the ground that there was no "capable and upright whig living in the place." [31]

Douglas' defense of manifest destiny in the debates over Texas, the Oregon boundary question, and the Mexican War had touched a responsive chord among Americans in the late 1840's. His advocacy of American expansion in the western hemisphere, and his reckless and often irrational diatribes against Great Britain, delighted those Americans who saw in the United States the great wave of the future. Douglas' deep faith in the Union, his frequent altercations with slave state Congressmen, and his denunciation of abolitionists brought him support from moderate and conservative men everywhere. His vigorous support of the Compromise measures and his successful leadership of the compromise forces stamped his name indelibly in the minds of many Americans as a defender of the Union against the destructive sectional tendencies of the time. His political acumen and his shrewd ability as a manipulator of votes and bills won the respect of friends and enemies alike. Spectators now flocked to the Senate galleries to hear Douglas speak, and the appellations which had been bestowed upon him, "Little Giant" or "the Young Giant of the West," found frequent mention in the nation's press.

Douglas' domestic life was as bright and promising as was his public life. With political success came social and economic success. His style of living assumed a new refinement and grace. Unfamiliar at first with the rules of etiquette, he soon adapted himself to the requirements of social life in the national capital, aided by a wife who had been raised on a southern plantation and who had been educated in a finishing school. Douglas retained some of the habits he had developed as a backwoods Illinois politician—a frequent recourse to profanity and coarse language, a taste for good American whiskey, the disgusting habit of chewing tobacco—but even these were affected by his new social position.

Douglas, recalled one contemporary, was "social to a degree, dining out almost daily when not entertaining his friends at his own hospitable home, visiting strangers at their hotels," always "with a pleasant smile or a kind word for everybody." His courtesy was "as knightly as if he had been born in the best society." Illinoisans visiting the capital were impressed with their Senator's popularity "in all the social circles." He always took time from his busy schedule to show his constituents the sights of the capital and, to their delight, to introduce them to some of the "bears and lions that infest the national 'fodder pen.' " They invariably returned to Illinois with the kindest feelings toward him "for his civility and old fashioned politeness." Douglas' taste for whiskey was gradually supplemented, in equally immoderate amounts, by brandy, cognac, and champagne. He ordered port and madeira wine by the cask directly from Portuguese wine merchants and entertained lavishly at receptions that offered a wide variety of potables. Meals in his home were served on decorated French chinaware, and his Washington tailor outfitted him in silk and striped Valencia vests and doeskin pants. His consumption of chewing tobacco declined as he found smoking expensive Havana cigars more socially acceptable and easier on the carpets.[32]

On November 3, 1850, a second son was born at the Martin plantation in North Carolina, and he was named Stephen Arnold after his father. Martha and the children continued to spend a considerable amount of time, especially during the recesses of Congress, in North Carolina, partly to be with Martha's widowed mother and partly to avoid the unhealthy atmosphere of Washington. When Martha did remain in Washington during the sitting of Congress, the children were usually left behind with their grandmother. Only rarely did Martha accompany her husband on his trips to Illinois. Separation from his wife and family weighed heavily on Douglas. "I need not say to you as a husband & father," he wrote to his wife's uncle, Thomas Settle, "how anxious I am to have my family with me and how slowly the time passes while waiting for the letter which shall fix the day for me to meet them."

It was not only the demands of his new social position, but the strong desire to have his family about him, more acute now that his second son had arrived, that impressed Douglas with the need for more permanent living quarters than the Washington hotel suites he and Martha had been occupying. In April 1851, he purchased two squares (blocks) and a large family residence at the intersection of New Jersey Avenue and I Street North, about one mile from the capitol and situated on a small rise in an as yet undeveloped area. The Douglas home soon became known as "Mount Julep"—"a resort for those who are fond of good eating & drinking." [33]

These were exciting years for the national capital as the city experienced a dramatic population growth that was matched by an unprecedented material prosperity. Real estate values increased, and Douglas was aware of the wisdom of investing in house and property. Gas lamps would soon be installed on Washington streets, and a city water system was being planned. On July 4, 1851, the cornerstone was laid for an extension of the capitol building. Construction on a new and magnificent dome would soon start. The destruction of the Library of Congress in a disastrous capitol fire the following December only emphasized the need for improvement in the building. Beautification of the city came more slowly. The removal of the slave pens and auction houses, following the 1850 legislation, was a decided advance. City streets, however, remained deep in dust in the summer and became quagmires in the winter. Garbage was still dumped in the streets and alleys, pigs roamed at will, and the lack of proper sanitation facilities greatly increased the unhealthy aspect of the city. In order to speed the paving of the city streets, Douglas, as a new property-owner, suggested in 1852 that the carriageway be narrowed, the sidewalks widened, and the remaining land along the streets devoted to ornamental courts or gardens.[34]

With a permanent residence in Washington, Douglas turned his thoughts to his own booming home town of Chicago. During his brief visits there he had always stayed in the local hotels, principally the Sherman House. He now desired more settled living quarters to which he could bring his growing family. In 1849, Douglas made his first purchase of lakefront land, some four miles south of the center of the city, and within a few years he increased his tract to nearly seventy-five acres. A portion of the land along the beach was sold to the Illinois Central Railroad for right-of-way (at a price of $21,300—about ten times what he had paid for the entire acreage), but he retained the higher ground to the west for his own estate. It was on this site, in a grove of oak trees and with a commanding view of the lake, that Douglas decided to build his Chicago home. His plans called for a spacious mansion with separate stables and a gatekeeper's lodge set amidst winding drives. The remaining portion of the tract would be subdivided into two parks and smaller lots to be known as Oakenwald. Until these grandiose plans could be realized, Douglas in 1851 erected a modest one-story home that reminded one visitor of a "Swiss country cottage house." Douglas' plans

were never fulfilled. He lived in the cottage only briefly, if at all, and it
was occupied by a tenant during most of the 1850's. His intention to develop an estate on the property was still a dream at the time of his
death.[35]

No small factor in Douglas' pursuit of politics and in his adjustment
to the social status that accompanied political leadership was his freedom from pecuniary worries. The costly political campaigns that would
drain his financial resources were still in the future. He was not wealthy,
but his means were sufficient to allow him to live comfortably, even os-
tentatiously. His law practice was no longer a major activity, of course,
although he still occasionally argued cases before the Illinois supreme
court. Unlike many of his colleagues, he maintained no law office at
home. Except for his admission to practice before the United States Supreme Court in the summer of 1850 and his argument of suits involving
property against the Trustees of the Illinois and Michigan Canal in the
following year, he engaged in little legal activity. He owned some railroad stock and held a quantity of Illinois state bonds, but speculation of
this type had never appealed to him and represented but a small part of
his means. Douglas' two major sources of wealth were his Chicago land
holdings and the Mississippi plantation that technically belonged to his
wife.

Besides his lakefront property, Douglas acquired several thousand
acres located in the western part of Chicago, as well as along the south
branch of the Chicago River and in the vicinity of Lake Calumet. The
value of his land, especially those tracts in and near Chicago, increased
drastically, so that Douglas was able to dispose of parts of it at great
profit. His Chicago property, he recalled in 1855, had cost him $11,300.
Yet the Illinois Central Railroad had paid him almost twice that sum
for just the right-of-way along his property's lakefront. In 1856, his
nearly seventy-five acres of lake shore was valued at $60,400 for tax pur-
poses, and sixteen acres of lake front property further north was valued
at $20,000 during the same year. One hundred acres on the western lim-
its of Chicago were said to have been sold by Douglas in 1856 for an
even $100,000. When government land sales in the Chicago land office
were terminated in 1855, he went on a buying spree, securing vast tracts
of land near Lake Calumet and along the Calumet River for $2.50 per
acre. While Douglas' land provided him with some income, he was
forced in later years to borrow against it in order to finance his political

campaigns, and by the time of his death most of it was heavily mort-gaged.[36]

The Mississippi plantation, almost 3000 acres along the Pearl River, provided a steadier source of income. As its manager, he received 20 per cent of its annual proceeds, enough, according to one opponent, to enable him "to adopt the luxurious habits of the Southern aristocracy." Although subject to periodic flooding, during the decade the plantation produced bumper crops of cotton and corn and, occasionally, enough surplus pork to sell to near-by markets. A small portion of the land along the river was planted in sugar cane. Douglas took his managerial duties seriously, visiting the plantation himself on frequent occasions and receiving reports from the New Orleans commission houses which handled the cotton crop. He also received detailed letters regularly from the plantation's overseer, discussing the nature of the crop, the problems with neighboring plantations, and the condition of the Negro slaves, who numbered about 140 by mid-decade. Because of the eagerness with which his political opponents attacked his plantation connection, Douglas was particularly concerned that the slaves be well-treated. He insisted that they be accorded regular worship services, and his custom of providing an annual barbecue for the entire group became widely known in the area. "The negroes are in fine helth," wrote the overseer, "children increasing very fast & doing well." The youngsters "get just as much butter milk as they can eate & they are just as fat as you ever saw hogs." "As to the negroes," he wrote, "they is no likeler or better in no country ginerally." Still, as the overseer reported, all was not idyllic on the plantation. "The negroes will steel hogs to sell to mean white folks," Douglas was informed in 1849, and later, "Nezer is yet in the woods . . . he will always give us troughble, he ran away almost for Nothing." Especially troublesome slaves were hired out; one "beged so harde to come back & that he never would give me eany more troughble."

Although as early as 1850 Douglas wrote of his intention to concentrate all his family's property in Illinois, he never did so. Instead, discouraged by the land's declining productivity and its seasonal flooding by the Pearl River, he determined to sell the plantation and find another site in Mississippi for the operation. In 1857 the plantation was broken up and sold, and in the same year Douglas, on behalf of his sons, entered into a partnership with James A. McHatton of Baton Rouge for the establishment of a new plantation south of Greenville, not far from the

Mississippi River. McHatton provided some 2000 acres of rich, unculti-
vated land, and Douglas furnished 142 slaves, as well as a quantity of
mules, cattle, and wagons. The profits of the new enterprise were to be
divided in proportion to the valuation of the property contributed by
each partner.[37]

Douglas' outlook at the beginning of the decade was encouraging. His
worries were few. The delicate state of Martha's health and her recurring sickness did cause concern (in 1851, Douglas employed a nurse to
look after her), and his indebtedness as he expended over $3000 on im-
provements to his Washington house and property gave him slight
pause. "I have already borrowed so much that I don't know where to
apply," he complained in December 1851, in response to a financial appeal.[38] But political leadership, social position, relative financial security,
and a happy family life all seemed good omens for the future.

# XV
## "Young America"
### 1852

i

If Douglas' prospects seemed bright in the early 1850's, those of his party were less than encouraging. The struggle over the Compromise of 1850 left a legacy of discord and dissension which mirrored the divisions in the Union itself. Anger over the passage of the Fugitive Slave Act strengthened the hands of freesoilers, who in several northern states controlled the Democratic party. In the south, elections were fought between opponents and supporters of the Compromise, and party lines were virtually obliterated. The south, declared the famous Georgia Platform, would agree to no further compromises; the existence of the Union would depend upon the faithful enforcement of the Fugitive Slave law by the north. Secession, it was reported, was still being talked of in South Carolina. "Nothing but the Providence of God," wrote an anxious North Carolinian, "can save the present Union." An Illinois Congressman predicted that "there is much danger of some kind of a fuss in the course of a year or two." [1]

The Fugitive Slave Act became the new target of antislavery men. Abolitionists, appealing to a "higher law," openly counseled resistance to it, and a series of dramatic slave rescues in northern cities followed. When Congress met in December 1850, it was clear that efforts would be made to repeal the obnoxious legislation. The attacks on the Compromise of 1850 were highly disturbing to Douglas, even though he was positive that any attempt to repeal the Fugitive Slave Act would be soundly defeated. In February 1851, when the slave Shadrach was rescued in Boston, Douglas angrily denounced the abolitionists. They

formed a conspiracy against the government and against the Constitution and should be held fully responsible for all that any of their number might do in resisting the law. Speaking in the Senate, he pointed the
finger of guilt at some of his northern colleagues. "I hold white men
now within the range of my sight responsible for the violation of the
law at Boston," he shouted. "It was done under their advice, under their
teaching, under their sanction, under the influence of their speeches."
Their only purpose, Douglas warned, was to "fan the flames of discord
that have so recently divided this great people." [2]

To meet this new crisis, pro-Compromise Union meetings were held
in several northern cities where bankers and businessmen particularly
wished to retain good relations with the south, and there was talk of organizing a new Union party that would unite the supporters of the
Compromise against the extremists in both sections. A movement toward this end appeared in Congress, led, it was said, by Henry Clay,
when forty-four Senators and Representatives, in January 1851, signed a
pledge to maintain the Compromise and to support no one for President
or Vice President who did not regard the settlement as a finality. Of the
signers, only five were Democrats, all of them from southern states.
Northern freesoilers and southern states' rights men resisted the suggestion, but so did the large body of national Democrats in the north.
Douglas was among those who refused to sign, even though he had been
one of the principal architects of the Compromise. If every Democratic
member of Congress should sign, he declared, he would still withhold
his support. For Douglas, the slavery question had been settled. No good
purpose could be served by continuing its discussion or by linking it
with the next presidential election. Any attempt to organize a new party
on the basis of the Compromise, he warned, would receive his strong opposition. "The Democratic party is as good a Union party as I want," he
later told the Senate, "and I wish it to preserve its principles and its organization, and to triumph upon its old issues." If the object of the signers should succeed, the slavery question would of necessity continue to be
the subject of debate and controversy. "That is the very thing which we
wish to avoid, and which it was the object of the compromise to prevent." He agreed that the Compromise was a final settlement, but he opposed all efforts to make its finality a matter of formal resolution. In any
case, he was confident that no attempt to disturb the Compromise could
possibly succeed.

Douglas' response to the movement was regarded as "best calculated to allay excitement and bring men back to a proper sense of their duties as citizens of a great confederacy." The idea, however, persisted. In November 1851, a group of New York businessmen known as the "Union Safety Committee" proposed that a mixed presidential ticket based on the finality of the Compromise be organized. Henry Clay and Lewis Cass were to be the candidates. Clay displayed some interest when approached, but Cass, on the advice of Douglas and New York's Daniel Dickinson, rejected the overture. Attempts were made to secure endorsement of the Compromise's finality in the Democratic caucuses of the House and Senate, but with Douglas' lieutenant, William A. Richardson, in the chair, the Democratic members of the House voted to table the resolution. The proposal was not even submitted to the Senate caucus. "The attempt to make the Compromise the basis of the Democratic creed failed as it ought," reported Senator Shields.[3]

For his stand, Douglas was accused of acting like a "cautious, calculating" politician, fearful that he might be injured "in future trading and bartering" with the "abolitionists of the north, and the secessionists of the south." Douglas *was* acting like a politician. The return of both northern and southern dissidents to the Democratic party was of special concern to him. The approaching presidential election made the problem of party unity all the more acute. Always the pragmatist, he did not wish to preclude freesoilers and southern radicals from serving the interests of the Democratic party; rather he hoped to preserve a broad, national character that could unite all the party's former elements. In addition, by avoiding hard commitments and party tests, he would maintain the flexibility that his own party role seemed to demand.

Douglas sought to remove a lesser source of discord within the party when, risking his popularity in the west, he opposed a river and harbor bill in the waning days of the short session of Congress. Internal improvements policy had been a source of serious dissension in the Democratic party since Polk's controversial veto in 1846 and had contributed in part to the disaffection of northern Democrats during the campaign of 1848. Northern and western Democrats adopted a softened line toward the question, while southern Democrats clung to their strict construction principles. An open party split was threatened in February, when some southern Democrats, led by Jefferson Davis, demanded that opposition to a pending river and harbor improvement bill be made a party principle on constitutional grounds. While some Democrats argued that internal improvements could be good Democratic doctrine, Douglas and Cass (both presidential hopefuls and therefore anxious to avoid a party split on any issue) sought a way out of the dilemma.

While voting to keep the bill under consideration, Douglas also urged a close and careful scrutiny of all its items in order to determine which of the appropriations were of a national character and which were not. He made an impassioned plea for improvements to the Illinois River as the link which "makes most of the States of this Union an island." "If there is any work that is entirely national in its character it is the Illinois river," he argued. But, he warned, if the bill was not put in "a proper shape" he would have to vote against it. Frantic efforts to bring the bill to a vote before the end of the session failed, so a crisis was at least temporarily averted. Had the bill passed the Senate in precisely the shape given to it by the House, one reporter predicted, the Democratic party "would have been demoralized, dissolved, annihilated for the next twenty years." Douglas, whose eagerness to improve the western waterways was tempered by "the more distant prospects of harmony and peace to the whole Union," was credited with an important part in the result.[4]

The struggle impressed Douglas with the need for some other way for handling internal improvements than the logrolling tactics that had prevailed in the past. The policy of granting public land to the states to aid in the construction of new projects, as in the case of the Illinois Central Railroad, was already an integral part of his program. Now he put forth another suggestion for overcoming party discord. Enable the states to improve their own rivers and harbors, he proposed, by granting them power to levy tonnage duties on vessels using the waterways. Improvements would be paid for from the money collected. His plan would provide a "regular system" for the improvement of rivers and harbors and, avoiding the pitfalls of constitutional interpretation, be one on which all sections could unite.

Douglas offered his proposal in the next session of Congress, in August 1852, and he spoke at length on its behalf. He protested the niggardly provisions for western improvements in past legislation—"a mere pittance for the Mississippi" and not one dollar for the whole Pacific coast—and argued that the improvements that had been made by the government on the western rivers "have done no perceptible good." He insisted that the money be put in the hands of those who had a practicable knowledge of the problems involved in order to guarantee its wise expenditure. But, more importantly, the collection of tonnage duties by the states would remove the question of internal improvements from national politics. "For the last nine years," he told the Senate, "it has been a death struggle in the last nights of the session—a trial of physical strength—whether the river and harbor bill should be defeated, or should be passed, by all possible combinations." Projects were approved or defeated not on their merits, but by "who should sit out the longest" or by how many votes could be traded. The strain on the party had often been well-nigh disastrous. His plan, he declared, would do more for the protection of inland commerce and for the preservation of life and property than all the appropriations that had ever been made from the national treasury, besides removing from Congress a troublesome and divisive question. Douglas had already sought the removal of the explosive slavery issue from the national councils. His proposed tonnage duties applied popular sovereignty to the issue of internal improvements.

Douglas encountered a storm of opposition both in Congress and in Illinois. Leading the Senate attack was Truman Smith of Connecticut, whose denunciation caused Douglas to lose his temper, driving him "into a very unseemly exhibition of himself." Smith, posing as a defender of Illinois' farmers, charged Douglas with attempting to defraud the west. *The New York Times* expressed surprise the plan could come from one who was usually so zealous for western interests. Pointing out how New York and the eastern commercial states could tax the western trade as it sought seaboard markets, the *Times* argued that the western states would be helpless under Douglas' plan. Even Lewis Cass deserted Douglas. Douglas also found little support for his scheme at home. It was both impractical and absurd, maintained one Illinois river town newspaper, since the whole cost of improving the rivers and harbors would be borne by westerners rather than by the nation as a whole. It would be "a system of direct taxation on the producers and consumers of the country, bearing more immediately and more onerously on western farmers than on any one else," protested another Illinois paper. Douglas' plan was rejected by the Senate, but he continued to advocate a system of tonnage duties as a replacement for existing internal improvements legislation. Early in 1854, in a letter to the governor of Illinois, he presented his case once again, but other issues very quickly overshadowed his efforts.[5]

During the months between the Compromise of 1850 and the 1852 presidential election, Douglas was busy attempting to persuade his fellow Democrats to overcome their factional differences. To many observers, his efforts seemed less concerned with the health of the Democratic party than with promoting his own ambitions as a party leader. His opposition to a declaration of the Compromise's finality as a party creed, his behavior on the internal improvements question, and even his softened tone toward Kossuth and the matter of intervention in Hungary all struck suspicious northerners as a blatant appeal for southern support. In 1848, his name had been proposed for the presidency by Illinois friends, but no one (not even Douglas) took the suggestion seriously. By 1851, however, he was more widely regarded as having the best chance of winning not only the Democratic nomination but the election as well. A united party was a prerequisite to his success.

ii

Almost as soon as the last vote was counted in 1848, the Democrats began speculating about the next election. The election campaign had revealed severe cracks and strains in the party, and many of its members felt that only new and vigorous leadership could restore it to its former strength. Of the party leaders, few seemed suited to the task. Cass was a loser, Buchanan would not do, Woodbury might be a possibility. "As between these *old fellows,* there is no great choice here," wrote an Illinois Congressman from Washington early in 1850, "but the feeling seems here to be for a new man." The feeling soon became a conviction. The old leadership, it was said, had grown stale, and the spirit of reform and change, so vital in earlier days, had been lost. Politicians seemed more interested in the outward forms of political power than in utilizing that power as an instrument for the improvement of the nation and of the world. The Mexican War and the acquisition of vast new lands in the southwest had quickened the belief in American manifest destiny. The liberal European revolutions of 1848 focused attention on the American experiment and suggested a more vigorous world role for the young nation. The Compromise of 1850 removed the most serious threat to the Republic since its founding and, with the slavery agitation muffled, opened the way for America's social and economic expansion. Business and commercial interests joined in the demand for bold youthful leadership. Territorial expansion, economic growth, and the promotion of progressive democracy everywhere became the tenets of this increasingly vocal element.

In 1845, Edwin De Leon, a South Carolina editor, published *The Position and Duties of Young America,* in which he argued that nations, like people, experience "infancy, manly vigor, and decrepitude." The United States, standing at the threshold of "exulting manhood," required the leadership of its young men, who would express their faith in the nation's glorious destiny and utilize their political power to achieve that destiny. The label "Young America" came to identify the movement of ardent, evangelical nationalism that included in its ranks reformers, businessmen, newspaper editors, and political figures. In 1851 and 1852 it had a more specific application to the group within the Democratic party that was determined to restore the party to its former Jacksonian vigor.[6]

That Stephen A. Douglas should become the candidate of Young America was logical. He possessed all the necessary qualifications. He was young (only thirty-eight years old), energetic, pugnacious, bold, and courageous. A man of firm convictions, he shared the faith in national destiny and from his seat in Congress had done much to promote it. He was well known for his expansionism, and his crucial role during the hectic days of 1850 and his interest in railroads and support of steamship subsidies had brought him into close contact with national financial circles. The Democratic candidate, it was predicted, would be someone from the "great northwest" who was not distasteful to any particular portion of the Union. "There is but one man who answers to this description." Douglas, wrote a New Yorker, "with his eastern birth, his western residence and his southern marriage will be regarded in those different sections as a less sectional man than any other . . . and the one most likely to be elected." [7]

It is not known precisely when the first serious suggestions of Douglas' candidacy for the presidency in 1852 were made. In January 1851, a Democratic meeting in Illinois' Jo Daviess county endorsed Douglas for the party's nomination, and Democrats in other counties quickly followed suit. At the same time, an upstate New York newspaper proposed Douglas' name, and other papers in the area joined in. That the suggestion had already been planted in Douglas' mind was evident. In February, Ohio Senator Salmon P. Chase noted that "Douglas is figuring" on the presidency. Douglas' efforts to consolidate his support immediately following the adjournment of the short session of Congress indicate that the suggestion was not new to him. In fact, the extent to which plans and strategies had been perfected by the adjournment in March demonstrates that a movement on his behalf was already well under way.

In his bid for the Democratic nomination, Douglas received the support of a motley group of lobbyists, claims agents, newspaper editors, frustrated politicians, and ambitious merchant capitalists. Aggressive and often indiscreet, they were all Young Americans who saw opportunities for their own advancement in the new order which they preached, and some of them apparently would stop at little to ensure the success of their movement. They blamed their own troubles, as well as those of the country, on the political stagnation that characterized national government, and they protested the stultifying leadership of the older professional politicians, whom they indiscriminately labeled "Old Fogies." " 'Young America' is to speak out," wrote one, "& is to be *heard* & *heeded* too at the coming election and *we* intend to prove . . . that it is not necessary to be professional men in *Politics* or *science* to be felt in the country." They were joined by sincere and well-intentioned men who saw in Douglas the symbol of America's own youthful vigor and who, with Douglas, argued that the nation's future lay in transcending sectional interests and in following broad national, progressive, and uniquely American policies both at home and abroad. Douglas accepted whatever support came his way and sought to broaden his popularity through behind-the-scene negotiations. He was with the Young America movement more than he was of it, and much of his later difficulty lay in his inability to maintain a tight control over the very elements he had marshalled in his behalf. In spite of his experience and success, Douglas still exhibited an eagerness and naïveté that his adversaries had long since overcome.[8]

A central figure in Douglas' campaign was the bizarre and enigmatic George Nicholas Sanders, a Kentuckian who had made a career as a political schemer, business agent, and revolutionary. Thoroughly imbued with the ideals of Young America—"the nerve and energy of the movement"—Sanders was a visionary whose enthusiasm and volatility frequently carried him beyond the bounds of sound judgment, often resulting in actions which injured the very causes he was promoting. His picturesque bombastic rhetoric was mixed with a deep and sincere faith in American democracy. The European revolutions of 1848 aroused him, and he went abroad to sell muskets to the revolutionaries. Several years later, from his consular post in London, he publicly advised the assassination of Louis Napoleon. Early in 1851, Sanders turned to Douglas as the man best suited to rescue the nation from "fogeydom" and to lead it onward and upward to its destiny. Viewed with suspicion by the old guard, Sanders' identification with Douglas' campaign was a handicap which Douglas discovered too late. In the meantime, Douglas outlined his campaign plans to Sanders and was pleased that they received his approval. "I have great confidence in your judgment & discretion," Douglas asserted. "I proffit more by your letters than any I receive," he wrote later, but he added cautiously, "By this you must not infer that I adopt all your views, for I am not yet fully convinced that you do not know how to make a mistake in politics." Serving with Sanders in the campaign were others of similar ilk: J. Knox Walker, notorious lobbyist, kinsman and former private secretary of President Polk; Francis J. Grund, an Austrian immigrant and political correspondent to several newspapers; Beverley Tucker, a Washington claims agent and nephew of the novelist of the same name; and William M. Corry, a Cincinnati newspaper editor.

To strengthen his candidacy, Douglas made the unprecedented decision to select his own vice presidential candidate. He chose forty-two-year-old Virginia Senator R. M. T. Hunter. Shortly after the adjournment of Congress, in mid-March, a group of young Democrats ("having a jollification at the National Hotel") proposed as an antidote to southern disunion sentiment "the election of Douglas and Hunter President and Vice-President of the United States." A few days later, Douglas, on his way to North Carolina, stopped in Richmond, where he proposed that a ticket be formed consisting of a Compromise northerner and a southerner who opposed the Compromise. It was an obvious bid for southern support, and Senator Hunter, staunch defender of southern rights, seemed the logical choice. Hunter, who thought Douglas was "one of the coolest observers even when he himself is concerned, that I ever saw," was willing to cooperate, and henceforth Sanders and his associates worked assiduously for the success of what became known as "the Ticket." Douglas hoped that all factions within the Democratic party would be able to "come together upon the basis of *entire silence on the slavery question* and support 'the Tickett.' " By offering the party a complete ticket, Douglas introduced a variation in presidential campaigning, while at the same time he recognized a new concern in the public mind (since Taylor's death in 1850) for the vice presidential office.[9]

Douglas' campaign for the Democratic nomination began in earnest fourteen months before the party convention. Grund commented that "Douglas is going it with a rush" and thought that the candidate ought not be pushed too fast so early. He hoped that Douglas would not commit his "fortunes to men whose hearts are too far in advance of their brains." Sanders, impetuous and impatient, disagreed. The ticket, he believed, should be brought before the country as soon as possible, and the northwest "should know that they are expected to bring forward Douglass." He dispatched letters to the west and south and conferred quietly with certain members of Congress. Douglas hoped to attract northern freesoilers to his side as well as the extreme southern states' rights wing. Preston King, freesoil member of the House from New York, told Sanders that he thought well of the ticket, but that he was not ready to commit himself. "I think Douglass can secure him on his return," Sanders wrote confidently. There also seemed to be a possibility that David Wilmot could be brought into the camp, although Sanders warned that it would not be wise to let Wilmot "be very open" in his support.

Sanders was also mindful of the importance of press support for the ticket. The Washington *Union* was in new hands. Old Thomas Ritchie had been eased out (with Douglas' active encouragement), and he had been replaced by two Tennesseans with strong Jacksonian ties, Andrew Jackson Donelson and Robert J. Armstrong. Armstrong, whose son-in-law, Arnold Harris, had steamship connections and had served as a claims lobbyist, was "all right," but Donelson, although a friend of Douglas', remained a question mark. Donelson, a true servant of the party, announced his neutrality, but he found it increasingly difficult "to steer my course so as to please all our aspirants to the Presidency." Privately, he expressed his belief that Douglas was stronger than any of the other contestants.[10]

Douglas' candidacy, pushed so openly and brazenly so early, seemed the height of impudence to some of his opponents. "Mr. Douglas," commented the *New-York Tribune* caustically, "is a young man of abilities by no means imposing—is opposed to the interests of his own great section of the country—has distinguished himself only as a faithful follower of Gen. Cass, and yet is actually aiming at the Presidency upon the strength of his having married in the South and acquired slave property." After having spent time "dining and speechifying" at Richmond, Douglas traveled to New York City in late April. Sanders, Knox Walker, and Tucker had been at work in the metropolis, and they had done their job well. Among Douglas' supporters was George Law, promoter of the United States Mail Steamship Company and a recognized power in the city's financial circles, who had used his influence to bring some of the nation's leading capitalists into the campaign. Douglas, commented one veteran observer, had "the money bags of the monopolists" behind him. The Empire Club, which had as members some of the city's leading businessmen, promised financial support, and Tammany Hall endorsed his candidacy. A round of private dinners and conferences caused the *Herald* to ask, "What is in the wind?" Douglas' position on Cuban annexation appealed to commercial men anxious to expand their interests, while men like John L. O'Sullivan, erstwhile editor of the *Democratic Review,* and Thomas Devin Reilly, an exiled Irish revolutionary, found Douglas' flamboyant notions of manifest destiny especially attractive. During his visit Douglas personally inspected one of Aspinwall's new steamships, christened *Illinois* in his honor, and, with the director of the city's charitable institutions, he visited the orphanage on Randall's Island, the immigration depot on Ward's Island, and the Blackwell's Island penitentiary. He found his prospects in New York highly encouraging, reporting to Hunter that "everything looks well—much better than either of us had a right to expect." Douglas' organization in the city, Tucker added, had begun under the most favorable auspices and would, "if judiciously managed," extend throughout the state.[11]

Before he left New York, Douglas declined an invitation from 600 of the city's prominent Democrats to attend a public dinner in his honor. In a carefully worded reply, he emphasized the "paramount duty of every democrat" to work tirelessly for the "peace, glory, and prosperity of the whole country." Referring to the recent sectional crisis, Douglas declared, "The necessity for confining the federal government clearly within the limits of its legitimate functions—for preserving the rights of the states in their original purity and vigor—for maintaining the supremacy of the laws—and for a strict observance of every provision of our constitutions—state and national—has never been rendered more manifest than by our recent experience." Having declined similar invitations in North Carolina and Virginia, however, he feared that an acceptance in New York might offend his southern supporters. When he learned that a similar invitation would be sent to Hunter, Douglas advised his running mate to decline "in a well considered & judicious letter, but at the same time notify them that you intend to visit the city in a quiet way during the hot weather . . . when you will be pleased to meet them in the social circle." At this stage of the campaign, Douglas wrote, "I doubt the policy of a public demonstration." [12]

On his way westward toward Illinois, Douglas made a long-overdue visit to his mother in upstate New York and joined the celebration marking the completion of the Erie Railroad, an occasion he turned to his own advantage in spite of the presence of such dignitaries as President Fillmore, Dickinson, Marcy, Seward, Webster, and John J. Crittenden. Douglas joined the group in Elmira, where he was greeted by a procession and made an extemporaneous speech. The Erie Railroad, he told the cheering crowd, was not solely a New York project. He regarded it as a segment of a great transcontinental railroad that would someday extend from New York to San Francisco, and he humorously referred to it as the New York branch of the Illinois Central Railroad. Its prosperity, he emphasized, would depend upon "the union of all the States." As the train traveled westward, Douglas was frequently called out to deliver impromptu remarks.

Among those captivated by the Illinois Senator were the newspaper correspondents who chatted with him on the train. He entertained them with detailed descriptions of the railroads that would soon traverse the nation and predicted that within twelve years a person might travel from one ocean to the other in five days' time. His proposals, noted one reporter, were "stated with the arithmetical precision of a mathematician and statesman instead of being the excited dreams of a poet." But it was not Douglas' plan for a transportation network that attracted notice; it was his character and personality. "It was curious to see in Senator Douglass the genuine American statesman," commented the correspondent of the *New-York Tribune.* "We Eastern men are all more or less mongrel. We have an English education and French manners. Our models and types are usually from the other side of the sea. . . . But the Western man is as original as the Indian. He is especially American; and a Senator of great ability and fame, sets curled up on a seat, smoking his friendly cigar, chatting with every one about everything— having no separate atmosphere of dignity, and wishing to be among the first intellectually, by no other right than he would claim the place physically—that is, by actual superiority. As a gentleman very happily said, 'Mr. Douglas has plenty of loose change—Mr. Webster has nothing but £50 notes.'" No description could have warmed the heart of Young America more. After a festive banquet at Dunkirk, the party embarked on a steamer for Buffalo, where the celebration was terminated with more speeches. Douglas' youth, contrasted with the grey heads about him on the platform, captivated the younger members of his audience. Encouraged, Douglas wrote Sanders that "things look well wherever I have been." His effort to reunite all Democrats was promising, for "both sections of the Party treat me kindly." Marcy, his own eye cast toward the presidential nomination, conceded that Douglas had rolled up "something of a wave as he passed through our state." [13]

When Douglas arrived in Chicago he found his friends busily at work on his behalf. Several Democratic papers in the state had already hoisted his name to their mastheads, and more would follow in the ensuing weeks. His candidacy was received enthusiastically, and there were signs that support from outside the party could be developed. Immediately upon his arrival, he conferred with John Wentworth, and apparently their discussion bore fruit. Wentworth's paper, the *Chicago Democrat*, moved from a reluctant admission that Douglas would be acceptable to the Van Buren–Free-Soil wing only as a last resort to a cordial support of his candidacy. By July, Wentworth was convinced that Douglas' prospects were better than those of any other candidate. The rapprochement between Douglas and the freesoilers took root as other freesoil organs in the state followed Wentworth's lead. Whig journals became more conciliatory in their attitude towards Douglas and spoke favorably of "the pet of the 'young democracy.'" Prominent Whig leaders in the state were said to have promised that if Douglas should be nominated for the presidency they would make no serious fight against him. From neighboring Indiana came the prediction that Douglas, "a western man in feeling and action," would be that state's first choice. A citizen of St. Louis reported that the "current is setting strong for Douglas, as the best means of rallying the whole democracy next year."

Douglas was aided by a wave of Union sentiment which swept his home state, inspired by feelings of relief that the crisis of the previous year had passed. The uncertainty of party lines was replaced by a return to party loyalty in 1851. Douglas, youthful and identified with the cause of Union, was "suited to the times and exigencies of the age." He was "one of the most orthodox of our statesmen," with a renown gained from his role in the Compromise "that will be as enduring as our institutions." Douglas filled the need for a young leader, for "a 'live man'— one who belongs to the present order of things—who will not have to be 'resurrected' before he can make a race." These were heady sentiments for a young politician not yet turned forty. "The only difficulty with Douglass," warned one editor, "is, that flattery may, and probably will, spoil him." [14]

Before he left Chicago, Douglas confided to an Indianapolis editor that he had initially preferred Cass for the presidency and had resolved to discourage the use of his own name. "But recent events indicate a determination on the part of other states to bring out new men," he added, "& the movement in my behalf having become so much more respectable & general than I anticipated I have concluded to allow things to take their course." Almost in the same breath, however, he indicated that that was precisely what he would not do. Concerned that his name might be brought too prominently before the public, Douglas proposed that private correspondence "with our friends in other states" would accomplish more than any other manner of operation. Particular attention, he suggested, should be paid to the south in order to ward off Buchanan's efforts there. He urged that letters be written to North Carolina, Virginia, Kentucky, and Tennessee. Encouraging reports were being received from Ohio, New York, and Pennsylvania, where he was confident that he could unite the party "after Mr Buchanan & Gen'l Cass shall have destroyed each others chances." Even in far-off California, Democrats pledged their support. Since none but friends were reporting to him, he wrote to Sanders, the news was good as a matter of course. "Probably all the others have equally as good grounds for thinking that their prospects are now bright and brightening every day." [15]

If Douglas intended to keep his name out of the public eye and to work quietly behind the scenes, his actions belied his words. Late in July, he announced he would go to the seashore in order to restore his wife's health. An invitation to attend a dinner in New York honoring Archbishop John Hughes was declined with a letter praising the Roman Catholic prelate. He would visit New England, where it was reported that the movement to "drop the fogies" had settled on him as the favorite, stopping at Niagara Falls, Saratoga, and finally Newport—all popular gathering places for politicians escaping the summer heat. En route, he stopped briefly in Detroit, where he was the house guest of Lewis Cass. What the two Democratic leaders said to each other is not known, but Douglas happily, and perhaps naïvely, reported that "the old General is all right & seems to understand things well & is perfectly reconciled to them."

During the third week of August, Douglas was in his native state of Vermont. He stopped briefly at his birthplace in Brandon and attended the commencement exercises at Middlebury College, where he was awarded an honorary Doctor of Laws degree (for which he later donated $500 to the college). To his Middlebury audience, he recalled his carpenter's apprenticeship in that town many years before. Turning to more serious topics, he proposed that the slavery controversy could best be settled in a way approved by Vermonters on other subjects—"by every man minding his own business, and abstaining from all interference with the concerns of his neighbor." In his commencement address, he cautioned "the learned professors" to teach obedience to the Constitution and to the laws and "the duties of one section of the Union toward another." Liberty, he declared, rested upon law; under all circumstances, the supremacy of law must be maintained.

By the end of August Douglas was in Newport, meeting with political figures from north and south and no doubt plotting further strategy for the campaign. He served as a patron of the "Grand Dress Ball" at the Ocean House on August 29, the event which officially closed the season, where Martha, "dressed in a white brocade dress, trimmed with lace and flowers" with a "head dress of gold and fawn," received the attention due the wife of a presidential aspirant. Returning to New York, Douglas continued to play the role of reluctant candidate, but few were fooled. He was initiated into the Society of Saint Tammany and, after a champagne supper, spoke to the sachems and members on the Union, the principles of democracy, and the western Indian tribes. A letter from a Boston editor, offering to support Douglas if the latter would, when elected, grant administration patronage to his newspaper and offices to his friends, aroused the Senator's ire. Favors to friends, he stated, must be subordinated to public interests. He had made no promises, nor had he intimated to anyone that their personal advantage would be served by his election. It was a principle, he declared, from which he could in no instance depart. Still, Douglas could write, while recovering at the Astor House from the rigors of his tour, that "I do not consider myself a candidate in the field canvassing for support." [16]

For a non-candidate, Douglas was remarkably active during the rest of the year. He was soon on the move again, this time traveling the state fair circuit. A host of dignitaries had been invited to attend the New York State Fair in Rochester, including Van Buren, Winfield Scott, ex-President Tyler, and Jenny Lind, but it was Douglas who was selected to deliver the principal address—a proper selection, commented one Rochester paper, since it was in western New York that Douglas "laid the foundation of his fame as a citizen and statesman." In his remarks, he appealed to the farmers of the nation, emphasizing again the theme of his campaign, that all sections of the Union were interdependent. Although addressing a northern audience, he pointed out the immense value of the southern staple crops—cotton, rice, sugar, and tobacco —to the commerce of the country and boldly argued the desirability of annexing new areas suited to sugar production in order to eliminate the dependence of the United States on foreign countries for this crop. He dwelt at length on the superiority of the nation in wheat and corn production and predicted that wool would soon become as important to American trade as cotton. The very diversity of the nation, in products, climate, and soil, should serve as a common bond, imparting strength and stability to its institutions. The Rochester speech was a major effort. Douglas was particularly anxious that it be widely published in the press, especially in the southern states. One correspondent regarded it as an "adroit move . . . towards an inaugural at Washington." There was no better way for "mixing good under-crust for political puddings than by pleasantly identifying oneself with the great company of voters who sow wheat."

From Rochester Douglas traveled to the Ohio State Fair in Columbus, where, in a drenching rainstorm, he was also called upon to speak. With the wide variety of products grown in the United States, its "inexhausti-bly fertile" soil, the expanding agricultural production, the easy availability of land, and the development of agricultural machinery, who can predict, he asked the Ohioans, "the destiny and greatness" of the American people? "With such vast resources, and such infinite materials to open them up, with our free and happy government, guarantying to the yeomanry and artisan the control of the lands they till and of the capital they create, there is no height of national and individual prosperity beyond the scope of our reasonable hopes, or the reach of a wise and peaceful employment of our energies."

By late October Douglas was in Baltimore for the Maryland State Fair, where, at the last minute, he agreed to substitute for Daniel Webster, who was unable to attend. He strongly urged an increased application of science to agriculture and took Marylanders to task for abandoning, rather than improving, their exhausted lands. It was the farmer's "religious duty," he charged, "to leave the ground from which he obtained his sustenance in life in the condition at least in which he found it, for the benefit of posterity." Geology, botany, and mineralogy should be studied with reference to the improvement of agriculture. Science must be practical, "adapted to the use and capacity of the plain farmer, the mechanic, the laborer." To facilitate a more scientific agriculture,

Douglas proposed the establishment of a national agricultural society that could disseminate information and stimulate "American genius and agricultural pride." The popular and practical applications of science, he argued, were "quite as useful and beneficial as discoveries in the moon, or attempts to establish abstract theories in science without practical results." A national society, with an annual national agricultural fair that would bring together the farmer of the north and the planter of the south, "would do more to bind this Union" than the laws of Congress could ever accomplish. Sincere, frank, and even scholarly in tone, with the theme of national unity running throughout, Douglas' state fair addresses were impressive performances, and the reception given his statements supported the claim that no national figure was more popular with the nation's "agriculturalists." [17]

Further conferences with supporters in New York and a quick trip to North Carolina preceded Douglas' arrival in Washington for the opening of Congress in December. The previous nine months had been exhausting. He had worked hard to heal the ruptures within the Democratic party, but he had worked equally hard to persuade northerners that the national interest lay in the union of all sections and in the submergence of sectional prejudices and hostility. One of the key reasons for the sectional crisis was the ignorance and misrepresentation that prevailed in the various parts of the country. "Why is it that you have a prejudice against the South?" he asked a Buffalo audience. "Is it because you do not know them? Why is it that South Carolina desires to sever the sacred bonds of the Union, and cut loose from you? Because they do not know you." If northerners and southerners could know each other better, they would find that all their prejudices were unfounded. "The South would be ashamed of the misrepresentations which they daily make against the North, and you would blush from misrepresentations which you utter every day against them." He earnestly hoped, he declared later, that the United States would present "not only a union of states, but a union of hearts." [18]

iii

Douglas returned to Congress encouraged and optimistic. The earnestness of his campaign and the "celerity of his movements" had attracted wide notice and seemed to give him a decided edge in the race. "It looks very much as if he were spreading his nets wide," commented the *Washington Republic,* "and if he does not catch as many larks when the skies

fall as most any one of his Democratic friends, it will not be his fault."
To Lanphier Douglas gleefully reported at the end of December that
"things look well & the prospect is brightening every day."

In the meantime, his friends had been busy. Sanders made a hurried
visit to his native state of Kentucky to stifle a movement there on behalf
of William O. Butler, and he reported success—Kentucky would go
for Douglas. The influential Louisville *Democrat* declared for the Illinoisan. From New York, Sanders confidently predicted that "the Ticket"
would sweep the state and boasted that even John Van Buren had promised support. "The young men here south & West are nearly all for
Douglas." Knox Walker was in Tennessee, where he was aided by William H. Polk, and the state's Democratic press was reported to be "leading off indirectly for Douglas." In Louisiana, Pierre Soulé, states' rightist
and expansionist, argued Douglas' cause, and the New Orleans *Delta,*
purchased by Douglas supporters, contributed its voice. In Ohio, where it
was said that Douglas fever "rages with considerable intensity," Samuel
Medary was clearing the track. Pennsylvania's Simon Cameron promised
Douglas that "we will in good time, help you along." William H. English's efforts in Indiana evoked Douglas' gratitude, and Douglas was especially pleased "that Indiana will be found with Illinois when the day
of trial arrives." As the time for the selection of convention delegates approached, Douglas urged that "all that is necessary now to enable me to
succeed is to show that the West is ready to unite on me." The "Little
Wizard of the West," observed one opponent, had captivated the hearts
of many Americans. Another contended that Douglas was "the most formidable of all the candidates now before the country for the nomination
and most likely to receive it." [19]

At the Democratic party's annual Jackson Day celebration on January
8, Douglas was toasted as "a noble specimen of the young democracy,"
and he used the occasion to deliver a ringing tribute to progress and the
national mission, striking a keynote for Young America. The mission of
"the democracy," he insisted, "is the great mission of progress . . . in the
development and advancement of human rights throughout the world."
Developments in "science and the mechanic arts" and the rapid strides
in the improvement of transportation and communication demonstrated
conclusively that "no matter how rapid may be our growth, or how wide
may be the expansion of our territory, our country will never be too
large for one republic, even if we should include the entire continent."
He sounded the call for a truly American foreign policy, "in accordance

with the spirit of the age," that would not shrink from carrying out the national mission. Turning to the foremost domestic problem, Douglas hailed the "Great West" as the nation's unifying force. Had it not been for the west, he suggested, the Union might long since have dissolved. "The North and South may quarrel and wrangle about a question which should never enter the halls of Congress; but the Great West will say to the South, You must not leave us; and to the North, You must faithfully observe the constitution—with all its compromises." Finally, he provided an insight into his own pragmatic political philosophy:

> The man is not consistent who supports a question of expediency now, merely because he advocated it a quarter of a century ago; for, if it was wise then, the probabilities are that the change of circumstances in the development of our resources has rendered it inexpedient and unwise at this time. The man is only consistent who follows out his principles and adapts his measures to them in view of the condition of things he finds in existence at the period of time when it is necessary to make the application. Hence I care not if a man says I have been inconsistent upon a measure of expediency, provided he will admit that I have always been faithful to my principles, and regulated all questions of expediency by them. Measures of policy are in their nature temporary, and liable to be abandoned whenever the necessity ceases which called them into existence; but democratic principles are immutable, and can never die so long as freedom survives.

The speech displayed all the confidence of a man about to taste success. The Douglas movement had reached its peak.[20]

Then clouds began to gather on the horizon. Andrew Johnson was convinced in December 1851 that Douglas' rise had been too rapid, and that he "has had his run." "Douglas has been pushed too fast," warned Illinois Congressman William H. Bissell. By appearing in the field so early he had given his opposition more time to organize against him. The "props and pillars of the party," or "old fogies," were not prepared to concede the race to the "Young Giant." Lewis Cass, James Buchanan, Sam Houston, William O. Butler, Thomas Hart Benton, and William L. Marcy, all seasoned politicians, eyed the nomination and viewed Douglas' highly organized and aggressive campaign with increasing consternation and disgust. No candidate had so openly and so determinedly sought the nomination before, and the spectacle seemed degrading both to Douglas and to the lofty position toward which he aspired. The men who surrounded Douglas were not held in high repute, and there was a tendency to judge him by the company he kept. John Slidell, pushing Buchanan's candidacy, described Douglas' supporters as "trading politicians and adventurers, with a very slight sprinkling of well meaning men." If Douglas should succeed in gaining the nomination, Slidell would "despair of the republic." The financier August Belmont charged Knox Walker, Sanders, and the "Lobby interest" with seeking Douglas' advancement in order to realize "the wildest schemes for appropriations for Railroads, Public works, distribution of public funds &c." "Every vulture that would prey upon the public carcass," wrote William R. King, "and every creature who expects the reward of office, are moving heaven and earth in his behalf," while Gideon Welles concluded that "the vicious influences of the party, the jobbers for claims, the plunderers of the National Domain, are urging Douglass, as well as those who go for Internal Improvements, Ocean Steamers, &c." Old Francis Preston Blair, reporting political developments in the capital to Van Buren, wrote that "the Lobby of Jobbers at Washington move Douglas as a puppet & draw around him all their forces." Perhaps no one expressed this revulsion so well as the young Tennessee Congressman Andrew Johnson. Douglas, he declared, was the candidate of "the cormorants of our party." "He is a mere hotbed production, a precocious politician warmed into, and kept in existence by a set of interested plunderers that would in the event of success, disembowel the treasury, disgrace the country and damn the party to all eternity that brought them into power. Their arms thrown about his neck along the street—reading pieces to him in the oyster cellar of a complimentary character which are to be sent off to some subsidized press for publication, then a drink, next a haugh, haugh, then some claim to be discussed by which they expect to practise some swindle upon the government." Douglas' followers were better suited "to occupy places (or cells) in the penitentiary than places of state." [21]

Yet among some of his critics there was a grudging recognition of Douglas' abilities. He had simply enlisted the aid of the wrong people and thus placed his own future in jeopardy. Blair was emphatic that if it came to a choice between Douglas and Buchanan, his sympathies would be with the former. "Although it would be a desecration of the whole House to nominate Douglas to it [the presidency]," he wrote, "yet with all his dissoluteness he is so much honester as a Democrat than Buck, I would take him." Even Buchanan admitted that if Douglas could succeed in uniting the various elements of the party it would be a worthy feat, but, he added, "I think he is strange timber from which to fabricate a President." Welles conceded Douglas' qualifications, but thought that the presidency required a man of more mature years and greater experience. Douglas would make an even better President twelve years hence and still be a young man for the post.[22]

Douglas tried to remain on friendly terms with his rivals. He was determined not to interfere with local candidates or favorite-son movements, in the hope that he could secure the second-choice preference of the delegates. When an attempt, mysterious in its origin, to link Sam Houston with northern freesoilers, ostensibly to promote his candidacy but in fact to discredit him in the south, was charged to Douglas, his denial was marked by a violent outburst of temper. His two most formidable rivals were Cass and Buchanan, but Douglas was reasonably certain that neither would be able to muster sufficient convention strength to secure the nomination. In that case, the convention would be deadlocked, and Douglas, with his second-choice strength, could come forth as a compromise candidate. It was a risky strategy and required cordial relations with the two Democratic leaders as well as with the lesser candidates, a relationship that was becoming more and more difficult to maintain as Douglas' friends became more aggressive in their campaign.

Some political veterans regarded Douglas' obvious maneuvering with suspicion and distaste. "Douglas tells Cass he is recruiting for him in case his force can nominate him with what he can himself throw into convention," wrote Blair, with some exaggeration. "He tells Bucks friends the same thing, & if neither of the great men can get the two thirds vote, then they are to unite on the recruiting Sarjeant." In Indiana, Douglas carefully advised English not to bring his name into opposition with that of the state's favorite-son candidate, Joseph Lane. To instruct the state's delegates for Lane, with himself as the second choice, he wrote, would "do equally as well" as to instruct for him in the first place. Informants in Pennsylvania wrote Douglas that his name would unite the state after Buchanan and Cass had destroyed each other's chances. John W. Forney, a Philadelphia newspaper editor and strong Buchanan backer, promised support to Douglas should Buchanan fail. The Van Buren wing of the party preferred Kentucky's William O. Butler, in spite of the oft-repeated hope that the ex-President's influence might be brought to bear on behalf of Douglas. The movements for Marcy in New York, William Allen in Ohio, and Franklin Pierce in New Hampshire, Douglas was convinced, were fronts for Butler. Marcy, already disturbed over Douglas' show of strength in his state, expressed

friendship for the Illinois Senator and, through an intermediary, concluded an arrangement whereby Douglas would cease his campaign in
New York in return for a clear field in the west. Presumably, Marcy also
promised Douglas New York's second-choice vote. When the Butler
movement subsequently collapsed, Douglas asked Blair for his support.
When Blair warned that his support might kill Douglas' chances, the
latter replied, "I've got a strong constitution, I can stand anything." But
Blair declined.[23]

Douglas' constitution, however, was not as strong as he supposed. In
December, Sanders, relentless in his efforts to promote Douglas' candidacy, purchased the *Democratic Review* "for the purpose of controlling
its columns until after the Presidential election." The magazine, he informed Hunter, would be used "with a vengeance to push forward our
ticket." In its first issue, Sanders warned, the lead article would take
strong ground for Douglas. Douglas had earlier been approached for
funds with which to buy the magazine but was unable to comply with
Sanders' request, although he promised he would attempt to raise the
money if it became necessary. It was not necessary, for Sanders, it was
said, received advances from New York's steamship interests. Douglas
lauded Sanders' intention and expressed his gratitude for "the service you
are rendering me." He should have known better. When the January
number of the *Review* was issued, it fell like a bombshell on the Douglas camp.[24]

The tone of the *Review*'s new management was established by the initial article, a testament to Young America entitled "Eighteen-Fifty-Two
and the Presidency." The article heralded 1852 as a year of liberation
for the oppressed masses of western Europe and for the United States.
The work of liberation in the United States would be carried out by a
new generation of American statesmen. "The statesmen of a previous
generation, with their personal antipathies, and their personal claims,
with personal greatness or personal inefficiency, must get out of the
way." The older politicians, by their "lack of statesmanship, lack of
temper, lack of discretion, and, most of all, by lack of progress," had
plunged the Democratic party into discord and dissension. The party, the
nation, and even the world, the *Review* exhorted, must be rescued by
one who can bring "young blood, young ideas, and young hearts to the
councils of the Republic." He must be a man unidentified with any section, "who has lived and thought for the whole," who can unite the
party "into one indomitable, invulnerable American power," and who

can guide the party and "the destinies of the Republic, to their just position and development." Failure to nominate such a man would bring ruin to the party and to the hopes of mankind.

Douglas was shocked. When Caleb Cushing wrote doubting the wisdom of Sanders' course, he replied, "Our friend Sanders is a noble fellow and a man of remarkable vigor of intellect, but I fear he lacks the requisite prudence to conduct the Review safely at the present time." Admitting that the article had given him much uneasiness, Douglas hoped that the magazine would refrain from attacking any Democrat, much less Democratic candidates for the presidency. "I have repeatedly expressed these opinions & pressed them upon our friend Sanders" but "it seems that my wishes in this respect are disregarded by him." Douglas questioned both the policy and propriety of the *Review's* assaults. "While I am a radical & progressive democrat," he continued, "I fear the Review goes too far in that direction—especially in regard to European affairs." A second article in the issue, a severe indictment of Louis Napoleon, would, Cushing feared, offend American Catholics. Douglas agreed; "its profane allusions to our Saviour & to religion" would be shocking "to any moral & religious man."

Sanders, unchastened, warned that there was more to come. "The more fire the better as we intend to make the times hot," he wrote to Cushing. To Douglas, he announced that "I shall make an attack on Genl Butler more terrific than was ever made against mortal man before. I'll finish him . . . dont be scared it will not be thunder, but it shall be an earthquake." [25]

Sanders' hostility toward William O. Butler was said to have originated with the latter's refusal to support the editor's father for a Kentucky political office. At any rate, Sanders was true to his promise, for the February issue of the *Review* contained a savage and vitriolic attack against the Kentuckian. General Butler was "a good sample of the no-policy statesman." Sanders charged him with "almost total lifelessness in public affairs . . . without known or fixed political principles." He scored Butler's "inertness and exclusivism, and his habit of voting for whigs" and declared that even in his military career, he had never shown "capacity beyond that of a brave subaltern." Sanders warmed to his task, and in the succeeding issues of the *Review* he continued his attacks. In March, he turned on John C. Breckinridge, another Kentuckian and a defender of Butler. Breckinridge, "the young fogy," had contrived during his short political life to commit more mistakes than any other member of the Democratic party. He has, wrote Sanders, "an avidity for mistakes—he flounders from mistake to mistake with a courage the most imperturbable." From Breckinridge he moved on to Marcy, "spavined, wind-blown, strained, ring-boned." Denouncing "our beaten old fogy hacks," Sanders finally urged the nomination of Douglas, "very democratic, very Young American, and very go-ahead." In the next issue, Cass was attacked as "a human contradiction" following a "winding, tortuous, cork-screw course." The *Review* charged that the "hierarchy of imbecility" had formed a conspiracy to attack, misrepresent, and prejudice the voters against Stephen A. Douglas.[26]

Douglas' shock increased with each issue. When informed of Sanders' intention to attack Butler, he immediately telegraphed the editor in an attempt to dissuade him from his course. Sanders spurned the effort. Douglas protested against the "impolitic & unjust" assaults. "The man whose active friends will try to advance his interests by assaulting others is sure to be defeated." "You may tell me in reply as you have done on a former occasion," he continued, "that you are a free man and have a right to do as you please, and that I had better mind my own business. This is all very true & would do very well if nobody was to be effected by your acts but yourself. But when your active support of me leaves the world to suppose that I instigate these assaults, I submit to you whether my appeals to you to desist ought not to be respected." Sanders publicly absolved Douglas from responsibility for the *Review*'s statements, but he refused to cease his attacks. "Dont be scared," he cautioned, "I hope to turn the tables on all our enemies." As Douglas persisted in his protests, Sanders turned his bitterness against him. "Politicians are all cowards and you are at the head of the list," he wrote, "I am sick." Douglas had obviously been corrupted by the "fogy atmosphere of Washington." [27]

The damage had been done, and Sanders' disclaimers had little effect. Douglas was convinced the public would still hold him responsible for the attacks. Sanders' unrestrained and ill-advised course had rendered Douglas' chances for the nomination nearly hopeless, and if the attacks continued he believed he would be forced to retire from the field. He protested vigorously against being placed in the position of "an Ishmaelite with my hand against everybody." "If you must assail others," Douglas advised Sanders, "also assail me . . . and at the same time select somebody else as your candidate." The relations between the two men were brought to the breaking point, and Douglas' thrust for the presidential nomination was severely blunted.

Douglas' opponents were not displeased with the consternation in the Douglas camp. The "bullying and domineering course" of his followers, they predicted, would result in a combination against him; the "old fogies" would bury Douglas "without benefit of clergy." Sanders' assaults, however, also intensified differences within the Democratic party and nullified Douglas' efforts to unite the party. The impact on Douglas' candidacy was serious enough, but the effect of Sanders' "terrible ebullition and sudden effervescence" on the party could be disastrous. All signs pointed to a "beautiful row" at Baltimore, where the Democrats were scheduled to convene on June 1. The Washington *Union* moaned that Douglas' brilliant offensive had been suddenly transformed into a defensive struggle.[28]

Kentucky's young Congressman John C. Breckinridge carried the issue to the floor of the House of Representatives, when he defended Butler from the *Review*'s "gross misrepresentations." Warning that an influence had appeared within the party "to promote particular interests by traducing the most honored names in our ranks," Breckinridge demanded that Douglas himself bear responsibility for the attacks. Douglas' friend William A. Richardson defended the Senator, denying that he was implicated in the editorial policy of the *Review,* but he was followed by California's Edward C. Marshall, who endorsed many of the *Review*'s sentiments in a vigorous panegyric on Douglas. The party, Marshall insisted, needed a "man who is able to create national sympathy—who can understand the people, and can make the people understand him." That man was Douglas.[29]

Douglas' determination carried him through the crisis, but Sanders' continuing attacks in the *Review* presented greater odds than he could easily overcome. His repeated warnings fell on deaf ears. Sanders was confident that nothing could stay the onward march of youth and progressive democracy, and that Douglas, with true "American pluck," would surmount the combinations of "senile 'old fogies' " that were forming against him. Even his rivals conceded that he might still go into the convention with considerable strength.

Encouraging reports from different parts of the country still came in, helping Douglas to maintain his optimism. In Virginia, the Richmond *Enquirer* continued to puff his chances for the nomination. A former Virginia Congressman urged Douglas' nomination because he was "at least as honest and more firm" than any of the other candidates, and another prominent Virginian assured Douglas that his campaign would yet succeed. From Florida came word that he would most certainly be the choice of that state's delegation, and the Jackson Association of New Orleans strongly recommended his nomination. Georgia's Herschel V. Johnson declared that "by judicious means" the Georgia delegation could be carried for Douglas. From California to Maine, Democrats were reported to be leaning toward the Little Giant. There was speculation again that the strongest candidates (presumably Cass and Buchanan) would "break down each other," thus providing Douglas with "a very good chance as the ultimate choice." Six weeks before the convention was scheduled to meet, Edmund Burke informed his New Hampshire friend, Franklin Pierce, that Cass, Buchanan, and Douglas were the three most prominent candidates for the nomination.[30]

Douglas did little open campaigning during the last months before the Baltimore convention. Congress was in session, and his legislative duties consumed most of his time. It was rumored that in desperation he was promising executive appointments in wholesale fashion in order to strengthen his position, but such reports were unsubstantiated. The announcement in the *New-York Tribune* that Douglas had already selected his cabinet, including George Sanders, Knox Walker, New York merchant Hiram Walbridge, and Pennsylvania's Native American Congressman Lewis Levin, was hardly calculated to aid his cause. A public dinner sponsored by Washington's Irish element enabled Douglas to blast England once again in an hour-long speech on behalf of Irish freedom. When the editor of the Richmond *Enquirer* solicited responses from fifteen presidential hopefuls to three questions dealing with the Fugitive Slave Act, Douglas promised that no attempt to alter its provisions or to render the Act inoperative would ever receive his approval. An eight-page biographical sketch, comparing Douglas with Andrew Jackson and hailing him as the most popular statesman "of that region which may now be considered as holding the sceptre of empire," was extensively circulated. The second generation of eminent American statesmen, the writer declared, must now give way "to new men, not because they have failed to perform their work . . . but because it is the order of nature that they should give place to others."

Douglas was also concerned with the action his own state would take. As early as December he had urged that Illinois Democrats select their delegates to the national convention "as soon as convenient," and insisted that they express their preference for the presidential nomination "in clear & unequivocal terms." Later he suggested that a large number of delegates be chosen in order to "ensure the attendance of most of our leading politicians at Baltimore." If five delegates were selected from each congressional district and twenty from the state at large, the Illinois delegation, fifty-five strong, "would exert a great moral influence on the other delegates." Douglas conferred frequently with the Democratic members of Illinois' congressional delegation, and they in turn reported his sentiments to the leaders at home. The Baltimore convention would look to Illinois for an indication of the platform on which Douglas was willing to stand, so it was imperative that the state's action reflect his views.

The Democratic state convention met at Springfield on April 19. The alliance between the freesoilers and the rest of the party, carefully worked out by Douglas and Wentworth, was immediately in evidence. The gubernatorial nomination went to Joel A. Matteson, a moderate antislavery man from the northern part of the state. The platform adopted by the assemblage, however, was not as simple as Douglas had hoped. Devotion to the national party platforms of 1840, 1844, and 1848 was declared, but the delegates went on to hit hard at the recent disturbances involving the Fugitive Slave Act. Strict adherence to the Compromise of 1850 was urged. Other resolutions admonished citizens and states to refrain from meddling with the institutions of other states. Douglas was given a strong endorsement, and the state's delegation was instructed to vote for him in the national convention.[31]

iv

Delegates to the Baltimore convention began to arrive in Washington late in May to have their opinions "moulded into permanent form" by the various candidates. Rumors, reports, and speculations circulated in abundance. One day, Douglas and Cass were the candidates to beat; on another, Douglas and Buchanan led the field; on still others, Buchanan and Cass had successfully pre-empted the race. Douglas, it was reported, would throw his support to Buchanan and against Cass, for the nomination of Cass would prevent the northwest from receiving the prize in 1856. In fact, Buchanan's managers had approached Douglas with the offer of the vice presidential nomination, but Douglas refused to consider it, still optimistic that his chances were best if the convention should deadlock. Few observers would venture any serious predictions as to the outcome of the race. "There is so much smoke now in the political atmosphere," wrote Donelson to Howell Cobb, "that it is difficult to see pre-

cisely the places of the objects the most prominent." Francis Preston
Blair found the friends of the candidates "all at sea without rudder or
compass." The rivalries were so keen that he thought "all union impossible among them except in favor of a new man—no party to the
brawl." Others had come to the same conclusion. Quietly assessing the
situation, Edmund Burke informed his friend Franklin Pierce that "if at
the proper time at the Convention, you will allow your name to be used
as a compromise candidate, you stand as good a chance for the nomination as any man I can now think of." [32]

On Tuesday, June 1, the Democratic national convention opened to
the booming of cannon. Congress was virtually deserted as its members
swarmed to the convention city. Baltimore was mobbed with noisy partisans, its streets "one moving mass." The confusion was so great that
some delegates complained that it was almost impossible "to find out
what is going on." Among the noisiest were Douglas' supporters. Young
America was there in force. From New York, a train load of "rowdy and
grogshop politicians," armed with champagne and caviar and accompanied by Lola Montez, had arrived to lend support to their reluctant,
and probably dismayed, champion. Six hundred Buchanan supporters,
with a bountiful supply of refreshments, had made the short journey
from Pennsylvania. Douglas, whose stock never seemed higher than on
the eve of the convention, remained in Washington. His campaign in
Baltimore was entrusted to a "private committee" led by Richardson and
David L. Yulee of Florida. Louisiana's Pierre Soulé was also on hand to
render advice. Disappointingly few Illinoisans had made the trip, and
the state's eleven votes would be cast by a fraction of the sixty-odd delegates that had been chosen.[33]

The convention opened auspiciously for Douglas. Romulus Saunders
of North Carolina was elected temporary chairman and Indiana's John
W. Davis was chosen as permanent chairman—both reputed to be
Douglas men. The vote to postpone the platform until after the balloting was considered a Douglas victory. "Young America has it all her
own way," wrote one correspondent. Some of the "high toned chivalry"
of the south complained that Douglas was "entirely too free and easy
with all sorts of people in the bar rooms and oyster cellars" to suit them,
but among southern delegates generally his position on Cuban annexation seemed to carry considerable weight. On the second day of the convention Douglas' nomination seemed certain. The impression that he

would succeed was gaining ground among the delegates. "Tell all our friends to keep cool—& not to become restive—or brag or bet on the result, and to do nothing to irritate anybody & to speak well of everybody," Douglas advised Yulee. "This caution will be necessary to many of my ardent young friends." The rumors that reached Washington obviously pleased him, although he wrote, "I do not allow myself to be either elated or depressed." By the evening of the second day, however, more sobering reports began to come through. Southern supporters of Buchanan threatened to secede from the convention rather than submit to Douglas' nomination, and the "old fogies" began "moving heaven and earth" to crush him. Yulee quickly advised Douglas to seek out Cass and "reconcile matters with him." [34]

Balloting began on June 3, the third day of the convention. By the adoption of the two-thirds rule, 197 votes were necessary for a nomination. On the first test of strength, Cass led with 116 votes, Buchanan received 93, and Douglas 20 (Illinois' eleven votes and a scattering from six other states). Eight ballots were taken in the morning and nine more before the day ended. By evening, it was apparent that Cass' support was beginning to fall off, Buchanan was holding his own with only a slight drop, while Douglas had more than doubled his strength, taking Missouri and Vermont out of the Cass column, Arkansas away from Buchanan, and gaining votes in Ohio, Tennessee, and Wisconsin. After a night of caucusing, the delegates assembled again on June 4 for another full day of balloting. Cass plunged to a surprising low; Buchanan, after a brief spurt, also dropped back. Douglas showed a steady increase until, on the thirtieth ballot, he secured 92 votes, a plurality of the convention, gaining Maine, Connecticut, Rhode Island, Mississippi, Louisiana, and a majority of Massachusetts. Douglas' Virginia friends, bound by the unit rule to vote for Buchanan, appealed for a release, and a similar movement developed in the Georgia delegation. Delegates from Ohio, Iowa, Tennessee, and North Carolina switched to Douglas. This steady show of strength alarmed Douglas' rivals. The delegates were weary, and a landslide to the Little Giant threatened. Southern Buchananites frantically sought to adjourn, but without success. Cass was suddenly revived, jumping from 27 votes on the twenty-ninth ballot to 123 votes on the thirty-third, gaining California and recovering Missouri, Louisiana, Rhode Island, and Massachusetts from Douglas. Maine switched to Pierce, Mississippi to Marcy, and the crisis seemed to be past. Douglas was uncertain how to interpret the results of the day's voting, but he was not yet discouraged. "I see no reason for alarm," he wrote Yulee, "and remain in good spirits."

After two days of fruitless balloting, the convention, tired and angry, was in a quandary. The Douglas drive had been headed off, Buchanan's chances were hopeless, and Cass, although he had been used to stop Douglas, was clearly unacceptable to large portions of the party, especially in the south. The opinion grew that all three candidates were now out of the question, and that a new candidate must be found. Young America, it was reported, would turn to Sam Houston, but there were more important movements afoot. Buchanan's supporters, recognizing the futility of their cause, determined in caucus to experiment with new candidates in order to ensure Cass' defeat. On the thirty-fifth ballot, Virginia's delegation, after a gesture toward Dickinson, turned to Franklin Pierce. Desperation mounted in the Douglas ranks. Some of his supporters were "profuse in money, promises & other appliances to insure success." It was all to no avail. Georgia came over to Douglas for two ballots, "to testify our admiration of his talents" and to prevent his friends from rallying upon Cass, but after that Douglas dropped to 33 votes, his hard-core support, and remained there during the rest of the balloting. Marcy enjoyed a brief surge, but his followers were unable to persuade the Cass and Buchanan men to switch to him. Pierce remained dormant until the forty-sixth ballot, when he began to pick up strength. Three ballots later, North Carolina, with an oratorical flourish, cast its vote for the New Hampshire candidate, and the stampede began. State after state joined the movement. The Illinois delegation withdrew for consultation. When its members returned, Richardson took the floor and announced, "We are rejoiced that the time has come when our bickerings have all ceased, and we unite with the great Democratic party in casting our votes for Franklin Pierce, of New Hampshire." The travail was over, and the party had at last found a candidate.[35]

Curiously, Pierce's nomination seemed to please almost every group in the party. Douglas, taken by surprise, immediately dispatched a telegram to Richardson, congratulating the party on "the fortunate result of the nomination," which was subsequently read to the convention amid tremendous cheering. Young America regarded the nomination as a triumph; the "old fogies" had been beaten and the reins turned over to a forty-eight-year-old whose ideas, as yet generally unknown, would surely be new. The "old fogies" breathed a sigh of relief and rejoiced that

Douglas had been turned back. On the night of the nomination, Buchanan's supporters held one final meeting in a back room of the Pennsylvanian's headquarters. There Henry A. Wise of Virginia solemnly declared, "Thank God, the Brandy bottle is smashed, the Champagne Bazaars are closed, and Douglas has crept out of town like a whipped dog with his tail between his legs." Freesoil Democrats were content, while southern Unionists congratulated themselves on a "safe deliverance."

There was little doubt that Douglas' chances had been killed by the over-zealous exertions of some of his followers and by his own early entrance into the race. "Douglas' case had been *overworked* and thus was spoiled," explained Congressman Bissell. "With one fourth the effort on the part of his friends, and no more, he would have been the nominee." "Henceforth he will have to *struggle,* like other aspirants to the Presidency, and like them take his *chance,*" Bissell concluded. The prestige of *"universal good feeling"* which Douglas had enjoyed was now "gone from him, and forever." Douglas' identification with the turbulent and impetuous elements in the young democracy of the north, his suspicious association with certain aggressive capitalist groups, and the support he received, toward the last, from the extreme southern states' rights wing of the party had provided serious handicaps to his campaign. Following the convention, Cave Johnson reported to Buchanan, "The associations of Douglas and his active supporters, jobbers, and so on, lost him ground every day for two weeks before the convention—and had they secured his nomination I could not have voted the ticket." But Douglas had also not received the strong show of support from the northwest on which he had counted so heavily. Only Illinois, half the Iowa delegation, and a minority of the Ohio and Wisconsin delegations stuck with him to the bitter end. Michigan and Indiana remained committed to Cass. The failure of his own section to "unite & speak out" revealed a significant weakness in his effort.[36]

On the fifth and last day of the convention, the delegates, eager to return to their homes, nominated William R. King of Alabama for the vice presidency. As the number of delegates quickly dwindled, the platform was rushed through. A colorless document, it recited the usual Democratic principles and skirted the problem of the Compromise of 1850 by promising faithful adherence and execution without declaring its finality. The party further pledged resistance to all attempts to renew the agitation of the slavery question either in Congress or out of it. Before the gavel fell to close the meeting, the delegates resolved to hold the next convention in the west, at Cincinnati, a move to get "beyond the reach of the Washington politicians and the speculators." [37]

Satisfaction with Pierce's nomination was increased when the Whigs, true to prediction, nominated another Mexican War hero, General Winfield Scott, on a platform that endorsed the Compromise as a finality. After the prolonged and bitter struggle for the Democratic nomination, the presidential campaign seemed anticlimactic. Democrats were confident of victory, while the Whigs were gloomy and pessimistic. The choice of Pierce by the Democrats, though unexpected, was not considered to be a weak one, for his nomination had the effect of closing the ranks and uniting the various elements of the party.

Douglas, as usual, took an active part in the campaign, embarking once again on a strenuous round of speech-making. Through a mutual friend, he informed Pierce that he would "spend the whole vacation upon the stump," boasting that he would visit twenty-eight of the thirty-one states (a prediction that fell far short of fulfillment). While Congress remained in session, he spoke within easy range of Washington, but following the adjournment on August 31 he traveled extensively through the north and west. His themes had by this time become familiar and even hackneyed, revealing the lack of real issues in the election campaign, but they still evoked enthusiastic responses from his audiences. He charged the Whig party and its administration with inefficiency, corruption, and the careless expenditure of money, and he hit hard at the Whig conduct of foreign policy, especially with respect to Cuba and Central America. "The time has arrived," he shouted at a giant rally in Washington, "when America should take her position among the nations of the earth, and assert those principles which her destiny and her mission demand she should maintain." The Caribbean Sea and the Gulf of Mexico "are AMERICAN WATERS, and *should be treated as closed seas to the exclusion of all European powers."* Lauding Pierce as the embodiment of Democratic principles, he called on the voters to join "this great work of reformation" and place the Democratic candidate in the executive chair. Douglas' emphasis on America's destiny in this and subsequent speeches was so sharp that *The New York Times* feared the Democrats had an extensive plan of annexation under consideration.

Before the end of July Douglas addressed similar meetings in Wilmington, Richmond, and Newburgh, New York. In Richmond he charged that Scott's nomination had been forced by northern freesoilers and asked whether it would be wise and patriotic to convert "a good General into a bad President." Loosing a stream of invective at the Whig party, which he claimed was being manipulated by Seward and his abolitionist allies, he accused Taylor of having followed a policy that, but for his death, would have plunged the nation into civil war. Douglas' attacks evoked a response in far-off Illinois, where Abraham Lincoln, angered by the remarks and "seized with a strong inclination" to answer them, asked the Springfield Scott club for permission to make a formal reply to the charges.[38]

Douglas spent most of the summer in Washington. Late in June he served as a delegate to a National Agricultural Convention, summoned to influence Congress in favor of the establishment of an Agricultural Bureau, and, as a member of the committee to prepare an agenda, he promised to support Jonathan Baldwin Turner's proposal for state industrial universities. As soon as Congress adjourned at the end of August, Douglas took to the stump with a vengeance. Accompanied by Lewis Cass, he addressed a "monster meeting" in Baltimore on August 31 and, a few days later, spoke to his "fellow citizens of Old Tammany" in New York. Cass had preceded Douglas with a statement in which he referred to himself as an "old fogy," but Douglas set matters right by assuring the crowd that Cass could never be an "old fogy," even if he should live a thousand years, describing Cass' speech as "a pure young American democratic speech." Douglas catalogued once again the sins of the Whig party and linked Scott with the Native American party, a telling charge before an audience composed in part of immigrants. Tearing into "proud, haughty, and insolent England," Douglas recalled, amid loud cheers, how the schooner *America* had "sailed round the English Yacht Club." "The whigs," he concluded, "don't understand the doctrine of progress."

Heading westward, Douglas spoke in Reading, Pennsylvania; Cleveland; Indianapolis; Louisville; Cincinnati; Columbus; and Monroe, Michigan, before arriving in Chicago. As he traveled, returns from state elections forecast a Democratic victory in November. On September 25, Douglas opened the campaign in Illinois at a mass meeting in Chicago, where he covered ground that had by this time become well-trodden. He "showed up" the inconsistencies of the Whig party and expounded his views on the extension of American territory and influence, adding that if Canada ever tired of her colonial vassalage to Great Britain he would extend her a cordial welcome. Chicagoans seemed more interested in his remarks on river and harbor improvements and on his scheme for the collection of tonnage duties. After a quick visit to Milwaukee, Douglas set out on a tour of his own state that would involve speeches in sixteen cities before election day.[39]

Accompanied by Richardson, Shields, and the Democratic nominee for lieutenant governor, Gustave Koerner, Douglas was received by Illinois Democrats with all the pomp and ceremony accorded returning heroes. Captivating fellow passengers in the cars or on the steamboats with "his impressive, almost enthusiastic, conversation," Douglas repeated his message to the voters at each stop until Koerner "wondered that these orators did not become sick of their eternal reiteration." Democrats exulted in his pointed jabs at the Whigs, while many Whigs, recalling their earlier support of the Senator, felt genuinely aggrieved at the level of invective to which his campaign had descended. But even the Whigs had little hope that they could turn the Democratic tide. When the votes were counted in November, Illinois, which had consistently voted for Democratic presidential candidates, maintained its reputation as the Democracy's "banner state." It gave Pierce a 15,000-vote majority. The state Democratic ticket was easily elected, and the new legislature would be overwhelmingly Democratic. Only in the state's congressional races could the Whigs find some solace. A redistricting of the state and the strength of freesoil sentiment in the north resulted in the election of four Whig Congressmen, an increase of three seats. The gains, however, did not offset the gloom into which Whigs were plunged by the national results. Scott was crushed, winning only 42 electoral votes (four states) to Pierce's impressive 254 electoral votes.[40]

The triumph of the Democrats in Illinois was all the sweeter to Douglas because it assured his own re-election to the Senate. His first senatorial term would expire with the adjournment of the thirty-second Congress the following March, and one of the new state legislature's first responsibilities would be to fill the Senate seat for another six years. The overwhelming Democratic majority—20 to 5 in the state senate and 56 to 19 in the lower house—placed the matter beyond any doubt. Douglas' friends promised swift action. Chicago's freesoil Democrat John Wentworth, elected to Congress with Douglas' help, sent his instructions to his legislator friends, confident that Douglas could not be beaten. On January 4, Douglas was nominated by acclamation in the Democratic caucus, and on the following day he was easily elected over a small and dispirited Whig opposition, who cast their ballots for state senator Joseph Gillespie more as a gesture than as an expression of dissatisfaction with Douglas. The latter's "wide-spread fame and his popularity with the Democracy throughout the country," observed one Whig, "was a sufficient reason for his return to Congress." Douglas' re-election to a second term in the United States Senate was duly celebrated, according to custom, at a brilliant "levee" in the statehouse. Music, food, and quantities of stimulating beverages attracted more than 1500 persons. The next morning the senate chamber looked as if a regiment of soldiers had camped there for a fortnight, cooking their own rations, and a new carpet had to be laid. When Douglas' friends sent him the bill for the "entertainment," they apologized for its high cost.[41]

The conclusion of the presidential campaign closed one of the most hectic periods in Douglas' career. As he surveyed the election returns and observed the shambles to which the Whig opposition had been reduced, he undoubtedly considered what might have been if his own campaign had followed a different course. "The Democratic spirit is entirely in the ascendant," moaned one Missouri Whig. "Even the whigs, for lack of moral courage, court it & bow to it." Douglas took comfort in the signal triumph of his party and congratulated himself that he had played no small part in bringing about the result. But the real prize, the only thing that could have made the triumph more complete, had been denied him. "Pierce is President-Elect," wrote one of his close friends after the election, "as you this day would have been but for some indiscreet (or pretended) friends." Circumstances would never be the same for him again, for the politicians were not likely to forget. Even Young America drifted away. Sanders, it was reported, was not "quite so much of a friend to Douglas, as he used to be."

There was work to be done, and the powerful voice of the Democratic party, with its new mandate, stood ready to accomplish it. To a Washington audience gathered to celebrate the election returns, Douglas proudly recalled the speed with which the party had closed its ranks after the nomination had been made. "The moment the voice of the party was pronounced," he declared, "all complaints, all murmurs, all heart-burnings ceased, and all rivalries and personal preferences were merged in the united effort and desire for the success of the party." Let the unity continue and the triumph will be complete. "Let not a man be found within our ranks who will ever dare for a moment to revive a remembrance of the rivalries and jealousies which may have existed in the party prior to the nomination." [42]

# XVI
## "The organization of Nebraska is a national necessity"
## 1852—1853

i

Inauguration day, 1853, was cloudy and dark. A heavy snow, driven by an "angry wind," fell all day, but in spite of the miserable weather the streets were filled with people. "A motley crowd of men, women, and children, foreigners, government clerks, and negroes" gathered along the line of procession; cannon boomed, bands played martial music, and platoons of soldiers paraded. Defying the elements, the President-elect, "the youngest, handsomest President we had ever elected," rode in an open carriage, his "weary sadness" contrasting sharply with the cheers of the waiting throng. Pierce had not wanted to be President, and his wife dreaded the new responsibilities that awaited them; two months before, his only son had been killed in a railroad accident, a tragedy that hung like a pall over the early days of his administration.

His inaugural address, delivered without notes or manuscript, seemed to promise an administration of harmony and order, if not of achievement. Couched in generalities, Pierce's remarks offered no new measures or programs. His term, he declared, would not be "controlled by any timid forebodings of evil from expansion," a statement that warmed the heart of Young America. America's "position on the globe" required the "acquisition of certain possessions not within our jurisdiction," a veiled allusion to Cuba. American citizens would be fully protected "upon every sea and on every soil where our enterprise may rightfully seek the protection of our flag." The idea of interference or colonization in the

374

western hemisphere by any foreign power was "utterly inadmissable." In domestic affairs, Pierce promised rigid economy and "an efficient discharge of duty"; the Compromise of 1850 would be "unhesitatingly carried into effect." Like most Americans, he expressed the fervent hope that the question of slavery "is at rest, and that no sectional or ambitious or fanatical excitement may again threaten the durability of our institutions or obscure the light of our prosperity." [1]

The new President's first task was the dispensation of the government patronage, and his decisions were anxiously awaited by office-hungry Democrats. Soon after his election, Pierce had determined that party unity would be the principal goal of his appointment policy. The strife which had wrenched the party in years past would be obliterated by an attempt to conciliate all groups. The loyalty of no Democrat was to be questioned.

Douglas, exulting over the landslide which buried the Whigs and assured of another six years in the Senate, felt self-confident and secure. His unsuccessful campaign for the nomination had elevated him to the party's top echelon, and he was prepared to assume the role of presidential adviser. Friends encouraged him to begin preparations for the next presidential race. Pierce's election, he was told, was a triumph for his own principles and vindicated his struggle for new and progressive policies. "The events in the Baltimore Convention," wrote David Yulee, "turned the eyes of the country fully upon you. In the very cradle of your national popularity you had strength to crush all the old combinations and organizations, and to open the way to the dynasty of a new generation." The northwest's claim to the presidency, he added, was insuperable, and Douglas would receive "an instant and acclamatory nomination." In the meantime, his voice could hardly be ignored.

Douglas was easily persuaded. He had already begun to give serious thought to the patronage problems which the new administration would face. "Reform must begin," he had written in December, "with the incumbents in office." Friends must be rewarded and enemies punished. "Show me a man who has no friends to reward and no enemies to punish, and I will show you a man whose capacity and qualities as a public man render him incompetent to administer the government." Only the best men should be selected for public office, but "everybody knows that the best men voted for Pierce and King." Honesty, capacity, and sound principles were the essential prerequisites. However, it was clear to Douglas that not all Democrats would qualify. "The party has been demoralized &

weakened by requiring one set of men to spend the money & time & do the work while the offices were awarded to a set of droans. This shall no longer be the case with my consent." Instead, Douglas promised, "I shall act on the rule of giving the offices to those who fight the battles." Pierce's attempt to please everyone found scant support in the Little Giant.[2]

If Douglas expected that his advice would be sought by the new President, some of his friends were not quite so sure. "Will you be *fully* in Pierce's confidence?" asked Thomas L. Harris. Douglas was advised to have "strong & watchful friends" in Pierce's cabinet, especially in the Treasury and Interior departments, with their broad patronage networks. For a time there was speculation that Douglas himself might be invited to take a seat in the President's council. Ohio supporters proposed that either Samuel Medary or Henry B. Payne be urged as possible cabinet appointees, while Democrats in Illinois pushed John A. McClernand. John Wentworth, who visited Pierce after the election, suggested Douglas' cousin-by-marriage, Governor David Reid of North Carolina. From New York City, Edward C. West urged Douglas to take immediate steps to have "a man who will be with us" appointed to the cabinet, and he advanced the name of Francis Cutting as one who was least entangled in New York's factional politics. By mid-January, Douglas' followers were still in the dark regarding Pierce's intentions, but no more so than Douglas himself. Complaining that no hint of the President's views had yet become clear, Missouri's Samuel Treat appealed to Douglas for information.[3]

Pierce's thinking, however, ran in directions not anticipated by the Douglasites. Treat feared that the President-elect would attempt to form a "mosaic Cabinet—without unity or consistency of views or action," and he warned that such a policy could only have disastrous effects. Yet this seemed to be Pierce's intention. Barely a week after the election, *The New York Times* predicted that Pierce would turn to Douglas' rivals for advice, and by mid-December it was reported with some certainty that he would not seek Douglas' assistance. Douglas became increasingly troubled, and even the hostile *New-York Tribune* regretted that he was to be "over slaughed in the ranks of his victorious party." The *Tribune* correspondent thought he knew the reason for the snub. If Douglas "could divest himself of his rabid Filibusterism and the spice of Demagogism, he would rank respectably as a Legislator and Statesman." But "those whom he would style unprogressive drones" were destined to have more influence with the new administration than he. Young America was to be curbed, complained the *Herald,* and the government would "resume the quiet old jog-trot pace of the good old days of Mr. Monroe." Douglas' discomfiture was no less keen than the disappointment of his followers. "If the Administration is against you," asked McClernand, "would it not be advisable to let your friends . . . at home know the fact?" [4]

Pierce, in his determination to gloss over the divisions in the party, decided to invite both a New York Barnburner (to appease the freesoil wing) and a southern states' rights advocate to take places in his cabinet. His first choice for the former was John A. Dix, but the suggestion raised such a storm that he soon dropped it. Instead, he turned to William L. Marcy, Douglas' rival for New York's support before the nomination and no friend of the Illinoisan, who had followed a softer line toward the Barnburners than most of his fellow Hunkers. Marcy was appointed Secretary of State. For his southern states' rights man, Pierce offered the post of Secretary of War to Hunter, who declined; the appointment was then given to Jefferson Davis. James Buchanan, when approached by Pierce for suggestions, proposed the name of his fellow-Pennsylvanian, James Campbell. To offset the disappointment of the freesoilers, James Guthrie of Kentucky was appointed, partly on the recommendation of Blair. James C. Dobbin, the North Carolinian who had sparked the movement to Pierce in the convention, was added, and Robert McClelland, from Cass' home state of Michigan, received a place. Finally, Pierce turned to a New England friend and confidant, Caleb Cushing, to round out his selection. The cabinet, as finally determined, included no one who could be described as a "real friend" of Douglas, an omission that was widely noticed. However, some of the President's efforts had touched close to the Douglas camp. Hunter had been Douglas' running mate on the ill-fated "Ticket"; Cushing, a contributor to the *Democratic Review,* was sympathetic with the aims of Young America and with Douglas' views on foreign policy; and Jefferson Davis had been Illinois' unswerving choice for the vice presidential nomination. These connections proved to be highly tenuous, and, with the possible exception of Davis, the cabinet was regarded as unfriendly to Douglas.[5]

Douglas fared better in the disposition of the lesser offices in the administration. Following the election, he was deluged with letters from office-seekers who assumed that his would be an influential voice with the new President. Many of the appeals could not be ignored, especially if

Douglas wished to build support for his candidacy in 1856. From Missouri, James S. Green, a former Congressman, complained that Benton Democrats and Whigs had combined to defeat him in the recent election; he now sought "an endorsement by the National Democracy" in the form of a "good Office from the President." An old Springfield friend who had emigrated to California, James A. McDougall, urged Douglas to "do something for *my* California friends at Washington." An envoy brought recommendations for the offices in Florida and Douglas received appeals for help from North Carolina. The territories also looked to Douglas as their special spokesman in the new administration. Minnesotans were in close contact, while the Mormons in Utah hoped that Douglas' friendship would result in the appointment of men "of their own choice." [6]

Douglas sought rewards for those who had backed his candidacy in their states, including California's Edward C. Marshall, who had delivered a stirring defense against Breckinridge's charges in the House; S. M. Johnson, editor of the *Detroit Free Press*; John M. Daniel, editor of the *Richmond Examiner*; and Tennessee's Congressman Frederick P. Stanton. Only Daniel received a post. Of a more delicate character was Douglas' attempt to secure an appointment for his brother-in-law, Julius N. Granger, in the Treasury Department. Even the *Democratic Review* was not forgotten. Douglas urged the President to tender a foreign appointment to Thomas Devin Reilly, reputed author of some of the *Review's* obnoxious statements during the campaign, but without success. Douglas' Young American supporters, however, did surprisingly well, although this seemed due more to Pierce's sympathy with their policy of expansionism than to Douglas' influence. Pierre Soulé, Douglas' lieutenant in Louisiana, was appointed Minister to Spain, while Daniel Sickles, Edwin De Leon, and John L. O'Sullivan all received lesser diplomatic posts. Most notable was George Sanders' appointment to the consular post in London, where he soon proved as much an embarrassment to the administration as he had been to Douglas during the campaign. His London office became a meeting-ground for European revolutionaries, and when he issued a public "Address to the People of France" urging the overthrow of Napoleon III, he outraged even the Senate. When his appointment was not confirmed, Sanders heaped his wrath on Douglas, whom he accused of conspiring against his character, even though Douglas was one of the few Senators who did vote for his confirmation.[7]

Of primary concern to Douglas was the patronage in Illinois. He had succeeded in reconciling the party's divisions during the campaign, and his position of leadership was firm. Within the limits of his belief that the offices should go to those who had fought the battles, he now sought to strengthen his political base even further by exerting a tight rein over the disposal of the patronage. Assisting him was John Wentworth, whose role assumed greater significance as a result of the Douglas-free-soil alliance during the campaign. Wentworth visited Pierce following the election, and he apprised Douglas of the pressures to which the President-elect was being subjected by the friends of Marcy, Buchanan, and the southern Unionists. Wentworth assured Pierce that he, Douglas and Shields "should agree in every instance & so make him no trouble" on the Illinois appointments.

Douglas and Wentworth were forced to move swiftly in order to head off a challenge from others in the party. When the Democratic electors met in Springfield in December to cast the state's vote, they also drew up a slate of proposed appointments to the state offices. Needless to say, their own names were prominent on the list. Not all of the recommendations were approved by Douglas' friends. For example, John A. McClernand, who was suspected of leaning toward Thomas Hart Benton, was strongly proposed for a cabinet post, and Douglas was quickly warned that the recommendation would only advance Benton's interests to the injury of his own. Douglas, however, was not alarmed. "Benton is not particularly hostile to me," he wrote Lanphier. "He hates everybody and only regrets that every leading Democrat in America cannot be prostrated at once." Wentworth, fearing that the electors might take the initiative for proposing appointments out of his and Douglas' hands, was doing all he could to discourage petitions and to prevent men from going to Washington to talk with the new administration. The *State Register,* reflecting Douglas' concern, deprecated "the efforts of a few men in the state to foment discord in our ranks by creating two 'sections' here—one backing the delegation and another backing a set of men 'solicitous for these places.' "

In the end the Douglas-Wentworth effort to harmonize the party prevailed. Freesoilers were appointed to almost every office in northern Illinois. When Chicago's Thomas Hoyne, a Van Buren supporter in 1848, received the office of district attorney, Democrats howled that Douglas was encouraging treachery to the party. Douglas conceded that Hoyne had offended "grievously upon that question," but he insisted that he had good reasons for urging his appointment. Hoyne himself responded by pledging his continued support to Douglas. Wentworth acquiesced in the appointment of one of his political enemies, Isaac Cook, to the Chicago postmastership and agreed to support an appointment for Douglas' friend David Gregg, whom he accused of hostility toward Democrats suspected of freesoil leanings. Wentworth urged that Gregg be sent "off so far that he will not find his way back." Gregg, accordingly, was appointed Commissioner to the Sandwich Islands, a post he held for the next five years. Wentworth further promised to support Richardson for Speaker of the House of Representatives and to work for Shields' re-election to the Senate in 1854. The *Register* defended the appointments against the "sullen disapproval" of many Democrats. Party unity was the primary objective (although some disaffected members charged that Douglas' strategy would destroy party unity), so there was a strong determination to prevent the dissensions of New York Democrats from spreading to Illinois. "If Mr. Marcy and Mr. Dickinson cannot heal up old sores," Lanphier noted, "I can see no good reason why the democracy of other states of the Union should tear themselves to pieces about it." [8]

If Douglas felt reasonably content with the appointments in Illinois, his efforts to secure offices for his constituents outside the state fell far short of his expectations. His position in the party and the fidelity of his state to the party, he believed, entitled Illinoisans to a greater share of the spoils than they received. After Pierce's inauguration, he and Shields urged the President to give their state "just such a proportion of the general appointments as its population would give it a fair title to expect under any administration." They delicately spelled out the state's due: a share of the representatives abroad (two chargés or one full mission and three or four consulates), at least one comptroller, and a moderate proportion of the minor appointments in the departments at Washington. This, they implied, was a minimum request. If the President deemed their appeal unworthy, "we can assure you before hand that no neglect or injustice of this kind will drive Illinois from the Democratic fold or its senators from the support of your administration." The words were carefully chosen, but they had little effect. Shields, puzzled over Pierce's attitude, reported "a general impression that you are to be crushed." Buchanan received virtually all he asked for, while the President "is to give your friends nothing." "If I thought his object were to crush you," Shields continued, "I would think him more than mad."

While Shields remained skeptical of Pierce's motives, others recognized the influence of Indiana's crafty Senator, Jesse D. Bright. Bright, already jealous of Douglas' growing stature in the northwest, had tipped his hand at Baltimore, when he kept the Indiana delegation out of the Douglas column. A supporter of Buchanan, Bright sought to weaken Douglas as a candidate for 1856 by blocking the appointment of his friends. "He is your enemy," Yulee cautioned. "He does not mean that you shall rise if he can prevent it." Yulee's warning was timely, for in April Bright appealed to Buchanan for help in defeating Douglas' requests for political appointments.[9]

## ii

That Douglas would encounter difficulties with the new President over the patronage was hardly anticipated at the opening of the year. In January 1853 he was selected to deliver the principal address at the unveiling of Clark Mills' equestrian statue of Andrew Jackson in Lafayette Square, across the street from the White House. The event attracted a large number of people, including many veterans who had served under Jackson. Douglas compared the statue with the monuments of ancient Rome, and he closed his eulogy with the conviction that Jackson "lives in the spirit of the age—the genius of progress which is to ennoble and exalt humanity, and preserve and perpetuate liberty." That evening, at the annual celebration of the Democratic party, Douglas was himself eulogized. His name was linked with that of the Old Hero, as "the man who stands upon the broad platform of our common country, and proclaims to the world that we are a free and independent nation of the earth, marching onward in the cause of constitutional liberty." To be identified with Jackson was a tribute which could hardly be exceeded. In the same month, news arrived from Illinois that he had been re-elected to a second term in the Senate, and Martha gave birth to their third child and first daughter. His happiness, Douglas remarked, was now complete.

Douglas' elation was short-lived. The delivery of his daughter had been followed by complications. Martha grew steadily weaker until, on January 19, with her husband and mother at her bedside, she died. She was followed a month later by their infant daughter. Martha was only twenty-eight years old and had been Douglas' wife for less than six years.[10]

Martha's death plunged Douglas into deep despair. In deference to his bereavement, the Senate adjourned so that its members could attend the funeral. Later her body was conveyed to North Carolina, where she was interred in the family plot near the Martin plantation. Expressions of condolence poured in. Old Thomas Ritchie wrote from Virginia, "you have been so kind to me during our eight years' intercourse at Washington that I cannot but deeply sympathize with you on this sad & unexpected calamity." David Reid reminded Douglas that "the memory of your departed companion, and above all your dear little children, still hold out inducements to make life and exertion desirable." Douglas returned to the Senate almost immediately. Looking tired and careworn, he sought to recover some of his lost momentum, but he was clearly not himself. His former fire and zest for debate had given way to emotionalism, impatience, and shortness of temper that were not characteristic. Reid, with whom Douglas visited in Raleigh following his wife's burial, wrote that "he appeared more depressed in feeling than I ever saw him before." [11]

Some time during the spring Douglas determined on a change of scene. A journey to Europe would not only enable him to overcome his grief amid new surroundings, but it would also provide him added perspective on the nation's problems. His denunciations of Europe and things European, especially in connection with the Clayton-Bulwer Treaty, had peaked in the weeks following Martha's death, and it was perhaps from a desire to see for himself that he made his decision. A New York friend, Edward C. West, made the arrangements for his passage. Early in May Douglas left Washington. Before his departure from the capital, he installed his sister Sarah and her husband, Julius Granger (for whom he had secured an appointment in the General Land Office), in his house. The financier August Belmont provided him with letters of introduction to several European banking houses, including one to Baron Alphonse de Rothschild in Paris, and Robert J. Walker gave him a letter to John McGregor, member of the British Parliament, in which he described Douglas as "a most zealous and efficient advocate of free trade." On May 14, Douglas sailed for Liverpool on the Collins Line steamer *Pacific*.

Douglas' decision to visit Europe aroused wide interest, and his journey was followed closely in the press. A Cleveland paper hoped that he would be " 'seen of all men,' as a good sample of home manufacture— a thorough out and out American, unawed by the power, and uncaught by the splendor of royalty." Others, hailing him as the embodiment of Young America, were confident that he would find much in Europe to confirm his prejudices. Unlike some Americans who had taken the "grand tour," his head would not be turned "by the glitter of a star or the sound of an empty title." [12]

In London, where he spent the first few weeks of his trip, Douglas visited the usual tourist attractions, but he spent most of his time observing the British Parliament and talking with his English counterparts. His reputation for violent Anglophobia had preceded him, so he was coolly received and even ignored by some government officials and members of the nobility. English radicals, however, showed no hesitation in greeting him. Joseph Hume, Richard Cobden, and John Bright extended their cordial hospitality to the visitor. Bright, who met him at a party at Cobden's (at which Kossuth was also a guest), described Douglas as "a little, dark, but firm-built and intelligent-looking person, . . . evidently a man of superior mental power, distinct and logical in his style of speaking." The meeting had a business as well as a social purpose, for both Cobden and Bright had invested heavily in the Illinois Central Railroad. Through the good offices of Hume, a place in the gallery of the House of Commons was set aside for Douglas' use. Douglas dined with Thomas Baring, head of England's famed financial house, and, accompanied by former New York Congressman Gouverneur Kemble and Martin Van Buren, he socialized with the poet and man of letters, Richard Monckton Milnes. Shortly after his arrival in London he expressed an interest in an audience with Queen Victoria, but declined when he was informed that he would have to appear in "court dress." To the delight of his friends back home, he insisted that he could not see the monarch unless dressed in a manner appropriate to a visit with an American President. The Queen did not relent, and Douglas left England without seeing her. [13]

From England Douglas traveled eastward to Smyrna and Constantinople, by way of Le Havre, Marseilles, Genoa, Florence, Rome, and Athens. In Genoa he inspected a newly completed breakwater and acquired a detailed map of the harbor, perhaps for future use in America. He observed the Fourth of July in Messina with members of the American community. Douglas' visit to Rome touched off a brief flurry of speculation in the American press. A New York Catholic newspaper announced that "a distinguished Senator of the United States," visiting in Rome, had formally renounced Protestantism and was received in the Roman Catholic Church. The name of the convert, the paper continued, had not been ascertained. The report immediately circulated that the Senator in question was Stephen A. Douglas. Some Democrats were thrown into the "greatest tribulation" at the news, while opposition papers launched sharp attacks against Douglas' blatant attempt to capture the Roman Catholic vote for the next presidential race. The incident inspired more humor than concern among some editors. The New York *Herald,* doubtful that Douglas was the individual referred to, nevertheless speculated that the Little Giant, "descended from Scotch Covenanters, after having failed to reach the Presidency . . . in a single bound, is now aspiring to become the Pope of Rome." If the rumor were true, commented *The Providence Journal,* the Pope would do well to keep an eye on Douglas, for "he will be for making St. Peter's chair elective once in four years, and will present himself as a candidate for the next succession." The excitement subsided as quickly as it began when it was revealed that Pennsylvania's Congressman Joseph R. Chandler, not Douglas, had received the Apostolic blessing.[14]

Douglas arrived in Smyrna, Turkey, on the heels of the celebrated "Koszta affair," and he reported that the excitement was greater than any he had ever witnessed. Martin Koszta, a Hungarian refugee, some years before had gone to the United States, where he declared his intention of becoming an American citizen. Returning to Turkey in 1853, he was seized in Smyrna by Austrian authorities and placed aboard an Austrian warship. The protests of the American diplomatic representatives in Turkey were ignored, and plans were made to return Koszta to Austria. Under the instructions of the American chargé in Constantinople, Captain D. N. Ingraham of the sloop-of-war *St. Louis,* lying in Smyrna harbor, demanded Koszta's immediate release and cleared his ship for action against the Austrian vessels. The Austrians yielded, and bloodshed was averted. "No event has created so much enthusiasm in behalf of our country or created so violent a sensation among the despots of the old world," Douglas reported. It was a delicate question, but Douglas suggested that it could be justified by Turkish law, which allowed a foreigner to seek the protection of any country he wished while he was domiciled in Turkey. Koszta had made the necessary declarations before Turkish authorities; although he had not yet become an American citizen, he was thus entitled to American protection. It was a line later taken by Marcy in his formal note to the Austrian government.

The Koszta affair was a sidelight to a developing crisis in the east. Douglas felt the tension as he traveled, and his discussions with government officials invariably turned to the threat of war between Russia and Turkey. In Constantinople he talked with Reschid Pasha, the Turkish foreign minister, assuring him that American sympathies were on the side of Turkey. He received permission and a promise of protection for a visit to Syria, the Holy Land, and Egypt, but there is no evidence that he made the trip. Although an audience with the Sultan had been arranged, Douglas found it impossible to defer his trip longer and left without seeing the Turkish ruler.[15]

Sailing from Constantinople, Douglas landed at the Russian Black Sea port of Odessa, where he "enjoyed the delights" of four days' quarantine against the plague before continuing on to St. Petersburg. His journey took him to the Crimea, "the most charming country in all Europe," Kiev, and Moscow, which he described as "the most gorgeous & curious city in the world." A few days were spent at "the great Oriental fair" at "Niznia" (Nizhni Novgorod), "where I saw assembled about 300,000 people of all nations & races, religions & costumes . . . with their goods trying to cheat each other." Most of the journey across Russia was made in a "long carriage," containing a sleeping room and a kitchen, traveling day and night at a steady clip of ten miles per hour.

In St. Petersburg, Douglas conferred with Count Nesselrode, private secretary to Czar Nicholas I. Nesselrode made arrangements for him to see the Czar, who was conducting troop maneuvers outside the city at the time. Douglas was taken into the field, provided an elegantly caparisoned horse (the stirrups had to be shortened before he could ride it), and accorded a place alongside the Russian monarch. Douglas later recalled the ludicrous figure he cut as he sat uncomfortably astride his mount while thousands of Russian soldiers passed before him.

In spite of Douglas' earlier denunciations of Russia's intervention in the Hungarian revolution, and of Russia's protest against America's part in the Koszta affair, the conversation between the two men was cordial. Czar Nicholas questioned Douglas regarding preparations for war in Constantinople, and when Douglas reported that the Turks believed the possibility of war depended upon the Czar, the latter replied that he was really a man of peace. In the discussion that followed, the Czar remarked that Russia and America were the only two "proper governments" in the world. All other powers were "mongrels," destined to be absorbed some day by these two nations. With the Koszta affair still fresh, Douglas was on the defensive with some members of the Czar's party. When the Swedish ambassador condemned Captain Ingraham's action and denied the right of any government to naturalize the subject of another, Douglas quickly pointed to the example of Bernadotte, father of

the Swedish king. Douglas was much impressed by the attention paid
him and later noted that it had been a "proud day for my country." [16]

Leaving St. Petersburg, Douglas crossed Sweden to visit Copenhagen,
Berlin, Prague, Vienna, Munich, and Frankfurt before arriving in Paris.
There, in the company of Tennessee Senator James Jones, he was
granted an audience with Napoleon III, at which the Emperor's wife,
the Spanish-born Eugénie, questioned him closely and sharply concerning American designs on Cuba. With his stay in Paris, Douglas' European excursion came to an end. He returned to Liverpool, where he
boarded the *Arctic,* and, on October 30, he arrived in New York after
an absence of five months.

Douglas' trip had served its purpose well. He returned to the United
States in good health and spirits, "chock full of anecdote" and with
"fresh stores of varied and important information." His reception in Europe had been impressive and satisfying, not the least of his satisfactions
being the fact that the Emperors of Russia and France had received him
in his ordinary civilian dress, while the British Queen had denied him
that privilege. He was lauded by his friends and by the press for having
upheld "the honor and glory" of the United States in the midst of
"crowns and coronets." His faith in American progress and democracy
had been reinforced, and when he was invited, shortly after his return, to
speak at the ceremony marking the beginning of construction on Washington's new acqueduct, he undoubtedly had the contrast between America and Europe in mind. "We in America," he said, "are accustomed to
spend money for works of utility, not on those of mere ornament, pomp,
and show." [17]

### iii

Douglas returned immediately to Washington and threw himself once
again into the maelstrom of national politics. His absence from the
country placed him in a forgiving mood. Although Pierce had made mistakes in his appointments, he wrote to Lanphier, he would hold no
grudge. Principles were more important; if the administration "stands
firmly by the faith," he promised his "hearty & energetic support." The
party, he conceded, was in a distracted condition, and it would require
wisdom and energy to consolidate its power, but Douglas was confident
that "all is right." Out of touch with political developments for several
months, Douglas did not know how "distracted" the party really was. In
London he had learned of Buchanan's dissatisfaction with Pierce's

course, but he was unprepared for the severity of the storm that swirled about the President.

Lanphier cautioned Douglas against over-optimism. "Without having heard from us for six months you still express confidence that we are 'all right,' " he replied. "In these days six months is a long time to be confident that any body is 'right,' without knowing it." Lanphier pointed to the "everlasting, never-to-be-ended New York quarrel" as the source of a potential explosion that could split the party throughout the nation. Pierce's attempt to harmonize the contending factions, he thought, was ill-advised and unnecessary, "productive of anything but *the object intended.*" He strongly feared the quarrel would spread to other states and noted signs that such a development was indeed already taking place. The party press had tried valiantly to put a " 'harmonious' face upon the matter," but their efforts did not express "the *inside* reflections of the great popular heart."

New York's troubled Democratic politics had become more complex than ever, and in September they boiled over into a new crisis. For a time during the 1852 campaign there was hope that the party could be united, but Pierce's patronage policy plunged Democrats into chaos once again. Trying to appease the extremes, Pierce had given the lion's share of the state offices to the freesoil-leaning Barnburners (led by John A. Dix and the Van Burens, father and son) and to the "soft," or conciliatory, wing of the conservative Hunkers (represented by Marcy), leaving Dickinson's "hard" wing of the Hunkers with little satisfaction. The irreconcilable character of these divisions became clear when the state convention failed to agree, broke up, and presented two platforms and tickets for the minor state offices which were at stake in 1853. The breach was widened in the campaign that followed, during which both sides hurled bitter accusations and epithets. As soon as Douglas returned from Europe, he was apprised of the seriousness of the split. The division of the party, wrote Edward C. West, was of a most decisive kind. The result was "a war full of bitterness and personality, and looking to the extermination of one or the other of the parties." Nor was the war to be limited to New York state. The "hards" were determined to carry their quarrel with Pierce into Congress.[18]

The crisis in New York was symptomatic of deep dissatisfaction with the administration among Democrats in other states. The supporters of the Compromise of 1850, so-called "National Democrats" in the north and "Unionists" in the south, everywhere felt slighted, as they did in Illinois itself (partly through Douglas' own policy of conciliating the free-soilers). Reports of open party splits came from Missouri, where Thomas Hart Benton was leading the opposition to the President, and from Massachusetts. Even some of those who had engineered Pierce's nomination felt betrayed. Edmund Burke, writing to Douglas, expressed the alarm felt by some of the President's close associates. "In the notice of appointments," Burke wrote, "the Administration has repudiated the *Union sentiment* which dictated the Compromise measures, and upon the strength of which Gen. Pierce was elevated to power. In the north it has been the especial policy of the Administration to reward the traitors against whom we have been fighting for years, and to proscribe and put down the old, true, and faithful leaders of the party." Surprised and disturbed by the ferocity of the attacks, Douglas was reluctantly drawn into the quarrel. From New York, a Marcy supporter warned Douglas against siding with the "hards," while a member of the opposing faction urged him to follow a course which the "hards" could sustain. Western Democrats, "somewhat at a loss as to the policy we should adopt," turned to Douglas for guidance. "The country is looking with a good deal of anxiety to your course on the hard and soft question in New York," wrote a former Indiana Congressman who had just been appointed governor of Minnesota Territory. Douglas, however, remained silent, hoping that the opening of Congress would clarify the situation.

The meeting of the new Congress was attended by more than the usual excitement and interest. The New York *Herald* had earlier speculated on whether either party would survive the session. Whigs, still shaken by their recent defeat, spoke openly of abandoning their organization and re-organizing on a more "popular" basis. One group, early in 1853, proposed that the name of the party be dropped, suggesting in its stead the label "Republican." The Democrats were as disorganized as the Whigs, especially in New York. Washington, it was said, was thronged with New Yorkers of all stripes, and all determined to seek a resolution of their problem on the national level. "Hards" were eager for battle, while the "softs" worried at rumors that Pierce, seeing the error of his ways, would make drastic changes in his appointments, beginning with the cabinet. As battle lines were drawn, Democrats looked inquiringly to the Illinois Senator. "We should like to know the present party position of Judge Douglas." [19]

If Douglas had a position during the first weeks of Congress, it was in defense of the administration. Although he nurtured his own grievances against Pierce, he nevertheless remained loyal to the President. The first test of the administration's strength, and its first defeat, came with the election for Senate printer. Pierce insisted on the election of Robert Armstrong, proprietor of the Washington *Union,* but the Senate chose instead pro-southern Beverley Tucker, who had recently established the Washington *Sentinel.* Armstrong's support, it was noted, came from the extreme north, "where freesoil sentiments are a sort of religion," although the strong antislavery Senators Seward, Chase, Sumner, and Wade voted with the majority for Tucker. Douglas was on the losing side, but it was the side of the administration. Tucker's election was a blow to the President and revealed the depth of dissatisfaction among Democratic Senators. Before Congress met, Pierce had further outraged the New York "hards" by removing Greene C. Bronson from the collectorship of the port and replacing him with Heman Redfield, a "soft" and a friend of Marcy. A battle over Redfield's confirmation in the Senate loomed as a significant test of the administration's patronage policy and a trial of "the exact issue before the country, so far as the Van Buren free-soil dynasty are concerned." Douglas supported Redfield's appointment, and Redfield eventually won the office, although by the time of his confirmation the party was convulsed by even greater issues.

The Democratic party was clearly in serious trouble. The opening of Congress had compounded its difficulties, and the dissension, according to one opposition Senator, had become "incurable." The general feeling of the party leaders, concluded a Washington correspondent, was "far from favorable" to the administration. "The dissatisfaction is wide spread and deep seated." Douglas, to whom party unity was the *sine qua non* for national development, sought desperately for a solution. A passive defense of the administration was not the answer. Pierce was simply not capable of galvanizing the warring elements into united action. The President's hesitancy, timidity, irresolution, and bad advice, wrote Missourian Samuel Treat to Douglas, would have to be counteracted somehow if the party were to be saved. Unless Pierce "promptly marks out a line of sound national and Democratic policy, and boldly makes it known to the country by unmistakeable *action,* it will be utterly impossible for him to save his Administration from total Failure." Nothing but the "boldest and most decided action can turn the current." Without it the Democratic party would soon be "shivered to atoms."

Douglas agreed with that diagnosis, but the prospect of finding such a policy seemed bleak. In November, while he was still fresh from his travels and before he had become aware of the full seriousness of his party's problems, Douglas had predicted that the main questions before Congress would be those dealing with the tariff, river and harbor improvements, and the Pacific railroad. None of these would now meet the requirements. The President himself had proposed no new measures. An increasing number of friends, impressed by Pierce's weakness, were again urging Douglas to strike out for the presidential succession, but Douglas had learned his lesson and was not to be pushed. "I do not think I will be willing to have my name used," he wrote to Lanphier. "I shall remain entirely uncommitted & hold myself at liberty to do whatever my duty to my principles & my friends may require when the time for action arrives. Our first duty is to the cause." Still, the Democratic victory in 1852 had left a void in the party's top echelons. Cass was clearly out of the picture; Buchanan was out of the country. The responsibility for seizing the initiative devolved upon Douglas. Again, opportunity seemed to beckon. What was obviously needed was the kind of effort that had coalesced the parties four years before when the nation stood in peril. The crisis facing his party, the instrument of Union and national progress, was no less severe. In 1850, Douglas had repeatedly asserted, it was the great west that had rescued the nation from disunion. It was now time for the west to speak out again.[20]

iv

Douglas had introduced his first bill for the organization of Nebraska Territory in 1844, almost ten years before. It was then a part of a grand program of western development which included the establishment of government in Oregon and the construction of a Pacific railroad. His dream had never diminished. Expansion to the Pacific had been followed by the organization of government in Oregon and California, providing a new urgency for the development of the intervening territory. The vast area between the Missouri River and the Rocky Mountains, set aside earlier as a "permanent Indian reservation," assumed new significance, lying as it did athwart the heavily traveled emigrant trails. Its restriction to the use of the Indians, its lack of organization, became increasingly anachronistic. In the following years, Douglas brought his western plans closer to realization. A program of aiding railroad construction through government land-grants was introduced in his Illinois Central railroad bill and was further confirmed in legislation for railroads in Missouri and Arkansas, in which Douglas also played a part. In 1848, he reintroduced his bill for the organization of Nebraska Territory. In the following year he argued persuasively for a Pacific railroad over a central route at the St. Louis railroad convention. A free homestead policy was also winning support.

As a further step toward the achievement of both the Pacific railroad and the establishment of territorial government in Nebraska, Douglas urged Congress to provide for the colonization of lands along the trails by settlers who could not only protect the emigrants from marauding Indians, but who could also initiate the economic development of the Plains. Douglas' efforts, however, met with little success. He complained bitterly of the indifference of the Senate toward territorial legislation and beseeched his colleagues to cease postponing territorial bills until the end of the sessions, when there was no longer time to consider them. When his bill to open the area to settlement by establishing colonies along the emigrant routes, which provided also for a telegraph line and an overland mail service, was greeted by a chorus of objections from southern Senators in the summer of 1852, he charged them with a "direct, open hostility to that section of country." His warning that the lack of communication with the Pacific and the absence of organized government west of Missouri might result in disunion was greeted by ridicule and sarcasm. "It is utterly impossible," he declared, "to preserve that connection between the Atlantic and the Pacific, if you are to keep a wilderness of two thousand miles in extent between you." [21]

In a move to keep Douglas' effort alive, California's Senator William M. Gwin proposed, with Douglas' sanction, that the bill be recommitted to the territorial committee, hinting broadly that a Pacific railroad measure might soon be reported. A few days later, on July 23, a bill was submitted providing for two Pacific railroads, one over a southern route and the other over a central one, although Douglas was singularly unenthusiastic toward it. No action was taken on it before the end of the session.

The Pacific railroad issue was revived in earnest early in the short session of Congress that met in December 1852, and it virtually dominated discussion in the Senate until late in February. The question's entanglement with sectional rivalries became painfully evident. As a substitute to Douglas' emigrant route bill, Gwin proposed a measure based, he said, on the one submitted earlier by Douglas' committee, but differing in one important respect. Instead of establishing two railroads, Gwin provided for one line from California to Arkansas, with branches radiating to various points in the Mississippi valley. Proponents of more northerly routes were quick to voice their opposition. A way out of the difficulty was devised by Senator Rusk of Texas, who revived the emigrant route bill once again and suggested that it be submitted to a special committee for consideration. The Senate agreed and five members were designated, three of whom were committed to a southern route.[22]

This was a critical time for Douglas. His wife lay desperately ill during much of the debate, and she died on the day before Rusk's committee was appointed. Nevertheless, he managed to maintain contact with the developments. Reflecting their southern orientation, the committee members proposed a single line, along a route to be designated by the President. Obviously, the committee expected a southern route to be selected. Rusk had shown Douglas the bill before he reported it, and, while the latter expressed some reservations, he regarded it on the whole as a good measure. The important thing, Douglas said, was to get the question of a Pacific railroad moving toward realization. "I do not think there is any question that can come before us more worthy to occupy attention than that of a railroad to the Pacific."

Although Douglas warned that the bill might require some amendment, he defended its general outlines. To those who objected to the provisions for federal aid, he argued that the government's investment was perfectly protected, and he dismissed the contention that the scheme was unconstitutional. He took issue with those who maintained that no railroad which crossed such a vast and uninhabited wilderness could possibly be a profitable venture, and he denounced the long-prevalent notion that everything between the Missouri and the Rockies was desert. Such ideas originated, he told the Senate, with those who compared the land with what they had known in the east. He reminded his critics that even sections of Illinois and Kentucky had once been advertised as barren and desolate. "I am under the impression that the vast regions of desert in the slopes on either side of the mountains west of the Mississippi will disappear before investigation and settlement, in the way that other deserts have." Settlers will follow the line, will cultivate farms and will build settlements. The country will be transformed from a wilderness into "one of the most densely-populated and highly-cultivated portions of America."

It was clear from Douglas' arguments that he assumed the railroad would ultimately follow a central route, an assumption he tried to plant in the minds of his colleagues. Replying to the charge that a federally incorporated company would be operating within the limits of a state, Douglas pointed out that "according to the bill it is not necessary that one inch of the road should be in a State of the Union," and he hinted that amendments might so modify the bill "that there should not be any possibility of entering a State of the Union, but be confined to the Territories." Sensing Douglas' purpose, one southern Senator immediately retorted "that this is to be a northern road." Following out the line of Douglas' reasoning, he declared that Pierce, a good states' rights man, would never consent to locate the road in a state. "Then I understand he will be compelled to locate the road through the South Pass," the Senator continued. "That will bring it in the forty-second degree of north latitude, and bring it through the Nebraska Territory." Douglas denied that the bill gave either side any advantage, but he did concede that the President, if he wished to do justice to both north and south, would select a central route. Southern suspicions were further confirmed when Shields, after having consulted with Douglas and others, offered an amendment that would prevent any of the money advanced by the government in aid of construction from being spent within a state, a blow to the advocates of a southern route. Rusk moaned that it would "disjoint" the whole bill. When it passed by a narrow vote, Gwin pronounced the project destroyed, while Rusk maintained that his bill had been reduced to a "useless piece of paper." California's Senator John Weller moved a reconsideration of the vote by which Shields' amendment passed. When his motion carried he offered a substitute that hardly differed from the original, stipulating that the money could be expended only in the territories. Weller's substitute passed by the same slim margin.

Douglas defended the Shields-Weller amendment and fought for the passage of the amended bill, even though some of its original supporters now abandoned it. The Senators seemed more interested in assigning blame for the measure's sudden downfall. Douglas, his temper rising, sought vainly to bring the proposal to a vote. To Senator Gwin, who gave the amended measure a reluctant support, Douglas was one of the principal culprits in casting the "bomb shell" that proved so fatal to the Pacific railroad bill. He charged him with attempting to curry favor, with an eye to the next presidential race, among southern states' rightists whose constitutional scruples rebelled against the appropriation of federal money for a railroad project within a state. It was more likely that Douglas sought to head off a movement that would have resulted in the selection of a southern route and to keep the way open for either a central or northern route and for the organization of Nebraska Territory.[23]

The friends of the Pacific railroad sought to salvage something from the wreckage. Gwin, on the day after the railroad bill was set aside, offered an amendment to an Army appropriation bill, providing for a detailed reconnaissance and survey of all possible railroad routes. The amendment, which had originally been offered by Senator Brodhead of Pennsylvania as a substitute for the railroad bill, received Douglas' support, and it later passed, but only after a considerable amount of debate. Gwin had opposed Brodhead's move earlier, but, as he told the Senate, "a drowning man will catch at straws." Douglas then revived his proposal for the protection of the emigrant routes to Oregon and California as an additional amendment to the appropriation measure. It barely passed the Senate, but, unlike the survey amendment, it failed in the House of Representatives. In the last moments of the session Douglas and Weller proposed, as an amendment to a post office appropriation bill, the construction of a telegraph line to the Pacific. The suggestion was sharply assailed by southerners, who suspected that it was a move to predetermine the Pacific railroad route, and it was defeated by the same combination that had brought the earlier railroad bill to its demise. Countering the southern objections one by one, Douglas finally and in resignation concluded, "We cannot satisfy them in any way."

The approval of the proposal to survey possible railroad routes was well received by the proponents of a Pacific railroad. Douglas derived considerable satisfaction from the fact that Congress had finally taken a positive step toward the realization of his dream to link the Pacific coast with the rest of the nation. That he was interested in more than one transcontinental line was soon evidenced by the "special solicitude" he expressed toward the exploration of the less well known northern route. Selected to lead the exploration was Isaac I. Stevens, a young Army officer and Mexican War veteran who had just been appointed governor of Washington Territory. Before leaving for the west, Stevens conferred with Douglas, and the two men studied maps of the probable route the surveying party would take. Later, as he moved westward, Stevens sent detailed accounts of his progress to Douglas. Robert J. Walker, who had organized a private railroad company and stood ready to bid for the construction of a Pacific railroad, sent assurances that, from his point of view, a northern route from Lake Superior to Puget Sound was quite practical.[24] Before either a northern or a central Pacific railroad route could hope to receive congressional sanction, however, the vast area over which the line would run had to be granted governmental organization. Whenever the Pacific railroad issue was discussed, the proposal to organize Nebraska Territory was not far behind.

V

Pressure to organize the area west of Missouri had, in the meantime, mounted, and by now it was coming not only from the advocates of a Pacific railroad in Congress, but from the west itself. In April 1852, Douglas submitted a memorial from a group of his constituents, asking that a territorial government be established in Nebraska. In the following June, citizens of western Missouri urged the immediate organization of the region. Months before, western newspapers had reported the desirability of settlement in Nebraska, where "boomers" were actively promoting the area. One of these, Thomas Jefferson Sutherland, conducted a persistent campaign on behalf of Nebraska in the press. Writing to Douglas in May 1852, Sutherland argued in considerable detail for closing "the two flanks of civilization" by organizing the unoccupied space between. Small groups of settlers, he reported, had already entered Nebraska to establish their homes. Several months later a representative was selected by people in the area to carry their plea for the creation of a territory directly to Congress. The representative, Abelard Guthrie, won the support of Thomas Hart Benton, who grasped at the Nebraska issue as a means of regaining his lost position in Missouri politics, but he was rebuffed by Missouri's Senator David R. Atchison. Atchison based his opposition, he told Guthrie, on the ground that the Missouri Compromise would prevent slaveholders from settling in the area. Guthrie, persuaded that the Compromise could not bind the people in moulding their institutions, was hopeful that this restriction might be overcome. Reflecting these increased pressures, northwest Missouri's Congressman Willard Hall introduced a bill into the House, in December 1851, for the organization of the Territory of Platte. Nothing came of his proposal, but he persisted, reintroducing his measure a year later when chances for success seemed more optimistic. This time his bill was referred to the House Committee on Territories, whose chairman, William A. Richardson, was recognized as Douglas' spokesman in the House.

As the committee deliberated, the report circulated in the west that two new territories would actually be projected: Nebraska, lying on both sides of the Platte River, and Kansas, "from the large river of that name which runs through it." The rumor, however, was without foundation. As the Senate warmed to debate over the Pacific railroad in February 1853, Richardson reported a bill for the single Territory of Nebraska, with northern and southern boundaries at 42°30' and 36°30', respectively. The bill was without doubt shaped with Douglas' advice. Debate on the measure began a few days later, and on February 10 it passed the House by an easy margin. The bill followed the usual pattern for territorial organization and contained no unique features. Discussion centered chiefly on the status of Indian tribes in the proposed territory. Only once was the question of slavery alluded to. In answer to an inquiry, Joshua R. Giddings, Ohio abolitionist and a member of the territorial committee, assured the House that the Missouri Compromise, although not mentioned in the bill, applied fully to the territory. "This law stands perpetually," he declared, "and I did not think that this act would receive any increased validity by a reenactment." The Compromise measures of 1850, he continued, did not "affect the question." Perhaps for this reason, the Congressmen from the deep south states voted overwhelmingly against the bill.[25]

Douglas reported the House bill to the Senate in the midst of the railroad debate, on the day before Shields submitted his controversial amendment. It was not brought up for consideration until the last day of the session. In the meantime, another piece of territorial business was given precedence and disposed of without difficulty. The increase in population in that part of Oregon Territory that lay north of the Columbia River, and the remoteness of the settlements there from those south of the river, had resulted in a movement for a new territory. The house responded quickly to the demand by dividing Oregon Territory and organizing the Territory of Washington for its northern settlers. Douglas submitted the bill to the Senate at the same time that he reported the Nebraska bill. Referred to by one Senator as "one of the old-fashioned territorial bills," the measure was passed swiftly and without debate. The laws of Oregon Territory were to continue in force in the new territory, and as these included the decision to prohibit slavery (in which the northern settlers had, in fact, participated), that question was not even raised.

The course of the Nebraska bill was not nearly as smooth. Rusk, whose Pacific railroad efforts had just been shattered, and Hunter objected to its consideration on the grounds that it was a controversial measure and that it contained many debatable points. Douglas responded to the objections with impatience and anger. "For two years past the Senate has refused to hear a territorial bill," he shouted. "For two weeks past, I have sat here hour after hour endeavoring at every suitable opportunity to obtain the floor." He was joined on the last day of the session by Senator Atchison, who explained that he had changed his mind on the question of organizing Nebraska Territory and would now support it. His earlier objection, Atchison explained, had been based on the applicability of the Missouri Compromise to the new territory. He had found, however, "that there was no prospect, no hope of a repeal of the Missouri compromise, excluding slavery from that Territory." The Compromise had been a great error, but he was now convinced that it was "irremediable," so he was prepared to submit to it. The "tide of population" would soon engulf "every habitable spot in Nebraska Territory." Even with Atchison's support, however, the cause became increasingly hopeless. Southern Senators returned to the question of Indian rights in the proposed territory, indicating as they did so their unwillingness to act on the bill. As the morning of March 4 broke, with the Senate chamber nearly empty (showing, John Bell noted, "what interest the Senate takes in such questions"), Douglas made a final attempt to secure consideration of the measure.

"It is an act that is very dear to my heart," he began, besides being a measure of "immense magnitude" and of "grave import" to the entire nation. The country must be opened to settlement, and the emigrants, traders, and settlers must be placed under the protection of law. Every effort to bind the Pacific to the rest of the country—by railroad, by telegraph, by military colonization—had been defeated. The organization of Nebraska Territory was a last alternative. Douglas was bitter. "I have been struck with the zeal which burns in some gentlemen's bosoms in behalf of the poor Indian," he observed. The issue, he was certain, was not the real one, for "it is necessary for them to avail themselves of some argument by which to resist this bill, and sympathy for the poor Indian is the argument that is resorted to." He reminded the Senators once again of the neglect to which the territories were being subjected, but his appeals were ignored. His motion to take up the Nebraska bill was laid on the table by a vote of 23 to 17.[26]

The vote made it clear to Douglas where the opposition to the organization of Nebraska Territory lay. Of the seventeen who supported the bill, only two Senators, both from Missouri, were from a slave state. Of the twenty-three in opposition, nineteen represented the slaveholding south. The conclusion was inescapable. Until the south could be won over, there was no possibility that organized government could be brought to the central plains. Without it, Douglas' western program, his hopes for binding the settlements on the Pacific to the rest of the nation, for linking the two oceans with a railroad and telegraph—in short, for strengthening the United States through the development of its great western potential—stood no chance of success. Douglas was correct in his charge that the argument over Indian rights was a pretext for opposition to the bill. The Indian removal policy, which had provided eastern Indians with "permanent" homes in the area, had been suspended years before, when Douglas had made his first moves toward the organization of Nebraska. He had, moreover, pointed out that the Indians already in the area would not be disturbed by the creation of a territorial government, for a clause of the proposed bill offered explicit protection to their rights. The real problem, revealed in part by Atchison, was the Missouri Compromise. Many of the supporters of Nebraska's organization had already concluded that the Compromise of 1850 rendered the Missouri settlement obsolete, but to others the relationship between the two compromises was unclear. Atchison himself, in raising the question, conceded that "I am not now very clear on that subject." Douglas may have pointed a way out of this difficulty as early as November 1852, when he wrote privately of his intention to bring forward a bill that would "repeal altogether that compromise." [27]

Congress adjourned on March 4, and Douglas left for Europe soon afterward, but the Nebraska question was by no means dead. On the contrary, events during the remainder of the year brought it more sharply into focus. Atchison returned to Missouri and became involved in Benton's campaign to capture his Senate seat. He determined to speak "to the whole State" on the theme of "Nebraska and the road to India." Undoubtedly impressed, as Douglas was, with the solid southern opposition to the organization of Nebraska, Atchison returned to his former position. No bill would receive his support, he told a western Missouri audience, which did not leave the slaveholder and non-slaveholder on terms of equality. He would be content, he added, to allow the people who would settle in Nebraska to decide the question of slavery for themselves—the principle established in the Compromise of 1850. In the meantime, agitation in western Missouri and Iowa for the opening of Nebraska mounted. Pressure for the settlement of the area increased all along the border, and some settlers began moving into the area. In July, representatives of various Indian tribes and some of the settlers sought to establish a provisional government for Nebraska, in lieu of congressional action. Other meetings followed, and two rival delegates were selected to represent Nebraska's interests in Congress. At least one spokesman suggested a way out of the impasse when he proposed the outright repeal of the Missouri Compromise in order that settlers from all parts of the Union might have an equal right to settle in the area with their property.

The movement reached a climax when a Nebraska convention met in the western Missouri town of St. Joseph, early in January 1854. Douglas, as the champion of Nebraska Territory, was invited to attend. Congress having just convened, he declined the invitation, but on December 17 he wrote to the convention's planners of his support for their movement. He reviewed his efforts to secure the organization of Nebraska Territory and argued once again for its urgency. To withhold territorial government from the area was to fly in the face of national progress. "The Idea of arresting our progress in that direction, has become so ludicrous that we are amazed, that wise and patriotic statesmen ever cherished the thought." Not only was the organization of Nebraska Territory an important local measure to the citizens of Iowa and Missouri, but "to the interests of the Republic it is a national necessity."

> How are we to develop, cherish and protect our immense interests and possessions on the Pacific, with a vast wilderness fifteen hundred miles in breadth, filled with hostile savages, and cutting off all direct communication. The Indian barrier must be removed. The tide of emigration and civilization must be permitted to roll onward until it rushes through the passes of the mountains, and spreads over the plains, and mingles with the waters of the Pacific. Continuous lines of settlement with civil, political and religious institutions all under the protection of law, are imperiously demanded by the highest national considerations. These are essential, but they are not sufficient. No man can keep up with the spirit of this age who travels on anything slower than the locomotive, and fails to receive intelligence by lightning. We must therefore have Rail Roads and Telegraphs from the Atlantic to the Pacific, through our own territory. Not one line only, but many lines, for the valley of the Mississippi will require as many Rail Roads to the Pacific as to the Atlantic, and will not venture to limit the number. The re-

moval of the Indian barrier and the extension of the laws of the
United States in the form of Territorial governments are the first
steps toward the accomplishment of each and all of those objects.

Seldom before had Douglas expressed his hopes and plans for western
development so succinctly. The "slavery agitation," he wrote, had hindered the achievement of these goals. Public attention was distracted
and the interests "of our old territory" neglected. Now he was confident
that everyone would recognize the necessity and importance of the organization of Nebraska Territory. As for the problem of slavery, which had
already struck an ominous chord in the brief discussion at the end of the
previous session, Douglas hoped that "all will be willing to sanction and
affirm the principle established by the Compromise measures of 1850" in
the new territory.[28]

# XVII
## "I passed the Kansas - Nebraska Act myself"
## 1854

i

Promptly at noon on December 5, 1853, David Atchison, President *pro tempore* of the Senate, called the first session of the thirty-third Congress to order. On the following day Pierce's message was read to the assembled members of the two houses. Largely a review of the state of the nation, the President's words were tentative and indecisive with regard to future policy. He touched upon the troublesome questions of internal improvements and the Pacific railroad briefly, but without any positive suggestions for action. The nation was at peace with foreign countries, he announced, and tranquillity reigned at home. The Compromise of 1850 had "restored a sense of repose and security to the public mind throughout the Confederacy," and he optimistically promised that "this repose is to suffer no shock during my official term, if I have power to avert it." The President concluded with reference to the death of Vice President William R. King, and the first business of the Senate was to pronounce appropriate eulogies to the Alabaman's memory.

The message reflected the gap that had developed between the Chief Executive and his party. The Democrats enjoyed a heavy majority in the Senate and an even heavier one in the House, where they outnumbered the Whigs by more than two to one, but many Democrats had already expressed their disinclination to follow the President's lead. Like the President, most of the Senators lacked experience, only a small handful having served more than six years. Douglas, beginning his second term, was numbered among the "veterans." "The old order had just passed," one historian has observed, "and the new generation had not known power long." Unlike the men they displaced, whose national perspective had been born of long service, the new Senators were more inclined to follow their own personal and sectional dictates. Party splits in the states, Pierce's patronage policies, and the demoralizing defeat of the Whigs in 1852 had disturbed old allegiances. The time was ripe for new combinations. Following up their success in the election for printer, recalcitrant Senate Democrats consolidated their position in the new committee assignments. At the instigation of Jesse Bright, the membership of fourteen committees was increased from five to six, with a corresponding increase in the Democratic majority on each committee, and the election of committee members by ballot was dispensed with. Instead, a slate presented by Bright was accepted.

Douglas' chairmanship of the Committee on Territories was renewed, and he was again given a place on the foreign relations committee, in recognition of his interest and involvement in America's external affairs. His control over the territorial committee, however, was not as certain as it had been earlier. Serving with him was the independent Texan, Sam Houston, who had opposed the last session's Nebraska bill and was not prepared to subscribe blindly to Douglas' program for western development. John Bell of Tennessee, the ranking Whig on the committee, had also registered his opposition. Arkansas' Robert W. Johnson, just appointed to the Senate to fill a vacancy, and Iowa's George W. Jones were the two remaining Democrats. Massachusetts' Edward Everett filled out the roster. Except for Everett, it was a western committee. Three of its six members were from slave states, while five of the nine members of the House territorial committee were from slave states, an ominous sign according to one Illinois paper. With far less than half the population, the slave states could control the committees in which questions concerning slavery were most likely to rise. "Rely on it, these committees have not been so packed without an object," the paper warned. "Watch and see." [1]

No time was lost picking up where the previous session had left off. On the first day, Iowa's Senator Dodge announced that he would introduce a bill for the organization of a territorial government in Nebraska, the same measure that had been defeated the March before. Gwin followed with a homestead bill and a bill for a donation of lands to California to aid in the construction of a telegraph and railroad line in that state. The latter, he told the Senate, was "the commencement of a great national road between the Pacific ocean and the Mississippi river"; the former stemmed from his pledge to Dodge that he would assist with the homestead bill once the railroad measure had passed. Before the session was a week old, a western "package," following the lines of Douglas' earlier program, had been laid before the Senate. On December 14, Dodge's Nebraska bill was referred to the Committee on Territories.

While Douglas' committee deliberated, the nation's press speculated on the result. Douglas' own statement, written three days after the bill's referral, that the principle established in the Compromise of 1850 should apply to Nebraska, was mirrored in the comments of numerous papers. In an editorial undoubtedly inspired (if not written) by Douglas, the *Register* urged that "the people of the different territories should be permitted to enjoy their own views as to their local and domestic affairs." The American people, by endorsing the 1850 measures, have manifested "a desire to permit the territories to lay the foundation of their state policy to suit themselves." Demagogues, northern and southern, would undoubtedly seek to revive the agitation over slavery, but, the paper hoped, the good sense and patriotism of the masses would prevail. "The territories should be admitted to exercise, as nearly as practicable, all the rights claimed by the states, and to adopt all such policy regulations and institutions as their wisdom may suggest." It was a concise summary of Douglas' views and a clear forecast of the stand he would take in the months ahead.

While many newspapers argued that Nebraska Territory should be organized on the basis of the Compromise of 1850, some addressed themselves specifically to the problem posed by the Missouri Compromise, the same problem which had bothered Nebraska's supporters earlier. Opinion seemed much more settled in December than it had been nine months before. The Compromise of 1850, it was asserted, had superceded the Missouri Compromise; it had even, in effect, repealed the earlier adjustment. Northern opposition to the extension of the Missouri Compromise line in 1850 had, in addition, amounted to a repudiation of the principle established thirty years before. The Compromise measures of 1850, one paper noted, "embraced one precedent which their framers doubtless intended should stand as a guide and landmark for all time. . . . A precedent thus laid down can scarcely be departed from, without peril in the future." The people of Nebraska should be allowed the same rights as those already granted to the people of Utah and New Mexico.

Douglas' committee, commented the Washington correspondent of the New York *Journal of Commerce,* had "a very delicate duty to perform." To revive the old Missouri controversy would be undesirable. "The committee think that they can get over it by placing the new territories [the correspondent was convinced that Douglas' bill would provide for as many as three new territories, instead of one] precisely on the same basis with the territories of New Mexico and Utah—that is neither excluding nor admitting slavery." Other observers concluded that the real test would not be on the question of the applicability of the Missouri Compromise, but rather would hinge on the validity of the 1850 Compromise. The Nebraska bill, predicted the New York *Herald*'s capital correspondent, would require "a distinct vote now either for or against the principles of that adjustment." Those who had loudly insisted on their "acquiescence in the Compromise measures" would now be compelled "to show their hands." On December 21, one week after Douglas' committee received the bill, Georgia's Whig Senator Dawson reported that the organization of Nebraska Territory would include the repeal of "the Missouri restriction." The issue, he thought, was intimately tied with Democratic factionalism in the northern states and with the administration's effort to unite the party on the Baltimore platform and its endorsement of the Compromise of 1850. The quarrel, Dawson suggested, "will commence at the North." Another southern Whig, John Bell, suggested that the movement was related to Pierce's patronage policy, to divert attention from the fact that appointments had been given to freesoilers.

Among northerners who saw the organization of Nebraska as merely a further affirmation of the Compromise of 1850, there was little apprehension that the area of slavery would actually be enlarged. As in Utah and New Mexico, slavery would be effectively excluded from Nebraska by natural forces—the soil, climate, and "the necessary pursuits of the people." Douglas shared this view and was to argue it forcefully. Furthermore, to Douglas, Nebraska Territory was not an isolated question, but was rather part of a larger program for western development which he had been urging for many years. The construction of one or more Pacific railroads would bring commerce to the prairies and encourage the building of towns, and a free homestead policy would attract settlement by small independent farmers; there was little danger, Douglas believed, that slavery could at the same time be successfully extended to the new territory. That Douglas' views were not accepted by all who looked to the precedent of the 1850 Compromise was evident during the weeks of speculation that followed the opening of Congress. Concealed in the press' comments was a basic ambiguity concerning the interpretation of the Utah and New Mexico acts. Douglas and his followers spoke of the territories assuming the rights of states and determining the nature of their own institutions as territories, while others saw in the Compromise acts only the right to decide the slavery question when a territory became a state. It was an ambiguity that was to assume more serious proportions later.[2]

ii

Douglas reported his Nebraska bill from the territorial committee on January 4. It differed markedly from the bill Dodge had introduced earlier in the session, which had been referred to the committee three weeks before. In fact, for all practical purposes, it was a different bill. Accompanying the measure was a detailed committee report.

As anticipated, and as Douglas had already hinted, the bill was couched in the language of the Compromise of 1850. That this should be so seemed logical in the climate of opinion that existed at the time. Both northern and southern newspapers had proposed it, as had those western elements who insisted that the area west of Missouri and Iowa be organized. Senator Atchison, representing this frontier opinion, had warned that no bill would receive his sanction that did not recognize the principle of the 1850 measures. The fate of the Nebraska bill in the previous session had revealed the need for southern support. Douglas was the author of the Utah and New Mexico acts and had defended their provisions not merely as an expedient for settling the question of slavery in the Mexican cession, but as a new basis for territorial organization generally.

The boundaries of the proposed territory were vastly enlarged, extending from the parallel of 36°30′ to the northern limit of the United States, at the forty-ninth parallel. In the phraseology of the Utah and New Mexico acts, the bill provided that "when admitted as a state or states, the said territory, or any portion of the same, shall be received into the Union, with or without slavery, as their constitution may prescribe at the time of their admission." The bill further provided that the legislative power of the territory should extend to all rightful subjects of legislation, consistent with the Constitution; certain enumerated actions were exempted from this grant of power, but slavery was not among them. Appeals to the Supreme Court of the United States in cases involving "title to slaves" or "questions of personal freedom" were allowed, again following the 1850 example, and the provisions of the Fugitive Slave Act were extended to the territory.

The report which Douglas submitted with the bill was little more than an elaboration of the relationship between the Nebraska bill and the Compromise of 1850. The committee altered Dodge's measure in order that the terms of the Compromise might be "affirmed and carried into practical operation within the limits of the new Territory." Douglas' views on the significance of the Utah and New Mexico acts were given extended treatment. Those acts "were intended to have a far more comprehensive and enduring effect than the mere adjustment of the difficulties arising out of the recent acquisition of Mexican territory. They were designed to establish certain great principles, which would not only furnish adequate remedies for existing evils, but, in all time to come, avoid the perils of a similar agitation, by withdrawing the question of slavery from the halls of Congress and the political arena, and committing it to the arbitrament of those who were immediately interested in, and alone responsible for its consequences." Nebraska, moreover, "occupies the same relative position to the slavery question, as did New Mexico and Utah, when these territories were organized." Mexican law presumably prohibited slavery in New Mexico and Utah, while the Missouri Compromise similarly prohibited slavery in Nebraska. Both, however, were disputed points. The Missouri Compromise, insofar as it sought to prescribe the domestic institutions of the territories, was regarded by some as unconstitutional. Since Congress had refrained from deciding the question of the validity of Mexican law in the earlier instance, "so your committee are not prepared now to recommend a departure from the course pursued on that memorable occasion, either by affirming or repealing the 8th section of the Missouri act." [3]

Douglas' bill established popular sovereignty in the proposed territory, while skirting the problem of the Missouri Compromise. The territorial legislature presumably would have the power to legislate with regard to slavery, and the people of the territory would be free to enter the Union as a state "with or without slavery." The Missouri Compromise was neither repealed nor abrogated; it was simply ignored. Like Mexican law in the southwest, the Missouri Compromise would remain in effect in Nebraska until superseded by territorial legislation, as Douglas clearly intended, from the analogy in his report. Without resorting to direct repeal, Seward noted, Douglas had gone "as far as the Democrats dare, toward abolishing that provision of the Missouri Compromise which devoted all the new regions purchased from France, north of the line of 36°30′, to freedom." In doing so, the responsibility was primarily Douglas'. "It was written by myself," he later recalled, "at my own house, with no man present." President Pierce was not consulted, nor did the territorial committee play an important part in shaping the bill. Two members had failed to attend the committee sessions. Bell was looking after his mining interests in Kentucky, and Houston, who had just arrived in Washington, told Douglas that "he might report anything if he would only put in the Compromise of 1850." Everett dissented from the bill and the report.[4]

While the responsibility for the bill's terminology belonged to Douglas, there were others in the Senate who felt a keen interest in the manner in which it would dispose of the slavery restriction. Over eighteen months later, Atchison boasted that he had inspired the wording of Douglas' bill. He recalled having informed Douglas of his desire to assume the chairmanship of the Committee on Territories so that he might report a bill that would remove the slavery exclusion from Nebraska. According to his account, Douglas asked for twenty-four hours to consider the matter; if, at the end of that time, he could not prepare a bill satisfactory to Atchison he would resign his post and support Atchison's appointment to it. Douglas vigorously denied the Missourian's allegations at the time, and Atchison later retracted his statement. It is undeniable, however, that Douglas was under strong pressure from the Missouri Senator, whose political future seemed to rest in part on the shape of Douglas' bill. Aligned with Atchison were three of the most powerful members of the Senate, all from slave states and all chairmen of principal committees—Mason and Hunter of Virginia and South Carolina's Butler. The four Senators lived together, forming what was known as the "F Street Mess." Douglas knew that southern votes were essential to the passage of his bill, and he was acutely aware that these four Senators could deliver the needed support. His bill was in their hands, and its terms must meet their approval. Finally, Douglas had secured the prior endorsement of Senator Bright and one other northwestern Senator, probably Cass, before reporting his bill to the Senate.[5]

The role of these Senators in determining the form of the Nebraska bill has often been exaggerated. Their importance lay principally in developing a strategy for the measure's passage. Its provisions conformed to Douglas' well-known convictions, and it was a logical extension of his western program. By basing his bill on the Compromise of 1850 and by supplanting the Missouri Compromise without actually repealing it, he was acting characteristically, attempting to achieve his ends with a minimum of upset and agitation. His last-minute effort on behalf of Nebraska's organization, without popular sovereignty, in March 1853, and his introduction of the Nebraska bill, with popular sovereignty, in January 1854, reflect both his conviction that the slavery issue was secondary to other more important questions and his often frenzied, pragmatic efforts to secure the passage of western legislation. In the perspective of his developing support for territorial self-government, it is his effort in March 1853 that stands as the aberration, dictated by the importance of the legislation and by the shortness of time.

On January 7, the Nebraska bill was printed in the Washington *Sentinel.* Three days later it was printed again, but with an added section that had, it was noted, been omitted from the earlier draft because of a "clerical error." This new section, section twenty-one, merely incorporated into the bill the concluding sections of Douglas' report, in almost the precise wording, specifying the relationship between the bill and the territorial acts of the Compromise of 1850 and rendering even more explicit the principle of popular sovereignty. "In order to avoid all misconstruction," the section read, "it is hereby declared to be the true intent and meaning of this act, so far as the question of slavery is concerned, to carry into practical operation the following propositions and principles, established" by the Compromise of 1850: all questions pertaining to slavery in the territories were to be left to the decision of the people residing therein; all cases involving title to slaves and questions of personal freedom were to be adjudicated in the local courts, with the right of appeal to the Supreme Court; and the provisions of the Fugitive Slave Act were to be extended to the territories. The new section was clearly not a part of the original bill, but whether it was indeed a "clerical error" or whether it was added as an afterthought it is not possible to determine. Douglas contended that the copyist had inadvertently omitted the section from the version that was submitted to the Senate. In any case, it did not alter the nature of the bill, although some later commentators have argued (unpersuasively) that the added section gave the bill "an entirely new meaning." Section twenty-one merely repeated the points made in Douglas' report and recapitulated provisions that were already in the bill. In doing so it gave them added emphasis.[6]

Those who first responded to Douglas' bill emphasized its relation to the Compromise of 1850 and regarded it in part as a political maneuver to test the fidelity of Democrats to the principles of the Baltimore platform. As a move toward establishing a new party orthodoxy, the bill was seen as a direct challenge to those freesoilers who had benefited from Pierce's patronage, a means for testing the President's policy of including all elements of the party in his program. It seemed to emerge from the party's own particular problems. One of Pierce's close friends applauded Douglas' bill for the salutary effect it would have on the party. "I am . . . glad," wrote Edmund Burke to Douglas, "that there is now a measure before Congress which will test the sincerity of the late Free soil Democrats whom Gen. Pierce has taken to his bosom." Burke was also pleased that Douglas was "not disposed to treat the principles of the late Compromise Acts, as nullities,—mere expedients to escape the peril of the moment,—but as practical things to be sacredly observed whenever occasions arise which demand their practical application." Burke's comments were echoed in the press. Douglas, declared the *Union,* had presented "a practical test of the sincerity of the covenant entered into by the democratic party at Baltimore." The bill was an encouraging sign that the administration would recognize none as orthodox Democrats who did not faithfully abide by the Compromise of 1850 as a final settlement of the slavery issue. It was intended, noted the *New-York Tribune,* "to try the potentiality of Governmental power and patronage." [7]

For all the reports of its political purposes, the bill was immediately recognized as having a much more serious import. In spite of the care with which Douglas worded both the bill and his report, and in spite of his rather naïve intent to avoid discussion of the Missouri Compromise, he was denounced for his breach, "whether insidious or hesitant, or open and flagrant," of the solemn compact between the north and south. The Nebraska bill effectively repealed the Missouri Compromise. Douglas, "down on his marrow bones at the feet of slavery," was boldly attempting to convert free into slave territory. He was charged with subscribing to a "higher law" by which the 1850 measures took precedence over the "salutary restriction" on slavery's expansion. Senator Chase, noting that not all southerners were eager for the bill, commented that Douglas had "outSouthernized the South" in his eagerness, dragging "the timid & irresolute administration along with him."

Others sprang to Douglas' defense. The people of Nebraska were sim-

ply guaranteed the same right the people of every other state had enjoyed, "the right to control and designate their own social institutions."
Douglas, it was recalled, had sought the extension of the Missouri Compromise line earlier, "but the organs which now insist upon the inviolability of that compromise denounced his proposition as a base truckling
to the slave power." The principle of the Missouri Compromise had already been repudiated. The south had been excluded from that part of
California lying south of 36°30', and Douglas was merely changing the
"saddle to the other horse" by opening the area north of 36°30' to
southerners. Douglas' argument that the measures of 1850 had established a new pattern for territorial organization received favorable endorsement. His report defined the plan "upon which all Territories shall
be hereafter organized. It is, simply, to leave all matters of territorial
legislation to the people of the Territories themselves. When Congress
has organized a Territory—erected and set in motion the machinery
of its government—its duties have been performed and its legitimate
powers exhausted. Thenceforth the people are their own rulers in respect
to all their domestic affairs, and interference from any other power is
anti-democratic and arbitrary." In the few days that followed the bill's
introduction, the Senate debated most of the arguments that would
shake the nation in the months to come.[8]

Douglas was disturbed at the interjection of the Missouri Compromise
into the discussion and by the widespread assumption that his bill, while
not saying so explicitly, would in fact accomplish its repeal. Equally
disturbing was a growing conviction among some southerners that
Douglas, by not being more explicit, had produced doubts that the Missouri restriction would actually be overridden. One group maintained
that his bill would repeal the Compromise; the other argued that it
would not. It was not the first time that he was caught between the two
sectional extremes. To complicate matters further, some in both north
and south discovered that the Compromise of 1850, far from replacing
the Missouri Compromise, had reinforced it. A clause in the New Mexico bill expressly upheld the validity of that portion of the joint resolution annexing Texas which recognized the Missouri Compromise. Although the clause had been written by Mason, its discovery was said to
have increased southern solicitude for a direct repeal of the 1820 Compromise.

Douglas had hoped to find an accommodation between the Missouri
Compromise and popular sovereignty, without completely overturning

the former. Early in the session, he remarked to Everett that "no man was so wild as to think of repealing the Missouri Compromise." But while Douglas searched for a middle ground, others did not. On the day after Douglas made his report, a correspondent of *The New York Times* noted that "ultra Southerners" found the bill unsatisfactory, and that they were "concocting another one." On January 16, Kentucky's Whig Senator Archibald Dixon proposed an amendment that the Missouri Compromise "shall not be so construed as to apply to the Territory contemplated by this act, or to any other Territory of the United States; but that the citizens of the several States or Territories shall be at liberty to take and hold their slaves within any of the Territories of the United States, or of the States to be formed therefrom." Not to be outdone, Charles Sumner countered with a second amendment on the following day. Nothing in the bill, Sumner proposed, "shall be construed to abrogate or in any way contravene" the Missouri Compromise. The issue which Douglas had hoped to keep in the background thus emerged as the dominant question in the proposed legislation.[9]

Dixon's move took Douglas by surprise, but it was not wholly without warning. Two days before, the Washington *Sentinel* had urged that that portion of the Missouri Compromise relating to slavery in Nebraska be *"directly and positively repealed"* so as to remove all doubt as to the applicability of the 1850 Compromise to the new territory. The *Sentinel* proposed that "some distinguished statesman like General Cass" offer such an amendment; if Cass would do so, the editor was confident that Douglas would sustain him. Cass was apparently approached later (by whom it is not clear), but he rejected the suggestion. Although he was reported to have declared his intention of voting for the repeal if it should be introduced, Cass was also said to be satisfied with Douglas' bill as it was originally submitted. On January 15, the *New-York Tribune*'s Washington correspondent predicted that Douglas himself would offer an amendment that would repeal the Missouri Compromise directly and absolutely.[10]

Dixon, however, made the first move. Convinced that Douglas' bill would exclude southern slaveholders from Nebraska, he dictated his amendment to his wife on the evening of January 15. Before he introduced it the next day, he showed it to his friend and fellow-Whig, Tennessee's James C. Jones, who promised his support. As soon as the amendment had been presented, the startled Douglas went to Dixon's seat to protest it. He interpreted Dixon's statement as affirmatively legis-

lating slavery into the territories of the United States, a move he could
not accept. His object, he reminded the Kentucky Senator, was neither
to legislate slavery into the territories nor to legislate it out of them, but
to leave the people free to do as they pleased on the question, as well as
on other matters which affected their interests. He pleaded with Dixon
not to do anything that would call the Compromise of 1850 into question or weaken it before the country. Dixon assured him that he too was
committed to the 1850 measures and denied that he had any intention
of embarrassing the author of the Nebraska bill. The amendment created immediate alarm in the ranks of northern Democrats, who thought
it was a deliberate maneuver by a Whig to destroy the unity of the
Democratic party. Lending some credence to this fear were later claims
that the suggestion to repeal the Missouri Compromise was strongly
pushed by none other than William H. Seward. Anxious to make Douglas' bill as objectionable as possible to northern antislavery sentiment,
Seward, who was on close terms with both Dixon and Jones, saw political advantage in forcing a commitment to repeal on the Democratic
party. Seward himself made that claim, although Dixon's wife later
could not recall his part in the matter.[11]

Douglas hesitated to accept any such modification of his bill. Dixon
admitted that he did not think his amendment would succeed, but other
southerners were immediately attracted to the possibility. Southern Democrats, unwilling to concede the movement for repeal to Whigs, began
to exert pressure on Douglas. On January 18, Douglas asked Dixon to
ride with him in his carriage in order that they might discuss the situation without interruption. Persuaded that the question of repeal could no
longer be ignored, sensitive to the antislavery charges that his bill had
in effect already dealt the Missouri Compromise a deathblow, and aware
of the mounting pressure from southerners, without whose votes Nebraska could not be organized, he asked Dixon for permission to take
charge of the amendment in order to "engraft it" on the Nebraska bill.
He anticipated, as he told Dixon, "much stir and commotion in the free
States," but he undoubtedly preferred that the repeal be accomplished
under his direction and in his own way than to leave it to the southern
slave interest.[12]

In the meantime, pressure to repeal the Missouri Compromise came
from another direction. Early in January, Alabama's Philip Phillips, who
was serving his first term in the House of Representatives, and was a
member of the House Committee on Teritories, arrived at the same con-

clusion as Dixon, that the terms of the Nebraska bill were a "delusion" as long as the Missouri Compromise was not repealed. Phillips communicated his concern to Hunter, who in turn passed it on to Atchison. Atchison, surprised at the interpretation Phillips placed on the bill, arranged a conference with Douglas, and the three men discussed the matter further. Douglas, according to Phillips' later account, expressed his belief that the Nebraska bill had repealed the slavery restriction, but he was nonetheless impressed with Phillips' arguments. At Douglas' request, Phillips drafted an amendment that would receive the endorsement of the south. Phillips' proposition was less strongly worded than Dixon's and actually gave Douglas' popular sovereignty an added boost: "That the people of the Territory through their Territorial legislature may legislate upon the subject of slavery in any manner they may think proper not inconsistent with the Constitution of the United States, and all laws or parts of laws inconsistent with this authority or right shall, from and after the passage of this act, become inoperative, void and of no force and effect." Phillips' version was still not the direct repeal of the Missouri Compromise desired by some, and, by recognizing the power of the territorial legislature to determine the question of slavery, it ran counter to the old Calhoun argument that the question had to be left open until the territory moved into statehood. In spite of this, the statement was accepted by the members of the "F Street Mess"— Atchison, Hunter, Mason, and Butler—when he submitted it to them for their approval. Persuaded that slavery could never be established in the "high latitude" of Nebraska Territory, Phillips conceded that he was actuated by what he then regarded as a *theoretical right.*[13]

With the amendments of both Dixon and Phillips in hand, Douglas next sought the backing of the Pierce administration. He had no desire to bear the responsibility alone. Time grew dangerously short, for on January 17 Douglas gave notice that he would ask the Senate to take up the Nebraska bill on the following Monday, January 23. Pierce, who had previously given little thought to Douglas' bill, was not happy with the movement to repeal the Missouri Compromise. Cass had personally urged the President to oppose Dixon's amendment in the interest of preserving party harmony, especially in the north. With Marcy seconding Cass' warnings, Pierce assured Douglas that he would not support the move. Taking the cue, the Washington *Union,* on January 20, denounced both the Dixon and Sumner amendments as a Whig abolitionist plot to reopen the slavery agitation, and it reiterated its approval of Douglas' bill.

The movement for repeal, however, had gathered too much momentum to be so easily dismissed by the President. On January 21 Pierce called his cabinet together to discuss it further. Jefferson Davis, Secretary of War, and Navy Secretary James C. Dobbin were said to have favored Dixon's amendment, while Marcy and others preferred Douglas' original wording. The decision was made to prepare still another amendment to meet the increasing pressure for repeal without, at the same time, endangering the unity of the party. The cabinet proposal, which was based on the conviction of both Pierce and Attorney General Caleb Cushing that the Missouri Compromise was unconstitutional and would certainly be declared so by the Supreme Court, avoided direct repeal. It declared that "the rights of persons and property shall be subject only to the restrictions and limitations imposed by the Constitution of the United States and the acts giving governments, to be adjusted by a decision of the Supreme Court of the United States." The draft, awkward and vague in its wording, was carried by John C. Breckinridge to Douglas and the members of Atchison's mess. Douglas accepted it, but it was rejected by the latter. The cabinet action, however, revealed not only an administration commitment to the idea of repeal, but also a deep concern over its proper wording.[14]

Time was now of the essence. Only one day remained, Sunday, January 22, before the Nebraska bill would be taken up, and Douglas had to act quickly. Dixon's amendment was not acceptable to him. His task was to discover a form for repeal that would satisfy not only himself but also the southern leaders and the President. It was not an easy combination to please. Knowing that the President transacted no business on the Sabbath, Douglas sought the aid of Davis. Pierce was persuaded to see Douglas, and later in the day he received the Illinois Senator, accompanied by Atchison, Mason, Hunter, Breckinridge, Phillips, and some others. Atchison and Douglas first talked with the President alone; when the rest of the party joined them in the library, Phillips was struck by the "cold formality which seemed to prevail." It was a moment of crisis for Pierce. Confronted by some of Congress' most powerful members, he agreed to the direct repeal of the Missouri Compromise, but not without a cautious reminder of the seriousness of their undertaking. Douglas insisted that he express his assent in writing. With the help of the group, Pierce drafted a statement to the effect that the Missouri Compromise, having been superseded by the principles of the Compromise of 1850, was inoperative. The wording was still not as strong as the southerners would have desired, and the word "repeal" was not employed, perhaps as a concession to Pierce, but the statement clearly followed the argument Douglas had made in his report. The result apparently owed much to Breckinridge, who had helped arrange the conference, for the Kentucky Congressman wrote a short time later that he "had more to do than any other man here, in putting it [the Kansas-Nebraska Act] in its present shape."

At the conclusion of the meeting, the President urged the group to see Marcy, but Marcy was not available. Later, the cabinet, including the hesitant Marcy, endorsed Pierce's action. The bill became an administration measure and a party test. Almost as if to anticipate the events of the twenty-second, the *Union* shifted its ground and on that morning strongly urged a more direct repeal.[15]

On January 23, Douglas astounded the Senate by bringing forward a completely new bill. The amendment dealing with the Missouri Compromise which had been agreed upon in the White House conference, a meeting of which few people in Washington had any knowledge, was by no means the only surprise. Instead of providing for the organization of a single territory, two new territories were proposed, Kansas and Nebraska. The southern boundary of Kansas Territory was moved northward, from 36°30' to the thirty-seventh parallel, in order that the lands of the Cherokee nation not be divided. The application of the Fugitive Slave Act to the new territories was rendered more stringent, and the twenty-first section of the original bill (the "clerical error"), describing the manner in which the terms of the Compromise of 1850 were to be carried into practical operation, was dropped. Finally, and most importantly, Douglas incorporated the draft he had carried with him from the White House. To the section that declared "that the Constitution, and all laws of the United States which are not locally inapplicable, shall have the same force and effect within the said Territory as elsewhere in the United States" he now added the words, "Except the eighth section of the act preparatory to the admission of Missouri into the Union, approved March 6, 1820, which was superseded by the principles of the legislation of 1850, commonly called the compromise measures, and is declared inoperative."

Although Douglas had called the members of his territorial committee together in a hurried meeting earlier in the day, they were given little opportunity to discuss the new bill. Everett was able to give it only a hasty examination. John Bell, who complained that he barely had time to glance over its provisions, agreed to the inclusion of the section on the Missouri Compromise, but only after reserving the privilege of opposing the bill's passage if he felt obliged to do so. Another member, Arkansas' Senator Johnson, apparently had not been present, for he queried Douglas later in the day on the floor of the Senate concerning the shape of the new bill. Yet in presenting the bill, Douglas described it as a committee recommendation. The correspondent of a Philadelphia newspaper reported that the measure had been agreed upon by both the Senate and House territorial committees, and that Richardson, chairman of the House Committee, would soon introduce an identical bill into the House of Representatives. Both Bright and Cass, he wrote, had approved of the changes, and he denied that the section on the Missouri Compromise had resulted from a conference with the administration. (The news of the Sunday meeting had not yet leaked out.) It is unlikely that the bill had been so thoroughly cleared before its introduction. Certainly the Senate committee had not been kept fully informed, and of the House committee, probably only Richardson and Phillips were aware of all the changes. Cass, who had earlier urged the President to resist direct repeal, had not been included, for on the day Douglas presented the bill Cass complained to Chase that he was not consulted and "was decidedly against the renewal of the agitation." At the same time, however, he indicated that he would support the substitute.[16]

While the new section on the Missouri Compromise was not anticipated, the other changes in the original measure were. The change in the southern boundary to prevent the splitting of the Cherokee lands had been suggested by the chairman of the Committee on Indian Affairs, William Sebastian of Arkansas. The division of the area into two territories was not sudden; in fact, it had already been discussed in some detail. As early as December there were rumors that Douglas' committee would report a bill for three new territories, Kansas, Nebraska, and Cherokee. The project was discussed at the time at Douglas' house, but the idea of a third territory west of Arkansas was given up, primarily, it was said, because "certain parties of influence" would not agree to disturbing the Indians in that area. The notion that two territories should be organized instead of one, however, had strong western support, and it persisted. The unofficial agents elected by the settlers in Nebraska and sent to Washington to push for a territorial government petitioned for it, and elements in Iowa particularly regarded it as vital to their own local interests. Iowa's Senators Dodge and Jones (Jones was a member of Douglas' committee) pressed for a division of Nebraska into two territories. Dodge pointed out that with a single territory, "the seat of government and leading thoroughfares must have fallen south of Iowa." It is possible also that Douglas regarded two territories as essential to the promotion of both a central and a northern Pacific railroad route. When he presented his new bill, Douglas told the Senate that both the Iowa and Missouri delegations had agreed that two territories were better than one. The charge made by the bill's antislavery opponents that Douglas made the change as a concession to the south was without foundation.

Douglas preferred to take up his new bill for consideration immediately, but he agreed to postpone it until the next day in order that it might be printed and studied by the Senate. When he brought it up on January 24, he was further importuned to delay its consideration. Douglas protested that any additional posponement might jeopardize the legislation. "I find it generally to be the case with my territorial bills," he told the Senate, "that if I do not get them acted on early in the session they are crowded over by other business at the end of the session, and are always postponed for want of time." In deference to the wishes of several Senators, however, he agreed that the bill should not be brought up before Monday, January 30.[17]

The new bill was not as much of a jolt to the Senators as many implied. After the introduction of Dixon's amendment, a rewording of the measure appeared quite probable. Douglas' reluctance to interject the question of the Missouri Compromise directly into the discussion was tempered by the fact that his antislavery opponents had already decided that his original bill would repeal the 1820 agreement. There was no way to avoid the controversy in any case. This, plus the pressure exerted on him by the small group of southern Senators, overcame his hesitation. In his presentation on January 23, he passed over the new wording as merely clarifying and making more specific one of the "delicate questions" in the original measure. He took comfort in the fact that his principle of popular sovereignty remained undisturbed in the bill. The provision enabling the territorial legislatures to deal with the slavery question had been retained, and whether the Missouri Compromise was repealed directly or not did not alter its force. He knew, as he suggested to Dixon, that direct repeal would arouse a storm of protest, but he was prepared to face it.

iii

The storm was not long in breaking. On the day Douglas agreed to the bill's postponement, January 24, the *National Era,* Washington's abolitionist organ, published a long and strongly worded protest against the Nebraska Act, under the headline, "The Appeal of the Independent Democrats in Congress to the People of the United States." The protest was the work of several men, but Ohio's Senator Salmon P. Chase assumed primary responsibility for it. Representative Joshua R. Giddings of Ohio had penned a preliminary draft, but Chase had revised and rewritten it. Gerrit Smith, Congressman from New York, and Charles Sumner made additional verbal changes, The document was signed by Chase, Giddings, Smith, and Sumner, along with Edward Wade of Ohio and Alexander De Witt of Massachusetts, all men noted for their abolitionist views. That the protest had been several days in preparation and that it was completed before the introduction of Douglas' substitute bill was further indication that the new statement on the Missouri Compromise had not altered the opposition's stance. *The New York Times* correspondent alluded to it in his dispatch of January 18; when it appeared in the *National Era,* it bore the date of January 22, the same Sunday on which Douglas' conference with Pierce took place. Chase later boasted that the "Appeal" was "the *most valuable* of my works." [18]

The protest pulled no punches. Douglas' bill (the original January 4 version) was arraigned "as a gross violation of a sacred pledge; as a criminal betrayal of precious rights; as part and parcel of an atrocious plot to exclude from a vast unoccupied region immigrants from the Old World, and free laborers from our own States, and convert it into a dreary region of despotism, inhabited by masters and slaves." All of the unorganized territory of the United States would be opened to the "ingress of slavery." The consequences of this "bold scheme against American liberty" were painted in the bleakest colors. The settlement and cultivation of the territory would be retarded, the Pacific railroad rendered useless, the homestead law worthless. "The blight of slavery will cover the land." The whole country would be subjugated "to the yoke of a slaveholding despotism." "Shall a plot against humanity and democracy so monstrous, and so dangerous to the interests of liberty throughout the world, be permitted to succeed?" Appended to the "Appeal" was a note added after Douglas' substitute bill was introduced, branding the amendment dealing with the Missouri Compromise as "a manifest falsification of the truth of history." That the Compromise of 1850 should have superseded the Missouri Compromise was a "sheer afterthought." In any case, it was noted sarcastically, to declare the Compromise inoperative was "a most discreditable way" of achieving its repeal.

Douglas received the "Appeal" with anger and deep indignation. On the day of its publication, he exploded in a conversation with the son of his old friend Murray McConnel. Pacing nervously back and forth, alternately puffing and chewing a succession of cigars to shreds, he expressed his resentment at the vilification of his motives. "I am not pro-slavery," he was reported to have said. "I think it a curse beyond computation, to both white and black." But the only power that could destroy slavery "is the sword, and if the sword is once drawn no one can see the end." He was, he declared, unwilling to violate the Constitution to end slavery, for "to violate it for one purpose will lead to violating it for other purposes." The "integrity of this political Union," he added, was "worth more to humanity than the whole black race." He recounted his reluctance to accept a direct repeal of the Missouri Compromise in his bill and expressed surprise that the move had come from the south. The repeal of the Compromise, he believed, would be "a step toward freedom," for slavery could no longer "crouch behind a line which Freedom is cut off from crossing." If Douglas' words were not exactly as McConnel recalled them (for the conversation was not recorded until many years later), there is no reason to suspect the sentiment.[19]

Douglas saved his formal reply to the "Appeal" for the opening of debate on the Kansas-Nebraska bill on January 30. His remarks drew a capacity crowd to the Senate chamber; the galleries were packed, as was the space on the floor behind the Senators. So many Congressmen came to listen that the House of Representatives was left without a quorum. Obviously angered, and speaking in a state of great excitement, Douglas lashed out at those who had impugned his motives. His statements were reported as violent, abusive, and vulgar, with an "overgorge of slang phrases." He "lost his temper before he began," commented one correspondent. It was necessary, wrote another, to hear and see "his defiant tone and pugnacious attitudinization" in order to appreciate "the terrific tornado raging within him." On several occasions, Chase sought to interrupt the flow of words with explanations of his own, but Douglas, with intense feeling, refused to yield the floor. "I will yield the floor to no Abolitionist," he exclaimed. The extremity of his language aroused such dismay among those who listened that Douglas, in cooler afterthought, deleted many of the epithets from the published version of his speech. In spite of its caustic character, the effort was judged to be a powerful one and its arguments overwhelming.

Douglas charged the authors of the "Appeal," whom he referred to throughout as the "Abolition confederates," with having perpetrated a "base falsehood" in their protest. He expressed his own sense of betrayal, recalling that Chase, "with a smiling face and the appearance of friendship," had appealed for a postponement of debate on the ground that he had not yet familiarized himself with the bill. "Little did I suppose at the time that I granted that act of courtesy," Douglas remarked, that Chase and his compatriots had published a document "in which they arraigned me as having been guilty of a criminal betrayal of my trust," of bad faith, and of plotting against the cause of free government. While other Senators were attending divine worship, they had been "assembled in secret conclave," devoting the Sabbath to their own conspiratorial and deceitful purposes.

In his defense of the bill, Douglas employed arguments that would be heard many times in the ensuing weeks. The Missouri Compromise, he told the Senate, had not simply been an expedient solution for an immediate problem; it had established a "great principle," a dividing line between free and slave territory that would be extended and renewed for each additional acquisition of land. With this understanding, Douglas recalled, he had inserted the Compromise in the joint resolution for the annexation of Texas in 1845, and again, in 1848, he had sought extension of the line to the Pacific Ocean. On the latter occasion, however, his efforts were defeated—defeated "by northern votes, with Free Soil proclivities." This, he insisted, was "the first time that the principles of the Missouri Compromise were ever abandoned." This defeat "created the necessity for making a new compromise in 1850." The idea of a geographical line separating freedom from slavery was abandoned, and in its place Congress substituted "a great principle of self-government, which would allow the people to do as they thought proper." These were the vital elements in Douglas' defense, then and later. Both the Missouri Compromise and the Compromise of 1850 had had greater application than simply to the specific area in question at the time. Each had been intended to establish a general principle that would determine future legislation regarding slavery in the nation's frontier regions. When the former was struck down, the necessity for the latter was created. Therefore, the principle of the 1850 Compromise measures had, by intent and by legal effect, superseded the Missouri Compromise.

If this principle were wrong, then his bill was wrong; if it were right, his bill was right. It was useless, he argued, to quibble over phraseology. Laws of Congress had never effectively excluded slavery from areas where people had not agreed with them. Slaves, for example, had been held in Illinois in defiance of the Northwest Ordinance. "Let all this quibbling about the Missouri Compromise, about the territory acquired from France, about the Act of 1820, be cast behind you; for the simple question is, will you allow the people to legislate for themselves upon the subject of slavery?" If the people wish slavery, they have a right to it; if they do not want it, it should not be forced upon them. Douglas was confident that when settlers moved into Kansas and Nebraska, when labor becomes plentiful, "it is worse than folly to think of its being a slave-holding country."

> I do not like, I never did like, the system of legislation on our part, by which a geographical line, in violation of the laws of nature, and climate, and soil, and of the laws of God, should be run to establish institutions for a people; yet, out of a regard for the peace and quiet of the country, out of respect for past pledges, and out of a desire to adhere faithfully to all compromises, I sustained the Missouri Compromise so long as it was in force, and advocated its extension to the Pacific. Now, when that has been abandoned, when it has been superseded, when a great principle of self-government has been substituted for it, I choose to cling to that principle, and abide in good faith, not only by the letter, but by the spirit of the last Compromise.

In conclusion, Douglas argued his own higher-law doctrine. He adhered, he said, not only to the Compromise of 1850, but also to "a higher and a more solemn obligation," to "that great fundamental principle of Democracy and free institutions which lies at the basis of our creed, and gives every political community the right to govern itself in obedience to the Constitution of the country." [20]

It was a dramatic opening for a debate that would soon engulf the nation. Chase, answering Douglas, contented himself with a few explanations regarding the preparation of the "Appeal" and asked for another postponement on the ground that he required still more time to study the bill. Douglas opposed further delays. Friends of the bill soon came to suspect that the opposition was deliberately seeking to put off the debate until a public reaction against the legislation could be developed. Their suspicions were well founded. One influential opponent of the bill advised a Senator, "The great object is delay. The bill must be kept in the Senate as long as possible. Meantime hell must be raised in the North. The ear of Congress is open. It must be deafened with a roar of condemnation." Earlier in the month, Benton had suggested to Seward that Douglas could yet be thwarted if the people in the north would demonstrate against the bill in public meetings and legislative resolutions. Chase, in the "Appeal," urged protest "against this enormous crime" by correspondence, through the press, in public meetings, and in legislative bodies. Douglas was charged with an eagerness to force the bill through the Senate, and, when he objected to the reading of the resolutions of an anti-Nebraska meeting in New York, he was accused of an unwillingness to hear any public judgment adverse to his measure.[21]

While Chase and his "Abolition confederates" had made up their minds on the bill, there were many who had not. Delay and postponement enabled them to gauge the direction of the wind before jumping into the fray. Douglas' bill produced an effect on some political nerves "much resembling the shock of a galvanic battery." Nowhere was the confusion more evident than among the Democratic factions in New York state. "We are in a fog here," wrote one New Yorker to Marcy, "what the Nebraska business means—what Douglass is driving at—whether the administration acts on compulsion or con amore." The *Union*'s announcement that fidelity to the Compromise of 1850—that is, to the principles of the Kansas-Nebraska bill—was an "essential requisite to democratic orthodoxy" placed the freesoil-leaning "softs" in a quandary. Recipients of presidential patronage, they had professed loyalty to Pierce. Now they were not so sure. John Van Buren, a leader of the Barnburners, was alternately declared to be a supporter and an opponent of Douglas' bill; in mid-February he confided his opposition to the bill to Marcy, but he did not state his position publicly. Members of both factions wrote to Douglas of their support, while New York's Governor Horatio Seymour reported that the bill had brought political affairs in the state "into a singular position." Others thought it to be a cunning and desperate scheme by Douglas to destroy Marcy's prospects for the presidency in 1856 by creating new divisions in New York's Democratic party.[22]

Uncertainty regarding the bill among politicians became painfully evident. Even the administration was said to be concerned lest the measure "make Douglas President." "No man really likes it," wrote a Washington correspondent, "and all are afraid of it." Some who supported the measure were convinced of its impropriety, but they feared to oppose it. Most agreed that a major result of the issue would be "to rally afresh the 'agitators' on both sides." The abolitionists would be given "a new fulcrum" upon which to "move the deepest prejudices of northern people." Seymour complained that the freesoil movement in the Democratic party, which except for the infusion of presidential patronage would have been dead a year before, would now be revitalized, and one editor predicted a "thorough reconstruction of the party organizations" for the next presidential contest. No better recipe for "reinflating Free Soilism and Abolitionism, which had collapsed all over the country," could have been chosen, observed Massachusetts' Robert Winthrop. If Douglas' bill should pass, Gideon Welles warned, "the floodgates would be open for a deluge of excitement." [23]

Like many of Douglas' critics, old Francis Preston Blair saw the hand of the southern slave power behind the bill. "The whole work was done by the Southern plotters," Blair wrote, "operating through their automaton whom they pull with a string and move with the ease of a supple-Jack." Blair was further convinced that the same "jobbers and plunderers," lobbyists and claims-agents, who had supported Douglas in 1852 were part of the conspiracy. Douglas' "ownership" of slaves in Mississippi was offered by others as an explanation for his action. "To engraft the gamecock airs of the Southern bully upon the Western demagogue," commented Greeley's *Tribune,* "is anything but an improvement." Even in the south reaction was mixed. Howell Cobb lauded Douglas' speech and hoped that all true Democrats would see their duty. "He who dallies is a dastard & he who doubts is damned." Not all southerners agreed. "The movement is madness and must result injuriously to the South," wrote a former Tennessee Congressman. Alabama's ex-Senator Jeremiah Clemens, suspicious of Douglas' interpretation of popular sovereignty, argued that the Kansas-Nebraska bill was not the boon many southerners believed it to be. "Squatter sovereignty," Clemens warned, would prove as effective in excluding slavery from the territories as the Wilmot Proviso. He was surprised that there should be opposition to the bill in the north. The ultra-southern *Charleston Mercury* issued a similar warning, and Alexander H. Stephens confided that the bill "is a bitter pill for Southern Fire eaters." [24]

iv

Debate on the Kansas-Nebraska bill in the Senate was characterized by persistent and frantic caucusing, impassioned and lofty oratory, and a flurry of amendments, some designed to improve the bill, others to delay it. Douglas was anxious that the bill be moved along to its final vote without distraction, and to this end the "friends" of the legislation met frequently to map their strategy. Both Whigs and Democrats, comprising a majority of the Senate, took part, a cooperation that did not pass unnoticed in the discussion. Although the meetings were not always harmonious, as Douglas sought to persuade the Senators that the measure should be pressed with a minimum of debate, there was a strong determination "to carry the bill as it stands on the slavery issue." [25] There was never any real doubt that the bill would pass the Senate. The debate changed few minds, merely affording a forum for the exposition of the principal arguments, both pro and con. Most of the addresses were published and widely circulated. Douglas took little part in the actual debate, delivering only the opening speech and the final summation. He played the role of floor manager for the bill, opposing distracting issues, objecting to delay, and moving postponement when it seemed in the best interest of the legislation. His counterpart for the opposition was Salmon P. Chase, Ohio's shrewd antislavery Senator.

The debate proceeded with regularity, a part of virtually every day in February being devoted to it. Many of the arguments were repetitious to the point of tedium, burdened with statistics and long quotations from a variety of authorities, spiced occasionally with sharp outbursts of personal rancor annd enmity. The legislative history of the Missouri Compromise was given an intensive review by both sides, and each dipped deeply into the early history of the Republic in order to demonstrate the policy of the "fathers" toward the slavery question. As Douglas had feared, the repeal of the Missouri Compromise became the principal focus of argument. Some Senators were led down distracting byways by the discussion. Dixon, defending his early effort to repeal the Compromise, sought to prove the inequality of the white and black races and recounted slavery's blessings to north and south alike. Jones of Tennessee and Badger of North Carolina (like Dixon, both Whigs) followed the cue, only to be answered by the abolitionist phalanx, Wade, Chase, and Sumner. Everett took a middle ground, pointing out that what had been done in three and a half centuries could not be undone quickly, and he looked forward to the day when America's Negroes would return to Africa as voluntary missionaries of civilization and Christianity. In answer to the argument that the Missouri Compromise represented a sacred and inviolable compact ("assumed beyond recall") between the sections, the bill's supporters pointed to the efforts of Chase and others to repeal the Fugitive Slave Act, likewise part of a sectional compromise. Both sides searched the debates on the Utah and New Mexico acts for evidence that they had established a precedent and a new principle for the organization of territories.

Critics of the Kansas-Nebraska bill argued that it would make of America's heartland—in Wade's words, "large as an empire . . . pure as nature . . . beautiful as the garden of God"—a dreary region inhabited by slaves and masters, discouraging the emigration of freemen and free labor. A large number of the debaters—Everett, Weller of California, Houston, Badger, Pettit of Indiana, Hunter, and Dodge— thought the issue abstract, agreeing implicitly with Douglas that slavery would never gain a foothold in the territories. Houston in fact declared that the Missouri Compromise protected the south from the extension of freedom. It was essential to the existence of slavery in the south, "a wall of fire to us" and a "guarantee for our institutions." Repeal the Compromise, he warned, and the south would soon be overwhelmed. Connecticut's Truman Smith, with whom Douglas had clashed before, declared that there were too many territories already and that there was no need for more, poking fun at Douglas' "remarkable fecundity in the line of Territories." [26]

One disturbing element in the debate was the ambiguity of the precise meaning of Douglas' popular sovereignty. Toombs read the measure as providing protection to all persons and property on an equal basis during the territorial period until such time as "this dormant sovereignty" sould become a state. Cass, on the other hand, argued Douglas' position, that the bill granted "full legislative power to these Territories over all questions of human concern, including slavery, unless restrained by the Constitution." The last phrase was the key one. Clayton warned the south that the bill in effect abandoned non-intervention by allowing the territorial legislature to legislate on the subject of slavery, and he feared that the effect of the bill would be to discourage slaveholders from taking their property to the new territories. Hunter hoped the issue would not be raised. Happily, he said, the bill was so worded that it could be maintained by both groups. If the territories should assume powers which were considered inconsistent with the Constitution, the courts would decide the question. But, Hunter conceded, "There is a difference of opinion amongst the friends of this measure as to the extent of the limits which the Constitution imposes upon the Territorial legislatures." The real issue behind the bill, as Chase and Cass pointed out, was one of constitutional interpretation. Did the Constitution of the United States allow the territories to exercise power of legislation over slavery?

To force a clarification of this ambiguity, Chase introduced his amendments to the bill. Dissatisfied with the vagueness of the repeal, Chase proposed a rewording that omitted all reference to the Compromise of 1850. "If you wish to break up the . . . Missouri compromise," he stated, "do it openly—do it boldly." Others, including Wade, Cass, and Stuart of Michigan, objected to the use of the word "supersedes" in Douglas' version. How, they asked, could an act of legislation be superseded by a principle? Douglas, after conferring with the bill's supporters, brought in his own amendment, which he thought would obviate the objections and at the same time reinforce popular sovereignty. Instead of declaring that the Missouri Compromise was "superseded" by the principles of the 1850 Compromise, Douglas now substituted the words: " [The Missouri Compromise,] being inconsistent with the principles of non-intervention by Congress with slavery in the States and Territories, as recognized by the legislation of 1850, commonly called the compromise measures, is hereby declared inoperative and void, it being the true intent and meaning of this act not to legislate slavery into any Territory or State, nor to exclude it therefrom; but to leave the people thereof perfectly free to form and regulate their domestic institutions in their own way, subject only to the Constitution of the United States." The new wording met Chase's desire for a more direct repeal, it carefully preserved the ambiguity regarding the power of the territorial legislatures over slavery, and the all-important reference to the Constitution, that is, to the courts, was retained. The last was clearly the bond that linked the supporters of the bill from both sections.[27]

Still Chase was not satisfied, and he persisted in his efforts to pin Douglas down. As soon as Douglas' amendment was accepted by the senate, Chase introduced a new change. To Douglas' words, he would add, "Under which the people of the Territory, through their appropriate representatives, may, if they see fit, prohibit the existence of slavery therein." The addition was in harmony with Douglas' interpretation of popular sovereignty, but its effect would be to split the supporters of the bill, since southerners denied that slavery could be tampered with during the territorial period. Chase's objection to the section as it stood, he said, was simply that it allowed opposite interpretations, it "carries a double aspect" and "leaves everything open to dispute." This was, however, precisely Douglas' intention. The further suggestion was offered that Chase's amendment be altered by adding after "prohibit" the words "or allow." Although this coincided exactly with Douglas' idea of popular sovereignty, he was quick to see that it would unite the antislavery and proslavery elements against the bill and thus defeat the organization of the territories. For this reason, Douglas defended the ambiguity and opposed Chase's attempts at clarification. The amendment was easily defeated, but Chase had made his point and southern apprehension over the bill's effects was by no means eased.[28]

One of the checks against territorial action on slavery, some southerners pointed out, was the provision for congressional review and disallowance of territorial legislation, traditional in territorial acts and included in the Kansas-Nebraska bill. This, too, came under fire. Both supporters and critics of the bill charged that congressional disallowance and the absolute veto of the territorial governor were inconsistent with popular sovereignty. Chase warned that he would move amendments to take care of these restrictions, but Douglas anticipated him by moving the appropriate amendments. Congressional disallowance was deleted and provisions added to give the territorial legislatures power to override the governors' vetoes. With the approval of these changes, the Kansas-Nebraska bill departed from the traditional pattern of territorial organization and moved significantly in the direction of self-government. Territorial settlers had long demanded the removal of these restrictions on their legislative actions, and Douglas, as their principal spokesman in Congress, had been sympathetic to their appeals. On the frontier, the slavery issue was much less real than the question of territorial self-government was. Douglas' insistence on popular sovereignty in Kansas and Nebraska, and his additional efforts to broaden the area of self-government, brought him strong support from the territories.

Chase made yet another effort to amend the bill by moving that all territorial officers be popularly elected, rather than appointed. Although Douglas was sympathetic to the change, he recognized Chase's move as an attempt to defeat the bill. Southerners became alarmed lest he accept this further extension of self-government, but Douglas had gone as far in this direction as he intended. The officers, he argued rather unconvincingly, were charged with the performance of national rather than territorial duties, and their popular election would be inappropriate.

Concern that the repeal of the Missouri Compromise would revive slavery in the two territories automatically, since that was the condition of the Louisiana Purchase before 1820, was eased by an amendment, proposed by Senator Badger and passed by the Senate, disclaiming any such effect. Of greater import was an amendment, introduced by Clayton, that would restrict the suffrage and the right to hold office to citizens of the United States. Clayton's proposal, reflecting the growing feeling against the foreign-born in the early 1850's, appealed especially to southerners, who numbered few immigrants among their constituents and who feared the power of their antislavery opinions if allowed to vote in territorial elections. The amendment narrowly passed, 23 to 21; all but one of the majority represented slave states and all of the opposition, including Douglas, came from free states.[29]

Anxious to terminate the debate and bring the bill to a vote, Douglas announced on February 24 that he intended to deliver his concluding argument on March 1, but his schedule proved to be overly optimistic. On March 2 the discussion entered its final stages. The tension was unrelieved. The exhaustion of the Senators took its toll as they became increasingly impatient and irascible, quick to take affront and magnifying small details into major issues. Insults were hurled and denied, and quarrels broke out even among the friends of the bill. Of the debate on that day Seward wrote, "It was a painful and disgraceful scene. Southern men were imperious, and Northern men abbetted them. Personalities disgraced the advocates of the bill. There is no longer any dignity or honor in serving our country in the Senate of the United States." There was, noted Everett, "on the part of many members evident excess in liquor," including one Senator who made himself obnoxious by continually interrupting the debate to make explanations.

After an overnight adjournment, debate resumed at 1 p.m. on March 3. Bell opened with a long speech opposing the bill, and a number of Senators followed with lengthy statements. The debate showed no signs of subsiding. Discouraged, Douglas offered to waive his summing up in the interest of time, but his offer was greeted by cries of "Oh, no; go on." At 11:30 p.m., he finally secured the floor. Despite the lateness of the hour, the galleries were thronged with visitors, and their frequent interruptions tested the patience of the Senate's presiding officer. Douglas' speech was an impressive intellectual and physical effort, lasting over three hours. His oratory had by this time become so well known that his major Senate speeches were considered events of some importance, although their popularity was sometimes due less to admiration of his ideas than to anticipation of his often sensational outbursts. Yet he had the reputation of being extremely thorough and "severely logical"; his mastery of the arguments, his almost total recall of past events and policies, and his originality of mind were the envy of many of his colleagues. "Not attractive nor plausible in delivery, not eloquent, and seldom entertaining," wrote a contemporary, "his oratory has few admirers, and has not heretofore been appreciated. . . . He seizes the great points of a subject, and these he presents without any attention to the impression they are likely to make upon an auditory, but only in reference to their bearings upon his argument, and the conclusions he wishes to establish."

Douglas had listened patiently to all the arguments against his bill and had received with equanimity the personal charges that had been hurled against him. He now replied in kind. The brunt of his attack fell on Seward and on the "trio of abolitionist senators." "His arrowy words were keen and burning, and kindled as they flew," commented one correspondent. "He showered upon them a perfect torrent of invective, argument, satire and ridicule." To the hostile *New-York Tribune,* Douglas' tone was "sneering" and "vulgar" and his "God damns" and "by Gods" were heard distinctly in the galleries. Everett, while conceding that Chase, Sumner, and Wade had given Douglas great provocation, thought the latter's replies to be "coarse and ungentlemanlike." Even so, the galleries frequently responded with applause, and some of the Senators "were scarcely less obstreperous," Senator Gwin pounding on the floor with his double-headed cane in delight at Douglas' remarks.[30]

Douglas responded first of all to the arguments of Bell and Houston, both of whom objected to the bill because of its alleged violation of Indian treaty rights. He pointed out that none of the tribes with which the government had treaty stipulations were embraced within the territories, and he reminded his critics that all of Congress' previous territorial bills had included Indians within their boundaries. If the policy toward Indians was to be altered it was not the business of the Committee on Territories to do so; that responsibility belonged to the Committee on Indian Affairs, with whom he had been in close communication throughout the formulation of the bill. In its provisions relating to the Indians, the measure followed the same policy as that which was in force in every one of the territories. To those who had urged that the organization of Kansas and Nebraska was unnecessary, Douglas reiterated the arguments he had made many times before. Emigrants to the Pacific coast required protection, and communication with the far west must be facilitated. All his earlier efforts to meet these needs, he recalled, had been defeated. Settlers had already moved into the area; whether or not they were legal inhabitants was a question which did not bother him. "It is enough for me that they are a part of our own people—that they are settled on the public domain—that the public interests would be promoted by throwing that public domain open to settlement, and that there is no good reason why the protection of law and the blessings of government should not be extended to them."

Douglas reserved his main thrust for a defense of the "great principle" contained in the bill. He had been censured because he had written and had introduced the measure, but as chairman of the territorial committee, he said, "I was not a volunteer in the transaction." Responsibility to the people of the territories and adherence to the legislation of 1850 which had supplanted congressional sovereignty with popular sovereignty dictated the terms of the Kansas-Nebraska bill. He denied that the repeal of the Missouri Compromise, with its "old exploded doctrine of congressional interference," was the main object of the bill. It was, he insisted, "a mere incident" in the recognition and establishment of popular sovereignty. His original bill had effectively nullified the Missouri Compromise because it was phrased in the same language as the 1850 acts. Later additions dealing with the Missouri Compromise, which Douglas had not initially thought necessary, were made "to avoid all misconstruction, and make the true intent of the act more explicit." "It is only for the purpose of carrying out this great fundamental principle of self-government that the bill renders the eighth section of the Missouri act inoperative and void."

To those who had charged him with being a northern man with southern principles, he replied that he had not brought forward popular sovereignty as either a northern or a southern man. "I have presented it especially as an act of justice to the people of those Territories, and of the States to be formed therefrom, now and in all time to come." The principle violates the rights of no state or territory, but "does equal and exact justice to the whole Union." He would have insisted on its inclusion in the unsuccessful Nebraska bill of the previous session had not lack of time persuaded him to press simply for the organization of the territory.

Popular sovereignty, he repeated, also had a broader significance, for he hoped that self-government for the territories would "destroy all sectional parties and sectional agitations." If the slavery question were withdrawn from Congress and committed "to the arbitrament of those who are immediately interested in and alone responsible for its consequences, there is nothing left out of which sectional parties can be organized." The peace, harmony, and perpetuity of the Union required it. The issue was closely related to his vision of national destiny. "You cannot fix bounds to the onward march of the great and growing country. You cannot fetter the limbs of the young giant. He will burst all your chains. He will expand, grow, and increase, and extend civilization, christianity and liberal principles. . . . You must provide for continuous lines of settlement from the Mississippi valley to the Pacific ocean. And in making this provision, you must decide upon what principles the Territories shall be organized; in other words, whether the people shall be allowed to regulate their domestic institutions in their own way . . . or whether the opposite doctrine of congressional interference is to prevail. Postpone it, if you will; but whenever you do act, this question must be met and decided."

Douglas' anger at the charges that had been leveled against him was obvious. His remarks were interspersed with personal retorts and slurs, especially against Seward, Sumner, and Chase. By focusing on the repeal of the Missouri Compromise, he shouted, they had diverted attention away from "this principle of self-government and constitutional right." With Seward he quarreled over whether the 1820 agreement was actually a compact, maintaining that a second compromise, made in 1821, had been necessitated by northern opposition, and pointing to New York's resolutions in 1820 against the admission of Missouri under its terms. His detailed review of the events of 1820 and 1821 moved the New York Senator to concede that "I have never had so much respect for him as I have to-night." Shifting his attack to Chase and Sumner, he reverted once again to the charges made in the "Appeal." Reminding the Senate that both Chase and Sumner had been elected by legislative coalitions in their respective states, Douglas boasted that "I did not obtain my seat in this body either by a corrupt bargain or a dishonorable coalition!" Both Senators were quick to reply to the affront. Chase later explained that he had not meant to impugn Douglas' motives in the "Appeal," but Douglas was unimpressed, suggesting that there seemed to be a wide difference between them as to the meaning of words.

"It is vain to attempt a description of this really great effort of the Illinois senator," commented the *Union* in a special Sunday edition brought out following the debate. "No one slept while *he* spoke." Even his friends were surprised at his "exhibition of logic and genius," and his opponents conceded its effectiveness. Years later, one of them recalled that Douglas' speech was "able, adroit, defiant, and denunciatory." [31]

Houston, noting that "this unusual night sitting" was without precedent, followed Douglas with a final plea to maintain the Missouri Compromise. "Stir not up *agitation!* Give us peace!" At five o'clock in the morning, after a continuous session of over seventeen hours, the vote on the Kansas-Nebraska bill was finally taken. The result demonstrated what had been known all along. The bill was approved by an overwhelming majority. Thirty-seven Senators voted in favor, fourteen against. Twenty-nine Democrats, fourteen from free states, voted with the majority; the eight affirmative Whig votes were all from the south. Five Democrats, seven Whigs, and the two Free-Soilers (Chase and Sumner) opposed the bill. Only two southerners, Bell and Houston, voted in the negative. The free states were almost evenly divided, fourteen for and twelve against. The Democratic party, though shaken, had maintained its discipline; it was the Whig party that had lost its unity. Seward, expecting the worst, moaned, "We have no longer any bond to Southern Whigs." The vote, commented the *Union,* fully established the nationality of the Democratic party and should quiet all doubts of the stability and perpetuity of the federal Union.[32]

The fight, however, was not yet over. From the beginning there had been doubts that the bill could be carried through the House of Representatives. Although the Democratic party held a majority, there was no assurance that it could be mobilized, even in the face of White House pressure. Most of the members represented free state constituencies and were decidedly more sensitive to the popular outcry against the measure than were the Senators, whose elections were both less frequent and more indirect. Illinois Congressman Richard Yates, after witnessing the all-night debate in the Senate, expected "such times as this House has never seen." Douglas, however, never lost faith that his bill would ultimately succeed. To Howell Cobb he wrote in April that the bill would surely triumph and "impart peace to the country & stability to the Union. I am not detered or affected by the violence & insults of the Northern Whigs & abolitionists. The storm will soon spend its fury, and the people of the north will sustain the measure when they come to understand it." "Our Southern friends," he advised Cobb, "have only to stand firm & leave us of the North to fight the great Battle. . . . The great principle of self government is at stake & surely the people of this country are never going to decide that the principle upon which our whole republican system rests is vicious & wrong." Still, it was only the shrewd management of House leaders and the constant direction of Douglas behind the scenes that finally dispelled the doubts that the bill could clear the lower house.

On March 21, William A. Richardson, Douglas' right-hand man in the House, moved the bill's referral to his territorial committee. He was immediately challenged by a New York "hard," Francis B. Cutting, who insisted that the measure be referred to the committee of the whole instead, where it would stand fiftieth on the calendar. Richardson charged Cutting with seeking to kill the bill "by indirection" and denounced the motion as an effort to defeat the legislation. Nevertheless, Cutting succeeded by a vote of 110 to 95, a margin narrow enough to show the friends of the bill the size of the task that lay before them. Opponents of the measure were exultant. All the bills preceding it on the calendar would have to be disposed of before the Kansas-Nebraska bill could be reached; if that should happen, its opponents could "readily talk it to death." Those who rejoiced, however, had not reckoned with the strength and determination of the bill's sponsors. Severe pressure was brought to bear on House members by Douglas, the President, and members of the cabinet, and their efforts paid off. On May 8, Richardson, in the committee of the whole, succeeded in laying aside eighteen bills which preceded an earlier House version of the Kansas-Nebraska bill. He then sought to substitute the Senate bill, without the Clayton amendment, unleashing a storm of opposition. For the next three weeks debate raged in the House with all the fury and bitterness that had characterized discussion in the Senate. Tempers flared and more than once physical violence was threatened.[33]

Douglas was present in the House almost constantly. "He has every man in the House of Representatives marked and numbered, and firmly believes the bill will go through by a decisive majority," commented a correspondent. He was accused of tampering with the Speaker and of seeking to alter the House rules, and many Congressmen bitterly resented this example of Senate direction. Richardson was at his side, insolent and domineering in his dictation. "No slave-driver was ever half so absolute on his own plantation." Parliamentary maneuvering became incredibly complicated, and the House seemed in danger of bogging down in a state of hopeless confusion. Alexander H. Stephens, Georgia's small and frail Whig Congressman, came to the rescue, and in a series of shrewd parliamentary moves he was able to bring the issue to resolution. On May 22, the substitution of the Senate bill was made and the vote finally taken. The act, minus the Clayton amendment, passed by a narrow margin, 113 to 100. The result was greeted with "prolonged clappings of hands and hissings." In far-off Springfield, Illinois, 113 guns were fired to announce "a moral victory more glorious than can be achieved upon the bloody fields of Europe." [34]

The rest was anticlimax. The bill was returned to the Senate, where the deletion of the Clayton amendment was quickly accepted. After midnight on May 25, following a last heated exchange between Douglas on the one hand and Chase and Wade on the other, the Kansas-Nebraska bill passed. Booming cannon almost immediately announced the result, and a "delirium of joy" passed through the ranks of those who had fought so hard for its passage. Five days later, on May 30, President Pierce signed the measure into law.

The act was another triumph for Douglas; its true dimensions and significance for him and his career would only become apparent with time. "I know the Bill is right," he had written a month before; he never wavered from this conviction in spite of the intensity of the attacks against him. Later he boasted: "I passed the Kansas-Nebraska Act myself. I had the authority and power of a dictator throughout the whole controversy in both houses. The speeches were nothing. It was the marshalling and directing of men, and guarding from attacks, and with a ceaseless vigilance preventing surprise." The struggle was over, but in a larger sense it had really only begun.[35]

# XVIII
## "By the light of my own effigy"
## 1854—1855

i

The organization of Kansas and Nebraska territories represented only one part of Douglas' western program, for territorial organization was closely related to the construction of a Pacific railroad and the establishment of a free homestead policy. In spite of the intensity of the debate on the Kansas-Nebraska Act, Douglas did not lose sight of these additional measures. "The Douglas bill," Atchison correctly declared, "was a Western measure. It was designed to add to the power and wealth of the West." But it was only one of the measures to which Douglas dedicated himself.

The Pacific railroad surveys that Congress had ordered in 1853 had not yet been completed, but Douglas was unwilling to await their final reports before resuming his agitation for a rail link with the Pacific coast. He had maintained close contact with the leader of the northern survey, Isaac I. Stevens, and was regularly apprised of its progress. A northern railroad route became as important to him as a central route. In 1852, he urged a land grant to aid in the construction of a ship canal around the falls at Sault Ste. Marie which would open Lake Superior to navigation.[1]

In the following year, Douglas became involved in a real estate venture at the far western tip of Lake Superior. He and Minnesota editor Daniel A. Robertson established a townsite claim in northern Wisconsin, at the mouth of the St. Louis River opposite what is now Duluth, Minnesota. When Henry M. Rice, Minnesota's territorial delegate, attempted to establish a rival claim he was invited to join Douglas and

Robertson. A syndicate was formed that eventually claimed 6000 acres, including the site of Superior City, divided into twenty-seven shares and held originally by nineteen people. "How would you like to buy a share in Superior City?" Douglas asked Philadelphia editor John W. Forney, and before Forney could reply Douglas was standing on a chair pointing to a map and predicting that "the greatest railroad in the world" would start from that point. Forney was persuaded. Douglas' enthusiasm was contagious, and shares were purchased by Jesse Bright, R. M. T. Hunter, John C. Breckinridge, Robert J. Walker, William A. Richardson, Pennsylvania Congressman John L. Dawson, Representatives William W. Boyce and William Aiken of South Carolina, and others, giving the syndicate a highly political character. The group was backed by Washington banker W. W. Corcoran, who also was a shareholder. Douglas was one of the few to hold two shares, for which he received loans from Corcoran of $5000 (on joint account with Bright) in 1854 and another $5000 in 1855. The shares appreciated in value quickly. By the fall of 1854 Douglas was asking $10,000 for half a share, convinced that "it is worth double that sum today as an investment."

With the opening of the ship canal and the construction of a railroad over a northern route, a new opportunity for commerce between the Atlantic states and the Pacific would develop and the entire northern half of the west would be opened to settlement. The town of Superior, Bright boasted, would in time outstrip Chicago. Douglas was not concerned over rivalry between Superior and his home city; there was potential enough, he felt, for at least two great arteries of commerce and transportation across the continent. Indeed, he supported legislation in the Senate that would donate lands for the construction of a railroad from Dubuque, Iowa, to Superior, thus establishing a connection between his townsite speculation and the Illinois Central Railroad.[2]

On January 4, the day that Douglas reported his Nebraska bill, the Senate, at Gwin's insistence, created a select committee to consider proposals for a Pacific railroad. Douglas was one of nine Senators appointed to the committee. The committee reported a railroad bill in March, but it excited little interest. Of greater import was Douglas' proposal to the committee, never formally reported, that three Pacific railroads be built, following northern, central, and southern routes, a plan endorsed by railroad promoters and western opinion. He was one of only a handful of northwestern Senators to vote for the ratification of the Gadsden Treaty with Mexico, a move that not only accorded with his belief in territorial expansion but also announced his support of a southern rail route. With the Nebraska bill demanding so much attention, however, and with the railroad surveys yet incomplete, the Senate had no inclination to take up the railroad issue. Douglas contented himself with an effort to suspend duties on the importation of railroad iron, in anticipation of Pacific railroad construction.

When the railroad issue was revived in the short session of the thirty-third Congress, Douglas' three-route proposal was given priority by select committees in both houses. The bill ran into a snag in the House, but when Douglas introduced it in the Senate he found its members in a receptive mood. In February 1855 it narrowly passed the Senate, the first Pacific railroad measure to be approved in either house of Congress, but without House action the bill died with the session. Before adjournment, the Senate also finally approved the construction of a telegraph line to the Pacific, but the terms were hardly satisfactory to private capital.[3]

To Douglas, a free homestead policy was as closely related to the organization of Kansas and Nebraska as was the Pacific railroad, but the efforts to enact a homestead law were hardly more successful. A Pacific railroad was one important inducement for the settlement of the new territories, free homesteads were another. The latter, Douglas thought, would ensure the peopling of the prairies by independent northern farmers, thus assuring the extension of freedom rather than slavery to the area. Some southerners were aware of this, pointing out that a homestead bill would be a blow to those who had supported Douglas on Nebraska. The House approved a homestead bill, but the Senate could not agree, even though Senators from both the free and the slave states of the west supported it. Douglas' efforts to complete his program of western legislation proved unavailing.[4]

When he wrote to Lanphier in November 1853 about the problems Congress would face in the coming session, Douglas predicted that the Pacific railroad question would be a "disturbing element." It was, in fact, given little consideration. A second issue, he noted, would be the perennial one of internal improvements. "The River & Harbor question must be met & decided," he wrote. "Now, in my opinion is the time to put those great interests on a more substantial & secure basis by a well devised system of Tonnage duties." His suggestion that internal improvements be financed by tonnage duties levied by the states had won some administration support; Secretary of War Jefferson Davis endorsed the plan, and Pierce was said to be leaning toward it. Two days before he reported the Nebraska bill, Douglas urged Illinois' Governor Joel A. Matteson to consider laying the question of tonnage duties before the state legislature. In a long letter—his most complete review of the question of internal improvements—Douglas called attention to the "uncertain, vascillating, and partial policy" which had in the past proved ruinous to western interests. Those parts of the nation most deeply concerned with internal navigation, he maintained, had been not only neglected, but paralyzed. Internal improvement bills, insofar as they dealt with the northern lakes and western rivers, had usually been characterized by "a death struggle, and a doubtful issue." Four times out of five, western interests had been defeated in one or the other of the houses of Congress or by presidential veto. Where improvements were approved, progress had "not been sufficiently rapid to keep pace with the spirit of the age." The answer, he repeated, was in a system of tonnage duties that would convert "a partial and fluctuating policy into a permanent and efficient system."

Douglas' letter excited considerable comment. The *Union* called it "one of the most important documents that has issued from any of our statesmen for many years," and one constituent regarded Douglas' proposal as equal in importance with the Nebraska bill. As before, however, many in the west were skeptical, if not openly hostile. Tonnage duties, some feared, would adversely affect commerce on the Great Lakes. Again the scheme was denounced as an effort to tax western interests for the accommodation of eastern capitalists. Douglas' proposal still encountered sufficient opposition to defeat its consideration. The traditional pork barrel system, with all its partisanship and local jealousy, was still preferable. When a new rivers and harbors bill came up late in the session, Douglas again described the traditional appropriations system as a "total failure in its practical operation." Too little, he charged, had been appropriated for improvements on the Great Lakes and the upper Mississippi, and the funds that had been allocated had been squandered. The bill passed Congress, but Douglas voted against it, convinced that it was contrary to every principle of sound judgment. Pierce promptly vetoed the measure.

Douglas' negative vote and Pierce's veto were received with indignation by many westerners. Flags flew at half-mast in Chicago harbor in protest. The interests of the west, it seemed, had been singularly ignored during the session. The Pacific railroad, free homesteads, and internal improvements had all been rejected. Offsetting these losses, there stood only the Kansas-Nebraska Act, but even this began to appear of questionable value by the summer of 1854.[5]

## ii

Almost from the moment he introduced the Nebraska bill, Douglas was assailed, and as the bill's passage became more certain the attacks increased in number and intensity. Perhaps the basic question involved in the story of the Kansas-Nebraska Act is not that of Douglas' motivation. Douglas' stand in the spring of 1854 was a logical extension of positions he had espoused and actions he had taken in earlier times. The important question may well be why the response to the bill and its author became so intense and volatile so quickly. Douglas was both surprised and dismayed at the reaction. His attempt to ascribe it to a small group of abolitionist conspirators was not convincing, and he soon was forced to recognize that opposition to the bill had a wider scope. Persuaded that his action had been necessary and his motives pure, he reacted with sensitivity and emotion.

The years since the 1850 Compromise had witnessed a growing antislavery feeling in the north, the depth and sincerity of which Douglas was not properly appreciative. Douglas believed that the passage of the Compromise measures, with their acceptance of popular sovereignty, meant freedom for the nation from a troublesome and potentially explosive problem. He felt that the nation could now get on with the more important questions of national development and expansion. Many Americans, however, were not so easily persuaded that the slavery issue had been settled. The Fugitive Slave Act aroused a bitter northern opposition, and the widely publicized "slave rescues" kept the question alive. The publication of Harriet Beecher Stowe's *Uncle Tom's Cabin* both reflected and encouraged a mood in the north that far overshadowed the lip service paid to the 1850 settlement by both political parties. The slavery issue had not been settled, and the acquiescence in the Compromise, which Douglas thought to be final and effective, proved deceptive. A large segment of northern opinion was ripe for protest against Douglas' bill.

Most of Douglas' critics, however, were not moved by moral indignation over slavery. Since the mid-1840's northerners had watched the growth of southern influence and power in the national government with apprehension and dismay. Such feelings were particularly acute in the west, where the failure of western measures was invariably blamed on the south. The commercial and cultural ties that had bound the two sections in earlier years had lost their strength; west and south had drawn apart. Douglas sought desperately to maintain a working alliance between the two, but his actions were always predicated on the belief that real power in the nation should reside in the west. To Douglas, the Kansas-Nebraska Act was a western measure, and he bristled at the charges that he had bowed to southern dictation in its formulation. The slaveholder, he repeatedly pointed out, could not compete successfully with the free western farmer in the new territories, so that slavery, he was convinced, could never gain a foothold there. While his belief was echoed by many in both the north and the south, others feared that an extension of southern power would result. The freesoil revolt in 1848 in the west reflected a fear of southern domination more than it revealed an antipathy toward slavery, and opposition to the Kansas-Nebraska Act followed the same pattern. Southern leaders did little to allay this apprehension, confident that the new states to be carved out of the territory would take their places "with those recognizing and cherishing the condition of African slavery."

Popular sovereignty, like the Kansas-Nebraska Act closely identified with the west, was a nebulous and complicated principle, never too closely defined and always ambiguous. To Douglas it was an expedient as well as a principle, frequently tailored to meet the exigencies of the moment but always based on his fundamental belief in local self-government. His faith in popular decision was great, and he felt that somehow everything would turn out all right if only the people could be allowed to determine the questions which closely affected them. Thus he was not bothered by the ambiguity of his doctrine—indeed, he preferred it that way—nor was he ruffled by the charges of inconsistency that were frequently leveled against him. "The man is only consistent," Douglas had said, "who follows out his principles and adapts his measures to them in view of the condition of things he finds in existence at the period of time when it is necessary to make the application." At another time, he denied that he had any "such pride of consistency" that should prevent him from modifying his views, if he thought such modification were both necessary and justifiable.[6]

As the Kansas-Nebraska Act made its way through the two houses of Congress, Douglas received encouraging words and congratulations from individuals throughout the country, especially from the north. Democratic newspapers flocked to his side. "You have made Cords of friends here, notwithstanding all that is said," wrote Samuel S. Cox from Ohio. An army officer in Kansas complimented Douglas on the "augmentation of the area of free republican institutions" which would result from the act. An Indianan sent his congratulations, confident that as the measure became better known it would win increasing approval. A traveler through Iowa and Illinois reported a "strong pro-Douglas feeling" based on the bill's recognition of popular sovereignty and "the absolute right of the people." In a different vein, a former colleague and friendly enemy, Robert Winthrop, wrote from Boston in laudatory terms of the ability and energy with which Douglas had conducted himself; Winthrop hoped, rather wistfully, that "we shall find something to agree about one of these days." "I can honestly say," he added, "that I had rather have you for a friend than an opponent." The press hailed the high principle upon which the act was based and predicted that its practical effect would be "future peace and quiet" and the "downfall of sectionalism in the halls of the national Capitol." Slavery, some maintained, would be barred from the territories as effectively by Douglas' popular sovereignty as by the Missouri Compromise. Other papers gave the act only lukewarm support, recognizing the validity of Douglas' movement but deploring its introduction into politics at this time. Still others heaped praise on Douglas for his fearless stand against "the whole horde of abolition harpies." Lest Democrats forget, the *Union* continued to emphasize that fidelity to the principles of the Kansas-Nebraska Act remained a test of Democratic orthodoxy.[7]

Reaction in the southern states, on the other hand, was marked by little excitement. "It is difficult for us to comprehend, or credit, the excitement that is said to prevail in the North, on account of the Nebraska question," wrote an Alabaman to his Senator. While the act received general approval, there was "no excitement, no fever, on the subject." In fact, much of southern opinion viewed the act with a moderate skepticism. Ex-President Tyler publicly supported popular sovereignty as a reasonable solution to the slavery problem, but he had little company among southern spokesmen. While the west hailed popular sovereignty as one of the act's great achievements, the south preferred simply to concentrate their approval on the removal of the Missouri Compromise restriction. One southern Congressman was convinced that his section would gain no practical good from the act, but with the removal of the "Stigma placed upon her by the Missouri restriction . . . we can say truly that in any event we are not worsted." Senator Hunter later made it clear that southern support of Douglas did not imply support of his doctrine of popular sovereignty. It was only because the act removed "an unjust and odious discrimination against her domestic institutions" that the south sided with Douglas. The ultra-southern *Charleston Mercury,* while offering support "in a moderate way," maintained that popular sovereignty was unconstitutional. Only the act's reference to the Constitution made it palatable. The union of Whigs and Democrats in the south was regarded as an encouraging omen, demonstrating the priority of sectional interests over those of the parties. Another Charleston paper charged that northern opposition to the bill revealed the true nature of the Compromise of 1850 as a "hollow hearted truce." [8]

Early in the discussion of the bill, a Maryland editor denounced the opposition as "mere figments of a morbid and restless imagination" and predicted that Douglas' arguments would soon silence the "croaking, carping, hypocritical enemies of popular sovereignty." Douglas was confident that "the storm will soon spend its fury." How far these statements missed their mark soon became apparent. The northern antislavery press attacked Douglas in rising crescendo, but few papers reached the heights of invective attained by a Detroit freesoil organ. "The bill introduced by S. A. Douglas, the Illinois man stealer—the mean wretch who misrepresents a nominally free State in the American Senate, while upon his southern plantations the bloody scourge is daily falling by his command upon woman's shrinking flesh—who trades in little children, and overtasks and scourges gray-headed men, that the stock of wines and brandies which his depraved appetite demands may be abundant—the bill which this slaveholder and supple slave of slaveholders has introduced, is the most impudent insult to legislative integrity ever conceived in the corrupt Congress of this slavery ridden nation." One hundred Ohio women sent him thirty pieces of silver as a reward for his action, "more brutal than Jewish crucifiers," and Benton's bitter prediction that the north would beat Douglas' brains out was widely reprinted. Reports of effigy hangings and burnings multiplied to such an extent that some feared that they might ultimately win sympathy for the Illinois Senator.[9]

Douglas took little public notice of the mounting attacks, but on three occasions he was moved to reply in kind through the press. To a statement in the Concord, New Hampshire, *State Capitol Reporter,* said to have been written by Edmund Burke, that the repeal of the Missouri Compromise would revive and re-establish slavery in the region, he penned an immediate and angry response. Reiterating his familiar argument that the Nebraska bill was based on "the great fundamental principle of self-government," Douglas charged that it was as valid to say that the measure opened the country to freedom by leaving the people *"perfectly free* to do as they please." The bill assumed, he added, that the people of the territories were as intelligent, wise, patriotic and conscientious as their brethren in the states and "as they were before they emigrated to the Territories." Why not, then, acknowledge their capacity to legislate for themselves? To conclude that the effect of this recognition of self-government would be the establishment of slavery was, Douglas argued, a wicked misrepresentation of the act. In a letter published in the *National Intelligencer* at about the same time, Edward Coles, an early settler of Illinois who had served as governor of the state from 1822 to 1826 before he returned to the east, challenged Douglas' assertion that slavery had never been successfully excluded from Illinois by congressional legislation. Douglas' reply, severe and sarcastic, included long quotations from territorial and state laws, some of them on the statute books when Coles was governor, that recognized the existence of slavery in defiance of the Ordinance of 1787. Not content with legal arguments, Douglas also directed his barbs at Coles personally, accusing him of having abandoned the state following his governorship because "the inducements which took you there could no longer be made available." Both letters were published in the press and distributed in pamphlet form.[10]

Most galling to Douglas were the attacks of the clergy. On March 14, Senator Everett presented a memorial to the Senate, 250 feet long and signed by over 3000 New England clergymen, protesting "in the name of Almighty God" the passage of the Kansas-Nebraska bill. The bill, they declared, was a moral wrong which would expose America to the "righteous judgments" of God. Douglas, bristling at the imputation, was on his feet immediately denouncing the effort. A man of no deep religious convictions himself, he resented the interference of the pulpit in matters of government. "Individually, I care nothing about this matter," he declared. "To me it is a very small affair, compared with the sort of treatment which I am receiving every day." But his reaction belied the disclaimer. The signers, he charged, had committed an atrocious falsehood and calumny against the Senate, had "desecrated the pulpit, and prostituted the sacred desk to the miserable and corrupting influence of party politics." They should be rebuked and required to confine themselves to their vocation, instead of neglecting their flocks and bringing holy religion into disrepute. He denied that clergymen had a peculiar right to determine the will of God in relation to legislative action. If they did, why not simply refer all political questions to them? Douglas' outburst was received with both shock and amused comment by the press, but the Illinois Senator was deadly serious. Words of consolation came from one New Englander, who pointed out that not one of the signers of the protest was a clergyman of the Roman Catholic Church.

When a meeting of twenty-five Chicago clergymen similarly protested the bill, Douglas replied in a long, carefully worded, and milder toned public letter—"Stephen's Epistle to Chicago," according to one editor. In more restrained and respectful language, he made essentially the same points he had offered in his Senate statement. "I must be permitted to say to you, in all Christian kindness," Douglas asserted, "that I differ with you widely, radically, and fundamentally, in respect to the nature and extent of your rights, duties, and powers, as ministers of the Gospel." He sought to vindicate himself, he informed the ministers, with "extreme reluctance" and added, in a tone replete with uncharacteristic humility, "My respect for your holy calling would induce me to submit, in silence, even to an unmerited rebuke, in preference to engaging in a controversy with ministers of the Gospel in any case where duty did not compel me to speak." But since he had been arraigned for carrying out the high public trust to which he had been called, he had no choice but to defend the "great principle" of the Kansas-Nebraska Act.

In spite of his soothing tones, Douglas had not heard the last from the clergy. In early May he received another protest, signed by over 500 clergymen in the northwest, couched in virtually the same language as the New England remonstrance. Instead of registering their objections "in the name of the Almighty God," however, the ministers protested in their own names as "citizens and ministers of the Gospel," a minor victory for Douglas. As before, Douglas chose to notice the protest on the floor of the Senate, utilizing the opportunity to review the many sermons that had been delivered from the pulpit against the Kansas-Nebraska Act during the preceding months. Reading the more colorful extracts from some of the sermons, he asked, "who is the best friend of our Christian religion: he who assumes the sacred place to convert it into a meeting where angry passions shall be aroused, and epithets of calumny and slander hurled on others; or he who would keep the politician within the sphere of his own proper limits, and the preacher within the sphere of his religious and clerical duties?" The Sabbath had been converted "into the great day of the hustings" when a man's character could be blackened "with security and impunity." Returning briefly to his earlier form, Douglas charged the ministers with being tools and instruments in a political crusade, fomented by "conspirators on this floor." Douglas tried hard to present himself as a defender of the "holy religion of our fathers" against corruption, but his efforts were not as convincing as he thought. Relations between the Illinois Senator and the pulpit remained strained.[11]

Aside from these public replies to his critics, which only embroiled him in additional controversy, Douglas held aloof from the groundswell of opposition to the Kansas-Nebraska Act, confident that it would soon subside. Although urged to call a meeting that would endorse the bill, he spurned the advice. He accepted invitations to speak in New York and Philadelphia during the summer, however, and at that time he took his arguments directly to the urban voters. He made two brief appearances in New York early in June, reiterating his familiar defense of popular sovereignty. "This is the issue upon which I intend to stand before the American people, and to meet either their approval or disapproval." He insisted that the principle had a wider application than that provided in the controversial act. Those who accepted it for Kansas and Nebraska must also support it "in all time to come" for other territories, whether "Oregon, Mexico, Cuba, or the Sandwich Islands." Douglas' statements were punctuated with groans and cat-calls; when he stopped at Trenton on his return he was jeered by an audience at the railway station, an incident for which New Jersey's governor later apologized.

In Philadelphia, Douglas delivered the Fourth of July address. The Know-Nothings had recently triumphed in the municipal elections, not because of the popularity of their nativist and anti-Catholic views, but because the voters had registered a protest against the two major political parties. Douglas accepted the challenge with alacrity. Speaking in Independence Square, he linked popular sovereignty with the colonial protests against British authority. Indeed, he traced his principle back to the beginning. With the charges of the clergy still fresh in his mind, Douglas argued that it was in accordance with divine law. "The Almighty breathed the principle into the nostrils of the first man in the garden of Eden, and empowered him and his descendants in all time to choose their own form of government, and to bear the evils and enjoy the blessings of their own deeds." As for the abolitionist contention that slavery was a monstrous evil, Douglas simply replied, "It is no part of my purpose to discuss the merits of slavery as a domestic or political institution." He tied the Know-Nothings to the anti-Nebraska movement and delivered one of his first blasts against the nativist crusade. "To proscribe a man in this country on account of his birthplace or religious faith is subversive of all our ideas and principles of civil and religious freedom," he shouted. "It is revolting to our sense of justice and right." [12]

While Douglas tried to shrug off many of the protests as inspired by a radical element, he was seriously concerned with the impact of the Kansas-Nebraska Act on party organization. Always devoted to his party and a persistent advocate of rigid party discipline and regularity, he was now faced with a growing political revolt whose true dimensions he little appreciated. By insisting that the act serve as a test for Democratic orthodoxy, the administration had deprived the anti-Nebraska Democrats of a place within the party, forcing them to find new vehicles for political expression. Predictions that the passage of the bill would result in new political alignments were frequently made during the congressional debates. Douglas recognized the threat that northern Whigs, freesoilers, and abolitionists might join ranks in a new sectional party, but he was confident that "enough patriotic men" would be found to meet this development.

While the battle in Congress was being fought, five free state legislatures—Maine, Rhode Island, Massachusetts, New York, and Wisconsin—passed resolutions condemning the Kansas-Nebraska Act, while Democratic majorities in four others—Pennsylvania, New Jersey, Ohio, and California—refused to commit themselves on the bill. Equally disturbing were signs of strife within the Democratic ranks. A Democratic convention in Connecticut opposed the bill, while a state convention in Pennsylvania, despite the entreaties of Douglas' friends, withheld an endorsement of the measure. From Ohio came word that anti-Nebraska Democrats were combining with Whigs and freesoilers in a fusion movement against the bill. Democratic majorities were drastically reduced in an election in Pierce's own state, and a Whig was elected mayor in normally Democratic Detroit. The split in New York was deepened. Preston King, a former Democratic Congressman said to be anxious for a general break-up of the old party organizations, was suggesting a Benton-Seward ticket for the next presidential election. Benton, beside himself with wrath, continued to denounce Douglas. "His legs are too short," he declared with reference to the presidential race. "That part of his body, sir, which men wish to kick, is too near the ground." Opposition did not subside with the final approval of the bill, as many Democrats expected; instead it grew worse. The successes of the Know-Nothings in the state elections added to the confusion. "Parties are now in a state of disorganization—rather of utter anarchy," reported one New Yorker to Martin Van Buren, "What is to come out of it, none can foresee." [13]

As the storm raged about him, Douglas looked to his own state for vindication. Since Democrats throughout the north were poised on the brink of revolt, the reaction of Douglas' party in Illinois became increasingly important to him. Not only was his own political future involved, he thought, but that of the party in the west. Illinois and the west could serve as an essential stabilizing influence in a rapidly disintegrating situation.

iii

Reactions to the Kansas-Nebraska Act in Illinois reflected the pattern in other parts of the north. Whigs strongly opposed the measure, while the Democrats, in spite of Douglas' power in the party, split. The Senator had not been home for well over a year and, even before the Kansas-Nebraska Act had been introduced, he had been warned that he had been out of touch with his constituents for too long. A hasty visit to Illinois, a friend had advised, would "inspire them with confidence in the future," but Douglas had neither the time nor the inclination to leave the national capital. The task of defending the act fell to his friend Charles H. Lanphier, editor of the influential *Illinois State Register*. Throughout the year the *Register* presented Douglas' arguments, lauded his supporters, and castigated his critics. Popular sovereignty, the "doctrine of domestic independence," received strong endorsement. The principle, wrote the editor, was established in the Compromise of 1850 and, overriding "all temporizing legislation," was irrepealable. It might "meet with contumely and rebuff, but it can never encounter overthrow." The question of slavery, he assured his readers, was not part of the issue, for advocacy of the act "commits no one in favor of slavery." Indeed, he continued, "we have no right to speculate on the morality or immorality of slavery in any such connection." While all powers of persuasion might be exerted to induce the people of Kansas and Nebraska to reject slavery, "we have no right to declare that they *must* reject it."

Douglas, following reactions in his state closely, expressed his gratification at the *Register's* course and was confident that all the Democratic papers in the state would follow its lead.[14]

Much of the Democratic press fell into line, but few papers reflected the *Register's* thorough commitment to the act. One exception was the *Quincy Herald,* which had been devoted to Douglas' advancement ever since his first election to the House, and which now vied with the *Register* in its zealous defense of the act and the "sacred principle" on which it was based. The question of slavery, the editor argued, had been settled forever by the measure. Since slavery could not flourish in the new territories, Douglas' act was actually one to extend freedom. Other journals merely acquiesced in the legislation, and some, like the Ottawa, Illinois, *Free Trader,* endorsed the act while expressing regret that its passage had aroused a new agitation over slavery. More serious signs of unrest and dissatisfaction within the Democratic ranks soon appeared. Murray McConnel warned Douglas that the Whigs and Free-Soilers, with some Democrats, were uniting in opposition to the Nebraska bill, while defections among the Democratic press became evident. Wentworth's *Chicago Democrat* assumed a strong anti-Nebraska tone, although, true to the truce made with Douglas earlier, Wentworth refrained from attacking the Senator personally. Chicago's *Democratic Press* abandoned Douglas, charging him with having committed an error that "will always be an incubus upon him in his future political history." It was the repeal of the Missouri Compromise, not popular sovereignty, that incited the paper's opposition. Popular sovereignty, the editor maintained, was "abstractly correct" and ought to be incorporated in all territorial organizations where no prior surrender or compromise of that principle had been made. The *Chicago Tribune* branded Douglas a traitor and a knave, and his action a betrayal of liberty in favor of slavery. Linking the Nebraska question with the temperance issue, the *Tribune* urged that the banners of Douglas' party be inscribed with a new motto, "Rum, Slavery and Democracy." Democratic papers in northern and central Illinois gradually joined the swelling ranks of criticism.[15]

Opposition from the press in his own home town concerned Douglas. Once again he turned his thoughts to the establishment of a new Chicago paper that could be relied upon to advance his position in the controversy. Isaac Cook, one of Douglas' Chicago lieutenants, had urged a new paper as early as February, and by the summer Douglas had made his decision. James W. Sheahan, a Washington newspaper correspondent, was induced to assume the editorial responsibility of a new Douglas organ in Chicago. In early September Douglas was circulating the prospectus of the *Chicago Times*, "the only true and reliable Democratic Paper published in this City." Money for the operation was provided by Cook and Douglas, although Sheahan complained immediately that it was not nearly enough to accomplish the desired results. The *Democrat*, the *Press*, and the *Tribune*, Douglas advised Sheahan, should be portrayed as allies and organs of the "great abolition Party." The *Times*, although it continued publication through the remaining years of Douglas' life, was almost constantly beset with financial difficulties and dissension within its management, and it never became the effective organ Douglas had envisioned.[16]

While the state's Democratic papers were divided, the Whig press was virtually unanimous in its denunciation of the Kansas-Nebraska Act. The *Illinois State Journal* warned that the act would "rouse up every sleeping energy of abolition fanaticism in the land." It was "a piece of wrong and treachery," and Douglas in proposing it had proved himself to be "the tool of designing, faithless and unprincipled southern men." It was, the paper charged, part of a plot to enable the south "to control the government of this great people." Some critics viewed the act simply as an attempt to enhance the value of the slaves on Douglas' Mississippi plantation.

The ranks of the opposition were further swelled by mass meetings, which sharply protested the repeal of the Missouri Compromise and the threat that slavery would be expanded to an area dedicated to freedom. Joseph Gillespie, speaking at Edwardsville, carefully disclaimed any intention to interfere with slavery where it already existed, but he denounced the bill which would establish "slavery in territory now free, thus retarding the settlement of the country, and placing an incubus upon every department of industry and enterprise." Douglas' popular sovereignty was right, one meeting resolved, except when it involved laws that would establish human slavery where it did not then exist. The popular reaction to the bill was most acrimonious in Chicago, where mass meetings dominated by freesoil Democrats angrily denounced Douglas. Only a small number of Douglas' friends were on hand to defend the Senator's action, and their efforts were in vain. Isaac Cook, almost alone in his support of the act, reportedly warned in desperation, "When Douglas comes home, he will make you take your tails between your legs and sneak off."

Among the more outspoken critics of the Kansas-Nebraska Act in Illinois were the Germans. Reflecting a widespread dissatisfaction with the bill, especially with the Clayton amendment, which discriminated against aliens, the Germans in Chicago met in March to express their opposition. The enthusiasm of the audience and the impassioned oratory of the leaders, only temporarily stilled by the efforts of some Douglas supporters to turn off the gas in the meeting hall, culminated in the passage of several caustic resolutions. Douglas was denounced "an ambitious and dangerous demagogue." The bill was seen as an "attempt to import Southern aristocracy and Southern contempt of free labor, into the North." When the meeting broke up, a procession marched to the public square, where Douglas was burned in effigy "amid the jeers and groans of a vast assemblage." [17]

Douglas took little public notice of the protest meetings in Illinois and, aside from his letter to the Chicago clergymen, made no attempt to defend his position. He was more concerned with the threat posed by the opposition to the stability and power of the state's Democratic organization and to his own leadership in the party. When Governor Matteson summoned the legislature into special session to consider the state's railroad development, Douglas feared that his critics would seize the chance to proclaim their reaction to the Kansas-Nebraska Act through legislative resolutions. Word had reached him in Washington of a plot of "Whigs, Abolitionists, & some disappointed office-seekers" to instruct him on the Nebraska question. Their ultimate purpose, he was convinced, was to divide the Democratic party and elect a Whig to succeed Shields in the Senate. To forestall the movement and at the same time to give the act Illinois' official endorsement, a sanction Douglas desperately needed in the face of mounting criticism in the north, resolutions approving the measure were introduced into the legislature on the first day of the called session. The resolutions, it was later charged, had been ordered by Douglas himself, while opposition among Democratic members was quickly overcome by the Senator's intervention. Party drill and a rumored "threatening telegraphic dispatch" from Douglas produced the desired results; only a small number of legislators opposed the resolutions, although the number of Democrats who cast negative votes or abstained was significant. Douglas could point to Illinois' action in the face of opposition from other northern legislatures, but it was hardly the clear-cut vote of confidence he had hoped for.[18]

More important tests were to follow—the legislative and congressional elections in the fall of 1854 and the selection by the new legislature of a United States Senator at the expiration of Shields' term—that demanded Douglas' presence in Illinois. When he paid a brief visit to New York in June, rumors circulated that he was in fact on his way to Chicago, but Douglas had no intention of returning to Illinois until after the adjournment of Congress. The Senator, crowed the *Chicago Tribune*, had "doubtless felt that Chicago is too hot for him, just now, and that it were better to wait until the indignation of the people somewhat subsides." Congress adjourned on August 7, and soon afterward Douglas was on his way west. His journey was clearly not the triumphal procession he had experienced in previous years. He appeared in excellent health and spirits, but his confidence was soon shaken as he encountered hostile demonstrations in the communities along his route. "I could travel from Boston to Chicago by the light of my own effigy," he related. "All along the Western Reserve of Ohio I could find my effigy upon every tree we passed." On August 24, he arrived in Chicago amid warnings against attempting any public defense of his position. Although disturbed, he appeared unruffled by the signs of hostility which he encountered. Few believed that Douglas would heed the warnings. "He will give them another specimen of his undaunted mettle," commented one paper, "such as he exhibited in 1850 when the negroes of Chicago and their white allies essayed to terrify him because of his support of the fugitive-slave law." [19]

The Illinois to which Douglas returned in the late summer of 1854 was troubled. Party leaders, sharing the Senator's anxiety, showed deep concern for the condition of the Democratic organization. None knew more clearly than Douglas that the challenge to Democratic leadership in the state was the most serious ever faced. The outcry against the Kansas-Nebraska Act continued to mount, aided by a succession of speakers from outside the state. Salmon P. Chase, Joshua R. Giddings, and Cassius Clay traversed the state, while local abolitionist leaders, notably Ichabod Codding of Chicago, joined the attack. Calls for a new political organization were issued. Throughout the summer, Whigs and dissident Democrats in the northern part of the state protested the extension of slavery. Some, influenced by similar movements in other states, adopted the name "Republican" to identify their cause. The election of a freesoil Whig, James W. Grimes, to the governorship of neighboring Iowa, which had been a staunch Democratic state, encouraged the movement in Illinois and demonstrated the seriousness of its impact. In Ottawa, Illinois, early in August, resolutions were approved calling for a state convention of all opponents to the Kansas-Nebraska Act to meet later in the fall. The inauguration of a new epoch in the history of political parties had been forecast, and there were unmistakable signs that the prediction would soon be fulfilled.

The loosening of party ties provided an opportunity for other political groups to gain a foothold in state politics which might otherwise have been denied them. The Know-Nothings enjoyed a remarkable increase in strength in many Illinois communities, and, after Douglas' denunciation of the movement in his Philadelphia speech, they raised their voices against the Senator. Many anti-Nebraska Whigs and Democrats, for want of a more effective vehicle, drifted into the Know-Nothing camp, adding a strong antislavery character to the party's nativistic platform. Douglas instructed Sheahan to maintain an unceasing attack against the Know-Nothings in the columns of the *Times*. Other Democratic journals followed suit in the hope that the state's German population might be wooed back into the fold. Instead, Douglas faced the opposition of both the nativists and the immigrants, a situation that puzzled the party strategists. The attacks of the German press gathered strength, and calls were issued for a statewide convention of Germans to make a formal protest. Lieutenant Governor Gustave Koerner, who had been a strong partisan of Douglas, broke with the Senator to lead the movement among his countrymen. Joining the nativists in their anti-Nebraska stance were the advocates of temperance reform, who also urged the adoption of statewide prohibition on the model of Maine's 1851 Liquor Law. Whigs, freesoil Democrats, Know-Nothings, German immigrants, and temperance reformers formed an anti-Nebraska coalition that soon assumed formidable proportions.

Further complications added to the chaos of party politics in Illinois. A drought during the summer of 1854 resulted in crop failures. Economic distress, keenly felt in parts of the state in that year, added to the resentment against the party in power, and by the end of the year signs of the financial depression that would grip the nation a few years later began to appear. The commercial interests in the northern part of the state, dependent on lake shipping, complained that Douglas' vote against the rivers and harbors improvement bill and his insistence on a system of tonnage duties was a deliberate attempt to punish the section for its political opposition. When President Pierce vetoed the bill, it was charged that he had done so at Douglas' request. The disappointment of the lake region found ready expression in the growing revolt against Douglas and the Kansas-Nebraska Act. Finally, events outside the state dramatized the slavery issue in a way the politicians could not. The popularity of Harriet Beecher Stowe's *Uncle Tom's Cabin* and the capture and return of fugitive slaves to slavery, culminating in the arrest of Anthony Burns early in the summer of 1854, produced an angry reaction against the south and seemed to substantiate the threat of southern slave expansion. It was against such odds that Douglas prepared to do battle.[20]

Although warned against it, Douglas decided to open his campaign with an address in Chicago on September 1, confident that he could overcome his opposition in the very heart of their camp. "They threaten a mob," Douglas wrote to Lanphier, "but I have no fears. All will be right." His opponents feared that resolutions endorsing the Kansas-Nebraska Act, purporting to reflect Chicago opinion, would be passed. In order to frustrate this strategy, newspapers urged Chicago's "order loving citizens to 'go early' and prepare to sit through if it takes till midnight." As if anticipating trouble, they asked that Douglas be given a patient and respectful hearing. "The honor of our city is at stake," wrote one editor. Any attempt to interrupt the meeting "would injure the cause it might be designed to promote, as well as leave an indelible stigma upon our city, which many long years could not eradicate." Early in the day, the flags of ships in the harbor were lowered to half-mast to protest Douglas' vote against the rivers and harbors bill, and shortly before the talk was scheduled to begin church bells began to toll a doleful dirge. Rumors that Douglas had recruited an armed Irish bodyguard, anathema to the Know-Nothings, and that trainloads of supporters were arriving from the country flew through the city during the day. A platform had been erected before the North Market Hall, and at the appointed hour, in spite of the oppressive heat, the streets were jammed with people.

Following a few brief remarks by the mayor of Chicago, Douglas announced that he would elucidate the principles of the Kansas-Nebraska Act because, he was convinced, so few people in Chicago really understood its provisions. Before he was able to launch into his argument, however, he was interrupted by an uproar of shouts, groans, and hisses. Each time he tried to speak the tumult was renewed. According to eyewitnesses, a few "missiles" were thrown at the platform, and on one occasion the mayor stepped forward to order the police to arrest those who were responsible. It was clear that Douglas was not to be allowed to speak. Persons in the audience called upon him to explain his vote against the rivers and harbors bill, but he could not have done so even if he wished. To the delight of the crowd, Douglas lost his temper, denouncing the assemblage as a mob and replying to their taunts by shaking his fist, which only intensified the din. Waving off the assistance of others on the stand, he attempted to stare the audience into silence, but to no avail. After enduring the insults and jeers for over two hours, he gave up, stalking off the platform with a parting shout of defiance. The crowd followed his carriage to the Tremont House, where Douglas was staying, and, after howling before the hotel for a time, finally dispersed.

The *Tribune* was delighted with the turn of events. By refusing Douglas, with his "Irish rowdies" and "grog-house politicians," the opportunity to speak, Chicagoans had in fact preserved their honor and self-respect; the incident was but just retribution for the crimes which lay "thick upon him." News of the incident would "carry joy and strength to the hearts of the lovers of freedom, and dismay and panic into the ranks of the slaveocracy."

Douglas later charged the Know-Nothings with responsibility for the disruption, an accusation that was probably not without some foundation, while the *State Register* regarded the action as characteristic of abolitionism. "It is but natural that men who deny to the people of the territories privileges which they claim for themselves, should deny, by mob violence, the privilege of free speech to those who differ with them in matters of public policy." Repercussions extended far beyond the boundaries of the state. The New York *Herald* emphasized the inconsistency of the abolitionists; "here we find the members of a party which has inscribed on its banners the motto, 'free speech—free labor—free men,' uniting to put down the exercise of a right guaranteed by the constitution, and adopted as one of their own cardinal points of faith." Even Greeley's *New-York Tribune* found the crowd's action indefensible. Mississippi's Senator Albert Gallatin Brown immediately wrote Douglas, "If your *friends* failed to make you President in 1852 your enemies will succeed in making you the first man in the Republic in 1856." [21]

His reception in Chicago was a deeply moving experience to Douglas; for once he had encountered a situation which he could not master. The seriousness of the rebuff was evident. If allowed to go unanswered, its impact on the party in the impending elections would be disastrous. Retreat was out of the question, nor could he quietly ignore the incident.

The true proportions of the opposition were for the first time revealed to him. He immediately began to make plans for an extensive campaign throughout the state on behalf of Democratic candidates for the state legislature and for Congress. If Chicago would not listen to him, he was certain the rest of the state would. It was not long before his old confidence returned. "In Illinois we will make all right," he wrote to John C. Breckinridge a few days after the Chicago incident, "The row at Chicago is doing us immense good." If anything, his experience in Chicago had toughened his resolve.

After a brief visit to Indianapolis, where he had been invited to address a state Democratic convention, Douglas returned to Illinois, where he threw himself into the campaign with an intensity that revealed his determination. It promised to be an uphill fight. Of Illinois' nine Congressmen, five had voted against the Kansas-Nebraska Act—the delegation's four Whigs and John Wentworth—while a sixth, Democrat William H. Bissell, prevented from voting by illness, had gone on record as opposing the bill. The Democratic party held a substantial majority in the state legislature, but in view of the lukewarm support given by many Democrats to the Kansas-Nebraska resolutions in February and the bitter splits that had developed in the party during the summer, Democratic strength in the local contests was no longer a source of confidence. The races for the state's legislative seats assumed a greater significance, for the new legislature would have the responsibility of filling Shields' Senate seat. Fortunately for Douglas, only one major state office, that of the state treasurer, was at stake in 1854.

The task of the Douglas Democrats was rendered more difficult by the numerous defections among party leaders on the Kansas-Nebraska issue. John Wentworth had been discreet and temperate in his opposition, fearing that attacks on Douglas in his district might very well result in his own defeat, but as far as Douglas was concerned the brief reconciliation between the two men was over. Douglas asked the editor of the *Chicago Times* to "make war on Wentworth every good chance you get, for . . . he must be beaten at all hazards." Bissell, whose opposition to the Kansas-Nebraska Act had surprised Douglas, announced that he would not seek re-election. Douglas' candidate for his seat was immediately challenged by Lyman Trumbull, an anti-Nebraska Democrat and former member of the state supreme court. Trumbull, who had first tilted with Douglas years before when the latter was appointed secretary of state, had returned to active politics as a vigorous opponent of the

Kansas-Nebraska Act and, with Whig encouragement and the solid support of the district's large German population, seemed well on his way to election.[22]

Other prominent Democrats followed suit. John M. Palmer, a member of the legislature's upper house, sought re-election on an anti-Nebraska platform. Palmer's revolt was encouraged by at least one leading Whig. "You are, and always have been, *honestly* and *sincerely* a democrat," wrote Abraham Lincoln to Palmer early in September, "and I Know how painful it must be to an honest sincere man, to be urged by his party to the support of a measure, which on his conscience he believes to be wrong." In a meeting with Palmer later in the campaign, Douglas angrily denounced his opposition and charged him with having joined the abolitionists. Among the Democrats defecting with Palmer were Norman B. Judd of Chicago and Burton C. Cook of Ottawa, both of whom played important roles in moulding opinion against Douglas' act in northern Illinois. Former Governor John Reynolds, influential among old-line Democrats in the southern part of the state, went over to the opposition. Sidney Breese, still nurturing his pique against Douglas and anxious to regain his Senate seat, opposed Douglas for personal reasons, and such long-time Douglas partisans as Ebenezer Peck and E. D. Taylor now joined the outcry against the Senator.

Douglas' insistence that the act be made a party test in the campaign aroused the ire of some who thoroughly approved its principles. Chief among these was John A. McClernand, who had represented Douglas' interests in the House of Representatives until his retirement in 1851. Recognizing the party split as an obstacle to his own efforts to return to national politics, McClernand refused to insist on the endorsement of the act. He wrote the *State Register* that he repudiated "this new test as unauthorized and inimical to the harmony and success of the democratic party" and criticized Douglas for attempting to read out of the party all who disapproved the act.[23]

iv

For two months following his return from Indianapolis, Douglas stumped the state in a speaking tour that carried him first through the unfriendly counties of northern Illinois. His audiences were openly hostile, and his speeches were frequently interrupted by expressions of displeasure. Still Douglas could write from LaSalle, with amazing confidence, that his meetings had been "glorious." "The party are all right everywhere," he asserted. "We will carry our Legislative Tickets all along the Canal line and also this Congressional District if we make the right kind of a fight."

Everywhere his message was the same. He reviewed the legislative history of the Kansas-Nebraska Act and defended its provisions with arguments that by now had a familiar sound. He charged into his adversaries, accusing his opponents with having become victims of an abolitionist plot, but he reserved his sharpest attacks for the Know-Nothings, whose nativistic and anti-Catholic platform was, he shouted, a clear violation of the Constitution. His arguments did not go unanswered. Douglas was followed from place to place by a variety of opposition speakers, the most persistent of whom was the abolitionist Ichabod Codding. In Bloomington Douglas encountered Abraham Lincoln for the first time during the campaign. The two men met in Douglas' hotel room, where, according to report, Lincoln refused to drink with the Senator, avowing his temperance principles and thereby delighting the temperance reformers. Douglas, declining an invitation to meet Lincoln in a joint debate, spoke in the afternoon, and Lincoln replied in an evening speech.[24]

Douglas arrived in Springfield on October 2. The state fair was then in progress, and people from all over the state were in the capital. His appearance marked the climax of the campaign. Assisting him was John Calhoun, a former mayor of Springfield who had just been appointed surveyor general of Kansas and Nebraska Territories at Douglas' behest, and James W. Singleton, a Whig who had come over to Douglas' side. Lincoln was on hand to counter Douglas' arguments, along with a procession of the Senator's Democratic opponents, including Sidney Breese, E. D. Taylor, and Lyman Trumbull. Forced to move into the statehouse by a heavy rain which had reduced the fair grounds to a quagmire, Douglas spoke for two and a half hours, delivering the same speech he had already given on many occasions. The pace of the campaign had begun to have its effect. His voice was hoarse, and he seemed fatigued and not well. Even so, much of the old fire remained. One devoted member of the audience later wrote that he could understand why the Chicagoans had not allowed Douglas to speak, "for he would most assuredly have turned the *Current* against them."

Lincoln followed with a formal reply on the following afternoon. Aroused "as he had never been before" by the repeal of the Missouri Compromise, Lincoln in 1854 not only sought election to the state legislature; he also was advertising his availability for election to Shields'

Senate seat. While he disavowed any intention of interfering with slavery where it existed and declared his willingness to sustain fugitive slave legislation, he insisted that Congress was pledged to prevent slavery from expanding into the territories. When he had concluded, Douglas, who was present in the audience, spoke for an hour and a half in reply, "in a most vehement and excited manner." Following the speeches, the local Republican editor gave rare tribute to Douglas' talent for persuasion: he wrote that the Senator "has power . . . He is the grand master of human passion and rules the crowd with an iron rule, because he governs them by and through their passions." [25]

Eight speeches in as many towns followed during the next ten days. On October 16 Douglas was in Peoria. Lincoln, urged by his friends to follow Douglas, was on hand, and both men delivered essentially the same speeches they had made in Springfield. Douglas was to close the discussion, as he had on the earlier occasion, but his hoarseness prevented him from doing so. William H. Herndon, Lincoln's law partner, later recalled that Douglas, fearing the effect of Lincoln's replies, asked for a "truce," offering to make no further speeches during the campaign if Lincoln would also desist. Lincoln was supposed to have agreed and returned home, only to discover that Douglas had broken his promise with a speech in Princeton. The story was denied by contemporaries, has been discounted by scholars, and probably never happened. Both Douglas and Lincoln traveled to Lacon following their Peoria confrontation. Douglas canceled his scheduled speech because of the condition of his voice, and Lincoln, not wishing to take advantage of the Senator's indisposition, canceled his own appearance. By the time Douglas reached Princeton, his voice had recovered sufficiently to enable him to debate with Owen Lovejoy, but a scheduled appearance the following day in Aurora, where the Negro abolitionist Frederick Douglass was prepared to answer him, was canceled. On October 19, Douglas returned to Chicago, unwell and tired. Except for a few speeches in the hostile First Congressional District later in the month, his campaign had closed.[26]

Douglas was as discouraged as he was fatigued. His leadership, so recently strong and unquestioned, was under serious challenge in much of the state. The opposition he had encountered away from Chicago, and the arguments against the Kansas-Nebraska Act, were more impressive and persuasive than he had anticipated. The movement to fuse his Democratic and Whig opponents into a new political coalition continued to gain momentum, although it became clear that the leaders of the opposition in the two parties were not yet ready to stake their political futures on a new organization. An effort to organize a state-wide Republican party proved abortive, although a Republican candidate for state treasurer was nominated.

Attacks on the Kansas-Nebraska Act were easily converted into attacks on Douglas personally. His strictures against the Know-Nothings led to charges that he had entered into an unholy alliance with the Irish against the native-born, favoring "foreigners" over the "descendants of revolutionary sires." He sought, it was said, to establish Roman Catholicism as the only true religion. Douglas' replies to the New England and Chicago clergymen seemed to bear out the charges. "Douglas cursed the Christian in the United States senate," claimed one opponent, and now "he cursed the true American." These were telling arguments among the voters of rural Illinois. The specter of Mormon polygamy was raised when it was suggested that, under Douglas' popular sovereignty, polygamy would be given legal recognition. One paper recalled that it had been Douglas, as a Judge, who had turned "Joe Smith, that pestiferous wretch loose among our people." Illinoisans were reminded once again of the Mississippi slaves which belonged to Douglas' sons, and the Senator was accused of introducing the Nebraska bill for his own financial advantage. Efforts were made to counteract the opposition arguments by importing out of state speakers to assist Douglas, but they were feeble and ineffective in comparison to the similar strategy employed by the anti-Nebraska element.[27]

News of Democratic disasters in Indiana, Ohio, and Pennsylvania arrived in mid-October and deepened the gloom in the Democratic camp. "I fear all is lost here," Richardson confided to Douglas. "The disasters in Penn Ohio & Indiana have drawn from us every doubtful vote." Lanphier became physically ill worrying about the outcome of the election. Jesse Bright, whose party had been defeated in his own state, was resigned to the loss of Illinois as well. "Illinois may follow the example of Ind. in the Election," he wrote to Douglas, "but if so, *I know* you are a man of to much nerve to be discouraged by such a result." Disturbing news also came from the state's congressional districts. Richardson, the man who had engineered the Kansas-Nebraska Act through the House, fully expected to be defeated. "I see plainly before me all the pleasures of private life, to which I go with the approval of a maj [ority] of my District." Richardson's defeat, speculated one Whig, would signal Douglas' downfall. Writing from Belleville, where Lyman Trumbull was running for Congress as an anti-Nebraska Democrat, Shields reported, "There is no hope for this district. All is perfect chaos, and the feeling is such that no effort can accomplish anything." Even in southeastern Illinois, an area presumed safe for Democrats, incumbent Congressman J. C. Allen was reported to be in trouble.[28]

The election results were not as bad as some Democrats feared, but they were bad enough. The party elected only four of the state's nine Congressmen, a loss of one seat. Lyman Trumbull was easily elected over his regular Democratic opponent, while Allen carried his district by so slim a majority that his victory was immediately contested. Three of the successful opposition candidates were elected as Republicans, all of them in northern districts. There were some bright spots. The two Democrats for which Douglas had campaigned especially hard won victories. Richardson was re-elected in spite of his misgivings, and in the Springfield district Thomas L. Harris ousted the Whig incumbent. Equally gratifying to Douglas was the defeat of John Wentworth. The Chicago district had been plunged into unprecedented confusion when Democrats not only challenged Douglas and the Kansas-Nebraska Act, but also Wentworth's political power. When an anti-Nebraska fusion convention nominated freesoil Democrat James Woodworth, Wentworth withdrew from the competition. His followers made their own nomination, and when the Whigs and Douglas Democrats followed suit, a four-cornered race developed in which Woodworth was the easy victor. On the statewide level, the Democrats elected their candidate for state treasurer, but it was clear that the victory could not be interpreted as an endorsement of the Kansas-Nebraska Act.

There was little to cheer the Democrats in the legislative returns. The anti-Nebraska fusionists carried both houses of the general assembly, shattering the Democratic majority of previous years and administering a long-threatened rebuke to the leadership of the Little Giant. The Democrats were naturally reluctant to interpret the results as a protest against the Kansas-Nebraska Act, preferring to assign their defeat to "a torrent of abolitionism, whigism, free-soilism, religious bigotry, and intolerance, all joined in a wild and wicked foray upon the democratic party and the constitution." The Know-Nothings were an easy scapegoat. Speaking in the Senate in the following February, Douglas saw in the elections "a crucible into which . . . [was] poured Abolitionism, Maine liquor law-ism, and what there was left of northern Whigism, and then the Protestant feeling against the Catholic, and the native feeling against the foreigner." "That crucible," he continued, "in which these various elements were melted, solved, and united was, in every instance, a Know-Nothing lodge." James Shields saw matters more realistically. "Two things have contributed to put the seal upon distraction," he wrote to Lanphier. "The *test* as they call it of Douglass to make men acknowledge that the act was all right, and the other the exposition of Atchison that he wanted a slave state back of Missouri, and that Douglass consented to be his instrument to effect this." Expressing what many Democrats hesitated to concede, he concluded, "The Anti Nebraska feeling is too deep—more than I thought it was." [29]

v

The Democrats in Illinois were staggered by their defeat, and when the election returns from other states began to come in their gloom became deeper. State after state had fallen to the new anti-Nebraska fusion movement. In some, notably Massachusetts, the Know-Nothings had swept the field. The shock of defeat produced rumblings of dissatisfaction with Douglas' leadership in the state party.

An invitation to speak in Chicago following the election provided Douglas with an opportunity to reassure the party faithful. It was not to be a public appearance, but rather a banquet sponsored by his friends to show "their profound admiration" for Douglas. His arguments were the familiar ones, but he delivered them with a calm restraint and persuasive eloquence that had been lacking in his earlier stump speeches. He reviewed the events leading up to the enactment of the Compromise of 1850, as he had so many times before, and recalled that he had been as fiercely and bitterly denounced for his support of the Missouri Compromise as he was now for securing its repeal. "Should the people of each State and Territory be allowed to form and regulate their own domestic concerns in their own way?" he asked. "If the principle be right, it will hardly be contended that it was wrong to carry it out when the acknowledged time for action had arrived."

Referring to the recent elections, Douglas assured his audience that there was nothing in their results "which should dampen our ardor or induce us to relax our energies." "Let us be of good cheer," he counseled, "all is well. Though the heavens are partially overcast, the clouds are passing away." [30]

But the clouds were not passing away. The new legislature would soon meet, and its first task would be the election of a United States Sen-

ator. Although he had returned to Washington, Douglas charted the
course he expected his supporters to follow. The strategy was to find a
new issue which could distract attention away from the Kansas-Nebraska Act and at the same time divide the new opposition coalition.
Lacking a majority in the legislature, there seemed to be little other
choice. As Lanphier put it, "They outnumber *us*—we must outmanage
*them.*" The new issue had already been suggested in Douglas' campaign
speeches. "The Nebraska fight is over," Douglas wrote to Lanphier, "and
Know Nothingism has taken its place as the chief issue of the future."
Irish-born Senator Shields was admirably suited to this new issue. "Our
friends in the Legislature," Douglas advised, "should nominate Shields
by acclamation, and nail his flag to the mast, and never haul it down
under any circumstances nor for any body." If Shields should be beaten,
it would be apparent "to the people & to the whole country that a gallant Soldier & a faithful public servant has been stricken down because
of the place of his birth." Douglas did not think that Shields could be
re-elected by this strategy, but he was hopeful "that this line of policy
will probably lead to a postponement of the election." In that event, constant pressure must be maintained on Shields' behalf until the next election. "I prefer no election under the circumstances," Douglas commented
to Sheahan, "to the election of any other man but Shields."

Anti-Nebraska leaders were also concerned lest their legislative majority fail to hold together. Trumbull, a candidate for the Senate in spite
of his election to the House, feared that "some of those who agree with
us in principle and ought to act openly with us, are . . . inclined to cooperate with the Nebraska men in carrying out their views . . . under
the delusive idea that by so doing they can maintain their former good
standing with Nebraska men." Lincoln, who declined his election to the
legislature in order that he might advance his candidacy for the Senate
more effectively, feared that some anti-Nebraska members would insist
on a platform "which I can not stand upon." With the Douglas forces
clearly in the minority, a number of other candidates appeared ready to
compete for the prize, threatening further splits in the anti-Nebraska
ranks. Sidney Breese was busy in the south developing support, while
Bissell was reported to be a candidate of both the Nebraska and anti-
Nebraska forces.[31]

Shields was worried, although he hoped that he might garner some
anti-Nebraska support. His vote for the Kansas-Nebraska bill had not
been enthusiastic, and he had taken little part in the state's legislative

campaign. It was not Shields' performance, however, that divided the legislators, but Douglas.' Not all Democrats supported Douglas' strategy. Some were convinced that his stubborn endorsement of Shields would result in certain defeat. Sheahan protested that to stick with Shields too long might cost the Democrats the election. "A new man should be talked of at once," he wrote, proposing the name of Governor Matteson. Harris insisted that Matteson be held in reserve in case Shields' election proved impossible. "The prospect of preventing an election of Senator," one legislator informed Douglas, "is very faint." Douglas was implacable. He instructed Harris to "take personal charge of everything" and cautioned him not to leave Springfield "even for a day" during the session. Shields should be supported to the bitter end.

As anticipated, the legislature was organized by the anti-Nebraska coalition, but the unity of the movement showed signs of cracking. Anti-Nebraska Democrats, anxious to wrest control of the party from Douglas, were unwilling to support a Whig for Senator, while many Whigs, quietly encouraged by Douglas Democrats to remain loyal to their ancient name and principles, refused to abandon their candidate, Abraham Lincoln. The common resentment against the repeal of the Missouri Compromise seemed to be losing some of its binding force. "They don't care two pence about Nebraska," Shields observed, "but Douglass they have sworn to destroy." Resolutions instructing Illinois' Senators to support the restoration of the Missouri Compromise stalled on their way to final passage. Finally, Douglas' strength was unexpectedly augmented. In a special election to fill Lincoln's seat in the lower house, an election which Lincoln curiously ignored in his eagerness to promote his candidacy for the Senate seat, a Douglas Democrat was victorious. Sensing the possibility of defeat, the anti-Nebraska leadership desperately offered to exchange Shields' re-election for the passage of the instruction resolutions.

The balloting began before a capacity crowd on February 8. For the first six ballots, Shields' support remained relatively stable. Lincoln, leading on the first ballot, steadily lost strength, while a handful of anti- Nebraska Democrats were steadfast behind Trumbull. The deadlock could not be broken. The Democrats were certain that Shields could not be elected. At this point, Harris, acting on his own authority, ordered Shields to be dropped in favor of the governor. Matteson provided the Democrats with a way out of their dilemma. He was popular, a member of the regular party organization, not objectionable to Douglas, and apparently acceptable to many Whigs. More important, he had remained discreetly silent on the Kansas-Nebraska Act. By the ninth ballot, Matteson had moved to within four votes of election, Trumbull had gained considerably, while Lincoln's support had dwindled badly. Lincoln, despairing of his own election and preferring Trumbull to Matteson, instructed his followers to switch their support to the former. On the tenth ballot, Trumbull was declared the victor.

Trumbull's election was anathema to the Douglasites. "The Neb. men," Lincoln wrote, "confess that they hate it worse than any thing that could have happened." His own defeat was bitter, but, he continued, "it is a great consolation to see them worse whipped than I am." Sheahan informed Douglas that "the severest blow we could have received has been given us." Douglas vainly sought to make political capital out of the setback. Answering the taunts of the antislavery Senators, he angrily declared that Shields had been doomed to defeat whether he voted for or against the Nebraska bill, for "he had been guilty of the crime of being born in Ireland!" For Trumbull he had choice words. Trumbull's claims to membership in the Democratic party, he told the Senate, "will be news to the Democracy of Illinois . . . How can a man who was elected as an Abolition-Know-Nothing, come here and claim to be a Democrat, in good standing with the Democracy of Illinois?" To make such a claim, he shouted, was to libel the state.

When he learned of Shields' defeat, Douglas impulsively urged Sheahan to announce Shields' candidacy for the governorship, but the Chicago editor wisely demurred, for the election was over eighteen months off. Shields, disappointed and disgusted at the turn of events, left Illinois in search of better opportunity in Minnesota Territory.[32]

It had been a rough year for the Little Giant.

# XIX
## "We must make a fight for principles"
### 1855

i

Douglas' political stock had dropped to a new low by the end of 1854, when he returned to Washington. He seemed almost subdued. The fierce opposition he had encountered and the rebuke administered to his leadership in the legislative elections had dealt a sobering blow to his confidence. His conviction that his position was right, however, remained unshaken; in fact the onslaughts against him had aroused an uncompromising defense of his past actions that seemed to leave little room for flexibility and pragmatic adjustment. The journey, down the Mississippi to New Orleans and thence to the east, was quiet in contrast to the noisy demonstrations that had attended his trip to Illinois only a few months before. An invitation to address a public reception in New Orleans was respectfully declined with a brief letter reiterating his familiar position on popular sovereignty. Douglas' arrival in the national capital in mid-December was without fanfare.

Although the political excitement of the year just past had demanded his full attention, Douglas felt the loss of his wife keenly. He had become careless in his dress and manners, and when he returned to Congress in December 1854 he was sporting whiskers. The long separation from his children was an additional source of anxiety to him. Robert had been sent to Rockingham County, North Carolina, to live with his grandmother during most of the year, while the younger "Stevie" remained in Washington with Douglas' sister and brother-in-law. During the trying days of the Kansas-Nebraska debate, he sought, with the help of the Grangers, to maintain his social life, entertaining lavishly on several occasions, but his efforts seemed forced and indifferent. There were rumors that he would soon marry again, but this was actually far from his mind.[1]

Financial problems also began to concern Douglas. The expense of his campaigns on behalf of the Kansas-Nebraska Act and the Democratic party had been a heavy drain on his resources. Thousands of copies of speeches delivered in Congress, his own as well as others, were printed and mailed to constituents in Illinois. His interest in the *Chicago Times* was more than just political, and when the paper ordered a new steam press Douglas accepted responsibility for the payments. To meet his obligations he borrowed money from his New York banker, sold part of his share of the Superior townsite, and contemplated selling some of his Chicago property. When Ohio's abolitionist Senator Wade charged Douglas with mercenary motives in his authorship of the Kansas-Nebraska Act —a charge echoed by Wentworth, who implied that profits from the Mississippi plantation were being used to buy Chicago property—the Senator was irate. He sent Sheahan an accounting of his Chicago real estate investments, to be made public at the appropriate moment. When a report was published that Douglas and John W. Forney were engaged in an extensive land speculation in Nebraska, Forney vehemently denied the allegation, and Douglas publicly repeated his determination never to purchase or own property in any of the territories as long as he served as chairman of the Senate Committee on Territories.[2]

Although preoccupied with political matters, Douglas still maintained his interest in the advancement of arts and letters and in the dissemination of scientific knowledge. He encouraged one minor novelist of the period to travel in Europe and financed the Italian education of one of America's promising young sculptors. Leonard Volk, who is remembered principally for his sculptures of Lincoln, was a kinsman of Douglas'. In 1855, Douglas was instrumental in sending Volk to Rome, where the latter attended "the finest school for advancement in the Art of Sculpture in the World." Later in the year, Volk wrote Douglas that he was expecting "a remittance from you as soon as it may be convenient for you to make it. . . . Perhaps I ask it too soon, but you desired me to let you know in time when I wanted more money, and I have now done so." Douglas continued to subsidize Volk during the rest of the decade.

As a member of the Board of Regents of the Smithsonian Institution,

Douglas was drawn into the controversy over the allocation of funds that troubled the institution during its early years. Joseph Henry sought to channel funds primarily into experimentation and publication, while a minority of the Regents, including Douglas, argued that the development of a scientific library should be given priority. Although most of the discussions were conducted behind closed doors, the issue reached the floor of the Senate. Douglas, regretting that the Regents' differences should have become a matter for congressional concern, reiterated his belief that the library should be the principal feature of the organization. When some bad feeling erupted in the debate, Douglas reminded the Senate that "a charitable fund for such high and noble purposes, ought to be administered in a spirit of kindness and charity." [3]

In contrast to the stormy scenes of the year before, the short session of the thirty-third Congress was anticlimactic. President Pierce's message was innocuous, and Congress seemed to be in a chastened mood. Routine territorial business occupied much of Douglas' time—appropriations for public buildings in the territories, the regulation of fees for territorial officers, the construction and improvement of military roads in the territories. He resisted an effort to separate the office of superintendent of Indian affairs from that of the territorial governor and sought to integrate the territorial courts into a larger plan for judicial reform. Among the questions with which he had to deal was the desire of some of the older territories for an extension of the provisions of the Kansas-Nebraska Act, particularly those that stressed popular sovereignty, to their own areas. The act was hailed in the territories as a significant step toward "the emancipation of the Territories" from the rigid and odious colonialism under which they had previously been governed. Federal restrictions on territorial legislation and congressional disallowance of territorial laws had long been primary targets of the frontiersmen. Oregon's territorial legislators had consistently petitioned Congress for the removal of these disabilities, and when Douglas deleted them from the Kansas-Nebraska Act they renewed their efforts. Failing in this, Oregonians turned to the alternative of statehood. Douglas responded by submitting a bill to admit Oregon as a state, but he encountered strong opposition from both northern and southern Senators. A petition was received from Minnesota Territory asking that the provision for congressional disallowance be removed from its organic act, but no action was taken on it. [4]

Outside Congress, Douglas was busy with matters dealing with the territorial patronage, an area where he claimed special influence. Pierce had already been receptive to the Senator's suggestions. Shortly after his inauguration, the President had nominated a former Illinoisan, Orville C. Pratt, to the supreme bench in Oregon Territory. Douglas' urgent objections, however, caused Pierce to withdraw the nomination. The organization of Kansas and Nebraska Territories opened a new field for the patronage, and Douglas was quick to take advantage of it. At Douglas' request, Pierce appointed John Calhoun, one of Douglas' strongest allies in Illinois, to the post of surveyor general of the two combined territories, probably the most powerful of the territorial offices because of the patronage it commanded. Douglas was equally successful in securing the appointment of his nominees to several lesser posts in Kansas. In the spring of 1855 he and Henry M. Rice, Minnesota's territorial delegate and a partner in the Superior speculation, sought the removal of Willis A. Gorman from the governorship of Minnesota Territory. Gorman, it was charged, had attempted to block legislation that would have enhanced the value of the Superior investment. Rice and Douglas proposed that Pierce replace Gorman with John C. Breckinridge, also interested in Superior, but the President vacillated and eventually did nothing.[5]

Although the national capital was relatively quiet in the spring of 1855, it was obvious that trouble was brewing. The confusion into which the parties had been plunged by the Kansas-Nebraska Act was an inescapable fact. Old alignments had been shattered, and new ones were taking shape. The most serious casualty of Douglas' advocacy of popular sovereignty in Kansas and Nebraska was the party system as it had developed over the preceding decades. "The Democratic party," moaned one southerner, "has been literally slaughtered in the Northern, Middle and Western States, whilst of the Whig party there is not left even a monumental remembrance."

The results of the state elections demonstrated the truth of this assertion. In October, when Pennsylvania, Ohio, and Indiana had been captured by the anti-Nebraska fusion movement, half of the Democratic majority in the House of Representatives was lost. The work was completed in November. New York fell to the fusionists and returned a congressional delegation that was overwhelmingly anti-Nebraska in composition. Most of New England was lost to the Democrats, while Democratic candidates in the remaining states of the northwest went down to defeat. When the final votes were tallied, the Democrats found they had lost their hold on the lower house of Congress for the first time in many years.

Stephen A. Douglas, about 1845

John A. McClernand, Illinois
Congressman, 1843-51, 1859-61; Douglas
leader in the House of Representatives

Charles H. Lanphier, editor of the
*Illinois State Register* and close friend
and supporter of Douglas

William A. Richardson, Illinois
Congressman, 1847-56; Douglas leader
in the House and at the national
conventions

Lyman Trumbull, Senator from Illinois
and political opponent of Douglas

Abraham Lincoln, at the time of his debates with Douglas, October 1, 1858

James Buchanan, during his presidency

Alexander H. Stephens, Georgia Congressman, 1843-59; Southern supporter of Douglas

John Slidell, Senator from Louisiana and Southern opponent of Douglas

John J. Crittenden, Senator from Kentucky, and advocate, with Douglas, of compromise, 1860-61

Herschel V. Johnson of Georgia, Douglas' vice-presidential running mate in 1860

John C. Breckinridge, Vice President, 1857-61, and candidate for the presidency, 1860

John Bell of Tennessee, candidate for the presidency on the Constitutional Union ticket, 1860

Martha Martin, Douglas' first wife (from a painting)
*Courtesy Illinois State Historical Library*

Stephen A. Douglas, about 1857-59
*Courtesy Illinois State Historical Library*

Adele Cutts, Douglas' second wife (from a portrait by G. P. A. Healy)

*Courtesy Illinois State Historical Library*

Stephen A. Douglas, 1860-61
*Courtesy Chicago Historical Society*

Illinois State Capitol, Vandalia, where Douglas began his legislative career

Illinois State Capitol, Springfield, in the 1850's

Stephen A. Douglas, about 1859-60

While the shifting party alignment was most dramatic in the House of Representatives, the political revolution also strengthened the opposition to Douglas and the Democratic leadership in the Senate. William H. Seward, a vigorous opponent of Douglas, was re-elected in New York. In Iowa, Douglas' friend and supporter Augustus Caesar Dodge was replaced by James Harlan. John P. Hale, who had tilted with Douglas in earlier years, was elected again by the New Hampshire legislature to fill a vacancy, a rebuke to the party in the President's own state. From Massachusetts came the outspokenly antislavery Henry Wilson, a man of Know-Nothing proclivities who owed his election to a combination of Free-Soilers, Know-Nothings and dissident Democrats. Finally, there was Lyman Trumbull, against whose election Douglas' followers in the Illinois legislature vainly protested on the questionable ground that Trumbull was ineligible to sit in the Senate. While old Francis Preston Blair could still write in February 1855 that Douglas was "really the great man at one end of the Avenue," the future of that greatness was clouded.

Democratic reverses in the north led to an exaggeration of the party's successes in the southern states. When Henry A. Wise successfully put down a determined Know-Nothing challenge in his race for the Virginia governorship, Pierce wrote Douglas that a "new face" had been put upon "the prospects of the Democratic party." The setback suffered by Douglas and the party, some hoped, would only be temporary. "Our columns are broken," commented John W. Forney, "but thank God, we have not lost our colours. Now our giant has touched Mother Earth, I expect him to recover strength again. . . . We shall have a smaller party than usual for a few brief months, but our devotion to principles will soon fill our ranks with bold and energetic Democrats." [6]

The question whether Douglas could quickly recover his lost ground was partially answered in February, when the calm of an otherwise dull congressional session was broken briefly by a foretaste of things to come. A bill that would allow cases arising under the laws of the United States to be transferred from state courts to federal courts, a response to increasing opposition in some northern states to the enforcement of the Fugitive Slave law, resulted in a confrontation between Douglas and Benjamin F. Wade. Before the outburst subsided, Fessenden and Wilson had joined in the attack on the Illinois Senator. Douglas defended the measure, arguing the primacy of federal law in areas that fell within the scope of the Constitution, a corollary of his belief in states' rights. "The laws of the United States," he maintained, "adjudged by the Supreme Court to be constitutional, are declared to be the supreme law of the land, anything in the constitution or laws of any State to the contrary notwithstanding." Wade disagreed. Curiously, he invoked the Virginia and Kentucky Resolutions, which, he said, provided the states with the right to judge the constitutionality of federal law. His state, Ohio, therefore had every right to declare the Fugitive Slave Act unconstitutional. The discussion soon left the area of constitutional interpretation as Wade pressed Douglas for an explanation of the recent Democratic defeats.

Douglas replied without hesitation, but also without credibility. The issue had not been drawn clearly between Nebraska and anti-Nebraska men, he shouted, for all the anti-Nebraska men who had been elected really owed their election to the Know-Nothings. Secret conclaves, meeting at "the dark hour of midnight," administering the "most horrible oaths," determined the election results. "Thus, by strategem and terrors, men personally hostile, were forced to act together—men who were the advocates of adverse and irreconcilable political theories, were apparently moulded into one common brotherhood . . . bound by oath to obey orders and vote as they were directed." In such colorful terms did Douglas rationalize the anti-Nebraska fusion movement. Henry Wilson fumed and William P. Fessenden objected. Turning to Fessenden, Douglas charged heatedly that "a Know Nothing cannot be a Know Nothing without swearing to tell a lie," a remark which Fessenden took personally. Subsequently, Douglas thought better of his statement. He informed Fessenden that he had stricken the offending remark from the official report of the discussion, and it did not appear in the *Congressional Globe.*

The debate continued as Douglas, driven to anger, accused his opponents once again of seeking the dissolution of the Union, of stimulating the passions of the sections, and of arraying the north against the south. "We are called . . . doughfaces and cowards because . . . we stand between the Constitution and those who seek to trample upon its provisions." "They tell us," Douglas went on, "that we are in vain attempting to resist an overwhelming torrent of northern sentiment; that our course is rushing us to inevitable self-destruction; that we are destined to be swept from the face of the earth, and sunk to the lowest depths of obloquy and infamy, from which there is no resurrection." Douglas' reaction made it clear that he did not regard the groundswell of opposition to the

Kansas-Nebraska Act and the subsequent Democratic defeats as demonstrating the error of his ways. "We calmly look the storm in the face, defy its mutterings and howlings about our heads, and hold on firmly to the Union and to the Constitution as the surest and only means of preserving it." Finally, Wade's reference to Douglas' Mississippi plantation as providing motives for his actions drew forth a detailed account of the manner in which the property had been received, with a sharp and bitter reference to those who would invade "the circle of my private relations in search of materials for the impeachment of my official action." The rebuke suffered in the elections obviously irritated Douglas more than he admitted.[7]

The "overwhelming torrent of northern sentiment" to which Douglas alluded was only one facet of the problem he had to face. If the rise of a viable antislavery opposition in the northern states spelled trouble for the Democracy, the events in Kansas were to prove equally disturbing.

ii

When Kansas and Nebraska territories were organized in 1854, the white population within their boundaries was small and scattered, consisting principally of a few hundred Army soldiers, missionaries, and Indian traders. The terms of the policy that had established this area west of the Missouri River as a great Indian reservation forbade permanent settlement, and those who wished to penetrate the region for commercial purposes were technically required to secure licenses from the national government. By early 1854, settlers from western Iowa and Missouri began to spill over into the prairies on the west bank of the Missouri, but their numbers were small and their presence frequently temporary. The organization of the territories, then, departed from what had become the normal course of frontier development. Prior to that time, territorial governments had been created in response to demands from already existent populations. Kansas and Nebraska were different. No significant local population clamored for their recognition as territories; the pressure for their organization came from outside.

This difference created certain problems in the development of the two new territories. First, when the territories were officially opened to settlement, the land for the most part was locked up by Indian titles that had not yet been extinguished. In Kansas land was not available to the incoming settlers under the normal operation of national land policy. Second, the absence of settlement in the territories meant that their local institutions would be established by a population that had not yet arrived. Under normal circumstances, this might not have been a problem. But the Kansas-Nebraska Act went beyond earlier territorial legislation, reducing the degree of national control over territorial affairs and expanding the area of self-government, including the power of decision over the slavery question. It is unfortunate that popular sovereignty, to which Douglas had become committed in territorial matters and which had worked well in other frontier areas, should have received its greatest and most publicized test in this abnormal situation. These two problems—the confused land situation and the fact that the slavery issue would be decided by a prospective population—forecast trouble from the very beginning.

Antislavery northerners quickly perceived that slavery could be kept out of the territories only by a population numerous enough to outvote its proslavery opposition. For Nebraska this was no problem. Lying west of a free state, it would be settled by people who had no taste for the institution. For Kansas, however, there was no such assurance. Missourians had been especially active in urging the opening up of Kansas' prairies to settlement, and they looked forward to moving in with their slave property. They regarded Kansas as their own area for expansion and came to resent the intrusion of others who would establish institutions there contrary to their own. Many of Missouri's leaders, in fact, insisted that the security of slavery in Missouri depended upon their ability to extend slavery into Kansas.

During the debates on the final passage of the Kansas-Nebraska bill, Seward warned the south that any attempt to extend slavery into Kansas would be challenged. "We will engage in competition for the virgin soil of Kansas," he told the Senate, "and God give the victory to the side which is stronger in numbers as it is in the right." A month before, a group of Massachusetts reformers had already accepted the challenge with the chartering of the Massachusetts Emigrant Aid Company, an organization that would soon be recast as the New England Emigrant Aid Company. The prime mover behind the effort was Eli Thayer, a Worcester schoolmaster, who hoped not only to save Kansas for freedom but also to reap monetary rewards by investing in the economic development of the new territory. Financial support for Thayer's enterprise came from Boston merchants and industrialists, the most important of whom was Amos A. Lawrence, who also was anxious to prevent slavery from spreading into Kansas. Similar organizations were formed in other parts of the north.[8]

The influence of the emigrant aid companies on Kansas settlement has been exaggerated, for their success in promoting an antislavery emigration from the free states was in the long run negligible. However, the companies were launched in 1854 amidst great fanfare and grandiose claims, designed partly to frighten southerners and partly to attract investors. Such claims proved to be more progagandistic than accurate, but their impact on Missourians was profound. Senator Atchison warned his constituents that not only Kansas but all the territories were to be "abolitionized" by the northern efforts, and he suggested that countermeasures be taken. "We must meet organization with organization," he advised. "We must meet those philanthropic knaves peaceably at the ballot-box and outvote them." Like his free state counterparts, Atchison urged the south to act quickly, "to go peacefully and inhabit the Territory, and peacefully vote and settle the question according to the principles of the Douglas bill." Thus the stage was set early for the contest in Kansas, and for the inhabitants of western Missouri the stakes were especially high.[9]

The task of organizing Kansas' territorial government fell to Pierce's choice for governor of the new territory, Andrew Reeder, an inexperienced Pennsylvania attorney whose appointment was dictated primarily by local political considerations. After a brief tour of Kansas, Reeder scheduled the election for territorial delegate to Congress for the end of November, postponing the first legislative elections until the next year over the vehement protests of the Missourians. Taking advantage of the fact that the Kansas-Nebraska Act failed to define voting qualifications precisely, illegal voters on both sides participated in the November election, and the proslavery candidate was easily elected.

The pattern of the delegate election was repeated with a vengeance in the legislative elections the following spring. During the winter, exaggerated reports that thousands of antislavery immigrants were on their way to Kansas persuaded the inhabitants of western Missouri that drastic measures were necessary in order to assure a majority in the territorial legislature. Protective associations were formed in Missouri's river counties, and the call went out to the south for assistance. As election day neared, Missourians began to pour over the border. A crude census, taken under Reeder's direction, had revealed a population in the territory of 8500, or which about 2900 were judged to be legal voters. When the polls closed on March 30, it was discovered that over 6300 votes had been cast and that the proslavery candidates had won easy victories. Writing to Senator Hunter shortly afterward, Atchison exulted in the decision. "The pro slavery ticket prevailed everywhere as far as heard from, by overwhelming majorities. . . . We had at least 7,000 men in the territory on the day of the election and one third of them will remain there."

The proslavery forces acted quickly to consolidate their victory. The new legislature, meeting during the summer, quickly adopted the revised statutes of Missouri as the general law of the territory and promulgated a harsh slave code by which slavery was not only legally recognized in Kansas but protected under the threat of extreme and unnecessarily stringent penalties. Reeder protested, but his position had been weakened by some unfortunate land speculations in central Kansas. The legislature petitioned the President for the governor's removal, and later in the summer Pierce obliged.

Reactions against the illegal seizure of power in the territory by the proslavery Missourian element were not long in forming. During the previous year, permanent settlers had been arriving in Kansas in large numbers, coming not from New England nor from Missouri, but from the states of the Ohio and Mississippi valleys. They came, for the most part, to build new homes, to make fresh starts and to participate in the economic development of the new territory. Few of them were anxious to engage in conflict over the slavery issue; for most slavery was an abstraction that had little or no bearing on their effort to improve their own condition. The spring election frauds and the adoption of the slave code rankled, not so much because the settlers were opposed to slavery but because they had been deprived of a voice in the government of the territory. By the summer of 1855, it was obvious that these settlers comprised a majority of Kansas' inhabitants.[10]

In September a group of settlers gathered at Topeka to protest the "bogus" legislature and its "bogus" laws and to invoke the only remedy available to them, "that of forming a government for themselves." Among those present was a former Illinois editor and friend of Douglas', Mark W. Delahay. Delahay, through the columns of his Leavenworth newspaper, conceded the right of the territorial legislature to extend protection to the slave property in Kansas, but he strongly objected to the "oppressive and *inquisitorial* laws" actually passed by that body. The legislature, he charged, had "trampled underfoot the organic act, and *assumed* the right to decide the complexion of the institutions of Kansas." The meeting determined to bypass the territorial government by scheduling a convention to draw up a state constitution. Delahay, representing Douglas' views, proposed that the constitution should make no mention of slavery. In the constitutional convention that gathered in Topeka later in the fall, Delahay introduced a resolution approving "the principles of non-intervention in local affairs of Kansas, as enunciated by the Nebraska-Kansas act, and that this Convention recommend to the people of Kansas a strict observance of the principles laid down in said act." The resolution was narrowly defeated.

Leadership in the Topeka convention was assumed by Charles Robinson, an agent of the New England Emigrant Aid Company, and James H. Lane, a political adventurer and former Congressman from Indiana who had earlier supported the Kansas-Nebraska Act. The partisans of popular sovereignty were overridden, although some, like Delahay, were later accorded positions of influence in the Topeka movement. After several days of discussion, a constitution was produced that in many ways was as rigid as the action of the territorial legislature. Slavery was to be prohibited in the proposed state after July 4, 1857, the foreign-born were to be excluded from the franchise, and (by a separate schedule approved in a special vote) free Negroes were to be excluded from the state. Most curious was the provision stipulating that the constitution was unamendable until after 1865, with only one amendment allowed during the five years thereafter.

The action at Topeka provided Kansas with two alternative governments, the regularly constituted but fraudulently elected proslavery territorial government and the illegal, unauthorized, Topeka free state government. Each ignored the other, and the partisans of each boycotted the actions and elections of the other. It was not a situation conducive to peace and tranquillity. The existence of two governments, each with its own constituency, and the unfortunate situation respecting land titles resulted in sporadic acts of violence that were promptly given magnified treatment in the nation's press. The Kansas-Nebraska Act did not cease to be an issue, as Douglas had predicted it would; instead, aggravated by what seemed to be the practical operation of popular sovereignty, the issue grew until the "Kansas Question" dominated political thinking in the nation.[11]

iii

During most of 1855 the Kansas issue was argued principally in the press and in a few local political contests. The territorial elections and the enactment of a strict slave code provided grist for the journalistic mill and arguments for the emerging Republican party. Antislavery newspapers early recognized the opportunities offered by the turmoil in Kansas, and they sent special correspondents to the scene. Those correspondents were, for the most part, zealous men committed to the cause, and the reports they filed were unabashedly designed to arouse northern passions against an elaborately described southern plot to capture Kansas for slavery. The beginnings of the Topeka free state movement provided a focus for their energies, and a dramatic (though highly exaggerated) struggle for the prairies soon became standard fare for many northern newspaper readers. "Freedom, Truth and Righteousness" were combating "Despotism" in Kansas, according to the *Chicago Tribune,* and the south was warned that "an army of New England boys" would soon be ready to defend Kansas "with their blood." "Border ruffians," the name attached indiscriminately to the partisans of slavery, were charged with all manner of atrocities against freedom-loving settlers.[12]

Congress had adjourned in March, thus depriving the Kansas issue of a national forum, and the new Congress would not meet until December. The interval provided the nation's lawmakers with a much-needed respite. The repercussions of the previous year continued to be felt. Atchison, who assumed a personal part in the proslavery campaigns in Kansas, failed in his bid for re-election to the Senate from Missouri, and his place was taken by James S. Green, a man whose hostility toward Douglas was to become more manifest in later years. In Ohio, Douglas' antagonist Salmon P. Chase was elected to the governorship, the first real success of the new Republican party on the state level. Chase's victory demonstrated the durability of the new party, and by the end of the year many prominent antislavery Whigs had made the transition into its ranks.

The year, however, had its brighter aspects for Douglas. The Know-Nothings suffered decline as the Republican party was strengthened, and in the local fall elections the nativist crusade lost much of the ground it had gained the year before. More importantly, the Democrats made small but encouraging gains. Chase's Senate seat was filled by a former Congressman, George E. Pugh, who was soon to become a loyal Douglas supporter, and in a special election in Illinois a Douglas follower was elected to Congress from Lyman Trumbull's district, thus restoring the Democratic edge in the state's House delegation. Local elections in Maine, Pennsylvania, Indiana, Wisconsin, and New Jersey resulted in gains for the Democratic party. Continued Democratic victories in the south brought an encouraging, if premature, response from the Little Giant. "Victories are crowding upon us on all sides," Douglas wrote dramatically in October. "The torrent of fanaticism has been rolled back almost everywhere." The prospects for a Democratic triumph in 1856 brightened. "I do not see how we can fail to elect the Dem nominee for President next year," Douglas informed Lanphier in mid-summer. From Mississippi a friend of Jefferson Davis wrote optimistically to Douglas, "I was a little afraid of the Nebraska question whilst the whole North was in a ferment and parties in the South unsettled, but it is now the great question and will bear you in triumph over all opposition." His preference for 1856, he concluded, was a presidential ticket of Douglas and Davis.[13]

If the presidency was in Douglas' mind, he did not announce the fact. He had learned well the lesson of his 1852 experience and was determined that he would not make the same mistake of appearing in the field too early. Some newspapers had proposed his candidacy as early as November 1853. "I do not wish to occupy that position," he wrote Lanphier at the time. "I do not think I will be willing to have my name used." Douglas did not, however, rule out the possibility. He would remain uncommitted, "at liberty to do whatever my duty to my principles & my friends may require when the time for action arrives." The outburst of indignation following the Kansas-Nebraska Act forced a reappraisal of his plans. "I do not intend to do any act which will deprive me of the control of my own actions," he had informed Lanphier, but his authorship of the controversial bill had precisely that effect.

Following the disastrous elections in the fall of 1854, Douglas felt that any speculation about his presidential candidacy would be presumptuous. In late January 1855, he authorized the Washington *Sentinel* to announce that he neither desired nor would accept the presidential nomination. Douglas urged Sheahan to copy the statement in the *Chicago Times*. "My determination not to be a candidate for President in '56 is well known to you and remains inflexable." The Democratic party must be restored to its former strength, and this, Douglas was well aware, could best be done if his name were not prominently displayed. "Avow the willingness of the Democracy of Illinois," he counseled Sheahan, "to unite cordially on Gen'l Pierce, or General Cass, or Mr. Buchanan or any other good man from the north, or on Mr. Hunter of Va. or Gen'l Houston of Texas or any other sound and reliable man from the South for the next Presidency; deprecating however the agitation of the question at this early day." Any other strategy at this point, he was convinced, would only deepen the party divisions and damage his own chances.[14]

In the meantime, Douglas took to the stump and spent most of the year speaking, arguing, and cajoling in an effort to revive the party's fortunes and to refurbish his tarnished image. Following the adjournment of Congress, he traveled to Richmond to assist Henry A. Wise in his campaign for governor. The national Democracy in the north and west, he explained, had been overwhelmed by a fusion of Know-Nothings, abolitionists, "and other advocates of the monstrous *isms* of the day." The real villains were the abolitionists, he pointed out, whose dictates the Know-Nothings invariably followed. Reporting the speech, one influential northern paper expressed surprise that Douglas was "still alive." "Political death takes as little hold on some men as drowning does on cats." Douglas soon demonstrated that any attempt to write his political obituary was premature.[15]

Territorial business kept Douglas in Washington until mid-April, when he departed for Illinois. His arrival in Chicago a few days later was in striking contrast to his reception there the previous September. Politics had become quiet, and his return home was greeted by some of his opponents with rare tribute. Part of it was the result of Douglas' own more optimistic demeanor. Douglas, reported the *Chicago Tribune,* was seen on the streets "bearing a less care-worn countenance, and looking in better health and spirits than when he was here last year." His appearance, the paper noted, belied reports that he had become "addicted to dissipation." "Certainly, he looks well, and we are pleased to see it, for however hostile he may have been of late years to measures of public policy which we deem essential to the perpetuity of our free institutions and Republican government, we cannot forget that as a Senator he has done much to advance the interests of our state and city." "Douglas is here and looking better than I have lately seen him look," wrote Charles H. Ray, the *Tribune*'s editor, to a friend, "He does not drink as much wiskey as usual."

Douglas' return coincided with a campaign for a prohibitory liquor law, to be decided by the Illinois voters in a referendum early in June, and some of the *Tribune*'s generosity resulted from Douglas' wise decision to remain aloof from the campaign. Supporters of the measure charged that "Free Whiskey constitutes a corner stone of the great Democratic party." Douglas himself had earlier inveighed against the movement as one of the "isms" involved in the fusion of his opposition. Now, however, he maintained a discreet silence on the question and, if the report may be credited, reduced his own alcoholic consumption. The referendum was defeated without his intervention, for only the northern antislavery counties solidly upheld it.[16]

Of greater import to Douglas was the election of judges to the state supreme court. Not long before, Wisconsin's supreme court had intervened in the execution of the Fugitive Slave Act, and antislavery leaders in Illinois hoped to elevate like-minded judges to the Illinois court. Politics entered the contests in spite of the tradition that judicial elections should be fought on a nonpartisan basis. In the northern part of the state, Judge John D. Caton was savagely attacked for his commitment to "the doctrines of Douglas, and the partisan school to which Mr. Douglas belongs." Besides being a "radical, thorough-going, uncompromising Nebraska man," it was charged, Caton would be an exponent of the Fugitive Slave Act. In central Illinois, where the issue was not so clearly drawn, Onias Skinner, a friend of Douglas', was opposed by Stephen T. Logan, one-time law partner of Abraham Lincoln. Both Caton and Skinner were successful, and Douglas took comfort in these small but important gains of the Democratic party.[17]

A series of excursions celebrating the completion of new rail lines enabled Douglas to talk to masses of people in what were ostensibly nonpolitical gatherings. In mid-May he rode the newly completed Chicago branch of the Illinois Central to Urbana, where he delivered a banquet address. A few days later he traveled in a special excursion train to Burlington, Iowa, where he spoke of the indissoluble connection between Chicago and Burlington and reminded his audience that the obstacles in the way of the completion of the Pacific railroad were more imaginary than real. Two months later he spoke at a railroad festival in Dubuque, and later in the same month he visited the northwestern Illinois town of Sterling to celebrate the completion of a railroad to that point.[18]

With this promising start, Douglas undertook his effort to reunite the party and restore it to state leadership. It was as much a personal struggle as a party one, for, as one opposition paper commented, "The Democratic party here is Stephen A. Douglas and his followers." Douglas' targets were the Whigs and those dissident Democrats who had broken with him over the Kansas-Nebraska Act. The choice he placed before both groups was association with the abolitionists on the one hand or membership in the regular Democratic organization on the other. In his effort he enjoyed the questionable assistance of the state's radical press, which attacked the anti-Nebraska Democrats as "disappointed and jaundiced politicians who have no more sincere love for freedom than Stephen A. Douglas has, but who oppose him and his Kansas-Nebraska schemes, . . . because they are jealous of his power." The "more honest and sincere" members of Douglas' opposition joined the Republican party, the "more crafty and insidious" returned to Douglas, while those that remained constituted "a feeble, blind and foolish band." [19]

The fusion movement, which reached its peak during the legislative session, lost its effectiveness as soon as the legislature adjourned. The radicalism of northern Illinois newspapers and leaders discouraged the more conservative Whigs and Democrats from continuing in the coalition. Many anti-Nebraska Democrats desperately sought to retain an identity with the Democracy, while most Whigs preferred to play a waiting game, not fully persuaded as yet that their party had ceased to exist. When the abolitionist Owen Lovejoy proposed a state convention to strengthen the move toward a new party, Lincoln replied that "the political atmosphere is such just now, that I fear to do any thing, lest I do wrong." Responding to the same proposal, Lyman Trumbull declined to participate, suggesting instead a meeting of Democrats who were opposed equally to slavery, abolition, and Know-Nothings. With the disinclination of such leaders as Lincoln and Trumbull, the attempt to found a Republican party in the state languished.

The political situation in Illinois remained sufficiently fluid through most of 1855 to encourage Douglas that some of his lost ground could be regained with a little effort. The impact of events in Kansas, however, remained an imponderable factor. His opponents eagerly pounced on news from Kansas for its value in strengthening their challenge to Douglas' leadership. As reports of border ruffians, fraudulent elections, and free state conventions west of the Missouri became more widely known, the prospects of fusion in the state brightened, but not until after Douglas made his appeal.[20]

In August Douglas returned to the east briefly on what must have

been a politically motivated visit. Stopping in Washington, he dined at
the White House with President Pierce. According to the report of the
meeting, at which Virginia's Senator Mason and probably others were
present, the topic of conversation was Kansas. Quite possibly Pierce consulted with the group on the selection of a new governor for Kansas to
replace Reeder, for on the following day the appointment of Wilson
Shannon, former Ohio governor, was announced. During the discussion,
Douglas was said to have denounced, "in no flattering terms," the involvement of Atchison and his Missouri followers in the territory's border troubles. On his way back to Illinois he stopped in Buffalo, where he
met with John Van Buren and the editor of the radically anti-slavery
Buffalo *Republic,* stirring speculation in the press. "What's in the
wind?" queried one editor. The *Chicago Democrat* headlined the story
"Douglas Turning Abolitionist," while the *State Journal* thought a division of the "spoils" had occasioned the meeting. Douglas was undoubtedly seeking to smooth over the party schism.[21]

Campaigning as if it were an election year, Douglas placed his message before the people. The results were mixed. An invitation from a
group of Boston abolitionists to deliver a lecture on slavery at Boston's
Tremont Temple elicited a review of his position on the institution. Declining the invitation on the ground that his "tastes" would not permit
him to accept, he once again emphasized slavery's local character. Neither the federal government nor the citizens of other states have any
right to interfere with slavery where it exists. "I have never deemed it
my duty, as a citizen of a non-slaveholding State, to discuss the supposed
advantages or evils, with the view of sustaining or destroying the domestic institutions of sister States, with which, under the Constitution and
laws of the land, I have no right to interfere, and for the consequences
of which I am in no wise responsible." It was an involved way of administering a slap at abolitionism, and his remarks won passing approval
even from some of his opponents. In Springfield, Douglas pointedly
stressed the sanctity of the Constitution, a position which the Whig
*State Journal* suggested would meet "the hearty concurrence of good
men of all creeds." He denounced the radical "isms" which had combined against him, and, in an effort to press his audience to a choice, he
branded all who opposed popular sovereignty as acting in league with
abolitionists and fanatics.

Crossing the Mississippi, Douglas confronted the Kansas troubles before a St. Louis audience. He was, he insisted, opposed to any interfer-

ence by any state or people in the internal regulations of the territory, denouncing both the wrongs inflicted on Kansas by the Missourians and the intervention by "regular organized societies" from New England. One St. Louis reporter was more fascinated with Douglas' appearance than interested in his argument. "A little man, with a big head, and a tolerable display of abdominal rotundity," Douglas did not "convey any impressions of the terror or senatorial might which he has at certain periods excited in certain portions of the country." Nattily attired in a black dress coat, black cravat, white vest, and white breeches, he conveyed his argument "with a loud voice and slow accent, shaking his head and fore finger when desirous of being emphatic." [22]

In the southern Illinois town of Salem, Douglas learned that Lyman Trumbull was on hand to reply to his speech. A debate on the Kansas-Nebraska Act was immediately arranged, but when Trumbull, in his opening remarks, did not even refer to the act, and instead seemed anxious to prove himself the better Democrat, Douglas angrily canceled the arrangement. He later challenged Trumbull to join him in a letter of resignation from their Senate seats, allowing the voters in the state to decide between their positions, but Trumbull declined to accept what was obviously an unequal suggestion. Douglas continued his tour through southern and central Illinois, defending popular sovereignty, attacking the Know-Nothings, and urging the Democracy to unite for the coming political struggles.[23]

Looking more and more like a presidential candidate in spite of his disclaimers, Douglas interrupted his tour to attend a Democratic mass meeting in Lexington, Kentucky. The meeting, which would serve as an important opener to the presidential campaign, had been planned many weeks before with his friend John C. Breckinridge, with whom Douglas had been in correspondence most of the summer. Conferring with men from Indiana, Ohio, Tennessee, and Missouri, Douglas prepared a series of resolutions "with the view of producing unity of action between the free & slave states" at the forthcoming national convention. They were adopted by the Lexington meeting, but their purpose transcended the immediate situation. "Illinois takes the lead," he informed Lanphier, "& will have the honor of making the national Platform." The resolutions, he wrote, "should be treated as the 'Illinois Platform,' " and he urged the Springfield editor to have them adopted at county meetings and at the state convention. Those who had assisted him in the preparation of the resolutions, Douglas wrote to Iowa's Senator George W. Jones, "agreed to have them passed in all of those states as original, without stating where they come from, in order to show that Democracy was the same everywhere, in the free & slave states alike." What Douglas left unsaid was that the resolutions, if adopted, would effectively bar anti-Nebraska Democrats and Know-Nothings from any participation in the party, would open the gates of the party to old-line Whigs, and, by endorsing his own position, would strengthen his candidacy for the Democratic nomination in 1856. They constituted his formula for restoring order and stability to American politics through the agency of a national, conservative Democratic party.

The resolutions declared the Constitution of the United States to be "a political contract between the people of independent sovereignties" and strongly urged a "vigilant guard" against the centralization of the powers reserved to the states or to the people as essential "to the preservation of our institutions." Congress had no rightful authority "to establish, abolish, or prohibit slavery in the states or territories." The only sure guarantee for "public tranquility" was through a strict adherence to the provisions of the Constitution and "non-intervention upon the subject of slavery" as provided in the Compromise of 1850 and in the Kansas-Nebraska Act. The Fugitive Slave Act and the Nebraska Act "are wise and just measures, and should remain undisturbed for the preservation of the national peace and union of the states." The "fundamental principle of entire and absolute equality among all the states" rendered Congress incompetent to impose conditions or restrictions upon the admission of new states that had not been imposed upon the original states. States' rights, popular sovereignty, a strict construction of the Constitution, and equality of the states under the Constitution—these were to be the basic elements in the Democratic platform for 1856. The language was carefully considered and, in the case of popular sovereignty, indirect, suggesting an ambiguity, perhaps unintentional at this point, that would cover both Douglas' and the southerners' view of the power of territories to deal with the slavery question. Additional resolutions were aimed at the Know-Nothings. They affirmed a natural right to religious freedom, rejected any distinction between naturalized and native-born citizens, and warned that any secret association or brotherhood for political objects was dangerous to free institutions. Finally, the administration of President Pierce was approved, both in its principles and in the practical operation of its leading measures. Douglas, aware that with the demise of the Whig party the Democracy was the only major national political party and hence the last bulwark of the Union, stressed the national character of the resolutions. "They are such as the democracy on the Aroostook and on the Rio Grande may repeat," commented the *State Register*.[24]

The "Illinois Platform" was enthusiastically adopted by the crowds at Douglas' remaining speaking engagements. On October 27, the Senator was in Paris, on the state's eastern edge, and was beginning to show the effects of his stumping tour. His voice had become hoarse, and he was physically tired. Following his Paris appearance, a group from Terre Haute, across the boundary in Indiana, insisted that he gratify local Democrats with a speech, and, although his remaining appointments in Illinois were tightly scheduled, he agreed to accommodate them. Appearing before the assembled crowd, he discovered that his hoarseness had become so aggravated that he could not speak effectively. A severe cold added to his problem, and early the next day he was seized by coughing spasms. He immediately took to bed and placed himself under the care of a local physician. He was suffering from an acute case of bronchitis. His remaining engagements were canceled, and he received strict orders to do no further speaking until his lungs and throat had healed. Recovery, however, did not come as expected, and his condition steadily worsened. Three weeks later, his physician reported no significant change, adding that it was impossible to predict when it would be safe or prudent for Douglas to leave his room. Deep solicitude was expressed throughout the nation, and at one point rumor of his death was circulated.

Illinois' Democratic leaders made frequent trips to Douglas' Terre Haute sickroom and sent back full reports on his condition, although they found him unable to converse. By December 1, improvement had begun. Thomas L. Harris, who remained with Douglas for much of the period, wrote to Lanphier, "Judge Douglas is slowly recovering, he now sits most of the day. He is still very hoarse, talks with difficulty, and has much soreness in the chest, and at intervals a hard cough. His attack was very severe. There was a general inflammation of the throat and respiratory organs, so much so, that suppuration has taken place, and the membranes sloughed off." There was hope, Harris noted, that Douglas might be able to start for Washington by mid-December. The hope proved vain. Although he resumed his correspondence with friends and relatives, he was still unable to return to his normal activities. As a final measure, throat surgery was recommended. In late December, he traveled by easy stages to Cleveland, where a series of operations on his throat was performed by Dr. Horace Ackley, a professor of surgery at the Cleveland Medical College. Early in January, Douglas wrote that his throat "is now very sore in consequence of the surgical operations recently performed, the last of which was a few days ago to cut off the *Uvula* or lower pallate." The doctor "delights in running Probings down the windpipe, and cutting off pallates, & clipping Tonsils, and all such amusements. I confess that I do not enjoy the fun quite as well as he seems to do." More worrisome than his physical condition was his absence from the Senate. "I have been shut out from the political world," he complained. With each day of convalescence his impatience to return to Washington mounted, but it was not until early February that he was back at his home in the capital and even later before he felt strong enough to appear in the Senate. It was not a convenient time to be out of circulation.[25]

#### iv

Douglas' purpose in stumping his state was revealed in a long and unusually informative letter to Georgia Congressman Howell Cobb, in response to Cobb's suggestion that Douglas might be rewarded with the presidential nomination for his contribution to the party's successes in the states in 1855. "In regard to the reward which you so generously offered," Douglas wrote, "I can only say that my position on that question is . . . I do not seek the nomination—do not ask it at the hands of our friends." The Democratic party must first be consolidated and provided with "a sound, national, constitutional platform." His Lexington resolutions, presumably the model he had in mind, allowed a wide range of interpretation with reference to popular sovereignty, to the point even of ambiguity. Douglas now seemed to follow an opposite tack. "Our Platform," he contended, "must be bold, unequivocal, & specific on all controverted points. There must be no highsounding phrases meaning nothing—no equivocal terms—no doubtful meanings—no double dealing for the benefit of timid & tricky politicians. We must say precisely what we mean and say it in such language that it cannot be construed one way south and another way north." For Douglas, at least at the moment, principle outweighed pragmatism. "We must make the next fight a fight for principles." In a veiled reference to Pierce, he insisted that the next administration "must not be a coalition of discordant materials nor a futile attempt to harmonize the principles avowed in the

Platform." Without ruling out the presidential nomination, he modestly concluded, "I desire our Party to assign me whatever position will make me most serviceable to the cause." The circumstances of the struggle over the Kansas-Nebraska Act and the subsequent assaults that he had endured "will render the triumph of the cause my perfect & complete vindication. . . . I ask no other reward—I seek no higher triumph."

Publicly, Douglas persisted in his declaration that he would not be a candidate for the nomination. Most people took him at his word. "The Illinois Senator has deferred his claims upon the White House until 1860," speculated *The New York Times,* "wisely judging, perhaps, that even the best and most popular candidate whom the Democracy can present will be floored in 1856." Douglas' goal, wrote Sheahan in the *Chicago Times,* was simply the endorsement of his principles. Once that was achieved he could allow "his seniors in age—Cass, Marcy, Buchanan, Pierce and others—to compete with friendly strife for the nomination." The contrast with 1852 was striking. Although skepticism was still expressed in some quarters, Douglas had apparently closed the door on any movement on his behalf.[26]

The reaction among Douglas' friends was varied. One disappointed Ohio supporter urged that if he did not want the nomination he should dictate the choice of the convention in order to protect his interests and those of his friends. The men who were closest to Douglas refused to accept the public announcements as final. After spending a few days at Douglas' bedside in Terre Haute, former Illinois Congressman Robert Smith proposed that the state's Democratic papers raise Douglas' name as their candidate for the presidency. "I do not think one word should be said against any other aspirant," Smith wrote to Lanphier, "or any insinuation that Douglas authorizes the announcement of his name, but I believe it good policy for the National Democratic papers of Ills, to let other portions of the Country know that we think the coming contest should be fought under the Banner of Stephen A. Douglas." When Douglas passed through Indianapolis on his way to Cleveland late in December, one Indianan who talked with him concluded that "he is no doubt a candidate, contrary to his previous declarations.

That Douglas had no intention of adhering to his public pronouncements became increasingly evident to his closest associates. As early as October, in his letter to Cobb, he suggested that "if my name shall be connected with the Presidential election it must be the voluntary act of our friends, prompted by an eye single to the success of the cause & the permanent triumph of our principles, without any reference to my personal wishes or aggrandizement, and especially without any agency on my part directly or indirectly, by word or deed." His letter was written from Lexington; not only had his conference there produced a platform for 1856, but it is likely that he also discussed his prospects for the nomination. Later, as he convalesced in Cleveland, he conferred with Ohio's Democratic leaders. The contests preceding the Ohio state convention had just been concluded, and he was gratified with the results. "Our friends have the entire and absolute control of the Delegation from this state," he informed Sheahan. "Ohio is as sure for us as Illinois. Our plan will be now to combine the whole North West as a unit if possible." When he returned to Washington he talked with David Reid, who promptly confided to his wife that Douglas' position in regard to the presidency had changed. "He is now in the hands of his friends, or in other words before the people." [27]

Douglas' efforts in Illinois during 1855 had borne fruit, for without strong backing in his own state he could hardly have sought the larger prize. The Democratic party, he was convinced, had been strengthened and a solid base established from which he would be able to mount a national campaign.

# XX

## "No compromise with the enemy"
## 1856

i

Douglas lay on his sickbed in Terre Haute on the day the first session of the thirty-fourth Congress formally opened. The outlook for orderly and harmonious deliberations was not encouraging. A presidential election year was at hand, and, as usual, partisan political considerations assumed an urgent and disquieting priority over any desire to provide the nation with sound legislative leadership. New faces and new political alignments were immediately in evidence. Flushed by their success in the turbulent months that followed the passage of the Kansas-Nebraska Act, members of the fledgling Republican party were determined to exploit and advance their new position of power. Southerners, gripped by an increased sense of desperation, were equally determined to halt the movement, which could only undermine their own power in the national councils. Hanging like a pall over the national capital were the developments in far-off Kansas, their outcome and significance still uncertain. "Every thing is in excitement & confusion," observed the wife of an Alabama Senator.

Signs of dissension soon appeared. In the House, a long and frustrating attempt to select a Speaker began. The Democrats, in a minority for the first time in many years, nominated William A. Richardson, a tribute to Douglas and an endorsement of his position, but anathema to the Republican plurality. Republicans, however, were as divided in their own choice as they were determined to prevent Richardson's election. To complicate the situation, the balance of power was held by a group of Know-Nothings. The balloting dragged on, day after day, and the House

488

remained in unprecedented and hopeless deadlock. Not until the members agreed that a plurality, instead of a majority, should elect a Speaker was the deadlock broken. Early in February, Nathaniel P. Banks of Massachusetts, a former Democrat who had passed through the Know-Nothing party on his way to Republicanism, was declared the winner. Republicans were jubilant; their new party, they enthusiastically reported, had been inaugurated. The victory, predicted abolitionist William Lloyd Garrison, was the first gun in the new revolution.[1]

While Republicans rejoiced, others counted the cost. "People will begin to think that if Congress cant elect a speaker, the government is nearly gone, and not worth preserving," moaned Howell Cobb. The apparent amity between Banks and South Carolina's William Aiken, who escorted the victor to the rostrum, did not erase the bitterness which the long struggle had aroused. Among the most impatient observers of the delay had been President Pierce, who waited to present his annual message to Congress. After consulting with a group of House members, he finally submitted his message on the last day of December, taking both houses of Congress by surprise.

Pierce's message, heavily weighted in the direction of foreign affairs, gave only brief attention to Kansas. Conceding that "acts prejudicial to good order" had been committed in the territory, he assured the members of Congress that nothing had yet occurred that would justify his intervention. The peremptory dismissal of Kansas' difficulties inflamed many northerners, but it brought words of praise from the south. Speaking of the message, one southern Senator found merit in its "bold proslaveryism." No President had ever "talked as plainly or as harshly to the sectionalists and fanatics." [2]

Antislavery Senators were unwilling to let the matter drop. As if anticipating Pierce's position, John P. Hale introduced a resolution on December 5, asking the President to inform the Senate whether he had received any evidence of "such resistance to the execution of the laws in Kansas" as would require the interposition of military force to preserve law and order in the territory. Douglas was immediately apprised of the news by George E. Pugh, Ohio's new Senator. A caucus, he wrote, had been called at which "some agreement will be made, among ourselves" as to the disposition of Hale's resolution. "I wish you were on hand to lead us."

It was not Hale's effort, but rather new developments in Kansas that forced Pierce to modify his stand. On December 3, the day that Congress met, the President received a telegram from Wilson Shannon, who had succeeded Reeder as governor of Kansas, appealing for soldiers to maintain peace in the territory. That was the communication to which Hale's resolution likely had immediate reference. Shannon's request had followed a threatened attack on the town of Lawrence by a proslavery posse, recruited largely in Missouri. The incident, known popularly as the "Wakarusa War," had been provoked by the murder of a free state settler, in turn setting in motion a train of incidents that revealed the solidarity of opposition to the territorial government. The "War," greatly exaggerated in the press, was settled by negotiation before any blood was shed, and Shannon's request for federal troops was canceled. A few days later, the Topeka free state constitution was ratified in an election in which only freesoilers participated, and early in January, the officers for the new "state" were chosen; both elections were accompanied by disorder, and more violence seemed in the offing. Pierce could no longer ignore the turmoil that gripped the new territory.[3]

On January 24, the President sent a special message to Congress that dealt exclusively with Kansas. Reviewing the events of the preceding year, Pierce placed the blame for the trouble on "local mal-administration" and on the "unjustifiable interference of the inhabitants of some of the States foreign by residence, interests, and rights to the Territory." The northern emigrant aid companies, proclaiming their purposes "in language extremely irritating and offensive to those of whom the colonists were to become the neighbors," had incited "illegal and reprehensible counter-movements" from Missouri. "Interference, on the one hand, to procure the abolition or prohibition of slave labor in the Territory has produced mischievous interference on the other for its maintenance or introduction." The legality of the territorial government was upheld and the Topeka movement denounced as revolutionary. Fearing that disorders in Kansas would continue, "with increasing tendency to violence," Pierce warned that the whole power of the executive branch would be exerted to support public order. He recommended that Congress pass legislation enabling the inhabitants of Kansas to frame a state constitution, thus preparing through regular and lawful channels for admission into the Union.

Reports of continuing trouble in Kansas impelled Pierce to issue a second, more decisively worded warning against violence in the territory. In a proclamation issued on February 11, the day that Douglas resumed his seat in the Senate, the President noted that combinations had been formed to resist territorial authority (the Topeka movement), persons residing in Missouri contemplated armed intervention in the territory, and inhabitants of more distant states were collecting money, engaging men, and providing arms for the same purpose. He commanded all persons engaged in "unlawful combinations" to disperse and threatened those who contemplated armed invasion or insurrection with suppression by federal troops.

The President's words were little heeded; his influence and prestige were at rock bottom. Horace Greeley prescribed "the spirit of martyrdom and Sharpe's rifles" for the ailing territory, while southerners urged their section to rush to Kansas' rescue. "This struggle in Kansas is the very turning point of the battle between the North and South which has raged for 35 years," wrote a Georgian to his Congressman. Which way the battle would go seemed to depend not upon national legislation, but upon the force and determination of the warriors.[4]

One who would not accept a violent solution to Kansas' difficulties was Douglas. He returned to the Senate in mid-February, weak, feeble, and unable to speak for any length of time. Almost at once he was plunged into the Kansas maelstrom. Pierce's recommendations had been referred to the Committee on Territories, where Douglas, selected as its chairman once again, set to work on a committee report. The membership of Douglas' committee had changed, but it was still essentially a western committee. Two newcomers to the Senate had been elected to its roster, North Carolina's Asa Biggs and Vermont Republican Jacob Collamer, former Postmaster General in Taylor's cabinet. William K. Sebastian replaced Robert Johnson, retaining Arkansas' representation on the committee, and John Bell and George W. Jones were holdovers from the previous session. The Democratic edge on the committee was enhanced by the fact that the two minority members, Bell and Collamer, did not share the same political faith; the membership was equally divided between the free and slave states.

That the committee would submit a detailed report on Kansas and, accepting Pierce's challenge, would propose a bill enabling the territory to take steps toward statehood soon became common knowledge. Rumors of friction between Douglas and Collamer were published early in March, when it was reported that the Vermont Republican had been deprived of an opportunity to see a draft of the committee's report. Douglas denied the allegation in a personal explanation to the Senate, pointing out that "perfect freedom of communication" existed between the two men and that, inasmuch as he had not yet completed it, the report had not been seen by any members of the committee. Indeed, Douglas was more careful to keep Collamer informed than he was to apprise the other members of the committee of his progress. Two southerners, Senator Albert Gallatin Brown and Representative John A. Quitman, both from Mississippi, were said to be exerting pressure on Douglas "to make a new pro-slavery issue" in the report, and one politico, with an eye to the presidential election, feared that Douglas might be persuaded "to play a desperate game for the Southern vote." Douglas was aware of the impact his statement would have on the race for the Democratic nomination, and he used the opportunity to strengthen his position. Harris, whom Douglas did consult, wrote, five days before the report was presented, that it "will be a crusher. It will cut down Pierce completely." The effort, again, was Douglas' rather than the committee's; as portions of it were completed, he read them aloud to his committee members, but it is probable that few if any changes were suggested.[5]

The report, which filled over forty printed pages, took Douglas two hours to read to the Senate; a minority report, submitted by Collamer, was half as long. Much of the ground covered by Douglas was familiar. Some of it followed Pierce's reasoning in his special January message. The organization of the Massachusetts Emigrant Aid Company was reviewed in detail, and much of the blame for Kansas' difficulties was placed on this "vast moneyed corporation" and its effort to control "the domestic institutions of a distinct political community fifteen hundred miles distant." New England's action, Douglas pointed out, aroused Missouri to a similar course; the difference between the two rival movements was the aggressive purpose of the former and the defensive policy of the latter. He did not consider it germane to inquire into the validity of the laws passed by the territorial legislature—this was "a judicial question, over which Congress can have no control"—but he did devote considerable space to the Topeka statehood movement as a revolutionary attempt to overthrow the territorial government in defiance of the authority of Congress. Douglas' review was manifestly one-sided, for while he traced the troubles to "foreign" intervention in the affairs of Kansas and criticized both sides in the struggle, he put the onus of responsibility on the north.

The report was also a significant step in the development of Douglas' view of popular sovereignty. No longer satisfied merely to defend it as an expedient, or even as a moral right, he now sought a legal and consti-

tutional basis for his position. Congress' power to create territories derived from the power to admit new states; in organizing a territory,
Congress must not impose any limitation that would destroy or impair
the equality of the proposed state with the original states. To influence
the character of a territory's institutions would be to influence the institutions of the state to be formed from the territory, thus destroying
"equality among all the states." Hence, Douglas concluded, the organic
act of a territory must "leave the people entirely free to form and regulate their domestic institutions and internal concerns in their own way."
In his analysis of the Topeka statehood movement, he further defined
the status of a territory in the federal system, drawing a distinction between sovereignty and the right of self-government. The sovereignty of a
territory, he suggested, "remains in abeyance, suspended in the United
States, in trust for the people, until they shall be admitted into the
Union as a State." In the meantime, the people in a territory are entitled
to enjoy and exercise all the rights and privileges of self-government,
subject to the Constitution of the United States and in obedience to the
organic law of the territory. Douglas' argument was strained; he seemed
on less sure ground than before. His attempt to find a constitutional justification for popular sovereignty in the long run weakened his stand
that it was a desirable expedient and was right, for he now indicated an
entire new direction for debate and disagreement. "The constitution,"
commented one editor, "threatens to be a subject of infinite sects, like
the Bible." Some concluded that Douglas' discussion of territorial sovereignty and self-government marked "the theoretical abandonment of the
whole doctrine of popular sovereignty," a result which Douglas certainly
never intended.

Collamer's minority report, predictably, defended the activities of the
emigrant aid companies and justified the Topeka movement. Douglas
had announced that he would soon bring in a bill enabling Kansas to
take the proper steps toward statehood. Collamer, on the other hand,
proposed that the only solution, without violence and without obedience
"to tyrranical laws made by foreign force," was the admission of Kansas
to the Union as a free state under the Topeka constitution.[6] The lines
were drawn for another round of debate on the Kansas question.

As soon as the reports were read, both Sumner and Seward were on
their feet, the former praising Collamer's statement as a "pillar of fire to
guide the country." The majority report, they contended, had smothered
the true issue. Douglas, wisely refusing to be drawn into debate, briefly

summarized the issue between the reports, as he saw it, and then suggested that all further discussion be postponed until the documents could be published and studied. "The minority report," he declared, "advocates foreign interference; we advocate self-government and non-interference. We are ready to meet the issue; and there will be no dodging."

But while Sumner and Seward were willing to abide their time, Douglas' new colleague Lyman Trumbull was not. Trumbull had just successfully weathered a challenge against his eligibility to sit in the Senate. He was eager to make his mark against the Little Giant. On the opening day of the session, the protest against Trumbull's election had been laid before the Senate, alleging that Trumbull, a judge on the state supreme court, was bound by the provision of the state constitution forbidding judges from seeking any other public offices during the term for which they were elected. The case aroused little discussion, and when Trumbull was admitted to his seat on March 5, Douglas was not even present to vote. His throat still bothered him, and he saw little point in expending energy in a hopeless fight. "My throat is no better & I could not have said a word had I been there," he wrote to a close friend. "No power on earth could have changed the result." [7]

Two days after the report was presented, Trumbull, feeling that it ought not to go before the country without his dissent, sought to answer it in a speech that consumed nearly four hours. Still maintaining his ties with the Democratic party, Trumbull's was an awkward position. He felt compelled not only to extricate himself from the abolitionist label which Douglas had applied to anti-Nebraska Democrats, but also to deny any affiliation with the "new parties" of the day. The report, he declared, contained unwarranted assumptions, inconsistencies, false deductions, and erroneous propositions. He challenged Douglas' constitutional argument, emphasized the differences between the north and south in the interpretation of popular sovereignty, defended the emigrant aid companies, and assailed the actions of Missouri's border ruffians. Douglas was absent from the Senate during most of Trumbull's speech. When he entered the hall and found himself under attack, he expressed considerable surprise, especially since there had been tacit agreement that no debate would occur until the report was printed and the bill which the territorial committee was preparing had been presented. Trumbull's retort that he was unaware that Douglas was not in his seat seemed lame and ineffective, particularly since he had been reminded of the Senator's absence during his speech. Douglas denied that his colleague was in fact a Democrat and that his sentiments reflected those of the people of Illi-

nois. A bitter exchange with Sumner ensued, and when Sumner castigated him for reviving the debate over the Kansas-Nebraska Act, he reminded the Massachusetts Senator that he had not first brought up the
subject. But the attack against Douglas was on. It was clear that his opposition was trying to seize the initiative against him before he was fully
prepared to meet it.[8]

On March 17 Douglas reported his bill for the admission of Kansas to
statehood. Its terms were ordinary and routine, conforming to the pattern usual to congressional enabling acts. Douglas simply followed his
view that a legal, authorized, territorial government did exist in Kansas,
and that the irregularities that marked territorial politics were the results of outside interference. According to the bill, a census would be
taken under the direction of the governor; when the territory should
contain in excess of 93,000 inhabitants (the number required by the ra-
tion for representation in Congress), the legislature was to provide for
the election of delegates to a convention for the purpose of forming a
constitution and state government. Significantly, no provision was made
for the submission of the constitution to the voters of the territory for
ratification or rejection. The bill was hardly acceptable to Kansas' free
state inhabitants and their congressional allies. The machinery of government would be left in the hands of a governor and legislature that
had been repudiated by an important element in the territory, and since
Kansas could not yet meet the population requirement, the authority of
the hated territorial government would be sustained for an indefinite period.

Following Douglas' opening speech in defense of his bill, Seward announced that he would offer a substitute bill providing for the immediate admission of Kansas under the Topeka free state constitution, a bill
that would follow the recommendation in Collamer's minority report.
This was equally unacceptable as a solution to the Kansas problem.
Drawn up in haste, imbued with partisanship, the Topeka document was
itself the result of irregularity. It was a situation appropriate to an election year. Douglas' bill, speculated one editor, could not pass the House,
and Seward's would never be approved by the Senate. The whole problem would then be referred to the people in the presidential election.[9]

ii

Douglas opened the debate on the Kansas question on March 20. His
speech had been well advertised, and the galleries were full. Hale, noting that a large number of ladies were in attendance, proposed that they

be allowed seats on the Senate floor. His suggestion was greeted by "sour looks and murmurs of disapprobation" from the gentlemen present, and when Hunter objected Hale's motion was withdrawn. Douglas' status as an eligible widower, it was said, had attracted a large female audience; many of the ladies occupied seats in the reporters' gallery, to the discomfort of the men of the press. After some preliminary business, Douglas rose, "dressed in a suit of black, with his frock coat buttoned to the chin, and his thick, dark hair swept negligently back from his massive forehead." His throat, protected by his coat, had so far improved as to allow him to address the Senate for two and a half hours "in a clear distinct voice."

Douglas' thrust was three-pronged. He answered Trumbull's charges, severely castigating him for his lack of propriety in attacking Douglas during the latter's absence from the Senate and repeating his charge that Trumbull had been carried "captive into the Black Republican camp." Moving to a defense of his report, Douglas reviewed the events in Kansas in detail. He lashed out at Reeder for having certified a majority of the members elected to the Kansas legislature, only to concede later that he had been deceived in doing so, and he characterized the Topeka statehood movement as illegal and revolutionary. He reminded the Senate that the Topeka government forbade free Negroes from settling in Kansas and taunted his opposition with professing to be the "especial friends of the negro" at the same time that they favor a proposition to deny the Negro the right "to enter, live, or breathe, in the proposed State of Kansas." The "unfortunate difficulties" in Kansas, he maintained once again, were the natural results "of two rival and hostile systems of emigration, organized in and prosecuted from the opposite and extreme sections of the Union, for the purpose of controlling the domestic institutions of the Territory—the one having for its paramount object the prohibition, and the other the protection, of the institution of slavery in Kansas." He rejected both efforts as gross violations of the Kansas-Nebraska Act, although he continued to place primary responsibility with New England for initiating the rivalry.

Douglas' speech merely elaborated and underscored the conclusions he had drawn in his report. He wisely avoided being drawn into a constitutional discussion by making no further mention of his attempt to base popular sovereignty on legal and constitutional grounds, nor did he discuss his Kansas statehood bill beyond a brief summary of its terms. Douglas resumed his seat exhausted, his voice showing the strain of his effort. When South Carolina's Senator Butler had interrupted earlier to propose an adjournment so that Douglas might continue his speech the next day, Douglas replied that if he should stop he would not have the strength to continue on the morrow. Still, the force of his oratory aroused admiration and praise, if not always agreement.[10]

Two weeks later Collamer defended his minority report, and Douglas answered him immediately. He took issue with the Vermont Senator's narrative of the Topeka movement and charged him with suppressing the more inflammatory statements and threats made by Kansas' free state settlers. The two Senators quibbled over the number of illegal votes that were cast in the territorial elections. Many settlers from the Ohio and Mississippi valleys, Douglas argued, had tried to enter Kansas before the organization of the territory in 1854, only to be discouraged by Indian agents seeking to enforce the Indian intercourse laws. Taking up temporary residence in western Missouri, these settlers bided their time. When Kansas was opened to settlement, they, along with many others from the western states, moved into the territory to select and stake out their claims. Finding themselves without proper shelter when winter arrived, large numbers returned to their old homes or to temporary abodes in Missouri and Iowa, there to await the spring. Governor Reeder's census was taken in mid-winter, during their absence, and the first territorial legislative election was scheduled before their return. Many settlers crossed into Kansas to vote, returning to their temporary homes to collect their families and to await the coming of warmer weather. Not all of the votes cast by these people on election day, in Douglas' judgment, had been illegal or fraudulent. He objected to the blanket indictment leveled by the Republicans. He did not excuse those Missourians who had clearly engaged in vote frauds, but he did question whether all those persons who marched into Kansas to vote were citizens of Missouri bent on controlling the election by fraud. Some of them, he suggested, were even from New England, detained by the winter in western Missouri. Douglas' statement was supported by Iowa's Senator Jones, with respect to emigrants from that state, and it was a fairly accurate summary of the facts of Kansas' settlement. Alluding to Collamer's statement that Kansas could have been admitted either as a slave or free state under the Missouri Compromise, and taunting Seward for his support of the Topeka constitution's Negro exclusion clause, Douglas charged his opposition with deliberately trimming its position for the benefit of the impending presidential race. He concluded his remarks amid a prolonged burst of applause from the galleries.[11]

The debate over Kansas continued off and on for several weeks, its sometimes sporadic character belying the intensity of feeling. On April 9, Seward defended the admission of Kansas as a free state under the Topeka constitution. He was answered by a procession of slave state Senators. Douglas took little further part in the discussion except to prod his colleagues to a more speedy consideration of the problem. He grew impatient with the slow progress of the Senate in considering his Kansas statehood bill. There seemed, he observed, no real desire to resolve the issue before the meeting of the national party conventions. While emphasizing his desire for a fair and open discussion of the question, he strongly opposed "the system which has been pursued of taking it up occasionally, making one speech on it, and then postponing it for a week; hearing another speech, and again postponing it for a week." At that rate, he predicted, the question would not be settled for another twelve months. He would not, he warned, agree "to have the bill lingering here during the whole summer." Other important measures demanded attention, but none of them, he felt, could be properly dealt with until the territorial question was disposed of. By the latter part of May, Douglas suggested that the Kansas bill either be postponed "for some time" or that it be taken up and pursued to its conclusion without further interruption. "In the way in which we now proceed with it, the subject loses all its interest." His admonitions went unheeded. The presidential election was on everyone's mind, and the Kansas discussion provided the Senators with a valuable sounding board. For Douglas, whose candidacy for the nomination would be advanced by the bill's passage, the delay was maddening.[12]

During the spring months of 1856, Douglas commanded considerable national attention. His recent illness and his late arrival in Washington had been more than compensated for by his energetic immersion once again in congressional politics. The winter was an unusually severe one, and members of the Senate sat wrapped "head and all" in enormous shawls, making frequent trips to the open grates in the corridor behind the Vice President's desk for momentary warmth. With Douglas' arrival, the need for warmth outside the chamber seemed less urgent. His oratory had long had its admirers. Laudatory descriptions of Douglas' power as a speaker had been offered by foe as well as friend, although his talent was not always employed to present arguments in the clearest possible light. "With the rapidity of lightning," recalled one witness to his performance, "his alert mind perceived the strength or weakness of a point, and when he was unable to turn an argument to his own advantage he would hopelessly befog it for anyone else." Douglas' fiery eyes, his deep voice, and his mastery of "rugged English," heightened the impression and made his listeners forget for the moment that he was, to put it mildly, "a little below the average height."

One day, in the midst of the Kansas debate, Harriet Beecher Stowe took a seat in the gallery. Her report of Douglas' part in the discussion captured the full impact of the Senator's power. He was, she wrote, the "very ideal of vitativeness." His figure was one of constant animation, "every inch of him has its own alertness and motion." From his first sentence, it was obvious that he possessed the "two requisites of a debator —a melodious voice, and a clear, sharply-defined enunciation," always accompanied by "the most off-hand assured airs in the world, and a certain appearance of honest superiority." "His forte in debating," Mrs. Stowe continued, "is his power of mystifying the point." His speeches, "instead of being like an arrow sent at a mark, resemble rather a bomb which hits nothing in particular, but bursts and sends red-hot nails in every direction." They were devoid of humor (Douglas possessed a sense of humor, but he was peculiarly inept in utilizing it) for which Mrs. Stowe was thankful, for if he had been witty as well he might have been "too irresistible a demagogue for the liberties of our laughter-loving people, to whose weaknesses he is altogether too well adapted now." The Republicans, she warned, had reason to fear him, for "they have pitted against them a leader infinite in resources, artful, adroit, and wholly unscrupulous."

Not all of Douglas' opponents were as charitable as Mrs. Stowe. His opening address in March prompted a scurrilous personal attack in the columns of the *New-York Tribune.* Any characterization of Douglas, the paper commented, required "the use of a vocabulary not highly esteemed in good society." "Douglas has brains," but so has the Devil, so had Judas and Benedict Arnold. "His is a bulldog mentality, a combination of the swineherd and the Caliban. . . . He can blackguard his betters like a fish-selling harridan. . . . He can run through the whole dispason of political falsehood with unrivaled skill, from the delicate note of suggested pervarication down to the double-bass of unmitigated lying. . . . In fact, Douglas has a jolly affection for a lie." To the reporter for *The New York Times* he had all the "swagger and slang of a shoulder-striker." [13]

On April 7, Lewis Cass presented a memorial from the "self-styled Legislature of Kansas" (the Topeka state legislature) asking that the territory be admitted to the Union as a free state. The incident provoked some of the most angry exchanges in the Kansas debate. The memorial had been placed in Cass' hands by James Lane, who had recently been named United States Senator by the Topeka movement. Douglas' suspicions were immediately aroused. The signatures appended to the memorial, he pointed out, were all in the same handwriting; moreover, the document contained many interlineations and erasures. Although suggesting that the memorial was not genuine, he urged that it be printed simply out of curiosity "to know what these men say in their own vindication." Cass' motion to print the memorial, however, was immediately challenged by slave state Senators, and an extended discussion of the question commenced. When various Republicans supported the motion on the ground that the Topeka movement was a legitimate authority, Douglas altered his position. "When the decision is to test a great principle," he informed his colleagues, "I am compelled to give my vote with a view to that principle." After a lengthy debate over the character of the Topeka government, the Senate rescinded its earlier decision to refer the memorial to Douglas' committee.

A week after its first presentation, the memorial, in somewhat different form, was resubmitted by Iowa's Senator Harlan, accompanied by an explanation from Lane himself. Harlan's action touched off a five-hour debate, with Douglas in the middle of the fight. Still doubting the genuineness of the memorial, Douglas charged Lane with couching his explanation in such equivocal and evasive language as to cast suspicion on the whole proceeding. Douglas went further. He accused Lane of materially altering the wording of the memorial after it had been passed, and he branded the document as an unquestionable forgery. In addition, the copy of the Topeka constitution which had been presented to the Senate lacked the Negro exclusion clause which had been approved by Kansans as a separate schedule. An imperfect and incomplete copy of the constitution, Douglas declared, "has been palmed off on the Senate," accompanied by "garbled and mutilated papers." It was now Douglas' turn to shout fraud.

Douglas came under immediate and vicious attack by Benjamin Wade and Henry Wilson. Referring to an earlier statement of Douglas' that the "revolutionary" Topeka movement would be reduced to subjection to the Constitution and laws, Wade shouted that "this talk about subduing us and conquering us will not do. . . . You may vote us down, but we shall live to fight another day." Wilson took up the cry, warning that "if we fall, we shall fall to rise again." "We shall vote for the admission of Kansas into this Union as a free State; if we fail, if you vote us down, we shall go to the country with that issue." Douglas, unawed, launched a diatribe of his own against the Republican party and the abolition movement which pushed the details of Lane's petition into the background. "We do not believe in the equality of the negro, socially or politically, with the white man," he declared as he compared Illinois' Negro exclusion law with that passed in Kansas. "Our people are a white people; our State is a white State; and we mean to preserve the race pure, without any mixture with the negro." His remarks, reflecting widely held views at the time, were greeted with loud applause from the galleries.

Although the debate had moved beyond the authenticity of Lane's memorial, Lane, whose character excited little admiration either then or later, decided he could not let the matter drop. Rumors that he would challenge Douglas to a duel circulated freely, confirming earlier reports that Douglas' opposition would attempt "to get him into a personal difficulty." On April 18, Lane asked Douglas "for such an explanation of your language . . . as will remove all imputation upon the integrity of my action or motives in connexion with that memorial." He arrogantly reminded Douglas that he had a certificate of election to the Senate from the Topeka government, was Douglas' peer, and therefore deserved better treatment. Before replying, Douglas sought the advice of a group of Congressmen, including Robert Toombs, John Weller, James Orr, Joseph Lane, and Bright. He then penned a long letter to the messenger whom Lane had employed to deliver his note. Taking cognizance of the rumors that Lane intended to challenge him, Douglas described Lane's note as so equivocal and contradictory that he was unable to determine whether "it is intended as a hostile message or a friendly note." He reviewed the debate over the memorial and repeated the statements he had made in the Senate, concluding that "my reply is, that there are no facts within my knowledge" which could remove the imputations that had been made on the integrity of Lane's actions or motives. With Douglas' reply, the matter was closed. Lane did not press his demand. When he charged that Douglas had shielded himself behind his "privilege" as a Senator, even Douglas' opponents denounced Lane's unwarranted inference and praised the Illinois Senator for his part in the exchange. Lane's attempt to bring a "forged and mutilated document" before the Senate was dismissed as an "egregious blunder." [14]

The most violent personal attack against the Little Giant came late in the following month. On May 15, Charles Sumner wrote Chase, "I have the floor for next Monday on Kansas, when I shall make the most thorough & complete speech of my life. My soul is wrung by this outrage, & I shall pour it forth." His speech, begun on May 19, had been carefully prepared, committed to memory and regularly rehearsed. Stung by Douglas' interpretation of the events in Kansas, he sought to present the truth about the "Crime Against Kansas." This outpouring of his tortured soul, however, was not limited to a discussion of developments in a territory 1500 miles distant; it was also a ferocious personal assault against Douglas and two southern Senators, Andrew P. Butler of South Carolina and James Mason of Virginia.

Sumner's speech was sprinkled with sexual imagery. Kansas' travail did not have its origin "in any common lust for power," he began. "It is the rape of a virgin Territory, compelling it to the hateful embrace of Slavery; and it may be clearly traced to a depraved longing for a new slave State, the hideous offspring of such a crime, in the hope of adding to the power of Slavery in the National Government." He would strip the crime of its apologies, exposing its nakedness, "without a single rag, or fig-leaf, to cover its vileness." The remedy, he proposed, had already been suggested "by the aroused masses of the country," the immediate admission of Kansas as a free state under the Topeka constitution. Turning on Senator Butler, who was absent from his seat, Sumner unleashed the full fury of his rhetoric. Butler was likened to Don Quixote, tilting against the cause of freedom. "He has chosen a mistress to whom he has made his vows, and who, though ugly to others, is always lovely to him; though polluted in the sight of the world, is chaste in his sight—I mean the harlot, Slavery." In an unfortunate reference to Butler's slight speech impediment, Sumner charged the South Carolinian with "incoherent phrases, discharged [with] the loose expectoration of his speech." "He cannot ope his mouth, but out there flies a blunder."

Douglas, Sumner continued, "is the squire of Slavery, its very Sancho Panza, ready to do all its humiliating offices." The Illinois Senator's report and opening speech had been labored, "piling one mass of elaborate error upon another mass," a mortal man combatting an immortal principle. The Kansas-Nebraska Act was a "repugnant measure" pressed by "arguments mutually repugnant." The bill was "in every respect a swindle"; no other word could "adequately express the mingled meanness and wickedness of the cheat." Subsequent events in Kansas had revealed the true nature of Douglas' doctrine, as popular sovereignty became "Popular Slavery." Douglas proposed, in his Kansas statehood bill, the "Remedy of Injustice and Civil War"; by contrast, the admission of Kansas under the Topeka constitution was the "Remedy of Justice and Peace." [15]

As Sumner began to speak, Douglas feigned indifference, conversing with fellow Senators or writing at his desk, but he was soon compelled to give the Massachusetts Senator his full attention. Pacing the floor at the rear of the chamber, obviously agitated, he was heard to mutter, "That damn fool will get himself killed by some other damn fool." When Sumner had finished, Douglas secured the floor, not to reply to the Senator's arguments but to deplore the malignant personal assaults. The speech, he declared, was distinguished for its "lasciviousness and obscenity," its insults premeditated and carefully practiced. "Is it his object," Douglas asked, "to provoke some of us to kick him as we would a dog in the street, that he may get sympathy upon the just chastisement?"

But Sumner was not yet finished, for he had no intention of letting Douglas' comments go unanswered. He retorted that he would not leave the Illinois Senator "the last argument." "He has crowned the audacity of this debate by venturing to rise here and calumniate me. . . . I say, also, to that Senator, and I wish him to bear it in mind, that no person with the upright form of man can be allowed— [Hesitation.]"

"Say it," urged Douglas.

"I will say it—no person with the upright form of man can be allowed, without violation of all decency, to switch out from his tongue the perpetual stench of offensive personality. . . . The noisome, squat, and nameless animal, to which I now refer, is not a proper model for an American Senator. Will the Senator from Illinois take notice?"

"I will," Douglas replied, "and therefore will not imitate you, sir."

"Mr. President, again the Senator has switched his tongue, and again he fills the senate with its offensive odor."

With that, the exchange ended and the Senate quickly adjourned.[16]

Two days later, the tragic sequel was acted out on the Senate floor. Preston Brooks, a Congressman from South Carolina and a kinsman of Butler's, entered the chamber and, while Sumner was seated at his desk, proceeded to cane the Massachusetts Senator into insensibility, vowing as he did so to revenge the libel on South Carolina and on its Senator. Sumner, bleeding profusely, was helped to the anteroom where a doctor dressed his wounds. Several days later, he was sufficiently recovered to make a statement before the committee appointed by the House of Representatives to investigate the incident. When he regained consciousness following the attack, while still lying in the aisle, Sumner stated, he noticed Brooks flanked on either side by Douglas and Toombs. Douglas quickly denied the allegation.

Just prior to the attack, Douglas told the Senate, he had been engaged in conversation in the reception room with Richardson, Benjamin Fitzpatrick of Alabama, and Pennsylvania Congressman J. Glancy Jones. When an excited messenger burst into the room with the report that someone was beating Sumner, Douglas "rose involuntarily" to his feet. "My first impression was to come into the Senate Chamber and help to put an end to the affray, if I could; but it occurred to my mind, in an instant, that my relations to Mr. Sumner were such that if I came into the Hall, my motives would be misconstrued, perhaps, and I sat down again." When word came that the attack was over, he rushed with others into the chamber. His statement was verified by those with whom he had talked both before and after he entered the chamber.[17]

The reactions in the north and south to the assault on Sumner revealed the degree to which the nation had become polarized. To the one section, Sumner became a martyr to the cause of antislavery against the aggressions of the slave power; to the other, Brooks was the hero of the hour for having administered well-deserved punishment to an abolitionist. New violence in Kansas added dimension to the fear that a crisis of serious magnitude in American politics was not far off.

Earlier in the month, the chief justice of the Kansas territorial supreme court charged a grand jury to indict the leaders of the Topeka movement for treason, and soon afterward Charles Robinson, an agent of the New England Emigrant Aid Company and governor of the free state, was apprehended and imprisoned. In addition, the jury found bills of indictment against the outspoken free state newspaper and the Free State Hotel in the town of Lawrence. The hotel was built like a fortress, and it was a source of annoyance to the proslavery element. The local sheriff, with a posse of over 500 men from Kansas and Missouri, entered the town, destroyed the presses of the newspaper, and bombarded and finally burned the hotel. Robinson's house was also destroyed. The outbreak, labeled the "sack of Lawrence" by the northern press, occurred in the latter days of May, just as the Senate was convulsed by Sumner's speech and Brooks' assault.

News of the invasion of Lawrence reached the ears of a fifty-six-year-old fanatic who had recently emigrated to Kansas to join his sons. Outraged, John Brown raised a small body of men and prepared to march to the relief of Lawrence. Before he arrived, however, the sheriff had done his work and disbanded his posse. Not to be deprived of the vengeance he had sworn against the forces of slavery, Brown turned on a scattered community along Pottawatomie Creek and, in cold blood, murdered five peaceful (and proslavery) settlers.

Suddenly, it seemed, all the forces of sectional hostility had reached their explosive climax. The bitter debate over Douglas' Kansas statehood bill, Sumner's intemperate speech and the subsequent violence in the Senate, the destruction in Lawrence, and the Pottawatomie murders were grim portents of the difficulties faced by the nation's political leaders in that presidential year. On June 2, the Democratic national convention was scheduled to meet in Cincinnati; circumstances could hardly have been less auspicious than they were on the eve of this conclave.

### iii

Douglas, although technically a convalescent in the spring of 1856, again occupied the role he seemed to love so well—the center of controversy, the object of fear, admiration, scorn, and downright hatred, a man few Americans could ignore. Always neglectful of his physical condition, he modified his living habits only slightly. He was rarely seen on the avenues of the capital or in public places. When not in the Senate, he generally kept to his home, where he was always available to those who had business with him. Under unceasing attack in Congress and in the press, he was like a steamer, "dashing from its prow every impediment" and bearing down all opposition. Douglas seemed to thrive on conflict, for his strength gradually returned.

Douglas had never really been serious in his public pronouncements against being a candidate for the Democratic presidential nomination. As many of his friends had long since concluded, it would have been most unlike the Little Giant to remain on the sidelines. His struggle over the Kansas-Nebraska Act and the vilification he had endured afterward virtually demanded that he take an active part in the 1856 election. Kansas was the dominant issue and the terms of the Kansas-Nebraska Act still the center of bitter discussion; it would have been anomalous indeed if the champion of popular sovereignty were not in the front line of battle. One supporter insisted that Douglas must allow his name to be used "or be driven to ignore the great act of his life." But the Illinois Senator was by no means a reluctant candidate.

Douglas' strategy, to avoid the overexposure he had suffered in 1852, to work discreetly and quietly behind the scenes with a few well-selected lieutenants, and yet to maintain a position that would allow him to work effectively for the nominee should he fail to get the nomination, was both an asset and a liability. He kept his rivals within the party guessing, but he also enabled them to organize their own candidacies freely. Hunter, who had presidential aspirations of his own, was advised that "Douglas' position cannot be known too soon." James Buchanan wrote from London that he had no desire the become President, but no one believed him, since his friends had been building support for him months prior to Douglas' return to Washington early in 1856. Pierce's hopes for a renomination were revived, although he appeared to be the weakest of the candidates.[18]

Douglas recognized that the election of a regular Democratic President in 1856 would be an uphill fight. The "allied army of *isms*," whose annihilation he had so confidently predicted, had not left the field. On the contrary, the impetus of the national campaign gave it strength. Anti-Nebraska Democrats still claimed their party affiliation and hoped to gain control over the organization. They could, wrote one, muster a stronger group of better Democrats at the Cincinnati convention than the "pseudo Democracy" represented by the administration. The Republicans and those Know-Nothings who regarded the repeal of the Kansas-Nebraska Act as the paramount issue were urged to hold simultaneous conventions in Cincinnati. Douglas would give his opposition no quarter. "We must make no compromise with the enemy—no concession to the allied isms—no coalitions with factions." The threat, however, dictated the utmost care in the Democratic choice. A candidate had to be selected who could bring unity and stability to the country without at the same time sacrificing the position to which the party had committed itself. It was a large order in view of the heightened feeling aroused by the events in Kansas, but Douglas never doubted that he was the best man available.[19]

To assist him in his campaign, Douglas selected David T. Disney of Ohio and a long-time Illinois friend, James W. Singleton. Disney, "a discreet man, full of talent & resources," was ten years Douglas' senior. With a long record in the Ohio legislature, he had been a member of

Congress for six years until he was defeated for the Democratic nomination in his district in 1854. Singleton had known Douglas since the time of the so-called Mormon War, when they had both served with the state militia. An old-line Whig member of the state legislature from 1850 to 1854, he had supported the Kansas-Nebraska Act, and in the political realignment that followed, he had moved into Douglas' camp. Singleton's selection indicated that Douglas would make a strong appeal for support among northern Whigs.

It was Singleton who formally announced Douglas' candidacy. In a letter to the editor of the *Richmond Examiner,* written a few days after Douglas had arrived in Washington, Singleton stated that Douglas' name would be presented to the Cincinnati convention. Any suggestion that Douglas would not be a candidate, Singleton declared, imputed political cowardice to the Senator. "It in effect declares," he continued, "that he has raised an excitement in the country which has given strength to free-soilism, and that now, when in appearance his party is environed by difficulties, he wants to skulk and dodge the blows that might be struck at him if standing at the head of his party in a national political battle—that he fears to risk his political fortunes upon an issue made by *himself.*" Douglas could rally the young and old, uniting Whigs with the northern Democracy, in a battle for the principles of the Kansas-Nebraska Act. "It is upon this issue that we are now to make the final grapple with black republicanism." [20]

Singleton's letter, a surprise to few people, ended speculation regarding Douglas' role in the campaign. Douglas, it had been said, would not challenge Pierce, but would "cheerfully" support the President in any contest with Buchanan. Another report had stated that Douglas would support a southern man, presumably Hunter, on the ground that the northwest (and he himself) would then be in line for the nomination in 1860. Illinois Democrats greeted Douglas' decision enthusiastically, and the *State Register* hoisted his name to its masthead. Other Democratic papers in the state quickly followed. Pierce was disappointed, having undoubtedly counted on Douglas' backing; the President's prospects, particularly in the west, were now considerably reduced. "Shrewd, cunning Douglas!" commented one anti-Nebraska editor, "Poor, deluded, duped Pierce!" Beverley Tucker, editor of the Washington *Sentinel,* who had published Douglas' early disclaimer, vented his anger at the Senator's apparent change of mind. He had taken Douglas at his word, he complained, and had already committed his support to Buchanan.[21]

Douglas lost no time in organizing support for his candidacy. The Cincinnati convention was to meet on June 2, and the intervening months were devoted to a careful exploration of all possible avenues to the nomination. Before his efforts were fairly under way, however, Democratic prospects suffered their first setback. On Washington's birthday, the Know-Nothings convened in Philadelphia. Their session was a stormy one, divided between the northern and southern branches of the party, and the more extreme antislavery northern group eventually walked out. Ex-President Millard Fillmore was the overwhelming choice of the party for President, although he had never been a member of the order. The platform was as conservative as the nominee; one plank endorsed the unqualified maintenance of states' rights, while another gave support to Douglas' doctrine of popular sovereignty. The slavery question was not specifically mentioned. Fillmore's nomination, Disney informed Douglas, "will materially *weaken* us." Southern Know-Nothings, whom Douglas had always carefully distinguished from the northern antislavery Know-Nothings, and northern Whigs, referred to as the "Silver Greys," would now be prevented from joining the Douglas movement, Disney feared.

Equally worrisome was the danger that the old-line Whigs generally might "rally in union with the Know nothings on Fillmore" and that the Republicans might, like the Know-Nothings, avoid nominating "an *ultra* man." To forestall these developments, Disney suggested, the Republicans must be strengthened by forcing the Kansas controversy in Congress and by letting "the agitation come from the abolitionists." The fear of abolitionist success in the election would then "scatter the combination in favor of Fillmore & drive his supporters into our ranks." It was a dangerous game. There is no evidence that Douglas consciously followed Disney's advice. Perhaps his impatience with the slow progress of territorial bills in the spring of 1856 sprang from a desire to prevent the Kansas issue from cooling off and, at the same time, a wish to provide Republican leaders with a full opportunity to air their views. Seen in this light, Sumner's outrageous speech could hardly have disappointed Douglas.[22]

Of more immediate concern to Douglas' managers, however, was the need to unite the party behind his candidacy. This proved to be no simple task. Clearly, his most formidable opponent was James Buchanan. Although Buchanan remained at his post in London until late April, he had developed considerable support, partly because of Douglas' reluctance to become an open and avowed candidate. Masterminding his campaign was shrewd, calculating John Slidell. Rendering somewhat questionable assistance was the ubiquitous George N. Sanders, who apparently forgot for the moment his earlier strictures against "old fogies." Sanders' appointment to the consulate in London early in Pierce's administration had not been confirmed by the Senate, and for that Sanders blamed a senatorial conspiracy of which he was certain Douglas was a part. Douglas must have been happy to have Sanders aiding his rival.

Buchanan gained strength. To many Democrats his absence from the country during the Kansas struggle was an asset, giving him a unique opportunity to unite the party's warring factions. Lewis Cass expressed his cordial feelings toward the Pennsylvanian ("for some reason or other he feels sore about Douglass," wrote Slidell), and Lyman Trumbull, representing the anti-Nebraska element, was said to be a Buchanan man. There was some speculation that Buchanan's nomination would enlist the aid of southern Know-Nothings in the election. Slidell thought for a time that Douglas himself might be wooed into the camp. In March he wrote to Buchanan of his "very *strong hopes* that Douglass will come in," and as late as May he still thought that a clear endorsement of the Kansas-Nebraska Act by Buchanan would reconcile Douglas or "at least spike his guns." Southern leaders split on Buchanan's candidacy. Howell Cobb, whom Douglas may have been counting on, regarded Buchanan's nomination and election as so promising that he advised caution and restraint in his campaign, while Hunter viewed Buchanan's nomination as a disaster for the south. It would "sink the Nebraska Kansas issue" and elevate such Buchanan men as Trumbull and Reeder. "In the passage of the Nebraska Kansas bill the South gained the first & only victory on the negro question which is to be found in our legislative history," he declared. After a hard and difficult fight in the north, "our friends in that section are about to recover the fulness of the day." Shall we, Hunter asked, "destroy them by choosing a Northern man for the very reason that he had no active participation in that contest which gave rise to the present issue?" In spite of Hunter's concern, Buchanan was said to be ahead in Virginia, partly, Singleton wrote, because Douglas was understood to be out of the ring.[23]

In the face of Buchanan's mounting popularity, Douglas worried about the role of Indiana's powerful Senator, Jesse Bright. Relations between the two rivals for control of the northwest Democracy had always been strained. Following the passage of the Kansas-Nebraska Act, however, a rapprochement between the two had been achieved, an arrangement that Douglas apparently assumed would continue through the 1856 election. Douglas' managers counted heavily on Bright's support. But Bright was less committed than Douglas thought. He could never be satisfied with the secondary role in the northwest which support for the Illinois Senator would assign him. At first he hoped for a place of his own on a national ticket headed by a southern candidate, but it was soon clear that his sympathies were with Buchanan. When Slidell promised him control over patronage in the northwest, Bright began working actively but discreetly for Buchanan. "We can rely on Bright," Slidell informed the Pennsylvanian in March. Signs that Bright was moving away from Douglas appeared earlier. "Bright is acting in good faith toward you," Disney wrote reassuringly to Douglas late in February, but a trip made by Bright with Slidell to Philadelphia, where the two talked with New York Congressman Daniel Sickles, bothered Disney. When Louisiana's Judah P. Benjamin informed Disney that Bright was backing Buchanan, the alarmed Disney wrote to Douglas immediately. "Is there not some mistake about this in relation to Bright? *Look into this without delay."* Bright's defection was a serious blow to Douglas' prospects for uniting the party.[24]

Less critical to Douglas' campaign were the ambitions of President Pierce. The difficulties in Kansas, which many people regarded as indicative of the President's weakness, and his handling of the patronage early in his administration had made Pierce patently unpopular with large numbers of Democrats. Some southerners believed that Pierce favored a free state in Kansas. Southern Know-Nothings charged him with approving the Kansas-Nebraska Act in order to enlarge the area of freedom. On the other side, the President's name was anathema to free-soilers. Still, there was enough support for Pierce, especially in New England and the south, to force Douglas to take account of the President's role in the campaign. Only by combining Pierce's following with his own, Douglas was convinced, could Buchanan's drive toward the nomination be halted. He was assured that the President's friends would eventually come over to his side and that Pierce himself would support Douglas against Buchanan. By early May, there were reports that Douglas and Pierce had reached an agreement to this effect. The two men met frequently at the White House. Blair wrote that they were *"in Cahoot*—each calculating that the defeat of Buck in the Convention was essential to give the least Chance for either of them."

Douglas' strategy, unlike that of four years before, was to refrain from attacks against his competitors. Publicly he carefully maintained the fiction that his candidacy was solely the work of his friends and against his own initial wishes. His campaign followed the advice of an old St. Louis friend, offered long after Douglas himself had adopted it. It is "all important that you shall not suffer any ill-feeling to spring up between you and your competitors, or your respective friends," wrote Samuel Treat early in April. "You must take and keep the most magnanimous grounds towards them—saying all the time, that whilst your friends have insisted, against your first impressions and wishes, to bring your name forward, you will not prevent the party from concentrating upon Pierce or Buchanan, or Hunter or any one else named,—that your first and great object in the conflict is, to insure the triumph and permanence of the true constitutional principle embodied in the Kansas-Nebraska bill." Douglas must avoid any act that would "draw the fire" of either Pierce or Buchanan. That he was successful became evident; Slidell still thought as late as May that he might be reconciled to Buchanan's nomination, while at the same time reports of a Douglas-Pierce arrangement were circulating.[25]

Douglas was anxious that the states of the northwest, as he wrote to Sheahan, be combined as a unit behind his candidacy. Solid strength from his own section was essential; without it his efforts to develop support from other parts of the nation would be seriously hampered. "If the North West is divided," predicted an Indianapolis editor, "we have but little hope." Douglas' confidence was shaken, however, when he received disquieting reports from some of his worried followers. The greatest difficulty appeared unexpectedly in Indiana, where the true nature of Bright's role gradually became clear, but trouble also appeared elsewhere. Buchanan was reported to be making inroads in Wisconsin and Michigan. Disney was closeted in New York with an influential Buchanan man from Michigan, one of the proprietors of the Detroit *Free Press,* and he wrote Douglas that the publisher could "be got" if Disney were able to "bid high enough." A later interview disclosed that the Michigan delegation would probably give Cass a token vote on the first ballot, after which it would support Buchanan. Cass, who held the Illinois Senator responsible for drawing off his own northwestern support in 1852, seemed anxious that Michigan withhold its vote from Douglas. From Ohio came word that many Democrats were opposed to Douglas because of the turmoil in Kansas. "If quiet could be restored there, everything would go well in this and other states." Illinois was the only sure state in the northwest. It was hoped that Douglas' commanding influence there would sway neighboring states. In early March, an election for mayor of Chicago was suddenly transformed into a trial of strength for the Little Giant. The *Chicago Tribune* had declared that the real issue in the contest was Douglas and his "Border Ruffian act." When the Douglas ticket won, his supporters were willing to accept the *Tribune's* declaration, and they spread news of the triumph to all corners of the nation.[26]

Outside the northwest, the richest prize was New York, where the Democratic party remained as hopelessly divided as it had been in years past. New York would again send two delegations to the national convention. Douglas set out to woo both factions, in the hope that their united endorsement of his candidacy would in turn unite the party, thus ending an internal squabble that had had repercussions beyond New York's borders. His conversations with John Van Buren and his meetings with upstate freesoilers during 1855 were undoubtedly a part of his plan. Disney was dispatched to New York early in the campaign, and for a time Singleton worked there with him. In New York City Disney found Buchanan thoroughly entrenched; the activity of Buchanan's supporters, he wrote Douglas, far exceeded his anticipation. He asked Douglas to stir Pierce into action against the Buchanan sentiment, preferably through the patronage, in order that the wrath of the latter might be directed against the President rather than Douglas. Disney predicted that a majority of both delegations would favor Douglas, if only communication could be opened between them. He played upon the New Yorkers' political pride and ambition, arguing that a united New York could be the "arbiter" of the convention, dictating the choice of nominee. The state would "reassume her old position as the first state of the Confederacy & have a controlling influence in the government and the Democratic party." The "softs" (the freesoil faction) proved easier to convince than the "hards." Marcy, a leader of the "softs," moved by an intense dislike of Buchanan and a growing conviction that Pierce could not win, expressed his preference for Douglas, and others followed.

Singleton traveled throughout the state, reporting to Douglas that *"quiet management"* could secure New York's vote in the convention, while Disney aimed his efforts at the "hards." Several interviews with such prominent men as the wealthy Augustus Schell, steamship operator Edwin Croswell ("prudent, discreet," and friendly to Douglas), and

Greene C. Bronson, whom Pierce had removed as collector of the port, convinced Disney that no progress could be made until Daniel Dickinson, powerful leader of New York's Hunkers, could be swayed. To accomplish that end, Disney called for help. Both he and Singleton urged Douglas to send "some *Southern* man of standing" to New York. A southern person, Disney wrote, would weigh more heavily with Dickinson than someone from any other location. Douglas' response was disappointingly negative: "I do not know of any Southern man of the kind you wish whom I could send on." Disney then appealed to Douglas to "get *Bright* to write to *Dickinson* urging him to come into the move and to take the initiative in New York in your favor." Bright, however, had no intention of supporting Douglas. These failures placed Disney in a difficult position. Dickinson, he wrote, hated Pierce, but he hated Marcy more, "& here lies the trouble." "I have *hinted* that *Dickinson* may be assured that he will be cared for in case of your success," Disney continued; later the *Chicago Times* printed a glowing vindication of Dickinson's character, but all to no avail. The split in the party remained as acute as it had ever been and the Buchanan influence among the "hards" seemed impregnable.

One consolation for Douglas was the pledge of support from the New York "softs." Several of their leaders promised to canvass the state in Douglas' behalf, and Dean Richmond, one of Marcy's principal upstate lieutenants, traveled to Washington to carry the promise of support directly to Douglas. It is ironic that the freesoil wing of the party should have provided Douglas with his most important strength in New York, although one "hard" who declared for Douglas did so precisely because the Little Giant had stood against the freesoil Democracy. Without the support of the powerful "hards," however, his prospects for carrying the state were dim.[27]

Support for Douglas in New England, as in New York, was less than encouraging. Disney went to work on some of Connecticut's delegates, while another assured Douglas of his favor because he wished "to sustain those who do not fear to stand in front of the battle." Buchanan's strength, however, proved formidable. One New Englander wrote Douglas that "Websters mantel has fallen on you," but the idea was not widespread. The best Douglas could hope for was second choice among those delegates who favored Pierce.

The south proved equally uncertain. Disney, from his base in New York, expressed great concern for Virginia, where Buchanan was being aided by Governor Wise. He urged Douglas to alert both Pierce and Hunter "to this condition of things in that state so that they may be roused to defeat the movement." Douglas' friends enlisted the aid of Kentucky's young John C. Breckinridge in building strength in the slave states, and Pierre Soulé was active in Louisiana. Andrew Johnson was reported to be working in Tennessee, while some North Carolinians, probably under the lead of David Reid, were urging Douglas' candidacy. In Missouri, David Atchison seemed safely in the fold. Douglas' efforts were hampered by the belief in some quarters that the nominee should be a southern man. "If there ever was a time when the Northern democrats ought to yield to the Southern, it is the present," an Alabaman contended. Linn Boyd, Kentucky Congressman and former Speaker of the House, supported Hunter first and Rusk second. His hostility toward Douglas was said to be intense. More important was the southern preference for Pierce's renomination. Again Douglas had to settle for being the second choice of the President's supporters. With the exception of Virginia, the south favored Douglas after Pierce.[28]

Developments preceding the Cincinnati convention demonstrated to Douglas the importance of an accord with the President, for only by securing Pierce's delegate support could he hope to make a showing. The warfare seemed most fierce between Buchanan and Pierce, encouraged no doubt by Douglas' attempt to remain on good terms with both while at the same time promoting the split between them. As the weeks passed there was increasing speculation that none of the three candidates could win the nomination. With their strength apparently equally divided, they would "have to walk the plank for a new man," especially if the two-thirds rule should be enforced. Just who the new man might be was uncertain, but the names of Hunter, Andrew Johnson, Rusk, and Wise were prominently mentioned.

As convention time drew nearer, Douglas' supporters grew more optimistic. After the first ballot, they hoped to combine Pierce's strength with their own and, with the promise of success, overawe Buchanan. As if to bear out this hope, the opposition press concentrated its fire on the Illinois Senator, virtually ignoring the other two candidates. Douglas, declared *The New York Times,* "is the evil genius of his party." Lacking in all the qualifications for statesmanship, "he has made a certain busy cunning (with which he happens to be unsparingly gifted) a tributary to his ambition." He was guilty of "clever imposture" and a "conscienceless thirst for public attention."

Douglas' own self-confidence was as great as ever. When, at a chance meeting in the parlor of Washington's National Hotel late in May, Buchanan patronizingly offered his young rival some advice, Douglas cockily retorted, "I expect to choose my Constitutional advisers soon, and am most happy thus to receive your acceptance in advance." His self-confidence was bolstered by the dedication of some of his followers. Buchanan's nomination, wrote one, would be an abandonment of all the principles for which Douglas had fought; if that should happen, "I do not care how soon they have a Sumner or a Seward in the White House." [29]

iv

In the last days of May, delegates from all parts of the nation began to gather in Cincinnati, the "Queen City of the West," and the city soon took on the character of a "great political exchange." It was the first time that a major party's national convention met away from the Atlantic seaboard, a tribute to the growing power of the west in the country's political councils. With the delegates came the usual horde of hangers-on, the "buzzards and camp-followers—pimps and prostitutes, political and other gamblers, that are inseparable from such events." Advance men from the camps of the three candidates arrived, and they jockeyed for position. New York financier Edward C. West, representing Douglas, sought spacious quarters in the Burnet House and offered to bear part of the cost ($150 a day) out of his own pocket. "I have determined that the Western men *should* have it," he informed Douglas. "If we do not have those quarters . . . I shall put it down as an omen against us." Another agent sent for Douglas' brother-in-law, Julius Granger, in order to have someone on the scene "who is more immediately identified with your personal welfare."

Newspaper reporters gathered in force and were busy interviewing delegates, circulating rumors, and adding up votes in the hope that some trend might be discerned. John Slidell, who at first did not plan to attend the convention, hurried to Cincinnati to ward off the efforts of Douglas and Pierce. He was joined by a powerful Senate triumvirate —Judah P. Benjamin of Louisiana, James A. Bayard of Delaware, and Jesse Bright—and the four were determined to control the convention in favor of Buchanan. Philadelphia editor John W. Forney was there seeking to split the Douglas-Pierce combination, and Thomas Hart Benton arrived, venting his spleen against the Little Giant at the slightest provocation, and urging Buchanan's nomination. William A. Richardson, Douglas' faithful lieutenant and floor manager in the 1852 convention, was prepared to assume a similar role at Cincinnati. Promises of the vice presidency were dangled in front of wavering delegations. The nomination of Douglas or Pierce, it was said, would be a "simple re-indorsement by the party of its declared principles and authentic history." Buchanan stood high among those "who are willing to suspend their principles for the sake of a successful election." Hostility toward Buchanan, Douglas was informed, would increase among those who found that the Pennsylvanian's mere acquiescence in the territorial legislation of the past fall short of the vigorous approval they demanded. The four Senators, however, found Buchanan's nomination to be the only means for preserving the power of the Democratic party. Buchanan himself, still pleading disinterest in his own nomination, warned that Pennsylvanians would "never forgive those who conspire against them in the present emergency." [30]

Douglas, although remaining in a deserted Washington and publicly displaying a lack of concern for the convention's action, was in close contact with his supporters at Cincinnati. One of them sent assuring word that "there is an under current working which will I feel confident be the means of your receiving the nomination." Other dispatches were less encouraging. The outside pressure was said to be ten to one for Buchanan. Douglas' friends, Isaac Cook, former Illinois Congressman Robert Smith, Washington McLean of the Cincinnati *Enquirer,* and Ohio's James B. Steedman, were working night and day, hardly allowing themselves time to eat or sleep. An overture from the Buchanan camp to pledge Douglas' delegates to the candidate who received the largest first ballot vote was arbitrarily rejected. Douglas' strategy was to do nothing on the first two ballots, marshalling all possible strength for a breakthrough on the third, but Richardson warned him that the Illinois delegation was "wild for your name to be presented which I think wrong." Buchanan was strong, had "forty candidates for Vice & will cheat them all." Confirming Douglas' growing suspicion, Richardson wrote that "Indiana is all gone & wrong." The result was uncertain, he continued, "but of one thing be sure I will take things in my own hands if necessary and if you dont get the nomination you will be bourn from the contest without dishonor." The Douglas men, reported the press, were in caucus the day before the convention was to open, discussing the propriety of withdrawing their candidate's name.[31]

Douglas scored a minor triumph on the opening day, June 2, when Ohio's Samuel Medary was chosen temporary chairman on Richardson's motion; at the end of the day Douglas' stock was said to be on the rise. Shortly after Medary's selection, a fist fight—"a vigorous display of pugilism"—erupted on the floor as a group of Benton delegates from Missouri, who had not been recognized by the national party chairman, forced its way into the hall. Richardson denounced the incident as an insult to the convention with an emphasis that was greeted "with hearty approbation." That all was not going well, however, seemed indicated when the Illinois delegation held a long, private caucus amid speculation that the delegates were deliberating on how best to withdraw "Little Dug" without doing him damage. Richardson was seen in "anxious talk" with John C. Breckinridge. Tall, slightly stooped, and coarse-featured, Richardson was a center of attention throughout the proceedings. Alert and intensely devoted to Douglas' cause, he regarded even the slightest movement as important. "Great attention is paid to whatever he says," wrote one reporter, "and when he goes into a fight he generally fixes it his own way." But, this reporter added, "his face does not shine with the interior inspiration of victory."

Richardson's anxieties were well founded. A Buchanan man, John E. Ward of Georgia, was selected to be permanent chairman, and Buchanan supporters were said to be in control of the committees. When the credentials committee recommended that both delegations from New York, the "hards" and the "softs," be seated, each to cast half the state's vote, Douglas' chances dimmed perceptibly. The setback was hardly compensated for by the endorsement of the principles of the Kansas-Nebraska Act in the platform, an endorsement which the chairman of the resolutions committee, Benjamin F. Hallett of Massachusetts, carefully described as having received the committee's unanimous support.[32]

Reports of these developments reached Douglas in Washington, and he immediately wired new instructions to Richardson. Fearing that the bitterness aroused in the convention might endanger Democratic prospects for victory, he reminded his followers that he placed more importance on the "triumph of our principles" than he did on his own personal elevation. "If the withdrawal of my name will contribute to the harmony of our Party or the success of the cause," he urged, "I hope you will not hesitate to take the step." When news of the platform committee's unanimous endorsement of the Kansas-Nebraska Act reached him, Douglas again reminded Richardson that "all the objects I had in view

in permitting my name to be used before the convention" had been accomplished. Again he urged that his name not be used in such a way as
to disturb the harmony of the party.

With these instructions in his pocket, Richardson placed Douglas'
name in nomination in a simple statement without embellishment, a
contrast to the elaborate speeches that had been made on behalf of the
other candidates. The character of the statement was not lost on the delegates. "There was something like grandeur in the rigid simplicity of the
nomination," reported one observer. Nonetheless, Buchanan led on the
first ballot, with Pierce a close second. Douglas, carrying Illinois, Missouri, and Iowa, with parts of Ohio, Kentucky, and Wisconsin, received
only thirty-three votes. Fourteen ballots were taken before the day was
over. Picking up strength from both Pierce and Buchanan, Douglas'
strength stood at 63 votes; Buchanan was far in the lead with 152½,
while Pierce had dropped to 75. Vermont, Arkansas, and a majority of
Georgia had switched from Pierce to Douglas, while Tennessee's twelve
votes were transferred from Buchanan. That night, June 5, the long-ru-
mored arrangement between Pierce and Douglas was invoked. When
the fifteenth ballot was taken the next day, the President had been virtually ruled out of contention and his strength was added to that of
Douglas. On the sixteenth ballot, no votes were cast for Pierce, Buchanan had edged up to 168, and Douglas stood at 122. Tennessee, however, had switched back to Buchanan, a loss that was keenly felt by the
Douglas managers; if Tennessee had remained in the Douglas column,
the Little Giant would have been within easy striking distance of his
rival. It was obvious that the Pierce-Douglas combination was not sufficient to crack the solidarity of Buchanan's support.

The real rivalry between Buchanan and Douglas was now exposed.
Two alternatives faced the convention; either one of the two candidates
must withdraw or a stalemate would result, with the possibility that
some new person would be brought forward. Years later, a member of
the Massachusetts delegation charged that Pierce's votes were given to
Douglas on the understanding that Douglas would continue the contest
with Buchanan until a compromise candidate could be found. It was unlikely that Douglas had agreed to such a plan; he had no desire to prolong the decision and certainly did not wish to jeopardize party unity.
There was little question which of the two alternatives would be followed. Richardson had received new instructions the night before. "Mr.
Buchanan," Douglas wrote, "having received a majority of the conven-

tion, is, in my opinion, entitled to the nomination. I hope my friends will give effect to the voice of the Majority of the Party."

After the sixteenth ballot, Kentucky's William Preston, an old-line Whig who had gone over to Douglas, secured the floor, "evidently laboring under much mental agitation." He had talked with Richardson and had seen Douglas' latest telegram. The two men agreed that Douglas had probably reached the peak of his strength and that it would be better for him to end by a "splendid retreat than perish by the secession of faithless adherents." Preston told the convention of his devotion to Douglas but added that it had now become clear that Buchanan was the choice of the party. Calling on Douglas' supporters to put an end "to the useless contest," he yielded the floor to Richardson. The delegates were in an uproar; cries of "No! No! Sit down—ballots! ballots!" punctuated Preston's remarks. Richardson rose to his feet and with a wave of his hand silenced the body. As he began to speak, however, voices from the Kentucky and Missouri delegations cried "Don't withdraw Dug— Stop!" and when Richardson declared it was his duty to speak, someone yelled "D——n the duty, sit down there." Richardson persisted. Reading Douglas' letter of June 3, he withdrew the candidate's name. The reading was frequently interrupted with wild cheers for "Little Dug." The seventeenth and last ballot followed quickly, and Buchanan received the unanimous vote of the convention.

In the final analysis, Douglas' strength at Cincinnati had come not from the states of the northwest, where Douglas had tried to build united support, but from the slave states of the south. The loss of the northwest was a bitter pill for Douglas to swallow. What he did not appreciate was the seriousness of the split within the northwest Democracy over the Kansas issue; Buchanan was simply a "safer" candidate for those who wished above all to ensure victory in the coming election. Outside the south, only New Hampshire, Vermont, Illinois, and the New York "softs" gave the Senator a solid support on the last day of balloting; North Carolina, Alabama, Mississippi, Kentucky, Missouri, Arkansas, Florida, Texas, and a majority of Georgia formed the substance of Douglas' candidacy. When the delegates rose to cheer the unanimous nomination of Buchanan, the southerners "preserved their dignity and their seats, and held their hats." The opposition of the south to Douglas' withdrawal was described as "tempestuous." To mollify both Douglas and the south, Buchanan's managers agreed to Richardson's request that John C. Breckinridge be nominated for the office of Vice President.[33]

There is no doubt that Douglas had strongly desired the nomination. His ambition for the highest office had not diminished, and the intricate strategy which he had employed before the convention indicated his determination to get it. However, another consideration also loomed large in Douglas' thinking. Ever since the passage of the Kansas-Nebraska Act, the purity of his Democracy had been questioned in the north. Dissident Democrats had denounced him as an apostate, while his anti-Nebraska opponents declared themselves the true party. In his own state they had made a strong effort to seize control of the party from his hands. As he had written many times, Douglas looked to the national convention for vindication, both of his principles and of his standing in the party, either by the nomination or by an endorsement of the Kansas-Nebraska Act. While he failed in the former, he succeeded in the latter. The results of the Cincinnati convention could still be regarded as a triumph. Douglas consoled himself with one further thought. He had been responsible for Buchanan's unanimous nomination; surely he would play a large role in a future Buchanan administration.

# XXI

## "Buck and Breck, Douglas and Democracy" 1856

i

Douglas, deeply disappointed at not having secured the nomination, received reassuring words from his friends following the Cincinnati convention. When Richardson read his letter to the convention, one delegate wrote, "the hearts of the representatives of the Democracy melted at your magnanimity, and you are already determined upon as the successor of Mr. Buchanan in 1860." "It would have done your heart good to have seen how gloriously you retired from that Convention," commented an Illinoisan who was present, "how nobly 'old Dick' placed you on the record, and the almost idolatry with which your name was cheered, when it was announced that for harmony, conciliation, and brotherhood, you wished your name withdrawn." An Indianan felt doubly motivated to write Douglas since the latter had counted heavily on that state's support. "My heart was with Douglas," wrote John Pettit, "but my head was with Buchanan, or in other words I preferred you for President but him for a candidate," a feeling, he added, that was shared by other Indiana delegates.

Buchanan's availability, and his detachment from the strife of the last few years, were important factors in the convention's choice. "The general tone of the country is for *pacification*," Disney concluded, "and Buchanan's age & supposed experience as well as *moderation* brought that entire sentiment to his support." Moreover, the Pennsylvanian appealed to a wider political spectrum than Douglas did. "The whigs who desire to vote with us, the tender toed Democrats & all the unsound de-sired Buchanan," Disney observed bitterly. Pettit agreed with Disney's assessment. "The age and experience of Mr. Buchanan tended not a little to produce this result, and it was strengthened by a large infusion of National Whigs who agree with our platform & will vote for us, but who begged that we should give them a man of the olden time." More importantly, the growing strength of the Republican party demanded a conservative nomination. Douglas gathered little comfort from such observations.[1]

Southerners' reactions to Buchanan's nomination were mixed. The ticket, wrote Clement C. Clay, would be a strong one in the north, sweeping the national Whigs and a large number of anti-Nebraska men into the Democratic fold; it would get a broader support than either Douglas or Pierce could have achieved. Representing two tariff states, Buchanan and Breckinridge would attract voters who might have balked at Douglas' anti-protectionism. The candidates' liberal position on internal improvements would secure the northwest, and Douglas might even have failed in this. While it was a safe ticket for the south, Clay argued, with Buchanan the "issue will not be fairly fought with Abolition & our triumph will be incomplete." The prospect for party unity would be dimmed, since Benton, Reeder, and Trumbull would now claim position in the Democracy. "There is, now, no nationality in the party on former issues." A New Orleans supporter wrote Douglas that Buchanan's nomination was better for foreign policy, but he regretted that the real statesman—Douglas—had been passed over. Hunter, who had never given up hope that he might emerge as a compromise candidate, was disappointed. His friends now urged him to assume leadership in the south so that he might control the choice of future presidential candidates.

Douglas wasted little time pondering the past, for more urgent tasks were now at hand. Replying to Pettit's condolences, he insisted that he had "no grievances growing out of the Cincinnati Convention and nothing to regret so far as I am personal[ly] concerned." The duty of all good Democrats now demanded an "undivided effort" to ensure Buchanan's election.[2]

Douglas had not been nominated, but the party had, he thought, adopted a platform that not only vindicated his position, but also provided a statement of principles around which all Democrats could rally. It was a conservative platform, emphasizing the party's traditional stand on states' rights and the strict construction of the Constitution and directing sharp rebukes at those who would flaunt these "time-honored" principles. The Know-Nothing crusade was denounced as contrary to the "spirit of toleration and enlarged freedom," and the Republican party, "a sectional party, subsisting exclusively on slavery agitation," was severely censured. The "only sound and safe solution of the 'slavery question'" lay in the principles of the Kansas-Nebraska Act. Popular sovereignty was thus endorsed, but in a further statement the platform recognized the right of the people of all territories, "acting through the legally and fairly expressed will of a majority of actual residents, and whenever the number of their inhabitants justifies it," to form a state constitution "with or without domestic slavery." The plank was ambiguous, but, in spite of his private protests against "equivocal terms" and "doubtful meanings," it was an ambiguity that Douglas endorsed. To Douglas, popular sovereignty meant that the slavery question could be decided by the voters of a territory while yet in a territorial stage, although many southerners insisted that the decision could only be made when the territory moved into statehood. Both sides found support in the 1856 platform; Buchanan, in fact, rendered both interpretations.

The call for a vigorous foreign policy in Central America and the Caribbean completed the party's appeal. With a thinly veiled Anglophobia, the platform upheld the Monroe Doctrine as sacred, hinted at the need for abrogating the Clayton-Bulwer Treaty, and declared America's right to the freedom of transit across Central America to be paramount and inviolable. Every effort, the statement concluded, should be made to guarantee American ascendancy in the Caribbean, an allusion to the acquisition of Cuba.[3]

A few days after the adjournment of the Cincinnati convention, the Republicans met in Philadelphia. The new party had achieved amazing strength in the short time since its first appearance, and it was evident that the troublesome Kansas issue had been the significant factor in its growth. Turning away from the more obvious political leaders, the Republican delegates nominated John C. Frémont, Thomas Hart Benton's dashing son-in-law, and drew up a platform that demanded unequivocally the admission of Kansas as a free state. The enthusiasm of the new party for its candidate and platform was impressive, and the confidence of its members that they would triumph in November refuted the Democratic charge that the party was but a temporary political aberration. A third presidential candidate filled out the field. Early in the year, the

Know-Nothings had nominated ex-President Millard Fillmore in a convention torn by dissension over the Kansas issue. Later, in September, a remnant of the old and now-defunct Whig party gathered. They endorsed Fillmore's nomination. Few doubted that the real struggle would be between Buchanan and Frémont, but Fillmore's candidacy had just enough support to remain a question mark in the campaign. It was also clear that the turmoil in Kansas would provide the campaign with its most urgent and dramatic issue. Worried Democrats, including Douglas, were suddenly aware of the necessity for a Kansas settlement before election day.

ii

The national conventions in June produced a hiatus in congressional deliberations, but by late June discussion of the Kansas question was resumed. Douglas, his Kansas bill languishing in the Senate and impatient to take to the campaign trail, sought to push the Kansas issue to solution. First initiative, however, came from the south when, on June 23, Georgia's fiery Senator Robert Toombs announced that he would introduce a new bill for Kansas statehood.

Toombs proposed that a census be taken in Kansas, overseen by a special panel appointed by the president in order "to preserve and protect the integrity of the ballot-box," on the basis of which the apportionment of delegates to a constitutional convention could be determined. Delegates would be elected on the day of the presidential election in November, a date when people in the states would be so preoccupied with that election that they would be discouraged from interfering in Kansas. Kansas would be admitted as a state without regard to the size of its population, a condition which the supporters of the free state constitution had already decided to ignore. The differences between Toombs' bill and that of Douglas were immediately apparent. The census would be closely watched and supervised, outside interference in the election would be guarded against, and the territory would be speedily admitted as a state. Moreover, the entire operation would bypass the existing territorial government.

The Republicans were taken by surprise. Toombs had carefully met their objections to Douglas' bill, and in his presentation he reviewed in a disarmingly calm and rational manner the circumstances which had motivated him. When Seward later referred to the measure as a compromise, Toombs was quick to reply, "It is no compromise." It was, he in-

sisted instead, a settlement of the question. The bill marked a new stage
in the Kansas debate, a genuine effort to remove the Kansas issue from
politics while restoring order in that troubled territory. Unfortunately,
there were powerful elements that opposed the elimination of Kansas as
an election year issue. The Republicans had made a heavy investment in
the question and were not prepared to see it so easily settled.[4]

Toombs' bill was quickly referred to Douglas' committee. At the same
time, Douglas' measure, which had been debated since March, was recommitted to the committee, and a new examination of the Kansas
question was ordered. A series of conferences among Democratic leaders
was then held at Douglas' home, at which it was decided that Toombs'
bill would be made a party measure "on which to fight the presidential
election."

On June 30, Douglas brought the bill back to the Senate floor with
an accompanying committee report. Reviewing all the proposals that
had been offered for a settlement of the Kansas problem, including one
by Trumbull attaching Kansas to Nebraska Territory, he concluded that
only Toombs' bill would "insure a fair and impartial decision of the
questions at issue in Kansas, in accordance with the wishes of the *bona
fide* inhabitants of the Terrritory, without fraud, violence, or any other
improper or unlawful influence." Dropped by the committee was a
clause requiring the submission of the proposed state constitution to the
voters of Kansas for ratification or rejection, but, as Douglas later explained, this was assumed as a matter of course. "Such a clause was unnecessary," he declared, "of course the constitution would be submitted
to the people." "Whenever a constitution shall be formed in any Territory," Douglas noted in his report, "justice, the genius of our institutions,
the whole theory of our republican system, imperatively demand that
the voice of the people shall be fairly expressed, and their will embodied
in that fundamental law." The opposition noted but made no issue of
the omission. Inasmuch as Douglas' first bill contained a reference to
submission, all assumed he was correct when he maintained that submission was taken for granted. Still the point was not clear. At a time when
precise and explicit language was necessary, Douglas once again supported an ambiguity, no doubt in the interest of party unity. It was a
risk he ran, but its full meaning would not become a serious question
until almost two years later.[5]

Douglas' endorsement of Toombs' bill was greeted with sarcasm by
some Republicans. He had, they scoffed, finally recognized the "bogus"

character of the Kansas territorial government. *The New York Times,* in a more serious vein, argued that while the new bill appeared to be an abandonment of popular sovereignty, it was in fact but another concoction of the "Kansas conspiracy." Senate Republicans agreed; although they conceded that the bill's provisions seemed liberal and even fair, they regarded with suspicion and hostility any measure proposed by a southerner and supported by Douglas. Jacob Collamer, a member of Douglas' committee, made the point in his minority report. No fair election of delegates could be secured, he maintained, since most of Kansas' free state settlers had been harassed and driven from the territory. It was a feeble argument, unsupported by the facts. If Douglas had shifted ground because of his alarm over Republican strength in the election campaign, as charged, the desperation of the Republicans to keep the Kansas issue alive until after the election was equally clear.

Debate began immediately. Republican leaders, impassioned and bitter, ranged widely over the whole course of recent events, reigniting a discussion of the Kansas-Nebraska Act and reviewing in careful detail the developments in Kansas during the past two years. Reference to the bill under discussion seemed almost incidental. Wade charged Douglas with surrendering the territory to the slave power, and in his attempt to prove that Douglas had repudiated popular sovereignty he came close to defending that doctrine. Wilson and Seward argued the illegality of the Kansas legislature, and the former tried to replace Toombs' bill with one abrogating the acts of the territory. Seward, while extolling the virtues of his own scheme to admit Kansas under the Topeka constitution, inconsistently denounced the Toombs' bill as patently unfair and onesided. The two principal objections to the measure were that President Pierce could not be trusted to appoint impartial commissioners to carry out its provisions and that most free state men had been driven from Kansas. To meet the latter objection, Douglas proposed an amendment to extend the right of voting to those *bona fide* residents of the territory who had absented themselves, provided that they returned before October 1. The amendment was agreed to, but it did nothing to mollify the Republicans.

The bill was finally brought to its final vote early on the morning of July 3, after a continuous session of twenty hours. A flurry of amendments were disposed of, and Douglas waived the speech which he had intended to give. The Republicans mustered only twelve votes against the bill, while thirty-three Senators voted in favor of it. The victory was

short-lived. Sent to the House of Representatives, the measure was peremptorily set aside by the Republican majority. Douglas exploded in bitterness. "All these gentlemen want is to get up murder and bloodshed in
Kansas for political effect. They do not mean that there shall be peace
until after the presidential election. . . . Their capital for the presidential election is blood. We may as well talk plainly. An angel from
heaven could not write a bill to restore peace in Kansas that would be
acceptable to the Abolition Republican party previous to the presidential
election." The Senate had, he thought, made an honest effort to achieve
a "fair, just, and equitable" settlement in Kansas.[6]

As the Toombs bill lay rejected on the Speaker's desk in the House of
Representatives, the prospects for bringing peace and order to Kansas in
1856 diminished perceptibly. The House replied to the Senate action
with the passage of a measure that would admit Kansas as a free state
under the Topeka constitution. Sent to the Senate, Douglas disposed of it
by proposing the substitution of the Toombs bill, which passed the Senate once again.

With the issue stalemated, talk of a new Kansas compromise was reported, and speculation in the press increased. Douglas was seen in frequent consultation with George G. Dunn, a freesoil Know-Nothing
member of the House from Indiana, and by the end of July "a new
scheme for the pacification of Kansas" seemed imminent. The result
shattered all hopes for an end to the problem. Dunn sponsored a bill for
the reorganization of Kansas Territory, shifting the boundaries, restoring
the Missouri Compromise, and providing for the election of a new territorial legislature. Slavery was to be allowed in Kansas until January 1,
1858, and the Fugitive Slave Act was expressly extended to the territory.
If it was intended as a compromise, it missed the mark. Passed by the
House, the Dunn bill was referred to Douglas' committee. In mid-August, Douglas, who, contrary to speculation, had had no part in its drafting, reported against the bill and urged that the best mode of settlement
was still that proposed by Toombs. "No measure can restore peace to
Kansas," he reminded the Senate, "which does not effectually protect the
ballot-box against fraud and violence, and impart equal and exact justice
to all the inhabitants." Of all the proposals submitted, he remained convinced, only that of Toombs accomplished this end.

One last confusing and ineffectual foray on the Kansas issue was attempted before the election. A routine bill for army appropriations was
amended by House Republicans to forbid the use of the military to en-

force the laws of the Kansas territorial legislature, an amendment in which the Senate refused to concur. Two committees of conference were appointed (Douglas sat on both), but the differences remained unresolved. The session ended without the passage of the appropriation bill, and the army was threatened with paralysis. Pierce immediately summoned Congress into a special session during the last week in August; after days of fruitless wrangling, the House relented, and the army received its appropriation.

Douglas spoke often and forcefully during these latter days. During the summer he had revealed his overriding concern for peace in Kansas and had demonstrated a flexibility that was lacking among his opponents. Each concession to the arguments of the opposition was greeted by taunts and sarcasm rather than by the spirit of conciliation he had hoped to promote. The issue was dictated by the politics of an election year, but, he reluctantly concluded, it also transcended the maneuverings of an election campaign. It was, he said dejectedly, a deeper question of union or disunion, a contest "rising in importance and magnitude far above any other that this or any other country has ever witnessed." For Douglas, this was "a painful reflection." [7]

iii

In 1859, when Douglas jotted down a few autobiographical notes for the benefit of a prospective biographer, he noted that his views with regard to foreign policy had "seldom been in accordance with the policy of the administration." He recalled his opposition to the Oregon Treaty, to the Treaty of Guadalupe Hidalgo, and to the Clayton-Bulwer Treaty. In each instance, his opposition had sprung from the conviction that the natural growth of the United States demanded expansion. Each of these treaties, he had argued, placed untenable limits on national expansion. Since 1854, Douglas had been embroiled in controversy over the Kansas issue, but this involvement had by no means diminished his zeal for an aggressive, expansive American foreign policy.[8]

Douglas had always been a persistent advocate of the acquisition of Cuba, although he favored direct action only in the event that Cuba's people desired annexation or that some European power might seek to extend its influence over the island. He remained convinced, however, that Cuba lay clearly within the sphere of America's natural expansion and that the day was not far distant when it would be incorporated in the Union. When Edward Everett, as Secretary of State in the last days of the Fillmore administration, refused to join an Anglo-French guarantee of Cuba's status as a Spanish colony, Douglas had high praise for the Whig's declaration that such an agreement would be contrary to the law of American growth.

In view of Douglas' position on Cuba, it is ironic that it was his own insistence on the organization of Kansas and Nebraska with popular sovereignty that placed the Cuban question on the shelf, at least for the next few years. Having committed his administration to the Kansas-Nebraska Act, President Pierce, whose desires for Cuba were nearly as strong as Douglas', could not pursue an active policy in the Caribbean without courting disaster among northern Democrats. On the day the Kansas-Nebraska Act passed the Senate, Alexander H. Stephens suggested that "we shall soon have another question which will absorb all others . . . our relations with Spain growing out of the state of affairs in Cuba." This was precisely what many freesoilers feared, that the Nebraska bill was only a first step in the ascendancy of the slave power and that it would soon be followed by the seizure of Cuba.[9]

Southern pressure for action increased when Spain, in an attempt to make Cuba less desirable to the expansionists, announced a plan that would free large numbers of slaves on the island. In February 1854, an American vessel, the *Black Warrior,* was confiscated in Havana harbor on the charge that the ship's manifest was false, a show of authority that Spain hoped might discourage any attempt to take Cuba by force. For many southerners, especially in the Gulf states, the real gain was not in the extension of slavery to Kansas but in the acquisition of Cuba. In the face of administration inaction, there were those who would take matters into their own hands. It was common knowledge in 1854 that a filibustering expedition, encouraged by Cuban exiles and expansionists and to be led by Mississippi's former governor and friend of Douglas', John A. Quitman, was being organized.

The bitter reaction aroused by the Kansas-Nebraska Act persuaded Pierce that he could ill-afford any hint of tacit support to Quitman's plans. On the day after he signed the bill, he warned that all violations of the neutrality laws and treaty obligations would be prosecuted. Douglas shared the President's concern, although he probably was not opposed to Quitman's project. With Jefferson Davis, Slidell, and James Mason, he urged Pierce to announce that the administration would pursue "an energetic policy" toward Cuba, hoping that this would discourage the filibusters. Instructions were dispatched to Europe calling for a meeting of the ministers to England, France, and Spain, presumably to discuss ways of bringing pressure on Spain to relinquish Cuba to the United States.

The meeting, held in Ostend, Belgium, in October, resulted in the famous Ostend Manifesto. Signed by Buchanan, John Y. Mason, and Pierre Soulé, the document urged the United States to make an immediate effort to purchase Cuba. Failing in this, the country would be justified "by every law human and divine" in seizing the island, "if we possess the power." The manifesto could not have been drafted at a more inopportune moment. Sent immediately to Washington, it arrived on election day, November 1854, when the disastrous political effects of the Kansas-Nebraska Act on the Democratic party became fully known. There was no alternative but to rebuke the diplomats and repudiate their declaration. Soon afterward Quitman's filibustering plans collapsed. The Cuba issue was played down, and when the Democrats gathered in Cincinnati later in 1856 they wisely limited themselves to a weak and vaguely worded declaration for American ascendancy in the Caribbean.[10]

In the meantime a new crisis had developed in Central America, and again, to Douglas' dismay, the uproar over the Kansas-Nebraska Act caused the administration to react less aggressively than he thought appropriate. The extension of British authority in defiance (it was thought) of the Clayton-Bulwer Treaty, combined with a heightened interest in an Isthmian transmit between the oceans, aroused an indignant concern among the nation's more fervent expansionists. Filibustering expeditions were openly planned, but they were soon dwarfed by the operations of William Walker. Taking advantage of a civil war in Nicaragua, Walker sailed for Central America with a group of armed men in May 1855. Within a few months after landing in Nicaragua, he had captured the capital, defeated the opposing forces, and become the virtual dictator of the country. Anglo-American relations, already strained, reached a critical juncture.

Walker's Nicaraguan enterprise secured sympathy and support from expansionist Democrats. The administration, however, stood aloof. The recognition of Walker's government by the American minister was withdrawn, and when Walker's minister to the United States arrived in Washington Secretary of State Marcy refused to receive him. Douglas followed these developments from his sickbed, and he chafed at the inaction which his illness had forced upon him. When he returned to his Senate seat in February he lost no time in making his position known. He openly avowed his sympathy for Walker and lashed out, with all his former fire, at the British threat to American expansion in the western hemisphere. His resentment of the British had attained new dimensions as reports of British efforts to recruit soldiers in the United States for the Crimean War circulated, and as he became more convinced than ever of Britain's perfidy in Central America. As soon as he reappeared in the Senate, Douglas announced that he would oppose Pierce's Central American policy. The recognition of Walker's government in Nicaragua, he urged, should be followed by an offensive and defensive alliance with the adventurer, preliminary, if need be, to a war with Great Britain. His conviction was bolstered by detailed reports which he received from Americans in Central America.

Douglas continued to exert pressure on Pierce to recognize Walker's government. On May 1 he sought to arouse the nation to the British danger in a fiery speech from the Senate floor. British policy, he declared, had made it obvious that "all American interests in Central America are to be sacrificed and destroyed." How much longer, he wondered, must the nation submit to these repeated invasions of its rights? Douglas had high praise for Walker and his government. "I hold that that government is as legitimate as any which ever existed in Central America . . . the firmest, the most stable Government that has ever existed there since the Spanish yoke was thrown off." Pierce was in error when he forbade Americans to join in Walker's venture. "Nicaragua has as much right to become an asylum for emigrants from the United Sates as our country has to become the asylum for emigrants from Europe." Walker, he pointed out dramatically, was comparable to such other "liberty-loving heroes" as Lafayette, von Steuben, and de Kalb. The presence of so many Americans in the new Nicaraguan government was strong argument for recognition. "I believe that the cause of progress, of humanity, of civilization, will be promoted by the extension of that American influence." Douglas, however, would not stop with recognition. The logical goal of America's mission in Central America was annexation, for which Walker's movement was but a first step. When the people of Nicaragua should become "thoroughly Americanized, when they come to understand the principles of our Constitution, and of our system of government," he argued, then the time for annexation will have arrived.

It was a matter of fate. A movement "in which civilization and humanity, and especially American interests, have so deep a stake" could not be checked.[11]

Douglas went much further than even some of his fellow expansionists were willing to go. Coming on the eve of the Democratic convention, his remarks did not enhance his campaign for the nomination, except perhaps in the south. Walker's supporters, however, were delighted, and Douglas was shortly invited to address a mass meeting in New York "to aid and encourage the struggling patriots under *General William Walker* in their efforts for Freedom," an invitation he wisely turned down. His Senate speech also played a part in forcing Pierce to reappraise the administration's policy toward Walker. After a series of cabinet meetings at which the Central American situation was discussed, the President announced on May 15 that Walker's government would be recognized.

Pierce's announcement was followed by swift action. A war vessel was dispatched to Nicaragua to protect American interests, and at the end of May the British minister to Washington, John F. Crampton, was declared *persona non grata,* as much because of the Crimean recruiting issue as of the Central American situation. As the Democrats gathered in Cincinnati for their convention, relations between the two governments had reached a point of crisis. During the summer months, however, the tension subsided as quickly as it had arisen. A new attitude of conciliation on the part of the British resulted in the negotiation of the Dallas-Clarendon Treaty, which provided for a gradual British withdrawal from some of her Central American commitments. Douglas opposed the new accord as energetically as he had opposed the Clayton-Bulwer Treaty a few years before, on the ground that it still confirmed the British presence in the area. When the treaty was finally ratified by the Senate in March 1857, it was with an amendment demanding the immediate withdrawal of the British from the Bay Islands, an area Douglas had repeatedly charged they held in violation of the Monroe Doctrine.

By helping to force the confrontation between the two nations, Douglas injured his own chances for the presidential nomination and unwittingly aided those of Buchanan. If amicable relations had been established before the Cincinnati convention instead of after, wrote one Douglas supporter, Buchanan might not have been nominated. In the absence of a settlement, however, and meeting at the peak of the crisis,

some delegates felt that Douglas' nomination would cause a further dete-
rioration of Anglo-American relations. The nation needed Buchanan's
diplomatic experience.[12]

## iv

Congress remained in session until the end of August, its members
growing daily more impatient to return home to campaign among their
constituents. The attempt to resolve the Kansas issue kept them busy
until the very last day and left many, like Douglas, in a state of almost
hopeless frustration. With the issue unresolved, the outcome of the presidential campaign loomed larger. Following the Cincinnati convention,
Douglas spoke at Democratic rallies in Washington, Philadelphia, and
New York, and on each occasion he forcefully reminded his audiences
that the Democratic party was now the only remaining national party, a
conviction he would develop and repeat in later years. The mission of
the party was now the mission of the Union, for without the party there
would be no Union.

There was little that Douglas could do to advance the cause of the
party's nominee until after Congress' adjournment. Alarmed at the
heavy contributions being made to the Frémont campaign by northern
businessmen, he urged Washington banker William W. Corcoran to
warn the nation that Frémont's election would "ruin all the Commercial
and monetary interests of the U. S." At his own considerable expense,
he ordered the reprinting of speeches and reports on Kansas and sent
thousands of copies throughout the country under his frank. Letters were
sent to those who had supported him in the convention admonishing
them to spare no exertion for Buchanan's election; his pleas became so
insistent that some people marveled at his magnanimity toward the man
who had beaten him in the convention. In order to meet his financial
obligations to the campaign, he sold some of his Chicago property (one
hundred acres on the western limits of the city for the round sum of
$100,000, according to Sheahan). Additional funds were devoted to the
establishment of a Douglas Democratic German language newspaper in
Chicago. Douglas later estimated that he had spent about $42,000 on
Buchanan's campaign. Throughout the summer his relations with Pierce
were strained, probably because of Pierce's feeling that Douglas had betrayed him at Cincinnati, and he had no communication with Buchanan.
The nominee carefully refrained from acknowledging Douglas' efforts on
his behalf for fear it might imply the promise of future reward.[13]

While occupied in Congress, Douglas remained in close touch with party developments in Illinois. The state Democratic convention met in Springfield on May 1, and until that time the anti-Nebraska Democrats hoped that they might yet secure control of the party. Reluctant to abandon their old allegiances, men like Trumbull, Koerner, Wentworth, Bissell, Palmer, and others still worked to commit the party to a slavery restriction platform. The meeting of the state convention, however, dashed their hopes. Determined to give Douglas' bid for the presidential nomination a strong boost, the delegates supported the Kansas-Nebraska Act as a test of party fealty and endorsed Douglas' course on the Kansas question. Taking their cue from Douglas, they declared that Lyman Trumbull was no Democrat, in effect reading the junior Senator out of the party. William A. Richardson was nominated for the governorship, a choice that had been dictated by Douglas in a meeting of party leaders at his Chicago home months before. "The enthusiasm was unbounded," wrote Republican Charles H. Ray, "and the determination to beat us was apparent in all." [14]

The anti-Nebraska Democrats, cut loose from the Democratic party, had no alternative but to associate with the Republicans. The latter were equally anxious to woo them into their fold. When the Republican state convention met at Bloomington later in May, it was controlled by former Democrats. John M. Palmer was selected to chair the meeting, and William H. Bissell, a former Democratic Congressman, was nominated for governor. Lincoln, who was chosen as an elector-at-large, exerted an important influence on the meeting, and his stirring speech at the conclusion of the deliberations set a moderate tone for the new party. The same moderation was urged on the state's delegates to the Republican national convention, where, it was thought, Buchanan's nomination must be offset by the selection of a candidate who was not "ultra" and against whom there were no old political prejudices. "Do not let the abolitionists urge us too far," advised one former Democrat.

Frémont's nomination was well received in Illinois (except by abolitionists, who announced they would support New York radical Gerrit Smith for the presidency), but Republican optimism depended ultimately on the failure of Congress to settle the Kansas difficulties before the election. Mark Delahay, a former Douglas Democrat who had moved into the Republican ranks, expressed it well. "If the House bill for the admission of Kansas is rejected by the Senate and the Toombs bill defeated by the House," he wrote, "then let Congress adjourn and we have matters in the best fix that we can get them." [15]

In spite of the confidence of leaders on both sides, the campaign in Illinois was marked by uncertainty. The impact of Fillmore's candidacy was unknown. Some Republicans feared it would split the anti-Nebraska vote; others were hopeful that Fillmore would only draw old-line Whigs away from Buchanan. Chicago Democrats became involved in a senseless quarrel between Postmaster Isaac Cook and Sheahan which threatened to spread to the rest of the state. Both men held an interest in the *Chicago Times,* and each sought to dictate the course of the party in Chicago's politics. Cook attempted to oust Sheahan as editor, and failing that, he took the matter to the courts to force the suspension of the paper. Sheahan pleaded with Douglas to intervene lest Cook's course bring ruin not only to the paper, but to the party as well. Douglas, anxious to retain the loyalty of both men, tried to remain aloof, but in vain. Through an emissary, he arranged terms by which Cook agreed to sell his interest in the *Times.* At a time when his financial resources were strained by the expenses of the campaign, Douglas was forced to buy out Cook's share. The fracas at times threatened to get out of hand as Democrats in other parts of the state took sides. Sheahan, indignant at Douglas' reluctance to intervene on his side and outraged that Cook's dismissal from the postmastership had not been arranged, vented his resentment against the Senator. "The party here will burst, dissolve," he complained to Lanphier. "The name of Douglas will again fall into disrepute, and the labors of the last two years will be wasted forever. . . . I will *never again* put faith in political aspirants." Cook, unreconciled to the terms of the settlement that was forced upon him, became a bitter critic of Douglas. [16]

With the adjournment of Congress, Douglas hurried west. On the way he participated in a massive demonstration of support for Buchanan held on the Tippecanoe battlefield in western Indiana, a site designed to endear old-line Whigs to the Democratic ticket. Near-by Lafayette was inundated with people, and estimates of the size of the crowd on the battlefield ranged from 50,000 to 150,000. Douglas shared the stage with a host of luminaries, including Lewis Cass, Jesse Bright, Kentucky Whig William Preston, James L. Orr of South Carolina, and vice presidential candidate John C. Breckinridge. On the platform with the slave state men were freesoiler John Van Buren and Daniel Dickinson, representing the feuding factions of the New York party. In one corner of the field Francis Grund, whom Douglas had persuaded to campaign in the west, addressed a delegation of Germans in their own language. The party was casting a broad net to meet the challenge of Cass' prediction that "we have a hard contest north of the Ohio."

Douglas spoke in Chicago on September 9, and several days later he appeared at a great "outpouring of the democracy" in Springfield. His arrival in the state was none too soon. Impressed with Bissell's popularity, some Democrats were apprehensive lest Illinois be lost to the Republicans. Douglas did not have to be reminded of the stakes in the campaign, but one friend warned that "your future depends upon the perpetuity of your power in Illinois." Richardson and Harris were on hand in Springfield to support the state ticket, while Douglas concentrated on the dangers of a Republican victory to the Union. As at Tippecanoe, a special appeal was made to the foreign element. Speeches in German were delivered simultaneously with the main event, and Illinois' Irish Democracy was given a prominent place in the parade. The enthusiasm was impressive. "It was 'Buck and Breck,' 'Old Dick,' Douglas and Democracy everywhere." [17]

Following this kick-off, Douglas announced another grueling schedule of speeches, extending from Galena in the north to Carbondale in the south. By the end of September, he was optimistic that Buchanan would carry Illinois. "We are in the midst of the most exciting contest ever known in this State," he wrote the nominee. "The opposition are making desperate efforts, but I think you may rely upon this State with entire certainty." Both sides made use of outside speakers. John Van Buren, New York Governor Horatio Seymour, Henry A. Wise of Virginia, Cass, and Howell Cobb spoke for the Democrats, while the Republicans imported John P. Hale, Nathaniel P. Banks, Francis Blair, Jr., and Kansas' free state "governor" Charles Robinson. In spite of the Republican efforts to avoid the label, however, the air of abolitionism hung too heavily about some of their speakers to suit many Illinois voters, especially in the central counties. Frémont's nomination had not swayed conservative Whigs from their support of Buchanan, and without the old-line Whigs, Lincoln noted, the anti-Nebraska strength was considerably weakened. Fillmore's candidacy threatened to divide the opposition to Buchanan even further. One of Douglas' strategies was to persuade antislavery Know-Nothings to resist all Republican overtures and to vote the Fillmore ticket.[18]

Douglas was much less confident of success in the state election, where a split in the opposition vote was less likely. Richardson had to bear the full brunt of the Kansas troubles, while Bissell, as a former Democrat, enjoyed a wide appeal. By October, Douglas virtually gave up hope that his friend and close associate would win. Would it not be well, he asked Sheahan, to prepare for the worst? "We may have to fight against wind & tide after the 14th [of October, the date on which several state elections would be held] and hence our friends ought to be prepared for the worst." His anxiety, coupled with the exhausting effects of his campaign, left its mark. To Frank Blair, who met Douglas on the campaign trail, the Senator appeared "down hearted & broken in spirit," while Theodore Parker, who heard him speak in Galesburg, reported that Douglas had been drinking heavily. Douglas' concern was not limited to the Illinois state election. Indiana, he feared, was also in danger, and he urged Breckinridge to join him in an effort to save the state. Buchanan's own state of Pennsylvania was also crucial to Democratic success. "All the efforts of our Party should be concentrated on Penn [sylvania] at the State election," he advised Buchanan. If Pennsylvania should elect its Democratic slate, "the battle is over." Buchanan, breaking his silence and mistakenly (but deliberately) addressing Douglas as "Samuel," agreed but expressed his confidence that all would be right.[19]

As election day approached, the picture grew brighter. A resounding Republican victory in Maine's state election in September frightened some southerners into thinking that Frémont might win, and disunion talk increased. In October, both Pennsylvania and Indiana elected their Democratic state tickets, relieving Douglas' concern and assuring victory in November. When the votes were finally counted, Buchanan had won and the Democrats had regained control over both houses of Congress. The Democratic margin, however, was narrower than party leaders had expected. Douglas was elated that Illinois had cast its vote for Buchanan, but he found the national results were less than reassuring. With all but one of the slave states and five free states, including Pennsylvania, Indiana, New Jersey, and California, besides Illinois, the Democratic candidate had achieved a safe majority in the electoral college, but he had received only 45 per cent of the popular vote. Frémont carried all the remaining free states, a strength which surprised even some Republicans. The latter, Lyman Trumbull observed, were "in great spirits for a defeated party."

Buchanan carried Illinois, a result that was attributed to "the super-human efforts of Douglas & his true friends," but at a price. The returns in the state contest bore out Douglas' gloomiest predictions. Bissell won the governorship decisively over Douglas' good friend and loyal supporter Richardson, a loss that the Little Giant felt keenly. Rejoicing that they had wiped out the blot placed on Illinois by the passage of the Kansas-Nebraska Act and the repeal of the Missouri Compromise, Republicans boasted that Douglas had been stripped of power on his home ground. A pattern emerged from the election returns as Illinoisans voted for order and stability on both the national and state levels. Douglas and Richardson suffered equally from their close involvement with the critical Kansas question. But aside from the immediate issues of the election, it became clear that the grip of the Democratic party on state politics was no longer as tight as it once was. The distribution of party strength gave Douglas little comfort. The northern counties gave heavy support to Frémont, although not enough to offset Buchanan's advantage in the south. These same northern counties, however, constituted the fastest growing section of the state, and there was every likelihood that they would soon outstrip the southern counties in voting power.[20]

Even Buchanan's victory was not the clear-cut vindication Douglas hoped to achieve. The Democratic platform had endorsed popular sovereignty, but the campaign proved how susceptible its vague phrases were to conflicting interpretations. Was it Douglas' view of popular sovereignty or that of the south that was now mandated? There was no obvious answer. Buchanan, in his acceptance letter and his few campaign statements, had subscribed to each, a vacillation that did not go unnoticed. "What will Mr. Buchanan do?" asked the New York *Herald*. "Which horse will he ride up to the Capitol on the 4th of March? Will he take up the doctrine of the sovereignty of the Territory over niggers? or will he adopt the more convenient policy of leaving slavery an open question till the people . . . have entered upon the business of a State organization?" Douglas, celebrating the Democratic victory, was unaware that his adversary during the next four years would not be the "allied isms" of the Republican party, but the formidable power of the southern wing of his own party.

Buchanan quickly recognized the magnitude of his mission. "The great object of my administration," he wrote at the end of December, "will be to arrest, if possible, the agitation of the Slavery question at the North & to destroy sectional parties." Not all of the signs, however, were hopeful. Buchanan's election, commented a southerner, "secures us a four years truce; whether it shall be anything more depends upon whether the public opinion of the North is really undergoing a healthy change in regard to our institution, or whether . . . the anti-slavery feeling there is still growing." [21]

v

The few months following the election gave Douglas, as well as the nation, a much-needed breathing spell. Peace, however elusive and temporary, seemed to have been restored in Kansas. Responding to the pleas of Douglas and others, Pierce had taken positive steps "to quiet the Kansas excitement" by sending a new governor to the territory. John W. Geary, an impressive Pennsylvanian with a frontier background, called for "an honest return to the beneficent provisions" of the Kansas-Nebraska Act. Although he was determined to follow a neutral course in Kansas, his insistence that responsibility for much of the disorder belonged to "over zealous persons in Missouri" and their "dogged determination to *force* Slavery" into Kansas brought him into sharp disagreement with the territory's proslavery leaders and discredited him in the south. He was eventually forced to flee Kansas in fear for his life, but during the last months of Pierce's presidency, at least, Kansas was quiescent. The territory, Geary informed Pierce, was "like a sleeping volcano ready to burst forth at any moment." [22]

The short session of Congress reflected the mood of calm and hopeful anticipation that seemed to have settled on the nation. Douglas busied himself with an accumulation of routine territorial business. When the House of Representatives passed enabling acts for Minnesota and Oregon, he worked to secure their passage in the Senate. When some southerners objected to the admission of additional free states, Douglas angrily replied that the admission of new states should be completely divorced from sectional or partisan considerations. The attempt to maintain an equilibrium between slave and free states, he insisted, was contrary to the Constitution and "to the principles of State equality and self-government." He answered objections to a provision in the Minnesota bill that would allow aliens, under certain conditions, to vote by pointing out the American mission to serve as "the asylum of the oppressed of all nations on earth." The strength of the nation, he argued, was in its diversity; to urge that "we must have uniformity in our laws; uniformity in the elective franchise; uniformity in our institutions respecting labor" was to strike at the heart of the Union's first great principle, "that each State shall be sovereign over all things relating to its domestic concerns, with a right to do as it pleased." Douglas had made these points before in debate against the Republicans; he now turned them against southerners, while the Republicans remained discreetly silent.

The Minnesota bill was passed with the alien voting provision intact. For his part in the debate, Douglas won praise as "the friend and advocate of freedom in its broadest sense. . . . To emancipate the condition of his fellow man is the pride of his soul." He was less successful in his effort to move Oregon along the road to statehood.

When Cyrus Field, promoter of a transatlantic cable between Newfoundland and Great Britain, appealed to Congress for assistance, Douglas gave the project strong support. For once his Anglophobia was muted. The cable, he asserted, would cultivate better feelings between the United States and England and help to erase the prejudices that existed between the two nations. Moreover, the enterprise would bring honor and glory "to American genius and American daring." A new low tariff bill was passed in the last days of the session, but Douglas' role in the discussion was apparently limited to the typically nationalistic observation that American wines were superior to the common wines of Europe.[23]

It was not solely with political matters, however, that Douglas was concerned during the weeks following the election. For three years he had endured the solitary existence that was forced upon him by Martha's death. Political strife and struggle consumed all his energies; he was totally committed to his role as a national political and party leader. To those around him he seemed to have no relieving personal life. In November 1856, Douglas surprised his friends and created a sensation in Washington society when he married a second time. It is not clear just when or where he first met Adele Cutts, but a story that circulated in the press assigned the role of intermediary to Jesse Bright. During the summer, Douglas frequently visited Bright in his Washington home to discuss the strategy of the Presidential campaign. On one such occasion, he was introduced to Miss Cutts, whose family lived opposite the Bright residence. Later the Indiana Senator was supposed to have suggested that Douglas marry again, "and there's the lady for you." Romance blossomed, and soon all of Washington was talking of Douglas' new interest. Their engagement was announced before he left to campaign in Illinois.

Adele Cutts had not yet reached her twenty-first birthday when she agreed to become Douglas' wife. Born in 1835, she was the daughter of James Madison Cutts, a government clerk in Washington for most of his life, and a grand-niece of Dolley Madison; her mother was a member of a prominent Roman Catholic family in Maryland. Adele was educated at a Catholic academy in Georgetown, and by the time she was eighteen she took her place in Washington society. Her family was not well off; Adele's fortune, it was said, was the "dowry of beauty." She was seen often at Washington receptions and balls and made an unforgettable impression wherever she went, "beautiful as a pearl, sunny-tempered, unselfish, warm-hearted, unaffected, sincere."

Not everyone was pleased with Adele's decision to accept Douglas' offer of marriage. Since the death of his first wife, Douglas' personal habits had become careless, his drinking had increased, and his clothes had become shabby. Some of Addie's friends apparently thought that she was marrying beneath her own social position. Jefferson Davis' wife, whose reaction was probably motivated in part by political considerations, was resentful. "The dirty speculator and party trickster," she wrote, "broken in health by drink, with his first wife's money, buys an elegant, well-bred woman because she is poor and her Father is proud." Such reactions, however, were rare.

As the wedding date approached, the event became the "absorbing theme of conversation" in the capital. It was such a match as to excite comment. Douglas was twenty-two years older than Adele. She was the "very embodiment of youth, beauty and accomplishments," and one reporter glowingly described her as "tall, elegantly formed, with a sweet, oval face, large brown eyes, small Grecian forehead, around which are entertwined the heavy braids of her glossy and abundant chestnut hair." Even Douglas' opponents conceded his good taste. Adele had an air of refinement that Douglas, trained in the rough school of western politics, could not approach. One of her favorite pastimes was reading books in French, a language in which she was said to excel. She was a devout Roman Catholic; Douglas' religious affiliation was nebulous, but he leaned toward the Baptists.[24]

The marriage was solemnized by a Roman Catholic priest on November 20, Thanksgiving Day, in the home of the bride's father. Only a few of Douglas' close personal friends were present, including James Shields, who served as best man. The couple left immediately afterward on a wedding trip to upstate New York and a visit with Douglas' mother. On the way they stopped in Philadelphia and New York City, where the wedding party attended an operatic performance. At Clifton Springs, while visiting his mother, Douglas and his bride were tendered a public supper and ball, at which the Senator could not resist making a speech on "the true character of the Kansas-Nebraska bill." On leaving New York the couple made a quick trip to Chicago, and by Christmas they were back in Washington, settled in Douglas' house. Everywhere they went, they attracted attention. The costume of the new Mrs. Douglas and even the style of her hair—"after the fashion of the Empress Eugenie"—were recorded in detail in the press. At the opera, the "battery of lorgnettes" was trained as much on Adele as on the stage. Douglas, it was reported, "looked uncommonly well and cheerful." [25]

Marriage to Adele worked a remarkable change in Douglas. From a frequenter of "crossroads taverns and city oyster saloons," he had been transformed "as by a fairy, into quite a genial and courtly aristocrat." His new wife, commented Shields, was "a splendid person and will be a great benefit to Judge Douglas. . . . Her influence will improve his appearance and soften his manners." Adele took a deep interest in Douglas' political career, accompanied him on his campaigns, and frequently sat in the Senate gallery when he made a speech. On more than one occasion, she hurried to the Senate floor following a Douglas speech to wrap an overcoat about the perspiring Senator. As a result of her efforts, Douglas seemed a new man. "The greatest possible improvement is visible in his appearance since his marriage," wrote one reporter. Before, Douglas had worn poorly trimmed whiskers, long hair, and a seedy dress coat; he "had a decidedly shabby look." "Now his face is clean shaved, his collar stands stiff and glossy, his linen looks decidedly respectable, he wears his hair much shorter than usual, and, to crown all, he appears in a new suit of black, a neat-fitting frock, instead of the shabby old dress coat, and looks about ten years younger than ever." [26]

Douglas' home became a showplace of Washington society, rivalling the White House in importance during the administration of bachelor James Buchanan. The Douglases began almost at once to entertain on a lavish and exquisite scale, with dinner parties and receptions. Adele presided with such queenly grace and "high bred courtesy" that it was difficult to say "whether the genius of the husband or the beauty of the wife attracts the most homage." She was at once the envy and admiration of Washington wives, and her style of entertainment as well as her fashionable attire attracted imitators. She was the first to hold early afternoon receptions with drapes drawn and rooms lighted with gas. Her dress was simple, though elegant, and she wore no jewelry to distract the beholder (Douglas had told her that "diamonds are the consolation of old wives"). Other Senate wives often sought her advice on clothes. The attention Adele invariably received from their husbands was, however, not always appreciated, and Mrs. Jefferson Davis, still not reconciled, pouted because Adele was accorded a higher place than she at some dinner parties.

Among the responsibilities of the new Mrs. Douglas was the care of Douglas' two sons, Robert and Stephen. Their lives had been unsettled since the death of their mother three years before. During Douglas' frequent absences from the capital they were cared for by his sister and brother-in-law, the Grangers, or by the Martin family in North Carolina. Adele immediately took the boys under her wing, and they came to look upon her as a true mother. She expressed considerable solicitude over their education and, after securing Douglas' approval, placed them in a Catholic school.

When Douglas returned to Illinois in May 1857, following the short session of Congress, he took his wife and boys with him. In Chicago, as in Washington, Adele attracted a good deal of attention as she sought to play a similar social role, but the character and institutions of Chicago society mystified and depressed her. She wearied of talking herself "to death over some very stupid women who honored me by calling socially," of making social calls herself from morning till night, and of constantly entertaining at dinner. She longed to be back in Washington, she wrote her mother, "in the old house on the hill." "I shall never breath freely in this atmosphere," she complained, "you can never imagine until you come here how forlorn one feels after being accustomed to interesting & very refined people & how terribly ugly & dirty this City is." It was to be her life, however, and she tried to adjust. "I am trying to like this place but it is very difficult," she confided.[27]

Fortunately for Adele, Chicago was less a home to Douglas than was Washington. It was in the capital that Douglas developed his domestic life, and it was there that he spent most of his time. His marriage provided the occasion for a further expansion of his Washington interests. With John C. Breckinridge and Minnesota's territorial delegate Henry

M. Rice, Douglas purchased additional property adjacent to his home (an area known as Minnesota Row) in April 1857, and on one of the lots he decided to build a new home. Plans were approved, and in May, following his departure for Illinois, the foundation was laid. Detailed reports of the grading of the property and the progress of construction were sent to Douglas in the west throughout the summer. When he returned to Washington later in the year for the opening of the new Congress, it was to a new and splendid "mansion" that had been commenced, finished, and furnished in his absence. Douglas now boasted a home that was in keeping with the new social position his marriage to Adele Cutts had brought him.[28]

# XXII
## "Kansas, Utah, and the Dred Scott Decision" 1856—1857

The administration of James Buchanan opened on a gay and hopeful note. Washington was crowded with well-wishers, and the balmy weather on inauguration day helped to swell the size of the throng. The ball that evening was a more festive occasion than Washingtonians had seen in a long time. A temporary building had been erected to accommodate the hundreds of guests, its ceiling draped with white cloth and studded with twinkling gold stars. Enormous gas chandeliers provided a blaze of light. The most beautiful among the ladies present was the new Mrs. Douglas, dressed in "bridal white," her hair adorned with a cluster of orange blossoms. Punch, wines, and liquors were available in abundance, and the guests danced until daylight the next morning.[1]

Earlier in the day Buchanan had delivered an inaugural address that breathed optimism and serenity. The tempest stirred by the election campaign, he noted, had subsided. The territorial question had been settled on the principle of popular sovereignty—"a principle as ancient as free government itself"—and with its settlement, "everything of a practical nature has been decided." No other issue remained, for everyone agreed that slavery in the states was beyond the reach of the national government. Douglas could not have found fault with these statements, but Buchanan did not stop with this gesture toward Douglas' principle.

The ambiguity of popular sovereignty, the differing constructions given to it by north and south, demanded attention. During the waning days of the thirty-fourth Congress, the question had aroused heated discussion as Republicans gleefully pointed out the contradiction between Douglas' interpretation of popular sovereignty and that of the south. As each view was vehemently defended, it became apparent that Democrats were not as united as they appeared to be.

Both sides looked to the new President to settle the issue, an expectation that caused him no little anxiety. A way out of the difficulty was suggested by those who believed that the Supreme Court must be the final arbiter over cases involving slavery during the territorial period. Pennsylvania's Senator William Bigler had told Buchanan of an earlier conversation with Douglas in which the latter had agreed that the ambiguous nature of popular sovereignty could ultimately be treated as a judicial question. Taking the cue in his inaugural address, Buchanan noted that "a difference of opinion has arisen in regard to the point of time when the people of a Territory shall decide this question [slavery] for themselves." It was, he continued, "happily, a matter of but little practical importance." Inasmuch as it was a judicial question, it belonged legitimately to the Supreme Court of the United States. Before leaving the subject, however, Buchanan offered his own answer to the question. "It has ever been my individual opinion that under the Kansas-Nebraska act the appropriate period will be when the number of actual residents in the Territory shall justify the formation of a constitution with a view to its admission as a State into the Union." It was an announcement that he espoused the view of the south rather than that of Douglas, an ominous sign that the Little Giant could not have missed.

Buchanan's allusion to the Supreme Court had other serious implications. The judicial question to which he referred was, he pointed out, pending at that very moment before the Supreme Court and "will, it is understood, be speedily and finally settled." To the Court's decision, "whatever this may be," Buchanan pledged his cheerful submission. The President referred to the Dred Scott case. He could easily and confidently promise his support to the Court's ruling, because he had already been informed what it would be. When Chief Justice Roger B. Taney delivered the Court's opinion on March 6, two days after the inauguration, the import of Buchanan's remarks became clear.[2]

The Dred Scott case had been in litigation for almost eleven years. It began in 1846, when Scott, the slave of a recently deceased Army surgeon, sued for his freedom before a Missouri state court, contending that his earlier residence at Army posts in Illinois and in territory made free by the Missouri Compromise (later Minnesota Territory) had in fact brought freedom to himself and his family. A verdict was returned in Scott's favor, but the case was immediately appealed to the Missouri Supreme Court, which, in 1852, reversed the lower court's decision. By a complicated series of maneuvers, the case was brought into the federal courts, and it reached the Supreme Court of the United States early in 1856. As a test case (for Scott would be free regardless of the outcome), the suit assumed increasing political significance. A decision by the nation's highest tribunal on the constitutional questions involved in the issue of slavery in the territories was welcomed by both sides to the conflict. First argued in February 1856, the case was postponed until the following December, after the presidential election.

Technically, the only question before the Supreme Court was that of jurisdiction, but there were strong pressures for a broader judgment on the constitutionality of the Missouri Compromise. Because of the predominantly southern membership on the Court, some southern leaders were confident that such a judgment would coincide with their position. Alexander H. Stephens, writing to his brother in mid-December, described his efforts to force the Court to a decision without further postponement. He was fairly certain that the Missouri Compromise would be declared unconstitutional, a decision that, for the south, would also settle the "political question . . . as to the power of the people in their Territorial Legislatures." Stephens expected the court to remove the ambiguity from popular sovereignty and to set aside Douglas' interpretation of the doctrine. Buchanan shared this expectation.

Stephens' confidence in the outcome increased. The questions involved in the case, he wrote on New Year's Day, "will have greater political effect and bearing than any others of the day." He had heard that the decision would accord with his own opinions on every point; if this be so, "Squatter Sovereignty" would be dealt a deathblow. For Buchanan, the nature of the decision was of the utmost importance. Having resolved to deal with the ambiguity of popular sovereignty in his inaugural address, he was anxious that his statements should correctly reflect the Court's thinking. Correspondence between the President-elect and two of the Justices during February provided Buchanan with the information he desired. That a majority of the Court would declare the Missouri Compromise unconstitutional had, by the end of February, become common knowledge, and Douglas was as aware of this as anyone else. How far beyond this declaration the Court would go, however, was uncertain, except perhaps to Buchanan. The allusion to the forthcoming decision in the context of the President's discussion of popular sovereignty must have given Douglas some pause, but before he had time to probe its meaning, the decision itself was handed down. There is no record of Douglas' immediate reaction to the Court's statement—his first public comment on it was not made until three months later—but the verdict undoubtedly shook his expectation that relations with the new administration would be smooth and harmonious.[3]

Chief Justice Taney led off, delivering what he termed the opinion of the Court, although his was only the first of seven opinions presented over a two-day period. A majority of the Justices agreed with Taney's argument in its essentials, although they arrived at their conclusions by varying routes, while Justices McLean and Curtis delivered strong dissenting opinions. The first question dealt with the court's jurisdiction over the case, a question, in turn, depending upon the court's determination of Scott's citizenship. Free Negroes, Taney concluded, were not encompassed in the language of either the Declaration of Independence or the Constitution, and if free Negroes were not, those held in slavery were certainly not. Hence, Scott was not a citizen of the United States and not entitled to sue in its courts; the Supreme Court had no jurisdiction over Scott's case.

Having disposed of this preliminary question, Taney turned to Scott's status as a Negro. Was he still a slave or was he free by virtue of his sojourn on free soil? Scott's brief residence in Illinois was not applicable, for he had returned to Missouri and initiated his suit under the laws of that state. The argument that he was free because of his residence in territory north of the Missouri Compromise line received the most extended treatment, and Taney's statement became the heart of the Court's decision as far as the public was concerned. Congress' right to regulate the territories stemmed not from the much-discussed clause in the Constitution granting power to make all needful rules and regulations for the territory and other property of the United States, but was derived from the power to admit new states. In acquiring new territory and holding it in readiness for statehood, the government was acting as the trustee of all the people and therefore was obligated to hold the territory for the equal and common benefit of all the people. Inhibited by the Constitution from infringing upon the rights of persons or of property, the government could no more restrict slavery in the territories than it could in the states. The Missouri Compromise was unconstitutional, for Congress had no power to deprive a citizen of his property. The prohibition of slavery in the territories, for which the Republicans contended, was therefore a power denied to Congress.

With that much of the Dred Scott decision, Douglas could agree. Taney's argument that the power of Congress over the territories derived from the power to admit new states merely reiterated a position Douglas had expressed many times. That Congress could not (and should not) legislate with respect to slavery in the territories accorded with Douglas' view of popular sovereignty, although Douglas based his argument more on considerations of moral right than on constitutional restriction. He disagreed with Taney's contention that the "needful rules and regulations" clause applied only to the territory held by the United States at the time of the adoption of the Constitution, and he later declared that the Chief Justice was in error on this point. Otherwise, Douglas stated, Congress would have had no power to provide for the disposal of the public land in the territories acquired since the Constitution had been ratified. This, however, was a minor disagreement.

Taney did not stop with a discussion of the power of Congress over slavery in the territories. Southerners anticipated a statement dealing with popular sovereignty as well as with Congress, and the Chief Justice did not hesitate to oblige. By pointing out that Congress could not constitutionally prevent a slaveholder from taking his slaves into the territories of the United States he had endorsed the southern position. He now went one step further in this direction when he asserted that if Congress "cannot do this—if it is beyond the powers conferred on the Federal Government—it will be admitted, we presume, that it could not authorize a Territorial Government to exercise them. It could confer no power on any local Government, established by its authority, to violate the provisions of the Constitution." Here was Taney's answer to Douglas' position. While the language was tentative and its force as part of the decision questionable, it was clear that the Court's statement struck at the heart of Douglas' doctrine. In its decision, the Supreme Court countered the positions of both the Republicans and the Douglas Democrats. The Republicans rose to the attack immediately; Douglas bided his time.[4]

ii

The Dred Scott decision was but one of the signals of trouble ahead for Douglas' relations with the new administration. Indeed, by inauguration day Douglas already suspected that his voice would carry little weight with the Chief Executive, a bitter pill for a man of Douglas' temperament to swallow. A month before, he had had "a full & free conversation" with Buchanan on matters relating to the patronage. "The inference is irresistable," he wrote to Missourian Samuel Treat, "that the patronage for the North West was disposed of before the nomination. . . . At present, I am an out sider. My advice is not coveted nor will my wishes probably be regarded." It was not difficult for Douglas to identify the villains responsible for this situation. "Bright," he wrote, "is the man who is to control it if they dare to carry out their designs. Slidell, Bright & Corcoran (the Banker) assume the right to dispose of all the patronage." Douglas' prognosis aroused all his belligerent instincts. "If this purpose is carried out," he warned, "& I am the object of attack I shall fight all my enemies and neither ask nor give quarter." If the power of the administration should be used "either for plunder or ambition I shall return every blow they may give."

Douglas' quickness to resent what he regarded as an unwarranted affront from the President-elect was exaggerated by the nature of his own expectations. Long the dominant power in Illinois Democratic politics, he had sought to broaden his influence to include the entire northwest. That his efforts had not been altogether successful was made clear at Cincinnati, but the full impact of his failure to marshal support in the northwestern states was obscured by his strength in other parts of the Union. Through his convention maneuvering, Douglas had emerged as Buchanan's most formidable competitor for the nomination, and when he withdrew his name, he quite naturally regarded himself as having made Buchanan's selection possible. This alone, he felt, entitled him to a position of power in the new administration. Douglas' tireless and effective campaigning in Illinois, without which Buchanan might not have carried the state, only increased his expectations. No one else in the northwest could match his credentials, not even Jesse Bright.

Douglas was encouraged in his position by friends and supporters who now besieged him with requests for office. His withdrawal at Cincinnati in favor of Buchanan and the latter's endorsement of the Kansas-Nebraska Act, wrote one correspondent, should give Douglas a strong voice in the selection of the cabinet. Treat, whom Douglas was pushing for a seat in the cabinet, assured his friend that Buchanan owed both his nomination and election to his exertions. Assuming that his word would weigh heavily with Buchanan, a group of friends had even gathered at Douglas' home to assist him in preparing a program for the distribution of patronage in New York City.[5]

Douglas, however, had also been warned. He was reminded of Bright's "duplicity" at Cincinnati, and the Indiana Senator was blamed for his failure to secure the nomination. Bright had expectations of his own, according to one paper, because "he did not bow down before Juggernaut Douglas." The bitter feud between the two Senators, no longer concealed, was exposed in the press, and there was speculation that "important consequences in North-Western politics" would result from the quarrel. Illinois Republicans, closely watching the developments, were jubilant, as Douglas was informed "that you have lost your influence at Washington." Rumors flew through Chicago that all the federal officeholders would be removed and replaced by the new administration. Buchanan's confidant, John Slidell, whose calm appraisal of the problems faced by the President contrasted sharply with Douglas' attitude, apprised his chief of Douglas' anxiety. Douglas, he wrote in mid-February, "assumes that he is the proper representative not only of Illinois, but of the entire Northwest. He is just now in a very morbid state of mind, believing or affecting to believe that there is a general conspiracy to put him down. . . . he has been disposed . . . to 'run a muck' against any one who showed a disposition to defend Bright." Slidell warned Buchanan against appointing "in your cabinet any decided partisan of Douglass." [6]

Buchanan's relations with Douglas had never been close, and he regarded the Little Giant with distrust. The memory of the 1852 campaign, when Douglas' managers had singled him out as an "old fogy," was still fresh. Moreover, Douglas' ambition for the highest office was keen, and Buchanan was determined not to help promote it. His discussion with Douglas in February was merely a matter of courtesy extended toward a powerful political leader. Buchanan was just as wary of Bright, who had advertised his desire for a cabinet post in the event that he should be defeated for re-election to the Senate. The quarrel between the two Senators embarrassed Buchanan's efforts to provide for the northwest in his top-level appointments, inasmuch as both men were regarded "as intriguing aspirants for the succession." There were reports that

Douglas was even exacting pledges for support in 1860 from those of-fice-seekers who applied to him for assistance.

Buchanan's dilemma was soon resolved. Bright was returned to the Senate, thus removing him from contention for a cabinet post. Douglas had two candidates for cabinet positions, William A. Richardson, who had been defeated in his bid for the Illinois governorship, and Samuel Treat. In March Treat withdrew, having secured a Missouri judgeship, which he considered more desirable than a post in the cabinet. Buchanan, able now to bypass both Bright and Douglas, turned to Michigan's aged Lewis Cass and, with some misgiving, awarded him the State Department. Douglas accepted the decision, undoubtedly relieved that Bright had not been favored but apparently unaware that it was Bright who had proposed Cass as a way out of the difficulties. Unwilling to see Richardson left out completely, however, he promptly asked that his trusted lieutenant be appointed to a "first class mission" abroad. Douglas also urged Buchanan to provide a place in the cabinet for Robert J. Walker, the Pennsylvania-born Mississippian who had served as Polk's Secretary of the Treasury. Walker, an expansionist and railroad specula-tor, had the support of a number of radical southerners, including Jeffer-son Davis, who preferred him over the Georgia Unionist Howell Cobb. Cobb had presidential ambitions, and Douglas may have regarded him as a possible rival for the 1860 nomination. Buchanan again took Bright's advice, and Cobb was appointed.

Whatever expectations Douglas may have had following the election, Treat's comment that the cabinet had not been selected with reference to his wishes was accurate. Douglas bitterly resented the President-elect's course, and relations between the two men deteriorated from that time on. When informed of Douglas' attitude, Buchanan reportedly com-mented, "I like Douglas very much. He shall have no cause to oppose my administration, but if he should, whilst I shall deeply regret it, I must bear it with a patient and resolute spirit." [7]

Actually, Douglas fared better in the distribution of the patronage than perhaps even he realized. Buchanan, hoping to heal the divisions within the party in the various states, sought to apply his appointment policy with an even hand by employing a principle of rotation designed to strengthen the party at its weakest spots through the infusion of new blood.[8] In Illinois, most of the changes in office were made in the strongly Republican northern districts, most of them in Douglas' home town of Chicago. Whether or not Douglas acquiesced in this policy is not clear, but there was little he could do about it. At least one of the changes proved to be a source of embarrassment for the Senator. Philip Conly had been appointed collector of customs at Chicago in 1855, and he had every reason to believe that he would be continued in that office. Indeed, Douglas apparently assured Conly that this would be the case. Shortly after the inauguration, Douglas informed Conly that "the circumstances surrounding the Administration" necessitated his resignation. Conly protested the injustice of the request, but he obliged, later conceding that the matter was probably out of Douglas' hands.

Conly's removal was directly related to the division within Chicago's Democratic ranks resulting from the disastrous quarrel the previous year between Sheahan and Postmaster Isaac Cook. The feud flared again following the presidential election. His patience exhausted, Douglas angrily lectured Sheahan on the folly of Chicago Democrats. Realization that the difficulties would affect both his standing in the new administration and Buchanan's distribution of the patronage in Illinois heightened his indignation. "If our friends would cease their personal quarrels and fight the common enemy of our principles with the same zeal & energy that they now fight one another, our party would be in the ascendant," he wrote. "Never did a party throw away its favour & waste its strength so foolishly & uselessly by personal quarrels, resentments and desire for revenge. If this course is persisted in the consequences are obvious and inevitable. No party, no matter how patriotic its men, and how fine its principles can survive such a suicidal course."

In the same letter, Douglas informed Sheahan that he had not yet reached a conclusion "in regard to the Post Office," a reference to Sheahan's repeated demands that Cook be ousted. On March 3, however, the consequences of the split which Douglas most feared became reality. John Wentworth, now running as a Republican, soundly defeated the Democrats in the election for mayor. Before the month was out, Cook had been removed from his office at Douglas' insistence. To replace Cook, Douglas secured the appointment of William Price, who promised to provide financial assistance to the *Times*. These maneuvers did little to repair the rift in the Chicago party.[9]

Outside of Chicago and northern Illinois, little was done to disturb the incumbent officeholders. An exception was the postmastership at Springfield, held by Isaac R. Diller, a long-time associate of Douglas and chairman of the Democratic state central committee during the 1856 campaign. Although Diller had worked tirelessly in behalf of the Buchanan ticket, he had also become embroiled in a quarrel with Charles H. Lanphier, editor of the *Illinois State Register,* over the location of a new post office in Springfield. Douglas, informed in February that the controversy "promises to be fruitful of evil to the Democratic party," evidently felt that Diller's removal was desirable. When his commission expired, he was, at Douglas' insistence, appointed consul to Bremen. In the application of Buchanan's patronage policy in Illinois, Douglas remained the state's most powerful spokesman, and, despite appearances, it was evident that the President attempted to gratify his wishes.[10]

Douglas' influence was also felt in appointments outside Illinois. On his strong recommendation Buchanan offered Ohio's David T. Disney, Douglas' 1856 campaign manager, appointment as minister to Spain, but Disney declined the offer. Joseph Wright, leader of the Douglas forces in Indiana, was appointed minister to Berlin, but this was due as much to Bright's effort to "exile" an opponent as to Douglas' influence. It was in the territories, however, that Buchanan leaned most heavily on Douglas' advice. In Kansas, John Calhoun, former mayor of Springfield, was retained in his post as Surveyor General, while the offices of United States Attorney and Marshal went to men Douglas recommended. When Buchanan decided to offer the Kansas governorship to Robert J. Walker, he called on Douglas for assistance. Samuel Medary, representing Douglas' support in Ohio, was appointed governor of Minnesota Territory, and Kirby Benedict, an Illinoisan and friend of Douglas, was reappointed to the New Mexico supreme court. Unable to offer Richardson the foreign mission to which he had been recommended, Buchanan appointed him governor of Nebraska Territory. Richardson, disappointed that he would not be sent abroad, declined, to the President's surprise. "I am truly sorry that Mr. Richardson did not accept the appointment of Governor of Nebraska," Buchanan wrote Douglas, "& after what passed between us, I was astonished to learn that he had been offended at the office." The position was kept open, Douglas and others exerted pressure on Richardson, and he finally accepted the post.[11]

In spite of this evidence of success, Douglas' expectations remained unfulfilled. Buchanan's failure to take him into his confidence in the selection of the cabinet rankled, and Douglas' inability to secure a larger share of the national and foreign service appointments for his Illinois supporters persuaded him that the President had administered a deliberate snub. Douglas had, for example, insisted that Illinois was entitled to two first class foreign appointments out of the eleven at Buchanan's disposal; none were awarded to the state. In September, unable to remain silent longer, he complained directly to the President, charging him with an "apparent neglect of this State in the distribution of the Patronage under your administration." His attitude was shared by other members of the state's congressional delegation. Congressman Isaac N. Morris protested that "it is very evident that Illinois is to receive as few favors from the present administration as the last," and he declared, with exaggeration, that "our recommendations have been totally disregarded." Republicans made political capital out of Douglas' ill-concealed dissatisfaction. "Is 'Little Dug' laid aside by the new President?" queried the *Illinois State Journal*. The appointments in the state, commented another paper, "gall the withers" of many Democrats who "will not draw kindly in the traces hereafter" no matter how severely the "lash may be applied." [12]

As Douglas feared, grumbling among Democrats soon became a protest against his own party leadership. The removals in northern Illinois aroused opposition not against Buchanan, but against Douglas, who was held ultimately responsible. A group of Democrats in Freeport condemned Douglas' "hypocritical policy" respecting the patronage. The party feud in Chicago still smoldered, for neither side was satisfied with Douglas' stand. "I shall not become a party to these feuds nor suffer myself to become the instrument of any faction," he had informed Sheahan, but in trying to avoid taking sides he had satisfied no one. Reports began to reach him in Washington that some Democrats were organizing to challenge his re-election to the Senate in 1858. "It is very evident there is something in the wind in this quarter not altogether favorable to you or your interests," wrote an informant from Springfield. "The scheme on foot is to carry the Legislature against you at the next session—not by our enemies the Republicans—but by your enemies in our own ranks." Richardson thought it "a tempest in a teapot," but nonetheless he deemed it of sufficient importance to warn Douglas. Similar rumors of a revolt against Douglas were received from Chicago. When a false report began to circulate that Douglas would not be a candidate for re-election, James W. Singleton, one of Douglas' 1856 campaign managers, sent a hurried note to Washington. "Have you *declined* being a candidate for re-election to the U. S. Senate? If you have not it is proper you should advise your friends at once." Douglas, baffled and disturbed, replied that the report was untrue. "I am at a loss to know the meaning of your allusion and shall be glad to hear from you in full and in entire confidence." Clearly, something was brewing.[13]

To add to Douglas' woes, Sheahan again threatened to resign the editorship of the *Chicago Times*. Criticism of Sheahan's course in the Chicago quarrel had mounted. Douglas' new brother-in-law, writing from Illinois, declared that the editor was "daily doing the Democratic party incalculable harm." With Cook out of office, Douglas apparently agreed that Sheahan's withdrawal from the paper might restore harmony to the party. To Isaac Morris, he described Sheahan as "the most impractical and impolitic man he ever knew—that he was an injury instead of a benefit to the cause, and it was absolutely necessary to get rid of him." A number of people were sounded out as possible successors to the editorial chair, including Horatio King of Maine, Buchanan's First Assistant Postmaster General, but no decision was made, and Sheahan remained in the post.

The dissatisfaction with Douglas' part in the distribution of the patronage, the incipient movement against his leadership, and the resentment of Chicago Democrats against his course in the party quarrel quickly developed into a Douglas-Buchanan split within the state's Democratic organization, encouraged in no small way by Douglas' own displeasure with the President. John Wentworth drove the wedge between the two men deeper when he sent papers to Buchanan purporting to demonstrate that Douglas' enmity against the President pre-dated the Cincinnati convention. A letter to the *Chicago Times* opposing Buchanan's nomination in such strong language that it proved offensive to the Pennsylvanian's friends, Wentworth maintained, had been written by Douglas himself. The original manuscript, salvaged by Wentworth's friends from waste paper swept out of the *Times* office, was forwarded to the President with a statement that it was in Douglas' handwriting. The charge was denied by *Times* staff members, and the President apparently took little notice of it. Later, R. B. Carpenter, a minor Chicago office-holder, boasted that he had received his appointment because of his opposition to Douglas and pointed to the fact as evidence of the Buchanan administration's hostility toward the Senator. Douglas promptly asked for Carpenter's removal, a request that was just as promptly granted. The removal should have silenced critics who questioned Douglas' influence with the President, and it should have eased Douglas' own apprehensions. It did neither. Douglas continued to complain, still harboring the belief that Buchanan should have turned to him before anyone else for assistance in shaping the new government. A rift opened between the two which in turn brought Douglas' leadership under challenge.[14]

During the summer, Douglas first learned of Buchanan's decision to confer an appointment in the Treasury Department on his father-in-law, James Madison Cutts. Cutts held a clerkship in the comptroller's office, so his advancement to the office of Second Comptroller would normally have caused little comment. With Douglas' recent marriage to Cutts' daughter, the decision was immediately attributed to Douglas' desire to seek preferment for members of his family. Moreover, there were reports that Cutts' appointment would be at the expense of Illinois. Douglas was informed initially of Buchanan's intention by Julius Granger, his sister's husband, who was himself an officeholder in the General Land Office. "Do you know," asked Granger, "that it is in contemplation to give Mr. Cutts a Bureau Office and that report says that as Illinois cannot be entitled to two—that Murray McConnell will probably be displaced for him?" Granger's source of information was Secretary of the Interior Jacob Thompson, who maintained that Douglas had requested Cutts' appointment. Shortly afterward, another cabinet member, Secretary of War John Floyd, informed Adele of the decision to promote her father.

Douglas, his anger aroused, sent Buchanan a copy of Granger's letter and asked for an explanation. "I will not conceal the deep mortification I feel," he wrote, "in having very respectable gentlemen believe that I would for a moment consent to the removal of Gen'l McConnel or any other good Democrat in order to make room for any of my family relations." He protested the appointment if it should cancel any portion of Illinois' claim "to her just proportion of the federal patronage." He reiterated his complaint that his state had been neglected in the distribution of offices. "Under past administrations I have felt keenly & deeply the neglect and injustice with which Illinois was treated in the distribution of the patronage. Other States could receive a Cabinet office, Foreign missions and several Bureau appointments all at the same time, while Illinois, a state which has never deserted the Democratic Banner, has been treated with a neglect which could not fail to wound the pride of all her working Democrats." Buchanan responded with a cutting reply that exhibited the coolness which prevailed between the two. "You need entertain no apprehensions on the subject," he assured the Senator. "Should I make the appointment which is not improbable, it will be my own individual appointment proceeding entirely from my regard for Mr. Cutts & his family, & not because Senator Douglas has had the good fortune to become his son-in-law." Cutts' selection would not be charged to Illinois.[15]

Douglas' opponents had a field day with the incident. Cutts' appointment, it was said, would damage Douglas "with Western men" more than anything else the President could have done. Illinois Democrats, disappointed in their own quest for office, were irate at the implication that Douglas' relatives would take precedence over their own claims. When Douglas heard that inquiries had been made on how many relatives he had because the administration would be expected to provide for all of them, he decided to publish his correspondence with Buchanan. There were those who thought he should have left well enough alone, for Douglas' apprehensions were subjected to additional ridicule. Especially revealing was Buchanan's reply to Douglas' protest. It was, declared the *Chicago Tribune,* "unhandsomely curt. There is a sly sting in its tone; a dislike in its brevity; a disrespect in its terms, that must have had a most unsavory grace to his Cincinnati rival." Greeley's *Tribune* sarcastically commented, "He loved not papa less but the party more." The state of feeling between Douglas and the President was exposed for all to see.[16]

Douglas was on the defensive, a position he had hardly anticipated after his run at Cincinnati and his successful campaign for the Democratic ticket in 1856. All of the latent hostility to his domination of Democratic politics in Illinois was coming to the surface, and his Republican opposition, closely watching his activities, was quick to ascribe nefarious motives to his every move. Early in the year, the Illinois legislature granted a charter to the University of Chicago, a Baptist institution in which Douglas took a keen interest. To provide a site for the university he donated ten acres of his lakefront property, valued at $50,000. The act was immediately assailed as motivated by a desire to enhance the value of his adjoining property; he was additionally charged with seeking the political support of the Baptist Church. Dismayed by the persistence of the onslaughts, Douglas offered to withdraw the donation, repay the church for expenses incurred in improving the site, and subscribe $50,000 toward the construction of the university on another site. He feared that the attacks would injure and perhaps destroy the institution itself. The president and board of the university rejected the suggestion, "unable to see *any good reason* for the *abandonment* of the present location." A more modest benefaction to the building fund of a Washington Methodist church was similarly attacked, this on the ground that proslavery doctrines were to be preached from its pulpit, demonstrating, it was said, Douglas' sympathy for human bondage.[17]

During the summer Douglas made a brief trip to Minnesota with his wife. His colleague and Washington neighbor, Henry M. Rice, had long urged him to visit the territory. "It must be getting very warm & dusty in Chicago," Rice wrote in June, "but here it is delightful and we have an abundance of room & a hearty welcome awaiting you . . . a little quiet country life would be of great service to Mrs D & yourself." The journey also had political overtones. Minnesota was moving into statehood, and his presence there might strengthen the Democratic party. At an impromptu serenade in St. Paul, Douglas was praised for his work on behalf of the territories—"all the Territories of the Confederacy bear the impress of your Statesmanship." In reply, he reviewed his long association with territorial development. "It has been my fortune and my pleasure to have had, to some extent, the care of seven of the Territories of the Union, prior to their admission as States," he declared. "It was my duty, as chairman of the Committee on Territories, to make their interests my special care. Inasmuch as there was no delegate to represent them in the Senate . . . I have acted as delegate for these seven Territories." He declined further public appearances, pleading limited time and his resolution not to influence the deliberations of the constitutional convention then in session. At the invitation of the convention, he appeared in the hall and received a standing ovation from the delegates, but he made no speech.

Republicans were suspicious. The *Chicago Tribune* charged Douglas with "making the Democracy of Minnesota worse Border Ruffians than they are already," while the *Illinois State Journal* accused him of "making pro-slavery harangues" and of stumping the territory "in favor of slavery extension and amalgamation Democracy." Douglas could ignore these charges, but when his assailants maintained that he had pecuniary motives for visiting Minnesota he rose quickly to his own defense. Secretary of War John B. Floyd had just ordered the sale of the Fort Snelling military reservation under terms that aroused such considerable opposition that a congressional investigation was later ordered. Douglas, Republicans contended, was a party to the "swindle" and had made the trip for speculative purposes. Denying that he had any prior knowledge of Floyd's action, Douglas again explained his determination never "to purchase or own, or become interested in any land, town lots or other property in any of the territories" as long as he remained chairman of the Senate Committee on Territories, "for the reason that I would not allow an enemy even a pretext for saying that my public action was influenced or stimulated by my own private interest." His statement only invited disbelief and ridicule.[18]

While Douglas pondered the meaning of the Dred Scott decision and grappled with Buchanan over the patronage, he continued his efforts to bring the Kansas issue to resolution. No other issue so dominated the early months of the Buchanan administration nor demanded more immediate attention. The calm that had settled over Kansas proved illusory. The Republicans, for whom Kansas had become a prime political issue, anxiously awaited the first moves of the new President. Douglas, as the author of the Kansas-Nebraska Act and the chief link between Congress and the territories, felt a keen responsibility in the desperate search for a solution.

Douglas was perhaps better informed regarding Kansas developments than most other national leaders were. In his capacity as chairman of the Senate Committee on Territories, he received a voluminous correspondence from settlers, government officials, and travelers on the scene. All of his information pointed unmistakably to the conclusion that the proslavery partisans in Kansas, in spite of their tactics, formed a minority in the territory, that the majority of the settlers represented the free states of the north and west, and that the continued domination of the territorial government by proslavery men, in defiance of the majority, constituted a serious violation of popular sovereignty. How to rectify the situation, without encouraging new measures of violence, was a question that challenged all the resources he could muster. Douglas' earlier tendency to blame Kansas' difficulties on the recruiting efforts of abolitionist societies no longer rang true. "The settlers from the eastern & middle States," wrote one visitor to the territory a year before, "are not the shabby set of hirelings & fanatics their enemies would represent. . . . They are earnest men . . . seeking a home mainly for the purpose of bettering their condition." From Douglas' old friend James Shields, now living in Minnesota, came words worth noting. "It took a world of mismanagement to turn poor houseless squatters who have fences to make and corn to raise and wives and children to feed into rebels. . . . There must have been gross mismanagement. . . . Border Ruffians and Abolitionists could not do it." Douglas would not wait for the administration to correct the "mismanagement." Pierce had failed and Buchanan was yet a question mark; the initiative was his if he wished to seize it.[19]

Douglas' solution had been the passage of an enabling act for Kansas that would guarantee a smooth and orderly transition from territorial government to statehood. No amount of persuasion could induce the free state group to support the territorial government; the answer lay in by-passing that stage of government completely and providing statehood, even though some might think it premature. At the same time, the movement into statehood must be made under the aegis of Congress instead of the territorial government if it were to succeed. His own statehood bill, introduced early in 1856, had not sufficiently circumvented the territorial government. Toombs' bill, which he later supported in preference to his own, did seem to offer a way out of the difficulty, but it became entangled with election year politics and failed.

As an expedient and interim measure, Douglas sought to persuade the Kansas territorial legislature to repeal the obnoxious laws against which the free state movement had so strenuously protested. He was in an advantageous position to make his wishes felt. John Calhoun, the Illinoisan whose appointment as Surveyor General Douglas had secured, was probably the most influential and powerful person in the territory, "an out and out, straight forward *national* democrat" who was widely regarded as Douglas' spokesman in Kansas. Through Calhoun Douglas was informed of developments in the territory, and he, in turn, was able to exert some influence on their direction. Some of the so-called "bogus" laws, Calhoun reported, had already been repealed by the upper house of the legislature, in accordance with Douglas' wishes, and he expected the unanimous concurrence of the lower chamber. Earlier he had been promised that attempts to execute "the odious provisions of their fugitive slave law" would be abandoned by the territorial authorities. "Your wishes in this matter, as a northern man," Calhoun assured the Senator, "have been more consulted than all things else; and if you should have observed any other defects a suggestion from you would do more for its removal than could be done by the whole force of the administration." The legislators, however, balked at removing the laws relating to the protection of slave property, and they reminded Calhoun that Illinois had retained similar legislation even after its admission to statehood. This, Calhoun concluded, was "the only law which will remain for an abolitionist to object to." The concessions, if indeed they were such, were not convincing, and Douglas' attempts at persuasion failed.[20]

One other avenue seemed for a time to offer opportunity for success. Ever since the organization of the territory, Douglas had hoped that a strong and viable Democratic party might be developed in Kansas. Federal appointments were made with a view toward encouraging this end—a motive that was by no means unique to Kansas among the territories—and Calhoun seems to have had this among his charges. The Surveyor General sought to organize the party on a basis broad enough to include both free state and proslavery Democrats, but his plans were threatened almost immediately by the intrusions from Missouri. His greatest embarrassment, he reported to Douglas, was the persistence of the proslavery men in maintaining their own organization, thus discouraging others from acting with them. It was more important, he concluded, that Kansas be a Democratic state than a free or slave state. In November 1855, Calhoun optimistically announced that proslavery Democrats had finally been induced to abandon their organization and to join with states' rights Whigs and free state Democrats in a new party to be known for the time as the State Rights party. It was, he wrote, "a purely democratic organization" and would soon assume that name. He had also persuaded the proslavery men to repudiate "all foreign influence from every quarter in elections." "Thus order and consistency are established by the democratic party in Kansas and the extravagant follies of Atchinson and Co. are repudiated. . . . all the true democrats of the territory, whether for free or slave state, now stand on the same platform."

Calhoun's optimism was unfounded. The lines between the free state group and the proslavery men were too deeply drawn. The new party, supported by federal officeholders and identified with the territorial government, smacked strongly of the proslavery party under a different name. Buchanan's appointment of northern Democrats to territorial vacancies, many of them urged by Douglas, was designed to ease the fears of free state Democrats and to encourage a genuine party organization, but it was of no avail. Cooperation with those who controlled the territorial government, in any form, was out of the question. Because of their support of the Topeka movement and their opposition to Pierce's Kansas policy, many free state Democrats found little choice but to enter the ranks of the Republican party. Douglas' hopes that a strong, united Democratic party might provide the needed stability to the territory were frustrated. To southerners, the blow would be doubly felt, for it seemed likely that Kansas, if admitted, would be neither a slave state nor a Democratic state. "The elements composing the democratic party here," Calhoun finally conceded, "are of such a character that we cannot in any way make them harmonize." [21]

The resignation of Governor Geary and a change of tactics by the proslavery party brought the Kansas question to a new crisis early in 1857. In February, the territorial legislature, unwilling to wait longer for Congress to pass an enabling act, provided for a constitutional convention to meet later in the year for the purpose of drafting a state constitution. The proslavery men, already in the minority, concluded that admission as a slave state provided the last opportunity to fix slavery in the territory; Congress, or at least the Senate, they thought, would incline favorably to their appeal. Geary, in one of his last official acts in the territory, vetoed the bill on the ground that it made no provision for the submission of the finished constitution to the people for ratification or rejection, but the legislature easily passed the measure over his objections. Submission was clearly not part of the strategy, for, in a fair election, the majority would handily reject a proslavery constitution.

The movement was fraught with danger, and Douglas was among those who recognized it. A statehood movement that so blatantly ignored the wishes of the majority could only have disastrous consequences. An enabling act, with provisions for federal supervision, was still, he felt, the only feasible solution. Michigan's Senator Stuart agreed. With such men as the proslavery leadership to execute the law, Stuart wrote to Douglas, fairness would be impossible. Moreover, Kansas could never be admitted under a constitution formed "now and in this way." Not only was the integrity of popular sovereignty at stake, but the future of the Democratic party in the northwest would be threatened. There were both moral and political reasons, the two men agreed, for resisting the statehood movement in favor of a congressional enabling act. Douglas, however, also recognized the impossibility of securing an enabling act in time, for Congress was not in session and would not meet again until after the Kansas convention had accomplished its work.

There were two possible courses of action. First, a strong man of national reputation could be selected to succeed Geary, one pledged to a free and fair submission of the constitution to the people and authorized to use the strength of his office to achieve that end. Second, Douglas could exert his own influence, through Calhoun, on the direction of the statehood movement. Douglas' choice for governor of Kansas was Robert J. Walker, and, fortunately, in this he and the President were agreed.

Walker and Douglas had become close friends by 1857, and they shared a common view of the Kansas question. During the election campaign the year before Walker had published a pamphlet in which he stated that Kansas would ultimately be a free state. Geographic conditions, climate, and the course of immigration, he wrote, militated against the introduction of slavery there. "You have certainly argued this question with great power and boldness," Walker wrote Douglas in January, "and your views against the authority of Congress to abolish or establish slavery in Territories, being founded on truth, must ultimately prevail." [22]

Walker was reluctant to accept the appointment, but Buchanan persisted, finally asking Douglas to intervene. In a conversation with Walker, Douglas, "who was very earnest and very excited," made it clear that the success of the Kansas-Nebraska Act depended upon Walker's acceptance of the governorship. Following Douglas' visit, Walker accepted, but he insisted that he would not go to Kansas unless the administration backed him in his contention that the constitution, whatever it might be, should be submitted to the people for acceptance or rejection. He agreed with Douglas that the true construction of the Kansas-Nebraska Act demanded no less. Buchanan concurred "distinctly and unequivocally." Instructions were accordingly drawn up in which the President reiterated, more formally, his pledge to support the new governor in the matter of submission. In his letter of acceptance, Walker further emphasized his understanding that the President and cabinet concurred in his conviction "that the actual *bona fide* residents of the Territory, by a fair and regular vote, unaffected by fraud or violence, must be permitted, in adopting their State Constitution, to decide for themselves what shall be their social institutions." The question must be settled by an appeal to "the whole people of Kansas . . . by a majority of whose vote the determination must be made." To his sister Walker wrote a short time later that the Kansas issue "is reduced to the simple issue, of slave or free state, and must be decided by a *full* and *fair* vote of a *majority* of the people of Kansas. The same question has thus been decided peacefully in every other state, and why not in Kansas?" Douglas himself could not have stated it more emphatically. [23]

Douglas was highly pleased with Walker's appointment, although some of his friends, preferring a man of more clearly western antecedents, thought that he would be no more successful than his predecessors had been. Republicans, impressed with Walker's statements, displayed a guarded optimism. Passing through Chicago on his way to Kansas, the new governor conferred again with Douglas, the latter helping Walker to put the finishing touches on his inaugural speech. Delivered in Lecompton, Kansas' territorial capital, at the end of May, the address repeated Walker's (and Douglas') belief that the territory's climate rendered slavery impracticable there. Promising support to the laws of the territorial legislature, Walker also assured the free state settlers that "in no contingency will Congress admit Kansas as a slave state or free state, unless a majority of the people shall first have fairly and freely decided this question for themselves by a direct vote on the adoption of the Constitution, excluding all fraud or violence." The address aroused an immediate reaction among southern radicals. *"We are betrayed,"* wrote a Georgian to Alexander Stephens. Forgetting the role played by Pierce's proslave appointees in territorial politics, southerners now denounced the interference of federal officeholders in Kansas affairs. The outburst was revealing to the new governor, and it placed Buchanan, whose apparent endorsement of Walker's course outraged southern ultras, in a dilemma. Douglas minimized the southern reaction and sought to bolster Walker's determination. The outbreak in the south, he suggested, resulted more from dissatisfaction with the patronage than from hostility toward the governor's policy. They "seized upon the Kansas question as a pretext, and made you the scape goat." Douglas' support of Walker's position was unwavering. "I have never hesitated to express the opinion that the constitution ought to be refered to the people for ratification. . . . The object should be to refer the constitution to the bona fide inhabitants of the Territory for their free acceptance or rejection, and to exclude all such as have gone there temporarily, for the mere purpose of participating in the contest, without becoming permanent citizens. . . . It is all important that the convention shall make such a constitution as the people will ratify, and thus terminate the controversy." [24]

Before he formally accepted the appointment, Walker had also insisted that he have the aid and cooperation of the federal officeholders in Kansas, especially John Calhoun. Anxious that his friend be retained in his position, Douglas assured Walker that Calhoun would support the submission of the constitution to the vote of the people. In March, Calhoun and A. J. Isacks, former district attorney for Kansas, traveled to Washington, where Douglas further urged upon them the necessity for a full submission. Isacks, "a pro-slavery man but a true democrat," talked with Douglas about the possible wording of the constitution, probably in

relation to the slavery question. Although "strongly in favor of introducing slavery into Kansas," Isacks was "yet anxious to do every thing to secure your interests in the formation of the Constitution," Calhoun informed Douglas. Back in Kansas, Calhoun followed Douglas' lead,
taking "a firm stand in favor of the submission of the entire constitution
to the people for their ratification or rejection."

Douglas was hopeful that the formula for the settlement of the Kansas question had at last been found. In Walker he finally had an able
and trustworthy collaborator. The President had pledged his support to
the governor. Influential members of the cabinet, notably Howell Cobb,
agreed that "there was no alternative but that of submitting the constitution to the popular vote." It was apparent that submission could have
but one result. Walker estimated that free state Democrats and Republicans could muster as many as 17,000 votes, as against only 7000 proslavery Democrats and Know-Nothings. "Nobody thinks of making Kansas a slave-state," a traveler reported to the administration. "The only
question is—shall it be a national democratic—or an abolition
state?" The elements of a new crisis, however, were present, and such
optimism was woefully premature. The outcry of southern radicals was
an ominous sign of trouble ahead. The leaders of the proslavery party,
Walker conceded, "are against me on the point of submitting the constitution to the people." Calhoun's effectiveness as Douglas' mouthpiece
was severely hampered by his reputation as a leader of the proslavery
forces and by his own ambitions for political power in Kansas. Moreover, the machinery for carrying through the statehood movement was
in the hands of a territorial legislature that was unrecognized by the majority of Kansans. The leaders of the legislature took full advantage of
their position. The census, on which apportionment to the constitutional
convention would be based, deliberately omitted sizable portions of the
free state population; the election of delegates in June, ignored by the
free state majority, resulted in a convention that was overwhelmingly
proslavery in composition.[25]

iv

Douglas finally left the national capital with his family in May for a
leisurely return to Illinois. His mood was mixed—he hoped that the
difficulties in Kansas would soon be put right, but smarted from Buchanan's supposed slight in patronage matters. Stopping in Cincinnati, he enjoyed a cordial meeting with an old enemy, Governor Salmon P. Chase,

an example of amity that some found pleasing "in the present excited state of parties." A few days after his arrival in Chicago, he delivered one of the major speeches of his career before a large audience in the statehouse at Springfield. The Grand Jury of the United States District Court, then in session, had asked Douglas to express his views on three of the most important topics "now agitating the minds of the American people"—Kansas, the Dred Scott decision, and conditions in Utah Territory. Douglas, taken by surprise, spoke extemporaneously, later writing out his comments for publication.[26]

Douglas' comments on Kansas were brief and optimistic. Peace and prosperity prevailed in the territory, and its people were about to speak for themselves through their delegates to the constitutional convention. The laws under which the delegates would be chosen, he commented, with more wishful thinking than good sense, are believed to be "just and fair." He had "every reason to hope and believe that the law will be fairly interpreted and impartially executed, so as to insure to every *bona fide* inhabitant the free and quiet exercise of the elective franchise." (Either Douglas had not been informed of the questionable mode adopted by the Kansas legislature for the selection of delegates or he was deliberately distorting its character; his opposition had no difficulty deciding which.) There was no obstacle, he continued, to the admission of Kansas as a free state, provided the majority participated in the delegate elections. However, if significant numbers absent themselves from the polls "with the view of leaving the Free State Democrats in a minority, and thus securing a pro-slavery constitution in opposition to the wishes of a majority of the people," then the responsibility would rest on "those who, for partizan purposes, will sacrifice the principles they profess to cherish and promote," by which Douglas meant Republicans. If, as he hoped, the Kansas question should be settled peacefully and in accordance with the wishes of her own people, then popular sovereignty shall have been vindicated, and sectional strife will be forced to give way to fraternal feeling.

Douglas' remarks on conditions in Utah Territory were more extended. The Mormon settlements, far distant and isolated by poor communication, had been governed by Brigham Young, who ruled as both civil and religious leader in accordance with the Church's theocratic organization. As in Illinois earlier, the Mormons followed an independent course, paying little heed to federal authority except as Young represented it. Order was maintained by their own militia, justice was dispensed in their own courts, and the territory's economic life remained under the tight control of the Church. Rumors of Mormon defiance multiplied, and when lurid tales of the practice of polygamy began to appear in the nation's press a general outcry against the religious group was raised. The Republicans capitalized on the reaction in the 1856 election campaign by inveighing against the "twin relics of barbarism," slavery and polygamy; demanding the intervention of the federal government, they hoped to embarrass the Democratic administration, and especially Douglas, who stood pledged to popular sovereignty. Buchanan, bowing to public sentiment, decided on a show of force, and in late May he ordered a military expedition to the Salt Lake basin. He also determined to replace Brigham Young with a non-Mormon territorial governor. The problem was a difficult one for the President, and in his discussions with cabinet members and with army officers recently returned from Utah he showed a tendency to place the responsibility on Douglas because he was chairman of the Committee on Territories.

Douglas was swept up in the tide of denunciation. He gave credence to wild reports that nine-tenths of Utah's inhabitants were aliens who refused to become naturalized citizens, that the Mormons were "bound by horrid oaths and terrible penalties" to recognize Young's authority as paramount to that of the United States, and that the Mormon government was stimulating the Indians to acts of hostility as well as prosecuting "a system of robbery and murder upon American citizens." If investigation should prove these charges to be true, he shouted, then "the inhabitants of Utah, as a community, are outlaws and alien enemies." Douglas approved Young's removal and the dispatch of a military force, but he went further, calling on Congress "to apply the knife and cut out this loathsome, disgusting ulcer." To the immense applause of his audience, Douglas proposed that Utah's organic act be repealed and the territorial government blotted out of existence so that the offenders could be apprehended and punished. Strong words for an advocate of non-intervention! Douglas conditioned his proposal on the receipt of authentic evidence of Mormon behavior, but his tendency to credit the charges that were being made was surprising, especially in view of his long and close contact with the Mormons.

The main thrust of Douglas' remarks was aimed at the Dred Scott decision. He castigated the Republicans for their onslaughts against the Supreme Court and reminded his listeners of their obligation to defend this "highest judicial tribunal on earth." "The peculiar merit of our form of government over all others," he pointed out,

> consists in the fact that the law, instead of the arbitrary will of a hereditary prince, prescribes, defines and protects all our rights. In this country the law is the will of the people, embodied and expressed according to the forms of the constitution. The courts are tribunals prescribed by the constitution, and created by the authority of the people to determine, expound and enforce the law. Hence, whoever resists the final decision of the highest judicial tribunal, aims a deadly blow at our whole republican system of government—a blow, which if successful, would place all our rights and liberties at the mercy of passion, anarchy and violence.

In the Dred Scott case, the judges, being "honest and conscientious" men, had faithfully performed their duty by determining all the questions involved in the suit. If the Court had dismissed the case for want of jurisdiction, as many critics insisted it should have done, Dred Scott would have been remanded to perpetual slavery and the merits of his case would have remained unexamined.

Douglas, to the surprise of no one, found no conflict or contradiction between the decision and his doctrine of popular sovereignty, although it was clear that he had not come to this view easily. Far from settling the ambiguity of popular sovereignty, the decision had further emphasized it, for Douglas' interpretation only dramatized his differences with southern Democrats. The justices, Douglas felt, were correct in declaring the Missouri Compromise unconstitutional and void. His attempt to find a vindication of popular sovereignty in the decision required some circumlocution. The right of a master to his slave in the territory had never been extinguished by the Missouri Compromise, but, he carefully explained, that right "necessarily remains a barren and a worthless right, unless sustained, protected and enforced by appropriate police regulations and local legislation, prescribing adequate remedies for its violation. These regulations and remedies must necessarily depend entirely upon the will and wishes of the people of the territory as they can only be prescribed by the local legislatures. Hence the great principle of popular sovereignty and self-government is sustained and firmly established by the authority of this decision." The "wisdom and propriety" of the Kansas-Nebraska Act had not only been endorsed by the people in the recent presidential election, Douglas concluded with obvious satisfaction, but it was now upheld by the nation's highest judicial tribunal.[27]

Douglas' statement was a forecast of the position he would follow in the troubled days ahead, as he fought both the Republicans and an important and powerful element in his own party. The more perceptive observers of the political scene had no difficulty recognizing the widening gulf that was opening in the Democratic ranks. Douglas, to his credit, was consistent in his advocacy of the principle for which he had struggled for so long. His reference to "police regulations and local legislation" was new only in its emphasis. He had made the same argument before. Seven years earlier, in 1850, he had reminded the Senate that legislation passed by Congress "to operate locally upon a people not represented, will always remain practically a dead letter upon the statute book, if it be in opposition to the wishes and supposed interests of those who are to be affected by it, and at the same time charged with its execution." He had returned frequently to the example of his own section, which, he maintained, had been made free not by the Northwest Ordinance, but by the expressed will of the people. Nor had he been the only one to recognize the importance of local law in the struggle over slavery in the territories. Only a few months before, South Carolina Congressman James L. Orr had warned that slavery would be valueless without "local legislation and local police regulations." If a majority of the people in a territory were opposed to slavery, they need only decline to pass laws for its protection in order to prohibit it.

To Douglas the "main proposition" decided by the court, however, was its judgment that "a negro descended from slave parents . . . is not and can not be a citizen of the United States." Here his agreement with the decision was on more solid ground, for there was little doubt that Douglas fully shared the views expounded by the majority of the Court. He disagreed with the assertion of many Republicans that the proposition was "cruel, inhuman and infamous," and he launched a bitter attack against the notion of Negro equality with white men. To those who maintained that the Declaration of Independence guaranteed Negro equality, Douglas denied that the signers intended to place the Negro race on an equal footing with the white race. "No one can vindicate the character, motive and conduct of the signers of the Declaration of Independence, except upon the hypothesis that they referred to the white race alone, and not to the African, when they declared men to have been created free and equal." They were, he insisted, speaking only "of British subjects on the continent being equal to British subjects born and residing in Great Britain." Further, "the history of the times clearly shows that the negroes were regarded as an inferior race, who in all ages, and in every part of the globe, and in the most favorable circumstances, had shown themselves incapable of self-government and consequently under the protection of those who are capable of providing for and protecting them in the exercise of all the rights they were capable of enjoying consistent with the good and safety of society." As a final argument against Negro equality, Douglas appealed to what he called "the great natural law" which demonstrated that "amalgamation between superior and inferior races" brings their posterity "down to the lower level of the inferior, but never elevates them to the high level of the superior race."

While Douglas insisted on the Negro's racial inferiority, he did not accept slavery as his natural condition. In a statement which he would repeat many times in the future, he declared that "it does not follow by any means that because the negro race are incapable of governing themselves that therefore they should become slaves and be treated as such." The "safe rule" was the one he had been preaching for years—and with this he returned to popular sovereignty—"that the African race should be allowed to exercise all the rights and privileges which they are capable of enjoying consistent with the welfare of the community in which they reside, and that under our form of government the people of each State and Territory must be allowed to determine for themselves the nature and extent of those privileges." [28]

Douglas' remarks were clear and pointed, unembellished by flowery rhetoric; they were also sincere and deeply felt. His interpretation of the Dred Scott decision had long been awaited, and it met the expectations. If he persuaded himself that the decision and popular sovereignty were not incompatible, however, he convinced few others. The speech gave him the opportunity to define his position at a time when he was under attack from Republicans and when his relations with the administration seemed to be deteriorating. The issues of popular sovereignty, with its important "local legislation" corollary, and Negro inequality made up the platform on which he would stand in the ensuing years. In one sense, Douglas' appearance in Springfield marked the beginning of a new and significant stage in his career.

Reaction to the speech was widespread. The *State Register* carefully summarized its contents and made preparations at once for the publication of the address in an edition of 200,000 copies, before Douglas himself intervened and reduced the number to 20,000. Missouri Senator

James S. Green sent his approbation, along with advice on how Douglas might parry the attacks that would surely be made against him. Thomas A. Hendricks of Indiana thought Douglas' remarks, especially on the Dred Scott case, were clear, popular, and opportune. Writing from Washington, a friend stated that the speech was the subject of all the talk and gossip in the capital, where it was "deemed by all one of your best efforts." The Washington *Union* praised Douglas' "lucid statements, vigorous thoughts, and powerful arguments." To some the address marked the opening of Douglas' campaign for the presidency in 1860. "The curtain of 1860 is partially lifted," commented the New York *Herald,* "and we have a peep behind the scenes. . . . As a democratic Presidential aspirant, Mr. Douglas is now without a rival in the great Northwest."

Douglas' interpretation of the Dred Scott decision elicited little comment from the Democratic camp. The Mormon question was a mere nuisance, "a side issue of very little consequence," although the *Register* noted that Douglas' remarks on Utah took many people by surprise, since the opposition had freely predicted he would evade the question. On Kansas, however, comment was extensive. Douglas' plan, suggested the *Herald,* was clearly to make Kansas a slave state, for he had made no allusion to Walker's insistence on the submission of the constitution. Douglas was obviously bidding for the support of the southern ultras against President Buchanan's Kansas policy as revealed in Walker's instructions. As if to give credence to the *Herald's* charge, Douglas' speech was highly praised by some radical southern papers, which in their enthusiasm for his comments on Kansas completely ignored his more significant utterances on the Dred Scott decision and popular sovereignty. "The present attitude of Mr. Douglas," the *Herald* concluded, "is at best an attitude of *quasi* hostility to the administration, and the first month of the coming Congress will remove all doubts upon the subject, or we are not among the prophets." The forecast was correct, but the editor erred in his appraisal of Douglas' position.[29]

The Republicans seethed with indignation; their reaction to Douglas' speech was shrill and persistent, indicating that he had touched a sensitive nerve. By courting ultra southern support, they charged, in an echo of the *Herald's* analysis, Douglas would, if he could, make Kansas a slave state. "Poor tool of Southern despots!" Another Republican was just as positive that Douglas was trying to "worm himself into the confidence of the free people of Illinois" in anticipation of the "stern political fight" that awaited him in 1858. Much was made of his Utah proposal as a naked renunciation of popular sovereignty. Why had he not made a similar suggestion when Kansas "was overrun and subjugated . . . by Democratic ruffians, as fell in their designs and as bloodthirsty in their excesses as even the polygamous inhabitants of Utah"? Most of the Republican ammunition was reserved for Douglas' discussion of the Dred Scott decision. His attempt to reconcile the decision with popular sovereignty by referring to "police regulations and local legislation" was dismissed as nothing more than a "contemptible quibble." The strongest objections were leveled against Douglas' implication that all who opposed the decision were in favor of racial equality, that is, were seeking "to raise the negro to a political and social equality with white men." The charge, according to one Republican paper, was a "foul aspersion" on the "freemen of the Prairie State." The intensity of the Republican attacks (which continued virtually unabated throughout the summer) led the *Register* to conclude that "Judge Douglas has been the object of more fiendish and malignant abuse and detraction than any man now alive."

To the Mormons, who recalled an early prophecy of Joseph Smith that Douglas' career would prosper only so long as he remained on friendly terms with the Church, the Little Giant had sealed his own fate. "He is just as big a damned rascal as ever walked," one Church leader insisted. "He will not go into the chair of State, he will go to hell." [30]

As soon as Douglas had completed his speech, the call was raised for an address in reply. Abraham Lincoln, who had been in the audience when Douglas spoke, came forward, and two weeks later he answered Douglas in the same statehouse hall. *"It will be an answer,"* Lincoln's law partner had promised. "Lincoln is a gentleman; Douglas is . . . an unscrupulous dog." In his rejoinder, Lincoln was indeed the gentleman. His calm, effective discussion of the issues which Douglas had raised contrasted with the usual Republican onslaughts. It was not the kind of reply many Republicans had expected. It was, confided one party member, "too much on the old conservative order"; Lincoln, it was feared, was no match for the Senator. A few days later, Lyman Trumbull delivered a second reply that seemed to satisfy much better.

Lincoln took little issue with Douglas on affairs in Utah. Like Douglas, he credited most of the reports that purported to describe the "open rebellion" in that territory. Republicans could easily support Douglas' solution. Lincoln pointed out, however, that in making his proposal,

Douglas had backed down from "his much vaunted doctrine of self-government for the territories," proving what Republicans had always claimed, that popular sovereignty "was a mere deceitful pretense for the benefit of slavery." Douglas' assertion that the election laws governing the choice of delegates to the Kansas constitutional convention were fair and just was, Lincoln declared, "extraordinary." He agreed that if they were, the free staters in Kansas ought to have participated, but he properly contended that the majority of the territory's voters had been deliberately excluded from the franchise. The results of the election, which had been held after Douglas had spoken, bore out Lincoln's statement.

Like Republicans generally, Lincoln devoted most of his attention to the Dred Scott decision. He agreed with Douglas that the Court should command the respect and obedience of the citizens, but, he emphasized, "we think the Dred Scott decision is erroneous. We know the court that made it, has often over-ruled its own decisions, and we shall do what we can to have it to over-rule this." In his comments on Negro equality, Douglas was playing upon the "natural disgust of nearly all white people, to the idea of an indiscriminate amalgamation of the white and black races." It was, Lincoln speculated, a desperate strategy for political survival to which he would cling "as a drowning man to the last plank." Douglas was guilty of "counterfeit logic" when he concluded that "because I do not want a black woman for a *slave* I must necessarily want her for a *wife*." Protesting the "mangled ruin" which Douglas had made of the Declaration of Independence, Lincoln asserted that the Declaration "contemplated the progressive improvement in the conditions of all men everywhere." Douglas had shorn the document of its vitality and practical value. Lincoln joined Douglas in his horror of amalgamation, but he contended that slavery, not freedom, was the greatest source of amalgamation. The separation of the races, he insisted, "is the only perfect preventive of amalgamation" and this separation can best be achieved by an opposition to the spread of slavery and by the colonization of free Negroes.[31]

In all the tumult that followed Douglas' speech, Lincoln's criticism stood out, and Douglas must undoubtedly have been impressed by it. It was a foretaste of what he would have to face in 1858. Lincoln's ambition to succeed Douglas in the Senate was well known, and some commentators felt that the senatorial contest had begun in Springfield a year early. For Douglas, the suggestion simply added to his anxiety. He was being driven to the wall. His disappointment in the distribution of the patronage, the cool hostility of the President toward his effort to strengthen his leadership in the party, the almost pathological and frenzied opposition he faced from Republicans, the Dred Scott decision, and the disturbing developments in Kansas all seemed to point toward a crisis of unprecedented, and unimaginable, proportions.

# XXIII

## "This flagrant violation of popular rights"
### 1857—1858

i

Early in September 1857, delegates gathered in the shabby little town of Lecompton, Kansas' territorial capital, and on September 7 the much-publicized constitutional convention opened. The delegates, selected in one-sided election contests earlier in the summer, were proslavery in their sympathies, and several of them were, or had been, slaveholders in Kansas. They were, however, individuals who had been identified with the territory since its inception (some had lived in Kansas long before the territory's organization), and they approached their task with a strong sense of responsibility. The convention became a national issue even before it met. The delegate elections, at which less than one-fourth of the total number of voters and only one-tenth of the estimated adult male population voted, had been denounced throughout the north. Governor Walker's predictions that Kansas would be a free state and his assurances that Congress would not admit it under a constitution that had not been first ratified by the people raised a storm of protest in the south, first against Walker and then against Buchanan when it seemed that the President endorsed the governor's stand.

Walker had done more than warn Kansans that the constitution must be submitted. In his first utterances in the territory, he tried to persuade the free state group to abandon its boycott of territorial elections, promising that all elections henceforth would be fair and that fraud and intimidation would be quickly detected and rooted out. Impressed by

Walker's sincerity, free staters cautiously pledged their participation in the October legislative elections and proceeded to nominate candidates. The news proved disturbing to the proslavery group, including the members of the constitutional convention. Their course of action, they concluded, would depend upon the outcome of the October elections, and to Calhoun's despair the belief that the constitution could not be submitted to the people gained in popularity. Calhoun, who had been elected president of the convention, decided to buy time. After meeting four days, the convention adjourned until after the elections. Writing to Douglas, Calhoun stated the two objects in view were "to put our best men to work" on a preliminary draft and, more important, "to secure the benefit of the popular expression, so as to better enable us to shape our course in the future." A Democratic victory in October, he hoped, would overcome any reluctance to submit the constitution, but he was not confident. The difficulties in persuading proslavery Democrats to unite with free state Democrats, he confided to Douglas, seemed insurmountable. Although he was convinced that the Democrats held a majority in the territory, he warned Douglas that "we are likely to be beaten in the October election." [1]

The results of the election confirmed Calhoun's fears. For delegate to Congress, the Democratic candidate was decisively beaten by a Republican. In the returns for members of the territorial legislature, the Democrats appeared to have won until Walker threw out the obviously fraudulent votes of two election districts, thereby destroying the Democratic majority. Walker's action raised a storm of protest, but he remained steadfast. Democrats, in Kansas and outside the territory, refused to be discouraged. Party lines were fluid and even temporary. Once the slavery issue was discarded they were hopeful the Democratic party would be in control. The new delegate had been a free state Democrat, and many of the new legislators were less Republican than free state in their affiliations. One thing, however, was clear. The proslavery cause in Kansas could never succeed in a fair trial of strength; to the members of the convention the only alternative now was admission to the Union as a slave state. Under these circumstances, the submission of the constitution to the voters for acceptance or rejection was out of the question. [2]

If Walker had aroused the ire of radical southerners before, his actions following the territorial election raised southern opposition to a fever pitch. There were signs that Buchanan, sensitive to the attacks, was wavering in his support of the Kansas governor. "There is no danger that the right of the people of Kansas to frame their own constitution in their own way will be disturbed," Attorney General Jeremiah Black had written. "The President will stand on that rock." The rock, however, was becoming slippery and the President's footing less sure. Some members of the Cabinet, notably Howell Cobb, still insisted that the constitution be submitted in a fair referendum to all the voters. Cobb was convinced that a large majority of Kansans opposed slavery and that Kansas, if admitted, would be a free state. Like many others in his party, he believed that the state, even if free, must certainly be Democratic. Everything hinged upon the action of the Lecompton convention. If the delegates should refuse to submit the constitution, a development which Cobb hoped "with all my heart" would not "come upon us," their action "will produce the most dangerous crisis we have yet had on the Kansas question." When the convention reconvened in October no one knew what its action would be, but many feared the worst.

Calhoun's role as a spokesman for "out and out submission" was seriously undermined by the election results. Anticipating the defeat, he had earlier suggested to Douglas that both the Topeka constitution and a slave state constitution be submitted to the people, the one receiving the highest vote to be presented to Congress. He must have known how such a referendum would turn out and that the proslavery group would never accept the proposal. Many of the delegates, resuming their deliberations, were more determined than ever to flout Walker's will. From William Weer, whose appointment as United States Attorney in Kansas Douglas had secured, Douglas learned that the ranks of the "non-submission party" in the convention had more than doubled since the temporary adjournment, and that its members "loudly opposed Walker & declared their determination to favor no plan he proposed." [3]

In desperation Calhoun wrote to Douglas for advice, but no answer was forthcoming. In the meantime, pressures mounted for no submission at all, as letters arrived from the south urging that a slave state constitution be drawn up and sent directly to Congress without a referendum. To counter these pressures, Cobb and Secretary of the Interior Jacob Thompson dispatched a land office clerk, Henry L. Martin, to Kansas, ostensibly to investigate land records but actually to add administration weight to full submission. The effort availed little in the highly charged atmosphere of the territorial capital. Against formidable odds, Calhoun, still seeking to represent the Douglas-Walker position, argued forcefully for "out and out submission." While he condemned the principles of the

Republican party, Calhoun told the convention, he defended their right to a voice "in fixing the organic law of the new State" and insisted that "they should have a vote upon the constitution." When the question was finally brought up before the convention, the delegates voted, by a majority of one, to send a proslavery constitution directly to Congress without a popular referendum.

Although beaten, Calhoun determined to salvage as much of submission as possible. With Martin and two of the delegates, he perfected a plan for partial submission, a compromise which he strongly considered to be better than no submission at all. According to this scheme, Kansas' voters would be asked to vote on the "Constitution with slavery" or the "Constitution without slavery." In either case, the constitution itself would be accepted. Inasmuch as this document provided for the protection of slave property in Kansas, the new state would be a slave state at least for the time being. Only the prospective immigration of slaves into Kansas would be affected by the vote. If a majority of the voters favored the "Constitution without slavery," as seemed likely if everyone participated in the referendum, then no further slaves could be brought in, and Kansas would, in time, become a free state. Having developed the compromise, Calhoun secured a reconsideration of the convention's decision, and in a second vote his plan for partial submission was narrowly successful. Several of the extreme proslavery delegates could not accept even this much submission, and they bitterly refused to sign the constitution.

Calhoun assumed that this compromise would have the support of the administration, since Martin had helped to draft it, but he worried about Douglas' reaction. His appeal to Douglas for advice had not been answered. Grasping at straws to ease his mind, Calhoun found an editorial in the *Chicago Times* which he immediately, and erroneously, assumed was not only an indirect response from Douglas, but also an endorsement of his plan for partial submission. In his troubled state of mind, Calhoun apparently read into the editorial exactly what he wanted to find there. Any attempt, the *Times* declared,

> to force a pro-slavery constitution upon the people without the opportunity of voting it down at the polls, will be regarded, after the recent expression of sentiment, as so decidedly unjust, oppressive and unworthy of a free people, that the people of the United States will not sanction it. . . . As Kansas must be a free State, even those persons in the territory who are known as 'pro-slavery' men, must recognize in the late election a decision which must not be slighted

nor put at defiance. To that expression of the popular will there should be a graceful, if not a cheerful submission. . . . If any members of the Convention desire to prolong the controversy . . . let a Free State Constitution—the Topeka Constitution, divested of such of its provisions as time has shown to be unsuitable—and a Slave State Constitution be prepared. Let them both be submitted to the people.

Only by the most obtuse reasoning could the editorial have been interpreted as sanctioning Calhoun's plan, although by proposing that both the Topeka constitution and a slave state constitution be submitted the *Times* had echoed one of Calhoun's earlier suggestions. With this editorial in hand, Calhoun assured his colleagues that Douglas would approve and support the action of the convention.

Not all of those who supported full submission were so confident. Weer informed Douglas that, although he opposed Calhoun's plan, "I believe it the best submission we could get." The future, however, was not bright. "Nothing can save us here but a turn out of the Free State men to vote," he wrote. "If they do, it will be equivalent to an indorsement of the whole constitution." The action of the convention persuaded Weer that there was "but one escape" for the Democratic party and that was "to cut loose from the Pro-slavery Party." Isacks agreed that partial submission "was the very best that could be done considering the large number of members who were utterly opposed to a submission of the constitution to the people in any form whatever." Governor Walker criticized the convention's decision, but Isacks hoped Douglas would approve it, "for to you, more I may say, than to all others, the democrats of Kansas look for an honest support." Three years later, in the 1860 election campaign, an attempt was made by some Democrats to implicate Douglas in the adoption of Calhoun's plan for partial submission. Douglas, it was charged, had written Calhoun a letter in which he not only proposed the scheme finally adopted by the convention but promised that he would give it his full support in Congress. The weight of contemporary evidence is heavily against any such conclusion. Closer to the event was the charge that the plan had been dictated in Washington by members of the administration and dispatched to Kansas with Martin, a charge that was denied by Jacob Thompson, in whose Interior Department Martin served.[4]

The convention not only defied Walker on submission, but the delegates also went beyond this to manifest their displeasure with the governor. They voted to oust Walker and other unsympathetic officeholders and to place the territorial government in the hands of Calhoun. It was Calhoun who would canvass the returns in both the election on the constitution and on the first state officers, and it was Calhoun who would issue the election certificates and call the first state legislature into session. Presumably, the members of the convention had no fear that Calhoun would reject fraudulent returns as Walker had done in October. The convention, Isacks wrote in justification to Douglas, was "purely representative of the people," while Walker represented only the federal government. Besides, "no one knows how long he would remain as governor." To add to Walker's troubles, he now seemed to have been abandoned by the administration. The governor left Kansas in mid-November, following the adjournment of the convention, and returned to Washington to seek clarification of his position. On his journey eastward, he stopped in Chicago to discuss the situation with Douglas.[5]

If Douglas hesitated in his reaction to the Lecompton convention, it was not evident. On November 23, about two weeks after the adjournment and after he had talked with Walker, Douglas informed Weer that, while Buchanan would probably approve Calhoun's conduct, "I must confess that I do not. . . . I fear that he has made a fatal mistake, and got us all into trouble. I regret that present position of things in Kansas, and fear the consequences." He admitted that he had not yet seen the Lecompton constitution or the proceedings of the convention, but he declared that "my course is plain. I must stand on the principles of the Kansas act and go wherever it carries me, and defend it against all assaults from any quarter." On the same day, he repeated his determination to McClernand. "The only question is," he wrote, "whether the constitution formed at Lecompton is the act & will of the people of Kansas, [or] whether it be the act and will of a small minority, who have attempted to cheat & defraud the majority by trickery & juggling. If it be the will of the people freely & fairly expressed it is all right, if not it must be rebuked." While he awaited the official facts before making a final judgment, Douglas speculated that "trickery & juggling have been substituted for fair dealing. If this shall turn out to be true we have but one course to pursue, and that is vindicate the principle of the organic act and the Cincinnati Platform by refering the whole matter back to the people."

Although word reached Douglas from Kansas that full submission of the constitution would have triumphed in the convention had not Calhoun wavered in his stand, this was unlikely, for the delegates had voted against submission in any form before Calhoun forced a reconsideration and the acceptance of his compromise. At the moment of crisis, these were the only alternatives available. For Douglas, no submission apparently would have been better than the plan adopted, for the former could more easily have been discredited in Congress. In a private conversation with Calhoun early in 1858, when the Surveyor General visited Washington, Douglas expressed his indignation at the convention's action. Calhoun explained that he had done everything in his power to secure the submission of the constitution. When he failed, he had on his own authority proposed the compromise in the hope that Douglas would support him. Douglas was curt and emphatic in his censure of Calhoun's reasoning. The plan was the "worst thing," a "fraudulent submission" and a "mockery." He could not sanction it, he told Calhoun, without "repudiating all the acts of my life, and doing a political act that I did not believe was moral and just." [6]

As soon as the work of the Lecompton convention became known, the question was asked, "What will Douglas do?" His role as an outsider in the Buchanan administration was widely discussed—and exaggerated—and his differences with the south over the interpretation of popular sovereignty were emphasized. The events in Kansas now seemed to deliver a crippling blow to his position. Republicans found satisfaction in his discomfiture. "The fortunes of Senator Douglas seem just now to be waning," commented the *Illinois State Journal*. His prestige had evaporated, and the leaders of his party, especially in the south, had turned against him. The Democratic party, meeting in Charleston in 1860, would be firmly in the hands of the fire-eaters, and Douglas' chances for the next presidential nomination were nil. His only hope, the paper continued, was "to unite upon himself the free-soilish Democracy of the North, for the race of '64." Will Douglas "redeem his pledges . . . that the people of Kansas should be left free to regulate their own domestic institutions in their own way?" asked the *Chicago Tribune*. "Or will he, when he reaches Washington, stand coldly back while the South crams Slavery down the throats of the people of that Territory?"

Douglas had reached another decisive moment in his career. Two paths were open to him. He could support the action of the Lecompton convention as the best that could have been achieved and push for the immediate admission of Kansas as a state. By doing so, he would improve his position within the Buchanan administration, win the favor of southern radicals, and ensure his nomination in 1860. This was the easy path of ambition; his career had pointed toward the presidential nomination for years, and this would be a sure way to realize his goal. It would not be without its price, for undoubtedly he would lose support in the free states, but such losses would probably be more than offset by gains in the south. If Douglas were as unscrupulous as his enemies insisted, as dominated by a desperate and dangerous ambition, such a move would be in character. His other alternative was to reject the partial submission plan of the convention as a sham and to oppose the admission of Kansas under the Lecompton constitution. If he did, his relations with the President, already strained, would worsen and the south would move to cast him out of the Democratic party. Without southern support, the prize in 1860 would undoubtedly be beyond his reach. Yet the second alternative would be consistent with the position he had pursued since the debates that followed the Mexican War. It would be in keeping with his own policy for bringing peace to Kansas and for settling the troublesome question of slavery expansion; it was the course he had already marked out in his advice to Kansas' leaders and in his promise of support to Governor Walker. As a northern and western man, opposed to the institution of slavery and dedicated to the democratic principle of popular sovereignty, there was no real doubt which path he would follow.

Douglas also had partisan reasons for rejecting the action of the Lecompton convention. By doing so, he would strengthen his support in the free states, where his leadership had been under fire. At the same time, he could challenge the dominance of the proslavery south in his party, restore its national character, and seat its power in the section he still believed to be the hope for the Union's survival, the great west. Challenged by a northern sectional party, the Democratic party was in danger, especially under Buchanan's tutelage, of becoming a southern sectional party. It was a trend Douglas was determined to halt.[7]

Although Douglas had early indicated privately which path he would follow, public speculation continued until the moment he declared himself in the Senate. The volume of his correspondence grew as he was bombarded with advice. "Now that the sentiment has been declared in the way pointed out by your Kansas & Nebraska Act," wrote one visitor to Kansas after the October elections, "you should become its foremost champion." The fate of the party was in Douglas' hands. "The democracy of the North and . . . of the whole Union look to you," wrote a friend from Iowa. "The only fear I have [is] that the extreme men of the South may demand more of the North than we can possibly grant them." The question, Douglas was told, involved a point of honor, but the unity of the Democratic party was also at stake. The time had arrived for Douglas to relieve his principle of "the odium which it has unjustly incurred." Nor was the advice limited to members of his own party. One Republican declared that "your *Hour has come";* by opposing the action of the convention, Douglas would make "troops of *new* friends in all the land."

John McClernand applauded Douglas' decision to oppose the Lecompton constitution. "Hitherto you have contended for the sovereignty of the people as a *principle;* now it remains for you to contend for it as a fact—a practical reality." Writing from southern Illinois, John A. Logan, soon to be elected to Congress, added his words of encouragement, and Sheahan reminded Douglas of the importance of the issue to the party in Illinois. "To admit Kansas as a Slave State would be destructive of everything in Illinois. . . . Remember that the *only* fight of *1858* will be in Illinois." Both Sheahan and McClernand urged that Congress ignore the Lecompton convention and pass a new enabling act for Kansas. Finally, historian George Bancroft offered his aid, suggesting historical precedents which Douglas might employ in his stand against Lecompton. "I hear, and I trust I may believe, that you intend . . . to stand by your Nebraska Bill in its plain signification, and not to allow it to become in the hands of timid or unprincipled men an imposture and a sham," he wrote. "At this time, it needs nothing but firmness on your part, in which I never knew you to be wanting, to place your bill, yourself, and democracy in a proud position, a better one than it has occupied since Polk went out of office." [8]

Not all of the advice Douglas received coincided with his decision to oppose the Lecompton constitution. His friend Samuel Treat strongly advised that Kansas be speedily admitted under the Lecompton constitution. Treat distrusted Walker and criticized him for exceeding his federal authority in attempting to dictate to the convention. Only the convention, legally constituted and empowered to draft a frame of government, could determine the submission question and, Treat believed, the partial submission finally adopted was evidently a "prudent" course. To submit the entire document to the voters would be to prolong Kansas' troubles indefinitely. Treat's view was narrowly legalistic. "If Kansas is kept out of the Union merely because the whole constitution is not submitted, then a precedent is set subversive of all law and society because an unauthorized and illegal expression of popular will [the Topeka movement] is permitted to override that will expressed through the forms of law and authority." An Illinois supporter agreed that full submission would have been followed by "worse chaos than ever" and regarded the action of the convention as "about right." From Georgia came the warning that Douglas would lose all his southern friends if he voted to submit the constitution to the "Topeka *Traitors.*" [9]

Douglas' course on Lecompton was revealed in November, when Sheahan answered the *Tribune*'s queries in the columns of the *Chicago Times,* several days before Douglas expressed his displeasure with Calhoun in his letter to Weer. Douglas, Sheahan announced, would insist on the faithful execution of the Kansas-Nebraska Act and would not allow the south to cram slavery down the throats of Kansans. For its position against the action at Lecompton, the *Times* had been accused of assuming "Republican grounds." "Are we to understand now," Sheahan asked, "that to insist on the faithful execution of the Nebraska act, is to become a Republican?" Sheahan's comments were confirmed during the last days of November, when Douglas openly denounced the Lecompton movement, charging that the whole proceeding had been concocted by the administration to ruin him. As soon as Congress met, he stated, he would introduce a new enabling act for Kansas, modeled on his earlier Minnesota bill. He made no attempt to conceal his anger, and, as it became clear that Lecompton would receive administration support, he promised to fight the administration to the bitter end. "By G–d, sir," Douglas purportedly told a Chicago Republican, "I made Mr. James Buchanan, and by G–d, sir, I will unmake him!" Still, there was a reluctance to believe that he would stand boldly in opposition to the Lecompton constitution. "I can hardly conceive it possible that he will break with the South and the Administration," wrote a correspondent of the *Chicago Tribune*.[10]

Republican leaders in Illinois regarded Douglas' statements with anxiety. Lincoln advised members of his party to "stand clear" of the "'*rumpus*' among the democracy," but he conceded that Douglas was making an impression on some. Lincoln had good cause for concern. William H. Seward visited Chicago in mid-October, and on the twenty-second Douglas had called on him. Herndon later revealed that at that time Douglas not only met with Seward, but with Thurlow Weed and

Horace Greeley as well, "by accident or otherwise." The substance of their conversation was not divulged, but rumors were afloat soon afterward that Douglas had struck a bargain with the Republican leaders on the Lecompton question. Douglas was quite clearly trying to appeal to Republicans, hoping to woo those with Democratic antecedents back into the party, and Republicans were worried lest his efforts be successful. "I am afraid that he will get a good deal of capital out of his late movement if he is not headed off," wrote the editor of the *Chicago Tribune,* who also reported pressure on the *Tribune* to cease its attacks on Douglas. In private conversations with Republicans, Douglas "really made some of their eyes stick out at his zeal." Several leaders urgently asked Trumbull to introduce the enabling act into the Senate before Douglas should have a chance to do so, in order to force him "to follow *our* lead." [11]

Douglas left Chicago in late November, "leaving quite a smoke in his rear," and arrived in Washington on December 2. Walker had preceded him, and in a meeting with Buchanan he had learned to his dismay that the President would back the action of the Lecompton convention and urge the immediate admission of Kansas. Walker then journeyed to New York to intercept Douglas and to report on the results of his conversation. Although Buchanan's attitude had by this time become known, Douglas sought a meeting with the President in the White House on the day after his arrival in the capital. The interview, reported by the press as being friendly and courteous, confirmed Walker's report. Buchanan had committed himself to the support of the Lecompton constitution, had already prepared his message to Congress, and had dispatched his views to Kansas. Although Douglas, as chairman of the Senate Committee on Territories, would be responsible for Kansas legislation in Congress, the President had acted without seeking his views or advice. Shocked at being so peremptorily ignored, Douglas became angry with the President. Buchanan reminded him that Lecompton would be an administration measure and that the Senator should fall into line or suffer the consequences. He recalled the fate of those Democratic Senators who had flouted Andrew Jackson's will. "Mr. Douglas, I desire you to remember that no Democrat ever yet differed from the Administration of his own choice without being crushed. Beware of the fate of Tallmadge and Rives." "Mr. President," retorted Douglas, "I wish you to remember that Gen. Jackson is dead, sir."

That evening Congressman Thomas L. Harris, after talking with

Douglas, informed Lanphier, "On Kansas Old Buck, his cabinet, every body in office & every body wanting office, are for the constitution—but we will whip out the whole concern, & drive Administration & all from their ground or into a minority. Douglas will make the greatest effort of his life in opposition to this juggle." [12]

ii

The Lecompton issue was not the only problem facing the nation in the fall of 1857. Clear signs of economic difficulties had appeared earlier in the summer, and by September, as sudden as it was unexpected, the United States was in the grip of a full-scale panic. Banks and business houses were forced to the wall. Banks that did not collapse suspended payment, and some closed their doors temporarily. Loans were called in wherever possible, spreading the misery, while new ventures were brought to a halt. Douglas, who had made heavy investments in Illinois land and in improvements in Washington (including his own new house, which was then under construction) and had given advances to his political friends, weathered the storm, but he was hard-pressed. Illinois Central stock tumbled, and his income was sharply curtailed. When he found himself unable to meet some of his obligations, he revealed the precarious nature of his finances. "My means of paying punctually depend upon my receiving sums due me and on which I have relied with entire confidence," he wrote to his banker. "The sudden change of monetary affairs has taken us all by surprise, and deprives us of the power of doing as we would like to do." Reports that he had sustained heavy losses through the depreciation of western lands and stocks were publicly denied. Douglas' contributions to his party, his continued interest in purchasing fine wines and cigars, the accommodation of his bankers, and his healthy bank balances at the end of the year all indicate that he emerged from the crisis relatively unscathed. The uncertainty of the economic situation, however, added to his general touchiness as he faced the most important political crisis of his career. [13]

By December, signs of recovery had pushed economic questions into the background. The Kansas issue clearly overshadowed all else. Speculation on its outcome abounded, but there was wide agreement that Douglas was "the man of the crisis." The fate of the Lecompton constitution was in his hands. His position in the party, his leadership in territorial matters, his contribution to Buchanan's victory, and the weight of his ability, declared the usually hostile New York Times, "combine to give

him an influence which will be decisive in the settlement of this controversy." More than at any other time in his life he commanded the center
of national attention. Douglas, concluded one New England paper, "en-
joys a higher degree of popular regard than any other statesman in
America"; paradoxically, "he is also hated, feared and abused more
heartily than any other statesman."

There was no doubt that there would be a fight and that Douglas
would again be in the middle of it. His pugnacious qualities had become
almost legendary, and as the nation awaited the opening of Congress,
these qualities were the subject of much comment. "The metal used in
his composition," commented one reporter, "is of the sternest and most
impregnable stuff." His physical appearance, "short, stout and thick,"
was befitting his role as "a man of the people." Most of the comment
was reserved for the character of his speaking. "No one among the grey
beards in the United States Senate commands such instant attention
when he rises to speak." As members of Congress began to gather in
Washington, anticipation mounted for the "brilliant sledge-hammer
speeches" which had become Douglas' hallmark. "He is a bold and independent speaker," wrote a woman who observed Douglas from the Senate gallery, "and has the power of thrilling his hearers through and
through; indeed, rapidity and boldness of thought are his inseparable at-
tributes. . . . His language is always sharp, and clear, and strong, and
knotty; never soft; seldom beautiful." [14]

In the last days before Congress opened, final efforts were made to dissuade Douglas from his opposition to Lecompton. Acting on rumors that
Douglas would oppose the constitution, Alexander H. Stephens spoke
with him on two occasions. "He is against us—decidedly—but not
extravagantly as I had heard. . . . His course I fear will do us great
damage." When Secretary of the Navy Isaac Toucey warned him of the
disastrous consequences that would follow a party rupture on the Kansas
question, Douglas scornfully replied that "while the Constitution declares that *Congress* may admit new States, *it hasn't a word in it about*
CABINETS *admitting them!*" In a second interview with the President,
Douglas was again cautioned. "Mr. Senator," Buchanan asked, "do you
clearly apprehend the goal to which you are now tending?" Douglas allegedly retorted, "Yes, sir, I have taken a through ticket, and checked all
my baggage." The pressure only stiffened his determination. "The Battle
will soon begin," he wrote Lanphier on the day before the session
opened. "We will nail our colors to the mast and defend the right of the

people to govern themselves against all assaults from all quarters. We are sure to triumph." [15]

That the administration still hoped for some accommodation with Douglas was apparent in the organization of Congress. Fears that Lecompton would be introduced into the Democratic caucuses as a test of loyalty to the party proved groundless. Douglas was re-elected chairman of the Committee on Territories, to the dismay of some administration supporters and the surprise of even Douglas himself, but the membership of the committee was so constituted as to leave Douglas in the minority. In the House, the administration supported South Carolina's James L. Orr for Speaker and James C. Allen, a former Congressman from Illinois and friend of Douglas, for Clerk, a victory for Douglas in both instances. For House Printer, Douglas' candidate, James B. Steedman of Ohio, was selected in spite of the fact that Steedman had recently reminded Buchanan of his own preference for Douglas at the Cincinnati convention. Douglas deliberately absented himself from the caucus that nominated Arnold Harris of the Washington *Union* for Senate Printer, and when the ballot was taken later he refused to vote "for reasons satisfactory to myself, but which I presume it is not necessary to state here." [16]

On December 8, the President sent his first annual message to the waiting Congress. His remarks on Kansas surprised few people. He extolled the "great principle of popular sovereignty" and implied that it was being carried out in strict compliance with the Kansas-Nebraska Act. The term "domestic institutions" in that legislation was "limited to the family," but included the relation between master and slave. Thus, the Lecompton convention, a legal body, had referred the question of slavery to the people "fairly and explicitly," and he expected that it would soon "be peacefully settled." The provisions in the constitution protecting slave property (which were not submitted to the voters) were "just and reasonable." While he did not make a specific recommendation to Congress, Buchanan predicted that, as soon as Kansas should be admitted as a state, the excitement in the nation would pass away. If the opportunity to settle this issue be rejected, he warned, Kansas would be involved in domestic discord for years to come.

As soon as the clerk completed his reading, Douglas was on his feet. Proposing that extra copies of the message be printed, he announced his concurrence in most of the President's statement, "but in regard to one topic—that of Kansas—I totally dissent from all that portion of the message which may fairly be construed as approving of the proceed-

ings of the Lecompton convention." There were, he observed, "intima-
tions on both sides of the Chamber (for I seem to stand between the parties) that they are waiting to hear what I may have to say on this
point." He promised to state the reasons for his dissent on the following
day.

Efforts by administration supporters to persuade Douglas to postpone
his speech were unsuccessful, and on December 9 he made his first public statement on the Lecompton issue. The President, he charged, had
committed a serious and fundamental error in his interpretation of the
Kansas-Nebraska Act, an error which Douglas sarcastically attributed to
the fact that Buchanan was out of the country when the act was debated
and passed. Popular sovereignty demanded that all local and domestic issues, including institutions concerning all the relations of life, should be
submitted to the people, not merely the slavery question. "I have spent
too much strength and breath, and health, too, to establish this great
principle in the popular heart, now to see it frittered away." If it be
right to insist on the submission of the slavery question, then "it follows
inevitably that every other clause of the constitution must also be submitted to the people." But, Douglas continued, the Lecompton convention, unauthorized by Congress, had no power to establish a new government. In the absence of an enabling act, it was merely an assemblage of
citizens petitioning the government, in the form of a state constitution,
for a redress of grievances. It was important that the petition embodied
the will of the people of the territory, fairly expressed, and again the
question of submission became significant. Those who voted for the delegates as well as those who refused to participate in the delegate elections
(which, Douglas pointed out, was their right) all expected that the convention "had no power to make a government, but only to frame one for
submission." This expectation had been encouraged by the assurances of
Governor Walker and the admonitions of the administration.

Douglas warmed to his task, and his language became more heated
and insistent as he turned his attention to the partial submission provided by the convention. The plan adopted was a "system of trickery and
jugglery to defeat the fair expression of the will of the people." Whether
they liked it or not, Kansas' voters were required to vote for the constitution in order to vote on the slavery question, "but no man is permitted
to record a vote against it." Why, he asked, are opponents of the constitution not being allowed to vote? The answer was obvious and
undeniable—"if they allowed a negative vote the constitution would

have been voted down by an overwhelming majority." This very action was proof to Douglas that the constitution did not have the endorsement of the majority of Kansans. "Is that the mode in which I am called upon to carry out the principle of self-government and popular sovereignty in the Territories—to force a constitution on the people against their will?" Buchanan's assurance that the constitution was "not particularly obnoxious" was no justification for "this flagrant violation of popular rights in Kansas." Whether the document was good or bad was beside the point; "it is their business and not ours." Douglas did not care what provisions were in the constitution, so long as they did not violate the Constitution of the United States and the "fundamental principles of liberty upon which our institutions rest." He had nothing to say about the banking provisions, the system of taxation, or the "Know-Nothing" clause concerning qualifications for office. "It is none of my business which way the slavery clause is decided," he declared, in a statement that has often been quoted out of context. "I care not whether it is voted down or voted up."

Douglas strongly objected to the urgency with which the constitution, "so unfair, so unjust as it is in all its aspects," was being pressed upon Congress. He proposed that both the Lecompton and Topeka constitutions be ignored and that a new enabling act (the Toombs bill would do) be passed which would guarantee a fair vote in the territory. He concluded his speech on a note of defiance. "If this constitution is to be forced down our throats, in violation of the fundamental principle of free government, under a mode of submission that is a mockery and insult, I will resist it to the last." He would regret any "social or political estrangement" that might result, but he would stand on the principle of popular sovereignty. "I will follow that principle wherever its logical consequences may take me, and I will endeavor to defend it against assault from any and all quarters."

Douglas was immediately challenged by Pennsylvania Senator Bigler. Defending the President's message, Bigler objected to Douglas' implication that Buchanan shared the view that Kansas' territorial legislature had no power to establish a legal constitutional convention, that the Lecompton body was merely an assemblage for a redress of grievances. Douglas referred to a statement made by Buchanan years before, and Bigler claimed a statute of limitations. In response, Douglas revealed his own pragmatic position on the consistency of politicans. "I believe in a statute of limitations in regard to political opinions," he acknowledged.

"I need one very much myself, on many points. I am not one of those who boast that they have never changed an opinion. Sir, it is a matter of gratification to me that I feel each year that I am a little wiser than I was the year before; and I do not know that a month has ever passed over my head in which I have not modified some opinion in some degree, but I am always frank enough to avow it. Still, it is fair for any man to hold me to a former opinion until I have expressed a contrary one." He further taunted the Pennsylvanian with the reminder that Buchanan's failure to make a specific recommendation on the constitution indicated the President's own hesitation regarding its fairness. The absence of a recommendation "clearly shows that it is not an Administration measure." [17]

Douglas' speech, probably the most significant of his career, was received "with pain on one side, and with rapturous applause on the other." The galleries and lobby of the Senate chamber had been packed long before Douglas took the floor, and at the conclusion of his remarks they burst into such a tumult that one southern Senator insisted the dignity and decorum of the Senate had been grossly violated. Senator Wade of Ohio, to the "merriment" of those around him, had earlier remarked, *sotto voce,* that it was the first slave insurrection he had ever seen. Horace Greeley's correspondent was certain that the speech "would mark an important era in our political history." [18]

Douglas' decision to oppose the administration plunged the party into confusion and consternation. His move was greeted initially by a shocked and studied silence, as southern Democrats were stunned and the Republicans perplexed. There was no doubt that Douglas fully comprehended the seriousness of his position. One Republican Senator noted that Douglas' manner and appearance as he spoke were unmistakable. "There was an air, not only of decision, but a consciousness apparently of having taken a decisive & irrevocable step," wrote Connecticut's James Dixon. "There was a bitterness too, towards his former allies— not to be expressed in words—but manifested by tone, manner & look." Douglas' opposition sent shock waves through the ranks of southern politicians. There are strange moves on the political chessboard, observed a South Carolina Congressman, "Douglas has gone off from us though I hope not finally." "The defection of Douglas," wrote Hunter, "is a severe blow. . . . The administration will have to depend mainly upon the states rights men of the South to support and sustain him." Georgia's Herschel V. Johnson, who leaned toward Douglas more than most southern leaders, grieved over the Illinoisan's action and regretted his loss. "It was not necessary for his fame or the future success of his ambition. . . . But if *he will,* let him go." Southern extremists adopted a harsher view. Douglas was a traitor and a renegade; his separation from the party, they hoped, was final and irrevocable. "The President will have to take the animal that would gore him by the horns and Jackson-like cut off his head."

Douglas' future in the Democratic party was now a matter of wide-spread speculation. Only two northern Democratic Senators, Charles E. Stuart of Michigan and David Broderick of California, seemed ready to follow Douglas' lead. Southern Senators met in hurried caucus, and it was rumored that they had agreed to drive Douglas from the party, although it became clear in subsequent days that no such decision was reached. "A new and tremendous sectional revolution" in the party was imminent, and some feared that Douglas would not only take the northern wing out of the party, but some of the southern wing as well. "Have you left the party, or has the party left you?" Douglas was asked.[19]

Many Republicans found Douglas' motives to be "utterly inexplicable." Dixon was inclined to think that Douglas was finally "indulging in the luxury of a conscience." He urged his colleagues not to scrutinize Douglas' motivation too closely. "He is right now, & if he will but continue so, I am willing to forget the past & cordially act with him & his friends in the future." Illinois Republicans were caught off guard. "We are almost confounded here by his anomalous position and know not how to treat him and his overtures to the Republican party," wrote the editor of the *Chicago Tribune* to Trumbull. "Douglas may be capable of good," warned another, "but he has fellowshipped with wrong and outrage so long, that I have misgivings." Republicans should stay clear of the Senator and "profit by the treason without taking the traitor to its embraces."

Republican leaders in the east, sensing an opportunity to weaken the power of the Democratic party, felt no hesitation in taking Douglas to their embrace. Their frequent visits to Douglas' Washington home raised speculation that some kind of alliance between Douglas and the Republican party was in the making. On December 11, Horace Greeley, accompanied by Republican Congressmen Schuyler Colfax of Indiana and Clark B. Cochrane of New York, called on Douglas, and three days later Colfax returned for a second visit with Massachusetts Congressman Anson Burlingame. On the following day Douglas conferred with former House Speaker Nathaniel P. Banks, and later Senator Benjamin Wade of Ohio paid a friendly visit to Douglas' house. Douglas told the Republicans of his determination to follow the principles indicated in his recent speech "no matter where they led him . . . even if it drove him to private life." He was convinced, he added, that southern extremists were trying to break up the Union, and he expressed surprise that his simple plea for justice to the people of Kansas should have aroused so much opposition among members of his party. Douglas revealed his plans to reintroduce the Toombs bill, with an added provision for the submission of the constitution to the people, and if that did not succeed he would use the Minnesota bill as a model for Kansas. In either event, he was confident of success. Colfax warned him that the support he might receive from Republicans would be limited to the Kansas issue and made it clear that there would be "no committal in regard to the Presidency." The interviews closed on a note of optimism.

Douglas also conferred with the newly elected Republican delegate from Kansas. In mid-December it was reported that Republicans had ordered 100,000 copies of Douglas' speech for wide circulation throughout the north. Lyman Trumbull, like his Illinois friends, was cautious. "Douglas does not mean to join the Republican Party, I presume," he wrote, "and yet if the Kansas question should be kept open for a few months, he may be forced into that position." While the Republicans took the initiative in seeking a *rapprochement* with their erstwhile enemy, and some had high hopes of winning him over, Douglas had no intention of leaving the Democratic party. On the contrary, he may have hoped that his course would detach the northern freesoil Democrats from the Republican party and win them back to the Democratic fold as a necessary counterweight to the increasing southern influence.[20]

Amidst the excitement that followed Douglas' speech, Governor Walker returned to the capital. He immediately held a long conference with the Senator. On the following day Walker visited Buchanan for a last interview, and on the next day, December 15, he submitted his resignation, accompanied by a full "manifesto" which Douglas had helped him to draft. Walker felt aggrieved and betrayed by the President. How deeply felt this sense of grievance was has been a matter of some uncertainty. With the south arrayed against him, it was unlikely that Walker would have been confirmed by the Senate in any case. Popular sovereignty, speculated the New York *Herald,* was merely a pretext; "the whole meaning of this Walker-Douglas anti-slavery conspiracy . . . is a revolutionary *coup d'etat* for the Presidential succession." [21]

Douglas hoped to delay consideration of the Lecompton constitution until he could build up a powerful, and popular, phalanx in opposition to the administration policy. His position was soon aided by events in Kansas. Frederick P. Stanton, Kansas' territorial secretary and acting governor in Walker's absence, had summoned the new Republican legislature into a special session, an action that raised a constitutional question, since the members, elected in October, were not to begin their terms until January. Proslavery men feared the legislature would tamper with the Lecompton constitution, and their fears were soon justified. A referendum on the constitution was ordered for early January, on the same day that the elections for state officers under the constitution had been scheduled by the Lecompton convention. The action threw the proslavery element into turmoil and resulted in a curious change of heart. "Kansas is indeed a whirlpool," wrote Weer to Douglas. It now seemed likely that Kansas would be a slave state (if Congress should follow Buchanan's recommendation) with a Republican state government; what was worse from the proslavery point of view was that Charles Robinson and James Lane, the prime movers behind the Topeka free state movement, would probably be sent to Washington as United States Senators. Such a development was unthinkable, and Kansas' proslavery leaders began calling for the rejection of the Lecompton constitution by Congress. To forestall a Republican victory, Kansas Democrats, both freesoil and proslavery, supported Douglas' effort to secure the passage of an enabling act. Buchanan's reaction to this turn of events was the immediate removal of Stanton and the appointment of James W. Denver, the territory's Commissioner of Indian Affairs, as territorial secretary and acting governor. Douglas made an attempt to block Denver's confirmation in the Senate, but he was absent when the vote was taken, and Denver was confirmed.

On December 21, the day set by the Lecompton convention for the vote on its partial submission plan, the constitution "with slavery" received over 6000 votes to only 569 for the constitution "without slavery," but the election was boycotted by the free staters. Two weeks later, on January 4, in the election provided by the free state legislature, the constitution was rejected by over 10,000 votes, while only 162 votes were cast in its favor. Over 4000 more persons voted against the constitution in January than had voted for it in December, a clear indication of the anti-Lecompton majority in the territory. The returns for members of the new state legislature were so muddled as to defy clear interpretation. Evidence of gross irregularities and fraud were discovered. Calhoun, exercising the authority given him by the Lecompton convention, extricated himself by certifying the election of proslavery majorities in both houses, thus adding to the outcry against the constitution.[22]

Douglas' defiance of the administration was quickly answered by Bigler, Graham Fitch of Indiana (who proved a new and eager ally of the President), and James S. Green of Missouri. The remaining days of December witnessed a running debate between the three administration supporters and Douglas. Standing alone, Douglas bore the brunt of the attack, but he proved equal to the task. His opposition to the Lecompton constitution stiffened, and his charges against the administration became more pointed. "This question between us," he told Green, "is radical. It is whether that people shall be permitted to form their own constitution, and whether the constitution under which they are to live shall embody their will or not." The scheme of Lecompton's backers, he shouted, "is a scheme of civil war," threatening "the peace and perpetuity of the Union itself." He bristled at the charges in the southern press that he "had deserted the Democratic party and gone over to the Black Republicans!" "There are men here personal enemies of mine," Douglas insisted, "men who would be willing to sink an Administration if they could kill off northern men, and get them out of the way in the future; such men are getting their tools to denounce me as having abandoned the party. Why? Because I do not desert my principles as freely as the masters of these editors desert theirs. I have seen this attempt—not sanctioned by the President; he scorns it; but there are men under him busy at work to convince every one that I have betrayed my party and my principles, in order to see if they cannot crush me among my Democratic friends."

As Bigler sought, ineffectively, to argue the administration position, Douglas' anger mounted. "I do not recognize the right of any body of men to expel me from the Democratic party. . . . If gentlemen can tolerate differences of opinion, we can act in harmony, but I shall maintain my views of right, whether there be harmony or not. . . . If, in doing so, I shall happen to come in collision with any of my friends on this floor, I shall deeply regret it; but still, if they cannot tolerate differences of opinion . . . then I must maintain my independent course of action inside of the Democratic party, standing by its organization and its principles until the party shall reassert its true and original principles." To Fitch he reiterated his opposition to the "fraud" perpetrated by the Lecompton convention, and once again he threw down the gauntlet to his opponents. Dripping with perspiration and shaking his finger in the face of the Indiana Senator, who sat nearly behind him, Douglas shouted, "Call it faction; call it what you please; I intend to stand by the Nebraska bill, by the Cincinnati platform, by the organization and principles of the party; and I defy opposition from whatever quarter it comes. . . . I ask no mercy in relation to this matter." He half-suspected, he said, that these frequent personal attacks were designed "to weary me out—to exhaust my strength."

On December 18 Douglas introduced his bill authorizing a new constitutional convention in Kansas and providing for the submission of the constitution to a popular vote. Modeled on the Toombs bill of the previous session, Douglas' measure would create a five-member commission, appointed by the President, to take a census, make the apportionment, and provide for a fair and impartial election. On the same day, Banks presented a Republican-sponsored bill in the House, patterned on the Minnesota enabling act, which would leave the supervision in the hands of the territorial legislature. They were the two alternatives which Douglas had earlier proposed, and there was little doubt that Banks' move was part of Douglas' general strategy.[23]

Congress recessed for the Christmas holidays on December 23. During the respite, Douglas traveled with his wife to New York. Stopping in Philadelphia, he conferred with newspaper editor John W. Forney, a former intimate of Buchanan who had now moved to Douglas' side. In New York, he met with local Democratic and Republican leaders, and he was pleased with the cordiality with which he was received. He "feels in good spirits" and "is desirous to commend himself to Republicans," wrote Preston King. Speaking with a group of Republicans in Banks' hotel room, Douglas again revealed his hope that the administration might be defeated by delaying a vote on Lecompton until the anti-Lecompton forces both within and outside of Congress could be organized. One of those present testified to Douglas' sincerity and his bitterness toward southern members of his party. "Douglas does not disguise his conviction," wrote New York editor John Bigelow, "that he can never be forgiven by the South if he were so much disposed to ask forgiveness, and I thought I could perceive by the way in which he talked abundant evidence of an old hostility rankling in his bosom of which this outbreak about the Lecompton Constitution was as but the flash of the priming to the discharge." [24]

iii

When Douglas returned to Washington, it was to his new and spacious home on the so-called Minnesota Block, adjacent to the residences of Henry M. Rice and Vice President Breckinridge. Callers found the interior "imposing & showy." A large ballroom had been provided, flanked by a dining room and "flirtation gallery"; the drawing room was dominated by two full-length portraits of Douglas and his wife. The windows of Douglas' library afforded a grand view of the capitol, and the library itself was well stocked with books, reflecting Adele's literary tastes. The house was officially opened with a gala housewarming in mid-January, when two thousand guests jammed its "capacious saloons." No other dwelling in Washington could match it, wrote one correspondent. "The White House itself is not more visited." Douglas was clearly planning to remain in Washington for a long time to come.[25]

Douglas' mail reached avalanche proportions as letters poured in lauding his stand on the Lecompton constitution. "The bone & sinew of the Northern Democracy are with you," wrote one New Yorker. Hundreds of communications from throughout the north substantiated the claim. From Vermont came word that influential Republicans "are out in your support," a development that was also reported in other states, and from Pennsylvania Douglas learned that "conservative men of all parties" agreed with the correctness of his position. Republicans, Americans (Know-Nothings), old-line Whigs, and freesoil Democrats sent words of assurance and encouragement. "The Free State men of the nation earnestly look to you as their most formidable ally." "Were you now to pass through these Western States, your progress, at every town & village, would be attended with one continued ovation of the masses of the people," wrote an Ohio supporter. The contrast with the dark days following the Kansas-Nebraska Act was striking.

Kansas correspondents kept Douglas posted on the latest developments there. Free state Democrats, Republicans, and free state Americans, he was told, approved his course. Only the proslavery fanatics balked. Douglas was now "the great champion of free government"; the people of the territory "speak your name in praise . . . in you, they have a worthy friend, and protector." Only a new enabling act, such as that introduced by Douglas in December, would satisfy "all reasonable men of all parties."

There were also words of caution. "Don't in a moment of irritation," wrote a Kentuckian, "say or do aught that can be construed into the idea, that you are the least under the influence of the Black Republicans." Others thought it might already be too late. "I have no doubt you have gone over to the black republican party"; if Douglas did not soon retrace his steps, warned this Philadelphian, he would suffer the same fate as Martin Van Buren and David Wilmot, "politically buried . . . beyond the hope of any resurrection." "You are the last man in the Democratic Party I should have suspected of going over to this most *infamous* Black Republican party," moaned another correspondent. "I fear it is now too late & that you must be considered a *Dead Cock* in the Pit." [26]

Assurances of support were received from unexpected sources. Edwin M. Stanton, although sympathetic with Buchanan's position, expressed admiration for Douglas' bold stand. Gideon Welles recalled his dismay twenty years before when Douglas lost his first campaign for Congress by a handful of votes, traced the "process of disintegration and disruption" that had characterized party politics since 1848, and declared that it was Douglas' mission to rebuke his party's leadership and lead the Democracy back to the principles it professes. "You are the only man . . . whom we can elect in 1860," concluded Forney. John Van Buren lauded Douglas' "dignified & impartial" speech, and New York Republican Thurlow Weed assured Douglas that the people *"are with you."* Benjamin F. Butler wrote that it was "a far greater honor to have made this speech, than to be President of the United States." Historian George Bancroft continued to send encouragement, along with detailed citations of historical precedents which Douglas might use, and economist Henry Carey congratulated him on his efforts "in the people's cause." [27]

Voices from the past were also heard, as old acquaintances recalled their early contacts with Douglas' developing career. Cyrus Knowlton, who had known Douglas as a boy in Vermont, marveled that "a little stone knocked from the Green Mountain rocks should [have] become the Kohinoor of American politics." Douglas' doctrine was "true gospel . . . the best one delivered to us since the Angels sung over the Star of Bethlehem." Henry Howe, Douglas' teacher at Canandaigua Academy, praised the "moral grandeur" of his position. Kinsman Daniel P.

Rhodes observed that, if Douglas had now left the Democratic party, "Be kind enough to advise me when you get into another so I can come in too." [28]

Southern reactions were more mixed. While some bitterly assailed Douglas for his opposition to Lecompton, others adopted a cautious and waiting attitude. "His former eminent services to the South," declared the Richmond *Examiner,* "demand that he should not be denounced, before ample time has been allowed for an examination of the position which he occupies." "We have yet to be convinced that the gallant Douglas is a traitor," commented the Richmond *Enquirer.* Not all Virginians deferred their judgment. When Governor Henry A. Wise announced his endorsement of Douglas' arguments in mid-January, pro-administration southerners were both surprised and dismayed. The submission plan of the Lecompton convention, Wise wrote Douglas, was "all pro & *no con."* Suppose the sides had been reversed in Kansas? What would have been the attitude of the south, Wise asked, if a free-soil minority had so manipulated the movement as to prohibit slavery in Kansas without providing an opportunity for a proslavery majority to express its judgment in a fair and impartial manner? "Would they contend in that case a convention is absolute?" Border state sentiment generally reflected Wise's view, although Wise's move was attributed to a split with southern radicals and to an effort to promote his own ambition by fusing with Douglas "in the reconstruction of the Northern democracy upon a Northern platform."

From the deep south came ominous warnings of an approaching crisis over the Union itself. South Carolina radicals believed that the time had arrived to make an issue with the north over "the *total* of wrongs to the South," with the Lecompton question as a pretext, "even at the cost of the Union." Robert Barnwell suggested that South Carolina leave the Union on the issue of Lecompton, and Senator James H. Hammond asked "if Kansas is *driven out of the Union for being a Slave State,* can any Slave State remain in it with honor?" "A Slaveholding Confederacy should be . . . the *ultimate* aim of every Southern patriot," wrote one of Hammond's correspondents. Douglas' Kansas-Nebraska Act was now recognized as a "decoy duck to the confiding deluded South," intended "to create a Free Soil Democratic state." As Republicans saw new merit in popular sovereignty, southern radicals turned bitterly against it. Georgia's Governor Joseph E. Brown urged that his state's role in the Union be seriously reviewed; "when the Union ceases to protect our equal rights, it ceases to have any charms for me." Still, at least one South Carolinian wrote to Douglas in disbelief, urging him to express his "true views" on the Kansas issue as a favor to his southern supporters.[29]

It was to Illinois, however, that Douglas looked with special concern during the early weeks of 1858. His second term as United States Senator was in its last year. With a senatorial election in the offing, the political importance of his course in Washington could hardly be exaggerated. His travels throughout the state during the summer and fall of 1857 had persuaded him that his stand against the Lecompton constitution would receive wide support. Information reaching him after his opening statement in the Senate confirmed this impression. "I don't see how you could have taken any other course, and sustained yourself at home," wrote one constituent. "Had you gone the other way, the Dem party in the State would have been routed horse foot and dragoon." Republican charges of insincerity and expediency began to lose their force, and the possibility that Douglas would make significant inroads into the opposition party loomed larger. A close friend of Lincoln's conceded that Douglas' stand was consistent with his position in previous years, and he assured the Senator that "in my humble opinion you are right, and you have in this case my sympathies and well wishes." Republican leaders shifted their tactics and concentrated on widening the split between Douglas and the administration, becoming (to the amusement of many Democrats) zealous advocates of popular sovereignty. "A complete revolution can be made in the Republican party here in six months," confided a northern Illinois editor.

Democrats at first sought to gloss over the party division, maintaining a loyalty to the President while supporting Douglas. The great majority of Democratic newspapers in the state assumed an anti-Lecompton position but refrained from attacking the administration. In the northern counties, freesoil Democrats who had identified with the Republican party in 1856 were reported to be moving back. A Democratic mass meeting in Chicago, hitherto regarded as hostile ground, strongly and enthusiastically endorsed Douglas' course, while similar gatherings throughout the state added momentum to the movement. Much, however, depended upon Douglas' determination to continue the struggle against the administration. "If you fight the battle boldly even a defeat would be a victory," wrote John A. McClernand, "but if you yield an inch you are undone." Ex-Governor Matteson was less sanguine. "If you can defeat the passage of the Kansas Constitution, all will be right, but

if you do not I fear the result in our State, as the Republicans will turn
all your good intentions to their own benefit." Others agreed with
Matteson. "There is but one hope left and that is the defeat of the Lecompton constitution," warned one of Douglas' close friends. "If the constitution passes, the Democratic party as they have made it at Washington can not carry a Congressional district in the North. It will be utterly
dead. . . . The North West has become a power in the Country, and its
voice must be heard." [30]

Douglas' differences with the administration placed the officeholders
in Illinois in a quandary. Many of them, owing their positions to Douglas, supported his course, but it soon became evident that the administration was exerting pressure on them to break with the Senator. Threats of
removal were made, often without administration endorsement. Douglas'
rivals in the party, reported Sheahan, were promising places to anyone
"if they will only be anti Douglas." Sheahan blamed the effort on Jesse
Bright. John Slidell also recognized the opportunity to weaken Douglas
in his own state, and he actually received assistance from Lyman Trumbull, who not only spoke favorably to the administration in behalf of
Douglas' Democratic enemies, but also promised to support the confirmation of any of them to offices in Illinois.

The biggest prize was the Chicago Post Office, located in an area
where the Democratic party was already weakened by dissension. Douglas' chief rival for control of Chicago Democrats was ex-postmaster Isaac Cook, whom Buchanan had earlier removed from office at Douglas'
insistence, and it was logical that the administration would turn to Cook
for aid in combating Douglas' influence. When Douglas announced his
opposition to Lecompton, Cook hurried to Washington to declare his
loyalty to the President. He hinted that his trip was made at Buchanan's
invitation and boasted that he and the President would "arrange matters
for Illinois." Soon afterward, the incumbent postmaster William Price, a
"fierce Douglas man," was removed, and Cook's name was sent to the
Senate for confirmation. Douglas fought the appointment, but to no
avail. In a vote that some regarded as a test vote on the Lecompton
issue, the Senate confirmed Cook's appointment, 25 to 18. To Douglas'
outraged supporters, Buchanan's move was tantamount to a declaration
of war. "If old Buck commences war & proceeds to blows," Sheahan had
advised, "we had better hit back promptly." Many rank-and-file Republicans joined the Democrats in denouncing Cook's appointment as an "insult to the people of Chicago," but Republican leaders in the state were

ecstatic. The pressure on Douglas officeholders continued to mount with the hint of more removals to come.[31]

iv

Congress reconvened on January 4. The Senate, commented one member, "has a very *mobbish* look." Precisely how the battle lines would be drawn was a matter of speculation. The Kansas issue had become "a game of cross purposes in which neither party . . . comprehends where it stands." Southerners, while showering invective on Douglas, conceded that the admission of Kansas with a Republican governor and legislature would do the south little good. James W. Denver, Walker's successor as governor of Kansas, advised the President that admission under the Lecompton constitution would destroy the opportunity to build a Democratic organization in the new state, while even some of the territory's proslavery leaders doubted the desirability of establishing a slave state in opposition to the free state majority. Senator Hammond professed a new indifference to the whole issue. "The South here," he wrote from Washington, "is utterly unorganized & I fear demoralized." Douglas' "treachery" to the south became a greater issue, and there was a determination to force Lecompton through Congress if for no other reason than to establish his apostasy as a member of the Democratic party.[32]

At the same time, Douglas' stock was reported on the rise among northern members of Congress. Republicans continued to give him support, although some undoubtedly agreed with Sumner's observation that "our experience of Douglas . . . would prevent any strong confidence in his labors for the good cause." With Schuyler Colfax acting as intermediary, Republican Congressmen continued to confer with Douglas in his home. Frank Blair, representing St. Louis in the lower house, asked his colleagues to accord Douglas "fair and kind treatment"; Colfax himself, still hopeful that Douglas might move into the Republican ranks, urged his party to avoid building a platform so high that Douglas could not climb upon it if he wished. Republicans and northern Democrats alike feared that Douglas might be tempted to accept a compromise on the Lecompton issue.

Compromise, however, was far from Douglas' mind. Responding to invitations to address mass meetings in Philadelphia and New York, he reiterated his "determined and unyielding hostility to the consummation of a scheme so monstrous as to force a constitution at the point of the bayonet down the throats of an unwilling people." Nothing less than the complete repudiation of the Lecompton constitution would satisfy him, and he asked his friends to "arouse the country on the great issues of self government." "I will take no step backwards and abate not one iota of the position I have taken," Douglas assured McClernand, "let the consequences be what they may to me personally." It would be, predicted Thomas L. Harris, a "war to the knife." [33]

Members of Congress bided their time until the official returns from the December and January elections on the Lecompton constitution could be received and analyzed. In the meantime, Douglas made an effort to secure passage of Minnesota's statehood bill, which he and his committee had prepared and submitted, but southern Senators were unwilling to sanction another free state while Douglas balked on the Kansas issue. To the charge that he proposed different rules for Minnesota and Kansas, Douglas replied, "I will never apply one rule to a free State and another to a slaveholding State. I hold each of the States equal in this Confederacy, and apply the same rule to one as to the other." When the official copy of the Lecompton constitution arrived in the capital at the end of January, Minnesota's admission was pushed into the background. On February 2, Congress received a message from the President, transmitting the constitution and arguing forcefully that Kansas be speedily admitted. That evening, Senate Democrats met in caucus to map their strategy. The press had confidently predicted that Douglas would finally be driven from the party, but the group merely decided to push the Lecompton issue to a settlement, to the exclusion of all other business.[34]

Douglas' plan, however, was one of delay. There was little likelihood that the Lecompton constitution could be defeated in the Senate. Although the Democrats enjoyed a comfortable majority, the Democratic caucus was dominated by southern Senators and their northern, pro-administration allies. While Douglas could count on the Republicans and some of the Americans, he was not able to muster enough support among the Democratic members to ensure the defeat of the Lecompton movement. Things looked better in the House. With Richardson and McClernand no longer members of the lower house, Douglas relied on Harris to lead the anti-Lecompton forces. By the time the President's message was received, an anti-Lecompton bloc had been organized, with Harris acting as its chairman. In its first trial of strength, the bloc narrowly succeeded in referring Buchanan's message to a select committee, thus avoiding the southern-dominated Committee on Territories. In the

Senate, the message was referred to Douglas' committee. If Douglas felt that he and Harris were in a position to direct the fate of the Lecompton constitution, he was soon disappointed. Harris' plans went awry when his select committee was packed with pro-Lecompton members, while Douglas faced formidable opposition in his own committee.

On February 4, Douglas introduced resolutions asking the President to transmit full information concerning the election returns in Kansas along with all correspondence between the executive departments and Kansas territorial officials, but this attempt to launch an investigation of the Lecompton movement failed. Engaged in almost daily debate, persistent, but showing the effects of the strain, Douglas was unable to breach the administration phalanx. His position in the Senate became increasingly difficult. A Democratic caucus, it was reported, had decided that Senators opposed to the administration's Kansas policy would not be expected to attend future caucus meetings. Harris complained that "nothing avails here now but *submission to administration or southern dictation.* . . . We must vote to admit Kansas under the Lecompton constitution, or we are Black republicans, renegades, demagogues, and all that." Douglas became convinced that the administration was bent on his destruction even at the expense of party unity.[35]

As a further blow, control over the territorial committee was taken from Douglas' hands. The administration majority on the committee turned to Missouri Senator James S. Green for leadership in preparing a Lecompton report and bill. Relations between Green and Douglas were far from amicable, and the former was not inclined to give the committee chairman even a modicum of consideration. Originally assured that he would be given ample time to prepare a minority report, Douglas was abruptly informed by Green on February 16 that the final action of the committee would be reported to the Senate on the eighteenth. He was given this much warning, wrote Green, "so as to prevent surprise." The announcement could not have come at a worse time. Adele had given birth prematurely and lay gravely ill. The baby survived only a few hours, and for a number of days Adele's own life was despaired of. Douglas remained at her bedside almost constantly until she was reported out of danger. Worn out by his exertions in the Senate and anxiety over his wife's condition, weakened by a succession of sleepless nights, Douglas worked steadily for one day and two nights on his report. Green undoubtedly hoped that Douglas would lack sufficient time to prepare a report, but the chairman completed his statement early on the morning of February 18 for submission to the Senate later that day. The two Republican members of the committee also submitted a minority report. None of the minority members were given the opportunity to read Green's report before it was presented as a committee document.[36]

In spite of the haste with which it had been drawn, Douglas' report was thorough and incisive, emphasizing the proslavery election frauds in Kansas, the illegality of the Lecompton convention's assumption of sovereign power, and the complete lack of satisfactory evidence that the constitution reflected the will of the people in the territory. George Bancroft thought the statement "could hardly have been better, had you had till Doomsday to prepare it." With the submission of the reports, the debate on Lecompton was ready to begin. "Winter will close and spring will come and go, and summer too for that matter, before the abomination will have passed over the Senate," predicted one paper. "The debate will be the most scorching which ever took place in Congress." [37]

Although the Senate galleries were daily thronged with spectators, the debate actually proved anticlimactic. A multitude of speeches was delivered, but the arguments had all been expressed before, and little that was new was advanced. In the meantime, the issue was further confused by developments in Kansas. After considerable vacillation, Calhoun certified the election of a Republican legislature under the Lecompton constitution. His action, it was said, had been dictated by the administration, in the hope that additional votes for the constitution might be secured. It succeeded only in revealing the administration's dilemma and the uneasiness of the southerners as they faced the prospect of admitting a slave state with a Republican legislature. Efforts to tie Lecompton with Minnesota, a free state for a slave state, were unsuccessful and were dropped.

Douglas "put on his 'battle face'" and threw himself into the debate, reviving his resolutions for full information on the Kansas elections and still hoping for an investigation that would delay final consideration of the Lecompton bill. Within a short time, however, the exertion of the previous weeks began to take its toll. He suddenly seemed pale and dispirited and complained of feeling unwell. By mid-March he was confined to his bed, unable to attend Senate sessions. His absence did not prevent the opposition from attacking him, and Douglas chafed at his inability to respond personally. When it was rumored that Douglas would appear on March 15, the galleries filled early, but Broderick, who had been answering the charges on his behalf, announced that Douglas' physician refused to allow him to speak. When he unexpectedly appeared in the anteroom later that night, it was obvious that he was too sick to participate. "Douglas is quite unwell," wrote Republican Senator Dixon. "He came into our night session, about midnight . . . but we sent him home. He was not fit to be there. He is very nervous, though he does not show it at all in his looks or appearance. His wife was dangerously sick for some days . . . & from this cause, & the anxiety natural to his position, he became nervous & sleepless. For ten days & nights he did not sleep at all—and for four days last week he was confined to his bed." The Lecomptonites, Dixon added, hoped to force a vote on the bill in Douglas' absence, but the minority, "determined & resolute," caused them to abandon the effort. "My opinion is they wish to avoid that last speech by Douglas." [38]

On March 22, unable to remain away any longer, Douglas appeared in the Senate to make his final speech on the Lecompton bill. A "prodigious multitude" crowded the capitol "beyond all precedent." An hour before he was to speak it had become "impossible to crowd another person into the galleries." Adele, unable to find a place in the ladies' gallery, was accorded a seat in the reporter's gallery. Douglas' arrival was greeted "by an outburst of wildest applause." At seven he began a speech that would consume three hours. "He looked pale and care worn," observed one reporter, "and his voice at first was feeble and uncertain. As he went on it acquired its customary ring and force, and he spoke with all his wonted animation." [39]

The moment was dramatic, but his address brought forth nothing that was not already known. He reviewed his course on the slavery question since he first entered Congress in 1843 before launching his attack on the Lecompton bill. The recent election returns, he maintained, formed conclusive evidence that the constitution did not embody the will of the people. Judged by "the technical rules of law," the constitution became null and void when it was voted down by a majority of the electorate; approached from the "spirit of statesmanship, in the spirit of justice and fairness," the conclusion was just as unmistakable since the constitution did not embody the popular will. On no account could its approval be justified. Congress was now being asked to give vitality to a "void, rejected, repudiated constitution." Such a violation of the "fundamental principles of free government" would establish a dangerous precedent for unscrupulous men in the future to "subvert all the other great principles upon which our institutions rest."

Elaborating on the arguments presented in his minority report, Douglas attacked the view that the people of Kansas could alter their constitution after admission. Buchanan had suggested that Congress insert such a clause in the act of admission. For Douglas, such an action would strike a fatal blow at states' rights. Whenever the government should recognize "the right of the people of a State to act in a different manner from that provided in their constitution . . . farewell to State rights, farewell to State sovereignty." If Buchanan's proposal should be approved, he asked, what would stop a future Congress from pronouncing judgment against the domestic institutions of a state in its act of admission?

Taking cognizance of the widespread reports that he would be driven from the Democratic party, Douglas concluded his address with a stirring testament of faith and principles. "I intend to vote, speak, and act, according to my own sense of duty, so long as I hold a seat in this Chamber. I have no defense to make of my Democracy. . . . The insinuation that I am acting with the Republicans, or Americans, has no terror, and will not drive me from my duty or propriety. . . . I stand firmly, immovably upon those great principles of self-government and State sovereignty. . . . I stand by the time-honored principles of the Democratic party, illustrated by Jefferson and Jackson; those principles of State rights, of State sovereignty, of strict construction, on which the great Democratic party has ever stood. I will stand by the Constitution of the United States, with all its compromises, and . . . I will stand by the American Union as it exists under the Constitution. If, standing firmly by my principles, I shall be driven into private life, it is a fate that has no terrors for me. . . . If the alternative be private life or servile obedience to executive will, I am prepared to retire." Even the *Chicago Tribune* expressed admiration for Douglas, the central figure in "one of the greatest [debates] in our history." Though pale and "attenuated by sickness," Douglas displayed a surprising physical vigor. "His manner was full of the old fire." [40]

Douglas' speech, for all practical purposes, closed the debate on the Lecompton constitution. On the next day, Green made one final appeal for passage. In a last desperate move, Kentucky's John J. Crittenden offered a substitute bill, proposing that the Lecompton constitution be resubmitted to a popular vote in a carefully supervised election; if it then be rejected, a new constitution was to be drawn up. Douglas supported Crittenden's substitute, but it went down to defeat. The decks were cleared for final action on the bill. Thirty-three Senators upheld the admission of Kansas under the Lecompton constitution, twenty-five opposed it. Joining the anti-Lecompton Democrats (Douglas, Broderick, and Stuart) was Ohio's George E. Pugh; two southern Whig-Americans (Bell of Tennessee and Crittenden) and nineteen Republicans completed the roster of Lecompton's opponents.[41]

While the Senate debated, House members engaged in a flurry of behind-the-scenes maneuvering designed to avert total administration defeat by promoting a compromise on the Lecompton issue. Anti-Lecompton members had succeeded in referring Buchanan's message to a special committee, rather than to the territorial committee, but their strategy availed them nothing when the Speaker packed the committee with administration supporters. The cause encountered a further setback when Harris, Douglas' lieutenant in the lower house, became desperately ill. Removed from his own lodgings to Douglas' house, it was shortly revealed that Harris was suffering the last stages of consumption. Alexander H. Stephens led the administration forces and worked tirelessly to crack the determination of the anti-Lecompton members. Douglas appeared frequently on the House floor, urging his followers to defeat the Senate bill and to accept Crittenden's proposal to return the Lecompton constitution to Kansas.

The key figure in the effort to split the anti-Lecompton bloc and to promote a compromise on which both sides could agree became Indiana's young Congressman, William H. English. A protégé of Jesse Bright, English had nevertheless maintained good relations with Douglas; although a supporter of the Lecompton constitution, his constituents stood on the other side, providing an incentive for compromise. Late in March, a Democratic caucus committee, chaired by English and including ten Lecompton men and ten anti-Lecomptonites, discussed means for uniting the two sides. The move alarmed some of Douglas' friends, but it encountered its stiffest opposition from intransigent pro-Lecompton southerners. Stephens, virtually conceding defeat in the House, fell back on a plan to force the appointment of a conference committee that could work out the differences between the two houses. English relayed the suggestion to the President, urging that it seemed "a safer course than to run the risk of a total defeat upon the naked senate bill," and Buchanan gave it his endorsement. Meanwhile, William Montgomery, anti-Lecompton Congressman from Pennsylvania, moved the adoption of Crittenden's proposal. On April 1 the House rejected the Senate bill, passing the Montgomery-Crittenden substitute by the close vote of 120 to 112.[42]

There was no hope that the Senate would concur in the House substitute. Douglas made a strong appeal for the Montgomery-Crittenden proposal, and Republicans became even more enamored of his leadership. When Trumbull, unwilling to defer to his colleague, charged that Douglas was seeking to build a great northern Democratic party, a number of Republicans, including William P. Fessenden, John P. Hale, Preston King, Israel Washburn, and Simon Cameron, announced their willingness to unite with him in that object. Although Douglas was accorded warm support by the Republicans, he was unable to persuade a majority of the Senators. The refusal of the Senate to accept the House substitute forecast the demise of the administration bill. "The agony is over and thank God, the right has triumphed!" wrote one Douglas Democrat. The agony was not over, but it was clear that the Lecompton bill, in the form in which the administration had presented it, was now dead. The way was now clear for Stephens to push his effort for compromise in a conference committee; it was the only way to save the administration from humiliating defeat and to break the deadlock on the Kansas question.

The Senate requested a conference committee on April 13 (Douglas voting in the negative), and on the next day the House agreed, but only after a tie vote had been broken by Speaker Orr. The results of Stephens' pressure became apparent as several anti-Lecompton members broke ranks to vote with the administration for a compromise. Senators Green, Hunter, and Seward and Congressmen English, Stephens, and Howard were appointed to the committee, three Lecompton members, one anti-Lecompton (if indeed English could be so clearly classified) and two Republicans. The burden of perfecting a compromise fell on English, although the plan that was finally adopted was initially proposed by Stephens and approved by the President. With the Republican members of the committee registering vigorous dissent, English submitted a compromise bill on April 23, and members of the administration went to work to persuade southern Democrats to accept it.

The English bill was an attempt to resolve the issue by subterfuge (using similar tactics to those employed by the Lecompton convention in the first place). By its terms, the controversial provisions of the Lecompton constitution were deliberately subordinated; the emphasis was placed, not on the slavery question, but upon the less vital matter of a land grant to the proposed state. Proslavery Kansans had demanded, as part of their statehood movement, a grant of land far in excess of that normally granted to new states, and a considerable number of Senators and Congressmen had balked at granting this liberality. The English bill scaled the grant down to normal size and coupled Kansas' admission under the Lecompton constitution to this reduced grant. An election was to be scheduled in the territory at which the voters would either accept or reject the revised land grant. If accepted, Kansas would be admitted as a slave state; if rejected, statehood would be indefinitely postponed. Although Kansas voters would ostensibly decide only the question of the land grant, they would in fact be voting on the Lecompton constitution. The subterfuge, it was hoped, would satisfy both the Lecompton and anti-Lecompton groups.[43]

The English bill placed anti-Lecompton Democrats in a dilemma. To accept it would be to endorse, at least implicitly, the Lecompton constitution; yet the bill provided, albeit indirectly, the referendum on the constitution proposed by the Montgomery-Crittenden substitute. There was little danger that the election proposed by the English bill would result in the acceptance of the land grant. Still, many of Douglas' followers in the House were reluctant to accept the compromise. "The English scheme is a miserable one," wrote Harris. "No one likes it." The bill was attacked by Republicans as a shameful bribe held out to the people of Kansas to accept a slave constitution, although this was patently untrue, inasmuch as the land grant was no larger than that usually offered new states. Nevertheless, pressure for its acceptance mounted.

On the day following the introduction of the English bill, the Washington *States* confidently reported that Douglas, Stuart, and Broderick would oppose it in the Senate. For Douglas, it was not an easy decision. Although inclined against the measure, he was aware that the bill would bring his warfare against the administration to a close, at the same time preserving popular sovereignty in Kansas. "If the English bill . . . passes, with the support of your friends," he was assured, "it will be regarded by the country as a magnificent triumph of the principles you have advocated." The bill appealed to the sense of pragmatic adjustment through compromise which he had urged many times before during periods of crisis. Pressures were brought to bear on the Illinois Senator to ensure his support. Robert Walker had come around, as had also the former territorial secretary and acting governor of Kansas, Frederick P. Stanton. Together they sought to persuade Douglas. At an evening conference with Douglas late in April, Walker and Stanton, joined by Forney, argued forcefully for the passage of the English bill as the only practical means for administering final and decisive defeat to the Lecompton movement. Their arguments must have been effective, for Douglas finally agreed, even offering to make a telegraphic announcement of his decision to the country.[44]

Still Douglas had doubts. Support for the English bill would be an acceptance of compromise with the southern and administration forces against whom he had fought so bitterly. His position had left little room for conciliation, and the abuse he had endured from the Lecompton camp would now make accord a hard pill to swallow. He was not prepared to risk losing the valuable Republican support he had gained, especially since he faced a crucial election contest in Illinois later in the year. The Illinois state Democratic convention had just passed strong anti-Lecompton resolutions at his insistence, and many of his followers in Illinois were urging him to stand firm against the compromise. Finally, the English proposition, if not a bribe, was unfair, for it established special rules for the admission of a slave state that were not extended to all proposed states, violating his long-held conviction that all new states should be admitted under the same set of conditions. Douglas' uncertainty remained in spite of Walker's convincing arguments.

All his doubts, however, were dispelled when he met with some of his anti-Lecompton colleagues to inform them of his decision to support the English bill. Broderick exploded. "Sir, I cannot understand it," he shouted, "you will be crushed between the Democracy and the Republicans. I shall denounce you, sir." Taken aback by the outburst, Douglas was convinced he now had no alternative but to follow his earlier inclination. He would oppose the English bill.[45]

Debate on the English bill was brief. On April 29, Douglas elaborated his opposition to the measure. He had been anxious, he said, to find provisions which he could support. Finding none, he had but "one line of duty"—to vote against the bill. He disliked the indirection by which the constitution was to be submitted, really no submission at all, and maintained that the people of Kansas were not free to accept or reject the constitution. "I insist," he told the Senate, "that where there are inducements on one side, and penalities on the other, there is no freedom of election." The bill did not bring "the question within that principle which I have held dear, and in defense of which I have stood here for the last five months, battling against the large majority of my political friends, and in defense of which I intend to stand as long as I have any association or connection with the politics of the country." On the next day, the bill passed the Senate, 31 to 22, and the House, where defections among the anti-Lecompton Democrats proved more numerous, 112 to 103. "Well its over—for the present," lamented Harris. "The progress of this business has been damnably corrupt. The Adm. has bought men like hogs in the market. It was impossible to cope with the money & patronage of the government." [46]

The passage of the English bill was an ignominious end to the crisis. Even in its resolution there was disagreement, and few were really happy with the result. Douglas, though he had opposed the method, regarded the submission of the Lecompton constitution as "virtually conceded" in the English bill. South Carolina's Senator Hammond, on the other hand, boasted that the south had made "no concession, no compromise." Buchanan congratulated himself on his success "in pacifying the Country on the Kansas question" and on his triumph over the Little Giant. If Douglas had succeeded in defeating the English bill, he wrote, "the country would have been in a terrible condition at the present moment." Perhaps the most striking reaction was a feeling of relief. "The country can breathe again," commented one editor. When the voters of Kansas Territory went to the polls in August and by a resounding margin rejected the land grant, the issue which had been agitating the nation since 1854 did indeed seem buried.[47]

Douglas' role in the Lecompton struggle was undoubtedly the most significant in his career. A new path was opened from which there would be no turning back. Both Democrats and Republicans were forced to reassess Douglas' position in national politics. Connecticut Senator James Dixon reflected the views of many Republicans when he wrote of Douglas, "My admiration for him increases with every exhibition he makes of his mental & moral strength. He was born to be the leader in some great enterprise . . . we are ready to sustain him for the Presidency in 1860—if circumstances shall then be favorable." Southerners who had supported him in years past regarded his course with sorrow and apprehension. If Douglas should ever be President, wrote Georgia's former governor Herschel V. Johnson, "it will be in despite of the South." The Lecompton crisis left a legacy of party disruption and sectional hatred from which the nation would not recover, and Douglas was the chief inheritor of that legacy.[48]

# XXIV
## "I shall have my hands full"
## 1858

i

While the drama of the Lecompton struggle monopolized public attention, and made outrageous demands on Douglas' time and energy, the Illinois Senator found himself embroiled in other, more peripheral controversies. His participation in the nation's business had never been narrowly restricted, and he made no exception during the vexatious Lecompton session. Although the battle against Lecompton sapped his strength, Douglas fought on other fronts as well. His concern lest the emphasis on Kansas and the slavery question result in the neglect of other territories and his eagerness to advance American interests abroad drew him into sharp exchanges with his Senate colleagues.

Three territories, including Kansas, drafted state constitutions in 1857. While Kansas dominated congressional deliberation, Minnesota and Oregon patiently awaited their turns, their appeals for admission as states entangled at times with the Lecompton issue. Southerners frequently demanded the approval of Kansas' slave state constitution as the price for their support of the two free states, and for a time Minnesota was linked with Kansas as part of a compromise bill. Douglas sought to gain consideration for Minnesota and Oregon on their own merits, but it was not until after the Senate had approved the Lecompton bill that he was able to bring them up for discussion. Emotions aroused by the Kansas issue carried over, and Lecomptonites were little inclined to gratify Douglas. Prolonged debate over details in Douglas' Minnesota bill and repeated postponements finally pushed him to the end of his patience. Why, he asked, was Kansas, with a smaller population, forced through the Senate in night sessions, while Minnesota's admission was subjected to constant delays? The urgency with which he pressed the Minnesota legislation was resented by Lecomptonites. One of them, Graham Fitch of Indiana, engaged in a shouting match with Douglas in which the two Senators bitterly accused one another of untruths. Tempers subsided, and on April 7 the Senate finally approved the bill by a large margin that contradicted the heated debate. The House concurred soon afterward, and Minnesota entered the Union as the thirty-second state.[1]

Douglas' efforts to secure Oregon's statehood proved even more complicated and frustrating. In the absence of an enabling act, Oregonians had taken the initiative. They ratified a state constitution late in 1857 and were preparing for their first state election, confident that Congress would act speedily and favorably on their admission. At the time they ratified their constitution, Oregon's voters also prohibited slavery (which aroused southern opposition) and overwhelmingly endorsed Negro exclusion (which provoked some northern opposition). Anticipating a struggle, territorial delegate Joseph Lane withheld the Oregon bill until both Kansas and Minnesota were disposed of. Again Douglas pressed his colleagues for quick action, noting the merits of Oregon's case in comparison with that of Kansas. The population was larger than that of Kansas; "it is a quiet, stable community . . . there has been no rebellion, no turmoil, no controversy there." He exposed the inconsistency of some northern Senators who had voted for Kansas' admission under the Topeka constitution (which had a similar provision excluding Negroes) and of southerners who had urged the approval of Lecompton. Their opposition, obviously based on narrowly sectional grounds, was "unjust, unfair, towards the people of Oregon." "Are we to be told," he asked, "that rebellion is to be rewarded; that civil war is a passport to speedy admission?" Attempts to postpone action until the next session were defeated, and on May 18 the Senate passed the Oregon bill. Action, however, came too late for consideration in the House, so Oregon, to Douglas' disappointment, remained a territory.[2]

The admission of new states was only a part of the western program which Douglas continued to urge on his colleagues. Responding to appeals from the frontier, he also sought the organization of two additional territories: Arizona, to be erected in the Gadsden Purchase area, and Dacotah, in the northern plains. That he had learned from the Lecompton debate was evident, for in both bills he provided for the submission of their state constitutions to a full vote of the people when the time came for their admission to the Union. Congress adjourned before any action could be taken on the new territories. Douglas also renewed his efforts to authorize the extension of a telegraph line to the Pacific, and in mid-April he delivered a long speech on behalf of the Pacific railroad. Denouncing the sectional arguments with which the railroad measure had become embroiled, he expressed his indignation that the bill should be lost merely because of disagreement over the route. It was, he declared, the greatest practical measure pending before the country. "The interests of commerce, the great interests of travel and communication —those still greater interests that bind the Union together, and are to make and preserve the continent as one and indivisible—all demand that this road shall be commenced, prosecuted, and completed at the earliest practicable moment." Finally, Douglas threw his support behind a measure that would provide land grants to the states for the establishment of agricultural colleges.[3]

Late in 1857, the notorious filibuster William Walker, expelled from Nicaragua earlier in the year, was arrested and charged with violation of American neutrality laws as he was about to lead another expedition into that Central American country. The arrest, carried out by Commodore Hiram Paulding in a Nicaraguan port, created another sectional issue and provided Douglas with another opportunity to voice his sentiments concerning American foreign policy. Southerners, faced with rising opposition on the Lecompton question, denounced the arrest, while the action was generally commended in the north. Buchanan censured Paulding, but at the same time he expressed his hostility to filibustering. Douglas, in the midst of his warfare against the administration and the south, suddenly found himself allied with his adversaries, a circumstance that aroused suspicion regarding the purity of his motives. The issue arose, he told the Senate early in January, "from the fact that in our anxiety to preserve the good opinion of other nations, by putting a stop to filibustering, we have gone beyond the authority of law." Such expeditions, he declared, should be stopped before they leave the United States; once they have escaped, "we are not responsible for them." Walker's arrest, in a foreign port, was "an act in violation of the law of nations and unauthorized by our own neutrality laws."

Douglas seized the occasion to detail his views on filibustering. "I have no fancy for this system of filibustering," he explained. "I believe its tendency is to defeat the very object they have in view, to wit, the extension of the area of freedom and the American flag. . . . I would like to see the boundaries of this Republic extended gradually and steadily, as fast as we can Americanize the countries we acquire and make their inhabitants loyal American citizens when we get them." The interests of commerce and of civilization demanded such expansion, but, he maintained, it should be carried out in a regular and lawful fashion. The Lecompton issue could not be kept out of the discussion. Douglas' stand against Walker's arrest, it was charged, was nothing more than an attempt to set himself right with the south, that the "fuss about Gen. Walker" had been raised "to cover up Douglas's sins on the Kansas question." Douglas ignored the charges, noting with satisfaction that southerners, too, opposed Buchanan's condemnation of filibustering. If he was to be read out of the party for differing with the President he would have plenty of company.[4]

Douglas' concern for a vigorous foreign policy had never flagged and would not now be muted by his deep involvement in the Lecompton crisis. He had been appointed to the Senate Committee on Foreign Relations once again, and as a member of that committee he spoke out freely and boldly. In the spring of the year alarming news arrived from the Gulf of Mexico, where British naval units had intercepted and searched American coastwise vessels suspected of being slavers. In several instances, American ships, refusing to show their colors, had been fired upon. Indignation swept the country, and it reached the Senate floor late in May. Douglas introduced a bill "to restrain and redress outrages upon the flag," authorizing the President to employ force to discourage future incidents. The bill won press support, and, when Douglas suggested further that letters of reprisal be placed in the hands of the Navy, he was widely praised. The Senate, however, was unwilling to act hastily. Secretary of State Cass lodged a formal protest with the British, and the foreign relations committee resolved that American vessels in time of peace were immune from visitation by ships of another power. Douglas' bellicosity toward Great Britain returned as he protested against these halfway measures. The time for discussion had passed; the time for action was at hand. England had been warned repeatedly against such depredations, with little effect. Another resolution would be meaningless. Douglas proposed that one of the offending British ships be captured and brought to an American port; "that will be a good time to negotiate."

Douglas had lost none of his fire. If England should not agree to respect American rights on the seas, he shouted, "then we will appeal to the God of battles." If war should be forced upon the United States, England's fate would be sealed. "I believe the moment England declares war against the United States, the prestige of her power is gone. . . . It will sink her to a second-rate Power upon the face of the globe, and leave us without a rival who can dispute our supremacy." The incident, however, closed without the resort to force which Douglas seemed so eager to adopt. The British government, replying to Cass' protests, disavowed the actions in the Gulf of Mexico and promised to halt the search of United States vessels.[5]

All in all, the session had been one of the most significant in Douglas' career, busy, fatiguing, and frustrating. He had been forced as never before to confront the full meaning of the principles on which he stood. His leadership in the party had been placed in jeopardy, but he now appeared before the people as a champion of principle, a role to which he was not altogether accustomed. Douglas found this altered image appealing, and in this sense the Lecompton crisis was a turning point in his career. He became more openly and unabashedly a defender of principle, struggling for popular sovereignty and the Union against increasingly vicious attacks from all sides. Less inclined to compromise than before, he was a man under fire, and the struggle brought out his best qualities. Douglas also became aware that political controversy was entering a new stage, one in which men would divide over essentially abstract issues. It was a development which he regarded as dangerous to the unity of the Republic. The practical needs of the nation would be submerged in abstractions which, he thought, could only result in bitter and irrepressible divisions.

Hanging over his activities in the winter of 1857-58, whether dealing with Lecompton, the territories, filibusters, or relations with Great Britain, was the struggle for re-election to the Senate which Douglas faced in Illinois. The campaign was very much on his mind, for on the day Congress adjourned he delivered what must have sounded to many like a valedictory address. Reviewing the political situation in Illinois and the opposition he faced there from both Republicans and administration Democrats, Douglas alluded to his part in the Lecompton controversy. "If this is to be the issue—if the great principle of self-government upon which all our institutions rest, the right of the people to form the constitution under which they are to live, and ratify or reject the same at a fair election, is to be the issue, my position is taken, and I am ready to maintain it." [6]

ii

Congress did not adjourn until mid-June of 1858, six weeks after the passage of the English bill had laid the Kansas struggle to rest. Douglas yearned for a respite. Concern for Adele's health, and his own illness, had sapped his strength, and the fight against Lecompton had brought him to the verge of exhaustion. Still, the pace of Douglas' social life had continued undiminished during the spring. Entertainments were held in his spacious new home, and Adele, in spite of her earlier confinement, reigned supreme, eliciting superlatives from social reporters and inspiring poems dedicated to her beauty. Not unmindful of her role, she faithfully attended the Senate when Douglas spoke, creating nearly as much stir in the galleries as did Douglas' words, and when Ohio's Congressman S. S. Cox, following Douglas' cue in opposition to the English bill in the House, was severely criticized for his stand, Adele made a point of visiting Cox's wife. Visits to New York City to purchase furnishings for his house and to enable Adele to shop for clothes provided Douglas with brief rest from the strain of debate, although such trips usually had political as well as domestic purposes. Photographers and engravers were busy on new portraits demanded by admiring supporters, and in Illinois Douglas' kinsman Leonard Volk prepared to execute a full-length statue of the Little Giant.[7]

Before his departure from Washington, Douglas had much to do in preparation for the senatorial campaign. Many of his friends in Illinois strongly urged that Adele accompany him. The presence of such "a sweet & beautiful woman" at his side, one of them wrote, would encourage his supporters and restrain his enemies. Arrangements were made for a full verbatim reporting of the speeches Douglas would deliver. James B. Sheridan, a reporter for Forney's Philadelphia newspaper and an expert in "phonography" (shorthand), left for Chicago ahead of Douglas to consult with Sheahan. Douglas' father-in-law, J. Madison Cutts, aided by Joseph Chandler, a former magazine editor and Whig Congressman from Pennsylvania, and Daniel McCook, who had held a subordinate clerical position in the House of Representatives, remained behind in Washington to handle the Senator's correspondence and to report on developments in the capital. Documents were ordered, notably the minority report on Lecompton and Douglas' several Senate speeches dealing with Kansas, and Cutts was instructed "to comply, in one shape or another, with every request from . . . Illinois constituents & friends—

and otherwise to make throughout the State as broad a distribution as possible." [8]

One of Douglas' concerns was his ever-present need for money. The demands of his creditors, more acute now because of the recent panic, and the expenses incurred in the construction of his Washington house left him hard-pressed. Notes that fell due had to be refinanced and bills for the improvement of the lots which he owned with Rice and Breckinridge taxed his resources. Friendly newspaper editors continued to appeal for funds, including John Heiss of the new Washington *States,* and Douglas dared not dismiss their requests too lightly. Most of all, he required considerable sums to finance his campaign for re-election. Some of his Illinois land was sold, but the proceeds fell short of meeting his needs.[9]

Douglas had been in negotiation with banks and financial houses since early in the spring. His role in the Lecompton struggle complicated matters, as pro-Buchanan bankers, for example, W. W. Corcoran, turned a deaf ear to his appeals. Additional efforts were required to prevent some of his notes from falling into Republican, and hence unsympathetic, hands. In the emergency, Douglas and his agents turned to New York. Cornelius Vanderbilt was approached, apparently without success; then August Belmont, one of New York's wealthiest financiers and a personal friend of Douglas', and Mayor Fernando Wood came to his rescue. Loans were arranged, but the details were not finally settled until months later. In the process, Douglas' already mortgaged Chicago property carried an even heavier burden of debt. At the same time, perhaps to forestall possible claims from his creditors, he transferred the title of his lands in Rockingham County, North Carolina, to Mrs. Martin, the mother of his late wife. Douglas' financial transactions became public knowledge, and the New York *Herald* estimated the extent of his "pecuniary raid on Wall Street" at $100,000.[10]

Douglas and his wife left for Illinois soon after the adjournment of Congress, but their trip was unhurried. After a number of days in New York City, during which time Adele attended the opera, they relaxed briefly at the home of his mother near Clifton Springs. The trip westward was attended by enthusiastic crowds. At several stops Douglas addressed large demonstrations in his honor, especially in Ohio, where he sought to strengthen his supporters in their contest with the administration wing of the party.[11]

Douglas appeared vigorous and confident, but his confidence masked a deep concern for the condition of the Illinois Democratic party. While his mail during the preceding months had brought him gratifying promises of support from party members, his course on the Lecompton issue had not left the party unscathed. Events during the spring severely shook his expectation that Illinois Democrats would unite behind him with a single voice. Party discontents from earlier years had never been fully quelled, and resentments against Douglas' control over the party still smoldered. His role in the distribution of patronage provoked additional hostility. Hard-liners resented the appointment of former free-soilers to office; those who were removed tended to blame Douglas. In Chicago, where party division was deepest and most worrisome, the feud between Cook and Sheahan had intensified when Cook regained his appointment to the post office. Danger signals appeared in other parts of the state. Lanphier's influence came under fire, and his position as Douglas' spokesman was challenged. Old-timers like John Reynolds, whose popularity in southern Illinois remained high, still regarded Douglas as an upstart, and they quite properly questioned the Senator's sincerity as a spokesman for the interests of the slave south. Sidney Breese, whose rivalry with Douglas was of long standing, was quick to bend dissatisfaction with Douglas to his own ambitions. As signs of discontent appeared, some of Douglas' friends tried to head them off. Former Congressman O. B. Ficklin insisted that "measures & not men are to be looked to if we would be a consistent party standing on right principles." Douglas, he urged, should be re-elected to the Senate and then presented for the presidency in 1860, "not because he is immaculate or without fault, but because the times & circumstances indicate him at present." [12]

That trouble lay ahead became obvious early in the Lecompton struggle. Soon after his opening attack against the President's policy, a large group of Democrats gathered in Chicago. Instead of giving Douglas' position the expected enthusiastic endorsement, the meeting passed resolutions praising both Buchanan and Douglas, an action that reminded one Lecomptonite of a circus performer trying to ride two horses at the same time. Chairing the meeting was Dr. Daniel Brainard, recently removed from his post as surgeon of the United States Marine Hospital. To the resolutions committee, Brainard appointed three other victims of Buchanan's patronage policy: Thomas Hoyne, former United States Attorney, Isaac Cook, former Postmaster, and Iram Nye, former United States Marshal. All held Douglas responsible for their removals and all soon became open supporters of the President, a nucleus for an administration party in Illinois that could effectively challenge Douglas' leadership. The *Chicago Democrat* concluded that the lukewarm resolutions were a "great rebuke" to Douglas, wishful thinking perhaps, but the editor was correct in his belief that the meeting augured ill for Douglas' plans.[13]

As the fight over Lecompton in Congress warmed, the tactics of the anti-Douglas, pro-administration Democrats became bolder. Joining their ranks was the notorious and erratic Dr. Charles Leib, engaged until recently in antislavery work in Kansas. Apparently experiencing a change of heart, Leib assumed an important role in the effort to build a Buchanan party in opposition to Douglas. Appointed a mail agent for the state, he traveled about Illinois, questioning federal officeholders about their Lecompton views and threatening removal if they sided with Douglas.[14] While Leib's threats may at first have been unauthorized, the strategy gained momentum. Demands for the wholesale removal of Douglas partisans reached Washington, and they soon had their effect. Isaac Cook's reinstatement in the Chicago Post Office, probably the most significant move toward strengthening the President's backers, marked Buchanan's recognition that his appointive power could be used effectively against Douglas. Cook became the leader of the Lecompton movement in Illinois, organizing anti-Douglas sentiment and freely offering his advice to Buchanan. That the President did not remove as many office-holders as Cook demanded reflected Buchanan's concern lest the strategy backfire, but enough Douglas supporters lost their positions to cause consternation among his followers. Government printing contracts became additional levers for the administration. Both the *Chicago Times* and the *Illinois State Register* lost government printing. There were remarkable conversions among some editors who hoped to receive the contracts.[15]

Douglas received frantic appeals for help in combating the opposition. Most of all, he was asked to clarify the impact of his anti-Lecompton stand on party alignments. "Are we to expect re-union of the Lecompton & anti Lecompton forces . . . or the organization of a new party, or the existence of three parties?" asked one of Douglas' correspondents. The Lecompton faction was increasing, Douglas was informed, not only from the patronage but also because of the belief that anti-Lecompton Democrats would leave the party to join with the Republicans. The solution was the formation of an anti-administration, anti-Lecompton party that would combine the leadership of Douglas, Seward, and Crittenden, for such an organization would be "overwhelming in Illinois." On the contrary, wrote another friend, "the only hope of beating you in Illinois is based on the expectation of making the Democracy there believe that you have deserted them." He urged Douglas to prove "that you are just as firm in the Democratic cause as ever, and under no possible contingencies can be made to quit your party associations and faith." [16]

The depth of the party split was exposed by the preparations for the Democratic state convention, scheduled to meet in Springfield in late April to nominate candidates for the only two state offices to be filled in 1858. Both sides struggled to control the local meetings which would name delegates to the convention, but, in spite of the fears of some Douglasites lest "traitors" find their way into the party councils, the Douglas wing easily triumphed. Undaunted, the Buchaneers (as they were soon called) determined to form a separate organization if they could not control the existing one. The Lecompton men, Douglas was warned, would break up the party if this were necessary to secure his defeat. Would not such a disruption be widely interpreted in the nation as rendering his re-election improbable? Isaac Cook laid his plans carefully. "If you cannot come to the convention as a *delegate,* which I trust you will be able to," he wrote to one postmaster, "*you* must at all events make your appearance there, as we intend there to organize the national democratic party, and it behooves the friends of the administration to be on hand with their armor on." If beaten in the choice of delegates, Cook advised the formation of contesting delegations. The inducement of presidential favor was held out. Writing to a newspaper editor, Cook added, "I . . . shall expect much to see you at Springfield, Ill. on the 21st, *when more will be done in relation to Postmasters and offices than at any other time, as I shall have an opportunity of then seeing most of the friends of the Administration who are applying for positions.*" Cook urged his correspondents to look not only to the interests of the party, but also to their "pecuniary profit and advantage." [17] For some Democrats, such arguments were difficult to resist.

The state convention, to no one's surprise, was organized by the Douglas Democrats. The Buchaneers, hopelessly outnumbered, declined to present their credentials to the convention, so the expected fight over the seating of contesting delegations did not materialize. Instead, they met separately near by, declared themselves to be the convention of the National Democratic party, listened to several caustic attacks on Douglas, and then adjourned to meet again in June. One delegate announced his preference in the coming election for Lincoln rather than for one "assuming the garb of a friend, while he deserts and curses the principles he has sworn to sustain."

Having taken the step to form a separate party organization, Cook and his associates needed time to build support from the party's rank and file as well as to secure the endorsement of the administration. Following the meeting, the National Democrats issued an address to the people of Illinois which revealed the true extent of their opposition to Douglas. Reviewing the Kansas struggle in detail, they concluded that Douglas' position on the Lecompton constitution violated the terms of his own Kansas-Nebraska Act. "Fealty to Senator Douglas," they declared, "is treason to the Democracy." Democrats must now choose "between our long cherished principles and his personal success." [18]

Lanphier feared that the machinations of the Lecomptonites would leave the majority of the party "too bitter for judicious or prudent action" in the convention. Several impassioned speeches were delivered, notably by Usher F. Linder and Richard T. Merrick—each "a rich, fervent & enthusiastic panegyric of Douglas"—but the resolutions were of a milder character. Douglas probably had a hand in their preparation. Affirming devotion to the Cincinnati platform and endorsing Douglas' Lecompton stand, the convention, in a conciliatory gesture, promised support to the President in all things that conformed to true Democratic principles (an implication, of course, that Buchanan had departed from party principles in his support of Lecompton). Significantly, a resolution denouncing Buchanan's removals from office was tabled. Nominations for state treasurer and superintendent of public instruction were made, and the delegates returned to their homes to prepare for the coming campaign. The *State Journal* reported that Douglas had sent several "vigorously written" resolutions, but that they were "cautiously and carefully hidden away in the breeches pockets of the committee and never saw the light." It is more likely that Douglas condoned the milder resolutions in an effort to minimize the differences between the two wings of the party, although he may have been disappointed that his own endorsement had not been more emphatic. [19]

The division in the Illinois party placed President Buchanan in a dilemma. The passage of the English bill and the settlement of the Lecompton controversy seemed to render the action of the National Democrats unnecessary. While Douglas had voted against the English bill, he had accepted its passage as final. The Buchaneers were clearly a small

minority, and even within their ranks there was some dissension, especially over the tactics of such men as Cook and Leib. To encourage a
party split in Illinois would run counter to the President's effort to maintain Democratic unity. Demands continued for the removal of Douglas
men from Illinois offices, and in some instances Buchanan obliged, but
his actions were neither fast enough nor sufficiently emphatic to persuade the leaders that their movement had full presidential support.
While he bowed to some of the pressure for removals, Buchanan balanced them with the appointment of several Douglas partisans, to the
extreme discomfiture of Cook and his followers. In late May, Sheahan,
through the editorial columns of the *Chicago Times,* directed a number
of questions to the Washington *Union* concerning Cook's boasts that the
administration desired Douglas' defeat even if it meant a Republican
victory and his threats that all officeholders must work for Douglas' defeat upon pain of removal. Obviously embarrassed, the *Union* simply
called upon all Democrats to unite against the common enemy. Although the editor made it clear that he could not speak for the administration, the statement was interpreted in Illinois as disapproval of the
National Democratic movement.[20]

Rumors of a reconciliation between Douglas and Buchanan began to
circulate. "It is understood that the administration will make no more
removals," reported Congressman Harris early in May. Republicans
viewed the possibility of a reconciliation with concern. "There seems to
be a sort of truce between the President and Douglas just now," reported
Trumbull from Washington. "The antagonisms in Illinois may have its
influence on Douglas," observed New York Republican Preston King. "I
hope he will be proved man enough to rise above them." The reports
caused consternation among some of Douglas' followers. Any reconciliation would place Douglas in the position "of begging pardon, and asking
to be restored to his original position of an humble follower of Buchanan." The most outspoken advice came from Linder, who had played a
leading role in the April convention. "You have passed the Rubicon
Douglas," he wrote in mid-May, "and you must march to Rome—you
cannot return to the administration without . . . political infamy." The
opportunity offered by the crisis must not be lost. "If we cannot reorganize the party, & thoroughly reform its ranks we are beat so bad that
burnt brandy will not save us. . . . Any reconciliation between you
and the Administration party *soils* you." [21]

The peace feelers reported by Harris were apparently premature, for he later informed Lanphier that "a general sweeping off is determined on, & Leib, Carpenter, Cook & Co are to be the dominant masters of Illinois." If the administration had cooled in its attitude toward a reconciliation, it may have been due to charges made by a minor Treasury official in St. Louis that Douglas contemplated joining the Republicans. Writing to Cobb, Isaac H. Sturgeon charged that Douglas, in an interview with Frank Blair, had revealed his intention "to be with the Black-Republicans in 1860." Sturgeon claimed that a friend had seen a letter, written by Blair to St. Louis editor B. Gratz Brown, describing the interview. An ardent supporter of the movement in Illinois to repudiate Douglas' leadership, Sturgeon later claimed to have evidence that Douglas favored emancipation in Missouri and that Douglas' entire Kansas-Nebraska policy had been to surround the slave states with free states in order to crush the institution of slavery. Douglas and Blair did meet during the Lecompton crisis, following which Blair observed that Douglas had "parted company with the negro Democracy forever," but Blair denied Sturgeon's charges. Sturgeon persisted in his accusations. "I tell you sir as sure as the Lord liveth," he informed Sidney Breese, "Judge Douglas is a traitor to the Democratic party as black as h—l itself or he is a deceiver of the Republicans." [22]

Reconciliation seemed even more remote when the *Union* denounced the "very hostile temper" which still existed among anti-Lecompton men. The editor questioned whether those who persisted in their antagonism toward the administration could be regarded as representing the Democratic party even though they might have a majority in their own locality. This time the National Democrats took heart. Sheahan believed that the *Union's* editorial was aimed at getting up a rival organization in the state that would support Howell Cobb for the next presidential nomination. He urged the great importance of securing a Douglas platform at the 1860 Democratic convention. If the Democrats at Charleston should "exclude your version of popular Sovereignty the Republicans will take it up, & sweep the country." Will there be peace or war? he asked Douglas. "If war I think we should meet it boldly." Cook continued to boast that the administration had given instructions to defeat Douglas for re-election to the Senate. If the administration intends to "make war," Douglas was informed, "it is high time the fact is known." [23]

If "war" against the Douglas Democrats in Illinois had become administration policy it still was not apparent by the time the National Democratic convention met on June 9. Isaac Cook had appealed to the

President for assistance on the ground that "the contest for the next two years with us must be fought and won *now*," but if Buchanan responded at all his response must have fallen short of expectations. The *Union*, in fact, proposed that the convention pass resolutions but make no nominations, suggesting that support of the Douglas nominations might be exchanged for an endorsement of the Buchaneer platform. While uncertainty still shrouded the administration position, there was no mistaking the attitude of the delegates who gathered in Springfield. Forty-nine counties were represented, a sizable increase over their April meeting but still less than half the state. One-third of the delegates, it was said, represented Cook County. In the opening speech, John Dougherty, a Jonesboro newspaper editor, denounced Douglas and predicted that he would be "crushed and ground to powder." Other speakers inveighed with equal eloquence against Douglas' "new abolition proclivities," condemned his association with Republicans, and charged him with selling out the party. Resolutions endorsed Buchanan's stand on Lecompton and attacked Douglas' "ruinous" course. Cook, as chairman of the new state committee, reported encouraging progress in organizing the party throughout the state. The meeting was closed with R. B. Carpenter's hopeful pronouncement that a new epoch had dawned. Dougherty and John Reynolds were nominated for state treasurer and superintendent of public instruction; both men, the *State Register* quickly pointed out, had opposed the Kansas-Nebraska Act in 1854. Dougherty had earlier urged the submission of the Lecompton constitution, but a trip to Washington and the subsequent appointment of his son as United States marshal for southern Illinois brought him to the administration point of view. No formal nomination was made for Douglas' Senate seat, but it was rumored that Sidney Breese would get the nod.[24]

Douglas Democrats were confident that the Republicans could be defeated in the election "even with this güerilla assistance," but the increased strength of the National Democratic movement caused them more anxiety than they admitted. Dougherty informed Republican leaders that his party would run a candidate in every county for every office. Francis J. Grund, administration wirepuller and office-broker, attended the Springfield convention as a Cook County delegate, heightening speculation that Buchanan would soon throw the full weight of his administration behind the effort to defeat Douglas. In Washington, preparations were made to send as many as one million copies of documents representing the administration's position to Illinois voters. Of greatest concern to the leaders of the Douglas party were the multiplying signs that the National Democrats were in close contact with the Republicans, in spite of the Buchaneers' charges that it was Douglas who was cooperating with the enemy.[25]

Less than a week after the Buchaneer's convention, Douglas took notice of the breach in the party in a formal speech before the United States Senate. Only rarely were a Senator's political problems at home brought before the Senate, but Douglas selected this means to present his case against the defectors. Obviously piqued by newspaper reports of the convention, he pointed out that the meeting had "no more authority to assume to be a convention of the Democracy of Illinois than any other equal number of citizens of the State who might get together irregularly." Moreover, the two "nominees" of the convention were not "uniformly consistent Democrats." The movement, Douglas charged, was the work of Dr. Leib, a man of questionable antecedents, a federal officeholder "who pretends that he is carrying out the policy and wishes of the Administration in his efforts to divide and defeat the Democratic party." Leib, he revealed, had been a prominent member of a secret military society in Kansas known as the Danite Society, which was led by the abolitionist James H. Lane. This connection "would naturally stimulate him to do everything in his power to destroy the Democratic party and build up the Republicans." Joined in his conspiracy by a "small squad of selfish and unscrupulous politicians," Leib had entered into an alliance with the Republican party. By concentrating on Leib, Douglas merely singled out the least popular, weakest, and most vulnerable of the Buchaneer leaders. Trumbull quickly denied the existence of any such alliance, but Douglas coolly replied that such a coalition did indeed exist and that he could prove it if pressed. Trumbull said nothing more.

Douglas also hinted that the door was still open for a reconciliation with the administration. In his charges, he carefully absolved the administration of responsibility. He did not believe, he declared, that the National Democratic movement had "any authority from the President, or any members of his Cabinet, to threaten honest Democrats with removal from office in the event they will not abandon their principles and betray their party, or to promise offices to others on condition that they will perform such an act of perfidy." On the other hand, a refusal to disavow those who would use the administration's name to further such nefarious purposes must in itself "be regarded and treated as an approval and indorsement of the act as having been done by authority." Douglas placed the issue squarely before Buchanan. There was yet time for peace, but Douglas made it clear it would have to be on his terms.[26]

Douglas' speech, Trumbull warned Lincoln, indicated the line he would take in the campaign. "He will seek to obtain Republican support by charging that some Republicans for the sake of beating him are in alliance with the Lecompton office holders." Like Trumbull, Republicans in Illinois denied that there was an "alliance" with the Buchanan Democrats. The *Chicago Tribune* went one step further, declaring its preference for the election of Douglas, "with his misty notions about slavery in the free Territories," over "any unqualified African Democrat of the Buchanan school." The *Union* defended Leib, although conceding that his appointment as mail agent may have been ill-advised. The leaders of the revolt against Douglas, however, looked for more than the rather half-hearted support which the *Union* provided. Appeals were again sent to Buchanan for the wholesale removal of Douglas' supporters from office. "How can we show our strength at the polls when such men are in place," asked Carpenter. "Our friends *cannot* allow Douglas to succeed." Two courses of action were open to the Buchaneers, he suggested: "To stand by our colors and our Chief or in case we should not be sustained to unite temporarily with the Republicans to defeat him." The latter course was repugnant, but "thousands of our friends" were prepared to adopt it. "The Democracy do not know that Douglas is out of the party," Carpenter informed the President. "Let it once be understood by the removal from office of Douglas men and we will sweep Egypt and give a good account of ourselves all over the state." [27]

At the moment, however, the administration seemed more interested in the possibility of a reconciliation. Support for Douglas in his quarrel with Illinois' Buchanan Democrats appeared from unexpected sources. The specter of a Republican victory in Illinois overshadowed disagreement in the party ranks. The differences between Douglas and his Democratic opponents, commented one southern newspaper, involved "more passion than principle," and if persisted in they would give Illinois to the Republicans. The Illinois split, if not discouraged by Buchanan, might encourage dissension in other states. Virginia Governor Wise and Secretary of War John Floyd urged a conciliatory policy on the President, while Missouri Senator James S. Green, Douglas' antagonist on the territorial committee, stopped in Illinois on his way home to pledge his support to Douglas in the coming campaign.[28]

Initiative in arranging a truce between Douglas and the administration was seized by James May, a friend of Buchanan and a confidant of government leaders. May approached Douglas at the Washington railway station as the latter was preparing to leave the capital, and thereafter he kept the Senator closely informed of his conversations with Buchanan's supporters. True friends of the Democracy, May urged, should be willing to sacrifice personal pride in the interest of saving the party. "I never did and hope never will advise even infringement of honor," he added, "but do as a friend advise *conciliation* as far as honor will allow and let pride go to h—— where it belongs." In the conversation at the station, Douglas, with a noticeable lack of enthusiasm, authorized May to inform the administration that he would do all in his power "to induce reconcilation and mutual support of the Administration if the leaders of the Administration would support the Nominations." May was disappointed that he had "so *little* to work on," but in the ensuing days he talked with prominent Democrats and reported the substance of his findings to Douglas.

May found enough interest in high places to encourage him in his efforts. Senator Bigler was well disposed, and Floyd promised to take an active part in carrying out the "conciliatory suggestions." Other cabinet members, and the President himself, May was informed, "can be conciliated." "I can safely say to you," May wrote Douglas, "that the *Gate is wide open.*" May's efforts were soon seconded by others. Douglas' old nemesis, George N. Sanders, with California Senator William M. Gwin, interceded with Buchanan and telegraphed that the President was satisfied with the position Douglas would take at home—"adherence to regular democratic nominations every where State and federal . . . Kansas Question left with people of Kansas English Bill rejected Kansas not to come in without representative ratio federal officials of Illinois to abandon their organization." Douglas' father-in-law, managing the Senator's affairs in the capital, lent his support. Sanders, it appears, was up to his old tricks, for Buchanan disavowed the telegram to Douglas as soon as he heard of it.[29]

Douglas, sensing the strength of his position and impressed with his enthusiastic reception as he journeyed west, reacted coolly to the negotiations and refused to go beyond his initial statement to May. In his last dispatch to Douglas, May revealed his embarrassment and humiliation, and he protested Douglas' "masterly inactivity." Nearly every prominent Democrat in Washington would help, he emphasized, "if encouragement is given that you desire conciliation." Douglas was unwilling to provide that encouragement. Any reconciliation, he had implied in his Senate speech, must be on his own terms. The next move must come from Buchanan. An overture to the administration, no matter how small, would cast doubt on the sincerity of his position during the Lecompton struggle and injure his following both within Illinois and across the nation. The challenge to his leadership mounted by the Buchaneers had left him angry and bitter, and he could not, in good conscience, negotiate with those who had assumed such a hostile tone against him. Furthermore, he was confident that he could win in Illinois without administration support; a victory under such circumstances would provide a strong power base from which to launch his own challenge of the party's leadership in 1860. Douglas, whose pragmatism had always dictated party unity above all other considerations, now refused to budge, further indication that the issues of national politics were assuming a new inflexibility.

Douglas' entry into Chicago had all the earmarks of a triumphal procession. A special four-car train met him in Michigan City, Indiana, and the route into Chicago was lined with cheering crowds, eager for a glimpse of the Senator. As the train pulled into the Illinois Central station, artillery boomed a 150-gun salute. Flags flew from the principal buildings and from the masts of ships in the harbor; banners hung from windows and were suspended across the street. Riding in an open carriage, Douglas followed a circuitous route to the Tremont House, where he would stay and from which he would later speak, acknowledging the shouts of the multitude that lined the streets. By early evening, people began to gather around the hotel. Omnibuses and trains arrived from all parts of the city and countryside. Windows and rooftops were jammed, guns continued to boom, and fireworks enlivened the scene.[30]

iii

While Douglas encountered the undisguised antagonism of the administration, he also faced his most serious challenge from the opposition party. Illinois Republicans, interested and even sympathetic bystanders to the Democratic split, had reason for optimism. The election of Lyman Trumbull to the Senate in 1854, the triumph of the Republican state ticket two years later, and the size of the Frémont vote attested to the rapid growth of the party. Abraham Lincoln, passed over for the Senate in 1854, had risen to party leadership and was regarded, by himself and others, as the logical person to challenge Douglas in 1858. The split in the Democratic state convention in April was an encouraging sign, and Lincoln, noting the "high spirits" among Republicans, concluded that "if we do not win, it will be our own fault." [31]

Douglas' course on the Lecompton question, however, while it threw the Democrats into turmoil, had placed Republicans in a difficult situation. His defiance of the administration had been applauded by many influential Republicans, some of whom even nurtured hopes that Douglas might be induced to switch parties. "The unexpected course of Douglas," Trumbull confided to Lincoln early in January, "has taken us all somewhat by surprise." Trumbull worried about the effect Douglas' position would have on Illinois Republicans. "Some of our friends here act like fools in running after & flattering Douglas. He encourages it & invites such men as Wilson, Seward, Burlingame, Parrot &c. to come & confer with him & they seem wonderfully pleased to go." Of utmost concern was the attitude of Horace Greeley, whose newspaper enjoyed a large circulation in the state. Greeley had high praise for Douglas' position on Lecompton. "His course has not been merely right," he argued, "it has been conspicuously, courageously, eminently so." For Illinois Republicans "to make the battle on him" in the election would be to court certain defeat. Greeley suggested instead that they tender their support to Douglas, thus ensuring his re-election to the Senate "with substantial unanimity." Not only did he counsel support to Douglas, he also urged Republicans in the Springfield congressional district to endorse the re-election of Thomas L. Harris. "Of the whole Douglas party, he is the truest and best." The attitude of the New York editor, Douglas was informed, created considerable consternation in the Republican press.[32]

No Republican was more disturbed with Greeley's advice than Abraham Lincoln. As the principal candidate for Douglas' seat, Lincoln had more to lose than anyone else from an alliance between Republicans and Douglas Democrats. "What does the New-York Tribune mean by its constant eulogising, and admiring, and magnifying Douglas?" he asked Trumbull as early as December 1857. "Does it, in this, speak the sentiments of the republicans at Washington?" Later in the spring, Lincoln dejectedly confessed to his law partner, William H. Herndon, that "Greeley is not doing me, an old Republican and a tried anti-slavery man, right." He implied that a trip by Herndon to confer with some of the Republican leaders might be helpful. Herndon took the hint, for he also wished to see Douglas—"I want to see Douglas's face: *I want to look him in the eye.*"

Herndon left for the east in March and called at Douglas' house soon after his arrival in Washington. Douglas was ill and confined to his room, but the two had "a pleasant and interesting interview." Lincoln, Herndon remarked, was not in anyone's way, "not even in yours, Judge Douglas." Calmly puffing his cigar, Douglas replied that neither was he in Lincoln's way, adding that it would not be he who invited conflict. When the conversation ended, Douglas asked Herndon to give Lincoln his regards "and tell him I have crossed the river and burned my boat." Herndon's visit with Greeley was less cordial. In reply to Herndon's questions, Greeley insisted, "Let the future alone; it will all come right. Douglas is a brave man. Forget the past and sustain the righteous." Herndon's only comment, as he reported the conversation to Lincoln, was, "Good God, *righteous,* eh!" Greeley had a different version; he later charged that Herndon had agreed with him and had deplored the "blind perverseness" of Illinois Republicans in opposing Douglas.[33]

Herndon's trip had not been reassuring, and when he returned to Springfield he exploded in a letter to Congressman Elihu Washburne. "Illinois," he contended, "was to be chaffered for, and *huckstered* off without our consent, and against our will. . . . *Illinois is not for Sale.* We here are not willing to be sacrificed for a *fiction*—national maneuvers." John Wentworth, just returned from New York, substantiated Herndon's impression. "I fear, Lincoln," he wrote, "that you are sold for the Senate by men who are drinking the wine of Douglass at Washington." Lincoln was inclined to be more charitable than his informants. While he believed that Greeley would be pleased to see Douglas re-elected, he did not attribute this attitude to a secret bargain between Greeley and Douglas, as so many Republicans were quick to charge. "It is because he thinks Douglas' superior position, reputation, experience, and *ability,* if you please, would more than compensate for his lack of a pure republican position, and therefore, his re-election do the general cause of republicanism, more good, than would the election of any one of our better undistinguished pure republicans." [34]

Herndon, however, believed that the support for Douglas among eastern Republicans was the result of a secret alliance concluded in the fall of 1857. Greeley, Seward, and Thurlow Weed had met with Douglas in Chicago, he charged dramatically, following which Douglas privately announced that he was a Republican. At that meeting, Douglas' opposition to the Lecompton constitution had been mapped, but more importantly, the men had agreed upon a strategy for the 1858 election. Greeley and Seward would support Douglas for re-election to the Senate, while Douglas would support Seward for the presidency in 1860. The arrangement fell through, Herndon added, when "Greeley found out that he could not rule us." Herndon's revelation was hardly news, for months earlier, rumors of such an alliance had circulated and had been denied. Over a year later, both Greeley and Douglas squashed a revival of the story with emphatic denials. A variation on Herndon's charge was offered by Iowa Senator George W. Jones, Buchanan supporter and avowed enemy of Douglas. Jones had reliable information, he informed Breese, "that a Union was effected at the last session of Congress, between Seward, Douglass & Crittenden, by which it was stipulated & agreed that Douglass was to be re-elected Senator . . . by a Union of the *Douglass* democrats with Republicans & Americans, thro' the influence of Seward & Crittenden; that Seward is to be made their candidate for Prest in 1860 & if elected that Mr. Crittenden is to form his Cabinet & that Douglass is to follow for the Presidency in 1864." [35]

While Douglas did not become a Republican as Herndon had predicted, he did expect Republican support in his campaign. Sheahan reported late in May that "we cannot expect a single Republican leader to join us, but may obtain large accessions from the rank & file." Further assurances of support came from some Republicans. Jonathan Blanchard, the antislavery president of Knox College, expressed his satisfaction that Douglas was now on the side of freedom and announced his support, a contrast with his earlier denunciations of the author of the Kansas-Nebraska Act. John M. Palmer conceded that his sympathies were "very strongly" with Douglas, and he declared his willingness to support the Senator, provided that Lincoln could somehow be mollified. (Palmer, however, soon recovered and by September was declaring his undying hostility to the Little Giant.)

The editor of the *Chicago Tribune* feared large-scale defections among Republicans in the northern part of the state, especially if Douglas should assume "steep free-soil ground" in his campaign, and concern was expressed for those old-line Whigs who continued to worry about the radical tendencies of the Republican party. This concern was highlighted when Judge T. Lyle Dickey, a close friend of Lincoln, announced his support for Douglas on the ground that Republicans were too closely allied with abolitionists. The Republican state chairman, Norman Judd, conceded that Greeley's attitude had injured the party, especially in the rural districts, but he saw no immediate cause for alarm. Republicans of Democratic antecedents, like Judd, were apparently standing fast. Some Republicans found it difficult to make a choice, and at least one county convention endorsed Douglas while expressing a preference for Lincoln for Senator.[36]

Republican leaders were keenly aware of their precarious position. Congressman Washburne urged that "the door of our party" be kept wide open so that all who wished could come in. He saw "no policy in abusing the Douglas men now—they are certainly not dangerous to us." A Republican of Whig antecedents, writing to Secretary of State Ozias M. Hatch, went much further. "If we run members for the Legislature pledged against him [Douglas]," he wrote, "we are gone." Douglas deserved Republican support: he rose from a poor boy to the champion of the United States Senate, he braved "the agitated *sea* of public indignation" following the Kansas-Nebraska Act and not only survived but helped to elect a Democratic President. He had denounced the "political rascality" that had been carried on in the name of the Kansas-Nebraska policy, and he was an Illinoisan of whom the people could justly be proud. Although guilty of temporary mischief earlier, Douglas had "done more to confirm, deepen & justify Free Soil principles than any & all other men." Republicans of more radical persuasion, on the other hand, warned against any coalition with the Douglas Democrats; Douglas' friends remained as before, "active and unscrupulous," and Republicans must be on their guard.

Lincoln was more sensitive to the dilemma than most others, probably because he had more at stake. He anxiously insisted that the differences between Douglas and the Republicans had not been diminished. Douglas' position on the Lecompton question was no reason for a re-appraisal of party policy; in voting together against the administration "neither Judge Douglas nor the Republicans, has conceded anything which was ever in dispute between them." The differences remained as sharp as before, the Republicans "insisting that Congress *shall,* and *he* insisting that Congress *shall not,* keep slavery out of the Territories *before & up to the time* they form State constitutions." [37]

The split between the Douglas and administration Democrats in Illinois was seen by the Republicans as an opportunity to offset possible losses. It was to their interest to see that the split was maintained and widened. In spite of all the denials of Douglas' charge that Republicans and administration Democrats had formed an alliance, Republican leaders were engaged in an informal cooperation with the Buchaneers. Trumbull feared that all the "so-called Democrats" would act together in the election, leaving the question of the senatorship to be settled later, and it was to prevent this kind of unity that Republicans worked. Every rumor of a reconciliation between Douglas and Buchanan was received with alarm and spurred them to greater efforts. The *New-York Tribune,* in an item widely copied by Douglas papers, offered proof "that the underhand coalition . . . of republicans with Lecomptonites to make a 'sure thing' of Judge Douglas' defeat, is . . . a veritable thing."

Early in 1858, John Wentworth advocated the separate organization of anti-Douglas Democrats so strongly that Sheahan wondered if he was about to turn the *Democrat* into a Lecompton organ, while Republican state chairman Norman Judd informed Trumbull that Isaac Cook's appointment as Chicago postmaster would be a certain step toward "dissolving Douglasism." He urged Trumbull to support Cook's confirmation, which the Illinois Senator did. The editor of the *State Journal* reported that "we have been encouraging the Buchanan men as much as possible and stimulating them to organize." Buchanan Democrats maintained close contact with Republican leaders, sending them reports of strategy and frequently conferring with them personally. One of the intermediaries between the two groups was the infamous Dr. Leib, whose Kansas antecedents probably made him more palatable to Republicans than others in the administration camp. Leib was in touch with Republicans Hatch and Judd and communicated in writing with Trumbull. "Leib," Trumbull was assured, "is drilling the faithful." In his capacity as mail agent, and with the tacit support of the Republicans, Leib was traveling over the state urging opposition to Douglas.[38]

One means of preventing the Democrats from uniting was to provide public evidence to the charge that Douglas was leaning toward the Republicans. Certain radical Republicans publicly endorsed Douglas, albeit temporarily, and some even made speeches in his behalf. One of these was Mark Delahay, an Illinoisan who had recently returned from Kansas to assist Lincoln in his canvass. In April, Delahay had congratulated Douglas upon the defeat of the Lecompton constitution in the House and offered his services "in doing honor to the champion of the rights of the People." Douglas did not respond, however, and Delahay apparently had a change of heart. In May, he joined Lincoln on the stump but deliberately conveyed the impression that he supported Douglas. "My speech did not please the Republicans," he revealed to Trumbull, " [but] by . . . Lincoln, it was understood what I should say beforehand; my policy is to back up Douglass until after the Buckhanan convention nominate their *state* ticket, then I am for Lincoln."

Herndon, whose father was acting with the National Democrats, had frequent conversations with the Buchaneers. "They make 'no bones' in telling me what they are going to do," he reported to Trumbull. When John Dougherty assured Lincoln that candidates would be run in every county and district, Lincoln replied, "If you do this the thing is settled —the battle is fought." It is fairly certain, however, that Lincoln knew little of the degree of cooperation that existed between the Republicans and the administration Democrats. He emphatically denied the existence of an alliance, unless "being rather pleased to see a division in the ranks of the democracy, and not doing anything to prevent it" could be termed an alliance. But then Herndon confided to Trumbull that Lincoln "does not know the details of how we get along." [39]

As Douglas Democrats sought Republican support and Republicans encouraged the Democratic split, rumors that political deals were being negotiated by the opposing sides became fairly common. Propositions were advanced and soundings were made by individuals who acted without the knowledge or approval of the leaders of either side. In mid-April, Daniel Brainard, whose loyalty to Douglas was by this time highly questionable, approached Charles H. Ray, editor of the *Chicago Tribune,* with the suggestion that Douglas be a candidate for the lower house of Congress from the Chicago district. With Republican support Douglas could be returned to Congress while leaving the way open for Lincoln's election to the Senate. Ray assumed that the suggestion had Douglas' sanction, concluding that Douglas despaired of re-election and was moving into the Republican party. "If he does come," Ray asked, "what are we to do with him?" "Shall we kill him off, and say that that shall be the fate of all Northern Democrats who come out against the Slave Power, or shall we use him to repair the mischief that he has wrought?" The suggestion seemed worthy of consideration if only because it would be a blow to John Wentworth, whom Ray despised. A few weeks later, Simeon Francis, a close friend of Lincoln's, reiterated the proposal in a slightly different form to Douglas himself. Lauding Douglas' position on the Lecompton constitution, he declared that he could not withdraw his support for Lincoln for Senator but did want to do something to help Douglas sustain his position. Inasmuch as Congressman Harris' health was poor, Francis proposed that Douglas be a candidate for Congress from the Springfield district.[40]

A greater flurry was caused in the Republican camp by an overture made by Sheahan in March. Douglas, he reported, was willing to retire from political life for a brief period "and take his chances by and by," conceding the senatorship to the Republicans. In return, the Republicans would not challenge the re-election of the anti-Lecompton Democratic Congressmen from the state, while the Douglasites would offer candidates in the four northern Republican districts but with no hope of success. The purpose was "to break the back of Buchanan in every county in Illinois." A caucus had been held in Washington, Sheahan announced, at which Douglas and his friends agreed "so to shape matters, if possible, with Republican aid, as to return to the next Congress an unbroken phalanx of anti-Lecompton men." Sheahan's plan was presented to Ray, who in turn sent it to secretary of state Hatch; a few days later, Jesse K. Dubois, Republican state auditor, reported its details to Trumbull. Both Ray and Dubois were inclined to take the offer at face value; they were confident that Sheahan spoke for Douglas. But, Ray added, "there is room for mistake after all, and we do not intend to throw up our caps until we see what's what." When apprised of the scheme, Lincoln counseled restraint—"we must never sell old friends to buy old enemies . . . let us all stand firm, making no committals as to strange and new combinations." Dr. Leib learned of the proposal almost immediately and cautioned Dubois and Hatch that they would be fools if they touched Douglas. That Douglas should try, through some such maneuver, to sound out the Republicans during the final stages of the Lecompton battle was entirely possible, but it is extremely doubtful that the details reported by Sheahan were presented with Douglas' approval. Sheahan had proved a somewhat erratic supporter before. It was not the first time that he spoke for Douglas without the latter's authority. Any offer that promised Douglas' retirement from politics should certainly have placed Republicans on their guard.[41]

Maneuvering apparently continued, and talk of deals persisted. "Our politics are getting warm, and Douglas sends out feelers to us to trade," Herndon wrote Theodore Parker in mid-April, "but as yet our men stand firm." While there may have been some wavering among rank-and-file Republicans, the party leaders stiffened in their determination to challenge Douglas' re-election. "One word about political trading," advised Republican Congressman William P. Kellogg, "I abhor it, detest it, and he that relies upon it for success is a trickster in *small* things." "Without offending or abusing unnecessarily the Douglasites," wrote former Democrat Gustave Koerner, "we ought to make no overtures." Lincoln, Koerner continued, "is our man." Washburne urged "that we have nothing to do in our State, but to go right ahead as republicans, putting forward our own men everywhere, and fight the battle on our own platform with energy and determination." [42]

The decision became easier when the Democratic convention met in Springfield in April. By endorsing the Cincinnati platform, the delegates, as Herndon put it, had cut every tie "that drew our good people *Douglaswards.*" Douglas, it was now clear, had no intention of joining with the Republicans. Several Republicans, including Lincoln, Ray, and Judd, attended the convention as observers. At its conclusion, they "went down stairs," where they issued a call for a Republican convention to meet in Springfield in June. "They were all glad that Douglas had called his convention and '*gladder*' that he had the Cincinnati platform made the substratum of his future action." In the ensuing weeks, a large number of county conventions endorsed Lincoln for the Senate, an unprecedented demonstration of unity which the *Chicago Tribune* attributed to a reaction against the "outside intermeddling" of some eastern Republicans. Ohio's Salmon P. Chase accurately summarized the party's position: "That Douglas acted boldly, decidedly, effectively, I agree. That he has acted in consistency with his own principle of majority-sovereignty I also freely admit. For his resistance to the Lecompton bill as a gross violation of his principle, and to the English bill, for the same reason, he has my earnest thanks. I cannot forget, however, that he has steadily avowed his equal readiness to vote for the admission of Kansas as a Slave or a Free State, in accordance with the will of the majority of the voters; that he has constantly declared his acquiescence in the Dred Scott decision . . . and that he indorses and maintains the platform lately adopted in Illinois, which is diametrically opposed to the declaration hitherto made by Republican conventions, State or national." Still, many Republicans thought conciliation the best policy toward Douglas, and as late as May 1 the editor of the *Illinois State Journal* confessed that "I begin to find myself somewhat embarrassed in reference to the treatment I should bestow upon our 'Douglas allies,'—I mean the Anti Lecompton Democrats." [43]

The Republicans met in Springfield on June 16, full of excitement and enthusiasm. Late in the afternoon, after having agreed on a platform of principles and nominated candidates for the state offices, the delegates "greeted with shouts of applause, and unanimously adopted" a resolution declaring that "Abraham Lincoln is the first and only choice of the Republicans of Illinois for the United States Senate, as the successor of Stephen A. Douglas." The nomination, unusual and unprecedented in the politics of the day, served notice that the Illinois party would follow an independent course. Lincoln responded later in the evening with the first statement of the 1858 campaign, his famous House Divided speech.

Lincoln tried to halt whatever influence Douglas might still have had on Republicans. The agitation of the slavery question, he insisted, allowed but two alternative courses of action. " 'A house divided against itself cannot stand,' " he declared. "I believe this government cannot endure, permanently half *slave* and half *free.*" He did not expect the Union to be dissolved, but he did feel that it would become all slave or all free. "Either the *opponents* of slavery, will arrest the further spread of it, and place it where the public mind shall rest in the belief that it is in course of ultimate extinction; or its *advocates* will push it forward, till it shall become alike lawful in *all* the states, *old* as well as *new—North* as well as *South.*" The gulf between Douglas and the Republicans was wide and deep and could not be bridged solely because he had had "a little quarrel with the present head of the dynasty" or because he had "voted with us, on a single point, upon which, he and we, have never differed." If Douglas and the Republicans could come together on principle, Lincoln would offer no obstacle, but, he warned, "he is not *now* with us—he does not *pretend* to be—he does not *promise* to *ever* be." [44]

The convention ended all speculation as to the course Illinois' Republicans would follow. "I want to see 'old gentleman Greely's' notice of our Republican convention," wrote Herndon. "I itch—I burn, to see what he says." Douglas' opportunity to woo Republicans into his camp had been lost. "He has raised our pride of opinion," Herndon continued. "He ought to say to the universal North, and the people thereof— 'Hush!' He should rock us to sleep. . . . He does not do this, but pinches us, and makes us fight back." The issue, commented the *State Register,* "is now plainly and squarely . . . before the people of the state." When informed of Lincoln's nomination, Douglas reportedly told John Forney that "I shall have my hands full. He is the strong man of his party—full of wit, facts, dates—and the best stump speaker, with his droll ways and dry jokes, in the West. He is as honest as he is shrewd, and if I beat him my victory will be hardly won." [45]

iv

Douglas' speech from the balcony of the Tremont House in Chicago on July 9 was his answer to Lincoln's charges and another notice to the Buchanan administration that there could be no reconciliation on any terms but his own. Apologizing for the "desultory manner" in which he spoke, and showing signs of fatigue, Douglas revealed the pattern of argument he would pursue in the campaign.

As expected, he emphasized "that great principle of self-government, to which my life for many years past has been, and in the future will be devoted" which he defined as "the exclusive right of a free people to form and adopt their own fundamental law, and to manage and regulate their own internal affairs and domestic institutions." It was not only the Republican party against which he fought in defense of this principle, but also the members of his own party who sought to force a constitution on the people of Kansas against their will. Douglas' first barbs were hurled at the Lecompton Democrats. He reminded his listeners that the battle against Lecompton had been won in large part because he had been impelled by honor, duty, fidelity, and patriotism to resist "to the utmost of my power the consummation of that fraud," even though the form of that victory failed to receive his endorsement. The English bill was not only unfair and discriminatory between free and slave states; it also was a mockery, for "any election is a fraud upon the right of the people which holds out inducements for affirmative votes, and threatens penalties for negative votes." Douglas' open criticism of the English bill effectively closed the door to reconciliation with the administration.

The defeat of the Lecompton movement was a "great moral victory," a reminder that, for Douglas, popular sovereignty was not only a pragmatic solution to a difficult problem but also now occupied a more lofty plane. He was careful, however, to credit success to "a large number of men of various and different political creeds" and expressed particular satisfaction that many Republicans had "manfully" sustained his principle. When the Crittenden-Montgomery bill, "as perfect an exposition of the doctrine of popular sovereignty as could be carried out by any bill that man ever devised," received support from Republicans, old-line Whigs and Americans, "I was rejoiced within my secret soul," for it meant the final vindication and triumph of popular sovereignty "as a permanent rule of public policy in the organization of territories and the admission of new states." Douglas read into the results of the Lecompton struggle much more than his opponents would concede, and in doing so he blurred his own definition of popular sovereignty. Most significantly, his interpretation left the administration Democrats outside the pale.

Lest his position be misunderstood, Douglas quickly pointed out that popular sovereignty was a two-edged sword. His opposition to the Lecompton constitution had been based solely on its violation "of the fundamental principles of free government" and bore no relation to the slavery issue. Congress had no right to force a slave state upon an unwilling people, but it also had no right to force a free state upon an unwilling people. "I deny their right to force a good thing upon a people who are unwilling to receive it." With Lincoln's recent emphasis on the slavery issue in mind, Douglas emphatically declared, "It is no answer . . . to say that slavery is an evil and hence should not be tolerated. You must allow the people to decide for themselves whether it is a good or an evil."

Douglas paid tribute to Lincoln as a "kind, amiable, and intelligent gentleman, a good citizen and an honorable opponent," but he took strong issue with Lincoln's contention that the nation could not endure half slave and half free, that it must become all one thing or all the other. Lincoln's statement, Douglas maintained, was nothing more than a bold and clear call for "a war of sections, a war of the North against the South, of the free states against the slave states." It argued a uniformity in institutions and local regulations that had never been contemplated by the framers of the government, a uniformity that was not only undesirable but impossible to achieve "in a republic as large as this" short of blotting out state sovereignty and erecting a despotism. "Diversity, dissimilarity, variety in all our local and domestic institutions" was, on the contrary, "the great safeguard of our liberties."

Douglas disputed Lincoln's attitude toward the Dred Scott decision and pointed out that on the question of Negro rights the judicial decision was in accord with his own position. Inasmuch as Lincoln raised the question, Douglas sought to strike a responsive chord in his audience by presenting his own unequivocal position. "I am free to say to you," he declared, "that in my opinion this government of ours is founded on the white basis. It was made by the white man, for the benefit of the white man, to be administered by white men, in such manner as they should

determine." He was, in short, opposed to Negro equality, "political or social, or in any other respect whatever." But he immediately qualified his
assertion by placing it within the context of states' rights and popular
sovereignty. A Negro, an Indian, or any other member of an inferior
race must "be permitted to enjoy, and humanity requires that he should
have all the rights, privileges and immunities which he is capable of exercising consistent with the safety of society." The extent of these rights
can only be determined by the local community. "Illinois has no right to
complain of Maine for conferring the right of negro suffrage, nor has
Maine any right to interfere with, or complain of Illinois because she
has denied negro suffrage." In making these assertions, Douglas appealed
to the prevalent and popular conception of race relations (one which he
shared to the fullest extent) in an effort to dramatize the radical character of Lincoln's arguments. At the same time he deliberately exaggerated
Lincoln's views, for he must have realized that even Lincoln would not
argue full equality for the Negro.

Before concluding his address, Douglas took one more swipe at the
Buchanan Democrats. They had entered into an unholy and unnatural
alliance with Republican leaders to divide the Democratic party and to
elect a Republican Senator, "as much the agents, the tools, the supporters of Mr. Lincoln as if they were avowed Republicans." Having been
defeated inside the party organization, this group of "unscrupulous federal officeholders" had gone outside in order to defeat and divide the
party in concert with the Republicans. They have, therefore, "ceased to
be Democrats."

Like Lincoln in his acceptance speech, Douglas reduced the issue of
the campaign to its simplest elements. "He goes for uniformity in our
domestic institutions, for a war of sections, until one or the other shall
be subdued. I go for the great principle of the Kansas-Nebraska Bill, the
right of the people to decide for themselves." The two opponents differed widely in their conclusions. Neither agreed that the other had correctly defined the issues, and this basic disagreement pervaded their arguments in the months thereafter.[46]

Reaction to Douglas' address followed partisan lines, but among those
most disappointed with his arguments were the spokesmen for the
Buchanan administration. His attack on the English bill was received
with "deep regret" by the Washington *Union,* whose editor suspected
that Douglas was attempting "to carve out of the public a new organization" with himself at its head. Douglas and Lincoln "belong virtually to

the same political party, and the race between them is simply a race between leaders of the same party for its nomination." All hope for a reunion between Douglas and the administration had evaporated.

Lincoln was in the audience when Douglas prepared to speak. As soon as Douglas learned of the fact, he invited his opponent to a seat on the balcony. On the next night, Lincoln delivered his reply to the Senator's attacks, taking the points one by one and subjecting them to his own keen analysis. The campaign had begun in earnest. Interest in its outcome transcended the political boundaries of the state in which it would be fought. Douglas, commented *The New York Times,* "goes into it with a degree of spirit that deserves victory, and in Mr. Lincoln he has a foeman worthy of his steel." The battle would be close, severe, and doubtful, and the *Times* would not predict the result. If Douglas should succeed, however, against the combined opposition of Republicans and administration Democrats, "it will be the most brilliant triumph of his life." Illinois, the *Times* concluded, "is from this time forward, until the Senatorial question shall be decided, the most interesting political battle-ground in the Union." [47]

# XXV
## "Glory to God
and the Sucker Democracy"
## 1858—1859

For Stephen A. Douglas, Illinois in 1858 was not only the battleground for the Union against the sectionalism of the Republican party; it was also a battleground for the "nationality" of the Democratic party, without which the Union could not survive. "The battle of the Union is to be fought in Illinois," reflected the Washington *States*. "In every respect, then, Illinois becomes, as it were, the Union for the time being." All the elements of the larger conflict were present in the contest. The stakes were high, for the nation, for the Democratic party, and for Douglas himself.

In this struggle it was the party that was most important, for the unity and "nationality" of the Democratic party was the key to both the Union and Douglas' own political advancement. The seeds of party disruption had been sown as far back as the mid-1840's, and since that time the party had become increasingly oriented toward the south, through its leadership as well as its policies. The conflict over the Lecompton constitution merely dramatized a trend that had been evident for years, revealing, as no other issue had, the dangers that beset the Democracy. Douglas' mission was to halt the party's drift into a sectional position and to assert, firmly and unequivocally, a national leadership and program—a task to which his energies had, in fact, been devoted for nearly a decade. "The integrity of the democratic party is at stake," declared the *State Register* during the campaign. It was appropriate that the effort be mounted from the west and by a westerner, for, to Douglas, this region was the least sectional and most national in the country. A victory for Douglas in Illinois would be "but a prelude to the reorganization of the Democratic party on the basis of the Cincinnati platform, as construed by that favorite of the Western Democracy." There were personal rewards involved as well, a fact Douglas never forgot. A victory over the combined opposition of the Republicans and Buchanan Democrats "would make him President by the spontaneous and irresistible demands of the masses of the Democracy." [1]

The determination of the administration to prevent such a result stiffened after Douglas' Chicago speech. Assaults against Douglas in the columns of the Washington *Union* increased, as the editors castigated the Senator for his "treachery" to the party. His language at Chicago was branded as "inimical . . . to the democratic party of the Union." As the weeks passed, the attacks became sharper. "The position of Mr. Douglas is one of essential hostility to the democratic party," the paper noted. "We maintain that he is a traitor by action, design and position." His hostility to the Lecompton bill, his praise for the Crittenden-Montgomery amendment, his opposition to the English bill, and his concert with Republicans marked him as a deserter. But Douglas had committed an even greater unforgivable crime, for he had abandoned the Democratic party to embrace the "scarlet woman of abolitionism." Upon the issue between Douglas and Lincoln, the editors confessed to a "serene indifference." [2]

The strictures of the *Union* reflected the attitude of the administration. Indeed, the President himself may have been personally responsible for some of the *Union*'s assaults. "He hates you in the most bitter and unrelenting manner," wrote the editor of the *States* to Douglas. The editors of the *Union* were frequent guests of Buchanan, and reports persisted that the paper's attacks on Douglas were hatched at these meetings. On one occasion, the President composed "a programme for an article for the Union" which would strip Douglas of his "pretension to be the great champion of popular sovereignty." Writing to an Illinois editor-postmaster, Buchanan based his hostility toward Douglas on the latter's attitude toward the English bill. Moreover, he was indignant with Douglas' failure to show a "repentant spirit" in his Chicago address. Attorney General Jeremiah Black summed up the administration's position on the contest between Lincoln and Douglas. Douglas, he contended, seemed more violently and bitterly opposed to the administration than to the Republicans. "Now, what should be the difference to us between such a man and an abolitionist, except such a man, elected by democratic votes, would do more injury to the democratic cause than an abolitionist would have it in his power to do?" [3]

Some of Douglas' friends questioned the wisdom of his effort to keep alive his differences with Buchanan. In the interest of political expediency, he was advised not to antagonize the President or his followers. Those who had supported the Lecompton bill "are your political brothers & comrades—they are composed for the most part of men on whom you must rely for future political elevation." There was no point in reviving a controversy that now lay dead. George Sanders, the quality of whose friendship Douglas might well question, expressed his utter disgust with Douglas' course, in terms reminiscent of 1852. "Why not a word from you of filial praise or of generous explanation of the entangled position of our glorious party? To whom are we to look for the tranquilizing oil upon the stormy waves of the present democratic agitation, if not to one whose name has been voiced so long in every state as the gallant champion of the democracy? . . . Continued harping upon the compromise measures of Fifty and Kansas is monotonous and retrograde. . . . I am tired of the constant prate of our public men about their deeds and political consistency, as if our country were finished and nothing left for us to do." [4]

As the administration's hostility toward Douglas became more intense, the National Democrats in Illinois (now derisively referred to by the Douglas Democracy as Danites) took heart and doubled their efforts to assume control of the party. Taking their cue from the *Union,* the few administration papers in the state, such as the Chicago *Herald* and Dougherty's *Jonesboro Gazette,* stepped up their attacks on Douglas. All portrayed the Senator as the ally of Black Republicans; he was, wrote Dougherty, "slowly sinking into the unfathomable depths of the filthy sea of Abolitionism." Stump speakers carried the same message across the state. "Force out every man that can talk at all," advised one administration supporter. "Hold frequent meetings. . . . Show that we are in *earnest* that we intend to conquer or die—this is the way to win battles." Carpenter canvassed the state, he later confessed, at the request of President Buchanan and upon the promise of a federal appointment. Outside assistance came from John Slidell, who stopped in Illinois after inspecting his property on Lake Superior.[5]

By late summer the campaign of the National Democrats entered a new stage, probably because its leaders thought they detected increasing popular support of their position. The Republican *State Journal,* eager to build up their confidence, declared that the National Democrats had mustered "a great army" that was destined to become *the* Democratic party in Illinois. "The signs all over the State are daily growing more and more adverse to the Douglasites." Conventions were held in most of the congressional districts, and candidates were nominated to challenge both the Douglas Democrats and the Republicans for seats in Congress. One of the most important was the Sixth Congressional District convention in Springfield on September 7. Both Vice President Breckinridge and former New York Senator Daniel S. Dickinson were promised as speakers, but neither made an appearance, although Dickinson sent his greetings. The gathering was the scene of violent attacks against Douglas by John Reynolds, who stated his preference for Lincoln over Douglas; Henry S. Fitch, a federal officeholder in Illinois and son of Indiana's anti-Douglas Senator; and old standbys Cook and Leib.[6]

The final step in the Danite campaign came shortly afterward when Sidney Breese, now a justice of the state supreme court, acceded to the pressure of his friends and announced his candidacy for the Senate, thereby relieving the Danites of the charge that by opposing Douglas they supported Lincoln. "There is no doubt in my mind—nor has there been—but that we can elect you to the U S Senate," exulted James J. Clarkson, although another warned Breese that the race was between Lincoln and Douglas, and a third candidate would fail miserably. Breese's decision came too late for his supporters to organize legislative tickets pledged to his election in all parts of the state, although the effort was made. Isaac Cook sent out word to the faithful that where such tickets were lacking, it was the true policy of the friends of the administration to cast their ballots for the Republican candidates.[7]

The Danites' most effective weapon against Douglas still remained the President's power over appointments and removals, and Buchanan began to wield the axe ruthlessly. Most spectacular was the removal of Douglas' friend and supporter, Austin Brooks, from the Quincy Post Office. Brooks had just been re-appointed to another term a few weeks before in a conciliatory gesture, but while expressing his gratitude to the President, he re-affirmed his loyalty to Douglas. Angered by the tone of Douglas' Chicago speech, Buchanan acted promptly to strip Brooks of his federal office.[8] Demands for the wholesale removal of Douglas partisans were combined with increased pressure on the officeholders to fall into line. John Slidell conferred with the Danite leaders in Chicago, and he reported to Buchanan that "they feel satisfied that if the policy you have indicated, of replacing Douglas office holders by friends of the administration be carried out promptly & effectively they will have it in their power to bring the State into line in '60." "It is the only course," Slidell added, "which will afford us a chance of success." Slidell, Bright, and J. Glancy Jones, Pennsylvanian and Buchanan leader in the House, dispatched confidential letters to Illinois officeholders urging them to do all in their power to ensure Lincoln's success. Attorney General Black followed suit. Local efforts supplemented those of the outsiders. Cook continued to remind all hopeful office-seekers that he had been empowered to dispose of the post offices in the state, and letters were sent to the incumbents to determine the direction of their loyalties. "Are you *for or against* the administration?" one postmaster was asked. "If against it, it is your duty to resign, and if you do not, at an early date you will be invited to do so!" Breese, even before the announcement of his candidacy in September, became an unofficial adviser to the administration on patronage matters in Illinois.⁹

While the National Democrats publicly charged collusion between Douglas and the Republicans, they not only urged support for Lincoln over Douglas, but also received covert aid from the Republican leadership. Iowa Senator George W. Jones, bitter in his denunciation of Douglas ("my connection with him in the Senate & as a member of the Comee on Territories has satisfied me, beyond a peradventure of his inordinate ambition, wrecklessness & treachery"), was convinced that the Republicans would come to Douglas' rescue if his election in the legislature seemed in doubt. Actually, the Republican leaders were anxious to strengthen the administration forces in the state against Douglas. Republicans joined with the Danites in an attempt to organize opposition tickets in some districts. Dr. Leib remained in close touch with Republican strategists, and Carpenter, one of the Danites' most effective orators, received at least some of his campaign instructions from the Republican central committee. "Carpenter will go wherever we want him," reported one Republican. One of the editors of the Republican *Chicago Journal* was contracted to write "Buchaneer, Anti-Douglas editorials" for the National Democratic press, for which he was assured he would receive payment from the Republican organization. The editor of a new Danite paper in Chicago, the *State Democrat,* divulged that Lincoln was to pay him $500, presumably to help finance the venture. Sheahan later charged that Republicans had spent as much as $60,000 in an effort to keep the Danite party on its feet.[10]

The National Democrats, abetted by Buchanan's open hostility toward Douglas and the less obvious assistance of the Republicans, caused Douglas little concern. Breese came into the field too late to pose any real threat, and the failure of the Danites to nominate more than a handful of legislative tickets indicated their lack of popular strength. The tactics of the Danite leaders, moreover, did not meet with the full approval of some administration supporters who, while making no concessions to Douglas, nevertheless supported the nominees of the April Douglas Democratic convention. Cook antagonized some of his followers with his dictatorial methods, while others in the Danite leadership proved difficult for the rank and file to swallow. Slidell reported a wide distrust of Brainard, and he personally found Leib to be disagreeable and indiscreet. The administration seemed sympathetic toward an effort to remove Leib but postponed action when others pointed out the effect it might have on the movement in Illinois.[11]

The more determined the opposition became, the sweeter would be Douglas' victory over it. To defeat both the Republicans and Buchanan would not only be personally satisfying, it would also gain him an advantageous position in the struggle for control of the national party. Douglas was not the only one to recognize this, as he received assurances of support from many elements outside the state. At the same time, Horace Greeley, reflecting substantial eastern Republican sentiment, was unreconciled to Lincoln's nomination and remained cool toward his campaign. In a classic letter to the editor of the *Chicago Tribune,* he lectured Illinois Republicans: "You have taken your own course— don't try to throw the blame on others. You have repelled Douglas, who might have been conciliated, and attached to our side, whatever he may *now* find it necessary to say, or do, and, instead of helping us in other states, you have thrown a load upon us that may probably break us down. You knew what was the almost unanamous desire of the Republicans of other states, and you spurned and insulted them. Now go ahead and fight it through. You are in for it, and it does no good to make up wry faces." Greeley continued to urge Republicans to support the re-election of Douglas Democratic Congressmen Thomas L. Harris and Isaac Morris. His attitude was as much a handicap and embarrassment to Lincoln as it was an asset and a delight to Douglas.[12]

To the annoyance of the administration, Douglas received sympathetic support from a number of southern Democratic leaders who feared not only the election of a Republican to the Senate, but also the impact a contest over Douglas might have on party organization in their own states. The bitter division between Douglas and the south over the Lecompton constitution, some suggested, was in the past and should be forgotten. That difference, wrote one Georgia Congressman, had been over facts, not principles. "Douglas is a true man to his country." James S. Green confided that "there are some things which I must condemn in Douglas, but as long as he defends the South and the Democratic party, and sustains the Constitution, against Black Republicans, I cannot hesitate in my preference for him over the opposition." South Carolina Congressman James L. Orr, Senator Robert Toombs of Georgia, and Mississippi Senator Albert G. Brown all declared their support of Douglas in the campaign. Tennessee's former Whig Senator James C. Jones traveled to Illinois to stump for Douglas among the state's old-line Whig element.[13]

In August, Alexander H. Stephens journeyed to Chicago with his brother Linton, and there were rumors that the trip had political purposes. Actually, the two Georgians went to the city to have their portraits painted by G. P. A. Healy, the noted artist, but while in Illinois they did not hesitate to declare their support for Douglas. "How any Southern man can wish to see his defiant plume go down in the conflict is passing strange to me," wrote Linton. From Virginia, Governor Henry A. Wise sent his endorsement. "Every impulse prompts me to rush to your side." Douglas' position was "a grand one . . . isolated by a tyrannical proscription, which would . . . lop off one of the most vigorous limbs of National Democracy—the limb of glorious Illinois!" Wise's pointed reference to administration policy in Illinois was interpreted as a move to secure the support of Douglas' friends for his own presidential aspirations in 1860.[14]

A number of influential southern newspapers gave Douglas editorial support, including the Richmond *Enquirer* (Wise's organ), New Orleans' *Delta* and *Courier,* the Mobile *Register,* the Memphis *Appeal,* the Augusta *Constitutionalist,* and the Montgomery *Confederation.* Those that did not were sometimes criticized for their stand. "Why don't you make those dam fools at the [Charleston] *Mercury* . . . stop their war on Douglas," protested one correspondent to South Carolina Congressman William Porcher Miles. "He is making now the boldest fight on abolition ever made in this country." The sympathy for Douglas in the south, commented *The New York Times,* might well astound the President and puzzle "superficial observers." It was, the paper speculated, a carefully calculated support, based on the realization that Douglas' course in Congress the previous winter had increased his strength in the free states. His defeat in Illinois would sap this strength and so weaken the northern Democracy as to destroy the party's chances for success in the 1860 election. It was the party's prospects that concerned the south; sympathy for Douglas did not imply an endorsement of his presidential ambitions or, for that matter, of his statements in the campaign.[15]

Members of the administration were perplexed by Douglas' southern support. Secretary of the Treasury Howell Cobb disagreed with Stephens, maintaining that neither the Democratic party nor the south would be served by Douglas' re-election. But while Cobb was protesting, cracks developed within the administration itself. A month before the election, Vice President Breckinridge, long a friend of Douglas, expressed his support for the Little Giant. The Buchaneers had counted heavily on backing from the Vice President, so his announcement was a hard blow to their effort.[16]

While the expressions of southern support heartened Douglas and weakened the Danite appeal, Douglas was more concerned with attracting the old-line Whig and American element to his side. Both candidates realized that the election might depend upon the votes of those who had supported Fillmore in 1856, and both tried to woo this group. Former Whigs, among them T. Lyle Dickey, James W. Singleton, Usher F. Linder, and John T. Stuart, declared for Douglas, and they used their influence to help swing the uncommitted. Of particular satisfaction to Douglas was Stuart's support, not only because Stuart had been a law partner of Lincoln's, but also because he had been Douglas' opponent in the hard-fought congressional race twenty years before. Since early in the spring, the Senator's friends had been at work among the Fillmore men, and by fall their efforts bore fruit. After conferring with Douglas and listening to his plans for securing the American party vote, one prominent American concluded, "I think it will be done as we are all violently opposed to Mr. Lincoln." [17] Douglas' appeal to the Whig-Americans also received a considerable boost from outside the state.

Early in July, Lincoln asked John J. Crittenden to clarify reports that the Kentucky Senator was anxious that Douglas be re-elected. "You have no warmer friends than here in Illinois," Lincoln stated. He was uneasy lest Crittenden's influence be exerted on behalf of his rival.

Rather bluntly, he warned the Kentuckian "that you would better be hands off!" There was enough substance to the report to give Lincoln cause for uneasiness. In the waning days of Congress the month before, Crittenden had urged Trumbull "to have no controversy with Douglas." Not long afterward, he assured Harris that he was prepared to express his views in Douglas' favor "in any mode in which they would be most effective." On the same day that Lincoln wrote Crittenden, Harris urged Douglas to consult with the Kentuckian as soon as possible, predicting that his support would be worth 20,000 votes to the Douglas campaign. Douglas moved quickly. Dickey recalled a conversation with Crittenden in which the latter lauded Douglas' "courage and patriotism" on the Lecompton question, "at the Sacrifice of old party associations [and] in the face of the bristling bayonets of the Republicans and defiance of the power and patronage" of the administration. Dickey wrote to Crittenden and asked him to confirm these sentiments.[18]

Crittenden promptly replied to both Lincoln and Dickey. To Lincoln he declared that Douglas' re-election was necessary "as a rebuke to the Administration, and a vindication of the great cause of popular rights & public justice." While he was not disposed to interfere in the Illinois campaign, he added, he could not forbear expressing his views when asked to do so. In his letter to Dickey, Crittenden confirmed the substance of their earlier conversation and reiterated his high opinion of Douglas, adding that Dickey was free to use the letter in any way he wished. The statement was widely circulated, and with good effect. Lincoln's disappointment was ill-concealed. Although their names lacked the magic which Crittenden's held for Illinoisans, other border state Whig-Americans, notably James Guthrie and Reverdy Johnson, also endorsed Douglas. James B. Clay, the son of Henry Clay, and Beriah Magoffin, soon to be elected governor of Kentucky, offered to speak for Douglas in Illinois.[19]

Douglas also made a strong effort to attract the support of Illinois' foreign-born, especially the Germans, whose voting strength was concentrated in Chicago and in the counties opposite St. Louis. While they had early affiliated with the Democratic party, many Germans, following the lead of such men as Gustave Koerner, had broken with Douglas over the Kansas-Nebraska Act. Attempts were made to win them back for the 1858 election. Richardson had reported that "time is thrown away upon any other Germans except the Catholics," but with the German Catholics there seemed to be some hope, especially if the Know-Nothings became closely tied with the Republicans. Douglas' opposition to the Lecompton constitution brought many Germans back to his side and caused others to question their allegiance to the Republican party. He remained in close touch with some of their spokesmen and met with delegations of Germans following his arrival in Illinois. In August, Douglas received a report "on the German press and German politics" which indicated that "two thirds of the Germans in Illinois are Republicans, but they are wavering and malcontent since your arrival and Mr. Lincolns speeches and the disclosures of his past." [20]

The senatorial campaign was undeniably an event of national significance, and it was Douglas who made it so. Not many people outside Illinois were acquainted with Lincoln, his record, or his position, but there were few who did not know Douglas' name. The impact of the election on party alignment was regarded as crucial. Much of the interest expressed in the campaign from outside Illinois sprang from party considerations. Republicans, anxious to stabilize their party organizations in the northern states, feared that a vigorous opposition to Douglas in Illinois might cast the party in a radical mould. Northern Democrats deplored the administration's assault on Douglas in Illinois and were concerned lest this policy divide the party in their own states. Let the administration continue its attacks on Douglas, predicted one editor, and the fall elections "will be the last gasp of the Northern democracy as an integral portion of the national democratic party." Southerners, aware of the increase in Republican strength in the free states, were not anxious to assist this trend by joining in the outcry against Douglas, even though this meant swallowing for a time Douglas' record. They would rather risk Douglas in the Senate than a Republican; the former, they thought, could at least be brought to heel by the power of a Democratic caucus. Over all loomed the next presidential election. To Douglas, re-election was necessary to restore the party to the viable national force it once was and to capture the party leadership two years hence. To Buchanan and his followers, Douglas was not only a formidable rival, he was a treacherous one, to be stopped at all costs. Southern leaders, aware that no Democrat could be elected without their support, were confident that Douglas' presidential aspirations could be thwarted. Some Democratic leaders saw the dilemma that faced the party. "The separation of Mr. Douglas from the Administration confuses everything," wrote Caleb Cushing. "If he fails, do we not lose the North West? If he succeeds, will he not presume too much?" Whatever the position, it was widely recognized that the result of the Illinois election would sharply clarify the prospects for 1860.[21]

ii

Douglas opened his campaign in Chicago, but it was in central Illinois that the real battle would be fought. "Do not spend much time in the North," where the Republicans had a strong advantage, wrote Harris. "The entire South as well as the Military tract," Douglas was assured, "is regarded by all as safe beyond all question." A *"severe"* canvass against Lincoln was in order, with a concentration on the crucial counties that lay in the center of the state. After remaining in Chicago for a week, he left for the state capital. At his side was Adele, who accompanied him during most of the campaign, adding her grace and beauty to her husband's effort. Everywhere she went she attracted attention, often meeting separately with the ladies (whose influence over their husbands' votes was not overlooked) and captivating the men. Her presence proved a valuable asset, for she won glowing words of praise from those who encountered her. One reporter was convinced that the Republicans regarded Adele's "queenly face and figure" as a "dangerous element," and another noted the contrast between "her youthful, blooming freshness and vivacity" and "her small, dark, sombre husband." [22]

The journey from Chicago to Springfield again assumed the characteristics of a triumphant procession. A special train was provided, colorfully decorated with flags and banners bearing the words "Stephen A. Douglas, the Champion of Popular Sovereignty." In Joliet a twelve-pound cannon, mounted on a flatcar, was added, and as the train moved across the prairie the cannon "belched forth in tones of thunder." No detail had been overlooked by Douglas' campaign managers. Careful preparations were made to greet the Little Giant along the way. Crowds gathered at the small stations, men cheered, ladies waved their handkerchiefs, and bands played. The train halted frequently to enable Douglas to acknowledge the receptions (and to replenish the supply of powder for the cannon). The first major stop was Bloomington, where Douglas made a speech and spent the night. Undaunted by rain showers, several thousand people greeted him at the station and joined the parade to his hotel. That evening, Douglas spoke to "an immense Concourse" from a platform erected in the courthouse square, while rockets and fireworks were discharged overhead. To the delight of the old-line Whigs, he in-

voked the memory of Henry Clay on behalf of popular sovereignty and
the Compromise of 1850 and vividly recalled the scene at the deathbed
of the "Great Compromiser." His words struck a responsive chord, for, as
one member of the audience wrote to Crittenden, "this is the pasture Whigs of Kentucky have always been used to." [23]

It was in Bloomington that Douglas responded to the charges, made
by Lincoln and the Republican press, that the Dred Scott decision had
negated popular sovereignty. Lincoln's fears that the decision would result in the spread of slavery to all the territories were unfounded, he declared, for "slavery will never exist one day, or one hour, in any Territory against the unfriendly legislation of an unfriendly people." Douglas
continued:

> Hence, if the people of a Territory want slavery, they will encour-
> age it by passing affirmatory laws, and the necessary police regula-
> tions, patrol laws and slave code; if they do not want it they will
> withhold that legislation, and by withholding it slavery is as dead
> as if it was prohibited by a constitutional prohibition, especially if,
> in addition, their legislation is unfriendly, as it would be if they
> were opposed to it.

The principle of popular sovereignty, in its practical operation, remained
unaffected no matter how the Dred Scott decision may have settled the
abstract question. Douglas' emphasis on "unfriendly legislation" and the
"police power" was not new. He had expressed the idea as early as 1842
and had used virtually the same language in 1857, when he spoke in
Springfield on the Dred Scott decision. He now used the argument primarily to win over the old-line Whig and German elements in the state.
"The Dred Scott Decision," he had been informed, "is the great bugbear
of the German republican leaders and must be answered on the stump."
Eighty thousand copies of the Bloomington address were printed and
distributed during the campaign.[24]

Elaborate preparations had been made to receive Douglas in Springfield. The Great Western and the Chicago, Alton and St. Louis railroads
ran special excursion trains to bring people in from outlying counties.
Members of the reception committee and other local dignitaries met
Douglas a few miles north, and, in a downpour of rain, they accompanied the Senator the remaining distance to the city. As the train
neared Springfield the cannon was fired at one-minute intervals. Douglas
alighted in a grove where a platform had been erected. The enthusiasm
of the waiting crowd was only slightly marred by the muddy condition

of the grounds and by the collapse of the stand under the weight of the official party. Douglas was introduced by Benjamin S. Edwards, a Republican who had declared for him, who was chairman of the reception committee.

In Springfield Douglas covered virtually the same ground as he had at Chicago and Bloomington, shifting his emphasis slightly to conform to the more conservative character of his audience. He reviewed his course on the Lecompton question, insisting once again that his objections to the Lecompton constitution rested solely on the fact that it was not the will and deed of the people. "I did not object to it upon the ground of the slavery clause contained in it." He brushed aside Lincoln's charge that he was a conspirator on behalf of slavery extension and instead invited close scrutiny of the revolutionary implications of his opponent's House Divided statements. Lincoln was again cast in a radical mould, desiring not only the abolition of slavery, but equality for Negroes. He is "a kind-hearted, amiable, good-natured gentleman . . . a fine lawyer, possesses high ability, and there is no objection to him, except the monstrous revolutionary doctrines with which he is identified and which he conscientiously entertains." [25]

The speeches at Chicago, Bloomington, and Springfield established a pattern for Douglas' later appearances: an emphasis on his course in the Lecompton crisis and an exposition of popular sovereignty as a sacred principle of free government, an attempt to place Lincoln on the defensive by linking him, and the Republicans, with radical and revolutionary doctrines, an explanation of the Dred Scott decision as it related to popular sovereignty, and an attack on the Danites for their efforts to secure his defeat by dividing the Democratic party and combining with the Republicans. He frequently shifted his emphasis to meet the differences in his audiences, directing his appeal principally to the uncommitted segments among the foreign-born, to the old-line Whig-American elements, and to members of his own party. Republicans found little in his speeches to substantiate the reports that Douglas sought to make inroads in their ranks, although some Republicans, attracted by the conservatism of his arguments, did give him support. Douglas acknowledged his Republican backing in the Lecompton fight, but he made it clear that the Republicans had come to him, he had not gone to them. Writing after the Springfield speech, Herndon noted that a few Republicans had "intended to take no sides against him" but that his statements had "roused the old fires and *now* they are his enemies." [26]

Although he maintained a residence in Chicago, Douglas had not actually lived in Illinois since 1843, when he first left the state for Congress, and in the fifteen years of his congressional service he had visited his constituents only between sessions. These were years of remarkable change in Illinois, in population growth, patterns of settlement, and economic development. Even so, Douglas displayed an unusual ability to judge the character of his audiences and to adapt his arguments accordingly. He knew his state, and this knowledge served him well during the campaign.

After conferring with the Democratic Central Committee in Springfield, Douglas issued the first of several schedules of appointments. By election day in November, three and a half months later, he had appeared in over sixty Illinois communities, almost two-thirds of which were in the important central counties. A year later he recalled delivering 130 speeches during the 1858 campaign, but his figure may have been inflated. A *New York Times* correspondent who covered the campaign reported after the election that Douglas delivered 59 set speeches, each of two to three hours' duration, 17 shorter speeches in response to serenades, and 37 speeches in reply to addresses of welcome. All but two of these were delivered in the open air, and seven were made in downpours of rain. Douglas, in the course of almost four months of strenuous campaigning, traveled over 5000 miles by railroad, steamboat, and horse conveyance.[27]

The extent of Douglas' campaign and the ease with which it was conducted was due in large part to the phenomenal railroad construction in the state during the preceding decade. For most of his travels he enjoyed the comfort of a private railroad car, which enabled him not only to rest between speaking engagements, but also to receive local delegations in style. The Republicans complained early of the assistance rendered by the state's railroads to the Democratic candidate, their "anxiety and interest" in his campaign, and their "extraordinary efforts" to swell the size of the demonstrations in his behalf. Special trains were run to many of the localities in which Douglas spoke, food was frequently provided to the excursionists free of charge, and posters and handbills advertising Douglas' appearances were circulated by the railroads. If these "huge corporations are thus going to make electioneering machines of themselves," observed the *State Journal,* "the people want to know it." The railroads were not unaware of the implications the election might have for their continued growth and development. Douglas had proved a good friend be-

fore, and, with his influence and power in both state and nation, they undoubtedly wished to cement their alliance with the Senator. Some of the
railroad officials, however, were also active partisans of the Democratic
party. Virgil Hickox, general agent of the Chicago, Alton and St. Louis
Railroad, was a member of the party's inner councils and would soon be
appointed chairman of the state central committee. George B. McClellan, a
vice president of the Illinois Central Railroad, was a strong supporter of
Douglas and did not hesitate to place the facilities of the railroad at
Douglas' disposal. The services of the railroads, however, were not provided without expense, contrary to Republican charges. Hickox noted
that his railroad "had agreed to perform certain work for a valuable consideration," so it is likely that Douglas had to pay for the use of the private car. Although no accurate figures exist, it was estimated that Douglas spent over $50,000 on his campaign, a large amount for that time,
and some of this probably found its way into the railroad coffers.[28]

Not only did the candidates utilize the opportunities offered by railroad technology, but they also employed the latest techniques in reporting. The campaign was one of the first to be reported in modern fashion,
as correspondents representing out-of-state as well as in-state newspapers
traveled with the candidates. No detail of the campaign was overlooked,
although the accuracy of the reporting frequently left something to be
desired, for the correspondents, like the papers that employed them, were
intensely partisan. Attendance figures fluctuated wildly depending upon
the politics of the paper in which they appeared, and the receptions
given the candidates by their audiences were often misrepresented and
exaggerated. The candidates' statements were usually reported faithfully,
even if quoted out of context at times. To provide accurate transcripts of
the speeches, both Lincoln and Douglas employed stenographers skilled
in "phonography." Two stenographers accompanied Douglas during
most of the campaign. Henry Binmore, a correspondent of the St. Louis
*Republican,* had been assigned by his paper to cover the campaign, but
his reports were so impressive that Sheahan employed him to provide
transcripts of Douglas' speeches and to travel with the Senator as part of
his official party. James B. Sheridan, "one of the most accomplished
phonographers in the United States Senate" and a reporter for John W.
Forney's Philadelphia *Press,* had also been assigned to cover the campaign in an official capacity. Following the election, Douglas retained
both Binmore and Sheridan as private secretaries.[29]

Douglas' talent as a campaigner and forensic speaker was well known.

He possessed what few orators of the day had, "a popular manner, under all circumstances adapting itself exactly to his audience, with just enough egotism to give his harangues the force and piquancy of personal appeal." He alternated between attack and defense, depending upon the character of those who had gathered to listen. In localities that were conceded either to the Democrats or Republicans, where the outcome of the election was in little doubt, he maintained an aggressive posture, bitterly attacking his opponent. In the questionable counties, Douglas concentrated his effort more on the defense of his past actions and record. Speaking usually without notes, his speeches had a spontaneous quality, although in fact they were carefully organized, and he had an "air of self-confidence that does not a little inspire his supporters with hope." He carried with him reference materials of various kinds from which he often read, including a small notebook in which he had pasted excerpts from Lincoln's House Divided speech and other items to which he constantly alluded. His deep voice had an explosive and staccato quality and, at least at the beginning of the campaign, had great carrying power. "Though not a pleasant speaker, his sentences are all compact and strong, his points are all clear, and every word he utters bears upon the doctrine he wishes to establish," wrote one correspondent. "He has no flights of fancy, no splendid passages, no prophetic appeals, no playful turns; he deals only in argument, and addresses only the intellect." One Republican admitted that "at times I was completely carried away with his masterful and fascinating manner." [30]

For many Illinoisans, it was their first glimpse of Douglas. Although he took some pains to disguise his short stature by standing behind a table while he spoke or by insisting that the platform be boarded along the sides, the contrast between Douglas and his lean, lanky opponent was striking. What he lacked in size he made up in energy. Square-shouldered, broad-chested, tossing his large head "with an air of overbearing superiority," Douglas was "the very embodiment of force, combativeness, and staying power." His appearance was commanding, whether bowing and smiling in response to the cheers or shaking his fist in wrath as he nervously paced the platform or graciously receiving the ladies in the many receptions that preceded his speeches. Persuaded that the people wished to see him dressed in a manner befitting a United States Senator, he appeared before his audiences in ruffled shirt, dark blue coat closely buttoned with shiny buttons, light trousers, and well-shined shoes. On his head he wore a wide-brimmed white felt hat.

The campaign was a long and hard one, and the strain soon began to tell on the campaigner. The weather throughout much of the summer was oppressively warm, interspersed with drenching summer showers, but by October blustery winds and cold days became the rule. Between engagements Douglas' railroad car was often filled with boisterous well-wishers whom the Senator entertained at the expense of sleep and relaxation, causing some concern among his aides lest his appearances on the platform be adversely affected by his "amusements." Republican correspondents were quick to note that "bad whisky" would soon take its toll. By the latter weeks of the campaign, Douglas' voice began showing the effects of his incessant speech-making, and he had increasing difficulty in making himself heard. A bronchial infection in late August temporarily slowed his pace. By the end of the campaign, his voice was so broken that only those close to the platform could hear him with ease.[31]

Douglas bore the full brunt of the campaign, and necessarily so, for no one could defend or justify his past actions as well as he. Pressures from the opposition, however, increased, so he felt it necessary to call on some of his friends for help. As the tempo of Republican attacks mounted, the number of Republican speakers in the field increased. In July, Lyman Trumbull, responding to the urgent appeals of the Republican organization, returned to Illinois to take an active part in the campaign against Douglas. Trumbull's entrance into the contest caused grave concern among Douglas' friends, for it was widely conceded that his reputation and experience exceeded that of Lincoln. In some circles, he was regarded as Douglas' real antagonist, and much publicity was given to his charges against the Little Giant. Douglas, urged to meet these new attacks without delay, was forced to alter the pattern of his speeches to take them into account. Richardson, John A. Logan, and even the newspaper correspondent Henry Villard took the stump to assist Douglas. In August, Douglas appealed to former Whig Usher F. Linder to assist him in northern Illinois in a letter that, if authentic, indicated his anxiety. "For God's sake, Linder, come up into the Northern part of the State and help me," he wrote. "Every *dog* in the State is let loose after me—from the bull-dog Trumbull to the smallest canine quadruped that has a kennel in Illinois." Douglas' confidence soon returned. "The Democracy are thoroughly aroused, and well united, and a glorious triumph awaits us as certain as the day of election comes," he assured one supporter. "Yet," he added, "our friends should not be idle but should put forth efforts that will overcome those that are made against us." [32]

A source of great irritation to Douglas early in the campaign was Lincoln's obvious intention to follow him about the state in an attempt to answer Douglas' arguments as soon after they were made as possible. Lincoln was present in the crowd when Douglas opened his campaign in Chicago and answered the Senator with a speech of his own the following day; at Bloomington, he was given a seat on the platform; in Springfield he spoke later the same day. In Springfield, handbills announcing Lincoln's speech were circulated in the crowd that had assembled to hear Douglas. The pattern was repeated in Clinton a few days later, when Lincoln himself told Douglas' audience that he would speak later that evening. The strategy had been planned by the Republican managers, and many of Lincoln's supporters had urged him to follow this course. "It is of great importance," advised one southern Illinoisan, "for you to be with Douglas at each one of his meetings." The tactic, however, aroused resentment among the Democrats. Douglas was urged to enlist the aid of other speakers to follow Lincoln if the latter "continues to hang about the tail-end of your meetings." The *Chicago Times* charged that Lincoln was unable to secure audiences of his own and facetiously suggested that the Republican candidate join one of the circuses then traveling about the state as a sure way of getting good audiences.

Lincoln responded to the Democratic charges by assuring Douglas in late July that "as matters now stand, I shall be at no more of your exclusive meetings." A few days later he wrote a series of letters to Republicans in various parts of the state announcing that he would not be in their towns at the time of Douglas' visits, as previously planned. "Judge Douglas considers my presence at his appointments as an intrusion; and so I have concluded to not be present at them." Lincoln's assurance, however, did not mean that he would follow a completely separate itinerary. When the Republican state committee issued Lincoln's schedule of appointments, it became clear that he would be dogging the Senator's heels, speaking in the same towns a day or two after Douglas' appearances. "My recent experience," Lincoln wrote on September 3, "shows that speaking at the same place the next day after D. is the very thing —it is, in fact, a concluding speech on him." [33]

In the meantime, the Republican organization, sensitive to the Democratic charges and not altogether happy with the defensive posture which Lincoln was assuming, sought ways of seizing the initiative from

Douglas. The suggestion that the two candidates speak together at a number of prearranged points in the state had been made earlier. The Republican managers now insisted that Lincoln challenge his opponent to joint debate, "in order that both speakers may address the people at the same places on the same day." This was "the usual, almost universal western style of conducting a political campaign." Lincoln acquiesced, traveled to Chicago to confer with state chairman Norman Judd, and promptly sent Douglas his challenge. "Will it be agreeable to you," he asked Douglas on July 24, "for you and myself to divide time, and address the same audiences during the present canvass?" Instead of following Douglas as the Senator met his appointments, Lincoln hoped to share the same platform with him.

Douglas hesitated. His first impulse was that he did not wish to get involved in a debate with Lincoln. He was known throughout the country; Lincoln was little known. Lincoln could only gain from a series of debates, while Douglas had little to gain, and possibly much to lose. Douglas had other concerns, which he conveyed in his reply to Lincoln's note. There was the matter of the Danites and the suggestion that Sidney Breese would soon announce his candidacy for the Senate. Reports had reached Douglas that plans were being made for Lincoln and Breese to canvass the state together "with no other purpose than to insure my defeat by dividing the Democratic party for your benefit." If Douglas should accept Lincoln's challenge, he feared that Breese would become a party to it and would insist on speaking from the same platform. His two opponents, working in concert, might be able to take the opening and closing speech in every instance. Douglas had no intention of allowing the Danites so great an opportunity. There were also some practical difficulties. The Democratic State Central Committee had already issued the list of Douglas' appointments, extending to late October, and plans for the meetings were well advanced. Besides, these meetings were intended to be Democratic affairs, with Democratic candidates for Congress and the legislature present to address the people on behalf of their own candidacies. There would be little time or opportunity for other speeches. Douglas was already annoyed with Lincoln for following him about; Lincoln's suggestion that he now share the same platform at each of Douglas' appointments heightened his resentment of the tactics of his Republican opponent.

The *Chicago Tribune,* in noting the challenge that was soon to be made, suggested that Douglas might not accept. He had, after all, refused to debate with Trumbull when the latter was a candidate for the Senate in 1854. If he should decline Lincoln's offer, the paper concluded, Douglas could have "no better reason than cowardice" for doing so. These were strong words and could not easily be ignored. "Douglas possesses one of those spirits," commented one observer, "which delight in storms, and love to battle and brave adverse elements." His political pugnacity soon overcame his doubts and hesitation. In fact, Douglas could not have hesitated long, for he replied to the challenge on the same day that Lincoln wrote him.

While he could not disrupt the plans that were already underway in the many localities on his list of appointments, Douglas found a way of accommodating his Republican opponent. Instead of sharing the platform at all of his scheduled meetings, he suggested that they speak together "at one prominent point in each Congressional district in the state," except the two (Chicago and Springfield) in which they had already delivered major addresses. He proposed that Freeport, Ottawa, Galesburg, Quincy, Alton, Jonesboro, and Charleston be selected as the sites for their discussions. At the same time, Douglas expressed some surprise that Lincoln had waited so long before making his move, especially since the two had seen much of each other during the first weeks of the campaign.[34]

Douglas' reply evoked an angry response from Republicans. "We do not think it argues very well for the courage of the Senator that he evades the challenge in the manner he does," retorted one editor. His effrontery in designating the places "where Mr. Lincoln must meet him, if at all," without consulting the Republican State Committee, surpassed the bounds of courtesy. Douglas should have agreed to discuss the issues with Lincoln "at every county, and in every town of any size or importance," but the seven proposed meetings "will be better than none." If Lincoln was disappointed with Douglas' reply there is no record of it. On July 29, the two candidates met along the road between Monticello and Bement. Lincoln informed Douglas that he had prepared his answer to Douglas' letter and needed only to compare the original with the copy. Rather than halt his procession while Lincoln made the comparison, Douglas suggested that Lincoln continue to Monticello, check his letter and then send it back to Douglas in Bement.

Lincoln accepted Douglas' proposition and left it to the Senator to decide on the details. The seven debates were immediately scheduled, the first, at Ottawa, to be held on August 21 and the last, at Alton, on October 15. Douglas agreed with Lincoln that they should alternate the openings and closings. "I will speak at Ottawa one hour, you can reply occupying an hour and a half and I will then follow for half an hour." The pattern would be reversed at the second debate in Freeport. "We will alternate in like manner at each successive place." The arrangement was agreeable to Lincoln, although he pointed out that Douglas had given himself four openings and closings to Lincoln's three.

The press reacted to the negotiations between Lincoln and Douglas in characteristically partisan fashion. There were "about one hundred points in the State where the candidates . . . ought to have held discussions," declared the *State Journal.* Lincoln had challenged Douglas to hold these hundred discussions, but Douglas had accepted only seven of them, a commentary on the Senator's courage and integrity. Douglas would, no doubt, continue "sneaking about the country by himself, assailing, misrepresenting and villifying the man whom he has so ignominiously refused to meet in open, manly debate, before the whole people." "The idea that a man who has crossed blades in the senate with the strongest intellects of the country . . . dreads encounter with Mr. A. Lincoln," argued the *State Register,* "is an absurdity that can be uttered by his organs only with a ghastly phiz." Standing on the sidelines were the National Democrats, serenely indifferent. Debate between Douglas and "black-republicanism," concluded the Washington *Union,* was the "most unprofitable thing imaginable." [35]

### iii

While the seven joint debates added a new dimension to Douglas' campaign, they elicited few arguments that had not already been expressed or that were not being expressed in his many individual appearances. Lincoln's attacks and charges were more keenly felt and required more immediate response, although there were still some Republicans who felt that Lincoln was not using his opportunity to full advantage. "When you see Abe at Freeport," *Tribune* editor Ray urged Elihu Washburne, "for God's sake tell him to 'Charge Chester! Charge!' Do not let him keep in the defensive. . . . Let us see blood follow every time he closes a sentence." Douglas lost his composure on occasion and sometimes replied to his opponent's charges in language that was less generous than that which he had used at the beginning of the campaign, bearing out Herndon's fear that personalities would creep into the debates. The accusations and denials exchanged by the candidates and their monotonously repetitive arguments became tedious, and one New York editor, far from the scene of excitement, dismissed the whole effort. "From Lincoln to Douglas, and from Douglas to Lincoln, their discussions have degenerated into the merest twaddle upon quibbles, 'forgeries,' falsehoods, and mutual recriminations of the most vulgar sort." [36]

Horace Greeley's *Tribune,* however, was convinced that the debates touched "some of the most vital principles of our political system." To one Illinois Republican, it was "a contest for the advancement of the kingdom of Heaven or the kingdom of Satan—a contest for an advance or a retrograde in civilization." Republicans argued that the principal issue was the extension or restriction of slavery to the territories, while Lincoln on at least one occasion placed "the real issue in this controversy" on a moral level—"the sentiment on the part of one class that looks upon the institution of slavery *as a wrong,* and of another class that *does not* look upon it as a wrong." To the Democrats, the contest was between popular sovereignty and congressional sovereignty, or democracy and "federalism." Douglas denied that moral arguments had any place in the discussion and insisted that he was fighting simply for the great principle of self-government. However lofty their sentiments, Douglas and Lincoln anxiously sought to establish their own political qualifications. The issue basically was that of the consistency and integrity of the two men and the degree to which their ideas, positions, and motives coincided with those of the Illinois electorate. Each defended his record, and each attempted to free himself from stigma and suspicion, Lincoln of association with the abolitionists and Douglas of association with southern slavery expansionists. Little time was devoted to discussions of future policy or to promises of future action except as these could be inferred from their general arguments. [37]

Douglas opened the debates at Ottawa with the announcement that he would discuss the important political topics that agitated the public mind. "I desire," he told his audience, "to address myself to your judgment, your understanding, and your consciences, and not to your passions or your enthusiasm." Having held the confidence of Illinois' citizens during twenty-five years of public service, while being exposed to more assaults and more abuse "than any man living of my age," Douglas was willing to trust their knowledge of his public conduct. Fighting both the Republicans and the National Democrats, he revealed a new inflexibility and a stiffening conviction that he was right. He denounced the sectionalism of his opponents. His political faith, Douglas repeatedly

Galena

★ Freeport

IOWA

Chicago

Turner Jc. ●

● Joliet

Rock
Island

● Geneseo

★ Ottowa

Kankakee

Toulon

● Hennepin

● Henry
● Lacon

Oquawka

★ Galesburg

● Pontiac

Burlington
Monmouth

● Metamora

● Onarga

Peoria ●

● Washington

Pekin ●

● Bloomington

Carthage
Macomb

● Lewistown

● Plymouth

● Havana

● Atlanta

Danville

Augusta ●

Walnut Hill

● Clinton

Urbana

Camp Point

Lincoln

● Monticello

★ Quincy

Beardstown

Springfield

● Decatur

Jacksonville

Pittsfield

● Winchester

Sullivan ●

Paris

Mattoon ●

★ Charleston

Carlinville ●

Gillespie ●

● Hillsboro

Mississippi

River

★ Alton

● Greenville

● Edwardsville

● Highland

M
I
S
S
O
U
R
I

● Belleville

● Centralia

● Waterloo

INDIANA

● Benton

● Chester

## Douglas' Speaking Dates
## in
## 1858 Senatorial Campaign

Douglas spoke in the towns marked ●

The seven debates are marked ★

★ Jonesboro

River

KENTUCKY

● Cairo

Ohio

Adapted from Harry E. Pratt; *The Great Debates* (1956).

maintained, was as broad and as liberal as the Constitution itself and could be proclaimed alike in all portions of the Union. He would not depart from his principles, he insisted, "either to the right or the left to flatter one section or the other," but would attempt to do justice to both north and south. Peace and Union demanded such a course. "By this I do not pretend that I have been, or am any more consistent than any other man," he added, "but I do insist that I have acted honestly and faithfully in my political course." The consequences of his course were well known—northern sentiment had run "in a torrent against me" and southern sentiment had come down "like an avalanche upon me" —but through all, he declared, "I knew I was right—I knew my principles were sound." [38]

Emphasis in the debates was given to popular sovereignty. Douglas spent much time tracing its development as the principal theme of his political career. The Compromise of 1850, the Kansas-Nebraska Act, and his opposition to the Lecompton constitution were stages in a logical and consistent progression, and he defended his role in all three by appealing to the unifying principle of popular sovereignty. Rejecting the Republican argument that Congress had an obligation to prevent the spread of slavery to the territories, he castigated those who would interfere with slavery in the southern states. In answer to one of Lincoln's questions, Douglas emphasized that he would never vote for a federal slave code in the territories, any more than he would support a code of laws against slavery in any territory. He meant, he said, to "knock in the head" the abolition doctrine that "there shall be no more slave states, even if the people want them" and assured his audiences that he had never inquired and never would inquire whether a new state had slavery as one of its institutions as long as the state's constitution was the act and deed of the people and embodied their will.[39]

Republican attacks on the Dred Scott decision elicited a strong defense of the Constitution and of the Supreme Court. "I stand by the Constitution as our fathers made it, by the laws as they are enacted, and by the decisions of the court upon all points within their jurisdiction as they are pronounced by the highest tribunal on earth." But when Lincoln asked him if he would submit to a Supreme Court decision that a state could not exclude slavery within its limits, Douglas scornfully rejected the possibility. Such a decision would be an "act of moral treason" to which no judge could stoop; Lincoln was insulting the bench by suggesting it. Devotion to the Constitution, he added, placed an obligation on every member of Congress to vote for an effective fugitive slave law. Although he supported the current law, he would not hesitate to replace it with more stringent legislation if it should prove ineffective.[40]

These same attacks, however, also forced Douglas to temper his strict constructionist stand by stressing what he called "the practical question" involved in popular sovereignty—"if the people of a territory want slavery they will have it, and if they do not want it you cannot force it on them." He had made the point early in the campaign, at Bloomington and at Springfield, but Lincoln's strategy forced him to return to the question repeatedly during the debates. Lincoln was urged to hit Douglas hard on the contradiction between the Dred Scott decision and popular sovereignty. By endorsing the decision, a friend wrote, Douglas "is in reality and beyond all doubt opposed to Pop Sov. & Self Govt." He proposed that the Republicans themselves adopt popular sovereignty "in reality," since Douglas had apparently discarded it. Popular sovereignty "is a very popular and pleasing idea with the massess"; besides, he added, there is no territory "either *north* or *south* of 36° 30', in which Slavery would ever be adopted, or allowed to exist for any length of time" if the question were left to the people (a point which Douglas had, in fact, made many times). Lincoln could not go that far, but the pressure on him to lay the issue directly before Douglas mounted. Would Douglas maintain, one Republican asked, "that if the people of the Territories dont like Slavery, they *will not* protect it by local laws?" If so, "will the South be content with the operation of a mere barren right?" Douglas, it was thought, was in a hard predicament and could easily be thrown on the defensive. Lincoln was hesitant at first. Douglas, he replied, cared nothing for the south; "he knows he is already dead there." He knew Douglas' position and correctly summarized the line the Senator would take if asked, "he will instantly take ground that slavery can not actually exist in the territories, unless the people desire it, and so give it protective territorial legislation." "If this offends the South he will let it offend them," Lincoln concluded, "as at all events he means to hold on to his chances in Illinois." Others saw an advantage in bringing the question directly into the campaign, and pressure soon came from Lincoln's own campaign managers. Just before the Freeport debate, Joseph Medill urged Lincoln to ask Douglas, "what becomes of your vaunted popular Sovereignty in Territories since the Dred Scott decision?" [41]

Lincoln followed Medill's suggestion. In his opening remarks at Freeport, he addressed a series of questions to the Democratic candidate, the second of which asked, "Can the people of a United States territory, in any lawful way, against the wish of any citizen of the United States, exclude slavery from its limits prior to the formation of a state constitution?" Douglas' reply was immediate and unhesitating. While Lincoln had not mentioned the Dred Scott decision, it was implied, and Douglas picked up the implication in his answer. He reminded the audience that he had already stated his position on many occasions and pointed out that Lincoln had "no excuse for pretending to be in doubt as to my position on that question." Consistent with his interpretation of the Dred Scott decision, Douglas denied that the question of the power of a territorial legislature to legislate on slavery had been decided by the Supreme Court. Reiterating what he had said on other occasions, he replied:

> It matters not what way the Supreme Court may hereafter decide as to the abstract question whether slavery may or may not go into a territory under the Constitution, the people have the lawful means to introduce it or exclude it as they please, for the reason that slavery cannot exist a day or an hour anywhere, unless it is supported by local police regulations. Those police regulations can only be established by the local legislature, and if the people are opposed to slavery they will elect representatives to that body who will by unfriendly legislation effactually prevent the introduction of it into their midst. If, on the contrary, they are for it, their legislation will favor its extension.

There was nothing new in Douglas' statement, but it created an immediate sensation in the nation's press. The *Illinois State Journal* found his answer unconvincing and likened Douglas to a circus rider who changes his apparel as he goes around the ring. To the Washington *Union*, Douglas had backed down from the Kansas-Nebraska Act, had abandoned the Cincinnati platform, and had repudiated the Dred Scott decision, "reasserting the odious *squatter-sovereignty* doctrine in its most radical and obnoxious form." Douglas' reply, coupled with his opposition to a federal slave code, was interpreted as a final and crushing blow to the rights of the south. "To this 'lame and impotent conclusion,' " railed the New York *Herald*, "has Judge Douglas' championship of the rights of the South come at last! Is this the feast to which the author of the Nebraska-Kansas bill invited the South?"

The "Freeport Doctrine" represented the ultimate stage for popular sovereignty from which there was no recourse. The Supreme Court, countered the Douglas press, had decided that Congress could not grant a territorial legislature the power to prohibit slavery, but it had not yet decided that the people of a territory do not possess that power independent of the action of Congress. But even if the Court should so decide, it would be a decision on the abstract question only; for all practical purposes, the power to exclude slavery would remain absolute through the instrument of "unfriendly legislation." Douglas' Freeport declaration, commented the Washington *States,* "is drawing the attention of the whole country to that matter; and . . . for the first time in their lives, many persons are beginning to completely understand the bearing of the Nebraska-Kansas bill." [42]

Whether or not the Republican campaign achieved any advantage from Lincoln's question and Douglas' answer is doubtful. Douglas, however, seized the opportunity provided by his opponent and returned to the "Freeport Doctrine" repeatedly in his later speeches. If anything, it placed him in an anti-slavery posture which may have appealed to some uncommitted voters. The emphasis given to the doctrine, however, overshadowed other elements in Douglas' popular sovereignty argument, among them his conviction that popular sovereignty was directly related to the future growth and destiny of the United States.

Douglas' manifest destiny had always been a comprehensive and deeply rooted faith, and now he carried its message to the Illinois voters. The essential element in America's growth was its commitment to democracy and states' rights, popular sovereignty in the broadest sense. Under the guidance of that principle, Douglas insisted, the United States had grown "with a rapidity unequalled in the history of the world." Population had spilled over the Allegheny Mountains to fill up the northwest, "turning the prairie into a garden, and building up churches and schools, thus spreading civilization and Christianity where before there was nothing but savage-barbarism." But the past paled before the achievements that were yet to come, for Douglas' vision of the future was intoxicating. By adhering faithfully to the principle of self-government, the United States would soon fulfill "that great mission, that destiny which Providence has marked out for us." The wilderness would be cleared, the prairies settled, railroads constructed, and cities established. The "stream of intelligence" from the Old World to the New would continue to flow as America provided asylum to the oppressed peoples of the world. Having grown from a feeble nation to "the most powerful on the face of the earth," the United States will continue increasing in power, strength, and glory until "the Republic of America shall be the

North Star that shall guide the friends of freedom throughout the civilized world."

Territorial expansion, Douglas argued, was irrevocably linked to popular sovereignty. Maintain that principle and the nation will last forever, expanding until it covers the entire continent. The United States was a young and growing nation for whom expansion was the law of existence. "It swarms as often as a hive of bees, and as new swarms are turned out each year, there must be hives in which they can gather and make their honey." [43]

The agitation of the slavery question, Douglas charged, slowed the progress of the nation toward its inevitable destiny, and if persisted in, it would weaken the nation's very existence. He became increasingly impatient with Lincoln's insistence that the moral issue of slavery was somehow involved in the campaign. The institution of slavery was to be dealt with in a practical political manner and must be left to the operation of popular sovereignty and states' rights. It was a local, or domestic, institution and hence dependent for its existence or non-existence on local law. Lincoln accused Douglas of refusing to argue whether slavery was right or wrong, a charge Douglas readily admitted. "I tell you why I will not do it," he told the audience at Quincy. "I hold that under the Constitution of the United States, each state of this Union has a right to do as it pleases on the subject of slavery." It would, therefore, avail the candidates nothing to discuss a question on which they would have no power to act as United States Senators. Morality was a matter of individual conscience and could not be imposed on people against their will and judgment. To bring questions of morality into political discussion, Douglas was convinced, would strike down the nation's political system, dangerously increase sectionalism at the expense of national interest, and ultimately destroy the Union. He would speak of "rights under the Constitution," he declared, "and not of moral or religious rights." The morals of the people in the slaveholding states were of no concern to him. They were civilized men, with consciences, "accountable to God and their posterity and not to us." [44]

While Douglas tried to avoid discussion of slavery and bristled at Lincoln's contention, especially in the latter weeks of the campaign, that the moral question was the primary issue of the contest, he did have much to say on the status of the Negro in American society. Lincoln's early assertion, that by the terms of the Declaration of Independence and natural rights the Negro was the equal of the white man, became a major target of Douglas' rhetoric. Lincoln, he charged again and again, was in league with the most extreme abolitionists. He accused the Republican of subscribing to a doctrine of full and complete racial equality, charges which Lincoln just as repeatedly denied. Douglas was insistent that the Negro ought not to be granted citizenship in any form, declaring bluntly at Charleston "that this government was established on the white basis. It was made by white men, for the benefit of white men and their posterity forever and never should be administered by any except white men." The Negro belonged to an inferior race and was incapable of self-government. Lincoln's conviction that the Declaration "and Divine Providence" provided equality was a "monstrous heresy." The signers of the Declaration of Independence, representing slaveholding constituencies without exception, "never dreamed of the negro when they were writing that document." They referred only to white men, to men of European birth and descent. "I do not believe," he said, "that the Almighty ever intended the negro to be the equal of the white man."

For all his emphasis, however, Douglas qualified his belief in the inequality of Negroes and whites by linking it with popular sovereignty. "I do not hold," he explained, "that because the negro is our inferior that therefore he ought to be a slave." On the contrary, both "humanity and Christianity" require that the Negro should be accorded "every right, every privilege, and every immunity consistent with the safety of the society in which he lives." To what degree Negroes should be given rights and privileges was a question which each state and territory must decide for itself, and he would not quarrel with the result. But where Negro rights or popular sovereignty were alternatives, he left no doubt as to his position. "I care more for the great principle of self-government, the right of the people to rule, than I do for all the negroes in Christendom," he declared in a concluding statement at the last debate. "I would not endanger the perpetuity of this Union. I would not blot out the great inalienable rights of the white men for all the negroes that ever existed." In the context of Illinois in 1858 (and, for that matter, in most of the United States), his position had much appeal.

The Republicans were sensitive to Douglas' attacks on the issue of Negro equality. While Douglas' charges against Lincoln were usually without foundation, they feared their impact on the voters. Toward the end of the campaign, a rather clumsy attempt was made to turn the issue against Douglas when the *State Journal* announced there was not a Republican in the state who advocated such an "odious doctrine" as "nigger equality." On the contrary, the *Journal* continued, it was the Douglas Democracy that favored Negro equality in order to promote an alliance between free Negroes and Douglas. The report was based on a proposal for Negro suffrage made by a Democratic De Kalb newspaper, as well as by the local Douglas Democratic candidate for the legislature. The charge was not followed up by Republican campaigners, and it soon disappeared from the public print.[45]

Other more effective charges were made against the Little Giant. One of the most serious resulted from Douglas' own failure to check the accuracy of his statements. At Ottawa, as he opened the debates, Douglas read a series of resolutions which, he said, had been passed at the first state convention of the Republican party in Springfield in October 1854. The resolutions urged the repeal of the Fugitive Slave Act, the restriction of slavery to the states in which it existed, the abolition of slavery in the District of Columbia, the prohibition of new slave states, and the application of the Wilmot Proviso to all new territory. Douglas hoped to demonstrate the radical character of the Republican party and, by implication at least, to connect Lincoln with radical doctrines. Prior to the debate, Douglas asked Lanphier to confirm the time and place at which the convention had been held and whether or not Lincoln was present; apparently he used Lanphier's subsequent information in his speech. Lincoln denied that he had been present at the Springfield meeting and, in fact, recalled having deliberately absented himself so as not to be identified with it. Further research by Republicans disclosed that the resolutions had not been passed by the Springfield convention at all, that they had in fact emanated from a meeting in Kane County, in the northern part of the state. Confronted with the evidence, Douglas conceded that he may have made an error "as to the *spot*" but insisted that his point remained—that the resolutions represented the Republican party platform when the party was first formed. Lanphier took the matter lightly. "I see that your quotation from our old file has made an uproar," he informed Douglas. "*I yet believe the resolutions there given* to be the genuine ones. Whether so or not, the point you made is not affected by their denial of the 'spot.'" The Republicans refused to let the matter drop, and they opened a barrage against Douglas for deliberately perpetrating a forgery.[46]

Lyman Trumbull's arrival in Illinois and his entrance into the campaign in early August (at the urgent request of the Republican committee) were enthusiastically welcomed by Republicans, and his first blasts

against Douglas caused the Senator no little anxiety. His attacks on
Douglas' role in Congress were sharper and probably more effective than
Lincoln's, for he spoke with a knowledge and authority which Lincoln
lacked. "He crowds his colleague very hard," reported one correspondent,
"harder, we think, than Mr. Lincoln has done in any of his published
speeches." Trumbull's initial speech, given in Chicago on August 7, was
reprinted and distributed through Douglas' audiences in order to give his
charges the widest possible circulation. Douglas was infuriated, and on
one rare occasion, in Beardstown, he lost his usual composure, referring
to his Senate colleague as "the miserable, craven-hearted wretch, [who]
would rather have both ears cut off than use that language in my presence, where I could call him to account."

Trumbull touched a sensitive nerve. He maintained that Douglas in
1856 had deliberately stricken from the Toombs bill for the admission
of Kansas a clause that would have required the submission of the proposed constitution to a vote of the people. This, Trumbull argued, revealed Douglas' true position; his later opposition to the Lecompton
constitution was a deceit, carried out for selfish political reasons. In spite
of the fact that the charge had been brought against Douglas during the
Lecompton debate in the Senate by Senator Bigler and had been answered at the time, the Republicans were gleeful. "There is abundant evidence," commented the *Chicago Tribune,* "to prove that Senator Douglas was himself a party to the original Lecompton fraud." The files of
the *Congressional Globe* and the *Chicago Times* were combed for indications that Douglas had opposed submission of the constitution in
1856. Democratic supporters of the Lecompton constitution were author-
itatively quoted to prove that Douglas' opposition to that document had
stemmed solely from his desire to be re-elected to the Senate. Lincoln
took the cue and confronted Douglas with Trumbull's statements at the
Charleston debate. Douglas, in his defense, reviewed his course in the
Senate once again, but both Lincoln and the Republican press found his
explanation unconvincing. The accusations were repeated during the remainder of the campaign, but with diminishing vigor and reduced effectiveness.[47]

Other issues were brought against Douglas during the campaign, but
none proved crucial to the final result. He was charged with promoting
the interests of the Roman Catholic Church. The Republican press railed
against the "union between the two despotisms—slavery and Catholicism" in an obvious attempt to prevent members of the American party

from joining Douglas' ranks. Douglas' wife was a Catholic and his two sons were being educated in a Jesuit preparatory school in Washington, facts which Republicans emphasized to demonstrate his attachment to the Church of Rome. Illinoisans were reminded that the Democratic party had for years been dependent upon the Irish Catholic vote. The Republicans hinted darkly that large numbers of Irishmen would be "colonized" in the doubtful districts to serve the cause of "the Pope, Slavery and Douglas." Douglas' role in the development of the Illinois Central Railroad, one of the sources of his popularity in the state, was questioned when Iowa Senator George W. Jones, a supporter of Breese and bitter enemy of the Little Giant, charged Douglas with having sacrificed the interests of Galena in favor of Dubuque as terminus for the line. A Galena editor, disturbed because the Republicans in northwest Illinois were making use of Jones' statement, wrote to Douglas for more information. Douglas denied Jones' charge of collusion, but he did admit that he had supported the extension of the road to Dubuque in order to save the land grant bill from defeat.[48]

On the eve of the election (too late for denials to affect the results), the Republicans charged that the slaves on the Mississippi plantation in Douglas' care were cruelly and inhumanly treated, "their backs scarred by the lash, their bodies pinched by hunger, their limbs bent by excessive work." Douglas, they asserted, "derives from their toil the cash with which he is endeavoring to convince the people that Slavery ought to exist forever." The information was said to have originated with John Slidell at the time of his Chicago visit and was relayed to the Republicans by Dr. Daniel Brainard, a member of the Danite faction of the Democratic party. There is little likelihood that the charge had any impact on the election returns. It was denied soon after the election by Slidell and by Douglas' partner in the plantation operation, J. A. McHatton, who released testimonial letters from the plantation physician and owners of neighboring plantations. Douglas took little notice of the incident.[49]

iv

Douglas' last debate with Lincoln occurred at Alton on October 15, but he continued his campaign up to the day of election. He addressed large crowds in Decatur, Springfield, and Bloomington, as well as groups in a number of smaller towns. In his last few engagements, he was forced to speak in a raw blustering wind and heavy rain showers. On October 30 he arrived in Chicago, physically exhausted, his voice hardly more than a whisper. On November 1, the night before the election, he made his last appearance, but a rainstorm added to his fatigue and prevented him from saying much.

In spite of the inclement weather, large numbers of voters went to the polls on November 2, more than had voted in the presidential election two years before. The results, although very close, were soon apparent. The Democrats won a majority of the legislative contests, which, with the holdover members of the legislature, assured Douglas of easy re-election to a third term in the United States Senate. In winning the legislature, however, the Democrats lost their state ticket. The Republicans elected their candidates for state treasurer and superintendent of public instruction, completing their hold on the state administration. In the vote for treasurer, which reflected most significantly the division between the parties, the Republicans received 125,430 votes to the Democrats' 121,609, a plurality of just under 4000 votes. The Danite ticket trailed with a pitiful 5071 votes, a painful reminder to Democratic leaders that their sweep of the election would have been complete had the party been united. Douglas, whose confidence had mounted in the latter days of the campaign, exulted in his victory "over the combined forces of the Abolitionists and the federal office holders." [50]

The Democrats focused their delight more on the rebuke which the election returns administered to Buchanan than on the defeat of Lincoln, for it was in this that they found the true significance of the campaign. While the vote had repudiated the "sectional hydra," commented the *State Register* in a burst of enthusiasm, it had also "condemned in thunder tones, treacherous demagogues, who would, in their envy of his [Douglas'] greatness, have crushed a noble champion of sound democratic principles, and a faithful public servant." In a more sober assessment of the election, *The New York Times* saw in the results "one of the most wonderful personal victories ever achieved by a public man." Douglas had returned to Illinois from Washington "a proscribed Democrat." He was compelled to fight the full strength of the Republican party with "such a portion of the Democracy as he could rescue from the influence of the Administration. A more unequal contest could not well be imagined, and . . . not another public man in the country . . . could possibly have achieved so brilliant a success." Douglas would now be more powerful at Washington than ever before, with "the whole Democratic Party of the North, and the conservative portion of that party at the South, at his back." [51]

The Republicans did not conceal their deep disappointment at Lincoln's defeat, although some of the leadership confessed that they had had little hope of victory anyway. The *State Journal* attributed the result to three factors. First, both parties had struggled to secure the old Fillmore vote, but Douglas had proved the more persuasive. Second, the apportionment to the state legislature, based on the 1850 census, had given Douglas a strong advantage. The population of the state had increased more rapidly in the northern Republican districts in the years since 1850, but this increase was not yet reflected in the composition of the legislature. Finally, the Republicans' most formidable obstacle was the relation in which Douglas stood to the national Democratic administration. Douglas' position on the Lecompton constitution had denied that important issue to the Republican party and brought him support from many who might otherwise have voted Republican. When all factors were carefully considered, the *Journal* concluded, the wonder was not that the legislature had been lost, but "that we made so strong a fight and came out of the contest so well." [52]

The Danite Democrats were not prepared to concede Douglas' re-election to the Senate in spite of their poor showing at the polls. The fight against Douglas, they announced, would continue. Several of the new members of the legislature and some of the holdovers, they predicted, would oppose Douglas' re-election. There might even be enough anti-Douglas Democrats, boasted Isaac Cook, to prevent a senatorial election until 1860. Several senate members assured Cook that they approved Buchanan's course on the Lecompton question and disapproved that of Douglas, encouraging the Danite leader to predict, *"The defeat of Douglas is certain."* Rumors circulated that the power of the administration would be exerted against Douglas in the legislature; foreign missions, it was said, had already been offered to three state senators. One officeholder (probably Cook) announced that he held blank commissions for federal offices and was prepared to insert the names of all Democratic legislators who refused to support Douglas. Most Republicans were skeptical, but some of Douglas' friends feared the reports might have substance in fact. Sheahan confessed to Lanphier that some Democratic members of the legislature might betray Douglas at the last minute, and he urged the Springfield editor to take action to prevent it.[53]

There were anxious moments on the opening day of the new session when the Republican members absented themselves in order to prevent a quorum, thus delaying the organization of the legislature. If the action resulted from an agreement with the Danites, as some suggested, it failed in its purpose, for all doubts of Douglas' re-election were dispelled when the Democratic caucus unanimously supported his nomination. The Republicans returned, agreed to a joint session, and on January 6, 1859, Douglas was re-elected, 54 votes to Lincoln's 46. There were no defections from the Democratic ranks, a unity which Cook had not expected. Lanphier immediately wired Douglas the good news: "Glory to God and the Sucker Democracy. Douglas 54, Lincoln 46. Announcement followed by shouts of immense crowd present. Town wild with excitement. Democrats firing salute. . . . Guns, music and whisky rampant." Douglas was in Baltimore when he received Lanphier's telegram. He replied tersely and with obvious relief, "Let the voice of the people rule." It was the end of a long and taxing struggle.[54]

# XXVI
## "I will make no sacrifice of principle"
## 1859

i

The conclusion of the 1858 campaign gave Douglas his first respite from political warfare in a long time. He was assured re-election and hardly took seriously the threats of the Danites that they might yet oust him from the Senate. Congratulatory messages poured in, and he took time to acknowledge the assistance which his friends had rendered in "the good cause." His success, wrote Reverdy Johnson, augured well for the true interests and safety of the nation. There were hints that greater rewards awaited him. "All honor is due to Judge Douglas," commented Charles Stuart, for "he has not only 'fought the fight' but he has also *'kept the faith,'* and there are rich treasures laid up for him in the hearts of the people of this confederacy." [1]

Following the election, Adele suffered a brief but painful illness and this, in addition to his own need for a rest, persuaded Douglas to plan a leisurely journey back to the national capital. His decision was reinforced by an unwillingness to resume his seat in the Senate until after the Illinois legislature had re-elected him. "I hope you will not find it necessary to be as active & untiring in your exertions to please this winter," Adele's brother cautioned her, and "that your good husband will have less to contend with and that you both will pass a more quiet winter than the last." [2]

While the fall election settled Douglas' immediate political future, it left open the more serious question of his relationship to his party, to President Buchanan, and to the southern leadership. The question was highlighted by the disastrous losses suffered by the party in the north, especially in the congressional races. The first reverses came in October, when Democratic candidates for the House of Representatives went down to unexpected defeat in Indiana, Ohio, and Pennsylvania. In November, New York was lost. A total of eighteen House seats were relinquished to the opposition, and Democratic control of the lower house in the next session was questionable. Administration supporters, unwilling to examine their own responsibility, blamed Douglas for the defeats. George W. Jones caustically remarked, "No patriot either in the North or the South should ever again place confidence in S. A. Douglas." Douglas' re-election and the success of a handful of anti-Lecompton Democrats was no comfort to the administration. Howell Cobb was "boiling over, more bitter than ever before," raving "like a wounded tiger." Douglas' success, Cobb charged, was "a hard blow upon the South" and would demoralize the party in the north. "In what does the attitude of Senator Douglas to-day differ from that of Mr. Van Buren in 1848?" asked the Washington *Union*. Van Buren had been "unhesitatingly plucked out and cast from" the party, and a like fate must now await the Illinois Senator. There was talk that the administration, prodded by the south, would settle on a congressional slave code as a new test of party affiliation.[3]

Still, hopes were high that the breach between Douglas and the administration could be healed. The *State Register* denied Republican charges that Douglas would be excluded from the party caucuses at the next session. From Washington, Douglas' brother-in-law observed that the warfare against the Senator would not be continued, "unless you exhibit a belligerent spirit." James May renewed his efforts to bring Douglas and the President together. Words of advice were offered Douglas by his supporters. "The party every where is keenly alive to the necessity of harmony," wrote Samuel Treat, "and he who contributes most to its restoration, will be most honored." Even the Washington *Union* modified its hostile attitude toward Douglas. The feeling, however, was not reciprocated. A clearer indicator of relations between Douglas and the President was a *Chicago Times* editorial in January, said to have been written by Douglas himself. A severe assault against Buchanan, the article shattered the prospect of a reconciliation, hoisting "the flag of rebellion . . . to this northwest wind." [4]

In any case, Douglas was too wise a politician to think that he could return in triumph to the party's inner councils, or that the animosities that had built up could so easily be erased. For him, the battle had not

ended; the party had still to be rescued from the sectionalizing tendencies that threatened its existence. The real struggle, he was convinced,
would take place in 1860. It was toward this crucial year that he now
bent his efforts. Illinois Republicans, quickly reconciled to his victory,
recognized his precarious position within the Democratic organization.
"He has a perilous rope-walk before him," predicted the Chicago *Tribune.* "Therefore Mr. Douglas must cast his lot decisively this winter, either with the Republicans or the pro-slavery Democracy. There is no
middle ground." That Douglas rejected this Republican appraisal became clear before he left Illinois, for it was precisely this middle ground,
the only national ground in his estimation, that he sought. Some anti-
Lecompton supporters urged him to carry on the fight outside the Democratic organization. John Forney feared Douglas would lose much of the
strength he had gained if he put himself in the hands of any party. The
abandonment of the Democratic party, however, was out of the question,
for Douglas still regarded the Democracy as his only hope for success.[5]

On the eve of his departure from Chicago, Douglas talked with
Charles H. Ray, *Tribune* editor and one of Lincoln's managers. When
asked about his relations with Buchanan, he retorted, "I have nothing to
ask for or grant in that quarter. He made the war; and by G–d! he
shall make peace if peace is to be made at all." Douglas promised to oppose the revival of the slave trade and the protection of slavery in the
territories with all the vigor he had mustered against the Lecompton
constitution. He would stand by the Dred Scott decision but would not
surrender his conviction that the people in the territories might still establish or prohibit slavery as they saw fit, the point made in his Freeport
debate. The administration, Douglas charged, had reduced Negroes "to
the status of mules"; so far as he was concerned, "they must be content
with the legislation which would protect mules—not persons owing
service or labor."

Douglas was more conciliatory in his last public statement before
leaving Chicago. Responding to a public demonstration in his honor, he
hailed his victory as "the triumph of the glorious principles of the Union
over fanaticism and sectionalism" and of the "principle of self government over Congressional interference and Executive dictation," a statement that covered both his Republican and Democratic opposition. He
hoped, however, that the heated feelings and angry passions of the campaign could now be buried. "It is neither just nor magnanimous to rejoice over a vanquished foe." He urged the nation to reject the "fatal

heresy" that the nation could not endure half slave and half free and called upon all national men, regardless of party, to join together to "drive back the dark, fatal cloud of sectional animosity." [6]

Douglas and his wife left Chicago for Washington late in November, traveling a circuitous route down the Mississippi to New Orleans and thence by sea to New York. The long journey, particularly the sea voyage, afforded them both a much-needed rest. A visit to the south also enabled Douglas "to try the pulse of the Southern people" and to test the many assurances of support he had received during his campaign. He ignored the advice that he should make no public statements or "accept no public demonstrations" on the way. Greeted by large crowds in St. Louis, Memphis, and New Orleans, he turned each occasion into a political rally, speaking with what one correspondent termed "his characteristic pluck and frankness." [7]

Douglas continued to harp on the theme of popular sovereignty. He conceded that the slaveholder had a right to take his slave property into a territory, a right confirmed by the Dred Scott decision, but insisted that once in a territory, slavery depended upon the territorial legislature for protection. As if to make certain that there should be no misunderstanding of his position, he reiterated his Freeport doctrine and warned his southern audiences that "it is folly for you to entertain visionary dreams that you can fix slavery where the people do not want it." He condemned Lincoln's House Divided doctrine and again called upon all national men to unite against the threatening tide of sectionalism.

He also linked popular sovereignty to the achievement of national destiny. "If that principle prevail," Douglas declared, "we have a future before us more glorious than that of any other people that ever existed." But peace and harmony between the free and slave states was essential to national progress. "The more degrees of latitude and longitude embraced beneath our Constitution, the better." America's strength was in its variety, its mission to become the greatest planting and greatest manufacturing, the greatest commercial and greatest agricultural power on the globe. With states' rights and territorial self-government, "America will fulfill the glorious destiny which the Almighty has marked out for her." In New Orleans, where the subject had special appeal, Douglas became more specific. He urged the acquisition of Cuba. "It is our destiny to have Cuba, and it is folly to debate the question. . . . Its acquisition is a matter of time only." He hinted of future acquisitions in Mexico and Central America but insisted that expansion must be peaceful and natural. "We live in a rapid age," he reminded his audience, "and things will come along naturally, soon enough." [8]

Embarking from New Orleans on the steamer *Black Warrior,* Douglas stopped briefly in Havana, where he talked with local officials and placed an order for 2000 cigars before continuing to New York. The trip continued to bear the earmarks of a triumphal procession. New York's common council declared him a guest of the city and provided a public reception in which an estimated 3000 people extended their greetings to the Senator and his lady. Douglas responded with a speech that evening in which he once again linked popular sovereignty with manifest destiny and expansion. Intermittent rain and the slushy condition of the streets hardly dampened the ardor of the crowd. Whether so intended or not, New York's official welcome was interpreted as a celebration of Douglas' victory in Illinois and as an endorsement of his platform. Needless to say, the federal officeholders in the city were conspicuously absent from the proceedings.

Douglas' New York reception moved the Washington *States* to comment on the mutability of human affairs. Less than a year before, during the Lecompton crisis, he had visited the city unnoticed except by a few personal friends. His fortunes had since taken an abrupt shift. "There can be no doubt," commented the *New-York Tribune,* "that Mr. Douglas is now, *par excellence,* the representative man of the Democracy of the Free States." A man of the people, "without much superfluous refinement of mind or manner," his pugilistic quality, quickness, and pluck made him a formidable figure, without a peer "in the unscrupulous rough-and-tumble conflict of partisan politics." Douglas' favorite principle had become "the living faith of the Democratic party of the North."

The adulation continued as Douglas approached Washington. Arriving in Philadelphia during a heavy snowstorm, he was greeted by a torchlight procession, a 200-gun salute, and a fireworks display. His friend Forney, in a speech to the crowd, praised Douglas as the hero who had stood against official power and had conquered. The guest of the city at a dinner in Independence Hall, Douglas recalled an earlier struggle for popular sovereignty. The scene was repeated in Baltimore, where the occasion became even more festive when he received Lanphier's telegram announcing his re-election to the Senate.[9]

If the signs were right, Douglas' stock was high, but how significant this would prove in his relations with Democratic leaders he had yet to discover. The real test awaited him in the capital. His enemies, who had followed his journey with increasing annoyance as news of his receptions circulated, were prepared to move to new lengths in their attempt to neutralize his influence and destroy his power.[10] Douglas was absent when the Senate convened early in December, and party leaders took advantage of the fact.

ii

The Democrats who gathered in Washington for the opening of the second session were in a quarrelsome mood. They were jittery and apprehensive of the party's future, full of resentment for the defeats they had suffered in the recent elections, and spoiling for revenge against the man they held responsible for them. From the first day of the session, it was obvious that a move would be made against the Illinois Senator. Rumor turned to fact when the Democratic members of the Senate met on December 9 to select committee members, normally a routine operation. The strategy soon emerged. Douglas was to be ousted from his chairmanship of the Committee on Territories, a radical move that was hotly debated for most of the day. The effort was sparked by Jefferson Davis, John Slidell, and Jesse Bright and had the support of, if indeed it was not dictated by, President Buchanan. The Chief Executive was reported earlier to have pronounced Douglas no Democrat and therefore ineligible to head a Senate committee. The move took some Senators by surprise; others stayed away from the caucus presumably because they refused to be involved in such a proscription. California Senator David C. Broderick was excluded from participation in the caucus because of his anti-Lecompton convictions.

Thomas Clingman of North Carolina insisted that all committee assignments remain the same as in the previous session, but his effort was in vain. Only seven of the twenty-four Senators present (out of a total of forty-four Democrats in the Senate) stood by Douglas, and those seven included some who had opposed him in the past: Clingman, Albert Gallatin Brown of Mississippi, William Bigler of Pennsylvania, James S. Green of Missouri, James Shields of Minnesota, Georgia's Robert Toombs, and Charles E. Stuart of Michigan. Stuart, like Broderick one of Douglas' anti-Lecompton supporters, had been admitted to the caucus, but there were hints that he too would be stripped of his committee power. His precarious position did not prevent him from denouncing the action as suicidal to the party. Bigler protested that Douglas ought not to be attacked while he was absent and unable to defend himself. Toombs, so enraged that he stalked from the room after the vote was taken, denounced the move as a vindictive action against an individual and therefore unworthy of men charged with governing a great country. Brown also opposed Douglas' removal, but on grounds of policy, reminding his colleagues that Martin Van Buren's rejection as minister to Great Britain had made him President not long afterward. Green, who was subsequently selected to succeed Douglas as chairman of the committee, voted against Douglas' ouster in the belief that it would "be prejudicially misconstrued by the country." [11]

Douglas' removal from the chairmanship of the Committee on Territories created a furor in Washington. Some Senators who had supported the caucus action maintained that they did so only because Douglas' absence from the Senate until January would inconvenience the committee in the discharge of its duties. "A more shallow defence could scarcely be devised," protested one editor, for it had been common practice in such a situation for the next ranking member to assume temporary charge of the committee. There were no real doubts about the motivation of the Senate Democrats.

The Committee on Territories had grown in significance since Douglas assumed its chairmanship eleven years before, partly because of the growing importance of the territories to the sectional conflict, but also because of the interest and energy with which he had promoted its responsibilities. By 1858, it had become "the great leading political committee of the Senate." The committee in turn served Douglas well, for it provided him with an effective power base, a vehicle for the advancement of his own views and ambitions. Earlier attempts to neutralize Douglas' power within the committee had had little effect. His stand in the Lecompton crisis and his insistence, in the bill creating Arizona Territory, that henceforth any territory seeking admission as a state must submit its constitution to the people for approval or rejection had embittered southerners in Congress. But it was the position he had taken in his senatorial campaign that brought the matter to its climax. California Senator William M. Gwin, who, as chairman of the Democratic caucus' committee on committees, played an important role in Douglas' ouster, charged that the doctrines Douglas had expressed in his Freeport speech demanded that immediate action be taken against him. The south, it was said, had temporized long enough and would no longer tolerate any halfway measures. Douglas had to be driven from the party. "How can any true state rights Southern man maintain that he should have been retained as the exponent of the Democratic party?" asked Senator Clement C. Clay of Alabama. "He antagonized all of that party in the Senate (except Stuart & Broderick) during the last session, on the Kansas issues, & he still opposes them upon a vital question—the rights of the South in the territories." Popular sovereignty had been exposed as more abhorrent to the south than the Wilmot Proviso, Clay insisted, and no southern man could support this "heresy." The chairman of a Senate Committee, he added, "should be the organ of the party that selects him." Douglas, it was obvious to Clay, could no longer claim to speak for his party.[12]

Not all southern Senators or administration supporters condoned the action of the caucus. Brown's warnings that Douglas' ouster would advance his campaign for the presidency by making him a martyr were widely repeated. James H. Hammond, who had absented himself from the caucus deliberations, agreed that Douglas must be read out of the party but felt it should have been done the year before. "I think it however very doubtful *policy* to disturb him *now.*" Minnesota's Henry M. Rice thought the action unwise and uncalled for. Douglas' own supporters reacted with a mixture of outrage that he had been ousted and confidence that the move would boomerang against the administration. Illinois Congressman James C. Allen leveled his anger against "the old 'Fossil' that presides at the 'White House,' " and he predicted that in 1860 "these same men will be getting down on their bellies in the dust before him [Douglas] and begging permission to lick his hand." Another Congressman, S. S. Marshall, was outraged "almost beyond endurance," suggesting that the "actors in this piece of low flung meanness and malevolence have raised a storm that they will find it difficult to allay." Most agreed that the caucus action had placed Douglas in a stronger position than before.[13]

Illinois Buchananites in Washington were gleeful; they freely predicted that Douglas' decapitation would defeat him in the Illinois legislature. Republicans, although hopeful, were not as optimistic. Speculation that Douglas would move into the Republican ranks was briefly revived, and some Republicans openly expressed sympathy for the Illinois Senator. Meeting in their own caucus, Republican Senators rejected the suggestion that they back Douglas in his fight with the Democratic party, although an unsuccessful attempt was made by Preston King on the Senate floor to force a separate vote on the composition of the Committee on Territories.[14]

Whether Douglas learned of the caucus action before he embarked from New Orleans on December 12 is not known. He certainly learned of it upon his arrival in New York, where a number of letters from political associates awaited him. All advised him to refrain from any impulsive public reaction to his removal. Regard the action and its perpetrators *"with dignified contempt . . .* as if nothing had occurred," wrote one friend. Daniel McCook urged him to continue to Washington without delay, and Morris advised him to say nothing about the caucus action until he could consult with his friends at the capital. "For God's sake, Judge," wrote James B. Steedman from Ohio, "don't evince any feeling about the petty persecution of the Senate in deposing you from the head of your committee. Bear it with Christian resignation—for I assure you that since the war of the Administration was commenced on you, nothing has been done which has given you greater strength [than] this miserable meanness and persecution." [15]

His friends had little cause for concern, for in his public addresses in Philadelphia and Baltimore Douglas gave no hint of a reaction to his removal. Nor did he refer to it when he arrived in Washington. A small but enthusiastic crowd greeted him as he alighted from his train, "looking fresh as the morning and firm as a pillar of iron," and accompanied him through the cold night air to his house. There, by the light of burning tar barrels, he made a brief speech, which was followed by a reception in his brightly lit mansion. A few days later, on January 10, Douglas resumed his seat in the Senate. The surroundings were unfamiliar, for just a week before the Senate had vacated its old chamber and moved into new and more commodious quarters. As he entered the room, he was greeted by scattered applause from the gallery, but his reception on the floor was "studiously cold and distant." A few, including some Republicans, shook his hand, and Seward conversed with him at some length. While Davis, Clay, and Gwin awkwardly extended their hands, it was apparent that administration Senators intended to "show him their cold shoulder." [16]

Douglas had returned to an atmosphere of ill-concealed hostility. "There are men here," reported Senator Hammond, "who will not spare him." Slidell, Bright, Fitch, Green, and Jones, to name only a few, "are keen for his blood." Buchanan, continuing his war against Douglas, sent

a number of anti-Douglas Illinois appointments to the Senate for confirmation, his haste, it was said, dictated by Douglas' absence. The ease
with which they were approved was interpreted as proof of the Senator's
fallen status. "If half of the infamy here could be known," moaned Morris, "it would startle the nation." [17]

Reports that administration supporters were trying to force Douglas
into personal quarrels convinced some observers that the question of the
Senator's role in the Democratic party might ultimately be settled on
the field of honor. Almost as soon as he landed in New York, Douglas
became embroiled in controversies with both Jones and Slidell. Jones,
blaming Douglas for his own defeat for re-election, persisted in his
charge that Douglas had sacrificed the interests of northern Illinois
when he agreed to extend the Illinois Central Railroad to Dubuque.
Douglas had branded Jones's insinuations as false early in August, but
Jones was not content to let the matter rest. In a letter written in November but not sent or made public until mid-December, Jones charged
that Douglas' statement was personally offensive and that he was compelled again "to fasten the lie" on the Illinois Senator. Douglas retained
his composure and wisely backed away but in doing so had the last
word. "I have no taste for this childish amusement," he wrote. The issue
between them had, in fact, already been settled by their respective states.
"I am entirely content with the verdict which the people of Illinois have
recently rendered upon my conduct and have no disposition to question
the propriety and justness of the judgment which the people of Iowa
have pronounced upon the services and conduct of Mr. Jones." [18]

Slidell's complaint against Douglas stemmed from charges made during the Illinois senatorial campaign that the slaves on Douglas' Mississippi plantation were mistreated. The source of the story was said to
have been Slidell, and, in a letter to a New Orleans newspaper, Douglas'
secretary James B. Sheridan attacked the Louisiana Senator for circulating a report he knew to be untrue. Slidell denied any connection with
the story but in doing so charged Douglas with having authorized Sheridan's attack and demanded a categorical explanation. The "famous Slidell difficulty" ended when Douglas denied that he had authorized Sheridan's attack and Sheridan himself conceded that he had written his
letter without consulting Douglas.

Douglas was being pushed, and there was no sign that the pressure
would ease. Late in January he became involved in a personal conflict
with Indiana Senator Graham Fitch, and once again rumors of immi-

nent physical violence began to fly. In an executive session of the Senate, while the body was considering certain presidential nominations to office, Douglas denounced recent appointments in Illinois, especially that of Isaac Cook, and declared that the federal officeholders in the state were incompetent and corrupt. Fitch immediately objected to Douglas' language on behalf of his son, who held the post of United States Attorney for the Northern District of Illinois. Douglas conceded that there were exceptions to his charge and that Fitch's son was one of these exceptions. The Indiana Senator, however, did not let the matter rest but continued in a vein so personal that he was repeatedly called to order. In a note to Fitch shortly afterward, Douglas protested "an affront so wanton, unprovoked, and unjustifiable" and asked Fitch for a retraction. Tension mounted when both individuals appointed friends to serve as intermediaries—Douglas selecting Roger Pryor, editor of the *States,* and Major Tom Hawkins, a Kentuckian known for his skill as a duelist —but after several more notes were exchanged tempers cooled and the matter was settled. All these incidents seemed to be part of a deliberate effort to bring Douglas to heel and to destroy his stature within the Democratic party.[19]

The effort seems even to have invaded Douglas' social life, although in a less dramatic way. Adele continued her reign over Washington society, winning compliments for her youthful beauty and easy grace and creating sensations whenever she appeared in public. A major social event of the winter season was a "grand ball" hosted by the Douglases in their new mansion in Minnesota Row; 1200 invitations were sent out, to friend and foe alike. The street became so jammed with carriages that guests had to alight several blocks away. Adele, "laboring under the effects of indisposition," received her guests seated, while her husband stood at her side to make the introductions. The affair was judged "one of the most brilliant" ever given in Washington, thanks to the "young and beautiful wife who was the great magnet of attraction." No cabinet member was present, each having forwarded regrets several days before.[20]

If Douglas' enemies expected that his removal from the committee chairmanship would provoke him to attack the administration, they were disappointed. The Senators who had engineered the removal hoped that Douglas would respond soon after his return to the Senate, providing them an opportunity to publicize his infidelity and to justify their action. Indeed, Gwin regarded it Douglas' duty "to give his reasons to the

Senate and to the country" for the position he had adopted in the Illinois campaign. But Douglas did not rise to the bait, acting instead as he would under normal circumstances. Why was it his duty to explain his views to the Senate? he later asked Gwin. The Senate was not his constituency, nor was he responsible to its members for his position. If it were his duty to provide the Senate with his "reasons," he added, then was it not also the duty of the Senators to hear them before they removed him from his chairmanship? Douglas departed from his usual routine only in his refusal to attend meetings of the territorial committee.

Douglas' strategy was revealed by A. J. Cass, Lewis Cass' brother, in a letter written in late January. "He will act with the democratic organization, as usual, upon all democratic measures—will attend their caucuses and go as far as the boldest in advocating the past and present policy of the party." At the same time, "he will not *seek* to open the issue" of his Freeport pronouncement or his removal and would avoid any action that could be construed as forcing a fight with the south or the administration. Southern and administration leaders in Congress, Cass continued, would like nothing better than to drive him into a hostile course that could be seized upon to falsify his position and "to create doubts in the minds of the democratic masses as to his future intentions." [21]

There were few bright spots for Douglas in the second session. He supported the bill providing land grants for the establishment of agricultural colleges, although at its final passage he paired off with Robert Toombs, one of the measure's opponents. The bill, passed by the House at the previous session, was vetoed by Buchanan. Oregon was finally admitted to statehood, but action on the organization of Arizona and Dacotah territories was defeated by the south. "Douglas is again on the Frontier for expansion," warned a South Carolinian, who feared "lest another *'Kansas fraud'* is sprung on the South." The homestead bill for which Douglas argued also perished for lack of action.

Two days after he returned to his seat, Douglas used the occasion of a Pacific railroad bill that had become stalled because of disagreement over the route to denounce sectionalism once again. Everyone agreed, he declared, that there ought to be a Pacific railroad, yet every bill brought before Congress had failed "because there are jealousies of section against section." Sectional rivalries had no place in the consideration of national legislation. "I do not wish, by law, to give an advantage to the

North or to the South. I hold that principle of legislation which treats all sections alike by the law, and leaves climate, soil, production, self-interest, the will of the people, to work out the result under our equal legislation." In the face of mounting sectional feeling, Douglas predicted that the passage of a railroad bill would be "utterly impossible" and the nation would be the loser. He was right.[22]

On January 17, spectators crowded the galleries of the new Senate chamber in the hope that Douglas would reply at last to the Senators who had stripped him of his committee position. His good friend Thomas L. Harris had died in his Illinois home shortly after being re-elected to Congress in November, and Douglas was scheduled to deliver the eulogy. The throng was disappointed, however, when he "declined to use the grave as a platform for the display of his eloquence." His comments were brief and simple. He lauded Harris for his faithful adherence to popular sovereignty, but beyond this he did not go in his appraisal of Harris' role in Congress. To some critics, it seemed that Douglas was keeping a small aperture open through which to crawl back into the party.[23]

Douglas further puzzled his enemies and disturbed his supporters when he continued to participate in Democratic party caucuses. One of them, dealing with Cuba, seemed to signal a reconciliation with Slidell. Following a recommendation in Buchanan's message to Congress, Slidell introduced a bill appropriating $30 million for the purchase of the Spanish island. While the bill was being considered in the foreign relations committee (of which Douglas was still a member), Democrats met to discuss its merits. Douglas was present to argue the case for annexing Cuba and to lend his support to Slidell's bill. He thought that the prospect of purchasing Cuba was, at the moment, remote, but he was willing to support the attempt. The only feasible way to secure Cuba, he suggested, was to await an incident that would justify the forcible seizure of the island. Negotiations for its acquisition could then be opened with Spain with some chance for success.

Douglas' endorsement of Slidell's bill was interpreted as a surrender "of his political fortunes into the hands of his enemies." Kentucky's former governor R. P. Letcher reflected a wider reaction when he expressed a loss of confidence in Douglas' firmness and self-respect. "Douglas will cling to the Democratic banner as long as a *shred* is *left;* his party may kick him, beat him, but as long as he has a hope of being taken up as a candidate for the Presidency he will humble himself *too low* to be respected by his party." If Douglas hoped to ingratiate himself with party leaders, Letcher asserted, he was mistaken, for they "won't honor him so much as to let him *wash up the dishes,* and eat in the kitchen of Democracy." But Douglas' presence in the caucus, aside from his eagerness to support a policy he had long advocated, stemmed precisely from his determination not to surrender to his enemies. He was unmoved by the criticism and, in fact, participated in a second party caucus (occasioned by a revolt of Pennsylvania Democrats on the tariff question) when he agreed that the party ought not modify its traditional stand on the tariff.[24]

Douglas' course continued to arouse speculation that his loss of power was real and complete. "Douglas is quiet," commented Preston King, "& out of all position." Southerners and supporters of the administration grew impatient with his restraint. When two Illinois Congressmen proposed that the territories be allowed to elect their own governors, judges, and other officials, a logical extension of popular sovereignty, it was assumed that Douglas had concocted "a new hostile device" to fling at the administration, "a wedge intended to split off a slice of the Northern democracy, as a sort of Van Buren balance of power for Mr. Douglas." The Washington *Union* immediately countered with editorials detailing the administration position on the prerogatives of territorial governments, but Douglas made no response.

Unwilling to wait longer, and anxious to gain support for their own views, southern radicals undertook to goad Douglas into a defense of his position. An early probing attack by Georgia Senator Alfred Iverson a few days before Douglas returned to his seat was a preview of things to come. "I do not consider the triumph of . . . [Douglas]," he protested, "as a victory of sound Democracy." It was instead a victory of freesoil Democracy over the constitutional rights of the south. The Wilmot Proviso, contended Iverson, was preferable to Douglas' popular sovereignty, for it was "an open and undisguised denial of right to the South," while the latter was "plausible, delusive, deceptive and fatal." He had words of warning for the south. "I believe that the time will come"— and he cited the election of 1860 as the moment of decision—"when the slave States will be compelled, in vindication of their rights, interests, and honor, to separate from the free States, and erect an independent Confederacy." [25]

The southern strategy was given an unexpected boost by New Hampshire's antislavery Senator John P. Hale, who threw the Kansas question into the Senate deliberations in the last days of the session, to the disgust and discomfiture of many of his colleagues. Hale offered an amendment to an appropriation bill which would withhold money for a census of Kansas, an effort to remove the restriction, imposed by the English bill, that Kansas not be admitted as a state until its population equaled the ratio of representation in the lower house of Congress. While he objected to the revival of the Kansas question, Douglas reiterated his opposition to the condition that had been attached to Kansas' admission. He reviewed his efforts to secure automatic admission for territories when their populations were sufficient for representation in Congress, and he reminded the Senate that the English bill had made Kansas an exception to this rule. Since Congress had been willing to waive the population requirement if Kansas "would take a particular constitution," Douglas argued that Kansas ought to be admitted with whatever constitution "she may desire to form." If and when Kansas came to Congress "with a constitution republican in form, and sanctioned by her own people," he would vote for her admission. "I am not willing to make the admission of a State dependent upon the condition that she will take such constitution as we may choose to impose upon her, instead of forming one to suit herself." [26]

Southern radical Senators grasped the opportunity to present their platform, make their points against Douglas, and force the Illinois Senator into an elaboration of his Freeport position. The Freeport Doctrine demanded a southern response, and in responding, southerners revealed the new position to which they now moved, in effect a platform statement for 1860. When the Senate convened on February 23, the first to rise was Mississippi's Albert Gallatin Brown, but Jefferson Davis and James S. Green soon joined the attack. Brown insisted that slave property in the territories was entitled to protection, not the kind of protection offered by "the mere naked Constitution," but *"adequate* protection, *sufficient* protection . . . suited to the nature and description of property to be protected." Such protection could only be provided by positive legislation; if the territorial legislature refuses to act, then the obligation to protect slavery is upon Congress. This, Brown made clear, would be the southern position in the 1860 election. If it should be denied, he warned, then "the Constitution is a failure, . . . the Union a despotism . . . [and] I am prepared to retire from the concern."

Brown's argument was buttressed by other southern Senators, who charged that Douglas' statement at Freeport revealed popular sovereignty in its true colors. It was, explained Davis, "a siren's song . . . a thing shadowy and fleeting, changing its color as often as the chameleon . . . a delusive gauze thrown over the public mind." None was more bitter than Virginia's James Mason, who spoke as one who had supported the Kansas-Nebraska Act. "You promised us bread, and you have given us a stone; you promised us a fish, and you have given us a serpent; we thought you had given us a substantial right; and you have given us the most evanescent shadow and delusion." [27]

It was a challenge which Douglas could not ignore. "If no other northern Democrat desires to be heard on the points presented by the Senator from Mississippi," Douglas opened, "I feel it incumbent on me to say something in vindication of my own position, reluctant as I am to occupy time at this stage of the session in a discussion of this question." He patiently repeated his views, gradually warming to the task until one correspondent thought that Douglas imagined himself on the stump in Illinois. Slaves are property, and the owner of a slave has the same right to emigrate to a territory with his slave property as does the owner of any other kind of property; whatever power the territorial legislature has over other kinds of property extends also to slave property. "I say that I leave all kinds of property, slaves included, to the local law for protection; and that I will not exert the power of Congress to interfere with that local law with reference to slave property. . . . If the people think that particular laws on the subject of property are beneficial to their interests, they will enact them. If they do not think such laws are wise, they will refrain from enacting them."

Douglas agreed with Brown that the failure of a territory to provide protection to slavery would exclude slavery as effectively as a constitutional prohibition, but he disagreed that it was therefore wrong for a territory to pursue that policy. When Senator Clay charged Douglas with holding that "squatter sovereignty is superior to the Constitution," Douglas denied that "sovereign power attaches to a Territory while a Territory." All the power possessed by a territory, he argued, was derived from the Constitution "under the organic act." He was unequivocal in his rejection of congressional intervention either for or against slavery in the territories and denounced the southerners' proposal for a federal slave code as contrary to the Democratic platform.

At last confronting those who would read him out of the Democratic party, Douglas contended that it was they, not he, who had jumped off the platform and who must go out of the party. "I have no idea of leaving," he declared to the applause of the galleries. "I intend to stand here in my place, for the next six years, battling for those principles to which so much of my life has been devoted, and to which I am ready to devote the balance." Again he repeated what he had said so many times before. Slavery ought not to be forced upon people who do not want it, nor should people who want it be deprived of it. He reminded the Senate that he had been assailed "first on one side and then upon the other, as if it was something extraordinary that I should hold the same opinions now that I so fully expressed in the great contests of 1850 and in 1854 and in 1856." Nothing had occurred that would require him to modify these opinions. "I have no such pride of consistency as would prevent me from modifying my opinions when convinced of an error; but upon this subject of congressional intervention I think I am right. I do not believe the peace of the Union can be maintained on any other principle." To which Jefferson Davis replied that Douglas was "full of heresy." [28]

The debate consumed virtually the entire day and threatened to continue unabated through the night. "They can go on here arguing against each other from this until doomsday, and I think it is high time the discussion should be put a stop to," complained one Senator. Another argued that "we are debating imaginary issues . . . and if this debate is to continue all night, I would rather go home." Others also recognized the abstract level of the discussion and they deplored the controversy the more because of it. The question which southern leaders put to Douglas was, according to one newspaper correspondent, "one of the most unprofitable, barren and impracticable slavery abstractions of the day." But because it was abstract, the issue also was dangerous, for from this time on, the question of slavery in the territories was debated without application to a real situation.

Douglas finally provided the Senate, and the country, with the "reasons" for which southern leaders had waited since the opening days of the session. While he made no direct reference to his removal from the committee chairmanship, it was very much in his mind, so his effort to trace the consistency of his views constituted his defense against the charge that he had suddenly become a heretic in the Democratic camp. Rumors later circulated that the debate sprang from a prior arrangement between Douglas and Brown. Brown denied their validity and explained to Douglas the purpose he sought to accomplish when he first challenged the Illinois Senator. "My object in bringing on the debate," he wrote, "was solely to show the Southern people . . . that most, if indeed not all the Northern Democratic Senators agreed with you, and while some of them were quite willing to see the denunciations against you in the South go on they were very reluctant to take issue with us, & against you before a Northern audience." It was Brown's intention to bring the differences between north and south into the open and especially to commit northern politicians on the issues that separated the sections. "I think the game of hide and whoop has been played long enough."

Throughout most of the discussion, the Republicans were silent. Hale was accused of forcing the fight in order to aggravate Democratic differences. "He has punctured the old Kansas sore of the democratic party very skilfully, and has . . . prevented by this untimely explosion between Mr. Douglas and the Southern fire-eaters, some expected reconciliation and treaty of peace." The *Union* likened the Senators to a pack of Newfoundland dogs. Hale "pitched in the chip, and all the high bloods of that august body have rushed into the water in full chase." In this sense, the issue was far from abstract, for its impact on the Democratic party and the Union would soon be measurable in some very real consequences.[29]

### iii

The end of the second session of the thirty-fifth Congress, a few days after the explosive exchange between Douglas and the southern radicals, left Democrats bitter, frustrated, and demoralized. The party, it was now apparent, was in a hopeless state of disarray. The gloss which many Democratic leaders, including Douglas, had tried to maintain was stripped away, and the seriousness of the party's schism was exposed for all to see. The events of the winter, concluded one Senator, pointed to "a thorough break up and dissolution of the democratic party." [30]

The struggle over the Lecompton constitution had earlier revealed the wide gulf separating northern and southern Democrats. But the English bill (as unsatisfactory as that measure was to some party members) and the course of events in Kansas seemed to settle the practical question involved, softening the impact of the disagreement and enabling the party to recover some of its equilibrium. Douglas' Freeport Doctrine, however, aggravated the ideological differences that had been so carefully concealed in the Cincinnati platform and forced the discussion to a level of abstraction where practical arguments held little weight. A dangerous polarization resulted that virtually ruled out concession and compromise. Although Douglas' views were neither new nor unexpected, their announcement, hard on the heels of the Lecompton crisis, pushed southerners into an extreme response. The demand of the southern radicals for positive protection of slave property in the territories became the only effective weapon with which to combat Douglas' popular sovereignty, with its disturbing corollary of unfriendly legislation.

Dissatisfaction of northern Democrats with the south had other manifestations than disagreement over the question of slavery in the territories. They were stung by widespread Democratic defeats in the 1858 elections; their resentment against the southern leadership mounted. Once again they had to return to their constituents (some for good) empty-handed and disappointed with the failure of measures for which many of them had been fighting for a long time. None felt the failure more keenly than Douglas and the western Democrats. The Pacific railroad had again been killed; homestead legislation had been frustrated, and the proposal to subsidize agricultural education with grants from the public domain had suffered a presidential veto. Appropriations for river and harbor improvements were not even considered. "Upon no single issue," the *States* had commented early in the year, "is there adequate agreement [among Democrats] for a common basis of action. . . . There is no such entity as a Democratic party." It was easy for western Democrats to place the blame for their failures; in each instance their measures were blocked by southerners or by the administration acting, it was thought, on behalf of the south. To many northerners, the southern demand for a federal slave code, coming at a time when southerners were beating down northern measures, was a last straw. Already facing repudiation by their constituents, they could hardly maintain a generous mood toward the south.

"We are not in a condition to carry another ounce of Southern weight," wrote James W. Singleton to Douglas. "We have essayed to vindicate their rights under the Constitution, we grant to them all we claim for ourselves, and we must now take our chances alike for the protection which the local laws will extend to our property in the territories; to go further and legislate for one or every species of property in the territories—would be *inexplicable inconsistency,* invoking the fatal acknowledgement *as error* all our preconceived notions of the right and capacity of the people to regulate their domestic affairs in their own way." If a "platform of Congressional intervention for the protection of slavery" should be forced on the north, Forney had written, "there will be no help for us."

The northern Democrats had their backs up, and their determination to resist southern demands stiffened. Douglas became more implacable as the stakes became more critical. No political creed, he insisted, was sound which could not be proclaimed throughout the United States. His doctrine of popular sovereignty, he still was convinced, was the only creed that met that criterion. "We must meet the issue boldly which has been presented to us by the Interventionists from the North and from the South, and maintain with firmness a strict adherence to the doctrine of popular sovereignty. ... There is no other salvation for the Democratic party." To defer to either the northern Republicans or the southern radicals would destroy the national character of the Democratic party and place the Union in jeopardy. It was still Douglas' mission to tread the middle ground, in the hope that both could yet be saved. "I do not intend to make peace with my enemies, nor to make a concession of one iota of principle, believing that I am right in the position I have taken, and that neither can the Union be preserved or the Democratic party maintained upon any other basis." [31]

Both sides looked to the Charleston convention for vindication, but the outcome of that meeting became less and less certain as time passed. Some Democrats were wholly pessimistic that party unity could be maintained in the face of the pressures that would come to focus there. Davis, Brown, and others had warned that if Douglas' position should be endorsed by the convention the south would withdraw; no candidate could secure a single southern electoral vote on a popular sovereignty platform. Douglas, on the other hand, insisted that a federal slave code platform not only was unacceptable to northern Democrats, but also could not carry a single northern state. An irrepressible conflict was developing within the Democratic ranks. The crisis, however, transcended the party, for without unity the Democrats would be powerless to prevent the election of a Republican President, and Iverson had already warned that the south would leave the Union in such an event. The nation depended upon the ability of the Democratic party to formulate a national platform, one that would be acceptable to all sections.

The results of the Illinois election foreshadowed the contest for the Democratic nomination in 1860 and, at the time, seemed to point to but one conclusion. Douglas could not fail in his bid for the presidential nomination, predicted *The New York Times,* "for it must be perfectly evident, even to Mr. Buchanan himself, that his [Douglas'] platform is the only one upon which the National Democracy can be rallied and reunited for the contest." In Douglas' criteria for success in 1860, the platform held top priority—"a bold, honest platform, avowing our principles in unequivocal language." The Democratic candidate should be someone "who is thoroughly identified with it and whose past gives assurance that he will honestly carry it out." He did not offer his name, although there was little doubt among northern Democrats that he was the only person who could satisfy the requirement.[32]

Shortly after Congress convened in December, a rumor spread that Douglas would withdraw his name from consideration. The report was later branded a "mischievous canard," but the question of his availability had been raised. Forney, who was eager to announce Douglas' name for the presidency, urged him to seek a nomination independent of the Charleston convention. The possibility was scotched immediately by an announcement in the *Chicago Times* that claimed the authority of Douglas himself. He would not seek a nomination at Charleston, but he would also not refuse the nomination if his friends should present his name there. The use of his name as a candidate "independent of and hostile to the nominations of the democratic party" was unauthorized and "wholly repugnant to his wishes and desires." [33]

Douglas' battle with the south in the Senate, however, revived speculation that he would organize an independent movement, converting the 1860 election into " a triangular contest, on the model of 1848." Forney persisted in his effort to persuade Douglas to adopt this course. Following Congress' adjournment, Douglas visited Forney in Philadelphia, finally impressing the editor with his determination to take his chances at Charleston. Still Douglas had apparently sounded out some of his supporters on the question of withdrawal, for in March A. D. Banks, the Virginia editor whom Douglas selected to assist him with his campaign, wrote, "The more I think of your suggestion that you should withdraw from the race the more I am averse to it." The northern Democracy expected Douglas to be a candidate, and he had no right to withdraw; he was not a free agent in the matter, a fact Douglas would soon learn from others.[34]

When Douglas announced that he would support the nominee of the Charleston convention, the inevitable reports of a reconciliation between Douglas and the President again appeared. The differences between them, according to the new administration organ, the Washington *Constitution,* were simply a "temporary alienation," such as the party was bound to experience on occasion. Negotiations were said to be underway to redefine popular sovereignty in a form that would be acceptable to all Democrats. In a trial effort, the *Constitution* denounced both the Freeport Doctrine and a federal slave code, arguing that slavery must remain unmolested in the territories until the moment of statehood—not a new definition, but the traditional Buchanan-southern view. The slavery question was a dead issue, and the demand for a slave code the "purest abstraction." When Buchanan met privately with Robert J. Walker, he stirred speculation that he would endorse the former Kansas governor for the nomination as a gesture toward reconciliation with Douglas.

No effort to find common ground between north and south could succeed that left Douglas out of the picture, yet that was what the administration seemed to be attempting. Senator Green suggested that all discussion of intervention and non-intervention be dropped as "non-essential" and that opposition to Kansas as a free state be withdrawn, but his proposals were also based on the southern view of popular sovereignty. George Sanders vainly tried to persuade Douglas to meet the administration on this ground. Obviously Douglas could be reinstated "as a regular member of the party" only at the price of his convictions. Overlooked in the administration's attempts to smooth the waters was the deepening commitment among northern Democrats to Douglas' position. "All reports of a coalition between Douglas & myself," wrote the President on May 1, "are so ridiculous that they are unworthy even of a denial." Douglas was equally emphatic, rejecting all suggestions that required the concession of "an iota of the principles he had all along avowed." Nevertheless, rumors of a reconciliation persisted throughout the summer.[35]

"I agree with you fully in regard to the necessity of thorough organization of our friends preparatory to the great battle at Charleston," Douglas wrote Singleton on the last day of March. Douglas began to lay the foundation for his presidential campaign as soon as his re-election to the Senate was sure. While he promised to abide by the results of the Charleston convention, he was determined that the platform be his and that he be the nominee. His response to the attacks of Brown and Davis in February were printed as a pamphlet, and 100,000 copies were sent out under the franks of various members of Congress.[36] Sheahan was at work on a campaign biography, sending the completed chapters to Douglas for revision and correction. Suggestions were made to publish a volume of Douglas' speeches. One Illinois editor wrote of his plans to bring out an edition of Douglas' debates with Lincoln in 1858. Arrangements were completed for the mass production of an "imperial photograph" and a new lithographed portrait that could be distributed during the coming months.[37] Douglas devoted considerable thought to his financial condition, corresponding with banks, appealing to friends, and traveling to New York in his quest for the resources necessary to a successful campaign. Notes that fell due were extended and mortgages refinanced; negotiations for the sale or lease of some of his Chicago land were undertaken. Douglas' already large debt burden became even larger as he looked ahead to the 1860 election. One report claimed that his Chicago property carried mortgages in excess of $160,000. An earlier investment in the Texan Emigration and Land Company was maintained; his allotment as a shareholder was seventy-five acres and it may have been this allotment, in "Peter's Colony" on the Brazos River near Fort Belknap, for which he received an offer from a Texas real estate agent. There is no record, however, that he sold his interest.[38]

In the spring of 1859, many state parties began moving toward the all-important selection of delegates to the Charleston convention. Douglas watched their movements with some anxiety. Demoralized by their defeats in 1858, Democrats in some northern states approached their task with diffidence. The state organizations reflected the same disagreements that divided the party nationally. Douglas received invitations to speak in Connecticut, New Hampshire, Massachusetts, Pennsylvania, Iowa, Ohio, and Minnesota, but he declined most of them. In an off-year election, Connecticut's congressional delegation was at stake, so he made plans to stump that state. The illness of his son caused him to cancel his tour, however, and he sent a public letter instead to a Hartford newspaper. "The Democratic party is the only political organization, which can preserve the peace and harmony of the Union," he wrote, and only a recognition of popular sovereignty could maintain "the integrity and ascendancy of the Democratic party." The statement did little good; the Republicans continued their sweep of the congressional elections.

In Pennsylvania, the Democratic state convention sided with the administration. Douglas hurried to Philadelphia, spoke with Forney, and shortly afterward a second convention met which offered a strong endorsement of the Senator's position. New York was the scene of frantic maneuvering as the party's factions sought to build strength for the state convention in September. Dean Richmond, Peter Cagger, the ubiquitous George Sanders, Erastus Corning, and other leaders of the "softs" attended informal caucuses in Douglas' Washington home, "deep in intrigues with the Douglas men." In July, Douglas was in New York, conferring with local politicians. Just where all this activity would lead was a matter of speculation.³⁹

Isaac Cook continued to plague Douglas in his home state. While the thrust of the Danites had been blunted by Douglas' easy re-election, Cook, encouraged and assisted by the administration, was using his position in the Chicago post office to rebuild his movement for the 1860 election. "I look upon Cook," wrote Slidell to Buchanan, "as by far the most influential friend you have in Illinois." Cook was soon sending optimistic reports of inroads made in the Douglas ranks. The Douglasites raised charges of corruption against the postmaster, but more serious to Douglas was the use of the post office to promote Danite strength. Clerks sympathetic to Douglas were dismissed, those who remained were forced to make financial contributions to the Chicago *Herald,* the Danite newspaper, printed speeches sent under Douglas' frank were not delivered, and in some instances Cook was charged with opening Douglas' letters. Douglas, annoyed to the extreme, began sending his communications with friends who traveled from Washington to Chicago or prepaying his letters in the hope that they might pass through the post office undetected. Formal charges were taken to Joseph Holt, the new Postmaster General, and the subsequent investigation not only confirmed most of them but also revealed that Cook was cheating the government out of thousands of dollars. Efforts to remove the troublesome postmaster, however, were frustrated by an administration which continued to find him useful politically.⁴⁰

Following Douglas' confrontation with the south in the Senate, he was bombarded with queries from apprehensive southern supporters who sought a clarification of his position. Douglas himself now wondered if the radicals spoke for a wide segment of southern opinion in their demand for a federal slave code. Some of his mail was reassuring. Southern opposition to Douglas, wrote a Virginian, was likely to give the impression that he had no strength whatever in the slaveholding states. The southern people must be convinced that the Democratic party could only be saved under Douglas' leadership. One southerner who was already persuaded was the Mobile newspaper editor John Forsyth. Just returned to Washington from Mexico, where he had served as minister, Forsyth questioned Douglas on the meaning of popular sovereignty. "I have an idea you are right, & I want to *know* it." He was prepared to waive the south's claim to the presidential nomination. "We must have a sound

Free State man to keep the issue from being purely sectional." Douglas, "a ray of light and hope" for the south, was that man. The Democratic party was the only barrier, he felt, to the designs of the abolitionists. "Break that down, and we are all at sea. . . . I am unwilling to risk this fearful future for an abstraction." [41]

Douglas first sent Banks on an extensive tour of the south, and then, in mid-May, he decided to examine his southern support at first hand. The need to draw up new articles of agreement with James A. McHatton, his partner in the Mississippi plantation enterprise, provided an excuse for the trip. It was a quick journey, but his pace was not so rapid that he did not have time to talk with southern friends along his route in Virginia, Georgia, Alabama, and Louisiana. He was anxious to test the impact not only of the slave code issue, but also of the disturbing question of the revival of the slave trade. Satisfied with the attitudes he encountered, he decided to end the speculation regarding his presidential plans, to strengthen his following among moderate southerners, and to ease the minds of his northern backers.[42]

J. B. Dorr, editor of the Dubuque *Express and Herald,* provided the opportunity. Douglas' supporters in Iowa, Dorr wrote the Senator, "feel somewhat embarrassed by the want of definite knowledge of your position in relation to the Charleston Convention of 1860." He asked for "an answer touching this subject." Douglas replied in a letter that was published in newspapers throughout the country, a formal announcement of his candidacy and the terms upon which he would accept it. He would allow his name to be presented to the convention only if the party adhered firmly to the "principles embodied in the Compromise measures of 1850 . . . re-affirmed in the Kansas-Nebraska Act of 1854, and incorporated into the Cincinnati platform in 1856, as expounded by Mr. Buchanan in his letter accepting the nomination," in other words, to popular sovereignty as Douglas interpreted it. He could not accept the nomination, he declared emphatically, if the convention should endorse "such new issues" as a congressional slave code for the territories, the revival of the African slave trade, or the doctrine that the Constitution either establishes or prohibits slavery in the territories beyond the power of the local population legally to control it.

Later in the summer Douglas wrote a second public letter in which he repeated his opposition to the revival of the slave trade, "in every form, and under any circumstances." The issue had been much on his mind since his return from the south. In private conversation, he had estimated that 15,000 African slaves had been landed illegally in the south during the previous year. He saw 300 of them, he said, in a slave pen in Vicksburg, and others in Memphis.

The publication of the letters produced a sensation throughout the country. Together they constituted a clear statement that the northern Democracy would settle for nothing less than the Douglas platform and a warning that the party could no longer be regarded as a vehicle for the advancement of southern interests at the expense of its national responsibilities.[43]

Some of Douglas' supporters were disturbed. "Your prospects for the Presidency brighten every day," wrote Steedman from Ohio. "But you must quit writing letters." From Tennessee, former governor James C. Jones advised, "I dont want you to write any more letters. . . . Stand on your present record and let the people do the rest." As he entered his campaign, however, Douglas insisted on being clearly understood. The letter to Dorr was not enough. The events of the spring persuaded him that his views needed still further explication and that his doctrine of popular sovereignty needed a firmer basis. The speculation in the press, the queries he received almost daily in his mail, the attacks of the radical south revealed a confusion and misunderstanding about his position that he felt must be dispelled. Ignoring the advice of his friends, Douglas prepared to issue yet another, more ambitious, and comprehensive statement of the ground on which he stood.[44]

iv

The administration charged Douglas with raising false issues in his letter to Dorr and denied that a federal slave code and the revival of the slave trade had any significant support among Democrats. Buchanan regarded the statement as "truly ridiculous," "an odd letter" filled with inconsistency and obscurity. "Like other men who have left the Democratic party," observed the President, "he has become bewildered & has involved himself in the most absurd contradictions." Douglas' letter, commented Slidell, "breathes that spirit of intolerable arrogance which has always characterized him." Even the *States,* a Douglas paper, questioned it. Under the editorship of Roger Pryor, a Virginian, the paper argued that territorial legislatures did not have the power to prohibit slavery, since Congress could not bestow authority on the legislature that it itself did not possess, a view maintained in the Dred Scott decision. A series of articles examined the territorial question in detail, generally assuming the administration stance which, because they appeared in a Douglas paper, raised new questions regarding the Senator's position. Probably because of this disagreement, Pryor left the paper in June.[45]

Southerners continued to ask Douglas for an elaboration of his views, "to avoid further misapprehensions of your position touching the *legal* power of a Territorial Legislature over the question of slavery." In reply, Douglas distinguished between the legal and political questions involved. All legal questions regarding the powers of a territorial legislature "must be determined by the Courts, whose decisions all must respect and obey"; the only political question was whether the slavery issue should be banished from Congress and referred to the people of the states and territories. Implicit in his reply was a denial that the Dred Scott decision had in any way answered the legal question; it would remain for a future court in a future case to do so. If unfriendly legislation against slavery were unconstitutional, it was up to the court to say so; in the meantime it could be exercised.[46]

As southerners questioned Douglas' popular sovereignty, Republicans moved to its support. Illinois Congressman William Kellogg argued early in the year that it was up to the Republicans to strip popular sovereignty of its deception and to "give it distinctiveness of character, and make it the real helper of popular institutions and popular rights." He proposed that voters in the territories be allowed to elect their own executive and judicial officers—an extreme to which even Douglas did not yet go—as a means undoubtedly of circumventing the appointive power of a possible proslavery administration. The Chicago *Tribune* hailed this new approach as "Republican Popular Sovereignty—the pure metal, with a clear and always recognizable ring!" Kansas had been saved for freedom by Douglas' doctrine, and Republicans now saw merit in it. Lincoln, disturbed by this novel tactic, warned that "no party can command respect which sustains this year, what it opposed last." Republicans as well as southerners were forcing Douglas to a new exposition of his political views.[47]

Douglas did not return to Illinois for the summer of 1859, but remained in Washington with his family. Adele was pregnant again, and her husband wished to be at her side since she had already suffered one miscarriage. Douglas also had political reasons for staying in the capital. His home was open to visiting Democratic leaders, and Washington's rumormongers were kept busy with the many conferences that were held there. It soon became common knowledge that Douglas was also spending his time on another "manifesto." As early as April he had written the historian George Bancroft of his plans to prepare an address "upon the right of the people of the Territories to govern themselves in all their domestic relations, without the interference of the federal government." Arrangements for its publication were concluded in July with the editors of *Harper's Magazine,* through the agency of a friend, William A. Seaver, who believed that the subject, "without reference to party politics," was of timely importance and "such paramount interest" that the public would welcome "the carefully elaborated views of a statesman whose public experience had necessarily familiarized him with territorial jurisprudence." Because its publication would be an innovation in magazine publishing, as well as in political expression, efforts were made to keep the arrangements secret.[48]

Douglas turned to early American history to find precedents for popular sovereignty, withdrawing from the Library of Congress such works as Elliott's *Debates,* Henry C. Carey's *Slave Trade,* Bancroft's *History of the United States,* and the histories of several of the colonies. Convinced that a parallel could be drawn between the colonies and the western territories, he appealed to Bancroft for help in tracing the principles involved in the struggle of the colonies against Great Britain. Douglas believed that the colonists claimed the exclusive right to legislate "in respect to their internal polity, slavery included," and he asked Bancroft for a list of colonial enactments which prohibited or excluded slavery. Bancroft, long a supporter of Douglas, obliged with copies of colonial documents, adding that "the entire control of the question of slavery by the respective colonial legislatures appears still more clearly from the laws relating to emancipation. . . . All such matters were always decided as the colonies pleased." Other friends sent Douglas additional evidence.[49]

Douglas completed the manuscript by mid-summer. "I am sure," he wrote to Seaver, "that my friend Fletcher Harper will never regret the favor to me in publishing it, while I claim it will help the magazine." The publication of his essay, "The Dividing Line Between Federal and Local Authority: Popular Sovereignty in the Territories," in the September issue created an immediate sensation. The fact that it was copyrighted caused consternation among newspaper editors, who were restrained from reprinting it without permission—"a revolution in modern systems of Presidential campaigning," complained the New York *Herald.*[50]

Douglas' purposes in the article were twofold: first, to demonstrate that popular sovereignty was firmly based on historical precedent, that the "fathers of the Revolution" had recognized the inalienable right of dependent political communities to local self-government, and that the slavery question was considered by them to be a matter of domestic and internal concern; and second, to provide a constitutional justification for popular sovereignty. Although he gave some attention to the Republican position, it was against his southern critics that his arguments were primarily directed. To those who maintained that a territorial legislature could not exercise a power over slavery not possessed by Congress—that the creature cannot be clothed with powers not possessed by the creator—Douglas pointed out that Congress, in creating territorial governments, did indeed confer power which it did not possess itself. In all such instances, he emphasized, the powers conferred were those which related to domestic affairs rather than to the general welfare of the nation. This, to Douglas, was the true "dividing line" between federal and local authority.[51]

Turning to history, Douglas found this "dividing line" clearly marked out in the "immortal struggle between the American Colonies and the British Government." He cited acts and petitions in which the colonists had insisted on the right to legislate with regard to slavery, and he found attempts to check the growth of slavery "by a system of unfriendly legislation." In all instances, slavery was regarded as a domestic question. Douglas discovered further background to popular sovereignty in Jefferson's 1784 plan for western government, although he ignored the prohibition of slavery originally included in Jefferson's scheme and made no mention of the Ordinance of 1787.[52]

Douglas' assertion that the word "States," as used in the post-Revolutionary period, encompassed both of the later concepts of "States" and "Territories" formed the crux of his constitutional argument. Although he had frequently spoken of the words as synonymous with respect to power over internal affairs, he had never developed the idea as fully as he did in this essay. During the Confederation and early national period, the temporary western governments were consistently referred to as "States" or "new States." Therefore, he maintained, both states and territories stand in the same relation to the Constitution as far as slavery, or any other domestic institution, is concerned. Popular sovereignty in the territories, he believed, was constitutionally justified beyond any reasonable doubt.

The members of the Constitutional Convention in 1787 had made a conscious effort, Douglas argued, to draft a new document modeled after the British constitution as interpreted by the colonies. It was inconceivable that these men would have withheld from the western governments the rights and privileges for which they themselves had fought as colonies. What had been claimed as the birthright of all Englishmen before the Revolution had become the birthright of all Americans by virtue of the Revolution. When the framers provided that "Congress shall have power to dispose of and make all needful rules and regulations respecting the territory or other property belonging to the United States" (Article IV, Section 3), they used the word "territory" to refer only to the unappropriated portions of the public domain, not to a political community or government. Advocates of the Wilmot Proviso had distorted the meaning of the clause, he wrote, in order to justify an absolute federal authority over the internal affairs of the territories. Douglas repeated that the authority of Congress to establish territorial governments was derived from the power to admit new states and to make all laws necessary and proper to that end.[53]

For judicial support, Douglas quoted the Dred Scott decision at length. He made free use of ellipses, however, citing only those portions which seemed to substantiate his position most fully, and at one point he transposed sentences in order to heighten the effect. His ground was less sure here, and his arguments became more involved and complicated. To those southern critics who maintained that slavery was among the areas of action forbidden to territories, Douglas replied that the Court was referring to powers forbidden to Congress, in states and territories alike; if slavery were included among these prohibitions, then the people of the states as well as those of the territories were powerless to control it by law.

As a final point, Douglas observed that the constitutional provision for the return of fugitive slaves defined a slave as a "person held to service or labor in one State, under the laws thereof." He maintained that, since the territories are encompassed within the meaning of the word "State," it would follow that the people of the territories have the same right to control the institution as do the people of the states. If "Territories" are not included within the meaning of the word "State," he pointed out, then the territories would become a refuge and sanctuary for fugitive slaves, a possibility which even the most radical southerner would not recognize.[54]

It is doubtful that Douglas secured many new converts with his essay.

The article was long and tedious, written in a turgid style that lacked the vibrancy of his speeches. Repetitious and often contrived, the effort perhaps weakened Douglas' case, for by seeking historical precedents and constitutional justification he removed popular sovereignty further from its pragmatic base by attempting to clothe it in theory. At the same time, Douglas' conclusions were unmistakable, and it was apparent to all just where he stood. Henry J. Raymond, editor of *The New York Times,* lauded Douglas for his courage in putting his ideas "in the broadest light of public opinion," noting that his doctrine of popular sovereignty was a "very fair compromise" between the Republican and southern positions. Douglas' mail was filled with letters of praise; even a few southerners registered a qualified approval. His senatorial adversary, Albert G. Brown, grudgingly observed that he had "made the best of a bad cause."

The southern reaction, however, was primarily one of indignation and protest. Douglas had now placed himself "outside the pale of the party," wrote an Alabama Congressman, and his essay gave him "a death blow in the South." John B. Floyd, Buchanan's Secretary of War, was confident that this "last exposition of squatter sovereignty will finally extinguish him." Alfred Iverson declared that an acceptance of Douglas would now be suicidal for the south. "All the heresies are in the manifesto," wrote the editor of the *Constitution* to Howell Cobb. To a Richmond editor, the essay was "an incendiary document" representing the "most dangerous phase which anti-slavery agitation has yet assumed"; there was no difference in principle between Douglas and Seward. And from Alabama came the demand that "the infection of his heresy" be halted before it destroyed the south. "A leprous limb may corrupt the whole body; but let the offending member be amputated and the whole system may be restored to health."

Banks informed Douglas that the article had "estranged" some of his southern friends. It had fallen on his apologists in the south, commented the Louisville *Courier,* like a "clap of thunder on a cloudless day." "His anti-Lecomptonism was bad, his Freeport speech was worse, but his 'copy-righted' Squatter Sovereignty essay . . . is worst of all." A few devoted southerners, like Forsyth, fought to keep pro-Douglas sentiment alive, but the odds against them were formidable.[55]

The publication of Douglas' essay unleashed a flood of answers; never before had the question of slavery in the territories been so thoroughly discussed. The editorial office of *Harper's* was swamped with communications from Republicans and southern Democrats asking for equal space to answer Douglas' arguments. Fletcher Harper conveniently sailed for Europe, but not before he received appeals from former Alabama Congressman Henry Hilliard; George Ticknor Curtis, the eminent constitutional historian; O. Jennings Wise, the son of Virginia's governor; Horace Greeley, and many others. "The scribblers of the American Union are in a stew," Seaver wrote Douglas. "They are after you with sticks whittled mighty sharp." None of the requests was granted, the magazine having decided earlier not to accept replies, and most of the answers to Douglas were published in the press or as separate pamphlets. Greeley tried to set the historical record straight in a long article in the *Tribune,* and Curtis, in a pamphlet publication, upheld Congress' power over slavery in the territories, amassing an imposing array of historical precedents and constitutional citations. The *National Intelligencer* published a series on "The Territorial Question" that extended over eight issues of the paper, and countless other replies appeared in print. Douglas was not without his defenders, among the most prominent of whom was Reverdy Johnson, former cabinet member, Whig, and a prominent constitutional lawyer who had argued against Dred Scott before the Supreme Court. "Your great reputation as a lawyer," Douglas wrote Johnson, "will give authority to your opinions throughout the Union." He felt "great pride in being sustained by one whose legal authority none feel disposed to question." [56]

The rush to counter Douglas' arguments was quickly overshadowed by the reaction of the administration. As soon as the essay appeared, Buchanan determined to answer it in an official way. He selected his Attorney General and fellow Pennsylvanian, Jeremiah S. Black, to accomplish the task. Black had played this role before, having polished presidential drafts for the press on previous occasions, and he now took his cue from Buchanan once again. On September 10, the *Constitution* published Black's answer anonymously, and shortly afterward it was brought out in pamphlet form. The statement simply reiterated the administration's position on the question of slavery in the territories—that popular sovereignty properly interpreted meant that a territory could act on slavery only when it was moving into statehood and that a slaveholder could hold his property during the territorial period without interference from either Congress or the territorial legislature. Douglas, Black charged, not only contradicted his own former views; he also rejected the Supreme Court decision when he argued his "unfriendly legislation" doctrine. Black's answer touched off a pamphlet war between Douglas and the administration that continued for the next two months.[57]

Douglas received a copy of Black's answer while he was in Ohio to speak in support of Democratic candidates in the state election. During the summer he had received appeals for help from Ohio supporters, as well as an official invitation from the state's Democratic central committee. Douglas had already planned to appear, with Kentucky's Senator John J. Crittenden, at the annual fair of the United States Agricultural Society in Chicago, and he agreed to stop in Ohio on the way west. The state was important to Douglas' plans, since his friends were convinced that they had a chance to win. "Ohio should lead the North West," Douglas wrote, and it was to encourage this leadership that he spoke at Columbus, Cincinnati, and Wooster. The announcement that Douglas would visit Ohio took the Republicans by surprise. On the same day Abraham Lincoln was invited to come "to head off the little gentleman." Lincoln spoke in Columbus and Cincinnati several days after Douglas had appeared there. The presence of Lincoln and Douglas in Ohio aroused considerable national interest, and their speeches were regarded as extensions of the 1858 debates. Douglas was admonished not to "make any severe attacks on the Republicans" nor to "make the Territorial question, the principal feature" of his speeches, but he did not follow the advice. His venom, however, was directed principally at the administration and the south.[58]

At Wooster on September 16 Douglas replied to Black with a bitterness that revealed his antagonism toward the administration. The author of the pamphlet, he charged, was a "calumniator" and his work a web of deliberate and insidious falsehoods, "put forth willfully and with bad intent." Douglas denied that he had ever regarded a territory as a sovereign power and bristled at Black's implication that he was at odds with the Dred Scott decision. In response to the Republican argument that slavery was immoral and therefore ought not to be allowed to exist in the territories, Douglas declared, "It is no answer to this argument to say that slavery is an evil or a crime, and therefore the people should not be permitted to ruin themselves for inflicting such a curse upon them. It is the right of every people to judge for themselves whether it be an evil or not. . . . I do not know of any tribunal on earth that can decide the question of the morality of slavery or any other institution. I deal with slavery as a political question involving questions of public policy." [59]

With Douglas' reply to Black at Wooster, the conflict became heated. Black promptly responded in an *Appendix* to his pamphlet in which he repeated his earlier arguments. Douglas accepted the challenge with a twenty-three page pamphlet, to which Black once again replied. In early November, Douglas made a final rejoinder. The controversy offered no fresh arguments. The pamphlets were repetitious, and neither Douglas nor Black wavered, while each accused the other of misrepresentation. There was scarcely a sentence in Douglas' argument, charged Black, "which does not either propound an error, or else mangle a truth." Douglas replied that Black's presentation was full of "disreputable imputations and equivocal disclaimers, nearly every alternate sentence [is] pregnant with offensive innuendoes." Douglas took issue particularly with some of Black's personal allusions, including Black's charge that he was struggling for the presidency. "I do not desire the presidency at this time. . . . I will take no steps to obtain the Charleston nomination. . . . I will make no sacrifice of principle, no concealment of opinions, no concession to power for the purpose of getting it." Douglas was convincing in the latter sentiment, but the public knew too much of his ambition and his plans to take the preceding disclaimer at face value.[60]

With the appearance of Douglas' last pamphlet in November, the controversy closed. His fight against Black had been carried on amid deep personal difficulties. On the last day of September, Adele gave birth to a daughter, Ellen, and congratulations poured in, but the joy was soon dimmed when Adele became desperately ill. For a time her life was in danger, and Douglas was almost constantly at her bedside. As her health improved by mid-November, he fell ill. He attributed his illness to the "variety of filth" and the "sluggish and nauseating 'goose creeks' " with which Washington was encompassed, but it was undoubtedly aggravated by his anxiety and loss of rest over Adele's difficulties. His last reply to Black was unfinished, but he authorized his secretary to publish what was written. "I am too feeble . . . to add more," he wrote. "Here let the controversy close for the present, and perhaps forever." By the first of December both Douglas and his wife were convalescent —Douglas looking "as if he had passed through a severe siege" and Adele not "less beautiful because a little paler than usual"—and their physicians strongly advised a southern trip to complete the recuperation.[61]

Douglas' decision to bring the controversy to an end came none too soon. Seldom had the American people been exposed so thoroughly to conflicting arguments over a political issue, in a flood of published pamphlets, in column after column of newspaper print, in repeated and repetitious speeches. By the end of 1859, the public was visibly tiring of the barrage. The feeling spread that the nation's leaders were losing themselves in a maze of abstractions. The entire question, observed *The New York Times,* "is rapidly passing out of the field of practical politics." The fears which this inspired had been expressed in midsummer by a Washington editor. "The territorial question has emphatically been the evil genius of the Democratic party. . . . This question has assumed as many phases, and originated more meaningless abstract political transcendentalisms, than there are, or probably ever will be, Territories within the bounds of the Republic." [62]

For all the verbiage, the issue within the Democratic party had narrowed to the question of when, or at what stage, the people of a territory could legitimately exercise authority over slavery. These differences were being challenged by the radical southern demand for positive federal protection of slavery in the territories, the force of which was yet uncertain. Conflict with the Republicans seemed insignificant compared to that which raged within the Democratic ranks. To Douglas the Union itself was at stake. Speaking in Chicago in September, he again called for an end to the sectionalism that threatened the country. "There is no point upon the whole continent, which reminds one more of the necessity of its preservation, than this Prairie where we now stand. . . . Our mission and duty . . . is to do justice to all sections, then demand and insist upon the preservation of the peace and harmony of this glorious confederacy." [63] Like many others, Douglas prepared for the confrontation that 1860 would bring.

# XXVII

## "There is no better Democrat than I"
## 1859—1860

The battle over the territorial question was interrupted in mid-October by startling news from Harper's Ferry. Those who wearied of the apparently endless controversy over abstractions were suddenly confronted with a very real crisis. Douglas had just published his first pamphlet reply to Black, but its notice in the press was delayed as the headlines screamed of John Brown and "servile insurrection." The news sent shock waves throughout the nation. Brown, convinced that southern slaves required only a leader to rise up and throw off their bondage, seized the federal armory and arsenal at Harper's Ferry, Virginia, on the night of October 16, and then waited for recruits to join his enterprise. Instead of recruits, state militiamen and federal troops moved on his base, and after a brief seige Brown and the survivors of his group were taken prisoner. For weeks the incident was the subject of almost daily newspaper comment. Brown was brought to trial and on November 2 was sentenced to death. A month later he was hanged. His last words provided an ominous prophecy to an already nervous and tense people. "I John Brown am now quite *certain* that the crimes of this *guilty land:* will never be purged *away;* but with Blood." [1]

Douglas would have much to say about Brown's abortive effort later, but at the time, deeply involved in the pamphlet war with Black and anxious over his wife's health, he simply drew the moral of the incident. The inevitable result of abolitionist agitation, supported by the Republican party, would be a bloody sectional conflict. This was the lesson of Harper's Ferry for the north; the lesson for the south was more urgent. The movement of northern fanaticism, "strong and conducted with desperation," required all the patience, forbearance, and firmness of the nation's conservative men to put down. The south must understand "how sensitive large numbers of professedly respectable citizens at the north are on this subject of slavery." For their own safety, southerners should drop the "wild and absurd notion" of a federal slave code, "meet the northern democracy on a middle tenable ground," and cease their "unreasoning hostility" to Douglas. John Brown had provided a dramatic and frightening taste of the consequences of any other course of action.[2]

The south, however, was not a willing pupil. Southern radicals used the incident to prove the danger of continued association with the north. They pointed to the rising strength of the Republican party as an unmistakable signal that the south would soon fall victim to northern fanaticism. Secession was urged as the only alternative. More moderate southerners clung to the hope that additional guarantees could still be secured within the Union. Far from being abandoned, a slave code now assumed a greater importance.

Although one southern correspondent reported that Douglas' stock had risen "far above par" as a result of Harper's Ferry, in many southern minds the Illinois Senator shared the odium with the Republicans. Brown had dealt a fatal blow at Republican prospects, wrote Bigler to Buchanan, but he had also thrown "a wet blanket over the shoulders of our friend Douglas." Southern hostility encompassed both Douglas' popular sovereignty and Seward's "irrepressible conflict" doctrine. All such "Northern trimmers" as Douglas and all such "trimming inventions as squatter sovereignty" must be swept away. The Democracy "must be prepared to reject all such half-way men and half-way expedients, and consent to stand by the South in 1860." The alternative was an independent southern Democratic party, but few doubted that disunion lurked in the background. "All the indications point to a fearful crisis on the slavery question," warned Howell Cobb. "I regret to say that the conviction is now forced upon me, that the days of the Union are numbered." [3]

Brown's raid could not have occurred at a worse time. Many states were involved in election campaigns, preparations were being made for the selection of delegates to the national Democratic convention, and Congress would soon meet. The fears, charges, and accusations put the nation's lawmakers in an ugly and anxious mood. When Congress met on December 5, only three days after Brown's execution, it was immediately apparent that its deliberations would be dominated by the sectional crisis, its course moulded by the approaching presidential election.

Trouble developed at once in the House of Representatives, where the struggle to elect a Speaker revealed the depth and seriousness of the sectional split. Predictions had been made as early as the summer that neither party would command a majority in the House and that a Speaker could be chosen only by adopting the plurality rule or by a coalition of some of the competing groups. The Republicans, with 109 members, were ten short of the majority necessary for organization. There were 101 Democrats in the House, but this number included thirteen anti-Lecompton Democrats whose support was not at all sure. Five of the anti-Lecompton Democrats were Congressmen from Illinois. The remaining twenty-seven members of the House, virtually all from southern states, were listed as Americans or as Whigs. The balance of power lay with the southern opposition members and the anti-Lecompton Democrats. The support of both groups would be necessary to elect a Democratic Speaker.[4]

The outcome of the speakership contest was of prime importance to Douglas, for he regarded it as a trial run for the Charleston nomination. He had first to persuade the anti-Lecompton Democrats to remain with the party and second to unite moderate southerners with the Douglas Democrats against the radical south. It was a course laden with problems. Before Congress convened, party members gathered in caucus to agree on candidates. Douglas urged his followers to participate in the Democratic caucus, but only the five Illinois Congressmen did so. Many of the other anti-Lecompton Democrats had been bitterly attacked by the administration during their election campaigns, and some owed their elections to Republican support, both factors which prevented them from following Douglas' advice. Douglas worried that some might drift into the Republican party.

The Democrats selected Thomas S. Bocock of Virginia as their candidate for Speaker and appointed a five-member steering committee to direct Bocock's campaign. On the committee was John A. McClernand, who had been elected to Congress from the Springfield district in 1859 in place of the deceased Harris, indication that Douglas still exercised some influence among party members. Bocock's selection was also a victory for moderation. "He is not one of the fanatical class of political recusants who are pledged to oppose Judge Douglas, for president, should he be nominated at Charleston," wrote McClernand. The Republican caucus chose John Sherman of Ohio.[5]

As soon as the balloting began on December 5, a new divisive element was thrust into the proceedings. Representative John B. Clark of Missouri introduced a resolution declaring that no member of the House was fit to be Speaker who had endorsed Hinton R. Helper's indictment of slavery, *The Impending Crisis of the South*, on the ground that the book contained doctrines that were "insurrectionary and hostile to the domestic peace and tranquillity of the country." Helper, with an impressive array of statistics, had attempted to prove that slavery was a burden to the south and the cause of the section's economic backwardness; implicit was an appeal to the southern yeomanry to overturn the institution. While southerners reacted to the book with outrage, Republicans regarded it as good campaign material. They sent out an appeal, soliciting funds to print a shorter version as a party document, and John Sherman was among the sixty-eight Congressmen who signed the appeal. The effort to organize the House was already complicated by the lack of a party majority and by John Brown's raid; the injection of this new issue rendered the selection of a Speaker almost hopeless.

Balloting continued through December and into the new year without result. In the meantime, the House remained unorganized, unable to conduct business, and the legislative branch of the government was virtually paralyzed. Tension in the chamber became heavy, tempers flared, and members armed themselves for protection.

The Illinois members were closely watched for clues to Douglas' strategy. In early January his plans were revealed by McClernand. "The policy of the Illinois delegation is plain and clear," he wrote. "It is to keep themselves within the party organization and to conciliate democrats of all shades of opinion so far as practicable—abating however not a jot or tittle of their principles."

Douglas' efforts to unite the opposition to the Republican party, however, faced enormous odds. He appeared often in the House to aid McClernand, but he was disappointed in the results. Three of the anti-Lecompton Democrats broke ranks and voted for Sherman. The southern members of the American party were divided, some arguing that they could never vote for a "squatter sovereignty democrat" and others refusing to support a Lecompton Democrat. The impossibility of uniting all three groups became increasingly clear. The southern radicals emerged as a fourth group, and overtures were apparently even made to them. Without Douglas' knowledge, George Sanders, who still insisted on promoting the Little Giant's presidential ambitions in his own way, wired two members of the South Carolina delegation that the inability of the House to organize was producing a conservative reaction in the north. "Dont organize," he advised on December 16. A few days later, Sanders wrote South Carolina Congressman William Porcher Miles, offering him both money and election to the speakership if the radical southerner would support Douglas. When Douglas himself was observed warmly greeting Miles' colleague, Lawrence Keitt, there was immediate speculation that he sought an accord with the radicals.[6]

When House members were not balloting they were engaged in an acrimonious debate that covered the whole range of the slavery question. The rhetoric played no small part in defeating Douglas' efforts, as the radicals pushed some of the Americans and anti-Lecompton Democrats into the Republican ranks and as Douglas Democrats alienated supporters of the administration. When Illinois Congressman Isaac N. Morris announced he would make a speech, several of his colleagues appealed to Douglas to stop him, fearing that he was "in a bad temper for the making of a judicious speech." "A hostile speech on his part now," they warned, "upon the heel of the defection of certain members wd. be most hurtful." Morris was not stopped. He delivered a caustic denunciation of the Buchanan administration in which he charged the President with hunting down Douglas Democrats "with unrelenting malignity."

President Buchanan, unwilling to wait longer for the organization of the House, sent in his message on December 27, partly in the hope that it might help speed a settlement. A lackluster document for the most part, the message attempted to soothe the fears and tensions aroused by Brown's raid. He could not, however, resist the opportunity to slap the Douglas Democrats. He declared again that the Supreme Court had established the right of every citizen to take slave property into the territories, but he now added that the slaveowners also had the right to have their property protected there. The statement seemed to put the administration on the side of a federal slave code. McClernand called the message "a national calamity." When Vice President Breckinridge, long regarded as a friend of Douglas, gave guarded support to a federal slave code in a Kentucky speech, Douglasites were convinced that the administration had joined the southern ultras. A conflict had appeared within the Democratic party, one correspondent observed, that portended "anything but harmony" for the Charleston convention.[7]

On the eleventh ballot, Bocock withdrew from the race, leaving the Democrats in a state of disarray. A number of candidates, including McClernand, rose and fell, dividing the vote of the loose collection of groups and factions that opposed the Republicans. Douglas had hoped that McClernand's candidacy could be avoided, thereby reserving his lieutenant for the important task of working behind the scenes to effect a coalition. McClernand withdrew his name, proposing instead that of Virginia's John S. Millson. Douglas tried to promote Indiana's anti-Lecompton Democrat John G. Davis and for a time endorsed Charles L. Scott, a Buchanan supporter from California, in the hope that Democratic strength could be combined on Davis when Scott failed. Later, Douglas turned briefly to the independent Texan Andrew J. Hamilton. By late January, he was busy on the House floor urging the candidacy of William N. H. Smith, a member of the American party from North Carolina, and on the thirty-ninth ballot Smith came within three votes of election, the first time that the Republican candidate slipped to second place. Sherman withdrew on January 30, and Republican strength was transferred to New Jersey's William Pennington, a former Whig. On the following day, Pennington lacked only one vote for election. The Democrats again concentrated on McClernand in a desperate effort to head off a Republican victory. One by one southern Democrats who had vowed never to vote for a Douglas man rose to give support to McClernand, but their numbers fell short. The southern Americans and a small group of southern radicals refused to join the movement, preferring party defeat to the endorsement of a Douglas Democrat. Pennington was elected and the House was organized at last.[8]

McClernand's failure was a grave disappointment to the Douglasites. The refusal of the southern Americans to back him rankled, in view of Douglas' efforts on behalf of their candidate Smith. "So the d——d South Americans would not come up on you, after all hands had supported their man," grumbled Lanphier. "Curse 'em." When Douglas' anti-Lecompton friend John Forney was elected clerk of the House some saw a move to placate Douglas, but it was hardly a victory inasmuch as Douglas had supported the incumbent clerk, Illinois' James C. Allen. Douglas, however, could salvage some satisfaction from the results. "We have gained something by our conciliatory course towards our fellow democrats," wrote McClernand. "We have, at least, facilitated their approach to our position" and knocked off some of "the edge and rancor of opposition to him in the South." John A. Logan, one of the loyal Illinois

Congressmen, was proud that McClernand had received the largest vote given to any Democratic candidate, "which shows how Douglas democracy stands here." Lanphier thought the opposition of the radicals would help Douglas in the north, for it was proof that "the worst ultra Southern men . . . have no sympathy with us,—indeed are deadly hostile, as their action shows." [9]

While Douglas may have found a ray of hope in the results of the speakership fight, he could not have been unaware of its deeper consequences. The struggle had aggravated the party's wounds in spite of the apparent amity at its conclusion. The divisions in the House, commented McClernand, reflected divisions in the country. "Our country for the first time is in serious danger of civil commotions." The intransigence of the southern radicals was an unpleasant reminder that feeling in the south ran deep. The south, shouted Congressman Keitt, "has no more compromises to make. She ought never to have made the first one. But she has made the last concession to save the Union; and, if pressed further, she will burst the bonds which unite her with faithless confederates; [and] will pull down the Federal temple." [10]

ii

Douglas, weakened by illness and looking gaunt and drawn, did not take his seat in the Senate until December 27, the day the President sent his message to Congress. During the following days he divided his time between the Senate and the floor of the House, where he directed his followers in the speakership contest. Again, in early January, his health failed, and he was unable to go to the capitol. "Douglas bears himself heroically. . . . His labors are Herculean," wrote McClernand, who worried that Douglas would soon be worn out if the pace continued.

In his absence from the Senate, the question of the chairmanship of the Committee on Territories was raised once more. Several Democratic Senators were in a more charitable mood than they had been the year before. Douglas' announcement that he would support the Charleston nominee and his instructions to his supporters in the House to join the Democratic caucus were viewed as conciliatory gestures. Green, who had replaced Douglas as chairman, extended the hand of forgiveness to the Illinois Senator, on the assumption that Douglas would thenceforth act with the administration. Douglas angrily spurned the overtures. When his friend Senator Yulee of Florida offered to relinquish his chairmanship of the Committee on Post Offices and Post Routes, Douglas made it clear that he would never accept the chairmanship of any Senate committee until he was reinstated as chairman of the Committee on Territories, a determination he repeated on the Senate floor. When Jefferson Davis denied that Douglas had been the victim of a proscriptive policy, Douglas displayed more sensitivity than he had publicly expressed before. It had been, he declared, a "proclamation to the world" that a man holding his views was not sound enough to serve as a committee chairman. "The courtesies of the Senate" had been violated, and self-respect required that he take no other place. When the new committee assignments were made, Douglas was given his customary seats on the territorial and foreign relations committees. He was dropped from the Committee on Public Buildings, to which he had been elected a year before, but Davis hastened to assure him that there was nothing personal in this action.[11]

Douglas was pressed hard throughout the session. As the leading candidate for the presidential nomination, he became the major target for enemies both within and outside his party. His position was more exposed than before, for he was without the assistance of two valued anti-Lecompton colleagues. California's David Broderick, who had stiffened Douglas' opposition to the English bill in 1858, had been tragically murdered in a duel, the sequel to a hard-fought state election. Charles E. Stuart had not been a candidate for re-election to the Senate from Michigan. Douglas' position was also more difficult, for he endeavored the impossible task of uniting the various elements of the party behind his own leadership. The Republicans were relegated at times to the role of bystanders as the battle raged among Democrats. The Senate became a forum for the debate of the issues that divided the party, "as much a presidential nominating convention as it was a legislative body." Not only did it seem likely that the Democratic platform would be hammered out during the session, but the nomination also might be determined. It was truly a "rehearsal for Charleston."

Although opportunity was at a minimum, Douglas was able on a few occasions to return to his long-standing effort to facilitate the settlement and development of the west. Miners occupying Indian lands in the central Rockies had organized a provisional government, and Douglas urged that their action be legitimized. The national government, he argued, must either enforce the Indian title and drive the settlers out of the area, or "we must extinguish the Indian title and organize a territorial government, and convert this squatter sovereignty into popular sovereignty." The former alternative was clearly out of the question. The Indians, he contended, "are fading away before the advance of civilization like snow before the vernal sun." These "barriers of barbarism, of savage ferocity" must be removed from the paths of progress. Douglas argued similarly for the organization of a Territory of Nevada, thus legalizing a miners' incursion into that area. Later in the session he again urged the passage of a free homestead bill, insisting that safeguards be provided to protect the settlers from the speculators, and recalling his early experience as a land officer. He was dismayed that the slavery question should continue to delay western legislation and hoped not only that the bill would pass, but that overland mail and Pacific railroad bills would follow quickly.[12]

The slavery question, however, dominated the deliberations of the Senate, so that Douglas practically abandoned his hopes for the achievement of constructive legislation. His thoughts too were fixed on the presidential election; his preparations for the Democratic convention held priority. Like the speeches of his colleagues, his utterances were carefully planned for their effect on the election. The fears aroused by John Brown's raid, the attempts to broaden the scope of popular sovereignty in the territories, the question of Kansas' admission as a state, provided the context for a comprehensive discussion of the issues that divided party and nation. There was an air of desperation about the proceedings, as if this were to be the last opportunity to ventilate these issues before their final resolution. Douglas was in the center of it all. Both southern Democrats and Republicans pressed him to reveal his plans and positions even more than he had done before. He had anticipated a full-scale debate on popular sovereignty at this session and had written his *Harper's* essay with this expected debate partly in mind.

The tone of the session was established on the day the Senate convened, when Senator Mason demanded an investigation of Brown's attack on Harper's Ferry. It was not until January 16, however, that Douglas joined the discussion. On that day he introduced his own resolution instructing the judiciary committee to prepare a bill that would protect each state and territory from "invasion by the authorities or inhabitants of any other State or Territory" and that would punish conspiracies to "invade, assail or molest the government, inhabitants, property, or institutions" of any state or territory. It was a far-reaching proposal, and one for which there were few precedents. He later added that he would also punish conspiracies to invade states or territories for the purpose of controlling local elections, "whether they be under the garb of Emigrant Aid Societies of New England or Blue Lodges of Missouri."

Douglas spoke in support of his resolution on January 23. Hours before the scheduled time, an estimated 2000 spectators crowded the floor and galleries of the Senate. It was "the insetting tide of the Presidential agitation," and Douglas, it was rumored, would "make the fur fly." His argument was legalistic, based on the larger question of the preservation of the Union against "this system of sectional warfare." During November, Governor Wise, responding to reports that a conspiracy to rescue John Brown was being organized, had appealed to the President for aid, but Buchanan had replied that he found no constitutional provision for taking action. Douglas disagreed with Buchanan. It was the responsibility of the national government, under the Constitution, "to insure protection and domestic tranquillity to each State and Territory," not only against foreign foes, but against domestic ones as well. Only by implementing this constitutional obligation, by suppressing such conspiracies in advance of the crime, could the course of disunion be stayed.

Douglas reserved most of his fire, however, for the Republicans, a reminder to Democrats that in their struggle with one another they should not forget their common enemy. Many of the southern states had not yet selected their convention delegates, and Douglas' remarks were directed as much to them as to the dangers that threatened the Union. The "Harper's Ferry crimes," he shouted to the applause of the spectators, "was the natural, logical, inevitable result of the doctrines and teachings of the Republican party." Republicans were pledged to violent and eternal warfare against slavery, "with the view of its ultimate extinction throughout the land." Sectional in its location, the party advanced a sectional appeal—"northern passion, northern prejudice, northern ambition against southern States, southern institutions, and southern people." Douglas warned that outbreaks like the Harper's Ferry raid would continue as long as Republican leaders persisted in their repugnant, subversive, and revolutionary doctrines. He was gratified that some of them had disavowed Brown's act, but he found the disavowals insufficient and unconvincing unless the doctrines that produced the act were also repudiated.

As Douglas hoped, his statements brought an immediate response from the Republican side. Senator Fessenden denied that the Republican party intended to interfere with slavery in the states where it existed.

Questioning Douglas' position on slavery, he asked if the Senator were really indifferent to the institution. If Fessenden thought he would elicit a sudden revelation of Douglas' innermost thoughts, he was mistaken, for Douglas simply reiterated his public view of slavery and tied it to his pragmatic outlook. "I hold the doctrine that a wise statesman will adapt his laws to the wants, conditions, and interests of the people to be governed by them." Slavery was simply a question of political economy, determined by climate, soil, production, and self-interest. "If I were a citizen of Louisiana I would vote for retaining and maintaining slavery, because I believe the good of that people would require it. As a citizen of Illinois I am utterly opposed to it, because our interests would not be promoted by it." Douglas chided the Maine Senator for his concern about slavery. "I have always noted that those men who were so far off from the slave States that they did not know anything about them, are most anxious for the fate of the poor slave."

Douglas' resolution immediately became entangled in the sectional debate. On January 31 it was tabled, but as late as June he still had hopes that it would be reconsidered and brought before the Senate.[13]

Douglas resumed his denunciation of the Republican party in late February, when he replied to a speech by Seward on the admission of Kansas, this time focusing on the question of racial equality. Seward's argument, he charged, like that of other members of the Republican party, rested on the assumption that the Negro and the white man were equal by Divine law, and that the Declaration of Independence itself recognized this equality. "For one," Douglas asserted, "I never held to any such doctrine." The Declaration of Independence referred only to white men and had no reference whatsoever to the Negro race. The government, he repeated again, "was made by white men, on the white basis, for the benefit of white men and their posterity forever, and should be administered by white men, and by none other whatsoever." He would not, he insisted, allow a Negro either to vote or hold office anywhere, if he had the power to prevent it.

Douglas brushed aside the protests of some Republicans that they did not subscribe to doctrines of racial equality and placed his finger on one of the Republican dilemmas. If Republicans persist in arguing that the Negro is made the equal of the white man, he reminded Seward, then let them implement this equality in their legislation by conferring all the rights of citizenship on the Negroes. If Republicans insist that Congress must prohibit slavery in all the territories, why do they not introduce bills to achieve this end? Douglas answered his own question. The Republicans were only interested in exciting the northern people against the south in order to get votes in the presidential election, but they shrank from carrying out their own pledges lest they lose some of the conservative voters who dislike the Democratic party. At the same time, they would lose their abolition allies if they did not hold out "the hope that it was the mission of the Republican party, if successful, to abolish slavery in the States as well as in the Territories of the Union." Using the Republican party in his own state to illustrate his point, Douglas asserted, "The creed is pretty black in the north end of the State; about the center it is a pretty good mulatto, and it is almost white when you get down into Egypt. It assumes paler shades as you go south." [14]

If some northerners feared that Douglas was bending too far toward the south in his attacks on the Republican party, they were soon reassured. His positions on slavery and racial equality were well known, and his statements simply repeated views he had voiced many times. Their repetition was necessary, he thought, for it was important that voters know precisely where he stood in relation to the Republican party. It was the anticipated debate over popular sovereignty that brought him into conflict with the south. He was on less sure ground there, for he wished to win over moderate southerners while confronting and isolating the radicals. In order to succeed, he had to prevent the moderates and radicals from making common cause on the territorial issue. Senator Hale jocularly observed that no member of the Senate had ever been elected President. The reason, Hale thought, was "owing to the introduction of these resolutions, and to making these fillibustering speeches, and drawing gentlemen out incautiously, so that they put their foot in it before they know exactly where they are going." The statement evoked laughter among the Senators, but there was a warning buried in the humor.

The debate was ignited, rather improbably, by a resolution of George Pugh, Senator from Ohio and Douglas' strongest ally in the Senate, asking that the congressional veto over territorial legislation be repealed for Utah and New Mexico territories. The resolution was innocuous enough (the veto had already been abandoned in the Kansas-Nebraska Act), but it became significant when it was reported that New Mexico had adopted a slave code. If the laws protecting slavery in New Mexico derived their validity from the approval of Congress, Pugh argued, then popular sovereignty was impaired. Pugh undoubtedly consulted Douglas on his resolution, so it may have been a deliberate move on their part to force a discussion of territorial policy. By presenting it in the manner he did, Pugh waved a red flag in the faces of those who advocated a federal slave code. The resolution was later amended by Iowa's Republican Senator James Harlan, who proposed that all territorial officers, executive, legislative, and judicial, be elected by the people. This further extension of popular sovereignty may also have had Douglas' sanction, for similar provisions were included in a bill which he had helped to prepare for introduction in the House by Isaac Morris.[15]

After an absence of a few days, Douglas returned to the Senate on January 9, just as Senator Iverson, responding to Pugh's resolution, began another of his fiery denunciations of the Illinois Senator. Charging Douglas with "plunging deeper and deeper into the abyss of political error," Iverson demanded the unmistakable recognition of southern rights as a precondition to affiliation with the northern Democracy. Popular sovereignty was as disastrous to the south as the Wilmot Proviso, and Douglas, its author, had forfeited all claim to the confidence and support of the southern people. He urged the formation of a southern confederacy and in a final outburst of radical fervor denounced those who would coerce the south to remain in the Union against its will. "Let those loud-mouthed, blood and thunder, braggadocio Hotspurs assemble their abolition army and come down . . . to *force* us back into the Union . . . [and] we should hang them up like dogs to the trees of our forests."

Iverson's intemperate blast was only the beginning. During the next few days, other southern Senators, notably Green, Davis, and Clay, joined the attack. After "a good deal of cross firing and sharp shooting" against the Little Giant, Douglas at last was drawn into the fray. His confidence bolstered by the news that Indiana had just pledged its delegates to his nomination, he calmly suggested that all who wished to assault him should do so. "When they get through," he added, "I will fire at the lump and vindicate every word that I have said." His opponents took great exception to his choice of words and responded immediately. Green exploded—"if he fires at the lump, he will find a Roland for his Oliver." Davis charged Douglas with magnifying himself if he thought there was a combination against him in the Senate. "He had better get through with one before he takes the lump." Clay accused Douglas of trying to invoke public sympathy on behalf of a persecuted and abused man.

Douglas was not to be outdone. To Davis he declared that he would "institute no comparison between him and me, on the modesty of my bearing and his in this body." Clay's remarks, he said, "only show that I was acting on the right principle in waiting until my assailants get through their bill of indictment, and then replying to them in a lump." Turning on Clay, Douglas insisted that the Alabama Senator had removed himself from the "pale of Democratic fellowship" when he indicated he would not support the Charleston nominee if that nominee were Douglas. But, Douglas went on, he had not asked Clay to support him, nor was he sure that he would do Clay the honor of accepting his vote. The Republicans sat quietly, enjoying the debate "hugely," as Douglas rebuked Clay's insolence "in an annihilating strain of sarcasm and contempt."

Douglas was not yet prepared to reply to the "lump," but he was ready to comment on his attitude toward the Charleston nomination. While he did not seek the nomination, he would accept it, but only if he could do so "on principles that I believe to be sound." He would not be a candidate on a platform that he could not execute in good faith. At the same time, he conceded that he could vote for a nominee with whom he disagreed on a platform which he could not approve, "for after having elected him, so far as we differed I would continue to differ from him as President, and so far as we agreed I would sustain him as President." In such a situation, it would clearly be "a choice of evils." Having said this much, he revealed his great annoyance that his record as a Democrat should be attacked by individuals whose labor for the party did not compare with his own. "I do not admit the fact that there is a better Democrat on earth than I am, or a sounder one on the question of State rights, and even on the slavery question." He would not, he asserted, arraign a fellow Democrat for his opinions, but "at the same time, I am determined never to surrender a conscientious conviction even to secure the highest place in the Government." With this, his assailants backed off, deploring personal controversies and denying that they meant to do any injustice to the Illinois Senator. Douglas had the last word when, in answer to a query, he summed up his position. "My belief is that Congress has no power over the subject of slavery in the States, or in the organized Territories of the United States, nor over any other municipal regulation, by a fair interpretation of the Constitution." [16]

It became obvious during the debate over Pugh's resolution that members of the Senate were seeking to shape the Democratic platform by their arguments. Radical southerners, challenged by the Ohio Senator and unwilling to allow the initiative to rest in the hands of the north, responded with resolutions of their own that were drawn with Charleston in mind. Brown had warned Douglas that the south would demand a slave code platform at Charleston. In mid-January he gave substance to his warning. The Committee on Territories, he proposed, must henceforth insert in every bill for the organization of a new territory a clause declaring it to be the duty of the territorial legislature to protect slave property; if a territorial legislature should fail to do so, the duty to protect slavery in the territories would devolve on Congress. The debate on territorial policy shifted immediately to Brown's resolution. But the Senate's platform-builders were not through. Two weeks later, Jefferson Davis introduced a less radical set of platform resolutions which made the same point in less direct and less offensive tones.

Davis' resolutions provided the most elaborate platform yet. Approved in advance by President Buchanan, they were addressed to the fugitive slave problem and the Harper's Ferry raid as well as to the territorial question, but it was the last that received greatest emphasis. Slashing at Douglas' Freeport Doctrine, Davis argued that neither Congress nor a territorial legislature, "whether by direct legislation or legislation of an indirect and unfriendly nature," could impair the right of a slaveholder to take his property into the territories. It was the duty of the federal government to afford "needful protection" to slavery in the territories, if not by the judiciary, then by Congress. The inhabitants of a territory could make no decision on slavery until they moved into statehood. The resolutions were an amalgam of Calhoun's views (indeed, Davis conceded they were based in part on Calhoun's 1837 resolutions), the Buchanan-southern interpretation of popular sovereignty, and the slave code demand. The discussion of Pugh's, Brown's, and Davis' resolutions became so entangled that it was difficult to distinguish them. In fact, it mattered little; as Senator Hale observed, "I find that it does not make the least odds under heaven what subject is up, any speech will answer for anything." [17]

Not all southern Senators looked favorably on the effort to anticipate the Charleston platform. Toombs concluded that "hostility to Douglas is the sole motive of movers of this mischief." While he did not wish to see Douglas nominated, he also did not want to alienate northern Democrats. Willard Saulsbury, from the border state of Delaware, thought the resolutions were bad policy for the Democratic party. The whole subject of slavery in the territories, he declared, was an abstraction, and the Senate was being converted into a debating society on abstract questions. Fearing the impact of the various motions and resolutions on the unity of the party, several border state Senators succeeded in having them referred to a caucus of Senate Democrats, where their discussion could be carried on away from the public view. The hope was that through negotiation the Senators would be able to "harmonize" the conflicting views of the territorial question by settling on some general statement to which they could all subscribe.

The caucus met on February 10. It was apparent from the outset that there would be no agreement. Some Senators, like Toombs, opposed the adoption of any resolutions; others supported those introduced by Davis. Douglas was present to argue his position and denounce Davis' resolutions. He proposed that the party simply stand on the Cincinnati platform, with the understanding that all questions concerning slavery in the territories be submitted to the Supreme Court for settlement. A growing number of Senators, recognizing the loopholes in Douglas' suggestion, insisted that the south was entitled to a federal slave code. To expedite the work of the caucus, a committee of five Senators was appointed to resolve the issue. Green, who had suggested the committee, was made its chairman. The members, chosen by the Douglas-hating caucus chairman, Jesse Bright, were Bright's Indiana colleague Graham Fitch, William Bigler, William Gwin, and James Chesnut of South Carolina. Whatever hopes Douglas might have had that the caucus would disavow the southern platform proposal were dashed when the membership was announced.

To many northern Democrats, the effort smacked strongly of an attempt to draw the Democratic platform in the Senate, where Douglas' strength was small, rather than to entrust the task to the Charleston convention, where the northern influence would be greater. Douglas' growing strength among northern state delegations was regarded with alarm by the south. In view of his repeated statements that he would not accept the nomination on principles he could not endorse, the platform became the means by which Douglas' drive toward the nomination could be stopped. A platform endorsed by a majority of the Senate Democrats would, it was thought, have a powerful influence on the convention, reducing the choice of candidate to secondary importance.

Douglas Democrats expressed considerable concern for the senatorial platform that would be adopted by "Bright Davis & Co." "Is it their design," asked an Ohio lieutenant, "to create a prestige for it which will incite the south at Charleston to insist upon it?" It was not difficult to perceive that Douglas was the real target. "The *platform* movement in the Senate," reported McClernand, "is designed to break down Douglas." To formulate a platform so odious that Douglas would feel honor-bound to denounce it was the quickest way to get rid of him.[18]

With Buchanan's approbation, Green's committee simply endorsed Davis' resolutions, splitting one of them into two parts and modifying the language only slightly. The key clause now read, "That if experience should at any time prove that the judiciary and executive authority do not possess means to insure adequate protection to constitutional rights in a Territory, and if the territorial government shall fail or refuse to provide the necessary remedies for that purpose it will be the duty of Congress to supply such deficiency." A prolonged debate in the caucus followed, as some Senators still voiced their opposition to any resolutions whatever. Douglas again forcefully expressed his dissent. Brown, disappointed that the committee had rejected his own slave code proposal, objected to the weak and general wording. Kansas Territory, he insisted, had already failed to provide the necessary protection to slavery, so that the contingency mentioned in the resolution had already happened. He proposed a substitute which declared that "it has become the duty of Congress to interpose" on behalf of slavery's protection in the territories; earlier he had introduced a bill in the Senate which would specifically and unequivocally provide protection to slavery in Kansas. Brown's objections were to no avail, for the revised Davis resolutions were adopted by a large majority.

On March 1, Davis introduced the caucus resolutions as a substitute for his earlier ones, explaining that "a conference with friends" in the meantime had persuaded him to accept certain modifications in the wording. The resolutions had one purpose, and one purpose only—to serve as both advice and ultimatum to the Charleston convention, now only about seven weeks away. They represented the only terms that would be acceptable to the south, and their endorsement became a condition for that section's participation in the Democratic national convention. It was the south's final answer to the Freeport Doctrine; its object, to defeat Douglas' nomination. Davis had no immediate plans to call up the resolutions for debate, nor did he anticipate that they would pass the Senate.

Douglas held his fire and made no public response to the resolutions.

While he had threatened to reply to the "lump," he did not do so during the few remaining weeks before the meeting of the convention. He was hampered in part by recurring illness, but he was also busy with his campaign and unwilling to make any statements that might jeopardize his progress. " 'Masterly inactivity' may be now the best tactic for Washington," wrote one of his advisers, and apparently Douglas agreed.[19]

iii

While members of the Senate attempted to thwart Douglas' candidacy, the Illinois Senator's campaign for the nomination moved into full swing. That a majority of the Democratic Senators felt it necessary to head off Douglas' drive was testimony to its success. Douglas Democrats became more confident of victory. Twice before, in 1852 and 1856, Douglas' plans had miscarried and he had suffered disappointment at the last moment. The prospect was for a different result in the spring of 1860. Douglas' changed role during the Buchanan administration played a large part in the difference, but Douglas had also learned from his earlier failures. He had developed an intricate and effective campaign machine which placed him far out in front of any competitors.

Douglas had begun to form his organization well over a year before. In the spring of 1859, he called to his side A. D. Banks, a Petersburg, Virginia, editor who had joined the staff of the pro-Douglas Cincinnati *Enquirer*. Banks, an enthusiastic and loyal supporter, opened an unofficial Douglas headquarters in New York and gathered about him a number of men as a kind of steering committee. One of them was Sanders, whose difficulties with the Little Giant seem to have been patched up. Sanders bombarded Douglas with advice, as always, suggesting arguments that might be made against Davis in the Senate, proposing that Douglas support a pay raise for the armed forces in order to bind the officers of the Army and Navy to his cause, and arranging appointments with politicians whom he thought Douglas should meet. Although he was considerably more subtle in his tactics than he had been eight years before, Douglas still watched him with a wary eye. Sanders' duties, sneered one New York editor, involved "the moral suasion of stewed oysters, Virginia ham and Bourbon whiskey," in the employment of which he was "without a peer." Another member of the committee was the New York financier August Belmont, who served as a fund-raiser for the campaign. Belmont had broken with Buchanan earlier, and his conversion to Douglas was complete. His contacts with New York's business houses and his meetings with the city's leading businessmen in his Fifth Avenue mansion brought financial support to the Douglas cause. Others involved in the Douglas organization were financiers Moses Taylor, Watts Sherman, and William B. Astor, and New York politician Dean Richmond.[20]

Supporters from other parts of the country traveled to New York to confer with members of the group and with one another. Douglas himself was an occasional visitor. The rest of the nation was not neglected either; Douglas developed a heavy correspondence with individuals in virtually every state of the Union. Douglas "has a camp . . . of partisans busy in his behalf," wrote Caleb Cushing to ex-President Pierce, and the press speculated that there were few localities in which there were not to be found "knots of his partisans" striving to forward his campaign.

Douglas, complained a Georgia Congressman, was "the most remarkable man in the Republic in making capital for himself and bringing men to his support." Banks made frequent trips to different sections of the country, including the west and south, and rumors flew that he was offering the vice presidential nomination to large numbers of unsuspecting aspirants. " 'Little fat Banks,' " commented the same Congressman, "seems to hold in the hollow of his hand the whole Presidential slate."

An expanded staff in Douglas' Washington office handled the increasing volume of correspondence and prepared copies of his speeches for mailing to lists of voters that were supplied by agents in many of the states. Three more-or-less official newspapers were maintained, with material as well as moral support—the Chicago *Times, Illinois State Register,* and the Washington *States and Union*—and countless other papers announced their support of Douglas. Appeals for financial help from editors throughout the Union became commonplace in his correspondence. Biographical notices were inserted in some of the nation's popular magazines, including *Frank Leslie's Illustrated Magazine.*

Sheahan's campaign biography of Douglas at last approached completion. Harper's offered to make it "their prominent spring book." The printing was rushed and the publication date set to coincide with the Charleston convention. Sheahan was less than pleased with the final result. Much material on the 1858 election had been condensed or omitted, and the Lecompton story had been generalized for political reasons. "Had there been no possibility of your nomination," Sheahan informed Douglas, "I would have written the naked truth in all its deformities, but pending the campaign I omitted everything calculated to provoke controversy, and substituted the wretched *fib* that Lecomptonism has been forgotten." While the Lecompton crisis was played down, the administration's role in the 1858 election was not. Douglas suggested to Sheahan that he had "no recommendations of mercy to make in behalf of the administration." [21]

Douglas' organizational efforts were uncommon in the politics of the 1850's, and for this reason they excited comment in the press. "Few persons have any just comprehension of the expensive and complicated machinery which prominent politicians of the present day invent and work to aid them in their ambitious schemes," observed the New York *Herald*. "In this respect . . . Senator Douglas is ahead of all competitors." As Douglas' political network became better known, attacks from the administration became more urgent. Douglas made no attempt to minimize his differences with the President; in fact, he insisted that his breach with Buchanan be stressed. Buchanan retaliated, and even Washington social life was drawn into the conflict when it was rumored that the President had persuaded the wives of his cabinet members "to cut Mrs. Douglas." Visiting lists were carefully screened to conform with the political divisions. Adele, sensitive to her husband's position, ostracized his opponents, treating them with a haughtiness that brought complaints of "rustic behavior" against her.[22]

Douglas' first concern was that his own section, the northwest, provide him with a solid base on which to build his candidacy. The lack of such a base had been a serious weakness in his 1856 campaign. Douglas' subsequent stand on Lecompton, his victory in Illinois in 1858 over a combined Republican and administration opposition, and his harassment by southerners all enhanced his popularity with rank-and-file Democrats in the northwest. By the presidential year he was widely received as their spokesman. His Ohio campaign in the fall of 1859 was partly an effort to strengthen this popularity. The Republicans won in Ohio and made gains in Indiana, Iowa, and Minnesota in the fall elections, prompting Frank Blair to observe that "all the chances the little rascal ever had" in the northwest had been destroyed. Douglas, however, was less interested in stopping the Republicans at this point than he was in capturing the state Democratic parties.

Douglas hoped that the Illinois Democracy would set the pace for the northwest and the nation. He suggested that the state convention meet early in the winter to select delegates to the Charleston convention, postponing the selection of presidential electors and the nominations for state offices until a later time. Douglas had no desire to run any unnecessary risks. If there should be a "violent contest" over the state nominations, he did not want to provide an opportunity for disappointed candidates "to make mischief" before the Charleston meeting. In selecting Illinois' twenty-two delegates, he advised, care should be taken to choose men with outstanding records on the slavery question who were well known nationally and favorably regarded by the south. In order that as many citizens of the state as possible make the trip to Charleston, Douglas suggested that assistant or consulting delegates be appointed. "In this way all of our friends can go in a quasi official capacity, and the more the better," although he did not think it would be "politic to announce to the world that a large number is expected to go."

The Danites, encouraged by Buchanan's backing of Isaac Cook, gave Douglas some concern. After failing to prevent his re-election to the Senate they began organizing for 1860, confident as usual that with administration help they could make deep inroads into the Douglas ranks. Douglas at first minimized their importance. "They can do no harm [for] the whole country understands their character & weakness." He later revised his impressions when the Danites scheduled a state convention for January a few days after the regular party. Changing his mind, Douglas now thought it advisable for the Democrat convention to appoint presidential electors as well as delegates, otherwise the Danites might form an electoral ticket and then demand that the party accept it. He not only wanted delegates pledged to his nomination; he also wanted electors who could be relied upon once he was nominated.[23]

Lanphier directed the arrangements for the state convention from his editorial office in Springfield. The resolutions, he wrote, would be regarded as Douglas' platform and therefore ought to be prepared with the greatest care. "Why not have [them] written under your own eye, just as you want them?" he asked Douglas. Douglas complied. Missing from the platform was a statement in regard to himself, which he thought could best be drafted by the convention. McClernand supplied the guidance in this instance. "I think there should be an emphatic expression in behalf of the nomination of Judge Douglas—that it should be terse and considerate in language but comprehensive in meaning." One of the questions facing the convention was whether the party should pledge its support to the Charleston nominee, whoever he might be. McClernand thought such a pledge might bring the Danites back into the organization. Douglas' view, aimed in part at his southern critics, was "that no man can honorably go into the Charleston Convention who is not willing to abide by its action." [24]

The Democratic state convention met at Springfield on January 4. Not all of Douglas' suggestions were followed. His proposal to appoint consulting delegates was left undone in the hurry and confusion that attended the meeting. Presidential electors were not chosen because of Lanphier's opposition. "I *knew* it would elicit *debate,* & reasons would have been given for not appointing which could have certainly done no good." Douglas' resolutions were all adopted, although the pledge to support the Charleston nominee, Lanphier confided, "was not the most popular of the series."

The resolutions provided a succinct statement of Douglas' position. The Cincinnati platform was reaffirmed and interpreted in the words and meanings with which it had been understood in 1856: that all questions pertaining to slavery be banished from Congress; that the people of the territories be free to make their own laws and regulations respecting slavery and all other matters of local concern; and that all questions affecting the constitutionality of territorial enactments be referred to the Supreme Court. The authority of the Supreme Court was upheld, and all good citizens were admonished to obey and respect its decisions. The charge that the Dred Scott decision decided against the right of the territories to determine the slavery question for themselves was indignantly rejected (a strike against the Republicans, but against the southern Democrats, as well, for they shared this view of the decision with the Republicans). John Brown and Harper's Ferry were denounced as natural consequences of Republican doctrine, and the obligation of Congress to enact an efficient fugitive slave law was endorsed. All new tests of Democratic faith were repudiated: the revival of the African slave trade; the congressional slave code; the doctrine that slavery is a federal institution, deriving its validity from the Constitution, rather than a mere municipal institution. Looking to Charleston, the state convention urged that the Cincinnati platform be readopted without any additions or deletions and that Douglas be nominated for the presidency.

The results of the convention were carefully studied, especially in Washington, as an indication of the direction in which Douglas and the northwest would go. The platform reaffirmed Douglas' convictions. It was now clear that he would not modify them in any significant manner. Consistent with the sentiments of the Dorr letter, the resolutions focused on popular sovereignty and rejected the demands of the southern ultras. Douglas' opposition to the Republican party was registered in forceful language; his critics within the Democratic party were attacked in more indirect and subtle ways. While refusing to budge from his commitment to popular sovereignty, however, Douglas made a gesture toward the south in his emphasis on the Supreme Court as the final arbiter of all questions relating to territorial policy, hoping perhaps to provide a bridge by which north and south could be joined. The thought was not new, but the emphasis was. Finally, Douglas now made positive what he had only hinted before, that the 1856 Cincinnati platform, interpreted his way, would suffice for 1860. Douglas hoped that he had found the formula that would bind both his party and the Union; in reality, he shut his eyes to much that had happened between 1856 and 1860.[25]

The Danites, or National Democrats as they called themselves, gathered in Springfield less than a week later to espouse the cause of the administration. They were as determined as ever to wrest party control from the hands of the Douglasites. The movement had clearly not prospered since the 1858 election. While the Douglas press dismissed the meeting as that of "a straggling and occasionally staggering office-holder" intent on keeping up the semblance of an organization, some Douglas leaders were privately worried. The Danites adopted resolutions repudiating popular sovereignty, maintaining the right of a slaveholder to hold his slaves in the territories, and reaffirming the Cincinnati platform "as expounded by the present administration." In what might have been a conciliatory gesture, they also pledged to support the nominee of the Charleston convention. A full set of delegates to Charleston was selected to compete for seats with the Douglas Democrats. *"They expect* to be admitted," one observer wrote anxiously to Douglas. Lanphier echoed the anxiety. "These rascals must have some hope of getting in, or they would not be pushing the matter as they do." As in 1858, the Danites enjoyed the encouragement of Republicans, who offered funds to defray expenses in Charleston.[26]

With a strong endorsement from Illinois, Douglas focused his efforts on the other northwestern states. His recent visit to Ohio and the hard work of devoted followers brought victory in the state Democratic convention, where Ohio's delegation to Charleston was instructed for Douglas by a large majority. "The Democratic thunder of Ohio will reverberate through the whole North . . . & its echo will be heard in the South," predicted one of the state's leaders. Their work completed, Ohioans offered to help in other states. Several attended the convention in neighboring Indiana. Douglas' victory over the desperate efforts of the Bright-Fitch organization in the Hoosier state brought him great satisfaction, as well as another delegation pledged to his nomination. "We have met the enemy and they are ours," an Indianapolis editor wrote to Douglas, "but it required much exertion, management, nerve and *pluck.*" In Michigan, where Stuart was at work, the Democratic convention gave the Little Giant a unanimous endorsement. Similarly, the Iowa and Wisconsin conventions gave Douglas their delegations. "Hurra for Michigan Iowa & Wisconsin!" exulted Lanphier. "Are we getting ahead!" Over the opposition of Henry M. Rice, the Minnesota convention declared Douglas its first choice (although binding instructions were defeated), and pro-Douglas resolutions prepared by James Shields were passed. By the end of February, Douglas had won the northwest. The section's seven states and sixty-six convention votes, rejoiced Ohio lieutenant Henry B. Payne, could be relied upon on all questions relating to organization, platform, and candidates. Many of the northwest's delegates, he added, would visit other states "to wake up some enthusiasm." [27]

Douglas' prospects were less sure in other parts of the country. In New York, whose thirty-five convention votes Douglas was anxious to secure, the situation was so tangled and confused as virtually to defy clear analysis. The effort to commit the New York delegation began early, but it was complicated by shifting alignments among the party's various factions. The state convention, meeting in Syracuse in September 1859, was controlled by the Albany Regency, the "softs" of former times, led by Dean Richmond and Peter Cagger, both strong Douglas men. An alliance was struck with the "hard" leader and enemy of Douglas, Daniel S. Dickinson, who favored conciliation and hoped for a Charleston delegation that would represent both groups. A slate of delegates was agreed upon, including twenty or so votes pledged to Douglas, with the remainder following Dickinson's lead. The unit rule was adopted, thus giving Douglas the entire delegation at least for the time being. The action was challenged by Fernando Wood, former mayor of New York City, and a group of "hards" who refused to acknowledge Dickinson's conciliatory gesture. A rival delegation was named. The effort to harmonize the New York party was thwarted, so the state would send two delegations to the national convention, as it had consistently in the past. The character of the regular delegation, however, remained fluid and required continuous attention. The actual preferences of the individual delegates were variously reported, and the number of uncommitted delegates rose and fell. Douglas made several trips to New York in the early weeks of 1860 to talk with party leaders, and his agents were constantly on the alert. Douglas repeated his "implicit confidence in the entire good faith of our friends in New York." Dean Richmond reported a week before the national convention that his delegation would be all right. Still, there were signs that administration pressure might be brought to bear on some of the wavering delegates, the Wood delegation won southern support, and Douglas himself was warned that his majority among the delegates might disappear if his nomination should prove unpalatable to the south.[28]

The situation in Pennsylvania was less hopeful. The schism of a year before, when two state conventions had met, was healed, and the administration wing had made its peace with John Forney. The price, however, was a delegation to Charleston that held a majority of anti-Douglas or uncommitted individuals. Douglas' interests in the state convention were advanced by Congressman William Montgomery, an anti-Lecompton leader in the House, and his selection as a delegate-at-large was regarded as a hopeful sign. Montgomery, on orders from the Douglas organization, followed a conciliatory line and muted his Douglasism in the interest of maintaining party harmony. If Douglas did not secure a majority, at least no other candidate was mentioned. From his headquarters in New York, George Sanders made arrangements for Douglas to confer with New Jersey officials and legislators as he passed through on his trips between the capital and New York. "I think we have New Jersey . . . but this will make it doubly sure," Sanders announced. His optimism was premature. The New Jersey convention endorsed no candidate and selected an uncommitted delegation to Charleston.

News from New England was more heartening. Maine, Vermont, and Rhode Island were pledged to Douglas; a Providence editor assured the Senator that the Rhode Island delegation "will remain in Charleston till November, if need be, and vote for you every time." In New Hampshire, Douglas' followers secured an endorsement for the Little Giant with the aid of the partisans of ex-President Pierce, who hoped that their man would receive the nomination if Douglas should falter. The delegation from Massachusetts was reported to be pro-Douglas, although not firmly so, and in Connecticut there was hope that at least a portion of the delegation would support Douglas.[29]

Douglas' northern strength was impressive, but whether he would be able to marshal it at the crucial moment in Charleston depended upon the attitude of the south. Many hesitant delegates looked to the south for signs that Douglas would be acceptable there. Even some of his devoted friends seemed reluctant to force him on an unwilling south; they feared that Douglas' nomination might lose that section to the Democratic ticket. Douglas' strength came from states in the north and west that were more likely than any others to cast their electoral votes for the Republican candidate; southern votes, it was thought, were necessary for election. Douglas was strongly urged to secure southern delegates who would be with him from the beginning, because a show of southern support early in the convention would reassure his northern friends. A comparable argument was put forth by his agents in the south. Let the north and west "stand firm & insist on your nomination as indispensable to Democratic success," wrote John Forsyth from Mobile, and "a break will be made in the phalanx of Southern opposition." Whatever the argument, it was indisputable that the south held the key to Douglas' success.

Douglas' friends in the slave states were joined in their task by members of his organization from the north. Hopeful reports detailing their progress filled his correspondence. The odds against which they struggled were formidable. John Brown's raid played into the hands of the radicals; they denounced Douglas and demanded a federal slave code with equal vehemence. Southerners were advised to shun Douglas' touch "as that of a leper." Some went further, openly advocating disunion and the formation of a southern confederacy. "There will be some difficulty," predicted a Mississippi politician, "In restraining the impetuosity of the fire eaters." Douglas needed southern support, and his course in the Senate during the early months of 1860 was designed in part to placate southern opinion. However, he was also aware that with every gesture toward the south he risked the loss of northern support. It was a situation to try the mettle of the shrewdest politician.[30]

Douglas found some encouragement in the south. He was informed repeatedly that the people were with him if their leaders were not, that he was "stronger, a thousand times, with the Southern People, than superficial currents set in motion by Politicians, would indicate." His national orientation, reported a southern correspondent, won him favor in the south in spite of the attacks of his enemies. Not all southern politicians were hostile. Louisiana Congressman Miles Taylor urged Douglas' candidacy as the only hope for the Union, although he did not concur in many of Douglas' opinions. While he preferred a southern candidate, wrote Representative Albert Rust of Arkansas, he would cheerfully support Douglas if he were nominated. Douglas' proscription by the south would mean the "denationalization" of the Democratic party, equivalent in Rust's mind to a disruption of the Union. A third Congressman, Texas' Andrew J. Hamilton, whom Douglas had supported for House Speaker for a time, added his endorsement, while arguing that the differences among Democrats had been magnified beyond their real importance.

The prospect of the vice presidential nomination was dangled before a number of southern political figures, including Alexander H. Stephens, whom Douglas himself favored for the post. Stephens, in private conversation with a Chicago friend of Douglas', was outspoken in support of the Little Giant. With others he was noncommittal, although he made no secret of his conviction that Douglas' patriotism and devotion to principle were unquestioned. Fellow Georgian Robert Toombs, anxious to prevent the government from falling into the hands of the Republicans, announced his support of Douglas, although he preferred some other candidate. Toombs felt Douglas had been in error, but he still regarded the Illinoisan as "a bold, manly, truthful, independent patriot." Alabama's Senator Benjamin Fitzpatrick refused to join the campaign against Douglas in his state and was thought to be friendly.[31]

Some of Douglas' hardest working southern supporters were newspaper editors. Foremost among them was John Forsyth, whose Mobile *Register* became a leading Douglas organ in the south. "I am doing my poor endeavor to breast the storm of sectionalism *here,*" he wrote Douglas, "as you have done in both sections of an exasperated union." His reports on developments in Alabama and elsewhere in the south were frequent and informative. Supplementing Forsyth's efforts was John J. Seibels, editor of the Montgomery *Confederation.* Henry Cleveland, of the Augusta *Constitutionalist,* placed his editorial columns at Douglas' disposal, and R. R. Collier, editor of a Petersburg, Virginia, newspaper, urged the view that Douglas' doctrine was "no worse, but better, than that of Southern men, for the South." [32]

As the southern state conventions selected their delegations to Charleston, the magnitude of Douglas' task became apparent. In spite of the efforts of his friends, the southern state parties shunned him. While they rejected him as their choice for the presidential nomination, however, they were unable to unite on any other candidate, naming instead a number of favorite sons. This lack of unity, plus the fact that he seemed assured of a scattered support from individual delegates of even the most hostile states, encouraged Douglas to believe that he might yet emerge as the south's second choice. Many southern leaders grudgingly conceded that he was the strongest candidate and probably the only Democrat who could be elected. Douglas relied on this concession to overcome whatever scruples they might have. It was a long shot, but the Little Giant remained hopeful.

To win southern support, a platform that would be acceptable to the slave states had to be found. There was little point in antagonizing the south, some supporters suggested, by insisting on a strongly worded popular sovereignty platform when a more general statement might satisfy both north and south. Douglas had pointed the way when he expressed his readiness to reaffirm the Cincinnati platform at Charleston "without the change of a word." The proposal appealed to many of his northern followers who were concerned over southern hostility, and it found increasing support among his southern friends. "We can meet you certainly upon the Cincinnati Platform & the Dred Scott decision, pure & simple," wrote Seibels, "and leave interpretations to the tribunals to which they belong." By following this strategy, no person or section would be asked "to sacrifice any preconceived opinion upon a point where we have agreed to disagree." Douglas would concede none of his principles; at the same time, he would be cast as a defender of traditional Democratic dogma while portraying the partisans of a slave code as apostates from the party. "If we can beat them on the Platform & re-adopt the Cin [cinna] ti Platform without amendment," Ohioan Payne predicted, "the victory is half gained." The suggestion received press support, and even the Buchanan administration, anxious to avert a north-south confrontation, saw merit in the idea.[33]

In the meantime, Douglas watched the southern conventions closely for their attitudes toward his candidacy. In Virginia, a heated struggle raged between Governor Wise and Hunter for control of the state's delegation. Douglas' campaign manager was on the scene trying to head off Wise in favor of Hunter, who was more likely to support Douglas. "The Hunter men must be made to feel that they have in your friends honorable and not factious opponents," Sanders advised Douglas, "so that when they leave H. they can easily go for you." Hunter was successful in securing an uninstructed, although friendly, delegation, and he began to pick up support elsewhere in the south. As the Charleston convention drew nearer, Hunter's friends were observed in frequent negotiation with Douglas' managers in Washington. In Georgia, Howell Cobb's presidential aspirations were supported, but his race left the state party so divided that nothing was sure. Toombs and Stephens leaned toward Douglas, while former governor Herschel V. Johnson stood aloof.[34]

In Louisiana an uninstructed delegation was appointed, although the state convention expressed its preference for John Slidell. Jefferson Davis was the favorite of Mississippi, even though one editor of a Douglas paper complained that the people of the state had been hoodwinked by men who desired a dissolution of the Union. Tennesseans expressed their support of Andrew Johnson, but Douglas was reported to be their second choice. In South Carolina the Unionists controlled the state convention, and they endorsed Douglas' friend and former Congressman James L. Orr, indicating a sympathy for Douglas in a state where he had little reason to expect it. Sanders, in contact with South Carolina leaders, was up to his old tricks, bargaining for support for Douglas and even offering the vice presidency to former Congressman Francis Pickens.

James Guthrie beat out John C. Breckinridge for the endorsement of Kentucky's convention, but the Vice President was favorably spoken of elsewhere in the south and gained strength among some northern Democrats. Breckinridge was thought to be Douglas' most serious competitor. Apparently Douglas shared this belief, for he made no effort to conceal his determination to prevent Breckinridge's nomination at Charleston. Sanders, who was confident that with a little tact the Breckinridge men could be brought to Douglas' side, pleaded with him to cease his attacks on the Kentuckian. Breckinridge's lukewarm support (as Douglas viewed it) in the 1858 senatorial campaign, the fact that he was being urged in the northwest by Douglas' enemies, and his endorsement of a federal slave code had brought the two friends to a parting of the ways.[35]

South Carolina's Senator Hammond worried about the fragmentation of southern strength among so many candidates, "*all* looking on Douglass as the great bug-a-boo—thereby elevating him at their own expense & equally ready to cut down any other person supposed to look that way." Efforts were made by administration supporters to identify a northern candidate on whom the south might unite, but without much success. President Buchanan had earlier removed himself from the race, but few were disposed to support him in any case. New York's Daniel

Dickinson was frequently mentioned. The "Senatorial clique"—Slidell, Bright, Fitch, Gwin, and others—for whom Douglas' nomination would be disastrous, advanced the name of Joseph Lane, the Indianan who had been elected one of Oregon's first Senators, but the south seemed little inclined to accept the suggestion.[36]

While there was little agreement among southern conventions on a candidate, there was clear and ominous agreement on their resolutions. Unequivocal in tone, they invariably denounced Douglas' "heretical" views and demanded the protection of slavery in the territories. Frequently they were accompanied by threats of party disruption if the Charleston convention should fail to adopt a southern platform. The resolutions and threats were warnings that even Douglas' willingness to reaffirm the Cincinnati platform would be unacceptable to the south. The Cincinnati platform was regarded as merely a shelter for Douglas' principles; the south would accept no platform that was capable of a double construction. The most dramatic action was that of the Alabama convention, which met soon after the Harper's Ferry raid. Led by the "prince of fire eaters," William Lowndes Yancey, the convention not only endorsed a federal slave code platform but also instructed its delegates to withdraw from the Charleston meeting if the plank were not included in the national platform. Although several of Douglas' friends in Alabama confidently expected a reaction against the radicals and in favor of Douglas to set in before Charleston, the mood of the state was more accurately summarized by one of Senator Clay's correspondents, who commented that "if Douglas & disunion were presented to their choice," Alabamans would "adopt the latter as the less evil!" The sentiment was by no means confined to Alabama. Mississippi joined in, and the fire-eaters began to lay plans for the secession of the two states from the convention "on the issue of squatter sovereignty and the construction of the Dred Scott decision." Texas, Douglas was told, would withdraw from the convention "if they cannot otherwise defeat your nomination," and other delegations were reported to be similarly inclined.[37]

Douglas' efforts to appease the south were severely damaged by the intransigent posture of the southern conventions. His hopes were further injured by a revival of the Lecompton issue during the early weeks of 1860. "Let the issue of Lecompton & anti Lecompton be for ever buried, as of no earthly practical importance at present," Seibels had advised Douglas. A congressional investigating committee, named for its Republican chairman, Representative John Covode of Pennsylvania, however, would not let the issue be buried. In an attempt to produce campaign material that could be used against the Democrats, the Covode Committee launched a thorough investigation of the Buchanan administration, including its handling of the Lecompton crisis. Among those interrogated was Robert J. Walker, who released, less than a week before the Charleston convention, Buchanan's letter supporting Walker's intention to guarantee a free and fair referendum on the Lecompton constitution. While the letter's publication probably aided Douglas in the north in his struggle against the administration, it also reminded southerners of Douglas' role in the crisis. By casting suspicion on the sincerity of Buchanan's motives, the revelation stiffened the southern demand for the protection of slavery in the territories. That southern leaders themselves were looking for ways of bringing Douglas' Lecompton role before the eyes of their constituents was revealed by the widow of John Calhoun, who informed Douglas that a relative of John.Slidell, among others, had tried to purchase all the letters that had passed between Douglas and her husband during the crisis.[38]

iv

As the state conventions completed their work, Douglas turned his attention to the delegates themselves. His correspondence swelled as reports from the newly elected delegates poured in, commenting on the current complexion of the delegations, pointing out weaknesses, offering aid, and seeking direction from the candidate himself. Some delegates appealed to Douglas for money to finance their trips to Charleston, confident that their votes were so valued that he would not hesitate to comply. Douglas and his staff, including his father-in-law, James Madison Cutts, were hard pressed to answer all the letters. Many of the delegates from the northern and northwestern states planned to stop in Washington on their way to Charleston, "for the purpose of taking soundings," as one editor put it, and some began to arrive as early as the first week in March. By mid-April, delegates were pouring into the capital. "Nothing is thought of or talked of but the Charleston Convention," observed Hammond.

Douglas and his managers were active among the delegates, seeking new support and bolstering those already committed. Some delegations received more attention than others. "The Douglas men," reported one correspondent, "are constant in their attentions to the New Yorkers." "All sorts of combinations are proposed & even to me," chuckled Hammond as he described an encounter with Banks and Sanders. They were "ready to offer terms," asking Hammond to talk up Douglas among New York and Pennsylvania delegates and hinting "that lightning might strike me in the Charleston Convention."

Administration pressure mounted in an attempt to reduce Douglas' strength. Efforts were made to counter this pressure, especially in the New York, Pennsylvania, and some of the New England delegations. A Massachusetts delegate, James G. Whitney, was appointed collector of customs in Boston by Buchanan, and he immediately altered his pro-Douglas stance. Douglas was informed that the administration would raise "Heaven and Earth to divide the several delegations in New England" and that the patronage-rich Boston customs house was one means to this end. Isaac Cook was in Washington at the request of the President (or so he boasted) to work whatever influence he might have on the visiting delegates. Erratic and obnoxious, he made the news primarily through his highly publicized wagers that Douglas would receive no support in his home state if nominated. John Slidell and the banker W. W. Corcoran, it was rumored, were in the market for delegates, offering to buy them up with either cash or offices.

Gatherings were held in Douglas' home, and delegates from many parts of the country were treated to Adele's gracious hospitality. The Douglas headquarters in the National Hotel was almost continually filled with delegates, members of Congress, governors, and other political aspirants, as well as "choice spirits." "We have meetings every night and talk matters over" as delegates mapped strategy with Douglas and his agents. On April 16, a week before the Charleston convention, a final gathering of Douglas delegates expressed complete confidence in the success of their cause. The speeches and liquor were abundant, and two southerners, Hamilton of Texas and Clingman of North Carolina, were loudly applauded when they pledged the south for the Little Giant.[39]

As they prepared for battle, the northwestern delegates became more resolute. No other result than Douglas' nomination would be acceptable. If a southern or slave code platform should be adopted, "the party may at once disband." Some of Douglas' followers admitted that they would sooner vote for the Republican candidate than endorse any other Democrat. What if Douglas should be defeated at Charleston on the platform question? Henry Payne and other northwestern leaders unhesitatingly proposed that the Douglas delegates withdraw from the convention in such an event. "To succumb would be destructive to us at home. . . .

Our men will be prepared to retire from the convention . . . and they will never in any event give even a complimentary vote for another than your-self." Their own political survival depended upon an acceptance of Doug-las and popular sovereignty. Smarting under repeated Republican charges of subservience to the slave power, they regarded a showdown with the south as imminent and desirable. Douglas' southern support was equally adamant. Forsyth suggested that Douglas would be "strong enough to control the nomination & platform" even if he were not the nominee, but he added that "the administration & the advocates of the 'slave code' must be beaten at all hazards." A Maryland delegate reflected the atti-tude of the Douglas forces as they prepared to leave for Charleston: "Rest assured of one thing there can arise no contingency in the Con-vention when your friends will agree to vote for any other man than yourself. The time for compromise and postponement upon that point has passed and so sure as the Convention will make a nomination—so sure will you be the man." [40]

Douglas encouraged as many of his followers as possible to make the trip to Charleston in order to offset the advantage of his southern en-emies. The "outside pressure" would have great influence on the conven-tion's deliberation, and Douglas was determined that as much of it as possible should be friendly to him. Lanphier predicted that between 200 and 300 Illinoisans would go to Charleston, but that number was exag-gerated. Lack of money discouraged large numbers of northwestern sup-porters from attending the convention, but there were other handicaps as well. Charleston was difficult of access and was poorly prepared to host the crowds that were normally attracted to a convention city. For weeks reports circulated throughout the north that lodging facilities were inadequate and that the hotel-keepers were determined to charge exorbitant prices. Some asserted that it was a trick "on the part of Doug-las' enemies to keep away northern outsiders." A movement to change the location of the convention won support in the north, and a number of other cities began bidding for the convention. Sanders proposed New Orleans, on the ground that it was more accessible to Douglas' friends than any other place, but Baltimore also received consideration as a city that would be more congenial to the maintenance of party unity. Acting in response to the complaints, the Democratic National Committee met in Washington early in April and, after examining the reports from Charleston, decided not to move the convention.[41]

In spite of the pressure to adjourn for the convention, Congress decided to remain in session. However, Representatives and Senators, many of them delegates, left for South Carolina, so there was little prospect that Congress would be able to conduct much business while the convention was in session. Washington was deserted, and an uneasy quiet descended on the city. Douglas remained in the capital, but he arranged for close telegraphic contact with his floor leaders. Earlier, in February, his agent Thomas Dyer of Chicago had visited Charleston, engaging quarters for several of the northwestern delegations and renting a hall to serve as the Douglas headquarters. The atmosphere of hostility was unmistakable. "Charleston is the last place on Gods Earth where a national convention should have been held," he informed Douglas. Richardson, who had managed Douglas' forces in the Cincinnati convention four years before, was once again designated to serve as Douglas' chief lieutenant. On April 18, Richardson and Dyer arrived in Charleston to organize their campaign.[42]

The stage was set for the final showdown between the warring factions in the Democratic party. The confidence of the Douglas men was matched by the threats of the fire-eaters. Any effort, wrote Virginia's Senator Mason months before, "to keep united, what God has sundered —the Slave states & the servile states" was doomed to failure no matter who should be nominated. To acquiesce in Douglas' nomination, maintained a Georgian, would be to abandon all the south had struggled for. "If we falter *now* and compromise our principles for party we seal our fate." As the delegates gathered, Robert Barnwell Rhett, Jr., Charleston's radical editor, wrote the obituary of the Democratic party. "The Democratic party, as a party, based on principles, is dead. It exists now only as a powerful faction. It has not one single principle common to its members North and South." [43]

# XXVIII

## "Secession from the Democratic party
## means secession from the Union"
## 1860

i

The Charleston convention opened on April 23, Douglas' forty-seventh birthday. Delegates had been arriving for days, and the hotels were swarming with politicians, all caucusing, cajoling, and speculating on the course the convention would take. Not as many visitors appeared as expected. Douglas supporters were particularly disappointed at the small turnout from the northwest, but conditions in the convention city were crowded enough. Douglas headquarters were located in the Hibernia Hall, where 132 cots were crammed into a single large room on the second floor. Meeting rooms had been furnished with long tables, plenty of chairs, and a large supply of Sheahan's *Life of Stephen A. Douglas,* just off the presses. At the Mills House, where several of the northwestern delegations, including Illinois, were lodged, there were four or five persons to a room. To add to the discomfort the temperature soared into the mid-nineties, unseasonably hot even for South Carolina.

Some delegates tried to beat the crowded conditions and high prices by providing their own accommodations. The Indiana delegation announced it would pitch tents, but the plan was abandoned. Other delegations chartered steamers which not only carried them to the convention but also served as floating hotels while there. The vessels, carrying the Pennsylvania, New York, and some of the New England delegates, were well stocked with liquor and beer, and one was said to have a contingent of "amiable females" on board. Few of the delegates were prepared for a long convention. As the days passed, lodging bills mounted, money ran low, and stocks of liquor were exhausted. The cramped quarters, the weather, and the "political caloric" resulted in frayed nerves and hair-trigger tempers, a poor prospect for the cause of party unity.[1]

Douglas men were noisily in evidence, and even their enemies conceded that they could probably muster a majority of the convention. Enthusiastic, "rampant and riotous," they were "brim full of the sound and fury of boastfulness," reported Cincinnati newspaper correspondent Murat Halstead. They were playing a conciliatory game, trying to "think and act upon the presumption that they have the Convention in their hands and wish to make all the friends they can in the South." The largest crowd, Halstead observed, was at the Mills House, where Douglas' friends swore they would stick to their candidate and refused to talk of a second choice. Some of them found it difficult to remain calm when they were harassed by southern radicals. One Illinois delegate complained to Douglas of "the bitterness of some of our Southern opponents. They go so far as to call us all abolitionists. . . . I assure you it is with great difficulty we can keep cool but we do so and with kind words turn away strife."

Early developments were encouraging. Some of the "outside pressure" from the south was clearly for Douglas. Sanders, burly and piratical looking, was at work on southerners and, it was thought, making progress. A close call came when the Democratic National Committee appeared ready to issue tickets to the contesting delegations from Illinois and New York, whereupon the northwest resolved they would "go out of the convention in a body." The timely arrival of a Douglas committeeman and the efforts of the Committee's chairman, Douglas supporter D. A. Smalley of Vermont, turned the tide. The southern delegations were in caucus almost constantly in an effort to agree upon a candidate, but they only exhibited their "incapacity to come together." Some charged the southern failure to "secret Douglas influences." [2]

On the question of Douglas' candidacy and platform, however, there was little disagreement among southerners. Yancey was on hand to see that the south did not falter in its stand against Douglas. With calm assurance, he carefully prepared for the moment when the south would speak out. Two days before the convention opened, the delegations of seven southern states—Georgia, Alabama, Mississippi, Louisiana, Florida, Arkansas, and Texas—agreed to remain firm in their demand for a slave code platform and to withdraw if their demand should be rejected. Portions of four other delegations were said to have joined in the pledge. "The ultra Southerners," wrote Halstead, "are becoming bitter." The publication of Buchanan's letter to Walker on Lecompton, "thrust in every delegate's face" to prove that Douglas had been right, stiffened the radicals' determination. Douglas men were surprised at the southern action, but they refused to take it seriously. A southern withdrawal, they asserted, might gain them strength in the north. One supporter later assured Douglas that only one or two states would probably leave the convention and that their departure could easily be turned to Douglas' advantage. Douglas reacted to the news from Charleston with apparent indifference. Appearing in the House chamber on the day the convention opened, he reiterated his hope that "his friends will make no compromises, ask no favors, will stand to their colors, and neither receive nor give quarter."

The fire-eaters were not the only ones working to frustrate Douglas' plans and ambitions. Representing the Buchanan administration was John Slidell, crafty and shrewd, "a matchless wire-worker," whose presence in Charleston meant a "war to the knife" against Douglas. Assisting Slidell were other members of the Senatorial Clique, Jesse Bright (whose hatred for Douglas was "the strongest passion of his soul"), William Bigler, and James A. Bayard, the last two serving as delegates from their states. Unlike the southern radicals, their war on Douglas was based on personal hostility, a motive they made no effort to conceal. The platform was of no consequence to them except as a means to stop Douglas.[3]

On April 23, after a morning of caucuses, the delegates pressed into the spacious hall of the South Carolina Institute for the opening of the convention at noon. The meeting's first actions were favorable to Douglas. T. B. Flournoy, a Douglas man from Arkansas, was elected temporary president. In the first test vote, Smalley's decision to exclude the contesting delegations from Illinois and New York was upheld, over the stiff resistance of several southern delegations, and the regular delegates from those states were given places on both the credentials and organization committees. Two days later the credentials committee reported in favor of their being permanently seated in the body. In a second test of strength, the convention approved a Douglas-sponsored rule change which would enable delegates in uninstructed delegations to cast their individual votes. The decision, "a great point gained" according to Stuart, would silence the anti-Douglas minorities on instructed delegations and secure the Douglas votes in the uninstructed delegations, most of which were from the south. Douglas' only setback in the preliminaries of the convention was the selection of Caleb Cushing, an anti-Douglas, pro-administration delegate from Massachusetts, as permanent president.

The actions of the first two days revealed the solidarity and discipline of the Douglas majority as well as the weakness of his opponents. The current seemed to be running toward the Little Giant. The "outside pressure" thus far was pro-Douglas, and one correspondent marveled at the number of southern supporters of Douglas who were on hand "to manufacture public opinion." The ultra southerners were indignant. At the end of the first day they met again in caucus, and again they resolved to stand firm on a slave code platform, citing Jefferson Davis' Senate resolutions as their demand. Still unable to agree on a candidate, their only hope for success was to force an issue over the platform. They were joined by the administration Senators, who saw in the slave code a weapon by which Douglas could be eliminated. As the delegates gathered on the second day, Halstead noted, "There is an impression prevalent this morning that the Convention is destined to explode in a grand row. . . . There is tumult and war in prospect." [4]

The decision to adopt a platform before balloting for a presidential candidate was supported by both the Douglas men and the southern radicals; each group hailed it as a victory and each thought it would prove an advantage. Some on the Douglas side were not so certain. Stuart was skeptical but allowed himself to be persuaded, although he anxiously observed that there were men in the convention who were "determined to resist us to the end by any and all means in their power," men, he added, who were "potent for mischief." The south could count on a majority of the platform committee, where each state was represented. Oregon and California lined up with the fifteen slave states to give the backers of a slave code platform a 17-to-16 edge. With a majority of the individual delegates, however, Douglas' supporters were confident that they would be able to determine the character of the platform on the convention floor, and they had little fear of a southern walkout. To some observers, the decision to adopt a platform first dashed the last hope for maintaining party unity.

To expedite their discussions and to ensure unified support, Douglas leaders appointed an "Executive Committee of the Friends of Douglas," consisting of two members from each state. The group conferred and agreed to press for the platform that had often been suggested earlier, a reaffirmation of the Cincinnati platform with an additional resolution endorsing the ultimate authority of the Supreme Court. Douglas himself advised his followers by telegraph not to go beyond these terms. It was crucial that the platform lend itself to a popular sovereignty interpretation, which was essential to political survival in the north, and the ambiguities of the Cincinnati platform and the Dred Scott decision provided the opportunity. The south, intransigent in its demand for the protection of slave property in the territories, rejected as a point of honor any platform capable of a "double construction." "Here, then," warned Halstead, "is the 'irrepressible conflict.' " [5]

The platform committee deliberated for several days as the delegates bided their time. Rumors of the committee's inability to agree sped through the hall. Some feared that the committee would be unable to report at all. As the days passed, the sense of crisis mounted, and the hopelessness of the committee's task became apparent. Its choice was limited; it must either "bring in a subterfuge" or "throw a bombshell." When the committee finally made its report, on April 27, it submitted not one, but three platforms, in effect inviting the convention to take its choice.

The majority, or southern, report endorsed the Cincinnati platform but added several new explanatory resolutions. One, proposed in the committee by Bayard on behalf of the administration Senators, forcefully denied the authority of a territorial legislature over slavery, including the power to impair slave property "by any legislation whatever," a response to Douglas' Freeport doctrine. Another declared it the duty of the federal government to protect "when necessary" the rights of persons and property in the territories—the slave code proposition. The minority, or Douglas, report followed the lines agreed upon earlier. The Cincinnati platform was affirmed on the ground that "Democratic principles are unchangeable in their nature when applied to the same subject-matters." Since all questions relating to the rights of property in the states or territories were judicial questions, read a second resolution, the party was pledged "to abide by and faithfully carry out" the determinations of these questions which had been or might be made by the Supreme Court. Both the majority and minority platforms included similar resolutions dealing with the enforcement of the fugitive slave law, the construction of a Pacific railroad, the acquisition of Cuba, and the protection of citizens abroad. A second minority report, submitted by Benjamin F. Butler of Massachusetts, simply endorsed the Cincinnati platform without the addition of any explanatory resolutions.

The Douglas platform was presented by Ohio's Henry B. Payne. He reminded the delegates that the fate of the Democratic party and the destiny of the Union depended upon the outcome of the convention, and he asked the south if it would risk both simply to secure an "abstraction." He emphasized the willingness to stand by the Dred Scott decision and appealed to southerners "to put no weights upon the North." On popular sovereignty, however, he insisted that there could be no compromise. "We never will recede from that doctrine, Sir; *never, never, never,* so help us God."

The presentation of the platforms and Payne's defense of the Douglas position produced the crisis for which the fire-eaters had waited. In an hour-and-a-half speech, Yancey mounted a vigorous attack against Douglas and his doctrines, to the ringing applause of delegates and visitors. He inveighed against Douglas' record on the Kansas question, his treachery during the Lecompton crisis, and his interpretation of the Dred Scott decision. Tracing the history of northern aggression upon the south, he insisted that new guarantees of southern rights were necessary. Defeat upon principle, Yancey exclaimed, was preferable to a victory won on ambiguous issues. His remarks were frequently interrupted by loud shouts of approbation and stamping of feet, clearly indicating that the "outside pressure" was now with the radicals. Ohio Senator George E. Pugh, "in a condition of considerable warmth," mounted the platform to answer Yancey. Pugh angrily denounced the demand that the northern Democracy bow to the southern ultimatum, that northern Democrats prostrate themselves with their mouths in the dust. "Gentlemen of the South," he roared, "you mistake us—you mistake us—we will not do it." The hall was quiet, "as it was understood that Pugh was the spokesman of Douglas, and that the fate of the Democratic party was in issue." [6]

Events moved rapidly following the presentation of the platforms. After a night spent in frantic maneuvering, a desperate attempt to avert an explosion was undertaken. Bigler, undoubtedly acting for the administration, moved that the reports be recommitted to the platform committee and suggested as a compromise a new set of resolutions which simply restated the southern platform in less precise language. The motion to recommit won by a single vote, against the strong opposition of the Douglas delegates, but Bigler's formula was turned down. The platform committee reported later, on April 28, again submitting three platforms. None of the three was significantly different from their earlier versions. The lines were drawn as rigidly as before; the disruption had only been postponed. Through all the confusion, Douglas men expressed confidence that all would eventually come out right. One wrote Douglas that Yancey's speech was merely the south's way of letting off steam, and that only Alabama and Mississippi would maintain their opposition to the Douglas platform. Sanders, appealing to Buchanan's patriotism and generosity, asked the President to forget past differences and support Douglas. The minority platform would be adopted, and only three southern states were likely to withdraw, leaving Douglas in command of the convention. The Little Giant, Sanders predicted, would receive the necessary two-thirds majority on the second or third ballot. The communication was telegraphed collect and cost the indignant President $26.80. Sanders sent similar appeals to the Vice President and members of the cabinet.[7]

Sanders' confidence was not widely shared. On Monday, April 30, the delegates gathered in the convention hall, many of them disheartened and discouraged at the prospects of mending the breach between Douglas and the south. The crowds had begun to melt away as trains and steamers carried the visitors back to their homes in the north, leaving the galleries to the Charlestonians, whose sympathies were wholly on the side of the radicals. There was more talk that the next President would be nominated at the Republican convention in Chicago.

In a mood of mounting despair, the convention addressed itself to the question of the platform. Butler's proposal, the Cincinnati platform pure and simple, was first rejected. A motion to substitute the minority, or Douglas, report for the majority report was then adopted, and the delegates prepared for the final crisis. Tensions that had been building for days now reached their peak. Each resolution, it was decided, would be voted on separately. The first, affirming the Cincinnati platform, was accepted, the voting interspersed with explanations, threats, and warnings. Douglas men pleaded for party unity; southerners denounced the "Cincinnati swindle" and asserted that they could never agree to stand on a court decision that was variously interpreted. As voting began on the second section of the minority platform, that pledging the party to abide by the decisions of the Supreme Court on questions of slavery in the territories, the Douglas men made their final move. Stuart called out that, if the south did not want the resolution, the north would not insist on it. Richardson unsuccessfully sought the floor to make an announcement, but as the balloting continued his strategy became clear. The northern states, voting at first in the affirmative, changed their votes to negative when they realized the south was not voting at all. The section was dropped, and the Douglasites fell back on a simple reaffirmation of the Cincinnati platform without explanation.

The south, however, continued to refrain from voting. The remaining planks, dealing with the Pacific railroad, the rights of naturalized citizens, the enforcement of the fugitive slave law, and the acquisition of Cuba, were adopted without the south's participation. Stuart, angered at the failure of the south to accept what was intended as a peace offering, concluded with an inflammatory speech that only irritated the southern delegates more. When Stuart had finished, delegates from Alabama, Mississippi, Louisiana, South Carolina, Florida, Texas, and Arkansas withdrew from the convention amid impassioned oratory and the applause of the gallery. The next morning, the Georgia delegation walked out.

The withdrawal of eight southern states staggered the Douglas men. They had expected the secession of a few delegates, the Alabama group and possibly one or two other states, and were convinced that "a little eruption" would strengthen them in the north and among moderate southerners. Indeed, the willingness of Douglas' friends to determine the platform before nominating a candidate was seen as an attempt to force a small southern withdrawal. The administration Senators saw through this strategy and urged the ultra southerners to remain in the convention. The real target, they argued, was not the platform, but Douglas himself. On the day before the explosion, Slidell, Bayard, and Bright persuaded Yancey to disregard his state's instructions and remain in the hall. Encouraged, Slidell assured others that the party would yet be saved if all the resolutions of the minority report, save the reaffirmation of the Cincinnati platform, were voted down. The Senators knew that Douglas could never be nominated with a two-thirds majority as long as the south continued to participate. Even some southerners agreed that a withdrawal would result in Douglas' nomination; the only way to stop him was to remain in the convention. The platform, however, was more important to the south than even Slidell realized. Yancey was unable to convince his delegation to remain; even the few Douglas supporters in the Alabama delegation insisted on a withdrawal, thinking that they were helping Douglas' cause.

A large number of Douglas delegates met on the evening of the withdrawal to take stock of the situation. Several border state southerners minimized the disruption, and Flournoy of Arkansas suggested conciliatory measures to bring the seceders back into the hall. Northern Democrats, however, had had enough of concession. If the seceding delegates wished to come back, argued Payne, they could do so without an invitation from Douglas' supporters. Like the ultra southerners, Payne and others now rejected any proposal that could be construed one way in the north and another way in the south. "The friends of Douglas," commented a correspondent, "were determined that there should be no misunderstanding or deception this time." [8]

The remaining actions of the convention were anticlimactic. Balloting for a presidential candidate began, but not until after there was a brief and acrimonious skirmish over the two-thirds rule. The New York delegation, with its thirty-five votes, became "the pivot on which things turn." With the support of the border states, the New Yorkers insisted that the nominee receive two-thirds of the full convention, or 202 votes, rather than simply two-thirds of those who remained. The adoption of the resolution was another blow to Douglas' managers, for it dashed their plans to nominate the Little Giant easily and quickly following the southern departure. The leader of the New York delegation, Dean Richmond, later explained to Douglas that the move was taken to prevent the remaining southern states from leaving the convention, to cast the bolters as disunionists and to strengthen Douglas' cause in the north. But New York was also motivated by the hope that Douglas, faced with the impossibility of nomination, might withdraw his name and that the convention could be reunited on a compromise candidate, to be selected by the New Yorkers.

Similar attention was given to the platform. A new resolution, supported by New York and the border states and introduced by a Tennessean, was proposed, which would, it was hoped, provide a bridge over which the seceders could return to the convention. A mild form of the federal slave code plank and a rebuke to the Freeport Doctrine, the so-called Tennessee Platform provided that all citizens "have an equal right to settle, with their property, in the Territories . . . and that under the decisions of the Supreme Court . . . neither their rights of person nor property can be destroyed or impaired by Congressional or Territorial legislation." Richardson responded with the emphatic declaration that there would be no retreat on either the candidate or the platform. The Tennessee Platform was not brought to a vote.

Douglas' name was placed in nomination by Austin King of Missouri. On the first ballot he received a comfortable majority of the votes, his opposition scattering among Guthrie, Dickinson, Hunter, Johnson, Lane, Davis, Toucey, and Pierce. But it was apparent to all that a two-thirds majority lay beyond his reach. Fifty-seven inconclusive ballots were taken on the first two days of May, Douglas' strength varying only slightly from his first ballot support. New York, which had just rendered Douglas' nomination an impossibility, voted consistently for him on all the ballots. Douglas' friends became increasingly obstinate. To suggestions that his name be withdrawn, they revealed Douglas' promise before the convention "that he would not repeat the Cincinnati despatch under any contingency." When it was rumored that he had telegraphed his followers to withdraw his name, Douglas himself issued the denial. "Not one word of truth in the report," he declared. "I have sent no message to Charleston, and shall send none." Like both Slidell and Yancey, Douglas was no longer able to control events; he would have failed even if he had asked to be withdrawn. "Douglas or nobody," wired Lanphier from Charleston. "His friends will never yield."

By May 3, the tenth day of the convention, the delegates became aware that further balloting would be simply an exercise in futility and frustration. Richardson, Stuart, and other Douglas leaders were nervous and worried, fearing defections from their ranks if the deadlock continued. There was reason for their anxiety. The New York delegation decided that, if Douglas were not nominated by the sixtieth ballot, their support would be withdrawn. Richardson was notified at once. The Tennessee Platform still remained a threat and if passed "would deaden Douglas." Rather than risk the loss of both the nomination and the platform, the Douglas leadership (at Douglas' own suggestion, it was said) adjourned the convention, to reassemble in Baltimore on June 18, six weeks later. In the interim, the parties "in the several States" were urged to make provision for filling "all vacancies in their respective delegations," which the Douglasites interpreted as applying to the seats of those delegates who had withdrawn from the convention. When the final tap of the gavel was sounded, there was a rush for the hotels and trains, and within a few hours of the adjournment, "Charleston was herself again." [9]

Following their withdrawal, the southern delegates gathered in a near-by hall and organized. Bayard, who had walked out with them in order that the administration might exert a restraining influence on their action, was chosen to preside. The majority platform was unanimously adopted, but the delegates declined to make a nomination. They fully expected that the regular convention would offer a compromise that would effect their return, and when the Tennessee Platform was introduced their hopes were boosted. Instead, the delegates were thrown into confusion by the unexpected news that the convention had adjourned. It was "a coup d'état upon the part of the Douglas men." Many of the southern delegates feared that they would be replaced for the Baltimore meeting, perhaps even cast outside the Democratic party. A resolution adjourning the meeting to Richmond on the second Monday in June was approved, and the seceders dispersed to return to their constituents.[10]

The Charleston convention was a tragedy of miscalculation. Each side gambled and each lost. Southerners were bitter. "The Douglas men came here rabid & reckless," wrote a South Carolinian, "like a gang of wolves or a flock of vultures, bent on spoil, without compromise or alternative, their howlings are for blood." A member of the Illinois delegation, on the other hand, complained that Douglas men encountered "a deep-rooted hostility and burning dislike" on the part of southerners which frustrated all attempts to arrive at a compromise. Illinois Congressman John Logan bitterly observed that "such a combination has never been met by any man on earth" as that Douglas had encountered at Charleston.[11]

ii

From his vantage point in Washington, Douglas remained cool and confident through most of the convention, displaying an outward attitude of indifference toward developments in Charleston. Politicians thronged his headquarters for the latest news, and his residence was crowded with well-wishers until late at night. As the convention approached its crisis, however, he became more worried and anxious; the strain began to tell. Among the first in Washington to learn of the southern withdrawal, he was startled and disappointed at the extent as well as the depth of the hostility toward him. His house became the scene of hurried conferences as his friends joined him in discussions of strategy. Pressure to withdraw his name increased. Administration efforts to defeat his nomination, while expected, weighed more heavily.

Douglas stood firm in the face of the pressure, for, as one editor put it, he had a heavy account to settle with both the radical south and the administration. But it was not an easy stance. Nervous and apprehensive, he took to drink, and when California Senator Milton Latham saw him on May 4, the day after the convention's adjournment, Douglas was under the influence of liquor, railing excitedly about his enemies and the bloodhounds who were after his life. A few days later, he appeared on the floor of the Senate, "his mouth closed up as if he was trying to bite a pin in two," fidgeting, drumming his fingers on the chair arms, clasping and unclasping his hands. He looked pale, and his hair had grayed; those who observed him were reminded that it had not been many weeks since he was lying on a sickbed, and that he was still not well.[12]

Advice poured in from all quarters. The adjournment of the convention, it was thought, could only result in "renewed zeal and courage" among his supporters. Border state men advised Douglas to accept the Tennessee Platform in order to strengthen his standing in the south. It was, they maintained, unobjectionable, and Douglas could afford to be liberal. When the Washington *States* urged the adoption of the Tennessee Platform as a fair compromise, it was assumed that it did so with Douglas' approval. Some were quick to charge him with duplicity and bad faith. Additional resolutions were proposed as solutions to the impasse in the party, all limiting in some way the power of a territorial legislature over slavery. One friend urged Douglas to drop the label "popular sovereignty" and to use the less controversial and more ambiguous phrase "non-intervention" instead. Northern supporters, on the other hand, made it clear that no concession on the platform could be accepted, that a retreat would result in the sacrifice of their careers and the abandonment of the northern Democracy.[13]

Douglas, however, had no intention of retreating. There was much to be done before the Baltimore meeting; new support had to be built in the south and the loyalty of northern delegates had to be strengthened. A large number of those who had attended the Charleston convention stopped in Washington to talk with the candidate, "to comfort and be comforted," and long lines of carriages were daily lined up in front of his residence. The Douglas headquarters took on new life.

The nomination of other presidential candidates brought new problems and new urgency to Douglas' efforts. On May 10, John Bell was nominated for the presidency by the Constitutional Union party, on a platform that simply stressed "The Constitution of the Country, The Union of the States, and The Enforcement of the Laws." Bell's selection was received in the Douglas camp as "the best thing that could have occurred for us." By cutting into Seward's strength, his candidacy would reduce the prospect of a Republican victory. From the first there was an element of compatibility between the Douglas and Bell forces. It was even suggested that Bell might resign his nomination in favor of Douglas.[14]

The Republicans, who gathered in Chicago later in the month, were watched by the Douglasites with a good deal more concern. All signs pointed to the nomination of Seward, a choice that Douglas' friends thought would bring the moderate and conservative southern strength to their side. The Republican strategists, however, concluded that a less controversial candidate was required to offset Douglas' probable nomination. Lincoln filled the bill. His race against Douglas two years before was still being talked about; his appeal would be to the same elements in the north that were attracted to Douglas. Lincoln's nomination was a victory for what Halstead called "the conservative expediency men." Douglas was in close touch with developments in Chicago, and he was one of the first in Washington to learn of Lincoln's selection. When he conveyed the news to delighted Republicans in Congress, he surprised everyone with his praise for the Republican nominee. Lincoln, he told several members of the House of Representatives, was the ablest debater he had ever faced, and no stronger nomination could have been made. Sanders and others in the Douglas organization boasted that Lincoln could easily be beaten, but most, like Douglas, anticipated "a devil of fight." [15]

Attention now focused on the south, particularly on those states whose delegations had withdrawn from the Charleston convention. The seceders returned to their constituents hoping to secure approval for their action, no difficult task, but they also had to counter the charges that they had withdrawn from the Democratic party. Douglas' southern supporters, on the other hand, seized the opportunity to call new state conventions and appoint new delegations. Some northwestern delegates offered their assistance, traveling through the south on their way home, making speeches, and conferring with politicians. There was more free and irresponsible talk of the vice presidential nomination as efforts were made to woo certain leaders into the Douglas fold. The erratic Sanders, without authorization, even sounded out Yancey for the position, providing the rumor mill with considerable grist later in the campaign.[16]

The struggle was narrowed to Alabama, Georgia, and Louisiana, where Douglas minorities were large and active. In Alabama, Forsyth, Seibels, and former governor John Winston tried to lay the foundation for a general movement toward Douglas. They called a state convention, which in turn named a set of Douglas delegates to replace the regular Yancey-led delegation. In Georgia, where Stephens continued to speak favorably of Douglas' nomination, a rump meeting selected a new delegation, and in Louisiana Pierre Soulé placed himself at the head of a Douglas delegation. Individual assurances of support came from other southern states, as men such as North Carolina delegate W. W. Holden decided that only Douglas' nomination could save the party and the country.[17]

The hastily called Douglas meetings were irregular and unauthorized, representing only a fraction of the southern party, but by selecting new delegations they forced the Charleston seceders to reconsider their plans to meet in Richmond instead of Baltimore. In the meantime, pressure was exerted upon the bolters from other quarters. Nineteen southern members of Congress, reflecting the administration's concern for party unity, appealed to the south to return to Baltimore, where "their presence might purge the party creed of its heresies and return it to unmistakable 'fidelity to the Constitution and the Union.' " To do otherwise, they urged, would be to destroy the "sole remaining conservative national organization in the country." To the fire-eaters, a return to Baltimore meant surrender to Douglas, and they balked at the advice. Yancey was unwilling to rejoin the convention unless an olive branch were tendered which, at the least, involved a reversal of the platform. The Charleston *Mercury* advised southerners not to be distracted by the congressional appeal. In the end, however, all of the seceding delegations except that of South Carolina were instructed to go to Baltimore.

The question was immediately raised whether the seceding delegates would be admitted to seats at Baltimore, especially those challenged by Douglas delegations. Douglas answered the question himself in a letter to August Belmont, two weeks before the convention would meet. The news from the south, he wrote, cheered him. "All we have to do is to stand by the delegates appointed by the people in the seceding States in the place of the disunionists." The issue had now been joined between union and disunion. "Of course," he continued, "we must stand by the Union men and redeem the implied pledge of the adjourning resolutions at Charleston by admitting the delegates appointed in pursuance of that invitation." Moreover, the bolters who may appear in Baltimore have no intention of abiding by the result, "but openly avow their object to be to bolt again and break up the convention. Of course no true Democrat will admit them to seats after such an avowal." Douglas was determined not to lose control at Baltimore, for a party test of his own was in the making. Belmont agreed "that we should not admit the seceding delegates unless regularly reelected by newly convened State Conventions & not participants of the Richmond Convention." [18]

While Douglas' prospects were being advanced in the south, his managers were also busy in the northeast, mending some of the cracks that had developed at Charleston. Hendrick Wright was active in Pennsylvania and hoped to add to Douglas' strength in that State. In Massachusetts, administration forces with money and office at their disposal were locked in a bitter struggle with the Douglas men, and attempts were under way to breach the Douglas lines in Maine and New Hampshire. Some Douglas delegates in New England complained that they did not enjoy the confidence of the Douglas leaders at Charleston and that the struggle in the convention appeared to be a vendetta between the northwest and the administration, "regardless of the rights, interests or feelings of the whole democracy whose votes must be secured." To check this attitude, Douglas was told, would require energy and money. "I am more than every satisfied," wrote a loyal New Englander, "that the fight must be made at Baltimore even to the breaking up of the convention. To retreat is but political suicide." [19]

It was New York that worried Douglas the most. Many New Yorkers still regarded themselves as potential President-makers, and they spoke of concessions that would bring the bolting southern delegates back. The Tennessee Platform was still mentioned as a compromise measure. It would be difficult, warned a New York delegate, to hold the state for Douglas at Baltimore unless Virginia or some other southern state "comes out flat-footed" for him. The administration redoubled its efforts to split the delegation, utilizing the force of patronage and promoting Governor Horatio Seymour as a compromise candidate. The Douglas forces suffered an embarrassing setback when Isaac V. Fowler, postmaster of New York City and a Douglas man on the state's delegation, fled the country after a shortage of some $160,000 was discovered in his accounts. Banks, Richardson, and Stuart were in New York conferring with delegates and assisting Dean Richmond, Peter Cagger, and August Belmont. Reports were sent to Douglas almost daily.

The reports were usually encouraging. Richmond's "blood is up," wrote Banks, and he would stand or fall with the northwest. Richardson and Stuart were confident that the delegation would stand by Douglas. "I feel pretty secure about this state," Richardson commented, "if there is any reliance in the word of men." Howell Cobb, alarmed at the tactics of Douglas men in the south, dispatched a fellow-Georgian and member of the Treasury Department, Junius Hillyer, to New York to encourage opposition to Douglas and to secure backing for the admission of the seceders into the Baltimore convention. Richardson quelled Hillyer's efforts, informing him bluntly that his self-respect would compel him to walk out of the convention if any seceder were admitted without first having been re-elected by his state. There would be no compromise with disunionists. Alabama delegate Leroy P. Walker was in New York on a similar mission.

Douglas was aided by the circulation of a long letter written by Alexander H. Stephens, urging the south to drop its demand for a slave code, to stand by non-intervention ("that Congress shall pass no law upon the subject of slavery in the territories, either for or against it"), and to rejoin the convention at Baltimore. Stephens stopped short of endorsing Douglas' popular sovereignty, but his statement was close enough. "Why should we desire or want any other platform of principles than that adopted at Cincinnati?" he asked. Desperately looking for signs of Douglas support in the south, New Yorkers were deeply impressed by Stephens' position. Sanders busily tried to patch up the differences with Fernando Wood. Richmond, daily more confident, promised to stop in Washington to receive Douglas' last-minute instructions before proceeding to Baltimore. With their own delegation apparently in order, New Yorkers began looking to the rest of the country. A "self constituted committee of seven" was organized to correspond with Democrats in other states and to raise money for Douglas' campaign. Included in the membership were such prominent citizens and financial leaders as August Belmont, George Law, John Jacob Astor, and Edward C. West.[20]

A great mass meeting at Cooper Institute in New York City on May 22 was organized to demonstrate New York's support of Douglas and to encourage the southern Douglasites in their struggle against the seceders. Some members of Congress, including southerners Rust, Hamilton, and Clingman, were on hand, and Richardson made one of the principal addresses. Resolutions were proposed declaring that Douglas could not be set aside without a betrayal of Democratic principles and pledging New York's vote for the Little Giant, and they were enthusiastically endorsed. A similar demonstration was held in Philadelphia on June 4.[21]

As Richardson labored among the New Yorkers, one of his principal worries was Douglas himself. There were hints that southern radicals would drag him into debate in the Senate in the hope that he might damage his own cause with his statements. Jefferson Davis had announced he would bring up his slave code resolutions for passage, a reaffirmation of the southern determination not to back down on the platform, and Douglas undoubtedly would become involved in the discussion. Richardson and others met with Douglas, who agreed that he would not participate in any debate except with Davis.

Davis began the discussion on May 7, and he was joined on the next day by Louisiana Senator Judah P. Benjamin, who maintained that Douglas' strength at Charleston was only the result of the unit rule's operation among some northern delegations. When Davis remarked that no individual had a right "to appropriate to himself exclusively all that belongs to a doctrine which he did not originate" (a reference to Douglas and popular sovereignty), Douglas was on his feet in reply. "I never pretended that I originated it," he declared, adding, "If one man is not the peculiar guardian of it, it is very evident that one man is the object of attack in regard to it." Implying that Davis was simply trying to influence the actions of the forthcoming convention, Douglas once again defended his position and indicated his readiness to respond to the attacks on his record. "I shall not reply to everybody in detail, unless I choose to do so."

Douglas formally replied to Davis on May 15. After speaking for three hours he was exhausted, and the Senate adjourned until the next day, when he concluded his remarks. The galleries were crowded as usual, a large number of the diplomatic corps was present, and at least a quorum of the House of Representatives was on hand to hear him. The crisis in the Democratic party had made him "the most conspicuous man . . . of the whole country." The effort was below his standard and reflected his weariness. By means of a tiresome and repetitious review of congressional debates, party resolutions, and state conventions since 1848, he sought to prove his consistency in supporting popular sovereignty. The party had repeatedly endorsed his position; it was the south, he insisted, that had shifted its stance. Inevitably he referred to his removal from the territorial committee chairmanship and to the charges that he was a heretic. Those charges had now been refuted, he pointed out, for the Charleston convention had affirmed his platform and had given him a majority vote for the presidential nomination. "I am no longer a heretic. I am no longer an outlaw from the Democratic party. . . . I want no further or higher indorsement." He read Stephens' letter on non-intervention to show that not all of the south was hostile to his position and then concluded with a call for the preservation of the party and of the Union. The "good old Democratic party" was the only organization left "sufficiently national and conservative in its principles and great in its numbers to preserve this Union." [22]

It was a gargantuan effort for Douglas. Already weakened and upset, the speech left him physically exhausted. Toward the end, his voice became thick and husky, signaling the return of his chronic throat problem. Some of his arguments were praised, but in general the speech was critically received. As one editor put it, it was "a discussion of the dead past, and not of the living present and coming future." Had the lengthy extracts and quotations come from "an ordinary Senator," they would soon have emptied the chamber.

Davis replied, and Douglas, on May 17, responded to some of his points. The slave code resolutions, he reminded the Senate, had been introduced "for the purpose of operating on the Charleston convention" but they had been rejected there. They constituted a disunion platform. "Congressional intervention South for slavery, congressional intervention North against slavery, brings the two sections into hostile array, renders a conflict inevitable, and forces them either to a collision or a separation." The southern platform, he urged with deep emotion, carried with it "not only a dissolution of the party, but a disruption of all those ties which bind the country together." Softening his own line, he repeated the formula that had been offered the south at Charleston. Stand by "non-intervention," Douglas counseled, cease quarreling over "these abstruse theories" about the power of a territorial legislature, and leave the question to the courts. "When we do that, there will be peace and harmony in the whole country." [23]

The debate continued, and Richardson's concern that Douglas would become more deeply involved increased. "Do not under any circumstances be drawn into a debate which will degenerate below the dignity of your position," he advised. Douglas should leave Washington with his wife and visit "some Springs." "Write no political letters not even to your most trusted friend." Richardson need not have worried, for Douglas' effort in the Senate prostrated him. He was not present for the remainder of the debate and was absent when the slave code resolutions were finally brought to a vote and passed. His throat affliction developed into a severe bronchial attack, and he was confined to his home; in June he feared he would have to go to New York for another operation on his throat. Early in the month, his eight-month old daughter, sickly since birth, worsened and died. Once again, deep personal crisis and tragedy coincided with mounting political pressures.[24]

### iii

It was clear from the beginning that Douglas would control the Baltimore convention. Paced by the northwestern delegates, the determination of Douglas' supporters had stiffened. "Unless he is nominated," one of them warned, "our party is gone for all time to come." A last-minute caucus met in Douglas' home, where Douglas reportedly agreed to let the northwest have its way. Richardson insisted that the northwestern delegates should withdraw from the convention rather than accept defeat, and he later declared that Douglas had endorsed this decision. There seemed little likelihood, however, that this strategy would be necessary. If Douglas could not receive a two-thirds majority, then he would be nominated by a simple majority. Douglas men had been threatening this for weeks. The northwestern leadership, Stuart, Richardson, Payne, George McCook, and Ben Samuels (the latter two from Ohio and Iowa, respectively), met in Baltimore two days early to lay their plans.[25]

Preparations for the convention had been underway long before the meeting day. Hotel accommodations were reserved for the Illinois delegation in the Gilmore House, the same hotel, oddly, in which Yancey and his followers were housed. The Douglas headquarters were established in the home of Reverdy Johnson, near the convention hall. Western trains arriving in Baltimore were jammed with Douglas partisans, and there was no question that the outside pressure would be with the Little Giant. Accompanying them were a number of bands. Impromptu concerts were given in Monument Square, on the steps of the Johnson house, and in the streets before the hotels. Special trains between Baltimore and Washington were chartered, enabling delegates to confer easily and quickly with Douglas. Workmen hastened to complete the remodeling of the Front Street Theater, where the convention would meet, extending the floor, cutting additional windows for ventilation, and installing chandeliers for night sessions.[26]

The outcome of the convention hinged on the status of those delegates who had walked out at Charleston. The week before, a number of southern delegations gathered in Richmond, but they were reluctant to make any move that would prejudice their role in Baltimore. Only South Carolina was adamant, refusing to recognize the Baltimore meet-

ing and remaining in the Virginia capital. Of the rest, all except Florida
had been instructed to seek admission in Baltimore; Florida's delegates
were there as observers, hinting that they would not join the convention
unless offered a special invitation. Debate on whether the seceding delegations should be allowed to take seats in the convention began immediately, and it was terminated only by the passage of a resolution referring
the credentials "of all persons claiming seats in this Convention, made
vacant by the secession of delegates at Charleston" to the credentials
committee. An attempt to bind all members of the convention to support the nomination, offered by a Douglasite from New York, was withdrawn at Douglas' own request, on the ground that such a pledge was an
innovation and not party usage.

As the credentials committee began its deliberations, the telegraph
wires to Washington were hot. Banks needed new instructions from
Douglas. "Will be in Washington by twelve o'clock. Do not go to Bed."
That New York's role was crucial and still somewhat doubtful was indicated by the reassurances that Douglas now received. "New York all
right give your self no trouble about the result," wired Illinois delegate
Thomas Dyer. From McCook came the advice, "Believe no adverse rumors Your friends steadfast and confident." [27]

While the convention marked time, maneuvering was frantic on the
credentials committee and behind the scenes. The Douglasites could not
possibly accept the readmission of all the bolting delegates, which would
have destroyed Douglas' chances for the nomination. The admission of
the contesting Douglas delegations from Alabama, Louisiana, and Georgia
was regarded as essential. Still, in spite of their bluff and bombast, they
were willing to compromise and trade, the readmission of the uncon-
tested delegations for the admission of the contested ones, but even this
willingness did not prevent the committee from submitting a majority
and a minority report.

The credentials committee reported on the fourth day of the convention to a crowded and tense hall, amid an atmosphere that was all the
more charged because part of the floor had collapsed just before. The
majority, or Douglas, report recommended the readmission of the original delegations from Texas and Mississippi and made concessions in the
cases of individual delegates from Arkansas and Delaware. The Douglas
delegations from Alabama and Louisiana were to be admitted, and the
vote of Georgia was to be divided between the bolters and the Douglas
men. The minority report called for the readmission of all the seceders.

The delegates at once became aware "that New York was shaky." Anxious to keep the party together but reluctant to offend Douglas, the New York delegates asked for an adjournment in order to discuss their next move. Rumors flew, the streets were filled with excited men, and the air was electric. From the steps of the Johnson house and from the balconies of the hotels, speakers harangued the delegates, sometimes within a few feet of each other, trying to outshout their opponents. Later that night, word that New York would support the majority report flew through the streets, and McClernand immediately wired the good news to Douglas.[28]

Voting on the reports began the following day. An effort to substitute the minority for the majority report was defeated, amid "the most profound and solemn silence," and the convention began consideration of each of the majority report's recommendations. The results surprised no one, as each of the recommendations was adopted, until the question of Georgia's delegation came before the meeting. New York switched from yea to nay, and Georgia's bolters were seated. New York also employed its thirty-five votes to defeat the routine motion to reconsider the report and lay it on the table, thus leaving the convention's action on the report open to reconsideration and subject to conciliation. The move probably was sanctioned by the Douglas leaders, but it had little effect on their southern opposition. The New Yorkers later offered to reconsider their vote on the Louisiana case in order to bring back the original seceding delegation from that state, but "the seceders and their friends would not hear to any such proposition." The Douglasites were unwilling to retreat on the Alabama decision, for that would bring the hated Yancey into the convention. "There was no longer any doubt about the disruption of the Convention," observed Halstead. "It was merely a question of time, and the time was short."

It was now Douglas' turn to offer a compromise. Late on June 20, the day before the credentials committee made its reports, he penned a letter to Richardson which contradicted all the assurances he had made to his followers before the conventions. "I learn there is eminent danger that the Democratic party will be demoralized if not destroyed by the breaking up of the Convention," he began. The nation would never be safe from the "perils of sectional strife" unless the doctrine of non-intervention by Congress should prevail over both the northern and southern interventionists. While he could never sacrifice the principle, "even to attain the Presidency," he could "cheerfully and joyfully" sacrifice himself "to maintain the principle." "If therefore you and any other friends who have stood by me with such heroic firmness at Charleston and Baltimore shall be of the opinion that the principle can be preserved and the unity and ascendancy of the Democratic Party maintained, and the country saved from the perils of Northern abolitionism and Southern disunion, by withdrawing my name and uniting upon some other non-Intervention and Union loving Democrat I beseech you to pursue that course." It was a hard letter for Douglas to write, and he must have realized that it would fall heavily on his supporters. At the same time, it is doubtful that he calculated the impact his withdrawal would have on the party in the north and northwest, but for the moment his fears for the country overshadowed sectional and partisan concerns.[29]

The suggestion that Douglas withdraw had been made many times before. Southern supporters had pleaded with him to withdraw in favor of someone like Stephens, and it was a close friend of Stephens' whose counsel Douglas now acted upon, at least in part. Indeed, Douglas later told a southern audience that he had Stephens in mind when he wrote of "some other non-Intervention and Union loving Democrat." Richardson pocketed Douglas' letter and vigorously denied its existence; he had no intention of giving up the struggle at this point, and his determination was stiffened by the seceders themselves. While they spurned New York's overtures on the credentials report, they demanded Douglas' unconditional withdrawal in a manner offensive to the Douglasites. At the same time they let it be known through Georgians Cobb and Toombs that Stephens was just as unacceptable as Douglas, ending all possibility that Douglas' followers would give up their candidate.

Two days later, Douglas, frustrated, sent Dean Richmond a dispatch in which he repeated the language of his letter to Richardson. It was an open invitation for the New York delegation to bring forth a compromise candidate, releasing the state to pursue its role as a peacemaker. But Richardson would not budge, and Richmond was unwilling to risk the political consequences that would follow an abandonment of Douglas.

Douglas' action was far too late. A New York delegate later wrote, "I knew your *real wishes,* & where you desired to stop, but it is difficult to arrest a hurricane." While much of the responsibility for the failure of conciliation stemmed from the unshakable position of the radical southerners, Douglas' northern supporters had also gone too far to retreat. The northwest was as implacable as the deep south. Northwestern Democrats had a large account to settle with the south and the administration. Memories of the Lecompton struggle, the interference in the Illinois election, Douglas' removal from the territorial committee chairmanship, the loss of patronage, all still burned; the charges of servility to the south on the one hand and of treason to the party on the other demanded vindication. If Douglas was willing to forget, even temporarily, his followers were not. "The Democracy of the Northwest," wrote Halstead, "rose out of the status of serfdom," and Douglas was the "implement" of the revolution.[30]

A few hours after the approval of the majority report of the credentials committee, the long-awaited crisis arrived, and neither Douglas nor anyone else could stay its course. After having left the question open for a reconsideration, the New Yorkers sought unsuccessfully to reach an accord with the south. Following their failure they returned to the hall and cast their votes to defeat the reconsideration. When a motion was made to proceed to the nominations, a Virginia delegate, "standing, very pale, nervous and solemn," announced the withdrawal of most of his delegation from the convention. The border south now joined the deep south and walked out. Virginia was followed by most of the North Carolina, Tennessee, Maryland, California, and Oregon delegations, while the Missouri and Kentucky delegates retired to consult. The next morning, June 23, the Kentucky delegates withdrew. They were joined by some from Missouri and Arkansas. Caleb Cushing resigned the presidency of the convention and left, followed by others from the Massachusetts delegation. As most of the delegates looked on in silence, the Democratic party destroyed itself. The action had a sobering effect. Calm prevailed, for "the deed was done." The case was now "beyond the power of medicine or surgery."

The convention was a shambles. Less than 200 votes (out of an original strength of 303) remained, and over half the states were either not represented or were represented by a fraction of their original delegations. With Ohioan David Tod in the chair, the delegates turned to the nomination of candidates. On the first ballot Douglas received all but eighteen votes, and when that margin was reduced on the second ballot he was unanimously declared to be the nominee. Douglas' long ambition was realized at last, but it was not at all as he had wanted it.[31]

The next step was the nomination of a vice presidential candidate. Although Douglas had made no secret of his preference for Stephens, his managers left the choice to the scattered southern delegates who remained in the convention. They passed over Stephens and proposed the name of Alabama's Senator Benjamin Fitzpatrick. Forsyth and Seibels insisted that with Fitzpatrick, Yancey could be beaten and Alabama carried for Douglas; in their eagerness to annihilate Yancey, the delegates endorsed the choice. It mattered little that Fitzpatrick did not support Douglas' position and that he had voted for Davis' slave code resolutions; Seibels had sounded him out in Washington and had received what he thought were firm assurances that he would accept the nomination.

Before adjourning, the convention put a finishing touch on the platform. The controversial plank interpreting the Cincinnati platform on the power of a territorial legislature was reworded in the hope that even more vagueness might attract southern votes. During the existence of territorial governments, the resolution stated, "the measure of restriction, whatever it may be, imposed by the Federal Constitution on the power of the Territorial Legislature over the subject of the domestic relations" would be finally determined by the Supreme Court. As one southern delegate pointed out, the resolution "did not mean anything at all." It is ironic that in its final wording the plank virtually met the position for which the Buchanan administration had always contended.

While the Douglasites were completing their business, the seceders were having a convention of their own in the Maryland Institute Hall, not far away. In an atmosphere of quiet relief, the delegates adopted the Charleston majority platform without dissent and nominated John C. Breckinridge and Joseph Lane for President and Vice President. To the irritation of many of the delegates, Yancey followed with a long-winded speech which some feared would identify their convention too closely with "the ultraism of Alabama" and with disunion. When he finished, the delegates, impatient and sick of oratory, hastily adjourned.[32]

In the late hours of June 23, the Douglas headquarters in Washington were brightly illuminated, and politicians gathered to celebrate. Delegates returning from Baltimore were met at the railroad station by crowds of well-wishers, and together they formed a procession to Douglas' home. Douglas acknowledged their enthusiasm with a short speech which reflected more anxiety than elation. The Union, he told them, was now in grave danger. It could only be saved by a strict adherence to popular sovereignty and the defeat of the interventionist extremes. His final words were sobering. "Secession is *disunion*," he declared. "Secession from the Democratic party means secession from the federal Union." The crowd cheered and moved on to serenade Fitzpatrick at his lodgings, but the Senator, it was said, suffered from indisposition and did not appear.

Four days later Douglas formally accepted the presidential nomination. "The Federal Union must be preserved," he wrote, and "the constitution must be maintained inviolate in all its parts." He recalled the preservation of peace and stability in the Union in 1850. If the country should be plunged into revolution by proslavery and antislavery interventionists, he wondered, "where shall we look for another Clay, another Webster, or another Cass to pilot the ship of State over the breakers into the haven of peace and safety!" [33]

# XXIX

## "To preserve the glorious Union against Northern and Southern agitators"
## 1860

i

Douglas did not record his feelings following the breakup of the Democratic party at Baltimore, but they were undoubtedly intense. His public concern for the maintenance of the Union was simply the surface manifestation of the deep fears he felt for the future of his country. His faith in the greatness of America's destiny, hitherto unshakable, was now suddenly threatened by forces which neither he nor anyone else seemed able to control. The threat was not new, but its dimensions were. If Douglas had expressed similar apprehensions before, he had always had the hope that the Democratic party would somehow recover its national role, submerging the divisive tendencies of the sectional quarrel over slavery in a burst of patriotism and devotion to the Union. As the party system drifted toward sectionalization, the Democratic party's role became more significant. Douglas recognized the stresses to which his party was subjected, but his fears had been tempered by a tendency to minimize the strength of his opponents and to exaggerate his own ability to overcome their opposition. When he became aware of the magnitude of his party's crisis, it was too late. Southern ultras ignored his pleas and insisted on their platform even at the expense of a united party. At the same time, Douglas' followers in the north and northwest could not be restrained from making frantic efforts to free themselves of the southern incubus.

With the disruption of the Democratic party at Charleston and Baltimore, an important vehicle for the accommodation of opposing interests and arguments had been removed from the nation's politics. Although he had frequently forecast dire consequences for the nation if his party should be destroyed, Douglas was now loath to believe that all hope for the Union was lost. He still looked to his southern followers to give his presidential candidacy a national character. Persuaded more than ever that his platform was the only Union platform, he nurtured hopes that the voters would recognize the momentous nature of the issues involved in the election and that he might yet be elected. But the election of 1860 would not only determine who was to be President; it would also decide the fate of the Democracy, and of Douglas' role in it. Party leadership was at stake. Douglas was grimly determined to win, if not the presidency then that other prize, control of the Democratic party. Either way, the nation could yet be saved.

The immediate task was to develop an organization for the presidential campaign. On its last day, the Baltimore convention appointed a twenty-eight-member National Democratic Committee, with representation from all but five of the states. August Belmont, who had impressed Douglas with his ability both as a fund-raiser and as a political organizer, was selected as national party chairman, an indication that Douglas placed high priority on the financial aspects of his campaign.

The National Committee was first called upon to choose a new vice presidential candidate. As soon as Fitzpatrick's nomination became known, the Alabama Senator was bombarded with telegrams demanding that he decline. Douglas' opponents convinced Mrs. Fitzpatrick that her husband would be "eternally ruined if he accepted" and asked her to intercede. Yancey paid Fitzpatrick a visit and sought to dissuade him from accepting. Seibels frantically urged the Senator to resist the pressure: "To refuse now would be to cower before your enemies disgrace your best friends and place yourself in a most unenviable position." Fitzpatrick, however, withdrew, explaining that Seibels had misunderstood him when the two had talked in Washington. To accept a place on a ticket with Douglas, whose views were "entirely opposite" to his own, he explained, would compromise his political integrity.[1]

Members of the National Committee hastily gathered in Washington to receive Fitzpatrick's declination and to select a replacement. Again Stephens' name was proposed, but there were strong doubts that he would accept. The committee turned to Herschel V. Johnson, a former United States Senator and governor of Georgia. A member of the Douglas delegation from Georgia that had unsuccessfully sought admission at Baltimore, Johnson had favored Stephens' nomination for the presidency on the ground that only someone friendly to Douglas' position, not Douglas himself, could patch up the party's wounds. He had been approached earlier by northwestern Democrats for the vice presidential nomination but had discouraged the suggestion. Now he felt he had no choice but to accept. "I was literally forced to take the V. Pret. nomination," he wrote Stephens, "purely as a matter of patriotic duty." Johnson had known Douglas since 1848 and had long admired both his frankness and his devotion to states' rights. He supported him for the presidential nomination in 1852 and 1856 and, like Stephens, argued that it was in the south's best interest to cement an alliance with Douglas in 1860. Also like Stephens, Johnson placed the blame for party disruption on the southern radicals who had rejected overtures on the credentials question and had withdrawn from the convention when their presence might have stopped Douglas' nomination. "Under these circumstances," Johnson wrote, "it is difficult to resist the Conviction that their fixed purpose was to break up the Democratic Party, regardless of consequences." [2]

The organizational network Douglas had created for his nomination now shifted its focus to the presidential campaign. The headquarters in the National Hotel in Washington were retained and placed in the charge of a resident executive committee, chaired by Louisiana Congressman Miles Taylor, which included several members of Congress. The party split, however, brought problems that Douglas had not anticipated. The state committees had to be persuaded that Douglas represented the regular Democratic organization; where they were committed to Breckinridge, new conventions had to be scheduled and new committees formed. Some states had selected their electoral tickets before the Charleston convention and had included both Douglas and Breckinridge men; if the tickets could not be pledged to Douglas, then new ones had to be chosen. The National Committee, in one of its early pronouncements, urged each state to secure an electoral ticket pledged to "the unequivocal support" of Douglas and Johnson. Taylor sent out a strongly worded warning against any compromise with Breckinridge supporters, emphasizing the incompatibility of popular sovereignty with the southern platform.

In spite of these efforts, Pennsylvania Democrats formed a combined electoral ticket with the understanding that the electors would vote for either Douglas or Breckinridge, depending upon which candidate had the better chance to defeat Lincoln. A "straight-out" Douglas ticket was later formed to compete with the combined slate, but it was obvious that its presence on the ballot would only confuse the voters. In New Jersey, the state committee also divided its electoral ticket between the two candidates. A delegation from the state waited on Douglas to explain the action, and Douglas tried unsuccessfully to dissuade them. He worried that similar efforts to present combined Democratic tickets might be made in other states. "Any Compromise with the Secessionists would be ruinous," he warned. "An amalgamation tickett with the bolters would disgust the people & give every Northern State to Lincoln." [3]

Douglas traveled to New York late in June to take soundings among political and financial leaders in the northeast. On the way he stopped in Philadelphia, where he responded to a serenade with a short statement. "I have no political speeches to make," he promised. "If my political opinions are not known to the people of the United States, it is not worth while for me to attempt to explain them now." A similar reception awaited him in New York. After a noisy parade up Broadway to his hotel, Douglas was again serenaded. Again he asserted his intention to play a passive role in the campaign. "It is the first time in my life," he said, "that I have been placed in a position where I had to look on and see a fight without taking a hand in it." The words had a strange ring coming from Douglas, and few people really believed that he would be content to remain on the sidelines for long.

Douglas stayed in New York until mid-July, receiving delegations and conferring with supporters from different parts of the country, while Adele reigned as "the social queen" of the Fifth Avenue Hotel. Richardson returned from a tour through New England and reported that prospects were brighter there than he had expected. To his friend Lanphier Douglas revealed his campaign strategy and speculated on the outcome of the election. "No time must be lost," he wrote, "and no effort spared. . . . We must make the war boldly against the *Northern abolitionists* and the Southern *Disunionists,* and give no quarter to either. We should treat the Bell & Everett men friendly and cultivate good relations with them, for they are Union men. . . . *We can have no partnership with the Bolters."* Breckinridge, he predicted, would not carry any states except South Carolina and perhaps Mississippi. Bell would carry Kentucky, Tennessee, North Carolina, Virginia, Maryland, and Delaware. "We shall probably carry Missouri, Arkansas, Louisiana, Texas, Alabama &

Georgia in the South, and hope to get enough more in the free States to be elected by the people." He urged Lanphier to organize the northwest; in Illinois "it is indispensable that our friends organize *every County* . . . thoroughly and open the canvass with vigor and energy." [4]

ii

Douglas was never so optimistic again. Convinced of the need for drastic action, he decided to enter the campaign personally, in a vigorous effort to carry the issues of the election directly to the people. To do so meant flouting a strong tradition, for it was not thought proper for a presidential candidate to electioneer. "But Mr. Douglas has no faith in standing still," observed one editor. The vindictiveness of his opponents compelled him to answer their charges, and the task of raising money would be eased if he appeared personally before the people. Although Douglas professed reluctance to abandon his passive role, he was convinced (partly at his wife's urgings) that the people must be apprised of the dangers faced by the nation. "The institutions and the happiness of this country," he believed, "are now in greater danger—in more absolute peril—than they have been at any other period in its history."

His campaign had a dual purpose, for he not only looked for votes, but also sought the endorsement of local Democratic organizations. The party had to be reshaped and its direction altered if it were to fulfill its broad national responsibilities; this could only be accomplished by denying the claims of the Breckinridge organization to legitimacy. Douglas was not fighting Lincoln so much as his enemies within his own party. He could wait for the presidency—he was only forty-seven years old —but he could not afford "to lose that place in the Democratic Party which was so long his," nor could he "consent to see the control of . . . the Democratic organization, placed in unfriendly hands." "He may not be elected," wrote one of his advisers, "but he will defeat the Vandals, and that will be glory enough for one man."

Douglas directed his first effort at New England. Aware that his decision to campaign would be severely criticized, he concealed the political purposes of his trip. He would visit his mother in upstate New York, attend the Harvard graduation of Adele's younger brother, James Madison Cutts, Jr., and return to the scenes of his childhood in Vermont to pay homage to his father's grave. Few people were fooled. As soon as his decision was announced, he was flooded with invitations to speak from local politicians, while hotel-keepers eagerly placed their facilities at his disposal. For a month following his departure from New York on July 14, he moved circuitously through the New England states, greeted by demonstrations, often speaking several times a day from railway platforms or hotel balconies and conferring with politicians in resort hotels. Notices of his itinerary preceded him, and posters announcing his schedule were circulated, but because his trip was supposed to be nonpolitical he always expressed surprise at the size of the crowds that greeted him. After haranguing his audiences on the merits of popular sovereignty, he customarily apologized for having been "betrayed" into making a political speech against his will.[5]

In Boston Douglas spoke from the balcony of the Revere House, the very spot, it was noted, where Daniel Webster had stood when he defended the Compromise of 1850. Douglas made the most of the analogy, to the disgust of many Republicans; to speak from the same balcony as Webster, he declared, "in defence of the same principle which Webster defended," was the "crowning act of his life." He toured the Lexington battlefield and spoke from the steps of the Bunker Hill monument. A high point of his visit was his participation in Harvard's commencement exercises, when he shared the platform with Governor Nathaniel P. Banks, Edward Everett, and Massachusetts' two Senators, Henry Wilson and Charles Sumner. Following the exercises Douglas was a guest at the alumni banquet, where he was introduced by Harvard's President Cornelius Felton as a man who had done much to found a University in Chicago. Douglas responded by wishing that he had been a son of Harvard, but he added that "if he was not her son, he might now at least claim to call himself 'a friend of the family.'" The banquet inspired one of the many vignettes of Douglas that appeared in the press during the tour. "He looks well enough," observed a reporter, "but not at all like a great man, intellectually, physically or morally. . . . He is a chunky man and looks like a prize fighter, though I am not sure as his arms are long enough for that. He has excellent prize fighting qualities. Pluck, quickness and strength; adroitness in shifting his positions, avoiding his adversary's blows, and hitting him in unexpected places in return."

Douglas' theme was always the same. Republicans and Breckinridge Democrats, all interventionists and representing sectional extremes, were locked in "an irrepressible conflict that can never be quelled until you decree that Congress shall not legislate in relation to private institutions anywhere." Everywhere he was reminded of popular sovereignty. It was not only the principle which Webster had defended, but it was also the principle for which "those immortal men" at Bunker Hill had fought and to which Massachusetts town meetings had been dedicated. "He has staked so much on the Squatter Sovereignty doctrine," one reporter complained, "that he seems to be falling into a monomania about it, and drags it about the country with him with as much assiduity as if it were a change of linen or a toothbrush." [6]

From Boston, Douglas traveled west to Albany, where a detachment of "Little Giants" marched in their drab and blue uniforms, and on July 21 he arrived in Saratoga. In spite of Sanders' warning that the proprietor was a Breckinridge man, Douglas and his wife stayed several days in a cottage on the grounds of the United States Hotel. Social life at the resort was in full swing, but the candidate spent most of his time "speaking, caucussing, and playing the agreeable" among those who partook of the springs' restorative waters. On July 25 he was again on the move, this time in the direction of his boyhood home in Vermont. The citizens of Brandon welcomed him in large numbers and responded with delight to his reminiscences. Speeches followed in Burlington, Montpelier, Concord (where he told his audience that he was enjoying a holiday and speaking a little "just for exercise"), Manchester, and Nashua. On August 2 he attended a mammoth clambake in his honor at Rocky Point, on Narragansett Bay near Providence, where he stood with a big cigar in his mouth, supported by a cane, shaking hands with people. The New England tour ended the next day, when he arrived in Newport. For twelve days he relaxed at the fashionable resort town, attending balls, going to formal dinners, and bathing in the surf. Adele won the admiration of all for her "vivacity and graceful courtesy." The American Association for the Advancement of Science was holding its annual meeting in Newport, and Douglas, in the company of the historian George Bancroft, visited some of its sessions.

Newport became a second headquarters while Douglas was there. Democratic politicos came and went, including national chairman Belmont, who chose this time to vacation in Newport. F. O. Prince, one of Douglas' Boston backers, A. D. Banks, and George Sanders were all on hand to discuss the problems of the campaign. [7]

There was little reason for Douglas to be disappointed with his reception in New England, but he realized that crowds at railway stations did not mean votes on election day. Some observers were puzzled why he should campaign so energetically in states that were certain to vote for Lincoln, but Douglas' contest was as much with the Breckinridge party as it was with the Republicans. "He cares nothing about his own personal success," wrote a reporter from Newport, "and comparatively little for the success of the Democratic party, as it stands at present. *But he intends to crush out utterly and forever the Disunion Party,* if it is in his power to do so." Everywhere Douglas counseled against union with the Breckinridge wing. When he was warned that a failure to unite would add to Lincoln's strength, he replied, "Then let it. It will give us the organization in 1864." To one Democrat who approached him in Boston, Douglas retorted, "If you voted against me [at Charleston] on principle, being for intervention, we cannot act together." [8]

Considerable criticism was aimed at Douglas by people who regarded a stump campaign by a presidential candidate to be humiliating and degrading. "It is not a seemly or a welcome sight to see any man whom a large portion of his countrymen have thought fit for the Presidency, traversing the country and soliciting his own election thereto." The high office of the presidency was reduced to the level of a county clerkship. Douglas' awkward attempts to disguise the purpose of his trip only invited ridicule. When he announced that he would visit his mother, a newspaper correspondent rushed to Clifton Springs to interview the lady. Douglas was expected on every train, she said, although she complained that "he never writes when we may expect him." Douglas' election to the presidency, she thought, would have one good result, for he would then stop endangering his health by making so many speeches.

Under the heading, "Stephen and His Anxious Mother," a Hartford editor wrote sarcastically of the "maternal pilgrimage." A broadside was widely circulated, advertising for information on the wayward son. Entitled " 'BOY' LOST," it reported, "Left Washington, D. C., some time in July, to go home to his mother, in New York. . . . He is about five feet nothing in height, and about the same in diameter the other way. He has a red face, short legs, and a large belly. Answers to the name of 'Little Giant.' Talks a great deal, and very loud; always about himself. He has an idea that he is a candidate for the Presidency. Had on, when he left, drab pants, a white vest, and blue coat with brass buttons; the tail is very near the ground." [9]

At Newport Douglas learned that his campaign was not going well. Belmont reported that efforts to raise money were meeting with little success. He encountered apathy and indifference; the opinion was gaining ground that nothing could prevent Lincoln's election and that it was useless to spend money in a hopeless cause. Many New York merchants feared the loss of their southern business if they contributed to Douglas' campaign. Men such as George Law and William H. Aspinwall, steamship operators who had backed Douglas in the past, now withheld their financial support. "If we could only demonstrate to all those lukewarm & selfish moneybags, that we have a strong probability to carry the State of New York," Belmont maintained, "we might get from them the necessary sinews of war." He urged Douglas to exert pressure on the New York Central Railroad interests for contributions, on the ground that a Republican victory in the state would damage their position. Miles Taylor seconded Belmont's plea. "The sinew of war, money, is absolutely wanting." An appeal for funds was sent out in Taylor's name, but two weeks later he reported that only Samuel Colt, the Connecticut arms manufacturer, had responded. The difficulties "on the subject of money" still remained. "We still go on, however, in the hope that something will turn up to help us." In mid-August Belmont's committee resolved to assess each congressional district in the nation $100 to help defray campaign expenses, but Douglas was informed that "there is little prospect, at present, of response." [10]

Lack of funds hampered an extensive pamphlet distribution, although it is inconceivable that many Americans did not know by this time where Douglas stood. In July, Taylor, with the help of Pugh and Rust, issued a document demonstrating that Douglas was the party's regular nominee and portraying the Little Giant as locked in combat with a conspiracy that was bent on destroying the Union. Believing the document to be needlessly aggressive, Belmont curtly informed Taylor that no money was available to support its publication and distribution. Complaints were received that German voters were being neglected because of a lack of German-language documents. Plans had been discussed early in the year for a German-language biography of Douglas, but they never materialized. A number of speeches were reprinted and sent out, but it was clear that this aspect of the campaign fell short of expectations.

More serious, according to some, was the absence of a strong Douglas paper in New York City. "The most influential papers here are against us, or what is worse, Janus-faced," wrote one New Yorker. For example, the support of the unpredictable New York *Herald* was worse than its opposition. Some efforts were underway "to supply the sad deficiency," but they were ineffective. In Illinois, Douglas lost crucial newspaper support in mid-campaign, when the Chicago *Times* was sold to Cyrus

McCormick and merged with its rival, the *Herald*. The sheriff was at the door, wrote Sheahan, and it was either sell or be sold. Although Douglas had put large sums of his own money into the paper in an effort to keep it alive, Sheahan blamed the Senator for his troubles. "To the party I owe nothing & feel less," he wrote. "Douglas has been cruel in his conduct towards me. . . . I owe him nothing in any way." There were hints that the *Times* might transfer its allegiance to Breckinridge.[11]

Sheahan's biography of Douglas, published on the eve of the Charleston convention, received wide publicity, and two other campaign lives appeared during the campaign. Henry M. Flint, associated with Sheahan on the *Times,* published an anonymous biography, and Ohioan Robert Bruce Warden brought out his life of Douglas later in the year. The publication of the Lincoln-Douglas debates as a Republican campaign document presented Douglas' important 1858 speeches to the voters at no expense to himself, but Douglas was not altogether happy with their appearance. He was convinced that Lincoln had been given an opportunity to revise, correct, and improve the texts of his speeches, while no similar opportunity had been granted to him. Douglas protested to the publisher and charged the publication with being partial, unfair, and "designed to do me injustice." The publisher denied that Lincoln had altered his speeches materially, but he conceded that more of Lincoln than Douglas had been put into the book because that was the way the Republicans wanted it. Douglas was given a chance to correct the plates, but he declined. Lincoln added his denial to that of the publisher; he had only made some minor verbal corrections, he wrote, not feeling justified in making any more substantial changes. The edition of the debates proved a best seller during the campaign, selling between 300 and 500 copies daily in mid-July.[12]

Douglas rarely referred publicly to his Republican opponent, but his New England tour convinced him that Lincoln's strength was formidable. He paid light-hearted tribute to Lincoln on a couple of occasions, telling one audience, "He is a very clever fellow—a kindhearted, goodnatured, amiable man. I have not the heart to say anything against Abe Lincoln; I have fought him so long that I have a respect for him." One thing was clear, he announced in Brandon, "you will have to go to Illinois for your next President." By midsummer, *The New York Times* was predicting Lincoln's election. "We think it not at all unlikely," the editor added, "that Mr. Douglas himself fully shares this opinion." There is some evidence that he did. While in Boston, Henry Wilson later recalled, Douglas expressed his belief that Lincoln would be elected. Massachusetts Republican Anson Burlingame later divulged a similar remark he said Douglas had made to him. According to Burlingame, Douglas said, in effect, "Burlingame, I am elected Senator for six years; I have got Joe Lane's head in a basket, and shall soon have Slidell's, Bright's and Fitch's. Won't it be a splendid sight, Burlingame, to see McDougal returned from California, Baker from Oregon, and Douglas and 'Old Abe,' all at Washington together—for the next President is to come from Illinois!" James McDougall and Edward D. Baker, both candidates for the Senate, had been active in Illinois politics before they moved to the Pacific coast. The conversation, reported in the press, damaged Douglas' southern support.[13]

Douglas' banter over the outcome of the election contrasted with the pessimism of his running mate. In July, Herschel Johnson confided his fears to his friend Stephens. "I have not much hope for the future," he wrote. "The sky is dark. The fires of sectionalism in the South are waxing hot and Black Republicanism in the North already exhibits the insolence of conscious strength. The South is in peril—the Union is in peril—all is in peril that is dear to freemen." He still regretted that Douglas' friends had not withdrawn his name at Baltimore. "I never saw such warm, devoted idolizing friends, as Douglas has," Johnson stated. "It is a pity that they have by their overwrought zeal put in jeopardy his fame & usefulness." Lincoln, Johnson was convinced, would be elected by the people. Like Douglas, Johnson saw other goals to be achieved than election to national office. He hoped that a fragment of the southern Democratic party, *"organized on the principle of non intervention,"* could be preserved as a nucleus "for reconstruction, at a future day." [14]

Miles Taylor was more optimistic. Much would depend, he wrote Douglas, on the state election in Maine in September. If Douglas Democrats won Maine, they would sweep the doubtful northern states in the early state elections, which in turn would concentrate southern Unionists on the Douglas ticket in November. There were a number of "ifs" involved, but Taylor was convinced that Douglas still had a strong chance to be elected "by a direct vote of the people of the United States in November." Strategy was planned at Newport. Belmont's committee agreed to concentrate on Maine and hoped to raise money by a special appeal to New England Democrats. Douglas interrupted his stay in Newport, left his wife behind, and made a rapid visit to Maine, speaking in Bangor, Augusta, and Portland.[15]

Douglas still believed that if he could not defeat the Republicans he could at least control the state Democratic organizations in most of the north. He had the energetic support of a group of state leaders and was able to rely on a large number of important journals with local circulation. The *States and Union,* although it did not fill the need for a nationally circulated paper, nevertheless served as a more-or-less official organ of Douglas' national headquarters. Attempts were made to counteract Douglas' strength by organizing the federal officeholders against him, and new appeals were made to President Buchanan for the removal of those suspected of sympathy with the Douglas party. Some were removed, notably the notorious George Sanders, who for some reason had been allowed to retain his post as Navy Agent until midsummer, but the effort hardly achieved the dimensions of a serious campaign movement.[16]

Desperate charges were dredged up against Douglas in an attempt to reduce his strength in some northern states, but they had little effect. One of the most persistent was the Republican attempt to link Douglas with the Catholic Church. From mid-July, when the Chicago *Tribune* charged Douglas with "unlimited submission to the spiritual and temporal authority of the wicked woman of Babylon," until October, editorials appeared under the query, "Is Douglas a Catholic?" The evidence, according to the Republicans, was overwhelming. Douglas' wife was a Catholic; his sons were attending a Catholic school in Georgetown; he was supported by the priests and laymen of the Church, as well as by the Catholic press; he had, according to rumor, been received by the Pope during his 1853 tour of Europe "as a lost sheep returning to the fold"; and he had rented a pew in a Washington Church. "Catholicism and Republicanism," noted the *Tribune* in its appeal to anti-Catholic sentiment, "are as plainly incompatible as oil and water. . . . The nation needs no Jesuits in the White House." Douglas was not a Catholic, but the denials of Democratic editors only tended to keep the issue alive.[17]

Under the headings, "Astounding Development" or "Startling Disclosures," Republican editors again charged Douglas with the authorship of the "Lecompton Swindle." John Calhoun was dead, but his widow was harassed for evidence that would tie Douglas with Kansas' proslavery party, and former members of the Lecompton convention were queried by a number of "investigators." The charge was taken up by the Breckinridge Democrats, who hoped to discredit Douglas' opposition to the Lecompton constitution and to transfer some of the odium attached to it from the Buchanan administration to Douglas.

Douglas did not respond to the charge until late in the campaign, when he alluded to the Lecompton crisis in a Milwaukee speech. "I never saw the Lecompton constitution until after it had been adopted in Kansas by the convention. . . . I never saw the schedule by which the slavery clause was submitted until after it was forwarded to the States for publication. I never heard, nor conceived, nor dreamed that any man on earth ever thought of such a scheme." His denials were bolstered when William Weer, former United States attorney in Kansas, published a letter Douglas had written him in November 1857, in which the latter took a strong stand against the action of the convention. Douglas, in his Milwaukee speech, also recalled his confrontation with Buchanan when he reminded the President that General Jackson was dead. "From that day to this," Douglas stated, "he and I have been trying the question, whether Gen. Jackson is dead. And one thing is certain—the people of Illinois decided in 1858, that James Buchanan was not General Jackson." [18]

### iii

With the New England tour at an end, Douglas next turned south. He had decided early to visit the border states, and a family matter provided an excuse. Mary Martin, the widowed mother of Douglas' first wife, died in June at her North Carolina home, and members of the family asked Douglas to assist them in the disposal of her property. The land, some 900 acres in Rockingham County, she bequeathed to her grandson, Douglas' elder son Robert. The residue of her estate was to be divided equally between Douglas' two sons; she had instructed that her slaves be divided between the two boys or that they be sold and the proceeds given to them in equal shares. [19]

There were compelling political reasons for his visit. Many slave state supporters appealed for aid in their struggle against the Breckinridge party. In Virginia, where the Douglasites steadfastly refused to compromise with the Breckinridge leaders, two party conventions were scheduled. Banks believed a visit to Virginia, where "our friends have become a little dispirited," was essential. Another Virginian added that "nothing would cheer us more in the fight with the Disunionists than a few words from yourself." From North Carolina came an invitation to address a

Douglas convention on August 30. "We greatly need your assistance," wrote his friend Robert Dick, "We are struggling against great odds." A strong conservative Union speech, with assurances that the rights of the south would be protected under his administration, would give Douglas the "Old North State" and would be "like the blast of a thousand bugles, throughout the South." [20]

A vigorous southern campaign, Douglas thought, would strengthen the cause of Union—a consideration that assumed greater importance as he witnessed Lincoln's growing popularity in the free states—and would challenge the power of the southern ultras. He was encouraged by the results of the state elections in Kentucky, North Carolina, and Missouri in the first week of August. In Kentucky, the Vice President's own state, the Breckinridge party was defeated by a Union ticket pledged to Bell. "How do you like the manner in which we cleaned out the vandals?" gloated a member of Kentucky's Bell-Everett committee to Douglas. In North Carolina, Democratic majorities were considerably reduced by a strenuous Bell campaign, "an awful damper to the B[reckinridge] & L[ane] party." Douglas was informed that Bell would probably carry North Carolina in November. Douglas candidates for state and national offices in Missouri were elected, and Republican Frank Blair won a seat in Congress from the St. Louis district; the Breckinridge ticket trailed the field. Union strength in the border south was impressive, and Breckinridge's supporters were dismayed. One Douglasite, writing from Georgia, eagerly observed that the elections "produced almost a revolution in parties at the South." Miles Taylor was elated by the results, confident that Douglas would win the presidency. But while the poor showing of the Breckinridge forces carried some encouragement into the Douglas camp, there was a more sobering aspect to the returns. The belief grew that no Democrat could carry the border states. As the Bell party demonstrated its power at the polls, it seemed likely that Douglas would trail the other three presidential candidates in November. Douglas was aware of this when he began his southern tour. His speeches assumed a new and different emphasis as he sought primarily to combat disunion in both party and nation.[21]

Douglas' relations with the Bell party were cordial. John J. Crittenden reflected the attitude of many Bell supporters when he spoke of Douglas in laudatory terms: "I can have no quarrel with him, he is a Union man. And a Union man I can always trust, when I believe him to be sincere and earnest, as I believe Douglas to be." Douglas, in correspondence with southern Bell leaders, had suggested early in the campaign that his followers cultivate friendly relations with Bell's supporters, a feeling that was reciprocated by Bell himself. There was talk of fusing the Bell and Douglas parties into a single Union ticket in the south, and similar proposals were made in some northern states. Bell men were advised not to nominate separate tickets in states where such action might injure Douglas, and Belmont even called on the Bell organization for financial help in fighting Breckinridge strength in New York.[22]

Douglas arrived in Norfolk, Virginia, on August 25 by steamer from Baltimore, with Adele at his side and appearing in fine health and good spirits. Soon afterward he addressed a large crowd from the courthouse steps. "I did not come here to purchase your votes," he declared. "I came here to compare notes, and to see if there is not some common principle, some line of policy around which all Union-loving men, North and South, may rally to preserve the glorious Union against Northern and Southern agitators. There is a larger feeling of self pride, of honest ambition, and of patriotism mingled with my efforts in the cause I have undertaken to carry out, than there is a desire or longing to be elected President of the United States. . . . I desire no man to vote for me, unless he hopes and desires to see the Union maintained and preserved intact."

Midway through his speech, he was afforded a dramatic opportunity to make his position clear. He was handed a slip of paper containing two questions propounded by a local Breckinridge elector. "If Abraham Lincoln be elected president of the United States," read the first question, "will the Southern States be justified in seceding from the Union?" Douglas replied, "To this I emphatically answer No." He acknowledged "the inherent and inalienable right to revolution whenever a grievance becomes too burdensome to be borne," but he insisted that the mere inauguration of a President whose opinions might be hostile to the Constitution, without an overt act, could never justify secession. "If they, the Southern States, secede from the Union upon the inauguration of Abraham Lincoln, before he commits an overt act against their constitutional rights," read the second question, "will you advise or vindicate resistance by force to their secession?" As the audience roared "No," Douglas again answered without hesitation. It is the duty of the President to enforce the laws, and he would do all in his power to aid the government in maintaining the supremacy of the laws against all resistance. "In other words, I think the President of the United States, whoever he may be, should treat all attempts to break up the Union, by resistance to its laws, as Old Hickory treated the Nullifiers in 1832." Douglas suggested that the same questions be asked of Breckinridge.[23]

Douglas' "Norfolk Doctrine" was immediately denounced in the south as counseling coercion against the states. Once again he was charged with treason, and southern radicals used his statements to bolster their arguments for secession. Some Douglas editors were embarrassed and minimized the importance of his answers. To the Washington *Constitution,* Douglas had completed his transition to the Republican party. He had, at Norfolk, issued some of the "boldest defiances and most pregnant warnings to the South that could be uttered." A new issue had been added to the campaign, the paper insisted: the power of the federal government to coerce a sovereign state. Breckinridge supporters in the north were confident that Douglas' answers could be turned to their advantage.[24]

Douglas did not relent in his attack against disunion. In Petersburg a few days later he struck hard again. "I did not come here to ask your vote, nor your suffrages for office," he explained. "I am not here on an electioneering tour. I am here to make a plea, an appeal for the invincibility of the Constitution and the perpetuation of the Union." The election of Lincoln, he stated, would be "a great public calamity," but if such a calamity should be inflicted on the nation, southerners must abide by the result. The constitutional election of a President could never be a pretext for secession. "There is no evil, and can be none, for which disunion is a legitimate remedy." In language reminiscent of earlier days, Douglas reminded his audience of the importance of the Union to the national mission. "The last hope of freedom in the old world is now centered in the success of the American Republic," he warned. "Tyrants have no hope of fastening their chains upon the necks of the people longer, unless they can sever this glorious Union." He called on all conservative men, lovers of the Union, and supporters of the Constitution to rally together against the disunionism of both northern abolitionists and southern secessionists.[25]

On August 30, standing next to a statue of George Washington outside the capitol in Raleigh, Douglas covered the same ground in an address to the delegates of the North Carolina state convention. "I love my children," he declared, "but I do not desire to see them survive this Union. I know of but one mode of preserving the Union. That is to fight against all disunionists. . . . The only mistake we Democrats made was in tolerating disunionist sentiments in our bosoms so long." Returning northward, he stopped for major addresses in Richmond and Baltimore, speaking in between at a number of towns in the Valley of Virginia. To his Richmond audience, he urged the importance of popular sovereignty, or self-government in the territories, as the only principle "upon which the peace and harmony of the country can be maintained and the perpetuity of the Union can be ensured." The Democratic party was the last hope for the Union, "the only historical party now remaining in the country, the only party that has its northern and southern support firmly enough established to preserve this Union," and he called on the people to repudiate the extremists who would destroy it.

In Baltimore, Douglas expressed his belief that the Union was being threatened by a southern secessionist conspiracy. "There is a mature plan throughout the Southern States to break up the Union." The election of Lincoln was the signal for action, and for that reason some southern leaders "desire the election of Lincoln so as to have an excuse for disunion." Not every Breckinridge man was a disunionist, Douglas maintained, but every disunionist was a Breckinridge man. "But for my apprehension on this subject," he explained, "I would not have taken the stump this year. I am not seeking the Presidency. I am too ambitious a man to desire to have my death-warrant signed now. . . . My object is to preserve this Union by pointing out what, in my opinion, is the only way in which it can be saved." [26]

Douglas completed his tour fatigued and hoarse. The pressure of the campaign was beginning to take its toll. When he arrived in Richmond, he "was roughly dressed—his enormous head being covered by an old slouch hat, and his general appearance more like that of a weary, wayworn, backwoods traveler, seeking repose from the toil and dust of the road, than like that of a distinguished statesman." Assessments of his campaign were mixed. Some, impressed by the large crowds that gathered to hear him, were convinced that significant inroads had been made into Breckinridge strength. Others doubted that very many people had been converted. Virginia's Governor John Letcher now endorsed Douglas' candidacy, but the electors chosen by the North Carolina Douglas convention were instructed to cast their ballots for either Bell or Breckrinridge if it became clear that Douglas could not command a majority of the electoral college. There was little doubt that Douglas' speeches had strengthened the Bell ticket in the border slave states. Many of his most enthusiastic auditors were Bell men, and one Breckinridge paper grumbled that Douglas' receptions in Virginia were in fact managed by the Bell organization.[27]

His boldness in carrying the campaign into the slave states won high praise in the northern press. That he should dare "to beard the lion of disunion in his own den" and to proclaim his principles in the very area where those principles had been "treated with contumely" was regarded with admiration and astonishment. Southern reactions were quite different. Following his Norfolk speech, Douglas was portrayed as Lincoln's ally; he should be stripped, "finally and hopelessly," of all southern sympathy. The south, warned a Mississippi paper, would "bristle with armed men" to repel the aggressions of Lincoln and Douglas, and Jefferson Davis reportedly advised his constituents to greet the invasion of Lincoln and Douglas with a gallows that took into account their difference in height. Southerners were urged to stand fast against Douglas' delusive and captivating remedy of territorial self-government. As Douglas concluded his tour, an Alabama newspaper hurled the final warning: "Douglas did well to turn his course Northward—there are some portions of the South where the utterance of such sentiments might have led to the hoisting of that coat tail of his that hangs so near the ground to the limb of a tree, preceded by a short neck with grapevine attachment." [28]

Douglas' visit to the border states was a turning point in his campaign. For the first time he confronted the question of secession, bringing it out into the open so that all could recognize it. Disunion was no longer simply an abstract threat; to Douglas, it had become a very real possibility. He was not yet ready to concede his own slim chances for victory, but from this time on the preservation of the union and the defeat of the southern radicals were of mounting concern to him.

The pace of his campaign hardly slackened as he moved northward. Pennsylvania, with its state election scheduled for early October, was a key state. In Harrisburg, like the good politician he was, he spoke on the tariff issue, skirting the question in such a way as to appear favorable to protection. Pointing out that the federal government was spending more than it was taking in, Douglas expressed his preference for increasing the nation's income by a tariff that was sufficient to defray its expenses. But while he did not depart from his traditional stand for a revenue tariff, he conceded that American industry deserved whatever protection a revenue tariff might afford. It was a way of standing on both sides of the issue. Republican papers had a field day as they charged Douglas with performing a "summersault" in order to bolster his failing cause. His journey through Pennsylvania was another triumphal procession, as he was greeted along the line of the Lebanon Valley Railroad by crowds of "expectant Democrats," with hearty cheers, booming cannon, and showers of bouquets from "patriotic ladies." His voice became increasingly hoarse and his speeches shorter. On September 10, he arrived in New York and checked into the Fifth Avenue Hotel for a few days of rest.[29]

On the following day, Herschel V. Johnson, summoned to campaign in the north, came to the city, and the two candidates conferred on strategy. The state elections in Vermont and Maine in early September were swept by the Republicans, to no one's real surprise, although the results in Maine shattered some of the hopes of the Douglas headquarters. There was more talk among Democrats of the need for desperate measures to stop Lincoln. Early in the summer suggestions were made for the withdrawal of Douglas and Breckinridge in favor of an acceptable compromise candidate. Jefferson Davis, no doubt acting with administration backing, proposed that all three opposition candidates, Bell, Breckinridge, and Douglas, withdraw, hoping that a compromise candidate such as New York's Horatio Seymour might be put forth in their places. Bell and Breckinridge reportedly agreed, but Douglas would not budge. Douglas was not convinced that his withdrawal at this point could stop Lincoln; he pointed out that his followers, if released from his support, would undoubtedly back Lincoln in preference to any candidate who would be acceptable to the Breckinridge party. It was, he said, an impracticable plan.[30]

Efforts to form fusion tickets took on new life in some states, particularly Pennsylvania and New York. In New York a combined Bell-Douglas ticket was formed, and Douglas leaders agreed that the state's electoral vote would be swung to Bell if that were necessary to prevent an election in the House. Douglas encouraged fusion with Bell, but he remained adamant against union with the Breckinridge ticket. In a speech in Reading, Pennsylvania, he warned against treating with Breckinridge. "I have fought twenty-seven pitched battles, since I entered public life, and never yet traded with nominations or surrendered to treachery." Early in September, New York's Douglas committee began to waver in the face of financial hardship and Lincoln's growing strength. Negotiations were opened with the Breckinridge forces, but disagreements over the shape of a combined slate and mutual distrust prevented any immediate progress. Dean Richmond, whose power over the party machinery in the state was virtually absolute, was willing to fuse with "the honest Breckites," but there was some question of identifying them. At an immense mass meeting and barbecue at Jones' Wood, outside New York City, Douglas lashed out against any effort to unite with the party of disunionists and traitors to law and the Constitution. He protested that under no circumstances would he endorse "a compact so devoid of rectitude." His comments left no doubt that his attitude was meant to apply to New York as well as to other parts of the country. "He is opposed to fusion all the way from Maine to California," commented *The New York Times*.[31]

Douglas' reaction to Davis' proposal and his opposition to fusion with Breckinridge stemmed from his belief that only he, of all the candidates, could beat Lincoln. Additionally, fusion with the Breckinridge party would in effect recognize the legitimacy of the Vice President's nomination and would seriously cloud Douglas' campaign for leadership of the Democratic party. "Should your friends unite with your common enemies—a mere faction—you will be defeated and will deserve it," wrote one New Yorker. Douglas still hoped that he might win the election, to the surprise of his running mate. Johnson talked at length with Douglas "about the condition of the country" and revealed his pessimism. Douglas was, Johnson wrote, "as usual frank and outspoken. He thought if he was not elected by the people, Lincoln would not be —nor Breckenridge and that neither of them could be, by the House of Representatives, if the election should be thrown before that body." Johnson disagreed. "I told him, he underestimated the power of Mr. Buchanan's army of office holders, in the Northern States; that although they could not carry a single one for Breckenridge, they would bring him enough votes to give them all to Lincoln, that he [Douglas] would not carry a single Southern State & that I regarded Lincoln's election as certain. I shall never forget the expression of deep sadness, at this announcement. He was silent & thoughtful, for a moment, but rallying said, 'If you be correct in your views, then God help our poor country.'"

Douglas was stung by Johnson's prediction that no southern state would go for him. He could not understand, he said, why the south was so hostile to him. Southerners had voted for him at the Cincinnati convention. Since that time he had not altered his views on "non-intervention." He had always been a friend to the south; indeed, he had, during his canvass with Lincoln, "endured threats, detraction & abuse, for his advocacy of the constitutional rights of the South." When Johnson explained that the "extreme men of the South" believed that popular sovereignty was as bad as abolition, Douglas replied, "Oh! little do they know of my heart. I am no advocate of slavery; but viewing it as a matter belonging to the people and protected by the Constitution, I would never consent for Congress to touch it in any way for any purpose. If I should be elected, I will give repose to the country—no abolitionist should participate in my administration—I should bring around me a new set of men & put the government on the old constitutional track." It was a pathetic hope, revealing both his attachment to his country and his unawareness of the depths to which sectional feelings had plunged by 1860.[32]

## iv

Douglas did not tarry in New York City; he soon left for the west, to continue speech-making in his own section. He was accompanied by his wife and by James B. Sheridan, the secretary and shorthand-expert who had served him so well in the 1858 campaign. On September 15, he arrived in Clifton Springs, near Canandaigua, and all the nation rejoiced that he had at last found his mother. "Third street is in a perfect whirl of excitement," reported a Philadelphia paper, "the bulletin boards around the several newspaper offices are crowded with anxious and interested readers. All the little sucker democracy are jubilant upon the receipt of the intelligence that 'Douglas has found his mother.' " He was greeted by a mass meeting in the small village, and he responded with a speech. A member of the audience asked, "Have the people of a Territory the right, according to the doctrine of non-intervention, to abolish or exclude slavery from a Territory while in a territorial condition?" Douglas was amazed that his views should be unknown to anyone. "I hold the people of a Territory," he replied, "and during a territorial condition, may introduce, exclude, abolish or regulate slavery just as they please." One southern friend feared the answer would further injure his cause in the south, but supposed that "he could not refrain from speaking out any longer, under the pressure." Large crowds continued to gather along the line of his route. He made major speeches in Syracuse, Rochester, and Buffalo before leaving the Empire State.[33]

It was almost a year since Douglas was last in the northwest. His followers had been working hard during the summer, but they regarded his presence as essential to their efforts. Indiana, like Pennsylvania, would go to the polls in October, and extra exertions were needed there. Criss-crossing Ohio and Indiana, Douglas spoke in Cleveland, Columbus, and Cincinnati before arriving in Indianapolis on September 28. The next day he re-entered the border south when he crossed the Ohio River to address an audience in Louisville. Herschel Johnson, who was with him in Indianapolis, was deeply impressed with the enthusiasm northwester-ners displayed for the Little Giant. "No living man has so deep a place in the hearts of the N. W. Dem as Douglas," he wrote, "The ground swell in the N West is tremendous." For a time, Johnson's pessimism waned. If Douglas could carry Ohio and Indiana, he predicted, he would gain considerable southern strength and might even carry Georgia.

As they expressed their loyalty to Douglas, people also marveled at his stamina and worried about his health. "The only wonder," wrote one editor, "is that his health does not give way under the trials and fatigue he is compelled to endure in order to meet the demands upon his strength." By the time he arrived in Cleveland, his voice was reduced to a "spas-modic bark," and only those nearest the platform could catch his words. He regularly kept a plate of lemons close at hand and frequently during his speeches he would "convulsively clutch" a lemon and squeeze the juice down his throat. "The Presidency," commented one observer, "is no compensation for the physical wear and tear he is suffering." There were reports that he was drinking heavily, and that at one Ohio stop he was so drunk he had to be helped from the train. Although Adele bristled at the charges and indignantly denied them, there was evidence of one con-vivial encounter with Seward, when the latter's eastbound train pulled into the station in Toledo while a reception for Douglas was in progress. Whiskey bottle in hand, Douglas noisily invaded the train, awakened the New York Senator, and urged him to share his reception. Seward tactfully declined.[34]

Still he went on, entering Chicago on October 4, where he was es-corted by a large torchlight procession to the Tremont House. The next day he addressed a multitude on the edge of the city, "over five acres of densely packed democrats," in a raw northeast wind. Seward had spoken in Chicago a few days before, and Douglas took the opportunity to an-swer him, charging the New Yorker with doctrines of racial equality. But once again the Union was uppermost in Douglas' mind. He linked Seward's "irrepressible conflict" with Lincoln's "house divided" and de-clared that "their propositions mean revolution—undisguised revolution," for they could not carry out their principles and preserve the Union at the same time. Both the Lincoln and the Breckinridge parties, "like the blades of a pair of shears . . . turn on a common pivot—that of intervention by Congress—and cut in opposition directions." With either, the Union was in peril. "I am no alarmist," he stated, but "I believe that this country is in more danger now than at any other moment since I have known anything of public life." The nation could not be maintained until northern abolitionism and southern disunion were buried in a common grave. The occasion was topped off with a spectacular fireworks display, and a number of buildings in downtown Chicago were illuminated especially for the event.[35]

Douglas rested in Chicago for a day, then he was off again, this time with speaking engagements in Iowa, Wisconsin, and Michigan. He emphasized his faith in western growth and development and spoke of his support of western measures in words his audiences wanted to hear. The rich and beautiful prairies over which he traveled, he told an audience in Iowa City, belied the once-popular view that much of the west was desert. He denounced the "ignorance which has prevailed throughout our country in respect to the resources and character of the Great West." He lauded the frontiersman's capacity for self-government, relating it to popular sovereignty, and recalled his own role in the creation of western territories and the admission of western states. To farmers for whom federal land policy was a vital issue, Douglas underscored his support of free homestead legislation. "If I had my way," he told a Dubuque audience, "there would never be another public land sale on the American Continent." He inveighed against the land speculator and branded any policy that allowed speculation as "vicious and defective." Land policy should be confined to the pre-emption system and the homestead bill, and none but actual settlers should be allowed to occupy the public land. "My policy always has been to make every inhabitant of the new states and territories a land-holder, as far as it was possible to do so, by our legislation."

On the subject of the Union and of the west's particular mission in its preservation, Douglas spoke with moving conviction. "We, in the Northwest, cannot permit this Union to be dissolved. We are emigrants from the East and from the South, from the free states and from the slave states. We have entered the wilderness together, and here upon the prairies have made our homes—marriages have taken place and children have been born—and our children have grand parents in the

Carolinas as well as in New York. . . . We are bound to the South as well as to the East, by the ties of commerce, of business, and of interest. We must follow, with our produce in all time to come, the course of the Mississippi River into the broad ocean. Hence, we cannot permit this Union to be dissolved." [36]

Douglas' admonition assumed a new urgency almost immediately. On October 9, voters in the three important states of Pennsylvania, Ohio, and Indiana went to the polls to elect state officers and members of Congress. Democrats were not confident of Ohio, but they regarded Pennsylvania and Indiana, carried by Buchanan in 1856, as essential to victory in 1860. Douglas received first word of the results while traveling in Iowa when Forney sent him a telegram with the grim announcement that the Republicans had swept Pennsylvania. Soon afterward he learned of a similar Republican sweep in Indiana. Ohio too went Republican, but that was expected. A crumb of comfort was derived from the defeat of several Republican Congressmen in Ohio and Pennsylvania, but the Republican gains in the statewide elections more than offset these losses. The results pushed fusionists to action, especially in New York, in a desperate effort to halt Lincoln. The prospect that the election might hinge on New York finally aroused New York City's merchants, and money was offered in support of a fusion ticket. Dean Richmond's Douglas committee relented, and a new slate of electors was drawn up, including men from the Douglas, Bell, and Breckinridge parties. In Pennsylvania, the Douglas committee bowed to pressure and withdrew its ticket, to the discomfiture of Forney, who defied the action and continued to support the Douglas electors. A fusion slate was also presented in New Jersey, over the protests of the Douglas committee.

Few people had any confidence that this last-minute activity would alter the course of the election. To Douglas, the results of the Pennsylvania and Indiana elections shattered his remaining hope for victory. Nothing now stood in the way of Lincoln's election by the people. With the certainty of Republican victory in November, Douglas feared, the Union was in more danger than ever. For weeks there had been talk of secession in the columns of southern newspapers, and with the state elections, earlier threats in South Carolina, Alabama, and Mississippi took on a new and ominous credence. Republicans scoffed at the possibility of secession and dismissed the threats as unworthy of serious consideration. Douglas, more familiar with southern attitudes and the character of the south's leadership, knew better. To his secretary Sheridan, he said, "Mr.

Lincoln is the next President. We must try to save the Union. I will go South." [37]

Douglas in fact had been planning another southern tour for some time. Urgent invitations from Georgia and Alabama had been pouring in. "Men would listen *to you*, & be 'converted,' that could not be induced to read a speech or hear an argument in your defence," wrote Seibels in August, and a month later Seibels' paper, the Montgomery *Confederation*, announced that Douglas would soon visit Alabama. Alexander H. Stephens wrote that a visit to Georgia "would change the opinions of thousands of our people who have been kept in the dark as to your views." "We are making a desperate fight against great odds," Stephens continued, "without any hope of carrying the state but with the view of maintaining sound principles and a sound national organization." On the day before the October elections, the *State Register* suggested that "in compliance with urgent solicitations" Douglas would extend his trip to the south, "perhaps as far as Mobile." He honored his remaining speaking engagements in the northwest, including stops in Milwaukee, Detroit, Kalamazoo, and a giant rally in Springfield (where he addressed over 5000 cheering Democrats), and on October 19, in St. Louis, he began his second southern campaign. He reiterated his concern for the Union—"How long can this agitation go on and the Union be saved?" he asked—and emphasized the role of "this great valley" in its preservation. For the benefit of St. Louisans, he spoke of his support of a Pacific railroad and pointed out that it was one of the casualties of the incessant "negro question." To one critic, Douglas' effort was "only a warming over of his *standing* speech on squatter Sovereignty, with some slight additional ingredients, to suit the local market." [38]

Douglas' decision to carry the cause of the Union into the heart of the south aroused bitter hostility in the southern Breckinridge party. A Memphis paper exploded with invective: "The bloated visage of Stephen A. Douglas is now turned toward the South. He commences his tramp to-day, and like an itinerant peddler of Yankee notions, will soon be hawking his pinchbeck principles over the South. He comes in our midst with no worthier motives than the incendiary." Lincoln would not be allowed to preach his "damnable" doctrines in the south, commented another paper, why should Douglas? Threats against Douglas were published, and Robert Toombs, in an inflammatory speech, warned that Douglas would not be permitted to repeat his Norfolk sentiments on Georgia soil. Some of Douglas' southern friends feared that he would be "grossly insulted" on his tour; others simply became defiant and challenged the radicals to make the attempt if they dared.[39]

Douglas was unruffled. His fears for the Union were borne out by the strident tone adopted by the southern press following the October elections. The returns were a "prophetic warning of the great disaster" that hung over the south; Lincoln's election was regarded as certain. Yancey's Montgomery organ reminded southerners that in November they would have to choose between "submission to the rule of a party whose avowed purpose is the abolition, not the restriction, of slavery, and a glorious career of uninterrupted prosperity as a separate nationality." "The Southern masses, almost to a man, regard the simple election of Lincoln as an 'overt act,'" observed an Atlanta editor, "and it is the solemn determination of the eight cotton states to secede immediately on his election." Secession became a matter of immediate decision as more and more southern editors joined the cry against submission to a Republican President. Whether Douglas really believed that he could reverse this sentiment is questionable, but he had enough faith in the good sense of the southern people to justify the effort. His tour would be an appeal to the people over the heads of their leaders.[40]

With Adele, her brother, James Madison Cutts, Jr., and Sheridan, Douglas traveled to Centralia, Illinois, where he and his party boarded a southbound Illinois Central train. In Tennessee he was met by Linton Stephens, brother of Alexander, who not only chaired the meeting in Memphis at which Douglas spoke, but accompanied the candidate to Atlanta. From Memphis, they journeyed to Huntsville, the center of Bell-Douglas strength in northern Alabama and the site of one of the state's few pro-Douglas newspapers. There Douglas addressed several thousand people from the Tennessee Valley counties. Speeches followed in Nashville, where some tension resulted when Douglas' path inadvertently crossed that of Yancey, in Chattanooga, and in Kingston, Georgia. In Kingston, he denied that the Constitution conferred on any state the right to secede and declared that if a state should secede the Chief Executive was obligated to resist it.

On October 29, Douglas arrived in Atlanta, and the next day he spoke to a large demonstration of Douglas and Bell supporters. He was introduced by Alexander H. Stephens. In his introductory remarks, Stephens recalled his sixteen-year friendship with Douglas. He asked Georgians to give the candidate "a careful, calm, and patient hearing. He comes to address not your passions, but your intellects." Douglas' principles, Stephens added, were the only ones upon which the Union could be preserved. Douglas responded with his insistence that disunion was no solution to the grievances felt by the south, and he denounced the radicals who would sacrifice the Union to achieve their ends. He repeated his answers to the Norfolk questions (by this time a standard element in his speeches) in spite of the warnings he had received, and he made much of Breckinridge's apparent unwillingness to face the same questions. The friendly editor of an Augusta newspaper was present to record his admiration for Douglas' boldness in carrying his appeal into the south. The man "who had faced the Abolition mobs in Chicago" was equally courageous before the threats of hostile crowds of the south. "He is certainly the greatest intellect of the western world," the editor commented.[41]

Stephens traveled with Douglas to the remaining Georgia appointments in Macon and Columbus. They were cheered along the way by supporters of the Bell ticket. In Macon, Douglas delivered "a plain, forceful speech—thoroughly national in spirit," and the local editor was relieved that "everything passed off pleasantly." Five days before election day, Douglas invaded central Alabama, and on November 2 he spoke from the steps of the state capitol in Montgomery. He was now in the heart of enemy territory, where disunion sentiment ran high. Just a week before, Toombs had delivered a fiery speech in Montgomery, in which "no form of appeal or invective was omitted which was calculated to urge on the masses to secession, and, if necessary, civil war." Threats against Douglas had been made. One ultra Montgomery paper wondered if he would have the audacity to speak in the city. While being escorted to his hotel following his arrival, several "addled" eggs were hurled at him, one of them striking his hat and splattering Adele, but otherwise he was received with courtesy. What enthusiasm he generated seems to have come primarily from the partisans of John Bell.

Douglas' speech in Montgomery followed the established pattern, although he gave greater emphasis to the machinations of the fire-eaters and singled out the Alabama delegation to the Charleston convention for special criticism. He hit hard against the threat of secession. "I believe there is a conspiracy on foot to break up this Union. It is the duty of every good citizen to frustrate the scheme." No one, he declared, was more anxious to see Lincoln defeated than he was. But, he insisted, "if Lincoln is elected, he must be inaugurated." The Constitution provided the means for punishing a President "if he attempts to violate any man's rights," but it also provided for the punishment of traitors. "I hold that the election of any man on earth by the American people, according to the Constitution, is no justification for breaking up this government." Douglas concluded with a call for Union men to "rally around the principle of non-intervention, and we will crush out Northern abolitionism and Southern disunion." His words were strong, and he had obviously been angered by some of the threats and charges made against him. He apologized for the harshness of his language, but he felt bound, he said, to repel the slanders that had been cast against him by his southern opponents. Following the speech, a planter in the audience was heard to remark, "Well, if Lincoln is elected, *perhaps* we can stand it for four years."

Yancey was among those who listened to Douglas, and that evening (Douglas spoke at mid-day) he delivered an answering speech. Douglas, however, did not stay to listen. He and Adele boarded a night boat for the trip down the Alabama River to Selma, where he was scheduled to speak the next day. A number of people gathered on the dock and crowded the steamer to hear his parting words. As he spoke, the deck gave way under the weight of the people, and he and Adele were thrown to the deck below. Both were badly bruised. Adele decided to remain in Montgomery to recuperate, while Douglas, hobbling on a crutch, continued on without her. (Five months later, long after Alabama's secession, Douglas received a bill for the crutch, with a reminder that he had forgotten to pay for it at the time.)[42]

On November 5, the day before the election, Douglas arrived in Mobile. On the advice of his friend Forsyth, he had boarded the steamer *Duke* in Selma for the last leg of his journey. The captain, Forsyth informed him, "is an ardent Douglas man besides being an *Irishman.* His countrymen are almost unanimously with us here." There was rivalry among steamboat operators to carry Douglas, and presumably some political capital could be gained by selecting the right one. On his arrival in Mobile, Douglas was formally greeted by former Governor John A. Winston, speaking from a pile of cotton bales, and that night he gave the last speech of his presidential campaign. The local Bell paper described it as "a triumphant vindication of his consistency since 1850."

As at Norfolk, Douglas was asked two questions by a Breckinridge supporter. First, if the election should be thrown into the House of Representatives and if it should be apparent that Douglas could not be elected, to whom would he throw his support, Lincoln or Breckinridge?

Second, if Lincoln were elected would Douglas accept a seat in his cabinet? Douglas was indignant. "There is no language with which I can express my scorn and contempt for this wretch who would intimate that in any contingency I would take office under Lincoln." He would in no event "accept office under Mr. Lincoln or Mr. Breckinridge or any other sectional candidate who advocates the doctrine of Congressional intervention." He was equally emphatic in his reply to the first question. Douglas had earlier insisted that an election in the House was to be avoided at all costs, for the crisis faced by the Union was so serious that the new President would require a stronger base of support than the House could provide. He had been reported in the press as telling a friend, "By God, sir, the election shall never go into the House—before it shall go into the House, I will throw it over to Lincoln." It was with this statement in mind that Douglas' interrogator in Mobile asked his question. Douglas answered, "No event or contingency could possibly happen in which I would advise any friend of mine to vote for Abraham Lincoln or could any event or contingency possibly happen in which I would advise any friend of mine to vote for John C. Breckinridge." Douglas had often declared that he would not be a candidate if the election were taken to the House, and he said so again in Mobile. He would not accept the presidency unless he were chosen by the people. He now added, "I scorn to accept the Presidency as a minority candidate." But Douglas had long known that the question would not arise.[43]

Election day, November 6, was a rare day of rest for Douglas; "he seemed to be less excited by the election and to think less of it than perhaps any other man in the city." His brother-in-law wired from Selma that "Addie" was well and cheerful and would join Douglas the next day. Arrangements were being made for their passage to New Orleans later in the week. He now had the time to read the mail that had somehow reached his hands in recent days. From August Belmont had come a frantic last-minute inquiry: "What is the feeling and danger at the South?" George Sanders reported impressive gains in New York. If the campaign would only last three more weeks, he wrote, Douglas would carry the state by 50,000 votes. From Huntsville, D. C. Humphreys sent congratulations on Douglas' Atlanta speech. "We may be defeated in your election to the Presidency, but whether you are chosen or not, the agitating question can be settled on no other principle than the one you propose."

Later that evening, Douglas joined Forsyth in the editorial office of the *Register* to receive the election returns. It was not long before both men knew that Lincoln had been elected President. Forsyth, in anticipation of the result, had already prepared an editorial endorsing the call for a state convention to deliberate on Alabama's course, and he asked Douglas to read it. Douglas immediately expressed his disapproval, but Forsyth argued that the only way to manage the secession current was to appear to go along with it and, by electing Unionists, to control the convention's action. Douglas warned of the risks involved and cautioned the editor that if they could not prevent the meeting of the convention they could not hope to control it once it was held, but Forsyth had made up his mind, the editorial would go into the paper. The impact of Lincoln's election was suddenly clear, and Douglas felt powerless to combat it. He returned to his hotel, according to Sheridan, "more hopeless than I had ever before seen him." [44]

v

Douglas regarded the election returns with mixed feelings. Lincoln was clearly elected with a substantial majority in the electoral college in spite of his minority popular vote. There were no doubts about the result, so Douglas' fears that the election might hinge on the House of Representatives were cast aside. Douglas was disappointed with his own poor showing in the electoral returns, but encouraged by the size of his popular vote.[45] He carried only the state of Missouri, and that by a very narrow plurality, and three electoral votes from New Jersey's fusion slate—twelve in all. He received 1,365,976 popular votes, slightly over 29 per cent of the total and over a half million votes more than Breckinridge. It appeared that his campaign for the leadership of the Democratic party had been successful and that the reconstruction of the party would be carried out under his tutelage. The distribution of his popular vote, however, gave him pause, for about 88 per cent of it was from the free states. Douglas had captured the Democratic party in the north, but it was clear from the returns that he was still unacceptable in the south. His popular vote in the slave states was just under 13 per cent of the total, the bulk of it in the border states. His drive to unite north and south under the national banner of the Democratic party and popular sovereignty had fallen disappointingly short.

There were some bright spots in the southern returns. Bell, with 515,973 slave state votes, was only 55,000 votes behind Breckinridge, and the combined Bell-Douglas vote, the Union vote, exceeded that of Breckinridge by 100,000 votes. Bell emerged as the chief beneficiary of Douglas' Union campaign in the slave states, and his ticket undoubtedly attracted the support of some of Douglas' own following. In the cotton states, where disunion sentiment was strongest, Breckinridge headed the field. In only two of them, Georgia and Louisiana, did the Bell-Douglas vote constitute a majority. If the Bell-Douglas vote were an indication, Union sentiment was strong throughout the south, a source for gratification to Douglas, but even this could not completely overcome his disappointment with the very poor showing his own candidacy made. Douglas was also aware, as his conversation with Forsyth had demonstrated, that the Union feeling evinced in the election might be quickly eroded by the pressures that followed Lincoln's victory.

Douglas derived his greatest satisfaction from the returns in his own northwest, where his challenge to Lincoln was most effective and his triumph over Breckinridge achieved avalanche proportions. He carried over 43 per cent of the vote in the northwestern states, compared to about 2 per cent for Breckinridge. The attempts of the Bright-Fitch forces in Indiana and of Isaac Cook's party in Illinois to weaken his ticket hardly made a dent in the final results. In Illinois, Cook was able to muster only a paltry 2400 votes for Breckinridge. In New England, where he had campaigned so vigorously, Douglas was disappointingly far behind Lincoln, receiving about 25 per cent of the popular vote, although his margin over Breckinridge was wide and impressive. It was evident that northern Democrats looked to Douglas and that his effort to consolidate his position within the party had not been in vain.

The movements to fuse the opposition to Lincoln, especially in the pivotal Middle Atlantic states, came too late to have any effect and only served to confuse the voters. In New York, the last-minute fusion of the Douglas, Breckinridge, and Bell tickets received 46 per cent of the state's popular vote, but Douglas' strong opposition to the effort undoubtedly pushed some of his supporters into the Lincoln column. If fusion had denied New York's electoral vote to Lincoln, the election would have been thrown into the House of Representatives, a prospect which Douglas dreaded. In Pennsylvania, a straight Douglas ticket remained in the field in addition to the Douglas-Breckinridge fusion agreed upon following the state election, presenting Douglas Democrats with an almost impossible choice. Douglas support disintegrated as some either did not vote or voted for Lincoln; the straight Douglas slate received less than 17,000 votes, while the 178, 871 votes cast in the state for the fusion ticket were credited to Breckinridge.[46] Because of the disarray created by the fusion efforts (in some states the opposition tickets were fused on the local level), the stringency of the Union issue in parts of the south, and the tendency of some Douglas Democrats to vote for Lincoln in the north and Bell in the south, the 1860 election returns hardly demonstrated the true strength of the parties.

Douglas was beaten. No matter what solace might be derived from the results, that fact remained. Defeat was imposed upon severe physical strain and fatigue. For three and a half months, from mid-July, when he left New York to campaign in New England, until early November, when he arrived in Mobile, Douglas had been on the move. There had been little respite as he visited twenty-three states in the northeast, the border south, the northwest, and the deep south. It was a killing pace. With only a few exceptions, each day was devoted to speech-making, and on some days he made several speeches within the space of a few hours. By the end of the campaign, his voice was shattered and his health was not much better. Some of his friends found bright spots in the election and sought to console him. "You have done your duty to your country and to our common country," wrote Humphreys, "and you have the proud consolation of feeling and knowing that your reputation is held dear by an *immense* multitude of your countrymen, and that your name is a tower of strength, and that you are really the choice of the people for President." Herschel Johnson had long expected defeat and was not surprised by the returns, but he added: "I think you made a magnificent race and though defeated, you have nothing for which to reproach yourself. You have fallen in a noble struggle for principle— but to rise again I trust, in the majesty of the same great principle." But, he wrote dejectedly, "I think the Union is gone." Richardson, returned to Congress by Illinois voters, informed his chief, "We are beaten but not conquered." Some northern newspapers, following the example of Lanphier's *Illinois State Register,* raised "the standard for Stephen A. Douglas in 1864." [47]

With Adele again at his side, Douglas left Mobile the day following the election, and on November 8 he arrived in New Orleans, where he was met by a large group of supporters led by Pierre Soulé. He appeared to be "totally indifferent so far as regards his defeat." He spoke from the steps of the St. Charles Hotel, to which he had been escorted. The street was jammed with people, the balconies and windows of adjacent buildings were crowded, and for a time Douglas seemed to be his old self again. "His eyes flashed, his brow knit, his lips became compressed" as he expressed his indignation at those who would pull down the Union. He saw better times coming, provided the people remained firm against the forces of disunion. It was raining when he arrived in New Orleans. The storm reminded him of the trial through which the nation was passing. "This is no time to despair or despond," he declared. "The bright sun will soon chase away these clouds and the patriots of the land, . . . will rally as one man, and throttle the enemies of our country." "Let us lay aside all partisan feeling," he urged, "and let us become patriots and lovers of our country. Let us unite to put down sectionalism and Abolitionism, and every other element of political and national discord. Let no grievances, no embittered feelings impair the force of our efforts." He thanked his audience for extending the same enthusiastic reception to him in defeat as they had two years before in victory.

Several days later he responded to the request of the city's monetary and commercial leaders for a statement "on the present condition of the affairs of our country." In a widely published letter, Douglas again expressed the hope that the passions and animosities of the campaign would give way to reason and patriotism. No man regretted Lincoln's election more than he, and no one was more prepared to resist, "by all the legitimate means," the policies which Lincoln and his party represented. But, he emphasized, the mere election of any man to the presidency, in accordance with the Constitution and the laws, did not provide a just cause for dissolving the Union. Lincoln, he told the south, was more to be pitied than feared. The Democrats had captured the House of Representatives and continued to control the Senate; the Supreme Court was safe from Republican influence. Lincoln "will be utterly powerless for evil, if he should have the disposition to do wrong." Even in his distribution of the patronage, he would be bound by a Democratic Senate. "What good or harm can he do to anybody?" Douglas asked. Does the election of a man who would be "thus tied hand and foot, powerless for good or evil . . . furnish sufficient cause for destroying the best government of which the history of the world gives an example?" Four years, he reminded southerners, would soon pass. In the meantime, he was confident that Lincoln would refrain from any act that would destroy the constitutional rights of citizens or that would invade the rights of states on the subject of slavery. Returning again to the danger which now beset the country, Douglas appealed for unity and patriotism. "I can perceive no just cause, no reasonable ground for such rash and precipitate action as would plunge into the horrors of revolution, anarchy and bankruptcy, the happiest people, the most prosperous country and the best government the sun of Heaven ever shed his genial rays upon." [48]

Douglas determined to make no further statements until he resumed his seat in the Senate early in December. He traveled slowly up the Mississippi, stopping to inspect his children's plantation along the way. The pressures of the campaign had been lifted, and the relief was evident in his appearance. Rumors that he had fallen ill after he left New Orleans were quashed by those who greeted him on his journey northward. His health appeared good. He had put on some weight, although he was still limping from the steamboat accident in Alabama. Douglas' mind was busy. Congress would soon meet, and it would be faced with more momentous questions than it had ever encountered before. Following the election, in Mobile, Douglas had talked with Forsyth about the future and had suggested a course which Congress might take to save the country. "I am exceedingly anxious to know what it is," wrote Herschel Johnson. Johnson was not the only one. Men in both the north and south now looked to Douglas for leadership. Virginia conservative Thomas H. Gilmer expressed the thought that was in many minds when he advised Douglas, "Your position now is more responsible than ever." [49]

# XXX

## "Compromise on the basis of mutual concession, or disunion and war"
### 1860—1861

i

Less than a month remained before Congress would convene, but in that short time the direction of events became clear. As Douglas left the south, the sparks of secession burst into flame in the cotton states. On the day after the election the Palmetto flag was raised over the offices of the Charleston *Mercury,* and soon afterward the South Carolina legislature summoned a secession convention. The conflagration spread rapidly to other states. While Douglas appealed to Union sentiment in New Orleans, his old enemy John Slidell was writing President Buchanan, "I see no probability of preserving the Union, nor indeed do I consider it desirable to do so if we could."

The conversion of Union sentiment to the support of secession was as rapid as it was unexpected. Politicians and editors who had urged Douglas' election not long before now joined the cry. John Forsyth, whose drift toward secession Douglas had painfully observed on election night, believed that submission to the Lincoln administration would be unconditional surrender. "It seems to me we must part," he wrote Douglas, although he had no illusions that it could be done peaceably. He had never believed that "a giant nation could die without a giant struggle." It was preferable to fight a long and bloody war, however, than to remain in the Union and "be stripped of 25 hundred millions of slave property & to have turned loose among us 4,000,000 of freed blacks."

"With your defeat," Forsyth commented, "the cause of the Union was lost."

Montgomery editor John J. Seibels, whose support of Douglas had been unwavering, had denounced secession as treason during the campaign; he now wrote of withdrawing from "an obnoxious and oppressive government" in order to establish a slaveholding confederacy. In Georgia, James Gardner, editor of the Augusta *Constitutionalist* and friend of Douglas', argued that Lincoln's election was intolerable for the south. "The hopelessness of preserving the Union," he observed, "has made disunionists, since the election, of thousands of Conservative and Union men." Another Douglas paper, the Memphis *Appeal,* found "an irrepressible conflict existing between the two sections, which it is impossible ever to reconcile." Douglas was still in New Orleans when the *Bee,* a paper which had strongly supported his election, called for a convention to consider Louisiana's secession from the Union. At the same time, the rival *Daily Crescent,* a Bell paper, chided Douglas for his belief that the south had little to fear from the Lincoln administration. Of Douglas' letter to the New Orleans citizens, the editor declared that "we never read anything from the pen of Senator Douglas which gave us so little satisfaction." The rush into the secessionist camp puzzled northern Democrats. "How can our friends in the cotton States," Belmont asked Forsyth, "reconcile their actions of to-day with their professions only a few months back?" [1]

Douglas arrived in Washington on December 1 and was immediately serenaded at his house by a large group of well-wishers. Again he urged all "Constitution-loving men" to unite for the preservation of the Union, and he expressed confidence that there was still a party strong enough in the south to save the country. Stephens had just spoken against secession before the Georgia legislature, and Douglas paid him high tribute. When he returned to the Senate, Douglas told his friends, he would do so "without prejudice or ill feelings towards any one except the foes of his country."

Douglas was aware of the political strength which almost a million and a half popular votes had given him. His popular support, though confined largely to the north, was impressive, and he was determined to use it to control the Democratic party. Some old foes within the party would not be returned to the Senate, so that the gains made in the congressional elections promised a substantial basis for party leadership in the next Congress. But that was a year away. Now everything depended upon the defeat of secession and the preservation of the Union by the short second session, the lame-duck Congress that would convene on December 3. Douglas had urged southern Senators and Congressmen to resume their seats, in spite of their views on secession, in order to check Republican strength, and he hoped that they would be willing "to sink their bickerings" at least until after the nation was saved. In fact, after caucuses and conferences, all but two Senators returned to Washington; only Hammond and Chesnut of South Carolina stayed away. Douglas' campaign for the Union during the presidential contest provided a foundation for the role he was prepared to play in Congress. "The whole country is looking to you," wrote a North Carolinian in late November.[2]

The mood in Congress would not make the task of conciliation easier. The Democratic party was a shambles, its members confused and demoralized, and there was small prospect that it could muster enough unity and strength to cope with the crisis. Nor was there any sign that Douglas' influence with party leaders in Congress would be any greater than before. Some southern and administration Democrats, in fact, again threatened to exclude Douglas from membership in the Democratic caucus.

"The absorbing, almost exclusive question of discussion here is 'secession' and 'disunion,'" wrote McClernand on the first day of the session. "A fanaticism, an infatuation has seized the minds of many, I believe most of the Senators and Representatives from the South. They are *fatally* bent on disunion." Slave state Senators and Congressmen met to discuss ways of promoting separation. Pressure was exerted on southern conservatives to accept "such measures as are desired by the revolutionists." Before the session was a week old, three deep south Senators—Brown, Iverson, and Wigfall—informed the Senate of the south's unshakable determination to secede. For them the crisis had moved beyond the point of conciliation. "We intend to go out of this Union . . . peaceably if we can, forcibly if we must," Iverson declared. A few days later, thirty southern members of Congress issued a statement to their constituents announcing that "the argument is exhausted" and that "all hope of relief in the Union . . . is extinguished." The goal of each slaveholding state, they advised, ought to be "speedy and absolute separation from an unnatural and hostile Union." One of the signers added that he would rather fall in battle against the south's enemies than submit to Black Republican rule and be murdered by the slaves. Another argued that "further remonstrance is dishonorable, hesitation is dangerous, delay is submission," and advised that "we ought to keep ourselves clean of all compromises."

Even moderate southerners, among them North Carolina's Thomas L. Clingman, who had sided with Douglas during the election campaign, spoke ominously of the south's future course. Clingman charged that Lincoln would make war upon the south until the section's social system were destroyed. While he spoke of the need for new guarantees, it was clear that he regarded their enactment as remote. Secession, he insisted, held no terrors for him.[3]

The Republicans, meanwhile, were as uncompromising as the southern ultras. They "are quiet, say nothing, promise nothing, threaten nothing," wrote an Alabama Congressman. The President-elect warned against any move that would compromise the party's stand. "Have none of it. The tug has to come & better now than later." Lyman Trumbull echoed Lincoln's sentiments. It would be wrong for Republicans to join in the effort to find "new compromises." Like others in his party, he minimized the seriousness of the crisis. "Republicans have only to stand firm acting firmly, but in a kind spirit & all will yet be well," he wrote the day after the southern address was issued. "Concession on our part or yielding anything of our principles would be fatal." [4]

Little help could be expected from the administration. Buchanan's message was read to the assembled lawmakers on December 4. The President disagreed with the southern extremists that Lincoln's election justified disunion, although he recognized the validity of their grievances, and he appealed to the south to remain in the Union. Secession, he argued, was unconstitutional; the framers of the government had not been "guilty of the absurdity of providing for its own dissolution." But while he branded secession as "neither more nor less than revolution," Buchanan also denied the power of Congress or of the President to "coerce a State into submission." There was no right of secession, but there was also no power to prevent it. It was a hopeless and helpless statement, and it satisfied neither the Unionists nor the secessionists, although it seemed to offer no obstacles to the latter. Buchanan proposed that the crisis be resolved by a constitutional amendment that would recognize the right of property in slaves in the states where it existed, protect slavery in the territories, and tighten the enforcement of the Fugitive Slave Act. Inasmuch as his proposal merely echoed the southern demands, Buchanan was hardly making a practical effort at conciliation.

"Seldom have we known so strong an argument come to so lame and impotent a conclusion," observed one Douglas paper.[5]

Immediately following the message, the House of Representatives appointed a special committee, one member from each of the thirty-three states, to consider the "present perilous condition of the country." This first step toward meeting the crisis, however, did not attract much confidence. Many of the slave state Congressmen declined to vote, on the ground that their states were already too far along the road of secession to be influenced by any compromise; the vote against the committee was solidly Republican. A Georgia Congressman denounced the stupidity of any effort to "patch up a peace between us," and another southerner predicted that the committee would be "thwarted at every step by systematic efforts on the part of the Ultra Secessionists." The move suffered a further loss of confidence when Speaker Pennington announced his choice of members. Not a single Douglas Democrat was appointed, an omission which McClernand termed a "parliamentary atrocity."

On December 6, Kentucky Senator Lazarus Powell moved the appointment of a similar committee in the Senate, to be modeled after the Committee of Thirteen, chaired by Henry Clay, which had reported the Compromise of 1850. Lacking the alacrity of the House, the Senate did not approve Powell's motion until December 18. Two days later, Vice President Breckinridge announced its membership. Douglas was one of three northern Democrats to be appointed, the others being Bigler and Rice. The five Republicans were Seward, Collamer, Wade, Grimes, and Doolittle, the latter three from the northwestern states of Ohio, Iowa, and Wisconsin, respectively. From the border states were Kentucky's two Senators, Powell and Crittenden, and Hunter of Virginia. Jefferson Davis and Robert Toombs represented the cotton states. Eight of the thirteen members were from states watered by the Mississippi and its tributaries.[6]

Douglas played a small part in the debate during the first weeks, but he was busy behind the scenes. On the day after his arrival in Washington, he conferred with Crittenden "on the policy to be pursued to save the Union." Crittenden, a true successor to Henry Clay, was expected to assume an important role in the search for a compromise, so Douglas quickly joined with him. The two men emerged as the leaders of the compromise forces, and the association between Douglas Democrats and border state Unionists, begun during the campaign, continued.

Douglas repeated his plea that party considerations be set aside until after "the questions upon which the fate of the country now hangs" could be resolved. He was ready to act with any party or individual devoted to the preservation of the Union, "in a spirit free from all committals of the past," as if he "had never given a vote or made a speech that would embarrass" him in his future actions. "I am ready," he wrote to Belmont, "to make any reasonable sacrifice of party tenets to save the country." In the Senate, Douglas had hard words for the southern fireeaters. He challenged the legitimacy of their grievances and became involved in an angry exchange with Iverson, Mason, and Wigfall. Ninetenths of the southern complaints against the enforcement of the fugitive slave law, he maintained, were false. While he argued that all personal liberty laws were unconstitutional and should be repealed, he believed that the fugitive slave law was enforced with as much fidelity as most laws. "If the grievance is that we have not passed laws to protect slavery in the Territories," he shouted, "why does not some one of you bring in a bill to protect slavery in the Territories?" Southern grievances were mere pretexts for disunion and had no substance that could not be met in a legal and constitutional manner.[7]

He expressed an equally hard line against secession, in terms that were reminiscent of Jackson. Only two alternatives faced the nation, "conciliation and concession, or civil war." National law must be enforced, including the collection of revenues in all ports, whether the states declare themselves out of the Union or not. "All govt is Coercion, and I go in for asserting this principle at every hazard," Douglas told a friend. "Better a million of men should fall on the battle field than that this govt should lose one single State!" He insisted that he could never "recognize or acquiesce in the Doctrine that any State can secede & separate from us without our consent." Coercion was not ruled out, but it was a last resort. He recognized the possibility of "civil war with our breathren in nearly one half of the States of the Union," but he informed Lanphier, "I will not consider the question of force & war until all efforts at peaceful adjustment have been made & have failed."[8]

That Douglas was identified with a policy of coercion was evident from the anxiety expressed by some of his southern supporters. His "Norfolk Doctrine" was still fresh in their memories. The northwest, they believed, was the seat of coercion sentiment, and Douglas was its spokesman. Rumors that he would make a strong coercion speech and that he intended to introduce a force bill aroused concern. If the reports were true, Herschel Johnson wrote, Douglas would drive every cotton state out of the Union. He begged Douglas "not to take ground for force" because of the cruel blow it would deliver to those southerners who had recently stood by him. A Marylander warned that such a speech would do irreparable harm in the border states. Still, Missouri secessionist Thomas C. Reynolds reported that after a four-hour interview with Douglas, in company with Arkansas Congressman Rust, he had strong hope that the government would acquiesce in South Carolina's secession. Douglas, however, simply hoped that a collision could be averted until all possibilities for compromise had been thoroughly explored. From his own state, Sheahan and Cyrus McCormick argued that if the south must go, "let them go in peace."

Disunion became reality on December 20, the day the membership of the Senate Committee of Thirteen was announced, when a South Carolina convention unanimously approved an ordinance of secession. The task of the committee became at once more complicated and more difficult as the question of government policy suddenly assumed a practical significance. An anonymous South Carolinian defiantly sent Douglas a copy of the Charleston *Mercury* which exultantly hailed the dissolution of the Union. Penciled in the margin was the comment: "Carolina has the spirit to determine and the courage to execute." The secession of three other states appeared imminent. Having failed to prevent the Union from breaking, the Unionists now faced the more arduous assignment of finding a way to mend it.[9]

ii

John J. Crittenden waited until the Committee of Thirteen was approved before he introduced his compromise plan. To a quiet, attentive chamber, he made an eloquent plea for the preservation of the Union. "This is a mighty empire. Its existence spreads its influence throughout the civilized world. Its overthrow will be the greatest shock that civilization and free government have received." The most notable feature of his proposal was the restoration of the Missouri Compromise line and its application to all territory "now held, or hereafter acquired." Slavery would be recognized and protected south of the line and prohibited north. States would be admitted (from both sides of the line) with or without slavery as their constitutions might provide. Further, Congress would be prohibited from abolishing slavery on government property in the slave states, from abolishing slavery in the District of Columbia as long as it existed in Maryland and Virginia, and from interfering with the domestic slave trade. Finally, slaveowners prevented from recovering their fugitive slaves by northern resistance would be compensated for their losses. No amendment to the Constitution could ever be made that would allow the government to alter the status of slavery in the states where it existed.

Crittenden's propositions, presented in the form of constitutional amendments, sparked brief optimism that the crisis might be settled. Douglas, in close touch with the Kentucky Senator, abandoned his plan to speak against secession lest it reduce the chances for conciliation. The southern fear that he would take strong ground in favor of coercion did not materialize. Among Republicans compromise sentiment seemed to gain ground, reflecting in part the concerns of the eastern business community over the effects of disunion. Political leaders such as New York's Thurlow Weed, newspaper editors, and a handful of Republican Senators were reported favorable to compromise. Seward privately assured a Virginia Unionist that he would support Crittenden's proposal.[10]

Although he preferred a plan of his own on which he had been working since the beginning of the session, Douglas gave the Crittenden compromise zealous support, even though it violated his cherished principle of popular sovereignty. August Belmont was certain that Douglas' self-denial and the sacrifice of popular sovereignty in the interest of saving the Union would increase his standing before the people. In the first meeting of the Senate committee to which the Crittenden compromise had been referred, Douglas spoke fervently of the necessity for constitutional amendments that would take the slavery question out of Congress. Again he emphasized his determination to act without commitment to any past policy, vote, or speech in his effort to save the nation. Not all committee members were as flexible. Seward was not in Washington, and in his place Wade expressed Republican opposition to compromise. Toombs, highly skeptical that any good could come out of the committee, attended with misgivings.

Crittenden's proposals were taken up on December 22. In a preliminary move, the committee members agreed that no proposition could succeed unless it was supported by majorities of both the Republicans and the other Senators, an example of Calhoun's concurrent majority. Davis insisted that the nation would be deceived if measures passed without Republican backing. Crittenden, Douglas, and Bigler argued warmly in favor of the compromise, but the Republicans (with Seward still absent) maintained that, since the election had decided the slavery issue, they had no concessions to make. Toombs and Davis were willing to accept the compromise, but they insisted that the proposals must first be accepted by the Republicans. They would not vote for it unless the Republicans did likewise. One by one the provisions of the compromise went down to defeat before the combined opposition of the deep south and Republican members.[11]

Douglas now came forth with his compromise plan. He submitted it to the Senate on December 24, and on the same day it was placed before the committee. Reflecting his conviction that all power over slavery should be taken from Congress, Douglas not only emphasized the territorial question, he also tried to include other possible points of friction between the north and south. The result was an unwieldy mixture of issues, embodied in two lengthy and diffuse constitutional amendments. Much of it was simply lifted from Crittenden's compromise.

Douglas' solution of the territorial question was complex, designed to provide security to the south while at the same time affirming popular sovereignty. Congress would be forbidden to legislate respecting slavery in any territory, and the status of slavery in each territory, "as the same now exists by law," would remain unchanged until the territory's population reached 50,000 white inhabitants. At that point the territory would pass into an intermediate stage, between territory and state; then the people would form a territorial constitution and would exercise all rights of self-government consistent with the Constitution of the United States. In this way Douglas recognized popular sovereignty, but by defining this stage precisely in terms of population, he sought to meet southern objections that power over slavery in a territory could be exercised by the first handful of settlers. As soon as the population was equal to that required for a member of Congress, the territory (or "new State," as Douglas confusingly termed it) would be admitted as a state with or without slavery, as its constitution specified. This, Douglas hoped, would take admission to statehood out of politics and provide for the automatic admission he had long advocated. Further, no additional territory could be acquired by the United States except by treaty or by a concurrent two-thirds majority in each house of Congress (Calhoun again), thus giving each section a check against territorial expansion. In all new territory, the status of slavery would conform to its status at the time of acquisition and could not be altered until the intermediate stage had been reached.

The second of Douglas' proposed amendments, except for its first two sections, merely repeated elements of the Crittenden compromise. The first two sections, dealing with the status of free Negroes in the United States, reflected Douglas' racial bias. First, the power of states and territories to legislate with respect to Negroes would be limited, a negation of his states' rights and popular sovereignty positions. The elective franchise and the right to hold office should never be exercised "by persons of the African race, in whole or in part." Second, free Negroes would be colonized at the discretion of the states and at federal expense in districts of Africa or South America acquired for this purpose. It is difficult to see what Douglas hoped to achieve by these propositions. They were not regarded favorably by southerners. One of Douglas' southern friends termed the colonization scheme "very objectionable" and protested the invasion of states' rights implied in the restriction of the political rights of free Negroes. "It would not be very safe for the South," he wrote, "to have the government clothed with such power." A prominent Republican organ took a similar view, arguing that it was an unwarranted interference in the rights of states, although this Republican editor had no objection if it were presented as a law rather than as a constitutional amendment.[12]

The principal advantages of his compromise, Douglas wrote Lanphier, were that it took the slavery question out of Congress forever, secured the rights of self-government in the territories, covered all the points in dispute between the sections, and gave "assurance of permanent peace." Most importantly, "by confirming the existing *Status* in the Territories it affirms Popular Soverignty by confirming what the people have already done." He sent copies of his amendments to a number of friends in north and south, but their reactions were mixed. "The South cannot ask for more," replied Belmont. He was sure the Republicans would recognize its merit, for it "would not add a foot of slave territory to the Union, except where climate and soil render it more profitable than free labor" (a curious reading of the Republican stand). Douglas was particularly interested in Stephens' reaction. The Georgian, however, was not encouraging. The south, he felt, would never agree to it. "Nothing can be made of any such scheme of adjustment." [13]

The committee brought Douglas' compromise to a vote four days after he introduced it, and they made short work of it. The territorial sections were supported by only two members, Crittenden and Douglas, while the remaining sections were defeated by solid Republican votes. The south, Douglas believed, would have approved his proposition if the Republicans had agreed to it.

The Republicans countered with a proposal of their own. Acting, he thought, with Lincoln's approval, Seward submitted several resolutions prescribing the limit beyond which his party would not go. Not one of them dealt with the territorial question. The Constitution would never be amended to authorize congressional interference with slavery in the states; the Fugitive Slave Act would be altered to allow the fugitive a jury trial (amended by Douglas to require the trial in the state from which the fugitive had fled); the states would be requested to repeal their personal liberty laws; and laws would be passed to punish individuals or "conspiracies" engaged in the invasion of one state from another (an echo of John Brown's raid). Douglas, consistent with his determination to support any feasible plan, voted for Seward's proposals, but the package was not successful. He refrained from voting on resolutions introduced by Toombs and Davis expressing the ultra southern position, on the grounds that they were merely abstract propositions and not designed to settle the controversy. The hopelessness of the committee's task became all too apparent. On December 28, after only a week's deliberation, its members gave up; they reported to the Senate that they had been unable "to agree upon any general plan of adjustment." [14]

On Christmas Day, Douglas wrote, "The prospects are gloomy, but I do not yet despair of the Union." Two days before, Toombs had addressed a telegram to the people of Georgia, declaring the work of the committee to be a failure. "The committee is controlled by Black Republicans, your enemies, who only seek to amuse you with delusive hope," he stated, "all further looking to the North for security for your constitutional rights in the Union ought to be instantly abandoned." In response, a group of Georgians headed by the mayor of Atlanta wired Crittenden and Douglas: "Is there any hope for Southern Rights in the Union? . . . You are looked to in this emergency. Give us your views." Douglas and Crittenden replied immediately: "We have hopes that the rights of the South and of every State and Section may be protected within the Union. Don't give up the Ship. Don't despair of the Republic." On the same day, Douglas dolefully observed that the two extremes, northern and southern, were "precipitating the country into revolution and civil war." Again he declared that he could never recognize or countenance the doctrine of secession, but he promised that he would not "consider the question of war until every effort has been made for peace, and all hope shall have vanished." The point had been reached where "a compromise on the basis of mutual concession, or disunion and war, are inevitable." [15]

The failure of the Committee of Thirteen added gloom to the holiday season. In the week before Christmas, conventions were elected in Florida, Mississippi, and Alabama, and the secession of those states seemed just a matter of time. On December 26, Major Robert Anderson, commanding a small force at Fort Moultrie near Charleston, moved his men to Fort Sumter. A furor followed that involved the President and his cabinet, southern Senators, and South Carolina commissioners in Washington. Buchanan refused to bow to the southern demands that Anderson be ordered back to Moultrie. "Christmas is over, and a sad one it has been," lamented one Washington observer. "A thick gloom pervades everybody's mind, and just now, no ray of hope cheers the heart of any one. Hope has flown and black despair has taken its place." A newspaper correspondent noted that "the reigning air is that of mourning." [16]

iii

Undaunted by the committee's failure, Crittenden and Douglas continued to press for conciliation. "From what dropped from Douglas at his bowl of Toddy on New Years day," wrote old Francis Preston Blair, "I suppose they are in *cahoot*." Douglas, Blair added, was "big with some great conceit" which he would soon bring forth. The "great conceit" was Douglas' long-awaited speech on the crisis. Anticipated for days, the moment arrived on January 3. On that day, the Senate not only received the report of the Committee of Thirteen but also considered Crittenden's compromise once again. Refusing to accept the committee action as final, the Kentucky Senator resubmitted his proposals with the addition of Douglas' two propositions concerning the political status and colonization of free Negroes. Because of the difficulty in securing the majorities in Congress required for constitutional amendments, Crittenden proposed that his resolutions be submitted to a national referendum. The compromise leaders were grasping at straws. "Private assurances" had been received that Seward would support the Crittenden compromise if it was brought before the Senate. A group of New York businessmen traveled to Washington to urge Republicans to make concessions, and Wall Street suddenly exhibited a "buoyant feeling."

Douglas' hopes rose. The Senate galleries were crowded "to suffocation," and for once he appeared in good health and spirits. Adele brought a group of friends early in the day to be sure of places, provided a cold luncheon "which was duly unfolded and devoured at noon," and waited five hours for Douglas to speak. His speech took two and a half hours and, according to one reporter, was "Websterian in its power, logic and eloquence." [17]

Douglas placed responsibility for the crisis at the feet of both the Republicans and the southern radicals, the latter for "rushing madly into revolution and disunion, as a refuge from apprehended dangers which may not exist," and the former for attempting to manufacture "partisan capital out of a question involving the peace and safety of the country." Whether southern fears were real or imaginary mattered little; they were believed, and the Republicans had done much to encourage them. He charged Republicans with advocating the exercise of federal power against slavery in the south, in spite of all their denials, and questioned whether this mode of ridding the nation of the evils of slavery could be justified in the name of civilization, humanity, and Christianity. Quoting passages from Lincoln's House Divided speech, he emphasized the "dangerous and revolutionary opinions" of the President-elect. Little wonder, he thought, that southerners were apprehensive.

At the same time, Douglas repeated his belief that the south had little to fear from Lincoln. Secession was madness, but, he pointed out, it was also wrong, unlawful, unconstitutional, and criminal. South Carolina had no right to withdraw from the Union. Moreover, the government unquestionably had the right "to use all the power and force necessary to regain possession" of South Carolina. "No man will go further than I to maintain the just authority of the Government, to preserve the Union, to put down rebellion, to suppress insurrection, and to enforce the laws." He shared none of the misgivings that had been expressed about coercion. "There can be no Government without coercion," he said. "Coercion is the vital principle upon which all Government rests." But, he asked, are we prepared for war? War means "disunion—final, irrevocable, eternal separation." He pleaded with the Republicans to join in supporting the only alternative to "civil war with all its horrors and miseries." Partisan politics should be submerged in the interest of saving the nation. "Better that all party platforms be scattered to the winds; better that all political organizations be broken up; better that every public man and politician in America be consigned to political martyrdom, than that the Union be destroyed and the country plunged into civil war."

Douglas reviewed the proposals he had placed before the Committee of Thirteen, but he did not push for their acceptance, knowing they had little chance for success. Instead he urged the adoption of the Crittenden compromise, especially the revival of the Missouri Compromise line, as a solution to the territorial question. Brushing aside the question of whether his support of Crittenden's proposal was consistent with his earlier record, Douglas commented, "The country has no very great interest in my consistency." The preservation of the Union was of infinitely more importance. He revealed that Davis and Toombs had been willing to support the Crittenden compromise and blamed the Republicans for the failure of the Committee of Thirteen. "Why cannot you Republicans accede to the reestablishment and extension of the Missouri compromise line?" he asked. "You have sung paens enough in its praise, and uttered imprecations and curses enough on my head for its repeal, one would think, to justify you now in claiming a triumph by its reestablishment." [18]

Neither the Republicans nor the southerners were happy with Douglas' views, although southern reactions were softer than those of their northern counterparts. Thomas Bragg, Senator from North Carolina, noted the aloofness of southern leaders following Douglas' speech. Although he opposed Douglas and disagreed with much that he said, Bragg lauded his conciliatory tone and found hope in his insistence that all possible efforts at compromise be tried. Striding over to Douglas, Bragg thanked the Illinois Senator. "It was the best speech for the South that he could have made," Bragg believed. "It is better to have such a man as Douglass with us, and for one I will forget the past and look to the future." Southerners, however, tended to distort Douglas' total argument as they emphasized only those portions of the speech which they wanted to hear. Little was said of his position on secession, but his "repudiation of force" as a means of preserving the Union was praised. Georgia secessionist Martin Crawford thought the speech would "do great good," and another Georgian interpreted it as sanctioning peaceable separation at least until the "abolition party" could be destroyed and the Union reconstructed.

Republicans responded angrily at the charges Douglas hurled at them and accused him of trying to justify southern treason. They made much of his lack of consistency in urging the restoration of the Missouri Compromise line, and they charged that by preferring conciliation to coercion he was making a virtue out of cowardice. Douglas' suggestion that they subordinate their party platform to the preservation of the Union was indignantly rejected. The speech, wrote Illinois Congressman Elihu Washburne to Lincoln, "was utterly infamous and damnable, the crowning atrocity of his life."

From New England, Douglas received reassuring words from an old adversary. "I rejoice at every manifestation of a spirit of conciliation & compromise," wrote Robert Winthrop, with whom Douglas had tilted over a decade before. "As I look back to the year 1848, under the light of later experiences & of existing dangers, I wish most heartily that your motion to run the Missouri Compromise to the Pacific, *pure & simple,* could have been carried." [19]

The efforts of the compromisers now became a desperate race against time. Events moved swiftly; each succeeding day brought new cause for despair. On January 2, Georgia's secession convention was chosen, and on the next day the governor ordered the state seizure of Fort Pulaski, near Savannah. On the fourth, Alabama occupied government installations in Mobile harbor. On January 5, the merchant vessel *Star of the West* sailed from New York with reinforcements and supplies for Major Anderson's command at Fort Sumter; four days later, on the ninth, the ship was fired on by shore batteries in Charleston harbor and driven off before it could accomplish its mission. Two days earlier, a secession convention was elected in Louisiana, and on January 8 Texas voters chose delegates to their convention. On the day that the *Star of the West* was fired on, Mississippi seceded from the Union. Florida followed on the tenth; the next day Alabama adopted its secession ordinance. A week had passed since Douglas made his appeal for the Union before the Senate. During that week three more states had seceded, secession was under consideration in three others, and the first shots had been fired against federal authority. It was apparent, commented the *Constitution,* that compromise between north and south was hopeless.

In the meantime, President Buchanan's attitude toward secession stiffened. Howell Cobb resigned from the cabinet early in December, and Secretary of War John Floyd departed in the wake of scandalous disclosures. On January 8, Mississippi's Jacob Thompson left his cabinet post. The changes strengthened the Union character of the executive branch. When Buchanan nominated a Pennsylvanian to the vacant post of collector for the port of Charleston, a sign that he would ignore secession and continue to enforce federal law in South Carolina, southerners bitterly denounced him. When his decision to reinforce the troops in Charleston harbor became known, the protests became even more vehement. "The South is sold out by him," wrote one southerner. "He has gone over body and breeches to the enemy."

Buchanan sent a special message on the crisis to Congress on January 8, but it was not read until the next day. Even in this time of emergency, the nation's lawmakers paid their homage to Andrew Jackson by adjourning on the anniversary of the Battle of New Orleans. The President emphasized again that neither he nor Congress had a constitutional power to make war against a state. However, he promised that the public revenues would be collected and the public property protected, insisting that the right to use military force against individuals who resisted federal authority was clear and undeniable. He appealed for prompt action to preserve the Union by compromise, and endorsed Crittenden's proposals. Buchanan had been guided in drafting his message by Jeremiah Black, and strong suggestions had been made that he sanction the conciliatory efforts of Crittenden and Douglas.[20]

On January 7, Crittenden spoke at length in defense of his compromise. Toombs followed with a fire-eating speech that the *New-York Tribune* dismissed as a "ferocious fulmination." Later in the week, the last week of a full Senate, Davis, Hunter, and Seward took the floor on three successive days. Speaking the day after Mississippi left the Union, Davis made an emotional appeal for peaceful separation, in the slender hope that a reconstruction of the Union might be achieved at a later date. But if separation be resisted by the north, he warned, the result would be "a war . . . the like of which men have not seen." With a note of sadness in his voice, he urged each of his colleagues to "act the patriot's part" so that the "angel of peace may spread her wings, though it be over divided States." The following day, Hunter, speaking for the upper south, produced an elaborate and complicated plan that called for a drastic alteration of the federal system and the adoption of such devices as Calhoun's concurrent majority and dual presidency. While he believed that his scheme would adjust the differences between the "two social systems," Hunter indicated in answer to a question that he would vote for Crittenden's compromise.[21]

Seward's speech had long been anticipated, for up to this time Republicans had said little except to express their strong opposition to compromise generally. Not only was it assumed that Seward spoke for the President-elect, but it was also believed that the New York Senator leaned favorably toward conciliation. He was reported to be in consultation with Crittenden and Douglas, and, a few days before, rumors that he and Thurlow Weed were hatching a compromise scheme had created consternation in Republican ranks. A group of New York businessmen, including Hamilton Fish, Erastus Corning, and William H. Aspinwall, had approached Douglas with a compromise suggestion that apparently had the sanction of Seward and Weed. Among its provisions was the stipulation that all of the territory south of 36°30′ (the Missouri Compromise line) would be admitted as a state with or without slavery as the people might decide. Douglas rejected the proposal because under its terms the territorial question would be "settled within six months, by excluding Slavery from every inch of our territory, and that will only add fuel to the present fire in the South." While he would be pleased with this result, the south would not. It could never be accepted by southerners and hence was no compromise at all.

Whether his reaction to the New Yorkers' plan was responsible for its modification or not, the proposal presented by Seward in his Senate speech reflected Douglas' argument. Seward did not endorse the Crittenden compromise, as some had thought he might. Instead, he merely reiterated the proposal he had placed before the Committee of Thirteen with the additional suggestion (like one made in the committee by Minnesota's Senator Rice) that all the territory except Kansas be admitted as two states, one to be free and the other (New Mexico) to be slave. Seward preferred, however, to wait until "the eccentric movements of secession and disunion shall have ended . . . and the angry excitements of the hour shall have subsided" before calling a national convention to consider amendments to the Constitution. If this was as far as Lincoln was willing to go, it was not nearly far enough for the south. Douglas, on the other hand, optimistically called Seward's effort a "great speech" and thought that as "an entering wedge, or basis of settlement," much good could result from it.[22]

When the Senate met on Monday, January 14, the Senators from the three recently seceded states, Alabama, Florida, and Mississippi, were absent (although they did not formally withdraw until a week later), leaving the Republicans in greater strength. On that day, Bigler introduced a bill that would implement Crittenden's call for a national referendum, and Crittenden pressed for the consideration of his resolutions. When

Republican Senators adopted delaying tactics in order to postpone the discussion, Douglas erupted. He pleaded for prompt action. If a majority of the Senators were determined to prevent a vote on the compromise, Douglas demanded that they avow their purpose openly and for the record, rather than trying to achieve their goal "by points of order and by giving it the go-by and taking up other questions."

After suffering another postponement on the following day, the resolutions were again before the Senate on January 16. Rice proposed a variation on the two-state plan which he and Seward had suggested, but discussion centered on Crittenden's compromise. Douglas proposed to amend the section dealing with the territorial issue by striking out the words "now held or hereafter acquired" in the hope that this might meet some of the Republican objections. The words were redundant, for the Crittenden amendment would automatically apply to any additions to the national territory. Other amendments were offered, but the Republicans would not budge from their opposition. Determined to prevent the Crittenden resolutions from coming to a vote, they proposed a distracting substitute, offered earlier by New Hampshire Senator Daniel Clark, which declared that the Constitution provided ample protection for all the interests of the country and that any attempt to reconstruct the Union was "dangerous, illusory, and destructive." To their great surprise, their tactic was successful. Clark's substitute passed by a close vote, 25 to 23. Douglas, in the anteroom of the Senate when the vote was taken, rushed back to the floor to cast his vote against the substitute.

Six southern Senators—Slidell and Benjamin of Louisiana, Hemphill and Wigfall of Texas, Iverson of Georgia, and Johnson of Arkansas—and Gwin of California deliberately withheld their votes, thus enabling the Republicans to defeat the Crittenden compromise. By abstaining, they wished to show the country, and especially the south, that the Republicans had no interest in conciliating the differences between the two sections. Had they voted, Crittenden's resolutions might ultimately have been accepted, but without Republican endorsement they could not have been implemented. No plan could succeed that did not have the sanction of the incoming administration, and the President-elect was emphatic in his opposition to any adjustment of the territorial question. Republican responsibility for the failure of compromise was clear and inescapable. The results of the vote were immediately telegraphed to the Georgia secession convention to prove that there would be no safety for the south in the Union. Two days later, on January 18, Georgia seceded. Similar advice was flashed to Louisiana by Senator Benjamin.[23]

The Senate vote on Clark's substitute left Douglas angry, frustrated, and disappointed. To one Washington correspondent, he appeared "very cross and crabbed . . . out of sorts with everybody." He had been convinced that compromise could succeed in spite of Republican opposition, and he now turned his wrath against the south. He denounced the abstaining southern Senators, charged them with being "in concert" with the Republicans, and took them to task for using the vote to hasten secession in their own states. The extremes had met, Douglas observed, both wished to defeat an adjustment, both preferred disunion to compromise. It was common knowledge, reported a North Carolina Congressman, that "Southern disunionists visit Northern Representatives at their rooms, talk with them & tell them to concede nothing, that nothing will be acceptable to the South, & they by concession will only humiliate themselves for no good." When the Senate met in executive session to confirm Buchanan's nomination of Joseph Holt as Secretary of War, Douglas and Crittenden warmly defended Holt's role in the attempt to reinforce Fort Sumter and upbraided the southern Senators for their part in the passage of Clark's resolution.

Time was running out, and the desperation of the compromise leaders mounted proportionately. On January 26, Louisiana seceded from the Union. Douglas was furious. Louisiana, he pointed out, had not been purchased for the sole benefit of its residents. It was purchased "with the national treasure, for the common benefit of the whole Union in general, and for the safety, convenience, and prosperity of the Northwest in particular." Illinois and the northwest, he warned, would never assent to the control of the Mississippi by a foreign power. (By "foreign power" he meant the south, but there were also reports that France stood ready to aid her former colony.) A few days later, on February 1, a Texas convention approved secession.[24]

iv

To people throughout the country Douglas had become a symbol of national union and reconciliation. Letters supporting his compromise efforts poured in. Maine's former Senator J. W. Bradbury regarded him as the last hope to save the nation from disgrace and ruin. Benjamin F. Hallett, a Boston editor who had opposed Douglas at Charleston, wrote of his "magnanimous spirit" and his "readiness to forget the past and unite on any reasonable measure that will preserve and restore the Union." Especially encouraging were the communications from the south. You are the only "living statesman," wrote a Mississippian, "with suficient influence to save the country from the horors that now stare us in the face." Douglas was the "brake water" to save the Union. Thousands of Georgians, he was assured, considered him the "greatest man now living." "It requires such men as you and Crittenden to save us," wrote a border state man, and to Crittenden a Virginian noted, "When you and Mr. D. have hope and a determination to 'hold on,' we must all hope." There were, however, somber words of warning as well. The issue, wrote Waddy Thompson from Florida, was not one of union or disunion, but one of peace or war. He urged Douglas to avoid "that direst scourge of humanity civil war. . . . forbearance & conciliation may induce the south to come again into the Union—rely upon it that coercion never will—after the shedding of seas of blood we may be reduced to submission—to be members of the Union again never." 25

A few days after the passage of Clark's substitute, there were signs that some Republicans wished to reconsider their stand. They had voted for it, it was said, in the belief it would not pass. Its unexpected adoption placed them in the false position of being unwilling to compromise. The reports had no substance, but their appearance at a time when other developments also seemed to point to a softer Republican position encouraged the compromise leaders. A motion to reconsider the vote on Clark's resolution was passed on January 18. The Crittenden compromise was before the Senate once more. That night Seward and Connecticut's moderate Republican Senator James Dixon conferred at length with Douglas and Crittenden. What they talked about was not divulged, but rumors spread that some new proposition that would meet Republican objections would soon be announced. The four Senators apparently continued to meet for several days afterward. Seward, an old friend in spite of their many disagreements, was Douglas' best hope for persuading the new President to follow a conservative line. Lincoln himself was said to have hinted to Edward Bates that he would be willing to accept an extension of the Missouri Compromise line under certain conditions.

On January 24, Douglas hosted a large dinner party at which Seward, Dixon, and Crittenden were among the guests, along with members of the foreign diplomatic corps. An atmosphere of optimism prevailed. Seward surprised all when, in a fit of enthusiasm, he offered a toast, "Away with all parties, all platforms, all previous committals, and whatever else will stand in the way of restoration of the American Union." Crittenden responded with such feeling that he shattered his glass when he replaced it on the table; Douglas admonished Seward not to forget in the morning what he drank at night. Later, at a small, more intimate gathering, Seward, Crittenden, and Douglas impressed the French minister with their confidence that the Union would be preserved. "I see indications every day of a disposition to meet this question now and consider what is necessary to save the Union," Douglas announced to the Senate. When pressed to reveal the grounds for his optimism, he replied evasively that "I have reasons satisfactory to myself upon which to predicate that firm hope that the Union will be preserved." [26]

The same hopeful outlook was conveyed by Douglas and Crittenden in dispatches to leaders in the border states. Voters in North Carolina, Virginia, Tennessee, and Arkansas would go to the polls in February to decide whether state conventions should be called. If compromise were to be successful, Douglas believed, it was imperative that secession be rejected in these states. While the North Carolina legislature debated its election bill, Douglas sent a draft resolution to Raleigh, endorsing the compromise proposals he and Crittenden had introduced, and he urged that it be promptly adopted. Its passage by North Carolina, he told Bragg, would have a strong impact on northern opinion and enable him "to hold the Republicans in check" until a compromise could be effected.

In Virginia, Republican defiance was said to be pushing conservative men into the secessionist ranks. Douglas and Crittenden joined Virginia's Unionist Congressmen in a special appeal to the state. Douglas wrote John S. Barbour, "I can say with confidence that there is hope of adjustment, and the prospect has never before been better than now since we first assembled." "All depends upon the action of Virginia and the border States," Douglas wrote another Virginian at the end of January. "If they remain in the Union and aid in a fair and just settlement, the Union may be preserved. But if they secede, under the fatal delusion of a reconstruction, I fear that all is lost. Save Virginia and we will save the Union." Virginia was saved when the February 4 election for convention delegates resulted in a victory for the Unionists; the assurances of Crittenden and Douglas were given considerable credit for the result.[27]

A few days before the Tennessee election, William H. Polk, a candidate for the convention, wired Douglas and Crittenden for advice. "Our hope for the Union firm," was the reply. "Take courage from old Virginia. Save Tennessee and the Union is safe." When Douglas was told of an editorial in the Memphis *Appeal* representing him as favoring secession "as a peace measure . . . with the view of a reconstruction on a constitutional basis," he responded with a sharply worded denial that was widely circulated. "In regard to secession," he wrote, "I have never had but one opinion . . . that of unqualified opposition." To secede, he insisted, would be to play into the hands of the northern disunionists "who believe that the disruption of the Union would draw after it . . . civil war, servile insurrection, and finally the utter extermination of slavery in all the Southern States." With compromise, on the other hand, "peace and fraternal feeling will soon return, and the Cotton States come back, and the Union be rendered perpetual." On February 9, Tennesseans turned down the proposal to call a convention. Appeals for help were also received from Arkansas, where, on February 18, a convention was approved and a majority of Unionists elected. Ten days later, North Carolina voters rejected the idea of a convention. The border states had been saved.[28]

If Douglas' optimism was based solely on his discussions with Seward and other Republicans, it was not justified. His hope that the Republicans were softening their stand against compromise gradually diminished. He was in a mood, however, to seize and exaggerate even the slightest encouragement. Douglas had other reasons for being hopeful. During the winter the suggestion that a national convention be summoned to deal with the crisis had been offered by a number of people, including Crittenden and Douglas, but it was the state of Virginia that seized the initiative. On January 19, the Virginia legislature passed resolutions inviting delegates from all the states to gather at a peace conference in Washington on February 4. As a basis for discussion, the legislature proposed Crittenden's compromise. It was the same date which the seceded states had selected for their convention in Montgomery. Even in the latter Douglas may have placed some hope, for one Alabama friend wrote that "if all the states invited shall send delegates [to Montgomery], much good may and will result especially if in the interim the olive branch is held out by the north." [29]

There also remained the possibility of congressional action. While much time was spent discussing specific plans of adjustment, Congress also dealt with other issues, and Douglas was hopeful that the seeds of compromise might be found there. On January 21, the day that the Senators from Florida, Alabama, and Mississippi formally withdrew, the Senate passed a bill admitting Kansas to the Union as a free state. Douglas had strongly supported the bill, and he became impatient as southerners delayed the legislation with amendments. "I do think we ought to admit Kansas promptly, without further delay, or further obstacle," he declared. "We have had controversies enough about Kansas." He chided his southern opponents for their objections to Kansas' admission now, "when none of them were presented in regard to the Lecompton constitution, three years ago." When the bill came to a vote, Douglas was one of several northern Democrats who joined the Republicans in its support. The bill was rushed through partly in the hope that Kansas' two Senators would arrive in Washington before March 4. "The fate of the country," wrote one Republican, "may depend on two votes." [30]

Three new territories were carved out of the west during the session, and Douglas pounced upon the action as evidence that Republicans were adopting a more flexible position on the territorial issue. Each of the territories—Colorado, Nevada, and Dakota—was organized without reference to slavery, a fact which Douglas found encouraging in view of his long battle for popular sovereignty. When the Colorado bill was taken up, Green of Missouri, still the chairman of the territorial committee, noted that a clause specifying the admission of the territory to statehood with or without slavery had been stricken to avoid controversy. Wade, a Republican member of the committee, later revealed that the wording of the bill resulted from an agreement between "the two sides of this Chamber." Neither side could organize the territory on the basis of its own principles. One wanted to make it a slave territory, the other wanted a prohibition of slavery. Yet both agreed that the organization of a territorial government "for the people of Pike's Peak" was essential, inasmuch as this area had been detached from Kansas when the latter attained statehood. An informal agreement, "nothing like a compromise," had been reached whereby no mention would be made of slavery in the bill, "one way or the other." It was obvious that Douglas, although a committee member, had not been a party to the negotiations.[31]

Douglas raised some objections to the legislation, particularly to provisions that would prohibit the territorial legislature from discriminating among different kinds of property in its taxing power (a blow against his Freeport Doctrine) and from impairing the rights of private property. The prohibitions, he was convinced, originated in the south's zeal to prevent the territory from excluding slavery, but he found them to be unwarranted infringements on the territory's right to self-government. In the last stages of debate on the Colorado bill, he offered a substitute with the startling provision that the people of the territory elect all of their officers, recalling Chase's similar efforts to amend the Kansas-Nebraska Act in 1854. Since that time, he argued, changes had been made in the duties of territorial officers so that they no longer were required to perform federal duties, making it possible now to achieve this logical extension of popular sovereignty. "I desire," he declared, "to deprive this Government of the power of having any Federal policy in regard to the politics of the Territories." It was a weak argument at best, and few took it seriously. Wade charged Douglas with introducing this extension simply because the appointing power would soon pass from Democratic hands, to which Douglas replied, "I repel the insinuation."

It is not clear why Douglas should have otherwise selected this moment to support the popular election of territorial officials. It had never occupied an important place in his view of popular sovereignty, and he did not press it now. When apprised of the agreement that lay behind the bill's wording, he dropped his opposition. "As it is a compromise, I do not want to disturb it." He could not refrain, however, from expressing his satisfaction that in passing the territorial bills "the two sides of the 'irrepressible conflict' " had finally endorsed popular sovereignty. He especially taunted the Republicans. They had "backed down from their platform and abandoned the doctrine of congressional prohibition. . . . They have abandoned the doctrine of the President elect . . . the whole doctrine for which the Republican party contended as to the Territories is abandoned, surrendered, given up; non-interference is substituted in its place." On the day of final passage, Edward Dickinson Baker, an old acquaintance from Illinois, a close friend of Lincoln, and now a Republican Senator from Oregon, indicated his commitment to Douglas' popular sovereignty and asked Douglas if a vote in favor of the territorial measures would be consistent with that stand. Douglas replied that it would. To one disgruntled Republican, it was "a day of triumph for Mr. Douglas." [32]

Douglas also used the debate on a Pacific railroad bill to argue for territorial rights in the hope of bringing north and south together. Pointing out that probably no Senator had devoted more time to securing a Pacific railroad than he had, he objected to the distinction made by some southerners between territories and states. "There seems to be a strong impression abroad that this Government, which has but few specified powers, so far as the States are concerned, is omnipotent in the Territories of the United States." The powers delegated by the Constitution to the federal government, he insisted, applied equally to the territories and states. "You have no more right to interfere with the domestic concerns of the people . . . or with their local institutions of any kind in a Territory than you have in a State." Douglas failed to persuade the south, and the Pacific railroad bill foundered, as it had so many times before, on sectional disagreement over routes.[33]

Following the withdrawal of southern Senators in January, the Republicans pushed the passage of the Morrill tariff bill, to Douglas' great dismay. He feared that the passage of a high protective tariff at this critical time would have a damaging effect on the efforts to bring the seceded states back into the Union. He reminded the Senate that the legislation, repugnant to the southern states, could only "increase that irritation and . . . alienate, in some degree, their affections to this Union, which have already been materially shaken." Douglas had always opposed the principle of protection, and he now reiterated his stand. The tariff question was not a simple one. "I have learned enough about it," he modestly proclaimed, "to know that I know scarcely anything about it at all; and a man makes considerable progress on a question of this kind when he ascertains that fact." A tariff, he pointed out, involved two conflicting principles that were constantly at war with one another, for while it would attempt to protect one branch of industry, it would strike a deathblow at another. "Every tariff involves the principles of protection and of oppression, the principles of benefits and of burdens."

Instead of a tariff, Douglas offered an alternate plan which would not only strengthen the nation's commercial system but also "facilitate a peaceful and satisfactory solution of all our difficulties with the seceding States." The plan, based on the German *Zollverein* which he had studied during his European trip in 1853, called for the creation of a North American customs union that would include Canada, Mexico, Cuba, and the Central American nations. All restrictions on internal commerce, he said, should be swept away "so that there should be entire free trade unrestricted between every State, province, or country upon the American continent and the adjacent islands."

Like everything else he undertook during the session, he related his scheme to the preservation of the Union and the adjustment of the sectional differences. One of the critical issues was the relationship between expansion and the extension of slavery; indeed, Republicans had objected to the Crittenden compromise because of the possibility that slavery would be extended as the nation expanded south of the Missouri Compromise line. The establishment of a customs union, Douglas contended, would bring all the commercial and economic advantages of territorial expansion without the problems of political union. Moreover, the slavery question would not arise. In a statement that reversed his earlier fervency for national expansion, Douglas now warned of the dangers involved in extending the country's political boundaries. "The difficulties we have had, growing out of this slavery question and the continual annexation of countries adjoining us to the American Union," he suggested, "ought to warn us of the dangers of trying to extend the same sort of domestic policy, the same system of political institutions, over countries and people who are not homogeneous with ourselves." Strange words from the Little Giant!

Douglas' suggestion was not an afterthought; it was one he had carefully considered and matured. Since he had returned from Europe in 1853, he had been intrigued with the possibilities of a North American customs union. The secession of seven southern states provided the opportunity to advance the plan in earnest. The passage of a protective tariff at this juncture, he thought, would be disastrous to the Union, and he no doubt shared August Belmont's fear that a high tariff would force Great Britain and France into a recognition of the southern Confederacy. Having provided a brief sketch in his Senate speech, Douglas began to collect statistics and to gather notes on the *Zollverein,* as well as on such subjects as Canadian reciprocity, for presentation in a detailed and elaborate paper which he may have intended to publish at some later date. A North American customs union would not only have commercial benefits, it might also serve as an element in a compromise with the seceded states; the thought also crossed Douglas' mind that it could provide a basis for relations between the United States and the deep south if secession should prove more than a temporary phenomenon. In private conversation, he commented that his plan was outlined "to shadow out the policy this Gov't would have to pursue" toward the seceded states. Perhaps, observed a member of the Senate, it was intended "as a *feeler.*" Douglas' proposal, however, attracted little attention, and the Morrill tariff was passed without difficulty.[34]

In each case—the creation of new territories, the Pacific railroad, and the tariff—Douglas sought clues to the settlement of the issues between the north and south, but in each case he was disappointed. At the same time, he was desperate to prevent the cleavage between the seceded states and the Union from widening. His goal was to maintain a delicate balance until some mode of adjustment could be agreed upon. "I do not desire to use words that are harsh and irritating on one side," he told the Senate, "and I will not use words that recognize the lawfulness of the doctrine of secession on the other." At the same time, he lashed out at those who would not follow the path of peace and compromise, those who would overturn the balance. "I regard no man as friendly to this Union," he exclaimed to the Republican members of the Senate, "who is unwilling to enter upon such a system of pacification and compromise as will preserve it." [35]

There was still time for Congress to agree upon a compromise, although it was fast running out. On January 28, Douglas introduced a new fugitive slave law which he thought would meet northern and southern objections to the existing legislation and, he hoped, strengthen the Union sentiment in the border states. A jury trial would be provided in a federal court if a fugitive continued to claim his freedom, and the slaveowner who was prevented from recovering his slave by violent resistance would be compensated by the government. Douglas also modified his compromise plan and stood ready to offer it as a substitute for the Crittenden resolutions. In its altered form it included many of the elements of his earlier proposal, but with the addition of clauses suppressing the African slave trade forever, requiring the rendition of all fugitives from justice regardless of whether the acts for which they were charged were crimes in the states to which they had fled, and limiting the President and Vice President to single six-year terms. With Crittenden, Bigler, and others, he tried to bring the Crittenden compromise to a vote in the Senate. The days, however, passed, and valuable time was consumed in seemingly endless, pointless wrangling. Delays and postponements added to his frustration, and the prospect that Crittenden's proposals would ever be acted upon grew increasingly dim. In an outburst that reflected his growing concern, Douglas shouted from his place in the Senate—"before high Heaven . . . [and] to the four corners of the Republic"—that there were disunionists on both sides of the chamber who preferred the destruction of the Union to the sacrifice of their political positions. It was time, he pleaded, for the Union men to come together and act in concert. The deliberations of the Washington Peace Conference became the last hope for compromise.[36]

On February 4, the day the Montgomery convention met and just a month before Lincoln would be inaugurated, the conference opened in Willard's Hotel. Only twenty-one of the thirty-three states were represented; the seven seceded states and several northern states sent no delegates. Ex-President John Tyler, seventy-one years old, was chosen to preside over the meeting. As the delegates arrived in Washington, Douglas invited Tyler to dinner and personally welcomed those from Illinois. One was John M. Palmer, a friend and former Democrat who had parted company with Douglas after the Kansas-Nebraska Act. Calling on Palmer at his hotel room, Douglas impressed the delegate with the gravity of the situation, referred to southern actions as a "rebellion" and expressed his fear that the "continent will tremble under the tread of a million armed men before the Rebellion is ended." Later in the month, he entertained the conference delegates in a lavish party at his home. Mrs. Tyler, flattered by the compliments paid her by Adele, noted that "people are catching at straws as a relief to their pressing anxieties and look to the Peace Commissioners as if they possessed some divine power to restore order & harmony. Here you can realize more than anywhere else the distracted state of the Country." [37]

The task of the Peace Conference was not only formidable. It was hopeless. The selection of delegates in some northern states was so manipulated by Republican governors and legislatures as to prevent an adjustment, and some delegates were instructed to resist compromise. The same delaying tactics that stalled compromise in Congress were invoked. Douglas appealed to Lincoln to intervene with the Republicans in order to save the conference, but his gesture was not successful. Under the circumstances, it was amazing that any report at all came from the gathering. The only plan upon which the delegates could agree (and then just barely) was the Crittenden compromise with some slight modifications. Tyler reported the plan to Congress, and on February 27 Crittenden brought it before the Senate.[38]

Only a few days remained in the session. The Peace Conference proposal was promptly submitted to a special five-member committee, which reported it back to the Senate the next day. The two Republican members (Seward and Trumbull) registered their opposition in a minority report, proposing instead that the question of a national convention be explored. Once again, the compromise forces encountered the delaying tactics of the Republicans. Crittenden substituted the Peace Conference plan for his own compromise, but his efforts to have it considered were frustrated by Republican insistence that the Senate rules be scrupulously observed. Consideration of the compromise would have to lay over until the next day, Friday, March 1. In anguish, Crittenden cried out, "a nation stands breathlessly looking on now to your proceedings to decide their doom; it may be either for peace or war, life or death to them; and the gentleman says our attempt to do something on the subject is out of order."

On March 1, Douglas proposed that a constitutional amendment just approved by the House of Representatives be considered at the same time as the Peace Conference resolutions. Discussed in the House Committee of Thirty-Three and offered by Ohio Congressman Thomas Corwin, the proposed amendment simply prohibited Congress from ever abolishing or interfering with slavery in the states. Similar to a suggestion of Seward's in the Committee of Thirteen, and endorsed by Lincoln, it was as far as the Republicans would go. (A second measure from the House committee, a bill to admit New Mexico as a slave state, was killed by Republican votes even though it was sponsored by Republicans; it never reached the Senate.) Three plans were now before the Senate—the Crittenden compromise, the Peace Conference substitute, and the House amendment. In the short time that remained, Douglas hoped that at least one of them might succeed. The day, however, was spent in fruitless debating, interspersed with points of order, and when it came to an end a Republican newspaper correspondent informed his paper that "the back of compromise I believe to be broken." [39]

Saturday, March 2, was the last regular meeting of the Senate except for a short two-hour session on the morning of March 4, the day the new administration would be inaugurated. Yet when the meeting opened and Douglas prepared to call up the House amendment for consideration, he was met with another Republican objection. Sumner argued that the amendment had not been read a second time and therefore could not be considered; the journal of the previous day's debate, he insisted, was in error. Douglas challenged Sumner's recollection, and the proceedings immediately degenerated into a noisy and confused exchange regarding the accuracy of the journal. The Senate finally voted that the journal was wrong, another delay and a blow to Douglas. Later, however, Bigler, with Douglas' support, succeeded in having the rules of the Senate relating to constitutional amendments suspended so that consideration of the amendments before them could be expedited without the constant challenges from the Republican side.

As the day continued, the range of options before the Senate narrowed. The House recessed at seven o'clock and would not meet again until Monday morning, when it would close its session. There would be no time for the consideration of any Senate-approved compromise. Douglas quickly realized that only the proposed Corwin amendment, already passed by the House, would have any chance of success. His motion to postpone all other orders of business and to consider the House amendment was approved, but only after a further wrangle with Mason of Virginia over rules and parliamentary procedure. Douglas' frustration mounted, reaching a peak when Ohio's Senator Pugh, who had been a friend to compromise, proposed changes in the amendment's wording on the ground that it was not expressed in good grammatical English. Douglas exploded. The resolution, he insisted, was clear and specific; no one could fail to understand it. Crittenden argued that he could "bear with bad English when it expresses a good thing." Pugh's changes, however, were approved by the Vice President's tie-breaking vote, and Douglas' hopes for the amendment's passage wavered.

To alter the wording of the amendment, Douglas urged, was to defeat the measure, for the House would have no time to act on an amended version. He secured a reconsideration, and after more debate (accompanied by noise and confusion in the galleries, as members of the House poured into the chamber to witness the Senate's last hours), Pugh's verbal alterations were voted down. Douglas had saved the amendment, but he was immediately challenged anew when Pugh now proposed to substitute the Crittenden compromise. Another flood of oratory was loosed, all the more impassioned for the flow of bourbon among the Senators. Douglas chafed and fumed. Again he insisted that debate could have little benefit. "We are now expending the whole night—all the time we have left of this session—in discussing these questions when certainly it can do no good, and may do great harm." Delay and debate could only mean defeat for the only compromise proposal that "is within our reach." The tide was finally stemmed at midnight, after a continuous session of twelve hours, when the Senate agreed to recess until the following evening, Sunday, March 3.[40]

Long before the meeting hour, spectators began to gather. By seven o'clock the galleries were crowded, people were standing in the aisles, and the Senate floor was packed. The ladies' gallery was a mass of color, like "some gorgeous parterre of flowers," while the gentlemen's side was "one dense black mass of surging, heaving men, pushing, struggling, and almost clambering over each other's backs in order to get a good look at the proceedings." One correspondent reported that the noise was like an immense beehive. It was soon apparent that the confusion among the spectators would interfere with the Senate's deliberations. Senators had difficulty making themselves heard over the din. Crittenden was interrupted in his opening remarks when a man in the gallery fainted from the heat and was carried out over the heads of the crowd. Douglas, on the edge of his patience, charged that the disruption came from Republican supporters who opposed compromise. He demanded that the aisles be cleared, and when no discernible movement followed, he threatened to call for the election of a new Sergeant at Arms who might be more effective in maintaining order. As the Senate debated a motion to clear the galleries, the noise subsided, those without seats left, and the Senators returned to their business.

Crittenden made a final eloquent plea for the preservation of the Union. Trumbull followed, urging that the government assume sufficient power to maintain itself and arguing the futility of compromise. Baker, the lone Republican who seemed to favor conciliation, confessed his willingness to make concessions in order to restore peace and union to the country. As midnight approached, Douglas asked that debate be stopped and that the Senate proceed to vote on the several propositions before it. First, he hoped all the attempts to amend them should be dropped. The House amendment should be brought to a vote in its original form. "Then let us take up the report of the peace conference, and have a vote for it or against it, without debate; and then take up the proposition of the Senator from Kentucky, and have a vote for or against it, without debate." Finally the Seward-Trumbull resolution calling for a national convention should be brought forward. He asked that his colleagues not consume the whole night, wearying the Senators with a "by-play of amendments, that will prevent a test vote upon any one of the questions."

As the hour of midnight passed and the Senate debate moved into the early hours of March 4, the galleries began to empty. On the floor, those Senators who were not engaged in the discussion napped. Douglas, responding to Mason's charge that the House amendment would do no good, that it was nothing more than a "bread-pill," defended the measure in his last statement of the session. "There is a want of confidence in the southern States," he declared, "in respect to the good faith of the North concerning the institution of slavery." The passage and ratification of the amendment would prove conclusively "that there is no such sentiment at the North as you apprehend." The amendment, he conceded, was not all that he thought should be done, but he found great virtue and security in it nonetheless. He charged southerners with harboring the fear that the amendment would pacify the people and thereby frustrate their disunion designs. Turning on the Republicans, he once again placed the responsibility for the defeat of compromise at their feet. The passage of the Crittenden compromise in December, he firmly believed, would have prevented the secession of all the states except South Carolina. The creation of the three new territories without mention of slavery ought, he felt, to allay southern apprehensions on the territorial question. The passage of the House amendment would have the same effect with respect to slavery in the states. "I think we ought to be satisfied with that until we can go to the people and procure proper constitutional amendments to make the security permanent." Douglas now became the focal point in the discussion, with both southerners and Republicans attacking him in turn.

Voting began at about five o'clock on the morning of the fourth. Pugh's attempt to substitute the Crittenden compromise for the House amendment was defeated, 25 to 14. The resolution for a national convention proposed by Seward and Trumbull was then beaten by an identical vote, and the proposition of the Peace Conference, presented also as a substitute, went down to defeat by the lopsided margin of 34 to 3. The way was at last clear for the House amendment; it passed the Senate by a precise constitutional majority, 24 to 12. As an afterthought, the Crittenden compromise was brought forth, and for the first time it was placed directly before the Senate, but it went down to narrow defeat before the united phalanx of Republican Senators. At seven o'clock, after another twelve-hour session, the Senate finally recessed. "The morning," wrote a reporter, "broke clear and beautiful." [41]

# XXXI

## "Tell them to obey the laws and support the Constitution of the United States" 1861

Douglas was exhausted. The strain of the presidential campaign and his plunge immediately afterward into the tensions and frustrations of the secession crisis had sapped his strength. Mentally as well as physically tired, he reflected in his appearance the stress under which he had been laboring. His face was furrowed more deeply, his eyes sunken, and his brow darker. There were reports that he was drinking heavily again. His temper was short and his patience thin.

Matching his fatigue was a deepening gloom as he watched the nation slip away. The optimism to which he had tenaciously clung was severely shaken by the obstructionist tactics of the Republicans and ultra southerners. The Montgomery convention, which some had thought might provide a basis for a reconstruction of the Union, was organizing a southern nation instead. Through his dogged persistence, the proposed thirteenth (or Corwin) amendment had cleared Congress at the last minute, the only positive evidence of the effort that had been invested in the cause of compromise. It was but a crumb, holding out little hope to the people. Dealing solely with the question of slavery in the states, it hardly met the issues that separated the north and south, and when Douglas tried to assure southerners that it was a meaningful move, surely even he must have known better. Still, as he pointed out, it was better than no action at all. He could look with greater satisfaction at the decision of the border states to remain with the Union; it was no small gain, and he had played a large part in its achievement. As the session closed, he received the gratitude of one who witnessed the final hectic scenes. But for his "noble & patriotic course," this observer was convinced, "Mason & Dixon's line would now be the boundary of the Southern Confederacy." [1]

Douglas, however, was still unwilling to concede that compromise had failed. With the expiration of the thirty-sixth Congress and the end of the Buchanan administration, he turned to the President-elect. His relations with the Republican President, with whom he had more in common than many thought, would, he hoped, be better than they had been with Buchanan, a member of his own party. What Lincoln's policy would be toward the seceded states was not known. The Republicans had rejected compromise as a means for restoring the Union, but they had offered no clear alternative. Many people in the country must have thought that Douglas would have a strong influence on the new President. The two men had long been acquainted and had shared many experiences (although most of them were marked by hostility). By late February and early March, the number of appeals from office-seekers asking Douglas' assistance became voluminous. There was little assurance, however, that Lincoln would take Douglas into his confidence. With the change of administrations, those who had looked to Douglas for leadership in the struggle for the Union, especially in the border states, became less sanguine of his success and more skeptical of his ability to influence policy.

Lincoln arrived in Washington unexpectedly in the early morning hours of February 23. Later that day, at his own request, he was visited in his quarters at Willard's Hotel by the Illinois congressional delegation, including Douglas, whom Lincoln had particularly asked to see. The interview between the two men was "peculiarly pleasant." On February 25, the President-elect, accompanied by Seward, visited both houses of Congress, and, while he was received with coolness by some Democratic Senators, Douglas was among those who extended a warm greeting. On the same day, Adele, "with graceful courtesy," called on Mrs. Lincoln.[2]

Douglas was anxious to talk with Lincoln about the crisis which beset the nation. On the night of February 26, he joined several members of the Peace Conference, including John Bell and Kentucky's James Guthrie, in an appeal to Lincoln for support. It was not until the following night, however, that Douglas was able to speak with Lincoln privately and at length. He feared that the Peace Conference had reached an impasse, unable to agree on a compromise plan, and was likely to adjourn without achieving anything. Its failure, he thought, might be used by the border states to justify their secession from the Union. "At the risk of being misunderstood," Douglas sought an appointment with Lincoln. He urged the President-elect to do everything in his power to prevent a dissolution of the Union and asked him to persuade his friends in the Peace Conference to do likewise. Douglas reminded him that they both had children and implored him "in God's name, to act the patriot, and to save our children a country to live in." He urged Lincoln to support with a strong recommendation Seward's proposal for a national convention.

For the first time, Douglas also indicated where he would stand in relation to the Republican administration. He was still, as he had ever been, Lincoln's political opponent, and he expected to oppose the political measures of his administration. But, Douglas assured Lincoln, he would take no partisan advantage nor manufacture any political capital out of any act of patriotism which Lincoln might adopt in order to preserve the Union. Lincoln listened "respectfully and kindly," told Douglas that the problem was much on his mind and thanked him for his visit. Douglas later commented that he had had no success "in getting Mr. Lincoln to a point on the subject." [3] The stalemate which Douglas feared was averted, as the Peace Conference finally agreed on a report, but there is no evidence that Lincoln interceded with the Republican delegates.

On March 4, Inauguration Day, military preparations in Washington added to the tension already created by the inability of Congress to agree on a compromise. There were rumors that Lincoln would be the target of a violent outbreak and that southerners would never allow him to take the oath of office. Reports that the city might be attacked brought troops to the streets, and from early morning "the drum and fife could be heard" as soldiers marched to their stations. When the flag was unfurled over the uncompleted capitol, one of the halliards broke, flinging the flag out like a pennant, an ill omen for the Union.

At ten o'clock, Congress met to bring the session to its final closing. Members of the Senate, after a twelve-hour meeting the night before, had had only three hours' rest. Most of the two-hour meeting that morning was consumed by Senator Bright, who droned on against a bill creating a metropolitan gas company in Washington, to the amusement of the Senators and the annoyance of the spectators who expected something more dramatic. Shortly before noon, Vice President Breckinridge entered the chamber with Hannibal Hamlin, the Vice President-elect, on his arm. As the hour of twelve approached, Breckinridge delivered a few parting remarks, administered the oath to Hamlin, and declared the thirty-sixth Congress to be officially adjourned.

The Senators quietly awaited the arrival of the presidential procession, talking in small groups. They were soon joined by members of the diplomatic corps, the Supreme Court, and the House of Representatives. A little after one o'clock, Buchanan and Lincoln entered the chamber arm in arm, the former "pale, sad, nervous" and the latter as "grave and impassive as an Indian martyr." The party was formed and filed out to the wooden platform that had been erected in front of the east portico of the capitol. Douglas accompanied the group and on the platform moved as far forward as he could, in order to leave no doubts that he would stand by the new administration in its effort to maintain the Union.[4]

As Senator Baker of Oregon prepared to introduce the President-elect, Lincoln fumbled awkwardly with his hat. Standing near by, Douglas took the hat from his hands and held it during the ceremony. Lincoln stepped forward, adjusted his spectacles and began reading his inaugural address. His opening sentence, "Fellow citizens of the United States," drew prolonged applause. The first public statement of policy by the new administration was brief, unequivocal, and conciliatory in tone. Lincoln, hoping to allay southern fears, disavowed any intention of interfering with the institution of slavery in the states where it existed and promised a faithful execution of the fugitive slave law. The southern people, he declared, need have no apprehensions that their property, peace, and security would be endangered by a Republican administration. He reduced the dispute between the north and south to its simplest expression: "One section of our country believes slavery is *right,* and ought to be extended, while the other believes it is *wrong,* and ought not to be extended." On the question of compromise, Lincoln recognized the authority of the people to amend the Constitution, adding that he "should, under existing circumstances, favor, rather than oppose, a fair opportunity being afforded the people to act upon it," preferably by means of a national convention. It was the mode formally proposed by Seward, Crittenden, and Douglas at various times in the previous weeks and pressed upon Lincoln by Douglas just a few days before.

Lincoln was also emphatic in his opposition to secession, insisting that "no State, upon its own mere motion, can lawfully get out of the Union." The Union was perpetual and could not be broken. He promised that the Constitution and laws would be enforced in all the states. "The power confided to me, will be used to hold, occupy, and possess the property, and places belonging to the government, and to collect the duties and imposts; but beyond what may be necessary for these objects, there will be no invasion—no using of force against, or among the people anywhere." Where hostility to the United States "in any interior locality" shall be so great and where the exercise of federal authority should be so irritating, no attempt would be made "to force obnoxious strangers among the people." His policies, Lincoln declared, would be carried out "with a view and a hope of a peaceful solution of the national troubles, and the restoration of fraternal sympathies and affections."

"In *your* hands, my dissatisfied fellow countrymen," Lincoln concluded, directing his remarks to the citizens of the seceded states, "and not in *mine,* is the momentous issue of civil war. The government will not assail *you.* You can have no conflict without being yourselves the aggressors." [5]

Douglas' reaction to Lincoln's address was immediately favorable. As Lincoln read, Douglas murmured such words as "Good," "That's so," "No coercion," and "Good again." He was among the first to congratulate the new President afterward; turning to a friend, he thanked God that Lincoln would not involve the nation in a war. When queried by a reporter, Douglas said, "He does not mean coercion; he says nothing about retaking the forts, or Federal property—he's all right." Douglas had had more time to think about the address when he commented to a second reporter, "Well, I hardly know what he means. Every point in the address is susceptible of a double construction; but I think he does not mean coercion." Correspondents continued to press him for his reactions. A day or so later, Douglas again responded. Some people had charged Lincoln with contradicting his party's Chicago Platform. "Well, what of it?" answered Douglas. If true, "it shows that Mr. Lincoln has the nerve to say what is right, platform or no platform. I defend the Inaugural if it is as I understand it, namely, an emanation from the brain and heart of a patriot, and as I mean, if I know myself, to act the part of a patriot, I indorse it." [6]

Following the inauguration, in a hall decorated with shields and flags and brilliantly lighted with gas, Douglas escorted Mrs. Lincoln to the inaugural ball, and at midnight he danced the quadrille with her. A few days later, Douglas and his wife were prominent among the guests at Lincoln's first White House reception. Adele was "the admitted belle" of the evening, her "tall and symmetrical figure," clad in a simple white dress, in striking contrast with the other guests. Apparently, she received more attention than the First Lady. Douglas "was there in all his glory," moving from one group to another, conversing, bowing, and shaking hands.

"What means this evident weakness of Mr. Douglas for Mr. Lincoln?" asked one correspondent. It was a question many people were asking. One suggestion held that Douglas was "playing a deep political game for the conservative sentiment of the country." Some were suspicious of his motives and hinted that he had already set his sights on the next presidential election. But Douglas had more immediate goals. Lincoln's inclinations, he believed, were basically peaceful and patriotic, but they needed reinforcing. For days he had been worried that Lincoln would fall under the influence of the Republican party's radical wing—those, he felt, who desired a civil war. He expressed as much concern for the formation of the new cabinet as did members of the President's own party, and he hoped that Seward would assume a primary role in it as a counterbalance to men like Chase and Montgomery Blair. Crittenden's term in the Senate had expired, and Douglas urged that the Kentuckian be appointed to the Supreme Court. The moral effect in the border states, he pointed out, would be great. There was even the remote chance that Douglas himself might be accorded a place of influence at the President's side. He regarded Lincoln with respect, but he was also aware that Lincoln's experience in governmental affairs could hardly match his own. To a friend, Douglas commented that the President "is eminently a man of the atmosphere which surrounds him." He was determined to be a part of that atmosphere.[7]

Douglas' first task was to persuade the south that his assessment of Lincoln's intentions was correct. It would not be easy. Texas Senator Wigfall, still in Washington even though his state had seceded, declared that war was now inevitable, and he telegraphed the information to his constituents; Senator Mason thought that Virginia would be dissatisfied with Lincoln's statements and would secede at once. Many border state southerners read coercion into Lincoln's statements. "Our people interpret the inaugural message as a message for war," wrote a Virginian to

Douglas; secession feeling had been running high in the state ever since its publication. From Kentucky, a friend wrote that many of Douglas' supporters had now become "the very hottest of the secessionists." "Are you not now satisfied that no honorable adjustment can be effected?" telegraphed an Arkansan to Douglas. And from Richmond, where the Virginia convention continued to sit, came the query, "Is there any hope? Can we remain in the Union?" Douglas and Crittenden shot back an answer: "Yes, there is hope. Stand firm and all will yet be right." [8]

ii

Following the expiration of the thirty-sixth Congress, the Senate continued to meet, in order to receive the appointments of the new administration and handle whatever other business might be necessary. A routine motion to print the inaugural address provided the first opportunity for southerners to express their reactions publicly. Lincoln's intention to treat the seceded states as though they were still in the Union, charged North Carolina Senator Thomas L. Clingman, could only lead to a collision of arms. The message, he believed, was a declaration of war against the south.

Clingman's statement provoked Douglas to reply. On March 6 he defended Lincoln's message as a "peace offering rather than a war message." He found much cause for hope in the President's assurance that his policy would be peaceful, not aggressive. Douglas pointed out that Lincoln had given "a distinct pledge that the policy of the administration shall be conducted with exclusive reference to a peaceful solution of our national difficulties." He had "sunk the partisan in the patriot" and was entitled to the thanks of all conservative men. Lest his interpretation be misconstrued, however, Douglas made it clear that he was not offering the administration his political support. "I do not wish it to be inferred from anything I have said or omitted to say," he concluded, "that I have any political sympathy with his administration, or that I expect that any contingency can happen in which I may be identified with it." He would oppose Lincoln's administration with all his energy on those issues which separate the parties, "but on this one question, that of preserving the Union by a peaceful solution of our present difficulties . . . if I understand his true intent and meaning, I am with him."

Douglas' defense of Lincoln's message created a sensation and inspired considerable speculation as to his motives. There was more to come. Clingman pressed for clarification of Lincoln's willingness to support compromise amendments and urged that Lincoln withdraw federal troops from the last southern forts that remained in government hands, Forts Sumter and Pickens. On the next day, Wigfall followed Clingman's lead. The Texan challenged Douglas' right to speak for Lincoln and called for a recognition of southern independence. He demanded that the troops be withdrawn and warned that war would result if it were not done. Wigfall's blast brought Douglas to his feet again. He reiterated his conviction that "the inaugural means peace" and rejoiced, because the Union was dearer to him than ever before, that peace would be maintained. Wigfall taunted him with references to his Norfolk speech during the presidential campaign, but Douglas brushed them aside with the statement that he had no reason to modify or change any part of that speech. The issues of the presidential election, however, were in the past. "I am now looking only to that line of public policy which will save this country from civil war and disruption."

Douglas startled the Senate when he announced that there was not food enough in Fort Sumter to last more than six weeks and, unless new supplies were sent, the garrison would be forced to evacuate the fort. He also maintained that the fort could not be reinforced without an army of at least 10,000 men on land to cooperate with the naval operations. The information, received with surprise and concern, had been known to the government for only a few days; that Douglas also knew of Major Anderson's situation implied that he held at least a degree of the administration's confidence. When Wigfall tried to elicit from Douglas the course which the government would follow toward Fort Sumter, Douglas replied sharply that it would hardly be wise for him to divulge information to one who would "soon be in the counsels of the enemy, and the command of its armies." Answering a later query from Mason, however, Douglas declared, "I take it for granted . . . that no attempt will be made to reinforce Fort Sumter, for the simple reason that it is impossible to do it, if even there was a disposition to do it." Although he added a disclaimer that he had "no knowledge of the views or purposes of anybody connected with the Government," it was assumed that he spoke for the President.[9]

Douglas' speeches were rushed to the printer and copies sent across the country. The response was heartening. If Douglas were correct in his assessment of the inaugural address, wrote Benjamin Rush, then Lincoln deserved the support of all conservative men. Douglas' speeches, the painter-inventor Samuel F. B. Morse assured him, would become the instruments for re-establishing national unity. More important was their impact on the south. Douglas' insistence that Lincoln's policy was peaceful, it was thought, would soothe the southern mind and have a salutary effect on the border states, where the new President's actions were being closely watched. When three commissioners sent by the southern Confederacy to negotiate with the Lincoln administration arrived in Washington, it was immediately reported that Douglas would act as a mediator between them and the President. One of the commissioners was Douglas' close friend John Forsyth, the Mobile editor with whom he had spent election night in November. Douglas did not serve as a mediator, but one who did convey the sentiments of Secretary of State Seward to the Confederate emissaries (on March 24) was the Russian minister in Washington, Baron de Stoeckl. The night before Stoeckl met with the southerners, he dined with Douglas.[10]

Border state Unionists were bolstered by Douglas' position in their fight against the secessionists. Their hands were strengthened by the widespread belief that Douglas had the ear of the President and would even be allowed to control the patronage in the border states. At least one cabinet member indicated that Douglas would be consulted before changes among the officeholders were made. Douglas' revelation that Fort Sumter would probably be evacuated "tended to nerve the hearts of the Union men" in Virginia. "The Seceders are *dismayed.*" In North Carolina, wrote Robert P. Dick, Union men placed great confidence in Douglas' "patriotism and judgment," and John A. Gilmer asked the Senator to place his views before the southern people as soon as possible. "I fully believe you can quiet the border states," wrote Gilmer. "You can place in the hands of the Union men weapons of offence and attack." Marylanders, it was reported, were sorry they had voted for Breckinridge instead of Douglas. Radicals were unmoved and skeptical of Douglas' motives. Resentful of his influence in the border regions, one Virginia secessionist spat, "The dirty, little scoundrel will I hope 'Link on' still more and expose his cloven feet." Douglas, to the ultras, had simply revealed his true Republican colors.[11]

The Republicans were ominously quiet in the face of Douglas' analysis of the President's intentions. The only person speaking for the Republican administration seemed to be Douglas, and some observers wondered if he knew what he was talking about. If Lincoln is really in favor of peace, asked the New York *Herald,* what has he done to secure it? Was he waiting for Fort Sumter to be attacked so that he could appeal "to the war spirit of the North" in order to invade the south? Southern Senators, noting that those who had a right to speak for the President "have been ominously silent," charged Douglas with encouraging Lincoln to follow a do-nothing policy of "masterly inactivity." The entire country, wrote a New Yorker to Douglas, was awaiting an answer to his interpretation of the inaugural address.[12]

None came. Douglas was out on the limb, and his perch became increasingly precarious. He conceded that his construction of the inaugural address was disputed and complained that "the Republican side of the Chamber remains mute and silent, neither assenting or dissenting." On March 13, in a dramatic move to smoke out the administration, he introduced a resolution calling on the War Department for information on the southern forts. He asked that the Senate be informed "what forts, arsenals, navy-yards, and other public works [in the seceded states] . . . are now within the actual possession and occupation of the United States, and by what number of men each is garrisoned and held, and whether reinforcements are necessary to retain the same." If so, he continued, does the government have the power and means to supply reinforcements "within such time as the exigencies and necessities of the case may demand?" Does the defense and protection of the United States even demand the retention of the forts? It was a bold attempt to draw forth the intentions of the administration, perhaps even to influence the development of policy, and to strike a wedge between the President and the radical members of his party. Lincoln had asked essentially the same questions of Winfield Scott, commanding general of the Army, a few days before, and Scott had delivered his answers on March 11. It is possible that Douglas knew of this exchange and wished to use it to promote a peace policy.

Douglas introduced his resolution, he said, for two reasons: to demonstrate that the President did not contemplate war, and to make it clear that he had no means for waging war even if he desired it. If the policy of the administration were one of peace, as Douglas expected it to be, the answers to his inquiries would relieve the nation's fears "and restore good will and good feeling among the people of the different sections." If the policy were war, then it was the people's due that the fact be known. Republicans objected strenuously to the resolution and tried to prevent its consideration.

Douglas challenged the Republicans to speak out on the question of Lincoln's policy. He had thrust himself between the secession movement and the "war construction" of the inaugural message in order to allay the fears of southern Union men. "I have taken this position as a Union man, as a friend of peace, from the conscientious conviction that I justly and correctly interpret the President's inaugural." If he was not correct, the Republican Senators had no right to remain silent and then deprive him of the means to get at the truth. A war to subjugate the seceded states would require a quarter of a million men and exorbitant taxation (he estimated $316 million a year to keep that number of men in the field). "Are we prepared for civil war, with all its horrors and calamities? Let your policy be proclaimed to the world, and let the people determine the question. Silence is criminal when we are on the eve of events like these." Douglas demanded to know.

Only three courses lay open, he continued, and the people must choose among them: the restoration and preservation of the Union peaceably, by constitutional amendment; the peaceful dissolution of the Union, the recognition of the independence of the southern states, and the "establishment of a liberal system of commercial and social intercourse with them by treaties of commerce and amity"; or war, with a view to the subjugation and military occupation of the south. The first was the best, the last the worst. Douglas, trying to press the Republicans, lauded their patriotism in organizing three territories on the basis of non-intervention and approving an amendment that would protect slavery in the states from congressional interference. Having gone thus far, he asked, why not embody the principle in the Constitution, denying the power of Congress over slavery everywhere? "Do this, and we shall have peace and harmony in the country."

The force of Douglas' appeal was marred by an unfortunate exchange with Maine's Senator Fessenden, who took personally what must have been a slip of Douglas' tongue. Douglas lost his temper, directing epithets at Fessenden that were "better adapted to a pothouse than the Senate Chamber." There were pointed references to settling the question "elsewhere" in accordance with the "code of honor," but both parties wisely backed away at the last moment. Turning to Wilson and Hale, who also attacked his resolution, Douglas defied them to marshal their arguments and make their attacks. "I expect to give these gentlemen some trouble during this Congress," he shouted. "I know their scheme. I do not mean that they shall break up this Union. I do not mean that they shall plunge this country into war." Douglas was under severe pressure, and the incident revealed how far he was being pushed by events.[13]

Republicans were extremely annoyed with Douglas' resolution, although few of them took any part in the debate. The information asked
for was sensitive and vital for national security; Douglas, they thought,
should know better. When Wisconsin Senator Timothy Howe attacked
him, Douglas noted that it was apparently impossible for a Republican
to make a speech without impugning his motives or assailing his character. "If I should die," he added in a jocular tone, "I would have the longest list of mourners that ever graced a funeral *cortège* in this country,
because there would be so many politicians deprived of the material out
of which they manufacture their speeches." When John C. Breckinridge,
now sitting as a Senator from Kentucky, tried to take the limelight from
Douglas by insisting that Republicans make new guarantees to the
south, Douglas replied that Lincoln's party had already abandoned its
position on the territorial question. It was his way of placing the Union
question squarely before the south and embarrassing the Republicans at
the same time.

The Republicans did not rise to the bait. Douglas virtually monopolized Senate debate, but he elicited no clear statements of policy from his
opposition. The President had declared that he would not make war
upon anybody, Fessenden contended, and the nation should be satisfied
with that. Douglas, more aware than ever before that there was little he
could do, fell into despair. "Seven States are out of the Union," he
moaned to the Republicans, "civil war is impending over you, commerce
is interrupted, confidence destroyed, the country going to pieces, just because I was unable to defeat you. . . . You can boast that you have defeated me, but you have defeated your country with me. You can boast
that you have triumphed over me, but you have triumphed over the
unity of these States."

On March 26, Douglas' resolution was tabled. Two days later, the Republicans, weary of Douglas' badgering, offered a resolution of their own
that was designed to stiffen Lincoln's resistance to conciliation. "The
true way to preserve the Union," the resolution stated, "is to enforce the
laws of the Union; . . . resistance to their enforcement, whether under
the name of anti-coercion or any other name, is encouragement to disunion; and . . . it is the duty of the President to use all the means in his
power to hold and protect the public property of the United States." The
resolution was never brought to a vote, for later in the day the Senate
adjourned, but Lincoln heeded the message.[14]

As Douglas's hopes faded, so did those of border state Unionists. Only the evacuation of Forts Sumter and Pickens would keep the northern slave states in the Union, wrote a North Carolinian to Douglas. If Lincoln's policy is peace and that policy is promptly carried out, "we can overwhelm the secessionists in this State—but if matters are kept in suspense & uncertainty much longer, I fear we are doomed to defeat." From Richmond, Thomas H. Gilmer pleaded, "What are the *real* prospects ahead? . . . I *hope* for the best but *fear* the worst." The vacillating policy of the administration, he continued, "is sorely perplexing the conservative men in this State." Expressions of concern also came from the north, especially from representatives of northeastern business interests, who insisted that "commerce, trade, manufactures & the arts are paralized & will be until this problem is solved." "The administration is now drifting," wrote a New York businessman. Another doubted that anything less than "a collision or loss of life" would awaken the Republicans to the danger which faced the nation. Douglas felt helpless, and it became clear that he could expect no aid from the White House.[15]

Desperate, Douglas turned in other directions. Failing in the first and best of the three alternative courses he described before the Senate, he now seems to have turned momentarily to the second. In a memorandum which he never made public, he reviewed his position on the crisis. Disunion, whether accompanied by war or carried out peaceably, would have disastrous consequences for the American people. Yet, he believed, peaceful separation was preferable to war; the former would leave the door open for a reconstruction of the Union, providing more time for the discussion of conciliation and compromise, while the latter would slam it shut. If separation could not be avoided, it was the responsibility of the people in both sections to agree on terms that would insure permanent peace.

As a suggestion, Douglas turned to his plan for a North American customs union, or *Zollverein*. He was worried, among other things, about the free flow of goods on the Mississippi River, a concern that was close to the interest of his own section. "There can be no peace so long as there be any restriction, hindrance or encumbrance upon commerce, trade, transit, and intercourse which is not common to the citizens of both [sections]." Douglas drafted a proposal for the union of north and south for commercial purposes as a condition for political separation, complete with provisions for the establishment and enforcement of uniform economic regulations in the two countries.

Early in April, he described his proposal to William H. Russell, corre-

spondent of the London *Times,* who stopped in Washington on his tour
of the United States. Russell had been urged to talk with Douglas, and
one of the latter's friends, who had seen Russell in New York, hoped
that Douglas would "impress him as you can, particularly with your
views of our actual position." The two men first talked on April 1, the
day after Easter. "He is called the Little Giant," wrote Russell, "being
*modo bipeduli staturâ,* but his head entitled him to some recognition of
intellectual height." Douglas summarized for him the sequence of events
which led to the crisis. He spoke "for more than an hour . . . with a
vigor of thought and terseness of phrase which, even on such dreary and
uninviting themes as squatter sovereignty and the Kansas-Nebraska
question, interested a foreigner in the man and the subject." Russell
thought that Douglas seemed to sympathize with the south on questions
of slavery and territorial extension, but "he condemned altogether the
attempt to destroy the Union." Three days later Russell attended a dinner party, given by Douglas, at which Salmon P. Chase and Caleb
Smith, two members of Lincoln's cabinet, and John Forsyth, one of the
Confederate commissioners, were also guests. Mrs. Douglas, reported
Russell, "did the honors of her house with grace and charming good-
nature." After dinner, Douglas described his plan for a customs union
which, he thought, would settle the controversy between the north and
the south. "Few men speak better than Senator Douglas," Russell continued, "his words are well chosen, the flow of his ideas even and constant,
his intellect vigorous, and thoughts well cut, precise and vigorous."

In case of separation, Douglas suggested, the north must fight the
south "on the arena of free trade." The tariff must be altered and the duties lowered "from point to point, in proportion as the South bids against
the North for the commerce of Europe, till the reduction reaches such a
point that the South, forced to raise revenue for the actual expense of
Government, and unable to struggle against the superior wealth of the
North in such a contest, is obliged to come to an understanding with its
powerful competitor and to submit to a treaty of commerce which shall
include all of the States of the North American Continent." [16]

Douglas was apparently leaving no possibility unexplored. His erstwhile friend, the notorious George N. Sanders, by now an ardent supporter of secession, turned up in Montgomery where debate on the proposed Confederate Constitution was under way. Professing to be an
agent of Douglas', he argued against excluding free states from joining
the Confederacy. "The game now," wrote one of the southern delegates,

"is to reconstruct [the Federal Union] *under our Constitution.*" The scheme apparently had the support of Douglas' southern supporters, but it was strongly opposed by the ultras. Sanders may also have placed Douglas' proposal for a commercial union before the Montgomery convention. "We cannot deny that there is a Southern confederacy, *de facto,*" Douglas had told the Senate. "I regret it most profoundly; but I cannot deny the truth of the fact, painful, mortifying as it is." Perhaps he thought that the fact could be used to effect a restoration of the Union.[17]

Douglas continued to receive mail from friends in the deep south, but it only added to his feeling of helplessness. Those who watched his efforts to mend the Union were convinced that he misread southern feelings and failed to appreciate the depth of emotion that lay behind the secession movement. The separation was permanent, he was told; a reconstruction of the Union was not only undesirable, it was impossible. "No compromise on earth can ever unite the cotton states with the old Union." The possibility of war swept closer and closer. If Lincoln did not evacuate the forts, wrote one former Douglas editor in Georgia, the south would take them "or sacrifice many lives in the attempt." And if war comes, what would be the result? "Subjugation is impossible," warned a Louisianan, "you may desolate our cities—sweep our commerce from the sea & fill the South with mourners but subjugation is impossible." [18]

### iii

As Douglas labored through the winter months to save the Union, he could not ignore his role as a party leader. He had been struggling hard during the past years to wrest control of the Democratic party from its southern leadership and to restore it to a sound national basis. Only by resisting the sectional drift of the latter 1850's could the party fulfill its traditional role as a force for Union and nationality. His campaign for the presidency was to a large extent a campaign for undisputed leadership in the Democratic party. The magnitude of his support in the election, and the subsequent secession of the seven deep south states, brought him the position he sought, but only after disunion had become a reality. Not only the Union had to be restored, but the party had to be rebuilt, and Douglas saw these as wholly compatible tasks. Democracy and Union were still one in his mind.

Not all Democrats shared Douglas' point of view. During the disturbing months of the secession crisis, many rank-and-file party members were confused and uncertain of their future. They were shocked by the withdrawal of the cotton states and literally did not know where to turn. To embrace the cause of Union too vigorously and to denounce the course of the south too emphatically seemed dangerously close to an espousal of Republicanism. Southern Democrats had for years charged Douglas with selling out to the Republicans, and northern Democrats were sensitive to the charge. On the other hand, to support southern secession was unthinkable.

In their dilemma, Democrats looked to Douglas for guidance. From New York came word that Douglas Democrats were waiting for their "cue what to do and how to act." Several members of the New York legislature suggested a meeting with Douglas. The Democratic party, a border state man wrote bluntly, was dilapidated, a ruined old edifice and an empty shell. "The question then with you is," he added, "how may you save yourself and friends and walk out of this scrape and leave the Republicans as the only living tangible evidence and representatives of the mischief which has been done." [19]

Through his leadership in the search for compromise, Douglas made it abundantly clear that the party could stand on no other basis than a firm repudiation of the disunionists, a denial of the right of secession, and an unequivocal avowal of the Union. His stand was mirrored in the advice which McClernand sent to party leaders in Illinois. "If we become entangled with disunionism we will be lost as a party. . . . We must train the public mind to look upon disunion with horror." Under no circumstances, he continued, would Democrats agree to any arrangement that returned the southern ultras to positions of party leadership. That leadership must now be seated in the northwest. Conceding that the course followed by Republicans might place the Democracy in a delicate position, McClernand suggested that the party in Illinois follow Douglas by placing the extremists, both Republican and southern, in the same disunion camp. "Our true and only policy is . . . to stand for the Union, boldly & explicitly." The Democratic party should sever its relations with southern disunionists, but at the same time its support of the Union should not be viewed as an endorsement of the Republican administration. It was a distinction Douglas had been careful to make in his defense of Lincoln's inaugural address.

The full implications of the Democratic dilemma were revealed in January, when Illinois Democrats met in a state convention to chart their course during the secession crisis. Because the meeting would reflect Democratic attitudes in his own state, the convention was important to Douglas; its actions were closely watched in other states. Douglas was in close contact with state leaders before the meeting, regarding it not only as an opportunity to present a model that other states could follow, but also as a means of reassuring the border states. Sheahan proposed that resolutions for the convention be drafted in Washington by Douglas and the members of the Illinois congressional delegation. Five "trial" resolutions were submitted to the state legislature, after their consideration in several stormy sessions of the Democratic caucus, as a test of Douglas support. Among them were statements declaring the Union to be perpetual, favoring a national convention for proposing amendments to the Constitution, and denouncing political organizations that seemed to prefer party to country. Some Democrats balked at two of the resolutions, one that denied a constitutional right of secession and another that declared that the federal government had the power and duty to use all necessary means for the enforcement of the laws. It became apparent that secession had some sympathizers in the state. The chairman of the Democratic state committee appealed to Douglas: "if it is important that we should take that position . . . you and our other members must write *immediately* to *all* of our leading men." He added, "Our friends are terribly disorganized." [20]

On the eve of the convention, the *State Register* declared that "for peace, democrats should be—are—willing to concede much." The delegates assembled, however, in an atmosphere of bickering and disagreement. Two of them had written to Douglas insisting that if peaceable measures failed to restore the Union, the south should be allowed to depart in peace. Others, like the former Whig James W. Singleton, Douglas' adviser and legislative spokesman, drifted toward sympathy with secession. The resolutions committee, chaired by William A. Richardson, overrode the opposition and presented resolutions that reflected Douglas' position. They were unequivocal in their declaration for the Union and in their denial of the right of secession, although in the latter case the committee expressed an equal opposition to the northern personal liberty laws. The convention endorsed the efforts to save the Union by compromise, and it warned that "the employment of military force by the federal government to coerce submission of the seceding states, will inevitably plunge the country into civil war." The delegates further declared it "the duty and power of the federal government

through the civil authorities within the jurisdiction of the states to enforce the laws," but they denied that the government had any constitutional power to employ the military to execute the laws "except in aid of
the civil authorities."

Some Democrats felt that the resolutions did not go far enough in
committing the party to the cause of Union; others were not convinced
that their stand could be easily distinguished from that of the Republican party. One of Douglas' friends reported, "They were afraid if they
were for the Union & the enforcement of the laws, that they would be
aiding the Republican cause." Douglas' party, in directing its appeal to
conservative men throughout the nation—in the seceded states, the
border states, and the free states—followed a risky and sometimes uncertain path. It was necessary, for Douglas still hoped to use a strong, rebuilt Democratic party as an instrument for the restoration of the
Union. McClernand again admonished Democrats to remain independent of "black republicanism" and "to keep clear of fire-eating disunionism. Identification with either would be fatal to us as Democrats." [21]

Douglas received suggestions for party reorganization on an even
broader scale. It was not inconceivable, wrote several supporters, that
conservative Republicans would become disenchanted with Lincoln's
leadership and would willingly join with Douglas in a new party structure. The name of the party would have to be changed. Transform it
into "a great and powerful Union party," let the word get out that the
Democracy of old is dead, and the Republicans would be robbed of the
"flower of their army." With Lincoln's inauguration, the proposals for a
new party under Douglas' leadership, including both Democrats and Republicans, increased. A new two-party system would emerge: the "irrepressible conflict-coercion" organization, represented by Lincoln, and the
new Union party, combining conservatives from both the Republican and
Democratic ranks. The new party could adopt as a platform, "A reconstruction of the government upon principles which will allow the
seceded States to return." Douglas, wrote one follower, was the one to
organize this new party and to be "the Candidate in '64." Moves in this
direction were actually being made in some of the border states, where
members of the Douglas and Bell parties coalesced in new Union organizations. Douglas, however, was not interested at this point in trans-
forming the Democratic party into a vehicle that would be acceptable to
conservative Republicans; he would accept Republican support, as always, but on his own terms.[22]

As the nation continued its drift, Douglas became discouraged that he would be able to build a strong Democratic party resting on a solid Union basis. Slave state Democrats were increasingly wary of his stand; Republicans regarded his course in the Senate as nothing more than unjustified harassment. He confided to a friend that the country was moving toward a collision, and he was not able to do anything about it. His attempts to rally the Democracy had failed; "the party was broken up." [23]

iv

Douglas' hope that Lincoln would withdraw the federal troops from the two southern forts was dashed during the last days of March. The President made tentative plans for the reinforcement of Fort Sumter but linked them with his more definite purpose to strengthen Fort Pickens, which lay off the coast of Florida, near Pensacola. The members of his cabinet had, on more than one occasion, advised him to evacuate Fort Sumter in the interest of avoiding a clash with the south. Only the radical members, Salmon P. Chase and Montgomery Blair (whose views Douglas had hoped to neutralize), voted consistently in favor of an expedition to Sumter. On the day after the introduction of the Republican resolution in the Senate, Lincoln issued orders to make ready a sea expedition that could sail for Charleston harbor by April 6. On April 4, he wrote to Major Anderson that the expedition "will go forward," and two days later, after he had learned of the failure of the attempt to reinforce Fort Pickens, he sent an emissary with a letter to South Carolina's governor, describing the plans to land provisions at Fort Sumter. Soon afterward the ships assigned to the expedition left New York and sailed southward. On April 8, the *New-York Tribune* blared forth, "Fort Sumter To Be Provisioned," and two days later the editor stated "with positive certainty" that the object of the expedition was the relief of Fort Sumter.

The nation nervously awaited news of the clash that now seemed inevitable. Douglas waited also. Riding with his wife on a Washington street, he spotted Lincoln's Secretary of the Navy, former Democrat Gideon Welles. Leaping from his carriage, Douglas told Welles "in a very earnest and emphatic manner" that the south was determined on war and was about to assault Fort Sumter. Without disclosing names, he indicated that his information had come from an authentic and reliable source. Immediate and decisive measures should be taken, he advised

Welles; for the government to persist in its dilatory policy was to invite "a terrible civil war." What these measures should be, whether for war preparation or for a last-minute avoidance of conflict, Douglas did not elaborate. Together, the two men conveyed the information to Seward, although Douglas by this time had begun to doubt whether Seward had a realistic grasp of the situation's real gravity. On April 12, two days after their encounter, the bombardment of Fort Sumter began.[24]

Sunday, April 14, was a day intense with excitement and agitation in the nation's capital. Telegraphic dispatches announcing the surrender of Fort Sumter's garrison to the Confederate States had been received the night before. Anxious eyes were turned toward the White House in anticipation of the President's reaction. Sharing the anxiety was George Ashmun of Massachusetts, a former Congressman who had served as chairman of the Chicago convention of the Republican party. Ashmun decided late that Sunday afternoon to persuade Douglas to make a public demonstration of his support of the administration in order to encourage national confidence in Lincoln.

Ashmun spoke with Douglas for an hour at the latter's house, finally suggesting that the President would welcome an interview with him. Douglas was doubtful at first. "Mr. Lincoln," he told Ashmun, "has dealt hardly with me, in removing some of my friends from office, and I don't know as he wants my advice or aid." After further discussion, during which Ashmun was joined in his effort by Douglas' "beautiful and noble wife," Douglas agreed to call on the President.

Lincoln was alone at the White House when Douglas arrived. Drawing from his desk a draft of the proclamation he intended to issue the following day, Lincoln opened the conversation. Douglas concurred in the policy the President would pursue, although he suggested that, instead of calling for 75,000 volunteers, "I would make it 200,000." Moving to a map on the wall, Douglas indicated the principal strategic points which he thought should be strengthened at once: Fortress Monroe, Washington, Harper's Ferry, and Cairo. He told Lincoln of the possibility of trouble in moving troops across Maryland to Washington and suggested that they be brought by way of Havre de Grace and Annapolis. The two men conferred for nearly two hours, their interview marked by a "cordial feeling of a united, friendly, and patriotic purpose."

Douglas later penned a report of his discussion with the President which he released to the press. "The substance of the conversation," he wrote, "was that while Mr D was unalterably opposed to the administration on all its political issues, he was prepared to sustain the President in the exercise of all his constitutional functions to preserve the Union, and maintain the government, and defend the Federal Capital. A firm policy and prompt action was necessary." Striking a note of concord, he added that he and Lincoln "spoke of the present & future, without reference to the past."

Douglas was more blunt and outspoken with a friend whom he met in the telegraph office. When asked what course he thought the President should pursue, he replied, "If I were President, I'd convert or hang them *all* within forty-eight hours. . . . I've known Mr. Lincoln a longer time than you have, or than the country has; he'll come out right, and we will all stand by him." When John W. Forney encountered Douglas on Pennsylvania Avenue and asked him, "What is now to be done?" he answered, "We must fight for our country and forget all differences." [25]

For Douglas, the attack on Fort Sumter ended all possibility that the Union could be restored peaceably. His efforts, begun so many months before, to forestall the separation of the south and north, to bind the sections with the bonds of party, to devise and implement a plan of conciliation and compromise, and to avoid an armed collision, all had now met with final failure. Of the three alternative lines of action which he had outlined to the Senate, only the last, the worst, remained. War was now a reality. On April 15, Lincoln issued his proclamation calling for 75,000 state militiamen to suppress the rebellion against the government and summoning Congress into a special session on July 4 to consider further measures that might be necessary. The outbreak of hostilities offered a new arena for Douglas, and his actions on April 14 indicated how surely he moved into it. His responsibilities, as he saw them, were with the government.

The report of Douglas' conversation with the President was published throughout the country. His position was lauded by Republicans and Democrats alike. "Let party lines go," wrote a Vermonter, *"Save our government."* Another writer believed that Douglas would now be consulted by Lincoln and that his "wisdom & large experience in public affairs" would influence the President's policy. A friend from Maryland assured him that that state would not secede, that he would fight Black Republicanism in the Union, not out of it. "We are satisfied that you are free of the crime of advising war & bloodshed, but as a loyal citizen you maintain the integrity of the Union & the majesty of Government even when administered on wrong principles." [26]

Douglas' announcement, however, fell hard on the border states, where Unionists still struggled against secession. He received urgent inquiries seeking to confirm the report that he would stand with the President. One of them, from St. Louis, elicited an immediate reply. "Without having been consulted or indorsing any particular measure," he explained, "I am for my country against all assailants." Finding the meaning of the response unclear, another St. Louisan wired Douglas, "Do you endorse Lincoln's war policy? Missouri will not." And again, Douglas sent back an immediate answer. "I deprecate war, but if it must come I am with my country and for my country, under all circumstances, and in every contingency. Individual policy must be subordinated to public safety." This exchange, too, received wide publicity.

Border state Unionists were angry, and they charged Douglas with undercutting their efforts. A Virginian was mortified at the news that Douglas was "now aiding and advising the Administration at Washington to attempt to carry out . . . coercion." He warned that "future generations will condemn you for the course you are now pursuing." Another friend recalled the hope that Douglas men in the north and conservative men in the border states "could by concert prevent a civil war." Since the publication of Douglas' statements, however, it was clear that the Douglas party would unite "with the abolitionists, in carrying on Mr. Lincoln's unholy, infernal war upon the South." No one was more upset and dejected than Thomas H. Gilmer, who had been working tirelessly on behalf of Douglas and the Union in Virginia. "The period for *words* is past," he wrote,

> The time of *war* is on hand. And may the God of battles *crush to the earth and consign to eternal perdition*, Mr. Lincoln, his cabinet and "aiders and abettors," in this cruel, needless, *corrupt betrayal* of the conservative men of the South. We would have saved the country, but for the fatuity and cowardice of this infernal Administration. . . . I hope you will not aid or countenance so detestable a *parvenue*. Should you do so, time will never heal the wound which you will thus have inflicted on as true friends as any man ever had. God forbid that I may ever live to see the day, when *S. A. Douglas* can stoop so low as to take by the hand, *such . . . as A. Lincoln and his cabinet*.

Conservative sentiment in the border states evaporated quickly, and Lincoln's call for troops was received with indignation and resentment. On the day that Gilmer wrote Douglas, April 17, Virginia adopted a secession ordinance. The machinery worked a little more slowly but no less effectively in other states. Arkansas seceded on May 6. On the same day the Tennessee legislature sent a secession ordinance to the people for ratification early in June, and on May 20 North Carolina left the Union.[27]

The fall of Fort Sumter deepened the Democratic dilemma. It became more difficult for many northern Democrats to distinguish between support of the Union and support of the Republican party. In Illinois, most Democrats followed Douglas' lead in urging bold action by the government against the south. Meetings attended by members of both parties were held throughout the state, and resolutions were adopted pledging an undivided support to the government. Democratic Congressmen John A. McClernand and Isaac Morris took strong ground "against treason and traitors, without a 'but' or an 'if.' " Lanphier was quick to join them.

Other members of Douglas' party in Illinois were hesitant and equivocal. Some held back, were silent, or "even talked secession"; others denounced Lincoln's proclamation as "a lawless act of usurpation." Sympathy for the south, it was reported, prevailed in the southern part of the state. As early as February, Douglas had been warned that secession sentiment there was on the increase. Richardson was conspicuously absent from the rallies and meetings, and he did not make his views public until early May, when he weakly urged that "every citizen owes it as a solemn duty to obey the law, to support the constitution, to repel invasion, and defend the flag." Singleton loudly opposed his chief's position, and southern Illinois Congressman John A. Logan, wavering in his attitude toward the crisis, strongly disapproved Douglas' course. Democratic Congressman James C. Robinson agreed with Logan "that the peace policy is the true policy for us." Another southern Illinoisan, a member of the legislature, believed that most of the Democratic members opposed the President's policy. He objected to the cry of some Democrats and Republicans that party considerations should be pushed aside in the interest of patriotism. "They are trying to grease us and swallow us."

Once again Douglas received appeals for advice. "Many who profess to be Union men," wrote one, "hesitate about coming out boldly against treason, fearing to be hereafter classed as Republicans. Will you not say, to all of us who are your *friends, first, last & all the time,* to stand by our Government, and sink party for the present." Douglas' reply was not long in coming.[28]

The Illinois legislature had been summoned to meet in special session on April 23, and Lanphier urged Douglas to be in Springfield when it met. According to a story told five years later, Douglas called on Lincoln again and apprised him of Lanphier's appeal. He offered to remain in Washington if needed, but the President agreed that he could probably do more good in Illinois. Whether the story is true or not, Douglas was anxious to carry his message to northwestern Democrats. In his effort to build the Democratic party into a strong but loyal opposition party, his own northwest would, as always, provide a key element. He later told an acquaintance that he had "come home to arouse the people in favor of the Union, so that all the people of Illinois should be united in favor of the country."

With Adele at his side, Douglas left Washington by train; it would be his last trip west. The capital he left, his only real home for the last eighteen years and the stage on which his career had unfolded, had all the appearances of a beleaguered city. Communication with the north was threatened; Confederate flags flew on the opposite bank of the Potomac, and rumors flew that southern soldiers were gathering for an attack on Washington. A local militia force had been hastily mustered to defend the city. Many residents had left for the north. On April 19, just before Douglas departed, troops of the Sixth Massachusetts, moving to reinforce Washington, had been attacked by a mob in Baltimore. The capitol itself was fortified. The Pennsylvania soldiers were quartered in the House chamber, the Massachusetts troops in the Senate chamber. Where Senators had but recently strained to avert civil war, soldiers now lounged. Privates sat at the Senators' desks, writing letters home.

The Baltimore and Ohio Railroad which carried Douglas and his wife westward ran for over a hundred miles through Virginia. The small arsenal town of Harper's Ferry, where the trains crossed the Potomac, had been seized by the Virginia militia the day after the state seceded. When Douglas' train arrived, it was halted and searched. Some of the soldiers recognized him and spoke of detaining him. Douglas quickly replied that a sojourn at Harper's Ferry might not be disagreeable, but he warned that, if he were kept prisoner, a force would soon arrive from the west larger than any that had ever been in Virginia before.[29]

Because of the delay at Harper's Ferry, Douglas missed a connection at the Ohio River town of Bellair, opposite Wheeling, and was forced to spend a day there. That evening he appeared on the balcony of the local hotel and addressed the citizens of both Ohio and Virginia who had gathered to greet him. He was gratified, he said, to find people on both sides of the Ohio River cheering the flag of their country, the "emblem of peace and union, and of constitutional liberty." The northwest could never recognize the right of states bordering the Atlantic, the Gulf of Mexico, or the Pacific to separate "from the Union of our fathers." Douglas' concern was with the disastrous consequences disunion would bring to travel and commerce in the nation's heartland. If the Gulf states were allowed to depart, how long would it be before New York "may set up for herself"? "The very existence of the people in this great valley," he emphasized, "depends upon maintaining inviolate and forever that great right secured by the constitution, of freedom of trade, of transit, and of commerce, from the centre of the continent to the ocean that surrounds it." This great valley, Douglas insisted, must never be divided, for it was "one and indissoluble." He denounced the "new system of resistance by the sword and bayonet to the results of the ballot-box" that would convert the nation into petty little confederacies.

The question, Douglas insisted, was not solely one of Union or disunion. It was also a question of order, stability, and "the peace of communities." The whole social system, he believed, was threatened with destruction. "I have almost exhausted strength, and voice, and life, in the last two years, in my efforts to point out the dangers upon which we were rushing." There was now no time to inquire into the causes of the crisis. "Unite as a band of brothers," he told the audience, "and rescue your Government . . . and your country from the enemy who have been the authors of your calamity."

Douglas repeated the same message at other stops along the way. In Columbus, he spoke from the statehouse steps, urging the citizens to stand by the flag. Would the people permit traitors to destroy the constitutionally elected government, he asked, or would they suppress the rebellion? He reiterated his intention to defend the political and property rights of the south; he would resist any attempt to interfere with southern domestic institutions. But the issue, he maintained, was no longer a question affecting the Negro. It was a question of the survival of the nation itself. "We must rally to the defense of the Government—to the reestablishment of the Union." The Democrats who had gathered "to get some light as to their duty" walked away reassured. Douglas spoke again in Indianapolis, where he conveyed the same sense of urgency, admonishing the people to turn aside from partisan quarrels and join together in support of the Union.[30]

Douglas arrived in Springfield early on the morning of April 25. The

Illinois capital, like Washington, had a martial spirit about it. Upon his arrival he addressed a company of volunteers from Vandalia who had come in on the same train. A short time later he returned to the station from his hotel and, standing in his open carriage, welcomed a company from northern Illinois, bidding them Godspeed in the work they were about to commence. The streets of the town were filled with soldiers, and one Democrat grumbled that it was unsafe for anyone to question the President's policy. Members of the legislature, apprised of Douglas' arrival, quickly adopted a joint resolution inviting him to address the assembly that evening.

During the day, Douglas talked with conservative Republican Orville H. Browning, whom he had beaten for Congress in 1843, and impressed him with the need for harmony and concert of action between Democrats and Republicans. Together the two men later met with Governor Richard Yates, Trumbull, Gustave Koerner, and others; at their behest Douglas and Browning "came to an understanding" which they hoped would result in the unanimous support of the various military bills pending in the legislature.[31]

Early in the evening, legislators and Springfield citizens crowded into the hall of representatives in the statehouse. When Douglas entered the chamber he was greeted by a long and deafening ovation. His speech was brief, as Douglas speeches went, but its effect was powerful. At ease among his constituents, he was more explicit and personal than on earlier occasions, speaking with an earnestness and emotion that carried his audience "to the highest point of patriotic excitement." Men were said to have wept and cheered by turns, and when someone entered the hall bearing an American flag the assemblage erupted in a frenzy of shouting and clapping.

His heart, Douglas began, was "filled with sadness and grief" as he contemplated the condition of his country. "For the first time since the adoption of the Federal Constitution," he declared, "a wide-spread conspiracy exists to destroy the best government the sun of heaven ever shed its rays upon." The dangers which threatened the nation were real and fraught with peril. Hostile armies were marching on the capital, the "piratical flag" had been unfurled against the commerce of the United States, the navigation "of our great river" was obstructed, and hostile batteries were planted on its banks. No one who had been in Washington during the last week, he contended, would consider his picture overdrawn. "A war of aggression and of extermination is being waged against the government established by our fathers." For what cause? Southern rights, he insisted, had never been more secure. For the first time in history, there was no congressional restriction on slavery anywhere in the country; the Fugitive Slave Act had never been enforced with more fidelity.

How then must this war be met? "So long as there was a hope of peaceful solution," Douglas asserted, "I prayed and implored for compromise." No effort had been spared, no opportunity missed. But when his efforts failed, only one course remained—to rally under the flag and around the government. Douglas' words, as he recalled his career and his lifelong devotion to the Union, were sadly reminiscent, a valedictory for both his country and himself. "It has been my daily avocation, six months in the year, for eighteen years, to walk into that marble building, and from its portico to survey a prosperous, happy and united country on both sides of the Potomac." He had been, he believed, as "thoroughly national" in his opinions and actions as any other man. If there had been error in his course, it was in leaning too far to the southern section of the Union against his own. He had never pandered to the prejudices of his section against the interests of the south, and, he declared, he would not now sanction any warfare upon the constitutional rights or domestic institutions of the southern people.

"The first duty of an American citizen," Douglas continued, "is obedience to the constitution and laws of the country." In the crisis, party creeds and platforms must be set aside, party organizations and partisanship must be dispensed with. Republicans, he warned, would not be true to their country if they made political capital out of the country's misfortunes. For the Democrats, Douglas had a special appeal. "Do not allow the mortification growing out of defeat in a partisan struggle," he advised, "and the elevation of a party to power that we firmly believed to be dangerous to the country—do not let that convert you from patriots to traitors to your native land." He hoped that no one would misunderstand his motives. "So far as any of the partisan questions are concerned," he assured his audience, "I stand in equal, irreconcilable, and undying opposition both to the Republicans and Secessionists." But not until the country has been rescued from its assailants would it be proper "for each of us to resume our respective political positions, according to our convictions of public duty." "Give me a country first, that my children may live in peace; then we will have a theatre for our party organizations to operate upon."

He urged every man to take a stand against this "crime against constitutional freedom, and the hopes of the friends of freedom throughout the wide world." The shortest way to peace, he declared, "is the most stupendous and unanimous preparation for war. The greater the unanimity, the less blood will be shed. The more prompt and energetic the movement, and the more imposing in numbers, the shorter will be the struggle." In conclusion, Douglas revealed the heavy impact the events of the spring had had upon him:

> I have struggled almost against hope to avert the calamities of war, and to effect a re-union and reconciliation with our brethren of the South. I yet hope it may be done, but I am not able to point out to you how it may be effected. . . .
>
> I see no path of ambition open in a bloody struggle for triumph over my own countrymen. There is no path of ambition open for me in a divided country, after having so long served a united and glorious country. Hence, whatever we may do must be the result of conviction of patriotic duty—the duty that we owe to ourselves, to our posterity, and to the friends of constitutional liberty and self-government throughout the world.
>
> My friends, I can say no more. To discuss these topics is the most painful duty of my life. It is with a sad heart—with a grief that I have never before experienced, that I have to contemplate this fearful struggle; but I believe in my conscience that it is a duty we owe ourselves, and our children, and our God, to protect this government and that flag from every assailant, be he who he may.[32]

The effect of Douglas' address was electric. Republicans vied with Democrats in their praise of his stand.

Douglas had more to say. On the day after his speech, he told Browning that "we ought to meet the traitors beyond the line, and fight the battles on their own soil." He was persuaded that the crisis stemmed from a conspiracy of southern leaders, and he informed Browning that plans had been made before the election to depose Lincoln if he should win. Douglas was convinced that Buchanan himself was involved. His bitterness toward the south mounted. His defense of southerners and southern rights during the 1850's, which he alluded to in his Springfield speech regretfully as a possible error, had been betrayed by the southerners' attempt to destroy the Union he loved so well.

On May 1, Douglas was welcomed back to his home city of Chicago like a conquering hero. Thousands of people gathered at the depot of the Chicago, Alton and St. Louis Railroad to await his arrival. Several bands entertained with music. When he stepped off the train a deafening cheer was raised, a parade was formed, and he was escorted through the streets to the National Hall, where he was scheduled to speak. "Partisan differences and the hot enmities of the old time," commented the Chicago *Tribune,* were forgotten, and both Republicans and Democrats united to honor the returning Senator.

Douglas returned to his criticism of the south. "I have struggled long for a peaceful solution of the difficulty," he contended. "I have not only tendered those States what was theirs of right, but I have gone to the very extreme of magnanimity." With what result? "The return we receive is War." He denied again that southerners had any legitimate grievances against the government. "The slavery question is a mere excuse," he continued, "The election of Lincoln is a mere pretext." The secession of the southern states resulted from "an enormous conspiracy" that was formed long before the last presidential election. He called on all people to resist secession to the utmost. Once secession is recognized, government is dissolved and the social order destroyed. "You have inaugurated anarchy in its worst form, and will shortly experience all the horrors of the French Revolution."

"There are only two sides to the question," Douglas emphasized. "Every man must be for the United States or against it. There can be no neutrals in this war, *only patriots—or traitors."* [33]

Douglas and his wife took their usual rooms at the Tremont House and prepared for a much needed rest. The hotel, at the corner of Lake and Dearborn Streets, had served as Douglas' Chicago home for several years. Although he had erected a cottage on his lakeshore property, it was rented to a tenant; his plans to build a permanent home in Chicago still awaited fruition. He now could look forward to two months of inactivity before the special session would meet on July 4, time enough to recoup his strength and map out a future course. Douglas ended his journey amid reports that he would soon be commissioned a major general by the President. He even received letters of application for positions on his staff if the appointment materialized; his friends were disturbed by the possibility that he would leave the Senate to assume a military role in the contest. The country needed him in the councils of government, not in the field. When Lincoln was asked to verify the rumor, he replied that he had not considered appointing Douglas to a military position. He added, however, that if generals were to be appointed from civil life, there were many who would be inferior to Douglas. [34]

Douglas was still concerned with the attitude that prevailed among some Democrats, in spite of the enthusiastic reception that was accorded his public statements. On April 29, he reported to Lincoln that "the state of feeling here and in some parts of our State [is] much less satisfactory than I could have desired or expected when I arrived." The information he received from local party leaders added to his disquietude. There was still hesitation among members of his party. As the Republicans continued to lavish their praise on Douglas, some Democrats began to look upon the Little Giant with skepticism and suspicion. The chairman of the Democratic state committee, Virgil Hickox, noted that members of the party in Illinois "distrust him on account of the great love that the Republicans profess now to have for him." They saw a discrepancy between the stand he took in the Senate on Lincoln's inaugural, his assurances that the President's policy would be one of peace, and his current support of reunion by force. "The democrats here have been educated by reading his [Douglas'] speeches to believe that Mr Lincoln has no constitutional right to pursue his present course," wrote Hickox to Douglas' father-in-law. "Hence they think the Judge in sustaining what is really thus the cause of his country & the flag of the Union, has gone over to the republicans." To remove these doubts, Hickox urged Douglas "to make a full explanation, either in a speech to be published or in a letter."

Douglas responded with an elaboration of his position in a letter to Hickox. "It seems that some of my friends," he began, "are unable to comprehend the difference between arguments used in favor of an equitable compromise with the hope of averting the horrors of war and those urged in support of the Government and Flag of our Country when war is being waged against the United States with the avowed purpose of producing a permanent disruption of the Union and a total destruction of its government." The issue now before the nation, he insisted, was not a party question, but was simply a question of "Government or no Government." He was not, as everyone supposed, in the confidence of the Lincoln administration. "I am neither the supporter of the partisan policy nor the apologist for the errors of the Administration. My previous relations to them remain unchanged." But he hoped the time would never come when he would not be willing to sacrifice his party feeling "for the honor and integrity of the country." In his final words of advice to his followers, Douglas wrote, "If we hope to regain and perpetuate the ascendancy of our party we should never forget that a man cannot be a true Democrat unless he is a loyal patriot."

Hickox expressed reservations about the letter—"What he has written is all right but is only in substance what he said in his speech here and does not accomplish what we desired"—but he forwarded it nonetheless to Douglas' father-in-law, James Madison Cutts, with instructions to have it published in the Washington newspapers. Shortly afterward, however, Hickox and Douglas conferred and decided to withhold publication. "Time alone will remove the impression on the true democrats minds, and we concluded that we had better let it take its course." Hickox wired Cutts, but the latter ignored the request. Douglas' letter was published in the *National Intelligencer* on May 17. It was his last statement to his party.[35]

V

The pressures of the secession winter had taken their toll on the Little Giant. He had not had a sustained respite from political activity for a long time. Physically run down, he had also suffered great emotional strain. The early months of 1861 were a time of anguish and frustration as he fought persistently and fruitlessly against disunion. With the failure of compromise and the outbreak of civil war, he fell into a severe depression and, while he was still able to whip up the enthusiasm of his audiences, his public statements revealed the sadness and grief with which he watched the Union die. Douglas' faith in his nation and in its democratic institutions was deep and fundamental to his thinking; his political career had been built upon an abiding belief in the progress, the manifest destiny, of the American people. Since the last years of the 1850's, however, he had had to shift his efforts from the promotion and expansion of America and its institutions to the task of preserving the very unity of the nation itself. It was a crushing blow, not only to this task but also to his faith in America's destiny, to witness the breakup of the Union and to stand by helplessly as the country rushed toward civil war. All he had worked and lived for seemed to crash about him.

Douglas also had more mundane concerns. During the last few years, financial pressures had increased. His senatorial campaign in 1858 and the extensive presidential tour in 1860 had plunged him deeply into debt. Much of his property in Chicago had been disposed of, and what was left was heavily mortgaged. He carried a heavy burden of indebtedness and had difficulty meeting his obligations. A last remaining source of income was the Mississippi plantation which he managed on behalf of his sons. Early in April, he wrote to his partner, James A. McHatton, of his need for money. "I am exceedingly oppressed for the want of money, and do not know where I can get enough to pay my little Bills and current expenses, unless it be got from our sales of cotton." He hoped that McHatton could send him $2000, but $1000 would do to relieve his "immediate necessities." McHatton's reply was not encouraging. The times were hard and cotton prices were low, but more importantly, the plantation was now in a foreign country and McHatton believed that "every house in N [ew]. O [rleans]. will stop payment." McHatton, who supported the Confederacy, wrote from the plantation that the people in the vicinity were "abusing" Douglas for his recent speeches. A Memphis newspaper proposed that Douglas' property be seized and sold "for the purpose of defending the south in a war which he and Lincoln has involved the country." [36]

On the evening of his reception and speech in Chicago, May 1, Douglas complained that he was not well, but he thought that a rest before his return to Washington would set matters right. He seemed to have a cold at first, but a fever set in and a physician was called. On May 10, he was forced to dictate his letter to Hickox to a secretary, being deprived of the use of his arms by a severe and painful attack of inflammatory rheumatism. He had been confined to his bed since the early part of the month. Few expressed concern that he might not recover, although Sheahan informed Lanphier on the 17th that "Douglas is very ill, and I am afraid is past all surgery." Douglas was a fighter, noted the editor of the *Tribune,* with a "constitution of wonderful recuperative force" and a will that had the strength of iron. He rallied, and on May 19 he was allowed to leave his room briefly to go into the open air. The next day his condition worsened, his physicians were hurriedly summoned, and there was some fear that he would die. Douglas' Washington physician, Dr. Thomas Miller, arrived, accompanied by Adele's mother and brother. Daniel P. Rhodes, a cousin from Cleveland, also arrived.

Douglas' illness was diagnosed as acute rheumatism. He had suffered this before, enduring prolonged and painful periods of illness particularly after times of unusual stress and crisis. This time, however, his strength was sapped and he was in a state of fatigue. The rheumatism assumed "a typhoid character" and was further complicated by an ulcerated sore throat, again an ailment with which he had had to contend before. "Torpor of the liver" and constipation were soon added to the other symptoms. Douglas had always smoked cigars heavily, and he drank more than was good for him, contributing perhaps to the difficulties in his throat and liver. From the early stages of his illness his mind wandered, and he alternated between periods of delirium and lucidity. The national crisis preyed on his mind. "Why do we stand still?" he called out on one occasion, "Let us press on! Let us to Alexandria quick!" At another time as one of his physicians "was administering a blister," Douglas asked, "What are you doing?" When told, he replied, "Stop, there are twenty against me, the measure is defeated."

Bulletins describing Douglas' condition were published daily in the press. One day he would sink and hope for his recovery was lost; the next he would rally and the danger seemed over. In one of his rational periods, he assured those around his bedside that he knew his constitution better than they and he was confident he should recover. On May 31 it appeared that Douglas was out of danger, but that afternoon "a bloody flux set in" and he declined rapidly. Hundreds of people gathered at the Tremont House for the latest word. On June 2, he seemed better, was rational, and appeared refreshed. At Adele's request, he was visited by Roman Catholic Bishop James Duggan, who asked him if he had ever been baptized according to the rites of any church. Douglas' reply was "Never." When the Bishop asked him further if he desired "to have mass said after the ordinances of the holy Catholic church," he responded, "No, sir; when I do I will communicate with you freely."

Early on the morning of June 3, it was apparent that Douglas' condition had worsened. His physicians—four from Chicago and Dr. Miller from Washington—conferred, and they agreed that the end was at hand. Adele and Rhodes, who had kept constant vigil, were at the bedside. Bishop Duggan returned, but Douglas again dismissed him. When asked if he desired the ministrations of any other clergyman, he replied negatively. Shortly after sunrise, as he was propped up on his pillows so that he could feel the fresh morning air, he suddenly uttered the words, "Death! Death! Death!"

Moving closer and placing her arm around his neck, Adele asked Douglas if he had any message for his sons, Robby and Stevie. "Tell them," he replied, "to obey the laws and support the Constitution of the United States." He then lapsed into a quiet although conscious state. Four hours later, at nine in the morning, Douglas died. He was only forty-eight years old.[37]

The news of Douglas' death spread quickly. Although it had been expected for days, it still fell with stunning effect. The bell in the Court House began to toll, flags were lowered to half-mast, and black drapery appeared on business fronts. Busts, portraits, and statuettes of Douglas, draped in black, were placed in shop windows; street cars, drays, and express wagons carried signs of mourning. The Board of Trade and the courts adjourned at an early hour, and the city's banks closed. People gathered quietly at the newspaper offices to read the latest bulletin. The scene was repeated in countless towns and cities throughout the nation. In Canandaigua, New York, Douglas' mother was overwhelmed with grief. The news was immediately telegraphed to the President. The White House and the Department buildings were draped in mourning, and many of the government offices closed. Secretary of War Simon Cameron issued an order directing all military units to observe a period of mourning for Douglas.

Douglas' body was removed to nearby Bryan Hall, where it lay in state; the Chicago Light Guard was posted as the guard of honor. For two days, a continuous stream of people, in double file, passed through to look on Douglas' face. Adele expressed the wish that her husband be buried in Washington, where their infant daughter lay. There was an immediate reaction. From Springfield, Governor Yates, with Lyman Trumbull, McClernand, Koerner, and several others, wired the mayor of Chicago that Douglas' remains ought not to be taken from the state. "Illinoisans claim a common interest in his fame & are unwilling that one whose life has been closely identified with the interests of the state should in death be separated from it." A committee was formed to wait on members of Douglas' family. William A. Richardson talked privately with Adele and later reported that she had acquiesced in the desire to bury Douglas in Illinois. She asked that the burial service be conducted by the Roman Catholic Bishop, inasmuch as Douglas had never affiliated with any particular faith.

Douglas' funeral was scheduled for Friday, June 7, in order to allow his sons time to reach Chicago from their Georgetown school. On the night before, members of Chicago's Masonic lodges, disturbed by the announcement that Bishop Duggan would conduct the funeral service, gathered in Bryan Hall to perform their own ceremony. On the morning of the seventh, the procession took form. Sixty-four pallbearers preceded the ornate hearse, which was followed by carriages carrying members of the family. Sixteen military companies were followed by public officials, members of organizations, and citizens. Five thousand people marched from the Bryan House to Douglas' lakeshore property, just south of the city limits, as church bells tolled and gun salutes were fired. The graveside ceremony was simple; there were no religious rites. Bishop Duggan delivered a brief eulogy. Douglas' last resting place was a temporary brick tomb on a slight rise overlooking Lake Michigan and, to the north across the sweep of shoreline, the city in which he had made his home. It was the site where he had hoped to erect a permanent residence some day.[38]

Douglas became the subject for countless eulogies throughout the land, as friends and foes alike hailed and extolled him. None, however, summed up his career so well as Douglas himself, in words he delivered in July 1849, on the death of President Polk: "He was the partisan of a principle—of a system of measures and policy which he believed to be essential to the purity and perpetuity of our republican institutions. Believing this, he consecrated his life to the cause, and staked his fortunes on the result." [39]

# Notes

## ABBREVIATIONS AND SHORT TITLES

*AHR*    *American Historical Review*

*CG*    *Congressional Globe*

CHS    Chicago Historical Society

*CWAL*    Roy P. Basler *et al.* (eds.), *The Collected Works of Abraham Lincoln* (9 vols., New Brunswick, N.J., 1953)

Douglas Papers, Chicago    Stephen A. Douglas Papers, University of Chicago Library

Douglas Family Papers, Greensboro    Stephen A. Douglas Papers, in the possession of the Martin F. Douglas Family, Greensboro, N.C.

DU    Duke University Library, Durham, N.C.

HSP    Historical Society of Pennsylvania, Philadelphia.

IHS    Illinois Historical Survey, University of Illinois, Urbana

IND    Indiana Historical Society, Indianapolis

ISHL    Illinois State Historical Library, Springfield

ISL    Indiana State Library, Indianapolis

*JISHS*    *Journal of the Illinois State Historical Society*

*JSH*    *Journal of Southern History*

KSHS    Kansas State Historical Society, Topeka

LC    Library of Congress, Washington, D.C.

*Letters*    Robert W. Johannsen (ed.), *The Letters of Stephen A. Douglas* (Urbana, 1961)

MHS    Missouri Historical Society, St. Louis

*MVHR*    *Mississippi Valley Historical Review*

NA    National Archives, Washington, D.C.

NCDAH    North Carolina Department of Archives and History, Raleigh

SHC    Southern Historical Collection, University of North Carolina, Chapel Hill

*TISHS*    *Transactions of the Illinois State Historical Society*

UG        University of Georgia Library, Athens
UV        University of Virginia Library, Charlottesville
WLC       William L. Clements Library, Ann Arbor, Mich.
WRHS      Western Reserve Historical Society, Cleveland, Ohio

## CHAPTER I

1   *Rutland Herald,* Aug. 2, 1860; Brandon *Northern Visitor,* Aug. 2, 1860; Alvin P. Stauffer, "Douglas in Vermont," *Vermont History,* XXVIII (Oct. 1960), 262.

2   Brandon *Northern Visitor,* Aug. 2, 1860; [Charles Spooner Forbes], "Illustrious Vermonters: Stephen Arnold Douglas," *The Vermonter,* II (Jan. 1897), 99.

3   *Springfield* (Mass.) *Republican,* July 21, 1860.

4   Autobiographical Sketch, Sept. 1, 1838, *Letters,* 57.

5   Timothy Dwight, *Travels in New-England and New-York* (4 vols., New Haven, 1821), II, 413; David M. Ludlum, *Social Ferment in Vermont, 1791–1850* (New York, 1939), 14–15, 29, 48; Zadock Thompson, *History of Vermont: Natural, Civil and Statistical* (Burlington, Vt., 1853), 117.

6   Thompson, *History of Vermont,* 95–96; William A. Robinson, *Jeffersonian Democracy in New England* (New Haven, 1916), 159.

7   The Douglass family name was spelled with a double "s" until 1846, when Stephen A. Douglas dropped the final letter. Except for references to Stephen A. Douglas, the old spelling has been retained. Material in the following paragraphs has been drawn from Charles Henry James Douglas (ed.), *A Collection of Family Records, With Biographical Sketches and Other Memoranda of Various Families and Individuals Bearing the Name Douglas or Allied to Families of That Name* (Providence, 1879).

8   Both of Douglas' grandmothers, Martha Arnold Douglass and Sarah Arnold Fisk, were said to have been descendants of William Arnold, an associate of Roger Williams' in Rhode Island. Douglas' older sister, Sarah Arnold, had been born on October 29, 1811.

9   Autobiographical Sketch, Sept. 1, 1838, *Letters,* 57. According to tradition, Douglas was sitting in his father's lap before an open fire when the final seizure came. Douglas fell into the fire, from which he was rescued immediately by a neighbor. See letter of Horatio L. Wait, June 14, 1911, in Edward S. Marsh (ed.), *Stephen A. Douglas: A Memorial* (Brandon, Vt., 1914), 35.

10   Abby Maria Hemenway (ed.), *The Vermont Historical Gazetteer: A Magazine Embracing a History of Each Town, Civil, Ecclesiastical, Biographical and Military* (5 vols., Claremont, N.H., 1877), III, 457, 471–72; Brandon *Vermont Telegraph,* Oct. 6, 1829; Probate Court Records, Rutland County, Vt., Vol. XIII, *passim,* Public Records Division, Montpelier, Vt.; Beriah Douglas to Stephen A. Douglas, June 10, 1832, Douglas Family Papers, Greensboro, N.C.; Douglas to Julius N. Granger, March 11, 1834, *Letters,* 5.

11   Autobiographical Sketch, Sept. 1, 1838, *Letters,* 57.

12   Theodore Johnson, "Did Stephen Douglas Attend the Arnold District

School?," *Vermont Quarterly,* XX (Oct. 1952), 306–7; [Charles Spooner Forbes], "Illustrious Vermonters: Stephen Arnold Douglas," *The Vermonter,* II (Jan. 1897), 94–95; Frank E. Stevens, "Life of Stephen Arnold Douglas," *JISHS,* XVI (Oct. 1923–Jan. 1924), 257–58.

13   "Reminiscences of Stephen A. Douglas," *Atlantic Monthly,* VIII (Aug. 1861), 205; [Forbes], "Illustrious Vermonters: Stephen Arnold Douglas," *Vermonter,* II, 95; *New York Times,* Aug. 2, 1860.

14   Autobiographical Sketch, Sept. 1, 1838, *Letters,* 57; Correspondence of the *Troy Whig,* New York *Herald,* July 14, 1860.

15   The principal source for this version, repeated by many of Douglas' early biographers, was Henry G. Wheeler, *History of Congress, Biographical and Political: Comprising Memoirs of Members of the Congress of the United States, Drawn from Authentic Sources* (2 vols., New York, 1848), I, 60–61. Allen Johnson (*Stephen A. Douglas: A Study in American Politics* [New York, 1908], 4) suggested that the information for Wheeler's essay was supplied by Douglas himself. The more credible version has been based on Douglas' autobiography, written ten years later, and on the recollections of his sister Sarah, who recalled the circumstances of Douglas' leaving home in a newspaper interview in 1860.

16   Autobiographical Sketch, Sept. 1, 1838, *Letters,* 57–58; Wheeler, *History of Congress,* I, 62; *History of Lee County* [Illinois], *Together with Biographical Matter, Statistics, Etc.* (Chicago, 1881), 194.

17   Autobiographical Sketch, Sept. 1, 1838, *Letters,* 58; Wheeler, *History of Congress,* I, 63; James W. Sheahan, *The Life of Stephen A. Douglas* (New York, 1860), 6; Nathaniel Harris to Douglas, March 28, 1858, Douglas Papers, Chicago.

18   "Reminiscences of Douglas," *Atlantic Monthly,* VIII, 206; Autobiographical Sketch, Sept. 1, 1838, *Letters,* 58; Thompson, *History of Vermont,* 143; Stevens, "Douglas," *JISHS,* XVI, 262.

19   Ludlum, *Social Ferment in Vermont,* 201–2; Lewis D. Stilwell, "Migration from Vermont (1776–1860)," *Proceedings of the Vermont Historical Society,* V (1937), 191–92.

20   Paul M. Angle (ed.), *Created Equal? The Complete Lincoln-Douglas Debates of 1858* (Chicago, 1958), 228–29.

21   Horatio Gates Spafford, *A Gazetteer of the State of New York: Embracing an Ample Survey and Description of its Counties, Towns, Cities, Villages, Canals . . .* (Albany, 1824), 80–82; James Stuart, *Three Years in North America* (2 vols., Edinburgh, 1833), I, 126; Whitney R. Cross, *The Burned-Over District: The Social and Intellectual History of Enthusiastic Religion in Western New York, 1800–1850* (Ithaca, 1950), 55–56, 114, 139–40.

22   Charles F. Milliken, *A History of Ontario County, New York, and Its People* (2 vols., New York, 1911), I, 281; "A History of Canandaigua Academy," *The Academian* (March 1916), 14; "Henry Howe," *ibid.* 30; *Catalogue of the Trustees, Teachers and Students of Canandaigua Academy . . . 1839,* Ontario County Historical Society, Canandaigua; Canandaigua *Ontario Phoenix,* July 27, 1831.

23 Autobiographical Sketch, Sept. 1, 1838, *Letters,* 58–59; Canandaigua Academy: Lists of Pupils, 1830–1836, MS, Ontario County Historical Society; Letter of George C. Bates, May 1, 1882, Canandaigua *Ontario County Times,* May 24, 1882; Stevens, "Douglas," *JISHS,* XVI, 265; Henry Howe to Douglas, Dec. 21, 1857, Douglas Papers, Chicago.

24 Sheahan, *Douglas,* 6; Stevens, "Douglas," *JISHS,* XVI, 265–66; Jefferson G. Thurber to Douglas, Jan. 31, 1845, Douglas Papers, Chicago.

25 For Tocqueville's visit to Canandaigua, see his *Journey to America* (ed. by J. P. Mayer, New Haven, 1959), 132.

26 Canandaigua *Ontario Freeman,* Nov. 21, 1832.

27 Autobiographical Sketch, Sept. 1, 1838, *Letters,* 59; Letter of L [evi]. H [ubbell]., Milwaukee *Morning News,* quoted in Washington *Union,* May 12, 1854; Letter of George C. Bates, May 1, 1882, Canandaigua *Ontario County Times,* May 24, 1882.

28 Sheahan, *Douglas,* 5.

29 Autobiographical Sketch, Sept. 1, 1838, *Letters,* 59.

## CHAPTER II

1 Douglas to Samuel Wolcott, April 26, 1854, *Letters,* 324.

2 Gustave Koerner, whose later political career in Illinois would bring him into contact with Douglas, traveled west over the same route, leaving Buffalo just a few days later. He described his journey in *Memoirs of Gustave Koerner, 1809–1896* (ed. by Thomas J. McCormack, 2 vols., Cedar Rapids, Iowa, 1909), I, 279–311.

3 Autobiographical Sketch, Sept. 1, 1838, *Letters,* 59; Sheahan, *Douglas,* 7; Wheeler, *History of Congress,* I, 63.

4 Douglas to Julius N. Granger, Sept. 20, 1833, March 11, 1834, Autobiographical Sketch, Sept. 1, 1838, *Letters,* 1, 4, 60. The exact character of Douglas' illness is uncertain. From his descriptions of the symptoms, it might have been rheumatic fever. In other places, he described it as "bilious fever," a term no longer used as it was in the 1830's.

5 Autobiographical Sketch, Sept. 1, 1838, *Letters,* 59–60.

6 Sheahan, *Douglas,* 8.

7 Koerner, *Memoirs,* I, 311; Autobiographical Sketch, Sept. 1, 1838, *Letters,* 60–61; Sheahan, *Douglas,* 9, 13. The book of travels that influenced Douglas' decision to settle in Illinois, written by a "Scotchman," according to Sheahan, may have been James Stuart's *Three Years in North America.* Stuart described a visit to Illinois in the spring of 1830.

8 Douglas to Samuel Wolcott, April 26, 1854, *Letters,* 324.

9 A. D. Jones, *Illinois and the West* (Philadelphia, 1838), 103–4; Jacksonville *Illinois Patriot,* Oct. 27, 1832, April 27, Aug. 31, 1833.

10 Douglas to Julius N. Granger, March 11, 1834, Autobiographical Sketch, Sept. 1, 1838, *Letters,* 4, 61.

11 *Ibid.* 62; Fritz Haskell, *Winchester Centennial Souvenir, Scott County, Illinois* (Winchester, 1930), 8, 22; *Proceedings of the Illinois Association, Sons of Vermont* (Chicago, 1877), 11–12. The records of the auction sale, while

indicating that Douglas was paid $2.50 for his services, also note that he spent $1.36 for two pen knives, one lot of newspapers, and three linen collars (Stevens, "Douglas," *JISHS*, XVI, 273).

12   William Henry Milburn, *Ten Years of Preacher Life* (Nashville, 1859), 133; Autobiographical Sketch, Sept. 1, 1838, Douglas to Julius N. Granger, March 11, 1834, *Letters*, 62, 4; *Proceedings of the Illinois Association, Sons of Vermont* (1877), 12.

13   Douglas to Julius N. Granger, March 11, 1834, *Letters*, 4—5; Speech in Winchester, Aug. 7, 1858, Angle (ed.), *Created Equal?*, 90; Douglas to Julius N. Granger, Nov. 14, July 13, 1834, Dec. 15, 1833, to Gehazi Granger, Nov. 9, 1835, *Letters*, 10, 8, 3, 21.

14   Autobiographical Sketch, Sept. 1, 1838, *Letters*, 63; *Proceedings of the Illinois Association, Sons of Vermont* (1877), 11—12; Frederick Gerhard, *Illinois As It Is: Its History, Geography, Statistics, Constitution, Laws, Government . . .* (Chicago, 1857), 69—70; Douglas to Julius N. Granger, March 11, 1834, *Letters*, 4; M. D. McHenry to John H. McHenry, June 20, 1834, John J. Hardin Papers, CHS.

15   Autobiographical Notes [April 17, 1859], *Letters*, 445; Daniel Roberts, "A Reminiscence of Stephen A. Douglas," *Harper's Magazine*, LXXXVII (Nov. 1893), 958; Autobiographical Sketch, Sept. 1, 1838, *Letters*, 62—63.

16   Sheahan, *Douglas*, 17; George Murray McConnell, "Recollections of Stephen A. Douglas," *TISHS*, 1900, 41—42; Roberts, "Reminiscence of Stephen A. Douglas," *Harper's Magazine*, LXXXVII, 958; Edmund Flagg, *The Far West: Or, A Tour Beyond the Mountains* (2 vols., New York, 1838), II, 57; Douglas to Henry Howe, Jan. 14, 1836, to Gehazi Granger, Nov. 9, 1835, *Letters*, 34, 23, 21.

17   Douglas to Julius N. Granger, May 9, 1835, *Letters*, 15; Vandalia *Illinois Advocate*, April 12, 1834; Springfield *Sangamo Journal*, April 5, 1834; Autobiographical Sketch, Sept. 1, 1838, *Letters*, 63; Sheahan, *Douglas*, 18—20. The preamble and the resolutions presented by Douglas were printed in full in the Vandalia *Illinois Advocate*, April 12, 1834.

18   Springfield *Sangamo Journal*, Dec. 14, 1833; Vandalia *Illinois Advocate*, April 12, 1834; Douglas to Julius N. Granger, May 9, 1835, Autobiographical Sketch, Sept. 1, 1838, *Letters*, 15, 63—64. Douglas' resolution favoring a national bank in principle was later used against him to prove his deviation from the Democratic position (*Quincy Whig*, Feb. 21, March 6, 1844).

19   Charles Manfred Thompson, *The Illinois Whigs Before 1846* (Urbana, Ill., 1915), 31, 43—45; Thomas Ford, *History of Illinois, from its Commencement as a State in 1818 to 1847* (Chicago, 1854), 104—5; Theodore C. Pease, *The Frontier State, 1818—1848* (*Centennial History of Illinois*, II, Chicago, 1922), 143, 147; James C. Finley to Joseph Duncan, May 27, 1834, Elizabeth Duncan Putnam, "The Life and Services of Joseph Duncan," *TISHS*, 1919, 150; Sheahan, *Douglas*, 18; Roberts, "Reminiscence of Stephen A. Douglas," *Harper's Magazine*, LXXXVII, 958.

20   *Chicago Democrat*, Aug. 27, 1834; Douglas to Julius N. Granger, Feb. 22, 1835, *Letters*, 12; Kinney to Elias Kent Kane, Dec. 27, 1834, Elias Kent

Kane Papers (transcripts), IHS; Douglas to Julius N. Granger, May 9, 1835, *Letters*, 16.

21   William C. Greenup to Kane, Dec. 20, 1834, Kane Papers, IHS; *Illinois House Journal, 1834–35,* 14–15, 213–16, 259–63; Ford, *History of Illinois,* 287–88.

22   Autobiographical Sketch, Sept. 1, 1838, Douglas to Julius N. Granger, May 9, 1835, *Letters,* 64, 16–17; Vandalia *Illinois Advocate,* Dec. 17, 1834, Jan. 21, 1835; Springfield *Sangamo Journal,* Dec. 13, 1834; Waller Jones to Hardin, Dec. 11, 1834, Hardin Papers, CHS; *Illinois House Journal, 1834–35,* 36, 63, 118, 127, 444, 448, 522; *Illinois Senate Journal, 1834–35,* 105, 262, 274, 289, 457.

23   Autobiographical Sketch, Sept. 1, 1838, Douglas to Julius N. Granger, Feb. 22, May 9, 1835, *Letters,* 12, 17; Sheahan, *Douglas,* 21–22.

24   Douglas to Julius N. Granger, Feb. 22, 1835, Autobiographical Sketch, Sept. 1, 1838, *Letters,* 12, 65; Roberts, "Reminiscence of Stephen A. Douglas," *Harper's Magazine,* LXXXVII, 959.

25   Douglas to Julius N. Granger, April 25, 1835, Autobiographical Sketch, Sept. 1, 1838, *Letters,* 13, 65–67; *History of McLean County* (Chicago, 1879), 345; Harry E. Pratt, "Stephen A. Douglas, Lawyer, Legislator, Register and Judge, 1833–1843," *Lincoln Herald,* LI (Dec. 1949), 13–14; Ford, *History of Illinois,* 82–86; Sheahan, *Douglas,* 22–25.

26   Springfield *Sangamo Journal,* Jan. 23, 1836; Wheeler, *History of Congress,* I, 78–80; John F. Snyder, "An Illinois Burnt Offering," *JISHS,* II (Jan. 1910), 23–35.

27   Douglas to Julius N. Granger, May 9, 1835, *Letters,* 15.

## CHAPTER III

1   Douglas to Julius N. Granger, July 13, 1854, *Letters,* 8.

2   Minor Rudd Deming to Stephen Deming, Nov. 28, 1835, Minor R. Deming Papers, IHS; Pease, *The Frontier State,* 175–77; Douglas to Julius N. Granger, May 24, 1835, Gehazi Granger, Nov. 9, 1835, *Letters,* 18, 19, 20, 23.

3   Douglas to Julius N. Granger, Jan. 7, April 8, 1836, *Letters,* 31, 35.

4   George W. Dowrie, *The Development of Banking in Illinois, 1817–1863* (Urbana, 1913), 60–61; Douglas to Julius N. Granger, April 25, 1835, *Letters,* 13.

5   Vandalia *Illinois Advocate,* June 3, 1835.

6   Douglas to Julius N. Granger, April 25, 1835, *Letters,* 14; Vandalia *Illinois Advocate,* April 15, 22, May 6, June 3, 1835.

7   *Sangamo Journal,* April 18, July 11, 1835; Vandalia *Illinois Advocate,* May 20, 1835.

8   *Ibid.* Dec. 17, 1835; *Sangamo Journal,* Feb. 6, 13, 20, Jan. 2, 1836.

9   *Illinois Senate Journal, 1835–36,* 76–78, 255–58; *Illinois House Journal, 1835–36,* 211–12, 233–40; Douglas to Julius N. Granger, Jan. 7, 1836, *Letters,* 32.

10   *Sangamo Journal,* Jan. 9, April 30, 1836; To the Democratic Republicans of Illinois, *Letters,* 24–30.

11   Sheahan, *Douglas,* 25–26; *Sangamo Journal,* April 9, 16, May 7, 14, 1836.

12   Sheahan, *Douglas,* 26–27; *Sangamo Journal,* May 7, 1836; Douglas to Julius N. Granger, April 8, 1836, Autobiographical Sketch, Sept. 1, 1838, *Letters,* 36, 67; Edmund Flagg, *The Far West; Or, A Tour Beyond the Mountains* (2 vols., New York, 1838), II, 60; Theodore C. Pease (ed.), *Illinois Election Returns, 1818–1848* (Springfield, 1923), 298.

13   Koerner, *Memoirs,* I, 414; Thompson, *The Illinois Whigs Before 1846,* 53–55; Pease, *Frontier State,* 239, 242; Vandalia *Illinois State Register,* Oct. 7, 1836.

14   Vandalia *Illinois State Register,* Dec. 8, 15, 1836; John J. Hardin to Sarah Hardin, Dec. 14, 1836, Hardin Papers, CHS; William Wilson to Mary Wilson, Dec. 29, 1836, William Wilson Papers, ISHL; Abraham Lincoln to Mary Owens, Dec. 13, 1836, Roy P. Basler *et al* (eds.), *The Collected Works of Abraham Lincoln* (9 vols., New Brunswick, N.J., 1953), I, 54; *Sangamo Journal,* Jan. 6, 1837.

15   *Illinois House Journal, 1836–37,* 19–26, 29, 102–117; Vandalia *Illinois State Register,* Dec. 23, 29, 1836; *Sangamo Journal,* Dec. 31, 1836.

16   Lincoln to Mary Owens, Dec. 13, 1836, *CWAL,* I, 54; *Sangamo Journal,* Dec. 17, 1836; *Illinois House Journal, 1836–37,* 48–49; John Bryant, quoted in Ida M. Tarbell, *The Life of Abraham Lincoln* (4 vols., New York, 1903), I, 145.

17   *Sangamo Journal,* Dec. 3, 1836; John F. Snyder, *Adam W. Snyder and His Period in Illinois History, 1817–1842* (Virginia, Ill., 1906), 215, 218; John H. Krenkel, *Illinois Internal Improvements, 1818–1848* (Cedar Rapids, Iowa, 1958), 65; *Illinois House Journal, 1836–37,* 17, 36; Autobiographical Sketch, Sept. 1, 1838, *Letters,* 67.

18   *Illinois House Journal, 1836–37,* 202–15; Krenkel, *Illinois Internal Improvements,* 67–69; J. P. Wilkinson, Jan. 19, A. H. Buckner, Jan. 28, Thomas W. Melendy to Hardin, Jan. 29, 1837, Hardin Papers, CHS; Autobiographical Sketch, Sept. 1, 1838, *Letters,* 68; Vandalia *Illinois State Register,* Feb. 24, 1837; *Sangamo Journal,* March 4, 1837.

19   James W. Putnam, *The Illinois and Michigan Canal: A Study in Economic History* (Chicago, 1918), 38–41; Wheeler, *History of Congress,* I, 69; Jacksonville *Illinoian,* Feb. 3, 1838; Autobiographical Sketch, Sept. 1, 1838, *Letters,* 67–68.

20   Dowrie, *The Development of Banking in Illinois,* 78–80; *Sangamo Journal,* Dec. 24, 1836, Jan. 27, 1837; Wheeler, *History of Congress,* I, 68; *Illinois House Journal, 1836–37,* 57, 199, 290–94, 485, 490, 493, 525.

21   Harry E. Pratt, "Douglas," *Lincoln Herald,* LII, 15; *Illinois House Journal, 1836–37,* 60–62, 143, 222; Autobiographical Sketch, Sept. 1, 1838, *Letters,* 68.

22   *Illinois House Journal, 1836–37,* 82–83, 752–59; Ford, *History*

*of Illinois,* 186–87; Krenkel, *Illinois Internal Improvements,* 72–74; Statement in Illinois Legislature, Feb. 15, 1839, *CWAL,* I, 144; Vandalia *Illinois State Register,* April 5, 1839; *Sangamo Journal,* Jan. 6, July 29, Aug. 5, Aug. 12, 1837; Douglas to the Editor of the *Illinois Patriot,* March 8, 1837, *Letters,* 37.

23    *Illinois House Journal, 1836–37,* 134, 241–44, 309–11, 824; Pratt, "Douglas," *Lincoln Herald,* LII, 15. Neither the details of the debate on the slavery resolutions nor the details of their amendments were recorded in the *Journal;* however, the resolutions as amended and finally passed apparently did not differ markedly in tone from those originally proposed.

24    Douglas to the Editor of the *Illinois Patriot,* March 8, 1837, *Letters,* 37–38; Surety Bond of Stephen A. Douglas, Records of the Bureau of Accounts (Treasury), Record Group 39, NA; Pease, *The Frontier State,* 245–46; *Sangamo Journal,* Feb. 11, 1837; William L. May to Levi Woodbury, Jan. 3, 1837, Richard M. Young to Woodbury, Feb. 14, 1837, Woodbury to Young, Feb. 23, 1837, General Records of the Department of the Treasury, RG-56, NA.

25    *Sangamo Journal,* April 1, 29, 1837; Pratt, "Douglas," *Lincoln Herald,* LII, 15–16; Douglas to Julius N. Granger, Dec. 18, 1837, *Letters,* 51; J. Madison Cutts, *A Brief Treatise upon Constitutional and Party Questions, and the History of Political Parties* (New York, 1866), 166–69; *Cincinnati Commercial,* Nov. 14, 1869.

26    Vandalia *Illinois State Register,* May 12, July 21, Sept. 15, Oct. 27, 1837; *Sangamo Journal,* June 10, 1837, March 27, 1840; Adam W. Snyder to Gustave Koerner, Oct. 18, 1837, "Letters to Gustav Koerner, 1837–1863," *TISHS,* 1907, 225; Jacksonville *Illinoian,* Jan. 20, 1838; Thomas Lord to James W. Stephenson, May 18, 1837, James W. Stephenson Papers, ISHL.

27    Vandalia *Illinois State Register,* May 12, 19, June 2, 1837; Pease, *The Frontier State,* 176–77; *Sangamo Journal,* April 29, May 6, June 3, 1837; To the Democratic Republicans of Illinois, [Nov. 1837], *Letters,* 42–50.

## CHAPTER IV

1    William L. May to Levi Woodbury, Sept. 15, 1837, *Sangamo Journal,* Nov. 4, 1837; Douglas to Woodbury, Oct. 6, 1837, *Letters,* 40–41.

2    Adam W. Snyder to James Semple, Aug. 8, 1837, Snyder, *Adam W. Snyder,* 236; Thomas Lord to James W. Stephenson, May 18, 1837, Stephenson Papers, ISHL; *Sangamo Journal,* Aug. 5, 1837; Douglas to Lewis W. Ross, Aug. 12, 1837, *Letters,* 39; Washington *Madisonian,* Oct. 27, 1837; *Illinois State Register,* Nov. 10, 17, 1837.

3    *Illinois State Register,* Sept. 8, Oct. 13, 1837; *Sangamo Journal,* Sept. 23, Oct. 14, 21, 1837.

4    *Sangamo Journal,* Nov. 25, 1837, Jan. 13, 27, Feb. 3, 10, 1838; Josiah Lamborn to Jesse B. Thomas, Dec. 1, 1837, Hardin Papers, CHS; Douglas to George R. Weber, Jan. 30, 1838, *Letters,* 51–55; Glenn H. Seymour, " 'Conservative'—Another Lincoln Pseudonym?" *JISHS,* XXIX (July 1936), 135–50; "Lincoln—Author of the Letters by 'A Conservative,' " *Bulletin of*

*the Abraham Lincoln Association,* No. 50 (Dec. 1937), 8–9; *Illinois State Register,* Dec. 8, 1837.

5   Bray Hammond, *Banks and Politics in America: From the Revolution to the Civil War* (Princeton, N.J., 1957), 496; Douglas to Lewis W. Ross, Aug. 12, 1837, *Letters,* 39; Richard M. Young to James W. Stephenson, Oct. 14, 1837, Stephenson Papers, ISHL; Adam W. Snyder to Koerner, Nov. 13, 1837, "Letters to Gustav Koerner, 1837–1863," *TISHS,* 1907, 228–29; *Sangamo Journal,* Dec. 23, 1837.

6   Lincoln to William A. Minshall, Dec. 7, 1837, *CWAL,* I, 107; David Davis to John Todd Stuart, Dec. 23, 1837, Stuart-Hay Papers, ISHL; *Sangamo Journal,* Dec. 23, 1837, Jan. 6, 1838; C. C. Brown, "Major John T. Stuart," *TISHS,* 1902, 109–10.

7   Douglas to Julius N. Granger, Dec. 18, 1837, *Letters,* 51; Jeriah Bonham, *Fifty Years' Recollections* (Peoria, 1883), 188–90; John M. Palmer, *Personal Recollections of John M. Palmer, The Story of an Earnest Life* (Cincinnati, 1901), 24; Harry E. Pratt, "Abraham Lincoln in Bloomington, Illinois," *JISHS,* XXIX (April 1936), 44; Milburn, *Ten Years of Preacher Life,* 132; Brown, "Major John T. Stuart," *TISHS,* 1902, 110.

8   Jacksonville *Illinoian,* March 31, June 30, July 21, 1838; *Quincy Whig,* June 2, 9, 30, 1838; *Chicago American,* quoted in *Illinois State Register,* Jan. 19, 1838; *Galena Gazette,* quoted in *Sangamo Journal,* March 31, 1838; *Sangamo Journal,* Aug. 4, 1838; Lincoln to Jesse W. Fell, [July 23, 1838], *CWAL,* I, 120.

9   *Sangamo Journal,* Aug. 11, 25, Sept. 1, 1838; *Illinois State Register,* Aug. 17, 1838; *Quincy Whig,* Aug. 25, 1838; Pease (ed.), *Illinois Election Returns,* 109–10; Douglas to Francis Preston Blair, Nov. 2, 1838, *Letters,* 69.

10   *Sangamo Journal,* Dec. 15, 1838, Sept. 11, 1840; A. H. Buckner to Hardin, Aug. 16, 1838, Hardin Papers, CHS; *Quincy Whig,* Sept. 22, 1838; Bonham, *Fifty Years' Recollections,* 189–90.

11   *Illinois State Register,* Sept. 21, 28, Oct. 12, 19, 26, Nov. 9, 23, 1838, Oct. 7, 1842; Douglas to Blair, Nov. 2, 1838, *Letters,* 69; Thomas Hart Benton to Douglas, Oct. 27, 1838, Douglas Family Papers, Greensboro; Charles V. Dyer to Hardin, Sept. 3, 1838, Hardin Papers, CHS; Usher F. Linder, *Reminiscences of the Early Bench and Bar of Illinois* (Chicago, 1879), 347; *Chicago Democrat,* Nov. 21, 1838; *Sangamo Journal,* Dec. 8, 1838, Jan. 12, Sept. 27, 1839.

12   Douglas to Stuart, March 4, 1839, *Letters,* 70–72; Stuart to Douglas, March 13, 1839, Stuart-Hay Papers, ISHL; Douglas to George R. Weber, March 12, Frederick R. Dutcher, Oct. 2, Lewis W. Ross, Oct. 14, 1839, *Letters,* 72–73; Lincoln *et al.* to the Editor of the *Chicago American,* June 24, Lincoln to Stuart, Nov. 14, 1839, *CWAL,* I, 151–52, 154; Hardin to Stuart, Nov. 28, 1839, Hardin Papers, CHS.

13   Paul M. Angle, *"Here I Have Lived": A History of Lincoln's Springfield, 1821–1865* (New Brunswick, N.J., 1935), 83–93; Paul M. Angle (ed.), *Herndon's Life of Lincoln* (Cleveland, 1949), 167–68; Carl Sandburg, *Lincoln Collector* (New York, 1949), 140; Ruth Painter Randall, *Mary Lin-*

*coln: Biography of a Marriage* (Boston, 1953), 9–10, 43–44; Stevens, "Life of Douglas," *JISHS*, XVI, 323.

14   *Illinois State Register,* Oct. 12, Nov. 23, 1839; Thompson, *Illinois Whigs Before 1846,* 63; *Sangamo Journal,* Oct. 11, 1839.

15   *Quincy Whig,* Aug. 31, 1839; *Sangamo Journal,* Aug. 30, Nov. 15, 1839; D. H. Rutledge *et al.* to Lincoln, Oct. 23, 1839, William Butler Papers, CHS; Lincoln to Stuart, Nov. 14, 1839, *CWAL,* I, 154.

16   *Illinois State Register,* Jan. 29, April 5, Nov. 23, Dec. 14, 18, 21, 1839; Sheahan, *Douglas,* 39; Ford, *History of Illinois,* 207.

17   Adam W. Snyder to James Semple, April 6, 1840, Snyder, *Adam W. Snyder,* 293–94; Thompson, *Illinois Whigs Before 1846,* 73–74; *Sangamo Journal,* Dec. 20, 1839.

18   Joseph Gillespie to William H. Herndon, Jan. 31, 1866, Herndon-Weik Papers, LC; Pratt, "Douglas," *Lincoln Herald,* LII, 38; *Illinois State Register,* Nov. 23, 30, 1839.

19   Pratt, "Lincoln—Campaign Manager and Orator in 1840," *Bull. Abraham Lincoln Assn.,* No. 50, 5; *Sangamo Journal,* Jan. 3, 1840; Lincoln to Stuart, Dec. 23, Speech on the Sub-Treasury, Dec. [26], 1839, *CWAL,* I, 159–79; *Illinois State Register,* Feb. 8, 1840.

20   *Illinois State Register,* March 27, May 29, Sept. 4, Oct. 2, 1840; *Sangamo Journal,* April 3, May 15, June 12, Oct. 2, 1840; Hardin to Stuart, April 13, 1840, Hardin Papers, CHS; Douglas to Lewis W. Ross, June 27, 1840, *Letters,* 93.

21   Emanuel Hertz, *The Hidden Lincoln, From the Letters and Papers of William H. Herndon* (New York, 1938), 380–81, 434–36; *Sangamo Journal,* April 24, Sept. 18, 1840.

22   Springfield *Old Hickory,* March 2, 1840; Lincoln to Stuart, March 1, 1840, *CWAL,* I, 206; *Sangamo Journal,* March 6, 1840; *Illinois State Register,* March 6, 1840.

23   *Sangamo Journal,* Feb. 21, 28, April 3, 1840; *Illinois State Register,* April 17, 1840; Call for Democratic County Convention, March 26, Douglas to Robert Allen, April 23, 1840, *Letters,* 81.

24   Ford, *History of Illinois,* 198; *Old Hickory,* Feb. 17, 1840; *Illinois State Register,* Feb. 14, July 10, 1840; *Sangamo Journal,* June 5, 1840; William Wilson to Mary Wilson, June 4, 1840, Wilson Papers, ISHL; To the Democratic Party of Illinois, May 13, To the People of Illinois, June 4, 1840, *Letters,* 82–92; *Chicago American,* Oct. 24, 1840.

25   *Sangamo Journal,* Nov. 29, 1839; *Illinois State Register,* Dec. 7, 1839, July 3, 1840; *Chicago American,* March 7, July 7, 1840; Sheahan, *Douglas,* 44–46; Wheeler, *History of Congress,* I, 76; Ford, *History of Illinois,* 215; Spraggins *v.* Houghton, *Illinois Reports,* III (2 Scammon), 211–14; Douglas to McClernand, Jan. 29, 1841, *Letters,* 95–96.

26   *Illinois State Register,* Jan. 11, March 8, April 26, July 26, Aug. 17, 1839, Dec. 4, 1840; John A. McClernand, Stephen A. Douglas *et al.,* Bond for Writ of Replevin, July 5, 1839, McClernand Papers, ISHL; *Sangamo Journal,* July 19, 1839; Alexander P. Field *v.* The People of the State of Illinois, *ex rela-*

*tione* John A. McClernand, *Ill. Reps.,* 2 Scam., 79–185; *Quincy Whig,* Aug. 20, 1839; Ford, *History of Illinois,* 214; John J. Duff, *A. Lincoln, Prairie Lawyer* (New York, 1960), 67–68; *Illinois Senate Journal, 1839–40,* 236–37; *1840–41,* 30–31. See Arnold Shankman, "Partisan Conflicts, 1839–1841, and the Illinois Constitution," *JISHS,* LXIII (Winter 1970), 337–67.

## CHAPTER V

1  Hertz, *The Hidden Lincoln,* 218; Application for Membership in Masonic Lodge, *Letters,* 81; George W. Warvelle (ed.), *A Compendium of Freemasonry in Illinois* (2 vols., Chicago, 1897), I, 27; Palmer, *Personal Recollections of John M. Palmer,* 30–31; Isaac N. Arnold, quoted in *History of Sangamon County* (Chicago, 1881), 94; R. H. Beach, quoted, *ibid.* 183; Stevens, "Douglas," *JISHS,* XVI, 351–54.

2  *Sangamo Journal,* April 14, 1838; *Illinois State Register,* Jan. 1, Dec. 4, 1840; Pratt, "Douglas," *Lincoln Herald,* LII, 38; Pratt, "Lincoln and Douglas as Counsel on the Same Side," *American Bar Association Journal,* XXVI (March 1940), 214; *Ill. Reps.,* 1 Scam., 576–79; *Illinois State Register,* June 30, 1837; Isaac Millar Short, *Abraham Lincoln, Early Days in Illinois, Reminiscences of Different Persons who Became Eminent in American History* (Kansas City, Mo., 1927), 34–37.

3  Duff, *A. Lincoln, Prairie Lawyer,* 53–57; Pratt, "Abraham Lincoln's First Murder Trial," *JISHS,* XXXVII (Sept. 1944), 242–49; Pratt, *Lincoln, 1809–1839: Being the Day-by-Day Activities of Abraham Lincoln from February 12, 1809, to December 31, 1839* (Springfield, 1941), 124, 140–41, 154; *Illinois House Journal, 1839–40,* 131–45, 150–51; *Illinois State Register,* Jan. 8, 15, 22, 1840; *Sangamo Journal,* Jan. 17, 1840; *Ill. Reps.,* 3 Scam., 273.

4  *Ill. Reps.,* 1 Scam., 185–86, 214–18, 498–500, 500–501, 524–25, 548–50; 2 Scam., 3–4, 79–185, 211–14, 222–23, 236–45, 348–51, 377–417, 444–48, 452–53; Pratt, "Douglas," *Lincoln Herald,* LII, 38–40; Orrin N. Carter, "Lincoln and Douglas as Lawyers," *Proceedings of the Mississippi Valley Historical Association,* 1910–11, 213–40.

5  Koerner, *Memoirs,* I, 449; *Illinois Senate and House Reports, 1840–41,* 137–40; *Illinois State Register,* Feb. 5, 1841.

6  Ford, *History of Illinois,* 217–20, 226; *Illinois Senate Journal, 1840–41,* 65, 148–49; *Sangamo Journal,* Feb. 5, 1841; Hardin to Stuart, Jan. 20, 1841, Hardin Papers, CHS; Albert G. Leary to John Wentworth, Jan. 25, 1841, *Chicago American,* Feb. 5, 1841; Adam W. Snyder to Koerner, Feb. 6, 1841, Snyder, *Adam W. Snyder,* 368; *Ill. Reps.,* 2 Scam., 377–417; *Illinois State Register,* Jan. 29, 1841; Douglas to McClernand, Jan. 29, 1841, *Letters,* 95–96.

7  *Illinois State Register,* Feb. 5, 12, 19, 1841; Breese to McClernand, Feb. 8, 1841, McClernand Papers, ISHL; A. W. Cavarly to Lincoln, Sept. 10, 1858, Abraham Lincoln Papers, LC; Snyder to Koerner, Feb. 8, 9, 14, 1841, Snyder, *Adam W. Snyder,* 368, 370, 371; *Quincy Whig,* Feb. 20, 1841; Ward Hill Lamon,

886 NOTES TO PAGES 96–103

*The Life of Abraham Lincoln* (Boston, 1872), 219; Ford, *History of Illinois,* 222.

8   *Illinois House Journal, 1840–41,* 406; McConnel to George T. M. Davis, Feb. 15, 1841, George T. M. Davis Papers, MHS; W. Smith to John Dean Caton, Feb. 16, 1841, John Dean Caton Papers, LC; Belleville *Great Western,* quoted in *Sangamo Journal,* March 19, 1841; Snyder to Koerner, Feb. 14, 1841, Snyder, *Adam W. Snyder,* 370; *Chicago Democrat,* quoted in *Sangamo Journal,* March 5, 1841; *Chicago American,* Feb. 18, 1841.

9   Douglas to Thomas Carlin, Feb. 16, Oath of Office, March 1, Douglas to Julius N. Granger *et al.,* April 3, 1841, *Letters,* 97, 98–99; Robert B. Warden, *Life and Character of Stephen Arnold Douglas* (Columbus, 1860), 56.

10   Douglas to James Shields, April 2, 1841, to Harry Wilton, March 27, 1842, *Letters,* 98, 101; *Sangamo Journal,* March 26, May 7, 1841; *Illinois State Register,* May 14, 1841; Nauvoo *Times and Seasons,* May 15, 1841; Stevens, "Douglas," *JISHS,* XVI, 343; *Chicago American,* July 19, 1842; Pratt, "Douglas," *Lincoln Herald,* LII, 41; *Quincy Whig,* March 6, May 29, 1841, July 12, 1843.

11   *Illinois State Register,* May 5, 26, 1843; Henry Brown, *The History of Illinois* (New York, 1844), 484; *Quincy Whig,* March 5, 1842, April 26, May 3, 10, June 7, July 5, 12, 19, 1843; W. A. Richardson, Jr., "Many Contests for the County Seat of Adams County, Ill.," *JISHS,* XVII (Oct. 1924), 373–77.

12   Penny *v.* Little, *Ill. Reps.,* 3 Scam., 304–5.

13   Stevens *v.* Stebbins, *Ill. Reps.,* 3 Scam., 24–25; King *v.* Thompson, *Ill. Reps.,* 3 Scam., 184–85.

14   Warren *v.* Nexson, *Ill. Reps.,* 3 Scam., 38–40; Gardner *v.* The People, *Ill. Reps.,* 3 Scam., 83–90; Penny *v.* Little, *Ill. Reps.,* 3 Scam., 301–5; Camden *v.* McKoy, *Ill. Reps.,* 3 Scam., 436–51. Other cases decided by Douglas, not previously cited, are found in the following volumes of the *Ill. Reps.:* Woodward *v.* Turnbull, 3 Scam., 1–3; The People *v.* Town, 3 Scam., 18; Pattison *v.* Hood, 3 Scam., 151–52; Roper *v.* Clabaugh, 3 Scam., 165–68; Campbell *v.* Quinlan, 3 Scam., 288–89; Dunn *v.* Keegin, 3 Scam., 292–98; Townsend *v.* The People, 3 Scam., 326–29; Carpenter *v.* Mather, 3 Scam., 374–76; Averill *v.* Field, 3 Scam., 389–92; Sellers *v.* The People, 3 Scam., 412–16; Heaton *v.* Hulbert, 3 Scam., 488–91; Cushman *v.* Dement, 3 Scam., 497–99; Bank of Illinois *v.* Stickney, 4 Scam., 4–7; Dawson *v.* Bank of Illinois, 4 Scam., 56–57; Grubb *v.* Crane, 4 Scam., 153–57; Eyman *v.* The People, 1 Gilman, 4–10.

15   Merton L. Dillon, The Antislavery Movement in Illinois, 1809–1844 (Ph.D. dissertation, Univ. of Michigan, 1951), *passim* (quotation from p. 329); Hermann R. Muelder, *Fighters for Freedom: The History of Anti-Slavery Activities of Men and Women Associated with Knox College* (New York, 1959), Chaps. VIII–IX.

16   Muelder, *Fighters for Freedom,* 212; Henry Asbury, *Reminiscences of Quincy, Illinois* (Quincy, 1882), 71–72; *Quincy Whig,* Aug. 27, Oct. 8, 1842, April 26, May 3, 1843; *Illinois State Register,* May 5, 1843; *Congressional Globe,* 36 Cong., 2 sess., 54; *Ill. Reps.,* 4 Scam., 498; Salmon P. Chase to "My dear Sir," Dec. 11, 1852, Salmon P. Chase Papers, LC.

17 Kinney *v.* Cook, Bailey *v.* Cromwell, *Ill. Reps.*, 3 Scam., 231–33, 70–72.

18 *Chicago American,* Nov. 16, 1840; *Illinois State Register,* Nov. 13, 1840.

19 Ford, *History of Illinois,* 262–65; *Sangamo Journal,* June 10, 1842; Robert Bruce Flanders, *Nauvoo: Kingdom on the Mississippi* (Urbana, 1965), 96–100.

20 Joseph Smith to the Editor, May 6, 1841, Douglas to John C. Bennett, [n. d.], Nauvoo *Times and Seasons,* May 15, 1841; Ford, *History of Illinois,* 263.

21 George R. Gayler, "Attempts by the State of Missouri to Extradite Joseph Smith, 1841–1843," *Missouri Historical Review,* LVIII (Oct. 1963), 24–26; Joseph Smith and Heman C. Smith, *History of the Church of Jesus Christ of Latter Day Saints* (4 vols., Lamoni, Iowa, 1908), II, 525–31; *Quincy Whig,* June 9, 1841; Monmouth correspondent of the *Joliet Courier,* quoted in B. H. Roberts, *A Comprehensive History of the Church of Jesus Christ of Latter Day Saints* (6 vols., Salt Lake City, 1930), II, 81–82.

22 A. R. Parker to Edward Warren, June 14, 1841, Edward Warren Papers, CHS; Entries, Oct. 14, 1841, Feb. 18, 1842, Journal History, Church of Jesus Christ of Latter Day Saints, Church Historian's Office, Salt Lake City; Nauvoo *Times and Seasons,* Jan. 1, 1842; *Illinois State Register,* Jan. 14, 1842.

23 Ford, *History of Illinois,* 267–69; *Chicago American,* July 5, 1842; *Sangamo Journal,* July 1, 1842; *Quincy Whig,* July 2, 1842; *Illinois State Register,* May 27, June 17, July 1, 1842.

24 *Sangamo Journal,* Aug. 12, Oct. 14, 21, 1842; Thomas Ford to Martin Van Buren, Sept. 11, 1843, Martin Van Buren Papers, LC; Gayler, "Attempts to Extradite Joseph Smith," *Missouri Historical Review,* LVIII, 27–32; Entry, Oct. 5, 1842, Journal History; Roberts, *A Comprehensive History,* II, 183.

25 *Illinois State Register,* May 14, 1841; Isaac N. Arnold, *Reminiscences of the Illinois Bar Forty Years Ago: Lincoln and Douglas as Orators and Lawyers* (Fergus Historical Series, No. 14, Chicago, 1881), 146; Jacksonville *Illinoian,* July 3, 1841; *Law Reporter,* IV (July 1841), 127; Pratt, "Douglas," *Lincoln Herald,* LII, 40–41; William Perkins to Lincoln, Nov. 1, 1859, Lincoln Papers, LC.

## CHAPTER VI

1 Douglas to William S. Prentice, Aug. 30, 1841, to Harry Wilton, March 27, 1842, *Letters,* 99–101; Samuel Treat to W. S. Prentice, Aug. 25, 1842, Samuel Treat Papers, ISHL; *Sangamo Journal,* Sept. 2, 1842.

2 *Illinois State Register,* Nov. 4, Dec. 23, 1842, Jan. 13, Feb. 3, April 7, 1843; *Chicago American,* Sept. 17, 1842; Don E. Fehrenbacher, *Chicago Giant: A Biography of "Long John" Wentworth* (Madison, 1957), 35–36; *Sangamo Journal,* Dec. 22, 1842; Hardin to Stuart, Dec. 28, 1842, Hardin Papers, CHS; Sheahan, *Douglas,* 54; Douglas to Breese, Nov. 6, 1846, *Letters,* 144–45.

3 Pease, *Frontier State,* 310–15; Ford, *History of Illinois,* 293–304, 309; Sheahan, *Douglas,* 48; Stevens, "Douglas," *JISHS,* XVI, 347.

4 Ford, *History of Illinois*, 289–90; Douglas to Prentice, Aug. 30, 1841, *Letters*, 100.

5 The new Fifth District included the counties of Jersey, Greene, Macoupin, Calhoun, Pike, Brown, Schuyler, Adams, Fulton, and Peoria; *Illinois State Register*, Jan. 27, Feb. 3, March 17, 31, June 16, 1843; *Quincy Whig*, May 24, 1843; Sheahan, *Douglas*, 55.

6 *Quincy Herald*, quoted in Peoria *Democratic Press*, June 14, 1843; *Illinois State Register*, June 9, 23, 1843; Carrollton *People's Advocate*, quoted in *Illinois State Register*, June 16, 1843; *Alton Telegraph*, quoted in *Quincy Whig*, June 28, 1843; *Quincy Whig*, June 28, July 19, 1843; *Peoria Register and North-Western Gazetteer*, quoted in *Quincy Whig*, June 28, 1843.

7 *Quincy Whig*, June 14, 21, 28, July 5, 12, Aug. 2, 1843; *Illinois State Register*, June 16, 30, 1843; Campaign Circular from Whig Committee, March 4, 1843, *CWAL*, I, 309–18; *Addresses on the Death of Hon. Stephen A. Douglas, Delivered in the Senate and House of Representatives on Tuesday, July 9, 1861* (Washington, D.C., 1861), 26–27; Koerner, *Memoirs*, I, 479.

8 *Quincy Whig*, July 5, 19, 1843; *Illinois State Register*, July 21, Aug. 25, Sept. 22, Oct. 27, 1843; Maurice Baxter, *Orville H. Browning: Lincoln's Friend and Critic* (Bloomington, Ind., 1957), 43–45; *Addresses on the Death of Hon. Stephen A. Douglas*, 26; Pease (ed.), *Illinois Election Returns*, 139; Hart Fellows to Hardin, Aug. 24, 1843, Hardin Papers, CHS; Ford, *History of Illinois*, 317–20.

9 *Illinois State Register*, Aug. 18, 1843; Jesse K. Dubois to Hardin, Aug. 24, 1843, Hardin Papers, CHS.

10 Stevens, "Douglas," *JISHS*, XVI, 362.

11 Douglas to Semple, [n.d.], *Letters*, 102; Charles Dickens, *American Notes* (New York, 1961), 139, 140, 144; Frances Trollope, *Domestic Manners of the Americans* (New York, 1960), 216; *New-York Tribune*, Dec. 15, 21, 1843.

12 *Chicago Democrat*, Dec. 20, 27, 1843, March 20, 1844; Hardin to D. A. Smith, Jan. 12, 1844, Hardin Papers, CHS; David S. Reid to R. Reid, Jan. 14, 1844, David S. Reid Papers, NCDAH; Hardin to Mrs. Browning, Dec. 26, 1843, Orville H. Browning Papers (typescripts), IHS.

13 *Congressional Globe*, 28 Cong., 1 sess., 3, 36, 315; John Wentworth to Walters & Weber, Dec. 3, 1843, *Illinois State Register*, Dec. 15, 1843; *Boston Daily Advertiser*, Dec. 15, 1843; Washington *Madisonian*, Dec. 11, 1843; Charles M. Wiltse, *John C. Calhoun: Sectionalist, 1840–1850* (Indianapolis, 1951), 147; Silas Wright to Van Buren, Dec. 6, 1843, Van Buren Papers, LC.

14 *New-York Tribune*, Dec. 15, 1843; Washington *National Intelligencer*, Dec. 19, 1843; Hardin to D. A. Smith, Jan. 23, 1844, Hardin Papers, CHS; John Quincy Adams, *Memoirs of John Quincy Adams, 1795–1848* (12 vols., Philadelphia, 1877), XI, 538.

15 Hardin to Editors of the *Journal*, Jan. 1, 1843 [1844], *Sangamo Journal*, Jan. 18, 1844; Amos Kendall to Van Buren, April 19, 1844, Van Buren Papers, LC.

16 *Illinois State Register*, Jan. 13, Feb. 24, 1843; *CG*, 28/1, 116–17,

123, Appendix, 43–46; Adams, *Memoirs*, XI, 478; Correspondence of the *Baltimore American*, quoted in *Quincy Whig*, Jan. 31, 1844; William H. Herndon to Hardin, Feb. 12, 1844, Hardin Papers, CHS; *Biographical Sketch of Stephen A. Douglas* [Washington, D.C., 1852], 5; Francis P. Blair to Jackson, Jan. 9, 1844, John Spencer Bassett (ed.), *Correspondence of Andrew Jackson* (6 vols., Washington, D.C., 1933), VI, 254; Jackson to Van Buren, Feb. 7, 1844, Van Buren Papers, LC.

17    *New-York Tribune*, Dec. 6, 9, 1843; Adams, *Memoirs*, XI, 443, 492, 509, 510–11; *Niles' National Register*, Feb. 17, 1844, 393–95; *CG*, 28/1, 36, 177, 282–84.

18    *CG*, 28/1, 9, 49–53, App., 23–24; Adams, *Memoirs*, XI, 453.

19    *CG*, 28/1, 549–52, 558–59, 567–68; Adams, *Memoirs*, XII, 11; *Sangamo Journal*, May 9, 1844; *Chicago Democrat*, May 29, 1844.

20    *CG*, 28/1, 507; Hardin to D. A. Smith, March 8, 1844, Hardin Papers, CHS; *Chicago Democrat*, March 27, 1844; Douglas to Jesse W. Fell, March 21, to Silas Reed, March 21, 1844, *Letters*, 103–104; Doctor bill, April 29, 1844, Douglas Family Papers, Greensboro.

## CHAPTER VII

1    *Illinois State Register*, June 6, 1845. Douglas' meeting with Jackson was later clouded by some uncertainty. Just before his death in 1846, Walters allegedly denied that Douglas had seen Jackson, but this claim was not recorded until 1860. Walters' relations with Douglas during his last years were not cordial, and there is reason to doubt his disclaimer, if, indeed, it was actually made. Jackson wrote late in August 1844 that he had talked with members of the "Illanoise" delegation to the Nashville convention, and Douglas referred to the incident three years later in a letter to Charles H. Lanphier. Theodore C. Pease and James G. Randall (eds.), *The Diary of Orville Hickman Browning* (2 vols., Springfield, 1925), I, 390–91; Jackson to Francis Preston Blair, Aug. 29, 1844, Blair Family Papers, LC; Douglas to Lanphier, Dec. 7, 1847, *Letters*, 155.

2    *CG*, 28/1, 6–7; *Chicago Democrat*, Jan. 10, 1844; "Documents," *Oregon Historical Quarterly*, IX (Dec. 1908), 394–95; *Illinois State Register*, Feb. 10, 17, 1843; *Sangamo Journal*, Feb. 16, 1843; *CG*, 28/1, 119, 345.

3    James Shields to Sidney Breese, April 12, 1844, Sidney Breese Papers, ISHL; John Reynolds to Hardin, May 4, 1844, Hardin Papers, CHS; *Illinois State Register*, April 19, May 24, 31, March 29, 1844 (in order of citation).

4    Orson Hyde to Council of the Church, April 25 (clipping), April 26, to "Dear Brethren," April 30, 1844, Journal History.

5    Herndon to Hardin, April 3, 1844, Hardin Papers, CHS; Ford, Feb. 10, 1844, Wentworth, Dec. 26, 1843, Walters to Van Buren, Jan. 29, 1844, Van Buren Papers, LC.

6    *Illinois State Register*, Feb. 24, March 3, 1843; *Sangamo Journal*, Feb. 23, 1843; Ford to Van Buren, Sept. 11, 1843, Van Buren Papers, LC; Wiltse, *Calhoun: Sectionalist*, 139.

7    Browning to Hardin, Feb. 14, 1844, Hardin Papers, CHS; *Illinois State Register*, May 2, 1845; Silas Wright, Feb. 20, Amos Kendall to Van Buren, April

19, 1844, Van Buren Papers, LC; *Illinois State Register,* May 17, 1844; Lucius Lyon to Lewis Cass, May 2, 1844, *Collections and Researches Made by the Michigan Pioneer and Historical Society,* XXVII (Lansing, 1897), 578–79.

8    Silas Wright, May 20, J. C. Rives to Van Buren, May 21, 1844, Van Buren Papers, LC; *Chicago Democrat,* June 5, 1844; Washington *Globe,* June 6, 1844; *Illinois State Register,* June 14, 1844.

9    *CG,* 28/1, App., 598–602; Adams, *Memoirs,* XII, 49; Justin H. Smith, *The Annexation of Texas* (New York, 1941), 273, 282–84.

10    *Illinois State Register,* May 17, 1844; A. R. Knapp to Hardin, Jan. 21, 1844, Hardin Papers, CHS; Washington *Globe,* Dec. 7, 1843, Feb. 4, 1844; S. Lisle Smith, Dec. 30, 1843, George T. M. Davis to Hardin, Jan. 6, Feb. 21, 1844, Hardin Papers, CHS.

11    Anson G. Henry, March 20, H. Lancaster, April 16, Charles Ballance to Hardin, May 12, 1844, Hardin Papers, CHS; Edward Dickinson Baker to Mrs. Orville H. Browning, Feb. 1, 1844, Browning Papers, ISHL.

12    *Illinois State Register,* July 12, 1844; *Quincy Whig,* June 26, July 10, 31, 1844; Koerner, *Memoirs,* I, 489; Pease (ed.), *Illinois Election Returns,* 146.

13    Herndon to Hardin, Feb. 12, 1844, Hardin Papers, CHS; *Quincy Whig,* July 10, 1844; *Illinois State Register,* Aug. 9, 1844; Henry to Hardin, Jan. 24, 1844, Hardin Papers, CHS.

14    James K. Polk to Cave Johnson, June 21, Aug. 20, 23, 26, 1844, St. George L. Sioussat (ed.), "Polk-Johnson Letters, 1833–1848," *Tennessee Historical Magazine,* I (Sept. 1915), 245, 248, 249; *Nashville Union,* Aug. 6, 17, Sept. 2, 1844; *Illinois State Register,* Aug. 30, 1844.

15    *Illinois State Register,* Sept. 20, 27, Oct. 4, Nov. 8, 1844; Douglas to Ezra Williams *et al.,* Oct. 7, to James Dunlap and Joseph Heslep, Oct. 7, 1844, *Letters,* 104–5.

16    Pease (ed.), *Illinois Election Returns,* 149–52; Calvin Brown to Douglas, Nov. 22, 1844, Douglas Family Papers, Greensboro; Hardin to Joseph Gillespie, Dec. 7, 1844, Joseph Gillespie Papers, ISHL; Justin Butterfield to John Quincy Adams, Nov. 23, Butterfield, Nov. 23, George T. M. Davis to Hardin, November 24, 1844, Hardin Papers, CHS.

17    Edwin A. Miles, " 'Fifty-Four Forty or Fight'—An American Political Legend," *MVHR,* XLIV (Sept. 1957), 291–309; Shields to Breese, April 12, 1844, Breese Papers, ISHL.

18    *Illinois State Register,* Feb. 7, 1845; Douglas to William Walters and George R. Weber, Feb. 16, 1845, *Letters,* 106; Isaac N. Arnold, Nov. 23, A. W. Cavarly, Nov. 26, Charles H. Larrabee, Nov. 27, James W. Keyes, Nov. 29, Josiah Lamborn to Douglas, Nov. 29, 1844, Douglas Family Papers, Greensboro.

19    Douglas to "Dear Colonel," Jan. 2, 1844, owned by James L. Norton, Jr., Galesburg, Ill.; George T. M. Davis to Hardin, Feb. 21, March 31, 1844, Hardin Papers, CHS; E. D. Taylor, Oct. 10, Thomas M. Hope, Dec. 2, E. A. Thompson to Douglas, Dec. 2, 1844, Douglas Family Papers, Greensboro.

20    *Chicago Democrat,* Dec. 25, 1844; Robert Seager II, *And Tyler Too: A Biography of John & Julia Gardiner Tyler* (New York, 1963), 252.

21    *CG,* 28/2, 4–5; Smith, *Annexation of Texas,* 320–21.

22   *CG,* 28/2, 26, 49, 65–66, 88; Aaron V. Brown to Polk, Dec. 29, 1844, James K. Polk Papers, LC; Jackson to Francis Preston Blair, Jan. 1, to William B. Lewis, Jan. 1, 1845, Bassett (ed.), *Correspondence of Jackson,* VI, 351, 352; *Speech of Senator Douglas at a Public Dinner given him by his Personal and Political Friends at Chicago, November 9, 1854* (Washington, D.C., 1854), 3–4.

23   *CG,* 28/2, 84–85, 90, 95, App. 65–68; Adams, *Memoirs,* XII, 139.

24   *Illinois State Register,* Jan. 31, 1845; *Chicago Democrat,* Jan. 22, 1845; *CG,* 28/2, 121, 125, 129–30, 171, 190, 193–94; Smith, *Annexation of Texas,* 327–32, 337–47. An early biographer of Douglas maintained that Douglas' extension of the Missouri Compromise to Texas represented the "germ" of his later doctrine of popular sovereignty, since all states admitted south of 36°30′ would come into the Union with or without slavery as their populations would decide (Allen Johnson, *Stephen A. Douglas: A Study in American Politics* [New York, 1908], 89). It is clear, however, that Douglas proposed the extension solely to quell an agitation over the slavery question, not out of any deep-seated conviction regarding the nature of local government.

## CHAPTER VIII

1   *Chicago Democrat,* May 14, 1845; *Illinois State Register,* Feb. 7, April 18, May 2, 9, 30, 1845; Douglas to Polk, April 17, 1845, *Letters,* 112–13; Shields to McClernand, Dec. 26, 1844, McClernand Papers, ISHL.

2   *Illinois State Register,* Feb. 7, April 4, 18, July 18, Sept. 5, 12, Oct. 24, 31, Nov. 7, 1845; George T. M. Davis to Hardin, July 27, 1845, Hardin Papers, CHS; James Shields to Breese, June 21, 1845, Breese Papers, ISHL; Douglas to the Editors of the *Illinois State Register,* June 28, 1845, *Letters,* 113–17.

3   Entries, June 30, 1844, Sept. 30, Oct. 1, 1845, Journal History; Ford, *History of Illinois,* 410–12; Douglas *et al.* to the President and Council of the Church of Latter Day Saints, Oct. 1, 3, to the Anti-Mormon Citizens of Hancock County, Oct. 4, to Thomas Ford, Oct. 4, 1845, *Letters,* 120–26; George Miller and Brigham Young, Dec. 17, Young to Douglas, Dec. 17, 1845, Douglas Family Papers, Greensboro; Almon W. Babbitt to Haywood and Fullmer, Feb. 3, 1847, Journal History.

4   *CG,* 28/2, App., 68; Shields to Douglas, Jan. 12, 1845, Douglas Family Papers, Greensboro.

5   *CG,* 28/2, 3, 226–27.

6   *CG,* 28/2, 218–19; Douglas to Asa Whitney, Oct. 15, 1845, *Letters,* 127–33. Douglas' letter was published under the title *Atlantic & Pacific Railroad. A Letter from the Hon. S. A. Douglass, to A. Whitney, Esq., N.Y.* (Quincy, Ill., [1845]); Whitney replied in *Atlantic and Pacific Railroad, A. Whitney's Reply to the Hon. S. A. Douglass* (Washington, D.C., 1845).

7   *CG,* 28/2, 21, 41, 104, 165, 173; Adams, *Memoirs,* XII, 121; *Illinois State Register,* Jan. 3, 1845; Washington *Madisonian,* Feb. 7, 1845.

8   *CG,* 28/2, 36–37; Robert Greenhow, *The History of Oregon and Cali-*

*fornia, and the Other Territories on the North-West Coast of North America; Accompanied by a Geographical View and Map of Those Countries, and a Number of Documents as Proofs and Illustrations of the History* (Boston, 1844); *CG,* 28/1, 292; 28/2, 197–201, 270.

9  *CG,* 28/2, 63, 225–27, 230, 236; Adams, *Memoirs,* XII, 159.

10  *New-York Tribune,* March 6, 7, 1845; *Inaugural Addresses of the Presidents of the United States from George Washington, 1789, to John F. Kennedy, 1961* (Washington, D.C., 1961), 89–98.

11  John T. Worthington to Hardin, July 21, 1845, Hardin Papers, CHS; *Sangamo Journal,* June 12, July 24, 31, 1845; *Illinois State Register,* June 13, July 25, 1845; *Chicago Democrat,* June 25, 1845.

12  *Sangamo Journal,* June 12, 1845; *Illinois State Register,* June 13, July 11, 1845; Douglas to Ford, Feb. 7, 1845, *Illinois State Register,* March 14, 1845; *Niles' National Register,* Aug. 9, 1845.

13  *Illinois State Register,* June 13, Nov. 28, 1845; *Sangamo Journal,* June 12, July 3, Oct. 16, 1845; J. D. B. DeBow, "Convention of Southern and Western States," *De Bow's Review,* I (Jan. 1846), 7–22; Pease, *Frontier State,* 331–32; Wiltse, *Calhoun: Sectionalist,* 235–39.

14  Edward J. Doherty, The Oregon Boundary Settlement, 1840–1846 (unpublished Ph. D. dissertation, Loyola Univ., Chicago, 1956), 299–307; Norman A. Graebner, "Polk, Politics, and Oregon," East Tennessee Historical Society *Publications,* XXIV (1952), 11–12.

15  Douglas to Augustus C. French, Feb. 20, 1846, *Letters,* 134; Washington *Union,* Nov. 6, 1845; *CG,* 29/1, 25, 6–7.

16  Washington *National Intelligencer,* Dec. 12, 1845; Calhoun to James Edward Calhoun, Dec. 14, 1845, J. Franklin Jameson (ed.), *Correspondence of John C. Calhoun,* American Historical Association *Annual Report, 1899* (Washington, D.C., 1900), II, 675; Douglas to French, Feb. 20, 1846, *Letters,* 135; *CG,* 29/1, 32.

17  *CG,* 29/1, 12, 26, 53, 85, 86, 122, 172; Adams, *Memoirs,* XII, 223; Calhoun to James Edward Calhoun, Jan. 16, 1846, Jameson (ed.), *Correspondence of Calhoun,* II, 676; R. L. King to Calhoun, Dec. 10, 1845, Chauncey S. Boucher and Robert P. Brooks (eds.), *Correspondence Addressed to John C. Calhoun, 1837–1849,* American Historical Association *Annual Report, 1929* (Washington, D.C., 1930), 310–11.

18  Washington *Union,* Dec. 20, 1845; *Illinois State Register,* Jan. 16, 1846; *CG,* 29/1, 124–27, 131.

19  *CG,* 29/1, 138, 258–60, 347–50; *New-York Tribune,* Feb. 6, 1846; Washington *National Intelligencer,* Feb. 6, 1846.

20  Milo Milton Quaife (ed.), *The Diary of James Knox Polk During His Presidency, 1845–1849* (4 vols., Chicago, 1910), I, 295–96; *CG,* 29/1, 395, 661, 685–87, 690–91.

21  John Hope Franklin, "The Southern Expansionists of 1846," *JSH,* XXV (Aug. 1959), 330–36; Robert Toombs to George W. Crawford, Feb. 6, 1846, Ulrich B. Phillips (ed.), *The Correspondence of Robert Toombs, Alexander H. Stephens and Howell Cobb,* American Historical Association *Annual Report,*

*1911* (Washington, D.C., 1913), II, 74; *CG,* 29 / 1, 497, 499, 686–87; *New-York Tribune,* March 16, 19, 1846.

22  *CG,* 29 / 1, 720–21; *Illinois State Register,* May 8, 1846; Charles Sellers, *James K. Polk: Continentalist, 1843–1846* (Princeton, 1966), 387–97, 410–12; Polk, *Diary,* I, 478.

23  *CG,* 29 / 1, 1200–1201, 1203–4; Washington *National Intelligencer,* August 15, 1846.

24  Cave Johnson to Polk, Dec. 6, 26, 1844, Polk Papers, LC; George M. Dallas to Philip N. Dallas, Dec. 1, 1845, Roy F. Nichols (ed.), "The Mystery of the Dallas Papers," *Pennsylvania Magazine of History and Biography,* LXXIII (July 1949), 20; Polk, *Diary,* I, 153–56, 280, 344–45.

25  *CG,* 29 / 1, 39–40, 43, 64–65, 559; Adams, *Memoirs,* XII, 222–23.

26  *CG,* 29 / 1, 559, 1053; *Illinois State Register,* April 24, 1845; Howell Cobb to Mrs. Cobb, June 14, 1846, Jameson (ed.), *Correspondence of Toombs, Stephens and Cobb,* II, 81–82; Washington *Union,* July 3, 7, 1846; Polk, *Diary,* I, 26–27.

27  Calhoun to Thomas G. Clemson, July 11, 1846, *Correspondence of Calhoun,* II, 700–701; *CG,* 29 / 1, 497–98, 518, 530–31, 1183–84.

28  *Illinois State Register,* April 3, Aug. 31, 1846; Polk, *Diary,* II, 62–63; *Quincy Whig,* Aug. 19, 1846; Washington *Union,* Aug. 14, 17, 1846.

# CHAPTER IX

1  Henry W. Hilliard, *Politics and Pen Pictures At Home and Abroad* (New York, 1892), 129; John W. Forney, *Anecdotes of Public Men* (2 vols., New York, 1873), I, 146; *Chicago Democrat,* Dec. 15, 1845; *Chicago Journal,* Oct. 30, Dec. 8, 1845; *Sangamo Journal,* Nov. 6, 1845; Polk, *Diary,* I, 479, II, 116, 119.

2  *Illinois State Register,* Jan. 16, May 8, 1846; *Quincy Whig,* June 3, July 15, 22, 1846; Pease (ed.), *Illinois Election Returns,* 157.

3  Semple, quoted in Stevens, "Douglas," *JISHS,* XVI, 393–94; George T. M. Davis to Hardin, Jan. 10, 1845, Hardin Papers, CHS; Douglas to Breese, Oct. 20, Nov. 6, 1846, *Letters,* 144–45.

4  Ford, *History of Illinois,* 390; Josiah McRoberts to Douglas, Nov. 16, 1846, Douglas Papers, Chicago; Douglas to Harry Wilton, Nov. 14, 1846, *Letters,* 146–47; Polk, *Diary,* II, 310–13.

5  Lanphier to Breese, Oct. 25, 1846, Breese Papers, ISHL; Caton to Douglas, Dec. 17, 1846, Caton Papers, LC; Douglas to Caton, Nov. 24, to William Martin, Nov. 19, to Hall Simms, Nov. 16, to Breese, Nov. 19, 1846, *Letters,* 147–50.

6  *Illinois State Register,* Dec. 18, 25, 1846; *New-York Tribune,* Dec. 25, 1846; *Chicago Journal,* Dec. 29, 1846; A. W. French, "Men and Manners of the Early Days in Illinois," *TISHS,* 1903, 73–74.

7  Douglas to Polk, Aug. 21, 25, 1845, *Letters,* 118, 119–20.

8  Polk, *Diary,* I, 34, 382; George L. Rives, *The United States and Mexico,*

*1821–1848* (2 vols., New York, 1913), II, 63–80, 118–19, 122–23, 157; Douglas to Hardin, May 2, 1846, *Letters,* 137; *CG,* 29/1, 783.

9   Dallas to Mrs. Dallas, May 12, 1846, Nichols (ed.), "The Mystery of the Dallas Papers," *Pa. Mag. of Hist. and Biog.,* LXXIII, 30; Wiltse, *Calhoun: Sectionalist,* 282–83; *CG,* 29/1, 791–804, 810.

10   *CG,* 29/1, 814–17, App. 903–8; Forney, *Anecdotes of Public Men,* I, 48, 52; *Illinois State Register,* June 26, 1846; John H. Dobson to David S. Reid, June 20, 1846, Reid Papers, NCDAH.

11   *Alton Telegraph & Democratic Review,* May 30, 1846; *Sangamo Journal,* July 2, 1846; Evarts B. Greene and Charles M. Thompson, *Governors' Letter-Books, 1840–1853* (Springfield, 1911), cv–cvi; Hardin to Douglas, Feb. 2, 5, May 14, 20, 31, June 3, 1846, Douglas Family Papers, Greensboro; Douglas to Hardin, May 15, 1846, *Letters,* 138; John H. McHenry to Hardin, June 27, 1846, Hardin Papers, CHS.

12   Polk, *Diary,* I, 478, 493; Hardin to Douglas, June 3, 1846, Douglas Family Papers, Greensboro.

13   Douglas to Hardin, June 16, 1846, *Letters,* 140; Polk, *Diary,* I, 482–83; Hardin to Douglas, June 16, 1846, Douglas Family Papers, Greensboro; Hardin to Douglas, June 28, 1846, Douglas Papers, Chicago; Polk, *Diary,* I, 484–85.

14   *New-York Tribune,* June 23, 1846; *Sangamo Journal,* July 9, 16, 1846; Douglas to the Editors of the *Alton Telegraph,* July 20, 1846, *Letters,* 143.

15   *Sangamo Journal,* Dec. 17, 1846, Jan. 21, 1847; Polk, *Diary,* II, 307, 368.

16   Polk, *Diary,* II, 275–76; *CG,* 29/2, 295–98; Washington *Union,* Feb. 1, 1847.

17   *CG,* 29/2, 13–15; Polk, *Diary,* II, 284–85; *Quincy Whig,* Feb. 24, 1847.

18   *CG,* 29/2, 452, 472; Polk, *Diary,* II, 211–12.

19   Fehrenbacher, *Chicago Giant,* 75–76; Washington *Union,* Feb. 3, 6, 1847; *New-York Tribune,* Feb. 9, 1847; *CG,* 29/2, 349–50, 360, 426.

20   Charles Buxton Going, *David Wilmot, Free Soiler: A Biography of the Great Advocate of the Wilmot Proviso* (New York, 1924), 94–102; Chaplain W. Morrison, *Democratic Politics and Sectionalism: The Wilmot Proviso Controversy* (Chapel Hill, N.C., 1967), 16–20; *New-York Tribune,* Aug. 10, 1846; New York *Herald,* Aug. 11, 1846; *CG,* 29/1, 1213–18.

21   *CG,* 29/1, 1217–18; *Illinois State Register,* April 2, 1847; New York *Herald,* Aug. 13, 1846; Polk, *Diary,* II, 75; Eric Foner, "The Wilmot Proviso Revisited," *Journal of American History,* LVI (Sept. 1969), 262–79.

22   *CG,* 29/2, 71, 166, 169–70, 188.

23   Washington *Union,* Jan. 4, 1847; Polk, *Diary,* II, 305; *Illinois State Register,* Jan. 29, 1847.

24   *CG,* 29/2, 303, 424–25; *New-York Tribune,* Feb. 3, 1847.

25   *CG,* 29/2, 573, App., 495–96.

26   *New-York Tribune,* March 8, 1847; Chicago *Western Citizen,* March 4, 1846; *Chicago Journal,* March 9, 1847; *Quincy Whig,* Jan. 27, 1847.

## CHAPTER X

1    Mary Jane Windle, *Life in Washington, and Life Here and There* (Philadelphia, 1859), 65–67; *New-York Independent*, May 1, 1856; Milburn, *Ten Years of Preacher Life*, 136.

2    *Sangamo Journal*, Feb. 25, 1847; *Chicago Democrat*, Feb. 21, 1844.

3    Stevens, "Douglas," *JISHS*, XVI, 362–63; Harry Z. Tucker, "The Story of Lucinda and Martha Martin," Greensboro *Daily News*, June 19, 1932; Martha Martin to Henrietta Settle, March 18, 1841, Robert Martin to Douglas, Sept. 26, 1846, Douglas Family Papers, Greensboro; *Sangamo Journal*, Feb. 25, 1847.

4    Douglas to David S. Reid, March 24, 1847, Reid Papers, NCDAH; George M. Davis to Douglas, May 9, 1847, Douglas Papers, Chicago.

5    Robert Martin to Reid, Dec. 17, 1844, David S. Reid Papers, DU; Stevens, "Douglas," *JISHS*, XVI, 641–42.

6    Stevens, "Douglas," *JISHS*, XVI, 637; *Quincy Whig*, May 19, 1847; *Illinois State Register*, March 17, 1848.

7    Bessie Louise Pierce, *A History of Chicago* (3 vols., New York, 1937–57), I, *passim; Norris' Business Directory and Statistics of the City of Chicago for 1846* (Fergus Historical Series, No. 25, Chicago, 1883), 6–7, 19.

8    *Norris' Business Directory*, 19; Pierce, *A History of Chicago*, I, 396–97, 425–28; Mentor L. Williams, "The Chicago River and Harbor Convention, 1847," *MVHR*, XXXV (March 1949), 607–26; Robert Fergus (comp.), *Chicago River-and-Harbor Convention, An Account of Its Origin and Proceedings* (Fergus Historical Series, No. 18, Chicago, 1882), 154.

9    Lucien P. Sanger to Douglas, Nov. 5, 1847, Douglas Family Papers, Greensboro; Illinois-Michigan Canal Records, Land Book R-2, Book D-10, Illinois State Archives, Springfield; Examination of Title . . . , Douglas Family Papers, Greensboro. I am indebted to Dr. Wayne C. Temple of the Illinois State Archives for assistance in locating Douglas' Chicago land purchases. George Fort Milton has asserted that Douglas began buying Chicago land even before he moved there (*Eve of Conflict: Stephen A. Douglas and the Needless War* [Boston, 1934], 7). No record of earlier purchases, however, has been found.

10    Last Will and Testament of Robert Martin, Lawrence County, Mississippi, June 26, 1848, James Strickland to Douglas, Oct. 15, Nov. 29, 1849, Douglas Family Papers, Greensboro; Brander Williams and Company to Douglas, Oct. 7, 1848, Douglas Papers, DU.

11    Springfield, *Illinois Journal*, Nov. 4, 1847; Washington *Union*, Nov. 1, 1847; Polk, *Diary*, III, 211.

12    *CG*, 30 / 1, 6–7; Polk, *Diary*, III, 236–37.

13    *CG*, 30 / 1, 21, 26, 92.

14    *CG*, 30 / 1, App., 221–27; *Illinois State Register*, Feb. 25, March 3, 1848.

15    *Sen. Exec. Jour.*, VII (30 / 1), 302–3; Polk, *Diary*, III, 371, 377–78.

16   *Illinois State Register,* Nov. 5, 1847; Douglas to "the Committee," Dec. 17, Washington *Union,* Dec. 24, 1847; Douglas to Samuel Treat, Feb. 19, 1848, *Letters,* 157.

17   *Sen. Exec. Doc.,* 30/1, No. 52, 4–36, 38–66; Rives, *United States and Mexico,* II, 633–37; Breese to Polk, Oct. 11, 1847, Polk Papers, LC; Treat to Douglas, April 8, 1848, Douglas Papers, Chicago.

18   New York *Herald,* March 10, 1848; Polk, *Diary,* III, 361, 446; John L. O'Sullivan to Polk, May 10, 1848, Polk Papers, LC.

19   *Illinois State Register,* April 10, 1851.

20   *CG,* 29/1, 126.

21   *CG,* 28/2, 284; Franklin A. Doty, "Florida, Iowa, and the National 'Balance of Power,' 1845," *Florida Historical Quarterly,* XXXV (July 1956), 30–59.

22   *CG,* 29/1, 789–90, 941, 1203; Douglas to George Manierre, July 15, 1846, *Letters,* 142.

23   *CG,* 30/1, 136, 309, 788–89, 804, 809.

24   *CG,* 30/1, 809, 875; Calhoun to James Edward Calhoun, July 9, 1848, Jameson (ed.), *Correspondence of Calhoun,* II, 759; Polk, *Diary,* III, 501–5.

25   *CG,* 30/1, 927–28, 950, 1002–5; Polk, *Diary,* IV, 20–21; Washington *Union,* July 19, 1848.

26   *CG,* 30/1, 1007, 1027, 1031, 1043, 1061, 1074, 1078; Polk, *Diary,* IV, 73–74.

27   J. Bragg to Van Buren, March 10, 1847, Van Buren Papers, LC; John Wentworth to Augustus French, Dec. 19, 1847, Augustus French Papers, ISHL; Calhoun to Duff Green, Nov. 9, 1847, Jameson (ed.), *Correspondence of Calhoun,* II, 740.

28   Wentworth to French, Dec. 19, 1847, French Papers, ISHL; D. L. Seymour to Douglas, March 25, 1848, Douglas Papers, Chicago.

29   Washington *Union,* Aug. 31, 1847; Wiltse, *Calhoun: Sectionalist,* 346–48.

30   New York *Herald,* Oct. 7, 1847; *CG,* 30/1, App., 86–88.

31   Lewis Cass to A. O. P. Nicholson, Dec. 24, 1847, in Washington *Union,* Dec. 30, 1847; Robert R. Russel, "Constitutional Doctrines with Regard to Slavery in Territories," *JSH,* XXXII (Nov. 1966), 472–74.

32   Charles Fletcher, Aug. 3, 1846, N. T. Rosseter to Douglas, Jan. 2, 1848, Douglas Family Papers, Greensboro; E. S. Kimberly to Douglas, April 10, 1848, Douglas Papers, Chicago; *Chicago Democrat,* March 12 [21], 1848.

33   Charles H. Lanphier to McClernand, Jan. 16, 1848, McClernand Papers, ISHL; McClernand to Lanphier, March 4, 1848, Charles H. Lanphier Papers, ISHL; Samuel Treat to Douglas, April 8, 1848, Douglas Papers, Chicago.

34   Washington *Union,* May 19, 1848; *New-York Tribune,* May 22, 1848; Douglas to Samuel Treat, Feb. 19, April 26, 1848, *Letters,* 157, 158–59.

35   J. Knox Walker to Polk, May 22, 24, 1848, Polk Papers, LC; Washington *Union,* May 27, 28, 1848; Kirk H. Porter and Donald B. Johnson (comps.), *National Party Platforms, 1840–1964* (Urbana, 1966), 10–12.

36　New York *Herald,* May 24, 1848; Porter and Johnson (comps.), *National Party Platforms,* 13.

37　Polk, *Diary,* III, 502, IV, 36–37; Fehrenbacher, *Chicago Giant,* 82–84; J. McRoberts to Lanphier, June 15, 1848, Lanphier Papers, ISHL; *Chicago Journal,* June 26, 1848; *Quincy Whig,* Sept. 12, 1848.

38　W. W. Holden to David S. Reid, April 19, 1848, Reid Papers, NCDAH; *Illinois State Register,* May 19, 1848; *Raleigh Register,* April 22, 1848, quoted in Paul Apperson Reid, Gubernatorial Campaigns and Administrations of David S. Reid, 1848–1854 (unpublished M.A. thesis, Univ. of North Carolina, 1938), 3.

39　Douglas to Cass, June 13, 1848, *Letters,* 160–61; Washington *Union,* June 24, July 13, 1848; John D. Freeman *et al.* to Douglas, June 22, 1848, Douglas Family Papers, Greensboro.

40　Douglas to Robert Smith, Sept. 20, 1848, *Letters,* 163–64; *Illinois State Register,* Nov. 3, 1848; Joseph G. Rayback, *Free Soil: The Election of 1848* (Lexington, Ky., 1970), 287; *Quincy Herald,* Nov. 17, 1848.

## CHAPTER XI

1　Polk, *Diary,* IV, 251; *CG,* 30/2, 5; Washington *Union,* Dec. 23, 1848; Calhoun to John H. Means, April 13, 1849, Jameson (ed.), *Correspondence of Calhoun,* II, 764; New York *Herald,* Dec. 19, 1848.

2　*Richmond Whig,* quoted in *Alton Telegraph & Democratic Review,* Aug. 10, 1849. See Morrison, *Democratic Politics and Sectionalism: The Wilmot Proviso Controversy.*

3　*CG,* 30/1, App., 506–7; 30/2, 208.

4　*National Whig,* quoted in *Illinois State Register,* April 10, 1849.

5　For detailed discussions of these constitutional arguments on the question of slavery in the territories, see Allan Nevins, "The Constitution, Slavery and the Territories," *The Gaspar G. Bacon Lectures on the Constitution of the United States, 1940–1950* (Boston, 1953), 97–141, and Russel, "Constitutional Doctrines with Regard to Slavery in Territories," *JSH,* XXXII, 466–86.

6　For a commentary on the development of the doctrine of non-intervention, see Milo M. Quaife, *The Doctrine of Non-Intervention with Slavery in the Territories* (Chicago, 1910).

7　Washington *Union,* Nov. 15, 1848; Polk, *Diary,* IV, 192–94.

8　Dallas to Mrs. Dallas, Dec. 7, 1848, in Nichols (ed.), "The Mystery of the Dallas Papers," *Pa. Mag. of Hist. and Biog.,* LXXIII, 47; Polk to Cass, Dec. 15, 1848, Lewis Cass Papers, WLC.

9　New York *Herald,* Dec. 12, 1848; McClernand to Lanphier and Walker, May 30, 1848, Lanphier Papers, ISHL; *Quincy Herald,* Nov. 10, 1848; John M. Clayton to John J. Crittenden, Dec. 13, 1848, John M. Clayton Papers, LC; New York *Herald,* Dec. 17, 1848; Dallas, Diary Entry, Dec. 13, 1848, in Nichols (ed.), "The Mystery of the Dallas Papers," *Pa. Mag. of Hist. and Biog.,* LXXIII, 55–56.

10　*CG,* 30/2, 1, 21; New York *Herald,* Dec. 11, 13, 14, 1848; *CG,* 30/2,

39, 71; Joshua R. Giddings, *History of the Rebellion: Its Authors and Causes* (New York, 1864), 294.

11   *CG*, 30/2, 46–47; Dallas, Diary Entry, Dec. 18, 1848, in Nichols (ed.), "The Mystery of the Dallas Papers," *Pa. Mag. of Hist. and Biog.*, LXXIII, 57; Polk, *Diary*, IV, 253–54; *CG*, 30/2, 191–92, 194.

12   *CG*, 30/2, 192–93; *Illinois State Register*, April 29, 1849.

13   *CG*, 30/2, 208.

14   Polk, *Diary*, IV, 232–33, 235, 236–37, 257.

15   *CG*, 30/2, 262; Polk, *Diary*, IV, 279, 286–87, 303–4; *CG*, 30/2, 340–42.

16   Polk, *Diary*, IV, 298; Wiltse, *Calhoun: Sectionalist*, 378–88; Calhoun to Mrs. T. G. Clemson, Jan. 24, 1849, Jameson (ed.), *Correspondence of Calhoun*, II, 762; Hilliard M. Judge to Calhoun, April 29, 1849, *ibid.* 1195; Polk, *Diary*, IV, 287–88; Alexander H. Stephens to Crittenden, Jan. 17, 1849, Alexander H. Stephens Papers, DU; Howell Cobb to Mrs. Cobb, Feb. 8, 1849, R. P. Brooks, "Howell Cobb Papers," *Georgia Historical Quarterly*, V (June 1921), 38; Robert Toombs to Crittenden, Jan. 22, 1849, Crittenden Papers, LC.

17   *CG*, 30/2, 381; Polk, *Diary*, IV, 312–13; Hopkins Holsey to Cobb, Feb. 13, 1849, Phillips (ed.), *Correspondence of Toombs, Stephens and Cobb*, II, 149–50; Washington *Union*, Feb. 4, 8, 1849; *CG*, 30/2, 435, 551, 552, 553.

18   *CG*, 30/2, 561, 562, 573, 668, App., 264, 267, 275 (the full debate may be found on pp. 253–309); Merle E. Curti, "Isaac P. Walker: Reformer in Mid-Century Politics," *Wisconsin Magazine of History*, XXXIV (Autumn 1950), 58–59.

19   *CG*, 30/2, 664–65, 666, 680, 682–91, 696; Washington *Union*, March 6, 1849.

20   *CG*, 30/2, 314–15; *Illinois State Register*, June 7, 1849.

21   *CG*, 30/2, 1, 68, 298–99, 635–36.

22   Washington *Union*, Nov. 7, 1849.

23   Oliver Dyer, *Great Senators of the United States Forty Years Ago (1848–1849), With Personal Recollections . . .* (New York, 1889), 129–31.

24   Stevens, "Douglas," *JISHS*, XVI, 637; Douglas to Adelaide Granger, May 30, July 28, 1849, *Letters*, 170–71; *Illinois State Register*, Aug. 22, 1849; Reid to Douglas, Sept. 3, 1849, William H. James to Douglas, Jan. 16, Feb. 27, 28, 1850, Douglas Family Papers, Greensboro. One newspaper report declared that Douglas had suffered an attack of cholera "followed by bilious diarrhoea," but it seems improbable that he had contracted the dread disease (*Illinois State Register*, September 10, 1849).

25   Arthur C. Cole, *The Era of the Civil War, 1848–1870* (*The Centennial History of Illinois*, III; Chicago, 1922), 61.

26   *Illinois Journal*, Nov. 15, Dec. 6, 1848; *Quincy Whig*, Nov. 21, 1848; *Illinois State Register*, Dec. 1, 1848; *Alton Telegraph & Democratic Review*, Jan. 12, 1849.

27   *Illinois House Journal, 1849*, 52, 55; *Illinois Senate Journal, 1849*, 38, 42–43.

28   *Illinois State Register,* Jan. 11, 20, 1849.

29   *Alton Telegraph & Democratic Review,* Jan. 12, 1849; *Illinois State Register,* Jan. 10, 1849. See also *Quincy Herald,* Jan. 19, 1849.

30   George T. M. Davis to Elihu Washburne, Jan. 14, 1849, Elihu Washburne Papers, LC; *Illinois Journal,* June 20, 1849; *Alton Telegraph & Democratic Review,* Jan. 19, March 16, 1849; *New-York Tribune,* Jan. 25, 1849; *Quincy Herald,* March 30, 1849; *Chicago Journal,* Feb. 13, 1849.

31   *Quincy Herald,* Jan. 26, 1849; *Illinois State Register,* Jan. 16, 1849; *Illinois Journal,* Jan. 17, 1849; L. P. Lacey to Douglas, Jan. 28, 1849, Douglas Papers, Chicago; *CG,* 30/2, 394; 32/1, App., 68.

32   *Illinois State Register,* June 14, Nov. 1, 2, 6, 1849.

33   *Alton Telegraph & Democratic Review,* Oct. 26, 1849; *Illinois Journal,* June 20, Oct. 31, 1849.

34   Douglas to Polk, April 17, 1845, *Letters,* 112–13; Breese to Polk, March 11, 1845, Polk Papers, LC; Shields to Douglas, June 6, 1848, Endorsement on McClernand to Douglas, May 1849, Douglas Papers, Chicago.

35   Shields to Douglas, July 12, 1848, Douglas Papers, Chicago; Polk, *Diary,* IV, 229–30; *Illinois Journal,* Jan. 17, 1849; Ottawa *Free Trader,* in *Illinois Journal,* Nov. 1, 1848; *Rockford Forum,* Jan. 17, 24, 1849; *Quincy Whig,* Jan. 30, 1849; Douglas to Charles H. Lanphier and George Walker, Jan. 7, 1850, *Letters,* 182.

36   *Illinois State Register,* Jan. 13, 1849; Arnold, *Reminiscences,* 142; Dallas to Mrs. Dallas, Jan. 17, 1849, in Nichols (ed.), "The Mystery of the Dallas Papers," *Pa. Mag. of Hist. and Biog.,* LXXIII, 66.

37   *CG,* 30/2, App. (Special Session), 326–29, 332–51; New York *Herald,* March 15, 20, 1849. In a letter to Breese earlier in the year, Darius B. Holbrook, writing from New York, reported that Douglas had said Shields was ineligible and that he could not therefore support him; in view of Douglas' later position as well as the lack of close relations between Holbrook and Douglas, little credence may be placed in this statement (Holbrook to Breese, Jan. 16, 1849, Breese Papers, ISHL).

38   Shields to Breese, Feb. 23, 1849, *Illinois State Register,* March 14, 1849; Shields to Augustus C. French, March 7, 14, 17, 1849, French Papers, ISHL; Lewis A. Birdsall to Douglas, March 18, 1849, Douglas Papers, Chicago; *CG,* 30/2, App. (Special Session), 333, 338.

39   Shields to French, May 3, 1849, Wentworth to French, May 20, 1849, French Papers, ISHL; *Illinois State Register,* May 28, Aug. 25, 1849; *Illinois Journal,* May 30, 1849; *Quincy Herald,* Aug. 3, 1849; Douglas to French, May 16, 1849, Douglas to Lanphier and Walker, Aug. 13, 1849, *Letters,* 167–69, 173.

40   *Illinois State Register,* Oct. 27, 1849.

## CHAPTER XII

1   New York *Herald,* Dec. 1, 1849, Jan. 16, 1850; David Outlaw to Emily Outlaw, Dec. 10, 1849, David Outlaw Papers, SHC; Henry L. Benning to Howell Cobb, July 1, 1849, Phillips (ed.), *Correspondence of Toombs, Stephens and Cobb,* 171.

2   Cleo Hearon, "Mississippi and the Compromise of 1850," *Publications of the Mississippi Historical Society,* XIV (1913), 62–68; Calhoun to Thomas G. Clemson, Dec. 8, 1849, Jameson (ed.), *Correspondence of Calhoun,* II, 776.

3   Stephens to Crittenden, Dec. 17, 1849, Stephens Papers, DU; Thomas L. Harris to Lanphier, Jan. 12, 1850, Lanphier Papers, ISHL.

4   William H. Bissell to Joseph Gillespie, Dec. 15, 1849, Gillespie Papers, ISHL; New York *Herald,* March 6, April 18, 1850.

5   *Illinois State Register,* Jan. 3, 1850; New York *Herald,* Dec. 3, 1849, Jan. 31, 1850; *CG,* 31/1, 311, 319, 320, 1330.

6   *CG,* 31/1, 71.

7   Baker to Clayton, March 20, 1849, Clayton Papers, LC; Holman Hamilton, *Zachary Taylor: Soldier in the White House* (Indianapolis, 1951), 178–80; Clayton to Crittenden, April 18, 1849, Crittenden Papers, LC; King to Clayton, June 20, 1849, Clayton Papers, LC.

8   Loomis Morton Ganaway, *New Mexico and the Sectional Controversy, 1846–1861* (Historical Society of New Mexico, *Publications in History,* XII; Albuquerque, 1944), 38–52.

9   Brigham Young, Heber C. Kimball, and Willard Richards to Douglas, May 2, 1849, Yale University Library; Young, Kimball and Richards to Douglas, July 20, 1849, Douglas Family Papers, Greensboro; Bissell to Gillespie, April 19, 1850, Gillespie Papers, ISHL; Dale L. Morgan, "The State of Deseret," *Utah Historical Quarterly,* VIII (April, July, Oct. 1940), 82–92.

10   Douglas to the Editors of the *Chicago Tribune,* Jan. 29, 1850, *Letters,* 184–86.

11   *CG,* 31/1, 110, 181–85.

12   *CG,* 31/1, 86–87, 211–13; Douglas to Lanphier and Walker, Jan. 7, 1850, *Letters,* 182–83; Douglas to C. R. N. Patterson, Feb. 4, 1850, quoted in Milton, *Eve of Conflict,* 51.

13   Clay to James Harlan, Jan. 24, 1850, Calvin Colton (ed.), *The Private Correspondence of Henry Clay* (New York, 1856), 600; Glyndon G. Van Deusen, *The Life of Henry Clay* (Boston, 1937), 399.

14   *CG,* 31/1, 244–46; Holman Hamilton, *Prologue to Conflict: The Crisis and Compromise of 1850* (Lexington, Ky., 1964), 53–54.

15   Speech of Douglas, Cincinnati, Sept. 9, 1859, Harry V. Jaffa and Robert W. Johannsen (eds.), *In the Name of the People: Speeches and Writings of Lincoln and Douglas in the Ohio Campaign of 1859* (Columbus, 1959), 160; *Illinois State Register,* Feb. 14, 1850; Washington *Union,* Feb. 7, 1850.

16   New York *Herald,* Feb. 8, 22, 1850; *New-York Tribune,* Feb. 11, 1850; Washington *Union,* Feb. 12, 1850; *Chicago Journal,* Feb. 11, 16, 1850.

17   *CG,* 31/1, 375–76; Alexander H. Stephens, *A Constitutional View of the Late War Between the States* (2 vols., Philadelphia, 1868–70), II, 201–4; Frank H. Hodder, "The Authorship of the Compromise of 1850," *MVHR,* XXII (March 1936), 527–28.

18   Edmund Burke to Douglas, Feb. 13, 1850, Douglas Papers, Chicago; Francis Preston Blair to Van Buren, March 24, 1850, Van Buren Papers, LC; Charles H. Ambler, *Thomas Ritchie: A Study in Virginia Politics* (Richmond, 1913), 282–83; Washington *Union,* March 24, 1850.

19   *New-York Tribune,* Feb. 8, 1850; *CG,* 31/1, 355, 356, 436–38, 592, App., 115, 127; Joseph H. Parks, *John Bell of Tennessee* (Baton Rouge, 1950), 244–46; Washington *Union,* Feb. 12, 1850.

20   *CG,* 31/1, 342–43, App., 151–52.

21   *CG,* 31/1, 451–55 (Calhoun), 476–84 (Webster), App., 260–69 (Seward); Wiltse, *Calhoun: Sectionalist,* 460–69; Peter Harvey, *Reminiscences and Anecdotes of Daniel Webster* (Boston, 1877), 219–20; Herbert D. Foster, "Webster's Seventh of March Speech and the Secession Movement, 1850," *AHR,* XXVII (Jan. 1922), 245–70; Glyndon G. Van Deusen, *William Henry Seward* (New York, 1967), 122–24.

22   *New-York Tribune,* March 15, 1850; New York *Herald,* March 16, 1850.

23   *CG,* 31/1, App., 364–75.

24   Buchanan to Douglas, March 22, 1850, Douglas Family Papers, Greensboro; *CG,* 31/1, App., 371, 373, 368, 375 (in order of citation).

25   *CG,* 31/1, 592, 628–29; 32/1, App., 67; Douglas to Lanphier and Walker, Aug. 3, 1850, *Letters,* 191–92; John M. Bernhisel to the "Brethren," March 5, 21, to Brigham Young, March 27, 1850, Journal History.

26   Washington *Union,* March 26, 28, 1850; Correspondence of the *Baltimore Sun, Alton Telegraph & Democratic Review,* April 5, 1850; Savannah *Georgian,* quoted in Washington *Union,* April 11, 1850; Thomas L. Harris to Lanphier, April 11, 1850, Lanphier Papers, ISHL; New York *Herald,* April 15, 1850.

## CHAPTER XIII

1   Bissell to Gillespie, Feb. 12, 1850, Gillespie Papers, ISHL; Shields to Lanphier and Walker, June 29, 1850, quoted in Milton, *Eve of Conflict,* 70; Richardson to an unknown correspondent, Feb. 19, 1850, quoted, *ibid.* 57; Cole, *Era of the Civil War,* 64–66, 68–70; Fehrenbacher, *Chicago Giant,* 97.

2   *Illinois State Register,* March 5, 7, 1850; Douglas to James H. Woodworth, March 5, 1850, *Letters,* 187–89; *CG,* 31/1, App., 370, 373; *Illinois Journal,* Feb. 27, 1850; Charles Sumner to Salmon P. Chase, Jan. 24, 1850, Salmon P. Chase Papers, LC. For an example of freesoil misrepresentation of Douglas' course in Congress, see Bureau *Advocate,* quoted in *Quincy Whig,* Jan. 22, 1850.

3   *New-York Tribune,* Feb. 2, 1850; Henry S. Foote, *Casket of Reminiscences* (Washington, D.C., 1874), 25–26; *Thomas Ritchie's Letter, Containing Reminiscences of Henry Clay and the Compromise* (Richmond, 1852), 9–10; *CG,* 31/1, 365–67, 368, 662, 757, 762–64, 774, 780; Douglas to Lanphier and Walker, Aug. 3, 1850, *Letters,* 191.

4   Sheahan, *Douglas,* 132–34; George D. Harmon, "Douglas and the Compromise of 1850," *JISHS,* XXI (Jan. 1929), 477–79. Clay's comments in this conversation were corroborated by Cass, a member of the committee, who had told the Senate earlier that it was quite possible the committee would simply recommend the passage of bills already before the Senate (*CG,* 31/1, 798).

5   *CG,* 31/1, 944–48; Douglas to Lanphier and Walker, Aug. 3, 1850, *Letters,* 192.

6   Avery O. Craven, *The Growth of Southern Nationalism, 1848–1861* (Baton Rouge, 1953), 95–98; *CG*, 31/1, App., 615; 31/1, 954; Clay to Thomas H. Clay, May 31, 1850, Henry Clay Papers, LC.

7   *CG*, 31/1, 1003, 1114–16, 1134, 1143.

8   R. M. T. Hunter to "Line," May 19, 1850, R. M. T. Hunter Papers, UV; *CG*, 31/1, 1134, 1145–46, App., 902, 911; Hodder, "Authorship of the Compromise of 1850," *MVHR*, XXII, 530–32; Robert R. Russel, "What Was the Compromise of 1850?" *JSH*, XXII (Aug. 1956), 300–03.

9   *CG*, 31/1, 1279, App., 958–60, 848–52; Thomas L. Harris to Lanphier, June 26, 1850, Lanphier Papers, ISHL; Washington *Union,* June 27, 1850; *New-York Tribune,* June 29, 1850; New York *Herald,* June 29, 1850.

10   Harris to Lanphier, July 19, 1850, Lanphier Papers, ISHL; *Illinois State Register,* July 30, 1850; *CG*, 31/1, App., 1266; Robert J. Rayback, *Millard Fillmore: Biography of a President* (Buffalo, 1959), 247–48.

11   *CG*, 31/1, 1160, 1481, App., 1420, 1456, 1458, 1460–61, 1463.

12   *CG*, 31/1, App., 1463–73; 36/1, App., 305–6; Hodder, "Authorship of the Compromise of 1850," *MVHR*, XXII, 532–33.

13   *CG*, 31/1, App., 1473–84, 1487; Rayback, *Fillmore,* 249–50; Hamilton, *Prologue to Conflict,* 110–14.

14   *CG*, 31/1, App., 1484; Robert C. Winthrop, Jr., *A Memoir of Robert C. Winthrop* (Boston, 1897), 134–35; Clay to Dr. F. Campbell Stewart, July 30, 1850, Clay Papers, LC; McClernand to Lanphier, July 31, 1850, Lanphier Papers, ISHL; David Outlaw to Emily Outlaw, Aug. 1, 1850, Outlaw Papers, SHC; Douglas to Lanphier and Walker, Aug. 3, 1850, *Letters,* 191.

15   *CG*, 31/1, 1503, App., 1483–85, 1505; Douglas to Lanphier and Walker, Aug. 3, 1850, *Letters,* 192.

16   *CG*, 31/1, 1503–4, 1573, 1589, 1520–21, 1555, 1791, App., 1485–1541, 1556–61.

17   New York *Herald,* Aug. 8, 13, 1850; Douglas to Lanphier and Walker, Aug. 3, 1850, *Letters,* 192–93; *CG*, 31/1, 1830.

18   *CG*, 31/1, 1660, 1830, App., 1664; 32/1, App., 66; *Chicago Journal,* Aug. 30, 1850; *Illinois State Register,* Sept. 4, 1850.

19   Hamilton, *Prologue to Conflict,* 155–60; New York *Herald,* Sept. 10, 1850.

20   *CG*, 32/1, App., 66; Harris to Lanphier, Sept. 25, 1850, Lanphier Papers, ISHL; Doctor bill, Oct. 2, 1850, Douglas Family Papers, Greensboro; *Illinois Journal,* Oct. 14, 1850; Douglas to Lanphier, Oct. 2, 1850, *Letters,* 196.

21   New York *Herald,* Jan. 29, 1850; Edward C. West to Douglas, May 11, 1850, Douglas Papers, Chicago; *New-York Tribune,* Oct. 11, 1850; *Illinois State Register,* Nov. 15, 19, 1850; Breese to Douglas, July 25, 1850, Douglas Papers, Chicago; Washington *National Intelligencer,* March 27, 1851.

22   O. C. Skinner, Sept. 11, S. S. Hayes to Douglas, April 13, 1850, Douglas Papers, Chicago; *Joliet Signal,* in *Illinois State Register,* Dec. 12, 1850; Harris to Lanphier, Sept. 21, 1850, Lanphier Papers, ISHL.

23   *Quincy Whig,* July 23, 1850; Douglas to Lanphier, Aug. 3, 1850, *Let-*

*ters,* 189–91; *Illinois State Register,* July 25, 1850; Douglas to Walker and Lanphier, Sept. 5, 1850, *Letters,* 194.

24   Augustus C. French, June 21, Isaac R. Diller, Sept. 16, Austin Brooks, June 9, 1850, Daniel Shaw to Douglas, Jan. 24, 1852, Douglas Papers, Chicago; Harris to French, July 27, 1850, French Papers, ISHL; *Chicago Journal,* March 27, 1851; Fehrenbacher, *Chicago Giant,* 102.

25   Cole, *Era of the Civil War,* 70–72; Muelder, *Fighters for Freedom,* 351; *Illinois State Register,* Oct. 28, 1850.

26   *Chicago Journal,* Oct. 23, 24, 1850; *Speech of Hon. Stephen A. Douglas, on the "Measures of Adjustment," Delivered in the City Hall, Chicago, October 23, 1850* (Washington, D.C., 1851), *passim;* New York *Herald,* Nov. 18, 1850; Washington *Union,* Oct. 29, 1850, March 11, 1851; *Illinois State Register,* Jan. 16, Feb. 8, 17, 1851.

27   *Illinois State Register,* Nov. 4, 8, 1850; *Illinois Journal,* Nov. 5, 1850; Adelaide Granger to Douglas, Sept. 18, 1850, Douglas Family Papers, Greensboro; New York *Herald,* Nov. 17, 1850; *CG,* 32 / 1, App., 68.

## CHAPTER XIV

1   Douglas to Whitney, Oct. 15, 1845, *Letters,* 127–33; *Illinois State Register,* Oct. 9, 15, 18, 22, 25, 27, 29, 1849; *Chicago Journal,* Oct. 22, 23, 1849; New York *Herald,* Oct. 30, 1849; R. S. Cotterill, "The National Railroad Convention in St. Louis, 1849," *Missouri Historical Review,* XII (July 1918), 203–15.

2   Paul Wallace Gates, *The Illinois Central Railroad and Its Colonization Work* (Cambridge, 1934), 24–32; Douglas to Breese, Jan. 5, Feb. 22, 1851, *Letters,* 199–202, 213; Breese to Douglas, Jan. 25, 1851, in William K. Ackerman, *Early Illinois Railroads* (Chicago, 1884), 80.

3   Gates, *Illinois Central Railroad,* 29, 33; Holbrook to Breese, Jan. 13, 16, 18, 25, 29, Feb. 2, 3, 5, 1849, Breese Papers, ISHL; *Illinois State Register,* Oct. 15, 1849; Douglas to French, Dec. 27, 1849, *Letters,* 178–81; Holbrook to French, Dec. 24, 1849, French Papers, ISHL.

4   *CG,* 31 / 1, 99, 344, 844, 851, 852, 904; Douglas to Thompson Campbell, June 7, 1852, Campbell to Editor, [n.d.], Washington *Union,* June 10, 1852; J. Madison Cutts, *A Brief Treatise upon Constitutional and Party Questions, and the History of Political Parties, As I Received It Orally from the Late Senator Stephen A. Douglas, of Illinois* (New York, 1866), 193–95.

5   *Illinois Journal,* May 16, 1850; *New-York Weekly Tribune,* May 11, 1850; Gates, *Illinois Central Railroad,* 41–42.

6   *Illinois Journal,* Feb. 14, June 7, 1850; Cutts, *A Brief Treatise upon Constitutional and Party Questions,* 196–98; Hamilton, *Prologue to Conflict,* 121; *CG,* 31 / 1, 1838. Douglas' version (as recorded by Cutts) has been challenged in some of its details by John Bell Sanborn, *Congressional Grants of Land in Aid of Railways* (Madison, 1899), 129–30. See also Milton, *Eve of Conflict,* 10–11.

7   Fehrenbacher, *Chicago Giant,* 107–8; John Wentworth, *Congressional Reminiscences: Adams, Benton, Calhoun, Clay, and Webster* (Chicago, 1882),

41–42; Harris to Lanphier, Aug. 5, 1850, Lanphier Papers, ISHL; Holbrook to French, June 20, 1850, French Papers, ISHL; Breese to Douglas, Jan. 25, 1851, in Ackerman, *Early Illinois Railroads,* 89.

8   Gates, *Illinois Central Railroad,* 36–41; Douglas to Lanphier, Oct. 2, 1850, to the Citizens of Chicago, [Oct. 1850], to W. W. Corcoran, Sept. 10, 1850, *Letters,* 196, 197, 195; Hamilton, *Prologue to Conflict,* 121; John F. May to French, Nov. 21, 1851, French Papers, ISHL; Holbrook to Douglas, June 17, 20, 1850, Douglas Papers, Chicago.

9   Douglas to Citizens of Chicago, [Oct. 1850], to Breese, Feb. 22, 1851, to Lanphier, Oct. 2, 1850, *Letters,* 197, 209, 213, 196; *Chicago Journal,* Oct. 15, 1850; Cutts, *A Brief Treatise upon Constitutional and Party Questions,* 192–93, 199; Breese to Lanphier, Dec. 23, 1850, Lanphier Papers, ISHL; Holbrook to French, Sept. 27, 1850, French Papers, ISHL; French to Holbrook, Nov. 1, 1850, Greene and Thompson (eds.), *Governors' Letter-Books, 1840–1853,* 235.

10   *Illinois State Register,* May 6, 1850; Julius Wadsworth to French, Sept. 23, 1850, Greene and Thompson (eds.), *Governors' Letter-Books, 1840–1853,* 344; *Illinois State Register,* Sept. 27, Oct. 23, 1850.

11   Gates, *Illinois Central Railroad,* 46–65; Holbrook to Breese, Oct. 10, Nov. 19, 27, Dec. 24, 1850, Breese Papers, ISHL; Robert J. Walker to Douglas, Sept. 21, 1850, Douglas Papers, Chicago; Shields to French, Dec. 11, 1850, French Papers, ISHL; Bissell to Gillespie, Dec. 12, 1850, Gillespie Papers, ISHL; James P. Shenton, *Robert John Walker: A Politician from Jackson to Lincoln* (New York, 1961), 133–36; *Illinois State Register,* Nov. 27, 1850; *Illinois Journal,* Oct. 11, 1850; Wadsworth and Sheldon to French, Oct. 11, Wadsworth to French, Oct. 23, 1850, Greene and Thompson (eds.), *Governors' Letter-Books, 1840–1853,* 355, 357.

12   *Illinois Journal,* Oct. 16, 1850; Polk to Mrs. Polk, Nov. 13, 1848, Polk Papers, LC; *CG,* 30/1, 964; 30/2, 20, 60–61; John L. Stephens to Douglas, Aug. 6, 1850, Douglas Papers, Chicago; P. M. Wetmore to William L. Marcy, Nov. 28, 1851, William L. Marcy Papers, LC; *New York Times,* March 15, 1852; Washington *Union,* March 16, 1852; Gates, *Illinois Central Railroad,* 63–64; Douglas to Robert Schuyler, Aug. 4, 1852, in possession of Kenneth Ward, Chicago.

13   Roy M. Robbins, *Our Landed Heritage: The Public Domain, 1776–1936* (Princeton, 1942), 105–9, 112–16; Cole, *Era of the Civil War,* 89–91; *CG,* 31/1, 87, 128, 210, 262, 263–64, 266; *Illinois State Register,* Jan. 10, 1850; *New-York Tribune,* Jan. 11, 1850; New York *Herald,* Feb. 11, 1850.

14   *CG,* 31/1, 1739–43, 1844, 1722–34; 32/1, 1683–86; *Illinois State Register,* Sept. 17, 1850; *New York Times,* July 16, 1852.

15   *CG,* 30/2, 45; 32/1, 984, 1756–57; 32/2, 1010–12.

16   *CG,* 30/1, 964; 31/2, 132.

17   Washington *Union,* March 13, 1851; *CG,* 31/1, 87; Richard Yates to Turner, June 23, July 10, 1852, Turner to B. Murray, Feb. 16, 1853, to Lyman Trumbull, Oct. 7, 1857, Jonathan Baldwin Turner Papers, IHS; *CG,* 32/1, 920.

18    *CG,* 29/1, 749–50; William J. Rhees (ed.), *The Smithsonian Institution: Journals of the Board of Regents, Reports of Committees, Statistics, etc.* (*Smithsonian Miscellaneous Collections,* XVIII; Washington, D.C., 1880), 179. For a discussion of these interests see Robert W. Johannsen, "Stephen A. Douglas and the American Mission," in John G. Clark (ed.), *The Frontier Challenge: Responses to the Trans-Mississippi West* (Lawrence, Kans., 1971), 111–40.

19    Washington *Union,* Jan. 31, 1852; *CG,* 30/1, 964; *Chicago Tribune,* March 22, 1853; *CG,* 32/Spec. Sess., App., 270, 273, 275–76. For the context in which Douglas developed his image of Europe, see Cushing Strout, *The American Image of the Old World* (New York, 1963).

20    *CG,* 30/2, 20–21, 60–61; Robert R. Russel, *Improvement of Communication with the Pacific Coast as an Issue in American Politics, 1783–1864* (Cedar Rapids, Ia., 1948), 57–59.

21    Mary W. Williams, *Anglo-American Isthmian Diplomacy, 1815–1915* (Washington, D.C., 1916), 54–66; Elijah Hise to Douglas, Feb. 14, 1853, Douglas Papers, Chicago.

22    *CG,* 31/1, 159, 356; 31/2, 94; 32/Spec. Sess., App., 268; E. George Squier to Douglas, April 9, 1850, Douglas Papers, Chicago; Williams, *Anglo-American Isthmian Diplomacy,* 97; Robert J. Walker to Douglas, May 4, 1850, Douglas Papers, Chicago; James Buchanan to McClernand, April 2, 1850, in George E. Belknap (ed.), "Letters of Bancroft and Buchanan on the Clayton-Bulwer Treaty, 1849–50," *AHR,* V (Oct. 1899), 100–101; Buchanan to McClernand, June 29, 1850, McClernand Papers, ISHL.

23    Richard W. Van Alstyne, "British Diplomacy and the Clayton-Bulwer Treaty, 1850–60," *Journal of Modern History,* XI (June 1939), 156–68; *CG,* 32/2, App., 170–73; 32/Spec. Sess., 257–59, 271–74.

24    Edward Everett to Douglas, Feb. 16, 1853, Douglas Papers, Chicago; Van Alstyne, "British Diplomacy and the Clayton-Bulwer Treaty," *Journal of Modern History,* XI, 167; Washington *Union,* Feb. 20, March 11, 1853; *Illinois State Register,* May 27, 1853; Everett Diary, March 21, 1853, quoted in Paul R. Frothingham, *Edward Everett: Orator and Statesman* (Boston, 1925), 342; *New York Times,* March 12, 1853.

25    *Chicago Tribune,* April 6, 1853; New York *Herald,* September 2, 1851.

26    Lester Burrell Shippee, *Canadian-American Relations, 1849–1874* (New Haven, 1939), 21–31; *CG,* 31/1, 261, 324, 701–2; New York *Herald,* Feb. 9, 11, 1850; Sir Henry Lytton Bulwer to Lord Palmerston, Feb. 18, 1850, quoted in Shippee, *Canadian-American Relations,* 32; Bulwer to Palmerston, April 16, 1850, quoted in Charles C. Tansill, *The Canadian Reciprocity Treaty of 1854* (Baltimore, 1922), 34.

27    New York *Herald,* Feb. 11, 1850; Douglas to Elisha Whittlesey, June 16, 1850, Elisha Whittlesey Papers, WRHS; *CG,* 31/1, 1908; 31/2, 202–3; T. W. Dimscourt to Bulwer, Sept. 26, 1850, quoted in Shippee, *Canadian-American Relations,* 34.

28    *CG,* 30/1, 569; Arthur J. May, *Contemporary American Opinion of the Mid-Century Revolutions in Central Europe* (Philadelphia, 1927), 21–64; Merle E. Curti, "The Impact of the Revolutions of 1848 on American Thought,"

*Proceedings of the American Philosophical Society,* XCIII (June 1949), 209–15; Curti, *Austria and the United States, 1848–1852: A Study in Diplomatic Relations (Smith College Studies in History,* XI, Northampton, Mass., 1926), 169–70.

29   May, *Contemporary American Opinion of the Mid-Century Revolutions in Central Europe,* 81–102; Shields to Koerner, Dec. 1, 1851, in "Letters to Gustav Koerner, 1837–1863," *TISHS, 1907,* 241; J. Addison Thomas to William L. Marcy, Dec. 18, 1851, Marcy Papers, LC; *CG,* 32 / 1, 70–71; Herbert Alan Johnson, "Magyar-Mania in New York City: Louis Kossuth and American Politics," *New-York Historical Society Quarterly,* XLVIII (July 1964), 237–49.

30   John W. Oliver, "Louis Kossuth's Appeal to the Middle West," *MVHR,* XIV (March 1928), 481–95; *New York Times,* Jan. 5, 1852; Washington *Union,* Jan. 8, 1852; *Illinois State Register,* Feb. 5, 1852.

31   Simon Cameron to Douglas, Nov. 30, 1849, Douglas Family Papers, Greensboro; Letter of George C. Bates, May 1, 1882, quoted in Canandaigua *Ontario County Times,* May 24, 1882; Bissell to Gillespie, Feb. 8, 1850, Gillespie Papers, ISHL; New York *Herald,* Aug. 26, 1850.

32   John W. Forney, *Anecdotes of Public Men* (2 vols., New York, 1873), I, 21, 146–47, 395; *Illlinois Journal,* March 27, 1850; Invoice, Jan. 16, 1848, Liquor bill, March 7, 11, 12, 13, 1851, Bill of W. Cowles & Sons, Dec. 1, 1852, Tailor bill, Aug. 18, 1851, Douglas Family Papers, Greensboro; C. H. de la Figanure to Douglas, June 13, 1850, Douglas Papers, Chicago.

33   Stevens, "Douglas," *JISHS,* XVI, 637; Douglas to Thomas Settle, Jan. 16, 1851, *Letters,* 207; *Alton Telegraph,* May 9, 1851; Washington *Union,* Nov. 29, 1851; Douglas to Board of Aldermen and Common Council, April 26, 1853, Washington *National Intelligencer,* May 5, 1853; John S. Williams to Gideon Welles, Nov. 26, 1852, Gideon Welles Papers, LC.

34   Constance McLaughlin Green, *Washington: Village and Capital, 1800–1878* (Princeton, 1962), chapters VII, VIII, *passim; CG,* 32 / 1, 2424.

35   Examination of Title . . . [n. d.], Map of Oakenwald Subdivision . . . July 1855, James Long to Douglas, Aug. 5, 1852, Douglas Family Papers, Greensboro; Douglas to James W. Sheahan, April 6, 1855, *Letters,* 338; Douglas to Robert Schuyler, Aug. 4, 1852, in possession of Kenneth Ward, Chicago; "Americus" to Mr. Bookwalter, March 15, 1862, undated clipping in possession of Joseph Eisendrath.

36   Washington *Union,* June 2, 1850; *Chicago Journal,* June 16, 1851; *Illinois Journal,* July 9, 1851; Douglas to Sheahan, April 6, 1855, *Letters,* 338; Tax receipts, Jan. 18, 1856, Douglas Family Papers, Greensboro; Sheahan, *Douglas,* 443; Chicago Land District, Tract Book No. 687, *passim,* Receiver's Quarterly Accounts, Book D, 1846–55, *passim,* Illinois State Archives.

37   *New-York Tribune,* Feb. 2, 1854; Brander Williams & Company to Douglas, Oct. 7, 1848, Jan. 9, 1851, Douglas Papers, DU; Brander Williams & Company to Douglas, Jan. 10, 1850, Douglas Family Papers, Greensboro; Washington *Union,* Aug. 19, 1853; James Strickland to Douglas, Oct. 15, 1849, Feb. 23, 1856, Feb. 21, April 14, Aug. 6, Nov. 1, 1857, Douglas Family Papers,

Greensboro; Douglas to Lanphier, Aug. 3, 1850, *Letters,* 190; A. Harris to Douglas, Jan. 3, 1853, Douglas Family Papers, Greensboro; Articles of Agreement, May 31, 1859, Records of the United States Court of Claims, Case No. 9192, Record Group 123, NA.

38  Douglas to George N. Sanders, May 18, 1851, to ——, July 27, 1851, to Sanders, Dec. 28, 1851, *Letters,* 219, 229, 233.

## CHAPTER XV

1  W. W. Holden to David Reid, Dec. 1, 1850, Reid Papers, NCDAH; T. R. Young to French, Dec. 23, 1850, French Papers, ISHL.

2  Douglas to Settle, Jan. 16, 1851, *Letters,* 207; *CG,* 31/2, App., 312; 32/1, 1952.

3  Roy F. Nichols, *The Democratic Machine, 1850–1854* (New York, 1923), 27–28, 37; Blair to Van Buren, Dec. 30, 1850, Van Buren Papers, LC; *CG,* 31/2, 304; 32/1, App., 68; *New York Times,* Dec. 6, 1853; New York *Herald,* Jan. 25, April 3, 1851; Henry S. Foote, *Casket of Reminiscences* (Washington, D.C., 1874), 83; Thomas D. Harris to Cobb, Nov. 29, 1851, Phillips (ed.), *Correspondence of Toombs, Stephens and Cobb,* 267; Shields to Koerner, Dec. 1, 1851, Greene (ed.), "Letters to Gustav Koerner, 1837–1863," *TISHS,* 1907, 241.

4  *Illinois Journal,* Sept. 26, 1851; New York *Herald,* March 2, 20, 1851; *CG,* 31/2, App., 344.

5  *CG,* 32/1, 350–51; App., 1127–31, 1142; *New York Times,* Aug. 24, 25, 1852; *Alton Telegraph,* Sept. 10, 1852; *Illinois Journal,* Sept. 23, 1852; Douglas to Joel A. Matteson, Jan. 2, 1854, *Letters,* 272–82.

6  Young to French, Jan. 13, 1850, French Papers, ISHL; Edwin De Leon, *The Position and Duties of Young America* (Charleston, 1845), quoted in Curti, "Young America," *AHR,* XXXII (Oct. 1926), 34. The best account of the Young America movement in both its general character and specific applications is Siert F. Riepma, Young America: A Study in American Nationalism Before the Civil War (unpublished Ph.D. dissertation, Western Reserve Univ., 1939).

7  New York *Herald,* March 22, 1851; *Illinois State Register,* April 14, 1851.

8  New York *Herald,* Feb. 3, March 5, 1851; *Illinois State Register,* Jan. 23, 1851; Chase to E. S. Hamlin, Feb. 24, 1851, *Diary and Correspondence of Salmon P. Chase,* American Historical Association *Annual Report, 1902,* II (Washington, D.C., 1903), 233; Beverley Tucker to R. M. T. Hunter, April 5, 1851, Hunter Papers, UV; Riepma, Young America, 97.

9  Curti, "George N. Sanders, Patriot of the Fifties," *South Atlantic Quarterly,* XXVII (Jan. 1928), 79–87; Curti, "Young America," *AHR,* XXXII, 37; Douglas to Sanders, April 11, July 12, 1851, *Letters,* 215, 228; New York *Herald,* March 20, 1851; Nichols, *Democratic Machine,* 110; Hunter to Sanders, May 9, 1851, Charles H. Ambler (ed.), *Correspondence of Robert M. T. Hunter, 1826–1876,* American Historical Assocation *Annual Report, 1916,* II (Washington, D.C., 1918), 127; Douglas to Hunter, May 6, 1851, *Letters,* 218.

10  Francis J. Grund to Sanders, March 20, Sanders to Hunter, March 20,

21, 1851, Hunter Papers, UV; Blair to Van Buren, March 15, 1851, Van Buren Papers, LC; Hunter to Sanders, March 27, 1851, Ambler (ed.), *Correspondence of Hunter,* 126; Andrew J. Donelson to Cobb, Oct. 22, 1851, Phillips (ed.), *Correspondence of Toombs, Stephens, and Cobb,* 263; Correspondence of the *Baltimore Clipper, Alton Telegraph,* March 28, 1851.

11  *New-York Tribune,* April 4, 1851; Riepma, Young America, 77, 104–6; Blair to Van Buren, Feb. 22, 1852, Van Buren Papers, LC; New York *Herald,* May 3, 1851; *Illinois State Register,* May 7, 1851; Douglas to Hunter, May 6, 1851, *Letters,* 218; Tucker to Hunter, April 5, 1851, Hunter Papers, UV.

12  *Illinois State Register,* May 22, 1851; Douglas to Francis B. Cutting *et al.,* May 3, to Sanders, April 11, to Hunter, May 6, 1851, *Letters,* 216–17, 215, 218; Hunter to Sanders, May 9, 1851, Ambler (ed.), *Correspondence of Hunter,* 127.

13  Washington *Union,* May 20, 1851; *Illinois State Register,* May 31, 1851; James Kendall Hosmer, *The Last Leaf* (New York, 1912), 7; Marcy to Archibald Campbell, May 28, 1851, Marcy Papers, LC.

14  *Illinois State Register,* May 19, 27, June 4, 11, 12, August 11, 1851; Fehrenbacher, *Chicago Giant,* 117–18; *Chicago Journal,* May 22, 24, 26, June 23, 1851; Wentworth to French, July 15, 1851, French Papers, ISHL; Cole, *Era of the Civil War,* 102; *Chicago Journal,* May 24, 1851.

15  Douglas to William J. Brown, June 21, to Sanders, July 12, 1851, *Letters,* 226–27, 228; *Illinois State Register,* August 2, 1851.

16  Douglas to ——, June 27, to ——, July 17, 1851, *Letters,* 229; New York *Herald,* July 14, 1851; Sanders to Hunter, Aug. 4, 1851, Hunter Papers, UV; *Illinois State Register,* July 7, 1851; *Brandon Post,* Sept. 4, 1851, quoted in Marsh (ed.), *Stephen A. Douglas: A Memorial,* 38–39; New York *Herald,* Aug. 28, Sept. 1, 3, 1851; Douglas to J. A. Beckwith, Aug. 12, 1854, to George Roberts, Sept. 8, 1851, *Letters,* 327, 230–31.

17  Washington *Union,* Sept. 13, 24, 27, 1851; *Illinois State Register,* Oct. 3, 1851; Douglas to Sanders, Sept. 22, 1851, *Letters,* 231–32; *New York Times,* Sept. 25, 1851; New York *Herald,* Oct. 24, 1851; *Illinois State Register,* Nov. 6, 1851.

18  Washington *Union,* May 20, 1851; *Illinois State Register,* Nov. 6, 1851.

19  *Washington Republic,* quoted in *Alton Telegraph,* Oct. 24, 1851; Douglas to Lanphier, Dec. 30, 1851, *Letters,* 235; Sanders to Caleb Cushing, June 12, 1851, Caleb Cushing Papers, LC; James Buchanan, Dec. 3, J. Addison Thomas, Oct. 27, Isaac Butts to Marcy, Nov. 25, 1851, Marcy Papers, LC; Louis M. Sears, "Slidell and Buchanan," *AHR,* XXVII (July 1922), 715; John P. Heiss, Jan. 11, 1852, Simon Cameron to Douglas, July 24, 1851, Douglas Family Papers, Greensboro; Douglas to Samuel Treat, Dec. 15, to William H. English, Dec. 29, 1851, *Letters,* 233, 234; Riepma, Young America, 121–23; Marcy to James G. Berret, Nov. 21, 1851, Marcy Papers, LC; Edmund Burke to Gideon Welles, Nov. 5, 1851, Edmund Burke Papers, LC.

20  Washington *Union,* Jan. 11, 1852; Riepma, Young America, 163–64.

21 Andrew Johnson to A. O. P. Nicholson, Dec. 13, 1851, LeRoy P. Graf and Ralph W. Haskins (eds.), *The Papers of Andrew Johnson* (2 vols. to date, Knoxville, 1967—), I, 630; Bissell to Koerner, Aug. 13, 1851, Greene (ed.), "Letters to Gustav Koerner," *TISHS,* 1907, 240; New York *Herald,* Nov. 8, 1851; Slidell to Buchanan, Feb. 26, March 19, 1852, quoted in Sears, "Slidell and Buchanan," *AHR,* XXVII, 715; Belmont to Buchanan, Dec. 6, 1851, quoted in Riepma, Young America, 119–20; King to Buchanan, March 6, 1852, James Buchanan Papers, HSP; Welles to William S. Pomeroy, Feb. 22, 1852, Welles Papers, LC; Blair to Van Buren, Dec. 21, 1851, Van Buren Papers, LC; Johnson to D. T. Patterson, April 4, 1852, Andrew Johnson Papers, LC.

22 Blair to Van Buren, June 1, 1852, Van Buren Papers, LC; Buchanan to Marcy, Sept. 30, 1851, Marcy Papers, LC; Welles to Burke, Nov. 3, 1851, Burke Papers, LC.

23 New York *Herald,* Aug. 22, Oct. 30, Nov. 4, 1851; John R. Peters, Oct. 6, 1851, J. Addison Thomas to Marcy, Jan. 20, 1852, Marcy Papers, LC; Blair to Van Buren, Dec. 21, 1851, Van Buren Papers, LC; Douglas to English, Dec. 29, to William J. Brown, June 21, 1851, *Letters,* 234, 227; Forney to French, Oct. 11, 1851, French Papers, ISHL; Douglas to Samuel Treat, Dec. 15, 1851, *Letters,* 233; Marcy to John Stryker, Sept. 30, John Slidell to Marcy, Oct. 10, Charles Eames to Marcy, Nov. 11, 1851, Marcy Papers, LC; Blair to Van Buren, April 30, 1852, quoted in Nichols, *Democratic Machine,* 116.

24 Sanders to Cushing, Dec. 25, 1851, Cushing Papers, LC; Sanders to Hunter, Dec. 24, 1851, Hunter Papers, UV; Douglas to Sanders, Dec. 28, 1851, *Letters,* 233–34.

25 "Eighteen-Fifty-Two and the Presidency," *Democratic Review,* XXX (Jan. 1852), 1–12; Cushing to Douglas, Feb. 1, 1852, Cushing Papers, LC; Douglas to Cushing, Feb. 4, 1852, *Letters,* 237; Sanders to Cushing, [Jan. 1852], Cushing Papers, LC; Sanders to Douglas, Feb. 3, 1852, Douglas Papers, Chicago.

26 "The Presidency and the Review," *Democratic Review,* XXX (Feb. 1852), 182–86; "Congress, the Presidency and the Review," *ibid.* XXX (March 1852), 202–24; "The Nomination—the 'Old Fogies' and Fogy Conspiracies," *ibid.* XXX (April 1852), 366–84.

27 Douglas to Sanders, Feb. 10, 1852, *Letters,* 239; Sanders to James Gordon Bennett, Feb. 10, 1852, New York *Herald,* Feb. 12, 1852; Sanders to Douglas, Feb. 20, 1852, *Democratic Review,* XXX (March 1852), 207; Sanders to Douglas, Feb. 9, 11, 1852, Douglas Papers, Chicago.

28 Douglas to Sanders, April 15, 1852, *Letters,* 246–47; New York *Herald,* Feb. 26, March 7, 27, May 25, 1852; Washington *Union,* March 5, 1852; Orlando B. Ficklin to French, April 23, 1852, French Papers, ISHL.

29 *CG,* 32/1, App., 302 (Breckinridge); 32/1, 711–14 (Richardson); 32/1, App., 383–86 (Marshall); B. F. Angel to Marcy, March 11, 1852, Marcy Papers, LC; Washington *Union,* March 16, 1852.

30 "Reminiscences of Washington: The Fillmore Administration, 1850–1853," *Atlantic Monthly,* XLVII (May 1881), 663; W. Grandin to

Douglas, Feb. 7, 1852, Douglas Papers, Chicago; Timothy Jenkins to Marcy, March 31, 1852, Marcy Papers, LC; *Illinois State Register,* Feb. 4, 1852; James A. Seddon to Hunter, Feb. 7, 1852, Ambler (ed.), *Correspondence of Hunter,* 137–38; John B. Floyd, March 17, David L. Yulee to Douglas, April 30, Herschel V. Johnson to O. B. Ficklin, May 17, Ferris Foreman to Douglas, Feb. 1, 1852, Douglas Family Papers, Greensboro; Washington *Union,* Feb. 14, 1852; *New York Times,* Feb. 18, 1852; Burke to Franklin Pierce, April 9, 1852, Franklin Pierce Papers, LC.

31  *New-York Tribune,* Feb. 28, 1852; *Illinois State Register,* Feb. 10, 1852; Douglas to Robert G. Scott, May 22, 1852, *Letters,* 247–48; *Biographical Sketch of Stephen A. Douglas, of Illinois* (Washington, D.C., 1852), *passim;* Douglas to Lanphier, Dec. 30, 1851, to Ebenezer Peck, [Feb. 1852], *Letters,* 235, 236; McClernand to Douglas, Dec. 16, 1851, Douglas Family Papers, Greensboro; T. R. Young to French, Jan. 18, 1852, French Papers, ISHL; Thompson Campbell to Lanphier, April 4, 1852, Lanphier Papers, ISHL; *Illinois State Register,* April 22, 24, 1852.

32  *New York Times,* May 26, 1852; *Alton Telegraph,* March 13, 1852; John Tyler, Jr., to Conway Whittle, April 8, 1852, John Tyler Papers, LC; Cave Johnson to Buchanan, May 6, 1852, James Buchanan Papers, HSP; Andrew J. Donelson to Cobb, May 10, 1852, Phillips (ed.), *Correspondence of Toombs, Stephens, and Cobb,* 294; Blair to Van Buren, April 30, 1852, Van Buren Papers, LC; Burke to Pierce, April 9, 1852, Pierce Papers, LC.

33  *New York Times,* May 31, June 2, 1852; J. Stryker, May 30, John V. L. Pruyn to Marcy, May 31, 1852, Marcy Papers, LC; New York *Herald,* June 2, 1852; Douglas to David L. Yulee, [May 1852], *Letters,* 249.

34  *New-York Tribune,* June 2, 3, 1852; New York *Herald,* June 3, 4, 1852; Douglas to Yulee, June 1, 2, 1852, *Letters,* 250; Yulee to Douglas, June 3, 1852, Douglas Family Papers, Greensboro.

35  Nichols, *The Democratic Machine,* 129–44; William Hincks and F. H. Smith, *Proceedings of the Democratic National Convention, held at Baltimore, June, 1852* (Washington, D.C., 1852), *passim;* New York *Herald,* June 5, 6, 7, 1852; Douglas to Yulee, June 4, 1852, *Letters,* 252; P. M. Wetmore to Marcy, June 5, 1852, Marcy Papers, LC; Herschel V. Johnson to Pierce, Nov. 8, 1852, Letter Press Book, Herschel V. Johnson Papers, DU.

36  *New York Times,* June 7, 1852; Douglas to Richardson, June 5, 1852, *Letters,* 252; New York *Herald,* June 9, 1852; Richard D. Arnold to John W. Forney, March 30, 1858, in Richard H. Shryock (ed.), *Letters of Richard D. Arnold, M.D., 1808–1876 (Papers of the Trinity College Historical Society,* XVIII–XIX; Durham, N.C., 1929), 87; John H. Lumpkin to Cobb, June 6, 1852, Phillips (ed.), *Correspondence of Toombs, Stephens, and Cobb,* 299; Bissell to Breese, June 10, 1852, Breese Papers, ISHL; Cave Johnson to Buchanan, July 23, 1852, Buchanan Papers, HSP.

37  Hincks and Smith, *Proceedings of the Democratic National Convention,* 40–43; New York *Herald,* June 8, 1852.

38  *New York Times,* June 7, July 3, 29, 1852; Charles H. Peaslee to Pierce, June 8, 1852, quoted in Milton, *Eve of Conflict,* 92; Washington *Union,*

June 11, 17, July 15, 18, 1852; Speech to the Springfield Scott Club, August 14, 26, 1852, *CWAL*, II, 135–57; *Illinois State Register,* Aug. 17, 1852.

39   *Illinois Journal,* June 14, 1852; Richard Yates to Turner, June 23, July 10, 1852, Turner Papers, IHS; Washington *Union,* Sept. 2, 5, 8, 1852; New York *Herald,* Sept. 3, 1852; *New York Times,* Sept. 6, 1852; Chicago *Democratic Press,* Sept. 27, 28, Oct. 1, 19, 1852.

40   Koerner, *Memoirs,* I, 590–97; *Illinois State Register,* Oct. 11, 12, 29, 1852; *Alton Telegraph,* Sept. 24, 1852; Cole, *Era of the Civil War,* 110–11.

41   Washington *Union,* Nov. 30, 1852; Isaac Cook to Douglas, Nov. 24, Dec. 17, 1852, Douglas Family Papers, Greensboro; Wentworth, Dec. 29, 1852, David L. Gregg to Douglas, Jan. 4, 1853, Douglas Papers, Chicago; *Alton Telegraph,* Jan. 7, 15, 17, 1853; Isaac R. Diller to Douglas, Feb. 2, 1853, Douglas Papers, Chicago.

42   Edward Bates Diary, 1846–52, entry of Nov. 3, 1852, MHS; Thomas L. Harris, Nov. 22, James O'Donnell to Douglas, Nov. 29, 1852, Douglas Papers, Chicago; David L. Gregg to Lanphier, Sept. 20, 1853, Lanphier Papers, ISHL; Washington *Union,* Dec. 5, 1852.

## CHAPTER XVI

1   Mrs. Roger A. Pryor, *Reminiscences of Peace and War* (New York, 1904), 16–17; Roy F. Nichols, *Franklin Pierce: Young Hickory of the Granite Hills* (Philadelphia, 1931), 234–36; James D. Richardson (ed.), *A Compilation of the Messages and Papers of the Presidents, 1789–1897* (10 vols., Washington, D.C., 1897), V, 197–203.

2   Nichols, *Pierce,* 220; Yulee to Douglas, Jan. 28, 1853, Douglas Papers, Chicago; Washington *Union,* Dec. 5, 1852; Douglas to Lanphier, Dec. 3, 1852, *Letters,* 258.

3   Harris, Nov. 22, 1852, Yulee to Douglas, Jan. 28, 1853, Douglas Papers, Chicago; *Alton Telegraph,* Nov. 19, 1852; *New-York Tribune,* Nov. 27, 1852; H. V. Willson, Nov. 18, Isaac R. Diller, Dec. 6, John Wentworth, Dec. 12, 29, 1852, Edward C. West, Jan. 18, Samuel Treat to Douglas, Jan. 17, 1853, Douglas Papers, Chicago.

4   Treat to Douglas, Jan. 17, 1853, Douglas Papers, Chicago; *New York Times,* Nov. 13, Dec. 16, 1852; *New-York Tribune,* Jan. 3, 1853; New York *Herald,* Dec. 20, 1852; McClernand to Douglas, March 24, 1853, Douglas Papers, Chicago.

5   Nichols, *Pierce,* 220–29; J. Addison Thomas to Marcy, Feb. 17, 1853, Marcy Papers, LC; Francis J. Grund to Cushing, Jan. 24, 1853, Cushing Papers, LC; McClernand to Douglas, March 24, 1853, Douglas Papers, Chicago.

6   James S. Green, Nov. 15, 1852, James N. McDougall, Jan. 28, Yulee, Jan. 28, Duncan McRae, Jan. 1, H. H. Sibley to Douglas, March 16, 1853, Douglas Papers, Chicago; Warren Bristol, Dec. 21, 1852, John M. Bernhisel to Pierce, March 23, 1853, General Records of the Department of State, Applications and Recommendations, 1852–61, RG-59, NA.

7   Douglas to Pierce, [n. d.], [March 1853], March 4, 8, 1853, *Letters,* 260, 261, 263; Douglas to Marcy, March 10, 1853, Marcy Papers, LC; Ivor Deben-

ham Spencer, *The Victor and the Spoils: A Life of William L. Marcy* (Providence, 1959), 230–31; Douglas to Sanders, March 27, 1854, *Letters,* 299; New York *Herald,* Feb. 15, 1854.

8   Wentworth, Nov. 14, Dec. 12, Isaac R. Diller to Douglas, Dec. 6, 1852, Douglas Papers, Chicago; Douglas to Lanphier, Dec. 3, 1852, *Letters,* 257–58; Wentworth, Dec. 29, 29 (second letter), 1852, Feb. 14, Thomas Hoyne, March 19, Lanphier to Douglas, Nov. 21, 1853, Douglas Papers, Chicago; Douglas to E. D. Taylor, July 20, 1853, in Thomas T. Hoyne, *Douglas as a Chicagoan* (Chicago, 1946), 7–8; Fehrenbacher, *Chicago Giant,* 121–22; *Alton Telegraph,* April 26, 1853; *Illinois State Register,* July 6, 1853.

9   Shields to Pierce, April 16, Yulee, Jan. 28, 1853, H. V. Willson, Nov. 18, 1852, Shields, [n. d.], Silas Ramsey to Douglas, Nov. 12, 1853, Douglas Papers, Chicago; Bright to Buchanan, April 20, 1853, Buchanan Papers, HSP; Wayne J. Van Der Weele, Jesse David Bright: Master Politician from the Old Northwest (unpublished Ph.D. dissertation, Indiana Univ., 1958), 123–24, 157–58.

10   Washington *Union,* Jan. 20, April 10, Jan. 9, 1853; *Illinois State Register,* Jan. 28, 1853.

11   *Alton Telegraph,* Feb. 3, April 27, Feb. 18, 1853; Thomas Ritchie, Jan. 25, Reid to Douglas, Feb. 2, 1853, Douglas Papers, Chicago; Reid to Thomas Settle, April 24, 1853, Thomas Settle Papers, SHC.

12   Edward C. West to Douglas, April 11, August Belmont to Baron Alphonse de Rothschild, May 13, to Douglas, May 14, 1853, Douglas Papers, Chicago; Stevens, "Douglas," *JISHS,* XVI, 640; Robert J. Walker to John McGregor, May 13, 1853, Douglas Family Papers, Greensboro; *Illinois State Register,* May 21, 25, 1853.

13   R. A. J. Walling (ed.), *The Diaries of John Bright* (New York, 1931), 146, 158; Joseph Hume to Douglas, June 1, Invitation of Thomas Baring, June 10, 1853, Gouverneur Kemble to Douglas, [n. d.], Douglas Family Papers, Greensboro; Cleveland *Plain Dealer,* Nov. 8, 1853, quoted in *New York Times,* Nov. 11, 1853.

14   Passport of Stephen A. Douglas (signed by William L. Marcy, May 4, 1853, with visa stamps and entries), Map of Genoa Harbor (inscribed "Purchased at Genoa/June 20th 1853/S. A. Douglas"), Douglas Family Papers, Greensboro; *Cincinnati Commercial,* Dec. 1, 1867; *Freeman's Journal,* quoted in *Alton Telegraph,* Aug. 9, 1853; *Illinois State Register,* Aug. 15, 1853; New York *Herald,* Aug. 5, 1853; *Providence Journal,* quoted in *Alton Telegraph,* Sept. 1, 1853.

15   Paris correspondent of the *Cincinnati Gazette,* quoted in *Illinois State Register,* Oct. 31, 1853; Douglas to John C. Breckinridge, Sept. 9, 1853, Breckinridge Family Papers, LC; Spencer, *The Victor and the Spoils,* 264–69; *Illinois State Journal,* Sept. 9, 1853; *Illinois State Register,* Sept. 9, 1853; Order of Sultan Abdul Mejid, Son of Sultan Mahmood Khan, Ever Victorious, Constantinople, 1853 (translation), Douglas Family Papers, Greensboro.

16   Douglas to Breckinridge, Sept. 9, 1853, Breckinridge Family Papers, LC; John Ralli to Douglas, Feb. 8/20, 1857, Gen. Rec. Dept. of State, Applications

and Recommendations, 1853–61, RG-59, NA; Douglas to Lewis Cass, April 1, 1857, *Letters,* 378–79; Washington *Union,* Nov. 10, 1853; Cleveland *Plain Dealer,* Nov. 8, 1853, quoted in *New York Times,* Nov. 11, 1853; Linder, *Reminiscences,* 80–82; "A Southerner's Estimate of the Life and Character of Stephen A. Douglas," *National Quarterly Review,* VI, Second Series (Jan. 1880), 189.

17  Cleveland *Plain Dealer,* Nov. 8, 1853, quoted in *New York Times,* Nov. 11, 1853; *Alton Telegraph,* Dec. 29, 1853; *Illinois State Register,* Nov. 2, 17, 1853; Isaac Diller to Douglas, Dec. 22, 1853, Douglas Papers, Chicago; Washington *National Intelligencer,* Nov. 10, 1853.

18  Douglas to Lanphier, Nov. 11, 1853, *Letters,* 267; New York *Herald,* Nov. 28, 1853; Lanphier, Nov. 21, Edward C. West to Douglas, Nov. 15, 1853, Douglas Papers, Chicago; Allan Nevins, *Ordeal of the Union* (2 vols., New York, 1947), II, 70–73.

19  Burke to Douglas, Jan. 9, 1854, Douglas Papers, Chicago; Thomas B. Carroll to Douglas, Nov. 22, 1853 (copy), Marcy Papers, LC; E. Darwin Smith, Nov. 13, Andrew Harvie, Nov. 14, Willis A. Gorman to Douglas, Nov. 25, 1853, Douglas Papers, Chicago; New York *Herald,* Nov. 20, Aug. 23, 1853; *Illinois State Register,* July 7, 9, 1853; *New York Times,* Dec. 5, 1853; Marcy to Cushing, Oct. 1, 1853, Cushing Papers, LC; New York *Herald,* Dec. 28, 1853.

20  Washington *Union,* Dec. 14, 17, 10, 1853; Heman J. Redfield to Douglas, Dec. 10, 1853 (copy), Redfield to Marcy, Dec. 23, 1853, Marcy Papers, LC; William C. Dawson to Linton Stephens, Dec. 21, 1853, Alexander H. Stephens Papers, LC; New York *Herald,* Jan. 2, 1854; Samuel Treat to Douglas, Dec. 18, 1853, Douglas Papers, Chicago; Treat to Cushing, Dec. 18, 1853, Cushing Papers, LC; Douglas to Lanphier, Nov. 11, 1853, *Letters,* 267–68.

21  *CG,* 32/1, 1683–84, 1762, 1760.

22  *CG,* 32/1, 1847, 1890; 32/2, 125–27, 280, 349; Russel, *Improvement of Communication with the Pacific Coast,* 96–98.

23  *CG,* 32/2, 469–70, 507–9, 708, 715, 741–42, 775; Russel, *Improvement of Communication with the Pacific Coast,* 99–107; William Henry Ellison (ed.), "Memoirs of Hon. William M. Gwin," *Quarterly of the California Historical Society,* XIX (June 1940), 173–74.

24  *CG,* 32/2, 798–99, 841, 845, 1010–12; Russel, *Improvement of Communication with the Pacific Coast,* 107–8; Robert W. Johannsen (ed.), "Reporting a Pacific Railroad Survey: Isaac Stevens' Letters to Stephen A. Douglas," *Pacific Northwest Quarterly,* XLVII (Oct. 1956), 97–106; Robert J. Walker to Douglas, Jan. 27, 1854, Douglas Papers, Chicago.

25  *CG,* 32/1, 967; James C. Malin, "Thomas Jefferson Sutherland, Nebraska Boomer, 1851–1852," *Nebraska History,* XXXIV (Sept. 1953), 181–214; Thomas Jefferson Sutherland to Douglas, May 24, 1852, Douglas Family Papers, Greensboro; Malin, *The Nebraska Question, 1852–1854* (Lawrence, Kans., 1953), 80–85; William E. Parrish, *David Rice Atchison of Missouri: Border Politician* (Columbia, Mo., 1961), 121–23; *Louisville Journal,* in *Illinois State Register,* Dec. 15, 1852; *CG,* 32/2, 7, 47, 474, 542–43, 565.

26   *CG*, 32/2, 540–42, 555, 658, 1020, 1113–17.

27   *CG*, 32/2, 1117, 1113; Douglas to Parmenas Taylor Turnley, Nov. 30, 1852, *Letters*, 255. Some doubts have been expressed of the authenticity of the Turnley letter.

28   Atchison to Samuel Treat, May 29, 1853, Treat Papers, MHS; Parrish, *David Rice Atchison*, 125–27; Malin, *Nebraska Question*, 154–206; Morton M. Rosenberg, "The Kansas-Nebraska Act in Iowa: A Case Study," *Annals of Iowa*, XXXVII (Fall 1964), 436–57; *Illinois State Register*, Dec. 12, 1853; Douglas to J. H. Crane, D. M. Johnson, and L. J. Eastin, Dec. 17, 1853, *Letters*, 268–71.

## CHAPTER XVII

1   *CG*,   33/1,   8–12,   19–21,   26–27;   Nichols,   *Franklin   Pierce*, 294–306; *Alton Telegraph*, Dec. 21, 1853.

2   *CG*, 33/1, 1, 5, 44; *Illinois State Register*, Dec. 16, 1853; P. Orman Ray, *The Repeal of the Missouri Compromise, Its Origin and Authorship* (Cleveland, 1909), 188–94 (for comments of the press); *Daily Albany Argus*, Dec. 14, 1853; New York *Journal of Commerce*, Dec. 30, 1853; New York *Herald*, Jan. 4, 1854; William C. Dawson to Linton Stephens, Dec. 21, 1853, Alexander H. Stephens Papers, LC; Joseph H. Parks, *John Bell of Tennessee* (Baton Rouge, 1950), 295.

3   *CG*, 33/1, 115; *Illinois State Register*, Jan. 11, 1854 (for a summary of the bill); Robert R. Russel, "The Issues in the Congressional Struggle Over the Kansas-Nebraska Bill, 1854," *JSH*, XXIX (May 1963), 192–95; *Senate Reports*, 33/1, No. 15, 1–4.

4   Russel, "The Issues in the Congressional Struggle Over the Kansas-Nebraska Bill, 1854," *JSH*, XXIX, 193; William H. Seward to Mrs. Seward, Jan. 4, 1854, quoted in Frederick W. Seward, *Seward at Washington, as Senator and Secretary of State: A Memoir of His Life, with Selections from His Letters, 1846–1861* (New York, 1891), 216; *CG*, 33/2, App., 216; Nichols, *Franklin Pierce*, 320; Diary of Edward Everett, Jan. 4, March 4, 1854, quoted in Paul R. Frothingham, *Edward Everett: Orator and Statesman* (Boston, 1925), 344–45, 353.

5   Ray, *Repeal of the Missouri Compromise*, 279, 282; *CG*, 34/1, 393; Roy F. Nichols, "The Kansas-Nebraska Act: A Century of Historiography," *MVHR*, XLIII (Sept. 1956), 201–04; Salmon P. Chase to E. S. Hamlin, Jan. 22, 1854, Chase Papers, LC.

6   Washington *Sentinel*, Jan. 7, 10, 1854; Johnson, *Douglas*, 232–33; Nevins, *Ordeal of the Union*, II, 95; Russel, "The Issues in the Congressional Struggle Over the Kansas-Nebraska Bill, 1854," *JSH*, XXIX, 193; Roy F. Nichols, *Blueprints for Leviathan: American Style* (New York, 1963), 289.

7   Burke to Douglas, Jan. 9, 1854, Douglas Papers, Chicago; Washington *Union*, Jan. 5, 6, 1854; *New-York Tribune*, Jan. 11, 1854. See also *New York Times*, Jan. 6, 1854; New York *Herald*, Jan. 11, 1854.

8   *New-York Tribune*, Jan. 6, 11, 1854; Chase to E. S. Hamlin, Jan. 22,

1854, Chase Papers, LC; New York *Herald,* Jan. 7, 21, 1854; Washington *Union,* Jan. 10, 1854; *Detroit Free Press,* quoted in Washington *Union,* Jan. 17, 1854.

9   New York *Herald,* Jan. 23, 1854; Everett Diary, March 4, 1854, quoted in Frothingham, *Edward Everett,* 353; *New York Times,* Jan. 6, 1854; *CG,* 33/1, 175, 186.

10   Washington *Sentinel,* Jan. 14, 1854; New York *Herald,* Jan. 18, 1854; Washington *Union,* Jan. 20, 1854; *New-York Tribune,* Jan. 16, 1854.

11   Mrs. Archibald Dixon, *The True History of the Missouri Compromise and Its Repeal* (Cincinnati, 1899), 442–43; Dixon to Henry S. Foote, Oct. 1, 1858, in Dixon, *True History,* 446; *CG,* 33/1, 240; Dixon to the Editor of the *Louisville Times,* Jan. 28, 1854, in Washington *National Intelligencer,* Jan. 30, 1854; Glyndon G. Van Deusen, *William Henry Seward* (New York, 1967), 150, 587; Seward to Mrs. Seward, Dec. 24, 1853, quoted in Frederick W. Seward, *Seward at Washington,* 213.

12   Henry S. Foote, *Casket of Reminiscences,* 93; George Murray McConnell, "Recollections of Stephen A. Douglas," *TISHS,* 1900, 47; James T. DuBois and Gertrude S. Mathews, *Galusha A. Grow: Father of the Homestead Law* (Boston, 1917), 144, 138–39; Dixon, *True History,* 444–45; Dixon to Foote, Oct. 1, 1858, in Dixon, *True History,* 447.

13   Extract from Notes of P. Phillips Left for His Children (typescript), Philip Phillips Papers, LC; Phillips to the Editor, Aug. 24, 1860, Washington *Constitution,* Aug. 25, 1860; Henry B. Learned, "The Relation of Philip Phillips to the Repeal of the Missouri Compromise in 1854," *MVHR,* VIII (March 1922), 303–17.

14   *CG,* 33/1, 186; Nichols, *Franklin Pierce,* 321–22; Washington *Union,* Jan. 20, 1854; New York *Herald,* Jan. 23, 1854.

15   Nichols, *Franklin Pierce,* 322–23; Extract from Notes of P. Phillips, Phillips Papers, LC; Jefferson Davis to Mrs. Dixon, Sept. 27, 1879, in Dixon, *True History;* DuBois and Mathews, *Galusha A. Grow,* 139–40; New York *Herald,* Jan. 24, 1854; Breckinridge to Robert J. Breckinridge, March 6, 1854, Breckinridge Family Papers, LC; Washington *Union,* Jan. 22, 1854.

16   *CG,* 33/1, 221–22, App., 408; *New York Times,* Jan. 25, 1854; Everett Diary, Jan. 23, 1854, quoted in Frothingham, *Edward Everett,* 345; "Observer" to Philadelphia *Ledger,* Jan. 23, in *Illinois State Register,* Jan. 31, 1854; Chase to Hamlin, Jan. 23, 1854, Chase Papers, LC.

17   *CG,* 33/1, 221, 239–40, App., 382; New York *Journal of Commerce,* Dec. 30, 1853; *New York Times,* Nov. 24, 1853; Washington correspondence of the St. Louis *Missouri Republican,* Jan. 13, 1854, quoted in Nevins, *Ordeal of the Union,* II, 97; Frank H. Hodder, "The Railroad Background of the Kansas-Nebraska Act," *MVHR,* XII (June 1925), 16–17.

18   Washington *National Era,* Jan. 24, 1854; George W. Julian, *The Life of Joshua R. Giddings* (Chicago, 1892), 311; *New York Times,* Jan. 19, 1854; Chase to Hamlin, Jan. 23, 1854, Chase Papers, LC; Chase to E. L. Pierce, Aug. 8, 1854, *Diary and Correspondence of Salmon P. Chase,* II, 263. Because of the charge that their work had "violated" the Sabbath, the signers altered the date of

the "Appeal" to January 19 when it was published in the *Globe* (*CG,* 33/1, 281–82).

19   *Ibid.;* McConnell, "Recollections of Douglas," *TISHS,* 1900, 48–49.

20   Washington *Union,* Jan. 31, 1854; McConnell, "Recollections of Douglas," *TISHS,* 1900, 45–46; *New-York Tribune,* Jan. 31, Feb. 1, 1854; *Illinois State Journal,* Feb. 8, 1854; *New York Times,* Feb. 1, 2, 1854; New York *Herald,* Jan. 31, 1854; *CG,* 33/1, 275–80.

21   *CG,* 33/1, 289–91, 282, 329; James Shepherd Pike to William Pitt Fessenden, Feb. 10, 1854, James Shepherd Pike Papers, LC; Seward to Thurlow Weed, Jan. 8, 1854, in Frederick W. Seward, *Seward at Washington,* 217; *New York Times,* Feb. 2, 6, 1854.

22   *Illinois State Register,* March 7, 1854; New York *Herald,* Jan. 25, Feb. 7, 1854; G. W. Newell to Marcy, Jan. 25, 1854, Marcy Papers, LC; Washington *Union,* Jan. 24, 1854; *New York Times,* Jan. 24, Feb. 4, 16, 1854; John Van Buren to Marcy, Feb. 12, 1854, Marcy Papers, LC; Greene C. Bronson to Douglas, Feb. 8, 1854, Douglas Family Papers, Greensboro; Edwin Croswell, Feb. 1, Heman J. Redfield, Feb. 27, Horatio Seymour to Douglas, April 14, 1854, Douglas Papers, Chicago.

23   Alexander H. Stephens to Linton Stephens, March 4, 1854, Stephens Papers, LC; *New York Times,* Jan. 28, Feb. 10, 16, 1854; F. L. Burr to Gideon Welles, Jan. 15, Welles to ————, Feb. 17, 1854, Welles Papers, LC; S. S. Nicholas to John J. Crittenden, Feb. 5, 1854, Crittenden Papers, LC; Seymour to Douglas, April 14, 1854, Douglas Papers, Chicago; New York *Herald,* Feb. 21, 1854; Winthrop, *Memoir,* 166 (under date of Feb. 24, 1854).

24   Blair to William Allen, Feb. 10, 1854, quoted in Reginald C. McGrane, *William Allen: A Study in Western Democracy* (Columbus, 1925), 136–37; John L. O'Sullivan to Douglas, [n. d.], Feb. 19, 1854, Douglas Papers, Chicago; *New-York Tribune,* Feb. 2, 1854; Howell Cobb to Douglas, Feb. 5, 1854, Douglas Papers, Chicago; George W. Jones to Cobb, Feb. 16, 1854, Brooks (ed.), "Cobb Papers," *Ga. Hist. Quar.,* VI, 150; Jeremiah Clemens to John Van Buren, Feb. 4, 1854, in Chicago *Democratic Press,* Feb. 18, 1854; Clemens to Nicholas Davis, Jr., Feb. 25, 1854, in *New York Times,* March 25, 1854; Charleston *Mercury,* quoted in *Alton Telegraph,* Feb. 28, 1854; Stephens to Linton Stephens, March 4, 1854, Stephens Papers, LC.

25   *New York Times,* Feb. 6, 1854; Robert Toombs to W. W. Burwell, Feb. 3, 1854, Phillips (ed.), *Correspondence of Toombs, Stephens and Cobb,* 342.

26   *CG,* 33/1, 339, 340–41, App., 144, 149, 163, 199, 206, 169–70. For an analysis of the issues in the debate, see Russel, "The Issues in the Congressional Struggle Over the Kansas-Nebraska Bill, 1854," *JSH,* XXIX, 187–210.

27   *CG,* 33/1, App., 347 (Toombs), 279 (Cass), 390–91 (Clayton), 224 (Hunter), 139 (Chase); 33/1, 343–44, 353.

28   *CG,* 33/1, 421, App., 280–81; James W. Taylor to Chase, Feb. 19, 1854, Chase Papers, LC.

29   *CG,* 33/1, 423, 474, App., 296–98.

30   Seward to Mrs. Seward, March 3, 1854, quoted in Frederick W. Seward, *Seward at Washington*, 224; Everett Diary, March 3, 1854, quoted in Frothingham, *Edward Everett*, 352; *CG*, 33/1, App., 325; Chicago *Democratic Press*, March 31, 1853; Washington *Union*, March 5, 1854; *Illinois State Register*, March 24, 1854; *New-York Tribune*, March 7, 1854; James S. Pike, *First Blows of the Civil War* (New York, 1879), 218.

31   *CG*, 33/1, App., 325–38; Washington *Union*, March 5, 1854; Henry Wilson, *History of the Rise and Fall of the Slave Power in America* (3 vols., Boston, 1872–77), II, 393.

32   *CG*, 33/1, 532, App., 342; Seward to Mrs. Seward, Feb. 16, 1854, quoted in Frederick W. Seward, *Seward at Washington*, 219; Washington *Union*, March 8, 1854.

33   New York *Herald*, Feb. 27, 1854; Richard Yates to Mrs. Yates, March 6, 1854, in Richard Yates and Catharine Yates Pickering, *Richard Yates: Civil War Governor* (ed. by John H. Krenkel; Danville, Ill., 1966), 93–94; Douglas to Howell Cobb, April 2, 1854, *Letters*, 300; *CG*, 33/1, 701–3, 1130–32; *Alton Telegraph*, March 24, 1854; *New York Times*, May 10, 1854; Nichols, *Blueprints for Leviathan*, 104–18.

34   *New-York Tribune*, May 15, 1854; Pike, *First Blows of the Civil War*, 220–21; *New York Times*, May 12, 1854; Stephens to W. W. Burwell, May 7, 1854, Phillips (ed.), *Correspondence of Toombs, Stephens and Cobb*, 344; D. A. Reese to Linton Stephens, May 20, 1854, Stephens Papers, LC; Stephens to Robert S. Burch, June 15, 1854, "Letter of Alexander H. Stephens, 1854," *AHR*, VIII (Oct. 1902), 95–97; Holt, "Political Career of Richardson," *JISHS*, XXVI, 235–37; *CG*, 33/1, 1254; *Illinois State Register*, May 24, 1854.

35   *CG*, 33/1, App., 755–88; DuBois and Mathews, *Galusha A. Grow*, 143; *New York Times*, May 27, 1854; Douglas to Ninian W. Edwards, April 13, 1854, *Letters*, 322; Cutts, *A Brief Treatise on Constitutional and Party Questions*, 122–23.

## CHAPTER XVIII

1   St. Louis *Missouri Republican*, June 21, 1854, quoted in Russel, *Improvement of Communication with the Pacific Coast*, 166; *CG*, 32/1, App., 951–52.

2   Henry Cohen, *Business and Politics in America from the Age of Jackson to the Civil War: The Career Biography of W. W. Corcoran* (Westport, Conn., 1971), 159–63; Philip R. Cloutier, "John C. Breckinridge, Superior City Land Speculator," *Register of the Kentucky Historical Society*, LVII (Jan. 1959), 12–19; John W. Forney, *Anecdotes of Public Men* (2 vols., New York, 1873), I, 19–20; D. A. Robertson to Douglas, Nov. 21, 1853, Douglas Papers, Chicago; Bright to Hunter, Sept. 2, 1854, July 29, 1855, Ambler (ed.), *Correspondence of Hunter*, 159, 168; Memorandum, Jan. 26, W. W. Corcoran to Douglas, July 2, to D. Cooper, April 26, 1855, Statement of Taxes, 1855, to William H. Newton, Jan. 8, 1857, to Douglas, Aug. 12, 1858, A. Hyde to Douglas, June 7, 1858, W. W. Corcoran Papers, LC; Douglas to Breckinridge, Sept. 7, 1854, *Letters*, 328.

3   *CG,* 33/1, 118–20, 144, 610; *Illinois State Register,* Jan. 30, 1854; Walker to Douglas, Jan. 27, Brigham Young to Douglas, April 29, 1854, Douglas Papers, Chicago; *Senate Executive Journal,* IX, 278; *New York Times,* April 12, 14, 1854, Jan. 12, 16, 1855; Russel, *Improvement of Communication with the Pacific Coast,* 191–98; Henry O'Reilly to Douglas, Jan. 20, Feb. 9, 1855, Douglas Family Papers, Greensboro.

4   Gerald Wolff, "The Slavocracy and the Homestead Problem of 1854," *Agricultural History,* XL (April 1966), 101–11; S. W. Johnston to Douglas, March 24, David S. Reid to Douglas, June 17, 1854, Douglas Papers, Chicago.

5   Douglas to Lanphier, Nov. 11, 1853, to Joel A. Matteson, Jan. 2, 1854, *Letters,* 268, 272–82; Washington *Union,* Jan. 17, 1854; M. McConnel to Douglas, Jan. 28, 1854, Douglas Papers, Chicago; *Chicago Tribune,* Jan. 26, 1854; *Illinois State Journal,* Feb. 2, Aug. 8, 1854; *Alton Telegraph,* Feb. 4, Aug. 12, 1854; Archibald Williams to James Knox, E. B. Washburne, Jesse O. Norton, and Richard Yates, Jan. 23, Washington *National Intelligencer,* Jan. 25, 1854; *CG,* 33/1, App., 1184–85; Nichols, *Franklin Pierce,* 295–96, 354–55; *New York Times,* Sept. 4, 1854.

6   James M. Mason to Editor of *The South,* July 22, 1857, in Virginia Mason, *The Public Life and Diplomatic Correspondence of James M. Mason with Some Personal History* (New York, 1906), 127; *Proceedings at the Banquet of the Jackson Democratic Association, Washington, Eighth of January, 1852* [n. p., n. d.], 10; *CG,* 35/2, 1256.

7   Samuel S. Cox, March 24, B. S. Beale to Douglas, June 2, 1854, Douglas Papers, Chicago; M. G. Bright to Douglas, March 10, Washington *Union,* March 18, 1854; Adam Gurowski to James S. Pike, June 8, 1854, in Pike, *First Blows of the Civil War,* 253; Robert Winthrop to Douglas, April 17, 1854, Douglas Papers, Chicago; New York *Herald,* Feb. 4, 9, 1854; Washington *Union,* Feb. 3, 7, 10, May 24, 1854. Both the *Herald* and the *Union* printed extensive press reactions from throughout the nation favorable to the act.

8   J. L. M. Curry to Clement C. Clay, July 5, 1854, Clement C. Clay Papers, DU; Seager, *And Tyler Too,* 407; William B. W. Dent to Herschel V. Johnson, June 13, 1854, Herschel V. Johnson Papers, DU; Hunter to Shelton F. Leake, Oct. 16, 1857, Ambler (ed.), *Correspondence of Hunter,* 238; Washington *Union,* March 1, 19, 1854; New York *Herald,* Feb. 4, 1854.

9   Annapolis *State Capitol Gazette,* Jan. 28, quoted in Washington *Union,* Jan. 31, 1854; Douglas to Cobb, April 2, to Ninian Edwards, April 13, 1854, *Letters,* 300, 322; Detroit *Democrat,* quoted in New York *Herald,* Feb. 4, 1854; *Chicago Tribune,* March 18, 1854; *New York Times,* Feb. 3, March 27, 1854.

10   Douglas to the Editor of the Concord (New Hampshire) *State Capitol Reporter,* Feb. 16, to Edward Coles, Feb. 18, 1854, *Letters,* 284–99.

11   *CG,* 33/1, 617–18; Thomas F. Carpenter to Douglas, April 15, 1854, Douglas Papers, Chicago; Douglas to Twenty-five Chicago Clergymen, April 6, 1854, *Letters,* 300–322; *CG,* 33/1, App. 653–57; *New York Times,* May 12, 1854; New York *Herald,* Sept. 19, 1854.

12   Bright to Douglas, Feb. 2, 1854, Douglas Family Papers, Greensboro;

New York *Herald,* June 5, 7, 1854; *New York Times,* June 10, 1854; Rodman M. Price to Douglas, June 9, 1854, Douglas Papers, Chicago; *Speech of Senator Douglas, at the Democratic Celebration of the Anniversary of American Freedom, in Independence Square, Philadelphia, July 4, 1854* [Philadelphia, 1854], *passim.*

13   New York *Herald,* June 7, 1854; Nevins, *Ordeal of the Union,* II, 146–49; J. C. Van Dyke, March 10, George W. Manypenny to Douglas, Feb. 22, 1854, Douglas Papers, Chicago; Gamaliel Bailey to Pike, May 30, 1854, in Pike, *First Blows of the Civil War,* 237; B. F. Butler to Van Buren, Dec. 2, 1854, Van Buren Papers, LC.

14   Andrew Harvie to Douglas, Nov. 14, 1853, Douglas Papers, Chicago; *Illinois State Register,* Jan. 11, 18, 31, July 26, 1854; Douglas to Lanphier, Feb. 13, 1854, *Letters,* 283–84.

15   Granville D. Davis, Factional Differences in the Democratic Party in Illinois, 1854–1858 (unpublished Ph.D. dissertation, Univ. of Illinois, 1936), 22, 19–20; McConnel to Douglas, Jan. 28, 1854, Douglas Papers, Chicago; Chicago *Democratic Press,* Feb. 16, May 24, 1854; *Chicago Tribune,* Feb. 10, 13, June 2, 1854; Cole, *Era of the Civil War,* 119, 120–21.

16   Isaac Cook to Douglas, Feb. 13, Announcement of *Chicago Times,* Sept. 4, 1854, Douglas Family Papers, Greensboro; Douglas to James W. Sheahan, Sept. 14, 1854, *Letters,* 330; Sheahan to Douglas, Sept. 29, 1854, Douglas Papers, Chicago.

17   *Illinois State Journal,* Jan. 13, 21, Feb. 18, May 24, Sept. 23, 1854; *Alton Telegraph,* April 6, 11, 1854; *Chicago Tribune,* Feb. 9, 17, March 17, 18, 1854; F. I. Herriott, "Senator Stephen A. Douglas and the Germans in 1854," *TISHS,* 1912, 156–58.

18   Douglas to Lanphier, Feb. 13, 1854, *Letters,* 283; Lincoln to Joshua F. Speed, Aug. 24, 1855, *CWAL,* II, 322; *Illinois State Register,* Feb. 20, 1854; *Alton Telegraph,* Feb. 22, 1854; Cole, *Era of the Civil War,* 121–22.

19   *Chicago Tribune,* June 9, 10, 12, 1854; Washington *Union,* Aug. 16, 30, 1854; Milton, *Eve of Conflict,* 175; New York *Herald,* Aug. 29, 1854.

20   Albert J. Beveridge, *Abraham Lincoln, 1809–1858* (2 vols., Boston, 1928), II, 227–30, 239–40, 264; Cole, *Era of the Civil War,* 123–24, 128, 202; *Alton Telegraph,* May 25, 1854; Douglas to Sheahan, Sept. 14, 1854, *Letters,* 330; Fehrenbacher, *Chicago Giant,* 131.

21   Douglas to Lanphier, Aug. 25, 1854, *Letters,* 327; Chicago *Democratic Press,* Aug. 29, Sept. 1, 4, 1854; *Chicago Tribune,* Sept. 2, 4, 5, 1854; *Alton Telegraph,* Sept. 4, 1854; Cutts, *A Brief Treatise on Constitutional and Party Questions,* 98; *Illinois State Register,* Sept. 4, 5, 1854; New York *Herald,* Sept. 5, 1854; *New-York Tribune,* Sept. 5, 1854; Washington *National Intelligencer,* Sept. 13, 1854; Albert Gallatin Brown to Douglas, Sept. 8, 1854, Douglas Papers, Chicago. Some of the myths respecting this incident have been effectively dispelled in Granville D. Davis, "Douglas and the Chicago Mob," *AHR,* LIV (April 1949), 553–56.

22   William H. English to Douglas, Aug. 6, 1854, Douglas Papers, Chicago; Washington *Union,* Sept. 14, 1854; Douglas to Ninian Edwards, April 13, to

Sheahan, Sept. 14, 1854, *Letters*, 322, 330; Fehrenbacher, *Chicago Giant*, 130–31; Bissell to Gillespie, Feb. 17, 1856, Gillespie Papers, ISHL; Mark M. Krug, *Lyman Trumbull: Conservative Radical* (New York, 1965), 89–92.

23   Lincoln to Palmer, Sept. 7, 1854, *CWAL*, II, 228; Palmer, *Personal Recollections*, 69; Breese to ————, March 20, 1854, Breese Papers, ISHL; Davis, Factional Differences in the Democratic Party in Illinois, 47–49; *New York Times*, July 17, 1854; McClernand to Lanphier and Walker, Oct. 14, *Illinois State Register*, Oct. 17, 1854.

24   Douglas to Sheahan, Sept. 14, 1854, *Letters*, 330; *Chicago Tribune*, Sept. 15, 19, 23, 25, 1854; Harry E. Pratt, "Lincoln in Bloomington," *JISHS*, XXIX (April 1936), 53; Beveridge, *Lincoln*, II, 241–42.

25   *Illinois State Register*, Oct. 4, 5, 6, 1854; *Alton Telegraph*, Oct. 5, 6, 1854; R. W. English to William H. English, Oct. 30, 1854, William H. English Papers, IND; Autobiography Written for John L. Scripps, [June 1860], Speech at Springfield, Illinois, Oct. 4, 1854, *CWAL*, IV, 67, II, 240–47; *Illinois State Register*, Sept. 28, 1854; *Illinois State Journal*, Oct. 10, 1854.

26   Herndon, *Life of Lincoln*, 300–301; B. F. Irwin, Feb. 8, E. M. Powell, Feb. 10, Robert Boal to Herndon, March 5, 1866, Herndon-Weik Papers, LC; Beveridge, *Lincoln*, II, 270–71; Paul M. Angle, "The Peoria Truce," *JISHS*, XXI (Jan. 1929), 500–505; Ernest E. East, "The 'Peoria Truce': Did Douglas Ask for Quarter?" *JISHS*, XXIX (April 1936), 70–75.

27   Cole, *Era of the Civil War*, 128–29; *Illinois State Journal*, Sept. 19, 22, 23, Oct. 11, 1854; *Illinois State Register*, Oct. 3, 1854; *Alton Telegraph*, Oct. 20, 1854; Cass to Andrew Harvie, Oct. 1, 14, enclosed in Harvie to Douglas, Oct. 18, 1854, Douglas Papers, Chicago; Richard L. Wilson to Lincoln, Oct. 20, 1854, Lincoln Papers, LC.

28   Richardson to Douglas, Nov. 5, 1854, Douglas Papers, Chicago; Davis, Factional Differences in the Democratic Party in Illinois, 57; Bright to Douglas, Nov. 7, 1854, Douglas Papers, Chicago; Abraham Jonas to Lincoln, Sept. 16, William H. Randolph to Lincoln, Sept. 29, 1854, Lincoln Papers, LC; Shields to Lanphier, Oct. 25, 1854, Lanphier Papers, ISHL; *Illinois State Journal*, Nov. 1, 1854.

29   Cole, *Era of the Civil War*, 130–31; Lincoln to Orville H. Browning, Nov. 12, 1854, *CWAL*, II, 286–87; Fehrenbacher, *Chicago Giant*, 132–33; *Illinois State Register*, Nov. 23, 1854; *Joliet Signal*, quoted in Davis, Factional Differences in the Democratic Party in Illinois, 62; Richardson to Douglas, Nov. 5, 1854, Douglas Papers, Chicago; *CG*, 33/2, App., 216; Shields to Lanphier, Oct. 25, 1854, Lanphier Papers, ISHL.

30   Thomas Hoyne *et al.* to Douglas, Oct. 23, 1854, Douglas Papers, Chicago; *Illinois State Register*, Nov. 21, 22, 1854.

31   Douglas to Lanphier, Dec. 18, 1854, to Sheahan, Feb. 6, 1855, *Letters*, 331, 333; G. F. Powers to Lincoln, Dec. 8, 1854, Lincoln Papers, LC; Lyman Trumbull to John M. Palmer, Nov. 23, 1854, George T. Palmer (ed.), "A Collection of Letters from Lyman Trumbull to John M. Palmer, 1854–1858," *JISHS*, XVI (April–July 1923), 20–22; Lincoln to Elihu N. Powell, Nov. 27, 1854,

*CWAL*, II, 289; Lewis Morrison to Breese, Dec. 15, J. L. D. Morrison to Breese, Dec. 27, 1854, Breese Papers, ISHL.

32 Shields, Jan. 14, Sheahan to Lanphier, Jan. 17, 1855, Lanphier Papers, ISHL; Douglas to Lanphier, Dec. 18, 1854, *Letters*, 331; Beveridge, *Lincoln*, II, 282–87; Harris, Jan. 25, F. D. Preston to Douglas, Jan. 21, 1855, Douglas Papers, Chicago; Lincoln to Elihu B. Washburne, Feb. 9, 1855, *CWAL*, II, 305–6; Sheahan to Douglas, Feb. 17, 1855, Douglas Papers, Chicago; CG, 33/2, App., 331; 34/1, 654–55.

## CHAPTER XIX

1 Washington *Union*, Dec. 14, 1854; *New-York Tribune*, Dec. 25, 1854; Richard Yates to Mrs. Yates, Feb. 3, 1854, in Yates and Pickering, *Richard Yates: Civil War Governor*, 92; Receipt for dinner parties, Jan. 5, 1854, Douglas Family Papers, Greensboro; *Chicago Democrat*, March 4, 1854; David S. Reid, June 17, J. N. Granger, Nov. 5, 1854, Franklin Pierce to Douglas, May 3, [1855], Douglas Papers, Chicago.

2 Bill for printing speeches, [May 1854], Horner and Crone to Douglas, Feb. 20, 1854, Douglas Papers, Chicago; Douglas to R. Hoe and Company, March 6, 1855, to John C. Breckinridge, Sept. 7, 1854, to Sheahan, April 6, 1855, to Editor of the *Chicago Times*, Aug. 29, 1857, *Letters*, 335, 328, 338, 394; Julius Wadsworth to Douglas, July 15, 1854, Douglas Family Papers, Greensboro; Cleveland *Leader*, Dec. 1, quoted in *New York Times*, Dec. 8, 1854.

3 Douglas to James Buchanan, Jan. 1, 1855, *Letters*, 332; Leonard Volk to Douglas, Nov. 2, 1855, Douglas Papers, Chicago; Douglas to Riggs and Company, May 31, 1856, Douglas Family Papers, Greensboro; *New York Times*, Jan. 13, 15, 16, 1855; *CG*, 33/2, 305.

4 Nichols, *Franklin Pierce*, 372–74; *CG*, 33/2, *passim*; Robert W. Johannsen, "The Kansas-Nebraska Act and the Pacific Northwest Frontier," *Pacific Historical Review*, XXII (May 1953), 129–42.

5 O. C. Pratt to Douglas, June 1853, Douglas Papers, Chicago; *Illinois State Register*, Sept. 10, 1853; Douglas to John Calhoun, Aug. 10, 1854, to Franklin Pierce, [n. d.], *Letters*, 326, 334; Nichols, *Franklin Pierce*, 404–5.

6 Howell Cobb to James Buchanan, Dec. 5, 1854, Phillips (ed.), *Correspondence of Toombs, Stephens and Cobb*, 348; Nevins, *Ordeal of the Union*, II, 341–46; Nichols, *Franklin Pierce*, 364–65; *Illinois State Journal*, Feb. 21, 1855; Trumbull to Palmer, Dec. 3, 1855, Palmer (ed.), "Letters from Lyman Trumbull to John M. Palmer," *JISHS*, XVI, 26; Blair to Van Buren, Feb. 9, 1855, Van Buren Papers, LC; Pierce to Douglas, May 28, 1855, Douglas Papers, Chicago; Forney to Breckinridge, Oct. 19, 1854, Breckinridge Family Papers, LC.

7 *CG*, 33/2, App., 214–17, 330–31; New York *Herald*, Feb. 24, 1855; Douglas to William P. Fessenden, March 2, 1855, *Letters*, 334–35.

8 *CG*, 33/1, App., 769; Samuel A. Johnson, *The Battle Cry of Freedom: The New England Emigrant Aid Company in the Kansas Crusade* (Lawrence, Kans., 1954), 7–15. For a discussion of land problems in Kansas, see Paul W.

Gates, *Fifty Million Acres: Conflicts over Kansas Land Policy, 1854-1890* (Ithaca, N.Y., 1954).

9   Atchison, quoted in James C. Malin, "The Proslavery Background of the Kansas Struggle," *MVHR,* X (Dec. 1923), 291, 292.

10   Nevins, *Ordeal of the Union,* II, 380-90; Malin, "Proslavery Background," *MVHR,* X, 295-97; Atchison to Hunter, March [April] 4, 1855, Ambler (ed.), *Correspondence of Hunter,* 160-61.

11   James C. Malin, "The Topeka Statehood Movement Reconsidered: Origins," *Territorial Kansas: Studies Commemorating the Centennial* (Lawrence, Kans., 1954), 33-69; Leavenworth *Kansas Territorial Register,* Sept. 22, 1855; John G. Clark, "Mark W. Delahay: Peripatetic Politician," *Kansas Historical Quarterly,* XXV (Autumn 1959), 301-2.

12   Bernard A. Weisberger, "The Newspaper Reporter and the Kansas Imbroglio," *MVHR,* XXXVI (March 1950), 636-42.

13   Nevins, *Ordeal of the Union,* II, 398-402; Nichols, *Franklin Pierce,* 426; Douglas to Howell Cobb, Oct. 6, to Lanphier, July 7, 1855, *Letters,* 342, 339; C. S. Tarpley to Douglas, Nov. 15, 1855, Douglas Papers, Chicago.

14   Douglas to Lanphier, Nov. 11, 1853, *Letters,* 267; Washington *Sentinel,* quoted in Washington *Union,* Jan. 27, 1855; Douglas to Sheahan, Feb. 6, 1855, *Letters,* 333-34.

15   *Richmond Enquirer,* quoted in Washington *Union,* March 30, 1855; *New York Times,* March 30, 1855.

16   *New York Times,* April 13, 1855; *Chicago Tribune,* April 18, 1855; Charles H. Ray to Elihu Washburne, April 21, 1855, Elihu Washburne Papers, LC; *Chicago Tribune,* April 2, 1855.

17   *Chicago Tribune,* quoted in *Illinois State Register,* June 1, 1855; Lincoln to Henry C. Whitney, June 7, 1855, *CWAL,* II, 313.

18   *Chicago Tribune,* May 17, 1855; Chicago *Democratic Press,* May 31, June 2, July 27, 1855; *Illinois State Journal,* July 21, 1855.

19   *Chicago Tribune,* May 1, April 24, 1855.

20   *Chicago Democrat,* May 5, 12, 1855; John Shup Wright, The Background and Formation of the Republican Party in Illinois, 1846-1860 (unpublished Ph.D dissertation, Univ. of Chicago, 1946), 178-84; Chicago *Democratic Press,* quoted in *Illinois State Journal,* July 18, 1855; Lincoln to Lovejoy, Aug. 11, 1855, *CWAL,* II, 316; Trumbull to Lovejoy, Aug. 20, 1855, Lyman Trumbull Family Papers, ISHL.

21   Washington *Union,* Aug. 10, 11, 1855; New York *Herald,* Aug. 19, 1855; *Buffalo Evening Post,* quoted in *Illinois State Journal,* Sept. 8, 1855; *Chicago Democrat,* Sept. 15, 1855.

22   Douglas to James W. Stone *et al.,* Sept. 11, 1855, *Letters,* 340-41; *Illinois State Register,* Sept. 14, 19, 1855; *Illinois State Journal,* Sept. 19, 1855; St. Louis *Missouri Democrat,* Sept. 22, quoted in *New York Times,* Sept. 26, 1855.

23   *Illinois State Journal,* Sept. 29, 1855; *Illinois State Register,* Oct. 2, 15, 1855; Chicago *Democratic Press,* Oct. 6, 1855; Davis, Factional Differences in the Democratic Party in Illinois, 77-78; Washington *Union,* Nov. 13, 1855.

24   Douglas to Breckinridge, May 25, Sept. 12, 22, 1855, Breckinridge to Douglas, Oct. 30, 1855, Breckinridge Family Papers, LC; Douglas to Lanphier and Walker, Oct. 15, to George W. Jones, Oct. 15, 1855, *Letters,* 344; *Illinois State Register,* Oct. 17, 1855.

25   W. D. Latshaw to Lanphier, Oct. 30, Nov. 9, 1855, Lanphier Papers, ISHL; Dr. Ezra Read to the Editor of the *Chicago Times,* Nov. 19, *Illinois State Register,* Nov. 23, 1855; New York *Herald,* Nov. 30, 1855; *Illinois State Register,* Dec. 1, 1855; Douglas to Cobb, Jan. 8, to David S. Reid, Jan. 11, 1856, *Letters,* 346–47; Washington *Union,* Feb. 9, 1856; *CG,* 34/1, 386.

26   Douglas to Cobb, Oct. 6, 1855, *Letters,* 342–43; *New York Times,* Sept. 13, 1855; *Chicago Times,* quoted in New York *Herald,* Dec. 17, 1855; *Illinois State Journal,* Dec. 21, 1855.

27   James B. Steedman to George E. Pugh, Nov. 29, 1855, Douglas Papers, Chicago; Robert Smith to Lanphier, Nov. 23, 1855, Lanphier Papers, ISHL; J. B. Norman to William H. English, Dec. 25, 1855, English Papers, IND; Douglas to Cobb, Oct. 6, 1855, to Sheahan, Jan. 11, 1856, *Letters,* 343, 348; David Reid to Henrietta Reid, March 3, 1856, Reid Papers, NCDAH.

## CHAPTER XX

1   Mrs. Clement C. Clay to Clement Comer Clay, Dec. 25, 1855, Clement C. Clay Papers, DU; Fred Harvey Harrington, " 'The First Northern Victory,' " *JSH,* V (May 1939), 186–205.

2.   Cobb to Mrs. Cobb, Jan. 13, 1856, Howell Cobb Papers, UG; Nichols, *Franklin Pierce,* 436–37; *CG,* 34/1, App., 4; Clement Claiborne Clay to Clement Comer Clay, Jan. 3, 1856, Clement C. Clay Papers, DU.

3   *CG,* 34/1, 5–6; George E. Pugh to Douglas, Dec. 5, 1855, Douglas Papers, Chicago.

4   *CG,* 34/1, 297–98; Washington *Union,* Feb. 12, 1856; *New-York Tribune,* March 19, 1856; Clement Claiborne Clay to Clement Comer Clay, March 10, 1856, Clement C. Clay Papers, DU; Thomas W. Thomas to Alexander H. Stephens, Feb. 25, 1856, Phillips (ed.), *Correspondence of Toombs, Stephens and Cobb,* 362.

5   *CG,* 34/1, 597; George N. Sanders to John Forney, March 10, 1856, Buchanan Papers, HSP; Harris to Lanphier, March 7, 1856, Lanphier Papers, ISHL.

6   *Senate Reports,* 34/1, No. 34, 1–41 (majority report), 42–61 (minority report); New York *Herald,* April 7, 1856.

7   *CG,* 34/1, 639–40; Trumbull to Palmer, Jan. 2, 1856, Palmer (ed.), "Letters from Lyman Trumbull to John M. Palmer," *JISHS,* XVI, 27; *CG,* 34/1, 1–2, 467; *Illinois State Journal,* March 12, 1856; Douglas to James W. Singleton, March 5, 1856, *Letters,* 349.

8   Washington *Union,* March 15, 1856; *CG,* 34/1, 652–58, App., 200–206.

9   *CG,* 34/1, 663, 693; Washington *Union,* April 19, 1856; *Illinois State Register,* March 27, 1856.

10   *CG,* 34/1, 693, App., 280–89; *New York Times,* March 22, 1856; *Illinois State Register,* April 8, 1856.

11   *CG,* 34/1, 821, App., 358–64, 376–77.

12   *CG,* 34/1, 1100, 1201, 1253.

13   Christian F. Eckloff, *Memoirs of a Senate Page (1855–1859)* (ed. by Percival G. Melbourne; New York, 1909), 5–6, 73; *New-York Independent,* May 1, 1856; *New-York Tribune,* April 11, 1856; *New York Times,* March 25, 1856.

14   *CG,* 34/1, 826–27, 851, 864, 893, App., 383–93; *Chicago Tribune,* April 22, 1856; New York *Herald,* March 20, 1856; James H. Lane to Douglas, April 18, in Washington *Union,* April 26, 1856; Douglas to Cooper Kinderdine Watson, April 19, 1856, *Letters,* 354–60; *New York Times,* May 1, 1856; New York *Courier and Enquirer,* quoted in *Illinois State Register,* May 15, 1856.

15   Sumner to Chase, May 15, 1856, Chase Papers, LC; *CG,* 34/1, App., 530–32, 535, 543.

16   David Donald, *Charles Sumner and the Coming of the Civil War* (New York, 1960), 283–88; *Cincinnati Commercial,* March 1, 1869, quoted in Milton, *Eve of Conflict,* 233; *CG,* 34/1, App., 544–47.

17   Donald, *Charles Sumner and the Coming of the Civil War,* 293–97; New York *Herald,* May 28, 1856; *CG,* 34/1, 1305; Douglas to J. E. Roy, July 4, 1856, *Letters,* 364.

18   St. Paul (Minnesota) *Pioneer and Democrat,* April 3, 1856; Henry M. Rice to John C. Breckinridge, Feb. 12, 1856, Breckinridge Family Papers, LC; A. D. Banks to Hunter, Nov. 23, 1855, Ambler (ed.), *Correspondence of Hunter,* 172; Buchanan to John Slidell, Dec. 28, 1855, Buchanan Papers, HSP.

19   Douglas to Cobb, Oct. 6, 1855, Jan. 8, 1856, *Letters,* 342, 346; Francis Preston Blair to Martin Van Buren, Jan. 25, 1856, Van Buren Papers, LC; Letter of Douglas, [n. d.], quoted in *Chicago Democrat,* Feb. 9, 1856.

20   Douglas to James W. Singleton, March 16, 1856, *Letters,* 351; Singleton to the Editor of the *Richmond Examiner,* Feb. 19, in *Illinois State Register,* March 11, 1856.

21   Samuel Treat to Caleb Cushing, Feb. 14, 1856, Cushing Papers, LC; New York *Herald,* Feb. 16, 1856; *Illinois State Register,* Feb. 28, 1856; Clement Claiborne Clay to Clement Comer Clay, March 10, 1856, Clement C. Clay Papers, DU; Chicago *Democratic Press,* March 10, 1856; Tucker to Douglas, April 19, 1856, Douglas Papers, Chicago.

22   Porter and Johnson (comps.), *National Party Platforms, 1840–1964,* 22–23; Disney to Douglas, Feb. 26, 28, 1856, Douglas Papers, Chicago.

23   Buchanan to Sanders, March 7, 1856, *The Political Correspondence of the Late Hon. George N. Sanders,* No. 20; Douglas to Sanders, March 27, 1854, *Letters,* 299–300; Slidell to Buchanan, Feb. 7, March 11, May 2, 24, 1856, Buchanan Papers, HSP; J. L. M. Curry to Clement C. Clay, May 10, 1856, Clement C. Clay Papers, DU; Cobb to ———, April 21, 1856, Phillips (ed.), *Correspondence of Toombs, Stephens and Cobb,* 364; Hunter to George Booker,

[n. d.], May 14, 1856, George Booker Papers, DU; Singleton to Douglas, March 30, 1856, Douglas Papers, Chicago.

24   Milton, "Indiana in the Douglas-Buchanan Contest of 1856," *Indiana Magazine of History,* XXX (June 1934), 126; Slidell to Buchanan, Feb. 7, March 11, 1856, Buchanan Papers, HSP; Disney to Douglas, Feb. 28, n. d. [probably March 1], n. d. [probably March 2, 1856], Douglas Papers, Chicago.

25   S. F. Butterworth to Douglas, April 30, May 3, 1856, Douglas Papers, Chicago; Rice to Breckinridge, May 1, 1856, Breckinridge Family Papers, LC; New York *Herald,* May 7, 1856; *New York Times,* May 5, 1856; Blair to Van Buren, May 17, 1856, Van Buren Papers, LC; Samuel Treat to Douglas, April 8, 1856, Douglas Papers, Chicago.

26   W. J. Brown to Richardson, Feb. 17, Sheahan, Feb. 19, Usher F. Linder, March 15, William H. English, May 30, Disney, n.d. [March 1], n. d. [March 2], H. V. Willson to Douglas, May 29, 1856, Douglas Papers, Chicago; *Chicago Tribune,* Feb. 20, 29, 1856; *Chicago Times,* quoted in *Illinois State Journal,* April 7, 1856.

27   Disney, Feb. 26, 28, 29, n. d. [March 1], n. d. [March 2], Singleton, March 5, Edward C. West, April 8, Willson to Douglas, May 29, 1856, Douglas Papers, Chicago; Douglas to Singleton, March 16, 1856, *Letters,* 351; Issac Bell, Jr., to Clay, May 17, 1856, Clement C. Clay Papers, DU.

28   Disney, Feb. 26, n. d. [March 1], Atchison, Feb. 28, Joel W. White, March 24, B. H. Cheever, April 29, 1856, Douglas Papers, Chicago; New York *Herald,* April 4, 19, 1856; H. V. Willson, Jan. 21, Henry M. Rice to Breckinridge, Feb. 3, 12, 1856, Breckinridge Family Papers, LC; *Illinois State Journal,* Feb. 9, 1856; James F. Grant to Clay, May 10, 1856, Clement C. Clay Papers, DU; George W. Thompson to Hunter, May 24, 1856, Ambler (ed.), *Correspondence of Hunter,* 195; A. J. Cass to Benjamin Butler, May 15, 1856, Benjamin Butler Papers, LC; Thomas R. R. Cobb to Howell Cobb, March 4, 1856, Phillips (ed.), *Correspondence of Toombs, Stephens and Cobb,* 363.

29   New York *Herald,* April 29, May 3, 14, 26, 1856; Toombs to George W. Crawford, May 17, 1856, Phillips (ed.), *Correspondence of Toombs, Stephens and Cobb,* 364; *New York Times,* May 3, 1856; St. Paul *Pioneer and Democrat,* May 27, 1856; Daniel McCook to Douglas, May 29, 1856, Douglas Papers, Chicago.

30   William B. Hesseltine and Rex G. Fisher (eds.), *Trimmers, Trucklers & Temporizers: Notes of Murat Halstead from the Political Convention of 1856* (Madison, 1961), 23—24; Edward C. West, May 22, Winslow Pierce, May 22, Daniel McCook to Douglas, May 29, 1856, Douglas Papers, Chicago; Slidell to Buchanan, May 26, 1856, Buchanan Papers, HSP; Roy F. Nichols, *The Disruption of American Democracy* (New York, 1948), 4—13; Buchanan to Corcoran, May 29, 1856, Corcoran Papers, LC.

31   New York *Herald,* May 31, June 2, 1856; Charles P. Button, June 1, T. M. Ward, June 1, Richardson to Douglas, June 1, 1856, Douglas Papers, Chicago.

32   Hesseltine and Fisher (eds.), *Trimmers, Trucklers & Temporizers,*

26–30, 33, 38–39, 45–46; John E. Ward to Cobb, June 3, 1856, Phillips (ed.), *Correspondence of Toombs, Stephens and Cobb,* 367.

33    Douglas to Richardson, June 3, 5 (two letters), 1856, *Letters,* 361, 362; Hesseltine and Fisher (eds.), *Trimmers, Trucklers & Temporizers,* 47, 51–52, 63; *Official Proceedings of the National Democratic Convention . . . June 2–6, 1856* (Cincinnati, 1856), 39–43, 45–46; Benjamin F. Butler, *The Candidature for the Presidency in Eight Years of Stephen A. Douglas . . . Speech of Gen. Benj. F. Butler, in Lowell, August 10, 1860* (Lowell, 1860), 8–9; William Preston to Douglas, June 7, 1856, Douglas Papers, Chicago.

## CHAPTER XXI

1    John S. Cunningham, June 6, Isaac Diller, June 10, Disney, June 7, John Pettit, June 10, Isaac Morse to Douglas, June 18, 1856, Douglas Papers, Chicago.

2    Clement Claiborne Clay to Clement Comer Clay, June 7, 1856, Clement C. Clay Papers, DU; Lewis Harvie to Hunter, June 16, 1856, Ambler (ed.), *Correspondence of Hunter,* 197; Douglas to Pettit, June 20, 1856, *Letters,* 363.

3    Porter and Johnson (comps.), *National Party Platforms,* 23–27; Roy F. Nichols, *The Disruption of American Democracy* (New York, 1948), 49–50.

4    *CG,* 34/1, 1439, App., 762.

5    *CG,* 34/1, 1467, 1475, 1506; 35/1, 22, 119; *Senate Reports,* 34/1, No. 198, 1–10 (quotations from 7, 9); Johnson, *Douglas,* 302–3.

6    *Illinois State Journal,* July 3, 1856; *New York Times,* July 4, 1856; *Senate Reports,* 34/1, No. 198, 1–3 (minority report); *CG,* 34/1, App., 749–805, 844.

7    *CG,* 34/1, 1567–74, 2230; 34/2, 53; Washington *Union,* July 9, August 14, 1856; New York *Herald,* July 10, 29, 1856; *Senate Reports,* 34/1, No. 282, 1–11.

8    Autobiographical Notes [Sept.-Oct. 1859], *Letters,* 472–73.

9    Stephens to J. W. Duncan, May 26, 1854, Phillips (ed.), *Correspondence of Toombs, Stephens and Cobb,* 345; *New York Times,* May 15, 1854.

10    Basil Rauch, *American Interest in Cuba, 1848–1855* (New York, 1948), 262–302; Sears, "Slidell and Buchanan," AHR, XXVII, 721.

11    *Illinois State Register,* Feb. 14, 1856; *CG,* 34/1, 1071–72.

12    Manuscript copy of handbill, Douglas to Isaiah Rynders *et al.,* May 7, 1856, Appleton Oaksmith Papers, DU; Williams, *Anglo-American Isthmian Diplomacy, 1815–1915,* 196–223; *Chicago Tribune,* May 19, 1856; New York *Herald,* Feb. 6, 1857; Isaac Morse to Douglas, June 18, 1856, Douglas Papers, Chicago.

13    Washington *Union,* June 7, 1856; *New York Times,* June 11, 1856; New York *Herald,* June 12, 1856; Bright to Corcoran, July 17, 1856, Corcoran Papers, LC; Printing bills, Aug., Sept. 1, 1856, Statement of amount due Cornelius Wendell, Jan. 1, 1857, Douglas Family Papers, Greensboro; Sheahan, *Douglas,* 443; Douglas to Sheahan, July 9, 1856, *Letters,* 365–66; "Life and Letters of Judge Charles Mason of Iowa," entry for March 27, 1857 (typescript), Charles Mason Papers, LC.

14   *Illinois State Register,* May 3, 1856; Chicago *Democratic Press,* July 13, 1855; Charles H. Ray to Elihu Washburne, May 4, [1856], Elihu Washburne Papers, LC; Ray to Trumbull, May 4, 1856, Trumbull Papers, LC.

15   James Knox to Richard Yates, March 17, 1856, Richard Yates Papers, ISHL; Bissell, May 5, Orville H. Browning, May 19, Norman Judd, June 7, Ebenezer Peck, June 10, Delahay, July 23, Yates to Trumbull, Aug. 3, 1856, Trumbull Papers, LC; Cole, *Era of the Civil War,* 145–47.

16   William H. Herndon, July 12, B. S. Edwards to Trumbull, July 24, 1856, Trumbull Papers, LC; Sheahan, Jan. 29, March 8, 16, 21, 31, D. Cameron, April 5, E. R. Hooper, April 12, Charles P. Button, May 15, 16, Thomas L. Harris to Douglas, May 18, 1856, Douglas Papers, Chicago; Isaac Cook, March 9, Sheahan to Douglas, May 19, 1856, Douglas Family Papers, Greensboro; Sheahan to Lanphier, May 6, 1856, Lanphier Papers, ISHL; Davis, Factional Differences in the Democratic Party, 83–85.

17   Washington *Union,* Sept. 3, 11, 13, 1856; Chicago *Democratic Press,* Sept. 8, 1856; Cass to Cobb, Sept. 9, 1856, Cobb Papers, UG; *Illinois State Register,* Sept. 11, 19, 1856; Daniel McCook to Douglas, Aug. 8, 1856, Douglas Papers, Chicago.

18   *Illinois State Register,* Sept. 20, 1856; Douglas to Buchanan, Sept. 29, 1856, *Letters,* 367–68; Cole, *Era of the Civil War,* 147; Lincoln to Trumbull, June 7, to Hezekiah G. Wells, Aug. 4, 1856, *CWAL,* II, 342–43.

19   Douglas to Sheahan, Oct. 6, 1856, *Letters,* 368–69; Francis P. Blair, Jr., to Montgomery Blair, Oct. 9, 1856, Blair Family Papers, LC; Theodore Parker to John P. Hale, Oct. 21, 1856, O. B. Frothingham, *Theodore Parker: A Biography* (Boston, 1874), 447–48; E. M. Burns to Breckinridge, Sept. 18, 1856, Breckinridge Family Papers, LC; Buchanan to Douglas, Oct. 4, 1856, Douglas Papers, Chicago.

20   Trumbull to Palmer, Dec. 2, 1856, Palmer (ed.), "Collection of Letters from Trumbull to Palmer," *JISHS,* XVI, 33; Bright to Edmund Burke, Nov. 12, 1856, Burke Papers, LC; *Illinois State Journal,* Nov. 14, 1856; *New York Times,* Nov. 12, 1856.

21   New York *Herald,* Dec. 28, 1856; Buchanan to John Y. Mason, Dec. 29, 1856, Buchanan Papers, HSP; M. R. H. Garnett to Booker, Nov. 13, 1856, Booker Papers, DU.

22   *New York Times,* June 14, 1856; John W. Geary to Pierce, Dec. 22, 1856, Jan. 12, 1857, Pierce Papers, LC.

23   *CG,* 34/3, 734, 851–53, 420–21, App., 353 (in order of citation); *Illinois State Register,* March 9, 1857.

24   Chicago *Democratic Press,* Nov. 25, 1856; Cincinnati *Commercial,* May 31, 1869; Mrs. Roger A. Pryor, *Reminiscences of Peace and War* (New York, 1904), 68; Varina Howells Davis to her parents, Sept. 15, 1856, Hudson Strode (ed.), *Jefferson Davis: Private Letters, 1823–1889* (New York, 1966), 80–81; New York *Herald,* Nov. 11, 21, 1856; Sister Marie Perpetua Hayes, "Adele Cutts, Second Wife of Stephen A. Douglas," *Catholic Historical Review,* XXXI (July 1945), 181–82.

25   *New York Times,* Nov. 25, Dec. 8, 1856; *Illinois State Journal,* Nov.

26, 1856; New York *Herald,* Nov. 25, 1856; *New York Express,* quoted in *Lecompton* (Kansas) *Union,* Dec. 25, 1856.

26  New York *Herald,* Dec. 20, 1856; Shields, quoted in Hayes, "Adele Cutts," *Catholic Historical Review,* XXXI, 183; Pryor, *Reminiscences,* 68; Correspondence of Boston *Traveller,* quoted in St. Paul *Pioneer and Democrat,* Jan. 7, 1857.

27  Harris to Lanphier, Jan. 20, 1857, Lanphier Papers, ISHL; Mary Jane Windle, *Life in Washington, and Life Here and There* (Philadelphia, 1859), 78; St. Paul *Pioneer and Democrat,* April 5, 1857; "The Hon. Stephen A. Douglas," *Harper's Weekly,* I (Dec. 26, 1857), 818; Pryor, *Reminiscences,* 69; Mrs. Henry M. Rice to Mrs. Douglas, Oct. 12, 1857, Douglas Family Papers, Greensboro; Varina Howells Davis to her mother, Dec. 16, 1857, Strode (ed.), *Jefferson Davis: Private Letters,* 97; Hayes, "Adele Cutts," *Catholic Historical Review,* XXXI, 185; Adele Cutts Douglas to her mother, June 24, 1857, *Letters,* 384–85.

28  Agreement with Henry M. Rice, April 13, House plans and sketches, J. F. Callan to Douglas, May 22, July 4, Aug. 8, 1857, Douglas Family Papers, Greensboro; David S. Reid to Henrietta Reid, Dec. 11, 1857, Reid Papers, NCDAH.

## CHAPTER XXII

1  Benjamin Perley Poore, *Perley's Reminiscences of Sixty Years in The National Metropolis* (Philadelphia, 1886), 515–16.

2  *CG,* 34/3, 100; John Bassett Moore (ed.), *The Works of James Buchanan* (12 vols., Philadelphia, 1908–11), X, 105–8; Nichols, *Disruption,* 60.

3  Stephens to Linton Stephens, Dec. 15, 1856, Jan. 1, 1857, Richard Malcolm Johnston and William Hand Browne, *Life of Alexander H. Stephens* (Philadelphia, 1878), 316, 318; Vincent C. Hopkins, *Dred Scott's Case* (New York, 1951).

4  *United States Reports,* 19 Howard, 399–454; Cutts, *A Brief Treatise Upon Constitutional and Party Questions,* 54.

5  Douglas to Treat, Feb. 5, 1857, *Letters,* 372; Ferdinand Kennett, Jan. 29, Treat to Douglas, Feb. 12, 1857, Douglas Family Papers, Greensboro; Edward C. West to Douglas, March 17, 1857, Douglas Papers, Chicago.

6  Daniel McCook to Douglas, Feb. 10, 1857, Douglas Family Papers, Greensboro; *New-York Tribune,* Dec. 5, 1856, Jan. 15, 1857; Charles P. Button to Douglas, March 14, 1857, Douglas Papers, Chicago; Slidell to Buchanan, Feb. 14, 1857, Buchanan Papers, HSP.

7  New York *Herald,* Jan. 30, 1857; A. Birdsall to Cobb, Jan. 29, 1857, Cobb Papers, UG; Douglas to Treat, Dec. 20, 1856, to Buchanan, [n. d.], *Letters,* 369–70; Treat to Douglas, March 10, 1857, Douglas Papers, Chicago; Toombs to Stephens, Feb. 14, 1857, Stephens Papers, LC; Robert McLane to Cobb, Feb. 14, 1857, Phillips (ed.), *Correspondence of Toombs, Stephens and Cobb,* 395; Nichols, *Disruption,* 57–58; Buchanan, quoted in Philip G. Auchampaugh, *James Buchanan and His Cabinet on the Eve of Secession* (Lancaster, Pa., 1926), 37.

8  I have been greatly assisted in the discussion that follows by David E.

Meerse, James Buchanan, The Patronage, and the Northern Democratic Party, 1857–1858 (unpublished Ph.D. dissertation, Univ. of Illinois, 1969).

9　Douglas to Conly, March 12, 1857, Collectors of Customs Applications, Illinois-Chicago, Philip Conly Papers, RG-56, NA; Conly to Douglas, March 13, 1857, Douglas Papers, Chicago; Douglas to Sheahan, Feb. 23, 1857, Letters, 374.

10　Davis, Factional Differences in the Democratic Party in Illinois, 133–34; William A. Richardson et al. to Douglas, Feb. 11, 1857, Douglas Family Papers, Greensboro; Diller to Douglas, Feb. 24, March 24, 1857, Douglas Papers, Chicago.

11　Douglas to Lewis Cass, March 9, 1857, Letters, 376; Isaac N. Morris to Douglas, March 14, 1857, Douglas Papers, Chicago; Buchanan to Douglas, Sept. 7, 1857, Douglas Family Papers, Greensboro.

12　Douglas to Buchanan, Aug. 31, Sept. 4, 1857, Letters, 397, 398; Morris to Horatio King, May 18, 1857, Horatio King Papers, LC; Illinois State Journal, March 21, 1857; Chicago Democratic Press, May 14, 1857.

13　Isaac Diller, Feb. 7, Richardson, Feb. 3, E. R. Hooper, Feb. 10, Singleton to Douglas, Feb. 9, 1857, Douglas Family Papers, Greensboro; Douglas to Singleton, Feb. 14, 1857, Letters, 373.

14　Sheahan to Douglas, April 4, 1857, Douglas Family Papers, Greensboro; J. M. Cutts, Jr., to Douglas, March 13, 1857, Douglas Papers, Chicago; Morris to King, June 10, 1857, King Papers, LC; Washington McLean to Douglas, June 14, 1857, Douglas Family Papers, Greensboro; D. Cameron, Jr., to Douglas, March 16, 1857, Douglas Papers, Chicago; Douglas to Horatio King, Oct. 9, 1857, Letters, 402.

15　Granger to Douglas, [n. d.], John B. Floyd to Mrs. Douglas, Sept. 24, 1857, Douglas Family Papers, Greensboro; Douglas to Buchanan, Sept. 4, 1857, Letters, 397–98; Buchanan to Douglas, Sept. 7, 1857, Douglas Family Papers, Greensboro.

16　C. W. C. Dunnington to Hunter, Oct. 6, 1857, Ambler (ed.), Correspondence of Hunter, 236; Douglas to Buchanan, Oct. 8, 1857, Letters, 401–2; Illinois State Register, Oct. 14, 1857; Chicago Tribune, Oct. 10, 1857; New-York Tribune, Oct. 13, 1857.

17　J. C. Burroughs to Douglas, Jan. 29, 1857, Douglas Family Papers, Greensboro; Washington Union, April 19, 1856; Chicago Tribune, July 7, 10, 30, 1857; Douglas to Burroughs, Aug. 8, 1857, Letters, 389–90; Resolution of the Board of the University of Chicago, Sept. 2, Burroughs to Douglas, Sept. 3, 1857, Douglas Family Papers, Greensboro; Illinois State Register, May 7, 1857; Chicago Tribune, May 5, 1857.

18　Rice to Douglas, June 26, 1857, Douglas Family Papers, Greensboro; Chicago Times, Aug. 21, 23, 1857; Douglas to Henry Hastings Sibley et al., Aug. 15, to Sibley, Aug. 18, 1857, Letters, 390–92; Chicago Tribune, Aug. 25, Sept. 1, 1857; Illinois State Journal, Aug. 28, 1857; Douglas to the Editor of the Chicago Times, Aug. 29, 1857, Letters, 396–97.

19　Samuel J. Mills, Feb. 22, Shields to Douglas, March 6, 1856, Douglas Papers, Chicago.

20　Calhoun to Douglas, Jan. 26, 1857, Douglas Papers, Chicago.

21    Calhoun to Douglas, Nov. 27, 1855, Douglas Papers, Chicago; Epa-phroditus Ransom to Cass, March 5, 1858, copy, KSHS; Calhoun, Sept. 28, Ransom to Douglas, May 19, 1857, Douglas Family Papers, Greensboro; Robert W. Johannsen, "John Calhoun: The Villain of Territorial Kansas?" *The Trail Guide*, III (Sept. 1958), 8–9.

22    Charles E. Stuart, March 29, Walker to Douglas, Jan. 9, 1857, Douglas Papers, Chicago; Nevins, *The Emergence of Lincoln* (2 vols., New York, 1950), I, 146.

23    *Chicago Times*, Oct. 17, 1860; *House Reports*, 36/1, No. 648, 105–6; Washington *Union*, March 31, 1857; Walker to "My Dear Sister," April 6, 1857, Robert J. Walker Papers, LC.

24    Isaac N. Morris to Douglas, April 1, 1857, Douglas Papers, Greensboro; Nevins, *Emergence of Lincoln*, I, 151–52; Thomas W. Thomas to Stephens, June 15, 1857, Phillips (ed.), *Correspondence of Toombs, Stephens and Cobb*, 400; Douglas to Walker, July 21, 1857, *Letters*, 386–87.

25    *House Reports*, 36/1, No. 648, 103, 111, 115, 161, 175; Calhoun to Douglas, April 2, 1857, Douglas Papers, Chicago; Johannsen, "John Calhoun," *Trail Guide*, III, 10–11; George A. Crawford to Horatio King, July 13, 1857, King Papers, LC; Robert W. Johannsen, "The Lecompton Constitutional Convention: An Analysis of Its Membership," *Kansas Historical Quarterly*, XXIII (Autumn 1957), 225–43.

26    *Illinois State Journal*, June 10, 1857; *Chicago Times*, quoted in Washington *Union*, June 20, 1857.

27    *Kansas, Utah, and the Dred Scott Decision. Remarks of Hon. Stephen A. Douglas, Delivered in the State House at Springfield, Illinois, on 12th of June, 1857* [n. p., n. d.], *passim;* Nichols, *Disruption*, 98–100; W. W. Drummond to Douglas, May 22, 1857, Douglas Family Papers, Greensboro.

28    *CG*, 31/1, App., 369–70; 34/3, 103–4; *Kansas, Utah, and the Dred Scott Decision, passim.*

29    *Illinois State Register*, June 15, 1857; Lanphier and Walker, June 23, F. D. Preston, June 24, Lanphier and Walker, July 16, James S. Green, June 16, Thomas A. Hendricks, July 11, Murray McConnel to Douglas, July 2, 1857, Douglas Family Papers, Greensboro; Washington *Union*, June 23, 1857; New York *Herald*, June 23, 24, 1857.

30    *New-York Tribune*, June 24, 1857; *Chicago Tribune*, June 16, 1857; Springfield *Republican*, June 15, 1857, quoted in Joseph Fort Newton, *Lincoln and Herndon* (Cedar Rapids, 1910), 118; *Chicago Daily Press*, June 16, 1857; *Illinois State Journal*, June 15, 19, 22, 23, 25, 26, 27, 1857; *Illinois State Register*, July 28, 1857; Salt Lake *Deseret News*, quoted in New York *Herald*, Dec. 25, 1857.

31    Gustave Koerner to Trumbull, July 4, 1857, Trumbull Papers, LC; William H. Herndon to Theodore Parker, June 17, 1857, quoted in Newton, *Lincoln and Herndon*, 119; Speech at Springfield, Illinois, June 26, 1857, *CWAL*, II, 398–410.

## CHAPTER XXIII

1 Johannsen, "Lecompton Constitutional Convention," *Kans. Hist. Quar.,* XXIII, 226–29, 234; Toombs to Cass, July 28, Aug. 11, 1857, Cass Papers, WLC; Washington *States,* Aug. 12, 22, 1857; Calhoun to Douglas, Sept. 28, 1857, Douglas Family Papers, Greensboro.

2 George A. Crawford to Horatio King, Oct. 12, 1857, King Papers, LC; Washington *States,* Nov. 7, 1857; Joel Fisk to Douglas, Nov. 13, 1857, Douglas Papers, Chicago.

3 Jeremiah Black to John Forney, [July 1857], Jeremiah Black Papers, LC; Cobb to Stephens, Sept. 12, 19, 1857, Phillips (ed.), *Correspondence of Toombs, Stephens and Cobb,* 422–24; Cobb to James L. Orr, Sept. 29, 1857, Orr-Patterson Papers, SHC; Calhoun, Sept. 28, William Weer to Douglas, Nov. 8, 1857, Douglas Family Papers, Greensboro.

4 *House Reports,* 36/1, No. 648, 162, 163, 171; Weer to Douglas, Dec. 21, 1857, Douglas Papers, Chicago; *Chicago Times,* Oct. 14, 1857; Weer to Douglas, Nov. 8, 1857, Douglas Family Papers, Greensboro; Isacks to Douglas, Nov. 16, 1857, Douglas Papers, Chicago; Washington *Constitution,* Oct. 6, 1860; *New York Times,* Dec. 4, 1857; O. Jennings Wise to Buchanan, Dec. 17, 1857, Buchanan Papers, HSP.

5 James P. Shenton, *Robert John Walker: A Politician from Jackson to Lincoln* (New York, 1961), 173–74; Isacks to Douglas, Nov. 21, 1857, Douglas Papers, Chicago; Buchanan to Black, Nov. 18, 1857, Black Papers, LC.

6 Douglas to Weer, Nov. 23, 1857, Washington *States and Union,* Nov. 1, 1860; Douglas to McClernand, Nov. 23, 1857, *Letters,* 403–4; Weer, Dec. 21, John Martin to Douglas, Dec. 27, 1857, Douglas Papers, Chicago; Weer to the Editor of the *Wyandotte* (Kansas) *Argus,* Oct. 22, quoted in Washington *States and Union,* Nov. 1, 1860.

7 *Illinois State Journal,* Nov. 4, 1857; *Chicago Tribune,* Nov. 19, 1857; New York *Herald,* Oct. 20, 1856 (for a statement by Douglas opposing slavery).

8 Joel Fisk, Nov. 13, James D. Eads, Nov. 19, W. W. Wick, Dec. 8, Ralph Leete, Dec. 5, J. Logan Chipman, Dec. 8, James A. Briggs, Nov. 28, McClernand, Dec. 2, Logan, Dec. 5, Sheahan, Dec. 4, George Bancroft to Douglas, Dec. 2, 1857, Douglas Papers, Chicago.

9 Treat, Dec. 2, 3, W. D. Latshaw, Nov. 23, S. T. Bailey to Douglas, Dec. 5, 1857, Douglas Papers, Chicago.

10 *Chicago Times,* Nov. 20, 1857; *New York Times,* Dec. 1, 1857; Charles H. Ray to Trumbull, Nov. 24, 1857, Trumbull Papers, LC; *Chicago Tribune,* Dec. 4, 1857.

11 Lincoln to Trumbull, Nov. 30, 1857, *CWAL,* II, 427; *Illinois State Register,* Oct. 26, 1857; Herndon to Theodore Parker, Sept. 20, 1858, Newton, *Lincoln and Herndon,* 215–16; Ray, Nov. 24, Judd, Nov. 21, Dec. 1, Charles Wilson, Nov. 26, Ebenezer Peck to Trumbull, Nov. 23, 1857, Trumbull Papers, LC.

12 Nichols, *Disruption,* 129–30; Harris to Lanphier, Dec. 1, 3, 1857,

Lanphier Papers, ISHL; *New York Times,* Dec. 4, 1857; Washington *States and Union,* Oct. 20, 1860.

13    Douglas to Riggs and Company, Sept. 28, 1857, *Letters,* 400; Washington *States,* Oct. 15, 1857; Canceled checks (Nov.–Dec., 1857), Bank statement of Chicago Marine and Fire Insurance Company, Dec. 1857, Riggs and Company to Douglas, Dec. 21, 1857, Douglas Family Papers, Greensboro; Isaac Moses to Douglas, Dec. 2, 1857, Douglas Papers, Chicago.

14    *New York Times,* Dec. 3, 1857; Springfield (Massachusetts) *Argus,* quoted in *Illinois State Register,* June 4, 1857; Newburyport *Herald,* quoted in *Illinois State Register,* Sept. 28, 1857; Mary Jane Windle, *Life in Washington, and Life Here and There* (Philadelphia, 1859), 65–66.

15    Stephens to Linton Stephens, Dec. 1, 3, 1857, Stephens Papers, LC; *New York Times,* Dec. 9, 1857; Horace Greeley, *Recollections of a Busy Life* (New York, 1868), 356; Douglas to Lanphier and Walker, Dec. 6, 1857, *Letters,* 405.

16    J. N. Granger to Douglas, Dec. 29, 1857, Douglas Family Papers, Greensboro; New York *Herald,* Dec. 21, 1857; *Chicago Times,* Dec. 16, 1857; James C. Allen to Douglas, Nov. 4, 1857, Douglas Family Papers, Greensboro; Daniel McCook, Nov. 30, Allen to Douglas, Nov. 30, 1857, Douglas Papers, Chicago; *New York Times,* Dec. 9, 1857; *New-York Tribune,* Dec. 4, 1857; New York *Herald,* Dec. 17, 1857; *CG,* 35/1, 63.

17    Moore (ed.), *Works of Buchanan,* X, 148–51; Preston King to Gideon Welles, Dec. 18, 1857, Welles Papers, LC; *CG,* 35/1, 5, 7, 14–18, 21.

18    New York *Herald,* Dec. 11, 1857; *New York Times,* Dec. 11, 1857; *New-York Tribune,* Dec. 15, 1857.

19    James Dixon to Welles, Dec. 15, 1857, Welles Papers, LC; Laurence Keitt to James H. Hammond, Dec. 18, 1857, James H. Hammond Papers, LC; Hunter to George Booker, Dec. 10, 1857, Booker Papers, DU; Herschel V. Johnson to Stephens, Dec. 24, 1857, Herschel V. Johnson Papers, DU; E. Banks to Black, Dec. 12, 1857, Black Papers, LC; New York *Herald,* Dec. 11, 18, 1857; R. P. Letcher to John J. Crittenden, Dec. 26, 1857, Crittenden Papers, LC; Edward C. West to Douglas, Dec. 8, 1857, Douglas Papers, Chicago.

20    Dixon to Welles, Dec. 15, 1857, Welles Papers, LC; Ray, Dec. 18, Bissell, Dec. 12, Charles L. Wilson to Trumbull, Dec. 14, 1857, Trumbull Papers, LC; Douglas to Colfax, [Dec. 1857], *Letters,* 405; Memorandum of interview, Burlingame & Colfax with Douglas, Dec. 14, 1857, Schuyler Colfax Papers, ISL; New York *Herald,* Dec. 11, 18, 1857; Trumbull to Lincoln, Dec. 25, 1857, Trumbull Family Papers, ISHL.

21    New York *Herald,* Dec. 14, 18, 1857; Washington *States,* Dec. 18, 1857; S. M. Johnson, Jan. 2, George N. Sanders to Buchanan, Jan. 21, 1858, Buchanan Papers, HSP; Nichols, *Disruption,* 154.

22    Weer to Douglas, Dec. 6, 25, 1857, Douglas Papers, Chicago; Weer to Douglas, Dec. 14, 1857, Douglas Family Papers, Greensboro; J. H. St. Matthew to Douglas, Dec. 29, 1857, Douglas Papers, Chicago; New York *Herald,* Dec. 11, 1857; Nichols, *Disruption,* 155; Johannsen, "Calhoun," *Trail Guide,* III, 14–16.

23    *CG,* 35 / 1, 50, 120, 121, 140; *Chicago Times,* Jan. 3, 1858; *New York Times,* Dec. 21, 1857.

24    New York *Herald,* Dec. 26, 28, 1857; Preston King to Welles, Jan. 2, 1858, Welles Papers, LC; John Bigelow to William Cullen Bryant, Dec. 28, 1857, quoted in Nevins, *Emergence of Lincoln,* I, 263.

25    Mrs. Levi Woodbury to Frances Lowery and Virginia Fox, Jan. 1858, Levi Woodbury Papers, LC; *Chicago Times,* Jan. 22, 27, 1858; Washington *States,* Jan. 18, 20, 1858.

26    J. Swain, Jan. 9, 1858, John Cain, Dec. 11, S. B. Benson, Dec. 12, 1857, A. Haines, Jan. 27, H. V. Willson, Feb. 28, A. M. Barnes, Feb. 1, 1858, A. G. Ege, Dec. 21, Alfred F. Goss, Dec. 24, 1857, L. Nash, Jan. 24, C. E. Blood, Jan. 18, John B. Cochran, Feb. 22, 1858, James B. Miller, Dec. 30, 1857, N. Brown to Douglas, Feb. 9, 1858, Douglas Papers, Chicago.

27    Edwin M. Stanton, Dec. 11, Gideon Welles, Dec. 12, 1857, March 16, 1858, Forney, Dec. 13, 1857, May 30, 1858, John Van Buren, Dec. 13, Thurlow Weed, Dec. 16, B. F. Butler, Dec. 18, George Bancroft, Dec. 31, 1857, Feb. 13, Henry Carey to Douglas, April 3, 1858, Douglas Papers, Chicago.

28    Cyrus Knowlton, Dec. 28, Henry Howe, Dec. 21, 1857, Gideon Granger, April 13, May 29, Daniel P. Rhodes to Douglas, Feb. 21, 1858, Douglas Papers, Chicago.

29    Richmond *Examiner,* quoted in Washington *States,* Dec. 17, 1857; Richmond *Enquirer,* quoted in *Illinois State Register,* Dec. 24, 1857; Henry A. Wise to Douglas, Jan. 14, 1858, Douglas Papers, Chicago; New York *Herald,* Feb. 11, 1858; John Cuningham, Jan. 26, Robert W. Barnwell, Jan. 18, Isaac W. Hayne, Jan. 6, James Gadsden to Hammond, Jan. 4, 1858, Hammond to William Gilmore Simms, Dec. 19, 1857, Hammond Papers, LC; Joseph E. Brown to Stephens, Feb. 9, 1858, Phillips (ed.), *Correspondence of Toombs, Stephens and Cobb,* 431; Warren D. Wilkes to Douglas, Feb. 5, 1858, Douglas Papers, Chicago.

30    Cole, *Era of the Civil War,* 157–59; C. Goudy, Dec. 20, 1857, Simeon Francis, Feb. 23, W. H. Bristol, Feb. 9, 1858, Seth Paine, Dec. 14, Isaac G. Wilson, Dec. 16, R. T. Merrick to Douglas, Dec. 15, 1857, Douglas Papers, Chicago; Herndon to Trumbull, Jan. 15, 1858, Trumbull Papers, LC; Ninian W. Edwards, March 5, McClernand, Feb. 12, Matteson, March 5, R. T. Merrick to Douglas, Feb. 22, 1858, Douglas Papers, Chicago.

31    George G. Swan, March 5, D. G. Salisbury, March 5, Sheahan to Douglas, Feb. 10, 1858, Douglas Papers, Chicago; George W. McConnell to Lanphier, [n. d.], Lanphier Papers, ISHL; Slidell to Buchanan, Feb. 17, 1858, Buchanan Papers, HSP; Harris to Lanphier, Feb. 27, 1858, Lanphier Papers, ISHL; *Chicago Tribune,* Jan. 27, 1858; New York *Herald,* March 10, 1858; Sheahan, *Douglas,* 386–87; Davis, Factional Differences in the Democratic Party in Illinois, 173–75; Sheahan, Dec. 31, 1857, William H. Adams to Douglas, March 15, 1858, Douglas Papers, Chicago.

32    Hammond to M. C. M. Hammond, Jan. 10, 1858, Hammond Papers, LC; Caleb Cushing to Franklin Pierce, Jan. 9, 1858, Pierce Papers, LC; Clement Comer Clay to Clement Claiborne Clay, [date mutilated], Clement C. Clay Pa-

pers, DU; Denver, Jan. 16, John H. Stringfellow to Buchanan, Jan. 5, 1858, Buchanan Papers, HSP; Samuel Treat to Douglas, Jan. 12, 1858, Douglas Papers, Chicago; Hammond to William Gilmore Simms, Jan. 20, 1858, Hammond Papers, LC; New York *Herald,* Jan. 8, 1858.

33   S. S. Marshall to John A. Logan, Jan. 13, 1858, Logan Family Papers, LC; Preston King to Welles, Jan. 15, 1858, Welles Papers, LC; Sumner to Chase, Jan. 18, 1858, Chase Papers, LC; Frank P. Blair, Jr., to Isaac H. Sturgeon, Oct. 25, Washington *States,* Oct. 29, 1858; King to Welles, Feb. 4, 1858, Welles Papers, LC; Colfax to Calvin Fletcher, Feb. 13, 1858, Calvin Fletcher Papers, IND; Daniel O. Morton to Douglas, Feb. 22, 1858, Douglas Papers, Chicago; Douglas to Forney *et al.,* Feb. 6, to "Gentlemen," Feb. 11, to George Bancroft, Feb. 15, to McClernand, Feb. 21, 1858, *Letters,* 408–10, 411–12, 417; Harris to Lanphier, Jan. 21, 1858, Lanphier Papers, ISHL.

34   *CG,* 35/1, 502, 521; Moore (ed.), *Works of Buchanan,* X, 179–92; *New-York Tribune,* Feb. 1, 1858; Asa Biggs to David Reid, Feb. 4, 1858, Reid Papers, NCDAH.

35   Nichols, *Disruption,* 156–62; *CG,* 35/1, 570–71, 641–43; New York *Herald,* Feb. 12, 1858; Harris to McClernand, Feb. 16, 1858, McClernand Papers, ISHL; Douglas to Treat, Feb. 28, 1858, *Letters,* 418.

36   Green to Douglas, Feb. 16, 1858, Douglas Family Papers, Greensboro; *Chicago Times,* Feb. 23, March 6, 1858; Forney to Douglas, Feb. 14, 1858, Douglas Papers, Chicago; Douglas to Forney, Feb. 15, 1858, *Letters,* 413; *CG,* 35/1, 755–56, 902–3.

37   *Senate Reports,* 35/1, No. 82, 52–76; Bancroft to Douglas, Feb. 20, 1858, Douglas Family Papers, Greensboro; *Chicago Times,* Feb. 26, 1858.

38   Nichols, *Disruption,* 163–64; *CG,* 35/1, 919–20; *Chicago Times,* March 7, 1858; Harris to Lanphier, March 11, 1858, Lanphier Papers, ISHL; *Chicago Tribune,* March 13, 1858; *New York Times,* March 15, 1858; Washington *States,* March 16, 1858; Dixon to Welles, March 17, 1858, Welles Papers, LC.

39   *New-York Tribune,* March 23, 24, 1858; Christian F. Eckloff, *Memoirs of a Senate Page (1855–1859),* 164–65; Washington *States,* March 23, 1858.

40   *CG,* 35/1, App., 194–201; *Chicago Tribune,* March 27, 1858.

41   *CG,* 35/1, 1260, 1264–65.

42   Nichols, *Disruption,* 166–68; *New-York Tribune,* March 25, 1858; New York *Herald,* March 27, 30, 1858; Washington *States,* March 29, 1858; J. B. Norman, March 5, John Cochrane to English, March 28, 1858, English Papers, IND; English to Buchanan, March 31, enclosed in Buchanan to Cobb, March 31, 1858, Cobb Papers, UG.

43   *CG,* 35/1, 1442–43, 1557–59, 1589–90, 1765–66; Dixon to Welles, April 2, 1858, Welles Papers, LC; Henry B. Payne to Douglas, April 9, 1858, Douglas Papers, Chicago; Johnston and Browne, *Life of Stephens,* 335; Washington *States,* April 16, 17, 19, 20, 21, 23, 1858.

44   Harris to Lanphier, April 29, 1858, Lanphier Papers, ISHL; Frank H. Hodder, "Some Aspects of the English Bill for the Admission of Kansas," Amer-

ican Historical Association *Annual Report, 1906,* I, 202–10; Washington *States,* April 24, 1858; J. Spencer to Douglas, April 23, 1858, Douglas Papers, Chicago; [Buchanan], Memorandum, April 30, 1858, quoted in Philip G. Auchampaugh, "The Buchanan-Douglas Feud," *JISHS,* XXV (April–July 1932), 19.

45   Edgar E. Robinson (ed.), "The Day Journal of Milton S. Latham, January 1 to May 6, 1860," *Quarterly of the California Historical Society,* XI (March 1932), 15; David A. Williams, *David C. Broderick: A Political Portrait* (San Marino, 1969), 178.

46   *CG,* 35/1, 1868–71, 1899, 1905–6; Harris to Lanphier, April 30, 1858, Lanphier Papers, ISHL.

47   Washington *States,* May 3, 1858; Hammond to William Gilmore Simms, May 3, 1858, Hammond Papers, LC; Buchanan to William B. Reed, July 31, 1858, Buchanan Papers, HSP; *New York Times,* May 1, 1858.

48   Dixon to Welles, March 6, 1858, Welles Papers, LC; Johnson to Hammond, May 1, 1858, Hammond Papers, LC.

## CHAPTER XXIV

1   James Shields to Richard G. Murphy, Feb. 8, 1858, St. Paul *Pioneer and Democrat,* Feb. 24, 1858; *CG,* 35/1, 1300, 1302, 1323–24, 1446, 1448, 1516.

2   *CG,* 35/1, 1324, 1415, 1963–64, 2204–7, 2209.

3   Sylvester Mowry to Douglas, July 1, 1857, Douglas Family Papers, Greensboro; *CG,* 35/1, 1415, 1531, 3042; *Chicago Tribune,* April 17, 1858; *New-York Tribune,* June 2, 1858; *CG,* 35/1, 252, 1563, 1644–46; Jonathan Baldwin Turner to Trumbull, Oct. 7, 1857, Trumbull Papers, LC.

4   James B. Steedman to Douglas, Dec. 28, 1857, Douglas Family Papers, Greensboro; *CG,* 35/1, 223–24; New York *Herald,* Jan. 4, 1858; Thomas W. Thomas to Alexander H. Stephens, Feb. 7, 1858, Phillips (ed.), *Correspondence of Toombs, Stephens and Cobb,* 431.

5   Washington *Union,* May 25, 1858; New York *Herald,* May 25, 1858; *New York Times,* May 31, 1858; *CG,* 35/1, 2451–52, 2496–97, 2746; R. W. Van Alstyne, "The British Right of Search and the African Slave Trade," *Journal of Modern History,* II (March 1930), 39–41.

6   *CG,* 35/1, 3057.

7   *New York Times,* April 12, 29, May 6, 1858; C. C. Leigh to Mrs. Douglas, April 8, A. T. Stewart and Company, April 21, C. H. Brainard, June 21, Leonard Volk to Douglas, April 14, 1858, Douglas Papers, Chicago; Volk to Mrs. Douglas, May 1, 1858, Douglas Family Papers, Greensboro.

8   R. T. Merrick to Mrs. Douglas, May 7, James B. Sheridan, June 15, Joseph R. Chandler, June 15, Daniel McCook to Douglas, July 24, 1858, Douglas Papers, Chicago; Statement of Cornelius Wendell for printing, [n. d.], Douglas Family Papers, Greensboro; J. Madison Cutts to Mrs. Douglas, July 12, 1858, Douglas Papers, Chicago.

9   James L. Woodward, July 1, 9, 10, Claggett and Dodson to Douglas, August 7, Statement of J. F. Callan, July 1, Callan, July 8, Richard Smith to Doug-

las, Aug. 5, 1858, Douglas Papers, Chicago; Bond for deed (DeWitt County, Illinois), April 19, 1858, ISHL.

10   T. Rush Spencer, Feb. 20, July 19, 20, 21, O. Bushnell, June 30, Aug. 25, John B. Murray, July 7, 15, Fernando Wood, July 8, Aug. 25, J. W. Ellington to Douglas, Oct. 5, 1858, Douglas Papers, Chicago; New York *Herald,* Sept. 15, 21, 1858.

11   Washington *States,* June 25, 1858; Chicago *Press and Tribune,* July 7, 1858; New York *Herald,* July 9, 1858; Clement L. Vallandigham to Douglas, June 13, 1858, Douglas Papers, Chicago.

12   O. B. Ficklin to Sidney Breese, Oct. 28, 1857, Breese Papers, ISHL.

13   *Chicago Times,* Dec. 20, 1857; *Chicago Democrat,* Dec. 21, 23, 1857.

14   Sheahan to Lanphier, Feb. 4, 1858, Lanphier Papers, ISHL; Norman Holm, April 14, G. W. McLane to Douglas, May 30, 1858, Douglas Papers, Chicago.

15   Harris to Lanphier, Jan. 21, 30, Feb. 27, 1858, Lanphier Papers, ISHL; J. H. Johnson to Douglas, June 2, 1858, Douglas Papers, Chicago; Cook to Aaron V. Brown, April 24, 1858, Horatio King Papers, LC; Washington *States,* Oct. 21, 1858. See also David E. Meerse, James Buchanan, The Patronage, and the Northern Democratic Party, 1857—1858.

16   William C. Goudy, March 21, Samuel Treat to Douglas, March 5, 1858, Douglas Papers, Chicago.

17   Harris to Lanphier, March 13, 1858, Lanphier Papers, ISHL; R. T. Merrick to Douglas, March 27, 1858, Douglas Papers, Chicago; Cook to N. Wright, April 8, and Cook to Elijah H. Eyer, April 8, 24, in *Chicago Times,* April 16, May 2, 1858.

18   Sheahan, *Douglas,* 392; *Illinois State Journal,* April 26, 1858; *Chicago Democrat,* May 10, 1858.

19   Lanphier, April 8, James A. Barret to Douglas, April 22, 1858, Douglas Papers, Chicago; *Illinois State Register,* April 22, 1858; *Illinois State Journal,* April 23, 24, 1858; *Chicago Tribune,* April 24, 1858.

20   *Chicago Times,* May 22, 1858; Washington *Union,* May 26, 1858.

21   Harris to Lanphier, May 7, 1858, Lanphier Papers, ISHL; Trumbull to John M. Palmer, May 20, 1858, Palmer (ed.), "Collection of Letters from Trumbull to Palmer," *JISHS,* XVI, 36—37; Preston King to Gideon Welles, May 29, 1858, Welles Papers, LC; R. P. Letcher to Crittenden, May 31, 1858, Crittenden Papers, LC; Linder to Douglas, May 15, 1858, Douglas Papers, Chicago.

22   Harris to Lanphier, May 8, 27, 1858, Lanphier Papers, ISHL; Isaac H. Sturgeon to Cobb, May 17, 1858, Cobb Papers, UG; Sturgeon to Breese, Sept. 11, 1858, Breese Papers, ISHL; Washington *Union,* Sept. 17, 1858; Frank P. Blair to James O. Brodhead, April 19, 1858, James O. Brodhead Papers, MHS; Blair to Sturgeon, Oct. 25, 1858, *CG,* 36/1, App., 163.

23   Washington *Union,* May 27, 1858; Sheahan, May 30, William Price to Douglas, June 9, 1858, Douglas Papers, Chicago.

24   Cook to Buchanan, May 10, 1858, Buchanan Papers, HSP; *Illinois State Journal,* June 10, 1858; *Illinois State Register,* June 11, 1858.

25   *Illinois State Register,* June 10, 1858; Herndon to Trumbull, July 8,

1858, Trumbull Papers, LC; William Weer to Douglas, May 14, 1858, Douglas Papers, Chicago; Chicago *Union,* quoted in *Illinois State Register,* June 10, 1858; Josiah M. Lucas to Abraham Lincoln, June 15, 1858, Lincoln Papers, LC.

26    *CG,* 35/1, 3055–58.

27    Trumbull to Lincoln, June 16, 1858, Lincoln Papers, LC; *Chicago Tribune,* June 21, July 2, 1858; Washington *Union,* June 18, 1858; R. B. Carpenter to Buchanan, June 23, 1858, R. B. Carpenter Papers, ISHL.

28    Augusta *Constitutionalist,* quoted in Washington *States,* July 12, 1858; Washington *States,* June 19, 22, 24, July 1, 6, 1858; John A. Parker, June 10, 19, W. A. Richardson to Douglas, July 27, 1858, Douglas Papers, Chicago.

29    James May, June 21, 24, 25, Sanders, July 1, J. M. Cutts, July 1, J. S. Wright to Douglas, Aug. 23, 1858, Douglas Papers, Chicago.

30    *Chicago Times,* July 10, 1858; Chicago *Press and Tribune,* July 10, 12, 1858.

31    Lincoln to Thomas A. Marshall, April 23, 1858, *CWAL,* II, 443.

32    Trumbull to Lincoln, Jan. 3, 1858, Lincoln Papers, LC; *New-York Tribune,* May 17, 1858; Horace Greeley, *Recollections of a Busy Life* (New York, 1868), 357–58; Greeley to Herndon, May 30, 1858, Herndon-Weik Papers, LC; R. W. Burton to Douglas, May 29, 1858, Douglas Papers, Chicago.

33    Lincoln to Trumbull, Dec. 28, 1857, *CWAL,* II, 430; Herndon to Weik, Dec. 23, 1885, Hertz, *The Hidden Lincoln,* 113–14; Herndon to Theodore Parker, March 4, 1858, Newton, *Lincoln and Herndon,* 150; Paul M. Angle (ed.), *Herndon's Life of Lincoln* (Cleveland, 1949), 321; Herndon to Lincoln, March 24, 1858, Newton, *Lincoln and Herndon,* 153; *New York Tribune,* Feb. 12, 1859.

34    Herndon to Washburne, April 10, 1858, Elihu B. Washburne Papers, LC; Wentworth to Lincoln, April 19, 1858, Lincoln Papers, LC; Lincoln to Charles L. Wilson, June 1, 1858, *CWAL,* II, 457.

35    Herndon to Theodore Parker, Sept. 20, 1858, Newton, *Lincoln and Herndon,* 215–16; New York *Herald,* April 13, 16, 1858; *Chicago Tribune,* April 30, 1858; James Watson Webb to George C. Bates, June 9, 1858, Lincoln Papers, LC; *Chicago Times,* Dec. 11, 1859; Douglas to McClernand, Dec. 7, 8, 1859, *Letters,* 479–80; George W. Jones to Breese, Sept. 17, 1858, Breese Papers, ISHL.

36    William C. Goudy, March 21, Sheahan, May 30, L. P. Paddock, May 20, Benjamin Kirk, June 4, Jonathan Blanchard to Douglas, May 1, 1858, Douglas Papers, Chicago; John M. Palmer to Trumbull, May 25, 1858, Trumbull Papers, LC; Palmer to Breese, Sept. 21, 1858, Breese Papers, ISHL; Lincoln to Washburne, May 27, to Stephen A. Hurlbut, June 1, 1858, *CWAL,* II, 455, 456; Norman B. Judd, June 1, John Wentworth, April 19, Thomas A. Marshall, May 1, Ward Hill Lamon to Lincoln, June 9, 1858, Lincoln Papers, LC.

37    Washburne to Lincoln, May 2, 1858, Lincoln Papers, LC; Nathan M. Knapp to Ozias M. Hatch, March 31, 1858, Ozias M. Hatch Papers, ISHL; B. Gratz Brown to Orville H. Browning, June 10, 1858, Browning Papers, ISHL; John H. Bryant to Lincoln, April 19, 1858, Lincoln Papers, LC; Lincoln to Jediah F. Alexander, May 15, 1858, *CWAL,* II, 446–47.

38   Trumbull to Palmer, June 19, 1858, Palmer (ed.), "Collection of Letters from Trumbull to Palmer," *JISHS,* XVI, 39; *New-York Tribune,* in *Illinois State Register,* June 4, 1858; Sheahan to Lanphier, Feb. 19, 1858, Lanphier Papers, ISHL; Judd, March 7, E. L. Baker, May 1, Leib, July 20, Mark Delahay to Trumbull, May 22, 1858, Trumbull Papers, LC.

39   Delahay to Douglas, April 7, 1858, Douglas Papers, Chicago; Delahay, May 22, Herndon to Trumbull, July 8, 1858, Trumbull Papers, LC; Lincoln to Trumbull, June 23, 1858, *CWAL,* II, 471–72; Herndon to Trumbull, June 24, 1858, Trumbull Papers, LC.

40   Charles H. Ray to Washburne, April 15, 1858, Washburne Papers, LC; Ray to Lincoln, April 14, 1858, Lincoln Papers, LC; Ebenezer Peck to Trumbull, April 15, 1858, Trumbull Papers, LC; Simeon Francis to Douglas, May 3, 1858, Douglas Papers, Chicago; Medill to Trumbull, April 22, 1858, Trumbull Papers, LC.

41   Ray to Hatch, March 20, 1858 (photostat), Hatch Papers, ISHL; Jesse K. Dubois, March 22, April 8, A. Jonas to Trumbull, April 11, 1858, Trumbull Papers, LC; Dubois and Hatch to Lincoln, March 23, Lincoln to Hatch, March 24, 1858 (photostats), Hatch Papers, ISHL.

42   Herndon to Parker, April 17, 1858, Newton, *Lincoln and Herndon,* 161; William P. Kellogg, May 4, Koerner to Hatch, April 20, 1858, Hatch Papers, ISHL; Washburne to Lincoln, May 31, 1858, Lincoln Papers, LC.

43   Herndon to Trumbull, April 12, 24, 1858, Trumbull Papers, LC; *Chicago Tribune,* June 14, 1858; Chase to James S. Pike, May 12, 1858, Pike, *First Blows of the Civil War,* 419–20; E. L. Baker to Trumbull, May 1, 1858, Trumbull Papers, LC.

44   *Illinois State Journal,* June 17, 1858; Don E. Fehrenbacher, *Prelude to Greatness: Lincoln in the 1850's* (Stanford, 1962), 68, 70–95; Paul M. Angle (ed.), *Created Equal? The Complete Lincoln-Douglas Debates of 1858* (Chicago, 1958), 1–9.

45   Herndon to Trumbull, June 24, 1858, Trumbull Papers, LC; *Illinois State Register,* June 17, 1858; Forney, *Anecdotes of Public Men,* II, 179.

46   Angle (ed.), *Created Equal?,* 12–25.

47   Washington *Union,* July 14, 15, 22, 1858; *New York Times,* July 12, 1858.

## CHAPTER XXV

1   Washington *States,* July 16, 1858; *Illinois State Register,* Oct. 2, 1858; Washington *National Intelligencer,* Oct. 6, 1858; St. Paul (Minnesota) *Pioneer and Democrat,* Oct. 27, 1858.

2   Washington *Union,* July 20, 27, Aug. 3, 8, 17, Sept. 3, 1858.

3   John P. Heiss to Douglas, July 15, 1858, Douglas Papers, Chicago; *New York Times,* July 31, 1858; Buchanan to Black, Aug. 4, 1858, Black Papers, LC; Buchanan to C. Farley, July 22, 1858, Buchanan Papers, HSP; Henry Payne to Douglas, July 26, 1858, Douglas Papers, Chicago; Jeremiah Black to J. W. Davidson, [Aug. 1, 1858], *House Reports,* 36/1, No. 648, 323–24.

4   A. D. Banks, Aug. 21, Sanders to Douglas, July 17, 1858, Douglas Papers, Chicago.

5   *Jonesboro Gazette,* Oct. 23, 1858, quoted in Davis, Factional Differences in the Democratic Party in Illinois, 213; Isaac H. Sturgeon to Breese, Sept. 19, 1858, Breese Papers, ISHL; Henry S. Foote, *Casket of Reminiscences* (Washington, D.C., 1874), 135.

6   *Illinois State Journal,* Sept. 15, 8, 1858; *Illinois State Register,* Sept. 10, 1858; Chicago *Press and Tribune,* Sept. 9, 1858; Archer G. Herndon to Breese, Sept. 9, 1858, Breese Papers, ISHL.

7   Breese to the Reverend W. F. Boyakin, Sept. 7, *Illinois State Journal,* Sept. 14, 1858; Cook, Aug. 27, Sept. 13, James J. Clarkson, Aug. 30, Sept. 9, 22, A. G. Herndon, Sept. 13, Philip A. Hoyne to Breese, Aug. 23, 1858, Breese Papers, ISHL; *Weekly Chicago Times,* Aug. 12, 1858.

8   *New York Times,* July 31, 1858; Buchanan to Horatio King, July 27, King to Aaron V. Brown, Aug. 3, 1858, King Papers, LC.

9   Slidell to Buchanan, Aug. 8, 1858, Buchanan Papers, HSP; New York *Herald,* Aug. 13, 1858; *Chicago Times,* Oct. 15, 1859; Thomas M. Hope to Alex Dunn, Sept. 12, enclosed in Dunn to Douglas, Sept. 22, 1858, Douglas Papers, Chicago; Black to Breese, Aug. 7, Sept. 17, 1858, Breese Papers, ISHL.

10   Jones to Breese, Oct. 17, 1858, Breese Papers, ISHL; Koerner, June 29, Leib to Trumbull, July 20, 1858, Trumbull Papers, LC; Charles S. Wilson to Richard Yates, July 25, 1858, Yates Papers, ISHL; A. Shuman to Ozias M. Hatch, Sept. 27, 1858, Hatch Papers, ISHL; Sheahan, *Douglas,* 416.

11   C. Farley, July 15, Slidell to Buchanan, Aug. 8, 1858, Buchanan Papers, HSP; Leib to Trumbull, July 20, 1858, Trumbull Papers, LC.

12   Greeley to Joseph Medill, July 24, 1858, Lincoln Papers, LC; Greeley to Herndon, Oct. 6, 1858, Herndon-Weik Papers, LC.

13   Augustus R. Wright to C. P. Culver, Aug. 23, 1858, Washington *States,* Aug. 27, 1858; James S. Green to Samuel Treat, Sept. 29, 1858, Treat Papers, MHS; Washington *States,* Aug. 2, 1858; Washington *Union,* Aug. 21, 1858; George W. Jones to Breese, Oct. 17, 1858, Breese Papers, ISHL; New York *Herald,* Sept. 25, 1858; Washington *States,* Sept. 22, 1858.

14   C. N. Pine to Buchanan, Aug. 17, 1858, Buchanan Papers, HSP; Linton Stephens to R. M. Johnston, Sept. 3, 1858, James D. Waddell (ed.), *Biographical Sketch of Linton Stephens, Containing a Selection of His Letters, Speeches, State Papers, etc.* (Atlanta, 1877), 154; Henry A. Wise to John Moore, Oct. 13, 1858, Washington *National Intelligencer,* Oct. 26, 1858; J. Letcher to Howell Cobb, July 29, 1858, Cobb Papers, UG.

15   A. D. Banks to Miles, Sept. 7, 1858, Miles Papers, SHC; *New York Times,* Sept. 7, Oct. 23, 1858; New York *Herald,* Aug. 31, 1858. Both the *Illinois State Register* and the Washington *States* printed extensive extracts from the southern press, demonstrating the extent of support for Douglas.

16   Cobb to Stephens, Sept. 8, 1858, Phillips (ed.), *Correspondence of Toombs, Stephens and Cobb,* 442–43; Breckinridge to John Moore, Oct. 4, James A. McHatton to Lanphier, Sept. 23, 1858, Lanphier Papers, ISHL; Isaac

Sturgeon to Buchanan, Oct. 22, 1858, Buchanan Papers, HSP; *New York Times,* Oct. 23, 1858.

17  S. H. Kerfoot, March 19, W. N. Coler to Douglas, May 25, 1858, Douglas Papers, Chicago; *Illinois State Register,* Oct. 8, 1858; Jediah F. Alexander to Lincoln, May 1, 1858, Lincoln Papers, LC; John Olney to Trumbull, [July 1858], Trumbull Papers, LC; J. S. Waterman to Mason Brayman, Sept. 6, 1858, Bailhache-Brayman Papers, ISHL.

18  Lincoln to Crittenden, July 7, 1858, *CWAL,* II, 483–84; Trumbull to Palmer, June 19, 1858, Palmer (ed.), "Collection of Letters from Trumbull to Palmer," *JISHS,* XVI, 39; Harris to Douglas, July 7, 1858, Douglas Papers, Chicago; Dickey to Crittenden, July 19, 1858, Crittenden Papers, LC.

19  Crittenden to Lincoln, July 29, 1858, Lincoln Papers, LC; Crittenden to Dickey, Aug. 1, 1858, Mrs. Chapman Coleman (ed.), *The Life of John J. Crittenden* (2 vols. Philadelphia, 1873), II, 164–66; Lincoln to Crittenden, Nov. 4, 1858, *CWAL,* III, 335–36; James Guthrie to Paul Washington, Oct. 3, 1858, James Guthrie Papers, SHC; Reverdy Johnson to Douglas, July 29, 1858, Washington *National Intelligencer,* Aug. 31, 1858; James A. McHatton to Douglas, Sept. 23, 1858, Douglas Family Papers, Greensboro.

20  Richardson to Douglas, May 30, 1857, Douglas Family Papers, Greensboro; Henry Greenebaum and Henry Bandt, Dec. 26, 1857, A. V. Hofer, March 17, Henry Bandt, March 31, Louis Didier to Douglas, [Aug. 1858], Douglas Papers, Chicago; *New York Times,* Aug. 12, 1858.

21  New York *Herald,* July 22 1858; Caleb Cushing to Franklin Pierce, Oct. 2, 1858, Pierce Papers, LC.

22  Harris, July 7, F. D. Preston to Douglas, May 14, 1858, Douglas Papers, Chicago; Horace White, quoted in Edwin Erle Sparks (ed.), *The Lincoln-Douglas Debates of 1858* (Springfield, 1908), 573; Henry Villard, *Memoirs* (2 vols., Boston, 1904), I, 91–92. For accounts of the 1858 campaign, see Sparks (cited above), Harry E. Pratt, *The Great Debates of 1858* (rev. ed., Springfield, 1956; originally published in *Illinois Blue Book, 1953–1954*), and Richard Allen Heckman, *Lincoln vs. Douglas: The Great Debates Campaign* (Washington, D.C., 1967).

23  *Illinois State Register,* July 19, 1858; Joel A. Matteson and Charles H. Lanphier to Douglas, July 10, 1858, Douglas Papers, Chicago; W. P. Boyd to Crittenden, July 17, 1858, Crittenden Papers, LC.

24  *Political Debates Between Hon. Abraham Lincoln and Hon. Stephen A. Douglas, In the Celebrated Campaign of 1858, in Illinois* . . . (Columbus, 1860), 34–35; Louis Didier to Douglas, [Aug. 1858], Douglas Papers, Chicago; Sheahan, *Douglas,* 417.

25  *Illinois State Register,* July 15, 19, 1858; *Illinois State Journal,* July 16, 19, 1858; Angle (ed.), *Created Equal?,* 43–66 (quotations from 44, 65).

26  Herndon to Trumbull, July 22, 1858, Trumbull Papers, LC. The three speeches with which Douglas opened his campaign have been analyzed in Forest L. Whan, "Stephen A. Douglas," in William Norwood Brigance (ed.), *A History and Criticism of American Public Address* (2 vols., New York, 1943), II, 807–10.

27   *Illinois State Register,* July 21, Aug. 2, Sept. 28, Oct. 15, 1858; Speech at Wooster, Ohio, Sept. 16, 1859, Harry V. Jaffa and Robert W. Johannsen (eds.), *In the Name of the People: Speeches and Writings of Lincoln and Douglas in the Ohio Campaign of 1859* (Columbus, 1959), 219; *New York Times,* quoted in *Illinois State Register,* Nov. 23, 1858.

28   *Illinois State Journal,* July 22, 24, 1858; George B. McClellan, *McClellan's Own Story: The War for the Union, The Soldiers Who Fought It, The Civilians Who Directed It and His Relations to It and Them* (New York, 1887), 36; Virgil Hickox to Editors, July 22, *Illinois State Journal,* July 24, 1858; Pratt, *The Great Debates of 1858,* 8.

29   Angle (ed.), *Created Equal?,* xxiv–xxv; Sparks, *Lincoln-Douglas Debates of 1858,* 80–81; *Chicago Times,* Aug. 25, 1858.

30   Portsmouth (N.H.) *Gazette,* quoted in *Illinois State Register,* July 29, 1858; Whan, "Douglas," in Brigance (ed.), *A History and Criticism of American Public Address,* II, 805, 806, 814–15; Correspondence of Boston *Daily Evening Transcript,* Oct. 13, 1858, quoted in Beveridge, *Lincoln,* II, 681; Joseph F. Evans, "Lincoln at Galesburg," *JISHS,* VIII (Jan. 1916), 562.

31   Interview of John W. Brown, Herndon-Weik Papers, LC; Evans, "Lincoln at Galesburg," *JISHS,* VIII, 562; Carl Schurz, quoted in Sparks, *Lincoln-Douglas Debates of 1858,* 448; Reminiscence of Ingalls Carleton, quoted, *ibid.* 207; Sheahan, *Douglas,* 432; McClellan, *McClellan's Own Story,* 36; Correspondence of the *Missouri Democrat,* quoted in Sparks, *Lincoln-Douglas Debates of 1858,* 443; Correspondence of the New York *Evening Post,* quoted, *ibid.* 499; Thomas W. Goodspeed, "Lincoln and Douglas With Some Personal Reminiscences," *JISHS,* XXVI (Oct. 1933), 192; *Chicago Times,* Aug. 28, 1858; C. R. Parke to P. D. Vroome, Oct. 26, 1858, C. R. Parke Papers, ISHL.

32   Dubois to Trumbull, July 17, 1858, Trumbull Papers, LC; Sheahan to Douglas, Aug. 13, 1858, Douglas Papers, Chicago; Linder, *Reminiscences of the Early Bench and Bar of Illinois,* 78–79, 344–45; Henry Villard to Douglas, Aug. 24, 1858, Douglas Papers, Chicago; Douglas to Linder, Aug. 22 [?], to Jacob I. Brown, Aug. 29, 1858, *Letters,* 427–28.

33   David L. Phillips to Lincoln, July 24, 1858, Lincoln Papers, LC; S. B. Buckner to Douglas, July 30, 1858, Douglas Papers, Chicago; *Chicago Times,* July 30, 1858; Lincoln to Douglas, July 29, to C. W. Michael and William Proctor, Aug. 2, to William Fithian, Sept. 3, 1858, *CWAL,* II, 530, 534, III, 84.

34   Beveridge, *Lincoln,* II, 628–29; Chicago *Press and Tribune,* July 22, 1858; Lincoln to Douglas, July 24, 1858, *CWAL,* II, 522; Stevens, "Douglas," *JISHS,* XVI, 553; Douglas to Lincoln, July 24, 1858, *Letters,* 423–24; *Illinois State Register,* July 29, 1858.

35   *Illinois State Journal,* July 29, 1858; *Chicago Times,* Aug. 1, 1858; Lincoln to Douglas, July 29, 1858, *CWAL,* II, 528–30; Douglas to Lincoln, July 30, 1858, *Letters,* 424–25; Lincoln to Douglas, July 31, 1858, *CWAL,* II, 531; *Illinois State Journal,* Aug. 3, 1858; *Illinois State Register,* July 31, 1858; Washington *Union,* Sept. 7, 1858.

36   C. H. Ray to Washburne, [n. d.], Washburne Papers, LC; Herndon to Theodore Parker, July 24, 1858, in Newton, *Lincoln and Herndon,* 196; New York *Herald,* Oct. 13, 1858.

37   *New-York Tribune,* Aug. 26, 1858; Abraham Smith to Lincoln, July 20, 1858, Lincoln Papers, LC; Chicago *Press and Tribune,* July 16, 1858; *Illinois State Journal,* Oct. 26, 1858; Angle (ed.), *Created Equal?,* 390 (Lincoln), 400 (Douglas); *Illinois State Register,* June 17, 1858; Whan, "Douglas," in Brigance (ed.), *A History and Criticism of American Public Address,* II, 795.

38   Angle (ed.), *Created Equal?,* 104, 256–57, 195, 180, 168 (in order of citation).

39   *Ibid.,* 347, 136, 203.

40   *Ibid.* 321, 154, 180.

41   *Ibid.* 231; J. H. Jordan, July 25, Henry Asbury to Lincoln, July 28, 1858, Lincoln Papers, LC; Lincoln to Asbury, July 31, 1858, *CWAL,* II, 530; Joseph Medill to Lincoln, [Aug. 27, 1858], Lincoln Papers, LC. The background to Lincoln's question at Freeport has been ably and definitively analyzed in Fehrenbacher, *Prelude to Greatness,* 122–26.

42   Angle (ed.), *Created Equal?,* 143–44, 152; *Illinois State Journal,* Sept. 13, 1858; *Illinois State Register,* Sept. 2, 1858; Washington *States,* Oct. 9, 1858.

43   Angle (ed.), *Created Equal?,* 202, 113–14, 352, 155.

44   *Ibid.* 343–44, 351.

45   *Ibid.* 111–12, 266–67, 294, 400; Charles L. Wilson to Trumbull, May 12, 1858, Trumbull Papers, LC; New York *Herald,* Aug. 16, 1868; *Illinois State Journal,* Sept. 28, 30, 1858.

46   Angle (ed.), *Created Equal?,* 105–6, 114–15, 131–33, 144–45, 157–58; Douglas to Lanphier, Aug. 15, 1858, *Letters,* 426–27; Lanphier to Douglas, Aug. 26, 1858, Douglas Papers, Chicago; *Illinois State Journal,* Aug. 25, 26, 27, 1858.

47   *New-York Tribune,* Aug. 18, 1858; Medill, Ray, and Scripps to Gentlemen, Aug. 24, 1858, Washburne Papers, LC; Mark M. Krug, *Lyman Trumbull, Conservative Radical* (New York, 1965), 141–42; Chicago *Press and Tribune,* Aug. 6, 1858; *Illinois State Journal,* Aug. 5, 1858; Angle (ed.), *Created Equal?,* 248–55.

48   *Illinois State Journal,* Aug. 30, Sept. 1, 1858; Chicago *Press and Tribune,* Oct. 12, 1858; Lincoln to Judd, Oct. 20, 1858, *CWAL,* III, 329–30; Ray to Hatch, [Aug.] 31, [1858], Hatch Papers, ISHL; H. G. Crouch to Douglas, July 28, 1858, Douglas Papers, Chicago; Douglas to Crouch, Aug. 7, 1858, *Letters,* 425–26.

49   Chicago *Press and Tribune,* Nov. 1, Dec. 24, 1858; J. A. McHatton to the Editors of the Baton Rouge *Advocate,* Dec. 8, 1858, quoted in Washington *States,* Dec. 21, 1858; Douglas to the Editor of the Washington *States,* Jan. 7, 1859, *Letters,* 433–34; A. L. Diket, "John Slidell and the 'Chicago Incident' of 1858," *Louisiana History,* V (Fall 1964), 369–86.

50   Sheahan, *Douglas,* 432; Fehrenbacher, *Prelude to Greatness,* 115; Douglas to Henry A. Wise, Nov. 7, 1858, *Letters,* 429. An analysis of the election re-

turns in relation to the counties in which Douglas and Lincoln spoke may be found in Whan, "Douglas," in Brigance (ed.), *A History and Criticism of American Public Address*, II, 823.

51   *Illinois State Register*, Nov. 6, 1858; *New York Times*, Nov. 5, 1858.

52   Judd to Hatch, Nov. 19, 1858, Hatch Papers, ISHL; *Illinois State Journal*, Nov. 8, 1858. Much was made of the apportionment issue as a factor in Lincoln's defeat, and charges of "gerrymandering" were leveled at the Democrats. Fehrenbacher has successfully laid this issue to rest in *Prelude to Greatness*, 118–20.

53   Chicago *Herald*, quoted in *Illinois State Journal*, Nov. 10, 1858; Cook to Buchanan, Jan. 11, 1859, Buchanan Papers, HSP; *Illinois State Register*, Dec. 28, 1858; Chicago *Press and Tribune*, Nov. 25, 1858; Sheahan, *Douglas*, 433; Sheahan to Lanphier, Dec. 28, 31, 1858, Lanphier Papers, ISHL.

54   *Illinois State Register*, Jan. 4, 1859; *New-York Tribune*, Jan. 5, 1859; J. W. Keyes, Jan. 7, Lanphier to Douglas, Jan. 9, 1859, Douglas Papers, Chicago; Cook to Buchanan, Jan. 11, 1859, Buchanan Papers, HSP; Lanphier to Douglas, Jan. [6], 1859, Lanphier Papers, ISHL; Douglas to Lanphier, Jan. 6, 1859, *Letters*, 433.

## CHAPTER XXVI

1   Sydney Myers to Douglas, Nov. 5, 1858, Douglas Papers, Chicago; Douglas to Myers, Nov. 7, 1858, *Letters*, 428–29; Reverdy Johnson to Douglas, Nov. 5, 13, Charles E. Stuart to F. H. Stevens, Nov. 16, 1858, Douglas Papers, Chicago. See also Edward Delaney, Nov. 8, Winston S. Pierce, Nov. 9, Henry A. Wise, Nov. 12, Archibald Dixon, Dec. 2, J. F. H. Claiborne, Dec. 5, J. J. Worley to Douglas, Dec. 12, 1858, Douglas Papers, Chicago.

2   Martin Ryerson to Douglas, Nov. 19, 1858, Douglas Papers, Chicago; J. M. Cutts, Jr., to Douglas, Nov. 30, to Adele Douglas, Dec. 4, 1858, Douglas Family Papers, Greensboro.

3   Nichols, *Disruption*, 219–21; Jones to Hammond, Nov. 19, 1858, Hammond Papers, LC; James B. Steedman to Douglas, Nov. 10, 1858, Douglas Papers, Chicago; Cobb to Dear Col, Nov. 4, 1858, Cobb Papers, UG; Washington *Union*, Nov. 6, 14, 1858; John Minor Botts to Washburne, Dec. 7, 1858, Washburne Papers, LC.

4   *Illinois State Register*, Dec. 8, 1858; J. N. Granger, Nov. 18, James May, Nov. 10, Samuel Treat, Nov. 17, Henry A. Wise, Nov. 12, A. O. P. Nicholson to Douglas, Nov. 10, 1858, Douglas Papers, Chicago; Isaac Cook to Buchanan, Jan. 11, 1859, Buchanan Papers, HSP; New York *Herald*, Jan. 10, 1859.

5   Chicago *Press and Tribune*, Nov. 9, 1858; James B. Sheridan to Douglas, Dec. 8, 1858, Douglas Papers, Chicago.

6   Ray to Douglas, Nov. 19, 1858, Douglas Papers, Chicago; Ray to Hatch, [Dec. 1858], Hatch Papers, ISHL; Ray to Washburne, Nov. 22, 1858, Washburne Papers, LC; *Chicago Times*, Nov. 18, 1858.

7   James Guthrie to Paul Washington, Dec. 31, 1858, Guthrie Papers, SHC; Chicago *Press and Tribune*, Dec. 6, 1858; Treat, Nov. 17, George R. B. Wilson to Douglas, Nov. 18, 1858, Douglas Papers, Chicago; *New York Times*, Dec. 6,

1858; Pierre Soulé *et al.* to Douglas, Dec. 2, 1858, Douglas Papers, Chicago; Douglas to Soulé *et al.,* [Dec. 1858], *Letters,* 430.

8   Washington *States,* Dec. 1, 4, 1858; *Speeches of Senator S. A. Douglas, on the Occasion of his Public Reception by the Citizens of New Orleans, Philadelphia, and Baltimore* (Washington, D.C., 1859), *passim; New-York Tribune,* Dec. 14, 1858.

9   Charles J. Helm to Douglas, Jan. 21, 1859, Douglas Papers, Chicago; *New York Times,* Dec. 20, 1858; Washington *States,* Dec. 20, 30, 1858, Jan. 1, 3, 1859; *New-York Tribune,* Dec. 31, 1858, Jan. 3, 1859; W. E. Lehman *et al.* to Douglas, Jan. 1, 1859, Douglas Papers, Chicago; John W. Forney and James B. Sheridan to Lanphier, Jan. 4, 1859, Lanphier Papers, ISHL; Washington *States,* Jan. 4, 6, 1859.

10   J. B. Baker, Jan. 4, Levi K. Bowen to Buchanan, Jan. 6, 1859, Buchanan Papers, HSP.

11   New York *Herald,* Dec. 9, 11, 1858; *New-York Tribune,* Dec. 9, 10, 14, 1858; *New York Times,* Dec. 10, 13, 1858; Chicago *Press and Tribune,* Dec. 14, 15, 1858; James S. Green to Treat, Dec. 14, 1858, Treat Papers, MHS.

12   *New York Times,* Dec. 13, 1858; Green to Treat, Dec. 14, 1858, Treat Papers, MHS; San Francisco *Daily National,* July 16, 1859; Clement Claiborne Clay to Clement Comer Clay, Dec. 11, 1858, Clement C. Clay Papers, DU.

13   Hammond to M. C. M. Hammond, Dec. 11, 1858, Hammond Papers, LC; Rice to C. W. Cottom, Jan. 1, 1859, St. Paul *Pioneer and Democrat,* Jan. 11, 1859; J. C. Allen, Dec. 12, S. S. Marshall to Lanphier, Dec. 9, 1858, Lanphier Papers, ISHL; Murray McConnel, Dec. 10, Marcius Willson, Dec. 14, James D. Eads to Douglas, Dec. 22, 1858, Douglas Papers, Chicago.

14   Trumbull to Lincoln, Dec. 19, 1858, Lincoln Papers, LC; Trumbull to Palmer, Dec. 19, 1858, "Collection of Letters from Trumbull to Palmer," *JISHS,* XVI, 41; Judd to Trumbull, Dec. 26, 1858, Trumbull Papers, LC; *Illinois State Journal,* Dec. 11, 1858; *New-York Tribune,* Dec. 10, 11, 1858; *CG,* 35/2, 44–45.

15   Albert Smith, Dec. 11, Daniel McCook, Dec. 18, Isaac N. Morris, Dec. 29, 1858, James B. Steedman to Douglas, Jan. 5, 1859, Douglas Papers, Chicago.

16   Washington *States,* Jan. 4, 7, 1859; *New York Times,* Jan. 13, 1859; Preston King to Gideon Welles, Jan. 10, 1859, Welles Papers, LC; *New-York Tribune,* Jan. 13, 1859.

17   Hammond to M. C. M. Hammond, Dec. 21, 1858, Hammond Papers, LC; Morris to Lanphier, Dec. 18, 1858, Lanphier Papers, ISHL; Chicago *Press and Tribune,* Dec. 22, 1858.

18   *New York Times,* Dec. 29, 1858; New York *Herald,* Dec. 27, 1858; Douglas to————, [Jan. 1859], *Letters, 432.*

19   Slidell to the Editors, Dec. 18, Washington *Union,* Dec. 19, 1858; Douglas to the Editor of the Washington *States,* Jan. 7, 1859, *Letters,* 433–34; Slidell to the Editors, Jan. 12, Washington *Union,* Jan. 13, 1859; *New-York Tribune,* Jan. 18, 1859; *Illinois State Register,* Jan. 22, 1859; *Illi-*

*nois State Journal,* Jan. 7, 1859; *New York Times,* Jan. 24, 25, 1859; Douglas to Fitch, Jan. 21, 22, 24 (2), 1859, *Letters,* 435–37; Stevens, "Douglas," *JISHS,* XVI, 658–59, 663. The entire correspondence between Fitch and Douglas was published in the Washington *Union,* Jan. 25, 1859.

20   New York *Herald,* Feb. 9, 1859; David Reid to Henrietta Reid, Feb. 4, 1859, Reid Papers, NCDAH; Replies to invitations, Douglas Papers, Chicago.

21   San Francisco *Daily National,* July 16, 1859; Douglas to the Editors of the San Francisco *National,* Aug. 16, 1859, *Letters,* 454–55; New York *Herald,* Jan. 14, 1859; A. J. Cass to Butler, Jan. 25, 1859, Benjamin F. Butler Papers, LC.

22   *CG,* 35/2, 334, 358, 626, 633; James Gadsden to Hammond, Dec. 13, 1858, Hammond Papers, LC.

23   *New York Times,* Jan. 19, 1859; *CG,* 35/2, 407; *Illinois State Journal,* Jan. 26, 1859.

24   Washington *States,* Jan. 17, 31, 1859; *New York Times,* Jan. 19, 1859; R. P. Letcher to John J. Crittenden, Jan. 20, 26, 1859, Coleman (ed.), *Life of Crittenden,* II, 170, 171.

25   King to Welles, Feb. 19, 1859, Welles Papers, LC; New York *Herald,* Dec. 12, 22, 1858; Washington *Union,* Dec. 22, 31, 1858; *CG,* 35/2, 242–43.

26   *CG,* 35/2, 1223–24.

27   *CG,* 35/2, 1241–43 (Brown), 1247 (Davis), 1249 (Mason).

28   *CG,* 35/2, 1244–47, 1255–58; *New-York Tribune,* Feb. 25, 1859.

29   *CG,* 35/2, 1260, 1264, 1247; New York *Herald,* Feb. 25, 1859; Brown to Douglas, Sept. 10, 1859, Douglas Papers, Chicago; Brown to the Editor, Sept. 10, Washington *States,* Sept. 19, 1859; Washington *Union,* Feb. 25, 1859.

30   King to Welles, March 14, 1859, Welles Papers, LC.

31   Washington *States,* Jan. 26, 1859; Singleton, Feb. 20, 1859, Forney to Douglas, Nov. 27, 1858, Douglas Papers, Chicago; Douglas to Singleton, March 31, 1859, *Letters,* 439.

32   *New York Times,* Nov. 5, 1858; Douglas to Singleton, March 31, 1859, *Letters,* 439.

33   *New-York Tribune,* Dec. 14, 1858; *Illinois State Register,* Dec. 21, 1858; Forney to Douglas, Dec. 1858, Douglas Papers, Chicago; *Chicago Times,* quoted in New York *Herald,* Jan. 7, 1859.

34   Chicago *Press and Tribune,* March 1, 1859; New York *Herald,* May 20, 1859; A. D. Banks to Douglas, March 20, 1859, Douglas Family Papers, Greensboro.

35   Washington *Constitution,* April 15, 23, 29, May 10, 1859; New York *Herald,* April 27, July 2, 1859; Buchanan to Cobb, May 15, 1859, Cobb Papers, UG; *New-York Tribune,* May 10, July 21, 1859; Sanders, Aug. 17, Thomas E. Dyer, Aug. 17, 1859, James B. Steedman to Douglas, Nov. 7, 1858, Douglas Papers, Chicago; Buchanan to J. B. Baker, May 1, 1859, Buchanan Papers, HSP; Washington *States,* May 31, 1859.

36   Douglas to Singleton, March 31, 1859, *Letters,* 439; New York *Herald,*

April 9, 1859; Washington McLean, April 4, A. D. Banks to Douglas, May 1, 1859, Douglas Papers, Chicago.

37  Douglas to Sheahan, April 8, 18, 1859, Autobiographical Notes, *Letters,* 441–42, 443–44, 444–46; D. B. Cooke to Douglas, March 26, 1859, Douglas Family Papers, Greensboro; D. B. Cooke, March 14, 29, A. A. Couch, April 6, Mathew B. Brady, [Feb.], C. H. Brainard to Douglas, March 14, April 2, 22, 1859, Douglas Papers, Chicago.

38  J. O. Jennings to Douglas, Jan. 30, 1859, Douglas Family Papers, Greensboro; Jennings, Feb. 21, James L. Woodward, March 8, Joseph Harrison, March 25, Forney, March 28, Robert H. Murray, March 30, John T. Soutter, May 9, Fernando Wood, Sept. 3, 1859, McCarty and Brown, Sept. 13, 1858, A. B. Fontaine to Douglas, Feb. 23, 1859, Douglas Papers, Chicago; M. Johnson to Buchanan, Aug. 13, 1859, Buchanan Papers, HSP.

39  *New-York Tribune,* Feb. 12, 1859; Washington *Union,* March 26, 1859; William D. Bishop, March 24, J. C. Palmer, April 5, Forney, July 23, John Peuman, July 25, P. M. Casady, Aug. 11, Sanders to Douglas, Aug. 18, 1859, Douglas Papers, Chicago; Douglas to [James M. Scofield], March 1859, *Letters,* 440; New York *Herald,* March 23, April 17, Feb. 1, July 9, 1859.

40  Slidell to Buchanan, Aug. 18, 1859, Buchanan Papers, HSP; Cook to Jeremiah Black, June 22, 1859, Black Papers, LC; Joseph Hartford, Jan. 28, April 20 (Deposition), April 23, Augustus F. Frizell to Douglas, March 20, 1859, Douglas Family Papers, Greensboro; Douglas to Sheahan, April 8, 1859, *Letters,* 441; *Illinois State Journal,* Aug. 9, 1859; Sheahan to Horatio King, April 26, 1859, King Papers, LC; I. Holbrook to Douglas, Sept. 20, 1859, Douglas Family Papers, Greensboro.

41  John L. Peyton, May 4, John Forsyth, March 26, 31, April 2, 1859, Douglas Papers, Chicago; Washington *States,* July 18, 1859; *Letters of John Forsyth, of Alabama, Late Minister to Mexico, to Wm. F. Samford, Esq., in Defense of Stephen A. Douglas* [Washington, D.C., 1859], 7.

42  Articles of Agreement, May 31, 1859, Records of the United States Court of Claims, RG-123, NA; Cobb to Dear Col, May 23, 1859, Cobb Papers, UG; *New-York Tribune,* May 25, 1859; Davis to Clement C. Clay, May 17, 1859, Clement C. Clay Papers, DU.

43  J. B. Dorr to Douglas, June 13, 1859, Douglas Papers, Chicago; Douglas to Dorr, June 22, to John L. Peyton, Aug. 2, 1859, *Letters,* 446–47, 451–52; *New-York Tribune,* Aug. 23, 1859.

44  James B. Steedman, Aug. 21, James C. Jones to Douglas, Sept. 1, 1859, Douglas Papers, Chicago.

45  Washington *Constitution,* June 25, 1859; Buchanan to Robert Tyler, June 27, to Slidell, June 24, Slidell to Buchanan, July 3, 1859, Buchanan Papers, HSP; Mem [orandum] of President [Buchanan], 1859, Black Papers, LC. The following section has been based on Robert W. Johannsen, "Stephen A. Douglas, 'Harper's Magazine,' and Popular Sovereignty," *MVHR,* XLV (March 1959), 606–31.

46  A. D. Banks to Douglas, Sept. 3, 1859, Douglas Family Papers, Greensboro; C. P. Culver, July 11, James T. Menefee, Aug. 9, Henry K. McCoy to

Douglas, Aug. 22, 1859, Douglas Papers, Chicago; Douglas to McCoy, Sept. 27, 1859, *Letters*, 468–69.

47  *CG*, 35/2, 565; *Chicago Tribune*, June 28, 1859; Lincoln to Samuel Galloway, July 28, 1859, *CWAL*, III, 394.

48  *New-York Tribune*, July 15, 1859; Douglas to Bancroft, April 11, 1859, *Letters*, 442; Harper and Brothers to O. Jennings Wise, Sept. 21, A. H. Guernsey, July 9, Fletcher Harper, July 30, William A. Seaver to Douglas, Aug. 4, 1859, Douglas Family Papers, Greensboro; Seaver to Douglas, July 15, 1859, Douglas Papers, Chicago; Memorandum, [n. d.], Adele Cutts Douglas to "My dear Sir," July 22, 1859, Douglas Papers, ISHL; Douglas to Seaver, July 17, 1859, *Letters*, 449.

49  Receipt Book J, 1857–1859, 303, Library of Congress Archives, LC; Douglas to Bancroft, April 11, 1859, *Letters*, 442–43; Bancroft to Douglas, April 19, 1859, Douglas Family Papers, Greensboro; James B. Sheridan, April 23, Ninian W. Edwards to Douglas, July 11, 1859, Douglas Papers, Chicago.

50  Douglas to Seaver, July 17, 1859, *Letters*, 449; New York *Herald*, Aug. 29, 1859; George I. Forrest to Douglas, Aug. 26, 1859, Douglas Papers, Chicago; Harper and Brothers, Sept. 6, 20, Seaver to Douglas, Sept. 23, 1859, Douglas Family Papers, Greensboro.

51  Douglas, "The Dividing Line Between Federal and Local Authority: Popular Sovereignty in the Territories," *Harper's Magazine*, XIX (Sept. 1859), 521. The essay has been reprinted in Jaffa and Johannsen (eds.), *In the Name of the People*, 58–125.

52  Douglas, "The Dividing Line Between Federal and Local Authority . . . ," *Harper's Magazine*, XIX, 521–26.

53  *Ibid.* 527–29.

54  *Ibid.* 529–33.

55  *New York Times*, Sept. 6, 12, 1859; Brown to Douglas, Sept. 10, 1859, Douglas Papers, Chicago; Eli S. Shorter to Franklin Pierce, Sept. 7, 1859, Pierce Papers, LC; John Floyd to Buchanan, Sept. 5, 1859, Buchanan Papers, HSP; Alfred Iverson, quoted in *New York Times*, Oct. 3, 1859; William M. Browne to Cobb, Aug. 26, 1859, Cobb Papers, UG; Richmond *Enquirer*, quoted in New York *Herald*, Sept. 9, and Washington *Constitution*, Sept. 16, 1859; *Southern Era*, quoted in Washington *Constitution*, Sept. 29, 1859; A. D. Banks to Douglas, Sept. 25, 1859, Douglas Papers, Chicago; Louisville *Courier*, quoted in *New-York Tribune*, Sept. 6, 1859.

56  Seaver to Douglas, Oct. 3, 1859, Douglas Papers, Chicago; Harper and Brothers to O. Jennings Wise, Sept. 21, 1859, Douglas Family Papers, Greensboro; *New-York Tribune*, Oct. 15, 1859; George Ticknor Curtis, *The Just Supremacy of Congress Over the Territories* (Boston, 1859); Washington *National Intelligencer*, Sept. 10, 13, 15, 17, 20, 27, Oct. 1, 6, 1859; Reverdy Johnson to Douglas, Sept. 16, 26, Oct. 16, 18, 25, 28, 31, 1859, Douglas Papers, Chicago; Douglas to Johnson, Oct. 21, Nov. 4, 1859, *Letters*, 477, 479. Johnson's pamphlet was *Remarks on Popular Sovereignty, as Maintained and Denied Respectively by Judge Douglas, and Attorney-General Black* (Baltimore, 1859).

57  Buchanan to Black, July 17, Aug. 4, 1858, Black Papers, LC; Washing-

ton *Constitution,* Sept. 10, 1859; *Observations on Senator Douglas' Views of Popular Sovereignty, as Expressed in Harper's Magazine, for Sept., 1859* (Washington, D.C., 1859).

58 Samuel S. Cox, Aug. 26, George E. Pugh, Aug. 13, George W. Manypenny to Douglas, June 27, 1859, Douglas Papers, Chicago; *New York Times,* Sept. 15, 17, 1859; Douglas to George W. Manypenny, Oct. 1, 1859, *Letters,* 476; William T. Bascom to Lincoln, Sept. 1, 1859, Lincoln Papers, LC; Washington McLean to Douglas, Sept. 6, 1859, Douglas Family Papers, Greensboro. For a detailed account of Lincoln and Douglas in the Ohio campaign, see Jaffa and Johannsen (eds.), *In the Name of the People,* 1–33.

59 Columbus *Ohio Statesman,* Sept. 20, 1859.

60 The sequence in this pamphlet war was as follows: (1) Douglas' *Harper's* article; (2) Black's *Observations;* (3) Douglas' Wooster speech; (4) Black's *Appendix* to his *Observations,* published in the *Constitution,* Oct. 6, 1859; (5) Douglas' *Popular Sovereignty in the Territories: Judge Douglas in Reply to Judge Black* [Washington, D.C., 1859]; (6) Black's *Rejoinder to Senator Douglas' Last,* published in the *Constitution,* Nov. 3, 1859; (7) Douglas' *Popular Sovereignty in the Territories: Rejoinder of Judge Douglas to Judge Black* [Washington, D.C., 1859]. The quotations are from the Washington *Constitution,* Nov. 3, 1859; Douglas, *Popular Sovereignty in the Territories: Rejoinder of Judge Douglas to Judge Black,* 1; Douglas, *Popular Sovereignty in the Territories: Judge Douglas in Reply to Judge Black,* 23.

61 Douglas to McClernand, Oct. 1, 1859, *Letters,* 474; Seaver, Oct. 14, H. B. Anthony, Oct. 17, J. Madison Cutts, Jr., to Douglas, Nov. 21, 1859, Douglas Papers, Chicago; S. C. Benham to Douglas, Nov. 29, 1859, Douglas Family Papers, Greensboro; *New York Times,* Nov. 12, 1859; *Chicago Times,* Nov. 17, 1859; Douglas, *Popular Sovereignty in the Territories: Rejoinder of Judge Douglas to Judge Black,* 15; *Chicago Times,* Dec. 2, 1859.

62 *New York Times,* Oct. 4, 1859; Washington *States,* July 16, 1859.

63 *Chicago Times,* Sept. 14, 1859.

# CHAPTER XXVII

1 Nevins, *Emergence of Lincoln,* II, 96.

2 Milton, *Eve of Conflict,* 396; *Chicago Times,* in *Illinois State Register,* Nov. 12, 1859.

3 *New York Times,* Nov. 23, 1859; Bigler to Buchanan, Oct. 22, 1859, Buchanan Papers, HSP; New York *Herald,* Oct. 19, Nov. 9, 1859; Cobb to John B. Lamar, Nov. 19, 1859, in Brooks (ed.), "Cobb Papers," *Georgia Hist. Quar.,* VI (Sept. 1922), 243.

4 Nichols, *Disruption,* 270–71; New York *Herald,* Aug. 31, Sept. 30, Oct. 2, 1859. The figures on party alignment in the House vary; I have used those provided by Nichols. Ollinger Crenshaw, "The Speakership Contest of 1859–1860," *MVHR,* XXIX (Dec. 1942), 323, lists slightly different figures.

5 New York *Herald,* Nov. 7, Dec. 2, 1859; Chicago *Press and Tribune,* Dec. 7, 1859; Nichols, *Disruption,* 273; McClernand to John Henry, Jan. 14,

1860, McClernand Papers, ISHL; Victor Hicken, "John A. McClernand and the House Speakership Struggle of 1859," *JISHS,* LIII (Summer 1960), 168.

6   *CG,* 36/1, 3; McClernand to Lanphier, Jan. 3, 1860, Lanphier Papers, ISHL; Nichols, *Disruption,* 273; New York *Herald,* Jan. 7, 1860, Dec. 30, 1859; Steven A. Channing, *Crisis of Fear: Secession in South Carolina* (New York, 1970), 107–8.

7   McClernand, John A. Logan, and J. C. Robinson to Douglas, Dec. 16, 1859, Douglas Papers, Chicago; New York *Herald,* Dec. 31, 1859; *CG,* 36/1, App., 64 (Morris), 1 (Buchanan); McClernand to Lanphier, Jan. 3, 1860, Lanphier Papers, ISHL; *New York Times,* Dec. 27, 1859, Jan. 20, 1860.

8   Hicken, "McClernand and the House Speakership Struggle," *JISHS,* LIII, 171–72; New York *Herald,* Dec. 31, 1859, Jan. 8, 29, 1860; Chicago *Press and Tribune,* Jan. 14, 1860. The last few ballots, from the thirty-ninth to the forty-fourth, are in *CG,* 36/1, 611–50.

9   Washington *States and Union,* Feb. 2, 1860; Lanphier to McClernand, Feb. 2, 1860, McClernand Papers, ISHL; McClernand to Lanphier, Jan. 3, 14, 1860, Lanphier Papers, ISHL; Logan to "Dear Bro," Feb. 5, 1860, Logan Family Papers, LC.

10   McClernand to John Henry, Jan. 14, 1860, McClernand Papers, ISHL; *CG,* 36/1, App., 97.

11   McClernand to Lanphier, Jan. 3, 1860, Lanphier Papers, ISHL; Chicago *Press and Tribune,* Dec. 19, 1859; New York *Herald,* December 21, 1859; *CG,* 36/1, 198, 425–26.

12   Nichols, *Disruption,* 270; *CG,* 36/1, 1247–48, 1660, 2040–41.

13   New York *Herald,* Jan. 25, 1860; Chicago *Press and Tribune,* Jan. 27, 1860; *CG,* 36/1, 448, 552–55, 558–59; Catherine M. Tarrant, "To 'insure domestic Tranquility': Congress and the Law of Seditious Conspiracy, 1859–1861," *American Journal of Legal History,* XV (April 1971), 113–16; Douglas to John F. Farnsworth, [June 1860], *Letters,* 488–89.

14   *CG,* 36/1, 915–16, 919–20.

15   *CG,* 36/1, 162, 190, 179; Morris to Douglas, Jan. 4, 1860, Douglas Papers, Chicago.

16   *CG,* 36/1, 379, 382, 421, 423–27; New York *Herald,* Jan. 15, 1860; Chicago *Press and Tribune,* Jan. 17, 1860; *Illinois State Journal,* Jan. 17, 1860.

17   *CG,* 36/1, 494, 658, 661.

18   Toombs to Stephens, Feb. 10, 1860, Phillips (ed.), *Correspondence of Toombs, Stephens and Cobb,* 461; *CG,* 36/1, 671; Nichols, *Disruption,* 284; New York *Herald,* Feb. 12, 13, 21, 1860; Chicago *Press and Tribune,* Feb. 21, 1860; Harrisburg *Patriot and Union,* quoted in Washington *States and Union,* Feb. 21, 1860; Henry B. Payne, Feb. 27, Murray McConnel to Douglas, Feb. 18, 1860, Douglas Papers, Chicago; McClernand to Lanphier, Feb. 23, 1860, Lanphier Papers, ISHL; *Chicago Times,* Feb. 18, 1860.

19   New York *Herald,* Feb. 27, 1860; *New York Times,* Feb. 27, 1860; *CG,* 36/1, 861, 935; C. P. Culver to Stephens, March 9, 1860, Stephens Papers, LC; Sanders to Douglas, Jan. 25, 1860, Douglas Papers, Chicago.

20    Sanders to Douglas, Jan. [two letters], Feb. 26, April 9, 1860, Douglas Papers, Chicago; New York *Herald,* Feb. 28, 1860; Irving Katz, *August Belmont, A Political Biography* (New York, 1968), 64–66; Sanders, April, Edward C. West to Douglas, April 16, 1860, Douglas Papers, Chicago.

21    Cushing to Pierce, Feb. 25, 1860, Pierce Papers, LC; New York *Herald,* Sept. 9, 1859; Martin J. Crawford to Stephens, March 14, 1860, Stephens Papers, LC; W. D. Shepherd, Feb. 17, Frank Leslie, March 2, April 16, William A. Seaver, Jan. 17, Sheahan, Jan. 16, April 14, Derby & Jackson to Douglas, April 3, 1860, Douglas Papers, Chicago.

22    New York *Herald,* Sept. 9, 1859, Jan. 12, 1860; Mrs. Roger A. Pryor, *Reminiscences of Peace and War* (New York, 1904), 98–99.

23    Frank Blair to Montgomery Blair, Oct. 20, 1859, Blair Family Papers, LC; Douglas to Lanphier, Oct. 1, to McClernand, Oct. 1, to Lanphier, Dec. 31, 1859, Jan. 1, 1860, *Letters,* 474–75, 481, 482; *Illinois State Register,* Dec. 21, 1859.

24    Lanphier to Douglas, Dec. 11, 1859, Douglas Papers, Chicago; Douglas to Lanphier, Dec. 31, 1859, *Letters,* 481; McClernand to Lanphier, Dec. 26, 27, 30, 1859, Lanphier Papers, ISHL.

25    Lanphier to Douglas, Jan. 5, 6, 1860, Douglas Papers, Chicago; Lanphier to McClernand, Jan. 6, 1860, McClernand Papers, ISHL; *Illinois State Register,* Jan. 5, 1860; McClernand to Lanphier, Jan. 10, 1860, Lanphier Papers, ISHL.

26    *Illinois State Register,* Jan. 11, 1860; Lanphier to McClernand, Jan. 10, 1860, McClernand Papers, ISHL; Virgil Hickox, Jan. 11, J. P. Campbell to Douglas, April 12, 1860, Douglas Papers, Chicago; Washington *States and Union,* April 20, 1860.

27    *Illinois State Register,* Jan. 6, 14, 1860; *New York Times,* Jan. 10, 21, 1860; H. V. Willson, Jan. 6, Daniel P. Rhodes, Jan. 7, Henry B. Payne, Jan. 9, Feb. 27, Ezra Reed, Jan. 12, Austin Brown, Jan. 13, Charles E. Stuart, Jan. 8, J. B. Dorr, Jan. 21, Willis A. Gorman to Douglas, Jan. 18, 1860, Douglas Papers, Chicago; Douglas to Stuart, Jan. 15, 1860, *Letters,* 482–83; Lanphier to McClernand, Feb. 24, 1860, McClernand Papers, ISHL; New York *Herald,* Feb. 23, 25, 1860.

28    Emanuel B. Hart to Cobb, July 2, 1859, Cobb Papers, UG; Sanders to Douglas, Sept. 15, 1859, Douglas Papers, Chicago; *New-York Tribune,* Sept. 14, 15, Oct. 3, 1859; *New York Times,* Sept. 16, 1859; John J. Taylor, Jan. 30, Cagger, Feb. 14, John Clancy to Douglas, April 12, 1860, Douglas Papers, Chicago; Douglas to Fernando Wood, Feb. 16, to Cagger, Feb. 19, 1860, *Letters,* 484–85; Dean Richmond to Douglas, April 16, 1860, Douglas Family Papers, Greensboro; J. T. Hatch to Buchanan, Feb. 7, 1860, Buchanan Papers, HSP; Nichols, *Disruption,* 257–59, 280.

29    Nichols, *Disruption,* 277, 279–80; McClernand to Lanphier, March 2, 1860, Lanphier Papers, ISHL; New York *Herald,* March 4, 1860; C[ornelius] W[endell], March 8, Sanders, Feb. 8, March 6, 21, Clement Webster, April 17, John Wells to Douglas, March 23, 1860, Douglas Papers, Chicago.

30    Hendrick B. Wright, March 30, John Forsyth to Douglas, April 5, 1860, Douglas Papers, Chicago; Toombs to Stephens, March 16, 1860, in Phillips

(ed.), *Correspondence of Toombs, Stephens and Cobb,* 465; New York *Herald,* Jan. 8, 1860; Atlanta *Southern Confederacy,* quoted in New York *Herald,* Jan. 23, 1860; D. H. Hamilton to William Porcher Miles, Feb. 2, 1860, Miles Papers, SHC; Powhatan Ellis to Charles Ellis, Jan. 31, 1860, Munford-Ellis Family Papers, DU.

31 Forsyth to Douglas, April 5, 1860, Douglas Papers, Chicago; *Illinois State Register,* Jan. 7, 1860; Miles Taylor to Louis Bush, Jan. 19, 1860, Albert Rust to My Dear Sir, Dec. 24, 1859, Andrew J. Hamilton to P. B. Fouke, March 10, 1860, in Washington *States and Union,* Feb. 3, Jan. 30, March 15, 1860; Thomas Dyer to Douglas, March 21, 1860, Douglas Family Papers, Greensboro; Stephens to J. Henly Smith, Feb. 24, Toombs to Stephens, Jan. 11, 1860, in Phillips (ed.), *Correspondence of Toombs, Stephens and Cobb,* 463, 455; C. P. Culver, April 18, John J. Seibels to Douglas, Jan. 17, 1860, Douglas Papers, Chicago; Stephens to Dear Sir, March 25, 1860, Stephens Papers, LC; New York *Herald,* Sept. 22, 1859.

32 Forsyth to Douglas, Dec. 12, 1859, Jan. 6, 13, 31, Feb. 4, 9, March 9, April 5, 1860, Douglas Papers, Chicago; Forsyth to Douglas, April 7, 1860, Douglas Family Papers, Greensboro; John J. Seibels, Jan. 17, 1860, Henry Cleveland, Sept. 16, 1859, March 25, 1860, R. R. Collier to Douglas, April 19, 1860, Douglas Papers, Chicago.

33 Douglas to Henry McCoy, Sept. 27, 1859, *Letters,* 469; Seibels, Jan. 17, Payne to Douglas, March 17, 1860, Douglas Papers, Chicago; Washington *States and Union,* Dec. 23, 1859, Jan. 7, 1860; New York *Herald,* Jan. 19, Feb. 9, 1860; Washington *Constitution,* July 8, 1859, Feb. 25, 1860.

34 Banks, March 14, Sanders, April 2, Gideon Pillow to Douglas, April 3, 1860, Douglas Papers, Chicago; New York *Herald,* Feb. 20, March 30, 1860; *New York Times,* April 5, 1860; Johnson to A. E. Cochran and J. M. Spullock, Dec. 3, 1859, Herschel V. Johnson Papers, DU.

35 H. Kennedy, Feb. 19, R. D. Shropshire to Douglas, April 16, 1860, Douglas Papers, Chicago; New York *Herald,* March 7, 1860; *Illinois State Register,* Jan. 24, 26, 1860; Channing, *Crisis of Fear,* 195, 202, 205; J. D. Hoover to Franklin Pierce, Feb. 25, 1860, Pierce Papers, LC; R. J. Haldeman, April 9, Sanders to Douglas, Feb. 5, 1860, Douglas Papers, Chicago; Toombs to Stephens, Jan. 11, 1860, Phillips (ed.), *Correspondence of Toombs, Stephens and Cobb,* 455.

36 Hammond to Harry Hammond, Feb. 12, 1860, Hammond Papers, LC; Buchanan to Cobb, July 23, 1859, Cobb Papers, UG; Washington *States and Union,* April 2, 1860.

37 J. T. Menefee, Feb. 14, W. B. Figures, Feb. 15, Forsyth, Feb. 20, Henry Hilliard, Feb. 21, George W. Paschal to Douglas, April 17, 1860, Douglas Papers, Chicago; Hugh Lawson Clay to Clement C. Clay, Jan. 19, 1860, Clement C. Clay Papers, DU; Robert Barnwell Rhett, Jr., to Miles, Jan. 29, March 28, 1860, Miles Papers, SHC.

38 Seibels to Douglas, Jan. 17, 1860, Douglas Papers, Chicago; Nichols, *Disruption,* 284–86; Oliver Diefendorf, April 26, June 6, Sarah Calhoun to Douglas, June 11, 1860, Douglas Family Papers, Greensboro.

39 R. W. Latham, April 13, W. K. Piper, April 16, Charles Halpine to

Douglas, April 14, 1860, Douglas Papers, Chicago; Washington *States and Union,* March 6, 1860; New York *Herald,* April 14, 1860; Hammond to M. C. M. Hammond, March 9, to Simms, April 8, 1860, Hammond Papers, LC; Moses Bates, March 5, E. D. Beach, April 12, John W. Mahan, April 17, Philip Hoyne to Douglas, April 12, 1860, Douglas Papers, Chicago; Logan to Mrs. Logan, April 16, 1860, Logan Family Papers, LC; *New York Times,* April 17, 18, 1860; Cleveland *Plain Dealer,* April 18, 19, 1860.

40    Payne, Jan. 2, March 17, Forsyth, April 5, T. M. Lanahan to Douglas, April 19, 1860, Douglas Papers, Chicago; New York *Herald,* Feb. 19, 1860.

41    Lanphier to McClernand, Jan. 17, March 15, 26, 1860, McClernand Papers, ISHL; Ezra Read, April 2, H. W. Harrington, March 24, W. W. Phelps, March 25, Sanders to Douglas, March 26, 1860, Douglas Papers, Chicago; *New York Times,* April 6, 1860; Washington *States and Union,* April 7, 1860.

42    Toombs to Stephens, April 20, 1860, in Phillips (ed.), *Correspondence of Toombs, Stephens and Cobb,* 467; Thomas Dyer to Douglas, Feb. 29, 1860, Douglas Papers, Chicago; *New-York Tribune,* April 20, 1860.

43    James M. Mason, July 1, 1859, Robert N. Gourdin to Miles, April 4, 1860, Miles Papers, SHC; *Charleston Mercury,* April 16, 1860, in Dwight L. Dumond (ed.), *Southern Editorials on Secession* (New York, 1931), 67.

## CHAPTER XXVIII

1    Washington *States and Union,* April 19, 1860; *New York Times,* March 8, April 23, 25, 1860; *New-York Tribune,* April 20, 1860; William B. Hesseltine (ed.), *Three Against Lincoln: Murat Halstead Reports the Caucuses of 1860* (Baton Rouge, 1960), 7; F. O. Prince to Mrs. Douglas, April 26, 1860, Douglas Papers, Chicago. See also Robert W. Johannsen, "Douglas at Charleston," in Norman A. Graebner (ed.), *Politics and the Crisis of 1860* (Urbana, 1961), 61–90.

2    Hesseltine (ed.), *Three Against Lincoln,* 9, 10–11; J. J. Jones, April 20, John Clancy, April 21, Murray McConnel to Douglas, April 22, 1860, Douglas Papers, Chicago; New York *Herald,* April 23, 1860; *New-York Tribune,* April 23, 1860.

3    Hesseltine (ed.), *Three Against Lincoln,* 8, 10, 11, 17–18; *New York Times,* April 25, 1860; New York *Herald,* April 23, 24, 1860; James E. Harvey to George Harrington, April 21, C. P. Culver to Douglas, April 25, 1860, Douglas Papers, Chicago; *New-York Tribune,* April 24, 1860; J. H. Clay Mudd to Stephens, May 22, 1860, Stephens Papers, LC.

4    *New-York Tribune,* April 23, 1860; *Official Proceedings of the Democratic National Convention, held in 1860, at Charleston and Baltimore* (Cleveland, 1860), 3–21; New York *Herald,* April 25, 1860; Stuart to Douglas, April 24, 1860, Douglas Papers, Chicago; Hesseltine (ed.), *Three Against Lincoln,* 18–32.

5    Stuart to Douglas, April 24, 1860, Douglas Papers, Chicago; Washington *States and Union,* April 26, 1860; *New York Times,* April 27, 1860; Hesseltine (ed.), *Three Against Lincoln,* 34–35.

6    Hesseltine (ed.), *Three Against Lincoln,* 44–55; *Official Proceedings,*

37–39; Washington *States and Union,* April 27, 1860; *New-York Tribune,* April 27, 1860; *New York Times,* April 28, 1860.

7   Hesseltine (ed.), *Three Against Lincoln,* 57–61; *Official Proceedings,* 41–45, 47–48; C. P. Culver to Douglas, April 28, 1860, Douglas Papers, Chicago; Sanders to Buchanan, April 27, 1860, Washington *States and Union,* May 21, 1860; Sanders to John B. Floyd, April 28, 1860, Cobb Papers, UG; *New York Times,* April 30, 1860; New York *Herald,* May 9, 1860.

8   Hesseltine (ed.), *Three Against Lincoln,* 64–85; *Official Proceedings,* 50–55; Toombs to Stephens, May 12, 1860, Phillips (ed.), *Correspondence of Toombs, Stephens and Cobb,* 477; Richard Taylor, *Destruction and Reconstruction: Personal Experiences of the Late War* (ed. by Charles P. Roland; Waltham, Mass., 1968), 4; *New-York Tribune,* May 2, 1860; D. H. Hamilton to Miles, April 26, 1860, Miles Papers, SHC; Washington *States and Union,* May 2, 1860; *New York Times,* May 2, 1860.

9   Hesseltine (ed.), *Three Against Lincoln,* 93–110, 118; *Official Proceedings,* 71–74, 89–90; New York *Herald,* May 2, 4, 10, 12, 1860; Washington *States and Union,* May 7, 1860; *Illinois State Register,* May 4, 1860; Dean Richmond, May 25, August Belmont to Douglas, May 7, 1860, Douglas Family Papers, Greensboro; *New York Times,* May 4, 1860; *New-York Tribune,* May 5, 1860.

10   Hesseltine (ed.), *Three Against Lincoln,* 111–17; William L. Yancey to Clay, May 4, 1860, Clement C. Clay Papers, DU; Martin J. Crawford to Stephens, May 11, 1860, Stephens Papers, LC.

11   Alfred Huger to Miles, May 7, 1860, Miles Papers, SHC; Linder, *Reminiscences,* 325; Logan to Mrs. Logan, May 7, 1860, Logan Family Papers, LC.

12   *New York Times,* April 27, 28, May 2, 1860; New York *Herald,* May 1, 3, 1860; Edgar Eugene Robinson (ed.), "The Day Journal of Milton S. Latham, January 1 to May 6, 1860," *Quarterly of the California Historical Society,* XI, 18; Hesseltine (ed.), *Three Against Lincoln,* 119.

13   E. C. Bailey, May 5, J. Haddock Smith, May 5, R. J. Brent, May 14, H. W. Miller, June 14, S. S. Marshall, May 20, S. S. Maffit, May 24, Hendrick B. Wright, May 7, J. L. Foster, May 7, Benjamin M. Samuels to Douglas, May 21, R. H. Glass to J. P. Heiss, June 7, 1860, Douglas Papers, Chicago; C. F. McCoy to Douglas, May 7, 1860, Douglas Family Papers, Greensboro; Washington *States and Union,* May 5, 1860; J. Henly Smith to Stephens, May 7, 1860, Stephens Papers, LC.

14   Banks, May 11, Henry S. Foote, May 11, Washington McLean to Douglas, May 24, 1860, Douglas Papers, Chicago.

15   New York *Herald,* May 5, 20, 1860; Schuyler Colfax to Lincoln, May 18, 1860, Lincoln Papers, LC; *New York Times,* May 21, 1860; S. C. Benham, May 14, T. J. Wright, May 18, Sanders, May 19, Sheahan, May 21, Blanton Duncan to Douglas, May 28, 1860, Douglas Papers, Chicago.

16   Gilbert Hathaway, May 6, Thomas Dyer to Douglas, May 12, 1860, Douglas Papers, Chicago; Washington *States and Union,* Oct. 19, 23, 1860.

17   Forsyth, May 9, 16, Seibels, June 5, Robert W. Simms, May 10, Thomas Dyer, May 12, James L. Seward, May 18, James Gardner, May 18, Thomas J.

Burke, May 28, W. W. Holden, June 1, Robert P. Dick, May 17, John P. Murray, May 9, R. W. Flournoy to Douglas, May 14, 1860, Douglas Papers, Chicago; Nichols, *Disruption,* 310, 313.

18   Washington *Constitution,* May 17, 1860; *New York Times,* June 2, May 29, 1860; Rhett to Miles, May 10, 1860, Miles Papers, SHC; Douglas to Belmont, June 4, 1860, in *Letters, Speeches and Addresses of August Belmont* (privately printed, 1890), 105–6; Belmont to Douglas, June 7, 1860, Douglas Family Papers, Greensboro.

19   Wright, May 14, Johnson Gardner, May 10, Moses Bates to Douglas, May 7, 18, June 5, 1860, Douglas Papers, Chicago.

20   D. A. Ogden, May 28, Payne, May 16, William H. Ludlow, May 21, 28, June 5, Peter Cagger, May 18, Banks, May 11, Richardson, May 13, 17, 22, 30, Stuart, May 14, T. M. Lanahan, May 22, Belmont, May 18, Sanders to Douglas, May 20, 25, 1860, Douglas Papers, Chicago; Richmond to Douglas, May 25, 1860, Douglas Family Papers, Greensboro; Stephens to Thirteen Gentlemen of Macon, May 9, 1860, in Henry Cleveland, *Alexander H. Stephens in Public and Private, with Letters and Speeches Before, During and Since the War* (Philadelphia, 1866), 661–68.

21   John Clancy, May 15, C. Webster to Douglas, May 19, 1860, Douglas Papers, Chicago; New York *Herald,* May 22, 23, June 5, 1860; James B. Sheridan to Douglas, May 31, 1860, Douglas Papers, Chicago.

22   Richardson to Douglas, May 22, 1860, Douglas Papers, Chicago; New York *Herald,* May 16, 17, 1860; *CG,* 36/1, 1971, 2100, App., 301–16.

23   New York *Herald,* May 18, 19, 1860; *CG,* 36/1, 2153, 2154, 2155.

24   Richardson, May 17, 22, George E. Pugh, May 28, Belmont, May 31, June 7, John A. Dix to Douglas, June 6, 1860, Douglas Papers, Chicago; New York *Herald,* June 1, 10, 1860; Logan to Mrs. Logan, Feb. 5, 8, 1860, Logan Family Papers, LC; Douglas to John F. Farnsworth, [June 1860], *Letters,* 488.

25   Logan to Mrs. Logan, May 5, 1860, Logan Family Papers, LC; New York *Herald,* June 18, 1860; A. Harris to Douglas, May 26, 1860, Douglas Papers, Chicago; James Love to John Bell, June 17, 1860, Polk-Yeatman Papers, SHC; Stuart to Douglas, June 16, 1860, Douglas Family Papers, Greensboro.

26   New York *Herald,* June 17, 1860; Washington *Constitution,* June 6, 15, 1860; S. J. Anderson, June 24, J. Henly Smith to Stephens, July 9, 1860, Stephens Papers, LC.

27   Hesseltine (ed.), *Three Against Lincoln,* 191–92, 208; *Official Proceedings,* 97–104; *New York Times,* June 20, 1860; Washington *Constitution,* June 21, 1860; Banks, June 19, McCook, June 19, Thomas Dyer to Douglas, June 19, 1860, Douglas Family Papers, Greensboro.

28   John F. Cowan to Douglas, June 21, 1860, Douglas Papers, Chicago; Johnson to Stephens, June 19, 1860, Herschel V. Johnson Papers, DU; Hesseltine (ed.), *Three Against Lincoln,* 211–22; *Official Proceedings,* 111–20; McClernand to Douglas, June 21, 1860, Douglas Family Papers, Greensboro.

29   Hesseltine (ed.), *Three Against Lincoln,* 224–28, 230–31; *Official Proceedings,* 132–40; Douglas to Richardson, June 20, 1860, *Letters,* 492.

30   S. J. Anderson, July 11, Linton Stephens, June 28, James Hambleton to

Stephens, July 2, 1860, Stephens Papers, LC; R. H. Glass, June 21, William H. Ludlow to Douglas, June 27, 1860, Douglas Papers, Chicago; Douglas to Dean Richmond, June 22, 1860, *Letters,* 493; *New York Times,* June 23, 1860; Hesseltine (ed.), *Three Against Lincoln,* 230–31, 262–63.

31   Hesseltine (ed.), *Three Against Lincoln,* 232–54; *Official Proceedings,* 163–70.

32   Hambleton to Stephens, July 2, 1860, Stephens Papers, LC; Seibels, June 23, William H. Ludlow, R. P. Dick, J. L. Seward *et al.* to Fitzpatrick, June 25, Benjamin Fitzpatrick Papers, SHC; Seibels to Douglas, June 25, 1860, Douglas Papers, Chicago; Hesseltine (ed.), *Three Against Lincoln,* 256–57, 265–77; *Official Proceedings,* 173–74, 176–77.

33   Washington *States and Union,* June 25, 1860; Douglas to William H. Ludlow, R. P. Dick, R. C. Wickliffe *et al., June 27, 1860, *Letters,* 494–96.

## CHAPTER XXIX

1   Hesseltine (ed.), *Three Against Lincoln,* 254–55; Katz, *August Belmont,* 70–74; Gabriel Duval, June 23, Thomas Walker, June 24, E. J. Fitzpatrick, June 25, J. L. M. Curry, June 25, Seibels to Fitzpatrick, June 24, Fitzpatrick to Seibels, July 9, 1860, Fitzpatrick Papers, SHC; J. Henly Smith to Stephens, Aug. 18, 1860, Stephens Papers, LC; Seibels to Douglas, June 25, 1860, Douglas Papers, Chicago; Fitzpatrick to J. L. M. Curry, July 12, to Seibels, July 27, to J. R. Powell, July 30, in Washington *Constitution,* July 26, Aug. 2, 9, 1860.

2   Hambleton to Stephens, July 2, 1860, Stephens Papers, LC; New York *Herald,* June 26, 1860; Johnson to Stephens, June 9, 29, 1860, Autobiography (Ms.), 134–38, Herschel V. Johnson Papers, DU; Stephens to J. Henly Smith, Sept. 12, 1860, Phillips (ed.), *Correspondence of Toombs, Stephens and Cobb,* 495.

3   Washington *States and Union,* June 30, 1860; New York *Herald,* June 28, July 8, 18, 26, 1860; Douglas to Nathaniel Paschall, July 4, 1860, *Letters,* 497.

4   New York *Herald,* July 3, 6, 1860; Washington *States and Union,* July 2, 1860; *New York Times,* July 3, 1860; Douglas to Paschall, July 4, to Lanphier, July 5, 1860, *Letters,* 497–98.

5   S. J. Anderson to Stephens, Sept. 2, 1860, Stephens Papers, LC; *New York Times,* June 25, July 12, 18, 28, Aug. 14, 1860; Oliver Stevens to Douglas, July 12, 1860, Douglas Papers, Chicago. See Robert W. Johannsen, "Stephen A. Douglas' New England Campaign, 1860," *New England Quarterly,* XXXV (June 1962), 162–86.

6   Cornelius C. Felton, March 20, 1858, James Dana to Douglas, July 19, 1860, Douglas Papers, Chicago; Boston *Daily Advertiser,* July 18, 19, 24, 1860; *New York Times,* July 20, 21, 24, 1860; Springfield (Mass.) *Republican,* July 21, 28, 1860.

7   Sanders, July 19, W. B. Sayles to Douglas, July 24, 1860, Douglas Papers, Chicago; *New York Times,* July 21, Aug. 1, 3, 4, 8, 16, 1860; Brandon *Northern Visitor,* Aug. 2, 1860; New York *Herald,* Aug. 4, 1860; Boston *Daily Advertiser,* Aug. 6, 1860.

8  *New York Times,* Aug. 16, 1860; Springfield (Mass.) *Republican,* July 28, Sept. 8, 1860; Quoted in Allan Nevins, *Emergence of Lincoln,* II, 291.

9  *New York Times,* Aug. 10, 1860; *Illinois State Journal,* July 24, 1860; Correspondence of the Troy *Whig,* New York *Herald,* July 14, 1860; Hartford *Evening Press,* quoted in Boston *Daily Advertiser,* Aug. 10, 1860; Broadside, Douglas Family Papers, Greensboro.

10  Belmont, July 28, Taylor, July 29, Aug. 13, Reid Sanders to Douglas, Aug. 10, 1860, Douglas Papers, Chicago.

11  Nichols, *Disruption,* 335–36; Taylor, July 29, Magnus Gross, Aug. 9, A. V. Hofer, Feb. 12, Reid Sanders to Douglas, Aug. 10, 1860, Douglas Papers, Chicago; Sheahan to Lanphier, July 28, Aug. 3, 1860, Lanphier Papers, ISHL; Chicago *Press and Tribune,* Aug. 1, 1860.

12  [Henry M. Flint,] *Life of Stephen A. Douglas, United States Senator from Illinois, With His Most Important Speeches and Reports, By a Member of the Western Bar* (New York, 1860); Robert Bruce Warden, *A Voter's Version of the Life and Character of Stephen A. Douglas* (Columbus, Ohio, 1860); *Political Debates Between Hon. Abraham Lincoln and Hon. Stephen A. Douglas, in the Celebrated Campaign of 1858 in Illinois* (Columbus, Ohio, 1860); Douglas to Follett and Foster Company, June 9, 1860, *Letters,* 489–90; H. M. Flint, April 30, Follett and Foster Company to S. S. Cox, May 23, July 16, Cox to Douglas, July 16, 1860, Douglas Papers, Chicago; Lincoln to Sheahan, Jan. 24, 1860, *CWAL,* III, 515.

13  *New York Times,* Aug. 4, 16, 1860; Brandon *Northern Visitor,* Aug. 2, 1860; Henry Wilson, *History of the Rise and Fall of the Slave Power in America* (3 vols., Boston, 1879), II, 699; *Illinois State Journal,* Sept. 11, 1860; J. Q. Smith to Douglas, Sept. 14, 1860, Douglas Papers, Chicago.

14  Johnson to Stephens, July 4, to A. E. Cochran, July 6, 1860, Herschel V. Johnson Papers, DU.

15  Taylor, Aug. 13, F. O. Prince to Douglas, July 28, Aug. 10, 1860, Douglas Papers, Chicago.

16  Nichols, *Disruption,* 336–37, 339–40; Isaac Cook to Buchanan, July 4, 1860, Buchanan Papers, HSP; New York *Herald,* June 29, 1860.

17  Chicago *Press and Tribune,* July 17, 21, 26, Sept. 18, Oct. 19, 1860; Washington *States and Union,* Aug. 27, 1860.

18  Chicago *Press and Tribune,* Oct. 12, 13, 1860; *Illinois State Journal,* Oct. 15, 18, 19, 1860; Washington *States and Union,* Oct. 20, 1860; Fred Emory *et al.* to John W. Martin, Sept. 13, 1860, Douglas Family Papers, Greensboro.

19  Thomas Settle to Douglas, June 30, 1860, Douglas Family Papers, Greensboro.

20  A. D. Banks, July 15, Aug. 2, A. M. Keiley, Aug. 8, Robert P. Dick, Aug. 2, 10, H. L. Hopkins to Douglas, Aug. 11, H. W. Miller to Hopkins, Aug. 8, William White to Miles Taylor, Aug. 17, 1860, Douglas Papers, Chicago.

21  Washington *States and Union,* Aug. 9, 14, 1860; Blanton Duncan, Aug. 14, Miles Taylor, Aug. 13, Seibels to Douglas, Aug. 14, H. W. Miller to H. L.

Hopkins, Aug. 8, 1860, Douglas Papers, Chicago; New York *Herald,* Aug. 8, 1860.

22 Washington *States and Union,* Aug. 9, 1860; Duncan to Douglas, Aug. 14, 1860, Douglas Papers, Chicago.

23 Washington *States and Union,* Aug. 25, 28, 1860; Norfolk *Southern Argus,* Aug. 27, 1860; Lionel Crocker, "The Campaign of Stephen A. Douglas in the South, 1860," in J. Jeffery Auer (ed.), *Antislavery and Disunion, 1858–1861: Studies in the Rhetoric of Compromise and Conflict* (New York, 1963), 263–68.

24 Donald E. Reynolds, *Editors Make War: Southern Newspapers in the Secession Crisis* (Nashville, 1970), 135–36; Washington *Constitution,* Aug. 31, Sept. 4, 1860; Franklin Pierce to Caleb Cushing, Sept. 5, 1860, Cushing Papers, LC.

25 Washington *States and Union,* Sept. 1, 1860.

26 New York *Herald,* August 30, Sept. 1, 1860; William W. Holden to Mrs. Holden, Aug. 30, 1860, William W. Holden Papers, DU; Emerson D. Fite, *The Presidential Campaign of 1860* (New York, 1911), 299; *New York Times,* Sept. 1, 5, 1860; George C. Rawlings to Charles Ellis, Sept. 4, 1860, Munford-Ellis Family Papers, DU; Washington *States and Union,* Sept. 3, 6, 7, 8, 1860.

27 *New York Times,* Sept. 1, 5, 1860; Washington *States and Union,* Aug. 30, 1860; New York *Herald,* Sept. 1, 1860; Washington *Constitution,* Aug. 30, 1860.

28 Providence *Post,* quoted in Washington *Constitution,* Sept. 4, 1860; Columbus (Ga.) *Daily Times,* Sept. 7, Natchez *Daily Free Trader,* Oct. 3, and Montgomery *Weekly Advertiser,* Sept. 19, 1860, quoted in Ollinger Crenshaw, *The Slave States in the Presidential Election of 1860* (Baltimore, 1945), 79, 82; Washington *Constitution,* Sept. 1, 1860.

29 Washington *States and Union,* Sept. 14, 15, 1860; Chicago *Press and Tribune,* Sept. 13, 1860; *Illinois State Journal,* Sept. 14, 1860; New York *Herald,* Sept. 11, 1860.

30 New York *Herald,* Sept. 12, June 30, 1860; Jefferson Davis, *The Rise and Fall of the Confederate Government* (2 vols., New York, 1881), I, 52; New York *Tribune,* Sept. 13, 1860; Franklin Pierce to James Campbell, Oct. 17, 1860, Pierce Papers, LC.

31 John Bell to Alexander R. Boteler, July 2, 30, 1860, Alexander R. Boteler Papers, DU; Washington Hunt to Bell, June 7, Aug. 19, Belmont to Blanton Duncan, Aug. 19, 1860, John Bell Papers, LC; Washington Hunt to Crittenden, Sept. 3, 1860, Coleman (ed.), *Life of Crittenden,* II, 217; *New-York Tribune,* Sept. 10, 1860; New York *Herald,* Aug. 31, 1860; J. Henley Smith to Stephens, Sept. 19, 1860, Stephens Papers, LC; *New York Times,* Sept. 14, 1860.

32 H. V. West to Douglas, July 12, 1860, Douglas Papers, Chicago; Autobiography (Ms.), 145–47, Herschel V. Johnson Papers, DU.

33 Philadelphia *Argus,* quoted in Washington *Constitution,* Sept. 26, 1860; Sarah Granger to Douglas, Aug. 8, 1860, Douglas Papers, Chicago; New York

*Herald,* Sept. 18, 19, 21, 1860; J. Henly Smith to Stephens, Sept. 19, 1860, Stephens Papers, LC; *Illinois State Register,* Sept. 19, 1860.

34   P. A. Hoyne, Sept. 2, Austin Brown to Douglas, Sept. 2, 1860, Douglas Papers, Chicago; Richardson, Sept. 12, Virgil Hickox to Douglas, Sept. 16, 1860, Douglas Family Papers, Greensboro; Johnson to Stephens, Oct. 1, 1860, Herschel V. Johnson Papers, DU; Washington *States and Union,* Sept. 19, 1860; *Illinois State Journal,* Oct. 4, 1860; *Illinois State Register,* Oct. 8, 1860; Charles Francis Adams, *Charles Francis Adams, 1835–1915: An Autobiography* (Boston, 1916), 65–66.

35   Chicago *Press and Tribune,* Oct. 5, 1860; Washington *States and Union,* Oct. 8, 11, 1860; *Illinois State Register,* Oct. 8, 1860.

36   Rita McKenna Carey, *The First Campaigner: Stephen A. Douglas* (New York, 1964), 73–85 (speech in Iowa City), 86–103 (speech in Dubuque).

37   Wilson, *The Rise and Fall of the Slave Power in America,* II, 700; Nichols, *Disruption,* 348–50; Washington *States and Union,* Oct. 10, 11, 1860; Washington *Constitution,* Oct. 10, 24, 1860; *New York Times,* Oct. 24, 1860.

38   James Gardner, Aug. 5, Seibels to Douglas, Aug. 14, 1860, Douglas Papers, Chicago; Montgomery *Confederation,* quoted in Washington *States and Union,* Sept. 21, 1860; Stephens to Douglas, Sept. 26, 1860, Douglas Family Papers, Greensboro; *Illinois State Register,* Oct. 8, 18, 19, 1860; Washington *States and Union,* Oct. 24, 25, 1860; Howard K. Beale (ed.), *The Diary of Edward Bates* (Washington, D.C., 1933), 154.

39   Memphis *Avalanche,* quoted in *New York Times,* Oct. 25, 1860; Crenshaw, *Slave States in the Presidential Election of 1860,* 83; J. A. Hambleton to Stephens, Oct. 25, 1860, in Myrta L. Avary (ed.), *Recollections of Alexander H. Stephens* . . . (New York, 1910), 55; Linton Stephens to Stephens, Oct. 16, 1860, in James D. Waddell (ed.), *Biographical Sketch of Linton Stephens, Containing a Selection of His Letters, Speeches, State Papers, etc.* (Atlanta, 1877), 234; Atlanta *Confederacy,* quoted in *New York Times,* Nov. 1, 1860.

40   Dallas *Herald,* Oct. 31, Montgomery *Weekly Advertiser,* Oct. 17, 1860, quoted in Reynolds, *Editors Make War,* 121; Atlanta *Confederacy,* quoted in *New York Times,* Oct. 29, 1860.

41   Linton Stephens to Stephens, Oct. 21, 1860, in Waddell (ed.), *Biographical Sketch of Linton Stephens,* 235–36; Crocker, "Campaign of Douglas in the South," in Auer (ed.), *Antislavery and Disunion,* 272–74; James Whelan to Douglas, Oct. 26, 1860, Douglas Family Papers, Greensboro; *Illinois State Register,* Nov. 23, 1860; Cleveland, *Alexander H. Stephens,* 146–48; Augusta *Constitutionalist,* Nov. 1, quoted in Washington *States and Union,* Nov. 3, 1860.

42   Macon *Daily Telegraph,* Nov. 1, 1860, quoted in Crocker, "Campaign of Douglas in the South," in Auer (ed.), *Antislavery and Disunion,* 275; Washington *States and Union,* Nov. 6, 1860; New York *Herald,* Nov. 14, 1860; *New York Times,* Nov. 9, 1860; David R. Barbee and Milledge L. Bonham, Jr. (eds.), "The Montgomery Address of Stephen A. Douglas," *JSH,* V (Nov. 1939), 527–52; F. M. Kohn to Douglas, April 1, 1861, Douglas Family Papers, Greensboro.

43    Forsyth to Douglas, Oct. 30, 1860, Douglas Papers, Chicago; New York *Herald,* Nov. 24, 1860; Crenshaw, *Slave States in the Presidential Election of 1860,* 85–86 (quoting the Mobile *Daily Advertiser,* Nov. 6, and the Montgomery *Confederation,* Nov. 16, 1860); *New York Times,* Oct. 17, 1860.

44    Mobile *Register,* quoted in *Illinois State Register,* Nov. 22, 1860; J. M. Cutts, Jr., Nov. 5, George A. Fosdick, Nov. 5, Belmont, Nov. 2, Sanders, Nov. 2, D. C. Humphreys to Douglas, Nov. 3, 1860, Douglas Papers, Chicago; James B. Sheridan to Henry Wilson, [n. d.], quoted in Wilson, *Rise and Fall of the Slave Power in America,* II, 700.

45    All election returns have been taken from *The Tribune Almanac and Political Register for 1861,* 39–64.

46    Alexander K. McClure to Lincoln, Oct. 15, 19, 1860, Lincoln Papers, LC.

47    Humphreys, Nov. 3, Johnson, Nov. 25, Richardson to Douglas, Nov. 27, 1860, Douglas Papers, Chicago; *Illinois State Register,* Nov. 16. 1860.

48    *Illinois State Register,* Nov. 14, 1860; *New York Times,* Nov. 15, 1860; Washington *States and Union,* Nov. 11, 1860; Douglas to Ninety-Six New Orleans Citizens, Nov. 13, 1860, *Letters,* 499–503.

49    *Illinois State Register,* Nov. 23, 1860; Chicago *Tribune,* Nov. 24, 1860; Johnson, Nov. 25, Thomas H. Gilmer to Douglas, Nov. 30, 1860, Douglas Papers, Chicago.

## CHAPTER XXX

1    Slidell to Buchanan, Nov. 13, 1860, Buchanan Papers, HSP; Washington *Constitution,* Dec. 6, 1860; Reynolds, *Editors Make War,* 147–59; Forsyth to Douglas, Dec. 28, 1860, Douglas Papers, Chicago; Augusta *Constitutionalist,* Nov. 16, New Orleans *Daily Crescent,* Nov. 15, 1860, in Dumond (ed.), *Southern Editorials on Secession,* 246, 238–42.

2    *New York Times,* Dec. 3, 1860; J. Henly Smith to Stephens, Dec. 2, 1860, Stephens Papers, LC; Nichols, *Disruption,* 392–93; Washington *Constitution,* Dec. 1, 1860; H. W. Miller to Douglas, Nov. 28, 1860, Douglas Papers, Chicago.

3    New York *Herald,* Dec. 7, 1860; McClernand to Lanphier, Dec. 3, 1860, Lanphier Papers, ISHL; Smith to Stephens, Dec. 9, 1860, Stephens Papers, LC; *CG,* 36/2, 10–14 (Iverson quotation on p. 11), 3–4 (Clingman); Edward McPherson, *The Political History of the United States of America, During the Great Rebellion . . .* (Washington, D.C., 1864), 37; Martin J. Crawford to Stephens, Dec. 8, 1860, Stephens Papers, LC; David Clopton to Clay, Dec. 13, 1860, Clement C. Clay Papers, DU.

4    Clopton to Clay, Dec. 13, 1860, Clement C. Clay Papers, DU; Lincoln to Trumbull, Dec. 10, to William Kellogg, Dec. 11, 1860, *CWAL,* IV, 149–50; Trumbull to Lincoln, Dec. 4, 1860, Lincoln Papers, LC; Trumbull to Mark Delahay, Dec. 14, 1860, Mark Delahay Papers, KSHS.

5    *CG,* 36/2, App., 1–4; Clopton to Clay, Dec. 13, 1860, Clement C. Clay Papers, DU; Cincinnati *Enquirer,* quoted in Nevins, *Emergence of Lincoln,* II, 353.

6   *CG,* 36/2, 6, 22 (Committee of Thirty-Three), 19, 116–17, 158 (Committee of Thirteen); David M. Potter, *Lincoln and His Party in the Secession Crisis* (New Haven, 1962), 89–91, 110–11; Crawford, Dec. 8, Smith to Stephens, Dec. 9, 1860, Stephens Papers, LC; McClernand to Lanphier, Dec. 10, 1860, Lanphier Papers, ISHL.

7   New York *Herald,* Dec. 3, 1860; Douglas to Belmont, Dec. 25, 1860, *Letters,* 505; *CG,* 36/2, 28, 52, 56–58.

8   *CG,* 36/2, 158; New York *Herald,* Dec. 8, 1860; Worthington G. Snethen to Lincoln, Dec. 13, 1860, Lincoln Papers, LC; *Chicago Tribune,* Dec. 18, 1860; Douglas to Lanphier, Dec. 25, to Belmont, Dec. 25, 1860, *Letters,* 504, 505.

9   Hunter to George Booker, Dec. 14, 1860, Booker Papers, DU; New York *Herald,* Dec. 15, 1860; Johnson to Stephens, Dec. 22, 1860, Herschel V. Johnson Papers, DU; R. J. Brent to Douglas, Dec. 17, 1860, Douglas Papers, Chicago; Reynolds to William Porcher Miles, Dec. 15, 1860, Miles Papers, SHC; Sheahan to Douglas, Dec. 17, 1860, Douglas Papers, Chicago; McCormick to Douglas, Dec. 29, Copy of Charleston *Mercury,* Dec. 20, 1860, Douglas Family Papers, Greensboro.

10   *CG,* 36/2, 112–14; New York *Herald,* Dec. 20, 1860; Albert D. Kirwan, *John J. Crittenden: The Struggle for the Union* (Lexington, 1962), 374–80; Potter, *Lincoln and His Party in the Secession Crisis,* 112–33, 182–84.

11   New York *Herald,* Dec. 22, 23, 1860; *Senate Reports,* 36/2, No. 288, 2, 5–6; Potter, *Lincoln and His Party in the Secession Crisis,* 171–72, 205–6; Belmont to Douglas, Dec. 31, 1860, *Letters, Speeches and Addresses of August Belmont,* 45.

12   *CG,* 36/2, 183; *Sen. Reps.,* 36/2, No. 288, 8–10; J. Henly Smith to Stephens, Dec. 26, 1860, Stephens Papers, LC; Chicago *Tribune,* Jan. 3, 1861.

13   Douglas to Lanphier, Dec. 25, to Belmont, Dec. 25, to Stephens, Dec. 25, 1860, *Letters,* 504–6; Belmont to Douglas, Dec. 26, 31, 1860, *Letters, Speeches and Addresses,* 40, 45; Stephens to J. Henly Smith, Dec. 31, 1860, Phillips (ed.), *Correspondence of Toombs, Stephens, and Cobb,* 526.

14   *Sen. Reps.,* 36/2, No. 288, 10–19.

15   Douglas to Lanphier, Dec. 25, 1860, *Letters,* 504; Toombs to the People of Georgia, Dec. 23, 1860, Phillips (ed.), *Correspondence of Toombs, Stephens, and Cobb,* 525; William Ezzard *et al.* to Douglas and Crittenden, Dec. 26, 1860, Douglas Family Papers, Greensboro; Douglas and Crittenden to Ezzard *et al.,* Dec. 29, 1860, *Letters,* 506; Douglas to S. S. Hayes, Dec. 29, 1860, Frankfort (Ky.) *Daily Commonwealth,* Jan. 26, 1863.

16   J. Henly Smith to Stephens, Dec. 26, 1860, Stephens Papers, LC; New York *Herald,* Dec. 23, 1860.

17   Blair to Frank Blair, Jr., Jan. 2, 1861, Blair Family Papers, LC; *CG,* 36/2, 237; Kirwan, *Crittenden,* 392; S. J. Anderson to Stephens, Jan. 2, 1861, Stephens Papers, LC; New York *Herald,* Jan. 1, 3, 4, 1861; *New-York Tribune,* Jan. 19, 1861.

18   CG, 36/2, App., 35–42.

19   Diary of Thomas Bragg, Jan. 3, 1861, SHC; Crawford to Stephens, Jan. 7, 1861, Stephens Papers, LC; James A. Nisbet to Douglas, Jan. 7, 1861, Douglas Papers, Chicago; Washington *Constitution,* Jan. 12, 1861; *New York Times,* Jan. 5, 1861; *Illinois State Journal,* Jan. 7, 12, 1861; Chicago *Tribune,* Jan. 8, 1861; Washburne to Lincoln, Jan. 4, 1861, Lincoln Papers, LC; Winthrop to Douglas, Jan. 11, 1861, Douglas Family Papers, Greensboro.

20   Washington *Constitution,* Jan. 10, 1861; J. Henly Smith to Stephens, Jan. 2, 1861, Stephens Papers, LC; Klein, *Buchanan,* 391; J. A. Campbell to Jeremiah Black, Jan. 4, 1861, Black Papers, LC.

21   *New-York Tribune,* Jan. 8, 1861; *CG,* 36/2, 306–12 (Davis, quotation from 312), 328–32 (Hunter).

22   Elihu Washburne to Lincoln, Jan. 7, 1861, Lincoln Papers, LC; *New-York Tribune,* Jan. 7, 1861; New York *Herald,* Jan. 7, 13, 1861; *CG,* 36/2, 341–44 (quotation from 344).

23   *CG,* 36/2, 351, 352, 360–62, 401, 402–4, 409, 410; Bragg Diary, Jan. 16, 1861, SHC; Nichols, *Disruption,* 444–47; Nevins, *Emergence of Lincoln,* II, 402–3.

24   *Illinois State Journal,* Jan. 28, 1861; *CG,* 36/2, 661, 668; John A. Gilmer to D. H. Albright, Jan. 8, 1861, John A. Gilmer Papers, NCDAH; Bragg Diary, Jan. 18, 1861, SHC; New York *Herald,* Jan. 20, 1861; *New-York Tribune,* Jan. 21, 1861; *CG,* 36/2, App., 39–40; Charles A. Davis to Douglas, Jan. 16, 1861, Douglas Family Papers, Greensboro.

25   Benjamin F. Hallett, Feb. 25, "A Georgian," [Jan.], John M. Huger, Jan. 4, John Hardy, Jan. 7, Philip Phillips to Douglas, Jan. 8, 1861, Douglas Family Papers, Greensboro; J. W. Bradbury, Feb. 4, E. Smith, Jan. 1, J. C. Napier, Jan. 3, C. B. Dodson, Jan. 7, J. M. Alexander, Jan. 12, Waddy Thompson to Douglas, Jan. 13, 1861, Douglas Papers, Chicago; W. P. Bond to Crittenden and Douglas, [Jan.], J. W. Paine to Crittenden, Jan. 5, 1861, Crittenden Papers, LC.

26   *New-York Tribune,* Jan. 19, 1861; *CG,* 36/2, 410, 443; Potter, *Lincoln and His Party in the Secession Crisis,* 305–6; New York *Herald,* Jan. 26, 30, 1861; *Illinois State Register,* Jan. 29, 30, 1861; Treat to Douglas, Jan. 18, 1861, Douglas Papers, Chicago; "A Table Talk with Seward" (clipping), Alexander Boteler Papers, DU; Daniel B. Carroll, *Henri Mercier and the American Civil War* (Princeton, 1971), 34–36; *CG,* 36/2, 669.

27   Bragg Diary, Jan. 14, 1861, SHC; Ellis B. Schnabel to Douglas, Jan. 5, 1861, Douglas Papers, Chicago; New York *Herald,* Jan. 27, 1861; Douglas to John S. Barbour, Jan. 27, *Illinois State Register,* Feb. 2, 1861; Douglas to My Dear Sir, Jan. 31, New York *Herald,* Feb. 6, 1861; James Barbour, Feb. 6, James Hicks, Feb. 6, Robert G. Green, Feb. 7, Richard P. Lott to Douglas, Feb. 23, 1861, Douglas Papers, Chicago.

28   William H. Polk to Douglas, Feb. 5, Douglas and Crittenden to Polk, Feb. 5 (copy), Thomas A. Blythe to Douglas, Jan. 30, 1861, Douglas Papers, Chicago; Douglas to the Editors of the Memphis *Appeal,* Feb. 2, 1861, Wash-

ington *National Intelligencer,* Feb. 7, 1861; S. F. Clark to Douglas, Feb. 8, David Walker and J. H. Stierman to Crittenden and Douglas, March 4, 1861, Douglas Papers, Chicago.

29   J. W. Lapsley to Douglas, Jan. 14, 1861, Douglas Papers, Chicago.

30   *CG,* 36/2, 445–46, 465–67, 473, 488–89; Bragg Diary, Jan. 19, 1861, SHC; Trumbull to Mark Delahay, Feb. 16, 1861, Delahay Papers, KSHS.

31   *CG,* 36/2, 641, 765.

32   *CG,* 36/2, 639–45, 763–66, 1206–8, 1391; James G. Blaine, *Twenty Years of Congress* (2 vols., Norwich, Conn., 1884–86), I, 271.

33   *CG,* 36/2, 428–30.

34   *CG,* 36/2, 953, 1051–53; Belmont to Douglas, Feb. 11, 1861, Douglas Papers, Chicago; Notes on the Zollverein, Notes and clippings in a packet labeled "Reciprocity," List of States composing the German Custom Union (dated April 2, 1861), Seward to Douglas, April 15, 1861, Douglas Family Papers, Greensboro; R. Hadfield, Jan. 14, J. Wadsworth to Douglas, Feb. 10, 1861, Douglas Papers, Chicago; Douglas, *An American Continental Commercial Union or Alliance* (ed. by J. Madison Cutts, Jr.; Washington, 1889); Bragg Diary, Feb. 19–22, 1861, SHC.

35   *CG,* 36/2, 1080–81.

36   *CG,* 36/2, 586; New York *Herald,* Jan. 29, 22, 1861; Kirwan, *Crittenden,* 405; *CG,* 36/2, 668–69; Bragg Diary, Jan. 31, 1861, SHC.

37   Julia Gardiner Tyler to her mother, Feb. 3, 13, 1861, John Tyler Papers, LC; John M. Palmer, *Personal Recollections of John M. Palmer, The Story of an Earnest Life* (Cincinnati, 1901), 89–90; *Illinois State Register,* Feb. 15, 1861; Douglas to John Tyler, Feb. 11, 1861, *Letters,* 507.

38   Robert Gray Gunderson, *Old Gentlemen's Convention: The Washington Peace Conference of 1861* (Madison, 1961), 33–42, 88; New York *Herald,* Feb. 28, 1861.

39   *CG,* 36/2, 1254–55, 1269–74, 1305–18; *New-York Tribune,* March 5, 1861.

40   *CG,* 36/2, 1338–39, 1342–56, 1359–74.

41   *CG,* 36/2, 1374–1405; New York *Herald,* March 4, 1861; *New-York Tribune,* March 5, 1861.

## CHAPTER XXXI

1   Britton A. Hill to Douglas, March 7, 1861, Douglas Papers, Chicago.

2   New York *Herald,* Feb. 24, 26, 1861; Washington *States and Union,* Feb. 25, 1861; *New-York Tribune,* Feb. 26, 1861; *Illinois State Register,* Feb. 28, 1861; Bragg Diary, Feb. 26, 1861, SHC; *New York Times,* Feb. 26, 1861.

3   *New York Times,* Feb. 28, 1861; New York *Herald,* Feb. 28, 1861; Blanton Duncan to Douglas, Feb. 6, 1861, Douglas Papers, Chicago; F. Lauriston Bullard (ed.), *The Diary of a Public Man* (New Brunswick, N.J., 1946), 65. Although considerable doubt has been cast on the authenticity of the Public Man's observations, they have been used where corroborative evidence is available. A highly embellished account of Douglas' meeting with Lincoln on Febru-

ary 27, written by a member of the Pennsylvania delegation to the Peace Conference who claimed to have been present, is in Esther Cowles Cushman (ed.), "Douglas the Loyal, A Hitherto Unpublished Manuscript by James Pollock, Previously Governor of Pennsylvania," *JISHS*, XXIII (April 1930), 163–70.

4   *New-York Tribune*, March 5, 1861; *New York Times*, March 5, 1861; *CG*, 36/2, 1413; Bullard (ed.), *The Diary of a Public Man*, 84–85.

5   Cincinnati *Commercial*, March 11, 1861, quoted in Allan Nevins, "He Did Hold Lincoln's Hat," *American Heritage*, X (Feb. 1959), 99; *New York Times*, March 5, 1861; First Inaugural Address—Final Text, March 4, 1861, *CWAL*, IV, 262–71. According to the Public Man, Douglas intimated the day before the inauguration that Lincoln had read parts of his address to him, Bullard (ed.), *The Diary of a Public Man*, 79.

6   *New York Times*, March 5, 7, 1861; "Reminiscences of Stephen A. Douglas," *Atlantic Monthly*, VIII (Aug. 1861), 211–12; *CG*, 38/1, 1499.

7   *New York Times*, March 5, 7, 11, 1861; New York *Herald*, March 10, 1861; Bullard (ed.), *The Diary of a Public Man*, 55.

8   *New York Times*, March 5, 7, 1861; James C. Taylor, March 18, Blanton Duncan, March 7, J. B. F. Curry to Douglas, March 5, 1861, Douglas Papers, Chicago.

9   *CG*, 37/Special Session, 1436–46; Philadelphia *Press*, quoted in *Illinois State Register*, March 19, 1861.

10   *New York Times*, March 9, 11, 1861; Joseph Mattingly, March 7, Benjamin Rush to Douglas, March 7, Invitation from Baron and Madame de Stoeckl, March 23, 1861, Douglas Papers, Chicago; Samuel F. B. Morse to Douglas, April 8, 1861, Douglas Family Papers, Greensboro.

11   R. M. T. Hunter to George Booker, Feb. 8, 1861, Booker Papers, DU; W. W. Holden and Quint. Busbee, March 13, J. M. Dent, March 11, Simon Cameron to Douglas, March 13, 1861, Douglas Family Papers, Greensboro; William C. Perkins, March 20, James B. Dorman, March 7, George Blow, Jr., March 13, Robert P. Dick, March 7, John A. Gilmer, March 8, 10, Samuel J. Handy to Douglas, March 22, 1861, Douglas Papers, Chicago; George Hume Steuart to W. J. Steuart, March 8, 1861, George Hume Steuart Papers, DU.

12   New York *Herald*, March 9, 1861; G. E. Irbell to Douglas, March 18, 1861, Douglas Papers, Chicago.

13   *CG*, 37/Special Session, 1452, 1457–65; Lincoln to Winfield Scott, March 9, 1861, *CWAL*, IV, 279; New York *Herald*, March 14, 16, 1861; *New York Times*, March 16, 19, 1861.

14   *CG*, 37/Special Session, 1464, 1501, 1503, 1511, 1519.

15   H. W. Miller to Douglas, March 24, 1861, Douglas Family Papers, Greensboro; H. W. Miller, March 31, T. H. Gilmer, March 28, April 1, Charles Upton, March 28, S. Churchill, March 22, W. H. Miller to Douglas, March 14, 1861, Douglas Papers, Chicago.

16   Milton, *Eve of Conflict*, 539–41; Douglas, *An American Continental Commercial Union or Alliance;* William Henry Hurlbut, March 27, Samuel Ward to Douglas, April 1, 1861, Douglas Papers, Chicago; William H. Russell to Douglas, [n. d.], Douglas Family Papers, Greensboro; William Howard Rus-

sell, *My Diary North and South* (Boston, 1863), 55, 62; Russell to the London *Times,* April 1, 1861, in Russell, *The Civil War in America* (Boston, 1861), 18.

17   Sanders to Douglas, Feb. 12, 1861, Douglas Papers, Chicago; Thomas Reade Rootes Cobb to Mrs. Cobb, March 6, 1861, quoted in Charles Robert Lee, Jr., *The Confederate Constitutions* (Chapel Hill, 1963), 113–14; *CG,* 37 / Special Session, 1459.

18   John Purcell, March 8, William M. Morton, March 21, E. W. Seibels, March 26, James A. Hambleton, Feb. 4, J. O. Harrison to Douglas, Jan. 31, 1861, Douglas Papers, Chicago.

19   Felix McCloskey, Jan. 17, Charles W. Baker, Jan. 17, B. F. Horan to Douglas, Jan. 17, 1861, Douglas Papers, Chicago. See Robert W. Johannsen, "The Douglas Democracy and the Crisis of Disunion," *Civil War History,* IX (Sept. 1963), 229–47.

20   McClernand, Dec. 21, 1860, Feb. 4, 1861, Sheahan to Lanphier, Jan. 4, 1861, Lanphier Papers, ISHL; *Illinois State Register,* Jan. 1, 10, 1861; Virgil Hickox to Douglas, Jan. 8, 1861, Douglas Papers, Chicago.

21   *Illinois State Register,* Jan. 15, 17, 1861; Frank M. Streamer to Douglas, Jan. 3, 1861, Douglas Papers, Chicago; Cole, *Era of the Civil War,* 256–57; Robert Smith to Douglas, May 17, 1861, Douglas Family Papers, Greensboro; McClernand to P. S. Read, Jan. 29, 1861, *Illinois State Register,* Feb. 18, 1861.

22   B. F. Horan, Jan. 17, G. L. Vliet, March 12, G. W. Renwick, March 20, Emory S. Foster, March 26, W. Kimmel to Douglas, April 3, 1861, Douglas Papers, Chicago.

23   Gideon Welles, *Diary of Gideon Welles, Secretary of the Navy under Lincoln and Johnson* (3 vols., Boston, 1911), I, 34.

24   Lincoln to Gideon Welles and Simon Cameron, March 29, to Robert Anderson, April 4, to Robert S. Chew, April 6, 1861, *CWAL,* IV, 301, 321–22, 323–24; *New-York Tribune,* April 8, 10, 1861; Gideon Welles to Mary Jane Welles, June 9, 1861, Welles Papers, LC; Welles, *Diary,* I, 32–34.

25   Cincinnati *Commercial,* Oct. 28, 1864; "Reminiscences of Stephen A. Douglas," *Atlantic Monthly,* VIII, 212; Statement, [April 14, 1861], *Letters,* 509–10; Forney, *Anecdotes of Public Men,* I, 224–25.

26   Proclamation Calling Militia and Convening Congress, April 15, 1861, *CWAL,* IV, 331–32; James M. Slade to Douglas, April 16, 1861, Douglas Papers, Chicago; H. V. Willson, April 18, R. J. Brent to Douglas, May 4, 1861, Douglas Family Papers, Greensboro.

27   Douglas to T. E. Courtenay, April 15, G [*sic*]. L. F. to Douglas, April 16, Douglas to James L. Faucett, April 17, *Illinois State Register,* April 22, 1861; Samuel A. Gordon, April 17, T. H. Gilmer to Douglas, April 17, 1861, Douglas Papers, Chicago; L. R. Barret to Douglas, April 23, 1861, Douglas Family Papers, Greensboro.

28   Joseph Medill, April 15, Orville H. Browning, April 18, 22, Trumbull to Lincoln, April 21, 1861, Lincoln Papers, LC; R. J. Smith to Douglas, Feb. 12, 1861, Douglas Papers, Chicago; Richardson to M. M. Bane, April 26, 1861,

*Illinois State Register,* May 7, 1861; *Illinois State Journal,* May 2, 1861; James P. Jones, *"Black Jack:" John A. Logan and Southern Illinois in the Civil War Era* (Tallahassee, 1967), 77–82; James C. Robinson, April 18, W. H. Green to Logan, April 25, 1861, Logan Family Papers, LC; Alfred Clapp to Douglas, April 15, 1861, Douglas Papers, Chicago.

29  Milton, *Eve of Conflict,* 564; Angle (ed.), *Herndon's Life of Lincoln,* 434n.; Shelby M. Cullom to Isaac N. Arnold, March 19, 1883, Shelby M. Cullom Papers, CHS; *New York Times,* April 24, 1861; Cincinnati *Commercial,* April 27, 1861.

30  New York *Herald,* April 25, 1861; *New-York Tribune,* April 26, 1861; Jacob Dolson Cox, *Military Reminiscences of the Civil War* (2 vols., New York, 1900), I, 5–6; *Illinois State Register,* April 25, 1861.

31  *Chicago Tribune,* April 26, 1861; Smith D. Atkins, "Patriotism in Northern Illinois," *TISHS,* 1911, 81; W. H. Green to Logan, April 25, 1861, Logan Family Papers, LC; *Illinois State Register,* April 26, 1861; Pease and Randall (eds.), *The Diary of Orville Hickman Browning,* I, 465; Koerner to Lincoln, May 17, 1861, Lincoln Papers, LC.

32  *Illinois State Journal,* April 26, 1861; Cullom to Arnold, March 19, 1883, Cullom Papers, CHS; *Speech of Senator Douglas Before the Legislature of Illinois, April 25, 1861* [n. p., n. d.], *passim.*

33  Pease and Randall (eds.), *The Diary of Orville Hickman Browning,* I, 466; *Illinois State Register,* May 3, 1861; *Chicago Tribune,* May 2, 1861.

34  Gordon Tanner to Douglas, May 4, 1861, Douglas Family Papers, Greensboro; *Illinois State Register,* May 15, 1861; *Chicago Tribune,* May 17, 1861.

35  Douglas to Lincoln, April 29, 1861, *Letters,* 511; Virgil Hickox to James Madison Cutts, May 13, to Douglas, May 4, 21, 1861, Douglas Family Papers, Greensboro; Douglas to Hickox, May 10, 1861, *Letters,* 511–14.

36  Douglas to James A. McHatton, April 4, 1861, *Letters,* 508; McHatton to Douglas, May 11, 1861, Douglas Family Papers, Greensboro; Memphis *Avalanche,* quoted in *Illinois State Register,* May 17, 1861.

37  "Death of a Patriot," *Chicago History,* VI (Spring 1961), 78; New York *Herald,* June 7, 1861; Douglas to Hickox, May 10, 1861, *Letters,* 511; *Chicago Tribune,* May 14, 18, June 1, 4, 1861; *Illinois State Register,* May 20, 28, June 1, 3, 1861; Sheahan to Lanphier, May 17, 1861, Lanphier Papers, ISHL.

38  *Chicago Tribune,* June 4, 5, 1861; "Death of a Patriot," *Chicago History,* VI, 78; New York *Herald,* June 4, 5, 8, 1861; R. T. Merrick to Lincoln, June 3, 1861, Lincoln Papers, LC; Richard Yates, Lyman Trumbull *et al.* to the Mayor of Chicago, June 3, Lanphier to Sheahan, June 3, 1861, Douglas Family Papers, Greensboro; *Illinois State Journal,* June 4, 5, 8, 1861.

39  Washington *Union,* Nov. 7, 1849.

# Index